REFERENCE GUIDES IN LITERATURE

Ronald Gottesman, *Editor*
Joseph Katz, *Consulting Editor*

Mark Twain
A Reference Guide

Thomas Asa Tenney

G. K. HALL & CO., 70 LINCOLN STREET, BOSTON, MASS.

Library of Congress Cataloging in Publication Data

Tenney, Thomas.
   Mark Twain : a reference guide.

   (Reference guides in literature)
   Includes index.
   1. Clemens, Samuel Langhorne, 1835-1910--Bibliography.
I. Title.
Z8176.T45 [PS1331] 016.818'4'09   76-41752
ISBN 0-8161-7966-2

To Margaret, Bob, Charles, and Will,

with love and gratitude.

Contents

Foreword by Hamlin Hill

"It is not worth the while," Thoreau observed, "to go round the world to count the cats in Zanzibar." But if Professor Tenney has had some stray felines to deal with among his 4900 entries, he also has the advantage of knowing that his Reference Guide to Mark Twain scholarship and criticism has a more vital significance than the census that Thoreau imagined.

Mark Twain has enjoyed a dual reputation (curiously harmonious with his dual personality) for over half a century. Highbrowed critics and harmless scholars have produced every conceivable "reading" of his works, from imaginative interpretations to definitive texts. They have explicated a single word and they have used Mark Twain to make grand syntheses of American thought and character. They have created, blindly followed, and sometimes vigorously attacked the "trends" in Mark Twain scholarship--trends which themselves have been both provocative and ultimately stultifying. The very quantity of academic research and publication about Mark Twain does much to bring into question the notion of an Establishment which, like eunuchs, protects its one-man harem from unauthorized violation. If such an arrangement does exist, it is the largest collection of eunuchs since Sollermun kept what Jim calls in Huckleberry Finn his "bo'd'n-house."

While academia has been fussing with Mark Twain's respectable image, his popular reputation has never suffered from fluctuations of any sort. Celebrities begin interviews with, "As Mark Twain once said..." He is the American touchstone for comparison with practically anything--the Mississippi, the Far West, post-Civil War New England, the debasement of the Protestant work ethic, even (in the recent Indo-China fiasco) as a rival to Thoreau on disobedience to law. Two idolatrous publications-- The Twainian and the Mark Twain Journal--are devoted almost exclusively to him; and it will not surprise anyone if, before long, the Reader's Digest begins printing direct quotations from him in red ink. At least ten documentary educational movies about Mark Twain were produced between 1946 and 1969 to carry the Sacred Relic down to junior-high-school level for Adoration by the next generation.

This is not the place to raise questions about what this dual reputation has done to Mark Twain--about the accuracy of either interpretation, or the conflict between the two images, or the wisdom of attempting to deflate the folk-hero concept of his life and literary career. But this volume is the foundation and starting-place for dozens of such investigations. Though Henry Adams was being facetious about plotting the curve of history into the future, it is possible with this bibliography at least to plot backward from 1974 the curves of Mark Twain's reputation.

If it is one of the most paradoxical literary reputations in our culture, it is also one of the most fundamental to try to comprehend. And the very elusiveness of the man heightens the challenge of attempting to find his essential qualities. That search must begin here.

If the editors of the Literary History of the United States were correct back in 1948 that "each generation must define the past in its own terms," maybe it will be possible to use Professor Tenney's scrupulous checklist to discern areas which are not yet examined and methods which have not yet been exhausted. This bibliography would be a Godsend if it only underscored those subjects of scholarly investigation which have been explored, mapped, meted and bounded, and subdivided to the point of contemptuous familiarity.

What can be said without the need of prophecy is that the flood will continue. However the next generation defines Mark Twain, it will find him as irrestible as earlier generations have; perhaps, with this survey of secondary materials before it, it can find not only more to say but also some important things which have not been said before. Scholarship should build upon its earlier insights, refining rather than merely repeating them. Here is the survey of what scholarship has done so far; and here, by implication at least, is the challenge to move ahead.

Hamlin Hill
University of New Mexico

Introduction

        This Reference Guide collects in a single volume all listings of books, reviews, and articles concerning Mark Twain in the major bibliographies through 1974. Except where indicated by an asterisk, the material for each entry has been personally examined; there are descriptive annotations, where possible noting any reprintings or abstracts published elsewhere. The index lists authors, topics, and works by Mark Twain, and also includes sections for the several hundred articles which contain his letters or photographs and drawings of him. The work here begun will be corrected, expanded, and kept up to date in an annual supplement in American Literary Realism.

        In the compilation I have tried to be objective and complete within the scope of coverage. The annotations are descriptions rather than abstracts, and as an aid to evaluation I have often quoted directly so authors might describe their own work; cross-references or the index will lead the reader to reviews of books listed and to replies in critical controversies. I have made no attempt to limit coverage to what I personally consider important: if a book or article appears in another bibliography the reader should be able to decide from my annotation whether he would find it useful. Some books and articles do not fulfill the promise of their titles (See 1949.B45 and 1964.B27, for example), and time need not be wasted on them again. I have excluded only dissertations (which ought to be treated in a volume of their own), ordinary editions of Mark Twain's works without significant editing or introductions, and appreciative poems by persons who did not know him. Finally, I have listed few newspaper interviews of Mark Twain, because Louis J. Budd has compiled a very full list, with summaries (scheduled for publication in January, 1977).

        This Reference Guide includes and extends the coverage of the major bibliographies. The original finding-list followed the Modern Humanities Research Association's Annual Bibliography of English Language and Literature, Roger Asselineau's The Literary Reputation of Mark Twain (1954.A2), Beebe and Feaster's checklist in Modern Fiction Studies (1968.B6), Lewis Leary's first two volumes of Articles on American Literature (1954.B35 and 1970.B51), and the bibliographies in Henderson (1911.A3) and the early issues of The Twainian (1939.B12, 1940.B10, and 1943.B3); there were also useful leads in the dissertations of Robert Rodney (1945.A2) and Webster L. Smalley (1948.A3). A full search of the abstracts in Abstracts of English Studies, American Literature Abstracts, and MLA Abstracts (all of which are cited in the annotations in this Reference Guide) revealed more articles. Finally, while waiting for printer's proofs I had time to check my text against the MLA Bibliography from the first volume, and the installments of "Articles on American Literature" in American Literature from 1951-1974; a few more items turned up, have been checked where possible, and are listed in the Addenda beginning on p. 397. The reader looking for material I might have missed should consult the "Bibliographies" heading in my index.

Mark Twain: A Reference Guide

The intended value of this guide to writings about Mark Twain has been twofold: not only to record the history of his popular and critical reputation, but also to codify a substantial body of factual data which would otherwise be difficult to trace. The major studies of Mark Twain are all listed here, but there are also many brief notes on sources and analogues, family history, and reminiscences by people who knew or met him; taken collectively, they add detail and insight to the picture of an important and complicated figure in our national literature.

In the beginning of my work I was sometimes impatient with the human limitations of my predecessors, but experience has bred respect for their accuracy and thoroughness in a task which only the foolhardy would attempt to expand. I am particularly grateful for the early work of Roger Asselineau, a remarkable achievement under pressure of time and one which proved to be so useful that it was later reprinted in this country; Professor Asselineau pointed the way to many items I should otherwise have missed.

A Reference Guide such as this could not have been produced without the facilities of numerous libraries and the skilled, patient help of their staffs. I am indebted to the libraries of Columbia University, Harvard University, the University of Pennsylvania, Bryn Mawr College, the University of North Carolina, and Duke University, and to the Boston, New York, Philadelphia, Chicago, San Francisco, and Oakland public libraries, and the Library Society of Charleston. I am particularly grateful for the hospitality and help I received in three summers in Redpath Library at McGill University; the time spent there was productive and thoroughly pleasant. In Montreal I also found useful material and kind treatment at Sir George Williams University.

No student of Mark Twain should overlook the Mark Twain Papers in The Bancroft Library at the University of California, Berkeley. In addition to the wealth of manuscripts, letters, photographs, scrap-books, newspaper clippings, early editions of Mark Twain's works, and books containing his marginal notations, there are extensive holdings in secondary materials; among the latter are books, offprints of articles, and a number of master's essays and doctoral dissertations. Unfortunately, I was able to spend only a week there, but the fine collection and the generous help of Frederick Anderson made it the most enjoyable week in the long period of compilation. The collection at Berkeley is still growing, and it should be the first thought for any person who has Mark Twain material of any sort and wishes to make it more accessible to scholars.

I would like to thank my colleague Robert Geraldi for his help with a number of articles in Italian, and Susan and Joanne Bogdanowicz for their accurate work in numbering the entries and typing the mass of index material. I also owe thanks to my sons Bob, Charles, and Will for their careful work on the finding list and the preliminary sorting of the 15,000 index slips.

My debt to the fraternity of Mark Twain scholars is incalculable, both for the material they have provided and the insights they have shared; working with their published writing has been a continuing pleasure, and I have tried to repay them with as comprehensive and accurate a summary of their work as I could achieve. The task should be continued, and I earnestly solicit corrections and additions from those who use this guide.

List of Abbreviations

AES   Abstracts of English Studies (the statement "reprinted in Twainian" after the listing of an AES citation indicates a reprinting of the abstract, not the article abstracted)

ALA   American Literature Abstracts

CY   A Connecticut Yankee in King Arthur's Court (1889)

FE   Following the Equator (1897)

GA   The Gilded Age (1874)

"Hadleyburg"   "The Man that Corrupted Hadleyburg"; also, the book, The Man that Corrupted Hadleyburg, and Other Stories and Essays (1900)

HF   Adventures of Huckleberry Finn (1885)

IA   The Innocents Abroad (1869)

JA   Personal Recollections of Joan of Arc (1896); this should not be confused with the article, "Saint Joan of Arc" (1904)

LOM   Life on the Mississippi (1883)

MT   Mark Twain; this abbreviation is also used for Samuel Langhorne Clemens, who created Mark Twain. The purpose here is to provide an easily recognizable abbreviation for a bibliography, with no attempt to resolve the obvious absurdity of referring to MT's boyhood, and MT's mother, sister and brothers, and so on.

MS   The Mysterious Stranger (1916)

P&P   The Prince and the Pauper (1882)

PW   The Tragedy of Pudd'nhead Wilson and the Comedy of Those Extraordinary Twins (1894)

RI   Roughing It (1872)

TA   A Tramp Abroad (1880)

TS   The Adventures of Tom Sawyer (1876); also used as part of
                                    the titles of Tom Sawyer Abroad (1894) and Tom Sawyer,
                                    Detective (1896)

        Note: Where a journal lists a winter issue as for two years connected by a hy-
                phen (as: Winter 1972-1973) it has been my practice to list entries
                from that issue for the earlier year.

Writings about Mark Twain, 1858-1975

NO DATE A BOOKS

A1   ANON. Mark Twain: Biography-Reminiscence
     [undated scrap-book in Chicago Public Libra-
     ry].
        Magazine articles and mounted newspaper
     clippings (mainly portraits and obituaries);
     much is familiar material, but the present
     bibliography lists this as the source of
     items from the Hannibal Morning Journal for
     April 22, 24, 26, 1910; from the St. Louis
     Times for April 22, 1910; from the Politik-
     ens Kronik (n.p.) for April 23, 1910; and
     for the 1914 Catalogue of First and Other
     Editions of the Writings of "Mark Twain,"
     Samuel Langhorne Clemens, and of Lafcadio
     Hearn.

A2   ANON. Mark Twain Region of Missouri. Jeffer-
     son City, Missouri: Missouri State Division
     of Resources and Development.
        A pamphlet of photographs of the region,
     some showing MT's birthplace and the MT
     State Park, monuments, etc., but providing
     no new information.

A3   *DUNCAN, CAPTAIN CHARLES. [Manuscript log of
     the Quaker City trip; in the Patten Free Li-
     brary, Bath, Maine.]
        [Source: Charles Shain, in "The Journal
     of the Quaker City Captain" (1955) and in
     Ganzel (1968), p. xiii and passim.] Pro-
     vides the captain's perspective on the tour
     on which IA is based.

A4   LAUTREC, GABRIEL DE. Contes Choisis par Mark
     Twain Traduits de l'anglais par Gabriel de
     Lautrec et précédés d'une étude sur l'hu-
     mour. Paris: Nelson, Editeurs [Londres,
     Edimbourg et New-York]. "Introduction:
     Mark Twain et l'Humour," pp. 9-20.
        MT is the best representative of American
     humor in France because his pleasantries
     are of more general interest than those of
     such countrymen as Artemus Ward, but like
     all great writers he has become universal
     while remaining national; he has painted a
     society and a period. Much of the essay is
     given over to general discussion of humor.
     [Year of publ. not given, but Lautrec men-
     tions MT's death in 1910]

NO DATE B SHORTER WRITINGS

B1   ANDERSON, CARL L. "Strindberg's Translations
     of American Humor," Americana Norvegica,
     pp. 152-94.
        [Source: undated photocopy in Mark Twain
     Papers; a preceding article cites sources as
     recent as 1964.] August Strindberg trans-
     lated two volumes of sketches and stories by
     MT, Artemus Ward, and others, published in
     Stockholm in 1878 and 1879; "perhaps the ac-
     tual work of translation had not been his at
     all, but that of his wife, a writer of ver-
     satile talents." The MT works translated
     were "Alonzo Fitz Clarence' och Rosannah
     Etheltons Kälekshistoria," "Berättelser om
     ädla handlingar," and "About Magnanimous-
     Incident Literature." "The Swedish transla-
     tion is, in fact, quite uneven; some parts
     are fairly literal and accurate, but most
     have been treated cavalierly."

B2   COVENEY, PETER. Poor Monkey.
        [Source: Winfield Townley Scott, "Mark
     Twain Revisited" (1961).] Contains a chap-
     ter on MT, reflecting the Brooks thesis and
     attributing the despair and frustration of
     MT's later years to his dichotomy between
     rebellion and conformity.

1858 A BOOKS - NONE

1858 B SHORTER WRITINGS

B1   *ANON. "A Sad Meeting," St. Louis News and In-
     telligencer, June 19, reprinted from Memphis
     Eagle and Inquirer.
        [Source: Reprinted in Twainian, IX
     (January-February, 1950), 2.] On SLC's
     grief at seeing his brother Henry, fatally
     scalded in the explosion of the steamboat
     Pennsylvania.

1862 A BOOKS - NONE

1862 B SHORTER WRITINGS

B1   *WRIGHT, WILLIAM [pseud. DAN DEQUILLE]. "Re-
     porter in California," California Monthly,
     IV, 170.

1862 - Shorter Writings

(*WRIGHT, WILLIAM [pseud. Dan DeQuille])
[Source: Edwin A. Ford, A Bibliography
of Literary Journalism in America. Minneapolis: Burgess Publishing Company, 1937.]

1866 A BOOKS - NONE

1866 B SHORTER WRITINGS

B1 *HARTE, BRET [signed F. B. H.] [Estimate of
     Mark Twain's October 2, 1866 lecture on the
     Sandwich Islands.] Springfield (Mass.)
     Daily Republican, (November 10).
     [Source: Quoted in Stewart (1941).]

1867 A BOOKS - NONE

1867 B SHORTER WRITINGS

B1   [Announcement of the Quaker City excursion.]
     American Agriculturalist, XXVI (March), 86.
       Mostly straightforward description of the
     projected itinerary. Captain Duncan is de-
     scribed as "the captain who has been eight-
     een years at sea, about half the time as
     master of large ships--who never swore an
     oath--never drank a glass of liquor, and
     though he has crossed the Atlantic fifty-
     eight times, never suffered a shipwreck,
     nor lost a man by accident. The company is
     to be select--every applicant's name is
     submitted to a committee."

B2   *[Reports of Mark Twain's Sandwich Islands
     lecture at St. Louis.] Missouri Republican
     (St. Louis), March 24, 26, 28.
       [Source: Quoted in Lorch (1947),
     pp. 299-307.] Includes text of speech
     (March 28) and a letter to the editor by
     MT (March 24).

B3   WEBB, CHARLES HENRY. "Advertisement," in
     MT's The Celebrated Jumping Frog of Cala-
     veras County, and Other Sketches (New York:
     C. H. Webb).
       MT is known not only as a humorist, but
     also as a moralist, "and it is not unlikely
     that as such he will go down to posterity,"
     although the present volume consists of
     humorous writings. "Mark Twain never re-
     sorts to tricks of spelling nor rhetorical
     buffoonery for the purpose of provoking a
     laugh...there are few who can resist the
     quaint similies, keen satire, and hard good
     sense which form the staple of his writ-
     ings." Reprinted in Scott (1955), p. 12;
     (1967), p. 12.

1868 A BOOKS - NONE

1868 B SHORTER WRITINGS

B1   [HARTE, BRET.] [Review: John Franklin Swift,
     Going to Jericho; or, Sketches of Travel in
     Spain and the East.] Overland Monthly, I
     (July), 101-103.

This book "is in legitimate literary succession to Howell's [sic] Venetian Life,
Ross Browne's multifarious voyages, and Mark
Twain's Holy Land letters. It is somewhat
notable that three of these writers are Cal-
ifornians, and all from the west." Comments
on MT's use of "brickbats on stained glass
windows with damaging effect" and his "lawless humor and lyric fire." [Note that this
precedes the 1869 book publication of MT's
newspaper letters in IA.]

1869 A BOOKS - NONE

1869 B SHORTER WRITINGS

B1   *ANON. [Review: Innocents Abroad.] Buffalo
     Express, October 16.
       [Source: Reprinted in Anderson (1971),
     pp. 25-26.] MT was a part owner of the Ex-
     press when this review appeared; it is com-
     mendatory.

B2   ANON. [Review: Innocents Abroad.] Nation
     (New York), IX (September 2), 194-95.
       Some of this imitates other writing in the
     genre and it is padded for sale by subscrip-
     tion, "but if some of the book is needless,
     none of it is really poor, and much of it
     very good." It is of some value as descrip-
     tion, and fresh and well-told. Reprinted in
     Anderson (1971), pp. 21-22.

B3   *ANON. [Review: Innocents Abroad.] Packard's
     Monthly, II (October), 318-19.
       [Source: Reprinted in Anderson (1971),
     pp. 23-24.] Places MT "first among American
     humorists. It is, indeed, doubtful if he
     has ever had an equal; he certainly has not
     had in his line--that of dry, self-contained,
     unobtrusive and pervading fun."

B4   *CLEMENS, SAMUEL L. [Letter, satirizing a snob-
     bish American family just returned from Eu-
     rope.] Boston Transcript (December 29),
     p. 1.
       [Source: Quoted by Arthur L. Vogelback
     (1948), p. 111, n. 1.]

B5   *"FOLIO, TOM." [Review: Innocents Abroad.]
     Boston Evening Transcript (December 15),
     p. 1.
       [Source: Reprinted in Anderson (1971),
     pp. 31-32.] Praises MT's humor and keen ob-
     servation.

B6   [HOWELLS, WILLIAM DEAN.] [Review: Innocents
     Abroad.] Atlantic Monthly, XXIV (December),
     764-66.
       The humor is "droll," "good-natured,"
     "not always delicate," but reflecting human
     nature. The book will give MT a reputation
     as more than a newspaper humorist. Reprint-
     ed in his My Mark Twain (1910), pp. 107-12;
     also in Anderson (1971), pp. 27-30.

1870 A BOOKS - NONE

1870 B SHORTER WRITINGS

B1   *ANON. [Brief biography of MT.] Frank Les-
     lie's Illustrated Newspaper, July 16.
          [Source: Twainian, II (February, 1940),
     7.]

B2   ANON. [Review: Innocents Abroad.] Athe-
     naeum, No. 2239 (September 24), 394-95.
          Recognizes MT's satire as encompassing
     not only the sights and experiences of his
     trip, but also the limitations of his fel-
     low-tourists. Reprinted in Anderson (1971),
     pp. 36-38.

B3   ANON. [Review: Innocents Abroad.] Saturday
     Review (London), XXX (October 8), 467-68.
          Compares MT and his companions to the
     Cook's tourist type of traveler, although
     MT is frank and original in his remarks.
     "In short, his pages may be turned over
     with amusement, as exhibiting more or less
     consciously a very lively portrait of the
     uncultivated American tourist, who may be
     more obtrusive, but not quite so stupidly un-
     observing as our native product. We should
     not choose either of them for our compan-
     ions on a visit to a church or a picture-
     gallery, but we should expect most amuse-
     ment from the Yankee as long as we could
     stand him." Reprinted in Scott (1967),
     pp. 17-21; in Anderson (1971), pp. 36-43.

B4   *BIERCE, AMBROSE. "Town Crier" page, San
     Francisco News-Letter, February 19.
          "Mark Twain, who, whenever he has been
     long enough sober to permit an estimate,
     has been uniformly found to bear a spotless
     character, has got married. It was not the
     act of a desperate man--it was not committed
     while laboring under temporary insanity;
     his insanity is not of that type, nor does
     he ever labor--it was the cool, methodical,
     cumulative, culmination of human nature
     working in the heart of an orphan hankering
     for some one with a fortune to love--some
     one with a bank account to caress. For
     years he has felt this matrimony coming on.
     Ever since he left California there has
     been an undertone of despair running
     through all his letters like the subdued
     wail of a pig in a wash-tub." [Source:
     Quoted by Carey McWilliams in Ambrose
     Bierce: A Biography (1929), p. 88.]

B5   *CABLE, GEORGE WASHINGTON. "Drop Shot," New
     Orleans Picayune, July 17.
          [Source: Reprinted in Turner (1960),
     pp. 4-5.] A regular column, here comparing
     MT and Josh Billings (Henry Wheeler Shaw):
     MT may have "the superior weight of mind,"
     although Cable is more drawn to Josh, "such
     a blessed old fool."

B6   *EGGLESTON, EDWARD. "The November Magazines,"
     The Independent, October 27.
          Eggleston said he was amused by an MT
     sketch in the Galaxy, but was more impressed
     by a poem by Helen Hunt in the same issue.
     [Source: William Peirce Randel, Edward Eg-
     gleston (1947), p. 109.]

B7   [HARTE, BRET.] [Review: Innocents
     Abroad.] Overland Monthly, IV (January),
     100-101.
          Note's MT's fresh vision, although he
     "seems to have followed his guide and guide-
     books with a simple, unconscious fidelity."
     He shows a "serious eloquence," though lack-
     ing "that balance of pathos which we deem
     essential to complete humor." Reprinted in
     Scott (1955), pp. 13-16; (1967), pp. 13-16;
     Cardwell (1963), pp. 1-4; Anderson (1971),
     pp. 32-35.

B8   *HINGSTON, EDWARD P. [Introduction.] The In-
     nocents Abroad. London: John Camden Hotten.
          [Source: Henderson (1911), p. 215;
     Asselineau (1954), No. 1.]

B9   *WARD, WILLIAM. "American Humorists," Macon
     (Mississippi) Beacon (May 14), p. 2.
          [Source: Reprinted in Anderson (1971),
     pp. 44-45.] "But, since Irving, no humor-
     ist in prose has laid the foundation of a
     permanent fame, except it be Mark Twain,
     and this, as in the case of Irving, because
     he is a pure writer. Aside from the subtle
     mirth that lurks through his compositions,
     the grace and finish of his more didactic
     and descriptive sentences indicate more than
     mediocrity, though much of his writing has
     a dash of Bulwer in it."

1871 A BOOKS

A1   *GRISWOLD, MRS. STEPHEN. A Woman's Pilgrimage
     to the Holy Land; or, Pleasant Days Abroad.
     Hartford: J. B. Burr & Hyde.
          [Source: Ganzel (1968), p. xiii and
     passim.] Reminiscences by a fellow-traveler
     on the Quaker City tour on which IA was
     based. See 1907.B21.

1871 B SHORTER WRITINGS

B1   ANON. "American Humour," Graphic (London)
     III (April 1), 295.
          MT, "who does not equal either 'Josh Bil-
     lings' or 'Orpheus C. Kerr,' has rather a
     forced sense of humour"; the writer likes
     MT "best when he is serious, and he can be
     both earnest and poetical," though he lacks
     the genius of Bret Harte.

B2   ANON. "The Literature of the United States in
     1870," Athenaeum, No. 2254 (January 7),
     p. 15.
          Briefly mentions IA, which shows "real
     travels in the East, as they impressed one
     of the drollest of voyagers. But the palm

1871 - Shorter Writings

(ANON.)
must this year be awarded to Mr. Bret Harte, author of The Luck of Roaring Camp, and Other Sketches..."

B3   ANON. "Mark Twain," Leisure Hour (London), No. 1039 (November 25), 752.
     Reprints from the River Column of the St. Louis Republican (n.d.) an account of MT's writing a sketch of Captain Sellers, steamboat pilot. "After he had written the article, he inquired of John Morris, now steward of the Belle Memphis, what name he should sign to it," and at that moment heard a leadsman sing out "Mark Twain." "This sketch...was subsequently placed in the hand of Mr. T. E. Garrett, who was at that time River editor of this journal, and it found a place in the River department of the Republican. It proved to be a decided hit, and was extensively copied by Western journals." [MT's real name is given as "Clements."]

B4   *CLEMENS, SAMUEL L. [Letter on Ruloff murder case.] New York Tribune, April 29.
     [Source: Cited in Vogelback (1948), p. 112, n. 2, and by Paine in Mark Twain, I, 436-37; text appears ibid., III, as Appendix K, 1628-29. Signed "Samuel Langhorne."]

1872 A BOOKS

A1   WARNER, CHARLES DUDLEY. Backlog Studies. Boston: James R. Osgood and Company (Reprinted Boston and New York: Houghton, Mifflin and Company, 1899).
     Conversations in the Nook Farm community in Hartford; MT is "Our Next Door," Joseph Twichell is "The Parson," etc.

1872 B SHORTER WRITINGS

B1   ANON. "Literary Notes," Book Section, The Academy, III (August 1), 283.
     Item in full: "M. [sic] Th. Bentzon begins a series of sketches of American humorists with an account of Mark Twain in the Revue des Deux Mondes (July 15). His criticisms are quite unexceptionable, but he seems to have been misled by the advertisements of a certain type of publisher, so that he exaggerates the popularity of his author, while expressing surprise at its extent."

B2   *ANON. "Mark Twain's Pipe," San Francisco Chronicle, n.d.; reprinted in Cleveland Herald Supplement, November 2.
     [Source: Quoted in Fatout (1964), pp. 36-37.] On a small, convivial group who first called themselves the "Companions of the Jug," and later "The Visigoths."

B3   ANON. "Uncivilised America," Manchester Guardian (March 6), p. 7.
     Includes a review of Roughing It; largely descriptive, setting MT's humor below that of Artemus Ward: "Mark Twain, too, often falls into the slang of transatlantic journalism, and displays also its characteristic inability to distinguish between the picturesque and the grotesque." Reprinted in Anderson (1971), pp. 46-47.

B4   ANON. [Review: Roughing It.] Overland Monthly, VIII (June), 580-81.
     The rollicking humor is "genuine, and thoroughly enjoyable," but there are also "fresh descriptions of natural scenery" and "impressive narrative." Reprinted in Anderson (1971), pp. 49-51.

B5   ANON. [Review: Screamers, an unauthorized edition of short pieces by MT (some signed "Carl Byng"). London: John Camden Hotten.] Spectator, XLV (May 18), 633-34.
     Places MT below Bret Harte, John Hay, and Artemus Ward in subtlety; "yet Mark Twain ranks high, and is much more certain to be understood and appreciated by a general public, especially in countries where the politics, manners, customs, and tone of thought of Americans are comparatively little known." "The book is rather a hotchpotch, and of very unequal merit. The tales are not all 'screamers.' Some even have a distinctly serious purpose, though put humorously."

B6   BENTZON, TH[ÉRÈSE] (MME. MARIE-THÉRÈSE BLANC). "Les Humoristes Américains: I. Mark Twain," Revue des Deux Mondes, C (July 15), 313-35.
     An introduction of MT to French readers, including a translation of "The Jumping Frog" (pp. 314-319) and discussions of IA and RI. Concludes by expressing the hope that although Bret Harte and MT are still strong fare for the French, "bientôt nous serons accoutumés à une langue américaine dont la verdeur savoureuse n'est pas à dédaigner, en attendant les qualités plus délicates et plus relevées que le temps lui apportera sans doute."

B7   [Caricature of MT.] Once-A-Week (London), XXVII (December 14), 519, 521.
     MT is depicted astride his jumping frog on p. 519, and there is a brief, descriptive appreciation of him on p. 521 (one of a series of caricatures of public figures).

B8   CLEMENS, SAMUEL L. "Mark Twain and His English Editor," Spectator, XLV (September 21), 1201-1202.
     A letter to the editor, accusing John Camden Hotten of having produced a pirated edition of his work as Screamers, with the addition of material attributed to "Carl Byng"--a nom de plume MT disavows. [See Hotten's reply, 1872.B12.]

B9 *____. [Letter, describing a rescue at sea by the crew of the Batavia, together with commentary by the editors.] Boston Transcript (November 26), p. 1.
     The account also appeared in the New York Tribune (Nov. 27), p. 1, and there is further MT correspondence on the topic and editorial commentary there in 1873 (January 27, p. 4; April 11, p. 5).
     [Source: Discussed and quoted by Arthur L. Vogelback in "Mark Twain: Newspaper Contributor," AL, XX (May), 114-17.]

B10 *____. [Letter.] Spectator (London), September 20.
     On Routledge as his authorized English publisher. [Source: Reprinted in Grenander, (1975), p. 2; p. 4, n. 8 adds: "Reprinted in Charles Meeker Kozlay, The Lectures of Bret Harte (Brooklyn--New York: Charles Meeker Kozlay, 1909), p. 51. This letter was picked up and commented on by The Nation, 15 (October 10, 1872), 234-35."]

B11 *EGGLESTON, EDWARD. "H.G.," Hearth and Home, (February 24).
     On Horace Greeley. Eggleston had joined Bret Harte, John Hay, and MT in celebrating his sixty-fifth birthday. [Source: Cited by William Peirce Randel in Edward Eggleston: Author of "The Hoosier School-Master" (1946), p. 131.]

B12 HOTTEN, JOHN CAMDEN. "'Mark Twain' and His English Editor," Spectator, XLV (September 28), 1237.
     A letter to the editor, defending himself against MT's charges a week before (1872-B8). Attributing the "Carl Byng" material to MT simply follows the prevalent belief that it is his work. Hotten denies that he is a pirate: the material he has taken has no copyright protection in England, if it succeeds anybody can bring out a cheaper edition; moreover, three letters to MT (one offering payment) have gone unanswered.

B13 [HOWELLS, WILLIAM DEAN.] [Unsigned Review: Roughing It.] Atlantic Monthly, XXIX (June), 48-49.
     Descriptive and appreciative. Reprinted in his My Mark Twain (1910), pp. 113-14. and in Anderson (1971), pp. 48-49.

1873 A BOOKS - NONE

1873 B SHORTER WRITINGS

B1 ANON. "Cracking Jokes," Once-A-Week (London), n.s. XII (November 8), 402-405.
     A review of MT's Hanover Square lectures ("Our Fellow Savages of the Sandwich Islands"); chiefly descriptive, followed by quotations from his books, "brimming over with fun."

B2 ANON. "Mark Twain," Every Saturday (Boston), IV (November 15), 555-56.
     On MT's lecture on the Sandwich Islands and on the nature of his humor, which is lesser than that of Artemus Ward but may bring him even greater popularity. [Reprinted from London Spectator, according to Twainian, II (February, 1940), 6.]

B3 ANON. "The Sandwich Islands," Saturday Review (London), XXXVI (October 18), 503-504.
     Chiefly on the interest of the history of the islands, with passing reference to MT's current lecture on the subject.

B4 ANON. "Twain Can Do't," Punch, LXV (December 20), 248.
     Various plays on MT's name, regret that his stay in London will be brief; readers are urged to go hear him lecture.

B4a *ANON. [Account of MT's "Our Fellow Savages of the Sandwich Islands" lecture.] The Brooklyn Eagle, February 8.
     [Source: Listed in Lorch (1958), p. 54, n. 12.]

B5 ANON. [Advertisement of MT's lecture on "Our Fellow Savages of the Sandwich Islands."] Graphic (London), VIII (October 11), 335.

B6 ANON. [Review of MT's lecture on "Our Fellow Savages of the Sandwich Islands."] Graphic (London), VIII (December 6), 539.
     A brief account of a successful evening, marked by MT's "quaint humour" and "curious anecdotes and bits of sly satire...The peroration...was a splendid piece of word-painting."

B7 ANON. [Brief comment on MT's new London lecture on the "Silver Frontier."] Graphic (London), VIII (December 13), 534.
     It would be "a hopeless task" to give a condensation of the lecture, since "his quaint conceits follow each other with so little intermission that one has scarcely time to straighten one's features ere they are puckered o'er by some fresh jest or tall story."

B8 *ANON. [Reports on MT's arrangements for London publication of GA.] New York Daily Graphic, November 5, p. 29; November 8, p. 54.
     [Source: Grenander (1975), p. 4, n. 10.]

B9 *CLEMENS, SAMUEL L. [Letters, praising the crew of the Batavia for a rescue at sea he witnessed and urging the establishment in America of a Humane Society like England's; also, editorial commentary.] New York Tribune, January 27, p. 4; April 11, p. 5.
     MT's eyewitness account of the rescue appeared in the Boston Transcript (November 26, 1872), p. 1, and New York Tribune (November 27, 1872), p. 1. [Source: Vogelback (1948), pp. 114-17.]

1873 - Shorter Writings

B10   *[Commentary supporting MT's proposal that
        ships be equipped with life-rafts instead
        of life-boats.] Chicago Tribune, April 26,
        p. 4.
          [Source: Quoted in Vogelback (1948),
        p. 119. Also see New York Tribune for this
        period, as discussed by Vogelback.]

B11   *[Discussions of Foster murder case in New York
        Tribune.] Editorial (March 6, p. 6); MT
        letter to editor (March 10, p. 5); letter
        by "H.K." criticizing MT's "ghastly flip-
        pancy" (March 11, p. 5).
          [Source: Quoted in Vogelback (1948),
        pp. 112-13.]

B12   HART, JOHN S. A Manual of American Litera-
        ture: A Text-Book for Schools and Colleges.
        Philadelphia: Eldredge & Brothers,
        pp. 437-42. (Reprinted New York, London:
        Johnson Reprint Corporation, 1969.)
          In a section on American humorists, pre-
        sents a purely uncritical biographical sum-
        mary, followed by excerpts from IA.

B13   *[HOTTEN, JOHN CAMDEN.] [Introduction.] The
        Choice Humorous Tales of Mark Twain. Lon-
        don: John Camden Hotten.
          [Source: Henderson (1911), p. 215.]

B14   *[Sandwich Islands annexation debated in New
        York Tribune.]
          MT describes the Islands (January 6, p. 4);
        editorial on the annexation question
        (January 9, pp. 4, 5); MT letter on Prince
        Lunalilo and the native drinking habits, and
        a scathing portrait of Harris, one of the
        "Royal Ministers" (ibid., pp. 4, 5); further
        Tribune comment on the issue and MT's in-
        volvement (January 10, p. 4; January 22,
        p. 4; February 5, p. 4; February 8, p. 4).
        [Source: Discussed and quoted by Arthur L.
        Vogelback (1948), pp. 119-25. Vogelback
        takes issue with the treatment of the MT
        letters of January 6 and 9 by Paine and
        Frear (p. 123, n. 24).]

1874 A BOOKS - NONE

1874 B SHORTER WRITINGS

B1   ANON. "American Literature," Saturday Review
        (London), XXXVII (January 24), 125-28.
          A review-article, with brief notice on
        p. 128: "The name of Mark Twain will be a
        sufficient recommendation of The Gilded
        Age, a three-volume novel of the English
        form, purporting to be jointly written by
        him and Mr. C. D. Warner."

B2   *ANON. "Mark Twain Toasts the Scotch," Lafay-
        ette (Indiana) Daily Courier, January 14.
          [Source: Reprinted in Twainian, XVI
        (November-December, 1957), 4 (1957.B2).]

B3   *ANON. "Mark Twain's Trails in London," New
        York Daily Graphic, January 15, p. 499.
          [Source: Cited in Grenander (1975),
        p. 4.] On MT's lectures; reprints a humor-
        ous MT letter to the London Post.

B4   ANON. [Review: The Gilded Age.] Athenaeum,
        No. 2411 (January 10), 53.
          "We think it is just possible that the
        authors, one or both, may have it in them to
        produce a story which we may read without
        fatigue, and without constant jars to our
        taste, while it shall have no lack of humour;
        but we cannot say that in The Gilded Age
        they have reached this desirable consumma-
        tion."

B5   ANON. [Review: The Gilded Age.] Graphic
        (London), IX (February 28), 199.
          "If any Englishman had ventured on a pic-
        ture of American manners and institutions
        half as highly coloured, he would at once
        have been loudly accused of the most rancor-
        ous spite and the grossest misrepresenta-
        tion." As a novel, the book is occasionally
        clever, but a failure because of poor con-
        struction; "The best character is decidedly
        the speculative 'Colonel' Eschol Sellers."

B6   ANON. [Review: The Gilded Age.] Old and New
        (Boston), IX (March), 386-88.
          "There is great power in the book, and of
        an uncommon kind. It is a determined and
        bitter satire," but "without comment and
        moral explanation." The review barely men-
        tions Colonel Sellers and describes the
        portrayal of Senator Dilworthy as crude and
        over-close, but "For two men situated as the
        authors of The Gilded Age are situated, it
        is a remarkably well-executed work; and
        without any relative or qualifying expres-
        sion, it is a book of real and high purpose,
        much graphic and portrait power, much knowl-
        edge of men and things, and uncommon swift-
        ness and force of action."

B7   *[BURLINGAME, EDWARD.] [Review: The Gilded
        Age.] Appleton's Journal, XI (January 10),
        59.
          [Source: Identified by John W. Crowley in
        "A Note on the Gilded Age," 1972.]

B8   FERRIS, GEORGE T. "Mark Twain," Appleton's
        Journal, XII (July 4), 15-18.
          A popular account, with portrait, largely
        biographical. MT's humor is "so genial, so
        charged with rich and unctuous [sic] humor,
        that we forget the lack of finesse and deli-
        cacy in its breadth and strength." Reprint-
        ed in Scott (1955), pp. 17-22; (1967),
        pp. 22-27.

B9   *LIKENS, MRS. J. W. Six Years Experience as a
        Book Agent in California. San Francisco:
        Women's Union Book and Job Printing Office.
          Mrs. Likens found GA sold very well.
        [Source: Cited by Bryant Morey French in
        Mark Twain and "The Gilded Age" (1965),
        pp. 6, 9.]

1875 A BOOKS - NONE

1875 B SHORTER WRITINGS

B1　BENTZON, TH[ÉRÈSE] (MME. MARIE-THÉRÈSE BLANC). "L'Age Doré en Amérique," Revue des Deux Mondes, VIII (March 15), 319-43.
　　　A review of GA (1874), which, as the work of MT and Charles Dudley Warner ("talent plus sage et moins original"), is difficult to read, with "une exubérante confusion, un mélange de bon sens et de folie" attributable to MT's audacious humor.

B2　*CLEMENS, SAMUEL L. "Mark Twain on Spelling," Saint Louis Republican, May 23.
　　　[Source: Reprinted without comment in Missouri Historical Review, XXV (April), 532-33.] Text of an introductory speech by MT before a spelling match at the Asylum Hill Congregational Church, Hartford, Connecticut.

B3　*_____. [Letter, urging American support for a Shakespeare theater at Stratford-on-Avon (reprinted by several papers around the country), and editorial comments.] New York Times, April 29, p. 6; Boston Transcript, May 1, p. 6; Chicago Tribune, May 7, p. 4 (editorial).
　　　[Source: Discussed and quoted in Vogelback (1948), pp. 124-25.]

B4　*HOWELLS, WILLIAM DEAN. [Review: Sketches, New and Old.] Atlantic, XXXVI (December). 749-51.
　　　[Source: Reprinted in his My Mark Twain (1910), pp. 120-24; also in Anderson (1971), pp. 52-55.] Notes MT's growing seriousness in this book, especially in "A True Story," in which "the rugged truth of the sketch leaves all other stories of slave life infinitely far behind, and reveals a gift in the author for the simple dramatic report of reality which we have seen equaled in no other American writer."

1876 A BOOKS - NONE

1876 B SHORTER WRITINGS

B1　ANON. "American Literature," Saturday Review (London), XLI (January 29), 154.
　　　A review of Sketches, New and Old (1875). The sketches "are nearly all capital, and all of them worthy of the author; short and lively, for the most part free from vulgarity and offence, raising a smile more often than provoking a roar of laughter, but always amusing."

B2　ANON. [Review: Tom Sawyer.] Athenaeum, No. 2539 (June 24), p. 851.
　　　MT is already known in England as a popular comic like Artemus Ward, but in this new book "The humour is not always uproar-

ious, but it is always genuine and sometimes almost pathetic, and it is only now and then that the heartiness of a laugh is spoilt by one of those pieces of self-consciousness which are such common blots on Mark Twain's other works. The Adventures of Tom Sawyer is an attempt in a new direction. It is consecutive, and much longer than the former books," though not strictly a novel or "even a story, for that presupposes a climax and a finish; nor is it a mere boys' book of adventures." Reprinted in Anderson (1971), pp. 64-65.

B3　ANON. [Review: Tom Sawyer.] British Quarterly Review, LXIII (October), 264.
　　　"The book is full of roaring fun, interspersed with true pathos.... It might... have given more emphasis to truth and straightforwardness. But it is irresistible; fully up to the mark of the 'Innocents Abroad.'"

B4　*ANON. [Review: Tom Sawyer.] Times (London), August 28, p. 4.
　　　Praises the humor in this story of a boy whose "eventful career exhibits an unprecedented precocity." [Source: Reprinted in Anderson (1971), pp. 66-68.]

B5　*[CONWAY, MONCURE D.] [Review: Tom Sawyer.] Examiner (London), June 17, pp. 687-88.
　　　[Source: Reprinted in Anderson (1971), pp. 62-64, noting another Conway review of TS June 26, in the Cincinnati Commercial.] Praises MT's humor and vivid, apt description; regrets the book is not longer.

B6　*HOWELLS, WILLIAM DEAN. [Review: Tom Sawyer.] Atlantic, XXXVII (May), 621-22.
　　　[Source: Reprinted in his My Mark Twain (1910), pp. 125-28, giving original Atlantic publication as December, 1875; also reprinted in Cardwell (1963), pp. 4-5, and in Anderson (1971), pp. 59-61.] Praises the portrait of boy-nature.

B7　LITTLEDALE, RICHARD F. "New Novels," Academy, IX (June 24), 604-605.
　　　On p. 605, a brief description of TS, ending: "The book is designed primarily for boys, but older people will also find it worth looking through."

B8　*TURNER, MATTHEW FREKE. "Artemus Ward and the Humourists of America," New Quarterly Magazine, No. 11 (April), pp. 208-12.
　　　[Source: Reprinted in Anderson (1971), pp. 55-58.] Probably based on Eye Openers (1875). Only MT and Bret Harte deserve "any kind of public criticism," and MT's is a low humor, ridiculing sacred things, forced, long-winded, tedious in his parodies. "It will be seen that Mark Twain is, by no means, a genial, kindly humourist, like his predecessor, Artemus Ward; that, though he hits the same blots, his mode of attack is altogether different. Mark Twain is a jester,

1876 - Shorter Writings

(TURNER, MATTHEW FREKE)
and very little more. When he is not on the trail of some joke, he is apt to be insufferably tedious."

B9 WHIPPLE, EDWIN P. "The First Century of the Republic (Seventeenth Paper)," Harper's Monthly, LII (March), 514-23.
Describes popular humorists such as Artemus Ward and John Phoenix, pp. 525-26. "Mark Twain, the most widely popular of this class of humorists, is a man of wide experience, keen intellect, and literary culture. The serious portions of his writings indicate that he could win a reputation in literature even if he had not been blessed with a humorous faculty inexhaustible in resource."

B6 [JOHNSON, ROBERT UNDERWOOD.] "A New Book by Mark Twain," Scribner's Monthly, XIII (April), 874-75.
A tongue-in-cheek review of Mark Twain's Adhesive Scrap-Book (1873). Reprinted in Twainian, VII (July-August, 1948) attributing the review to Johnson on the basis of a statement in his Remembered Yesterdays (1923).

B7 *[Sketch, by or of MT.] World (London), December 20.
[Source: Dixon Wecter, "Frank Finlay; or, The Thameside Tenderfoot in the Wooly West," Twainian, VI (July-August, 1947), 1-4. A letter from Finlay of that date refers to "a well-meant but imperfect sketch of one Mark Twain in the World of today."]

1877 A BOOKS - NONE

1877 B SHORTER WRITINGS

B1 *ANON. "The Ship-Owners and Mr. Duncan," New York Times (date not available).
On the accusations against Captain Duncan of the Quaker City, involving misuse of funds. [Source: Reprinted in Twainian, XI (July-August, 1952), 3-4.]

B2 ANON. "Twain and Harte's New Play: Its First Production in Washington," Argonaut (San Francisco), I (May 19), 5.
A long, descriptive review of the play Ah Sin. "The plot of the play and cast of characters is decidedly Californian, so much so as to suggest that it is but a re-vamping of 'The Two Men of Sandy Bar,' written by Bret Harte and brought to grief by the same unkind means that brought Anna Dickinson low--dramatically speaking."

B3 *ANON. [Review: Tom Sawyer (1876).] New York Times, January 13, p. 3.
[Source: Reprinted in Anderson (1971), pp. 69-72.] Praises MT's humor and accurate portrayal of Tom's world (although he is somewhat precocious), but finds the violence rather strong for young readers.

B4 *CASSIDY, GEORGE W. [Statement that the pseudonym "Mark Twain" was derived from S. L. C.'s custom of asking a Virginia City bartender to chalk up drinks for himself and a friend.] Eureka, Nevada Sentinel, May 8.
[Source: Quoted in Fatout (1964), pp. 35-36.]

B5 *CLEMENS, SAMUEL L. "Mark Twain on His Muscle. Emulating MacBeth, He Kills Duncan Over Again. The 'Innocent' at Home Tells the Story of His Crimes Abroad," New York World, February 18.
Letter to the editor, criticizing the captain of the Quaker City. [Source: Reprinted in Twainian, XI (July-August, 1952), 3-4.]

1878 A BOOKS - NONE

1878 B SHORTER WRITINGS

B1 ANON. "Mark Twain at Home," Leisure Hour, No. 1389 (August 10), 510-11.
Briefly describing an interview with MT, notes "the excellency of his literary taste" and calls him not a "professional humorist," but "a constitutional humorist," in his point of view toward any subject.

B2 *ANON. [Description of MT's Hartford house.] English World, January, 1878.
[Source: Quoted in Blair (1960), p. 16.]

B3 WAKEMAN, CAPTAIN EDGAR. The Log of an Ancient Mariner. Being the Life and Adventures of Captain Edgar Wakeman. Written by Himself, and Edited by His Daughter [Minnie Wakeman-Curtis.] San Francisco: A. L. Bancroft & Co., Printers.
Wakeman was the "Ned Blakely" of RI, and appeared elsewhere under various names, including "Hurricane Jones" and "Captain Stormfield."

1879 A BOOKS - NONE

1879 B SHORTER WRITINGS

B1 ANON. "Table Talk." Gentleman's Magazine, CCXLVI (April), 505.
Brief mention of an MT story.

B2 *ANON. [Interview.] Hartford Courant, May 14, p. 1, col. 8.
MT comments that what can be satirized in England can also be found nearer home. [Source: Quoted in Baetzhold (1970), pp: 76-77.]

B3 *CLEMENS, SAMUEL L. Letters to Hartford Courant, concerning new postal order requiring more complete addresses on letters; as reprinted by the Boston Transcript (November 28, p. 3; December 11, p. 4;

(*CLEMENS, SAMUEL L.)
December 12, p. 4) and the Chicago Tribune (November 29, p. 13). Also, a reply to MT by the private secretary to the Postmaster-General (Boston Transcript, December 11, p. 4).
[Source: Discussed and quoted in Vogelback (1948), pp. 126-27. The private secretary to the Postmaster-General mentioned having read MT's letter in the Cincinnati Inquirer (date not given).]

B4   *YATES, EDMUND. "Mark Twain at Hartford," in his Celebrities at Home, n.p. Reprinted from The World (London). Third Series.
[Source: Henderson (1911), p. 216.]

1880 A BOOKS - NONE

1880 B SHORTER WRITINGS

B1   ANON. "Mark Twain and Dan De Quille," Argonaut (San Francisco), VI (January 31), 6.
An apocryphal story, reprinted from the Carson Appeal, of an attempt by Dan De Quille (William Wright) and MT to start a paper in Mendocino County; on their way there they were attacked by Indians and used up their type as shot in defending themselves--so they went on to Virginia City and took jobs on the Enterprise.

B2   ANON. "Mark Twain on Plagiarism," Leisure Hour, No. 1482 (May 15), p. 320.
Quotes MT's account of having unconsciously borrowed a dedication to a book from Oliver Wendell Holmes; provides no new information or perspective.

B3   ANON. [Review: A Tramp Abroad.] British Quarterly Review, LXXII (July), 228-29.
"Mr. Mark Twain is a lively companion. He indulges in the kind of facetiae which luckily, to a great degree, please the cultured and uncultured alike," but "he is apt...to practice his trick too often; so that it is not advisable to read too much of him all at once.... But Mr. Mark Twain is delightful. No more pleasant and airy pages, or fuller of sudden and playful antitheses, have recently been given to the public."

B4   ANON. [Review: A Tramp Abroad.] Graphic (London), XXI (May 1), 451.
"Writing pleasantly about well-known things...Mark Twain's charm is that he puts things so unexpectedly--says the very thing which nobody would ever think of saying"; some of his topics are briefly listed.

B5   ANON. [Review: A Tramp Abroad.] Saturday Review (London), XLIX (April 17), 514-15.
The book contains some good things, among them Jim Baker's story about the blue-jay and the "Tale of the Fishwife and Its Sad Fate," but as a whole is too long, often

dull, and carelessly put together; it should be read in snatches, with judicious skipping, and will then "furnish a good deal of genuine amusement." Reprinted in Anderson (1971), pp. 76-80.

B6   [HENLEY, WILLIAM ERNEST.] [Unsigned Review: A Tramp Abroad.] Athenaeum, No. 2739 (April 24), pp. 529-30.
"He has a keen, sure sense of character and uncommon skill in presenting it dramatically; and he is also an admirable storyteller, with the anecdotic instinct and habit in perfection." Reprinted in Anderson (1971), pp. 73-76, with attribution to Henley.

B7   [HOWELLS, WILLIAM DEAN]. [Review: A Tramp Abroad.] Atlantic Monthly, XLV (May), 686-88.
Attempts by others to imitate MT have failed, and this new book is enlightening and delightful. Reprinted in his My Mark Twain (1910), pp. 129-33, and in Anderson (1971), pp. 81-84.

1881 A BOOKS - NONE

1881 B SHORTER WRITINGS

B1   ANON. Facts. By a Woman. Oakland, California: Pacific Press Publishing House.
On her experiences in selling TS by subscription in the area of Oroville, California, pp. 34-53.

B2   ANON. "Personating Mark Twain," The Californian: A Western Monthly Magazine, IV (July), 97-98.
From an exchange copy of another journal (not named), an anecdote of the Honorable DeShane Hornet, a temperance lecturer who was asked to substitute when MT could not keep a lecturer engagement in Gloucester; not realizing a change had been made, the audience greeted Hornet's every remark with laughter and he angrily walked out.

B3   ANON. [Brief Review: The Prince and the Pauper.] Athenaeum, No. 2826 (December 24), p. 849.
"A heavy disappointment...some four hundred pages of careful tediousness, mitigated by occasional flashes of unintentional and unconscious fun...if to convert a brilliant and engaging humourist into a dull and painful romancer be necessarily a function of the study of history, it cannot be too steadily discouraged." Reprinted in Anderson (1971), pp. 91-92 (quoting what MT later said about the reviewer).

B4   ANON. [Review: The Prince and the Pauper.] Critic, I (December 31), 368.
This is not a complete change of direction: "What has made Mark Twain's extravagant humour so effective has been (apart from its

(ANON.)
more glaring qualities) the skillfully
painted background of more subdued and often
delicate description."

B5 *[BOYESON, H. H.] "Mark Twain's New Departure," Atlantic, XLVIII (December), 843-45.
[Source: Reprinted in Anderson (1971),
pp. 85-89).] A review of P&P; praises MT
in his new role "as the author of a tale
ingenious in conception, pure and humane in
purpose, artistic in method, and, with
barely a flaw, refined in execution."

B6 *HOWE, E. W. [On MT.] Atchinson (Kansas)
Globe, December 31, p. 3.
"Mark Twain's career is nearly at an end.
The paragraphists have commenced to pelt
him, and they will finish him before they
get through. His wit has been watered until it is without flavor." [Source: Quoted by S. J. Sackett in his E. W. Howe (New
York: Twayne Publishers, Inc., 1972),
p. 74.]

B7 PURCELL, E. [Review: The Prince and the
Pauper.] Academy (London), XX
(December 24), 469.
"A ponderous fantasia on English history,"
in which "a few smart sayings relieve the
monotony of a prolix work singularly defi-
cient in literary merit." Reprinted in
Anderson (1971), pp. 90-91.

1882 A BOOKS - NONE

1882 SHORTER WRITINGS

B1 *ANON. "California Writers: Mark Twain,"
The Occident (Berkeley, California)
November 10.
[Source: Twainian, II (April, 1943).]

B2 ANON. "Mark Twain Tries to Pull Wool Over
the Marines, But Doesn't," Vicksburg Daily
Herald, April 26.
[Possibly reprinted from the Memphis
Ledger.] On MT's attempt to revisit his
old haunts incognito while gathering material for the expanded LOM: he registered
at the Peabody Hotel as "C. L. Samuels."
Also tells apocryphal stories about MT
as cub pilot on the old Aleck Scott, under
Captain Bart Bowen: "he used to play
pranks on the celebrated Captain Isaiah
Sellers, the pilot on the other watch, who
was hard to awaken." [Transcript provided
by William Van S. Carhart.]

B3 ANON. "Mark Twain Visits the Historic City
and Takes Some Views of Things as They
Exist in These Parts. How He Looked to a
Casual Observer," Vicksburg Daily Herald,
April 27.
General description. MT "looked yester-
day, like a man who had just escaped from
a lunatic asylum, whose only sense was in

the perfect realization of that fact, and
whose every energy was concentrated in an
effort to dodge its keeper." [Transcript
provided by William Van S. Carhart.]

B4 ANON. [Review: Innocents Abroad.] British
Quarterly Review, LXXV (January), 101.
This book is too well-known to need
lengthy description. MT "always avoids irreverence" in his description of Palestine
and skillfully balances between exaggeration
and subtlety. "It consitiutes a type; and
the wisdom is as much as the wit, the serious meaning as the outrageous extravagance."

B5 ANON. [Review: The Prince and the Pauper.]
British Quarterly Review, LXXV (January),
118.
MT "has written a story which gives a vivid idea of a historical period, but which
outrages history at every point in the most
daring and barefaced manner.... We do not
think that this sort of writing in ordinary
hands would be advisable for the young of
any age...but Mr. Mark Twain's fun and satiric chaff, his mingled humour and pathos,
his fine perception of human nature, and his
nimble fancy make him an exception," as has
been shown by the experience of young readers.

B6 *ANON. [Review: The Prince and the Pauper.]
Century, XXIII (March), 783-84.
[Source: Reprinted in Anderson (1971),
pp. 92-94, with the suggestion that it may
be a response to the 1881 Boyeson review.]
"So far as it was the author's purpose to
produce a work of art after the old models,
and to prove that the humorous story-teller
and ingenious homely philosopher, Mark
Twain, can be a literary purist, a scholar,
and an antiquary, we do not think his 'new
departure' is a conspicuous success."

B7 ANON. [Review: The Prince and the Pauper.]
Graphic (London), XXV (March 25), 306.
"This delightful story" is for all ages,
with its "subtle plot, marked by the crisp
incisiveness of a clever, though not quite
faultless, style, and...the quaint and shad-
owed mystery--perhaps, too, the barbaric
horror--of medieval times. Its humour is
delicate; its fun joyously real; and its
pathos tender and deep."

B8 ANON. [Brief Review: The Prince and the
Pauper.] Spectator, No. 2795 (January 21),
p. 95.
"An ingenious idea, which has been well
worked out"; the new lives of the two boys
"make a contrast both humorous and pathetic,
and consequently very effective."

B9 ANON. [Review: The Prince and the Pauper.]
Westminster Review, n.s. LXI (April), 576.
"The story has its merits, though it is a
little long, and at times threatens to be
tedious. On the whole, Mr. Mark Twain is
more at home in his earlier efforts."

B10   ANON. [Brief Review: The Stolen White Elephant.] Athenaeum, No. 2852 (June 24), p. 795.
       The title story "is really good work. With 'The Invalid's Story' it is enough to make the book a success, and to compensate for the pompous dulness and the wooden morality of The Prince and the Pauper."

B11   ANON. [Brief Review: The Stolen White Elephant.] British Quarterly Review, LXXVI (October), 247.
       Of these short stories, "some are satirical, others grotesque, a few merely fanciful and touched by sentiment.... Mark Twain is always ingenious, funny, and dashing, but sometimes in satire he overdoes it, and is too much on the 'broad grin.'"

B12   ANON. [Brief note on The Stolen White Elephant.] Critic, II (June 17), 163.
       Among "Minor Notices"; primarily descriptive.

B13   ANON. [Review: The Stolen White Elephant.] Graphic (London), XXVI (July 15), 62.
       "A sad falling-off from the works which have made Mr. Clemens' reputation in two continents" this book has as its "funniest story, 'The Recent Carnival of Crime in Connecticut'...but what slight humour there may be in 'The Invalid's Story' is quite lost in the inherent repulsiveness of the incident."

B14   ANON. [Brief Review: The Stolen White Elephant.] Nation (New York), XXXV (August 10), 119.

B15   ANON. [Review: The Stolen White Elephant.] Westminster Review, n.s. LXII (October), 576-77.
       "It is difficult to choose where all is good, but perhaps the 'Gossip about old Captain Hurricane Jones of the South Pacific' and 'The Invalid's Story,' are the most irresistibly funny of all." "The American Language" is discussed at length by the reviewer.

B16   ARNOLD, MATTHEW. "A Word about America," Nineteenth Century, XI (May), 680-96.
       "The Quinionian humour of Mr. Mark Twain, so attractive to the Philistine of the more gay and light type both here and in America, another French critic fixes upon as literature exactly expressing a people of this type, and no higher. 'In spite of all its primary education,' he says, 'America is still, from an intellectual point of view, a very rude and primitive soil, only to be cultivated by violent methods. These childish and half-savage minds are not moved except by very elementary narratives composed without art, in which burlesque and melodrama, vulgarity and eccentricity, are combined in strong doses'" (pp. 689-90).

B17   *BENTZON, THÉRÈSE (MME. MARIE-THÉRÈSE BLANC). Littérature et Moeurs Étrangères: Études. Paris: G. Lévy, 2 vols.
       Reprints her essays on MT from Revue des Deux Mondes, 1872, 1875 (II, pp. 1-38, 231-71). [Source: Asselineau (1954), No. 4.]

B18   HAWEIS, H. R. "Mark Twain," in his American Humorists: Lectures Delivered at the Royal Institution. (London: Chatto & Windus), pp. 163-96. (Source: Third Edition, 1890.)
       Praises MT's vivid observation, ability not to bore his readers, noting that he is not very profound. "In freshness and fertility Twain resembles poor ARTEMUS, and rises above BRET HARTE, though he is less intense and pathetic than the latter." Reprinted in Scott (1955), pp. 29-33 and (1967), pp. 34-38.

B19   HOWELLS, WILLIAM DEAN. "Mark Twain," Century Magazine, XXIV (September), 780-83.
       A general study of his life and works, noting the autobiographical quality of his writing, which is at once American and universal. He is a gifted story-teller and painter of character; it is his artistry that will make his humor last. Frontispiece sketch of MT. Reprinted in his My Mark Twain (1910), pp. 134-44, and abridged in Anderson (1971), pp. 98-103 and Kesterson (1973), p. 13.

B20   NAST, THOMAS. [Cartoon of MT.] Harper's Weekly, XXVI (January 21), 37.
       Shows MT in Canada to arrange for copyright of his books. Also, Anon., "Canadian Copyright," a brief comment on the cartoon and on MT's problem with foreign copyright. Cartoon reprinted in Meltzer, 1960, p. 153, and on front cover of Mark Twain Journal, XVI (Winter, 1971).

B21   NICHOL, JOHN. American Literature: An Historical Sketch 1620-1880. Edinburgh: Adam and Charles Black, pp. 426-32.
       "It is probable that, to the lower class of British Philistines, American prose is, at this day, represented not so much by Irving, Emerson, or Hawthorne, as by 'Mark Twain,' who has done perhaps more than any other living writer to lower the literary tone of the English-speaking people." In LOM, a beautiful book, he spoke of the loss in freshness of vision suffered by a pilot or doctor as he learns to turn a professional eye toward his subject, and to them must be added "the professional humorist, who has lost the power of seeing the beauty of the universe, because he has come to regard it as a mere text-book for his sadly incessant and ultimately wearisome jests." Reprinted in Anderson (1971), pp. 94-97; in Scott (1955), pp. 23-28 and (1967), pp. 28-33. Excerpted in Kesterson (1973), pp. 15-16. In 1902

1882 - Shorter Writings

(NICHOL, JOHN)
Nichol dismissed MT with an oblique reference in his Encyclopaedia Britannica article (1902.B21).

B22   NOBEL, JAMES ASHCROFT. [Brief Review: The
       Stolen White Elephant.] Academy (London),
       XXII (July 1), 6.
          This resembles MT's other works, and will
       be popular with those who like them. "Sev-
       eral of the sketches are quite amusing...
       the volume as a whole is quite up to its
       author's average."

1883 A BOOKS - NONE

1883 B SHORTER WRITINGS

B1   ANON. [Review: Life on the Mississippi.]
       Athenaeum, No. 2901 (June 2), pp. 694-95.
          "Mr. Clemens's new book is a disappoint-
       ment." Much of it is derived from books,
       except for the chapters recalling actual
       experience, where "we come in contact with
       Mark Twain at his best." Reprinted in An-
       derson (1971), pp. 113-16.

B2   ANON. [Review: Life on the Mississippi.]
       Atlantic Monthly, LII (September), 406-408.
          Descriptive and appreciative; gives no
       indication of a falling-off in the second
       half.

B3   ANON. [Review: Life on the Mississippi.]
       British Quarterly Review, LXXXVIII (July),
       123-24.
          Discusses the book in terms of its humor,
       which is not of the highest order.

B4   ANON. [Review: Life on the Mississippi.]
       Congregationalist (British), XIII (August),
       702-705.
          "There are passages in this book which
       are equal to anything he has ever written,
       if, indeed, they are not superior. For if
       the humour is less condensed in its charac-
       ter, being spread over a larger surface, it
       has lost nothing of its old richness of
       flavour; while the purely descriptive parts
       of his narrative are marked by even more
       than his customary sprightliness and spir-
       it."

B5   ANON. [Review: Life on the Mississippi.]
       Graphic, XXVIII (September 1), 231.
          MT's earlier chapters contain "an admir-
       able specimen of his powers as a serious
       writer of history," but he "soon slips into
       his accustomed style," moving from "the
       graphic to the grotesque." This will prob-
       ably not be as popular as some of his other
       works; "nevertheless, it is well worth
       reading." Reprinted in Anderson (1971),
       pp. 118-19.

B6   ANON. [Review: Life on the Mississippi.]
       Nation, XXXVII (August 30), 192.

A minor review: The book is important as
the record of a period, and MT should not
be burdened with the title of professional
humorist.

B7   BROWN, ROBERT. [Review: Life on the Missis-
       sippi.] Academy (London), XXIV (July 28),
       58.
          "The fun in Mr. Clemens' Tramps Abroad is
       frequently forced, and sometimes quite un-
       suited to the subject in hand. His American
       experiences have rarely this fault; the
       writer seems to feel the ground he is tread-
       ing more secure.... The book is indeed the
       best account of social life on the Missis-
       sippi with which we are acquainted," and
       also gives a valuable account of the river.
       Reprinted in Anderson (1971), pp. 116-18.

B8   *[Counterfeit MT letter.] Discussed in Arkan-
       saw [sic] Traveler (August 4), p. 4.
          [Source: Quoted by Vogelback (1948),
       pp. 127-28.]
          On a bet, an 1859 MT letter was concocted
       and published, "and was immediately repro-
       duced by many of the leading newspapers in
       the country."

B9   *HAWEIS, H. R. "Mark Twain," Elzevir Library,
       March 12.
          [Source: Twainian, II (February, 1940).]

B10   *HEARN, LAFCADIO. [Review: Life on the Mis-
       sissippi.] New Orleans Times-Democrat
       (May 30), p. 4; Hearn, Essays on American
       Literature, ed. Sanki Ichikawa (Tokyo, 1929),
       pp. 127-33.
          [Source: Parsons (1969), 10-11. "In
       some respects...the most solid book that
       Mark Twain has written."] Reprinted in An-
       derson (1971), pp. 109-12.

B11   *MILLER, "JOAQUIN" (CINCINNATUS HINER MILLER).
       [His description of a dinner in his honor,
       attended by MT.] Somerville (New Jersey)
       Unionist, reprinted in Hartford Courant,
       January 9.
          [Source: Anon. "Mark Twain and Anthony
       Trollope, Equestrians," (1951), 14-15.]

B12   *PERRY, THOMAS SERGEANT. "An American on Amer-
       ican Humour," St. James's Gazette, VII
       (July 5), 5-6.
          [Source: Reprinted in Anderson (1971),
       pp. 103-108.] Sees MT's humor as representa-
       tive of a democratic, serious, ironic quali-
       ty in the American national character, re-
       acting against Europe, though not indepen-
       dently and perhaps not in hostility.

B13   READE, A. ARTHUR. Study and Stimulants; or,
       The Use of Intoxicants and Narcotics in Re-
       lation to Intellectual Life, as Illustrated
       by Personal Communications on the Subject,
       from Men of Letters and of Science. Phila-
       delphia: J. B. Lippincott and Co.,
       pp. 120-22.
          Contains a letter from MT beginning, "I

(READE, A. ARTHUR)
have not had a large experience in the matter of alcoholic drinks." MT goes on to
say that two glasses of champagne stimulate
the tongue and go well before an after-dinner speech, but "wine is a clog to the pen,
not an inspiration." The greater part of
the letter concerns his immoderate smoking,
his conviction that it does not injure his
health, and one or two occasions when he
stopped.

1884 A BOOKS

A1   *GAUTHIER-VILLARS, HENRY (WILLY). Mark Twain.
Paris: Gauthier-Villars.
[Source: Asselineau (1954), No. 5.]

1884 B SHORTER WRITINGS

B1   ANON. "Mark Twain," Leisure Hour (London),
p. 510.
Retells MT's own account of the origin
of his pen-name; adds no commentary or new
information.

B2   ANON. "Mark Twain in Bronze," Critic, n.s.
II (October 18), 184-85.
About the bust of MT by Karl Gerhardt.
Includes a description of it by Charles
Dudley Warner in the Hartford Courant (date
not given).

B3   *ANON. "Mark Twain in a Dilema [sic]--A Victim of a Joke He Thinks the Most Unkindest
Cut of All," New York World (November 27),
p. 1.
An illustration in the first edition of
Huckleberry Finn was rendered obscene by
somebody in the electrotyper's office.
[Source: Major portion of text reprinted
in Vogelback (1939), pp. 262-63.]

B4   *ANON. "Mark Twain's Altered Book," New York
Herald, November 29.
On the mutilated cut on p. 283 of HF;
gives the caption as "What [sic] do you
reckon it is?" [Source: Reprinted in
Twainian, V (March-April, 1946), 2.]

B5   ANON. "Tampering with Mark Twain's Book,"
New York Tribune, November 29, p. 3.
[Source: Reprinted in Twainian, V
(March-April, 1946), 2; cited in Vogelback
(1939), 263, n., indicating that this is a
modified reprinting from the New York World,
November 27, p. 1.] On the mutilation of
the cut on p. 283 to render it obscene.

B6   *ANON. [Story of the mutilation of a plate in
first edition of HF to produce an obscene
effect.] Boston Transcript, December 2,
p. 6.
[Source: Cited by Vogelback (1939),
p. 263, n. Vogelback indicates this is a
reprinting, possibly with variations, of an
account in the New York World (November 27),
p. 1.]

B7   *ANON. [Story of the mutilation of a plate in
first edition of HF to produce an obscene
effect.] Chicago Tribune, November 30,
p. 23.
[Source: Cited by Vogelback (1939),
p. 263, n. Vogelback indicates this is a
reprinting, perhaps with variations, from
the New York World, November 27, p. 1.]

B8   ANON. [Brief item: 150 "people of distinction in literature and the arts" sent requests for MT's autograph, timed to reach
him April 1st.] Critic (New York), IV
(April 5), 163.

B9   *ANON. [The rambling narrative style of Twain,
Riley, and Artemus Ward is the pose of "innocence victimized by the world, flesh, and
devil."] Washington Post, November 25.
[Source: Quoted by Henry Nash Smith,
introduction to HF, Riverside edition (1959),
p. xviii.]

B10 ANON. [Brief Review: The Adventures of Huckleberry Finn.] Athenaeum, No. 2983
(December 27), p. 855.
Laudatory and descriptive. "For some time
Mr. Clemens has been carried away by the am-
bition of seriousness and fine writing. In
Huckleberry Finn he returns to his right
mind and is again the Mark Twain of old
time.... Jim and Huckleberry are real creations, and the worthy peers of the illustrious Tom Sawyer." Reprinted in Anderson
(1971), pp. 120-21, with a suggestion that
the reviewer may be William Ernest Henley.

B11 PEASE, THOMAS H. [Letter to the editor of the
Palladium, from New Haven, April 23; here
reprinted.] Literary Era (Philadelphia),
II (July), 207.
Describes the book, The Enemy Conquered;
or, Love Triumphant, subject of the Hartford
Courant article (here attributed to Joseph
Twichell); the dealer's remaining copies of
the book were eventually sold for scrap.

B12 *SHIRLEY, JAMES. "Some Verses by Mark Twain,"
The Wasp (San Francisco), January 19.
[Source: Reprinted in Twainian, V
(July-August, 1946), 4.]

B13 STEPHENS, H. B. "Mark Twain's 'Dorg,'" Every
Other Saturday (Boston), I (December 20),
457-58.
On MT's dog "Burns," with an MT letter to
Stephens containing an obituary poem to the
dog. Article reprinted in Twainian, XII
(July-August, 1953), 3.

B14 [TWICHELL, JOSEPH.] "Mark Twain's Quest. The
Efforts of a Humorist to Secure a Rare Book--
A Long Search," Literary Era (Philadelphia),
II (June), 185-86.
Reprints an article from the Hartford Cour-
ant on the attempts by MT and Twichell to lo-
cate a copy of The Enemy Conquered; or, Love
Triumphant; for further comment see letter by

1884 - Shorter Writings

([TWICHELL, JOSEPH])
Thomas H. Pease reprinted in July issue
(1884.B11), where this article is attributed
to Twichell.

1885 A BOOKS - NONE

1885 B SHORTER WRITINGS

B1   ANON. "The American Humorists," Critic, VII
(December 5), 274 ("From the London Daily
News").
    Mostly about MT: "His gravity in narrat-
ing the most preposterous tale, his sympathy with every one of his absurdest characters, his microscopic imagination, his
vein of seriousness, his contrasts of pathos, his bursts of indignant plain speaking
about certain national errors, make Mark
Twain an author of the highest merit, and
far remote from the mere buffoon."

B2   ANON. "Modern Comic Literature," Saturday
Review (London), LIX (March 7), 301-302.
    A reply to Mr. Cowle's intemperate attack
on Modern Comic Literature in the Melbourne
Review, this includes a lengthy defense of
MT, and of Huckleberry Finn in particular.
Reprinted in Anderson (1971), pp. 127-28;
notes the conjecture of Brander Matthews
"that it is the work of...Mr. Andrew Lang."

B3   *ANON. [Banning of HF by the Concord Public
Library.] Boston Transcript, March 17.
    [Source: Long passage reprinted in Marks
(1959), p. xi.] The committee do not call
the book actually immoral, but it "contains
but little humor, and that of a very coarse
type"; it is "the veriest trash...rough,
coarse and inelegant, dealing with a series
of experiences not elevating, the whole
book being more suited to the slums than to
intelligent, respectable people." Also excerpted in Gerber (1971), p. 8, and Kesterson (1973), p. 17.

B4   *ANON. [Banning of HF by Concord Public Library.] Springfield (Massachusetts) Republican, as quoted in The Critic, VI
(March 28), 155.
    [Source: Reprinted in Gerber (1971),
pp. 8-9.] "Mr. Clemens is a genuine and
powerful humorist, with a bitter vein of
satire on the weaknesses of humanity which
is sometimes wholesome, sometimes only grotesque, but in certain of his works degen-
erates into a grotesque trifling with every
fine feeling. The trouble with Mr. Clemens
is that he has no reliable sense of propriety. His notorious speech at an Atlantic
dinner, marshalling Longfellow and Emerson
and Whittier in vulgar parodies in a Western miner's cabin, illustrated this, but
not in much more relief than the Adventures
of Tom Sawyer did, or these Huckleberry
Finn stories, do..."

B5   *ANON. ["A discursive and ill-argued attack on
the vulgarity of 'modern' humour."] Melbourne Review, X (January), 94-100.
    [Source: Headnote to Item No. 37 in Ander-
son (1971), p. 127.]

B6   NO ENTRY

B7   ANON. [Interview with Jane Clemens, MT's
mother.] Critic (New York), VII (December 12), 276.
    The boy avoided school, though he enjoyed
reading history (clipping from an undisclosed
source).

B8   *ANON. [MT's lectures in Keokuk, Iowa, and
greetings to his mother.] Keokuk Daily Gate
City, January 15, Weekly Gate City,
January 22.
    [Source: Reprinted in Twainian, XXIV
(November-December, 1965), 2-3.]

B9   ANON. [Notice, which follows in full.]
Graphic, XXXI (May 23), 530.
    "Humourists will delight in 'The Mark
Twain Birthday Book,' edited by 'E. O. S.'
(Remington), which contains excerpts from
Mr. Clemens' writings. Each day is allotted
several sentences, presumably summarising
the character of the person who writes his
name on the opposite page, such as 'A Med-
dling Old Clam,' or 'She was attractively
attired in her new and beautiful false
teeth.'"

B10   *ANON. [Recitation by MT and Cable in Paris,
Kentucky, New Year's night.] Paris Kentuckian, January 3.
    Praises their performance, describes the
visit, but says nothing new about topics or
performance. [Source: Reprinted in Twainian, XXIV (November-December, 1965), 1-2.]

B11   ANON. [Reprinted item from The Summary, "A
weekly journal published in the interests of
the New York State Reformatory"], Critic, VI
(May 30), 264.
    "The Reformatory Library also procured
Huckleberry Finn," was impressed with it as
irreligious, as the Concord (Massachusetts)
library had been, "and the fact came under
the notice of Professor Sanborn, who was
visiting us." He wrote the Superintendent:
"I have read 'Huckleberry Finn,' and I do
not see any reason why it should not go into
your Reference Library, at least, and form
the subject of a debate in your Practical
Morality Class. I am serious in this."
Reprinted in Gerber (1971), pp. 9-10.

B12   ANON. [Review: Huckleberry Finn.] British
Quarterly Review, LXXXI (January-April),
465-66.

(ANON.)

Although MT "is sometimes a little coarse, sometimes a little irreverent, and inclined to poke fun at the Old Testament," his humor redeems him and "Huckleberry Finn's adventures are told with a prevailing dryness and sense of reality which do much to compensate for offences against taste." The book is discussed as a successful sequel to Tom Sawyer, with no reference to the events after Huck escaped from his father's cabin.

B13 *ANON. [Review: Huckleberry Finn.] Boston Transcript, March 19.
     [Source: Quoted by Blair (1960), p. 2: the book is "so flat, as well as coarse, that nobody wants to read it after a taste of it."]

B14 ANON. [Review: Huckleberry Finn.] Westminster Review, n.s. LXVII (April), 596.
     "'The Adventures of Huckleberry Finn' are good even for Mark Twain.... There is abundance of American humour of the best sort; plenty of incident, sometimes thrilling, at others, extravagantly burlesque; charming descriptions of scenery, and admirable sketches of character."

B15 *[BRIDGES, ROBERT.] "Mark Twain's Blood-Curdling Humor," Life, V (February 26), 119.
     A hostile review of Huckleberry Finn.
     [Source: Reprinted in Durant da Ponte (1959); Anderson (1971), pp. 126-27; Lettis (1962), p. 275; and Gerber (1971), pp. 7-8.]

B16 CLARK, CHARLES H. "Authors at Home, V. Mark Twain at 'Nook Farm' (Hartford) and Elmira," Critic, VI (January 17), 25-26.
     A general account of his homes and his current activities, among them bicycling, billiards, the Monday Evening Club, and smoking cigars. [Reprinted in J. L. Gilder and J. B. Gilder, eds., Authors At Home (New York: Cassell Publishing Company), according to Henderson (1911), p. 217.]

B17 *CLEMENS, SAMUEL L. [Letter.] Critic, VI (April 11), 180.
     To Concord (Massachusetts) Free-Trade Club, on being elected an honorary member. "A committee of the public library of your town have condemned and excommunicated my last book [HF]--and doubled its sale"; also criticizes a decision by a Boston judge allowing sale of an unauthorized edition of his work. [Source: Reprinted in Gerber (1971), p. 9.]

B18 "Mark Twain's Semi-Centennial," Critic, VII (November 28), 253.
     Consists of a poem by Oliver Wendell Holmes ("To Mark Twain [On His Fiftieth Birthday]"); a note from Frank R. Stockton (congratulating him on his first half-century: "May you repeat the whole performance and 'mark twain!'"); a note from Charles Dudley Warner; and a letter to the editor from Joel Chandler Harris, praising MT and singling out Huckleberry Finn: "There is not in our fictive literature a more wholesome book." Harris letter reprinted in Gerber (1971), pp. 12-13; excerpted in Kesterson (1973), p.118. Holmes poem reprinted in Scott (1955), pp. 34-35; (1967), pp. 39-40; Kesterson (1973), pp. 19-20.

B19 [MATTHEWS, BRANDER.] [Review: Huckleberry Finn.] Saturday Review (London), LIX (January 31), 153-54.
     Superior to Tom Sawyer, because of the skill and self-restraint with which MT tells the story through Huck, this is the work of "a literary artist of a very high order." (Unsigned, the review is attributed to Matthews by Walter Blair in Mark Twain and Huck Finn (1960), p. 5, and by Anderson and Sanderson in Critical Heritage (1971), where it is reprinted as Item 35, pp. 121-25.) Also reprinted in Bradley, et al. (1962), pp. 275-79, and in Gerber (1971), pp. 2-7.

B20 PERRY, THOMAS SERGEANT. "Mark Twain," Century, XXX (May), 171-72.
     A review of Huckleberry Finn. The use of Huck as narrator lends unity and truthfulness; the ending seems contrived. Considers in terms of humor questions now taken somewhat differently, as in Huck's "mixed feelings about rescuing Jim, the negro, from slavery. His perverted views about the unholiness of his actions are most instructive and amusing." Reprinted in Lettis (1962), pp. 276-77; in Anderson (1971), pp. 128-30; in Gerber (1971), pp. 10-12.

1886 A BOOKS - NONE

1886 B SHORTER WRITINGS

B1   *ANON. [Account of the "Sir Robert Smith of Camelot" reading at Governors Island, November 11, 1886.] Hartford Courant, November 13, p. 1.
     MT describes the early stages of his Connecticut Yankee. Reprinted from the New York Sun of November 12. [Source: Quoted by Baetzhold, (1970), pp. 104-107; also see his "The Autobiography of Sir Robert Smith of Camelot: Mark Twain's Original Plan for A Connecticut Yankee," (1961), 456-61. Also noted in Mark Twain's Fable of Progress (1964) by Henry Nash Smith (p. 111, n. 11), who says this Sun and Courant version uses the name "Sir Robert Smith," but the New York Herald report of November 12 used the name "Sir Bob Smith."]

B2   *ANON. [Account of the "Sir Robert Smith of Camelot" reading at Governors Island, November 11, 1886.] New York Herald, November 12, p. 10.
     Another account of the reading reported in

1886 - Shorter Writings

(*ANON.)
the Hartford Courant for November 13; the
Courant entry gives details mentioned by
Baetzhold (1961, 1970) and Henry Nash
Smith (1964).

B3 FORGUES, EUGÈNE. "Les Caravanes d'un Humoriste," Revue des Deux Mondes, LXXIII
(February 15), 879-918.
    A review of Life on the Mississippi,
which is summarized and quoted at length,
together with a discussion of MT as a writer and a defense against accusations of
mere poor taste and vulgarity: "Mark Twain
n'est pas uniquement un amuseur incorrigible
et perpétuel.... C'est un observateur
sagace et pénétrant, qui voit bien et
raconte juste." Most of his writing has
concerned travel, by land and sea, with
the exception of "son exquise idylle," Tom
Sawyer. Unfortunately, his works have not
been successful in France.

B4 *LANG, ANDREW. "For Mark Twain," Longman's
Magazine, VII (February), 445-46.
    [Source: Anderson (1971), pp. 146-47).]
A conventional ode honoring MT on his 50th
birthday.

B5 RICHARDSON, CHARLES F. American Literature
1607-1885. New York: G. P. Putnam's Sons.
2 vols. I, 521, 523-24.
    Brief mention. "The reigning favorites
of the day are Frank R. Stockton, Joel
Chandler Harris, the various newspaper
jokers, and 'Mark Twain.' But the creators
of Pomona and Rudder Grange, of Uncle Remus
and his Folklore Stories, and of Innocents
Abroad, clever as they are, must make hay
while the sun shines. Twenty years hence,
unless they chance to enshrine their wit in
some higher literary achievement their unknown successors will be the privileged
comedians of the republic. Humor alone
never gives its masters a place in literature; it must coexist with literary qualities, and must usually be joined with such
pathos as one finds in Lamb, Hood, Irving,
or Holmes." Artemus Ward, like MT, made
his lampoons "either for the sake of fun
alone, or for the ridicule of solemn pre-
tence and hypocrisy." Bret Harte is
praised passim in both volumes.

1887 A BOOKS - NONE

1887 B SHORTER WRITINGS

B1 *BARNES, GEORGE E. "Mark Twain," San Francisco Morning Call, April 17.
    Barnes was the editor who asked Clemens
to resign from the Call in 1866. Fatout
quotes this article in Mark Twain in Virginia City (1964), concerning MT's investments in mining stock (p. 21), his unpopu-
larity in Nevada (p. 46), and his (and Artemus Ward's) dullness in conversation
(p. 126).

B2 *BOLTON, SARAH H. "Mark Twain," in her Famous
American Authors (New York: Thomas Y.
Crowell.)
    [Source: Henderson (1911), p. 216.]

B3 *HAWEIS, HUGH REGINALD. [Introduction.] Innocents Abroad (abridged ed.). London:
Routledge's World Library.
    [Source: Asselineau (1954), No. 7.]

1888 A BOOKS - NONE

1888 B SHORTER WRITINGS

B1 ALLEN, GRANT. "Genius and Talent." Fortnightly Review, n.s. CCLX (August 1),
240-55.
    Brief reference to MT as a leader among
the western American humorists, approached
only by Artemus Ward, Josh Billings, and
Orpheus C. Kerr. Quoted in Anderson (1971),
p. 12.

B2 ANON. "The Great American Language," Corn-
hill, n.s. XI (October), 363-77.
    Briefly mentions MT, passim.

B3 *ANON. [MT accepts honorary M.A. from Yale and
defends American humorists against the attacks of Matthew Arnold.] Hartford Courant,
June 22.
    [Source: Quoted in Baetzhold (1970),
pp. 120, 342, n. 33.]

B4 ARNOLD, MATTHEW. "A Word about America," in
his Civilization in the United States:
First and Last Impressions of America.
(Boston: Cupples and Hurd), pp. 92-93.
    "The Quinionian humour of Mr. Mark Twain,
so attractive to the Philistine of the more
gay and light type, both here and in America," reflects an elementary taste in literature. "But now it seems doubtful whether
America is not suffering from the predomi-
nance of Murdstone and Quinion herself--of
Quinion at any rate." [Quinion was the
warehouse manager of Murdstone and Grinby in
David Copperfield.]

B5 GRIPENBERG, BARONESS ALEXANDRA. "Mark Twain,"
in her A Half Year in the New World: Mis-
cellaneous Sketches of Travel in the United
States (Source: Trans. and ed. by Ernest
J. Moyne, Newark: University of Delaware
Press, 1954), pp. 67-72.
    Describes a visit to MT's Hartford home.
For further details see Moyne (1973).

B6 LANG, ANDREW. "International Girlishness,"
Murray's Magazine (London), IV (October),
433-41.
    On MT, briefly comments that not all Amer-
icans appreciate Lang's praise of him "as
one of the greatest of living geniuses
(perhaps it is not saying much) who now use
the English language." Some Americans "are
not as proud of Mark Twain as one could
wish."

B7   MATTHEWS, BRANDER, and CLEMENS, SAMUEL L.
     "American Authors and British Pirates,"
     New Princeton Review (London), V (January),
     46-65.
         In "A Private Letter and a Public Post-
     script" (pp. 46-54) MT tells Matthews that
     American law gives foreigners less protec-
     tion than British law does, and Americans
     are as guilty as anybody of literary theft.
     In the following "An Open Letter to Close a
     Correspondence," Matthews argues that pro-
     tection for a foreigner's books under Brit-
     ish law is less easy to obtain than MT rep-
     resents. This correspondence led to an es-
     trangement described by Matthews in his
     "Memories of Mark Twain" (1920).

1889 A BOOKS - NONE

1889 B SHORTER WRITINGS

B1   *ANON. [Interview.] New York Times,
     December 10, p. 5.
         MT praises Dan Beard's illustrations for
     A Connecticut Yankee. [Source: Cited in
     Mark Twain's Fable of Progress (1964) by
     Smith, who adds that MT "complicated the
     task of future critics by unqualified
     praise of the illustrations as a whole"
     (pp. 81, 115, n. 23).]

B2   *[BAXTER, SYLVANUS.] [Review: Connecticut
     Yankee.] Boston Sunday Herald,
     December 15, p. 17.
         [Source: Reprinted in Anderson (1971),
     pp. 148-52.] "Of all the extraordinary
     conceits that have germinated in his fruit-
     ful imagination, nothing more delicious has
     ever occurred to Mark Twain."

B3   GOULD, E. W. Fifty Years on the Mississippi;
     or, Gould's History of River Navigation.
     St. Louis: Nixon-Jones Printing Co.
         Generally praises LOM and its recognizable
     portraits of individuals, but says MT ex-
     aggerated the authority of pilots and their
     independence of the captains (pp. 489-96).
     A section of biographies of old steamboat-
     men includes a discussion of Captain John
     Klinfelter of the Pennsylvania (pp. 612-17)
     and of the explosion in which Henry Clemens
     died. Both accounts are heavily padded
     with extracts from LOM.

B4   LANG, ANDREW. "American Humour," in his Lost
     Leaders. (New York: Longmans, Green and
     Co.), pp. 70-77.
         Finds Bret Harte's humor "more humane, on
     the whole, than the laughable and amazing
     paradoxes of Mark Twain, or the naïvetés of
     Artemus Ward" and notes MT's exaggerations
     and dry delivery, his turning his material
     to comic account, but also his healthy out-
     spokenness. The copy of the book examined
     is a second edition with no indication of
     the original date, and there was earlier
     publication in the Daily News (London).

B5   *"TWARK MAIN," "Archimedes," Australian Stan-
     dard, VI (July), 2-3.
         On the power of land monopoly. [Source:
     Reprinted in Twainian, XII (November-
     December, 1953), 2-3.]

1890 A BOOKS - NONE

1890 B SHORTER WRITINGS

B1   *ANON. "Didactic Humorists," Speaker, I
     (January 11), 49-50.
         [Source: Reprinted in Anderson (1971),
     pp. 158-59.] Includes a review of Connecti-
     cut Yankee: "Mr. Clemens is not only dull
     when he is offensive; he is perhaps even
     more dull when he is didactic." The illus-
     trations are badly done and ill-placed:
     "We hope--we may even believe--that we have
     seen the artist at his worst; we certainly
     have not seen the author at his best."

B2   ANON. "Mark Twain's Camelot," Spectator,
     LXIV (April 5), 484.
         Deplores its portrayal in CY: "Is it not
     written in this coarse and clumsy burlesque,
     of which America in general, and Mark Twain
     in particular, ought to be heartily ashamed?
     Mr. Howells, however, is in raptures over
     this sorry performance."

B3   *ANON. "Mark Twain's New Book. A Crusher for
     Royalty." Sydney (Australia) Bulletin,
     March 8.
         "The one most favorable British review"
     of CY, according to Baetzhold (1970),
     pp. 353-54, n. 2.

B4   *ANON. "Modern Men: Mark Twain," Scots Ob-
     server, IV (September 20), 454-55.
         [Source: Smalley thesis (1948), pp. 41,
     61, 70.]

B5   ANON. "The Way Mark Twain Impressed England,"
     Critic, n.s. XIV (November 29), 286-7.
         From The Scots Observer (date not given).
     On MT's incomparable humor.

B6   *ANON. [Excerpt from Connecticut Yankee, with
     comment.] Nationalist, February 2, p. 116.
         [Source: Reprinted in American Literary
     Realism, 1870-1910, V (Winter, 1972),
     87-88.] Praises MT's emphasis on "loyalty
     to one's country, not to its institutions
     or its office-holders," and his appeal for
     human equality.

B7   ANON. [Review: Connecticut Yankee.] Athena-
     eum, No. 3251 (February 15), p. 211.
         This "rather laborious piece of fun with
     a sort of purpose in it" is mechanical and
     too long, but harmless: "Sir Thomas Malory
     and Lord Tennyson will survive." Reprinted
     in Anderson (1971), pp. 170-71.

1890 - Shorter Writings

B8   ANON. [Review: Connecticut Yankee.] Critic, n.s. XIII (February 22), 90.
      "We do not at all approve of Mark's performance; it is very naughty indeed: but-- and that is all he and his publishers want-- we cannot help laughing at it."

B9   *ANON. [Review: Connecticut Yankee.] Daily Telegraph (London), January 13.
      [Source: Reprinted in Anderson (1971), pp. 160-63.] "It is quite possible that a serious purpose underlies what otherwise seems a vulgar travesty," but there was an idealism in Arthurian legend as there is today; and today there are still oppressors: "Which, then, is to be the most admired-- the supremacy of the knight or the success of the financier? Under which King will the American serve--the ideal or the real? Will they own allegiance to King ARTHUR or JAY GOULD?"

B10   *ANON. [Review: Connecticut Yankee.] Literary World (Boston), XXI (February 15), 52-53.
      [Source: Anderson (1971), pp. 172-72.] We can laugh at MT's exaggerations in LOM, "When he prostitutes his humorous gift to the base uses of historical injustice, democratic bigotry, Protestant intolerance, and nineteenth-century vainglory, we must express the very sincere animosity we feel at such a performance. If anything could be less of a credit to our literature than the matter of this book, it certainly is the illustrations which disfigure it."

B11   *ANON. [Review: Connecticut Yankee.] Quincy (California) Plumas National (July 5), p. 2.
      [Source: Reprinted in Anderson (1971), pp. 174-76.] Praises CY as "one long satire on modern England and Englishmen, under the clever guise of an attempt to picture the England of the sixth century and of Arthurian legend."

B12   *ANON. [Review: Connecticut Yankee.] Scots Observer, January 18.
      [Source: Reprinted in Anderson (1971), pp. 164-66.] "As for Mark Twain, he has turned didactic, and being ignorant is also misleading and offensive."

B13   *ANON. [Review: Connecticut Yankee.] New York Standard, VII (January 1), 10.
      [Source: Smith (1964), pp. 80, 115, n. 20.] Smith quotes the reviewer in Henry George's journal as commenting that MT supplied the feeling for democracy in general, and the Dan Beard illustrations pointed out fundamental causes and cures for wrongs; Smith observes that in some instances Beard went beyond the text, as in advocating his own single-tax doctrine.

B14   ANON. [Review: The Prince and the Pauper (play).] Critic (New York), XIII (January 25), 43.
      Mrs. Richardson, who prepared the play for the stage, "has done her part of the work as well, perhaps, as could be expected; but the piece, as it stands, has no real value, and would have but a poor chance of success without a public favorite like Elsie Leslie to play the two principal characters.... The improbabilities, not to say absurdities, of all this are much more apparent in a play than in the original story .... The best act, artistically, is the last, in which a good deal of the original dialogue is preserved, including some happy examples of Mark Twain's peculiar humor."

B15   AUSTIN, L. F. [Review: Connecticut Yankee.] New Review (London), II (February), 187-88.
      Treats the book as a joke, along with the praise of it by Howells in his Harper's review.

B16   BAINTON, GEORGE, comp. and ed. The Art of Authorship: Literary Reminiscences, Methods of Work, and Advice to Young Beginners, Personally Contributed by Leading Authors of the Day. New York: D. Appleton and Company.
      On pp. 85-88, quotes an undated letter from MT, who describes an author's method of composition as the unconscious accumulation of sentences that please him, as models, collected for "the building, brick by brick, of the eventual edifice which we call our style." Reprinted in Twainian, IX (March-April, 1950), 1-2.

B17   HOWELLS, WILLIAM DEAN. [Review: Connecticut Yankee.] Harper's Monthly, LXXX (January), 319-21.
      Praises MT's social satire and Dan Beard's illustrations, which reflect "the wrath and the pathos as well as the fun of the thing." Reprinted in his My Mark Twain (1910), pp. 145-49, and (with some material not in My Mark Twain) in Anderson (1971), pp. 152-56. Abridged in Cardwell (1963), pp. 6-8.

B18   *KIPLING, RUDYARD. [MT Interview.] New York Herald, August 17.
      "Kipling had included a paragraph of shocked disbelief that Mark Twain had written such a book as A Connecticut Yankee. But the glittering encomiums of the rest of the account evidently offset its ending," according to Baetzhold in Mark Twain and John Bull (1970), p. 188; he adds that the interview was published in two Allahbad, India papers, The Pioneer (March 18) and The Pioneer Mail (March 19) before it appeared in the Herald. According to Baetzhold, the interview is reprinted in Kipling's From Sea to Sea (1899) without the last paragraph, with its comments on CY (p. 358, n. 18).

B19 *KRIEGER, G. [Introduction: Tom Sawyer.]
Leipzig: G. Freytag.
[Source: Henderson (1911), p. 217.]

B20 NOBLE, JAMES ASHCROFT. [Brief review: Connecticut Yankee.] Academy (London),
XXXVII (February 22), 130.
"MT's "new book is utterly unworthy of
him. Though burlesque is the cheapest kind
of humour which can be produced by men
whose humorous facility is of the slenderest sort," it has a proper field. Arthurian legend is not this field, and "if we
laugh at the new book we are ashamed of
ourselves."

B21 *O'BRIEN, DESMOND. [Review: Connecticut
Yankee.] Truth, XXVII (January 2), 25.
[Source: Reprinted in Anderson (1971),
pp. 157-58.] "A Yankee at the Court of
King Arthur is a bizarre book, full of all
kinds of laughable and delightful incongruities--the most striking of its incongruities, however, being unconscious, grim,
and disenchanting.... His fooling is admirable, and his preaching is admirable,
but they are mutually destructive."

B22 [STEAD, WILLIAM T.] "Mark Twain's New Book;
A Satirical Attack on English Institutions,"
Review of Reviews (London), I (February),
144-56.
Selects CY as the Novel of the Month:
for all its many faults, "to those who endeavour to understand what the mass of men
who speak English are thinking, as opposed
to those who merely care about what they
ought to be thinking, this book of Mark
Twain's is one of the most significant of
our time." MT attacks the present as well
as the past, and America as well as England; CY "is the latest among the volumes
whereby Americans are revolutionising the
old country," together with Henry George's
books and Edward Bellamy's Looking Backward. Reprinted in Anderson (1971),
pp. 167-70 (without the extensive quotation
from CY, identification of the author as
Stead is by Anderson).

1891 BOOKS - NONE

1891 B SHORTER WRITINGS

B1 ANON. "American Fiction," Edinburgh Review,
CLXXIII (January), 31-65.
Mentions MT's name in a list of humorists, observing that "the humorous drama
with a single character in different situations is one which American humourists
have made peculiarly their own"; the critic's own preference is for Lowell.

B2 ANON. "The Luck of Arthur Scoresby: One of
Mark Twain's Stories," Review of Reviews
(London), IV (August), 153.

Summarizes and extensively quotes MT's
story, "Luck," from the August Harper's.

B3 ANON. "Mark Twain Among the Prophets," Review of Reviews (London), IV (December),
590.
Summarizes and extensively quotes MT's
article on "Mental Telegraphy" in the
December Harper's.

B4 ANON. "To an Old Humorist," Bookman (London),
I (November), 61-62.
Passing references: MT is grouped with
Rabelais, Swift, Sterne, Dickens, and
Holmes, but "If Mark Twain had to be judged
summarily by his Connecticut Yankee at the
Court of King Arthur, he would have but an
indifferent reputation with at least half
the English-speaking race."

B5 BEERS, HENRY A. Initial Studies in American
Letters. New York: Chautauqua Press.
The material touching on MT is virtually
the same as in Beer's earlier An Outline
Sketch of American Literature (New York:
Phillips and Hunt, 1887). In 1891 Beers
still groups MT with Artemus Ward and the
other popular humorists of the age (pp. 188-89), though conceding that "his humor has a
more satirical side than Ward's, sometimes
passing into downright denunciation. He delights particularly in ridiculing sentimental humbug and moralizing cant" (p. 194).

B6 *CLEMENS, WILL M. "Life of Mark Twain, I,"
Library and Studio, July-December.
[Source: Twainian, II (November, 1940),
4.]

B7 COFFIN, WILLIAM A. "J. Carroll Beckwith,"
Harper's Weekly, XXXV (September 26), 734.
On Beckwith's life and paintings; his
portrait of MT is reproduced as a woodcut
frontispiece, p. 717.

B8 GOODMAN, ARTHUR JULE. [Full-page portrait of
MT]. Half-tone reproduction of sepia
sketch; no text.

B9 HAWTHORNE, JULIAN, and LEONARD LEMMON. "Mark
Twain," in their American Literature: An
Elementary Text-Book for Use in High Schools
and Academies. (Boston: D. C. Heath & Co.,
Publishers), pp. 313-15.
He has keen eyes and describes both scene
and character vividly. "Whether in jest or
in earnest, [MT] is always and instinctively
an artist; it is a necessity of his nature
to perfect his work."

B10 LANDON, MELVILLE D. ("ELI PERKINS"). Eli
Perkins: Thirty Years of Wit and Reminiscences of Witty, Wise and Eloquent Men.
New York: Cassell Publishing Company.
MT said he liked HF best of all his books
"because it has the truest dialect" (p. 76);
Landon describes MT as "both a humorist and
a wit" (p. 81).

1891 - Shorter Writings

B11 LANG, ANDREW. "The Art of Mark Twain," Illus-
     trated London News, XCVIII (February 14),
     222.
          A general defense of MT as a serious writ-
     er in addition to being a gifted humorist.
     "I have abstained from reading his work on
     an American at the Court of King Arthur,
     because here Mark Twain is not, and cannot
     be, at the proper point of view. He has
     not the knowledge which would enable him to
     be a sound critic of the Middle Ages." But
     in TS and HF he reveals himself as "one
     among the greatest contemporary makers of
     fiction" and HF is "a masterpiece." Re-
     printed in The Critic (London), XVIII
     (March 7), 130; XIX (July 25), 45-46 (as
     "Mr. Lang on the Art of Mark Twain," mis-
     takenly attributed to Illustrated News of
     the World). Reprinted in Anderson (1971),
     pp. 131-35 ("This article is apparently
     Lang's response to Clemens' request for
     support in the face of adverse criticism.")
     Also reprinted in Scott (1955), pp. 36-40;
     (1967), pp. 41-45.

1892 A BOOKS

A1   CLEMENS, WILL M. Mark Twain: His Life and
     Work, A Biographical Sketch. San Francis-
     co: The Clemens Publishing Company. Also
     Chicago, New York: F. Tennyson Neely,
     Publisher.
          A note by Isobel Lyon, MT's secretary,
     indicates that this contains facts not in
     the Paine biography (Note in New York Pub-
     lic Library; photocopy in Mark Twain Pa-
     pers, Berkeley).

1892 B SHORTER WRITINGS

B1   ANON. [Review: The American Claimant.]
     Bookman (London), III (November), 60.
          Brief, noting the humor, "But there are
     dull patches, and misplaced serious patches,
     and indeed Mulberry Sellers has carried
     away his biographer to regions where extra-
     vagance and exaggeration are no longer
     wholesome farce, but wearisome and fatuous,
     occasionally something worse."

B2   ANON. [Brief Review: The American Claim-
     ant.] Review of Reviews (London), VI
     (October), 399-400.
          A bare reference: those who have enjoyed
     MT will like this, and this time "he has
     refrained from hurting the feelings of
     those who were distressed by the travesty
     of the Arthurian legend."

B3   ANON. [Review: The American Claimant.]
     Spectator (Supplement), No. 3360
     (November 19), p. 714.
          Chiefly descriptive and only moderately
     enthusiastic, noting that "There is some
     satire in this book, good humoured and
     reasonably effective, and there is plenty

of fun, the quality of which is beyond all
question." The elaborate scheme of Colonel
Sellers "is one of the most characteristic
pieces of the American humour of extravagance that we have ever seen."

B4   ANON. [Brief reference.] Review of Reviews
     (London), V (February), 188.
          Mark Twain is a valuable asset to the new
     Idler.

B5   *CLEMENS, WILL M. "Life of Mark Twain, II,"
     Library and Studio, January-June.
          [Source: Twainian, II (November, 1940),
     4.]

B6   FAIRBANKS, MARY MASON. "The Cruise of the
     Quaker City. With Chance Recollections of
     Mark Twain," Chautauquan, XIV (January),
     429-32.
          The author was a traveling companion on
     the tour on which IA was based, and a life-
     long friend and confidante. The trip was
     more successful than MT represented; she
     appreciates his account and speaks warmly
     but judiciously of MT and his works. Quotes
     a lengthy "extract from a letter written by
     him to a young friend on the occasion of
     her début" on the change from childhood and
     the building of a mature life, and quoting
     from Thomas Fuller, whose pithy "pemmican
     sentences" he admires. Lengthy excerpt re-
     printed in Review of Reviews (London), V
     (January), 43.

B7   *GOODMAN, JOSEPH T. "Artemus Ward," San Fran-
     cisco Chronicle, January 10.
          Describes Ward's famous visit to Virginia
     City. [Source: Quoted by Fatout (1964),
     pp. 123, 129, 131, 133.]

B8   RANKIN, SCOTT. "People I Have Never Met:
     Mark Twain," Idler, II (October), 339.
          A cartoon of MT, dressed as a sailor, on
     the bridge of a ship; a life-ring reads
     "Quaker City."

B9   SHARP, LUKE. "Mark Twain: A Conglomerate In-
     terview, Personally Conducted by Luke
     Sharp," Idler, I (February), 79-92.
          Contains "Good Stories of Mark Twain in
     London" by Bruce Hatton; an account of his
     smoking; an excerpt from the interview Kip-
     ling published in his From Sea to Sea (1899)
     and MT's recollections of Kipling; a refer-
     ence to a passage in MT's "Mental Telegra-
     phy" as foundation for his The American
     Claimant [beginning as a serial in this is-
     sue of Idler]; and a reprinting of the poem
     to MT on his fiftieth birthday, by Oliver
     Wendell Holmes. There is also an extract
     from an interview in which MT expressed his
     admiration for Thomas Bailey Aldrich. The
     article is illustrated by eight snapshots
     of MT taken on board the French liner, La
     Gascogne as it neared Havre, and the issue
     has a sketch of MT as frontispiece.

B10   SLADEN, DOUGLAS. "New York as a Literary
      Centre," English Illustrated Magazine, X
      (October), 136-44.
          Brief and superficial description of MT
      as seen by the (N.Y.?) World; portrait
      (pp. 142-43).

B11   *STUART, J. "Mark Twain," Literary Opinion,
      July.
          [Source: Twainian, II (December, 1940),
      6.]

B12   TOWNER, AUSBURN. "Langdon, Jervis," in his
      Our County and Its People: A History of
      the Valley and County of Chemung (Syracuse,
      New York: D. Mason & Co., Publishers),
      pp. 609-17.
          On MT's father-in-law, noting his concern
      for his business, home, and religion, and
      describing his benefactions. The volume
      also describes other prominent citizens.

B13   WALLACE, WILLIAM. [Brief review: The Ameri-
      can Claimant.] Academy (London), XLII
      (October 29), 386.
          "Quite up to its author's usual standard.
      It is well balanced and well written,"
      though somewhat monotonous in its humor.

1893 A BOOKS - NONE

1893 B SHORTER WRITINGS

B1   *ANON. "Mark Twain at the Lotos," Critic,
      November 18.
          [Source: Henderson (1911), p. 217.]

B2   ANON. "Stockton on Mark Twain," Critic,
      n.s. XX (August 12), 111.
          Summary of Stockton's "Mark Twain and his
      Recent Work" in the August Forum.

B3   ANON. [Brief Review: The American Claimant.]
      Athenaeum, No. 3407 (February 11), p. 184.
          "Only rather amusing."

B4   ANON. [Brief Review: The £1,000,000 Bank-
      Note, and Other Stories.] Athenaeum,
      No. 3432 (August 5), p. 191.
          Faintly praises the title story and
      "Playing Courier"; "Petition to the Queen
      of England" is in the fading tradition of
      Artemus Ward.

B5   ANON. [Brief Review: The £1,000,000 Bank-
      Note, and Other Stories.] Bookman (London),
      IV (June), 91.
          "There is one good thing in this volume
      ["The Enemy Conquered; Or, Love Trium-
      phant"], and that apparently is not Mark
      Twain's. What of the remainder is passable
      is Mark Twain's commentary on the good
      thing." The rest of the book is disap-
      pointing.

B6   *ANON. [Sketch of MT at banquet honoring Henry
      Irving.] Once-A-Week (London), December 2.
          [Source: Twainian, n.s. II (April, 1943),
      6.]

B7   *DAGGETT, ROLLIN M. "Daggett's Recollections,"
      San Francisco Examiner, January 22.
          Description of MT's appearance on first
      arrival in Virginia City. [Source: Quoted
      by Fatout (1964), pp. 7-8.]

B8   *"DE QUILLE, DAN" [WILLIAM WRIGHT.] "Artemus
      Ward in Nevada." The Californian, IV
      (August), 403-406.
          [Source: Quoted by Fatout (1964), pp.
      pp. 128-29.] For MT's version see his
      "First Interview with Artemus Ward" in
      Sketches New and Old. Twainian, I (Decem-
      ber, 1939), 6, erroneously gives the name
      as "Dan Quille."

B9   *_____. "Reporting with Mark Twain," Califor-
      nia Illustrated, July, 170-78.
          [Source: Quoted by Fatout (1964), pp. 31,
      114, 117, 173, 174. Twainian, I (December,
      1939), 6, lists this as having appeared in
      The Californian for July, 1893.]

B10   *_____. "Salad Days of Mark Twain," San Fran-
      cisco Examiner, March 19.
          [Source: Quoted by Fatout (1964), p. 166.]

B11   *McEWEN, ARTHUR. "In the Heroic Days," San
      Francisco Examiner, January 22.
          [Source: Quoted by Fatout (1964),
      pp. 17-18.] Quotes MT's complaint that "to
      write a burlesque so wild that its pretended
      facts will not be accepted in perfect good
      faith by somebody, is very nearly an impos-
      sible thing to do." Describes the imagina-
      tive reporting of MT and Dan De Quille, who
      "often did the better work."

B12   MIGHELS, ELLA STERLING (CUMMINS). The Story
      of the Files: A Review of California Writ-
      ers and Literature. San Francisco: World's
      Fair Commission of California, Columbian
      Exposition, pp. 103, 123-25.
          Derived chiefly from RI and other MT
      works, and the Will Clemens biography, and
      generally superficial. "He is not particu-
      larly amiable nor generous personally, but
      he is endowed with a sense of justice, and
      he knows exactly what he is about." There
      are chapters on the Californian, Sacramento
      Union, and other periodicals for which MT
      wrote.

B13   SAINTSBURY, GEORGE. [Brief Review: The
      £1,000,000 Bank-Note, and Other Stories.]
      Academy (London), XLIV (July 8), 28.
          A dull book. "If there is fun in this
      volume of Mark Twain's (except a certain
      faint and overwrought strain of it in the
      mock romance of 'The Enemy Conquered') this
      reviewer avows himself a conquered enemy."

B14 STOCKTON, FRANK R. "Mark Twain and His Recent
     Works," Forum, XV (August), 673-79.
          Largely on MT's humor, praising his
     "courage"--the audacity of his conceptions
     and expression; also praises him as a story-
     teller, "a man of broad sympathies," while
     recognizing that "the figure with the trag-
     ic mask stalks through much of Mark Twain's
     work." Reprinted in Scott (1955),
     pp. 41-48; (1967), pp. 46-53.

B15 *VEDDER, HENRY C. [Article in series on "Liv-
     ing American Writers."] New York Examiner,
     April 6.
          [Source: Anderson (1971), pp. 176-81.]
     A conventional view, noting MT's serious
     purpose, and integrity, praising his his-
     torical novels, and, still more, those
     about the Mississippi Valley. Unfortunate-
     ly, MT is insufficiently understood and
     appreciated, especially in England. See
     also Vedder's American Writers of To-Day
     (1894.B10).

1894 A BOOKS - NONE

1894 B SHORTER WRITINGS

B1   [ALDEN, WILLIAM LIVINGSTONE.] "The Book
     Hunter," Idler, VI (August), 213-24.
          Contains a brief review of PW (pp. 222-23)
     as primarily a novel, containing "a care-
     fully painted picture of life in a Missis-
     sippi town in the days of slavery," although
     the twins "are as little like Italians as
     they are like Apaches." The extracts from
     "Pudd'nhead Wilson's Almanac" leave the
     reader wanting more. Reprinted in Anderson
     (1971), pp. 182-83.

B2   ANON. "Test Readings of Mark Twain's Hands,"
     Borderland (London), I (October), 558-60.
          In the previous issue, experts in palmis-
     try were invited to read the character of
     an unidentified person from pictures of his
     hands. Readings by "Miss Ross," "J. E.,"
     "Lucis," and "E. L. C." are given, showing
     partial success in describing the subject,
     now revealed as MT, who had been debating
     with friends over whether palmistry was a
     superstition not to be taken seriously even
     in fiction. "In our next Number I hope to
     be able to publish his opinion upon the ac-
     curacy or otherwise with which strangers
     have hit off his distinguishing character-
     istics." [The September and November issues
     were not available in the libraries where
     this bibliography was compiled, but MT's
     comments are in the January, 1895 issue
     (1895.B2).] There are clear photographs of
     the front and back of MT's right hand.
     [Henderson (1911), p. 218 lists an article
     by this title for January, 1894; I have not
     checked it--T.A.T.]

B3   ANON. [Brief Review: Tom Sawyer Abroad.]
     Athenaeum, No. 3474 (May 26), p. 676.
          A dull book, and "a grievous disappoint-
     ment to admirers of The Adventures of Tom
     Sawyer and of his friend Huckleberry Finn...
     it is a pity that [MT] should squander him-
     self on such a book as this."

B4   ANON. [Review: Tom Sawyer Abroad.] Bookman
     (London), VI (June), 89-90.
          "Tom was a promising boy in the old days.
     He is mostly conceited and sententious now.
     He says a shrewd thing or two, but all his
     adventures with balloons, and lions, and
     tigers, and dervishes, and the incongruity
     of American new humour meeting African bar-
     barism and strangeness, hardly do more than
     provoke a wearied smile."

B5   ANON. [Review: Tom Sawyer Abroad.] Saturday
     Review (London), LXXVII (May 19), 535-36.
          "The humour is genuine and characteristic,
     but it is thin." Chiefly a summary, con-
     demns the ending: "anything more flat and
     unprofitable or more shabby to the reader
     was never devised."

B6   CHAMBERS, E. K. [Brief Review: Tom Sawyer
     Abroad.] Academy (London), XLVI (July 14),
     p. 27.
          This is not offensive, as was CY: "It is
     more decent to parody Jules Verne than Sir
     Thomas Malory, and Mark Twain may therefore
     be said to have returned in his latest
     flight of humour to the limits of legitimate
     burlesque." Unfortunately, this is not a
     very funny book.

B7   CLEMENS, SAMUEL L. "Private History of the
     'Jumping Frog' Story," North American Re-
     view, CLVIII (April), 446-53; briefly sum-
     marized and quoted in "Mark Twain as Pla-
     giarist," Critic, XXIV (March 31), 221.
          Begins by telling of the stir created a
     few years ago when "a lady from Finland"
     [Baroness Alexandra Gripenberg] mistakenly
     attributed to him a story by Hopkinson
     Smith, using a plot previously used by
     Boccaccio; and now a version of the "Jumping
     Frog" story has turned up in Sidgwick's
     Greek Prose Translation. [The passage later
     turned out to have been adapted by Sidgwick
     from MT's story--T.A.T.]

B8   *FREEMAN, WILLIAM H. The Press Club of Chica-
     go: A History, with Sketches of Other
     Prominent Press Clubs of the United States.
     Chicago: The Press Club of Chicago.
          [Source: Material on MT (including a note
     by him) is quoted by George Hiram Brownell
     in "Mark Twain Lauched the Chicago Press
     Club of which George Ade Later Became a
     Member," Twainian, IV (March, 1945), 1-2.]

B9 *WILLIAMS, MARTHA McCULLOCH. "In Re 'Pudd'n-head Wilson,'" Southern Magazine (February), pp. 99-102.
    [Source: Quoted in Rowlette (1971), p. vii.] Describes the book (as serialized in the Century) as "tremendously stupid," and malicious and misleading."

B10 VEDDER, HENRY C. American Writers of To-Day. New York, Boston, Chicago: Silver, Burdett and Company, pp. 94, 124-40.
    Vedder's article in the New York Examiner for April 6, 1893, here titled "Mark Twain" and augmented by a sketchy biographical introduction (pp. 124-29) and a conclusion praising MT's business sagacity, ending with a comment on reports that his best is reserved for private conversation: "Pity it is, if this be true, that there is not a chiel amang them to take notes and prent 'em" (pp. 139-40). Scott reprints the article without the added material in Selected Criticism (1955, pp. 49-54 and 1967, pp. 54-59).
    Also see Vedder's "Charles Dudley Warner" (pp. 87-103): "Mr. Samuel L. Clemens has published certain books in serious literature, without in the least persuading the public to take him seriously. Many read The Prince and the Pauper through with misgiving, lest a huge jest might after all be concealed beneath the apparently sober tale. They failed to enjoy the story, because they were continually and nervously looking for some hidden snare. It is only when, as 'Mark Twain,' he writes some such trash as The Adventures of Huckleberry Finn that this really capable writer can make sure of an appreciative hearing" (p. 94).

B11 ZANGWILL, I. [Review: Tom Sawyer Abroad.] Pall Mall Magazine, IV (November), 524-25.
    Chiefly descriptive. "There are no so many good things" as in TS and HF, "but there are not a few memorable passages."

1895 A BOOKS - NONE

1895 B SHORTER WRITINGS

B1 ALDEN, W. L. "The Book Hunter," Idler, VII (May), 565-76.
    On p. 575 Alden comments on Personal Recollections of Joan of Arc, which has begun serial publication in the April Harper's Magazine as the work of the Sieur Louis De Conte, translated by Jean François Alden: "Every student of French literature knows that the 'Personal Recollections' in question were written by the Sieur Uquel Berri-Finn, and that they were originally translated into English by M. Marc Touêne. Nothing that the Sieur Uquel Berri-Finn has written is more characteristic of that charming author than are the opening chapters of this new romance."

B2 ANON. "Character Reading by Palmistry and Otherwise: The Story of the Tell-Tale Hands of Mark Twain," Borderland (London) II (January), 60-64.
    Contains poorly reproduced photographs of the front and back of MT's left hand, a letter to the editor by MT commenting on the accuracy of the readings in the October, 1894 Borderland (1894.B2), and a reproduction of the envelope in which the letter was mailed. In turn, there are character readings by graphologists, using his handwriting on the envelope: "The result will probably convince Mark Twain that he had better be judged by palmistry than by graphology."

B3 ANON. "A Frenchman on Mark Twain and His Criticisms of Bourget," Literary Digest, X (March 2), 10-11.
    A translated portion of an article by M. Labadie-Lagrave in Le Figaro (Paris, February 2), defending Paul Bourget, whom MT had recently attacked in North American Review, and comparing their approaches to a topic. MT "begins by choosing a thesis, and he then invents a series of adventures, generally very interesting, which are built up so as to throw into full light a truth that he has previously formulated in his mind."

B4 ANON. "Mark Twain's Serious Stories," Review of Reviews (London), XII (September), 231.
    Briefly summarizes MT's "Mental Telegraphy" article in the September Harper's.

B5 *ANON. [Interview.] Cleveland Daily Leader, July 16.
    [Source: Quoted by Fatout (1964), p. 215.]

B6 *ANON. [Interview.] Portland Oregonian, August 11; reprinted there February 8, 1925.
    Contains MT's comments in favor of governmental monopolies, on travel, and on his characters (and their names), not created, but recollected as combinations of people he had known. [Source: Reprinted in Twainian, XXIV (January-February, 1965), 1-2.] This, together with a review in the New Whatcom, Washington Reveille (1895.B13), is incorrectly listed by the 1965 MHRA Annual Bibliography as "FATOUT, PAUL. Mark Twain on the Lecture Circuit; Newspaper Accounts Concerning Mark Twain's Lectures..."; in fact these are reprintings of articles cited by Fatout in his 1960 book.

B7 *ANON. [Interview.] Sydney Morning Herald (September 17).
    MT describes Lewis Carroll as "a true and subtle humorist" and comments on The Mikado. [Source: Quoted by Baetzhold (1970), pp. 36, 115-16, with notes on pp. 328, n. 9 and 341, n. 26.]

B8 *ANON. [Interviews in which MT praises Kipling.] Adelaide South Australia Register
and Advertiser (October 14); Minneapolis
Penny Press (July 23), and Times (July 24);
Sydney Morning Herald and Daily Telegraph
(September 17); Bombay Times of India
(January 24, 1896).
     Baetzhold (1970, p. 358, n. 21) lists
these as clippings in the Mark Twain Papers.

B9 ANON. [Review: The Prince and the Pauper.]
London Quarterly Review, LXXXVIII (July),
388.
     Brief and descriptive. "The adventures
of the two boys in their new worlds keep
one amused and interested throughout."

B10 ANON. [Brief Review: Pudd'nhead Wilson.]
Athenaeum, No. 3508 (January 19),
pp. 83-84.
     "The story in itself is not much credit
to Mark Twain's skill as a novelist," and
few of the characters are striking, but
"If the preface [with its tasteless humor]
be skipped, the book well repays reading
just for the really excellent picture of
Roxana." Reprinted in Anderson (1971),
p. 183.

B11 ANON. [Review: Pudd'nhead Wilson.] Bookman (London), VII (January, 1895), 122.
     Brief and descriptive: MT's use of the
fingerprint device is "ingenious," and by
the long confusion of the children "the end
is prevented from being a very cheerful
one."

B12 ANON. [Review: Pudd'nhead Wilson and Those
Extraordinary Twins.] Critic, XXVI
(May 11), 338-39.
     Among the American humorists, "the one
accomplished artist...is Lowell, whose
university traditions were very strong and
controlled his bubbling humor. The others
are pure 'naturalists'--men of instinctive
genius who have relied on their own conscious strength to produce delight in the
reader, irrespective of classicity of
form, literary grace or any other of the
beloved conventions on which literature as
literature has hitherto depended." PW is
"admirable in atmosphere, local color and
dialect, a drama in its way, full of powerful situations, thrilling even; but it cannot be called in any sense literature."
Reprinted in Anderson (1971), pp. 184-85.

B13 *ANON. [Review: MT lecture.] New Whatcom
(Washington) Reveille, August 16.
     Notes his bad cold, solemn, severe man-
ner; the same issue carries what is apparently a reprint from a Portland newspaper,
noting his blend of humor and pathos;
there was a large audience. [Source: Reprinted in Twainian, XXIV (January-February,
1965), 2-3.]

B14 ELDERKIN, JOHN. A Brief History of the Lotos
Club. New York: Lotos Club, pp. 112-18.
     On the 1893 dinner honoring MT.

B15 HANNIGAN, D. F. "Mark Twain as a Critic,"
Free Review [later The University Magazine
and Free Review], V (October), 39-43.
     In response to MT's "The Literary Offenses
of Fenimore Cooper" in the July North American Review, defends Cooper but concedes that
"Mark Twain possesses a gift which Cooper
lacked."

B16 KIMBALL, ARTHUR REED. "Hartford's Literary
Corner," Outlook (New York), LI (June 1),
903-906.
     A popular account, with pictures of MT,
Charles Dudley Warner, Harriet Beecher
Stowe, and their homes, and also a picture
of Richard Burton; notes that MT is considerably more than a mere jester.

B17 MATTHEWS, BRANDER. "Of Mark Twain's Best Story," in his Books and Play-Books: Essays
on Literature and the Drama (London: Osgood, McIlvaine & Co.), pp. 184-92.
     On the truth and vitality of HF. On
pp. 160-61, writing of Robert Louis Stevenson, he recalls Stevenson's "hearty praise
of Mark Twain's Huckleberry Finn, and his
cordial belief that it was a great book,
riper in art and ethically richer than the
Tom Sawyer of which it is the sequel."

B18 O'RELL, MAX. "Mark Twain and Paul Bourget,"
North American Review, CLX (March), 302-10.
     A reply to MT's "What Paul Bourget Thinks
of Us," which appeared in the January issue,
attacking the picture of America in Bourget's Outre-Mer. O'Rell concedes that Bourget's main appeal is stylistic, and lost in
the English translation MT read; he adds a
spirited defense of French morality.

1896 A BOOKS - NONE

1896 B SHORTER WRITINGS

B1 ANON. "Mark Twain Up-to-Date," Idler, IX
(July), 901-906.
     A brief, general discussion containing no
new information, but with fourteen photographs of MT at different ages and an excellent photograph of his birthplace at Florida, Missouri before restoration.

B2 ANON. "Portraits of Mark Twain." McClure's,
VII (June), 73-78.
     Fifteen halftone portraits and a picture
of MT's Florida, Missouri birthplace; also,
a brief, conventional biographical sketch.

B3 *ANON. [Interview.] The Englishman (February 8).
     [Source: Baetzhold (1970), p. 184.] MT
"told a Calcutta reporter that on the basis
of progress in industry, education, security, and prosperity one must inevitably judge
British rule to be best for India.

B4 ANON. [Review: Joan of Arc.] Bookman (London), X (July), 124.
"It is all very fresh, and much finer in texture than, we confess, we had expected from its writer," and there is only one serious flaw: "Joan was argumentative, it is true; but he makes her arguments into long-winded discourses."

B5 *ANON. [Review: Mark Twains humoristische Schriften.] Beilage z. Allgemeinen Zeitung (May 6).
[Source: Henderson (1911), p. 218.]

B6 B., R. C. "Mark Twain on the Platform" (Reprinted from The Sketch), Critic (New York), XXVIII (April 25), 286.
On MT's world lecture-tour, with a description of his choice of material and of his platform appearance and manner. Followed by an excerpt from the Tribune, quoting an MT letter of February 16 to Charles Henry Webb, and by brief comment on Twichell's sketch of MT in the May Harper's.

B7 *CABLE, GEORGE WASHINGTON. "Samuel L. Clemens, 'Mark Twain,'" The Letter (a publication of the Home Culture Clubs of Northampton, Massachusetts), (February 1).
[Source: Reprinted in Turner (1960), pp. 122-24.] Praises the entertaining quality of MT's humor, and the way it bears rereading.

B8 HOWELLS, WILLIAM DEAN. [Review: Joan of Arc.] Harper's Weekly, XLI (May 30), 535-36.
MT was more restricted by historical facts here than in CY, and his attempts to portray language and attitudes of the age are less successful than passages in which he forgets and writes in his own idiom: "I am not at all troubled when he comes out with a good, strong, downright American feeling; my suffering begins when he does the supposed medieval thing." Reprinted in his My Mark Twain (1910), pp. 129-35.

B9 LE GALLIENNE, RICHARD. [Review: Personal Recollections of Joan of Arc.] Idler, X (August), 112-14.
Compares the historical approach to that of Carlyle's French Revolution, adding: "The man who has inaugurated a great epoch in the history of humour--and the whole of modern humour is the invention of Mark Twain--must have a great imagination, as he must also have a great heart. We have not waited for Joan of Arc to find these important gifts in Mark Twain, but certainly they are here once more, with even more than their ancient vitality." [Much of the review consists of long quoted passages.]

B10 MATTHEWS, BRANDER. "The Penalty of Humor," Harper's Monthly, XCII (May), 897-900.
MT's writing is uneven, but the best of it is very good; critics do an injustice if they dismiss him as merely a humorist. Reprinted in Twainian, XXX (March-April, 1971), 1-4.

B11 "ROUNDABOUT, ROBERT" (pseud.), "Roundabout Readings," Punch, CX (January 4), 4.
High praise for HF. Extensively quoted in Linneman (1965).

B12 TRENT, WILLIAM PETERFIELD. "Mark Twain as an Historical Novelist," Bookman (New York), III (May), 207-10.
Chiefly on JA. MT has failed in his effort, and Joan and the other characters (with the exception of the narrator) are not truly brought to life. Fortunately, MT has made his contribution elsewhere, as in TS, and "is something far more than a mere man of letters, even a great one; he is something more than a mere humorist, even a thoroughly genial and whole-souled one--he is a great writer." Reprinted in Anderson (1971), pp. 186-90.

B13 TWICHELL, JOSEPH H. "Mark Twain," Harper's Monthly, XCII (May), 817-26.
A survey of MT's career and works, with personal recollections, by MT's Hartford minister and friend of many years. There is a frontispiece portrait of MT, "Engraved by Florian from a photograph by Falk and Company, Sydney, October, 1895." Text extensively quoted by Chester L. Davis in Twainian, XXIX (September-October, 1970), 1-4; (November-December), 1-3. A summary, with quotations, may be found in Anon., "Mark Twain: A Character Sketch by a Friend," Review of Reviews (London), XIII (May, 1896), 442.

1897 A BOOKS - NONE

1897 B SHORTER WRITINGS

B1 ANON. "Facts versus Fun," Academy (London), LII (December 11), 519-20.
A review of More Tramps Abroad (Following the Equator), "a good-humoured, instructive, entertaining, careless, ill-considered, and rather disappointing book." Reprinted in Anderson (1971), pp. 207-209.

B2 ANON. "Mark Twain," in Charles Dudley Warner, ed., Library of the World's Best Literature (New York: R. S. Peale and J. A. Hill), VII, 3787-89.
An introduction to excerpts from LOM, CY, and P&P, emphasizing MT as an important writer as well as "the first of living humorists." The passages are selected to support the claim for his place as a writer who, "if the fashion of humor changes...will remain for other qualities--certain primordial qualities such as are exhibited in his work on the Mississippi--a force to be reckoned with in the literature of this century."

B3   ANON. "Mark Twain, Benefactor," Academy, LI
(June 26), 653-55.
        Before Kipling, MT was "the ideal of mas-
culine writers" in his direct approach to
his subject, but "in the early eighties....
He abandoned his zest in lawless life and
the records of his personal impressions in
the serious places of the earth, and he
turned to satire and romance"; Kipling "is
a finer artist than Mark Twain, his sympathies are wider, his genius is more comprehensive, and yet, when all be said, the
fact remains that Mark Twain is his literary
progenitor." Reprinted in Anderson (1971),
pp. 195-98.

B4   ANON. "Mark Twain's Home in the Temple of
Fame," Literary Digest, XIV (April 10),
701-701.
        Summarizes the estimate of MT by Charles
Miner Thompson in the April Atlantic
(1897.B28).

B5   ANON. "Mr. Stead on Mark Twain," Academy
Fiction Supplement (London), LII
(August 28), 58-59.
        An excerpt from the sketch of MT (here
attributed to William T. Stead) in the Review of Reviews, 1897.B27.

B6   *ANON. [Review: Mark Twains humoristische
Schriften.] Illustrierte Zeitung,
Nr. 2843.
        [Source: Henderson (1911), p. 219.]

B7   ANON. [Summary of reviews of More Tramps
Abroad (Following the Equator).] Academy
(London), LII (December 25), 580.

B8   ANON. [Review: More Tramps Abroad (Following the Equator).] Athenaeum, No. 3661
(December 25), pp. 883-84.
        "It is too long, and there are passages in
it that are too diffuse; but none of his
works would stand better for a sample of all
his wares--humour, good sense, good nature,
genuine good fun, shrewd observation, and
bits of description which would be hard to
equal in the writings of the most serious
travelers."

B9   *ANON. [Review: More Tramps Abroad (Following the Equator).] Speaker, XVI
(December 11), 671.
        [Source: Reprinted in Anderson (1971),
pp. 209-10.] A disappointing book, though
"distinctly worth reading," it contains
prosy and labored sections as well as some
good specimens of MT's humor and some "quick-
witted and caustic social judgments."

B10   ANON. [Brief review: Tom Sawyer, Detective;
and Other Tales.] Academy (London), LI
(January 2), 18.
        "On the whole, this is a bright, readable
book, with nothing of that detestable tendency to parody the wrong things which we
have occasionally regretted in the author."

B11   ANON. [Review: Tom Sawyer, Detective.]
Bookman (London), XI (February), 151-52.
        "We have liked Tom Sawyer and Huck Finn
better in other circumstances," but there
are ."much feebler things" in the book: "In
'Adam's Diary' Mark Twain is at his feeblest
and vulgarest; he fell no lower in 'A Yankee
at the Court of King Arthur.'"

B12   ANON. [Review: Tom Sawyer, Detective, and
Other Tales.] Athenaeum, No. 3617
(February 20), p. 244.
        The title story is a disappointment, "How
to Tell a Story" does not make its case, and
the chapters on Paul Bourget "hardly seem
worth reprinting."

B13   ANON. [Editorial comment.] Academy, LI
(June 26), 652.
        On the mistaken rumor that MT was in ill
health in London, and on the subscription
established by the New York Herald to relieve his financial distress.

B14   ANON. [Several brief items.] Critic (New
York), XXXI (November 20), 307.
        On MT in Vienna, his speech before the
Concordia literary association in broken
German, narrowly escaping being photographed
while inspecting the royal box at the new
Burgtheater, and his plans to remain in
Vienna for approximately eight months.

B15   BIGELOW, POULTENEY. "Foreign Notes," Harper's
Weekly, XLI (May 8), 463.
        MT finished his new book (FE) last night;
he and his family are well and happy in London, the daughters enjoying their bicycles.

B16   CLEMENS, SAMUEL L. "Mark Twain on Empire-
Building. A Philosophy of Clothes-Lines,"
Review of Reviews (London), XVI (November),
468.
        Excerpts from a portion of FE in McClure's,
November.

B17   ELLIS, ALFRED. [Photograph of MT in London.]
McClure's, X (November), 2.
        Precedes "From India to South Africa," an
excerpt from FE.

B18   *ENGEL, E. "Die Humoristen," in Geschichte der
nordamerikanischen Literatur. Leipzig: J.
Baedaker.
        [Source: Henderson (1911), p. 219.]

B19   FLAGG, CHARLES NOËL. [Full-page (frontis-
piece) portrait of MT, from portrait by
Flagg.] McClure's, VIII (March).
        This is the painting commissioned by Mrs.
Clemens in 1891, and hung in the house in
Hartford.

B20   *HAMMOND, MRS. JOHN HAYS. A Woman's Part in a
Revolution. New York and Bombay: Longmans,
Green and Company.

(*HAMMOND, MRS. JOHN HAYS)
On p. 152, describes MT's visit to the prisoners at Pretoria. [Source: Twainian, XVII (January-February, 1958), 1-3.]

B21 MARTIN, E. S. "This Busy World," Harper's Weekly, XLI (May 8), 462.
A brief note describes MT's original plan to dedicate JA to his wife Olivia as a silver-wedding present; through oversight the dedication was omitted from the first copies sold, but it will be on an inserted slip in copies sold in the future.

B22 ____. "This Busy World," Harper's Weekly, XLI (November 20), 1146.
A brief note on MT cites a newspaper story on a banquet in his honor in Vienna and quotes a Times (London, n.d.) story on his attendance at a stormy all-night session of the Austrian parliament.

B23 MASTERS, DAVID. "Mark Twain's Place in Literature," Chautauquan, XXV (September), 610-14.
MT has worked to overcome the handicap of his early reputation as a comic writer, and has done significant serious work. "While not a master of literary technique," he surpasses his contemporaries in the directness, clarity, and vividness of his prose. Reprinted in Anderson (1971), pp. 199-204.

B24 *MATTHEWS, BRANDER. "Mark Twain--His Work," Book Buyer, n.s. XIII (January), 977-79.
[Source: Reprinted in Anderson (1971), pp. 191-94.] A general estimate of MT, whose true worth has yet to be recognized by a public that still thinks of his early humor--which, good though it is, has been far surpassed by his later work.

B25 *____. [Review: The Gilded Age play.] Scribner's (July).
[Source: George B. Odell, Annals of the New York Stage, IX (1870-1875), New York: Columbia University Press, 1937, p. 556.] This review could not be found in examination of Scribner's at several libraries. Scribner's reviews at the beginning and ends of issues were sometimes cut out by binders, and it is possible that the Odell listing is correct. (T.A.T.)

B26 MURRAY, DAVID CHRISTIE. "My Contemporaries in Fiction. XII.--The Americans," Canadian Magazine, IX (October), 497-98.
MT is distinctively American, as Henry James and Mary Wilkins Freeman are not. Although he can be eloquent, "the medium he employs is the simplest and plainest American English." His creed is "manly, and clean, and wholesome." MT shows his limitations in CY: "Apart from its ethics, the book is a mistake, for a jest which could have been elaborated to tedium in a score of pages is stretched to spread

through a bulky volume, and snaps to pieces under that tension." Excerpted in Anderson (1971), pp. 205-206.

B27 [STEAD, WILLIAM T.] "Character Sketch: Mark Twain," Review of Reviews (London), XVI (August), 122-33.
[Unsigned; attributed to Stead (an editor of Review of Reviews) in Anon., "Mr. Stead on Mark Twain," Academy Fiction Supplement, 1897.B5.] Praises MT's works, and describes the man in part on the basis of meetings with him at which MT spoke of his books, Mississippi River water, clothing, bicycling, the type-setting machine, and the effect on employment of introducing new industrial processes. Includes several photographs of MT, including one "taken in 1890 by Peter Mapes Dodge" [Apparently at Onteora, New York--T.A.T.] Also appeared in Review of Reviews, Australasian ed., in September, according to Henderson (1911), p. 219.

B28 THOMPSON, CHARLES MINER. "Mark Twain as an Interpreter of American Character," Atlantic Monthly, LXXIX (April), 443-50.
"He is not a great or a skillful writer," and lacks the taste of an Oliver Wendell Holmes. His character Tom Sawyer is inferior to the Bad Boy of Thomas Bailey Aldrich, but the character Huck rises above the conventional vagabond in "his essential honesty, his strong and struggling moral nature." Despite the artistic flaws in MT's work the reflection of his life is appealing: "If a man can thoroughly express the individuality of a nation, he may fairly be called great." Reprinted in Scott (1955), pp. 55-64; (1967), pp. 60-69.

1898 A BOOKS - NONE

1898 B SHORTER WRITINGS

B1 *ANON. "The Anecdotal Side of Mark Twain," contributed by friends of Mark Twain. Ladies Home Journal, October.
[Source: Twainian, II (November, 1940), 4.]

B2 ANON. "Facts About Mark Twain," Review of Reviews (London), XVIII (September), 254.
Summarizes Carlyle Smythe's "The Real Mark Twain" (1898.B27) and quotes passages on "His Literary Tastes" (MT once told Smythe, "I have no really literary taste, and never had"), and "His Love of Children."

B3 ANON. "Following the Equator in Zigzag," Overland Monthly, XXXI (April), 378-80.
A review, using abundant quotation to illustrate an estimate of Following the Equator as "a happy and interesting jumble...a traveler's miscellany."

B4 *ANON. "Lettres Anglaises," Mercure de France, February.

1898 - Shorter Writings

(*ANON.)
Contains a review of More Tramps Abroad (Following the Equator). [Source: Henderson (1911), p. 219.]

B5   ANON. "Mark Twain as a Globe-Trotter," Literary Digest (New York), XVI (January 22), 115-16.
A review of Following the Equator; consists largely of excerpts showing MT's observation and humor, but little on his social commentary.

B6   *ANON. "Mark Twains Lebengeschichte," an unauthorized and offensive biography in a six-volume edition of MT's works published in Stuttgart by Robert Lutz.
[Source: Discussed in Twainian, VI (March-April, 1947), 1.] Also listed for 1899 (1899.B9).

B7   *ANON. [Review: Following the Equator.] Critic, XXXII (February 5), 89-90.
[Source: Reprinted in Anderson (1971), pp. 212-14.] Praises the description, social commentary, and humor: "One reads as if traveling with a shrewd, kindly, sincere, and humorous man of the world who has kept only illusions enough to make life really living.... With less of broad farce, this latest book has more wit, and more literary value, than any other volume of the author's work."

B8   ANON. [Review: More Tramps Abroad (Following the Equator).] Bookman (London), XIII (February), 164.
Brief and descriptive: MT's manner has been often imitated and this will not be as popular as his earlier travel books. The reader will find MT "an agreeable fellow-tramp, observant, thirsty for information, unprejudiced, and unconventional, often flippant in the wrong place, but not obtrusively playing the funny man."

B9   ANON. [Review: More Tramps Abroad (Following the Equator).] Review of Reviews (London), XVII (January), 79-82.
Chiefly summary and extensive quotation of "a first-class book of travel, entertaining, interesting, up-to-date, genial, full of Mark Twain's descriptive charm, and richly spiced with his extravagant nonsense."

B10   ANON. [Review: More Tramps Abroad (Following the Equator)]. Saturday Review (London), LXXXV (January 29), 153.
At his best, MT is "the Great American Spirit, tongue in cheek, strolling irresponsibly around the universe. And, between its wads of padding, 'More Tramps Abroad' does afford us this spectacle," but too often it is merely labored and contrived. Reprinted in Anderson (1971), pp. 210-11.

B11   ANON. [Brief item, praising the industry with which MT repaid the debts from his business failure.] Academy (London), LIII (March 5), 259.

B12   ANON. [Brief reply to Carlyle Smythe's "The Real Mark Twain" in the September Pall Mall Magazine.] Academy (London), LIV (August 27), 197.
Smythe belabors that point that MT is more than a humorist: "Who, it may be asked, doubted it?"

B13   ANON. [Brief item.] Literary Digest (New York), XVI (February 5), 163.
Quotes a Westminster Gazette citation of correspondence in the (British) Methodist Times recommending MT's New Pilgrim's Progress [the British title of IA], but only for "the reader who understands the difference between American humor and lying"; he will find beneath the joking "the mind of a 'cute, observant, and--yes--reverent traveller in the Holy Land.'"

B14   ANON. [Brief item, noting the unanimous praise by the British press for MT's paying off the last of the Webster and Company debts.] Literary Digest, XVI (April 16), 463.

B15   BARR, ROBERT. "Samuel L. Clemens: Mark Twain; A Character Sketch." McClure's X (January), 246-51.
Also in Idler (1898.B16).

B16   _____. "Samuel L. Clemens, 'Mark Twain.'" A Character Sketch by Robert Barr. With a Reproduction of Mark Twain's Latest Portrait," Idler (London), XIII (February), 23-29.
MT is a greater man than the label of popular humorist would suggest: "I am convinced that in Samuel L. Clemens America has lost one of its greatest statesmen; one of its most notable Presidents." Among MT's works, "The Prince and the Pauper is certainly one of the very best historical novels that ever was [sic] written, and if it had not appeared, some popular books which might be mentioned would not now be in existence. Joan of Arc has been hailed by several of the most distinguished critics of Europe as a distinct gain to the serious literature of this country. In A Connecticut Yankee at the Court of King Arthur the author ran counter, not only to his own label, but to a labelled section of history. The age of Arthur has been labelled 'sentimental,' and the iconoclast who stirred it up with the inflexible crowbar of fact, and showed under what hard and revolting conditions the ordinary man then existed, naturally brought upon himself the censure of the Slaves of the Label. But these are three books which, aside from their intrinsic interest, cause a man to think; and I hope

(BARR, ROBERT)
that some day Mr. Clemens will turn his attention to American history and give us a
volume or two which will be illuminating."

B17   BENTON, JOEL. "Reminiscences of Eminent Lecturers," Harper's Monthly, XCVI (March),
603-14.
Contains a rather conventional description
of MT's manner on the lecture platform,
pp. 610-11.

B18   BESANT, SIR WALTER. "My Favorite Novelist
and His Best Book," Munsey's Magazine,
XVIII (February), 659-64.
Praises HF for the pleasure it gives a
reader, as an adventure story and for a picture of its time and place, "because, you
see, there is no moral in this book; and no
motive; and no plot." Reprinted in Anderson
(1971), pp. 136-45.

B19   BROOKS, NOAH. "Early Days of the Overland,"
Overland Monthly, XXXII (July), 3-11.
Contains passing reference to MT, pp. 7-9,
as one of the contributors to the Overland
Monthly.

B20   _____. "Mark Twain in California," Century,
LVII (November), 97-99.
Repeats the familiar history of MT's early days in California; interesting only for
the weight lent by the fact that Brooks was
managing editor of the Sacramento Alta California, which sent MT on the Quaker City
tour. (P. 96 is an engraving by T. Johnson
from a photograph by Sarony).

B21   DE LAGUNA, THEODORE. "Mark Twain as a Pros-
pective Classic," Overland Monthly, XXXI
(April), 364-67.
Praises MT as story-teller rather than
novelist, his style "historically...of in-
finite import. Aesthetically, it has been
seriously undervalued. Quite unpretentious,
it is none the less admirably adapted to
its content." Summarized in "Mark Twain
as a Word-Painter," Literary Digest (New
York), XVI (May 28), 642. Reprinted in
Anderson (1971), pp. 216-20.

B22   HILLIER, ALFRED P. [Passage from his "newly
published Raid and Reform."] Academy (London), LIII (January 22), 96.
An extract from his diary, describing
MT's visit to the prison camp in Pretoria
during his world lecture tour. MT told
the prisoners that prison life provides
valuable leisure, and promised to ask the
president to extend their sentences.

B23   PANCOAST, HENRY S. An Introduction to American Literature. New York: Henry Holt and
Company.
Briefly discusses MT in a section on American humorists (pp. 328-30), criticizing
the "cynical levity" of IA; concedes in a
footnote: "It is but just to remind the

student that Mark Twain has done some excellent work of a quite different character.
He is here alluded to simply as a humorist."

B24   *POTTER-FRISSELL, E. "Americans in Vienna:
Mark Twain," Musical Courier, December 7.
[Source: Twainian, II (February, 1943),
6.]

B25   *SCHLIECH, K. L. "Psychophysik des Humors,"
Zukunft, XXV, pp. 374-93.
[Source: Henderson (1911), p. 219.]

B26   SCOLIK, CH. "Mark Twain Sitting for His Portrait, March, 1898." McClure's, XI (May),
2.
Photograph by Ch. Scolik, Vienna: MT
sitting for a bust by Miss Theresa Feodorowna Ries.

B27   SMYTHE, CARLYLE. "The Real Mark Twain," Pall
Mall Magazine, XVI (September), 28-36.
A general discussion of the man and his
works, noting that his reputation as humorist sometimes proved burdensome; includes
personal reminiscences of MT in India, and
three photographs of him. An extensive excerpt appears under the same title in Literary Digest (New York), XVII (September 24),
372-73. Summarized in "Facts About Mark
Twain" (1898.B2).

B28   *STANLEY, HIRAM M. [Review: Following the
Equator.] Dial, XXIV (March 16), 186-87.
[Source: Reprinted in Anderson (1971),
pp. 214-15.] "A first-rate specimen of
that eminently sagacious mixture of sense
and nonsense which is so characteristic of
him."

B29   *STEUART, JOHN A. "American Fiction in England," Outlook, I (June 25), 658-59.
[Source: Rodney dissertation [1945],
p. 281).

B30   *T., S. "Mark Twain," Monatblätter für
deutsche Literatur, III, pp. 33-35.
[Source: Henderson (1911), p. 219.]

1899 A BOOKS - NONE

1899 B SHORTER WRITINGS

B1   *ANON. "Lettres Anglaises," Mercure de France,
December.
A review of Mark Twain's Collected Works.
[Source: Henderson (1911), p. 220.]

B2   *ANON. "Mark Twain as a Cub Pilot," Saturday
Evening Post (December 16).
[Source: Twainian, n.s., II (June, 1943),
6.]

B3   ANON. [Brief comment on the reminiscences
which MT says he has been writing.] Academy
(London), LVI (May 27), 572.

1899 - Shorter Writings

B4   ANON. [Brief comment on MT's graceful, natu-
      ral way of accepting the praise given him
      and his works.] Academy (London), LVI
      (June 17), 648.

B5   ANON. [Brief comment on the forthcoming
      Author's Edition of MT's works, and on his
      "Concerning the Jews."] Academy (London)
      LVII (September 9), 243.

B6   ANON. [Brief quotation from MT on topic of
      Christian Science, in the current Cosmo-
      politan.] Academy (London), LVII
      (October 21), 445.

B7   ANON. [Quotations from More Tramps Abroad
      (Following the Equator).] Academy (London),
      LVII (November 18), 560.
         Editorial comment notes MT's scant sympa-
      thy for the Boers.

B8   *ANON. [Article identifying the original of
      Colonel Sellers (in The Gilded Age) as
      James W. Wardner.] Utica (N.Y.) Saturday
      Globe, February 11.
         [Source: letter to Chester L. Davis from
      George H. Town in Twainian, XVI (January-
      February, 1957), 4.]

B9   *ANON. [Introduction: Mark Twains humoris-
      tische Schriften.] Stuttgart: Lutz.
         [Source: Henderson (1911), p. 220.]
      Also listed for 1898 (1898.B6).

B10   ARCHER, WILLIAM. America Today: Observa-
      tions and Reflections. New York: Charles
      Scribner's Sons.
         On MT, pp. 212-13: "If any work of in-
      contestable genius, and plainly predestined
      to immortality, has been issued in the Eng-
      lish language in the past quarter century,
      it is that brilliant romance of the Great
      Rivers, The Adventures of Huckleberry Finn.
      Intensely American though he be, 'Mark
      Twain' is one of the greatest living mas-
      ters of the English language." [Apparently
      this may have appeared previously in Pall
      Mall Gazette or Pall Mall Magazine, accord-
      ing to a note on p. vii.]

B11   BROOKS, NOAH. "Noah Brooks on Mark Twain,"
      Overland Monthly, XXXIII (April), 379-80.
         An excerpt from Brooks's recent article
      in The Century, on MT's connection with the
      Overland in its early days.

B12   *DOTEN, ALF. "Early Journalism in Nevada."
      The Nevada Magazine, (Winnemucca, Nevada), I
      (October), 182-84.
         Includes the account of a joke Steve Gil-
      lis played, presenting MT with an imitation
      Meerschaum pipe. [Source: Benson (1938),
      pp. 88, 90, 162.]

B13   DOUMIC, RÉNÉ. "Revue Littéraire: Nos Humor-
      istes," Revue des Deux Mondes, CLV
      (October 15), 924-25.

Brief mention of MT (p. 932), citing The
Stolen White Elephant as an example of his
works famous in the English- and German-
speaking countries: "Cela est puéril et
long. On a l'impression d'une farce pour
grands enfans qui aiment à être secoués d'un
gros rire. L'impression n'est pas juste,
évidemment; et il est clair que, pour avoir
conquis une si grande réputation, Mark
Twain doit être un fantaisiste éminent.
Mais de cette fantaisie rien ne passe dans
la traduction."

B14   FIELDER, ELIZABETH DAVIS. "Familiar Haunts of
      Mark Twain," Harper's Weekly, XLIII
      (December 16), 10-11.
         A description of Hannibal, Missouri, with
      several photographs, including "Laura Hawk-
      ins as a girl" and the "The Hannibal of Fif-
      ty Years Ago."

B15   *HARLAND, HENRY. "Mark Twain," London Daily
      Chronicle, December 11.
         [Source: Reprinted in Anderson (1971),
      pp. 227-31.] Primarily on IA, which typi-
      fies MT's work: "The qualities and defects
      of The Innocents Abroad are the qualities
      and defects of Mark Twain's temperament, and
      they are present in varying proportions in
      all his books: vulgarity, naturalness, ir-
      reverence, freshness of vision, honesty,
      good-humor, wholesomeness." RI, TS, and HF
      are better books.

B16   HIGGINSON, THOMAS WENTWORTH. Cheerful Yester-
      days. Boston, New York: Houghton, Mifflin
      and Company, pp. 284-85.
         Visiting Darwin, in 1872, learned of his
      "hearty enjoyment of Mark Twain, who had
      then hardly begun to be regarded as above
      the Josh Billings grade of humorist; but
      Darwin was amazed that I had not read 'The
      Jumping Frog,' and said that he always kept
      it by his bedside for midnight amusement."

B17   *HUNEKER, J. G. [Mention of MT.] Musical
      Courier, XXXVIII (June 28), 23.
         [Source: Quoted by Robert Falk in The
      Victorian Mode in American Fiction, 1865-
      1885 (1965), p. 165.] "Mr. Clemens is one
      of the most original writers America has
      produced and more of an artist than is gen-
      erally believed. Being a humorous soul the
      public was slow to recognize his power in
      other fields. I pin my faith on Huckleberry
      Finn. For me it is the great American novel,
      even if it is written for boys."

B18   *KEELING, ANNE E. "American Humour: Mark
      Twain," London Quarterly Review [Not the
      same as Quarterly Review], XCII (July),
      147-62.
         [Source: Asselineau (1954), No. 18; re-
      printed in Anderson (1971), pp. 221-27.]
      Discusses the joking in IA, the irreverence
      in CY, the indictment of slavery in PW and
      FE, calling MT "this sturdy foe of oppression

(*KEELING, ANNE E.)
and injustice, this lover of the heroic and
the magnanimous...who still continues to
provide clean, wholesome food for laughter,
under the familiar style of Mark Twain."

B19   KIPLING, RUDYARD. "An Interview with Mark
Twain," in his From Sea to Sea: Letters of
Travel. New York: Doubleday & McClure
Company and Toronto: George N. Morang &
Co., Ltd. II, pp. 167-81.
[Originally published in The Pioneer
(Allahbad), March 18, 1890 and The Pioneer
Mail, March 19, 1890, according to Asselineau (1954), No. 8. In his "Preface" to
Vol. I, Kipling says the material in the
two volumes "was written by me for the Civil and Military Gazette and the Pioneer
between 1887-1889" (p. v.)]. After pages
on his reverence for MT and the difficulty
of finding his Elmira home, quotes him on
copyright, and on a possible sequel to TS:
"Suppose we took the next four and twenty
years of Tom Sawyer's life and gave a little joggle to the circumstances that controlled him. He would, logically and according to the joggle, turn out a rip or an
angel" (p. 175). Also gives MT's views on
the impossibility of candid autobiography,
the nuisance of conscience, his lack of interest in current novels, and his distinction between public and private opinions.
Describes MT's grey hair and corncob pipe.

B20   LEVY, M. S. "A Rabbi's Reply to Mark Twain,"
Overland Monthly, XXXIV (October), 364-367.
An answer to MT's "Concerning the Jews"
in the September Harper's, lists Jewish
patriots and their contributions to American
freedom, and points to brave Jewish soldiers
in American and other armies.

B21   LIVINGSTONE, LUTHER S. "The First Books of
Some American Authors: V.--Mark Twain,
Bret Harte, and Artemus Ward," Bookman (New
York), VIII (February), 563-67.
On The Celebrated Jumping Frog of Cala-
veras County, and Other Sketches (1867), re-
producing the title page and with comments
by MT on the book (pp. 563-64).

B22   MOFFETT, SAMUEL E. "Mark Twain: A Biographical Sketch," McClure's, XIII (October),
523-29.
"Editor's Note.--Owing to the number of
unauthorized and largely apocryphal accounts of his life that have appeared in
various countries, Mark Twain asked his
nephew, Mr. Samuel E. Moffett, to write a
sketch of him that should be authentic.
The result was the present article, of
which Mark wrote, when it was submitted for
his opinion, 'this biographical sketch suits
me entirely--in simplicity, directness, dignity, lucidity--in all ways.' It so completely satisfied him that he has chosen it
to appear in the collected subscription
edition." In the Authorized Edition (New

York: Harper & Brothers, 1925) it appears
at the end of In Defense of Harriet Shelley
(XVI, 387-96).

1900 A BOOKS

A1   *LAUTREC, GABRIEL DE. Contes Choisis de Mark
Twain, traduits par G. de Lautrec et pré-
cedés d'une étude sur l'humour. Paris:
Mercure de France, 2e éd.
[Source: Asselineau (1954), No. 20:
"First dated edition of Twain's Sketches in
French translation, preceded only by a se-
lection published by Nelson."]

1900 B SHORTER WRITINGS

B1   ANON. "General Gossip of Authors and Writers," Current Literature, XXIX (December),
708-10.
On pp. 708-709, summarizes "a tribute in
the New York Times" by Major J. B. Pond,
who describes MT's world lecture tour and
praises his personal traits.

B2   ANON. "The Lounger," Critic (New York),
XXXVII (November), 398.
Includes brief comment on MT's return from
London, where he told a reporter he had
"done more regular, systematic work here
than in any other city."

B3   ANON. "Mark's New Way," Academy (London),
LIX (September 29), 258-59.
A review of The Man that Corrupted Hadleyburg. "The new Mark Twain--the Mark Twain
of this book in particular--is not a whit
less readable than the old, and he is more
provocative of thought."

B4   ANON. "Mark Twain, American," Harper's Weekly, XLIV (December 15), 1204.
A short editorial praising MT "for his humor, for his integrity, for the glorious example he has set, for his philosophy, his
kindness of heart, and his gentleness of
manners, but, above all...the incarnation of
all the virtues of civic life."

B5   ANON. "Mark Twain, American Citizen," Nation, LXXI (November 29), 419-20.
Praises MT's attacks on American corruption at home, policy in Philippines and
China.

B6   ANON. "Mark Twain's Aftermath," Outlook
(London), VI (September 29), 280.
A review of The Man that Corrupted Hadleyburg. There are a few good parts, but "most
of this volume reads like a third-rate imitation of the Mark Twain whom we knew and
loved of old."

B7   ANON. "Mr. Kipling and Mark Twain," Academy
(London), LVIII (March 17), 237.
On Kipling's interview with MT, as re-
printed in his From Sea to Sea. Here quoted

1900 - Shorter Writings

(ANON.)
extensively, it "is in some respects the best interview that we have ever read," revealing Kipling's profound admiration for MT.

B8   ANON. [Brief Review: The Man that Corrupted Hadleyburg.] Athenaeum, No. 3805 (September 29), p. 410.
      This collection includes some good things, but "diffuseness...spoils most of the matter in this book." The title story is not mentioned.

B9   ANON. [Review: The Man that Corrupted Hadleyburg.] Blackwood's, CLXVIII (November), 733-34.
      Nothing on the title story, and the other stories and sketches in the volume are dismissed as "nothing very great," but TS, HF, LOM "form as conspicuous and valuable a contribution to the literature of the United States as has been made since the days of Poe" and "Mark Twain at his best is as good, in his own line, as any living writer of English prose." At times he is "too fond of being didactic, of pointing morals, of teaching the old world how to conduct its affairs," and he "is conspicuously defective in the historical sense." See 1900.B11.

B10   ANON. [Brief notice: The Man that Corrupted Hadleyburg.] Critic (New York), XXXVII (November), 468.

B11   ANON. [Review: The Man that Corrupted Hadleyburg.] Living Age, Seventh Series, IX (from beginning, CCXXVII; December 15), 695.
      After TS, HF, and LOM it would be wrong to reproach MT for this new book. There are glimpses of his old humor, but now "He is too fond of being didactic, of pointing morals, of teaching the old world how to conduct its affairs." His sense of history is weak. See 1900.B9.

B12   ANON. [Review: The Man that Corrupted Hadleyburg.] Review of Reviews (London), XXII (September), 398.
      Mostly extracts.

B13   *ANON. [Review: Gabriel de Lautrec, trans., Contes Choisis de Mark Twain.] Mercure de France (September).
      [Source: Henderson (1911), p. 221.]

B14   ANON. [Brief summary and quotation of J. E. Hodder Williams's illustrated article on MT in the current Bookman (London).] Academy, LIX (September 8), 184.

B15   ANON. [Brief Notice: Vols. VI-XII of the Chatto collected edition.] Bookman (London), XVIII (April), 30.
      Comments on the pleasure in looking again on RI, TS, GA, and LOM.

B16   ARCHER, WILLIAM. "'The Man that Corrupted Hadleyburg'--A New Parable." Critic (New York), XXXVII (November), 413-15.
      "A parable pure and simple...were we to take it as a story, as a representation of life, its cynicism would be intolerable." MT has given us moral lessons "translated into modern terms of almost Swiftian sternness." (More a discussion of this one tale than a review of the book.)

B17   BEACH, E. E. [Review: The Man that Corrupted Hadleyburg.] Harper's Weekly, XLIV (August 25), 806.
      A general and largely uncritical description of several stories in the new book.

B18   *BELEZZA, PAOLO. Humour. Strenna a Beneficio del Pio Instituto dei Rachitici. Milan: P. Agnelli.
      [Source: Reviewed by Howells in "A Modern Italian View of Mark Twain" (1901.B18), also Asselineau (1954), No. 21.]

B19   BIGELOW, POULTENEY. "God Speed Mark Twain!" Independent, LII (October 25), 248-50.
      On MT's return to New York from his world lecture tour, and on his kindness to other authors. Sketch of MT by Bigelow.

B20   *BRIDGMAN, L. J. "To Mark Twain," Harper's Weekly (December 8).
      [Source: Listed in Twainian, II (March, 1940), 3 as "poem illustrated by author"; a search of this issue was unsuccessful, and the citation appears to be incorrect.]

B21   BRONSON, WALTER C. [Discussion of MT] in his A Short History of American Literature, Designed Primarily for Use in Schools and Colleges. (Boston: D. C. Heath & Co., Publishers), pp. 286-87.
      Calls MT "the greatest writer of the West," noting both his vigor in books dealing with the Mississippi, and in another group of "his better works...an historical imagination and a finish of manner hardly to be expected in the author of the rougher books.... Time will winnow much chaff from his pages, but much of great merit will remain."

B22   BURTON. "Aldine Club Dinner to Mark Twain, December 4, 1900," Harper's Weekly, XLIV (December 15), 1203.
      A photograph of MT and other guests at the dinner, with identifications but no other text.

B23   CLEMENS, WILL M. "Mark Twain on the Lecture Platform: The story of an unwilling orator, with extracts and unpublished letters written by the famous humorist," Ainslee's Magazine (New York), VI (August), 25-32.
      Contains a number of MT letters to James Redpath, and reprints the reactions of Joel Benton and H. R. Haweis to his lectures;

(CLEMENS, WILL M.)
tells of the time when the Hon. Demshain [De Shane?] Hornet gave a temperance lecture when MT failed to arrive, but left in disgust when the audience mistook him for MT and laughed at every word he said. Frontispiece photograph of MT by Sarony, p. 2.

B24 *D. "Mark Twain," Alte und Neue Welt, XXXIV, p. 700.
A review of his Ausgewählte humorist. Schriften. [Source: Henderson (1911), p. 221.]

B25 *FORD, JAMES L. "An American Humorist," Collier's Weekly (November 3).
[Source: Twainian, I (December, 1939), 6.]

B26 H., W. J. [Quotations from letter.] Critic (New York), XXXVII (November), 398-400.
Extensive quotations from a letter from W. J. H. on possible bombshells in MT autobiography to be published a hundred years after his death--but "how slender is the possibility" that his reputation will endure.

B27 HAWLEY, B. F., M.D. "A Further Glimpse of Mark Twain's Hero," Century, LX (May), 157-58.
A letter to the editor, occasioned by MT's "My Debut as a Literary Person" in the November Century; describes an 1876 sea-trip on which Captain Josiah Mitchell was Hawley's fellow-passenger, with a cabin across the corridor. Although Mitchell was weakened by the ordeal MT described, and now terminally ill, by will-power he remained alive long enough to reach New York and see his wife a day before he died.

B28 HOLLISTER, WILFRED R., and HARRY NORMAN. Five Famous Missourians. Kansas City, Missouri: Hudson-Kimberley Publishing Company.
On MT, pp. 7-85; basically biographical. "The data relating to the subjects has been furnished the authors almost entirely by members of the families and personal friends of the subjects, and has been authenticated by reference to them, in order that apocryphal matter might not be used" (Preface, p. 3). Contains anecdotes of MT's early years, some of which may be useful; refers to Pamela Clemens as "Parmelia" (pp. 13, 29).

B29 HOWELLS, W[ILLIAM] D[EAN]. "The Surprise Party to Mark Twain," Harper's Weekly, XLIV (December 15), 1205.
Howells' imaginary conversation with a number of the characters created by MT, who plan a party in his honor; Howells, asked to help in the festivities, remembers and liberally quotes his tribute to MT at a Lotos Club dinner as a text which might be used again.

B30 LANS, MATTHEW IRVING. "Biographical Sketch," in English as She Is Taught, by Mark Twain. (Boston: Mutual Book Company) [pp. iii-v.]
A brief review of the salient events in MT's life as they were generally known at the time.

B31 NICHOLSON, WILLIAM [Color sketch of MT.] Harper's Weekly, XLIV (December 15), 1201.
Front-cover portrait, without text.

B32 *POND, JAMES B. "Across the Continent with Mark Twain," Saturday Evening Post (September 29), p. 6.
[Source: Twainian, n.s., II (June, 1943), 6; Harnsberger (1960), p. 281, n. 4.]

B33 ____. Eccentricities of Genius: Memories of Famous Men and Women of the Platform and Stage. New York: G. W. Dillingham Company, 197-233 (preceded by portrait), and passim.
Extensive account of MT on lecture tours, but very little on his actual lecturing. The page numbers given in the index are not entirely accurate. Contains MT letters.

B34 REGAN, W. A. "A Surprise Party to Mark Twain by His Characters," Harper's Weekly, XLIV (December 15), 1215-16.
A two-page drawing of MT and his characters; there is a brief description in Anon., "Mark Twain and His Characters," p. 1219, also noting MT's enjoyment of the dramatization of P&P.

B35 SHINN, EVERETT. [Portrait.] Critic (New York), XXXVI (March), facing p. 193.
Full-length, "from a pastel drawing by Everett Shinn." Also, brief note on p. 193: MT will return to America in April; where he will live is uncertain.

B36 WASHINGTON, BOOKER T. Up from Slavery: An Autobiography. [The copy examined was Garden City, New York: Doubleday, Doran & Company, 1938, with a 1900 copyright notice], p. 284.
Reports that his first meeting with MT was in London in 1899, at a reception given by Ambassador Choate; he does not elaborate.

B37 WHITING, LILIAN. Kate Field: A Record. Boston: Little, Brown and Company.
Contains text of an MT letter of March 8, 1886 in which he agrees with her hostility toward the Mormon religion: "I would like to see it extirpated, but always by fair means, not these Congressional rascalities. If you can destroy it with a book,--by arguments and facts, not brute force,--you will do a good and wholesome work." MT would be willing to publish such a book, if his publishing company were not already committed by contracts for the next few years.

B38 WILLIAMS, J. E. HODDER. "Mark Twain," Bookman (London), XVIII (September), 169-74.
A very general sketch of MT's life and

1900 - Shorter Writings

(WILLIAMS, J. E. HODDER)
works, providing no new information and
very little critical comment.

1901 A BOOKS - NONE

1901 SHORTER WRITINGS

B1   ANON. "Mark Twain and the Missionaries: The
      Parable of the Watermelons," Review of Re-
      views (London), XXIII (February), 467.
         Extract from MT's reply to Dr. Ament in
      North American Review, February. No signi-
      ficant commentary.

B2   ANON. "Mark Twain on M'Kinley," Nation,
      LXXII (February 7), 104-105.
         Editorial on "To the Person Sitting in
      Darkness" in the February North American
      Review: "delicious though biting satire."

B3   *ANON. "Mark Twain--The World's Greatest Hu-
      morist. Twenty Reasons Why We Say So.
      From a Personal Examination," Phrenologic-
      al Journal and Science of Health, CXI
      (April), 103-106.
         [Source: Reprinted in Madeline B. Stern,
      "Mark Twain Had His Head Examined" (1969).]

B4   ANON. "A Sketch of Mark Twain. The Veteran
      Author Returns to America," Review of Re-
      views (New York), XXIII (January), 37-41.
         A popular account of MT's life, travels,
      and works; laudatory and largely descript-
      ive, illustrated with photographs of MT and
      his Hannibal and Hartford homes.

B5   ANON. "To a Person Sitting in Darkness,"
      Outlook (New York), LXVII (February 16),
      386-87.
         MT's article in the North American Review
      "will have no effect on the opinion of the
      fairly informed, unprejudiced, and inde-
      pendently thoughtful student of current af-
      fairs.... Most Americans will think that
      American soldiers and Christian missiona-
      ries are as much entitled as Satan not to
      be condemned without a hearing."

B6   ANON. [Anecdote concerning an MT lecture in-
      troduced by a local minister's lengthy
      prayer.] Book Buyer, XXII (April), 179.
         Includes photograph of MT, facing p. 179.

B7   ANON. [Portrait of MT in Harper's Magazine
      advertisement.] Harper's Weekly, XLV
      (November 16), verso of front cover.
         [Mistakenly reported as a full-page
      portrait in Twainian, II (March, 1940),
      4.]

B8   ANON. [Selections from Extracts from Adam's
      Diary in April Harper's Magazine.] Review
      of Reviews (London), XXIII (April), 378-89.
         Commentary says it is amusing.

B9   ANON. [Summary of "To the Person Sitting in
      Darkness" in North American Review,
      February.] Review of Reviews (London),
      XXIII (February), 254-56.
         A few words of praise are given, but no
      significant analysis.

B10   DOUMIC, RENÉ. Études sur la Littérature Fran-
      çaise, Quatrième Série. Paris: Perrin &
      Cie., p. 257.
         In a chapter titled "Nos Humoristes," says
      the Anglo-Saxon humor does not readily trans-
      late into French because of different cus-
      toms and attitudes. An example is MT, with
      his le Vol de l'Éléphant blanc: "Cela est
      puéril et long."

B11   ELDERKIN, JOHN, CHESTER S. LORD, and HORATIO
      N. FRASER, eds. After Dinner Speeches at
      the Lotos Club. New York: Privately Print-
      ed.
         Contains the text of MT's speech at the
      dinner in his honor, November 10, 1900
      (pp. 374-79); without editorial comment,
      but with group photograph facing p. 374.

B12   "EPHE, UNCLE." "To Mark Twain: A Southern
      Tribute," Harper's Weekly, XLV (March 16),
      301.
         An affectionate poem in Negro dialect.

B13   FRANCE, CLEMENS J. "Mark Twain as Educator,"
      Education, XXI (January) 265-74.
         Sympathy, insight into human nature, and
      freedom from prejudice qualify MT to speak
      as an educator, and his works embody "a
      common sense philosophy of life." TS shows
      how a real boy can mature through experience
      if allowed to do so, and has the further
      value of reminding adult readers of the im-
      portance of boyhood.

B14   HALSTEAD, MURAT. "Happenings to Humorists:
      Tales of Three of the Old Masters," Criteri-
      on, II (August), 15-18.
         Anecdotes of Artemus Ward, Ned Sothern,
      and MT.

B15   HARKINS, E. F. "Mark Twain," in his Famous
      Authors (Men). (Boston: L. C. Page &
      Company), pp. 43-57.
         An admiring but superficial biography
      for the general reader.

B16   *HEIM, H. "Mitteilungen a. d. gesammten
      Gebiete d. engl. Sprache u. Literatur,"
      Beibl. z. Anglia, pp. 28-31.
         (Contains a review of TS, in gekürzten
      Fassg.; W. K. Krüger, Leipzig: Freitag,
      1900.)
         [Source: Henderson (1911), p. 222, also
      listing another review "by J. Ellinger.
      Same journal, s. 148."]

B17 HOWELLS, WILLIAM DEAN. "Mark Twain: An In-
     quiry," North American Review, CLXXII
     (February), 306-21; also CXCI (June, 1910),
     836-50.
          A general discussion of his career and
     works, noting their seriousness and import-
     ance but also the delight and entertainment
     they bring readers. Discusses MT's delib-
     erate avoidance of purely logical structure
     in his writing: "He would take whatever
     offered itself to his hand out of that
     mystical chaos, that divine ragbag, which
     we call the mind." His language is straight-
     forward, with words used in their common ac-
     ceptance and without regard for derivation.
     "The result is the English in which the
     most vital works of English literature are
     cast, rather than the English of Milton and
     Thackeray and Mr. Henry James." Reprinted
     in his My Mark Twain (1910), pp. 165-85,
     and (almost in full) in Scott (1955)
     pp. 65-78; (1967), pp. 70-83; excerpted in
     Simpson (1968), pp. 103-105.

B18 _____. "A Modern Italian View of Humor
     (Second Paper)," North American Review,
     CLXXIII (November), 709-20; on MT,
     pp. 710-11, 714-17, 720.
          A review of Paolo Bellezza, Humour (Stren-
     na a Beneficio del Pio Instituto dei
     Rachitici, 1900). Generally agrees with
     Bellezza's general discussion of humor, es-
     pecially in calling MT the greatest living
     humorist. Reprinted in Howells' My Mark
     Twain (1910), pp. 157-64.

B19 *HUBBARD, ELBERT. "Heart to Heart Talks with
     Philistines by the Pastor of His Flock,"
     The Philistine, XII (April), 146-49.
          [Source: reprint of an anecdote in Abe
     C. Ravit and Norris Yates, "Mark Twain,
     Cable, and The Philistine," Mark Twain Jour-
     nal, X (Summer, 1955), 14, 23.]

B20 LEUPP, FRANCIS E. "Mark Twain as Inventor,"
     Harper's Weekly, XLV (September 7), 903.
          Describes patents assigned to MT for a
     buckle strap, self-pasting scrap-book, and
     history game.

B21 LUTHER, MARK LEE. "Mark Twain and the First
     Nevada Legislature," Land of Sunshine [later
     became Out West: A Magazine of the Old
     Pacific and the New], XV (August-September),
     144-49.
          Describes a copy of the Territorial Enter-
     prise, quotes extensively from RI, defends
     the Legislature against "the implication of
     selfish incompetence," comparing Nevada
     legislative records with MT's account, but
     gives little other new information.

B22 McARTHUR, JAMES. "Notes of a Bookman," Harp-
     er's Weekly, XLV (October 19), 1058.
          Briefly notes Paul Kester's dramatization
     of Tom Sawyer, now in the hands of Charles
     Frohman. "Mr. Kester has taken his own time

in making the play, and the result will, I
believe, be highly satisfactory."

B23 *MANN, MAX. [Biographical Introduction to A
     Tramp Abroad (selected chapters for use in
     the schools).] Leipzig: Freytag.
          [Source: Henderson (1911), p. 222.]

B24 NEWCOMER, ALPHONSO G. American Literature.
     Chicago: Scott, Forasman and Company,
     277-79, and passim.
          Praises MT as storyteller, satirist, moral-
     ist, and for his portrayal of character.
     [A textbook.]

B25 [PECK, HARRY THURSTON.] "As to Mark Twain,"
     Bookman (New York), XII (January), 441-42.
          [Incorrectly listed as "Mark Twain: A
     Humorist Only," in Twainian, I (November,
     1939), 3.] Takes issue with the lavish
     praise given him: "Mark Twain is first and
     last and all the time, so far as he is any-
     thing, a humourist and nothing more." Photo-
     graph of MT, p. 440. Reprinted in Anderson
     (1971), pp. 231-34, with the attribution to
     Peck. Anderson adds that the Washington
     Times answered Peck in "A Little Man and a
     Great Subject" (January 31).

B26 PHILLIPS, R. E. "Mark Twain: More than Humor-
     ist," Book Buyer, XXII (April), 196-201.
          Praises his keen observation and his dedi-
     cation to "justice, absolute democracy and
     humanity" in a discussion of MT as a serious
     writer. Reprinted in Anderson (1971),
     pp. 234-42.

B27 *RAMSAY, W. "Mark Twain: A Biographical
     Sketch," Great Thoughts (December).
          [Source: Twainian, II (February, 1940),
     7.]

B28 TRENT, W. P. "A Retrospect of American Humor,"
     Century Illustrated Monthly Magazine, LXIII
     (n.s. XLI; November), 45-64.
          A very general discussion of a number of
     humorists, including MT; includes drawing
     and photograph of MT.

B29 *WAGNER, PH. [Review: The Adventures of Tom
     Sawyer. In gekürzten Fassg. (W. G. Krüger,
     Leipzig: Freytag, 1900).] Englische Studi-
     en, p. 164.
          [Source: Henderson (1911), p. 222.]

B30 WENDELL, BARRETT. A Literary History of Ameri-
     ca. New York: Charles Scribner's Sons, and
     London: T. Fisher Unwin.
          Comparatively little on MT, but only be-
     cause the book emphasizes authors no longer
     living. Compares MT to Franklin and Irving,
     despite lesser grace, for his sober confu-
     sion of fact and nonsense (pp. 101, 173,
     508), and says that his power "would have
     been exceptional anywhere" (p. 513). HF,
     with its dialect, is a "masterpiece, that
     amazing Odyssey of the Mississippi," the

1901 - Shorter Writings

(WENDELL, BARRETT)
product of "an artistic conscience as stren-
uous as Irving's, or Poe's, or Hawthorne's"
(p. 477); it is "a book which in certain
moods one is disposed for all its eccentric-
ity to call the most admirable work of literary art as yet produced on this continent"
(p. 503).

1902 A BOOKS - NONE

1902 B SHORTER WRITINGS

B1   ABERNETHY, JULIAN W. American Literature.
New York: Charles E. Merrill Co. [A text-
book; Source: 1908 Reprinting.] On MT,
pp. 469-72.
Sees MT as essentially a humorist and de-
cries his supposed vulgarity, though praising his clear vision and "clean-cut, effective expression." TS and HF are "astonishingly clever studies of the American bad
boy," and LOM is his "best autobiographical
narrative."

B2   ANON. "American Booksellers Entertained by
Harper & Brothers," Harper's Weekly, XLVI
(June 28), 814.
A group photograph of authors and other
guests at the American Booksellers' Convention; MT appears prominently in the left
foreground.

B3   ANON. "A Banquet of Sensations" [Review of
A Double-Barrelled Detective Story], Outlook (London), IX (July 5), 717.
"Starting with an idea sombre enough to
satisfy a tragic dramatist of ancient
Greece, he suddenly becomes farcical and
fizzles...not only does the inventor of
tragic 'situations' destroy their dignity,
but the humorist...turns giggler" in his
Sherlock Holmes burlesque.

B4   ANON. "In Honor of Mark Twain: Verses at a
Dinner Celebrating His Sixty-Seventh Birthday," Harper's Weekly, XLVI (December 13),
1943-44.
Includes William Dean Howells, "A Double-
Barreled Sonnet to Mark Twain (Written to
be Heard, Not Read)"; John Kendrick Bangs,
"Mark Twain (A Post-Prandial Obituary)"
[with passing mention of the "Gyascutus,"
which has been compared to the "Royal Nonesuch" in HF]; Henry Van Dyke, "A Toast to
Mark Twain!" All are comic, laudatory, and
affectionate. Also, on p. 1927, F. M. Ashe,
"In Honor of Mark Twain's Sixty-Seventh
Birthday," a full-page drawing of the group
at the Metropolitan Club, November 28.

B5   ANON. The "Man in the Street" Stories. From
"The New York Times." Containing Over Six
Hundred Humorous After-Dinner Stories about
Prominent Persons. New York: J. S. Ogilvie
Publishing Company.
Anecdotes Nos. 1, 87, 203, 208, 263, 344,
419, 492, and 596 concern MT.

B6   ANON. "Mark Twain and His Career," Review of
Reviews (London), XXVL (July), 54.
Summarizes and quotes W. B. Northrop's "A
Day with Mark Twain" in the July Cassell's,
(1902.B22).

B7   ANON. "Mark Twain on Christian Science,"
Harper's Weekly, XLVI (December 27), 2022.
An editorial on MT's article in the December North American Review; chiefly descriptive, but suggests that MT exaggerates the
likelihood of Christian Science becoming a
new religion: it is merely another new
sect.

B8   ANON. "Mark Twain Unveils a Tablet to Eugene
Field," Harper's Weekly, XLVI (July 5), 851.
Describes MT's unveiling of a tablet at
Field's birthplace in ceremonies on June 7;
MT had come to receive an honorary LLD from
the University of Missouri. Includes two
photographs of MT at the unveiling, and his
brief remarks.

B9   *ANON. "The Sixty-Seventh Birthday of Mark
Twain," The Critic, November 30.
[Source: Twainian, II (January, 1940),
5. The article is not in the November, 1902
issue of The Critic: An Illustrated Monthly
Review of Literature Art and Life (G. P.
Putnam's Sons).]

B10   ANON. "Was Mark Twain Tom Sawyer?" Review of
Reviews (London), XXVI (September), 272.
A summary of Henry M. Wharton, "The Boy-
hood Home of Mark Twain," (1902.B26).

B11   ANON. [Review: A Double-Barrelled Detective
Story.] Academy, LXIII (June 26), 14.
A short review, briefly describes the beginning; then: "The story thus launched is
of breathless interest, and it is short."

B12   ANON. [Review: A Double-Barrelled Detective
Story.] Athenaeum, No. 3901 (August 2), p. 152.
"The hand of the master is not easy to
recognize."

B13   ANON. [Brief Review: A Double-Barrelled Detective Story.] Saturday Review (London),
XCIV (August 2), 147.
The book is "hopeless...an odd jumble:
there is very nearly a serious plot, arising
out of a very disgusting incident, and then
the story tails off into a feeble burlesque
of detective fiction."

B14   *ELLINGER, J. "Altertümliche Sprache in d.
Roman: The Prince and the Pauper."
[Source: Henderson (1911), p. 223, listing with 1903 entries, but with facts of
publication thus: "Beiträge zur neuer.
Philologie J. Schipper z. 19 Juli 1902,
ss. 88-107."]

B15   *ANON. "Mitteilungen a. d. gesamten Gebiete d.
engl. Sprache u. Literatur," Beibl. z. Anglia, p. 149.

(ANON.)
A review of A Tramp Abroad, edited by M. Mann (Leipzig: Freytag, 1901). [Source: Henderson (1911), p. 223.]

B16   FARMER, A. O., and ALICE G. HOWLAND. "Obituaries of Mark Twain," Harper's Weekly, XLVI (November 29), 1791.
A review of A Tramp Abroad, edited by M.
Letters to the editor, offering humorous obituaries in response to MT's request in "Amended Obituaries" in the November 15 issue, p. 1704.

B17   HALSEY, FRANCIS W. "Some Books to Read this Summer," Review of Reviews (New York), XXV (June), 700-707.
Portrait of MT and brief mention of A Double-Barreled Detective Story (p. 707), without critical comment.

B18   *HOWE, E. W. [Apparently on MT's Autobiography, appearing serially in Harper's.] Atchinson (Kansas) Globe (June 2).
[Source: Quoted by Calder M. Pickett in his Ed Howe: Country Town Philosopher (Lawrence and London: The University Press of Kansas, 1968, p. 123).] MT, "scraping the moss of his memory," would find turning backward brings "only a great shaking up of stiff limbs and illusions."

B19   HOWELLS, WILLIAM DEAN. "Mr. Howell's [sic] Literary Appreciation of Mark Twain," Connecticut Magazine, No. III-IV (December), pp. 409-12.
A condensation of his "Mark Twain: An Inquiry" (1901.B17), with only minimal editorial comment added.

B20   MATTHEWS, BRANDER. "The Penalty of Humor," in his Aspects of Fiction, and Other Ventures in Criticism. (New York: Charles Scribner's Sons), Third ed., enlarged, pp. 43-56; pp. 54-56 on MT.
Franklin, Lincoln, Canning, and Disraeli were taken less seriously than they deserved, and the same fate has befallen MT. Praises parts of TS, HF, PW, and MT's story-telling and mastery of English prose in the highest terms. He is uneven, to be sure, and has written some poor things, but it is chiefly because of his humor that he is not ranked at his true value.

B21   NICHOL, JOHN. "American Literature," Encyclopaedia Britannica (Akron, Ohio: Werner Company), I, 718-35.
Under "Travels," p. 727, mentions Nathaniel Parker Willis as holding "a respectable place" among the numerous American authors who have published their impressions of the Old World, with every variety of good and bad taste, from Old Home to the Innocents Abroad." Discussing humor (pp. 727-28), shows moderate approval for Bret Harte and Artemus Ward, but apparently includes MT with the worst of Ward's imitators, who "have caught the trick of his phrase and

who are unrestrained by his good feeling and good sense, an easy descent to the lowest level of light literature--that which panders to the vice of moral scepticism and thrives on the buffoonery of making great and noble things appear mean or ridiculous. The names of those who habitually feed on mental garbage should be left to sink into the oblivion from which they have unfortunately emerged." There is no other mention here of MT, whom Nichol attacked in his 1882 book, American Literature, (1882.B21).

B22   NORTHROP, W. B. "A Day with Mark Twain," Cassell's Magazine, XXXIV (July), 115-21.
On a visit to MT at Saranac Lake, New York; consists largely of familiar biographical data, with five photographs. Summarized in Anon., "Mark Twain and His Career," (1902.B6).

B23   PATTEE, FRED LEWIS. "American Literature," Encyclopaedia Britannica, New American Supplement. Akron, Ohio: The Werner Company, XXV, 168-69. (Copyrighted 1896; a note refers to the "earlier account of this subject" by John Nichol in Vol. I [1882.B21])
"His descriptions, sometimes even approaching the realms of poetry, his accurate characterizations, his powers of minute observation and of narration, his facility and his sense of proportion, give [his books] their truest value." His humor, from IA on, "has ever been leveled against sham and hypocrisy." "His later works have been growing more and more serious, and it is more than probable that the critics of the future will rank him as a strong and intensely original writer who was incidentally a humorist."

B24   PERRY, BLISS. A Study of Prose Fiction. Boston: Houghton Mifflin Company (Source: 1920 reprint with only minimal alterations.)
On pp. 338-39, cites Fenimore Cooper, Poe, and Hawthorne as "American fiction-writers who have won a secure place in the world's literature." One might also consider "Bret Harte...Mark Twain, Howells, Aldrich, Stockton, James, Cable, Crawford, and many another living writer of admirable craftsmanship and honorable rank. But I suppose that there are few critics who would deliberately select among these later men a fourth to be placed in equality of universal recognition with that great trio who more than a century ago were in the fullness of their power."

B25   PHILLIPS, ROLAND. "Mark Twain and the Chat Noir," Book Buyer, XXIV (June), 379-82.
Concerns a joke played on M. Salis, cabaret-owner, friend of poets, and admirer of MT; contains nothing bearing directly on MT.

B26   WHARTON, HENRY M. "The Home of Mark Twain," Century, XLIV (September), 674-77.
A popular description of Hannibal, with five photographs; briefly summarized in Anon., "Was Mark Twain Tom Sawyer?" (1902.B10)

1902 - Shorter Writings

B27 *[WHITELOCK, WILLIAM WALLACE.] "The Literary
        Guillotine," The Reader, issues of late
        1902 and early 1903.
          [Source: Twainian, II (May, 1943), 6,
          identifying Whitelock as "presumed author."]

1903 A BOOKS

A1   ANON. Mark Twain's Birthday. A Report of the
        Celebration of the Sixty-Seventh Thereof at
        the Metropolitan Club, New York,
        November 28th, 1902. N.p., Copyright by
        George Harvey, 1903.

1903 B SHORTER WRITINGS

B1   *ANON. "Fiftieth [sic] Birthday of Mark
        Twain," Critic (January).
          [Source: Henderson (1911), p. 223.]

B2   ANON. "Mark Twain's Audiences," Harper's
        Weekly, XLVII (December 19), 2071.
          A brief, undocumented anecdote of MT's re-
        ply to a question of what audiences make the
        most responsive and sympathetic listeners:
        "college men and convicts." Also, p. 2030,
        photograph of MT, without comment, in "A
        Group of Our Harper Authors and Artists."

B3   ANON. "More from Mark Twain about Christian
        Science," Harper's Weekly, XLVII
        (January 24), 145.
          Summarizes from the current North Ameri-
        can Review the second installment of MT's
        writing on Christian Science.

B4   ANON. "Will Christian Science Rule the
        World?" and "The Future of Christian Sci-
        ence," Review of Reviews (London), XXVII
        (January), 35-36; (March), 280.
          Summaries of articles by MT in North Amer-
        ican Review, December, 1902 and March, 1903.

B5   ANON. [Two caricatures of MT, who "has an-
        nounced his intention of leaving America
        and making his permanent home in Italy."]
        Bookman (New York), XVII (July), 449.

B6   *CATANI, UGO. [Portrait of Mark Twain, from
        the miniature of Ugo Catani.] Studio,
        (September 15).
          [Source: Henderson (1911), p. 223.]

B7   CHESTERTON, G. K. "Bret Harte," in his Varied
        Types. (New York: Dodd, Mead and Company),
        pp. 179-95.
          Chesterton regards American humor as
        based on exaggeration. Passing references
        to MT as lacking Harte's subtlety and rev-
        erence, pp. 182-84.

B8   *DIEDRICH, B. "Mark Twain u.d. amerikanische
        Humor," Der Türmer (Stuttgart), July,
        pp. 434-45.
          [Source: Henderson (1911), p. 223.]

B9   *FITCH, THOMAS. "Recollections and Reflections
        of Thomas Fitch." San Francisco Sunday Call,
        October 4, 1903.
          [Source: Quoted by Fatout (1964, pp
        pp. 173-75) concerning a continued novel in
        the Occidental (cf. RI, Vol. II, Ch. X).]

B10 *HAMMERTON, J. A., ed. Stevensoniana. London,
        pp. 88, 293-94.
          Stevenson's praise of MT's books. [Source:
        Quoted by Baetzhold (1970), pp. 204-205,
        361, n. 17.]

B11 HIGGINSON, THOMAS WENTWORTH, and HENRY WALCOTT
        BOYNTON. A Reader's History of American
        Literature. Boston, New York, Chicago:
        Houghton, Mifflin Company, pp. 246-48.
          Sees MT as primarily a humorist, but rec-
        ognizes a somewhat different achievement in
        HF.

B12 KELLER, HELEN. The Story of My Life by Helen
        Keller. With Her Letters (1887-1901) and A
        Supplementary Account of Her Education, In-
        cluding Passages from the Reports and Letters
        of Her Teacher, Anne Mansfield Sullivan by
        John Albert Macy. New York: Doubleday,
        Page & Company, passim.
          Recollections of MT are affectionate but
        not illuminating. There were several meet-
        ings, one of them March 31, 1895 when she
        was fourteen (pp. 227-28). Photograph of
        Helen Keller with MT facing p. 138.

B13 LEVERING, ALBERT. "The Man Who Corrupted Eddy-
        ville. Being Some Account of the Troubles
        which Beset Mark Twain During His Quest for
        Mrs. Eddy's Book," Harper's Weekly, XLVII
        (February 7), 215.
          A cartoon sequence in which several Chris-
        tian Scientist booksellers and Mary Baker
        Eddy herself refuse to sell or give a copy
        of Science and Health to MT, who appears dis-
        guised as various characters from his books.

B14 MABIE, HAMILTON W[RIGHT.] "The Best-Known
        American Humorist," Ladies' Home Journal, XX
        (March), 17.
          Brief item, noting the lasting importance
        of his works; with photograph of "Mark Twain,
        with his Wife and Daughter."

B15 STODDARD, CHARLES WARREN. "A Humorist Abroad,"
        in his Exits and Entrances: A Book of Es-
        says and Sketches (Boston: Lothrop Publish-
        ing Company), pp. 61-74.
          On MT when he was lecturing in London,
        1873-74, and they shared rooms.

B16 *SWOBODA, WILHELM. [Review: A Tramp Abroad,
        edited by M. Mann (Leipzig: Freytag, 1900).]
        Die neueren Sprachen, (July), pp. 223-35.
          [Source: Henderson (1911), p. 223.]

B17 WOODBERRY, GEORGE EDWARD. America in Litera-
     ture. New York and London: Harper & Broth-
     ers. Republished Upper Saddle River, N.J.:
     Literature House/Gregg Press, 1970,
     pp. 159-61.
       [According to a note facing the verso of
     the t.p., "The papers in this volume origi-
     nally appeared in Harper's Magazine and
     Harper's Weekly."]
       MT was the climax of Western humor, "al-
     though, fun for fun's sake being his rule,
     he often goes sprawling, for fun seldom
     stands alone; for long life it has to mate
     with something, to blend with other ele-
     ments, as in the great humorists." The
     picturesqueness of the West called for the
     artist, and "the artist came in Bret Harte."

1904 A BOOKS - NONE

1904 B SHORTER WRITINGS

B1   ALDEN, W. L. "Mark Twain; Samuel L. Clemens,"
     English Illustrated Magazine, n.s., XXXII
     (November), 182-84, 188.
       "Mark Twain is essentially an enthusiast,
     and his enthusiasm is always for the things
     that are noble, and heroic, and right."
     Photo of MT by Walter Barnett, and bibliog-
     raphy of his works and secondary material
     concerning him.

B2   ANON. "Mark Twain's Latest," Spectator, XCII
     (June 11), 925-26.
       A review of Extracts from Adam's Diary.
     "Not only is this little book to be acquit-
     ted of the charge of any real irreverence,
     but...its audacity is so tempered by deli-
     cacy, and even tenderness, of feeling that
     no broad-minded reader can arise from its
     perusal without enhanced admiration for the
     great and kindly humourist who, since Dick-
     ens's death, has done more than any other
     writer to promote the gaiety of the two
     great branches of the Anglo-Saxon race."

B3   *ANON. [Interview with MT in Florence.]
     [Source: Reprinted in James McArthur,
     "Books and Bookmen," Harper's Weekly,
     XLVIII (May 14), 753.]
       Describes MT's appearance and quotes his
     views on copyright and Christian Science;
     photograph: "Mark Twain in the Garden of
     the Villa di Quarto, near Florence." Fol-
     lowed by James McArthur's brief, uncritical
     description of Adam's Diary.

B4   ANON. [Portrait of MT, "From a photograph
     recently taken in Italy."] Review of Re-
     views (New York), XXX (July), 122.

B5   *BURTON, RICHARD. Literary Leaders of America.
     New York: Charles Scribner's Sons.
     [Source: Andrews (1950), p. 273.]

B6   "A CONSTANT READER." "The God of Battles,"
     Harper's Weekly, XLVIII (November 26), 1814.
       Incorrectly ascribes to MT a letter in the
     previous issue. Also, p. 1820, a brief MT
     anecdote on an occasion when the missed his
     steamboat and made no excuse in his report:
     "My boat left at 7.20. I arrived at the
     wharf at 7.35 and could not catch it."

B7   CONWAY, MONCURE DANIEL. Autobiography: Memo-
     ries and Experiences. Boston and New York:
     Houghton, Mifflin and Company. 2 vols. II,
     142-45.
       Describes an 1872 MT lecture in St.
     George's Hall (London), MT at a Savage Club
     dinner, where he praised the Albert Memorial
     "which will stand in all its beauty when the
     name it bears has crumbled into dust." De-
     scribes a visit to the Hartford home in
     1876, and MT as master of ceremonies in an
     entertainment for Harriet Beecher Stowe.
     It was Conway who took the MS of Tom Sawyer
     to England. Also, describes MT and Olivia
     visiting Stratford-on-Avon, MT's amusement
     in London when shown a mechanical "leaping
     frog," which he followed around the room on
     hands and knees. Describes MT reading aloud
     from the MS of A Tramp Abroad in Paris in
     1879, "and the tact and insight displayed by
     his wife in her comments were admirable."
     Much of this is reprinted in Twainian, XII
     (September-October, November-December, 1953);
     XIII (January-February, 1954).

B8   *FIELDS, MRS. JAMES T. Charles Dudley Warner.
     New York: McClure, Phillips & Co.
       [Source: Bryant Morey French, ed., The
     Gilded Age (1972), "Selected Readings,"
     p. xli: "A contemporary memoir of Warner by
     the wife of the publisher of the Atlantic
     Monthly."]

B9   GELLI, E. "A New Portrait of Mark Twain,
     Painted by the Italian Artist E. Gelli, to
     be Exhibited at the World's Fair at St.
     Louis," Harper's Weekly, XLVIII (September 3),
     1347.
       The portrait is reproduced, full-page,
     without further comment.

B10 GILDER, RICHARD WATSON. "Mark Twain: A Glance
     at His Spoken and Written Art," Outlook (New
     York), LXXVIII (December 3), 842-44.
       The two forms of his art overlap; both are
     marked by strong convictions and a dramatic
     presentation. On p. 843, a full-page por-
     trait of MT, "Drawn from life for The Out-
     look by Kate Rogers Nowell."

B11 *M'ARTHUR, J. [Interview with Mark Twain.]
     Harper's Weekly (May 14).
       [Source: Henderson (1911), p. 223.]

B12 *MORRIS, CLARA. "An Interview with Mark Twain,"
     Metropolitan Magazine (March).
       [Source: Twainian, II (February, 1943),
     6.]

1904 - Shorter Writings

B13   PARROTT, T. M. "Mark Twain: Made In America," Booklovers' Magazine (February),
pp. 145-54.
[Source: Scrapbook, Mark Twain: Biography-Reminiscence in Chicago Public Library; also, listed in Twainian, I
(November, 1939), 3.] An extensive, general discussion of MT's writing, which is
characterized by a sweet sunniness, across
which no shadow of impurity ever falls."
Reprinted in Anderson (1971), pp. 243-53.

B14   *[PECK, HARRY THURSTON.] "Mark Twain at Ebb
Tide," Bookman (New York), XIX (May),
235-36.
A review of Extracts from Adam's Diary as
showing "just how far a man who was once a
great humorist can fall. We thought when
we read A Double-Barrelled Detective Story
that Mark Twain could do no worse. But we
were wrong." [Source: Reprinted in Anderson (1971), p. 254, with attribution as
"quite probably" by Peck.]

B15   SIMBOLI, RAFFAELE. "Mark Twain from an Italian Point of View," Critic, XLIV (June),
518-24.
Primarily on MT at the Villa di Quarto in
Florence, with photographs of the Villa,
two photographs of MT, and one of Jean
Clemens on her horse. There is only brief
comment on MT, as a writer whose humor is
not much understood in Italy although JA
"met with considerable success."

B16   THOMAS, FREDERICK MOY. Fifty Years of Fleet
Street. Being the Life and Recollections of
Sir John R. Robinson. London and New York:
Macmillan, pp. 157-58.
Far from joking all the time, "As a matter
of fact he is, or was some ten years ago, a
sad, slow, somewhat ponderous man. He
spoke with a deliberation that was almost
irritating. He was greatly interested in
labour questions, and would tell in a deliberate, matter-of-fact way the story of
the Knights of Labour and similar organiza-
tions in the United States. Of humour there
was none in his conversation.... His hair
some years ago was wild and bushy, his eyes
had a kindly but plaintive expression."
When MT dined at a London club, all the
waiters found pretexts to come to his table
and he recognized one of them and chatted
with him.

B17   TRENT, WILLIAM P. "Mark Twain," in his A
Brief History of American Literature. (New
York: D. Appleton and Company), pp. 235-36.
TS raised MT to a place "as one of the
greatest living writers of the fiction of
blended humour, adventure, and realistic
description of characters and places....
So thoroughly American a career and two
such masterpieces as Tom Sawyer and Huckleberry Finn seem to assure [MT]...an abiding
reputation not surpassed by that of any of
his fellow writers of the modern period."

B18   *WURM, A. "Mark Twain als Mensch u. Humorist,"
Alte und neue Welt (Einsiedeln), p. 718.
[Source: Henderson (1911), p. 224.]

1905 A BOOKS - NONE

1905 B SHORTER WRITINGS

B1   ANON. "If Emperors Were All Stripped Naked,"
Review of Reviews (London), XXXI (April),
375.
Summary of "The Czar's Soliloquy," which
appeared in North American Review in March.

B2   ANON. "Mark Twain at Seventy," Outlook (New
York), LXXXI (December 2), 808.
Notes the uneven quality of MT's work:
"some of it is distinctly slovenly and lacking in spontaneity, with grave defects not
only of conventional but of fundamental
taste; but much of it is fresh, vivid, original, and of a quality not yet fully appreciated by cultivated Americans." Life on
the Mississippi, Tom Sawyer, Huckleberry
Finn "are likely to be kept with the real
books from American hands two or three centuries hence, when a whole world of well-
bred, scholarly, and cultivated writing will
have passed into that oblivion which awaits
everything except life expressed in terms of
beauty, freedom, humor, and power."

B3   ANON. "Mark Twain on Copyright," Review of
Reviews (New York), XXXI (February), 213-14.
A summary of his article in the January
North American Review.

B4   ANON. "Mark Twain on Copyright," Review of
Reviews (London), XXXI (February), 165.
Summarizes and quotes his article in the
January North American Review.

B5   *ANON. "Mark Twain u. d. amerik. Humor,"
Beilage zur Allgemeinen Zeitung (München),
Nr. 77.
[Source: Henderson (1911), p. 224.]

B6   *ANON. "Mark Twain's Autobiography, 1872,"
Connecticut Magazine (April).
[Source: Henderson (1911), p. 224.]

B7   ANON. "Mark Twain's 70th Birthday. Souvenir
of Its Celebration," Supplement to Harper's
Weekly, XLIV (December 23), 1883-1914.
An extensive record of the dinner in MT's
honor at Delmonico's, December 5, with the
guest list (p. 1884), and with full-page
photographs of those seated at each table
(pp. 1894-1914); gives texts of speeches,
poems, and messages honoring MT by Theodore
Roosevelt, William Dean Howells, Brander
Matthews, John Kendrick Bangs, Kate Douglas
Riggs [Wiggin], Richard Watson Gilder, An-
drew Carnegie, George Washington Cable,
Amelia E. Barr, Weir Mitchell, Virginia
Frazer Boyle, Joel Chandler Harris, Wilbur
D. Nesbit, Louise Morgan Sill, Hamilton W.

(ANON.)
Mabie, Agnes Repplier, Irving Bacheller, Rex E. Beach, Hopkinson Smith, Carolyn Wells, and Henry Van Dyke, and a list of signers of a telegram of birthday greetings from Europe. The text of MT's speech appears on pp. 1885-86.

B8 *BRUNI, LIVIA. "l'Umorismo americano, Mark Twain," Nuova Antologia (Rome), ser. IV, CXV (CXCIX), 697-709.
[Source: facts of publication are from Asselineau (No. 27, 1954); summarized in Review of Reviews (New York), XXXI (June), 743-44, with long quotations (and the author's name rendered as "Livia Pruni").] The article contains Italian translations of several short stories; the only major work already available in translation was The Prince and the Pauper. There is a discussion of the nature of humor and the loss in translation. MT's humor has none of the obscenity all too common in Italy and France. His harsh words for Italy in the early travel books were justified, and he now is in sympathy with the new government.

B9 CLEMENS, SAMUEL. "Mark Twain for Jerome," Harper's Weekly, XLIX (August 26), 1238.
A brief letter to the editor, concluding: "Out of respect for him, his morals, and his principles, I mean to vote for him only once on election-day, but if I were free from this restraint I would make it a hundred."

B10 CRILLY, DANIEL. "The After-Dinner Oratory of America," Nineteenth Century, LVII (May), 853-68.
References to MT, passim, but purely derivative.

B11 *DE LEON, DANIEL. "An Irrepressible Humorist," Daily People (New York), September 7.
[Source: Foner (1958), p. 329.]

B12 *DIEDERICH, B. "Mark Twain," Tägl. Rundschau (Leipzig), Nr. 280.
[Source: Henderson (1911), p. 224.]

B13 EATON, CHARLOTTE. "Mark Twain on Copyright," Harper's Weekly, XLIX (February 11), 214.
A letter to the editor, supporting MT's article on copyright in the current North American Review.

B14 *HUENDGREN. [Review: A Tramp Abroad, edited by M. Mann. Leipzig: Freytag, 1901.] Gymnasium (Paderborn), p. 49.
[Source: Henderson (1911), p. 224.]

B15 HUTTON, LAURENCE. Talks in a Library with Laurence Hutton. Recorded by Isabel Moore. New York and London: G. P. Putnam's Sons, passim.
Contains silhouette of MT by Alice I. Bunner (facing p. 6); MT a dinner guest (pp. 22, 326); MT and Helen Keller's first meeting: "He was peculiarly tender and lovely with her--even for Mr. Clemens--and she kissed him when he said good-by" (pp. 390-91). On the night when the death of Bret Harte became known, "he was discussed in a most feeling way in a monologue talk of an hour or two by Mark Twain," who referred to him as "Frank" Harte, thereby losing his audience, who did not realize he was talking about Bret Harte (p. 407); also, tells of Harte's hearing the "Jumping Frog" story and urging MT to publish it (p. 409). MT's introduction of Cable to a Hartford audience, anecdotes about Jean Clemens and Harriet Beecher Stowe, and two MT notes (pp. 419-21).

B16 JOHNSON, CLIFTON. "Mark Twain's Country," Outing Magazine, XLV (January), 433-40.
On a visit to Hannibal and Florida, Missouri; illustrated with several photographs, including one of the front of the home of Tom Blankenship ("when he left home, it was to go to the penitentiary"). One old acquaintance called MT "the most over-rated man in America.... As a boy, Sam was just like other boys, except he might have been a little slower. He was considered blamed dull, to tell you the truth." Another acquaintance remembered him as solitary, not interested in hunting and fishing with the other boys, although fond of exploring the cave. Both remembered his slow, drawling speech.

B17 *KELLNER, L. "Mark Twain (zum siebzigsten Geburtstag)," Neue Freie Presse (Literaturblatt), December 3, pp. 31-32.
[Source: Henderson (1911), p. 224.]

B18 [LAMONT, HAMMOND.] "Mark Twain at Seventy," Nation (New York), LXXXI (December 14), 478-79.
MT has won respect as a writer, here and in England, although he does not belong to the coteries of Boston and New York. "He knows America and knows it whole," writing with power rather than fine academic distinctions. He is "a humorist of the first rank," to be sure, but also a humanist. Reprinted in Anderson (1971), pp. 255-57, with attribution to Lamont.

B19 *SALOMON, LUDWIG. "Mark Twain (zu seinem siebzigsten Geburtstage)," with portrait. Illustrierte Zeitung (Leipzig), November 30.
[Source: Henderson (1911), p. 224.]

1906 A BOOKS - NONE

1906 SHORTER WRITINGS

B1 ANON. "Further Anecdotes of Mark Twain," Harper's Weekly, L (March 24), 421.
Chiefly on MT in Hartford, with texts of some brief MT notes.

B2   ANON. "Mark Twain's Life of Samuel L. Clem-
        ens," Current Literature (October).
        [Source: Henderson (1911), p. 225.]

B3   *ANON. "A Playmate of Mark Twain's," Human
        Life (May).
        [Dixon Wecter (1952), pp. 52-53, 282-83,
        reports that this contains "a garbled inter-
        view with [MT's] cousin Tabitha Quarles
        Greening," with a variant account of the
        incident in which little Sam was almost
        left behind when the family moved from
        Florida, Missouri to Hannibal.]

B4   ANON. "Writing His Autobiography," Harper's
        Weekly, L (December 22), 1845.
        A full-page cartoon, showing MT, in furs,
        writing and leaning against a mile-post
        reading "71 Years Young"; nearby is an
        overturned automobile on which the front
        license plate reads "Serious Life."

B5   ANON. [Comment on MT's Autobiography.] Put-
        nam's Monthly, I (November), 217-20.
        Spurred by current publication of MT's
        reminiscences in the North American Re-
        view, describes and quotes his 1871 bur-
        lesque autobiography and reprints a long
        portion of his discussion of simplified
        spelling. There is almost no editorial
        comment.

B6   ANON. [Full-page drawing of MT receiving a
        laurel wreath from a girl dressed as Joan
        of Arc, at a dinner of the Society of
        American Illustrators.] Harper's Weekly,
        L (January 6).

B7   BARNES, L. CALL. "Fresh Light on the Dark
        Continent," American Journal of Theology,
        X (January), 192-99.
        A review-article, discussing a number of
        books about Africa. On p. 198: "Several
        succinct statements of the case against
        the Congo State are available in this coun-
        try. But the brochure which is likely to
        do the most popular execution is King Leo-
        pold's Soliloquy, by Mark Twain. The
        great humorist never wielded his pen more
        pointedly in behalf of honesty and humani-
        ty. It is significant, too, that he puts
        added emphasis in his second edition, is-
        sued since the publication of the report of
        the king's commission."

B8   *DIEDERICH. B. "Mark Twain: Neues v. Alt,"
        Der Türmer (May), pp. 173-78.
        [Source: Henderson (1911), p. 225.]

B9   GODDARD, HENRY P. "Anecdotes of Mark Twain,"
        Harper's Weekly, L (February 24), 280-81.
        Recollections by Goddard, who knew MT in
        the 1870's. Notes MT's generosity in sign-
        ing over a lecture fee to Colonel Richard
        Malcolm Johnston; describes MT's comments
        on lecturing and his gradual reduction of
        lecture notes to a few marks on his finger-
        nails.

B10 KING, FREDERICK A. "The Story of Mark
        Twain's Debts," Bookman (New York), XX
        (January), 519-22.
        Reprinted in issue of June (1910.B101).

B11 MERRILL, W. H. "When Mark Twain Lectured,"
        Harper's Weekly, L (February 10), 199, 209.
        Describes an MT lecture "in the early
        seventies...in a thriving village in west-
        ern New York."

B12 ORR, CHARLES. "An Unpublished Masterpiece,"
        Putnam's Monthly, I (November), 250-51.
        Three letters, dated June 21, June 24,
        and July 7, 1880, from John Hay to Alexan-
        der Gunn, concerning MT's 1601; there is no
        clue as to the topic, although its racy na-
        ture is vaguely suggested.

B13 SIDGWICK, ARTHUR, and ELEANOR MILDRED SIDG-
        WICK. Henry Sidgwick: A Memoir by A. S.
        and E. M. S. London and New York: Mac-
        Millan, p. 406.
        Quotes the Cambridge professor's journal
        (March 29, 1885), praising HF: "Huck Finn
        is a kind of boyish, semi-savage Gil Blas,
        of low--the lowest--Transatlantic life,
        living by his wits on the Mississippi. The
        novelty of the scene heightens the romantic
        imprévu of his adventures: and the comic
        imprévu of his reflections is--about once
        every three times--irresistably laughable."

B14 STOKER, BRAM. Personal Reminiscences of
        Henry Irving. London: William Heinemann.
        2 vols.; I, 166; II, 324.
        MT was a guest at a supper with Sarah
        Bernhardt one night in 1899 when she was
        playing Hamlet at the Adelphi; F. P. Dunne
        was also present (I, 166). Among those
        listed as having dined with Irving are
        "S. L. Clemens ('Mark Twain')" and "Mrs.
        and Misses S. L. Clemens" (II, 324).

1907 - A BOOKS - NONE

1907 B SHORTER WRITINGS

B1   ANON. "Are We Standing at the Birth of a
        Great Religion?" Current Literature, XLII
        (March), 321-24.
        In part a descriptive review of MT's
        Christian Science, but chiefly devoted to
        a broader treatment of the topic, giving
        background on Mary Baker Eddy and newspaper
        discussion of her work.

B2   ANON. "The Innocents Abroad and How Mark
        Twain Came to Write It," Review of Reviews
        XXXVI [?] (London), 167.
        Summarizes MT's own account in the in-
        stallment of his autobiography in the July
        North American Review; also summarizes
        William Lyon Phelps, "Mark Twain" in the
        same issue, and includes comments on what
        MT could do at his best and most serious

(ANON.)
from the unsigned "Musings without Method" [by Charles Whibley] in the August Blackwood's.

B3   ANON. "Mark Twain," Living Age, Seventh Series, XXXVI (from beginning, CCLIV; July 6), 60-62.
      General praise: "Mark Twain will always be remembered first and foremost as a humorist; but it is only because his claims as a humorist are overwhelming that he had not been acclaimed as a serious student of character, a novelist, and a charming writer of whimsical historical romance." Praises many of MT's books, even CY as "an extremely clever and imaginative tour de force." (Reprinted from Spectator, n.d.; Henderson [1911], p. 225 gives Spectator printing as May 25). See 1907.B4.

B4   *ANON. "Mark Twain," Spectator, XCVIII (May 25), 825-26.
      [Source: Reprinted in Anderson (1971), pp. 258-61.] An enthusiastic but rather superficial survey of MT's life and works for English readers when MT came to England to receive an honorary doctoral degree from Oxford. See 1907.B3.

B5   ANON. "Mark Twain, Doctor of Letters," Harper's Weekly, LI (July 13), 1010.
      Editorial comment on MT's honorary Oxford degree, awarded not just because he is a celebrity, but because he is an able and recognized author.

B6   ANON. "Mark Twain, En Route for Oxford to Receive the Degree of Doctor of Letters, Besieged by Reporters on His Steamship in England," Harper's Weekly, LI (July 13), 1034.
      Photograph, without commentary.

B7   ANON. "Mark Twain's Publicity R. I. P.," Bookman (New York), XXVI (September), 9-10.
      "'Mark Twain's work,' said one British writer when British applause was at its loudest, 'has absolutely no connection with literature,' and some of it 'has for sheer concentrated vulgarity never been beaten'; and it was a pity, said another, that Oxford did not honor Henry James instead." The American press reported only England's praise when MT visited. The trouble with these journalistic orgies of praise is that they "always look the week after like public funerals of common sense."

B8   ANON. "Social and Anecdotal" page. Illustrated London News, CXXXI (July 6), 10.
      Describes MT's friendly meeting with a porter.

B9   ANON. "To a Master of His Art" (Cartoon). Punch, CXXXII (June 26), 453.

MT with cigar, Mr. Punch offering him glass from "The Punch Bowl." Text (in full): "Mr. Punch (to Mark Twain): 'Sir, I honor myself in drinking to your health. Long life to you--and happiness-and perpetual youth!'"

B10   ANON. [Review: Christian Science.] Athenaeum, No. 4147 (April 20), pp. 466-68.
      Mostly summary; favorable, calls MT "one of the sanest, least prejudiced of men."

B11   ANON. [Review: King Leopold's Soliloquy.] Athenaeum, No. 4153 (June 1), p. 664.
      Very brief review. Declares that "Mark Twain is a serious writer of considerable courage as well as a humorist," and his pamphlet is "a trenchant satire."

B12   ANON. [Review: King Leopold's Soliloquy.] Bookman (London), XXXII (July), 150.
      Brief, notes that "There has not in our time been a fiercer satire or a finer instance of the value of humour as an instrument of reform."

B13   ANON. [Comment on King Leopold's Soliloquy.] Punch, CXXXII (June 19), 439.
      Text in full: "We are glad to see MARK TWAIN taking part in the campaign against the owner of the Congo Free State. Mark II is ammunition which has done good service in the past."

B14   ANON. [Comment on King Leopold's Soliloquy.] Punch, CXXXII (June 26), 451.
      Text in full: "It is rumored that MARK TWAIN has received a communication from the King of the BELGIANS offering to defray the entire expense of the obsequies referred to by the American humorist upon his arrival in this country. The only provision that His MAJESTY makes is that the funeral shall take place at once."

B15   ANON. [Account of MT at the Royal Garden Party.] Illustrated London News, CXXX (June 29), 983, 985.
      At a party for 8,000, MT was "prominent among the distinguished guests." Illustrated.

B16   ANON. [Portrait of MT in Oxford gown.] Burr McIntosh Monthly (New York), XIV (September), [47].
      No significant text.

B17   BLAND, HENRY MEADE. "Mark Twain," Overland Monthly, XLIX (January), 22-27.
      Praises MT's tenderness and his "sternly philosophical side," notes his friendship with Charles Warren Stoddard; a popular account providing no new information or unusual critical perception. Illustration (p. 22): "Mark Twain, drawn by Alice Resor from latest copyrighted portrait by Rockwood, N.Y."

B18 BROOKS, SYDNEY. "England's Ovation to Mark Twain," Harper's Weekly, LI (July 27), 1086-89.
    On MT's cordial reception when he received an honorary degree from Oxford, with an account of his speech at a Pilgrims' Club banquet. Includes sketch of MT chatting with King Edward at Windsor, and photograph of MT in the procession at Oxford just after the degree was awarded.

B19 _____. "Mark Twain in England," Harper's Weekly, LI (July 20), 1053-55.
    On MT's popularity, and his reception when he was there to receive his Oxford degree. Cartoons of MT from London Daily Chronicle by David Wilson (p. 1053) and P. Richards (p. 1054), and photograph of MT after receiving his degree (p. 1055).

B20 *GOULD, STUART. "Samuel L. Clemens," Broadway Magazine (later Hampton's Broadway Magazine) (February).
    [Source: Twainian, I (December, 1939), 6.]

B21 GRISWOLD, STEPHEN. "Quaker City Excursion," in his Sixty Years with Plymouth Church (New York: Fleming H. Revell Company), pp. 153-66.
    Describes the tour on which IA was based; briefly mentions MT. Quotes at length (pp. 156-64) the account of the visit to the Czar at Yalta in Mrs. Griswold's A Woman's Pilgrimage to the Holy Land (1871).

B22 KIMBALL, EDWARD A. "Mark Twain, Mrs. Eddy, and Christian Science," Cosmopolitan, XLIII (May), 35-41.
    A reply to MT's Christian Science by "a prominent Christian Science author."

B23 LANG, ANDREW. "At the Sign of St. Paul's" [literature page]. Illustrated London News, CXXX (May 25), 798.
    Brief note (in full): "The great American humorist, who has just passed his seventieth birthday, comes to Oxford this summer to receive the degree of D.C.L." Portrait.

B24 _____. "Mark Twain," Albany Review (London), L (April), 35-43.
    A general account of MT's works, which Lang first encountered while riding on a train with his friend and tutor Benjamin Jowett (later Master of Balliol); Lang "shrieked and exploded with laughter" over "The Celebrated Jumping Frog," then handed it over to his companion. "He read through it with perfect solemnity combined with disapproval, and returned it to me without a word." Of MT's works, TS is the Iliad, HF "the Odyssey, of life, not of boy's life only," but "I have never read, and never will read," CY.

B25 MABIE, HAMILTON W. "Mark Twain the Humorist," Outlook (New York), LXXXVII (November 23), 648-53.
    A general, admiring discussion of the man and his works, generally uncritical though noting the ephemeral quality of some of his writing. On p. 648, full-page photograph of MT.

B26 MATTHEWS, BRANDER. "Mark Twain," in his Inquiries and Opinions. (New York: Charles Scribner's Sons, 1907), pp. 137-66.
    A biographical and critical account by one of MT's early advocates in the academic world. This was written as the introduction to a complete edition of MT's works, and appears in Innocents Abroad in the Author's National Edition. Asselineau (1954), No. 28 gives a cross-reference to Matthews's "Mark Twain--His Work," Book-Buyer, XIII (January, 1897), 977-79.

B27 MOFFETT, SAMUEL E. "Mark Twain, Doctor of Letters," Review of Reviews (New York), XXXVI (August), 167-68.
    General praise of MT on the occasion of his receiving an honorary degree from Oxford; no new information. Includes photograph of MT.

B28 PEARSON, E[DMUND] L[ESTER]. "The Children's Librarian versus Huckleberry Finn: A Brief for the Defense," Library Journal, XXXII (July), 312-14.
    "Extreme Respectability" in the children's departments of public libraries is excluding TS and HF, which Pearson defends for honest portrayal: "Not Henty's wooden heroes, nor golden-curled, lace-collared Fauntleroys; but real boys." Reprinted in his The Library and the Librarian (1910.B114).

B29 PHELPS, WILLIAM LYON. "Mark Twain," North American Review, CLXXXV (July 5), 540-48.
    Discusses the growth of MT's standing and declares him now "our foremost living American writer," not only for his humor, but for his literary art in the creation of characters and in his dramatic power. Reprinted in his Essays on American Novelists (New York, 1910), pp. 99-114; in Anderson (1971), pp. 262-70; in Scott (1955), pp. 79-88, and (1967), pp. 84-93.

B30 SEAMAN, OWEN. "To Mark Twain," Punch, CXXXII (June 27), 463.
    A poem honoring MT, guest of the Pilgrims Club, June 25th.

B31 SIMBOLI, RAFFAELE. "Mark Twain and His Double," Ladies' Home Journal, XXIV (May), 59.
    While living in Florence MT was often mistaken for Professor Borzi [later director of the Botanical Gardens at Palermo]. In turn, when Borzi visited Sweden and Norway in 1899 he was widely mistaken for MT and "even Ibsen fell into the error and came to call on me," said Borzi.

B32 *TEICHMANN, E. [Review: The $30,000 Bequest and other Stories.] Neue Philologische Rundschau, p. 503.
[Source: Henderson (1911), p. 225.]

B33 THOMPSON, VANCE. "The Yarns of a Traveler," Outing Magazine, LI (October), 16-22.
Stories about murder told by a group of men on an ocean liner; MT suggested the topic, but told no story and made no significant comments.

B34 *WATSON, AARON. "Artemus Ward and Mark Twain," and "Mark Twain's Own Account," in his The Savage Club (London: T. Fisher Unwin), pp. 119-35.
[Source: Henderson (1911), p. 226.]

B35 [WHIBLEY, CHARLES.] "Musings without Method: The Hilarity of London--Mark Twain's Message of Mirth--The Limitations of Humour--an Obvious Incongruity--The Example of the Eighteenth Century--Cotton and Bridges--Life on the Mississippi--The Talent of Mark Twain--The Sin of Exaggeration..." Blackwood's Edinburgh Magazine, CLXXXII (August), 279-86.
A generally unsympathetic response to the adulation MT was receiving on his last visit to England; praises the beauty of LOM, but condemns CY as "such a masterpiece of vulgarity as the world has never seen. His book gives you the same sort of impression which you might receive from a beautiful picture over which a poisonous slug had crawled." Reprinted in Scott (1955), pp. 89-97; (1967), pp. 94-102, with a note: "Authorship revealed in note from Wm. Blackwood & Sons, Ltd., October 12, 1953." Also reprinted in Anderson (1971), pp. 271-76.

B36 WILBUR, SIBYL. The Life of Mary Baker Eddy. New York and London: Concord Publishing Company, pp. 216-18.
Cites MT's charges in Christian Science that Mary Baker Eddy's Science and Health is absurd, unoriginal, and not her work; gently disagrees.

1908 A BOOKS - NONE

1908 B SHORTER WRITINGS

B1 ANON. "Four Distinguished Americans. From a Photograph Taken at Lakewood, N.J., Where a Luncheon Was Given to Mr. Howells to Bid Him Godspeed on His Journey to Europe," Harper's Weekly, LII (January 18), 13.
Full-page photograph of Howells, MT, Henry M. Alden, and Mayo W. Hazeltine.

B2 ANON. "Mark Twain's New Home at Redding," Harper's Weekly, LII (July 4), 24, 29.
On the purchase of the land, building of the house, and the neighbors. Illustrated with photographs of the house, local scenes, and MT playing billiards with Albert

Bigelow Paine. Attributed to Paine in Henderson (1911), p. 226.

B3 *ANON. "Mark Twain's Pastor: Some Stories of Samuel L. Clemens," Daily Graphic (London), July 11.
[Source: Leah A. Strong (1966), p. 178.]

B4 ANON. [Portrait of MT and daughter Clara.] Burr McIntosh Monthly (New York), XV (March), [57-58].
Accompanying text states that MT had approximately $50,000 on deposit at the Knickerbocker Trust Company in New York at the time of the crash; he opposed establishing a permanent receivership on the grounds that it would be as expensive to maintain as a harem: "Anybody who has had experience in this line will endorse my statement."

B5 ABERNETHY, JULIAN W. "American Humor," in American Literature. New York: Charles E. Merrill Co. [copyright 1902 by Maynard, Merrill & Co.], pp. 465-72.
The book is a broad survey, intended for use in the schools, and the treatment of MT is superficial, though laudatory (except for regretting his frequent coarseness). TS and HF are "astonishingly clever studies of the American bad boy, and LOM is "his best autobiographic narrative," a product of the river which inspired him. Abernethy appears to be guided primarily by Brander Matthews and H. R. Haweis, both of whom he quotes in praise of MT (the attributions are unclear, but the sources seem to be Aspects of Fiction, Harper, 1892, and American Humorists, Funk, 1883, respectively).

B6 BRERETON, AUSTIN. The Life of Henry Irving. London: Longmans, Green, and Co., 2 vols.; II, 37, 42. 68.
MT a guest at a dinner given in Irving's honor at the Somerset Club by Charles Fairchild and James R. Osgood; Howells and Aldrich were also present, 1884 (p. 37); Irving a guest at MT's home in Hartford, 1884 (p. 42). MT's name was among over a hundred signatures on a letter dated 14th March, 1885, inviting Irving to a banquet in his honor at Delmonico's, April 6 (p. 68).

B7 GREENSLET, FERRIS. The Life of Thomas Bailey Aldrich. Boston and New York: Houghton Mifflin Company.
Includes the correspondence with MT that followed Aldrich's attribution in Every Saturday of the "Carl Byng" and "Hy Slocum" sketches in the Buffalo Express to him, with MT's tribute to Harte's influence as literary mentor, although their friendship had ended (pp. 94-99); correspondence in which MT deluged Aldrich with photographs in response to a request for one (pp. 112-17, including a self-portrait sketch, facing p. 114); anecdote on their comparative popularity in France (p. 117); quotes MT declaring "that if he was a fool, he was at least God's fool, and entitled to some

1908 - Shorter Writings

(GREENSLET, FERRIS)
respect" (p. 192); on MT as so well known
that "little donkey-boys on the Nile...will
tell you that they were 'Mark Twain's' don-
key boys" (p. 220).

B8 *MATTHEWS, BRANDER. "American Humor," Saturday Evening Post (November 21).
[Source: Twainian, II (June, 1943), 6.]
Reprinted in his The American of the Future,
and Other Essays (1910, B105).

B9 *PEMBERTON, T. EDGAR. Life of Bret Harte.
London: C. Arthur Pearson.
[Source: Henderson (1911), p. 226.]

B10 SEDGWICK, HENRY DWIGHT. "Mark Twain," in his
The New American Type, and Other Essays
(Boston, New York: Houghton, Mifflin and
Company), pp. 281-313.
On MT as the embodiment of a democratic,
American spirit in literature.

B11 STEWART, WILLIAM M. Reminiscences of Senator
William M. Stewart of Nevada, ed. George
Rothwell Brown. New York and Washington:
The Neale Publishing Company.
"Chapter XXIII. Mark Twain becomes my
secretary--Back from the Holy Land, and he
looks it--The landlady terrorized--I inter-
fere with a humorist's pleasures and get a
black patch--Revenge!--Clemens the hero of
a Nevada hold-up" (pp. 219-24). An unsympathetic portrayal of MT, who briefly was
Stewart's secretary in Washington. Concludes: "Clemens remained with me for some
time. He wrote his book in my room, and
named it The Innocents Abroad. I was so
confident that he would come to no good
end, but I have heard of him from time to
time since then and I understand that he
has settled down since then and become respectable.

B12 *_____. "A Senator of the Sixties," Saturday
Evening Post (February 15).
[Source: Twainian, II (June, 1943), 6.]

B13 STODDARD, CHARLES WARREN. "In Old Bohemia,
II, The Overland and the Overlanders,"
Pacific Monthly, XIX (March), 261-73.
Contains anecdotes of MT in California
and recollections of sharing rooms with
him in London in the winter of 1873-74.
Includes photograph of MT.

B14 WHIBLEY, CHARLES. "American Literature,"
Blackwood's, CLXXXIII (March), 414-22.
On MT, pp. 419-20: "There is but one
author who represents with any clarity the
spirit of his country, and that author is
Mark Twain. Not Mark Twain the humourist,
the favourite of the reporters, the facile
contemner of things which are noble and of
good report, but Mark Twain, the pilot of
the Mississippi, the creator of Huck Finn
and Tom Sawyer. He, indeed, is national as
Fielding is national. Future ages will

look upon Huck Finn as we look upon Tom
Jones,--as an embodiment of national virtue."

1909 A BOOKS - NONE

1909 B SHORTER WRITINGS

B1 ANGERT, EUGENE H. "Is Mark Twain Dead?"
North American Review, CXC (September),
319-29.
A spoof, purporting to demonstrate that
MT died in 1906 in Europe and his subsequent
public appearances are those of an impostor,
and works bearing his name are those of a
person lacking humor: he could not have
written either the scholarly Is Shakespeare
Dead? or Christian Science, and even if he
could have written the latter, he would not
have chosen to. Significantly, he did not
sign the articles of incorporation of the
Mark Twain Company. Angert proposes Elbert
Hubbard as the author of works attributed to
MT in recent years.

B2 *ANON. "Horace Ezra Bixby, Mark Twain's Boss,"
Broadway Magazine (later Hampton's Broadway
Magazine), January.
[Source: Twainian, I (December, 1939),
6.]

B3 ANON. "The Lounger," Putnam's Magazine, VII
(December), 369-70.
Brief comment on Clara's wedding to Ossip
Gabrilowitsch, quoting MT's answer when
asked whether the marriage pleased him:
"Yes, fully as much as any marriage could
please me or perhaps any other father.
There are two or three tragically solemn
things in this life, and a happy marriage
is one of them, for the terrors of life are
all to come. A funeral is a solemn office,
but I go to them with a spiritual uplift,
thankful that the dead friend has been set
free. That which follows is to me tragic
and awful--the burial. I am glad of this
marriage, and Mrs. Clemens would be glad,
for she always had a warm affection for
Gabrilowitsch, but all the same it is a
tragedy, since it is a happy marriage with
its future before it, loaded to the Plim-
soll line with uncertainties." Also contains comments by MT at a musicale in Redding (Sept. 21). The writer mentions having
"spoken of Mr. Clemens's country home more
than once in these pages."

B4 *ANON. "Mark Twain from a New Angle," Current
Literature (August).
[Source: Henderson (1911), p. 227.]

B5 *ANON. "Mark Twain's House at Redding, Connec-
ticut," American Architect & Building News,
(February 10).
[Source: Twainian, I (October, 1939), 4.]

B6   ANON. "Mark Twain's New Book and a Commenta-
       tor," Bookman (New York), XXIX (June).
          MT's Is Shakespeare Dead? is a comic
       piece which "can be read through cheerfully
       in an hour"--yet a writer for the Boston
       Evening Transcript finds "depth and subtle-
       ty" in it!

B7   ANON. "Stormfield, Mark Twain's New Country
       Home. How the Humorist Built a House With-
       out Seeing It--An Italian Villa in the
       Connecticut Hills--The Second in a Series
       of Articles on Country Homes of Notable
       Americans." Photographs by A. Radclyffe
       Dugmore. Country Life in America, XV
       (April), 607-11, 650-51.
          A description of the house at Redding,
       Connecticut, illustrated by pictures of the
       house and MT at his ease there, and a fac-
       simile of his "Notice. To the next Bur-
       glar" warning that hung in the billiard-
       room.

B8   BAILEY, ELMER JAMES. "The Essayists and the
       Humourists," in Theodore Stanton, ed.,
       A Manual of American Literature (New York:
       G. P. Putnam's Sons), pp. 321-59; on MT,
       pp. 357-59.
          Regrets that MT was burdened by his repu-
       tation as a humorist and predicts that
       "future critics may come to regard The
       Prince and the Pauper (1882) and Personal
       Recollections of Joan of Arc (1896), two
       serious and dignified pieces of writing, as
       Mr. Clemens's best work." The Oxford de-
       gree awarded him, though a surprise to
       many, was evidence that "humour at last
       seems to be coming into its own."

B9   *FISCHER, M. "Mark Twain on Christian Sci-
       ence," Die Neueren Sprachen, pp. 206-28.
          [Source: Henderson (1911), p. 227.]

B10   GILMAN, ARTHUR. "Atlantic Dinners and Di-
       ners," Atlantic Monthly, C (November),
       646-57, on MT, pp. 651-53.
          A brief account of his Whittier Birthday-
       Dinner speech, with no indication that it
       gave offense.

B11   HENDERSON, ARCHIBALD. "Mark Twain," Harper's
       Monthly, CXVIII (May), 948-55.
          Praises MT's robustly national qualities,
       although "he is America's greatest cosmo-
       politan." "But, after all, Mark Twain's
       supremest title to distinction as a great
       writer inheres in his mastery in that
       greatest sphere of thought, embracing re-
       ligion, philosophy, morality, and even
       humor, which we call sociology." Reprinted
       in Scott (1955), pp. 98-106, and (1967),
       pp. 103-11. This appears to be the "Philos-
       opher, Moralist, Sociologist" chapter in
       Henderson's 1911 book (1911.A3) and trans-
       lated into German in Deutsche Revue
       (1911.B9).

B12   *____. "Mark Twain--Wie Er Ist. Eine Skizze
       nach dem Leben," Deutsche Revue, XXXIV
       (November), 195-205.
          [Source: Henderson (1911), p. 227;
       Leary (1954), p. 49.

B13   *____. "The Real Mark Twain. The Man and His
       Work," Charlotte (North Carolina) Observer,
       Sunday, May 16.
          [Source: Henderson (1911), p. 226.]

B14   HOWELLS, WILLIAM DEAN. "The Editor's Easy
       Chair," Harper's Monthly, CXIX (July),
       313-16.
          On the debate over the authorship of
       Shakespeare's plays; praises MT's knowledge
       of the details, and his Is Shakespeare Dead?
       as "his humorous exposition of the mock
       combat," in which "the controversy is for-
       ever destroyed, and only the miracle of
       Shakespeare remains."

B15   LUCY, HENRY W. "Mark Twain," in his Sixty
       Years in the Wilderness: Some Passages by
       the Way. (London: Smith, Elder & Co.),
       pp. 220-29, (364).
          Reminiscences of MT at a dinner in his
       honor at the Punch offices, and a scheme
       MT and Lucy had jokingly concocted to
       blackmail wealthy persons with scurrilous
       obituaries supposedly to be published on
       their death; also, two letters from MT to
       Lucy and an MT letter to the editor to be
       sent out to newspapers, offering to pay a
       good price for "access to my standing obit-
       uaries, with the privilege...of editing,
       not their facts, but their verdicts"
       (p. 226). Also, tells the story of MT at
       a dinner given in his honor by the American
       Ambassador, Whitelaw Reid; MT had prepared
       a speech, but was not called on to give one,
       and later confided to Lucy that he had sold
       it for two hundred dollars (p. 228).

B16   *LUX, JACQUES. "Mark Twain," L'Indépendence
       Belge, July 16.
          [Source: Henderson (1911), p. 227.]

B17   *MENCKEN, H. L. [Review: Is Shakespeare
       Dead?] Smart Set, XXVIII (August), 157.
          [Source: Conclusion reprinted in Anderson
       (1971), p. 277.] An inaccurate, unsuccess-
       ful book by "the most noble figure America
       has ever given to English literature. Hav-
       ing him, we may hold up our heads when
       Spaniards boast of Cervantes and Frenchmen
       of Moliere." He has given us HF, "But since
       Following the Equator, his decline has been
       almost pathetic."

B18   NORTHRUP, CLARK SUTHERLAND. "The Novelists,"
       in Theodore Stanton, ed., A Manual of Amer-
       ican Literature (New York: G. P. Putnam's
       Sons), pp. 115-240; on MT, pp. 187-88.
          "Artistically defective his work is in-
       deed, but it cannot be denied the qualities
       of eloquence, naturalness, and sincerity.
       The work, like the man, is genuine."

1909 - Shorter Writings

B19   PAINE, ALBERT BIGELOW. "Mark Twain at Storm-
        field: The House of Many Beatitudes,"
        Harper's Monthly, CXVIII (May), 955-59.
              On MT's home at Redding, Connecticut, and
        his life there.

B20   PENN, PETER. "Some American Humour," English
        Illustrated Magazine, XLI (June), 299-301.
              Contains passing and superficial refer-
        ences to MT; praises his "variety."

B21   THOMPSON, PAUL. "A Day with Mark Twain,"
        Burr McIntosh Monthly (New York), XVII
        (March) [22-24].
              Superficial description of a visit to MT
        at his "Stormfield" home in Redding, Con-
        necticut; illustrated with two photographs
        of MT and two of the house.

1910 A BOOKS

A1   CHUBB, PERCIVAL, ed. Travels at Home. New
        York and London: Harper & Brothers.
              Selections from MT's works for school
        use in 6th, 7th, and 8th grades. The in-
        troduction is conventionally laudatory and
        biographical, and contains no new informa-
        tion or significant criticism.

A2   EPUY, MICHEL. Le legs de 30.000 Dollars et
        autres contes, traduits et préfacés d'une
        étude sur l'auteur par Michel Epuy. Paris:
        Marcure de France.
              [Source: Asselineau (1954), No. 41.]

A3   HOWELLS, WILLIAM DEAN. My Mark Twain: Rem-
        iniscences and Criticisms. New York and
        London: Harper & Brothers Publishers.
              A collection of Howells' writings on MT
        and reviews of his books, with minor re-
        visions or none at all. The first section
        is the material which appeared as "My Memo-
        ries of Mark Twain" in Harper's Monthly
        (August-October), with the change of an
        occasional word or paragraph division, and
        the second part consists of reviews of MT's
        books and some more general discussions,
        "allowed to follow here in the order of
        their original publication, with no sort of
        correction or effort to reconcile them with
        one another." Reprinted 1967, ed. Marilyn
        Austin Baldwin, with introduction, notes,
        and index. See 1967.A3.

A4   *HYATT, EDWARD (Superintendent of Public In-
        struction). A Calaveras Evening with Mark
        Twain and Bret Harte, a diversion for the
        English class. Sacramento: W. W. Shannon,
        Supt. State Printing.
              [8-page pamphlet. Source: Asselineau
        (1954), No. 34.]

A5   *JOHNSON, MERLE. A Bibliography of the Works
        of Mark Twain. New York and London: Harp-
        er & Brothers.

[Source: Asselineau (1954), No. 29.]
Now superceded by Revised and Enlarged edi-
tion, 1935 (A12), reprinted 1972, Westport,
Connecticut: Greenwood Press, Publishers.

A6   KENDALL, C. N. Travels in History. New York
        and London: Harper & Brothers.
              Extracts from P&P, CY, and JA for school
        use in 6th, 7th, and 8th grades. Introduc-
        tion (pp. vii-ix) notes the importance of
        "authors who interpret life with vitality
        and reality" for young readers and (follow-
        ing Howells) points out the "national spir-
        it" in MT. P&P is "largely imaginative,"
        with "variety, pathos, and abundant humor."
        In CY "The ignorance and savagery beneath
        the ancient pomp and glitter are well con-
        trasted with the resourcefulness and human-
        itarianism of to-day." "The tone of Joan of
        Arc is devout, the humor subdued, and the
        treatment dignified and elevated."

A7   *LIVINGSTON, LUTHER S. The Works of Mark
        Twain. The description of a set of first
        editions of his books in the library of a
        New York collector (R. F. Pick). With Fac-
        similes.
              [Source: Asselineau (1954), No. 30; he
        adds: "only 75 copies were printed accord-
        ing to Wilfred Partington (cf. Bookman,
        March 1933)."]

A8   PAINE, ALBERT BIGELOW. The Ship-Dwellers: A
        Story of a Happy Cruise. New York and Lon-
        don: Harper & Brothers Publishers.
              Paines's account of his own trip forty-
        two years after the cruise of the Quaker
        City and covering much the same itinerary.
        In some respects this is an admiring
        (though pale) imitation of IA, to which
        there are frequent references. On
        pp. 51-53 Paine describes a meeting at
        Gibraltar with Michael Benueñes, who said
        he had been the local guide for MT's party.

1910 SHORTER WRITINGS

B1   ADE, GEORGE. "Mark Twain and the Old Time
        Subscription Book," Review of Reviews (New
        York), XLI (June), 703-704.
              Reminiscence of the bulk and appearance
        of the books; unlike most of the others,
        MT's were a delight for a boy to read.
        Reprinted in Anderson (1971), 337-39.

B2   _____. "Mark Twain as our Emissary," Century,
        LXXXI (December), 204-206.
              A popular appreciation of MT's popularity
        at home and abroad.

B3   ALDEN, HENRY M. "Mark Twain--An Appreciation,"
        Bookman (New York), XXXI (July), 366-69.
              A general and popular appreciation, noting
        MT's imagination and sensitivity. Photo-
        graph: "Mark Twain at Oxford."

B4 _____. "Mark Twain: Personal Impressions,"
Book News Monthly, XXVIII (April), 579-82.
On the autobiographical element in MT's
work, and his "openly dramatized personality." Praises "the profound spiritual implications of some of his short stories,
like The Man Who Corrupted Hadleyburg and
"Was It Heaven or Hell?" All these show
the finest lines of his art, of his humor,
of his large but delicately sensitive personality." Photograph of MT as frontispiece to issue (facing p. 573).

B5 ANON. "Chesterton on Mark Twain," New York
Times, May 7, "Saturday Review of Books and
Art," p. 262.
Summarizes and quotes G. K. Chesterton's
assessment of MT in T. P.'s Weekly
(1910.B77).

B6 ANON. "Comment," Harper's Weekly, LIV
(April 30), 4.
MT was probably the world's greatest
living writer; irreverent toward shams but
of the highest honor and integrity. (Photographs of MT, front cover, p. 3).

B7 ANON. "A Correspondent Writes," Athenaeum,
No. 4305 (April 30), p. 527.
Note from a reader who wrote MT in 1900:
"Who is your favorite novelist, and what is
your favorite novel?" MT's reply: "Q. My
favorite novel? A. 'Huckleberry Finn.'
Very truly yours, Mark Twain."

B8 ANON. "The Death of Mark Twain," Chautauquan,
LIX (June), 9-10.
Obituary praise for his humanity and wis-
dom.

B9 ANON. "Fashions in Humor," Emporia (Kansas)
Gazette, April 28, p. 1.
Quotes Franklin P. Adams in the New York
Evening Mail (n.d.), predicting that HF
and "The Jumping Frog" will last, but much
of MT's other work will not; because of
changing tastes; the writer uses this as a
point of departure for a general discussion
of this change in taste.

B10 ANON. "French Sneer at Mark Twain," New York
Times, April 24, p. 3.
Reports that the French press generally
has expressed sympathetic notice of MT's
death, reflecting "an extraordinarily
widespread knowledge of the subtleties of
the English language among Frenchmen. A
surprising exception is to be found in Ernest Charles, a critic much in the public
view, who in a short article on Mark Twain
seems determined to convince every reader
possessing any degree of penetration that
the views which he expresses are the product
of ignorance and anti-Americanism combined.
This article is published in Gil Blas...
Mr. Charles says in effect that Mark Twain
did well to die, and that it was not his
fault if while he was all his life the most

laborious humorist, he was totally lacking
in wit. 'Mark Twain's humor,' M. Charles
adds, was painful, his fantasies dense and
difficult to follow. By them one may estimate the exact distance which separates the
Yankee country from the civilized world."
[The New York Times is the best single
source for American and foreign tributes
during the period following MT's death.]

B11 ANON. "The Frontiersmen," T. P.'s Weekly
(London), XV (June 24), 793.
Summarizes the unsigned article by Frank
Jewett Mather in The Nation (N.Y., April 28,
1910.B104) on MT and Henry James. Questions
Mather's suggestion that the prospects of
survival as a major author are good for MT
but uncertain for James.

B12 ANON. "His Career as Soldier: Captain Grimes
Tells of First Battle--It Was with a Mule,"
St. Louis Times, April 22.
[Source: Scrapbook, Mark Twain: Biography-Reminiscence, n.d., in Chicago Public
Library.] Reminiscences by Captain Horace
Ezra Bixby and Captain A. C. Grimes ("former proprietor of Grimes' Clubhouse, King's
Lake, Lincoln County"). The brief account
by Grimes adds nothing to MT's own "Private
History of a Campaign that Failed." Bixby
said that "Clemens was a good pilot, in
spite of what the rest of the profession
said about him. I soon saw that he was a
smart fellow, and it was his brains that
made the other pilots jealous and led them
to say that he did not know the river, that
he was just an inspired loafer, or something of that sort. He was a good pilot,
and he learned it from me...Mark never was
jolly exactly, always serious, but he
showed the gift of humor, even at that time.
He was not entirely popular with his fellows,
as I have said, and maybe his tongue had
something to do with that." Bixby interview
reprinted (as "Special to the World") in New
York World, April 24, p. 3.

B13 ANON. "In the Interpretor's House" [A regular
section of the magazine], American Magazine,
LXX (July), 428-32.
Presented as a discussion between the Observer and the Poet of MT's originality,
integrity, kindliness, contempt for sham.
Gives considerable space to the familiar
biographical details, and says little specifically about MT's works.

B14 ANON. "A Land of No Laughter?" The British
Weekly, XLVIII (April 28), 81-82.
Title is taken from the first lines of
James Rhoades's 1867 poem on the death of
Artemus Ward: "Is he gone to a land of no
laughter,/ This man that made mirth for us
all?" Reprinting the entire poem, the article takes up the question of whether there
can be a place for laughter in heaven, and
is primarily devoted to a discussion of humor and religion. The occasion is the death

1910 - Shorter Writings

(ANON.)
of Mark Twain, who had won a place in the world's heart. "Mark Twain was certainly much more than a mere jester. He had an intensely serious side."

B15   ANON. "Last Honors to Mark Twain. Scenes at the Services Held over the Body of the Dead Author at the 'Brick Church,' Fifth Avenue and Thirty-Seventh Street, New York," Harper's Weekly, LIV (May 7), 11.
Five photographs.

B16   *ANON. "The Late Mark Twain (Samuel L. Clemens)," Phrenological Journal and Science of Health, CXXIII (June), 190.
[Source: Reprinted in Madeleine B. Stern, "Mark Twain Had His Head Examined" (1969).]

B17   ANON. "Learned River for $500," St. Louis Republic, April 22, p. 3.
Interview with Captain Horace Bixby, who taught MT to be a river pilot. "While he was with me on the boats he was writing all his spare time. He wrote for some of the magazines, but I don't know which ones."

B18   ANON. "Mark Twain," Athenaeum, No. 4305 (April 30), pp. 524-25.
In the past twenty years he has built a reputation as a fearless spokesman on public affairs. "He was one of the most serious-minded of men, though his serious writing was not effective. But his humour had wholesome teaching behind, and keen, though kindly criticism of human foibles and weaknesses."

B19   ANON. "Mark Twain," Century, LXXXI (June), 315.
"Chivalrous as he was in his championship of causes in his more serious work, he had no false shame about writing pure fun, with no other purpose but to amuse."

B20   ANON. "Mark Twain," Collier's XLV (April 30), 9.
Short editorial, praising the writer and man.

B21   ANON. "Mark Twain," Dial, XLVIII (May 1), 305-307.
His best works are TS, HF, RI, and others in which he draws on western experience, and his next best are the travel books, which reveal an increasing sophistication and corresponding decline in naturalness. By transplanting himself in the East he cut off his sources. "Over some of his later flounderings in the alien elements of literary criticism, history, and metaphysics, it were best discreetly to draw a veil" (p. 306). Reprinted in Anderson (1971), pp. 281-84.

B22   ANON. "Mark Twain," Independent, LXVIII (April 28), 934-35.
A general discussion, much of it bio-

graphical; declines to predict whether his fame will endure.

B23   ANON. "Mark Twain," Outlook, XCIV (April 30), 971-72.
A general and somewhat derivative obituary account.

B24   ANON. "Mark Twain," The Public (Chicago), XIII (April 29), 385-86.
An editorial praising MT's democracy. "The death of this man at his age calls for no tears of grief. He passes out of his life normally, after doing a life's work so well that it will be a wholesome influence with many a generation yet to come." Gives the text of a brief note thanking the editor of The Public for sending him a book, "which I prize for its lucidity, its sanity & its moderation, & because I believe its gospel" (from Villa di Quarto, Firenze, January 7, 1904). The issue of May 13 contains a letter to the editor from Daniel Kiefer praising MT for speaking out against the wrongs committed by his own country in the Philippines, as well as the wrongs of other nations (pp. 439-40).

B25   ANON. "Mark Twain," Punch, CXXXVIII (April 27), 306.
Short farewell poem, unsigned.

B26   ANON. "Mark Twain," Spectator, CIV (April 30), 720-21.
On MT's dry humor, gentle satire, portrayal of life and character. TS and HF "will live always in the first rank of American literature. They are great because they are simple."

B27   ANON. "Mark Twain," (London) Times Literary Supplement, April 28, p. 153.
Much of the obituary is biographical and general, with the usual praise for TS and HF for their portrayal of boy-nature. "A Yankee at King Arthur's Court is a book which we have sedulously avoided as we would avoid a book on Sir Lancelot at the Court of Mr. Taft," but "his heart was in the right place" in JA. Reprinted in Living Age, CCLXV (May 28), 564-67.

B28   ANON. "Mark Twain: An American Pioneer in Man's Oldest Art, Whose Death Is Mourned by the World at Large," Collier's XLV (April 30), 10-11.
A general discussion, intelligent but not original. Photograph p. 11.

B29   ANON. "Mark Twain and Christian Science," The British Weekly, XLVIII (May 12).
A brief note, concerning an article on MT in "The New York Christian Advocate--a most reputable journal," which praised his attack on Christian Science. This note is followed by "Mark Twain's minister," on the death of the wife of Joseph Twichell.

B30   ANON. "Mark Twain as a Serious Force in Lit-
      erature," Current Literature, XLVIII
      (June), 663-67.
          Summarizes and extensively quotes recent
      discussions of MT as a serious writer by
      Archibald Henderson, William Dean Howells,
      William Lyon Phelps, Henry M. Alden, and
      by anonymous writers in the New York Times
      and the San Francisco Argonaut; all but the
      Argonaut article are listed in this bib-
      liography, and the article adds nothing to
      them. Includes photograph, copyright by
      Gessford.

B31   ANON. "Mark Twain Commemorated," Outlook,
      XCVI (December 10), 801-802.
          Brief account of a meeting held in Car-
      negie Hall the previous week; the account
      in Harper's Weekly (December 17) is con-
      siderably more extensive.

B32   ANON. "Mark Twain in Memoriam. Interesting
      Passages from the Tributes Paid to the
      Great Humorist at the Memorial Meeting in
      Carnegie Hall, New York," Harper's Weekly,
      LIV (December 17), 8-10.
          Includes list of a number of the distin-
      guished guests, a large photograph, and
      texts of the remarks of several, among
      them Howells, Twichell, Joseph G. Cannon,
      Champ Clark, George Washington Cable, and
      Henry Van Dyke (who wrote a poem to MT for
      the occasion, 1910.B134).

B33   ANON. "Mark Twain Moraliste," La Revue
      (Paris, old Revue des Revues), LXXXVI
      (15 Mai), 278.
          Brief summary of Régis Michaud, "L'Envers
      d'un Humoriste: Mark Twain" (Revue du
      Mois, 10 April, 1910.B108).

B34   ANON. "Mark Twain's Estate," Bookman (New
      York), XXXI (June), 339.

B35   ANON. "Mark Twain's Gold and Dross," Liter-
      ary Digest, XL (June 11), 177.
          Summarizes and quotes Harry Thurston
      Peck's "Mark Twain a Century Hence" (Book-
      man, N.Y., June); briefly quotes William
      Lyon Phelps (Review of Reviews, June), who
      places RI above IA.

B36   ANON. "Mark Twain's Investments," Collier's,
      XLVI (November 12), 32.
          A list of the securities in his estate.

B37   ANON. "Mark Twain's Mysterious Book,"
      T. P.'s Weekly (London), XV (May 27), 675.
          On What is Man? Consists almost entirely
      of summary and quotation, and contains no
      critical estimate.

B38   ANON. "Mark Twain's Pessimistic Philosophy,"
      Current Literature, XLVIII (June), 643-47.
          On What is Man? Almost entirely descrip-
      tion of the book and quotation from it.
      Includes a photograph of MT in bed (copy-
      right by Van der Weyde) and one of him

looking out a window at Redding (copyright
by Paul Thompson).

B39   ANON. "Mark Twain's Religious Book," Liter-
      ary Digest, XL (May 7), 920.
          A description of What is Man? with exten-
      sive quotation and no added interpretation;
      based on an account in the New York Trib-
      une, it concludes with a quotation from
      The Outlook on MT's serious purpose and
      broad popularity (dates not given). In-
      cludes photograph of MT by Paul Thompson,
      copyright 1909.

B40   ANON. "Mark Twain's Secret Book Gives Start-
      ling Views," New York Times, May 1, Magazine
      Section, p. 2.
          Summary and extensive quotation of What
      Is Man?

B41   ANON. "More About Twain," Bookman (New York),
      XXXI (July), 458-59.
          Anecdotes about a letter addressed "Mark
      Twain, God Knows Where" which reached him,
      and MT's comment that the Ah Sin play (writ-
      ten in collaboration with Bret Harte) "had
      a run of one consecutive week."

B42   ANON. "Mr. Twichell's Praise," Hartford Times,
      April 22, p. 11.
          An interview with MT's friend of many
      years' standing, providing a number of sto-
      ries and insights, not all of which may be
      available elsewhere; mentions MT's lack of
      relish for Dickens and enthusiastic readings
      from Browning, and visits to the Farmington
      Avenue house by Henry Irving, Bret Harte,
      Charles Kingsley, and [Joe] Jefferson.
      When his coachman Patrick [McAleer] died,
      MT wired, "explaining that he wished to be
      a bearer, but the coachman's family, while
      appreciating the sympathy, decided that this
      service was out of place. The author at-
      tended the funeral and was, outside of the
      family, the principal mourner." The Hart-
      ford Times, like the Courant, reported MT's
      death and his career at length, making full
      use of local and wire-service material.

B43   ANON. "News for Bibliophiles," Nation (New
      York), XCI (September 22), 260.
          Describes the bibliography of MT's pub-
      lished works being compiled by Merle John-
      son, to be published shortly by Harper's.

B44   ANON. "News Notes," Bookman (London),
      XXXVIII (May), 53.
          "Whatever may be the ultimate fate of his
      other books, there is no doubt that in Tom
      Sawyer and in Huckleberry Finn he has done
      work that will endure."

B45   ANON. "Obituary Notes: Mark Twain," Pub-
      lishers' Weekly, LXXVII (April 30), 1796-97.
          Chiefly biographical, but contains a
      statement by Albert Bigelow Paine on MT's
      connection with Charles L. Webster & Company
      and one by Colonel George Harvey, president

1910 - Shorter Writings

(ANON.)
of Harper & Brothers, on the offer MT accepted from that firm: "It was proposed to take over all his books, guarantee him an income from royalties of not less than $25,000 per annum, and pay him 30 cents a word for all he should write, whether published or not for five years."

B46   ANON. "One of Twain's Final Letters Sent to Ambitious Little Girl," New York American, April 27, p. 5.
Quotes part of a letter from MT in Bermuda to Sulamith Ish-Kishor, then a girl of thirteen (and later a writer herself), who had written him of a dream she had after reading P&P.

B47   ANON. "The Originals of Some of Mark Twain's Characters," Review of Reviews (N.Y.), XLII (August), 228-30.
A summary, with quotations, of Homer Croy's "The Originals of Mark Twain's Characters" in Bellman (1910.B81).

B48   ANON. "Portland Woman Bitter at Twain," Portland Oregonian, April 22, p. 4.
An interview with Nina Larowe, who was on the Quaker City tour and has nothing good to say for the young MT: "he drank and he swore...Twain was mean and he had no idea of what that trip meant--that it was a trip of influence. But then he was a nobody then and could not understand such things." In a letter to the editor on April 23 (p. 5), Mrs. Larowe says that in a hurried interview "the reporter extracted apparently all the bitter and none of the sweet, making me seem very narrow and unable to appreciate genius." She summarizes the trip and describes some of the passengers, speaking more charitably of MT than she had according to the earlier news story. The interview angered Harriet Oxer, whose letter to the editor (April 25, p. 6) condemns Nina Larrowe's lack of Christian charity and argues that the cruise would have attracted little attention if MT had not immortalized it in IA.

B49   ANON. "Quelques Anecdotes sur Mark Twain," La Revue (Paris, old Revue des Revues), LXXXVI (1 Juin), 423.
Only a few anecdotes, which originally appeared in Alexander McD. Stoddart's "Twainiana," Independent, May 5 (1910.B127).

B50   ANON. "Real and Unreal Propriety," Chicago Tribune, April 24 (Drama-Editorial Section), p. 4.
Quotes from President Taft's tribute to MT, disseminated through the wire services: "He never wrote a line that a father could not read to a daughter" and uses this as a point of departure: "As applied to Mark Twain the comment was without value, but as explanation of American literature it could not be excelled." The attitudes

behind such statements as Taft's reflect a national cultural immaturity.

B51   ANON. "Recollections of His Life Here," San Francisco Examiner, April 22, p. 2.
Includes those of Alf Doten, apparently recorded indirectly, observing that MT had a few close friends but did not seek wide popularity. Retells the story of the pretended holdup of MT at Gold Hill, and also gives an unusual version of the origin of the "Mark Twain" pseudonym: "Doten delighted in pretending to their new acquaintances that it originated from Clemens using the expression in the booming days of Virginia City on such occasions as he found it convenient to 'stand off' a friendly bartender for drinks for Doten and himself." Other reminisicences reflect (and may be derived from) MT's own accounts of his western years. The whole issue of the Examiner is rich in tributes to MT, most of them from the wire services.

B52   *ANON. ["Some very good pictures," apparently relating to MT.] Portland Sunday Oregonian, July 3.
[Source: Letter from S. L. Severance to Albert Bigelow Paine, March 13, 1912, printed in Twainian, XXVI (March-April, 1967), 3.]

B53   *ANON. "The Spirit of American Humor," The Nation (London?), VII (April 30), 149.
[Source: Smalley thesis (1948), pp. 63, 70.]

B54   ANON. "Topics of the Day: Mark Twain," Literary Digest, XL (April 30), 857-58.
Summary of press comments on MT.

B55   ANON. "Tributes to Mark Twain," Harper's Weekly, LIV (May 14), 35.
In Harper & Brothers advertisement for the Author's National Edition of MT's works, tributes by President Taft, Theodore Roosevelt, President Woodrow Wilson [of Princeton University], Dr. Van Dyke, Mrs. Julia Ward Howe, James Whitcomb Riley, Booth Tarkington. All of these tributes may be found elsewhere, distributed by the newspaper wire servies (the Boston Globe printed most of them).

B56   ANON. "Twain Nearly 80, Says Goodwin," Sacramento Union (April 23), p. 4.
Reminiscences by C. C. Goodwin, who joined the Territorial Enterprise after MT's departure, and heard a number of MT stories. He based his estimate of MT's age on a book of biographies erroneously giving his year of birth as 1830. This interview with Goodwin, distributed by the press services and widely reprinted, is anecdotal and contains no new or valuable information. Surprisingly, the coverage of MT's death in the Union is rather thin, with nothing of value concerning his former connection with that paper.

B57 ANON. "A Western Word on Mark Twain," New
York Times (May 7), "Saturday Review of
Books," p. 253.
Briefly summarizes his eulogy in the San
Francisco Argonaut.

B58 ANON. [Brief obituary notice.] Spectator,
CIV (April 23), 655.
More than a humorist, a great humanist.
"Though not a man of learning, he had in
him the spirit of letters.... The mass of
his literary work was very great, but he
never wrote a line that he had cause to be
ashamed of."

B59 ANON. [Obituary.] Illustrated London News,
CXXXVI (April 30), 640, 643.
Brief commentary, praises MT and compares
him to Dickens for sympathy and sense of
fun, and for a "reforming and philanthropic
spirit" which, however, was more prominent
in the works of Dickens. Portrait, p. 643.

B60 ANON. [Obituary Notice.] Saturday Review
(London), CIX (April 23), 516. MT was
MT was comic on a lower level, "first among
the comic men of America--a country which can
never become seriously minded or reflective
enough to produce a humourist." Despite
his crudity, he forced his readers to
laugh. "With his faults he had the supreme
excuse that condones many of the artistic
blemishes in Shakespeare's early farces--
he was vital." Reprinted in Anderson
(1971), p. 278.

B61 ANON. [Untitled brief biographical summary.]
Nation (N.Y.), XC (April 28), 440.

B62 ANON. [Untitled notice.] Literary World,
LXXVI (May 15), 131-32.
Brief, biographical and anecdotal;
treats MT primarily as a humorist.

B63 ANON. [Photographs of MT.] The World's Work,
XX (June), 12976-77.
MT at the billiard table, in bed (reading The World's Work), and sitting in a
large wicker chair.

B64 ANON. [Review: Captain Stormfield's Visit
to Heaven.] Book News Monthly, XXVIII
(May), 717.
"No better demonstration of the untruth
of dead liberalism exists. No better hit
at the weakness of narrowness and ultra-
conservatism has appeared.... Yet there is
nothing in it which ought to offend the
most orthodox fair mind."

B65 *ANON. [Review: Captain Stormfield's Visit
to Heaven.] Harper's Weekly (January 22).
[Source: Twainian, II (March, 1940), 4.]

B66 ANON. [Brief Review: Captain Stormfield's
Visit to Heaven.] Literary Digest, XL
(January 1), 33.
"Mark Twain treats his subject in a good-

natured, liberal, and rollicking manner and
with a daring extravagance, somewhat ma-
chine-made, and always banal, which is absolutely lacking in humor, but he does not
make any moral or political point." There
is nothing offensive, but also nothing
interesting in the picture of Stormfield's
destination.

B67 ANON. [Review: Mark Twain's Speeches.]
Athenaeum, No. 4322 (August 27), pp. 229-30.
Criticizes the editing.

B68 *ANON. [Review: Merle Johnson, A Bibliogra-
phy of the Works of Mark Twain.] Nation,
XCI (December 22), 601.
[Source: Twainian, II (March, 1943), 5;
Asselineau (1954), No. 32.]

B69 BEARD, DAN. "Mark Twain as a Neighbor," Review of Reviews (New York), XLI (June),
705-709.
Reminiscences of MT at his "Stormfield"
home, with an account of his first arrival
there and his greeting. Photographs of MT,
and of the house and grounds.

B70 _____. "Mark Twain, the Man, as Dan Beard
Knew," San Francisco Examiner, April 25,
p. 16.
At this time Dan Beard was living near
MT's "Stormfield" home at Redding, Connecticut; years before, he had illustrated CY,
and here he quotes MT's description of the
hero: "Now, Mr. Beard, you know the character of the Yankee. He is a common, uneducated man. He's a good telegraph operator;
he can make a Colt's revolver or a Remington
gun--but he's a perfect ignoramus. He's a
good foreman for a manufacturer, can survey
land and run a locomotive; in other words
he has neither the refinement nor the weakness of a college education. In conclusion
I want to say that I have endeavored to put
in all the coarseness and vulgarity into
the Yankee in King Arthur's Court that is
necessary and rely upon you for all the refinement and delicacy of humor your facile
pen can depict." [There is an unconfirmed
report that a shorter version of this feature story by Beard may be extant in a copy
of the New York American of about this period either in the New York Public Library or
at the Library of Congress, but that not
all editions of the American carried the
story.] Paine (1912.A3) gives an abbrevi-
ated account of these words (II, 887-89),
but does not cite a source.

B71 "BRITANNICUS" [BROOKS, SYDNEY.] "England and
Mark Twain," North American Review, CXCI
(June), 822-26.
England has had no national author since
the death of Dickens (Tennyson was not as
generally beloved), and "we have perforce
claimed Mark Twain as the representative
'racial' author of his day and have felt for
him only a little less admiration, gratitude

1910 - Shorter Writings

("BRITANNICUS" [BROOKS, SYDNEY.])
and affection than his own countrymen."
Reprinted in Anderson (1971), 286-90, where
"Britannicus" is identified as Brooks (also
so identified in Asselineau [1954], No. 52).

B72   BROADLEY, A. M.   Chats on Autographs. Lon-
       don: T. Fisher Unwin, pp. 229, 341.
          Contains the conclusion of a letter in
       which MT says that the Atlantic notice of
       RI is entirely satisfactory, "and I am as
       uplifted and reassured by it as a mother
       who has given birth to a white baby when
       she was awfully afraid it was going to be
       a mulatto" (p. 229). Autograph letters by
       MT are listed as having sold for $150 and
       $100 (p. 341).

B73   [BURTON, RICHARD.] "Mark Twain--R.I.P.,"
       Bellman (Minneapolis), VIII (April 30),
       541.
          Vague and general praise. Unsigned:
       identified from cover list of contents.

B74   CARMAN, BLISS. "The Last Day at Stormfield,"
       Collier's, XLV (May 7), 9.
          A poem on the death in springtime of the
       weary humorist; "haply...In Avalon, Isle of
       Dreams," Chaucer, Shakespeare, Molière, and
       Cervantes are enjoying his humor. (With
       full-page half-tone portrait of MT.)

B75   CARNEGIE, ANDREW, et al. "Tributes to Mark
       Twain," North American Review, CXCI (June),
       827-35.
          Carnegie, Andrew. Says MT credited him
       with the inspiration for CY through his
       Triumphant Democracy and with the author-
       ship of a chapter heading in PW. Praises
       his business integrity (pp. 827-28).
          Paine, Albert Bigelow. Compares MT to
       Halley's Comet (p. 828).
          Washington, Booker T. Saw MT several
       times at his Hartford and New York homes,
       and at the Lotos Club. Praises MT's sym-
       pathetic portrayal of Jim in HF and his
       work for Congo reform, and "the flavor of
       the South" in his works (pp. 828-30).
          Tarkington, Booth. MT was "the American
       Spirit.... Everything seemed safer because
       he was with us" (pp. 830-31).
          Gompers, Samuel. "He was a deep student
       of men and events, a philosopher" (p. 831).
          Nesbit, Wilbur D. "He is Cervantes and
       Carlyle and Hugo and Dickens all in one"
       (pp. 831-32).
          Ade, George. MT knew better than to pub-
       lish too much, or too much of the same
       thing, and so he never lost public favor
       (pp. 832-33).
          Garland, Hamlin. On MT as a westerner
       and "a great fictionist and a rough-hewn
       stylist uttering himself in his own way,
       which was a large, direct and forceful
       way" (pp. 833-34).
          Bangs, John Kendrick. "I sometimes won-
       der if he were not quite the most command-
       ing literary personality of this period"
       (p. 834).

          Matthews, Brander. Much of MT's work may
       be forgotten, but much is great and will
       survive: TS, HF, RI, LOM, TA, "Hadleyburg."
       "Mark Twain was great...as a humorist, as a
       story-teller, as a stylist, and as a moral-
       ist" (pp. 834-35).

B76   CASTELLANOS, JESÚS. "Mark Twain," Reprinted
       in his Los Optimistas: Lecturas y Opiniones
       Críticas de Arte. Collección Póstuma Publi-
       cada por la Academia Nacional de Artes y
       Letras. (Habana: Talleres Tipográficos del
       "Avisador Comercial," 1914), pp. 169-73.
          An obituary summary, dated "Abril 1910"
       at the end but without facts of original
       publication. "La obra de Mark Twain se
       comparaba en vida suya con la de Cervantes
       y Molière" (p. 173). Asselineau (1954),
       No. 199 cites a 1918 Madrid ed. of Los
       Optimistas, pp. 115-20.

B77   CHESTERTON, G. K. "Mark Twain," T. P.'s
       Weekly (London), XV (April 29), 535-36.
          In part, this is more interesting as an
       example of Chestertonian paradoxes than as
       a discussion of MT, although it contains
       his views of the American culture and MT's
       relation to it. On CY says MT failed to
       understand what Arthur stood for: "But all
       these limitations of his only re-emphasize
       the ultimate fact: he never laughed at a
       thing unless he thought it laughable. He
       was an American; that is to say, an unfath-
       omably solemn man." Reprinted in Scott
       (1967), pp. 112-17.

B78   "CLAUDIUS CLEAR" [SIR ROBERTSON NICOLL.]
       "Mark Twain," The British Weekly, XLVIII
       (April 28), 93.
          In part a conventional tribute, this
       notes MT's tenderness toward his wife and
       daughters, and grief at their loss. Praises
       him as a writer: "Perhaps the criticisms
       that have appeared, excellent as some are,
       have scarcely done justice to Mark Twain's
       exceeding care in his style. He was a most
       precise and painstaking writer, and attached
       the greatest importance to the music of
       words and the harmonious ordering of claus-
       es"; MT's strictures on Fenimore Cooper are
       quoted to illustrate his concern for lan-
       guage. The account is entirely sympathetic,
       more so than required by courtesy toward
       the dead, and contrasts with the words of
       "Claudius Clear" in 1912.B21. [Attributed
       to Sir Robertson Nicoll by The Literary
       Digest (November 30, 1912).]

B79   CLEMENS, SAMUEL L. "Mark Twain's Address
       Before Hannibal High School Class of 1902.
       Delivered in the Park Theatre Friday Even-
       ing, May 30, 1902--He Presented Diplomas to
       Members of the Class," Hannibal Morning
       Journal, April 23 (copy in scrapbook: Mark
       Twain: Biography-Reminiscence in Chicago
       Public Library).
          Consists largely of MT's remarks, with
       very brief description of the event.

B80   COLBY, F. M. "Mark Twain's Illuminating Blunder," Bookman (New York), XXXII (December), 354-58.
      Defends MT's Whittier Birthday Dinner Speech, and condemns the cold audience: "Reading the speech nowadays we can think only of the inhumanity of that awful group of diners toward Mark Twain. No other motive than the desire to amuse them is discernible in a single line of it.... Whether Mark Twain's joke was good or bad it was at least vivacious and therein lay its blasphemy. Suddenly and without warning he burst out talking in a group of deeply dyed New Englanders as if among men."

B81   CROY, HOMER. "The Originals of Mark Twain's Characters," Bellman (Minneapolis), VIII (June 25), 804-805.
      Superficial discussions of several friends, acquaintances, and relatives of MT's; provides no new information. The identification of Laura Fraser as Becky Thatcher and B. C. M. ("Barney") Farthing as Huckleberry Finn was common in the April, 1910 newspapers, although Farthing's claims have since been passed over in favor of Tom Blankenship (identified by MT). Summarized and extensively quoted in Review of Reviews (N.Y.), August (1910.B47).

B82   DE QUILLE, DAN [WILLIAM WRIGHT.] "His Life in Virginia City as Reported Was Full of Wild Pranks and Merriment. Active in Stirring Days of Old Mining Camp," Rocky Mountain News (Denver), April 22, p. 3.
      Somewhat conventional reminiscences of rooming with MT at the Daggett & Meyers building, and of the practical jokes played on them; also, describes MT as a fencing enthusiast: "Twain became quite an expert with the foils. In attack he was fiery and particularly dangerous, for the reason that one could not watch his eyes, which he habitually wears about half closed. In defence he was not so good, and would nearly always give ground when hotly pressed."

B83   DICKIE, J. F. "Mark Twain," in his In the Kaiser's Capital (New York: Dodd, Mead and Co.), pp. 182-90.
      On his acquaintance with MT in New York and Berlin; anecdotal.

B84   DREDD, FIRMIN. "Mark Twain's Biographer," Bookman (N.Y.), XXXI (June), 363-65.
      On Albert Bigelow Paine and his association with MT. In preparation for the monumental biography, "No trouble or expense has been spared. For example, a year or two ago Mr. Paine made a long pilgrimage, following step by step the Innocents Abroad" (p. 365; cf. Paine, The Ship-Dwellers, 1910.A8). Two photographs of Paine, one showing him playing billiards with MT at Stormfield.

B85   EGGLESTON, GEORGE CARY. Recollections of a Varied Life. New York: Henry Holt and Company.
      Contains personal recollections of MT, mostly at public meetings; indexed.

B86   *EPUY, MICHEL. Antholgie des humoristes anglais et américains. Paris: Delagrave
      [Source: Asselineau (1954), No. 40: "On Mark Twain, pp. 422-423; extracts pp. 423-481."]

B87   _____. "Mark Twain (Samuel Clemens)," Grande Revue, LXI (10 Mai), 66-75.
      Largely biographical, but notes his fine character, and the serious tone in some of his books. Was he a heavy-handed buffoon, lacking art, as some of the recent notices of his death have charged? Yes, he was that at the beginning of his career, but he was capable of pity and tenderness, as in "A Dog's Tale" or "Was It Heaven or Hell?" and in "Eve's Diary" "il a atteint la perfection d'un Homère ou d'un La Fontaine."

B88   GAINES, CLARENCE H. "Mark Twain the Humorist," Book News Monthly, XXVIII (April), 583-88.
      Humor gave MT perspective. "While Samuel Clemens has jested more tremendously than any of his contemporaries, he is perhaps the sincerest writer in America. So that, on the whole, one does him the greatest injustice ever to call him (merely) a humorist." Illustrations: photographs of "Stormfield" home, and of MT and a bust of MT.

B89   *GRISWOLD, STEPHEN. [Letter or interview, in which he apparently criticized MT. Griswold had been a shipmate on the Quaker City tour on which IA was based.] Brooklyn Eagle, June 5.
      [Source: Ganzel (1968), pp. 260n, 266n.]

B90   Hannibal Morning Journal. [Source: Scrapbook, Mark Twain: Biography-Reminiscence in Chicago Public Library, n.d.], April 22.
      RoBards, John L. "Tribute to Mark Twain." Affectionate, general. "Mark Twain's Last Visit to Hannibal." Reprints of news stories in the Journal, May 29-June 3, 1902: MT honored by schools, local dignitaries. April 24.
      "Prophetic Words of Hon. George A. Mahan, Uttered October 24, 1906." Someday there will be a monument to MT in Hannibal.
      "Characteristic Mark Twain Letters." In 1903 Mr. T. F. Gatts requested permission to set a "Mark Twain Day" at the St. Louis World's Fair; MT replied in part: "I hope that no society will be named for me while I am still alive, for I might at some time or another do something which could cause its members to regret having done me that honor." In reply to further urging he repeated his thanks, but "I am a Missourian and so I shrink from distinctions which have to be arranged before hand and with my

(Hannibal Morning Journal)
privity, for I then become a party to my
own exalting."
April 26.
"Hannibal's Tribute to Samuel L. Clemens,
'Mark Twain.'" Describes the meeting at
the Presbyterian Church the previous afternoon, quoting tributes by local dignitaries,
among them MT's boyhood friend John L. Ro-
Bards; like the rest he was laudatory but
general.

B91   HENDERSON, ARCHIBALD. "The International
Fame of Mark Twain," North American Review,
CXCII (December), 805-15.
Surveys some of the more significant
critical commentary on MT in France, Ger-
many, Italy, and elsewhere. Reprinted in
Anderson (1971), 302-12; revised as "The
World-Famed Genius" in Henderson's Mark
Twain (London, 1911), pp. 127-76.

B92   HERON, HERBERT. "Mark Twain," Harper's Weekly, LIV (June 11), 24.
On the laughter MT gave the world, and
the falsehoods he exposed; he will be
mourned.

B93   HOWELLS, WILLIAM DEAN. "A Critical Comment
on Mark Twain's Work," Harper's Weekly,
LIV (April 30), 10, 27.
Excerpts from his "Mark Twain: an Inquiry" (North American Review, 1901; reprinted there 1910 and in Howells, My Mark
Twain).

B94   _____. "Mark Twain: An Inquiry," North
American Review, CXCI (June), 836-50.
Reprinted from North American Review,
February, 1901; also reprinted in his My
Mark Twain (1910.A3). Photograph of MT,
p. 720.

B95   _____. "My Memories of Mark Twain," Harper's
Monthly, CXXI (July), 165-78; (August),
340-48; (September), 512-29.
Admiring discussion of author and man by
a professional colleague and close personal
friend of more than forty years; reprinted
with only minor changes in his My Mark
Twain, pp. 1-100 (1910.A3). Summarized,
with excerpts, as "Mark Twain as William
Dean Howells Saw Him," Current Literature,
XLIX (October), 445-47.

B96   _____. [Introduction: Mark Twain's Speeches.] New York and London: Harper & Brothers Publishers.
A rather general, two-page introduction
without new information. "I never heard
Clemens speak when I thought he quite
failed," but he was at his best when he
carefully prepared his apparently spontaneous performances. [This edition differs
significantly from that of 1923 in the
selection of speeches.]

B97   JAMES, GEORGE WHARTON. "Mark Twain and the
Pacific Coast," Pacific Monthly, XXIV
(August), 115-32.
On MT in Nevada and California, with recollections by acquaintances, some from
published works and some apparently from
conversations. Repeats a story that MT was
twice captured in the Civil War, the second
time escaping and fleeing to Nevada to escape punishment for violating parole after
the first capture. Also quotes accounts by
Ella Sterling Cummings, and, at length, from
recollections (some apparently given orally)
by Charles Warren Stoddard, on MT's lack of
self-confidence while lecturing in London
in 1873. Quotes at length an interview of
Nina Larowe and her letter to the editor
(1910.B48) on MT as she saw him on the Quaker City tour. Includes photograph of MT by
Major J. B. Pond on the world lecture tour,
and four photographs by A. F. Bradley.

B98   JENSEN, JOHANNES V. "Mark Twain," Politikens
Kronik (n.p.), (April 23).
[Source: Scrap book, Mark Twain: Biogra-
phy-Reminiscence in Chicago Public Library.]
A memorial tribute, in Norwegian.

B99   JEROME, JEROME K., et al. "Mark Twain. Some
Personal Recollections and Opinions," Bookman (London), XXXVIII (June), 116-19. Portrait and Cartoon.
"Jerome's First Meeting with Him." After
MT had dined with him in London, Jerome was
struck by the fact "that neither of us had
made a single joke or told a funny story."
Struck by MT's "deep feeling and broad sympathies" (p. 116).
"E. V. Lucas and Twain at a 'Punch Dinner.'" Praises TS and HF; describes MT as
"visibly touched, almost melted" by the reception (pp. 116-17).
"Walter Emanuel's Opinion of Mark Twain's
Humour." An original, an example to other
humorists; his best work will endure
(p. 117).
"J. J. Bell and a Twain Joke." Bell never
met MT, but appreciated his joke about Noah
(pp. 117-18).
"Leonard Henslowe on Interviewing Mark
Twain." "Mark Twain was always kind to the
interviewer, and showed tact even in putting
him off." A holograph note from MT is reproduced in facsimile (p. 118).
"Arnold Bennett Considers Twain Was a Divine Amateur." Never met MT. Best work in
first half of LOM. "Episodically, both
Huckleberry Finn and Tom Sawyer are magnificent, but as complete works of art they are
of quite inferior quality.... He had no
notion of construction, and very little
power of self-criticism. He was great in
the subordinate business of decoration....
The praise poured out on his novels seems
to me exceedingly exaggerated" (p. 118).
[Reprinted in Anderson (1971), p. 285.]

(JEROME, JEROME K., et al.)
"Owen Seaman's Welcome to Mark Twain in 1907." A reprint of the "To Mark Twain" poem in Punch (1907.B30), without added commentary (p. 118).
"Mr. Pett Ridge on the Charm of Mark Twain." After a busybody introduced him to MT as the MT of London, Ridge told MT: "What he intended to say was that you were the Pett Ridge of America!" MT replied, "Ah, now I can see we shall get along well together" (p. 118).
"F. Anstey in Praise of Mark Twain." No personal recollections; likes HF (p. 119).

B100   JERROLD, WALTER, "Mark Twain, the Man and the Jester," Bookman (London), XXXVIII (June), 111-16.
On the deep feeling behind MT's humor, and the distinctively American quality of his writing. Quotes Bret Harte's account of his first meeting with MT. Includes portraits of MT by George Hutchinson and by Spiridon.

B101   KING, FREDERICK A. "The Story of Mark Twain's Debts," Bookman (New York), XXXI (June), 394-96.
A superficial popular account, somewhat inaccurate ("His popularity with Englishmen had never been great, owing to the liberties he had taken with that nation's people in Innocents Abroad"); chiefly descriptive and based on secondary sources. ["Reprinted from THE BOOKMAN for January, 1906."]

B102   *LANCASTER, CHARLES. "Mark Twain," Liverpool Daily Post and Mercury, May 5.
[Source: Cited in letter by W. E. Benjamin to Albert Bigelow Paine in Twainian, XXVI (November-December, 1967), 4.]

B103   [Mark Twain Number.] Bookman (London), XXXVIII (June).
Cover photograph of MT by E. H. Mills.

B104   [MATHER, FRANK JEWETT.] "Two Frontiersmen," Nation (New York) XC (April 28), 422-23.
MT and Henry James are both frontiersmen with fidelity to their vision; MT's reputation will probably endure, "while the fate of Mr. James's delicate art seems to be involved in the hesitancy that afflicts his own heroes." Also appeared in New York Evening Post, April 23, p. 6. Reprinted in Anderson (1971), where this unsigned article is attributed to Mather (pp. 279-81).

B105   MATTHEWS, BRANDER. "American Humor," in his The American of the Future, and Other Essays (New York: Charles Scribner's Sons), passim.
MT, here described as a great humorist, is in a class with Cervantes and Molière. There is a strong implication that MT is more than simply amusing, but the article does not lend itself to exploration of other aspects of his writing. Reprint of 1908.B8.

B106   MAURICE, ARTHUR BARTLETT. "Best Sellers of Yesterday. II--Mark Twain's The Innocents Abroad," Bookman (New York), XXXI (June), 374-79.
Second in a series on such best-sellers by various authors; chiefly descriptive, based on secondary sources, with extensive quotation and illustrations from IA. Praises MT's "keen observation, clear perception and a remarkable freshness of the point of view"; the book remains a best Seller of To-day."

B107   *MENCKEN, H. L. [On his admiration for HF.] Smart Set, XXXI (June), 153-54.]
[Source: Cited in Anderson (1971), p. 277.]

B108   MICHAUD, RÉGIS. "L'Envers d'un Humoriste: Mark Twain," Revue du Mois, IX (April 10), 430-44.
Notes the serious element in MT's work, his literary art, concluding: "Au point de vue artistique, Mark Twain est, après Dickens, un des plus grands caricaturistes des lettres anglaises. Ainsi que l'auteur de Gargantua et celui de Don Quichotte, il a plus de fois donné à satire la forme d'une épopée.... Mark Twain en est l'Homère, plus sérieux qu'on ne pensait, sous son travesti d'humoriste."

B109   MILLARD, BAILEY. "Mark Twain in San Francisco," Bookman (New York), XXXI (June), 369-73.
Superficial, dependent on secondary sources, and not wholly accurate. Reports that MT worked for a time for the San Francisco Morning Call before three months of pocket-mining for gold in Calaveras County, and quotes a conversation between Noah Brooks and MT [who was in New York at the time], in which MT won reluctant approval for the Quaker City tour at the expense of the San Francisco Alta California.

B110   MURRAY, ADA FOSTER. "To Mark Twain," Harper's Weekly, LIV (May 7), 27.
A short poem on the enchantment in MT's humor, and his "exquisite and true" touch for "the deeper things" as well.

B111   NESBIT, WILBUR D. "Samuel Langhorne Clemens, 1835-1910," Harper's Weekly, LIV (May 7), 30.
Reprints a poem which appeared "at the time of Mark Twain's death" in the Chicago Evening Post. His monument will be "a boy who hugs a well-thumbed book,/ Wherein dwell the companions of his heart."

B112   PAIN, BARRY. "The Humour of Mark Twain," Bookman (London), XXXVIII (June), 107-11.
Largely hostile, by an acquaintance of Bret Harte. "Mark Twain's humorous writing at its best does bear some resemblance to Bret Harte's, but Bret Harte made far fewer inartistic blunders." Much of MT's humor

(PAIN, BARRY)

is now dated; and "if we make this allow-
ance, it may be said that when Mark Twain's
humour fails, it is because his taste fails.
It was his misfortune to hate all that was
old and established.... I do not allude
only to that dismal failure, his Yankee at
the Court of King Arthur. Many instances
of this dullness of perception may be found
in his travel books." Even HF is marred
by MT's inability to maintain a consistent
esthetic distance from his material. Pain
agrees, however, with MT's condemnation of
The Vicar of Wakefield as insincere.

B113   PAINE, ALBERT BIGELOW. "Mark Twain: A Biographical Summary," Harper's Weekly, LIV
(April 30), 6-10.
A useful brief biography, but superseded
by Paine's extensive 1912 life of MT
(1912.A3).

B114   PEARSON, EDMUND LESTER. "The Children's Librarian versus Huckleberry Finn: A Brief
for the Defense," in his The Library and
the Librarian. (Woodstock, Vermont: The
Elm Tree Press), pp. 26-32.
Reprinted from Library Journal
(1907.B28).

B115   PECK, HARRY THURSTON. "Mark Twain a Century
Hence," Bookman (New York), XXXI (June),
382-93.
"I should say that the first two books--
The Jumping Frog (1867) and The Innocents
Abroad (1869) are never likely to go out of
print or out of favour. Roughing It (1872)
will be valued both for its humour and for
its history for many years. The Adventures
of Tom Sawyer (1876) and Huckleberry Finn
(1885) will remain for perhaps two decades.
All the rest of Mr. Clemens's books may
perhaps be sold by subscription agents among
his 'complete works' for a certain time,
but they will not be read." Includes several photographs of MT, and one of Theresa
Feodorowna Ries working on a bust of him.
Reprinted in Anderson (1971), pp. 291-95.

B116   PHELPS, WILLIAM LYON. "Mark Twain," in his
Essays on Modern Novelists (New York: Mac-
Millan), pp. 99-114.
Originally in North American Review,
1907.B29.

B117   _____. "Mark Twain, Artist," Review of Reviews (New York), XLI (June), 702-703.
"Mark Twain was a greater artist than he
was humorist; a greater humorist than he
was philosopher; a greater philosopher than
he was thinker. Goethe's well-known remark
about Byron, 'The moment he thinks, he is a
child,' would in some respects be applicable
to Mark Twain,'" but MT "was a profoundly
serious artist." Reprinted in Anderson
(1971), pp. 296-98.

B118   _____. "Some Notes on Mark Twain. With Some
Unpublished Letters," Independent, LXVIII
(May 5), 956-60.
"Some Rambling Notes of an Idle Excursion"
parallels Sir Thomas Browne's Religio Medici
in suggesting that Elijah kindled a fire on
a wet altar because he soaked it in petroleum rather than water; an MT letter on the
subject to Phelps (April 24, 1901) is here
printed, together with one to Bret Harte
(May 1, 1867) on the recent publication of
the Jumping Frog book, Also includes miscellaneous comments on MT's hesitating agreement
that HF is his best work, his support for the
Japanese side in the war with Russia, his
visible distress over the final illness of
his wife, and his popularity among German
readers; cites an unnamed French journal
which in 1907 ranked him at the head of the
day's leading authors. Sketch of MT by
Poulteney Bigelow. Reprinted with minor revisions in Phelps's Essays on Books (1914).

B119   RIDEING, WILLIAM H. "Mark Twain in Clubland,"
Bookman (New York), XXXI (June), 379-82.
Anecdotes of MT when he stayed for a few
months at the Players Club in New York; describes his manner of speaking, when at ease
or angry, and his reaction on being shown a
Greek version of his "Jumping Frog" story
(which later turned out to be a translation
for classroom use by Henry Sidgwick).

B120   RILEY, JAMES WHITCOMB, et al. "Indiana School
of Authors, in Deep Grief, Drops Tender
Praise at Bier of the Humorist," Indianapolis
Star, April 22, p. 7.
Somewhat conventional appreciations, without added editorial comment, by Riley, George
Ade, Meredith Nicholson, Charles Major, and
Newton Booth Tarkington. The general tenor
of the remarks is that MT was lovable, sane,
and distinctively American; although this
appears to be the first and fullest publication, these authors' remarks were widely
quoted through the wire services.

B121   _____. "Tribute of America's 'Funny Men' to
the King of Them Who Has Passed Away," Boston Post, April 23, p. 7.
"Yesterday the Post wired the leading humorists of the country, asking for express
sions upon the death of the dean and most
famous of the corps, Mark Twain. The love
and admiration in which Mr. Clemens was held
is told in the following tributes," by James
Whitcomb Riley, Frank L. Stanton, George
Ade, Sewell Ford, R. F. Outcault, C. B. Lewis (M. Quad), Paul West, S. E. Kiser, Newton
Newkirk, Walt Mason, Wilbur D. Nesbit, Wallace Irwin, Samuel G. Blythe, and Franklin
P. Adams. The Boston Post also contained a
rich sampling of tributes by public figures
as reported by the wire services.

B122 SHERMAN, STUART P. "Literary News and Reviews: The Humor of Mark Twain," New York Evening Post, May 14.
      [Source: clippings in Mark Twain--Biography-Reminiscence scrapbook in Chicago Public Library.] Extensive, biographical, and laudatory, noting the American quality of his works. "Handicapped by uproarious laughter, he produced two or three pieces of fiction which deserved serious attention; but his leonine head had grown gray before he lived down his record as a 'platform humorist.'"

B123 _____. "Mark Twain," Nation (New York), XC (May 12), 477-80.
      On MT as a big-hearted, unsubtle, robust American, and on his humor. Reprinted in Cardwell (1963), 9-14; Scott (1955), 107-16; Scott (1967), 118-27. Asselineau (1954), No. 169 reports a reprinting in Gustav Pollak, ed., Fifty Years of American Idealism (Boston, 1915, pp. 388-400); revised and expanded as "The Democracy of Mark Twain" in Sherman's On Contemporary Literature (New York: Henry Holt, 1917, pp. 18-49); Asselineau (1954), No. 519 reports reprinting of the book in 1931, and (No. 330) of the essay in Kenneth Allan Robinson, et al., Essays Towards Truth (New York: Henry Holt, 1924, pp. 368-95). The revision also discusses the Paine biography as "a part of the prose Odyssey of the American people," which "will continue to be read when many of Mark Twain's writings are forgotten" and concludes with a postscript on MS, which a boy of nine can read "with delight and without undesirable stimulation," despite the irony and atheism in "a book written at his elders."

B124 SMITH, H. B. [Review: Mark Twain's Speeches.] Bookman (N.Y.), XXXII (September), 78-79.
      A descriptive review, mostly summary and quotation.

B125 STEDMAN, LUCY, and GEORGE M. GOULD. Life and Letters of Edmund Clarence Stedman. New York: Moffat, Yard & Co. 2 vols.
      Contains partial text of Stedman's letter to MT (July 7, 1889), praising CY but with a number of criticisms of details, by page-number (II, 370-72).

B126 STERN, CAROLINE. "Mark Twain (A Nocturne of the Mississippi)," Harper's Weekly, LIV (July 2), 32.
      A poem on MT and the river.

B127 STODDART, ALEXANDER McD. "Twainiana," Independent, LXVIII (May 5), 960-63.
      Anecdotes, most of them not apocryphal but also not new; one, apparently not printed elsewhere, describes MT's participation in charades, as told by T. Max Smith, music critic of the New York Press.

B128 [STRUNSKY, SIMEON]. "Serious Humorists," Nation (New York), XC (June 30), 645-46.
      Through the "certain paradoxical habit we have fallen into when passing judgment on the illustrious dead," we praise their less salient qualities: MT had a serious side, but this is not what made him a great humorist and "There was no fundamental pessimism in Mark Twain." Reprinted in Anderson (1971), pp. 299-301, with attribution of this unsigned article to Strunsky.

B129 TAFT, WILLIAM HOWARD, et al. "Honor His Memory," Boston Globe (April 22), pp. 1-2.
      A number of brief and generally conventional tributes, of which those by Taft, Hamlin Garland, and William Dean Howells appeared in many or most American newspapers; also includes tributes by Thomas Wentworth Higginson, Julia Ward Howe, Thomas Nelson Page, Henry Cabot Lodge, Sam Walter Foss, Woodrow Wilson, William Lyon Phelps, and Charles Follen Adams.

B130 THOMPSON, JAMES WESTFALL. "Mark Twain," Harper's Weekly, LIV (May 14), 34.
      A poem, evoking the great Mississippi River and mourning MT's death.

B131 TORREY, CHARLES L. "Mark Twain, Sir Thomas Browne, and the Old Testament," Nation, XC (June 2), 553-54.
      A letter, commenting on William Lyon Phelps, "Some Notes on Mark Twain" (Independent, May 5, 956-60); begins by drawing a parallel between Sir Thomas Browne's Religio Medici and MT's Captain Ned Wakeman suggesting naphtha as the source of the altar fire which discomfited the prophets of Baal. Torrey points to a still older parallel in II Maccabees, i, 19 ff., in which "Nehemiah watered the grand altar with petroleum."

B132 TWICHELL, JOSEPH H. "Mark Twain: Mr. Twichell's Tribute to His Old and Very Dear Friend," Hartford Courant, April 23, p. 8.
      A letter to the editor which notes his "big, warm and tender heart," and, beneath his "exterior roughnesses...exquisite refinements of taste and sentiment." "He was quickly responsive to any appeal to his sympathy, especially to his pity. I have seldom known a person so easily moved to tears. He could sometimes be of an unsparingly hostile temper toward a fellow man, but he could never bear to see an animal in pain." Leah A. Strong reproduces the entire text of this letter in Joseph Hopkins Twichell: Mark Twain's Friend and Pastor (1966.All), pp. 68, 89-90.

B133 VALE, CHARLES. "Mark Twain as an Orator," Forum, XLIV (July), 1-13.
      Chiefly obituary praise of the man and works, of which "Huckleberry Finn is his supreme and incontestable masterpiece." Describes MT's speech at a 1907 dinner

(VALE, CHARLES)
given in his honor by the Lord Mayor of London, presided over by T. P. O'Connor, and his presence years earlier at a party at which the guests included Wagner, Liszt, Turgenev, Browning, Rosetti, Sir Frederick Leighton, Burne-Jones, William Morris, Bret Harte, and Joaquin Miller. Quotes the last part of Augustine Birrell's speech in his honor at a Pilgrims' dinner given for MT, and concludes with a reprinting of Owen Seaman's poem to him in Punch. "Acknowledgments are especially due to Mr. William Archer and Mr. T. P. O'Connor, M. P., for valued assistance."

B134 VAN DYKE, HENRY. "We Knew You Well, Dear Yorick of the West" [poem], American Academy and the National Institute of Arts and Letters, Public Meeting, Held at Carnegie Hall, November 30, 1910, in Memory of Samuel Langhorne Clemens (New York, 1922).
[This attribution by Scott, who reprints in (1955), p. 117, and (1967), p. 128]; poem also in "Mark Twain Commemorated," Outlook, XCVI (December 10), 802, and "Mark Twain in Memoriam..." Harper's Weekly, LIV (December 17), 10.

B135 WATTERSON, HENRY. "Mark Twain--An Intimate Memory," American Magazine LXX (July), 372-75.
MT originally meant the part of Colonel Sellers in the GA play for Edwin Booth, and resented the purely comic interpretation of the part by John T. Raymond; describes but does not reprint an MT letter on the original of Sellers, described in some detail, and Raymond's reaction to reading a letter from him to Watterson: "'Do you know,' said he, 'it makes me want to cry. That is not the man I am trying to impersonate at all.' Be sure it was not; for there was nothing funny about the spiritual being of Mark Twain's own Mulberry Sellers; he was as brave as a lion and as stern and upright as a covenanter." Describes a joke he and MT played on Murat Halstead by giving a cub reporter an interview in his name, repudiating his well-known principles.

B136 WHITE, FRANK MARSHALL. "Mark Twain as a Newspaper Reporter," Outlook, XCVI (December), 961-67.
White was responsible for engaging MT to write an account of the 1897 Diamond Jubilee for the New York World. It was at this time that a reporter called, having heard that he had died; MT sent him this note (here reproduced in facsimile): "James Ross Clemens, a cousin of mine, was seriously ill two or three weeks ago in London, but is well now. The report of my illness grew out of his illness; the report of my death was an exaggeration." Also publishes the texts of several MT notes to White. Includes photograph of MT.

B137 WILLIAMS, C. "Mark Twain," Harper's Weekly, LIV (August 20), 21.
A poem on the death of MT: he was kind, wholesome and wise in his humor. [Reprinted from Sunset (San Francisco), XXV (July), 58, according to Asselineau (1954), No. 82.]

B138 WOOLF, S. J. "Painting the Portrait of Mark Twain. The Humorist's Character as It Became Unfolded to the Artist," Collier's, XLV (May 14), 42-44.
Includes quotations from MT (from memory?) and sensitive observation of his character, based on meetings and sittings in February, 1906.

1911 A BOOKS

A1 *ANDERSON AUCTION COMPANY. Catalogue of the Library and Manuscripts of Samuel L. Clemens...to be Sold Feb. 7 & 8, 1911. New York: The Anderson Auction Co.
[Source: Asselineau (1954), No. 104.]

A2 *ANON. Mark Twain: Autograph Manuscripts and First Editions Offered by Dodd & Livingston. New York.
[Source: Asselineau (1954), No. 103.]

A3 HENDERSON, ARCHIBALD. Mark Twain. London: Duckworth & Co. [Also New York: Frederick A. Stokes Company, 1912, and reprinted Folcroft, Pa.: The Folcroft Press, Inc., 1969.]
A major study of man and works, reflecting some personal acquaintance. The chapter titled "The World-Famed Genius" appeared in somewhat different form as "The International Fame of Mark Twain" (North American Review, December [1910.B91]), and "Philosopher, Moralist, Sociologist" appeared as "Mark Twain als Philosoph, Moralist und Soziologe" (Deutsche Revue, 1911.B9). Contains an extensive bibliography of articles and reviews concerning MT (pp. 215-30), incorporated in the present bibliography. Illustrated.

1911 B SHORTER WRITINGS

B1 ADAMS, JOHN. "Mark Twain As Psychologist," Bookman (London), XXXIX (March), 270-72.
A review of What Is Man? as a depressing work, and one ill-suited to MT's literary style. MT fails to observe the dualism he creates in distinguishing between the part of man that does things and the inner force that impels him to do them, and his purely mechanistic view of man disregards the undeniable existence of remorse.

B2 ANON. "Mark Twain as the Embodiment of American Romance," Current Literature, LI (November), 566-68.
A review of Archibald Henderson's Mark Twain. Summarizes parts and quotes freely,

(ANON.)
but does not make a critical estimate.
Full-page photograph of MT, p. 566.

B3   ANON. "Mark Twain's European Fame," Bookman
      (New York), XXXIII (June), 347-50.
         Summarizes the chapter in Archibald Hen-
      derson's Mark Twain on European translations
      and estimates of MT: he is not greatly ap-
      preciated in France and Italy, but very
      popular in the Scandinavian countries and
      in Germany, where the two American authors
      most widely read are MT and Emerson.

B4   ANON. [Review: Archibald Henderson, Mark
      Twain.] Bookman (London), XL (April),
      37-38.
         MT indeed "belongs among the immortals of
      his generation," although Henderson tends
      to over-state the case because he was per-
      sonally charmed by an acquaintance with
      him; hence his criticism is "unreliable";
      nonetheless, he vividly shows "the breadth,
      the height, the depth, and the ingrained
      humanity" of MT's character.

B5   C., M. B. "Mark Twain as a Reader," Harper's
      Weekly, LV (January 7), 6.
         A letter written to William Dean Howells
      from one of the women who used to meet in
      MT's home in Hartford to listen to him read
      from Browning.

B6   CAMPBELL, KILLIS. "From Aesop to Mark
      Twain," Sewanee Review, XIX (January),
      43-49.
         "A Dog's Tale" follows ancient tradition
      in its account of a dog wrongly punished
      after saving the master's child.

B7   *FROHMAN, DANIEL. Memories of a Manager. New
      York: Doubleday, Page & Co., p. 50.
         Comments on the play, Colonel Sellers as
      a Scientist, written in collaboration with
      William Dean Howells. [Source: Quoted by
      W. J. Meserve in The Complete Plays of
      William Dean Howells (1960), p. 208.]

B8   HALLECK, REUBEN POST. History of American
      Literature. New York: American Book Com-
      pany.
         On MT, pp. 355-64 and passim. Recognizes
      HF as "Mark Twain's masterpiece." MT will
      survive because of his artistry; his humor
      is "a preservative salt, but salt is valu-
      able only to preserve substantial things."

B9   HENDERSON, ARCHIBALD. "Mark Twain als Philo-
      soph, Moralist un Soziologe," Deutsche Re-
      vue (Stuttgart und Leipzig), XXXVI, Erster
      Band (Januar bis März), 189-205.
         A German translation of the concluding
      chapter of his Mark Twain [1910.A3].

B10   *____. "Mark Twain Seen in Three Aspects,"
      NCR, II (March 5), 6-7, 10.
         [Source: Leary (1954), p. 49.]

B11   *HERTS, ALICE MINNIE [HENIGER]. The Children's
      Educational Theatre, with an introduction
      by Charles W. Eliot. New York and London:
      Harper & Brothers.
         [Source: Asselineau (1954), No. 106,
      noting that it "contains a few pages on The
      Prince and the Pauper"; a copy of this book
      is listed in the card catalogue of the Oak-
      land (California) Public Library, but not
      on the shelf.]

B12   *HOWELLS, WILLIAM DEAN. "In Memory of Mark
      Twain," American Academy Proceedings, I
      (November 1), 5-6.
         [Source: Leary (1954), p. 50.] This may
      be the same as the item listed for 1913.B8.

B13   JAMES, GEORGE WHARTON. "How Mark Twain Was
      Made," National Magazine (Boston), XXXIII
      (February), 525-37.
         An enthusiastic popular account of MT's
      early years as a writer, molded by Califor-
      nia and the great West. Based primarily on
      familiar published accounts, but the source
      of the story of MT and his imitation meer-
      schaum pipe is given as Dan de Quille in
      private conversation. MT in London in 1873
      with Charles Warren Stoddard is described
      as homesick, and, when in his cups, lachry-
      mose, pessimistic, and convinced that he
      will die in the poorhouse. James contends
      that his account of MT reading to Stoddard
      from the book of Ruth is more complete and
      less expurgated than Stoddard's in the
      chapter "A Humorist Abroad" in his Exits
      and Entrances.

B14   MATTHEWS, BRANDER. "'Mark Twain' (Samuel L.
      Clemens)," in An Introduction to American
      Literature revised ed. (New York: American
      Book Company), pp. 220-31.
         This is a text-book, with questions for
      students at the ends of chapters. Matthews
      remains essentially unchanged in his esti-
      mate of MT, though more frankly acknowledg-
      ing his willingness to satisfy the public
      demand for humor, even at the expense of
      art.

B15   PAINE, ALBERT BIGELOW. "Mark Twain: Some
      Chapters from an Extraordinary Life,"
      Harper's Monthly, CXXIII (November),
      813-28; CXXIV (December), 42-53.
         The first of thirteen installments of
      Paine's biography of MT, which appeared as
      a book in 1912; includes illustrations not
      used in the book.

B16   SMALLEY, GEORGE W. Anglo-American Memories.
      New York and London: G. P. Putnam's Sons.
         On MT dining with Edward, Prince of Wales
      (afterward Edward VII) at Bad Nauheim; MT
      "did not care to adapt himself to the cir-
      cumstances; considering, perhaps, that the
      circumstances ought to adapt themselves to
      him. The meeting was not a success, and,
      so far as I know, was never repeated. So-
      cially speaking, the Mississippi Pilot was

(SMALLEY, GEORGE W.)
an intransigeant at times, and this was one
of the times. He could not, I suppose,
overcome his drawling manner of speech nor
reduce his interminable stories to dinner-
table limits. He had the air of usurping
more than his share of the conversation and
of the time, which he certainly did not
mean to" (pp. 412-15).

1912 A BOOKS

A1   ANON. Saturday Morning Club of Hartford.
Hartford: The Case, Lockwood & Brainard
Co.
A pamphlet, including a list of 15 lec-
tures there by MT, 1876-1907.

A2   *CLEMENS, SAMUEL L. Cuentos Escogidos:
tradución directa y esmerada de A. Barrado,
precedidos de un prólogo de Angel Guerra.
Madrid: Noticiero-guía de Madrid.
[Source: Asselineau (1954), No. 114.]

A3   PAINE, ALBERT BIGELOW. Mark Twain: A Biography, The Personal and Literary Life of
Samuel Langhorne Clemens. New York and
London: Harper & Brothers Publishers.
3 vol. (Part of this biography appeared
in Harper's, 1911-1912; the texts are not
identical).
The authorized biography. Paine met MT
in late 1901, and in January, 1906 made
arrangements to become his official biographer. His account of the later years is
based on personal observation and information supplied by acquaintances of MT, and
on documentation provided by MT and his
friends and family. He took pains to ob-
tain material from surviving individuals
who had known MT, and but for his efforts
much of value might have been lost. Paine
was more dependent on MT's own recollections for the earlier period, but often
heard different versions of the same incident and conceded that MT's accounts ought
to be confirmed from other sources whenever possible.
Paine has justly been criticized for suppression of factual material and for a
somewhat casual attitude toward papers in
his charge and toward the responsibilities
of an editor. In his behalf it may be
argued that some information was withheld
out of concern for Clara Clemens, and that
as MT's literary executor he was interested in maintaining the value of MT's literary name as an asset which continued to
provide her support. As biographer and
editor Paine assembled and organized a
large amount of material, laying a substantial foundation for MT scholarship.
His great work is being supplemented and
corrected, but will never be entirely replaced.

B1   *ANON. "Busy Life of the Rev. Joseph H. Twich-
ell, Mark Twain's Friend," New York Sun,
February 4, p. 7.
[Source: Listed by Leah A. Strong in
Joseph Hopkins Twichell (1966), p. 176.]

B2   ANON. "The 'Cub' Days of Mark Twain," Literary Digest, XLIV (February), 305-307.
A popular account of MT on the "Orion
Enterprise" (sic) in Nevada; based on an
extract from Paine's biography serialized
in Harper's.

B3   ANON. "How 'The Players' Was Formed," Literary Digest, XLV (October 12), 621.
Excerpts from the Paine biography on MT's
part in the founding of the New York club.

B4   ANON. "Mark Twain," Athenaeum, No. 4433
(October 12), pp. 403-404.
A review of the Paine biography: it is
too long and English critics will question
the estimates of some of MT's works.

B5   ANON. "Mark Twain's Failures," Literary Digest, XLV (July 27), 150.
On works MT abandoned, sometimes on the
urging of Olivia Clemens--whose voice was
simply that of good judgment. Summary of
an installment of the Paine biography in
Harper's Monthly (July), with the greater
part of the text consisting of quotations
from it, adds no information or judgment.

B6   ANON. "Mark Twain's Lucky Failure," Literary
Digest, XLIV (February 24), 391-92.
A summary of part of the fourth install-
ment of the Paine biography in Harper's, on
MT's failure as a miner.

B7   ANON. "Mark Twain's Portrait," Outlook (New
York), CII (November 9), 528-29.
A general discussion, occasioned by the
three-volume Paine biography, which "is
much too long; but it presents the apology
of being interesting from cover to cover."

B8   ANON. "Mark Twain's Private Girls' Club,"
Ladies' Home Journal, XXIX (February), 23,
54.
A series of letters from MT to a little
girl in France, 1902-1909, and "Constitu-
tion and Laws of the Juggernaut Club."
Photograph: "Mark Twain Trying to Make the
Life of Joan of Arc Intelligible to a Young
Girl Friend."

B9   ANON. "Napoleon III in America," Bookman
(New York), XXXVI (November), 238.
Briefly notes MT's comment on Napoleon III
in IA; erroneously reported in Asselineau
(1954, No. 134) as dealing with MT's "con-
sultation of Cheiro, a famous chiromancer."

B10 ANON. "One Who Didn't Like Mark Twain," Literary Digest, XLV (November 30), 1014-15.
Sir Robertson Nicoll, writing as "Claudius Clear" in The British Weekly (1912.B21) criticized MT's hostility toward Christianity and his "habitual, incessant, and disgusting profanity"; Nicoll questioned MT's stature as a humorist and called him "a man absolutely destitute of culture, and incapable of consecutive thought.... There are signs that Mark Twain was occasionally very kind to people who needed help, but not many signs."

B11 ANON. "The Origin of Pudd'nhead Wilson," Literary Digest, XLV (October 26), 740-41.
An extract from the Memoirs of the palmist "Cheiro," recently published by Lippincott; he read the palm of MT, who was in a serious mood at the time. MT examined Cheiro's collection of hand-prints, and was especially impressed by the similar prints of a mother and daughter, whose lives were also similar; claims this suggested the theme for PW.

B12 ANON. "Punch, Brothers," Bookman (New York), XXXVI (November), 236-37.
Excerpts the background of MT's "A Literary Nightmare" from the new Paine Biography, and ends with a French version of the jingle said to be by Swinburne.

B13 *ANON. "Spiritual Tragedy of Mark Twain," Current Literature, LIII (November), 582-84.
[Source: Asselineau (1954), No. 136: MT's sense of failure grew out of public expectation of humor, not serious writing.]

B14 ANON. "The Story of Grant's Memoirs," Literary Digest, XLIV (September 7), 373-75
Summarizes part of the September installment of the Paine biography in Harper's.

B15 ANON. "A Typical American," Nation, XCV (November 14), 475-59.
Reviews the Paine biography as "The prose Odyssey of the American people...it will continue to be read when half of Mark Twain's writings are forgotten."

B16 ANON. [Review: Paine, Mark Twain.] Spectator, CIX (October 12), 557-58.
Paine wrote the last volume "on a different scale from the others"; the reader will enjoy this biography despite its length.

B17 BACHELLER, IRVING. "Mr. Paine's Biography of Mark Twain," Literary Digest, XLV (November 16), 909.
"Mark Twain was one of seven men who in the last sixty years have reconstructed America and voiced its spirit. [The others were Lincoln, Vanderbilt, Edison, Greeley, Whitman, and Howells.] This is less a review of Paine's biography, than Bacheller's own tribute to MT: "He found the East

still in the bondage of Puritanism. Lincoln freed the negro. Mark Twain freed the white man."

B18 BICKNELL, PERCY F. "Mark Twain," The Dial, LIII (October 16), 290-92.
A review of the Paine biography, mostly summary. "The authoritative life of the great humorist has been written."

B19 *BODINE, T. V. "Birthplace of Mark Twain. The Story of the Great Humorist and Philosopher and his Equally Whimsical Uncle--Judge John S. Quarles," Kansas City Star Magazine, May 19.
Draws heavily on published accounts by MT, but informed by familiarity with the region. [Source: Reprinted in Twainian, XVII (March-April, 1958), 1-4; Asselineau (1954), No. 125.]

B20 CAIRNS, WILLIAM B. A History of American Literature. New York: Oxford University Press.
[Source: Asselineau (1954), No. 486.] Examined: 1930 revised edition, apparently unchanged in the portion on MT (pp. 444-52). Describes his life and work, arguing that his writing matured but that the serious writing of the later years has been overrated. "He has left, however, a considerable amount of truly genuine work in which the humor is more than cleverness and the seriousness is without affectation; and it will be strange if American readers willingly let this die."

B21 "CLAUDIUS CLEAR" [SIR ROBERTSON NICOLL.] "Mark Twain," The British Weekly LIII (October 24), 109.
Begins with a hostile discussion of MT, most of which is excerpted in The Literary Digest, November 30 (1912.B10), but the article is primarily a conventional discussion of the man and his works, occasioned by the recent publication of the three-volume Paine biography. The attribution to Nicoll is made by The Literary Digest. The British Weekly's subtitle of "A Journal of Social and Christian Progess" may help explain the vehement exception taken to MT's irreligion.

B22 _____. "Mark Twain in Adversity and Prosperity," The British Weekly, LIII (October 31), 141.
A conventional biographical account which adds nothing to the Paine biography. The identification of "Claudius Clear" as Sir Robertson Nicoll is by The Literary Digest, November 30 (1912.B10), which, however, does not mention this account.

B23 KYNE, PETER B. "The Great Mono Miracle: An Echo of Mark Twain," Sunset: The Pacific Monthly, XXIX (July), 37-49.
A work of fiction with MT as a character.

1912 - Shorter Writings

B24   MARKHAM, EDWIN. [Review: Paine, Mark Twain.]
      Hearst's Magazine, XXII (December), 135-38.
            Summarizes MT's life and comments that
      Paine reports the facts more carefully than
      MT did.

B25   PAINE, ALBERT BIGELOW. "Mark Twain: Some
      Chapters from an Extraordinary Life," Harp-
      er's Monthly, CXXIV (January), 215-28;
      (February), 419-33; (March), 583-97;
      (April), 737-51; (May), 934-47; CXXV
      (June), 104-19; (July), 249-63; (August),
      405-17; (September), 593-605; (October),
      767-80; (November), 923-35.
            Concluding installments of Paine's biogra-
      phy of MT, which began in November, 1911;
      includes illustrations not used in the book.

B26   PERRY, BLISS. "Humor and Satire," in his The
      American Mind. Boston and New York: Hough-
      ton Mifflin Company, pp. 166-208; on MT,
      pp. 197-202.
            Asselineau (1954), No. 146, reports a
      1913 edition, London: Constable.
            MT embodies American extravagance and ir-
      reverence, but draws the line short of what
      the American mind reveres. His "hatred of
      pretence and injustice, his scorn at senti-
      mentality coupled with his insistence upon
      the rights of sentiment, in a word his
      persistent idealism, make Mark Twain one of
      the most representative of American writers.
      Largeness, freedom, human sympathy, are re-
      vealed upon every page," although perhaps
      his "extraordinary fantasies" are no more
      successful than "the delicate humor of
      Charles Lamb." [From the E. T. Earle Lec-
      tures delivered at the Pacific Theological
      School, Berkeley, in 1912, and later at the
      Lowell Institute, Boston, the Brooklyn In-
      stitute, and elsewhere, as "American Traits
      in American Literature."]

B27   RICHARDS, P. "Mark Twain," in his Zeichner
      und "Gezeichnete" aus den Erinnerungen eines
      amerikanischen Zeichners und Journalisten
      (Berlin: Reflektor-Verlag), pp. 9-20.
            Describes MT's trip to England on the
      S. S. Minneapolis in 1907, and his receiv-
      ing an honorary degree from Oxford; in-
      cludes sketches of MT by Richards, several
      photographs (one on front cover), and
      facsimile reproductions of a letter from
      R. W. Ashcroft informing Richards of MT's
      death and a note by MT that "Taking the
      pledge will not make bad liquor good, but
      it will improve it."

B28   RIDEING, WILLIAM HENRY. "Mark Twain and E.
      C. Stedman," in his Many Celebrities and a
      Few Others: A Bundle of Reminiscences
      (Garden City, New York: Doubleday, Page &
      Company, and London: Eveleigh Nash),
      pp. 153-72.
            On MT at the Players Club, describing the
      genesis of "The Jumping Frog," and on the
      difficulties in dealing with his contribu-
      tions to The Century. Notes that in an

evening of speech-making MT preferred to
speak late, in order to pick up cues from
those preceding him.

B29   *ROBERTSON, J. M. "The Positions of Mark
      Twain," in The Baconian Heresy: A Confuta-
      tion (n.p.), Chapter II.
            On MT's influence in favor of the thesis
      that Bacon wrote Shakespeare's plays: "He
      is apt to win the laughers--a thing not be-
      fore to be apprehended from Baconian propa-
      ganda." Apparently regards MT's Is Shakes-
      peare Dead? as moderately important.
      [Source: quoted by Henry M. Partridge in
      "Did Mark Twain Perpetrate Literary Hoaxes?"
      (1934.B22).]

B30   *SMITH, ALPHONSO. "Mark Twain und die ameri-
      kanische Humor," in his Die amerikanische
      Literatur (Verlesungen, geh. am. d. Kgl.
      Friedrich-Wilhelms-Universität zu Berlin).
      Berlin: Wiedmannsche Buchh. [Bibliothek
      der amerikanischen Kulturgeschichte]),
      pp. 312-37.
            [Source: Asselineau (1954), No. 118.]

B31   TRENT, W. P., and JOHN ERSKINE. "Mark Twain
      and Bret Harte," in their Great Writers of
      America. (Home University Library of Mod-
      ern Knowledge). Pp. 232-50; on MT
      pp. 243-50.
            Harte has greater delicacy, but MT has
      greater force; MT's honor led him to a lec-
      ture tour to repay his debts, while Harte
      "disappointed his countrymen"; also notes
      "the tragic decline of Bret Harte's char-
      acter." MT's humor may be forgotten as
      tastes change, but TS revealed him as "a
      novelist of the first rank." There is a
      "tragic contrast between the boy's simple
      point of view and the things he saw but did
      not understand"; in HF "this note of ele-
      mental tragedy is increased until certain
      passages...would be hard to overmatch in
      any literature."

1913 A BOOKS

A1   WALLACE, ELIZABETH. Mark Twain and the Happy
      Island. Chicago: A. C. McClurg & Co.
      Prefatory note by Albert Bigelow Paine.
            An adult's recollections of her friendship
      with MT, whom she met in Bermuda and later
      visited at Stormfield. Includes photographs
      and letters.

1913 B SHORTER WRITINGS

B1   ABBOTT, KEENE. "Tom Sawyer's Town," Harper's
      Weekly, LVII (August 9), 16-17.
            A popular account of Hannibal, Missouri,
      with reminiscences by local people. Photo-
      graphs include one of Laura Frazer at nine-
      teen; she says that for a time another wom-
      an (who moved to Hannibal after Sam Clemens
      had left) had claimed to be the original of
      Becky Thatcher.

B2   ANON. "Mark Twain as Publisher," Bookman,
       XXXVI (January), 489-94.
          On MT's ultimately unsuccesful connection
       with the Webster Company; there are several
       anecdotes but no significant new informa-
       tion.

B3   ANON. [Review: Paine, Mark Twain (1912).]
       North American Review, CXCVII (January),
       136-38.
          The book is important not only as the
       life of a man, but as a picture of his
       time.

B4   *CARUS, PAUL. "Mark Twain's Philosophy," in
       his The Mechanistic Principle and the Non-
       Mechanical. An Inquiry into Fundamentals
       with Representatives from Either Side
       (Chicago: The Open Court Publishing Com-
       pany), pp. 54-97.
          [Source: Asselineau (1954), No. 140;
       describes this as a reprint of his article
       in The Monist (1913.B5), consisting largely
       of quotations from What Is Man?]

B5   _____. "Mark Twain's Philosophy," Monist,
       XXIII (April 13), 181-223.
          Lengthy quotations from What Is Man?
       with occasional brief comments by the edi-
       tor.

B6   *GOODWIN, C. C. As I Remember Them. Salt
       Lake City: Published by a Special Commit-
       tee of the Salt Lake Commercial Club.
          [Source: Asselineau (1954), No. 141;
       notes: "Charles Carroll Goodwin was a
       friend of Mark Twain's during the latter's
       stay in Nevada. Cf. DeVoto's Mark Twain's
       America, p. 135, n. 2."]

B7   [HOWELLS, WILLIAM DEAN.] "Editor's Easy
       Chair," Harper's Monthly, CXXVI (January),
       310-12.
          Favorably reviewing the 1912 Paine bio-
       graphy, this is chiefly a description of
       MT's life as described by Paine and as
       known to Howells.

B8   * _____. "In Memory of Mark Twain," in Pro-
       ceedings of the American Academy of Arts
       and Letters and the National Institute of
       Arts and Letters. Vol. I: 1909-1913.
       New York.
          [Source: Asselineau (1954), No. 147.]
       This may be the same as the item listed
       for 1911.B12.

B9   *KELLNER, LEON. Geschichte der Nordamerikan-
       ischen Literatur. Berlin: G. J. Göschen.
       2 vols.
          [Source: Asselineau (1954), No. 142.]

B10   LONG, WILLIAM J. American Literature: A
       Study of the Men and the Books that in the
       Earlier and Later Times Reflect the Ameri-
       can Spirit. Boston, New York: Ginn and
       Company.
          Criticizes MT's crudity in IA, CY, but

also in TS, with its "dime-novel sensation-
alism," its emphasis on "the lawless, barbarous side of boy-life...its self-assertion
without its instinctive respect for authority" (pp. 466-67). HF "ends not with a
moral climax," but in Jim's rescue "by the
most approved dime-novel methods. The portrayal of all these astonishing scenes is
vivid and intensely dramatic; one needs
hardly to add that it is a portrayal, not
of the great onward current of American
life, but only of its flotsam and jetsam."
Still, MT portrayed character and scene
vividly, and "was at heart a reformer"
(pp. 467-68). Some critics believe his
"more dignified works," such as P&P and JA,
will last longest (p. 466).

B11   MACY, JOHN. "Mark Twain," in his The Spirit
       of American Literature (Garden City, New
       York: Doubleday, Page & Company),
       pp. 248-77, and passim.
          Laudatory, following Paine, Howells, Mat-
       thews, and Phelps. Attacks the critics who
       libeled MT with words about his "kindly wit
       and humor which never hurt any one."
       Notes his "lofty idealism" as in JA, "an
       eloquent book," its tone "sustainedly per-
       fect" (p. 269); also notes the sentimental-
       ism of "A Dog's Tale" (p. 252, n). Elsewhere
       in the book Macy cites MT's comments in his
       discussions of Cooper (pp. 39, 41, 44) and
       Howells (pp. 290-91). On William James,
       says only MT reaches "his stature and ori-
       ginality.... Even the fine novelists,
       Mr. Howells and Mr. Henry James, are not
       the human equals of those two" (pp. 297-98);
       the chapter ends by confessing that associa-
       tion was made partly to shock some people,
       but chiefly because it is just. Reprinted
       in Scott (1965), pp. 118-28; (1967),
       pp. 129-39; in Anderson (1971), pp. 313-26.

B12   *MENCKEN, H. L. "The Burden of Humor," Smart
       Set, XXXVIII (February), pp. 151-54.
          [Source: Reprinted in Anderson (1971),
       pp. 327-31.] Calls HF "one of the great
       masterpieces of the world," and praises
       MT's language and vision. HF, LOM, CY,
       and Captain Stormfield's Visit to Heaven
       "are alone worth more, as works of art and
       as criticisms of life, than the whole out-
       put of Cooper, Irving, Holmes, Mitchell,
       Stedman, Whittier and Bryant.... I believe
       that he was the true father of our national
       literature, the first genuinely American
       artist of the blood royal." Reprinted in
       A Mencken Chrestomathy, Edited and Annotated
       by the Author (New York: Alfred A. Knopf,
       1967), p. 485; also reprinted in Gerber
       (1971), pp. 15-19 (giving volume number as
       XXXIX, but with the same month, year, and
       pagination as reported by Anderson).

B13   MILLARD, BAILEY. "When They Were Twenty-One,"
       Bookman (New York), XXXVII (May), 296-304.
          On "California authors in their salad
       days"; describes MT writing for the Golden

1913 - Shorter Writings

(MILLARD, BAILEY)
Era and traveling in Europe with Charles
Warren Stoddard (p. 298).

B14 O'CONNOR, MRS. T. P. "Sir Walter Scott and
the Civil War," in her My Beloved South
(New York and London: G. P. Putnam's
Sons).
Defends Scott against MT's accusations in
LOM: "Mark Twain ought to have been a
Southerner, but he was born with a too
practical soul. His hardness made him understand the North, and he did it more
than justice; his want of romance made him
misunderstand the South, and he did it less
than justice."

B15 PHELPS, WILLIAM LYON. [Review: Paine, Mark
Twain (1912).] Independent, LXXXIV
(March 6), 531-33.
"This is assuredly a great biography,
probably the best ever written in America."
Chiefly descriptive, noting Paine's tact,
patience, and devotion in MT's last years.
The book's only flaw is careless proof-
reading.

B16 RICHARDSON, CHARLES F. [Review: Paine,
Mark Twain (1912).] Yale Review, n.s. II
(Spring), 563-67.
A good book because of the author's enthusiasm, and MT's role as a representative
man may justify the length; but MT does
not belong in a class with Poe and Hawthorne.

B17 *TWICHELL, JOSEPH H. "Mark Twain," in Dudley
Payne Lewis, ed., History of the Class of
1903, Yale College (New Haven), n.p.
[Source: Asselineau (1954), No. 143.]

B18 *URBAN, WILBUR MARSHALL. "Mark Twain, Pure
Fooling," Neale's Monthly, May.
[Source: Twainian, II (March, 1943), 5.]

1914 A BOOKS

A1 Catalogue of First and Other Editions of the
Writings of "Mark Twain," Samuel Langhorne
Clemens, and of Lafcadio Hearn. The Prop-
erty of The Tomlinson-Humes Company (In
Bankruptcy) and of Mr. Merle Johnson. To
Be Sold at Unrestricted Public Sale on
January Twentieth, 1914 Under the Manage-
ment of the American Art Association,
American Art Galleries, Madison Square
South, New York. Contains Foreword by
Merle Johnson, dated December 29, 1913.
[Source: Bound in scrapbook, Mark
Twain: Biography-Reminiscence, Chicago
Public Library, n.d.]

1914 - B SHORTER WRITINGS

B1 *BURTON, RICHARD. Little Essays in Literature
and Life (New York: The Century Company),

pp. 201-208.
[Source: Asselineau (1954), No. 158:
"A chapter on Twain, insists on his seri-
ousness and even sadness."]

B2 COLBRON, GRACE ISABEL. "The American Novel
in Germany," Bookman (New York), XXXIX
(March), 45-48.
MT was a close second to Bret Harte in
popularity, as measured by sales of the
Tauchnitz editions; TS and HF were his most
popular.

B3 FULTON, ROBERT. "Glimpses of the Mother Lode,"
Bookman (New York), XXXIX (March), 49-57.
On a visit in 1912 to the region made famous by MT and Bret Harte; with several photographs.

B4 HAWTHORNE, HILDEGARDE. "Mark Twain and the
Immortal Tom," St. Nicholas, XLII
(December), 164-66.
Very briefly describes meeting MT at his
"Stormfield" Home in Redding, Connecticut,
and summarizes his life and works for young
readers.

B5 HIGGINSON, MARY THACHER. Thomas Wentworth
Higginson: The Story of His Life. As reissued Port Washington, N.Y. and London:
Kennikat Press, 1971.
Higginson first saw MT at a farewell dinner to Wilkie Collins in 1874; thought him
"something of a buffoon, though with earnestness underneath; and when afterwards at
his own house in Hartford, I heard him say
grace at table, it was like asking a blessing over Ethiopian minstrels. But he had
no wine at his table and that seemed to
make the grace a genuine thing." The two
later became good friends (pp. 259-60).
Describes MT writing in bed in later years
(pp. 373-74).

B6 HOWE, J. OWEN. "Twichell, Chum of Mark
Twain," Boston Evening Transcript (April 4),
Part III, p. 5.
A half-page account of Joseph Hopkins
Twichell, with biography and a portrait;
describes his friendship with MT.

B7 *MURET, MAURICE. Les Contemporains étrangers.
Lausanne: Payot, 2 vols.
[Source: Asselineau (1954), No. 159:
"On Mark Twain, vol. 2, pp. 133-189."]

B8 PHELPS, WILLIAM LYON. "Notes on Mark Twain,"
in his Essays on Books (New York: The Macmillan Company), pp. 211-22.
Reprinted with minor revisions from Independent (1910.B118).

B9 *RICHARDS, P. Mark Twain Anekdoten, gesammelt
und mit einem Vorwort von P. Richards, mit
neun Bild-beigaben. Berlin: Reflektor-
Verlag.
[Source: Asselineau (1954), No. 157.]

B10 STREET, JULIAN. "Hannibal and Mark Twain,"
     in his Abroad at Home: American Ramblings,
     Observations, and Adventures (New York:
     The Century Company), pp. 237-52. Also in
     Collier's, LIII (August 29), 18-19, 31-34.
        An impressionistic and somewhat unsympa-
     thetic account of a visit to Hannibal. In-
     cludes five lines of verse MT wrote in the
     autograph book of his friend Ann Virginia
     Ruffner.

B11 TICKNOR, CAROLINE. "Mark Twain's Missing
     Chapter," Bookman (New York), XXXIX (May),
     298-309.
        On MT's writing of LOM, with extensive
     quotation of his marginalia in Mrs. Trol-
     lope's Domestic Manners of the Americans.
     The original Chapter XLVIII of LOM (here
     reproduced, pp. 306-309) was suppressed
     out of fear that unfavorable comparison of
     the South to the North would cost Southern
     sales; also here reproduced are the can-
     celled cuts from p. 356 showing a shrouded
     body and from p. 441 showing MT surrounded
     by flames.

B12 *UNDERWOOD, JOHN C. "Democracy and Mark
     Twain," in his Literature and Insurgency
     (New York: Mitchell Kennerley), pp. 1-40.
        [Source: Asselineau (1954), No. 161;
     Underwood compares MT to Grant and Lincoln
     as a democratic hero.]

1915 A BOOKS

A1   *WHITE, IDA BELLE. Spirits Do Return. Kansas
     City, Missouri: The White Publishing Com-
     pany.
        [Source: Asselineau (1954), No. 170;
     quotes: "This book was written through
     the inspirational spirit of the well-known
     writer, Samuel L. Clemens, Mark Twain."]

1915 B SHORTER WRITINGS

B1   *ANON. "Captain Horace E. Bixby; Who Taught
     Mark Twain How to Pilot," New England Maga-
     zine, n.s., LII (April), 281-83.
        [Source: Asselineau (1954), No. 173.]

B2   ANON. "Mark Twain's War Map," North American
     Review, CCI, (June), 827-29.
        MT's map of Paris (1870) and his accom-
     panying text, with a 40-word introductory
     note added.

B3   BALL, SIR ROBERT. Reminiscences and Letters
     of Sir Robert Ball, Edited by His Son, W.
     Valentine Ball. London, New York, Toronto
     and Melbourne: Cassell and Company, Ltd.
        Sir Robert Ball was Astronomer Royal of
     Ireland, 1874-1892. He mentions meeting
     MT in New York at a lecture by Mr. Seton-
     Thompson (January 1, 1902): "He is a most
     striking-looking man, and we had a nice
     little talk. I told him how fond we were
     of 'Mr. Bixby'" (p. 348; the editor mentions
     Sir Robert's enjoyment of LOM on p. 126).

B4   COREY, WILLIAM ALFRED. "Memories of Mark
     Twain," Overland Monthly, LXVI (September),
     263-65.
        "Herewith are set down some hitherto un-
     published incidents culled from the recol-
     lections of Mr. W. W. Barnes of Oakland,
     concerning Samuel L. Clemens while the
     great humorist was 'Roughing It' in Virginia
     City, Nevada." This is the Barnes of the
     rival newspaper, the Union, and he here re-
     lates several incidents from Roughing It,
     adding a few details; he applied the term
     "yellow journalism" to MT's "Massacre at
     Empire City" story [described in "My Bloody
     Massacre" in Sketches New and Old]. Ac-
     cording to Barnes, MT stole the "Jumping
     Frog" story, which "before Clemens ever
     heard of it, was written by Samuel Seabough,
     and was published in the San Andreas Inde-
     pendent, the leading newspaper of Calaveras
     County. Seabough...editor of the Independ-
     ent...got the story of the Jumping Frog
     from a man named Parker who was afterwards
     a member of the legislature from Mono
     County.... Clemens simply warmed it over,
     dished it up as his own, and got all the
     credit." Finally, Corey tells of Artemus
     Ward's visit to Virginia City on a speaking
     tour: "It was hardly fair in Clemens, with
     the lecture hour drawing near, to get Ward
     hopelessly drunk, black his face with burnt
     cork and then thrust him out before his
     waiting audience. In fact it was, as Mr.
     Barnes tersely characterized it, 'a damned
     dirty trick'" but typical of this stage in
     MT's and Artemus Ward's lives, and the audi-
     ence "probably regarded the matter as a
     great joke, and alone worth the price of
     admission."

B5   HOPKINS, R. THURSTON. Rudyard Kipling: A
     Literary Appreciation. New York: Frederick
     A. Stokes Company, n.d. (Preface dated
     November, 1915).
        Anecdotes involving MT, pp. 50-54; quotes
     an 1895 MT letter to Kipling on the possi-
     bility of a meeting in India: "I shall
     come riding my ayah with his tusks adorned
     with silver bells and ribbons, and escorted
     by a troop of native howdahs richly clad
     and mounted upon a herd of wild bungalows;
     and you must be on hand with a few bottles
     of ghee, for I shall be thirsty."

B6   JAMES, GEORGE WHARTON. "Mark Twain at Lake
     Tahoe" and "Mark Twain and the Forest
     Rangers," in his The Lake of the Sky: Lake
     Tahoe (Pasadena, California: G. W. James;
     reprinted with same pagination, Chicago:
     The Charles T. Powner Co., 1956),
     pp. 359-62, 363-65.
        These are two appendices, the first an ex-
     cerpt from RI and the second from "a quar-
     terly magazine published solely for the
     Rangers of the Tahoe Reserve," describing
     MT's accidental burning of a forest as he
     told it in RI and as the incident would
     have taken place in 1912: rangers would

(JAMES, GEORGE WHARTON)
put out the fire and a court would fine
him for carelessness.

B7   KELLNER, LEON. American Literature, translated from the German by Julia Franklin.
Garden City, New York: Doubleday, Page &
Company. Pp. 200-11.
MT's humor involves exaggeration, but its
essence is "the human...delight in the
weakness, perversity, folly, of a beloved
fellow-creature" (p. 207); the Germans appreciate his portrayal of character. "Our
American, in his fine humanity, in his
idealism, in his gentleness, is almost an
old-fashioned gentleman" (p. 210).

B8   PAINE, ALBERT BIGELOW. "A Boys' Life of Mark
Twain," St. Nicholas, XLIII (November),
2-11; (December), 146-47.
Begins the serialization of Paine's
1916 book; illustrated with drawings and
photographs.

B9   PATTEE, FRED LEWIS. "Mark Twain," in his A
History of American Literature since 1870
(New York: The Century Co.), pp. 45-62 and
passim (indexed).
"With Mark Twain, American literature became for the first time really national."
He is a droll comedian, social critic, and
author of romance, and his fame will endure
in this last capacity, in which his masterpieces are LOM and RI; in these, as in GA
("a few chapters of it"), TS, HF, and PW,
"he has done work that can never be done
again." "To turn from Mark Twain to Bret
Harte is like turning from a great river on
a summer night, fragrant and star-lit, to
the glamour and unreality of the city theater" (p. 65). Pp. 58-61 reprinted in
Kesterson (1973), pp. 54-56.

B10   WARD, LESLIE. Forty Years of "Spy." London:
Chatto & Windus.
On p. 129, describes drawing MT's portrait
for Vanity Fair: "The whole time I watched
him he paced the room like a caged animal,
smoking a large calabash pipe." MT wanted
to wear his Oxford academic gown, but Ward
preferred to depict him in the more familiar
white suit. "He struck me as being a very
sensitive man, whose nervous pacings during
my interview were the result of a highly
strung temperament."

B11   YOUNG, JOHN P. Journalism in California.
San Francisco: Chronicle Publishing Co.,
pp. 66, 71, 131.
Bare mention of MT, and no new information.

A1   PAINE, ALBERT BIGELOW. The Boys' Life of
Mark Twain: The Story of a Man Who Made
the World Laugh and Love Him. New York and
London: Harper & Brothers Publishers.
A revision for young readers of Paine's
1912 three-volume biography; serialized in
St. Nicholas, 1915-16.

B1   ANON. "Capitalizing Mark Twain," Literary
Digest, LIII (October 14), 959-60.
Undated excerpts from the St. Louis Post-
Standard on the exploitation of MT's name
by Hannibal, Missouri, and from the Newark
Star-Eagle on a spiritualist attempt to
communicate with MT, and on the "Jap Herron"
novel he supposedly dictated.

B2   BOWEN, EDWIN W. "Mark Twain," South Atlantic
Quarterly, XV (July), 250-68 [also listed,
incorrectly, under "Henderson, Archibald"
in several bibliographies].
A general discussion of MT as a great humorist and self-made man, with a summary of
his career and uncritical listing of his
works. "Certainly he has produced books
that will make his name live in American
literature because they themselves are genuine literature."

B3   *FITCH, GEORGE HAMLIN. "Mark Twain--Our Greatest Humorist," in his Great Spiritual Writers of America (San Francisco: P. Elder &
Co.), pp. 111-18.
[Source: Asselineau (1954), No. 176,
noting that Fitch "insists most unspiritually
on the success story."]

B4   GILDER, RICHARD WATSON. Letters of Richard
Watson Gilder. Edited by his Daughter,
Rosamond Gilder. Boston & New York: Houghton Mifflin Company, The Riverside Press,
passim on MT (indexed).
On MT's winning the Grant Memoirs from the
Century, pp. 124-25; at a reading for international copyright, introduction to the
President, pp. 195-96; on MT as next-door
neighbor, Summer 1904, pp. 361-62. Defends
MT against charge by "a superintendent of
schools in a distant part of the West" that
his works are "destitute of a single redeeming quality"; however, Gilder concedes (in
copy of letter he sent MT) that "Mr. Clemens
has great faults; at times he is inartistic-
ally and indefensibly coarse" (pp. 398-99).

B5   *JONES, DR. J. T. "The House Mark Twain's
Father Built," in his Prose and Poems, Col-
umbia, Kentucky, n.p.
[Source: Wecter (1952), p. 320.]

B6   McCLELLAND, CLARENCE PAUL "Mark Twain and
     Bret Harte," Methodist Review, XCVIII
     (Fifth Series, XXXII; January-February),
     75-85.
          Chiefly descriptive. Although Harte
     gives a graphic view of the West in stories
     "perfect in form and yet melodramatic and
     sentimental, still it is Mark Twain who
     will give us purer enjoyment, and, above
     all, a better insight into human nature."

B7   PAINE, ALBERT BIGELOW. "A Boys' Life of
     Mark Twain," St. Nicholas, XLIII (January),
     210-19; (February), 328-36; (March), 408-14;
     (April), 498-505; (May), 598-606; (June),
     696-704; (July), 801-809; (August), 881-90;
     (September), 998-1006; (October), 1078-88.
          Completes the serialization, begun in
     1915, of Paine's 1916 book. Illustrated
     with drawings and photographs.

B8   ROSEWATER, VICTOR. "How a Boy Secured a
     Unique Autograph of Mark Twain," St. Nich-
     olas, XLIII (March), 415.
          As a sixteen-year-old Senate page in
     1888, Rosewater got "Mark Twain" written
     in his album; then, on request, MT wrote
     "S. L. Clemens" diagonally across the
     first autograph. (Reproduced in facsimile.)

B9   YARMOLINSKY, ABRAHAM. "The Russian View of
     American Literature," Bookman (New York),
     XLIV (September), 44-48.
          MT is very popular, and has been trans-
     lated into both Russian and Ukranian.
     "The Prince and the Pauper was the first to
     appear, and it has to this very day re-
     mained the standard juvenile, more popular
     with Russian readers than The Adventures
     of Tom Sawyer or his Huckleberry Finn."
     His purely humorous works are widely avail-
     able, both in conventional volumes and in
     cheap paper-covered "brochures." Quotes
     an interview in Vienna by a Russian jour-
     nalist; MT comments on the failure to pay
     him royalties, and observes that the Rus-
     sian press is becoming Americanized.

1917 A BOOKS

A1   *BARRIE, JAMES M. Who Was Sarah Findlay? by
     Mark Twain with a suggested solution of
     the mystery by J. M. Barrie. London:
     Privately Printed by Clement Shorter.
     [11-page pamphlet. Source: Asselineau
     (1954), No. 183.]

A2   CLEMENS, SAMUEL L. Mark Twain's Letters,
     Arranged with Comment by Albert Bigelow
     Paine. New York and London: Harper &
     Brothers, 2 vols.
          Paine has been criticized for his edit-
     ing. These letters are only a small sel-
     ection from those left by MT, and they are
     not reprinted in their entirety nor are
     omissions always clearly indicated. Other
     parts of some of the letters may be found
     in Paine's 1912 Biography.

A3   HUTCHINGS, EMILY GRANT. [Introduction.]
     Jap Herron: A Novel Written from the Ouija
     Board. New York: Mitchell Kennerley.
          A novel attributed to the spirit of MT.

1917 B SHORTER WRITINGS

B1   ANON. "Editing Mark Twain," Literary Digest,
     XLIV (January 20), 127-28.
          Summarizes New York Times article on R. W.
     Gilder's experience with MT as a Century con-
     tributor; reproduces text of a Gilder letter
     to a western school superintendent, also
     quoted in 1916.B4.

B2   ANON. "Mark Twain's Pen Picture of His All-Too-
     Human Brother," Current Opinion, LXII (May),
     351-52.
          Quotes MT's letters to Howells (concerning
     Orion Clemens) recently published in Harper's;
     only brief commentary added.

B3   ANON. "The Saving of Mark Twain," Literary Di-
     gest, LV (November 24), 54-59.
          About Henry H. Rogers, who straightened out
     MT's financial affairs; a summary of MT let-
     ters currently appearing in Harper's.

B4   ANON. "Three Stories a Year Are Enough for
     a Writer. Ring W. Lardner, Humorist, Who
     Makes Fiction Out of Life of Baseball Play-
     ers, Thinks Fewer and Better Short Stories
     Needed," New York Times Magazine (March 25),
     p. 14.
          Speaking of authors, Lardner ranks George
     Ade above MT and prefers Booth Tarkington's
     "Penrod" books to HF. "No, I certainly
     don't believe that Mark Twain is our great-
     est American humorist. Some of his fun is
     spontaneous, but a great deal of it is not."

B5   ANON. "When Twain Conquered Grant," Literary
     Digest, LV (July 21), 57-60.
          Summarizes and quotes part of the July
     installment of MT's letters in Harper's.

B6   *AYRES, J. W. "Recollections of Hannibal,"
     Palmyra Spectator, August 22.
          Discusses Tom Blankenship (the original
     of Huck), who, rather than Sam Clemens, led
     the boys. [Source: Cited by Walter Blair
     (1960), p. 55.]

B7   CLEMENS, MILDRED LEO. "Trailing Mark Twain
     Through Hawaii. 'Roughing It' in the Is-
     lands, Fifty Years After," Sunset: The
     Pacific Monthly, XXXVIII (May), 7-9, 95-98.
          About a recent trip to the Islands, il-
     lustrated with recent photographs and en-
     livened with references to MT's descrip-
     tions in RI.

B8   [HYSLOP, JAMES H.]. "The Return of Mark
     Twain," Journal of the American Society for
     Psychical Research, XI (July), 361-65.
          On Jap Herron, recently published by
     Mitchell Kennerly and said to have been
     dictated by MT's spirit and recorded by
     Mrs. Emily Grant Hutchings, of St. Louis.

1917 - Shorter Writings

([HYSLOP, JAMES H.])
As confirmation, MT was consulted again, through other mediums, revealing "unmistakable evidence in the experiments with Mrs. Chenoweth that Mark Twain colored the facts quite as much as the psychic." [This journal is indexed, and several volumes contain numerous references to "Clemens," "Mark Twain," and "Twain, Mark" not listed in the present bibliography.]

B9   LINDSAY, VACHEL. "Mark Twain and Joan of Arc" and "The Raft," in his The Chinese Nightingale and Other Poems. (New York: The Macmillan Company), pp. 47, 71-74.
On Joan of Arc, shows MT's glorious portrait but mourns "at bloodshed caused by angels, saints, and men." "The Raft" is a more extensive tribute to MT, not limited to HF. "When the Mississippi Flowed to Indiana" appeared in his The Golden Whales of California (New York: Macmillan, 1920), on the world of Tom Sawyer and Becky Thatcher. These are now grouped as "Three Poems about Mark Twain," and may be found in Selected Poems of Vachel Lindsay, ed. Mark Harris (New York: Macmillan and London: Collier Macmillan, 1963), pp. 16-21.

B10   PAINE, ALBERT BIGELOW, ed. "Mark Twain's Letters" (title varies), Harper's, CXXXIV (May), 781-94; CXXXV (July), 177-86; (August), 378-88; (September), 569-77; (October), 638-47; (November), 812-19.
Includes photographs, and facsimile reproductions of some of the letters.

B11   SHUSTER, GEORGE NAUMAN. "The Tragedy of Mark Twain," Catholic World, CIV (March), 731-37.
About MT's pessimism as reflected in MS and elsewhere.

B12   WHITE, EDGAR. "Mark Twain's Printer Days," Overland Monthly, LXX (December), 573-76.
Contains recollections of MT in Hannibal by Jimmy Tisdale, Major Frank Daulton, and Alex Lacey, but adds no new information and appears to be indebted to MT's own published recollections. There are photographs of MT (by Paine), Hannibal, and Major Daulton, but nothing new or significant.

B13   WIER, JEANNE ELIZABETH. "Mark Twain's Relation to Nevada and to the West," Nevada Historical Society Papers, I (1913-1916). Carson City: State Printing Office, 99-104.
A general, popular account of MT's Nevada days, illustrated with photographs of cabins in which he lived in Aurora and Unionville, and of his sister-in-law, "Mrs. Orion Clemens, 1866." Facing this article (p. 98) is a picture of the flag-raising on Mt. Davidson described in RI (II, Chapter XIV), part of an article with contemporary accounts. On pp. 89-90 are a description and photo-

graph of "Mark Twain Relics": part of a pistol and a more serviceable pipe.

B14   WOODBRIDGE, H. E. "Mark Twain's Fatalism," Nation, CV (October 11), 399.
MT's view of life as a chain of events, in which a small change can have profound effects.

B15   WYATT, EDITH. "An Inspired Critic," North American Review, CCV (April), 603-15.
MT as philosopher and critic of his time.

1918 A BOOKS - NONE

1918 B SHORTER WRITINGS

B1   ANON. "Literature and Life Mirrored in Mark Twain's Letters," Current Opinion, LXIV (January), 50-51.
A review of Mark Twain's Letters (1917). Mostly extracts. Cites a New York Evening Post review (n.d.) that calls them a welcome change from "Maeterlinck, Wilde, Strindberg, Ibsen, and the Russian gloom artists."

B2   ANON. "Mark Twain's Childhood Sweetheart Recalls their Romance," Literary Digest, LVI (March 23), 70-75.
Summarizes, with lengthy excerpts, an interview of Laura [Hawkins] Frazer, the original of Becky Thatcher; from Kansas City Star (n.d.).

B3   ANON. "Mark Twain's Unedited and Unpublished Satire: 3,000 Years among the Microbes," Current Opinion, LXV (July), 48-49.
Summarizes and extensively quotes a review in New York Evening Mail (n.d.) by Edna Kenton, who considered MT a great satirist but a martyr to editing.

B4   BELDEN, H. M. "Scyld Scefing and Huck Finn," Modern Language Notes, XXXIII (May), 315.
Seeking a body with a floating loaf of bread was anticipated in "divination by shield, sheaf, and candle."

B5   *CASTELLANOS, JESÚS. Los Optimistas. Madrid: Editorial América, Biblioteca Andrés Bello. [Source: Asselineau (1954), No. 199: "On Mark Twain, pp. 115-120. Ranks Twain with Cervantes and Molière."]

B6   D[ANZIGER], S[AMUEL]. "Democracy of Mark Twain," Public (New York), XXI (February 23), 242-43.
On CY as "a textbook of democracy, economic as well as political," and on the economic implications of the magic tree in MS. [Signed with initials "S.D."; the name "Samuel Danziger" appears on the masthead.]

B7 HARRIS, JULIA COLLIER. The Life and Letters of Joel Chandler Harris. Boston and New York: Houghton Mifflin Company.
Contains letters revealing MT's interest in folk-tales of the slaves and in the manner of story-telling, mentioning "The Golden Arm" (pp. 167-70), and thanking Harris for praising HF in an interview in the Atlanta Journal (p. 566). Efforts to persuade Harris to give readings could not overcome his diffidence; letters show the two men planning to meet in New Orleans and for Harris to visit in Hartford, but there are no new details (pp. 170-72, 190-92).

B8 HENDERSON, ARCHIBALD. "A Laughing Philosopher," Bookman (New York), XLVI (January), 583-84.
A review of Paine's edition of Mark Twain's Letters (1917), with praise for "the entirely natural picture it presents of an almost miraculous development"; the influence of Olivia Clemens and Howells was beneficial.

B9 HOWELLS, W. D. "The Editor's Easy Chair," Harper's, CXXXVI (March), 602-604.
"Mr. Albert Bigelow Paine has ended his very faithful and intelligent labors on the biography of a man nearer and dearer to his generation than any other, in two volumes of Mark Twain's Letters. Unless more material should unexpectedly offer itself, these letters will tell us the last we shall ever be told of one who can never be told enough of, and who tells himself in them more explicitly and directly than in all his other work."

B10 HYSLOP, JAMES H. "The Return of Mark Twain," Journal of the American Society for Psychical Research, XII (January), 4-38.
Further discussion of the 1916 Jap Herron book and communications with the spirit of MT. Mrs. Emily Grant Hutchings, of St. Louis, was unfamiliar with MT's work at the beginning of the project, and Mrs. Hays, the psychic, was said to have read "a great deal of Mark Twain's work" but the statement was challenged by Mrs. Hutchings in the next issue (p. 74). (A sequel to "The Return of Mark Twain," 1917.B8.)

B11 *MATTHEWS, BRANDER. [Introduction.] The Adventures of Huckleberry Finn. New York & London: Harper & Brothers.
[Source: Asselineau (1954), No. 198.]

B12 MENCKEN, H. L. A Book of Prefaces. New York: Alfred A. Knopf (revised ed.), pp. 131-32, 203-34.
Cites William Lyon Phelps's Essays on Modern Novelists on the slow academic recognition of MT; praises MT as an artist but regrets his Philistine smugness and Puritan distrust of new ideas and beautiful things (as in IA).

B13 *MICHAUD, RÉGIS. "L'épopée humoristique de Mark Twain," in his Mystiques et Réalistes Anglo-Saxons, d'Emerson à Bernard Shaw (Paris: A. Colin), pp. 133-66.
[Source: Asselineau (1954), No. 200; describes this as "good second-hand criticism."]

B14 PERRY, BLISS. The American Spirit in Literature: A Chronicle of Great Interpreters. New Haven: Yale University Press; Toronto: Glasgow, Brook & Co.; London: Humphrey Milford, Oxford University Press. (The Chronicles of America Series, Vol. XXXIV), pp. 237-40.
RI, LOM, GA, TS, and HF are "books that make our American Odyssey, rich in the spirit of romance," and in the public eye "It is clear that Mark Twain the writer of romance is gaining upon Mark Twain the humorist." Notes his literary integrity, hatred of evil, and his pessimism as in Hadleyburg and MS.

B15 *SHOEMAKER, FLOYD CALVIN. "Samuel L. Clemens, Mark Twain, America's Greatest Humorist," in his Missouri's Hall of Fame: Lives of Eminent Missourians (Columbia: Missouri Book Co.), pp. 3-18.
[Source: Asselineau (1954), No. 202.]

B16 WHEELER, CANDACE. "Mark Twain," in her Yesterdays in a Busy Life (New York: Harper & Brothers), pp. 324-38.
On the Clemens family in Hartford and visiting the Wheelers in Onteora, N.Y., with one photograph of MT and one of his family, and two MT letters [August 30, 1885?] and October 31, 1890. There are also brief references to MT on pp. 307, 310-11 (not indexed).

B17 *WINKLER, EUNICE. "The Return of Mark Twain," Azoth (January).
[Source: Twainian, I (October, 1939), 5.] Apparently this is a spiritualist publication.

1919 A BOOKS - NONE

1919 B SHORTER WRITINGS

B1 ANON. "American Humour: Poor Samples," Saturday Review (London), CXXVII (September 27), 294.
A review-article, dismissing The Curious Republic of Gondour, and Other Whimsical Sketches as material MT himself had not considered worth reprinting. "Altogether we are quite content with the ample range of Mark Twain's works published in the uniform edition."

B2 ANON. "Mark Twain," Athenaeum, No. 4675 (December 5), pp. 1288-89.
A review of What Is Man? And Other Essays

(ANON.)
as less daring than MT thought: "It is difficult to understand what all the excitement is about."

B3   ANON. "When Mark Twain Petrified the Brahmins,"
Literary Digest, LXII (July 12), 28-29.
Summarizes an article by E. B. Osborn
in the London Morning Post (n.d.) about the
speech given by MT at the Whittier Birthday
Dinner. Osborne took MT's part, describing
those who criticized the speech as "a dreadful set of hard-shell prigs."

B4   ANON. "Belaboring the Brahmins Again," Literary Digest, LXIII (October 4), 31.
E. B. Osborn attacked the Boston literati
a second time in the London Morning Post
(n.d.) for their chilly reception of MT's
Whittier Birthday Dinner Speech. American
newspapers commented on Osborn's articles
and individuals wrote him letters generally
approving his stand.

B5   ANON. [Review: What is Man? And Other Essays.] Athenaeum, No. 4673 (November 21),
p. 1241.
Descriptive and very brief.

B6   *BOSC, R. "Mark Twain et l'humour américain,"
Revue de Synthèse Historique, XXIX, 181-87.
[Source: Asselineau (1954), No. 215:
"A discussion of Régis Michaud's chapter on
Twain in Les Mystiques et Réalistes Anglo-
Saxons."]

B7   BOYNTON, PERCY H. "The West and Mark Twain,"
in his A History of American Literature
(Boston, New York: Ginn and Company),
pp. 380-95.
For undergraduates. Begins with discussion of Bret Harte, who "seems like a trink-
et shop at the foot of Pike's Peak as Mark
Twain looms above him (p. 381)." Praises MT
as decent and serious, and notes the humor
in JA; IA is not irreverent toward what deserves respect. There is a discussion of
MT as a thinker on religion (with a quotation from What Is Man?), but nothing on his
major works.

B8   *BRIDGES, HORACE J. "The Pessimism of Mark
Twain," The Standard (Cooperstown, N.Y.),
July.
[Source: Twainian, II (July, 1943).]

B9   *CLEMENS, SAMUEL L. [Facsimile of letter from
MT, June 24, 1874, about appropriating his
pseudonym from Captain Isaiah Sellers.]
The Eighteenth Year Book 1919. Boston:
The Bibliophile Society, 1919, p. 124.
[Source: Quoted in Fatout (1964), p. 34.]

B10   ELLSWORTH, WILLIAM W. "Mark Twain--The Grant
Memoirs--Nicolay and Hay's Lincoln," in his
A Golden Age of Authors: A Publisher's
Recollection (Boston and New York: Houghton
Mifflin Company), pp. 221-42.

On MT in amateur dramatics (he tended to
go on talking after having spoken another
actor's cue lines), his part in founding the
Saturday Morning Club, the restraining influence of Olivia Clemens, MT on lecture
tour, his practical joke on Thomas B. Reed
and Richard Watson Gilder, and the advantage
to the Grant family of having the Memoirs
published by the Webster Company rather than
the less-experienced Century Company. Includes facsimile of MT letter to Ellsworth
(January 13, 1893) praising the advertising
for The Million Pound Bank-Note.

B11   *FITCH, TOM. [Quotes MT on his brief military
service in Missouri.] San Francisco Examiner, March 30.
[Source: Quoted in Fatout (1964),
pp. 66-67.]

B12   *FRANK, WALDO. "The Land of the Pioneer," in
his Our America (New York: Boni & Liveright), pp. 37-44.
[Source: Reprinted in Scott (1955),
pp. 129-33; (1967), pp. 140-44.] "Out of
the bitter wreckage of his long life one
great work emerges by whose contrasting fire
we can observe the darkness. This work is
Huckleberry Finn. It must go down in history, not as the expression of a rich natural culture like the books of Chaucer,
Rabelais, Cervantes, but as the voice of
American chaos, the voice of a pre-cultural
epoch.... Huckleberry Finn is the American
epic hero. Greece had Ulysses. America
must be content with an illiterate lad. He
expresses our germinal past. He expresses
the movement of the American soul through
all the sultry climaxes of the Nineteenth
Century." Frank describes MT as "a man of
genius.... The soul of Mark Twain was
great," but he anticipates Van Wyck Brooks
(1920.B12) in arguing that the frontier life
followed by Eastern respectability destroyed
the artist MT might have been: apart from
HF, "the balance of his literary life, before and after, went mostly to the wastage
of half-baked, half-believed, half-clownish
labor." What Is Man? is the work of MT's
last years, "the profane utterance of a defeated soul bent upon degrading the world to
the low level where it was forced to live."

B13   *HYSLOP, JAMES HERVEY (formerly professor of
logic and ethics at Columbia University).
Contact with the Other World; the latest
evidence as to communication with the dead.
New York: The Century Company.
[Source: Asselineau (1954), No. 213.]
Chapter XVI (pp. 249-81) concerns communication with MT's spirit, which claimed to have
spoken freely and without suppression in his
lifetime. [Several university libraries
which do not have this book do have a number
of other books by Hyslop on psychic matters--
T.A.T.]

B14   ____. "Mark Twain Returns?" Unpartizan Re-
       view ("Originally The Unpopular Review"),
       XII (October-December), 397-409.
          On psychic experiments involving Mrs.
       Emily Grant Hutchings and Mrs. Lola Hays of
       St. Louis, a Mrs. Chenoweth of Boston, and
       a Miss Burton of Toledo. There was appar-
       ent contact with MT's spirit, to which the
       books Jap Herron and Brent Roberts are at-
       tributed. Hyslop approaches his material
       cautiously but not skeptically.

B15   *JAMES, G. W. "Mark Twain: An Appreciation
       of His Pioneer Writing on Fasting and
       Health," Physical Culture (May).
          [Source: Asselineau (1954), No. 217.]
       According to Twainian, II (May, 1943), 6,
       the issue also includes a front-cover por-
       trait and other portraits of MT by Bradley.

B16   MARCOSSON, ISAAC F. Adventures in Inter-
       viewing. London and New York: John Lane,
       pp. 216, 244-47.
          On MT's friendship with Henry H. Rogers.
       Includes facsimile of an anecdote about
       Rogers that MT wrote out for Marcosson to
       incorporate in an article on Rogers (it
       could not be signed by MT, because of an
       agreement with his publishers for exclusive
       rights to material bearing his name); also
       photograph of MT.

B17   *MENCKEN, H. L. "The Man Within," Smart Set,
       (October) pp. 139-43.
          [Source: Reprinted in A Mencken Chresto-
       mathy, Edited and Annotated by the Author
       (1967), pp. 488-89.] On MT's combination
       of moral arrogance and hesitation to offend
       public opinion. Praises the honesty and
       excellence of What Is Man? but deplores
       MT's witholding it from print for many
       years. MT's timidity in speaking his mind
       has lessened his contribution to American
       letters--but there remains HF, with "some-
       thing that vastly transcends the merit of
       all ordinary books."

B18   MILBANK, ELIZABETH PALMER. "In Mark-Twain
       Land," St. Nicholas, XLVI (August), 934.
          Briefly describes Florida, Missouri for
       young readers. Includes photographs of MT
       monument and his birthplace.

B19   SCHÖNEMANN, FRIEDRICH. "Mark Twain and Adolph
       Wilbrandt," Modern Language Notes, XXXIV
       (June), 372-74.
          Finds MT's response to the Meister von
       Palmyra and "the ethical lesson of it in
       complete harmony" with his pessimism. "It
       is possible that this 'majestic drama of
       depth and seriousness' set his mind to
       work," resulting in What Is Man? and MS.

B20   ____. [Note.] Modern Language Notes, XXXIV
       (February), 128.
          Comment on Mark Twain's Letters (1917)
       and what it shows of "Mr. Clemens' relation

to the land and people of Germany." See his
longer article in Modern Language Notes,
XXXIV (June), 372-4, citing as his own this
note which was signed "F.S."

B21   SEITZ, DON C. Artemus Ward (Charles Farrar
       Browne). New York and London: Harper &
       Brothers Publishers, pp. 141-50.
          Describes Ward's visit to Virginia City,
       his friendship with MT, and MT's lecture on
       him; the sources of information seem to in-
       clude nothing not already familiar to stu-
       dents of MT (MT's own accounts are evident).
       His letter to MT from Austin (January 1,
       1864), is included, with regrets at having
       become so drunk one night (pp. 144-45).
       The book is unindexed, but includes an ex-
       tensive bibliography.

B22   WATTERSON, HENRY. "Mark Twain--The Original
       of Colonel Mulberry Sellers--The 'Earl of
       Durham'--Some Noctes Ambrosianae--A Joke on
       Murat Halstead," in his "Marse Henry": An
       Autobiography (New York: George H. Doran
       Company), I, 119-33.
          Watterson and MT were distantly related
       by marriage. This account describes several
       of their joint relatives, among them James
       Lampton, who, for all his folly, "was as
       brave as a lion and as upright as Sam Clem-
       ens himself" (p. 123). Tells of receiving
       a long, amusing letter from MT; "Two or
       three hours later came a telegram. 'Burn
       letter. Blot it from your memory. Susie
       is dead'" (p. 127). Concludes with the sto-
       ry of a joke on a New York World reporter:
       MT introduced his friend as Murat Halstead,
       and Watterson "lined out to him a column or
       more of very hot stuff, reversing Halstead
       in every opinion" (pp. 130-32).

B23   WOODBRIDGE, H. E. "Mark Twain and the 'Gesta
       Romanorum,'" Nation, CVIII (March 22),
       424-25.
          Shows parallels to MS in story of an angel
       changing human destinies.

1920 A BOOKS

A1   BROOKS, VAN WYCK. The Ordeal of Mark Twain.
       New York: E. P. Dutton & Co.
          One of the seminal works on MT, consider-
       ing him as a victim of his environment: the
       sterility of the frontier and the genteel
       influence of Eastern respectability (parti-
       cularly through Olivia Clemens and William
       Dean Howells) had a devastating influence on
       MT as a writer. This book established one
       pole of MT criticism, and led to a reply by
       Bernard DeVoto in Mark Twain's America
       (1932); Brooks slightly revised his own book
       (1933) in the light of DeVoto's criticisms,
       but left his argument basically intact. The
       1920 version of the book is excerpted brief-
       ly or at some length, either to catch the
       flavor of Brooks's thesis or his discussion

(BROOKS, VAN WYCK)
of MT's humor or of specific works, in
Marks (1959), pp. 1-18; Scott (1955),
pp. 134-47, (1967), pp. 145-58; Bradley
(1962), pp. 283-88; Leary (1962), pp. 35-61;
Lettis (1962), pp. 284-96; Cardwell (1963),
pp. 15-25; Smith (1963), pp. 13-28; Simpson
(1968), pp. 106-107; Gerber (1971),
pp. 19-29; Kesterson (1973), p. 29.

A2   *PAINE, ALBERT BIGELOW, ed.   The Letters of
Mark Twain. London: Chatto & Windus.
[Source: Asselineau (1954), No. 226;
also, several British reviews. The present
bibliography will use throughout the title
of the 1917 American edition, Mark Twain's
Letters--T.A.T.]

A3   _____, ed. Moments with Mark Twain. New
York and London: Harper & Brothers Publishers.
Selections in chronological order, taken
from MT's published work and introduced
briefly by Paine, who says his intent was
to show that MT "was something more than a
mere fun-maker" (p. vi). Contains no new
information or judgment.

A4   *_____. A Short Life of Mark Twain. New York
London: Harper & Brothers.
[Source: Asselineau (1954), No. 223.]

1920 B SHORTER WRITINGS

B1   ALDRICH, MRS. THOMAS BAILEY. Crowding Memories. Boston and New York: Houghton
Mifflin Company.
References passim to MT--who revealed in
his Autobiography and elsewhere that he detested Mrs. Aldrich. Gives a different
perspective to several stories involving
MT and the Aldriches, including the one
about MT's asking them, while visiting in
Hartford, not to make noise upstairs because it disturbed Livy, who had a headache.
According to Mrs. Aldrich, Livy told them
the next morning that she had no headache
and that their bedroom was in another wing
of the house (pp. 146-48.)

B2   ANON. "Business versus Genius," Freeman, I
(July 14), 412-13.
Van Wyck Brooks's The Ordeal of Mark
Twain has been misinterpreted as blaming
the failure of MT's later years on the
earlier ones and on his wife and mother;
rather, Brooks shows MT more broadly (and
successfully) as a product of his time,
the get-rich-quick epoch after the Civil
War.

B3   ANON. "Mark Twain," New Statesman, XV
(October 2), 707-10.
A review of Mark Twain's Letters (1917),
which reveal "his modesty, his quiet reserve of strength"; MT is more himself
here than in Paine's biography, which was
"written from the Boston angle." MT

"needed education; he needed 'showing'--but
he was shown the wrong things" by his wife
and Howells, who "wanted to help." Fortunately, MT "let culture go," and gave the
world IA, RI, TA, LOM, and HF.

B4   ANON. "Mark Twain's First Sweetheart, Becky
Thatcher, Tells of Their Childhood Court-
ship," in Willard Grosvenor Bleyer, How to
Write Special Feature Articles (Boston, New
York: Houghton Mifflin Company), pp. 299-
305.
The text of an interview in the Kansas
City Star (n.d.) with Mrs. Laura Hawkins
Frazer, with her recollections of Sam Clem-
ens in childhood.

B5   ANON. "Taming Mark Twain," Literary Digest,
LXVII (November 13), 34-35.
On Van Wyck Brooks's The Ordeal of Mark
Twain and on The New Statesman reviews
(liberally quoted) of the Paine biography
and edition of MT's letters.

B6   ANON. "Two Literary Shrines Menaced," Literary Digest, LXV (May 29), 36-37.
On plans to convert the MT house in Hartford into apartments (the other shrine was
the house of John Keats in London).

B7   ANON. [Review: Van Wyck Brooks, The Ordeal
of Mark Twain.] Weekly Review (New York),
III (August 4), 108-109.
"Mr. Brooks's bias is strong, but not
literary, and it appears to be the corrective or curative of the normal literary bias.
His theory obliges him to look for both
great abilities and for great disabilities
in Mark Twain, and this guides him unerring-
ly to the perfectly sound conclusion that
Mark Twain's force was far beyond his capacity." Brooks "owns a thesis which attracts
to its defense a large number of crisp facts
and observations. His book will interest
and serve even the unbeliever."

B8   ANON. [Review: Paine, ed., Mark Twain's
Letters.] Living Age, Eighth Series, XX
(from beginning, CCCVIII: November 27),
555-57.
(Reprinted from The Nation). Notes the
humanity and sincerity revealed in the letters; presumably, Paine has withheld "the
most unconventional of his musings."

B9   ANON. [Review: Paine, ed., Mark Twain's
Letters.] Times Literary Supplement,
September 23, p. 615.
MT is revealed as "a deeper, more complex
character than any he created...the most
laborious of writers, throwing into the fire
twice what he publishes." The reviewer
finds "this most generous man a prey to
money troubles that were the appropriate
punishment of something very like greed."

B10 *BOYNTON, PERCY. [Introduction.] The Adventures of Tom Sawyer. New York and London: Harper & Brothers. (Harper's Modern Classics, ed. for educational use by Prof. W. T. Brewster).
[Source: Asselineau (1954), No. 228.]

B11 BRADFORD, GAMALIEL. "Mark Twain," Atlantic Monthly CXXV (April), 462-73.
Using biographical data and basic interpretations from Paine, this appreciation sets MT outside of and above "the ordinary standards of mere literary men." Notes MT's melancholy and lack of religious faith. Reprinted in Scott (1955), pp. 163-74, and (1967), pp. 174-85.

B12 BROOKS, VAN WYCK. "The Genesis of Huck Finn," Freeman, I (March 31), 59-63.
HF succeeds because MT through Huck "was licensed to let himself go.... Huck's illiteracy, Huck's disreputableness and general outrageousness are so many shields behind which Mark Twain can let all the cats out of the bag with impunity." Eastern respectability had controlled MT but not changed his instincts: "You see what happens with Mark Twain when the lion-tamer turns his back."

B13 _____. "A Lost Prophet," Freeman, I (March 24), 46-47.
Chiefly on Horace Traubel and on his study of Walt Whitman; notes that MT's and Whitman's comments on each other were few and inconsequential.

B14 _____. "Mark Twain's Humour," Dial, LXVIII (March), 275-91.
Chapter VIII of The Ordeal of Mark Twain, abridged.

B15 _____. "Mark Twain's Satire," Dial, LXVIII (April), 424-43.
Chapter X of The Ordeal of Mark Twain, abridged.

B16 CARNEGIE, ANDREW. Autobiography of Andrew Carnegie. Boston: Houghton Mifflin, pp. 282-85.
Contains text of MT's letter requesting a dollar and a half to buy a hymn-book, and pays tribute to his warmth and integrity. Of first visit to MT after the death of Olivia: "I fortunately found him alone and while my hand was still in his, and before one word had been spoken by either, there came from his, with a stronger pressure of my hand, these words: 'A ruined home, a ruined home'" (pp. 284-85).

B17 *FARRAN I MAYORAL. Lletres a una Amiga Estrangera, Barcelona. [Critical study of MT, p. 84.] Reviewed in La Revista.
[Source: MHRA Annual Bibliography (1920), No. 197; other facts of publication on the book and the review in La Revista not available.]

B18 HEWLETT, MAURICE. [Review: Mark Twain's Letters.] London Mercury, III (December), 230-32.
An intelligent but minor review; praises MT as author and man, though not one of the great letter writers.

B19 *HOLT, HENRY. [Recollection of MT.] Unpartizan Review (October).
[Source: Reprinted in his Garrulities of an Octogenerian Editor (1923.B15).]

B20 JAMES, WILLIAM. The Letters of William James, Edited by His Son Henry James. Boston: The Atlantic Monthly Press. 2 vols. I: 333, 341-42; II: 264.
In a letter to Josiah Royce from Florence (December 18, 1892), described MT as "a fine, soft-fibred little fellow...I should think that one might grow very fond of him, and wish he'd come and live in Cambridge" (I, 333); to Francis Boot from Florence (January 30, 1893) mentions MT dining with him the night before, calls him "a dear man" (pp. 341-42). In a letter to his brother Henry and son William James, Jr. (Feb. 14, 1907) describes the aged MT at dinner as "good only for monologue, in his old age, or for dialogue at best, but he's a dear little genius all the same" (II, 264).

B21 JOHNSON, ALVIN. "The Tragedy of Mark Twain," New Republic, XXIII (July 14), 201-204.
In answer to Van Wyck Brooks, concedes that "Mark Twain yielded himself to his environment, to the prejudice of his best work"; but "Mark Twain was not in revolt against American institutions," and so could not be a satirist. He "was essentially a pioneer, with his character formed under pioneer discipline or indiscipline," and his pessimism was largely that of his generation.

B22 MATTHEWS, BRANDER. "Mark Twain and the Art of Writing," Harper's CXLI (October), 635-43.
Praises the directness and colloquial ease of MT's style, but his limitations as a critic. Reprinted in Scott (1955), pp. 148-62; (1967), pp. 159-73.

B23 _____. "Memories of Mark Twain," Saturday Evening Post, CXCII (March 6), 14-15, 77-81.
A friend's reminiscences for a general audience; notes that his "An Open Letter to Close a Correspondence" in New Princeton Review (1888) temporarily cooled their friendship. Illustrated with pictures of MT, including photograph taken on a porch at Onteora, New York, with Matthews, Lawrence Hutton, and Carroll Beckwith.

B24 MENCKEN, H. L. Prejudices, Second Series. New York: Alfred A. Knopf. On MT, p. 98.
Brief mention of MT, alternately striving for English approval and clowning for the public, "shrinking poltroonishly from his own ideas, obscenely eager to give no

1920 - Shorter Writings

(MENCKEN, H. L.)
offense," a greater artist than Poe or
Whitman but less of a man.

B25   O'DAY, CLARENCE. "Stories from the Files:
Famous Writers Who Contributed to the
Overland Monthly Fifty Years Ago," Overland
Monthly, LXXV (April), 326-28; (May),
407-409; (June), 517-519, 551.
    Reprints material MT wrote for the Over-
land and later used in Innocents Abroad,
the brief editorial comment by O'Day merely
provides necessary background for readers
of a later time.

B26   PECKHAM, H. HOUSTON. "The Literary Status
of Mark Twain, 1877-1890," South Atlantic
Quarterly, XIX (October), 332-40.
    A brief survey, drawing chiefly on Paine
and several reviews of MT's works in the
Atlantic, Academy, Athenaeum, Critic, etc.
"In the realm of pure literature perhaps
the most representative American author of
the eighties was Mark Twain."

B27   PHILLIPS, MICHAEL J. "Mark Twain's Partner,"
Saturday Evening Post, CXCIII
(September 11), 22-23, 69-74.
    On recollections left in manuscript by
Calvin H. Higbie, the friend to whom MT
dedicated RI; the manuscript is extensively
quoted, and there are photographs of Higbie,
MT's cabin in Aurora, Nevada, and of Aurora
as it was in 1920.

B28   *QUINN, ARTHUR HOBSON. [Introduction.] The
Prince and the Pauper. New York and Lon-
don: Harper & Brothers (Harper's Modern
Classics, ed. for educational use by
Prof. W. T. Brewster).
    [Source: Asselineau (1954), No. 227.]

B29   R., V. "Humorist and Moralist," Athenaeum,
No. 4719 (October 8), p. 470.
    A review of Paine, ed., Mark Twain's
Letters. More about MT, the man and au-
thor, than about the letters; favorable.

B30   *RICHEPIN, JEAN. "Les Humoristes--Marck
Twain," in his L'Âme Américaine (Paris:
Flammarion), pp. 155-74.
    [Source: Asselineau (1954), No. 234;
notes that the article is made up largely
of quotations, and Richepin misspells MT's
name and is unsure whether he is still living.]

B31   *SCHÖNEMANN, FRIEDRICH. "Amerikanischer Humor," Germanistisch-Romanistisch Monats-
schrift, VIII, 152-54, 216-27.
    [Source: Asselineau (1954), No. 250.]

B32   TEN EYCK, ANDREW. "Uncle Sam's Tin Halo:
Something about Mark Twain, Europe, and
the Poor American Diplomat," Outlook (New
York), CXXVI (December 22), 724-27.

On America's poorly paid and inexperienced
ambassadors; dramatizes the point with a
passing reference to MT's words on the subject. Includes photograph of MT.

B33   VAN DOREN, CARL. "The Fruits of the Frontier," Nation, CXI (August 14), 189.
    [Source: Reprinted in Leary (1962),
pp. 65-68.] A review of Van Wyck Brooks,
The Ordeal of Mark Twain. It "is so brilliant a book and comes so near the truth
in its general outlines that it seems almost an excess of seriousness to point out
certain excesses of seriousness into which
Mr. Brooks has been carried by his ardor
for the dignity of the literary profession.... If only Mr. Brooks were willing
to lay a little more stress upon the tragedy and a little less upon the guilt of his
offending author and nation!"

1921 A BOOKS - NONE

1921 B SHORTER WRITINGS

B1   ANON. "A Scotch Tilt against Mark Twain,"
Literary Digest, LXVIII (January 8), 35.
    Robert Blatchford, editor of The Clarion,
an English laborite paper, took issue there
with MT's comments on Scott; as excerpted
in Literary Digest it appears that Blatch-
ford was defending Scott, rather than attacking MT.

B2   ANON. "Tom, Mark, and Huck," English Journal, X (September), 403-404.
    Superficial description and praise of TS
and HF. "If the report that one of these
stories is soon to be available in a school
edition is correct, teachers should not be
slow to transfer it from 'home reading' to
class study."

B3   BOK, EDWARD W. The Americanization of Edward
Bok: The Autobiography of a Dutch Boy Fifty Years After. New York: Charles Scribner's Sons.
    In his distinguished career as editor and
publisher Bok is probably best known as
editor of the Ladies' Home Journal. There
are several references in his book to MT,
and two letters--one in response to a request from Bok in his youth for an autograph and one in response to a request for
permission to print an interview
(pp. 205-207).

B4   BURTON, RICHARD. "The Mystery of Personality,"
Bookman (New York), LII, No. 5 (January),
333-37.
    A review of Van Wyck Brooks, The Ordeal of
Mark Twain (1920). "The conclusion is unsound," because "He has succumbed to the
danger which always confronts the thesis-
maker who has to subdue data so they may
buttress his belief." [The pagination in

(BURTON, RICHARD)
the volume LII of Bookman examined was confused, but No. 5 (January) includes this
article on pp. 333-37.] Reprinted in Leary
(1962), pp. 69-75.

B5   CORTISSOZ, ROYAL. The Life of Whitelaw Reid.
New York: Charles Scribner's Sons. 2 vols.
I, 157, 248, 272-75; II, 380-81.
Reid was editor of the New York Tribune,
and, later, Ambassador to England. Vol. I
includes notes to him from MT (pp. 157, 248,
273-75) and from Charles Dudley Warner
(p. 273--about plans for GA). In Vol. II
there is a brief description of an MT
speech and the letter from Lord Curzon inviting Reid to receive an honorary Oxford
degree, and asking him to cable the same
invitation to MT and Thomas Edison (who declined with thanks, citing the pressure of
his work).

B6   HAM, GEORGE H. "Mark Twain, the Great Humorist," in Reminiscences of a Raconteur, Between the '40s and the '20s (Toronto: The
Musson Book Company, Limited), pp. 142-47.
Anecdotal. Ham speaks of frequent meetings with MT, and friendship with his former business manager, Ralph W. Ashcroft,
and Mrs. Ashcroft (formerly Miss Lyon, MT's
secretary); he notes that they "could give
the world a more realistic insight of the
dead author than has ever yet been presented," but gives no details and does not hint
at the acrimonious parting of the two from
the Clemens employment (pp. 142-43). Unreliable: describes MT as "a very shrewd
investor," who would put his money from a
book or lecture tour "into some sound enterprise" and "developed what is now the linotype, the first type-setting machine"
(pp. 145-46).

B7   *HARRIS, FRANK. "Memoirs of Mark Twain,"
Pearson's Magazine (November).
[Source: Twainian, II (May, 1943), 6.]

B8   HEWLETT, MAURICE. "Mark Twain and Sir Walter
Scott," Sewanee Review, XXIX (April),
130-33.
Defends Scott, though conceding his books
are "occasionally absurd."

B8   *HOLT, HENRY. [Brief mention of MT.] Unpartizan Review (January).
[Source: Reprinted in his Garrulities of
an Octogenerian Editor (1923.B15).]

B10   *MATTHEWS, BRANDER. "Mark Twain and the Art of
Writing," in his Essays on English (New
York: Charles Scribner's Sons), pp. 243-68.
[Source: Asselineau (1954), No. 255; de-
scribes this as a reprinting from Harper's,
(1920.B22).]

B11   MORRISSEY, FRANK R. "The Ancestor of the
'Jumping Frog,'" Bookman (New York), LIII
(April), 143-45.
An improbable analogue: suggests that
MT's story may derive from a similar compe-
tition in Virginia City, involving chloro-
formed grasshoppers.

B12   O'HIGGINS, HARVEY, and EDWARD H. REEDE, M.D.
"Mark Twain as Exhibit A," McClure's , LIII
(April), 12-13, 42-44.
A psychological interpretation of MT as
having developed his literary art to compensate for feelings of inadequacy which may
be traced to his childhood, beginning with
the weakness resulting from premature birth;
doubting his literary powers, "he compromised
on humor. He attacked only what it was safe
for him to attack: the injustices of the
feudal system...Christian Science in its in-
fancy, Tammany Hall in an election campaign...." Uses Paine extensively, but makes
no mention of Van Wyck Brooks.

B13   PAINE, ALBERT BIGELOW. "The Lost Napoleon,"
in his The Car that Went Abroad: Motoring
through the Golden Age (New York and London: Harper & Brothers Publishers),
pp. 72-78.
Following by car the course of MT's excursion down the Rhône, Paine rediscovered the
formation described in an MT sketch.

B14   RINAKER, CLARISSA. [Bibliography of MT.]
Cambridge History of American Literature.
Cambridge: Cambridge University Press, and
New York: The MacMillan Company [from 1931
reissue], IV, 635-39.
Uneven and incomplete; the bibliography in
the 1931 reissue lists nothing later than
1920.

B15   SCHÖNEMANN, FRIEDRICH. "Mark Twains Weltan-
shauung," Englische Studien, LV (January),
53-84.
Despite his reputation as a jester MT had
a serious outlook on life, as is reflected
in his letters and in such works as MS,
What Is Man?, JA, and CY. "Mark Twain,
'Gottes Narr,' ist um den Ausgang seines
Lebens nie besorgt gewesen, und ebensowenig
um Schluss und Ende seiner Philosophie."

B16   SHERMAN, STUART P. "Mark Twain's Place in
American Literature," in Cambridge History
of American Literature. (Cambridge: Cambridge University Press, and New York: The
Macmillan Company [from 1931 reissue]), III,
1-20.
Somewhat unsympathetic and superficial,
devoting considerable space to biography and
plot-summaries, and drawing on William Dean
Howells and Brander Matthews for a positive
view of MT as a writer.

1921 - Shorter Writings

B17 *STEARNS, HAROLD. "Van Wyck Brooks: Critic
     and Creator," in his America and the Young
     Intellectual (New York: George H. Doran
     Company), pp. 24-33.
        [Source: Reprinted in Leary (1962),
     pp. 76-80.] The Ordeal of Mark Twain
     (1920) is a serious and provocative work,
     though somewhat vacillating because Brooks
     lacks a clear central philosophy of life,
     writing at some times like a believer in
     free will, at others like a determinist.

B18 VAN DOREN, CARL. "Mark Twain," in his The
     American Novel. (New York: The Macmillan
     Company), pp. 157-87; passim.
        A "Revised and Enlarged Edition" appeared
     in 1940, but the changes in the treatment
     of MT are comparatively minor: Van Doren
     drops the charge that MT's failure to be-
     come a national satirist stems "partly from
     excess of patriotism, partly from a lack of
     the literary seriousness which might have
     enabled him to hold out against the influ-
     ence of his wife and his new environment"
     (p. 167; cf. p. 145 in the 1940 ed., where
     these words do not appear). Considers MT
     as a major author, though flawed, with HF
     his great work, in a class with The Scarlet
     Letter (pp. 170-75). Pp. 137-38, 160-62 of
     the 1940 revised edition are reprinted in
     Kesterson (1973), pp. 57-59.

1922 A BOOKS

A1   *ANON. Public Meeting under the Auspices of
     the American Academy and the National In-
     stitute of Arts and Letters Held at Carne-
     gie Hall, New York, November 30, 1910 in
     Memory of Samuel Langhorne Clemens (Mark
     Twain). New York: American Academy of
     Arts and Letters.
        [Source: Asselineau (1954), No. 266;
     See 1910 entries for details-T.A.T.]

A2   FISHER, HENRY W. Abroad with Mark Twain and
     Eugene Field: Tales They Told to a Fellow
     Correspondent. New York: Nicholas L.
     Brown.
        "Editor's Note" by Merle Johnson vouches
     for the substantial accuracy in "substance
     and manner, if not always the exact lan-
     guage" in these recollections of MT and
     Field in Berlin, Vienna, London, and Paris;
     some are recorded from memory, but Fisher
     also had diaries and notebooks to follow
     (pp. vii-x). Fisher's "Preface" begins:
     "To begin with, of course, I don't claim
     that all these stories are absolutely first
     hand. I sometimes jotted down what I
     heard Mark say, or stored his talk in some
     compartment of memory, only to hear him re-
     peat the yarn, after a space, in quite dif-
     ferent fashion" (p. xv).

A3   *LAUTREC, GABRIEL DE, trans. Mark Twain, Con-
     tes Choisis, traduits par Gabriel de Lautrec
     et précédés d'une étude sur l'humour.
     Paris: Nelson.
        [Source: Asselineau (1954), No. 268.]

1922 B SHORTER WRITINGS

B1   ADE, GEORGE. Single Blessedness and Other
     Observations, Garden City, New York: Dou-
     bleday, Page & Co.
        Reprints his 1910 essay, "Mark Twain as
     Our Emissary" without significant revisions,
     pp. 203-210.

B2   ANON. "Alas Poor Yorick!" Times Literary
     Supplement, October 26, p. 678.
        A review, chiefly descriptive, of Van
     Wyck Brooks, The Ordeal of Mark Twain.
     [The British edition appeared in 1922, ac-
     cording to Asselineau (1954), No. 264.]

B3   ANON. "On the Trail of Mark Twain," New York
     Times Book Review and Magazine (October 8),
     p. 7.
        On a tour of the Sierra Nevadas by Nicho-
     las Murray Butler, described at length and
     enlivened by MT's description of Mono Lake,
     quoted from RI. Includes photographs of
     Butler's party and of the King River Canyon.

B4   *ANON. "Tells of Mark Twain's Brief Soldiery
     in 1861," Hannibal (Missouri) Courier-Post,
     September 2.
        [Source: Asselineau (1954), No. 289.]

B5   ANON. [Review: Henry W. Fisher, Abroad with
     Mark Twain and Eugene Field.] Boston Tran-
     script, April 8, p. 10.
        Descriptive; includes picture of MT.

B6   ANON. [Review: Henry W. Fisher, Abroad with
     Mark Twain and Eugene Field.] Dial, LXXIII
     (August), 235.
        Makes short work of the book; concludes:
     "Mr. Fisher appears to have been assiduous
     without great success; his contribution to
     the bulk of Mark Twain's wit is hardly com-
     mensurate with the size of his book."

B7   ANON. [Review: Henry W. Fisher, Abroad with
     Mark Twain and Eugene Field.] The Literary
     Review ("Published by the New York Evening
     Post"), II (April 1), 550.
        MT would not be grateful for the editing,
     which makes this book "all droll waggish-
     ness," and therefore of a type that ulti-
     mately tires a reader. Fisher honestly
     concedes that the tales may not be exactly
     as he heard them from MT. "A remark of this
     kind was in order, for some of the things
     said about the ex-Kaiser, his troops, his
     U-boats, and his big guns, leave the im-
     pression that they were edited after, not
     before, the World War. The few pages de-
     voted to Eugene Field are less amusing but
     more informative."

B8   AYERS, COL. JAMES. "'Mark Twain' Doing the
      Islands--How He Discharged Himself from the
      Call--Mark as a Joker--Could Give But Could
      Not Take----His Intended Father-in-Law
      Makes an Awkward Proposition--He Disposes
      of It Handsomely," in his Gold and Sunshine:
      Reminiscences of Early California (Boston:
      Richard G. Badger), pp. 223-26.
          Ayers writes from personal acquaintance
      and says MT resigned from the San Francisco
      Call because of a tactful suggestion that
      he do so.

B9   B., L. [Review: Henry W. Fisher, Abroad with
      Mark Twain and Eugene Field.] Freeman, V
      (July 12), 429.
          "The record of many incidents, scraps of
      conversation, and bits of reminiscence;
      all lined up with their heels together and
      their eyes to the front, without a twinkle
      in them."

B10   BRADFORD, GAMALIEL. "Mark Twain," in his
      American Portraits.(Boston and New York:
      Houghton Mifflin Co.), pp. 1-28.
          "Somehow in Mark Twain the humor and the
      pathos are not essentially blended." Be-
      cause of a "lack of depth in thinking and
      feeling," Bradford is "reluctant to class
      Mark with the greatest comic writers of the
      world. His thought was bitter because it
      was shallow." Nonetheless, "He did more
      than make men laugh, he made them think, on
      practical, moral questions.... My final,
      total impression is desolating": MT's in-
      fluence in many ways is harmful, although
      "he was a big man and he had a big heart."

B11   "BURGLAR, A." "The Mark Twain Burglary," in
      his In the Clutch of Circumstance--My Own
      Story (New York, London: D. Appleton Com-
      pany), pp. 168-82.
          On the burglary of MT's "Stormfield" home
      in Redding, Connecticut. He believes that
      MT was influential in having the charges
      against him reduced, so that the sentence
      was ten years rather than thirty.

B12   CLEMENS, SAMUEL L. "Unpublished Chapters
      from the Autobiography of Mark Twain,"
      Harper's, CXLIV (February), 273-80;
      (March), 455-60; CXLV (June), 310-15.
          Each installment begins with a brief
      headnote by Albert Bigelow Paine, addressed
      to the general reader.

B13   *CLEMENS, WILL M. "The Genesis of Mark Twain,"
      The Biblio (Pompton Lakes, New Jersey).
      In eight parts, August 1922 to March 1923.
          [Source: Twainian, I (November, 1939),
      3.]

B14   *____. "The Genesis of Mark Twain," Genealo-
      gy Magazine (Pompton Lakes, New Jersey),
      October, 1922; January, April, 1923.
          [Source: Twainian, II (May, 1943), 6,
      with a note that this is probably the same
      text as that appearing in The Biblio.]

B15   DICKEY, MARCUS. The Maturity of James Whit-
      comb Riley. Indianapolis: The Bobbs-Mer-
      rill Company, Publishers.
          On p. 165, text of address on an envelope
      written by MT in Vienna to "Mr. James Whit-
      comb Riley/Poet & a dern capable one, too,/
      Indianapolis, Indiana,/ U.S. of America."
      On p. 231, text of MT letter (October 3,
      1888) to "Mr. W. D. Foulke and Others," re-
      gretfully declining an invitation to a din-
      ner honoring Riley, because "I am finishing
      a book begun three years ago. I see land
      ahead; if I stick to the oar without inter-
      mission I shall be at anchor in thirty days;
      if I stop to moisten my hands I am gone."
      Briefly mentions MT, passim (indexed).

B16   DREW, JOHN. My Years on the Stage. New York:
      E. P. Dutton & Company.
          Contains recollections of MT and the thea-
      ter passim (indexed).

B17   HOLMES, RALPH. "Mark Twain and Music," Centu-
      ry, CIV (October), 844-50.
          Following the Paine biography for factual
      data, discusses MT's early distaste for op-
      era, his love for Negro spirituals, fasci-
      nation with a music box, painful sensitivity
      to some sounds (such as ticking clocks and
      barking dogs), and his eventual solace in
      the music played on an orchestrelle in the
      New York home of his later years. In Vienna,
      according to Clara Clemens, "my father was
      always ill at ease among the musical people,
      for they were concerned with a form of art
      that left him wholly unmoved, and sometimes
      actually uncomfortable."

B18   HOWE, M. A. DEWOLFE. Memories of a Hostess:
      A Chronicle of Eminent Friendships Drawn
      Chiefly from the Diaries of Mrs. James T.
      Fields. Boston: The Atlantic Monthly
      Press.
          Describes visits to the Clemens home in
      Hartford. MT verses (a parody of Poe's
      "The Bells") and a letter from him to James
      T. Fields are reproduced in facsimile
      (pp. 248-49).

B19   ____. "Bret Harte and Mark Twain in the
      'Seventies: Passages from the Diaries of
      Mrs. James T. Fields," Atlantic Monthly,
      CXXX (September), 341-48.
          Entries for April and May, 1876 in the
      diary of the wife of the former Atlantic
      Monthly editor (pp. 344-48) describe MT's
      love for reading, dissatisfaction with Amer-
      ican government, support for women's suf-
      frage, apology for having spoken too quickly
      before Olivia. This is "part of a book to
      be published October 1," according to "The
      Contributors' Column," p. 428.

B20   HUNEKER, JAMES GIBBONS. [Brief mention of MT.]
      Steeplejack. New York: Charles Scribner's
      Sons, 2 vols, in 1; I, 100.
          Calls MT "our most American of writers,
      one who would outlive the pallid philosophy

1922 - Shorter Writings

(HUNEKER, JAMES GIBBONS)
of Emerson, the swaggering humbuggery of
Walt Whitman, or the sonorous platitudes of
Longfellow."

B21 *KWEST, DR. FRANZ. [Introduction.] Die Abenteuer Tom Sawyers und Huckleberry Finns.
Berlin: Mitteldeutsche verlangstalt, Leh-
mann und Fink.
[Source: Asselineau (1954), No. 267.]

B22 LUCY, SIR HENRY. The Diary of a Journalist:
Later Entries. London: John Murray,
pp. 231, 290, 315-16.
Briefly mentions MT, but provides no new
information beyond what he gave in his Sixty
Years in the Wilderness: Some Passages by
the Way (1909).

B23 MATTHEWS, BRANDER. "Memories of Mark Twain,"
in his The Tocsin of Revolt and Other Essays.
(New York: Charles Scribner's Sons),
pp. 253-94.
Personal recollections, including those of
a summer with MT at Onteora, N.Y. in 1890;
notes a temporary falling-out over copyright
laws and also comments on occasional failures as a speaker. Takes MT's word that
his primary resource for inspiration is
memory, and notes his life-long quality of
boyishness. The date "(1919)" appears at
the end, and this may well be a mere reprint
of the Saturday Evening Post article of the
same title (1920.B23).

B24 McCUTCHEON, GEORGE BARR. "When Mark Twain
Was a 'New' Writer," Literary Digest International Book Review, I (December), 16-17.
Portrait. An appreciative review of the
35-volume Gabriel Wells Definitive Edition,
noting that there is included "an appreciation written especially for each of the
main titles," by E. V. Lucas, Hamlin Garland, Mary E. Wilkins Freeman, Booth Tarkington, Hugh Walpole, Kate Douglas Wiggin,
Meredith Nicholson, William Allen White,
Stephen Leacock, G. K. Chesterton, Brander
Matthews, and William Dean Howells.

B25 MOORE, OLIN HARRIS. "Mark Twain and Don
Quixote," Publications of the Modern Language Association, XXXVII (June), 324-46.
"The purpose of this paper is to trace the
influence of Cervantes upon Mark Twain, with
particular attention to th supposedly autobiographical tales Huckleberry Finn and Tom
Sawyer." The humor of both authors "lies
to a great extent in the contrast between
imaginative and unimaginative characters,"
and MT, more widely read than is generally
recognized, parodied literary sources and
created characters misled by their reading.

B26 PEARSON, EDMUND LESTER. [Review: Fisher,
Abroad with Mark Twain and Eugene Field.]
Independent, CVIII (April 8), 353.3
"I suspect that there is more of Mr. Fisher than of Mark Twain" in this book, with
its "continual use of slang phrases which
were unknown until after Mark Twain's death
('hard-boiled,' for instance)."

B27 SCHÖNEMANN, F. "Amerikanische Mark Twain-
Literatur 1910-1920," Englische Studien,
LXVI (January), 148-53.
A survey of writing by and about MT pub-
lished since his death; essentially an an-
notated bibliography.

B28 _____. [Review: Bümmel durch Europa (A Tramp
Abroad.] Das literarische Echo: Halbmonat-
schrift fur Literaturfreunde (Stuttgart;
after Vol. XXV became a monthly, Die Literatur), XXII (November 1), 177.
Brief review, noting that a high point of
the book is the description of a journey in
the Black Forest [In German].

B29 TICKNOR, CAROLINE. "Mark Twain's 'Life on the
Mississippi,'" in her Glimpses of Authors.
Boston and New York: Houghton Mifflin Company (also London: T. Werner Laurie Ltd.--
but printed by The Riverside Press), 132-51
and passim on MT. Reprinted 1972: Free-
port, New York: Books for Libraries Press
(Essay Index Reprint Series).
Caroline Ticknor was the daughter of the
publisher Benjamin Holt Ticknor and her
reminiscences are at first-hand. In addition to giving a few details about the publication of LOM (and quoting MT's correspondence with the publisher), she describes
MT's seventieth birthday dinner, and the
train trip with him to the Thomas Bailey Aldrich home in Portsmouth. Elsewhere in the
book she notes MT's interest in Edward Bellamy's Looking Backward (p. 117), and a
tribute Howells at his own seventy-fifth
birthday dinner paid to the memory of his
friend (pp. 177-78).

B30 *WADE, MRS. MAY HAZLETON BLANCHARD. "Mark
Twain, Giver of Mirth," in her Real Americans (Boston: Little, Brown & Co.),
pp. 192-241.
[Source: Asselineau (1954), No. 276:
"merely a sentimental biographical sketch."]

1923 A BOOKS

A1 CLEMENS, SAMUEL L. Europe and Elsewhere, with
an appreciation by Brander Matthews and an
introduction by Albert Bigelow Paine. New
York: Harper & Brothers.
The first is a "'Biographical Criticism'...
prepared by Prof. Brander Matthews, as an
introduction to the Uniform Edition of Mark
Twain's Works, published in 1899." Paine's
introduction discusses MT's unpublished
writings and gives background on the materials published here.

A2 _____. Mark Twain's Speeches, with an Introduction by Albert Bigelow Paine and an Appreciation by William Dean Howells. New
York and London: Harper & Brothers.
   The Paine introduction is a biographical
summary, emphasizing MT's career as a
speaker; the Howells appreciation is reprinted from the 1910 edition of the Speeches (1910.B96), in which the selection of
speeches is somewhat different.

1923 B SHORTER WRITINGS

B1 ANON. "Miscellaneous Twain," Springfield
(Massachusetts) Daily Republican
October 26, p. 16.
   A review of the "lesser writings" in Eu-
rope and Elsewhere; descriptive and largely
indebted to the introductory "Biographical
Criticism" by Brander Matthews.

B2 ANON. "Missouri Honors the Prince of Humorists," Literary Digest, LXVIII (August 11),
30.
   Excerpts (n.d.) from the St. Louis Globe-
Democrat and the Quincy (Missouri) Whig
Journal on Florida, Missouri, on the house
there where MT was born, and on the proposed
state park.

B3 *ANON. [Review: Mark Twain's Speeches.] New
York World, May 27, p. 7.
   [Source: Asselineau (1954), No. 309.]

B4 ANON. [Review: Mark Twain's Speeches.] Outlook (New York), CXXXV (June 27), 287-88.
   "A great deal of the sparkle of the humor
is lost in the stolid printed page. Yet
there is good browsing in the book, and
there is what Mark Twain loved to call
'horse sense' as well as fun."

B5 ANON. [Review: Mark Twain's Speeches.]
Springfield (Massachusetts) Daily Republican, June 22, p. 16.
   Descriptive and based primarily on the
introduction.

B6 BERGENGREN, RALPH. "Mark Twain in Europe and
Elsewhere. The Great American Humorist Discourses on Many Things that Touch the Heart
of Humanity," Boston Evening Transcript
October 13, Book Section, p. 2.
   A review: "Europe and Elsewhere, opened
here and there, usually provides something
that catches the attention and interests
the reader though the timeliness of the
topic has gone past." Illustration: "Mark
Twain (From a Drawing by S. J. Woolf...)"

B7 *BRIDGES, HORACE JAMES. "The Pessimism of
Mark Twain," in his As I Was Saying--A Sheaf
of Essays and Discourses (Boston: Marshall
Jones Co.), pp. 35-51.
   [Source: Asselineau (1954), No. 295;
Bridges argues that pessimism is a product
of satire.]

B8 CANBY, HENRY SEIDEL. "Mark Twain," The Literary Review ("Published by the New York Evening Post"), IV (November 3), 201-202.
   Occasioned by the publication of the Gabriel Wells "Definitive Edition" of MT's works;
takes issue with Van Wyck Brooks: "Most
artists are suppressed in one way or another,
and not only in America. Yet it is arguable,
nevertheless, that Clemens was the kind of
spirit that needed a certain amount of suppression, without which he would have fizzed
his way through life like an uncapped soda
spring." Reprinted in Canby's Definitions:
Essays in Contemporary Criticism (Second Series). New York: Harcourt, Brace & Co.,
1924, pp. 157-65 (Reprinted Port Washington,
N.Y.: Kennikat Press, 1967).

B9 CLEMENS, CLARA. "How I Got Rid of Nervousness
in Public," Étude, XLI (May), 295-96.
   On her way of achieving mental serenity
before concerts; followed by extensive excerpts from Ralph Holmes, "Mark Twain and
Music" (1922).

B10 COOK, SHERWIN LAWRENCE. "Mark Twain as a Maker of Speeches," Boston Evening Transcript,
June 16, Book Section, p. 3.
   A review of Mark Twain's Speeches, noting
MT's development: "It is not often that a
literary man's ability to speak keeps step
with his progress as a writer," as did MT's.
On the Whittier Birthday Dinner speech,
cites contemporary newspaper accounts indicating that "certain of the diners must
have been amused." Portrait: "Mark Twain.
(From an Etching by Otto Schneider...)"

B11 *DUNN, HARRY H. "To Revive Pony Express to
Honor Mark Twain," Dearborn Independent,
July 14.
   [Source: Twainian, II (January, 1940),
5.]

B12 FISHER, SAMUEL J. "Mark Twain," Spectator,
CXXX (June 2), 922.
   A letter to the editor, from Pittsburgh,
Pennsylvania. Answers the charges in Kreym-
borg's favorable review of The Ordeal of
Mark Twain (p. 701), in particular noting
that MT was financially independent to write
as he pleased, and in their last years both
MT and his wife lacked religious convictions.

B13 *FITZGERALD, F. SCOTT. "10 Best Books I Have
Read," Jersey City Journal (April 24), p. 9.
Syndicated by the North American Newspaper
Alliance.
   [Source: reprinted in Fitzgerald/Heming-
way Annual (1972), 67-68.] Fitzgerald's
complete statement on MT: "'The Mysterious
Stranger.' (Mark Twain). Mark Twain in his
most sincere mood. A book and a startling
revelation."

B14　HARRIS, FRANK. "Memories of Mark Twain," in his *Contemporary Portraits, Fourth Series*, (New York: Brentano's), pp. 162-73.

Attacks MT for his hostility toward Bret Harte, calls *JA* "a dreadful book" that "makes a Puritan maiden of the great French-woman," and objects to his essay on Howells "in which that tedious person is praised as if he were one of the great writers."

B15　HOLT, HENRY. *Garrulities of an Octogenerian Editor*. Boston and New York: Houghton Mifflin Company. On MT, pp. 99-102, 129 (originally appeared in the *Unpartizan Review*, October, 1920 and January, 1921).

On meetings with MT, the last one at a dinner in the Times Tower honoring the edi-tor of the London *Times*. "If Mark said anything funny it was bitterly funny. His wife was dead. The burden of his talk was that he was growing old, that the future was dark, and that the heart was gone out of him." Holt was distressed that MT was not interested in Psychical Research, de-spite published evidence of psychical ex-periences in the family (pp. 100-101).

B16　HUTCHISON, PERCY A. "Dinner-Talk by Mark Twain," *New York Times Book Review* (June 10), p. 8.

A review of Paine's new edition of *Mark Twain's Speeches*; they give little evidence of the pessimism attributed to MT by recent critics [such as Van Wyck Brooks].

B17　JOHNSON, ROBERT UNDERWOOD. *Remembered Yester-days*. Boston: Little, Brown and Company.

On the loss of Grant's *Memoirs* by the Century Company to MT's publishing company, not quite suggesting unethical practice by MT (pp. 217-19); MT's lobbying for a strong-er copyright law (pp. 267-69); a probing ex-amination of his personality, noting both his tenderness and his hard hitting and hard hating: "His violence was almost unexampled among literary men" (pp. 319-25). Two pho-tographs: "Mark Twain at Onteora" and "Mark Twain in Tesla's Laboratory. Photo-graphed by phosphorescent light" (facing p. 324).

B18　JORDAN-SMITH, PAUL. "Mark Twain," in his *On Strange Altars: A Book of Enthusiasms*. (London: Brentano's, Ltd.), pp. 136-45.

A superficial over-view of several of MT's works, largely plot-summary. Praises MT's social satire and argues that humor saved him from bitterness.

B19　KREYMBORG, ALFRED. [Review: Brooks, *The Ordeal of Mark Twain*.] *Spectator*, CXXX (April 28), 701.

Praises Brooks for his "intellectual hon-esty and integrity of utterance," and shares his view of MT as having shrunk from the heights he might have achieved as a satirist to become a mere clown--but he created "at least one masterpiece: *Huck Finn*."

B20　MATTHEWS, BRANDER. "Mark Twain," in *An Intro-duction to the Study of American Literature* (Revised). (New York, Cincinnati, Chicago, Boston, Atlanta: American Book Company), pp. 215-26.

A policy of not including living authors kept MT out of the first edition of this school survey (1896); the essay in this late edition is primarily biographical and de-scriptive, and adds little to his judgments published in the earlier period when Matthews was among the first in the academic community to recognize the importance of MT.

B21　_____. "Mark Twain and the Theater," in his *Playwrights on Playmaking, and Other Studies of the Stage*. (New York, London: Charles Scribner's Sons), pp. 159-83.

On MT's appreciation of the theatre, and his efforts as a playwright. His dramatiza-tion of *GA* apparently owes something to Gil-bert S. Densmore's plotting in a version that was suppressed after a cash settlement by MT. MT failed as a dramatist because for all his dramatic genius in creating characters, he lacked the constructive skill the stage re-quires.

B22　_____. "Mark Twain Stands and Delivers," *Lit-erary Digest International Book Review*, I (August), 57.

A review of *Mark Twain's Speeches*, but in-cluding Matthews's own discussion of MT as a skilled speaker who prepared carefully and knew his audience--but Matthews cites two failures. This new edition of the speeches supercedes the carelessly edited 1910 ver-sion.

B23　MAVOR, JAMES. *My Windows on the Street of the World*. London and Toronto: J. M. Dent & Sons Ltd; New York: E. P. Dutton & Co., I, 197; II, 183.

William Morris read aloud from *HF* until past two in the morning, then stayed up until five to finish it (I, 197). Quotes a comic poem MT wrote in an album about Laurence Housman (II, 183).

B24　O'BRIEN, EDWARD J. "Bret Harte and Mark Twain," in his *The Advance of the American Short Story*. (New York: Dodd, Mead and Com-pany), pp. 98-116; on MT, pp. 112-16, (entry based on 1931 revised ed., apparently un-changed in content and pagination).

Charges Harte with personal irresponsibil-ity; his writings portray the vanished West, but they are shallow and sentimental and his tales of life in Europe are "rubbish." On MT, discusses only the short stories and leaves the general discussion of MT to "Van Wyck Brooks, who ranks with T. S. Eliot as the most intellectually mature of contempo-rary American critics."

B25 PHELPS, WILLIAM LYON. "The American Humorist: Mark Twain," in his Some Makers of American Literature (Boston: Marshall Jones Company), pp. 163-87.
    On MT as careful literary artist, interpreter of life, and "the incarnate spirit of America."

B26 _____. "Mark Twain, the American Humorist," Ladies' Home Journal, XL (May), 18, 208-11.
    A lengthy discussion of the man and his works, praising his artistry and a humor that kept him from being conceited.

B27 *RANKIN, J. W. [Introduction.] Life on the Mississippi. New York and London: Harper & Brothers (Modern Classics).
    [Source: Asselineau (1954), No. 291.]

B28 *ROBERTS, CARL ERIC BECHHOFER. The Literary Renaissance in America. London: William Heinemann, Ltd.
    On pp. 2-7, follows Brooks in accounting for MT's pessimism. [Source: Asselineau (1954), No. 294; family name "Roberts," according to card files at Duke University Library and Oakland Public Library.]

B29 SCHÖNEMANN, FRIEDRICH. "Mr. Samuel Langhorne Clemens," Archiv für das Studium der neueren Sprachen und Literaturen, CXLV (August), 184-213.
    On MT as revealed in the 1917 edition of his letters; notes the problem even in America of distinguishing between Clemens and the "Mark Twain" he created. [In German.]

B30 _____. [Review: MT's Tolle Geschichten.] Die Literatur (Stuttgart), XXVI (December), 179.
    Brief review, comments, "Mit solch einem tieferen Blick in Mark Twains Seele entdeckten wir auch ein Amerikanertum, zu dem uns die 'Tollen Geschichten,' so ergösslich und Mark Twainisch sie sein mögen, nicht führen können, was bei unserer recht magelhaften Einsicht in das Wesen der amerikanischen Kultur sehr zu bedauern ist."

B31 TASSIN ALGERNON, and ARTHUR BARTLETT MAURICE. "Mark Twain, Idol-Smasher," in The Story of American Literature. (New York: The Macmillan Company), pp. 318-27.
    Laudatory and rather superficial, intended for younger readers. A "Foreword" notes that the papers in this book originally appeared weekly, in serial form, but does not indicate where they were published.

B32 VAN DOREN, CARL. "The Lion and the Uniform," in his The Roving Critic, New York: Alfred A. Knopf [as reprinted Port Washington, N.Y.: Kennikat Press, 1950], pp. 45-55.
    On Van Wyck Brooks's The Ordeal of Mark Twain (1920), which in its arraignment of MT's times "exhibits instances of special pleading and a definite animus [that] must be admitted even by those who, like myself, agree that the picture here drawn of our greatest humorist is substantially accurate as well as brilliant."

B33 WIGGIN, KATE DOUGLAS. My Garden of Memory: An Autobiography. Boston and New York: Houghton Mifflin Company.
    Passim on public functions at which MT was present (indexed). Describes a serious and not wholly successful MT reading (pp. 240-41) and MT receiving his honorary degree from Oxford (pp. 304-307).

1924 A BOOKS

A1 CLEMENS, SAMUEL LANGHORNE. Mark Twain's Autobiography, edited and with introduction by Albert Bigelow Paine. New York and London: Harper & Brothers Publishers, 2 vols.
    The text of reminiscences written and dictated by MT and selected by Paine. "Perhaps it is proper to assure the reader that positive mistakes of dates and occurrence have been corrected, while, for the rest, the matter of mere detail is of less importance than that the charm of the telling should remain undisturbed." By MT's request, the order is that of composition, rather than chronology of events. Much is not included here, either because of Paine's judgment or because of MT's injunction that certain items not be published for a number of years after his death, but this version of MT's autobiographical material has not been replaced by DeVoto's edition of Mark Twain in Eruption (1940) and Neider's The Autobiography of Mark Twain (1959). MT's "Chapters from My Autobiography" had appeared in North American Review, 1906-1907; since they appeared before his death and he had approved the texts for publication they have a greater authority than this version by Paine, with several silent expurgations.

A2 *GILLIS, WILLIAM R. Memories of Mark Twain and Steve Gillis: A Record of Mining Experiences. Sonora, California: Printed by The Banner.
    [Source: Asselineau (1954), No. 321.]

A3 FINGER, CHARLES J. Mark Twain, the Philosopher Who Laughed at The World. Girard, Kansas: Haldeman-Julius Company.
    [Source: Asselineau (1954), No. 320: "Pays homage to Mark Twain's condemnation of mob-rule and anti-Semitism."]

1924 B SHORTER WRITINGS

B1 ANON. "Conrad Pays Tribute to Mark Twain," Mentor, XII (May), 45.
    From a Mentor interview. "'Mark Twain was a good pilot,' said Conrad. 'He must have been. No man who had not done the actual work could write of steamboat life as he did.'" The descriptions of life in America are what count. "'They have life--American life. They are authentic.'" "'Often,' says

1924 - Shorter Writings

(ANON.)
Conrad musingly, 'I thought of "The Missis-sippi Pilot" and of Twain while I was in command of a steamer in the Congo and stood straining in the night looking for snags. Very often I thought of him. He understood all that sort of job.'"

B2   ANON. "Gleams of Mark Twain Humor. Selected Incidents and Anecdotes Reflecting the Unique Character and Whimsical Quality of the Humorist," Mentor, XII (May), 56-58.
A few anecdotes apparently not reported elsewhere; also, three cartoon representa-tions of his 1907 visit to England and photograph of MT in Harper & Brothers office, New York.

B3   ANON. "Mark Twain," New Statesman, XXIV (November 8), "Additional Pages," x, xii, xiv.
A review of Mark Twain's Autobiography, which its random arrangement makes "a scrapbook...but this lack of order and pro-gression cannot spoil its chief charm, which is the companionship of Mark Twain himself; his fun and his honest angers, his tender affections...there is an exhilarating air of freedom blowing through these pages."

B4   ANON. "Mark Twain and General Grant," Mentor, XII (May), 46-47.
Anecdotes and the account of MT's involve-ment in publication of Grant's Memoirs; pro-vides no new information.

B5   ANON. "Mark Twain Memorial Park," Mentor, XII (May), 54-55.
The history of the park in Florida, Missouri.

B6   ANON. "Mark Twain--Radical," Saturday Review of Literature, I (November 1), 241.
MT spoke more freely on social issues than recent critics would admit, but "knew much more of America than his more scornful successors. Perhaps that is why he liked his country in spite of the deeds of his countrymen."

B7   ANON. "One Love of a Lifetime," Mentor, XII (May), 50.
On Olivia; adds little to the Paine bio-graphy.

B8   ANON. "Self-Revelation of our Greatest Humor-ist," Current Opinion, LXXVII (November), 578-80.
A review of Mark Twain's Autobiography. "His greatest tragedy lay in his inability to resist the moods which robbed him of faith and of happiness," but his writings brought "unmeasured delight to millions of readers."

B9   ANON. [Review: Mark Twain's Autobiography.] Times Literary Supplement, November 6, p. 701.
An evaluation of MT as he emerges in his book. Despite hatred for the human race, he was warm in his personal affections. He was a conscious literary craftsman, and it was his art rather than money-making that could charm his depressions away: "His most successful calculation must have been the miscalculation that led to his bankruptcy. In paying off his debts he was at his happiest." The book's deliberate absence of formal organization "gives the impulsive man, and when it has illumined President and coachman with an equal light abruptly shut off, they have fulfilled their function of reflecting Mark Twain."

B10   NO ENTRY

B11   BOYNTON, PERCY H. "Biography and the Personal Equation," in his Some Contemporary Ameri-cans: The Personal Equation in Literature. Chicago: The University of Chicago Press (Reprinted New York: Biblo and Tannen, 1967), pp. 242-64; on MT, pp. 244-57.
Discusses several interpretations of MT. The Paine biography contains an abundance of data, and Paine was aware of MT's creative memory, but inclined to hero-worship and "as keen about Twain's billiards as he was about his books" (p. 245). Howells' My Mark Twain "was by title and nature a per-sonal tribute which is only half read if Mr. Howells is not interpreted into every page" (p. 250). Brooks's The Ordeal of Mark Twain is written to a thesis, pompously sol-emn, and prone to regard opposing opinions as wrong because they are generally accepted. Boynton regards Gamaliel Bradford's portrait of MT as "bafflingly indeterminate" as to whether it praises or condemns. This essay is one of a group incorporating material which previously appeared in the Dial, the Freeman, the Independent, and the New Repub-lic (p. vii).

B12   CLEMENT, MRS. N. E. "Clement, Clements, Clem-ans. With a Notice of Mark Twain's Ances-try," Virginia Magazine of History and Bio-graphy [title also appears as Virginia His-torical Magazine], XXXII (292-98).
"In the Genealogy Magazine edited by Wm. M. Clemens, of Pompton Lakes, New Jersey, there appears an article beginning in Vol. X, No. 9, called 'The Genesis of Mark Twain,' in which the author treats of the Virginia ancestry of the distinguished American humor-ist and author." Numerous statements of fact in that article are here challenged in a detailed account.

B13 *FINGER, CHARLES J. "Mark Twain, the Philoso-
pher Who Laughed at the World," Life and
Letters, (April [Mark Twain Number]).
[Source: Twainian, II (November, 1940),
4; this is not the British Life and Letters--
T.A.T.]

B14 GABRILOWITSCH, CLARA CLEMENS. "My Father,"
Mentor, XII (May), 21-3.
Clara was somewhat overawed by her famous
and sometimes rather reserved father; tells
the story of his keeping the secret of her
destructive pet squirrels.

B15 LAROM, WALTER H. "Mark Twain in the Adiron-
dacks," Bookman (New York), LVIII
(January), 536-38.
Recollections of a visit to MT's bungalow
on Saranac Lake; includes texts of two MT
letters to Mr. and Mrs. George V. W. Duryee
(June 14, September 19, 1901).

B16 LEISY, ERNEST ERWIN. "Mark Twain," in his
American Literature: An Interpretive Sur-
vey. (New York: Thomas Y. Crowell Compa-
ny), pp. 170-78.
Biographical, broadly appreciative.
Notes his serious thought, pessimism.
"Mark Twain's reputation, however, does not
rest on his philosophy but on his portrayal
of life in mid-nineteenth-century America,
... He is the incarnation of democratic
America, best fulfilling Whitman's concep-
tion of the promise of American life....
He spoke the national idiom."

B17 LITTELL, ROBERT. [Review: Mark Twain's Autobiography.] New Republic, XL (October 29),
230.
"What we learn about Mark Twain from
himself is pleasant, or touching, or tedious, or explicit, or narrative, but not
very illuminating." The recollections of
his youth are the best, most vivid parts.

B18 "Mark Twain Number--Articles by His Biographer and Close Friends," Mentor, XII (May).
Articles are listed individually in this
section. Illustrated with photographs and
drawings.

B19 MARSHALL, ARCHIBALD. "Last Century's Literary Favorites: I, Huckleberry Finn," Literary Digest International Book Review,
II (January), 104, 106.
Appreciative: a masterpiece, though the
ending is weak.

B20 MATTHEWS, BRANDER. "Mark Twain as Speech-
Maker and Story-Teller," Mentor, XII (May),
24-28.
Insists on MT's artistry and careful
preparation; tells the anecdote of MT mis-
taking a guest for a book agent.

B21 ____. "The Truth about Mark Twain," Literary
Digest International Book Review, II
(November), 845-48.
An extended (and favorable) review of Mark
Twain's Autobiography by an old friend and
advocate. Includes a drawing of MT by Carroll Beckwith in Onteora, N.Y., 1890, and a
photograph of MT, Matthews, and friends,
also Onteora, 1890.

B22 MIEROW, HERBERT EDWARD. "Cicero and Mark
Twain," Classical Journal, XX (December),
167-69.
On the first Tusculan Disputation and "The
Death of Jean": "Each suffered the loss of
a daughter, and each sought refuge in writ-
ing. Some of the sentiments we find in
Cicero reappear in Mark Twain."

B23 *MITCHELL, EDWARD PAGE. Memoirs of an Editor.
New York: Charles Scribner's Sons.
[Source: Asselineau (1954), No. 328:
passim on MT.]

B24 *NELSON, W. H. "Mark Twain Out West," Methodist Quarterly Review, LXXIII (January),
65-83.
[Source: Asselineau (1954), No. 346;
Methodist Review, LXXIII (1891) and CVII
(1924) checked at Duke University without
success--T.A.T.]

B25 *O'HIGGINS, HARVEY, and EDWARD H. REEDE, M.D.
The American Mind in Action New York and
London: Harper & Brothers.
[Sources: Asselineau (1954), No. 329
("A Chapter on Twain, pp. 26-49, takes up
again Brooks's thesis: Mark Twain 'was as
profound a biological failure as America
has produced.'"). Also discussed in Claudia
C. Morrison, Freud and the Critic: The Early Use of Depth Psychology in Literary Criticism (1968), pp. 112-13 (the discussions of
Margaret Fuller and of MT "represent in
some respects more rounded treatments of
their subjects than the full-length Freudian
biographies of them written at the same
time."]

B26 PAINE, ALBERT BIGELOW. "Mark Twain--Boy and
Man. The Story of His Life," Mentor, XII
(May), 3-20.
Condensed biography, illustrated; contains
no new information.

B27 PEARSON, EDMUND LESTER. "Huckleberry and
Sherlock," Outlook (New York), CXXXVIII
(October 15), 256-57.
A review-article on Arthur Conan Doyle's
Memories and Adventures and Mark Twain's
Autobiography; the latter is "a great and
grievous disappointment...the book consists
of a great deal that was printed years ago
in the North American Review, together with
other pages which are superfluous after
Mr. Paine's magnificent biography."

1924 - Shorter Writings

B28 RAYMOND, E. T. "The Victorian Humorist," London Mercury, X (August), 374-86.
On MT, pp. 378-79: "Mark Twain offers perhaps the supreme illustration of this nineteenth-century complacency" in his views concerning language, morals, philosophy-- and foreigners.

B29 RICE, CLARENCE C., M.D. "Mark Twain as His Physician Knew Him," Mentor, XII (May), 48-49.
Chiefly anecdotal, on cigars, billiards, shirts, spelling, etc. As a speaker, "He had two voices, two styles of speech and delivery: the humorous, slow-spoken drawl, and, on rare occasions, the loud and sonorous voice of the eloquent orator." Notes MT's love for the word "gaudy."

B30 RODGERS, CLEVELAND. "The Many-Sided Mark Twain," Mentor, XII (May), 29-44.
A rather general discussion and a number of photographs of MT, his homes, and Missouri scenes.

B31 ROGERS, CAMERON. "In Which Mark Twain Reveals Himself," World's Work, XLVIII (October), 679-81.
A review of Mark Twain's Autobiography: appreciative, uncritical; concerned with content rather than form.

B32 *ROSENFELD, PAUL. [Essay on Van Wyck Brooks; speculates on his blind spot concerning MT.] Port of New York.
[Source: Cited in James R. Vitelli, Van Wyck Brooks (1969), p. 113.]

B33 SEABRIGHT, J. M. "A Shrine to the Prince of Humorists," Literary Digest International Book Review, II (November), 848-49.
On the Mark Twain Memorial Park at Florida, Missouri.

B34 SEITZ, DON C. "Mark Twain's Autobiography," Bookman (New York), LX (December), 446-48.
A review. Chiefly descriptive; enjoys the rambling. "It sometimes seems in reading Mark Twain that he was far too contemptuous of himself, and this fact the 'autobiography' emphasizes."

B35 SHAW, BERNARD. Saint Joan: a Chronicle Play in Six Scenes and an Epilogue. New York: Brentano's.
In "Preface," pp. xxv-xli, argues that MT's JA fails to put Joan in the context of her time: his portrait "makes her creator ridiculous, and yet, being the work of a man of genius, remains a credible human goodygoody in spite of her creator's infatuation"; moreover, MT misunderstands Joan's judges.

B36 *SPRINGFIELD, LINCOLN. Some Piquant People. London: T. Fisher Unwin.
Contains two MT anecdotes, one concerning Darwin. [Source: Starrett (1945), p. 1.]

B37 STANTON, THEODORE. "Mark Twain's 'Lost Napoleon,'" Stratford Monthly (Boston), VII (April), 36-41.
On the rock formation to be seen from the Rhône, resembling Napoleon, and described in "The Lost Napoleon" in Europe and Elsewhere. Stanton was unsuccessful in a search for the formation, undertaken at MT's request; Albert Bigelow Paine described his own successful search in a chapter in his book, The Car that Went Abroad, 1921.B13, and later wrote that he had seen the formation several times. Stanton quotes from a conversation with MT on the subject, and from an MT letter of October, 1901.

B38 STEINDORFF, ULRICH. "Mark Twain's Broad German Grin. New Translations Have Helped to Restore a Lost Sense of Humor," New York Times Book Review (July 13), p. 6.
On the growth of MT's reputation in Germany; he is an important writer.

B39 *STEUART, JOHN A. Robert Louis Stevenson: A Critical Biography. Boston, II, 135.
MT's description of RLS, after a meeting in New York in April, 1888. [Source: Quoted by Baetzhold (1970), pp. 203-204.]

B40 STRATE, JESSIE B. "Mark Twain and Geography," Journal of Geography, XXIII (March), 81-92.
She finds MT's work filled with passages she can read to her high-school classes in geology and commercial geography to give them a sense of a place, people, geographical features, or the passage of time.

B41 VAN DOREN, CARL. "Posthumous Thunder," Saturday Review of Literature, I (October 25), 225.
A review of Mark Twain's Autobiography, which "bears witness on many pages that Mark Twain was, for all his rough power, a man imperfectly schooled in any kind of knowledge or any kind of logic." Although the book contains no explosions "it crackles constantly, and now and then it stuns. The question remains: Is there more of it somewhere?"

B42 VAN DOREN, MARK. [Review: Mark Twain's Autobiography.] Nation, CXIX (November 12), 524.
No order, no stirring disclosures of MT's private opinions, but "first-rate writing," or, rather, "first-rate talk."

B43 WHITE, EDGAR. "The Old Home Town," Mentor, XII (May), 51-53.
Description of Hannibal, with anecdotes.

B44 WILSON, FRANCIS. Francis Wilson's Life of Himself. Boston and New York: Houghton Mifflin Company.
On MT at the Players Club in New York, and several anecdotes, pp. 298-301; includes MT photograph.

B45 WOOLF, LEONARD. "Mark Twain," Nation & Athenaeum, XXXVI (November 8), 217.
A review of Mark Twain's Autobiography, interesting for its "trenchant outspokenness," though "not quite so unreserved as one might be led to expect from the Preface." Praises MT's "literary craftsmanship.... But behind the clarity and exactness of style was something more--a very good brain. Mark Twain's humour is often very much on the surface; it covers an intense seriousness and a highly intellectual interest in things and ideas."

1925 A BOOKS

A1 *CLEMENS, SAMUEL L. Mark Twain, 1601, or Conversation at the Social Fireside as It Was in the Time of the Tudors, introduction by Charles Erskine Wood, and other letters by Mark Twain. New York: Grabhorn Press. [Source: Asselineau (1954), No. 363.]

A2 LAWTON, MARY. A Lifetime with Mark Twain. The Memories of Katy Leary, for Thirty Years His Faithful and Devoted Servant. Written by Mary Lawton. New York: Harcourt, Brace and Company.
A servant's view, as told to Mary Lawton, of persons and incidents in MT's life; useful for extending the perspective furnished by Paine and others. Illustrated.

A3 SCHÖNEMANN, FRIEDRICH. Mark Twain als Literarische Persönlichkeit. Jenaer Germanistische Forschungen, Heft 8. Jena: Verlag der Frommannschen Buchhandlung (Walter Biedermann).
Reveals the impressive breadth of MT's reading. Summed up, with the reviews it received, in Hemminghaus, Mark Twain in Germany (1939).

1925 B SHORTER WRITINGS

B1 ANDERSON, SHERWOOD. Dark Laughter. New York: Boni & Liveright, pp. 14-18, 100, 168.
A work of fiction. Anderson's John Stockton (alias "Bruce Dudley") thinks about MT in Hartford, on the river, piloting, writing HF; regrets that MT didn't describe the less glamorous things he had seen on the river, and when he returned to finish LOM, why didn't he write an epic of what had been destroyed, instead of filling the book with statistics and old jokes? (pp. 14-18). On "a kind of big continental poetry" of the river that "Mark Twain had almost got and didn't dare try to quite get" (p. 100). The character Aline remembers IA, which her father had loved but which "had really been nothing but a kind of small boy's rather nasty disdain of things he couldn't understand" (p. 168).

B2 ANON. "Mark Twain as a Billard Fan," Literary Digest, LXXXVI (July 25), 55.
Anecdotes and an MT note (to Mrs. Henry Rogers, thanking her for her husband's gift of a billiard-table), excerpted from Willie Hoppe's book, Thirty Years of Billiards.

B3 ANON. [Review: Mark Twain's Autobiography.] Edinburgh Review, CCXLI (January), 203.
"He has let imagination have as free a reign as memory. The result is a series of descriptions--humorous, satirical, or pathetic--in which the reader sees not so much the subject as the personality of the author developing from his sympathies or full-blooded hatreds."

B4 ANON. [Review: Mary Lawton, A Lifetime with Mark Twain.] Saturday Review of Literature, II (December 26), 452.
The book chiefly concerns minor domestic details, although it casts light on MT's view of the incident involving Maxim Gorki; it also shows that "native kindliness and unselfishness characterized both master and servant. Malice simply did not exist in either."

B5 BARRUS, CLARA. The Life and Letters of John Burroughs. Boston and New York: Houghton Mifflin; reissued New York: Russell & Russell, 1968. 2 vols. II, 87-88, 221-22.
Journal entry of November 8, 1905 says MT was "very diverting, as he always is" at the first dinner of the American Academy of Arts and Letters (p. 87); at the MT seventieth birday dinner in December, Burroughs sat by Mrs. Henry Rogers; "Her husband sat at Mark Twain's table.... How Mark Twain can accept favors from him is a mystery." MT's speech was amusing, but only because of the delivery (p. 88). When sitting for a bust by Pietro in 1915, Burroughs was kept still by friends reading to him from MT's Joan of Arc (pp. 221-22).

B6 BEERS, HENRY A. "Among the New Books," Yale Review, n.s. XV (Autumn), 162-65.
Includes a review of Mark Twain's Autobiography (1924): "The charm of the book is its informality."

B7 BIGELOW, POULTNEY. Seventy Summers. New York: Longmans, Green & Co.; London: Edward Arnold & Co., II, 156-165-68.
Describes MT in Johannesburg (1896), in poor health but courteous toward individuals who claimed to have known him in the West; but afterward: "I never thought there could be so many G--d d----d liars in any one town! They were not even intelligent liars-- they gave dates when I was not even in America and they named places that I never heard of before--the blank-blank damned liars!" (pp. 166-67). Also tells of MT in London (1899), tricked into attending a large dinner at the Goerz residence with the promise that it was to be a "family" party of four (p. 168).

1925 - Shorter Writings

B8   BIRON, CHARTRES. [Review: Mark Twain's Auto-
      biography (1924).] London Mercury, XI
      (January), 325-26.
          "A mere scrap-book of detached and inco-
      herent incidents"; "Yet to read the passages
      in this book about his wife and children is
      to realize how exquisitely he could write on
      occasion."

B9   *BRAGMAN, LOUIS J. "The Medical Wisdom of
      Mark Twain," Annals of Medical History, VII,
      425-39.
          [Source: Asselineau (1954), No. 382:
      "Made up of extracts from his works."]

B10   BRANDL, ALOIS. [Review: Friedrich Schöne-
      mann, Mark Twain als literarische Persön-
      lichkeit.] Die Literatur (Stuttgart),
      XXVII, No. 10, 627-28.
          Chiefly descriptive [In German].

B11   *[BROWNELL, GEORGE HIRAM (?)] "Sam Slick,
      The Connecticut Clockmaker, Original of
      Uncle Sam and Source of Inspiration for
      Dickens, Mark Twain and Other Humorists,"
      Dearborn Independent (The Ford Internation-
      al Weekly), XXV (October 10).
          [Source: Reprinted in Twainian, XVI
      (March-April, 1957), 3-4; (May-June), 4.]
      Contains very little on MT, except for argu-
      ing that CY and IA follow the example of
      Thomas Chandler Haliburton's "Sam Slick" in
      the Yankee's irreverent view of the glories
      of the old world. (Article somewhat vague-
      ly attributed to Brownell by Chester L.
      Davis in Twainian.

B12   CATHER, KATHERINE DUNLAP. "The Boy Who Went
      Back," in her The Younger Days of Famous
      Writers (New York and London: The Century
      Company), pp. 185-204.
          A children's account of MT's boyhood, pro-
      viding no new information.

B13   COLLINS, JOSEPH. "Litterateurs: American
      Writers," in his The Doctor Looks at Bio-
      graphy: Psychological Studies of Life and
      Letters (New York: George H. Doran Com-
      pany), pp. 63-97; pp. 73-79 on MT's Autobio-
      graphy.
          Appreciative; praises his warmth, humani-
      ty, and tenderness. "His was the antithesis
      of the Messianic complex. He had a simple
      heart, and an intricate soul."

B14   ELLINGER, JOH. [Review: Friedrich Schöne-
      mann, Mark Twain als literarische Persön-
      lichkeit.] Anglia Beiblatt, XXXVI
      (December), 372-74.
          Notes that Schönemann has revealed MT as
      better read and more influenced by his read-
      ing than generally realized; warmly recom-
      mends the book. [In German.]

B15   *FEDERICO, P. J. "Mark Twain as an Inventor,"
      Journal of the Patent Office Society, VIII,
      75-79.
          [Source: Asselineau (1954), No. 383.]

B16   GARBETT, A. S. "When Mark Twain Sang Spiritu-
      als," in his department, "The Musical Scrap-
      Book," Etude, XLII (December), 854.
          An excerpt from Mary Lawton's transcrip-
      tion of Katy Leary's recollections in Pic-
      torial Review (now more readily available in
      her A Lifetime with Mark Twain, 1925.B24),
      with only a very brief headnote.

B17   GESSFORD, J. G. [Photograph of Mark Twain.]
      Bookman (New York), LXI (March), facing
      p. 31.

B18   GILLIS, JAMES M. "Mark Twain," in his False
      Prophets (New York: The Macmillan Company),
      pp. 125-45.
          MT's early works are crude, and appeal,
      as Henry James says, to "rudimentary minds."
      His final despair is the product of life-long
      scoffing at sacred things: "If ever a man
      sowed what he reaped, it was Mark Twain."

B19   GOLDBERG, ISAAC. The Man Mencken: A Biograph-
      ical and Critical Survey. New York: Simon
      and Schuster, passim.
          The many references to MT in the index
      lead to statements of his influence on
      Mencken, who read HF at the age of seven,
      and comparisons of Mencken to MT.

B20   HARWOOD, H. C. "Mark Twain," Spectator,
      CXXXV (December 19), 1146, 1148.
          A review of the Florida Edition of The
      Works of Mark Twain. Ranks MT low as a hu-
      morist and satirist, who "only succeded in
      satirizing what he did not understand" and
      lacked the courage of a Voltaire or a Swift.
      "He need not, by the way, have been afraid
      of the effect on religion of his doubts; at
      his shrewdest, he would only have become the
      William Jennings Bryan of agnosticism. But
      it was not timidity that makes the mass of
      Mark Twain's work a desert of dullness. It
      was stupidity. He lacked any kind of philo-
      sophy." TS and HF, however, "deserve every
      one of the superlative praises lavished upon
      them. They are bright with the magic that
      only memories of boyhood can cast, and in-
      formed with the sympathies that could only
      be given by one who ever remained a child at
      heart as, alas! he did in mental develop-
      ment."

B21   HIGGINS, AILEEN CLEVELAND. "She Was Mark
      Twain's Sweetheart," Collier's, LXXV
      (June 27), 32.
          On Mrs. Laura Hawkins Frazer, in 1925 a
      cheerful, elderly lady; she had long been
      superintendent of Hannibal's "Home for the
      Friendless."

B22   HOPPE, WILLY. "Mark Twain, a Great Old Bil-
      liard Fan," in his Thirty Years of Billiards,
      (New York: G. P. Putnam's Sons), pp. 190-14.
          [Source: 1975 Dover Publications reprint.]
      MT attended Hoppe's 1906 match with George
      Butler Sutton; pressed to address the crowd,

(HOPPE, WILLY)
he told of losing a game to a Nevada shark who played him left-handed--and conceded afterward that he was a left-handed man. MT attended a number of championship matches.

B23 INGLIS, REWEY BELLE. "A Lesson on Mark Twain," English Journal, XIV (March), 221-32.
This lesson "was part of a three-months' course in American literature given to juniors in the University High School.... The students were not told that a stenographic record was being made, lest the spontaneity of the lesson be spoiled." Text of class discussion.

B24 LAWTON, MARY. [Excerpts from her A Lifetime with Mark Twain, as Told by Katy Leary to Mary Lawton.] Literary Digest, LXXXV (April 25: "A Maid's-Eye View of Mark Twain"), 36, 38, 40; LXXXVI (August 22: "Mark Twain's 'Glory Hallelujah!'"), 38, 40.
Reprinted from Pictorial Review, XXVI [(April-September, according to Asselineau (1954), No. 361.)]

B25 LUDEKE, HENRY. [Review: Van Wyck Brooks, The Ordeal of Mark Twain (1922) and Friedrich Schönemann, Mark Twain als Literarische Persönlichkeit (1925).] Deutsche Literaturzeitung für Kritik der internationalen Wissenschaft, XLVI:2 (12 September), 1802-1814.
Summarizes Brooks's thesis, but expresses some reservations; argues that Schönemann ought to have made more of MT's western backgrounds. [In German.]

B26 PAINE, ALBERT BIGELOW. "Innocents at Home: How Mark Twain Dictated His Life Story to Him in 'Cowboy' Billiard Games or Lying Comfortably in Bed, Told by His Biographer," Collier's, LXXV (January 3), 5-6, 45.
A popular account, with an amusing description of MT at the billiard table.

B27 _____. Joan of Arc: Maid of France. New York: The Macmillan Company, 2 vols., passim.
There are a few quotations from MT in the two volumes, and a tribute to his JA in the introduction, but nothing significant.

B28 * _____. "Who Wrote 1601?" Two Worlds, December.
[Source: Twainian, II (June, 1943), 6; describes this as an excerpt from his Biography, "also slightly-censored version of Twain's '1601.'"]

B29 RANDALL, A. W. G. [Review: Friedrich Schönemann, Mark Twain als Literärische Persönlicheit.] Saturday Review of Literature, II (September 5), 108.
"A very thorough, and yet very lively and challenging piece of criticism," which

should help correct the European misconception of MT as unliterary, a mere fun-maker.

B30 *SCHÖNEMANN, F. "Mark Twains Autobiographie," Hannoverscher Kurier, August 5; also in Magdeburger Zeitung, October 4.
[Source: Asselineau (1954), No. 387.]

B31 SINCLAIR, UPTON. "The Uncrowned King," in his Mammonart: An Essay in Economic Interpretation (Pasadena, California: Published by the Author), pp. 326-33.
"Mark Twain had in him the making of one of the world's great satirists.... But he was not allowed to express himself as an artist; he must emulate his father-in-law, the Elmira coal-dealer." Briefly describes a meeting with MT in Bermuda: "I saw that he was kind, warm-hearted, and also full of rebellion against capitalist greed and knavery; but he was an old man, and a sick man, and I did not try to probe the mystery of his life." Also passim on MT; indexed.

B32 TANDY, JENNETTE. Crackerbox Philosophers in American Humor and Satire. New York: Columbia University Press, passim.
A published doctoral dissertation, this also appears in a variant form without thesis note. The few brief references to MT are based on familiar sources and there is little critical discussion, but Miss Tandy anticipated later scholarship in her passing remark that "Mark Twain's indebtedness to Southwestern humor has never been fully acknowledged" (p. 94).

B33 VAN DOREN, CARL. "Mark Twain and Bernard Shaw," Century, CIX (n.s. LXXXVII; March), 705-10.
A comparison: Shaw is the more interested in pure ideas, MT in rounded characters; in their treatments of Joan of Arc Shaw portrays a clash of individual and institution, while for MT innocence ultimately loses to evil. Reprinted in Scott (1955), pp. 175-82.

B34 _____. "Two in One," Century, CIX (January), 429-30.
A review of Paine's two-volume edition of Mark Twain's Autobiography (1924) as "a work which with admirable flexibility fits itself to his strong, rich, casual nature."

B35 _____, and MARK VAN DOREN. American and British Literature since 1890. London and New York: The Century Company, p. 44.
Calls MT's last years "that fascinating chapter of his life which was to reveal him as a man of bitter thought as well as a humorist, a commentator upon the times in unstinted language, a kind of prophet who was to be listened to with more respect after his death than before it." Other references to MT in this school manual are minor.

1925 - Shorter Writings

B36 *WATKINS, LOUISE W. Four Short Stories and a
Play. Los Angeles, California: Privately
Printed.
[Source: Asselineau (1954), No. 371:
"Contains a short essay on Twain."]

B37 WATSON, AARON. A Newspaper Man's Memories.
London: Hutchinson & Co., pp. 281-83.
On MT's election to honorary membership
in the Savage Club in London, in 1899; although he had been making jokes about being
accused of stealing the Ascot Cup he apparently was not pleased at being presented
with a large replica. Says MT contributed
a chapter to Watson's book about the Savage
Club.

B38 WEBSTER, DORIS, and CHARLES WEBSTER. "Whitewashing Jane Clemens," Bookman (New York),
LXI (July), 531-35.
A portrait of MT's mother as a lively,
independent person with a good sense of
humor; she was not a Puritan (or any other
sort of Yankee), and certainly not the
blighting influence on her son that Van
Wyck Brooks and Harvey O'Higgins have depicted.

B39 WHITE, EDGAR. "Tom Sawyer and Huckleberry
Finn Memorial Statue. The Immortal Boys
Will Stand in Bronze in Mark Twain's Own
Home Town," Mentor, XIII (October), 54-55.

B40 WINTER, WILLIAM. The Life of David Belasco.
(As reissued, New York: Benjamin Blom,
Inc., 1972). 2 vols. I, 64-68, 365-67.
["Third Edition, First Published in New
York, 1925. Reissued 1972 by Benjamin
Blom, Inc. New York, N.Y."]
On the play of The Gilded Age, including
the text of a letter by John T. Raymond
(who played Colonel Sellers) to the New York
Sun, December 2, 1874, and a lengthy quotation from "W.W." in "The Wallet of Time," on
the contribution of Raymond to the success
of the play (pp. 64-68). On the dramatization of The Prince and the Pauper, suggested
by Elsie Leslie, who played both Tom Canty
and Prince Edward, and on Belasco's impatience with the cast (pp. 365-67). Margaret
Duckett lists a 1918 publication for this
book (New York: Moffett, Yard and Company)
in her Mark Twain and Bret Harte (Norman,
1964), p. 351.

B41 WOOLF, LEONARD. "Mark Twain," Nation & Athenaeum, XXXVI (September 26), 765.
A review of The Florida Edition of Mark
Twain (Chatto & Windus), with estimates of
TA ("first-rate journalism"), P&P (betrays
"a commonness and tawdriness, a lack of
sensitiveness, which do not matter to the
impetuous appetite of youth, but which cannot be ignored by the more discriminating
and exacting taste of middle-age"), and HF;
this, "in humour as in everything else, is
far the best thing Mark Twain wrote. Its
freshness, gusto, exuberant vitality are

astonishing," especially under the influence
of the river; there is a falling-off after
the King and Duke come aboard. Woolf feels
that MT's humor is losing its old charm,
and ranks it below that of "Mr. Dooley"
[Finley Peter Dunne].

1926 A BOOKS

A1 *CLEMENS, SAMUEL L. Rapporto della visita di
Capitan Tempesta in Paradiso, translated by
Laura Balini, preface by Conrado Alvaro.
Aquila: Vecchioni.
[Source: Asselineau (1954), No. 393.]

A2 _____, and BRET HARTE; ed. John Howell.
Sketches of the Sixties. Being Forgotten
Material Now Collected for the First Time
from "The Californian," 1864-67. San Francisco: John Howell.
Now superceded by the 1927 revised edition, (1927.A1).

A3 MAYFIELD, JOHN S. Mark Twain vs. The Street
Railway Co. Introduction by Charles Finger.
N.p.: Privately Printed.
A pamphlet containing two MT letters
(May 5, 13, 1906; reproduced in facsimile),
together with affidavits and correspondence
from the Metropolitan Street Railway Company involving MT's complaint that his
daughter Clara had been short-changed by a
conductor; he received a twenty-cent refund.

1926 B SHORTER WRITINGS

B1 ANON. "Sam Clemens in 'Sideburns' to 'Dear
Friend Annie,'" Literary Digest, LXXXIX
(May 8), 36, 38, 42, 44, 46.
On the discovery of five letters from MT
to Annie Elizabeth Taylor in May-June, 1857
when she was a girl of seventeen. Three of
these letters have since been lost; those of
May 25 and June 1 are printed here, together
with background material and photographs of
MT and Annie Elizabeth Taylor. [From Kansas
City Star Magazine, n.d.]

B2 BACHELLER, IRVING. Opinions of a Cheerful
Yankee. Indianapolis: The Bobbs-Merrill Co.
Recollections of visits to MT at his homes
in Hartford and on Fifth Avenue, and a luncheon with him "at a little Bohemian club organized by myself and Stephen Crane and Edward Marshall and Willis Hawkins, all editors or special writers on the metropolitan
press," pp. 6-11.

B3 *CESTRE, CHARLES, and B. GAGNOT. Anthologie de
la Littérature Américaine. Paris: Delagrave.
[Source: Asselineau (1954), No. 394.]

B4 CHILDS, MARQUIS W. "The Home of Mark Twain,"
American Mercury, IX (September), 101-105.
Describes Hannibal, Missouri of the later
day as ugly, commercial, and taken over by
the Rotary Club. Near Bird Street (with its

(CHILDS, MARQUIS W.)
three bordellos) is the Mark Twain Home.
"Within is a hodge-podge of relics of the
great man. Every citizen of Hannibal has
gone to his attic and brought forth a chair
on which Mark once sat, or a glass from
which he once drank. The front room, into
which one steps directly from the street,
has about it an air of mouldering decay,
filled as it is with a conglomerate array
of junk. Albert Bigelow Paine has contributed many of the pieces."

B5 DONOVAN, M. M. "Custodian of a Famous Cabin,"
Sunset: The Pacific Monthly, LVII
(September), 47.
Photograph of "William R. Gillis, Custo-
dian of the Mark Twain Cabin on Jackass
Hill," with reminiscences.

B6 FISCHER, WALTHER. [Review: Friedrich
Schönemann, Mark Twain als literarische
Persönlichkeit (1925).] Englische Studien,
LXI (December), 135-39.
This review is itself a thoughtful investigation of MT's thinking, taking into account a number of his published works; notes
the romantic element in MT, and suggests
that his pessimism was personal rather than
a result of literary influences.

B7 GARNETT, DAVID. "Mark Twain: 1835-1910,"
in Walter James Turner, ed., Great Names;
Being an Anthology of English and American
Literature from Chaucer to Francis Thompson
(New York: The Dial Press), pp. 261-62.
A brief introduction to selections from
IA and RI; follows the interpretation of MT
by Van Wyck Brooks.

B8 GOURMONT, RÉMY DE. "Études de Littérature
Américaine: II.--L'Humour et les Humoristes," Promenades Littéraires, 6e Serie,
pp. 87-138.
Notes MT's rare power of observation and
gift for language, and his understanding of
Negro speech and psychology. He could have
been an Aristophanes, but with the encouragement of the public he chose to play the
buffoon.

B9 GRIMES, ABSALOM. "Campaigning with Mark
Twain," in his Confederate Mail Runner,
Edited from Captain Grimes' Own Story by
M. M. Quaife. (New Haven: Yale University
Press; London: Humphrey Milford, Oxford
University Press), pp. 1-19.
Grimes claims to have been associated
with MT as a pilot and in the Confederate
irregular unit described by MT in "The
Private History of a Campaign that Failed."
Quaife's introduction describes the book,
written in 1910-1911, as "an old-age narra-
tion," with many possibilities for error
(p. xi). Asselineau (1954), No. 724 also
lists a 1926 edition of this book.

B10 *HALDEMAN-JULIUS, EMANUEL. Iconoclastic Liter-
ary Reactions. Kansas City, Kansas: Big
Blue Book, No. B-16.
[Source: Asselineau (1954), No. 399:
"Contains three articles on Mark Twain."]

B11 HOUSE, EDWARD M. The Intimate Papers of Colonel House, Arranged as a Narrative by
Charles Seymour. Boston and New York:
Houghton Mifflin Company, I, 21.
Paine took Captain Bill McDonald of the
Texas Rangers to dinner at MT's home on
Fifth Avenue; House came later, to see
McDonald shooting billiards awkwardly,
sighting his cue "just as if it were a
rifle.... It entertained Mr. Clemens immensely. When we went upstairs Clemens ran
and Bill ran after, as if to catch him, but
did not do so."

B12 HULBERT, MARY ALLEN. "Other Celebrities,"
Liberty, II (March 6), 12-14.
On pp. 13-14, recollections of MT and
Henry Rogers in Bermuda. MT's secretary,
Miss Lyon, always referred to MT as "The
King"--a sobriquet Mrs. Hulbert took to be
a reference to the disreputable character
in HF. On p. 12, photograph: "Mrs. Hulbert, at extreme left, and party of her
guests, with Mark Twain and H. H. Rogers in
the foreground."

B13 *JANTZEN, H. [Review: Friedrich Schönemann,
Mark Twain als literarische Persönlichkeit
(1925).] Zeitschrift für französischen und
englischen Unterricht, XXV, 368-69.
[Source: Asselineau (1954), No. 406.]

B14 JONES, HOWARD MUMFORD. [Review: Friedrich
Schönemann, Mark Twain als literarische
Persönlichkeit (1925).] Journal of English
and Germanic Philology, XXV (January),
130-31.
"The sole defects of the monograph" are
a European's occasional "misreadings of
Twain and the United States" and "a tendency
to mistake parallelism for indebtedness, or
at least to leave this impression with the
reader." With only these reservations, "no
summary or extract can do justice to the
brilliance and breadth of this monograph....
All future interpretations are bound to be
influenced by these essays."

B15 LAW, FREDERICK HOUK. "Samuel Langhorne Clemens (Mark Twain): Humorist," in his Modern
Great Americans: Short Biographies of Twenty Great Americans of Modern Times Who Won
Wide Recognition for Achievements in Various
Types of Activity (Students' Edition). (New
York, London: The Century Company),
pp. 77-91.
Provides no new information and is marred
by factual errors: states that the Clemens
house in Hannibal was made of brick, that
"mark twain" means "up to the mark of two
feet," that he briefly owned the Comstock
Lode, prospected for gold with Bret Harte,

1926 - Shorter Writings

(LAW, FREDERICK HOUK)
and made a profit of $100,000 from his
patented scrap-book.

B16 MUMFORD, LEWIS. The Golden Day: A Study in
American Experience and Culture. New York:
Boni and Liveright Publishers. Reprinted
by W. W. Norton & Company in 1934; in paperback, Boston: Beacon Press, 1957 (with different pagination).
    Chapter IV, "The Pragmatic Acquiescence,"
treats MT on pp. 170-79. MT felt contempt
for mankind as a result of the cheapening of
values in the miserable struggle for existence in Missouri and Nevada, took the com-
forts of his century and the society that
produced them too much to heart, and "did
not see that his Yankee mechanic was as absurd as Arthur himself." "In a different
fashion from Howells, Mark Twain was afraid
of his imagination," and turned to burlesque
his impulses toward poetry or beauty. His
despair was the result of accepting the values around him although he realized that
they were not central human values. Reprinted in Scott (1955), pp. 183-87; excerpt in
Leary (1962), pp. 81-82.

B17 ORCUTT, WILLIAM DANA. "Friends through the
Pen," in his In Quest of the Perfect Book
(Boston: Little, Brown & Co.), pp. 171-77.
    On a visit to MT at the Villa di Quarto
(Florence) three days before the death of
Olivia Clemens, and on MT moved to tears at
his seventieth birthday dinner in New York.

B18 PHELPS, WILLIAM LYON. As I Like It, Third
Series. New York, London: Charles Scribner's Sons.
    "This book contains selections from the
articles of the same name printed in Scribner's Magazine from September, 1924 to
January, 1926, inclusive." Indexed by
Dr. Frederick Pottle, passim on MT.

B19 *SHERWOOD, ROBERT EDMUND. "Regarding Tom Sawyer and Others," in his Here We Are Again:
Recollections of an Old Circus Clown (Indianapolis: The Bobbs-Merrill Co.),
pp. 213-18.
    [Source: Asselineau (1954), No. 403.]

1927 A BOOKS

A1 CLEMENS, SAMUEL L., and BRET HARTE, edited by
John Howell. Sketches of the Sixties, by
Bret Harte and Mark Twain. Being Forgotten
Material Collected for the First Time from
"The Californian," 1864-1867. San Francisco: John Howell.
    A revision of the 1926 edition (1926.A2).
The introduction by Howell gives background
of San Francisco in the 1860's, and of The
Californian and MT's and Harte's association
with it. There is also a list of all their
articles in The Californian, with dates of
publication. This 1927 revision includes
material not in the 1926 edition.

1927 B SHORTER WRITINGS

B1 BENNETT, JAMES O'DONNELL. Much Loved Books:
Best Sellers of Yesterday. New York: Liveright Publishing Company, pp. 210-22, 459.
    Chapter XXX, "Mark Twain's 'Adventures of
Huckleberry Finn,'" consists of quotations
from the book and appreciative words by Bennett (pp. 210-16). Chapter XXXI, "How Huckleberry Finn Was Written" includes information from the Paine biography and quotes
familiar praise of the book by several critics. Provides no new information or original
judgment (pp. 217-22). There is a brief
bibliography of secondary material on p. 459;
most of it is well known and all is included
in the present bibliography. The material on
HF was reprinted in Bennett's paperback Much
Loved Books (Greenwich, Connecticut: Faw-
cett Publications, Inc., 1959), pp. 128-40.

B2 BUSBEY, L. WHITE. "A Distinguished Lobbyist,"
in his Uncle Joe Cannon: The Story of a
Pioneer American as told to L. White Busbey,
for 20 years his private secretary (New York:
Henry Holt and Company), pp. 270-81.
    On pp. 270-75, describes MT's efforts in
behalf of stronger copyright legislation.

B3 BUXBAUM, KATHERINE. "Mark Twain and American
Dialect," American Speech, II (February),
233-36.
    In HF "The inconsistencies of Huck's
speech can hardly be attributed to anything
but carelessness," although it may have its
counterpart in the alternation between correct and incorrect usage by actual persons.
Nonetheless, MT's "admirable use of phonetic
spelling" is superior to that of Lowell and
others, and even his inconsistency adds to
the book's unstudied charm.

B4 ERSKINE, JOHN. "The First and Best Story of
Main Street: John Erskine Tells Why Huckleberry Finn has won a place among the Immor-
tals," Delineator, CX (February), 10, 94,
97.
    TS is "built up with anecdotes, each one
complete in itself, and none developed beyond the point of the joke"; in MT's better-
constructed book, Huck "tells us far more
than he knows; through his naive confessions
we see the panorama of his world and become
sophisticated. We are really studying ourselves." Reprinted in Erskine's The Delight
of Great Books (1928), pp. 263-74; also reprinted in Lettis (1962), pp. 297-304.

B5 ESPENSHADE, A. H. "Tom Sawyer's Fiftieth
Birthday: A Brief Sketch of Mark Twain's
Life," St. Nicholas, LIV (August), 808-809.
    Biography for young readers, containing no
unusual information.

B6 GRIMES, ABSALOM. "Campaigning with Mark Twain
Twain," Missouri Historical Review, XXI
(January), 188-201.

(GRIMES, ABSALOM)
   An excerpt from his Absalom Grimes, Confederate Mail Runner (1926), describing Civil War service with MT.

B7   *HARBECK, HANS. "Amerikanische Humor," Der
     Kreis: Zeitschrift für künstliche Kultur,
     IV, 276-84.
        [Source: Asselineau (1954), No. 427.]

B8   HAZARD, LUCY LOCKWOOD. "Mark Twain: 'Wild
     West Humorist of the Pacific Slope,'"
     "The Psychic Frontier," and "Mark Twain:
     Son and Satirist of the Gilded Age," in her
     The Frontier in American Literature (New
     York: Thomas Y. Crowell Company),
     pp. 198-200, 200-201, 220-30.
        "If the frontier of Bret Harte is melo-
     drama, the frontier of Mark Twain is farce"
     (p. 198). Criticizes Brooks for lacking
     humor (p. 201), and notes the freedom from
     convention on the frontier (p. 201). On
     MT's "compassion for failure," and therefore
     less worship of success than Brooks suggests
     (pp. 222-23); notes MT's affection for Colo-
     nel Sellers and contempt for Senator Dil-
     worthy (p. 227).

B9   *LESSING, O. E. Brücken über den Atlantik--
     Beiträge zum amerikanischen und deutschen
     Geistesleben. Stuttgart: Deutsche Verlags-
     Anstalt.
        [Source: Asselineau (1954), No. 419.]

B10 MEYER, HAROLD. "Mark Twain on the Comstock,"
     Southwest Review, XII (April), 197-207.
        A general account of MT in Nevada, adding
     nothing significant to Paine's 1912 biogra-
     phy. Not documented.

B11 NEVINS, ALLAN. The Emergence of Modern Ameri-
     ca, 1865-1878. Vol. VIII in A History of
     American Life, ed. Arthur M. Schlesinger
     and Dixon Ryan Fox (New York: The Macmil-
     lan Company), pp. 247-51 and passim.
        Nevins is interested in MT's "rapid con-
     quest of a half-reluctant national public
     and his success in presenting the remote
     frontier as well as the Mississippi Valley
     to the reading world" (p. 249), but his ac-
     count is essentially a repetition of materi-
     al from Paine and Howells and elsewhere his
     treatment is chiefly one of using MT's works
     to illustrate his own discussion of the
     age. There is no new information on MT and
     very little interpretation.

B12 QUINN, ARTHUR HOBSON. A History of the Amer-
     ican Drama from the Civil War to the Present
     Day. New York and London: Harper & Broth-
     ers Publishers, 2 vols., passim.
        On Ah Sin and the plays from The Gilded
     Age and The American Claimant, I, 110-16,
     with place and date of first performances,
     II, 299, 304, 332; also, brief note of
     other attempts at the drama by MT, and dra-
     matizations of his works by others, I,
     110-16. Briefly describes Augustin Daly's

Roughing It play, not a dramatization of the
novel, but burlesquing the West of MT and
Bret Harte in Act III (I, 20). Quotes a
long paragraph from MT's curtain speech at
the first night in New York of Ah Sin (I,
111-12).

B13 SADLEIR, MICHAEL. Trollope: A Commentary.
     London: Constable & Co., Ltd.
        On p. 285, quotes a Trollope letter of
     July, 1873: he will dine with MT and Joa-
     quin Miller the following week, at his
     club.

B14 SHERMAN, STUART. "Mark Twain's Last Phase,"
     in his The Main Stream (New York, London:
     Charles Scribner's Sons), pp. 80-88.
        A review of Mark Twain's Autobiography,
     originally in "Books," the literary supple-
     ment of the New York Herald Tribune, 1924
     or 1925 (p. ix). Bad autobiography, but an
     "interesting hodgepodge.... As far as I can
     make out, he grew in sympathy, insight, bit-
     terness, courage and passion to the end. At
     seventy he was a clear-eyed youth, pushing
     steadily forward toward a fresh conception
     of reality." MT had broken many of his
     chains, and is still "dangerous--like all
     free spirits."

B15 SPEAKMAN, HAROLD. "Becky and Ignition," in
     his Mostly Mississippi (New York: Dodd,
     Mead and Company), pp. 173-90.
        Describes a visit to Hannibal, where one
     local citizen told him MT had been a poor
     steamboat pilot. Speakman visited Laura
     Hawkins Frazer (sketch of her, p. 178); she
     told him she and MT had never been lost in
     a cave, as described in TS.

B16 WOOD, CHARLES ERSKINE SCOTT. Heavenly Dis-
     course. New York: The Vanguard Press,
     passim.
        A series of satiric conversations in the
     next world, originally written for the
     Masses; only a few appeared before the de-
     mise of that journal. The cast includes
     God, Jesus, St. Peter, Socrates, Buddha,
     Socrates, and others, and MT participates
     in a number of conversations on such topics
     as "Freedom," "Censorship," "God on Cathol-
     icism and the K.K.K.," "God Advises Peter
     as to the Church," and "Satan Recovers His
     Reason."

1928 A BOOKS

A1   CLEMENS, SAMUEL L. The Adventures of Thomas
     Jefferson Snodgrass. Edited by Charles
     Honce, with a Foreword by Vincent Starrett,
     and a Note on "A Celebrated Village Idiot"
     by James O'Donnell Bennett. Chicago: Pascal
     Covici, Publisher, Inc.
        Three travel letters in the Keokuk (Iowa)
     Post, November 1, 29, 1856; April 10, 1857.
     Bennett's "A Celebrated Village Idiot" is an
     anecdotal account of Orion Clemens, reprinted
     from the Chicago Tribune (n.d.)

1928 - Books

A2   *CLEMENS, SAMUEL L.   Selections, with notes by
      Vincenzo Grasso.   Palermo: R. Gino.
         [Source: Asselineau (1954), No. 431.]

1928 B SHORTER WRITINGS

B1   ANON. "Mark Twain's Masonic Record," Grand
      Lodge Bulletin, Grand Lodge of Iowa, A. F.
      & A. M., XXIX (May), 575-76.
         Describes a painting of MT at age 21,
      "presented by Mrs. Orion Clemens some years
      ago," and "now on display at the Iowa State
      Insurance Company's office at Keokuk, Iowa."
      [Reproduced on front cover, p. 561.] "Bro.
      Ray V. Denslow, Grand Secretary, Grand
      Council R. & S. M. of Missouri, gave an ac-
      count of Mark Twain's Masonic record in
      Scottish Rite Progress a few years ago,
      from which the following extract is taken."
      The lengthy extract tells of MT's election
      to Polar Star Lodge No. 79; he received his
      third degree in Masonry on July 10 [1861],
      but was out of touch with his lodge when he
      went to Nevada and "he allowed himself to
      be temporarily suspended. He was reinstated
      in April, 1867" before traveling on the
      Quaker City to Europe and the Holy Land,
      and while in the Holy Land he cut wood from
      a cedar in the Forest of Lebanon and had it
      made into a gavel for Polar Star Lodge No.
      79. After his marriage he appears to have
      ceased affiliation, although he and friends
      played billiards at the old Masonic Club in
      Elmira, New York. [Source: photocopy pro-
      vided by courtesy of Charles T. Jackson,
      Grand Secretary, Grand Lodge of Iowa, Iowa
      Masonic Library, Cedar Rapids.]

B2   *BARTON, SIR DUNBAR PLUNKET.   Links Between
      Shakespeare and the Law.   London: Faber &
      Gwyer Ltd.
         [Source: Asselineau (1954), No. 432;
      notes comments on MT's Is Shakespeare Dead?]

B3   BECK, WARREN. "Huckleberry Finn versus The
      Cash Boy," Education, XLIX (September),
      1-13.
         Compares HF to the turgid, shallow boy
      stories of Horatio Alger, Jr.: Huck is
      notable for his warmth, integrity, and wis-
      dom, and he could grow with a college edu-
      cation as the Alger hero could not.

B4   BIKLE, LUCY LEFFINGWELL (CABLE). "Readings
      with Mark Twain: Dr. Sevier (1884)," and
      "More Readings with Mark Twain: Home in
      Northampton (1885-1887)," in her George W.
      Cable: His Life and Letters (New York:
      Charles Scribner's Sons), pp. 114-36,
      137-53.
         Includes letters describing their joint
      lecture tours, and on visits to the Clemens
      home, with descriptions of the family.
      [Also, reissued New York: Russell & Rus-
      sell, 1967, with same pagination.]

B5   CHAPMAN, HELEN POST.   My Hartford of the Nine-
      teenth Century.   Hartford: Edwin Valentine
      Mitchell.
         Mentions Joseph Twichell teaching MT to
      ride a bicycle (p. 43), and MT presenting
      Tiffany pins to the Saturday Morning Club
      (p. 61).

B6   *COWPER, FREDERICK A. G. "The Hermit Story, as
      Used by Voltaire and Mark Twain," in Papers,
      Essays, and Stories by His Former Students,
      in Honor of the Ninetieth Birthday of Charles
      Frederick Johnson, ed. Odell Shepard and
      Arthur Adams (Hartford, Connecticut: Trini-
      ty College), pp. 313-37.
         [Source: MHRA Annual Bibliography (1929),
      No. 172; Asselineau (1954), No. 433; William
      M. Gibson, ed., Mark Twain's Mysterious
      Stranger Manuscripts (1969), p. 2.] Sug-
      gests that sources for MS may include Chap-
      ter XX ("L'hermite") of Voltaire's Zadig,
      and Goethe's Faust.

B7   CRAVEN, THOMAS. "A Cure for Critics: Paint-
      ing Defended from Both the Cynical and the
      Rapturous," Bookman (New York), LXVIII
      (October), 163-64.
         In IA MT ought to have attacked the pro-
      fessional critics, rather than the old mas-
      ters, about which both he and the critics
      knew "precisely nothing."

B8   ERSKINE, JOHN. "Huckleberry Finn," in his
      The Delight of Great Books. Indianapolis:
      The Bobbs-Merrill Company, pp. 263-74.
         A reprint of his 1927 article in Delinea-
      tor (1927.B4).

B9   FRENCH, MRS. DANIEL CHESTER. [Anecdotes.]
      Memories of a Sculptor's Wife (Boston and
      New York: Houghton Mifflin Company),
      pp. 159-61.
         Describes MT at the Richard Watson Gilders'
      in New York and repeats two stories he told
      on himself: of being introduced to a poet
      and telling her how funny her poems were
      (only to discover she was not the poet he
      had thought), and of sitting across the
      aisle on the elevated train from a man who
      stared, and finally told him he looked just
      like Mark Twain.

B10   HOPE, ANTHONY. Memories and Notes. London:
      Hutchinson & Co., pp. 172-73.
         [Also listed in Asselineau (1954), No.
      435 as Garden City: Doubleday, Doran &
      Co.] Describes a heated debate between MT
      and Lord Kelvin over whether any nation has
      the right to deny others freedom to travel
      or trade in its territory. Hope considers
      MT's slow, drawling speech a disadvantage.
      "At his best he is a great writer, but his
      worst is terribly far below his best"; it
      is a failing in humorists, as also in
      Sterne.

B11 HOWELLS, WILLIAM DEAN. *Life in Letters of William Dean Howells*. Ed. by Mildred Howells. New York: Doubleday, Doran & Company. 2 vols. passim.
The MT-Howells correspondence is now available in a well-edited two-volume edition (1960), but there is still much of interest in what Howells wrote about MT to others, as in his letter to Charles Eliot Norton about "that hideous mistake of poor Clemens's" in his disastrous speech at the Whittier dinner (letter of December 19, 1877, I, 243).

B12 *JAN, EDUARD VON. "Das literarische Bild der Jeanne d'Arc," *Beihefte zur Zeitschrift für Romanische Philologie*, Heft 76.
On MT's *JA*, pp. 139-43. [Source: Asselineau (1954), No. 441; MHRA *Annual Bibliography* (1928), No. 646.]

B13 *MICHAUD, RÉGIS. *Panorama de la Littérature Contemporaine*. Paris: Kra.
[Source: Asselineau (1954), No. 437: "On Mark Twain, pp. 78-79, 99-102."]

B14 PAINE, ALBERT BIGELOW. "*The Prince and the Pauper*. How Mark Twain Came to Write the Story in Which He Himself Took Such Keen Delight," *Mentor*, XVI (December), 8-10.
The inspiration came from *The Prince and the Page*, by Charlotte M. Yonge.

B15 PATTEE, FRED LEWIS. "On the Rating of Mark Twain," *American Mercury*, XIV (June), 183-91.
"Mark Twain must be rated as a thwarted creator like Melville, one ham-strung by his times and his temperament." He produced "glorious fragments," not "rounded masterpieces," but "he will endure long."

B16 ROSENBERGER, EDWARD G. "An Agnostic Hagiographer," *Catholic World*, CXXVII (September), 717-23.
MT's usual literary crudity and hostility toward conventional religious belief make the "reverential enthusiasm" of his *JA* a welcome surprise. "The depth of Joan's sanctity as described by this blustering agnostic is a most tender and beautiful thing," and one may hope and predict that *JA* will outlast *TS*, *HF*, and the rest of *MT*'s works.

B17 YORK, ALVIN C. "The Diary of Sergeant York, Part One," *Liberty*, V (July 14), 7-10.
Says his great-grandfather hunted with MT's father, "and his famous Tennesse Land Grant is where I live."

1929 A BOOKS

A1 *CLEMENS, CYRIL. *A Letter of Mark Twain to His Publishers, Chatto & Windus of London*, calling their attention to certain indiscretions of the proof-readers of Messrs.

Spottiswoode & Co., printed for the first time from the letter in the collection of James Hart, with an introduction by Cyril Clemens and a portrait by Valenti Angelo. San Francisco: The Penguin Press. [4-page pamphlet.]
[Source: Asselineau (1954), No. 448.]

A2 ____, ed. *Mark Twain Anecdotes: Tributes to Mark Twain by G. K. Chesterton & John Galsworthy, Members of the Society*. Webster Groves, Missouri: Mark Twain Society.
Contains two very brief "Tributes to Mark Twain" by Galsworthy and Chesterton, followed by a number of miscellaneous jokes "submitted in the Second Annual Contest of the Mark Twain Society."

A3 PAINE, ALBERT BIGELOW. *The Boy's Life of Mark Twain*. Ed. Walter Barnes. New York and London: Harper & Brothers Publishers. Harper's Modern Classics.
Walter Barnes has added a very brief "Preface" and a two-page "To the Student" at the beginning, and an outline, questions, a biography of Paine, and "To the Teacher" at the end; his suggestion is that as far as possible the book should stand on its own merits [sensible advice, since Paine's is at least as good as most biographies for younger readers that have appeared since--T.A.T.].

1929 B SHORTER WRITINGS

B1 ANON. "Albert Bigelow Paine's Biography of Mark Twain," *Overland Monthly*, LXXXVII (June), 190.
A review of the revised edition: laudatory and descriptive, with no mention of any specific revisions.

B2 ANON. "In School with *Becky Thatcher* and *Tom Sawyer*," *Literary Digest*, C (March 9), 60-64.
On the occasion of the death of Laura Frazer, the original Becky; summarizes and excerpts an interview of some years earlier from the Kansas City *Star*, a portion of *Tom Sawyer* dealing with Tom and Becky, and stories from the New York *Herald Tribune* and New York *World*.

B3 *ANON. "Tom Sawyer and Huckleberry Finn: Erronotts," *World Review*, VIII (May 6), 201-203.
[Source: Asselineau (1954), No. 478.]

B4 BAY, J. CHRISTIAN. "*Tom Sawyer, Detective*: The Origin of the Plot," in William Warner Bishop and Andrew Keogh, eds., *Essays Offered to Herbert Putnam by His Colleagues and Friends on his Thirtieth Anniversary as Librarian of Congress, 5 April 1929* (New Haven: Yale University Press), pp. 80-88.
MT's source was *The Minister of Veilby* (1829) by the Danish poet, Steen Steensen Blicher, and based on events of 1607-26 involving the execution of a man whose alleged

(BAY, J. CHRISTIAN)
"victim" had disappeared. Bay traces the steps by which MT could have become familiar with the account and notes that he had been periodically accused in Denmark of carelessness with his sources. MT's footnote in the original Harper's Magazine publication in 1896 gave his source as "an old-time Swedish criminal trial" (pp. 85-86).

B5   BRASHEAR, MINNIE M. "An Early Mark Twain Letter," Modern Language Notes, XLIV (April), 256-59.
Reprints from the Hannibal Daily Journal of September 10, 1853 a letter dated "New York, Aug. 31, 1853"; about his job as a printer in New York, and impressions of the city.

B6   [BRIGGS, JOHN ELY.] "Comment by the Editor," Palimpsest, X (October), 387-88.
On the General Directory of the Citizens of Keokuk, Iowa, compiled and published by Orion Clemens in 1856, followed by a Business Mirror in 1857.

B7   CLEMENS, CYRIL. "Becky Thatcher--Personal Reminiscences," Overland Monthly, LXXXVII (May), 142, 157.
On a visit to Hannibal and meeting with Laura Frazer, the original of Becky Thatcher; she said some incidents involving her in TS and in the Paine biography represented literary license.

B8   _____. "Map, drawn by Cyril Clemens, President Mark Twain Society, showing places associated with Mark Twain's first sojourn in the West," Overland Monthly, LXXXVII (April), 100.

B9   _____. "Mark Twain: 1835-1910," Overland Monthly, LXXXVII (April), 103-104.
A popular biographical account, appropriate to this special MT issue of the Overland Monthly but containing no new material.

B10   _____. The True Character of Mark Twain's Wife," Missouri Historical Review, XXIV (October), 40-49.
Beginning with the story of MT's "exaggerated" death and an excerpt from Mary Lawton's A Lifetime with Mark Twain, prints the texts of several letters from MT and Olivia Clemens to Cyril Clemens' parents in order to demonstrate "the happy family life of the Clemenses," and thereby show that Olivia Clemens had better sense than Van Wyck Brooks attributed to her.

B11   _____. "A Visit to Mark Twain's Country," Overland Monthly, LXXXVII (April), 116-117, 127; (May), 145-146, 158.
Describes Angel's Camp and Jackass Hill, local sights, a jumping-frog contest, etc. Two illustrations: "William Gillis in front of Mark Twain Cabin on Jackass Hill" (p. 116), and "Cyril Clemens, President Mark Twain Society" (p. 117).

B12   CLEMENS, J. R. [DR. JAMES ROSS CLEMENS.] "Some Recollections of Mark Twain," Overland Monthly, LXXXVII (April), 105, 125.
Anecdotes, including one about MT with Thomas Hardy, and a story by MT about experimenting with ants and little paper churches (they went to the one with honey in it). Makes the claim (justified) that "I was the innocent cause of Mr. Clemens' famous cablegram: 'The report of my death is greatly exaggerated.'"

B13   CLEMENS, SAMUEL L. "Some Unpublished Letters by Mark Twain," Overland Monthly, LXXXVII (April), 115, 122, 124.
"The following heretofore unpublished letters were written to Dr. and Mrs. James Ross Clemens, parents of Cyril Clemens through whose courtesy they are here printed for the first time." Fourteen postcards and letters, 1897-1910, chiefly on matters personal but not intimate.

B14   DEVOTO, BERNARD. "Brave Days in Washoe," American Mercury, XVII (June), 228-37.
Chiefly about Virginia City in its heyday; about MT pp. 236-37.

B15   ESKEW, GARNETT LAIDLAW. "Steamboats Come Back Despite Mark Twain," in his The Pageant of the Packets: A Book of American Steamboating (New York: Henry Holt and Company), pp. 161-74.
Only passing mention of MT, providing no new information or interpretation.

B16   "Excerpts of Letters written by Thomas A. Edison and G. Bernard Shaw, to be used in Cyril Clemens' forthcoming Biography of Mark Twain," Overland Monthly, LXXXVII (April), 102.
Edison tells of a visit by MT to his laboratory, where he was recorded telling several stories; the recordings were lost in a fire several years later. Shaw describes MT's "complete gift of intimacy which enabled us to treat one another as if we had known one another all our lives, as indeed I had known him through his early books, which I had known and reveled in before I was twelve years old."

B17   FEE, HARRY T. "Jackass Hill," Overland Monthly, LXXXVII (May), 146.
A poem about his thoughts on visiting a place made famous by MT and Bret Harte.

B18   GAITHER, RICE. "Steamboatin' Days on Our Rivers," New York Times Magazine (November 10), pp. 4-5, 20.
Almost entirely devoted to steamboats of the past and present, with only passing mention of MT (listed in several standard bibliographies).

B19   GORDON, GILBERT. "To Mark Twain's Shrine," Sunset Magazine: The Pacific Monthly, LXII (June), 16-17.

(GORDON, GILBERT)
On MT in Nevada and California, with brief description of a projected shrine, which "is not as yet completed. It will be located in Angel's Camp, Calaveras County." Photograph: "Twain's old shack at Virginia City, now preserved at Reno."

B20 HAWTHORNE, JULIAN. "Mark Twain As I Knew Him," Overland Monthly, LXXXVII (April), 111, 128.
Adding little information to what appears in MT's published works, expresses personal admiration. "He would never have been widely known but for his humor, and yet it was his humor that made him stop short of greatness. One felt in contact with him a largeness of nature which he failed to put into literary form. There was a 'kink' in his grain that gave him fortune, but denied him immortality.... His popularity kept him in a groove which, otherwise, he might have escaped from." Ends with credit-line: "(Courtesy of the Pasadena Star-News)."

B21 JAMES, OLIVER CLEMENS (FLORENCE CLEMENS). "The Everlasting Author," Overland Monthly, LXXXVII (April), 106.
Praises MT for his humor, tenderness, strength, and general sanity.

B22 JUDD, IDA BENFEY. "The Mark Twain Association," Overland Monthly, LXXXVII (April), 126, 128.
On the formation of the Association, which conducts a "yearly Prize Contest for the ten best quotations from Mark Twain's books"; William Lyon Phelps of Yale is chairman of the judges. Plans are being made for "the establishment of a Mark Twain Professorship of Humor and the Comic Spirit at one of our universities in 1935, which will be the hundredth anniversary of his birth."

B23 KELLER, HELEN. "Mark Twain, as Revealed by Himself to Helen Keller," American Magazine, CVIII (July), 50-51, 80, 82.
An excerpt from her Midstream: My Later Life (1929.B24). Photograph of MT.

B24 _____. "Our Mark Twain," in her Midstream: My Later Life. Garden City, N.Y.: Doubleday, Doran & Company, Inc., pp. 47-69 and passim.
A sensitive account of their meetings at Stormfield and elsewhere. Quotes MT on his loneliness after the death of Olivia (pp. 50-51). Also, tells of MT speaking at Princeton on the Phillipine situation, the killing of six hundred Moros, and Funston's capture of Aguinaldo by a stratagem. Woodrow Wilson, who was present, looked out the window during the talk and afterward commented to the effect that "much heroism does not always keep military men from committing follies" (pp. 48-49, 103-104). Helen Keller

concedes the difficulty of quoting MT exactly, but says she made notes after their conversations (p. 68).

B25 KENNEDY, KATHERINE. "Mark Twain," Overland Monthly, LXXXVII (April), 111.
A short poem about the success of the "Man of Mark."

B26 *LEISY, ERNEST ERWIN. American Literature: An Interpretive Survey. New York: Thomas Y. Crowell.
[Source: Asselineau (1954), No. 454: "pp. 170-179 on Mark Twain--very superficial."]

B27 LORCH, FRED W. "Adrift for Heresy," Palimpsest, X (October), 372-80.
On the expulsion of Orion Clemens from the local Presbyterian Church for heretical views expressed in a public lecture and reiterated in an examination before the minister and several members of the congregation; includes text of a letter from Orion to his mother (August 10, 1876) on his religious views (pp. 373-76) and a photograph: "Orion and Molly Clemens at Home" (facing p. 378).

B28 _____. "The Closing Years," Palimpsest, X (October), 381-86.
On the passing of Orion Clemens, and the affection in which he was held by his neighbors; includes a poem, "The Keokuk Pilgrim," probably by Orion Clemens.

B29 _____. "Lecture Trips and Visits of Mark Twain in Iowa," Iowa Journal of History and Politics, XXVII (October), 507-47.
On lecture trips in the 1860's and 1880's, his 1882 trip to gather material for LOM, and his last visit, in 1890, shortly before his mother's death. Includes MT's letter to his sister-in-law, Molly, on his brother Orion's death, and says that most of the correspondence to Orion and Molly was burned by the administrator after Molly's death in 1904.

B30 _____. "Literary Apprenticeship," Palimpsest, X (October), 364-71.
On the efforts by Orion Clemens as an author, and the gossip suggesting that he helped MT write some of his books.

B31 _____. "Mark Twain in Iowa," Iowa Journal of History and Politics, XXVII (July), 408-56.
On MT at Muscatine and Keokuk in the 1850's, with correspondence to his brother Orion's paper from Philadelphia and elsewhere, " "Thomas Jefferson Snodgrass" correspondence to the Keokuk Post, and a letter to his mother from Nevada, published in the Keokuk Gate City.

B32 _____. "Molly Clemens's Note Book," Palimpsest, X (October), 357-63.
Family history, including the death of MT's brother Henry, and the 1861 move to Nevada.

(LORCH, FRED W.)

"It is unfortunate that the note book consists so largely of mere chronology." Photograph of Orion Clemens (facing p. 362).

B33 _____. "The Tradition," Palimpsest, X (October), 353-56.

On the lasting popularity of MT's brother Orion, who was "witty, absent-minded, and often humorously inconsistent," but not ridiculous.

B34 McKAY, DONALD. "On the Vanishing Trail of Tom Sawyer," New York Times Magazine, (October 27), pp. 8-9.

Describes Hannibal, Missouri, as McKay saw it on a visit while he was working on illustrations for a new edition of TS.

B35 McWILLIAMS, CAREY. Ambrose Bierce: A Biography. New York: Albert & Charles Boni, pp. 87-88, 99-100.

Bierce's first meeting with MT, and text of his comment in the San Francisco Newsletter in 1890 (quoted in 1870.B4) on MT's marriage to a rich woman (pp. 87-88); also, Bierce, MT, and Joaquin Miller as dinner guests at the White Friars' Club, London, in the winter of 1873 (pp. 99-100).

B36 OLDER, FREMONT. "The Famous Jumping Frog Story. William Gillis, one-time associate of Mark Twain, tells Fremont Older the true story of the Jumping Frog. Told by William Gillis," Overland Monthly, LXXXVII (April), 101-102.

Older says Gillis heard the story from "an old man from Arkansas. The Arkansas man heard the story from old Dan Rice, the famous circus clown who owned a circus in the early sixties, and who used to tell the story in his circus work.... Samuel Sebaugh, a brilliant writer on the San Andreas Independent, hearing this story wrote it as a local happening, and the new version of it became very popular along the Mother Lode." There follows a version of the story, here told in dialect as by an elderly Negro, with frogs named Jim Polk and Henry Clay.

B37 *_____. "Russell K. Colcord," San Francisco Call-Bulletin, September 12.

Reminiscence by Colcord, who remembered MT in Aurora as "cold, selfish, and unsocial"--though conceding they had only a nodding acquaintance. [Source: Quoted by Fatout (1964), p. 45.]

B38 OVERTON, GRANT. "Howells: Twain," in his An Hour of the American Novel. (Philadelphia and London: J. B. Lippincott Company), pp. 37-43.

A popular account, describing the two men and their principal works. Compares MT, Melville in "their vitality and early adventurousness; they had minds of the same order. Success, world-wide popularity and

the restraints of Howells and Mrs. Clemens soothed and distracted Twain through most of his lifetime. But well before the end of it he put on paper a misanthropic bitterness that Melville probably suffered, too, but left unwritten" (pp. 39-40). In MS, MT's "moral nihilism finds frankest expression. His view of the cosmic spectacle is a good deal like that of Thomas Hardy in 'The Dynasts,' but without Hardy's dignity and courage." MT's best works are HF and "The Man that Corrupted Hadleyburg," but his Autobiography "is uninteresting in a few spots and trivial in many." Brooks's The Ordeal of Mark Twain "cannot be overlooked...but its argument must be received cautiously; it probably infers too much on too slender evidence" (p. 42).

B39 PHILPOTTS, EDEN. "On Mark Twain's Visit to England," Overland Monthly, LXXXVII (April), 106.

A poem praising MT and welcoming him to England (apparently on the occasion of his visit in 1907).

B40 [QUAIFE, M. M.] [Discussion of the unpublished autobiography of Orion Clemens.] Mississippi Valley Historical Review, XVI (December), 438-39.

The author of "Mark Twain in Iowa" [Fred W. Lorch, 1929] sought permission from Albert Bigelow Paine to examine Orion Clemens's autobiographical papers, but "It was not granted, and in this connection the information was vouchsafed that most of them have already been burned, while permission to examine any that may have escaped destruction is 'quite out of the question'"; legally, this may be proper, but Quaife condemns the action as wholly irresponsible. [Author identified as Quaife in Twainian, II (February, 1943), 6.] On p. 443 there is an unsigned note that Cyril Clemens has lent the Historical Society of St. Louis "a collection of Clemens family letters, most of which passed between Mark Twain and wife and the donor's parents in the years 1881-1908."

B41 RICHARDS, P. "Mark Twain als Wildwest-Journalist," Westermanns Monatshefte, CXLVII (October), 158-60.

A popular account of MT's frontier journalism, based principally on RI.

B42 SOSEY, FRANK H. "Palmyra and Its Historical Environment," Missouri Historical Review, XXIII (April), 361-79.

"In 1914 a great eastern magazine published a story purporting to have been written by Mark Twain in which he told of a thrilling incident of slavery days in Marion City," here retold and followed by a more complete and accurate account.

B43 VAN DOREN, MARK. _An Autobiography of America_.
New York: Albert & Charles Boni.
Contains passages from LOM (pp. 353-67)
and RI (pp. 432-45, 454-61), with very
brief headnotes; listed elsewhere (incorrectly) as containing "several chapters devoted
to Mark Twain."

B44 VAN DYKE, HENRY. "Mark Twain--A Memorial
Poem Given at Carnegie Hall, New York City,
November 30, 1910," _Overland Monthly_,
LXXXVIII (April), 104.
A reprinting of the poem originally pub-
lished in 1910, in "Mark Twain in Memoriam,"
Harper's Weekly, LIV (December 17), 10.

B45 _____, et al. "Tributes to Mark Twain, Written for this Number of the _Overland_ by Members of the Mark Twain Society," _Overland
Monthly_, LXXXVII (April), 107-108, 123.
Tributes by Henry Van Dyke, Hamlin Garland, H. M. Tomlinson, Rupert Hughes,
E. F. Benson, Sir Esme Howard (British Ambassador to the United States), Ida Tarbell, G. M. Trevelyan, Concha Espina, W. W.
Jacobs, Temple Bailey, E. V. Lucas, [Lord]
Dunsany, Knut Hamsun, Stephen Leacock,
William J. Locke, Arthur Pinero, Walter de
la Mare, and Anthony Hope Hopkins.

B46 WINTERICH, JOHN T. "Mark Twain and _The Innocents Abroad_," in his _Books and the Man_.
(New York: Greenberg: Publisher),
pp. 170-92.
About the publication and sale of IA,
based primarily on such familiar accounts
as MT's autobiography and Paine; gives interesting information on the illustrations
and a few first-edition points. "Acknowl-
edgements" (p. vii) says the papers in this
volume originally appeared in _Publishers'
Weekly_, but does not give specific issues.

1930 A BOOKS

A1 EDWARDS, FRANCES M., ed. and introduction.
_Twainiana Notes from the Annotations of
Walter Bliss_. Hartford: The Hobby Shop,
Publishers.
Annotations by Bliss in his copy of the
1910 bibliography of MT's works compiled by
Merle Johnson.

A2 GILLIS, WILLIAM R. _Gold Rush Days with Mark
Twain_. Introduction by Cyril Clemens. New
York: Albert & Charles Boni.
Anecdotes, some of which concern MT, by a
friend and mining partner.

A3 MARTIN, ALMA BORTH. _A Vocabulary Study of
"The Gilded Age."_ With an Introduction by
Robert L. Ramsay and a Foreword by Hamlin
Garland. Webster Groves, Missouri: Mark
Twain Society.
Lists 142 words not in the _Oxford English
Dictionary_ ("either altogether or in the
meaning used by Mark Twain"--p. 26) and 71

words for which _The Gilded Age_ provides earlier citations. In the foreword titled
"Mark Twain's Freshness of Diction" Garland
concludes: "With all his coarseness he was
essentially wholesome, and his vocabulary
was as wide and as varied as his almost un-
paralleled experience" (p. 3).

A4 *_Tributes to Mark Twain by Members of the Soci-
ety_. Paris [Kentucky?]: Printed for the
Mark Twain Society by H. Clarke.
[Source: Asselineau (1954), No. 483.]
Conventional tributes by Galsworthy, Ches-
terton, Hamlin Garland, W. W. Jacobs, E. V.
Lucas, Dunsany, Knut Hamsun, W. De la Mare,
Pinero, G. M. Trevelyan, A. E. Housman, and
others. [13-page pamphlet.]

A5 WEST, VICTOR ROYCE. _Folklore in the Works of
Mark Twain_. Lincoln: University of Nebraska Studies in Language, Literature, and
Criticism, No. 10.
There are chapters on "Ghostlore," "Demon-
ology," "Witchcraft," "Luck and Unluck,"
"Signs, Portents, Omens," "Proverbs," and
"Sundry Superstitions" in MT's works, but
this is basically a series of organized
lists. There is no attempt made to place
the material in a broader folklore perspective and the references are only to works
by MT and to the Paine biography.

1930 B SHORTER WRITINGS

B1 ARMSTRONG, C. J. "Mark Twain's Early Writings
Discovered," _Missouri Historical Review_,
XXIV (July), 485-501.
On the contributions to Hannibal newspapers by young Samuel Clemens, with texts
(among them "Love Concealed. To Miss Katy
of H--l," the "Rambler" and "Grumbler" correspondence, and "'Local' Resolves to Commit Suicide," illustrated by a clumsy woodcut by Sam).

B2 BLAIR, WALTER. "Burlesques in Nineteenth-
Century American Humor," _American Litera-
ture_, II (November), 236-47.
MT is among the authors treated. This article is reprinted as part of Blair's _Two
Phases of American Humor_, an excerpt from
his doctoral dissertation at the University
of Chicago (Private Edition, Distributed by
the University of Chicago Libraries, n.d.
The copy at McGill University is stamped as
having been received May 21, 1932); this reprint has the pagination of the _American
Literature_ printing).

B3 BRASHEAR, MINNIE M. "Mark Twain Juvenilia,"
American Literature, II (March), 25-53.
Includes texts of Hannibal newspaper
sketches by young SLC. "These early writings will not suggest the need of any new
rating of Mark Twain."

B4 *BROWN, GEORGE ROTHWELL. Washington, A Not
     Too Serious History. Baltimore: Norman
     Publishing Company.
          On pp. 417-18, says MT was a customer at
     James Guild's bookshop whenever he was in
     Washington. [Source: French (1965),
     pp. 36; 291, n. 30.]

B5 CHURCHILL, WINSTON S. A Roving Commission:
     My Early Life. New York: Charles Scrib-
     ner's Sons.
          On p. 360, very briefly describes a meet-
     ing with MT, who introduced him at his
     first public lecture in New York. MT auto-
     graphed a set of his books for Churchill
     and conversed pleasantly with him, but was
     unsympathetic toward England's position in
     the Boer War.

B6 CLEMENS, CLARA. "Recollections of Mark
     Twain. Part I--Her Childhood Memories,"
     North American Review, CCXXX (November),
     522-29; "Part II--Love Letters of the Humor-
     ist" (December), 652-59.
          Extracts from her forthcoming My Father,
     Mark Twain (1931); three-part series ends
     January, 1931.

B7 CLEMENS, CYRIL. "Mark Twain's Favorite
     Book," Overland Monthly, LXXXVIII (May),
     157.
          Years of research and painstaking compo-
     sition made MT prefer his JA for a time,
     but his real favorite, although the writing
     had been burdensome, was HF.

B8 GARLAND, HAMLIN. Roadside Meetings. New
     York: The Macmillan Company.
          On MT traveling and lecturing with the
     "gentle, religious, and rather effeminate"
     George Washington Cable (pp. 104-105). De-
     scribes interviewing MT in London for
     McClure's (on the Grant Memoirs, and the
     failure of the Webster Company); Mrs. Clem-
     ens asked that the interview not be pub-
     lished (pp. 449-53). The latter part ap-
     pears in Garland's "Roadside Meetings of a
     Literary Nomad" in Bookman (New York), LXXI
     (July), 425-27, and the comparatively brief
     comment on MT and Cable may have been in an
     earlier issue.

B9 HAPGOOD, NORMAN. "Mark Twain," in his The
     Changing Years: Reminiscences of Norman
     Hapgood (New York: Farrar & Rinehart, In-
     corporated), pp. 202-11.
          On acquaintance with MT, with anecdotes
     showing his "almost Quixotic" concern for
     the feelings of other people. Quotes MT
     in his late years: "I was happy in the ear-
     ly part of my life. I am happy now; but
     there was a stretch of years in the middle
     of my life when I was not happy...and that
     middle period was the only part that was
     worth anything."

B10 JOSEPHSON, MATTHEW. "Those Who Stayed," in
     his Portrait of the Artist as American (New
     York: Harcourt, Brace and Company),
     pp. 154-61.
          MT lacked the seriousness of a Whitman or
     of a Henry James (whom "he despised, and
     nicknamed 'Henrietta-Maria'"). Josephson
     rejects Brooks's notion that MT was sup-
     pressed: he liked the life he had chosen.
     Nonetheless, Brooks is correct about MT's
     dual nature, which reflects a duality in the
     national character. Reprinted (in part;
     pp. 158-61) in Leary (1962), pp. 83-84.

B11 KEMBLE, E. W. "Illustrating Huck Finn," Colo-
     phon, Part I (February; pages not numbered .
          Kemble was 23 when he illustrated HF, and
     was paid $2,000 for the job. He used one
     model, a boy named Cort Morris, for all the
     characters--including Huck, Jim, and all the
     men and women. When HF was filmed, the di-
     rector, William Desmond Taylor, made the
     characters fit the drawings.

B12 LORCH, FRED W. "A Mark Twain Letter," Iowa
     Journal of History and Politics, XXVIII
     (April), 268-76.
          A letter published in the Keokuk Gate City
     (June 25, 1862) to his mother, from Carson
     City, Nevada Territory, dated March 20, 1862;
     it does not appear in Paine's edition of MT's
     letters.

B13 MABBOTT, T. O. "Mark Twain's Artillery: A
     Mark Twain Legend," Missouri Historical Re-
     view, XXV (October), 23-29.
          Reprints from the Silver Cliff Daily Pros-
     pect (March 16, 1860, "printed from a photo-
     static copy without intentional emendations")
     an apocryphal tale there credited to the
     Carson Appeal: "Mark Twain's Artillery.
     How He Defeated a Band of Redskins in the
     Days of '49. Type as Grape Shot." By this
     account, MT and his friend "Dan de Quille"
     (William Wright) attempted to start a paper
     in Menocina County and after using up their
     type as shot, joined the Territorial Enter-
     prise together.

B14 MORRIS, HARRISON S. Confessions in Art. New
     York: Sears Publishing Company, Inc.,
     pp. 202-203.
          Describes MT at a dinner in his honor in
     New York, given by the illustrators when
     his Joan of Arc had just appeared. A girl
     dressed as Joan and accompanied by pages
     and trumpeters presented him with a crown.
     He was exuberant. Includes illustration:
     "Menu for a Dinner to Mark Twain," showing
     Pudd'nhead Wilson and bearing the date
     December 21, 1905.

B15 PARRINGTON, VERNON LEWIS. "The Backwash of
     the Frontier: Mark Twain," in his The Be-
     ginnings of Critical Realism in America
     1860-1920, Vol. III is his Main Currents in
     American Thought (New York: Harcourt,
     Brace and Company), pp. 86-101 and passim.

(PARRINGTON, VERNON LEWIS)

Completed only to 1900, due to Parrington's death in 1929. Sees MT as the irreverent frontier adolescent taken in hand by the East--but he remained boyish and clung to his integrity. His life is important as a reflection of his time, to which he only surrendered in part (p. 88). Agrees with Brooks that the later bitterness may be attributed in part to this surrender, but "a humane and generous spirit cannot long watch with indifference the motley human caravan hastening to eternity--cannot find food for laughter alone in the incredible meanness and folly of men cheating and quarreling in a wilderness of graves" (p. 89). Parrington notes MT's intellectual isolation: "If he had known Henry Adams as intimately as he knew Henry H. Rogers, very likely his eyes would have been opened to many things that would have done him good" (p. 90). HF shows MT's rebellion against the laws of society (pp. 94-95), and CY is an attack, not so much on chivalry, as on centuries of oppression (pp. 95, 97-98). Reprinted in Scott (1955), pp. 188-99; (1967), pp. 186-97; Leary (1962), pp. 87-98; brief excerpt in Lettis (1962), pp. 305-307.

B16 PATTEE, FRED LEWIS. The New American Literature 1890-1930. New York, London: The Century Co., p. 89 and passim.

Most of the brief references to MT are not illuminating, but on p. 89 Pattee quotes W. P. Trent's dismissal of JA as "a large piece of mosaic work," alternating history and fiction without a fusing process.

B17 POWELL, LYMAN P. Mary Baker Eddy: A Life Size Portrait. New York: The Macmillan Company, passim.

Several references to MT, with an attempt to show him as less hostile to Christian Science: "Mark Twain's final reversal of his previous judgment may come as news to many: 'Christian Science is humanity's boon. Mother Eddy deserves a place in the Trinity as much as any member of it,'" for her healing principle (p. 40, with a footnote on p. 81 giving the source as the 1912 Paine biography, III, 1271).

B18 *READ, OPIE. "Mark Twain and the Pilot," in his I Remember (New York: R. R. Smith, Inc.), pp. 155-65.

On a meeting with MT on a steamboat. [Source: Asselineau (1954), No. 491.]

B19 RILEY, JAMES WHITCOM. Letters of James Whitcom Riley, ed. William Lyon Phelps. Indianapolis: The Bobbs-Merrill Company. Passim on MT (indexed).

Texts of MT letters to W. D. Foulke, October 3, 1888, and to Riley, February 2, 1891 (pp. 329-30; MT praises Riley as more accomplished than most poets at reading his own poems aloud).

B20 VAN DOREN, MARK. "Clemens, Samuel Langhorne," in Allen Johnson and Dumas Malone, eds., Dictionary of American Biography (New York: Charles Scribner's Sons), IV, 192-98.

[Source: 1958 reprint, II, Part II, with the same pagination.] MT's best works are HF and the first part of LOM. Van Doren notes MT's limitations as a thinker, the uneven quality of his writing, and "the violence which frequently led him into burlesque so fantastic as to be dull"; but Howells and Olivia Clemens helped "to keep Mark Twain's genius within decorous bounds."

B21 WINTERICH, JOHN T. "The Life and Works of Bloodgood H. Cutter," Colophon, Part II (May), 8 pp. (not numbered).

Cutter wanted to be known as a humorous poet, did not mind the way he was depicted as the "Poet Lariat" in IA, and did not realize that he was himself portrayed as a comic object. Comparatively little on MT.

1931 A BOOKS

A1 *ANON. The Movie Story of Tom Sawyer. Racine, Wisconsin: Whitman Publishing Company.

"(Shortened to The Story of Tom Sawyer on the front cover but with the first wording on the title page). The book contains 24 pages, including pastedowns. Illustrations were color photographs taken from the Paramount motion picture starring Jackie Coogan as Huck." [Source: Asselineau (1954), No. 535; additional details quoted from letter (April 15, 1974) from William H. Larson, Senior Editor, Western Publishing Company, Inc. (Whitman/Golden Press), Racine, Wisconsin.]

A2 *ANON. The Story of the Paramount Picture "Huckleberry Finn." N.p.: Lubin Press, circa 1931.

[Source: Asselineau (1954), No. 534. Asselineau attributes this to a typewritten bibliography in Widener Library at Harvard University. The title suggests that this may have been a publicity release on the filming, or--more probably--a version of MT's book released at a time to cash in on the new film--T.A.T.]

A3 CLEMENS, CLARA. My Father, Mark Twain. Illustrated from Family Photographs with Hitherto Unpublished Letters of Mark Twain. New York and London: Harper & Brothers Publishers.

Contains reminiscences and useful primary materials; unindexed.

A4 *LEWIS, OSCAR. The Origin of the Celebrated Jumping Frog of Calaveras County. San Francisco: The Book Club of California.

[Source: Asselineau (1954), No. 505: "Gives the different versions of the tale."]

1931 - Books

A5 *WALL, BERNHARDT. In Mark Twain's Missouri,
etched and published by Bernhardt Wall,
Lime Rock, Connecticut.
[4 pp. pamphlet. Source: Asselineau
(1954), No. 506.]

1931 B SHORTER WRITINGS

B1 ANON. [Review: Clara Clemens, My Father,
Mark Twain.] Times Literary Supplement,
November 26, p. 937.
Long, but primarily descriptive.

B2 ARMSTRONG, C. J. "John L. RoBards--A Boyhood
Friend of Mark Twain," Missouri Historical
Review, XXV (April), 493-98.
Includes the text of several MT letters
(and one by Jane Clemens) to RoBards, chiefly on transferring the remains of MT's father and his brother Henry to one lot in Mt.
Olivet Cemetery in Hannibal. In one letter
from Hartford (April 17 [1876]), MT urged
simplicity: "I enclose check for $100. If
Henry and my father feel as I would feel
under the circumstances, they want no prominent or expensive lot, or luxurious entertainment in the new cemetery. As for a
monument--well, if you remember my father,
you are aware that he would rise up & de-
molish it the first night. He was a modest
man & would not be able to sleep under a
monument."

B3 *_____. "Sam Clemens Considered Becoming a
Preacher," The Christian (June 13).
[Source: Reprinted under this title in
Twainian, IV (May, 1945), 1; other facts of
publication and information about The Christian not given.] The Reverend Mr. Armstrong
was scheduled to retire May 31, 1945 as pastor of the First Christian Church in Hannibal.

B4 ASHTON, J. W. [Review: Victor Royce West,
Folklore in the Works of Mark Twain
(1930).] Philological Quarterly, X
(October), 416.
MT's interest "seems to differ very
slightly, if at all, from that of the ordinary intelligent person," and West errs in
trying to show more; he also reads too much
into such conventional locutions as "poor
devil" and "luck," which probably had little
folk significance. "The chapter on Signs,
Portents, Omens is perhaps the best since
it presents actual situations rather than
casual references."

B5 BALDWIN, CHARLES C. Stanford White. New
York: Dodd, Mead & Company.
An eccentric book, with references to MT
passim. He is described in the Index
(p. 397) as "potentially the greatest of
American writers, but (alas) cowed and
beaten by the prejudices and conclusions of
his contemporaries in society and the arts--
best remembered for Huckleberry Finn and
for the anecdotes attributed to him." This

description is not followed up in the text,
which says little about MT with relation to
White but does tell of his visiting White
and St. Gaudens in Paris; they counted the
black cigars he smoked.

B6 BLAIR, WALTER. "The Popularity of Nineteenth-
Century American Humorists," American Liter-
ature, III (May), 175-94.
Contains relatively little on MT.

B7 BLANKENSHIP, RUSSELL. "Lost in the Gilded
Age," in his American Literature as an Ex-
pression of the National Mind (New York:
Henry Holt and Company), pp. 457-76.
Discusses MT jointly with Henry Adams. In
"Mark Twain" (pp. 458-70) describes the man,
his works, and his inner conflicts.

B8 BURPEE, CHARLES W. A Century in Hartford.
Being the History of the Hartford County
Mutual Fire Insurance Company. Hartford:
The Hartford County Mutual Fire Insurance
Company.
On p. 81, quotes MT's reaction in 1878
when asked if he would have his house con-
nected to the telephone system: "No! I
want something to keep voices further away--
not bring them nearer."

B9 CESTRE, C. [Review: Alma Borth Martin, A
Vocabulary Study of Mark Twain's "The Gilded
Age" (1930).] Revue Anglo-Américaine, VIII
(June), 458-59.
Brief and descriptive. [In French.]

B10 CHAPIN, ADELE LE BOURGEOIS [MRS. R. W. CHAP-
IN.] "Their Trackless Way": A Book of
Memories, ed. by Christina Chapin. London:
Constable & Co. Ltd. Passim on MT (indexed).
On dining with MT in South Africa
(pp. 119-23) and in London (pp. 140-41);
on his meeting James McNeill Whistler in
London (pp. 180-82); on lunching with MT
at the Yale Bicentennial (pp. 211-12);
quotes a letter from Lord Gray, discussing
patriotism and citing a statement to him
by MT that America had left England's government rather than England itself, and it
would now be an honor to be a colony
(p. 220).

B11 CLEMENS, CLARA. "Recollections of Mark Twain:
Last Years of the Humorist," North American
Review, CCXXXI (January), 50-57.
Extracts from her My Father, Mark Twain,
concluding a three-part series begun in
1930.

B12 DAVIS, ARTHUR KYLE. [Review: Victor Royce
West, Folklore in the Works of Mark Twain
(1930).] Modern Language Notes, XLVI (May),
350.
"A commendable piece of extracting and...
interesting if essentially uncritical."

B13 DEVOTO, BERNARD, '18. "Mark Twain and the Genteel Tradition," Harvard Graduates' Magazine, XL (December), 155-63.

MT "was a humorist. He had had no formal education. His life had been spent in activity, away from what are known as aesthetic pursuits.... He came East and he accepted tuition," especially from Howells, and "accepted, to the small extent of which he was capable, without any awareness of surrender, the dominant criteria of his age." Richard Watson Gilder purified the language of HF for serialization in The Century, but MT accepted a similar service for PW, and kept Gilder's changes for the book publication. "This damage was purely verbal. The tradition may have wrought a greater damage by turning him from Pudd'nhead Wilsons and Huck Finns to knights, kings, and armored virgins," but such questions are conjectural.

B14 _____. "The Matrix of Mark Twain's Humor," Bookman (New York), LXXIV (October), 172-78.

Frontier humor in the newspapers gave MT a style, form, and themes.

B15 _____. "The Real Frontier: A Preface to Mark Twain," Harper's, CLXIII (June), 60-71.

Only tangentially on MT, this article defends the frontier against charges by Van Wyck Brooks and others that it was merely a region of violence, spiritual repression, and intellectual vacuity.

B16 DRAKE, ERIC. [Review: Alma Borth Martin, A Vocabulary Study of Mark Twain's "The Gilded Age" (1930).] Anglia Beiblatt, XLII (December), 364-67.

The thesis cannot be taken seriously, despite the interest of many of the words and phrases: a) the categories are too simple, and vaguely defined by inadequate criteria; b) "There is a naive assumption of the accuracy of the New English Dictionary"; c) Mrs. Martin is "confused between syntax and vocabulary" in treatment of some word-combinations as though they were single words, as with gawky-looking, canvas-covered, Bible class; d) "The running commentary is curiously child-like"; e) for about 120 Americanisms, century of origin is not given. "It is...surprising to find a study based on these rather naive and uncritical methods sponsored by a university professor. Surely the evident good will and sincerity of the author could have been turned to better account." [In English.]

B17 GARLAND, HAMLIN. "Mark Twain, Carnegie, and Roosevelt," in his Companions on the Trail: A Literary Chronicle (New York: Macmillan), pp. 192-207.

Describes a dinner with the Clemens family in 1903 at their home in Riverdale, New York; quotes MT's spoken remarks on Christian Science.

B18 GILBERT, ARIADNE. "Mark Twain: Sam, Sinner and Saint," in her Over Famous Thresholds (New York, London: The Century Company), pp. 230-62.

A biographical sketch, apparently based largely on Paine.

B19 GOODPASTURE, A. V. "Mark Twain, Southerner," Tennessee Historical Magazine, Series II, I (July), 253-60.

After a lengthy family history (pp. 253-56), argues that "every drop of Mark Twain's blood was Southern." "While in the East he wrote his stories of Southern and Western life, but he never wrote a story of Eastern life.... The fact is, he never understood nor appreciated the New England culture." MT's reason for leaving the Confederate military service was probably the appointment of his brother Orion as Secretary of the Territory of Nevada.

B20 GRATTAN, C. HARTLEY. "Mark Twain," in John Macy, ed., American Writers on American Literature, by Thirty-Seven Contemporary Writers (New York: Horace Liveright, Inc.) pp. 274-84; also, Hamlin Garland quotes MT on Howells, p. 289.

Notes MT's volatile temperament, uneven writing, emotional ambivalence: "His ordeal was an ordeal by temperament as much as by anything else," and his pursuit of wealth shows that he "was incapable of defying his age" (p. 277). Notes MT's clear, direct style (p. 283), his satire, his final pessimism, and concludes by contrasting him with Henry James, although "it is those two who are fast becoming the great figures in our literature for the period 1870-1900" (p. 284).

B21 *HAMON, LOUIS ("CHEIRO"). Fate in the Making. Revelations of a Lifetime. New York & London: Harper & Brothers.

[Source: Asselineau (1954), No. 513; notes that "Cheiro" once examined MT's hand but makes no specific comment on this book.]

B22 HARRIS, JOEL CHANDLER. Joel Chandler Harris, Editor and Essayist: Miscellaneous Literary, Political, and Social Writings, ed. by Julia Collier Harris. Chapel Hill: The University of North Carolina Press, pp. 253-54, 375.

Takes issue with MT's criticism of the The Vicar of Wakefield, but praises him as "not only our greatest humorist, but our greatest writer of fiction." [Originally in Uncle Remus's Magazine, February, 1908.]

B23 HEINEMAN, DAVID E. [Letter to the Editor.] Michigan History Magazine, XV (Winter), 136-42.

On "a receipt book...each page of which has the caption 'Young Men's Society, of Lansing.'" The entry for December 24, 1864 lists MT's lecture, "An American Vandal Abroad," at one hundred dollars (p. 137);

(HEINEMAN, DAVID E.)
his "Out West" lecture of December 15, 1871 brought one hundred twenty-five dollars (p. 139).

B24   HICKS, GRANVILLE. "Mark Twain's Pessimism," Nation, CXXXIII (October 28), 463-64.
A review of Clara Clemens, My Father, Mark Twain. "Certainly his daughter, though she prints a number of new letters, presents no information that will involve a new conception of his character."

B25   HUGHES, ROBERT M. "A Deserter's Tale," Virginia Magazine of History and Biography, XXXIX (January), 21-28.
A defense of "Governor John B. Floyd, of Virginia, Secretary of War in Buchanan's Cabinet. My mother was his adopted daughter, and one of her last requests of me was to defend his memory from the vile slanders against him," as in MT's "The Case of George Fisher." The actual case is here discussed in detail, with Hughes expressing sorrow that a Southerner should join Floyd's detractors--but MT's Confederate service was brief and undistinguished.

B26   LORCH, FRED W. "A Source for Mark Twain's 'The Dandy Frightening the Squatter,'" American Literature, III (November), 390-13.
With parallel columns, shows strong similarity to "A Scene on the Ohio" in the Bloomington (now Muscatine, Iowa) Herald of February 13, 1849.

B27   MASON, LAURENS D. "Real People in Mark Twain's Stories," Overland Monthly LXXXIX (January), 12-13, 27.
Attributes living originals to MT's characters, chiefly on the basis of what he wrote about them in his Autobiography and elsewhere.

B28   RAOUL, MARGARET LENTE. "Debunking a Famous Story," Bookman (New York), LXXIII (August), 607-608.
Reproduces in facsimile, with commentary, MT's note in which he stated that "the report of my death was an exaggeration." The story was also told by Mrs. Raoul's father, Frank Marshall White (1910.B136), and on several occasions by Cyril Clemens.

B29   ROURKE, CONSTANCE. Native American Humor. New York: Harcourt, Brace and Company, pp. 209-21, and passim (indexed).
MT was a story-teller with "a pioneer talent," a social critic only in the "instinctive and incomplete" way of the American comic tradition. "He was never the conscious artist, always the improviser." These pages on MT reprinted in Scott (1955), pp. 200-206; (1967), pp. 198-204; in Leary (1962), pp. 99-106; in Cardwell (1963), pp. 26-30; some reprintings are partial.

B30   STEWART, GEORGE R. Bret Harte: Argonaut and Exile. Boston and New York: Houghton Mifflin Company, passim.
The frequent references to MT are based on material already known in MT scholarship.

B31   UNDERHILL, IRVING S. "An Inquiry into Mark Twain's Latest Book! The Adventures of Huckelberry [sic] Finn," Colophon, Part 6, 10 pp. (including facsimiles; pages not numbered).
About the copies of the first edition of HF shipped to California, and there altered to replace the offensive cut on p. 283. See Underhill's "The Haunted Book" (1935.B75).

B32   WINSTEN, ARCHER. "The Intimate Twain," Scribner's, XC (November), 16, 18 (specially numbered section at beginning of issue).
A brief review of Clara Clemens, My Father, Mark Twain as a book which makes almost no attempt at interpretation, adds very little to the Paine biography, and supports rather than refutes Brooks's "penetrating study of Mark Twain."

1932 A BOOKS

A1   CLEMENS, CYRIL, ed. Mark Twain the Letter Writer. Boston: Meador Publishing Company.
Letters by MT, some of them reproduced in facsimile, together with biographical details and anecdotes.

A2   DEVOTO, BERNARD. Mark Twain's America. Boston: Little, Brown and Company.
One of the central critical works on MT, brilliant but pugnacious; DeVoto calls this reply to Van Wyck Brooks's The Ordeal of Mark Twain (1920) an "essay in the correction of ideas" (p. v, dedication). DeVoto made a broad study of the frontier and frontier humor, and insists on their salutory influence in developing MT and shaping him as a writer. Reprinted Chautauqua, New York: Chautauqua Institution, and often reprinted thereafter. Excerpts reprinted in Bradley (1962), pp. 288-97; Leary (1962), pp. 109-23; Lettis (1962), pp. 307-15; Cardwell (1963), pp. 31-35; Simpson (1968), pp. 7-15; Gerber (1971), pp. 32-41.

A3   LEACOCK, STEPHEN. Mark Twain. London: Peter Davies (Also New York: D. Appleton and Company, 1933).
A popular biography by a fellow-humorist; more enthusiastic than penetrating.

A4   POTTER, JOHN K. Samuel L. Clemens: First Editions and Values. Chicago: The Black Archer Press.
Gives prices as an approximation, based on auction records, booksellers' listings, etc., and lists points distinguishing first editions; superseded in the latter by Merle Johnson and Jacob Blanck.

1932 B SHORTER WRITINGS

B1   ANON. "Copyright in the Days of Mark Twain,"
     Publishers' Weekly, CXXI (February 27), 949.
     Describes and quotes a letter from MT to
     Kate Douglas Wiggin (date not given) about
     his attempts to lobby for an improved copy-
     right bill.

B2   ANON. "Mark and His Temper," Quarterly Jour-
     nal of the University of North Dakota (now
     North Dakota Quarterly), XXII (Spring),
     277-78.
     A brief, descriptive review of Clara
     Clemens, My Father, Mark Twain.

B3   ANON. [Review: Stephen Leacock, Mark Twain.]
     Times Literary Supplement, November 24,
     p. 886.
     "A clear and well-proportioned sketch,"
     primarily concerned with MT as an artist;
     English readers will assent to Leacock's
     praise of HF, but not his praise of CY:
     "He does not seem to be aware that in this
     book more than in any other Mark Twain ex-
     hibited his insensitivity to the ideal."

B4   ARVIN, NEWTON. "Mark Twain Simplified," New
     Republic, LXXII (October 5), 211-12.
     A review of Bernard DeVoto, Mark Twain's
     America, which distorts and misrepresents
     "what is perhaps the most remarkable piece
     of interpretive biography in our litera-
     ture, The Ordeal of Mark Twain," by Van
     Wyck Brooks. "Mr. DeVoto, in one chapter,
     has pointed out several details in which
     Brooks is fairly open to attack. But he
     has nowhere grappled with a serious inter-
     pretation on its own merits, and by dispos-
     ing not only of Brooks, but of such writers
     as Waldo Frank and Lewis Mumford, as roman-
     tic ignoramuses, he prejudices his own
     theory (for he distinctly has one) in the
     eyes of every fair-minded bystander." Re-
     printed in American Pantheon, ed. Daniel
     Aaron and Sylvan Schendler (New York: Dela-
     corte Press, 1966), pp. 135-41.

B5   BENNETT, ARNOLD. The Journals of Arnold Ben-
     nett, 1896-1910, ed. by Newman Flower.
     London, Toronto, Melbourne and Sydney:
     Cassell and Company, Ltd. [MT is not list-
     ed in the indexes of other volumes of Ben-
     nett's journals examined.]
     Robert Barr says MT once told him his
     average expenses were $35,000 per year;
     Pond once offered MT $50,000 for a lecture
     series, and Hearst offered him $52,000 for
     52 weekly articles in the Journal (p. 188);
     in 1905 Bennett was enjoying LOM (p. 206).

B6   BOYNTON, PERCY H. "Mr. Clemens' Family,"
     New Republic, LXIX (January 27), 302-303.
     A review of Clara Clemens' My Father,
     Mark Twain (1931). "The book of reminis-
     cences does not attempt character analysis
     or aesthetic criticism, but as an obvious-
     ly honest and candid piece of work it

provides data on which to modify or confirm
the abundant literature of this sort."

B7   BROWNELL, GEORGE HIRAM. "Mark Twain and the
     Hannibal Journal," American Book Collector,
     II (August-September), 173-76; (October),
     202-204.
     An "extract from a longer essay, by Mr.
     Brownell, entitled 'Mark Twain in Magazines
     and Newspapers'" (facts of publication not
     given). Extends and corrects MT's own ac-
     counts of his work on his brother Orion's
     newspaper. Sources include Minnie M. Brash-
     ear, "Mark Twain Juvenilia" (1930), articles
     by the Reverend C. J. Armstrong in Missouri
     Historical Review and Hannibal Courier-Post
     (dates not given), and "an extensive cor-
     respondence with Rev. Armstrong."

B8   *BUCKBEE, EDNA BRYAN. "Mark Twain's Treasure
     Pile," in her Pioneer Days of Angel's Camp
     (Angel's Camp, California: Published by
     Calaveras Californian), pp. 21-35.
     On the Origin of "The Jumping Frog."
     [Source: Asselineau (1954), No. 544.]

B9   CALVERTON, V. F. The Liberation of American
     Literature. New York: Charles Scribner's
     Sons, passim.
     The "liberation" is first from European
     models and later it is what is implied by
     Calverton's avowedly Marxist views. With
     the rise of America to world power came a
     change in psychology, so "that Whitman and
     Twain came to be looked upon as native gen-
     iuses instead of as isolated eccentrics"
     (pp. 31-32). "Products of the frontier
     force," they were "the first American poet"
     and "the first American prose writer of any
     importance." The two Mark Twains were the
     youthful frontier optimist and an older
     pessimist, disappointed in his dreams for
     America. Had he lived in our time he might
     have been a communist; as it was, he re-
     mained among the petty bourgeoisie, con-
     demning American imperialism because it in-
     fringed on the property rights of smaller
     nations (pp. 319-28, 338). Reprinted in
     Scott (1955), pp. 207-14; (1967),
     pp. 205-12.

B10 CANBY, HENRY SEIDEL. "Mark Twain Himself,"
     Saturday Review of Literature, IX
     (October 29), 201-202.
     A review of Bernard DeVoto's Mark Twain's
     America, a useful corrective to Van Wyck
     Brooks, who appeared "more concerned with
     the ills of America than with the truth
     about Mark Twain"; however, "I wish that
     Mr. DeVoto had thrown his stones in a pam-
     phlet and written his book afterward."

B11 CARPENTER, FREDERICK I. "Anent American Hu-
     mor," Saturday Review of Literature, VIII
     (March 12), 590.
     A letter to the editor, arguing the im-
     maturity of earlier American humor, such as

(CARPENTER, FREDERICK I.)
MT's: Neither Tom [Sawyer] nor Mark ever grew up. American humor remained a childish evasion."

B12 CHAPMAN, JOHN W. "The Germ of a Book: A Footnote on Mark Twain," Atlantic Monthly, CL (December), 720-21.
Text of two letters by MT (Hartford, 1887) to the Reverend Mr. Chapman, a charity hospital chaplain who had written him on behalf of a dying patient named Jesse Leathers. MT said he had sent only a small amount of money, having been warned that Leathers, a distant relative, was "inordinately selfish and self-seeking, and not very scrupulous," and that aid would do him little good. Chapman notes that in The American Claimant (1892) the claimant next before Mulberry Sellers was Simon Lathers.

B13 *CLEMENS, CYRIL. "The Ancestry and Birth of Mark Twain," in Susan Louise Marsh and Charles Garrett Vannest, eds., Missouri Anthology (Boston: The Christopher Publishing House), pp. 91-96.
[Source: Asselineau (1954), No. 542.]

B14 COOPER, LANE. "Mark Twain's Lilacs and Laburnums," Modern Language Notes, XLVII (February), 85-87.
The passage beginning Chapter IV of A Double-Barreled Detective Story parodies Walter Besant and James Rice's The Seamy Side, a Story (1880), pp. 168, 297.

B15 DEVOTO, BERNARD. "In re Mark Twain," Saturday Review of Literature, VIII (April 2), 640.
A letter to the editor, in reply to one by Frederick I. Carpenter, March 12. (1932.B11). Carpenter's assertion that repression by his wife kept MT's humor from maturing is unsupported, and "only a repetition of the ideas of Mr. Van Wyck Brooks, which are a compound of frivolous and superficial psycho-analysis and a theory about the obligation of the artist based on the sentimental politics and economics of pre-war 'Liberalism.' In common with everyone else who has written about Mark Twain since the publication of The Ordeal of Mark Twain, except Mr. Macy, Mr. C. Hartley Grattan, and Mr. Carl Van Doren, Mr. Carpenter has let Mr. Brooks's notions substitute in his thinking for an examination of what Mark Twain actually wrote."

B16 _____. "Tom, Huck, and America," Saturday Review of Literature, IX (August 13), 37-39.
"The following article will constitute part of a chapter to appear in Mr. DeVoto's Mark Twain's America."

B17 _____. [Review: Clara Clemens, My Father, Mark Twain (1931).] New England Quarterly, V (January), 169-71.
Chiefly an attack on Albert Bigelow Paine for his refusal to allow scholars access to

MT's unpublished manuscripts and letters: "About four years ago a writer who contemplated a critical discussion of Mark Twain was informed by Mr. Paine that no further book about him was necessary. The canon was established: whatever of Mark Twain's writing it was proper for the public to see was in print." Rumor has it that Paine is planning another book exploiting the materials, and now Clara has one of her own; but "she had all that precious stuff to dip into and she chose to publish some love-letters from Mark Twain to his wife.... Miss Clemens's taste is really dreadful. Katie Leary, the parlor maid, wrote a far more valuable, and far more understanding book about Mark Twain." [For Paine's reply, see Anon., "Mark Twain's Biographer Denies He Had a Shady Side" (1933.B2).]

B18 HENDRICK, BURTON J. The Life of Andrew Carnegie. Garden City, N.Y.: Doubleday, Doran & Company, Inc. II, 271, 277.
Anecdote of MT asking Carnegie for a dollar and a half to buy a hymn book (no new details in the familiar story) and brief mention of MT as a dinner guest; portrait of MT facing p. 278.

B19 KING, GRACE. Memories of a Southern Woman of Letters. New York: The Macmillan Company.
On MT and his family in Hartford (pp. 75-78, 82-88, 92-96) and in Florence (pp. 168-79), and on the deaths of Jean and Olivia Clemens (pp. 201-203). Grace King was close to the Clemens daughters and writes well about them. Includes the text of an MT letter. For further details, see Robert Bush article in American Literature (1972.B24).

B20 KNIGHT, GRANT C. "Mark Twain," in his American Literature and Culture (New York: Ray Long and Richard R. Smith, Inc.) pp. 358-67.
MT is important as an American voice for independence from Europe and for recording social history, as in TS, HF, and LOM. MT is remembered as humorist, rather than as novelist or essayist. Knight praises CY as "a masterpiece in irony," which exposes evils of the past and shows the advantages of living in a later time. HF "does not strike the bottom of human experience. All its events are seen through immature eyes," and it is not outstanding in dignity, humor, tragedy, or weight and power.

B21 LEWISOHN, LUDWIG. "Demos Speaks," in his Expression in America (New York and London: Harper & Brothers, Publishers), pp. 194-232; pp. 212-32 concern MT.
Views MT as folk-artist, "Huck Finn grown up," and not spoiled by false sophistication. "I gravely doubt whether he underwent any ordeal," although he may have chafed at some of Olivia Clemens's restrictions (some of which were needed); and some of the words and passages she removed were inserted in

(LEWISOHN, LUDWIG)
the manuscript for that purpose (pp. 217-18). [Asselineau (1954, No. 548) reports that "this book was later republished as The Story of American Literature."] Reprinted in Leary (1962), pp. 127-31.

B22   LODGE, SIR OLIVER. [Anecdote.] Past Years: An Autobiography. New York: Charles Scribner's Sons, pp. 219-20.
       At a dinner in London, Andrew Lang was introduced to Mr. and Mrs. Clemens but misunderstood the name as "Cummins" and paid no attention to them until Lodge told him afterward and Lang hastened to make amends. MT was displeased.

B23   *MARKOVITCH, M. "Servantes i Mark Tven," Venaz [The Crown, Belgrade], XVIII, No. 1.
       [Source: Asselineau (1954), No. 564*.]

B24   OLDS, NATHANIEL S. "A Mark Twain Retort," Saturday Review of Literature, VII (May 7), 722.
       Reviewing A Double-Barreled Detective Story (in "the Post Express, in Rochester, N.Y., then a highly respectable afternoon daily and now owned by Mr. Hearst"), Olds questioned the plausibility of the incident in which a pregnant woman is tied to a post and dogs are set on her; in a letter here published MT tells Olds that the fictional account is based on a real event.

B25   PHELPS, WILLIAM LYON. "As I See It," Scribner's Magazine, XCI (January), 54-55.
       Contains a descriptive and laudatory review of Clara Clemens' My Father, Mark Twain, "a book that should have an enormous circulation.... These pages are worth reams of serious criticism or heavy-handed attempts at psycho-analysis by those who never knew him and are devoid of a sense of humor."

B26   RASCOE, BURTON. "Mark Twain: The First American," in his Titans of Literature from Homer to the Present (New York, London: G. P. Putnam's Sons), pp. 421-29.
       The writing of HF, the first use of the native idiom in "an unquestioned work of genius," is "the most important single event in American literature." In later years MT gave way to pessimism couched in conventional literary language, worn out by his years of struggle against propriety. Accepts the view of Brooks that Mrs. Clemens was MT's censor--but says the autobiography gives no indication that he objected and some of MT's outbursts needed restraint.

B27   *SELDES, GILBERT. "American Humor," in his America as Americans See It (New York: Harcourt, Brace and Company, Inc.)
       [Source: Reprinted in James Dow McCallum, ed., The College Omnibus (New York: Harcourt, Brace and Company, Inc., 1934), pp. 272-81.] MT was too ready to accept the

"humorous habits of his time," and too dependent upon exaggeration. In Europe he defended America by belittling what he saw, but on the river and in the West he was more at ease, "neither defending the common man nor afraid of the superior man."

B28   SIEGEL, ELI. [Review: Bernard DeVoto, Mark Twain's America.] Scribner's, XCII (November), 5-6 (specially numbered at front of issue).
       DeVoto "goes, at times, critically wild and is unfair" to Brooks, Frank, and Mumford; our critical outlook ought to consider more than one sort of great American literature.

B29   SMITH, REED. [Review: Russell Blankenship's American Literature as an Expression of the National Mind (1931).] American Literature, IV (March), 78-82.
       The part on the treatment of MT merely paraphrases Blankenship.

B30   UNDERHILL, IRVING S. "A Dog's Tale," American Book Collector, I (January), 14-18.
       On his experience in obtaining several hundred copies of the pamphlet first edition of this work, and his inability to dispose of them all profitably without destroying the market for them as a rarity.

B31   _____. "Two Interesting Letters Pertaining to Huckleberry Finn," American Book Collector, II (November), 282-89.
       A short letter from William Gannon, New York book seller (September 15, 1932), inquiring about bibliographical points of HF, and a lengthy reply by Underhill (pp. 382-89), in the course of which he states that the English edition of TS preceded the American one, and gives his opinion that the first English edition of HF was set from a complete copy of the American edition.

B32   VAN DOREN, CARL. "Toward a New Canon," Nation (New York), CXXXIV (April 13), 429-30.
       Brief mention: "Mark Twain seems a great man of letters as well as a great man."

B33   VAN DOREN, MARK. "DeVoto's America," Nation, CXXXV (October 19), 370-71.
       A review of Mark Twain's America. "Mr. DeVoto thinks he is meeting a theory with facts, but as usual in such situations he only gets tangled in a profusion of data." To put matters in perspective will require "someone less cantankerous" than DeVoto.

B34   WARD, A. C. "Three Voices," in his American Literature 1880-1930. London: Methuen [also New York: Lincoln McVeagh, The Dial Press, according to Asselineau (1954), No. 550)], pp. 33-62; on MT pp. 52-62 and passim.
       The other two with independent vision and freedom from conventional habits of thinking were Whitman and Emily Dickinson

1932 - Shorter Writings

(WARD, A. C.)
(pp. 61-62). MT suffers from his tendency
toward horse-play and a strain of the Philistine. Eve's Diary and JA show his "insight
and a comprehensive sense of pity" (p. 57),
but he ended in the despair of Hadleyburg.
CY was one of MT's "aesthetic indecencies"
of which he was guilty only because the
public demanded them (p. 30), and the English feel about it "very much as a cathedral
custodian would if a boisterous holiday-
maker vomited over an exquisite medieval
carving" (p. 56). Links TS and HF as reflecting MT's "impatience with conventional
uses" (p. 58). On the insights of Brooks and
defects of the Paine biography, brief mention on p. 253.

1933 A BOOKS

A1   BROOKS, VAN WYCK. The Ordeal of Mark Twain.
New York: E. P. Dutton.
A new edition of his 1920 book, with re-
visions in the light of DeVoto's Mark
Twain's America (1932) but with the basic
argument unchanged.

A2   *CLEMENS, CYRIL. The International Mark Twain
Society: Its History and Members. Webster
Groves, Missouri: International Mark Twain
Society.
[Source: Asselineau (1954), No. 572.]

A3   PARTRIDGE, H. M., and D. C. PARTRIDGE. The
Most Remarkable Echo in the World. New
York: Privately Printed.
An elaborate spoof purporting to demon-
strate that MT wrote works attributed to
Poe, Hawthorne, and Lewis Carroll.

1933 B SHORTER WRITINGS

B1   *ANON. "Excerpt from a letter dated March 1,
1899," Autograph Album, I (December), 44.
[Source: Leary (1954), p. 43.]

B2   ANON. "Mark Twain's Biographer Denies He Had
a Shady Side," Literary Digest, CXVI
(July 29), 23.
In an excerpt from an interview in the
New York Herald Tribune Albert Bigelow
Paine says that while there is much left
behind by MT that remains unpublished,
there is no indecent writing being suppressed; rather, much of the material is of
inferior quality, and MT himself asked that
some things not be published until a hundred years after his death. "Because the
trustees of the estate and Clara Clemens
and I, who are the literary executors, have
not given all these papers to the public
we have been severely criticized. A young
man in an excellent book stated I had written him that I thought any further books
about Mark Twain were unnecessary. Of
course, I never said anything of the kind.
The more books written about Mark Twain the

better I am satisfied." [For one version of
DeVoto's accusation against Paine, see annotation to his review (New England Quarterly,
1932.B17) of Clara Clemens's My Father:
Mark Twain.]

B3   ANON. "Mark Twain's New Deal," Saturday Review of Literature, X (December 16), 352.
Reports that Franklin D. Roosevelt took
the phrase from CY, and discusses the similarities of the two New Deals.

B4   ANON. "Two Etymologies," Word Study (G. & C.
Merriam Co.), IX (November), 5-7.
Winston Churchill's novel The Crisis suggested that a stateroom on a river boat is
so called because the first ones were named
for states, and the texas, after the annexation of Texas, as a structure annexed to the
staterooms; the publishers of the Merriam-
Webster Dictionaries wrote MT for confirmation, and he called the theory far-fetched
in a letter from Ampersand, N.Y. (July 26
[1901], here reproduced, partly in facsimile). The other etymology concerns Hervey
Allen.

B5   ANON. [Review: Cyril Clemens, ed., Mark
Twain, the Letter Writer (1932).] Times
Literary Supplement, January 19, p. 38.
"These letters add nothing significant to
what is already known" about MT.

B6   ARVIN, NEWTON. "The Friend of Caesar," New
Republic, LXXIV (March 29), 191.
A review of Van Wyck Brooks, The Ordeal of
Mark Twain (New and Revised Edition: valuable, but to be more profound would require
"a genuinely dialectical history of the
development of American society") and Steph-
en Leacock, Mark Twain, which "rather surprisingly...shows that he has not read The
Ordeal of Mark Twain to no effect." Review
reprinted in Arvin, American Pantheon
(1966), 141-44.

B7   BLAIR, WALTER. [Review: Bernard DeVoto, Mark
Twain's America (1932) and Cyril Clemens,
Mark Twain the Letter Writer (1932).] American Literature, IV (January), 399-404.
Blair says DeVoto's book is "splendid" on
Clemens and his frontier background, but in
writing about the critics "his judgment is
as unsound as his judgment concerning Mark
Twain and his predecessors is sound." Cyril
Clemens's book is anecdotal, filled out with
"newspaper stories about Mark Twain and letters to and from the humorist. There does
not seem to be much system in the arrangement of the material."

B8   BOYNTON, PERCY H. [Review: Bernard DeVoto,
Mark Twain's America (1932).] New England
Quarterly, VI (March), 184-87.
"The virtue of Mr. DeVoto's book is that
it is definite and that it so concretely relates the shaggy realist, humorist, satirist
to a western way of life and a western

(BOYNTON, PERCY H.)
manner of expression," but DeVoto's attacks on Brooks and others are a distraction: "It is too bad that so otherwise clear, rational, and convincing an account should be thus becluttered."

B9   *BRADFORD, GAMALIEL. "Mark Twain," in his Portraits and Personalities (Boston and New York: Houghton Mifflin Co.), pp. 213-35; also on MT, pp. 265-66.
[Source: Asselineau (1954), No. 571.]

B10 BROWNELL, GEORGE HIRAM. "Kipling's Meeting with Mark Twain," American Book Collector, IV (September-October), 191-92.
On the publication of Kipling's interview of MT in the New York Herald, August 17, 1890.

B11 _____. "Mark Twainiana," American Book Collector, III (March), 172-77; (April), 207-12.
On MT's early writings in Missouri and Iowa, in Nevada and California, and elsewhere, with credit to Willard S. Morse for his part in uncovering much of the West Coast material.

B12 _____. "Mark Twain's First Published Literary Effort," American Book Collector, III (February), 92-95.
On Franklin J. Meine's discovery of "The Dandy Frightening the Squatter," and, briefly, on MT's writings on the West Coast, and in the Buffalo Express and the Galaxy.

B13 _____. "Mark Twain's Speech at the Whittier Banquet," American Book Collector, IV (August), 73-75.
A popular account, adding little or nothing to Paine's, about MT's unsuccessful speech; notes that the holograph manuscript of the speech is in the collection of Willard S. Morse.

B14 CHASE, MARY ELLEN. "Mississippi America," Commonweal, XVII (January 11), 303-304.
A review of DeVoto, Mark Twain's America (1932); criticizes the style and controversial tone, but finds "the virtues of Mr. DeVoto's book far over-balance its shortcomings. It is far more than a criticism, an interpretation of Mark Twain...it is a text-book of social history...a study in anthropology...a revelation in frontier religion; it is physiology, sociology, physiography, all in one."

B15 CLEMENS, CYRIL. "Mark Twain and Jane Austen: An Imaginary Conversation on a Transatlantic Steamer," Overland Monthly, XCI (January), 21.
An amusing fictionalized dialogue consisting of a heated exchange, chiefly about vivid characterization.

B16 CLEMENS, J[AMES] R[OSS.] "Mark Twain and the Ants," Atlantic Monthly, CLI (June), 34-36. [sic: end of issue].
"Dr. Jim" Clemens (Cyril's father) describes an MT story, from the unpublished papers, of experiments with ants. MT said he made them little paper churches, labeled for the different congregations, but they always went to the one with honey in it. Later, he put an ant family in a little paper cottage and made the eldest son drunk three nights; they accepted him twice, then threw him out, thus demonstrating more than human wisdom.

B17 DEVOTO, BERNARD. [Letter to the Editor.] Saturday Review of Literature, X (July 22), 4.
Answering Van Wyck Brooks's The Ordeal of Mark Twain, the Lewis Mumford review of it (May, pp. 573-75, 1933.B25) and a brief editorial comment in Saturday Review (July 8, p. 688), says that the Mississippi steamboating world was indeed materialistic, but "my melancholy quarrel with Messrs. Brooks, Frank, and Mumford proceeds from their insistence that pioneer life was somehow more 'materialistic' than life anywhere else in America, and that this same 'materialism,' somehow as a result of the frontier, suffused American life. My book expressed my dissent from that beautiful simplicity." In the preceding column appears "The Pipe of Peace," an unsigned editorial statement acquiescing in DeVoto's position but arguing that the frontier provided both temptation and opportunity for materialists.

B18 FENN, WILLIAM PURVIANCE. Ah Sin and His Brethren in American Literature. Peking: College of Chinese Studies, Co-operating with California College in China.
Briefly describes what MT wrote about the Chinese in America (pp. 33-35 and passim), making no attempt to go beyond the familiar sources.

B19 GARY, LORENA M. "Oh, Youth! Mark Twain: Boy and Philosopher," Overland Monthly, XCI (November), 154-55.
Biographical summary, apparently based on the Paine Biography and William Dean Howells' My Mark Twain (1910).

B20 *HICKS, GRANVILLE. "A Banjo on My Knee," in his The Great Tradition (New York: The Macmillan Co.), pp. 38-49.
[Source: Reprinted in Scott (1955), pp. 215-22; (1967), pp. 213-20; Leary (1962), pp. 132-40. Leary quotes a request by Hicks that he indicate "that it does not fully represent my present opinion. The chief difference is that I should make more today of what Mark Twain did accomplish, though I have much the same feeling about what he didn't and why." Also see Hicks, 1935.B43 entry.] "Because there was so little in his

1933 - Shorter Writings

(HICKS, GRANVILLE)
own preparation, and so little in the intellectual life of his time, to guide him,
Mark Twain could never satisfy himself that
a literary career adequately expressed the
powers that he felt within him." TS, HF,
PW, LOM, CY, and JA are "his chief contribution to American literature...it is
doubtful if he ever achieved all that he
had given promise of doing or really deserved the high rank that was so readily
accorded him."

B21   LEISY, ERNEST E., and JAY B. HUBBELL. "Doctoral Dissertations in American Literature,"
American Literature, IV (January), 419-65.
On p. 438, lists five completed dissertations on MT, and on p. 460 lists two dissertations in progress [later completed].
Supplemented by Leary (1948).

B22   LORCH, FRED W. [Review: Van Wyck Brooks,
The Ordeal of Mark Twain.] American Literature, V (May), 185-7.
In this revision of the 1920 edition
Brooks has not abandoned his thesis that
MT's creative life was blocked by the influence of time and place, and of those
near him. "In matters of detail, however,
Mr. Brooks has made a number of changes,
though few of these seem important enough
to have warranted the labor of bringing out
a revised edition." A few intemperate assertions have been dropped, but "the additions to the present volume are meager and
on the whole unimpressive." Sides with
DeVoto, and does not view restraint as necessarily harmful to MT's creative life.

B23   LOVEMAN, AMY. "The Clearing House," Saturday
Review of Literature, X (September 16),
120.
"A Study of Mark Twain" notes a request
by Edward Wagenknecht for pertinent information he might use in the book he is writing on MT.

B24   MATTHIESSEN, F. O. "Mark Twain and the
Jameses," Yale Review, n.s. XXII (Spring),
605-609; on DeVoto's Mark Twain's America,
pp. 605-607.
Brooks's Ordeal was "brilliant and challenging," but "too rigidly intellectual-
ized"; DeVoto's Mark Twain's America is
angry, often inaccurate, prone to oversim-
plify: "It furnishes a mass of not too
well-organized material that is useful for
interpreting him, but it is not the trenchant essay in social and intellectual history that was needed." [A review article;
also discusses books on Henry James.]

B25   MUMFORD, LEWIS. "Prophet, Pedant and Pio-
neer," Saturday Review of Literature, IX
(May), 573-75.
A review of Van Wyck Brooks, The Ordeal
of Mark Twain, defending it against Bernard
DeVoto, whose book "in itself generously

contains enough data to support every item
in Mr. Brook's characterization." To Mumford, "not merely as a writer but as a man
Mark Twain seems a small, spoiled effigy
of the person he might have been."

B26   PARKS, EDD WINFIELD. "Mark Twain Miscon-
strued." American Review, I (June), 363-67.
A review of Stephen Leacock's Mark Twain:
"Mr. Leacock has relied almost entirely
upon the compendious but uncritical biography by Albert Bigelow Paine, and the interesting but highly imaginative 'psychograph'
by Van Wyck Brooks, The Ordeal of Mark
Twain." What Leacock lacks is familiarity
with American frontier life, as revealed by
DeVoto.

B27   PARTINGTON, WILFRED. "Mark Twain--in Love,
in Anger, and in Bibliography," Bookman,
(New York), LXXVI (March), 313-14, iii-iv
[sic].
A rambling account of the collector's interest and problems with MT first editions
and letters; quotes MT's letters of
November 28, December 2, 1868, on his engagement to Olivia Langdon.

B28   PHELPS, WILLIAM LYON. "The Real Mark Twain,"
Scribner's Magazine, XCIII (March), 182-83.
A review of Bernard DeVoto's Mark Twain's
America (1932): "I think Mr. DeVoto over-
estimates the importance of Mr. Brooks's
work The Ordeal of Mark Twain (1920)." De-
Voto knows his material and has a sense of
humor.

B29   RICHARDS, P. "Reminiscences of Mark Twain,"
Library Review, No. 25 (Spring), pp. 19-22.
Richards, who "drew hundreds of caricatures of the great humorist," here records
MT's comments on teasing James McNeill
Whistler, what President Eliot of Harvard
told MT about Darwin's use of his books as
bedtime reading, on speaking in London before the Authors' Club and the Savage Club,
on his preference for short words (especially when he was paid by the word), and on a
humorist's difficulty in being taken seriously. "This article will serve to introduce Mark Twain by Stephen Leacock."

B30   RUSSELL, FRANCES THERESA. [Review: Bernard
DeVoto, Mark Twain's America (1932).]
University of California Chronicle, XXXV
(January), 157-61.
"Both as much needed counter propaganda
and as a mine of information displayed with
skillful artistry...a valuable addition to
the national garner."

B31   *TARKINGTON, BOOTH. [Introduction.] The Ad-
ventures of Huckleberry Finn. New York:
The Limited Editions Club.
[Source: Asselineau (1954), No. 569:
"Attacks Brooks without naming him."]

B32 UNDERHILL, IRVING S. "Diamonds in the Rough,
     Being the Story of Another Book that Mark
     Twain Never Wrote," Colophon, Part 13
     (February), 8 pp. (not numbered).
        Contains the text of an MT letter to J.
     H. Riley, proposing a business arrangement
     to send him to the South African diamond
     fields to collect information and impres-
     sions for another travel book like IA and
     RI.

B33 _____. "'Tempest in a Teapot' or 'Notes on
     Huckleberry Finn': Announcement of a New
     Book," American Book Collector, IV
     (September-October), 153-56.
        A rambling discussion of the first print-
     ing of HF, and of the mutilated cut on
     p. 283. "These notes will be a summary,
     with many additions and a few amendments,
     of articles that have appeared in The Colo-
     phon, Number Six, and The American Book Col-
     lector, November, 1932." [Apparently, Un-
     derhill's book never appeared--T.A.T.]

B34 *VAN DOREN, CARL. American Literature: An
     Introduction. Los Angeles: U. S. Library
     Association. On MT, pp. 58-62.
        [Source: Asselineau (1954), No. 576.]

1934 A BOOKS

A1   BRASHEAR, MINNIE M. Mark Twain: Son of Mis-
     souri. Chapel Hill: University of North
     Carolina Press.
        "This book is an attempt to verify an im-
     pression, formed from personal observation,
     that commentaries on Mark Twain which have
     pointed to his Middle West up-bringing as
     unfortunate, even tragic in its suppres-
     sions, are not true accounts." Includes
     chapters on MT's reading and the influence
     on him of eighteenth-century Europe, and a
     21-page bibliography (not systematically
     incorporated in the present bibliography).
     [Also, reprinted: New York: Russell &
     Russell, Inc., 1964.]

A2   *CLEMENS, CYRIL. Mark Twain and Mussolini.
     Webster Groves, Missouri: International
     Mark Twain Society.
        [Source: Asselineau (1954), No. 607:
     "The author recounts interviews with Musso-
     lini, Shaw, Galsworthy, Maurois, Chesterton,
     Drinkwater, and F. D. Roosevelt, on the sub-
     ject of Mark Twain's importance."]

A3   DECASSERES, BENJAMIN. When Huck Finn Went
     Highbrow. New York: Thomas F. Madigan,
     Inc.
        A pamphlet containing an MT letter to Mary
     Hallock Foote (December 2, 1887, reproduced
     in facsimile) on his readings from Browning.

A4   *VYGODSKAYA, EMMA OSIPOVNA. Marka Twena pied-
     zivojumi [The Adventures of Mark Twain.]
     Riga, Latvia.
        [Source: Asselineau (1954), No. 604.]

1934 B SHORTER WRITINGS

B1   ADAMS, SIR JOHN. "Mark Twain, Psychologist,"
     Dalhousie Review, XIII (January), 417-26.
        A discussion of What Is Man? and the light
     cast on MT's thinking by a letter to Adams
     (December 5, 1898) on his new book, The
     Herbartian Theory Applied to Education. The
     letter is reproduced in full in Lawrence
     Clark Powell, "An Unpublished Mark Twain
     Letter" (1942).

B2   ALTROCCHI, JULIA COOLEY. "Along the Mother
     Lode," Yale Review, n.s. XXIV (Autumn),
     131-45.
        Description of California gold fields and
     their history; MT is mentioned only in pass-
     ing. This marginal item probably attracted
     the attention of previous bibliographers be-
     cause it follows Stephen Leacock's essay on
     MT and Dickens (1934.B14).

B3   ANON. "Mark Twain Anticipates Roosevelt,"
     Word Study (G. & C. Merriam Co.), IX (April),
     4.
        Reprints a brief news item from the St.
     Louis Post-Dispatch (n.d.): Cyril Clemens
     presented the gold medal of the Internation-
     al Mark Twain Society to the President, who
     credited CY as his source of the term, "the
     New Deal."

B4   ANON. [Review: Van Wyck Brooks, The Ordeal
     of Mark Twain (revised edition, 1932).]
     Times Literary Supplement, June 28, p. 456.
        "Still the most striking study of the in-
     ner reality of its subject that has yet been
     published," but revised very little for the
     new edition. Regrettably, in his more recent
     critical works Brooks has not fulfilled his
     early high promise.

B5   ANON. [Brief, minor review: Minnie M. Brash-
     ear, Mark Twain, Son of Missouri.] Nation
     (New York), CXXXVIII (April 4), 395.

B6   ARVIN, NEWTON. [Brief Review: Minnie M.
     Brashear, Mark Twain: Son of Missouri.]
     New Republic, LXXVII (March 28), 194.
        "Miss Brashear is less shrewish than De-
     Voto and more concrete," but her idyllic
     picture of life in Hannibal must be taken
     with some reservation.

B7   BROWNELL, GEORGE HIRAM. "Mark Twainiana,"
     American Book Collector, V (April), 124-26.
        On the first publication of "The Jumping
     Frog," and on other early publications of
     MT's writings in the Sunday Mercury and Sat-
     urday Press.

B8   CLEMENS, CYRIL. "Mark Twain's Religion," Com-
     monweal, XXI (December 28), 254-55.
        MT has been accused of irreverence and
     atheism by critics who cite Captain Storm-
     field's Visit to Heaven and Eve's Diary to
     support their argument. These critics mis-
     represent MT's views, as is made clear in a

1934 - Shorter Writings

(CLEMENS, CYRIL)
letter from Dr. Henry Van Dyke (here published for the first time), who says that
"No one who heard him speak of the simple
faith of his dearly beloved wife (as he often spoke to me) could think of him as being
indifferent to religion."

B9   COMPTON, CHARLES HERRICK. "Who Reads Mark
Twain?" American Mercury, XXXI (April),
465-71; expanded in his Who Reads What? Essays on the Readers of Mark Twain, Hardy,
Sandburg, Shaw, William James, and the Greek
Classics (New York: The H. W. Wilson Co.),
pp. 11-34.
Records of book-borrowing at the St. Louis
Public Library, if typical of national patterns, suggest that "Mark Twain is the most
widely read American author, living or dead";
Compton tabulates the popularity of individual works, and adds comments by "a seamstress," "an unemployed telegraph operator,"
"a chemical engineer," "a contractor," and
"a musician" in response to a questionnaire
he sent out.

B10 *DOUGLAS, GILBERT. "Behind that Door," New
York World Telegram (August 15), p. 21.
Contains an unpublished MT letter from Ham-
ilton, Bermuda, January 26, 1910.
[Source: MHRA Annual Bibliography (1934),
No. 3853.]

B11 GRINSTEAD, FRANCES. "Mark Twain Biography,"
Southwest Review, XIX (Winter), 12-13.
A review of Minnie M. Brashear, Mark
Twain, Son of Missouri. Chiefly descriptive. "The author has unearthed a number
of facts which will be valuable to every
Mark Twain student of the future; but perhaps the most striking part of her book is
her contention that [MT]...was a product of
eighteenth-century ideals."

B12 *HARPER, JOSEPH HENRY. I Remember. New York
and London: Harper & Brothers.
Contains reminiscences of MT, pp. 134-49.
[Source: Asselineau (1954), No. 609.]

B13 HOWELLS, WILLIAM DEAN. "When Mark Twain
Missed Fire," Golden Book, XX (July), 97-98.
On MT's disastrous speech at the Whittier
Birthday Dinner; excerpted from his "My
Memories of Mark Twain," Harper's, CXXI
(August, 1910), 512-13 and his My Mark
Twain (1910), pp. 58-61.

B14 LEACOCK, STEPHEN. "Two Humorists: Charles
Dickens and Mark Twain," Yale Review, n.s.
XXIV (Autumn), 118-29.
Both authors show a kind of "divine retro-
spect" that blends humor and pathos.

B15 *LE BRETON, MAURICE. "Mark Twain: An Appreciation," Revue Anglo-Américaine, XII
(October), 401-18.
[Source: Reprinted in Smith (1963),
pp. 29-39; translated by Myra Jehlen. Note

that "Un Centenaire: Mark Twain" attributed
to Le Breton is listed for 1935, but the article could not be found; my source of bibliographical data may have been in error.]
Emphasizes MT's original, realistic, Western
quality, his feeling for "the deeper reality
beneath appearances." His feeling for the
beautiful "in no way implies conformity to
rules or canons. It is purely the emotion
of an imaginative man who, dissatisfied with
the commonplace, takes refuge in the unique.
It is a moment of happiness, not the goal of
a patient and rational search."

B16 ____. [Review: Minnie M. Brashear, Mark
Twain: Son of Missouri.] Revue Anglo-
Américaine, XII (October), 81-83.
Summarizes Miss Brashear's thesis that
Missouri was particularly important in shaping MT, and that there was a strong influence of European literature, and especially
of the eighteenth century. This would require a reshaping of conventional thinking
on MT and the question remains open. Miss
Brashear's research is especially useful and
original in the first part of her book. [In
French.]

B17 LYMAN, GEORGE D. The Saga of the Comstock
Lode: Boom Days in Virginia City. New
York, London: Charles Scribner's Sons. On
MT, pp. 202-15, 246-304.
Provides a vivid popular account of MT's
Washoe days, supported by copious notes
(pp. 380-95 on MT). Although Lyman is writing for a general audience and stresses the
more lively aspects of his material, he has
turned up a wealth of evidence which merits
further investigation; his sources have not
been systematically traced for the present
bibliography.

B17A MARQUIS, DON. Chapters for the Orthodox.
Garden City, New York: Doubleday, Doran &
Co., Inc.
[Source: Quoted by Christopher Morley in
"Hunting Mark Twain's Remainders" (1935.B63);
year and facts of publication are from National Union Catalogue.] God told a reporter
he had given MT a river of his own in Heav-
en, and tolerated the "gorgeous lyric" of
his profanity. MT was ready to accept Satan's offer to run the river in Hell for a
while, but "his wife and William Dean Howells
wouldn't let him."

B18 MILLER, JAMES MacDONALD. An Outline of American Literature. New York: Farrar & Rinehart, pp. 208-209, 234-35, and passim.
The greater part of this book is given over
to biographical outlines, lists of works,
and discussions of literary movements. Contrasts MT to the local colorists in that he
dug deeper, as Hardy did (pp. 208-209). He
is "the essential American, the complete
verbal expression of his age," and Whitman
prepared the way for him. Despite his artistic disorder and extravagance, his

(MILLER, JAMES MacDONALD)
irreligion, and the faults of his age, "he was generous and sympathetic and gentle... straightforward and passionately honest and altogether lovable."

B19 MILNE, JAMES. The Memoirs of a Bookman. London: John Murray.
Describes MT as being touched on hearing of John Bright's account of a Quaker funeral in London, and MT having conducted Charles Kingsley around Boston (pp. 59-60). Describes MT as representing the bond between England and America: "He had a curious old-worldism in his nature as well as the fresh, alert, untrammelled mentality of the country whose child he was to the end" (p. 121). Also, on his serious attitude toward writing, and his concern over copyright laws (pp. 122-24).

B20 O'FAOLÁIN, SEÁN. "The Slavery of Mark Twain," Spectator, CLIII, 137.
A review of the revised edition of Brooks's The Ordeal of Mark Twain (1933), which O'Faoláin summarizes and praises. "And yet there is Huckleberry Finn and at least half of Life on the Mississippi--all lovely and all real. One should read The Ordeal of Mark Twain if only to see how it was possible, by the grace of God, for these pure pearls to be saved from the corrosive of a cynic born without a will."

B21 OLDER, FREMONT. "Mark Twain and Jackass Hill," Overland Monthly, XCII (July), 118.
First appeared as an editorial in the San Francisco Call-Bulletin under this title; discusses the competition of various places where MT lived to establish an official shrine to him, with Hartford as a leading contender, ready to guarantee $500,000 for the purpose. Jackass Hill can make no such offer, but it was there that he wrote "The Jumping Frog."

B22 PARTRIDGE, HENRY M. "Did Mark Twain Perpetrate Literary Hoaxes?" American Book Collector, V (December), 351-57.
A literary spoof, attributing George Horatio Derby's Phoenixiana and Squibob Papers to MT. Also, cites his contribution to the debate over the authorship of Shakespeare's plays, as discussed by J. M. Robertson in The Baconian Heresy: A Confutation (1912.B29). "(To be concluded in next issue.)"

B23 PHELPS, WILLIAM LYON. "As I like It," Scribner's Magazine, XCV (June), 432-35.
Contains anecdotes of MT giving his own introduction at a lecture in Newark, New Jersey (described himself as "a tall, sparse man"), and of Joseph Twichell reproving MT for swearing, only to be told, "Oh, Joe, you and I use exactly the same words, you in your prayers and I in my conversation; but we don't either of us mean anything by it."

B24 *SMITH, ANNELLA. "Mark Twain--Occultist," Rosicrucian Magazine, XXVI, 65-68.
[Source: Asselineau (1954), No. 628.]

B25 TINKER, EDWARD LAROQUE. "Cable and the Creoles," American Literature, V (January), 313-26.
Contains comments on the strained relationship of Cable and MT on their lecture tour; quotes an MT letter in possession of Major Pond's son describing Cable as "a Christ-besprinkled, psalm-singing Presbyterian."

B26 WARFEL, HARRY R. "George W. Cable Amends a Mark Twain Plot," American Literature, VI (November), 328-31.
Consists of half-page introduction by Warfel and text of a letter from Cable to Richard Watson Gilder (May 9, 1884) concerning a scheme for a literary joke. "The charm lies in reading a story whose salient events are already known, & reading it told over & over in 1/2 doz ways." Involved, according to Warfel, were MT, Cable, Gilder, "and probably Howells and Aldrich."

B27 WEISS, H. B. "Mark Twain's Hidden Autography," American Book Collector, V (October), 289-93.
Summarizes the argument in D. C. Partridge and H. M. Partridge's The Most Remarkable Echo in the World (1933) that internal ciphers reveal MT's authorship of the works attributed to Poe, Howthorne, and Lewis Carroll; a letter from Irving S. Underhill suggests a hoax may be involved, and George S. Frisbee writes in to agree with the Partridges, adding passages from Alice's Adventures Under Ground and elsewhere, in support of the thesis.

1935 A BOOKS

A1 *ANON. In Commemoration of the 100th Anniversary of the Birth of Samuel Langhorne Clemens, Famed as Mark Twain, this book is affectionately dedicated by the citizens of his boyhood home, Hannibal, Missouri. Hannibal: Lithographed by the Standard Printing Co.
[24-page pamphlet. Source: Asselineau (1954), No. 651.]

A2 CLEMENS, CYRIL. Mark Twain's Religion, with a foreword by Russell Wilbur. Webster Groves, Missouri: International Mark Twain Society.
"This monograph originally appeared in the Commonweal for December 28, 1934" (1934.B8).

A3 _____, ed. Mark Twain Wit and Wisdom. New York: Frederick A. Stokes Company.
Consists of Mark Twain anecdotes from various sources (not listed). There is a rather conventional preface by Stephen Leacock, who concludes: "Of one or two stories in the present volume I have heard it said by the pedantic that they are as old as the

(CLEMENS, CYRIL)
Greeks. To which I can only reply that in that case the Greeks stole them from Mark Twain" (p. viii).

A4 CLEMENS, SAMUEL L. The Family Mark Twain. New York and London: Harper & Brothers Publishers.

A generous anthology of 1462 pages, containing four complete novels (LOM, TS, HF, CY) and many popular tales and sketches. Contains Albert Bigelow Paine's "Mark Twain: A Biographical Summary," a condensed version of an appreciative account which first appeared in Harper's Weekly, LIV (April 30, 1910), 6-10, and Owen Wister's "In Homage to Mark Twain," which also appeared in Harper's Monthly, CLXXI (October, 1935), 547-556. This would have been a fine gift book in the centennial year of MT's birth, but it contains nothing of special importance to the scholar.

A5 *____. Mark Twain's Notebook, prepared for publication with comments by Albert Bigelow Paine. New York and London: Harper & Brothers.
[Source: Asselineau (1954), No. 641; also in Authorized Edition.]
A selection of materials from MT's unpublished notebooks, from his days as a river pilot until 1906. Paine's brief introduction denies that there has been any deliberate suppression of racy material in MT's unpublished manuscripts: "Mark Twain had his say; as much as any author could have it, thirty, forty, fifty years ago. When restricted at all it was chiefly through his own expressed wish to observe the conventions and convictions of that more orthodox, more timid and delicate (possibly more immaculate) day."

A6 *____, (translator). Slovenly Peter; or, Happy Tales and Funny Pictures, freely translated by Mark Twain, with Dr. Heinrich Hoffmann's illustrations, adapted from the rare first edition by Fritz Kredel. New York and London: Harper & Brothers; also, "now printed for the first time for members of the Limited Editions Club," New York: The Marchbanks Press.
[Source: Asselineau (1954), Nos. 643, 644.]

A7 *CROSS, WILBUR L. A Statement [Regarding] the Centenary of Mark Twain. Hartford, Connecticut.
[Source: Asselineau (1954), No. 652.] A broadside: a proposal by the Governor of Connecticut to designate November 1 as Mark Twain Day.

A8 EMBERSON, FRANCES GUTHRIE. Mark Twain's Vocabulary: A General Survey. University of Missouri Studies, X (July 1), 1-53.
Includes a Preface by Robert L. Ramsay. Treats the development of MT's vocabulary,

and special aspects of it such as Americanisms, possible coinages, adoptions, revivals, and a miscellaneous category. The "major parts" were reprinted in Twainian, XI (November-December, 1952), 1-4; XII (January-February, 1953), 1-4; (March-April), 1-4; (May-June), 3.

A9 *HELLER, OTTO. The Seriousness of Mark Twain. Address at the Annual Dinner of the State Historical Society at Hannibal, Missouri, May 9, 1935. Hannibal: Hannibal Chamber of Commerce.
[Source: Asselineau (1954), No. 635; described as a 14-page pamphlet, "A protest against Brooks's thesis in the name of local patriotism."]

A10 HERZBERG, MAX J., ed. The Mark Twain Omnibus Drawn from the Works of Mark Twain and Edited by Max J. Herzberg. New York, London: Harper & Brothers.
Consists of PW, a number of stories, sketches, and letters, introductory material, and exercises, with a bibliography of secondary material (not annotated and apparently not selected according to a plan). A school anthology.

A11 HÜPPY, AUGUST. Mark Twain und die Schweiz. Dem Grossen Freund und Bewunderer unseres Landes zum 100. Geburtstag. Zurich: Reutimann & Co.
Concerned with MT's visits to Switzerland, rather than with Swiss interest in his works. Contains a discussion of A Tramp Abroad on pp. 52-60.

A12 JOHNSON, MERLE. A Bibliography of the Works of Mark Twain, Samuel Langhorne Clemens. A List of First Editions in Book Form and of First Printings in Periodicals and Occasional Publications of His Varied Literary Activities. Revised and Enlarged. New York and London: Harper & Brothers.
This has only been superseded in part by Jacob Blanck's Bibliography of American Literature (Vol. II [1957], 173-254) and is still extremely valuable. In addition to th the material listed in the descriptive title there is a wealth of notes, commentary, and information on material about MT. Of particular interest are "Books Containing Mark Twain Letters," discussion of MT's plays and of dramatizations of his work, discussion of newspaper interviews, "General Notes and Comment" (a miscellany of brief items which do not fit in elsewhere), "Several Items by Mark Twain" ("a selection of juvenilia and specimens of the later writings as a professional newspaperman"). There is an extensive and detailed index. [Reprinted Westport, Connecticut: Greenwood Press, Publishers, 1972.]

A13 *LANGDON, JERVIS. Mark Twain and Elmira, Mark Twain Centennial Committee of New York.

(*LANGDON, JERVIS)
[Source: Asselineau (1954), No. 635,
which describes it as a 6-leaf pamphlet by
a nephew of MT.]

A14   PATTEE, FRED LEWIS, ed. Mark Twain: Representative Selections. New York: American
Book Company.
        "Luckily he had a sensible wife. Care-
fully was he directed into the literary
areas where lay his great power. Assisted
by Twichell and Howells he was led to the
writing of Old Times on the Mississippi, a
marvellous classic. He was directed by Warner into the wonder area of The Gilded Age,
he was induced to add to it his Tom Sawyer
and best of all his Huckleberry Finn"
(p. xxxvi). Pattee also notes MT's power
as a satirist, but "What results from Mark
Twain's furious assaults upon his times?
Archibald Henderson has classed the man as
'the greatest sociologist in letters.'
Just why? He accomplished nothing"--people
read GA for amusement (pp. xlii-xliii).

A15   TAYLOR, COLEY B. Mark Twain's Margins on
Thackerary's "Swift." New York: Gotham
House.
        Contains text of MT's pencilled comments
in the section on Swift in Thackeray's English Humorists ("the Harper edition of
1868"-- p. 29). This is nominally a 55-
page booklet, in which the first 27 pages
are given over to the half-title, title-
page, and a very general preface on MT in
Redding by a neighbor who did not know him
well; the latter part of the book is valuable and has frequently been cited by students of MT.

A16   WAGENKNECHT, EDWARD. Mark Twain: The Man and
His Work. New Haven: Yale University
Press.
        Reflects thorough familiarity with the MT
scholarship of the time, and includes a ten-
page bibliography. A completely revised
edition appeared in 1961. Pp. 57-80 excerpted in Scott (1955), pp. 223-30.

1935 B SHORTER WRITINGS

B1   ALTICK, RICHARD D. "Mark Twain's Despair:
An Explanation in Terms of His Humanity,"
South Atlantic Quarterly, XXXIV (October),
359-67.
        "He was not a psychological wreck all his
life, tormented by a sense of guilt at having betrayed his artistic instincts. On
the contrary, he was more than ordinarily
happy during his best years," and, by his
own standards, a success; but he became a
pessimist and a cynic because of his growing materialism at the expense of "his
idealistic-intellectual-artistic side....
Mark Twain remained all his life immature,
socially, intellectually, or emotionally;
and thus when old age came he was totally
unprepared for it."

B2   ANON. "Ever this Twain Is Met. World-Wide
Tributes Paid on Centenary of Writer's
Birth; Hannibal, Missouri to Be Shrine;
Mussolini Heads Movement," Literary Digest,
CXX (November 30), 19.
        Contains no specific references, except to
an editorial in the Hannibal Courier-Post
urging the establishment of a memorial
shrine to MT in that city; includes pictures
of sculptures by Walter Russell of MT and
Tom and Huck for the memorial, and comments
on the oddity of Mussolini's part in sending
a $200 contribution and his selection to be
Honorary President of the fund for a memorial in St. Louis.

B3   ANON. "A Garland for Mark Twain's Centennial,"
New York Times Book Review (August 4), p. 5.
        A review of Cyril Clemens, ed., Mark Twain:
Wit and Wisdom, which brings MT "freshly and
vividly into the reader's consciousness...
it is a delightful book for casual reading."

B4   ANON. "Mark Twain," Saturday Review of Literature, XIII (November 16), 8.
        On MT's warm, kindly side, as exemplified
in the two letters on the following page
(1935.B25, as "Two Letters of Mark Twain,
Hitherto Unpublished").

B5   ANON. "Mark Twain," Times Literary Supplement, November 30, pp. 779-80.
        A review-article and general discussion of
MT, who was no novelist, but a humorist and,
still more, "a poet, even in his humor";
his lasting works are TS, HF, LOM, RI, and
parts of GA and PW. "All that Mark Twain
was and was not [was] inherent in his frontier origin." There is comparatively brief
discussion of Albert Bigelow Paine, ed.,
Mark Twain's Notebook (Contains "no sur-
prises...it is in fact incomplete and textually unreliable in addition to being inadequately edited"); Edward Wagenknecht,
Mark Twain: The Man and His Work ("Sums up
the outstanding facts and critical views,
stands so squarely in the centre of the
field as to suggest little need of further
discussion"); Minnie M. Brashear, Mark Twain:
Son of Missouri (1934; "Seeks to prove the
existence on the frontier of an 'authentic'
culture, but shows it as little more than
'an interest in the safe and reliable classics'--which is not culture but its simula-
crum, too partial and provincial to fulfill
the true function of culture"); Fred Lewis
Pattee, ed., Mark Twain: Representative
Selections (Briefly noted).

B6   ANON. "Mark Twain Centennial. Commemorations
Will Be Held Throughout Nation this Year,"
Literary Digest, CXIX (April 20), 31.
        On the Mark Twain Centennial Committee,
quoting a note to Nicholas Murray Butler,
the chairman, from Rudyard Kipling: "To my
mind he was the largest man of his time,
both in the direct outcome of his work, and,
more important still, as an indirect force

(ANON.)

in an age of iron Philistinism. Later generations don't know their debt, of course,
and they would be quite surprized if they
did." Other commemorative groups are also
mentioned, and there is a photo of MT (copyrighted by Paul Thompson).

B7   ANON. "Mark Twain Centennial to be Widely
       Celebrated," Publishers' Weekly, CXXVII
       (February 9), 697.
          A survey of plans: Nicholas Murray Butler
       is chairman of a centennial committee, and
       there will be formal dinners in the larger
       cities, radio programs, films, a special
       stamp issue, articles in national magazines,
       and interviews with people who knew MT.
       There are also plans for celebration of the
       centennial in England, and there will be
       showings of an early film showing him, as
       well as a commemorative medal and a special
       edition of his works.

B8   ANON. "The Mark Twain Commemoration," Colum-
       bia University Quarterly, XXVII (December),
       357-78.
          Nicholas Murray Butler presided over the
       ceremonies, held October 31, 1935. The ad-
       dresses were by James Campbell on "The Case
       of Clemens vs. Twain" (pp. 358-69) and
       Christopher Morley on "The Return of Huckle-
       berry Finn" (pp. 369-78). Butler praised
       MT's "many-sided and truly rich personality"
       and told several anecdotes. Campbell dis-
       cussed the changes in MT's critical reputa-
       tion and discussed the question of whether
       a great artist was stifled in him, conclud-
       ing that he was the man our national litera-
       ture needed to provide a regeneration, to
       blow the masses of stale air out, although
       his philosophy was mechanical and works such
       as MS were marred by a failure to keep psy-
       chic distance; his great achievement was
       "the perfect expression of the culture of
       western America" in such products of his
       personal experience as TS and HF. Christo-
       pher Morley commented on the dated quality
       of some of MT's humor and the way his minor
       works are being forgotten. The debunking
       by Brooks and others, though humorless and
       often mistaken, is a healthy preventive to
       adulation of MT. MT's great works are TS
       and HF, which, for all their flaws, contain
       "writing admirable and perfect for its pur-
       pose." [Morley covers much the same ground
       in his "Hunting Mark Twain's Remainders" in
       the Saturday Review of Literature,
       November 2 (1935.B63), and Campbell's speech
       is reprinted as "Twain Versus Clemens"
       [(1936.B8).]

B9   ANON. "Our Mark Twain," Scholastic, XXVII
       (November 23), 3.
          An editorial, discussing MT's fame, crit-
       ical views of him, and the importance of
       his work. Introduces a Mark Twain Number,
       containing the following, in addition to
       articles listed in the present bibliography:

a reprinting of Owen Wister's "In Homage to
Mark Twain," (pp. 6-7, 21); "Mark Twain Digs
for Gold," a Radio Play by Gladys Schmidt
(pp. 9-10); "Chronology of the Life of Mark
Twain" (p. 16, "From Mark Twain, by Stephen
Leacock"); "Mark Twain Bibliography" (p. 17,
selected from Wagenknecht's bibliography in
Mark Twain: The Man and His Work); "Twain
Poster Contest" (p. 35); and pictures of the
Arthur W. Woelfle portrait of MT, Walter
Russell's model of the center portion of a
sculpture group for the Mark Twain Memorial,
and a number of photographs of scenes in
Hannibal, Missouri.

B10   *ANON. "Princes de l'humour: Alphonse Allais,
       Mark Twain," Annales Politiques et Littér-
       aires, CLX (September 25), 316-17.
          [Source: Asselineau (1954), No. 715.]

B11   ANON. "Scattered Letters of Mark Twain, To-
       gether with Eulogistic Contributions for His
       Centennial" ("Published through the courtesy
       of Mr. Cyril Clemens"), Missouri Historical
       Society Glimpses of the Past (now Missouri
       Historical Society Bulletin), II (October),
       123-32.
          Includes an MT letter of April 14 (1868?)
       asking a person named Williams to "see that
       no reports or synopses (even the most meagre
       ones) are made of my lecture"; to P. D. Pel-
       tier (October 14 [1879]) on a lecture wel-
       coming Georgia veterans to Hartford ("Per-
       sonal contact & communion of Northerners &
       Southerners over the friendly board will do
       more toward obliterating sectional lines and
       restoring mutual respect and esteem than any
       other thing that can be devised"); to Sig-
       mund Schlesinger (Vienna, February 2, 1898
       about a play on which they had planned to
       collaborate); also several MT letters to
       James Ross Clemens. Tributes to MT from
       Lord Dunsany, Eugene O'Neill, Irvin S. Cobb,
       Carl Sandberg, David Warfield, and Hendrik
       Willem Van Loon.

B12   *ANON. [Interview with Mrs. W. E. Ireland.]
       Hannibal Courier-Post, March 6.
          MT renamed Holliday's Hill for Cardiff,
       South Wales because it reminded him of a
       similar hill there. [Source: Wecter (1952),
       pp. 157, 300.]

B13   ANON. [Review: Slovenly Peter, translated by
       MT from Dr. Heinrich Hoffman's Struwelpet-
       er.] Saturday Review of Literature, XIII
       (November 16), 26.
          "Mark's translation has the gay insouci-
       ance one would expect."

B14   ANON. [Brief, descriptive review: Slovenly
       Peter, translated from Dr. Heinrich Hoff-
       man's Struwelpeter.] Times Literary Supple-
       ment, November 30, p. 780.

B15 ARVIN, NEWTON. "Mark Twain: 1835-1935," New Republic, LXXXIII (June 12), 125-27.
MT won a great and lasting readership, but writing for such a large and uncritical audience was harmful to him as artist and critic of his time; nonetheless, for works such as his attacks on American imperialism, "and despite the vast wastage of his career, Mark Twain may well survive as a writer and in the affections of later generations and of a class to which he did not directly address himself." He will survive, "but surely far less as a writer, at the best, than as a folk-hero, a grand half-legendary personality." Reprinted in Scott (1955), pp. 231-35, and in Leary (1962), pp. 141-44.

B16 BECKER, MAY LAMBERTON. "Books: A Reading Menu for the Week," Scholastic, XXVII (November 23), 17.
A review of LOM as a "truly American" book some critics say will outlive all MT's books except TS and HF, and of DeVoto's Mark Twain's America (1932), which "can hardly be surpassed" as introduction to MT and "as a preface to the understanding of American literature and its differences from English literature."

B17 *BINGHAM, ROBERT WARWICK. "Buffalo's Mark Twain," Museum Notes, Buffalo Historical Society, II, No. 4-6.
[Source: Asselineau (1954), No. 672.]

B18 BORGES, JORGE LUIS. "Una Vindicación de Mark Twain," Sur, V (Noviembre), 40-46.
Supports DeVoto's view of MT as vigorously American, in opposition to "la depresiva tesis de Brooks." "Mark Twain (importa repetirlo) ha escrito Huckleberry Finn, libro que basta para la gloria. Libro ni burlesco ni trágico, libro solamente feliz."

B19 CANBY, HENRY SEIDEL. "Mark Twain: Anti-Victorian," Saturday Review of Literature, XII (October 12), 3-4, 14.
A review of Mark Twain's Notebook and Edward Wagenknecht, Mark Twain: The Man and His Work, which, "if it contributes nothing really new, is a sane and accurate discussion of a man hard to analyze, and very difficult to estimate without exaggeration either of his tragic pessimism or his boisterous humor. This writer's sensible handling of the wife-suppression theory is excellent, and indeed his volume is the most useful, if not the most brilliant or penetrating, short book on Mark Twain. The Notebook provides no startling evidence, and "the novelty is in a change in emphasis," stressing MT's "inmost thoughts." He was not suppressed, and managed to express radical ideas in his lifetime, as in HF and CY. Picture of MT and Olivia Clemens on front cover.

B20 _____. [Brief review: Mark Twain's Notebook.] Book of the Month Club News, November, p. 15.
The book refutes the Brooks view of suppressed genius but provides no starling revelations.

B21 CHARPENTIER, JOHN. "Humour Anglais et Humour Américain, À Propos du Centenaire de Mark Twain," Mercure de France, CCLXIV (15 Décembre), 475-500.
Consists of two somewhat distinct essays; the first ends (p. 488): "Nous allons voir, maintenant, en prenant pour exemple Mark Twain, comment l'humour révolutionnaire est devenu matérialiste de l'autre côte de l'océan." On the basis of photographs in the Paine biography and in Clara Clemens's My Father, Mark Twain Charpentier asks, "Mark Twain avait-il des origines juives, comme on l'a hasardé?" (p. 490).

B22 CLEMENS, CYRIL. "The First Book on Mark Twain," Commonweal, XXII (Ocober 11), 591.
A review of Fred Lewis Pattee's Mark Twain: Representative Selections, which are well chosen and come with "a scholarly and fascinating introduction." Pattee, as a college professor, errs in denying MT a place "among our few great literary masters."

B23 _____. "Mark Twain's Joan of Arc," Commonweal, XXII (July 26), 323-24.
A discussion for the general reader of JA and MT's admiration of Joan. (See letter by Walsh, August 23, p. 408, 1935.B80.)

B24 *CLEMENS, SAMUEL L. "Letter to the Hon. Secretary of the Treasury," dated October 13, 1902. Book News (American Book Company), Autumn.
[Source: MHRA Annual Bibliography (1935), No. 3744.]

B25 _____. "Two Letters of Mark Twain, Hitherto Unpublished," Saturday Review of Literature, XIII (November 16), 9, 29.
To twelve-year-old Margaret Blackmer (September 18, October 6, 1908), mentioning visits from several of his "Angel-Fishes," listing JA, P&P, HF, and TS as his favorite books, commenting on the recent burglary of his Redding, Connecticut home, and mentioning an expected visit from his childhood sweetheart [Laura Hawkins Frazer].

B26 COLUM, MARY M. "The Misunderstood Jester," Forum, XCIV (November), 277-78.
A review of Edward Wagenknecht's Mark Twain: The Man and His Work, which here receives little critical attention; instead, the reviewer praises MT as "a folk writer," in a picaresque tradition with which he was familiar, and a writer of genius although he had "from his intellectual side, an uninteresting mind." MT "had an immense audience, to which he was devoted, and which he did not wish to disturb in any of its convictions." There is passing mention of

117

(COLUM, MARY M.)
"that brilliant book of Van Wyck Brooks',
The Ordeal of Mark Twain."

B27 DAVIDSON, LOUIS B. "He Fell in Love with a
Picture," Liberty, XII (November 30), 48-50.
A popular account of MT's love for his
wife Olivia, adding nothing to the details
given by Paine and in other familiar sources.

B28 DEANE, THE REV. CANON ANTHONY. "Mark Twain,"
in The Right Hon. Earl of Lytton, ed.,
Essays by Divers Hands, Being the Transactions of the Royal Society of Literature of
the United Kingdom. n.s., XIV (London:
Humphrey Milford, Oxford University Press),
pp. 99-110. [Read March 7, 1935.]
Praises MT's courage in meeting his af-
flictions, and puts HF first among his
books. Despite occasionally forced humor
and uncertain taste, his work "caused a
vast amount of wholesome and hearty laughter" (pp. 109-10).

B29 DEVOTO, BERNARD. "The Greatness of Mark
Twain. A New Biography that Silences the
Frustration Theory--And His Notebook,"
New York Times Book Review, October 27,
pp. 1, 22.
A review of Edward Wagenknecht, Mark
Twain: The Man and His Work and Albert
Bigelow Paine, ed., Mark Twain's Notebook.
Wagenknecht's "sane, sound and tolerant
book" provides little new evidence, apart
from the Fairbanks correspondence, but
gives a useful survey of MT criticism--
rendering verdicts which are just but sometimes less scornful than the targets deserve. He rightly shows the careful artist
but errs in calling MT a thinker. The notebooks are good to have, but Paine is incorrect in saying that they are complete "and
he accompanies them with notes in his familiar piety."

B30 _____. [Review: Fred Lewis Pattee, ed.,
Mark Twain: Representative Selections.]
New England Quarterly, VIII (September),
427-30.
As an anthology it is flawed by the absence of anything written after 1877 (as a
result of copyright restrictions), and the
introduction, despite its "sound judgment"
and "critical sanity," overestimates the
beneficial influence of the East while suggesting that almost nothing written under
that influence will endure. Pattee misunderstands the influences of the popular
humor of the time; for example, in fact
"the influence of Artemus Ward on Mark
Twain was the influence of a man who finds
a publisher for a young writer and no more."

B31 DICKINSON, ASA DON. "Huckleberry Finn is Fifty Years Old--Yes; But Is He Respectable?"
Wilson Bulletin for Librarians, X (November),
180-85.
A general discussion of HF, followed by an
account of the difficulty of getting the
book into the children's section at the
Brooklyn Public Library. Dickinson wrote
MT, whose reply (December 21, 1905) is reproduced in facsimile; there is also a page
of photographs showing MT's grave, and several homes, including the one on Fifth Avenue, New York City.

B32 DREISER, THEODORE. "Mark the Double Twain,"
English Journal, XXIV (October), 615-27.
"From his grave he fairly yells: 'I was
restrained. I was defeated. I hate the
lying, cowardly world that circumvented me.
Man is not good. He is not honest. Life is
a lie! Life is a lie!' Read What Is Man?
Read The Mysterious Stranger. The truth is,
as you see, that Twain was not two people,
but one--a gifted but partially dissuaded
Genius who, in time, and by degrees changed
into his natural self." Reprinted in Leary
(1962), pp. 145-58.

B33 _____. "Mark Twain: Three Contacts. Revealing a Writer's Curiosity about the Sentiments
Another Writer Leaves Out of His Books," Es-
quire, IV (October), 22, 162-162B.
Dreiser twice met MT and tried unsuccess-
fully to interview him; the second attempt
almost succeeded after Dreiser mentioned
W. D. Howells (whom he regarded less highly:
"I was interested to see whether Twain...
was still overawed by this polished minor
realist, who had insinuated himself into
the sanctuary of eastern literary punditry.")
Finally, in 1907 or 1908, Dreiser achieved
a meeting in the back room of a New York
saloon with MT, who was "thanks to the magi-
cal release of a little alcohol--voicing
things never said in his published works or
public addresses," setting forth his pessimistic philosophy. Commenting on a breach
of promise suit then prominent in the papers,
MT commented [quoted from memory, and only
"approximately"] "that all men love their
wives, and are faithful to them, particularly if they're in the public eye; that you're
supposed to love your wife and be sexually
faithful.... Just the same, after the first
few years of marriage, men·don't love their
wives, and they are not strictly faithful....
The passion that brings about courtship,
marriage and the honeymoon is one thing, and
ends with the honeymoon, or a year or two
later. The sex desire is an unmanageable
thing, and can be aroused in any real man by
any young and attractive and sensuous girl."

B34 DUNSMOOR, KATHRYN. "Land of Tom and Huck,"
Scholastic, XXVII (November 23), 11-12.
Describes Hannibal, Missouri as it appeared in 1935 (based on the Hannibal Courier-Post of March 6 and on MT's Autobiography).

B35 ESKEW, GARNETT LAIDLAW. "Steamboating Again
     on Mark Twain's River," Rotarian, XLVII
     (November), 25-28, 50.
        On a recent steamboat trip, a popular ac-
     count apparently drawing on Paine and LOM;
     includes photographs of steamboats and of
     MT's pilot's certificate.

B36 *FEDERICO, P. J. [Article on MT Centennial.]
     Journal of the Patent Office Society.
        [Source: Twainian, XVI (November-Decem-
     ber, 1957), 1-4.]

B37 FISCHER, WALTHER. "Mark Twain (Zu seinem 100
     Geburtstage am 30. November 1935)," Neueren
     Sprachen, XLIII, Heft 11, 471-80.
        A survey of his works on the hundredth
     anniversary of his birth.

B38 FOOTE, E. B. "A Mark Twain Problem: The
     Mysterious Paragraph," Saturday Review of
     Literature, XII (October 26), 9.
        Letter to the editor, quoting a paragraph
     attributed to MS by "a San Francisco even-
     ing paper nearly twenty years ago" but not
     to be found in the book; can a reader pro-
     vide information? [For further comment see
     Wagenknecht, 1935.B79.]

B39 FROHMAN, DANIEL. Daniel Frohman Presents: An
     Autobiography. New York: Claude Kendall &
     Willoughby Sharp.
        On the P&P play and on litigation with MT
     ("During the day we sued each other in
     court. At night we played billiards togeth-
     er at the Players' Club"), pp. 141-44; also,
     brief references to MT, passim (indexed).

B40 HAIGHT, GORDON S. [Review: Edward Wagen-
     knecht, Mark Twain: The Man and His Work.]
     Yale Review, XXV (Autumn), 212-13.
        Praises Wagenknecht's thoroughness but re-
     grets "his lack of critical perspective."

B41 *Hannibal (Missouri) Courier-Post, Mark Twain
     Centennial Edition, March 6.
        [Source: Ferguson (1943), p. 334.]

B42 HEMINGWAY, ERNEST. Green Hills of Africa.
     New York: Charles Scribner's Sons. On MT,
     pp. 22-23.
        "All modern American literature comes from
     one book by Mark Twain called Huckleberry
     Finn. If you read it you must stop where
     Nigger Jim is stolen from the boys. That
     is the real end. The rest is just cheating.
     But it's the best book we've had. There
     was nothing before. There has been nothing
     as good since." MT and Henry James "both
     lived to be old men but they did not get any
     wiser as they got older. You see we make
     our writers into something very strange."
     Hemingway cites pressures that include the
     demands of an expensive standard of living,
     and the effect of the critics on an author
     who heeds them.

B43 HICKS, GRANVILLE. The Great Tradition: An
     Interpretation of American Literature since
     the Civil War. Rev. ed. New York: Macmil-
     lan (Reprinted New York: Biblo and Tannen,
     1967), pp. 38-49, 68-72.
        The frontier as it influenced MT was vital,
     but it was also provincial, and this accounts
     for the virtues and defects of IA (pp. 39-42).
     MT lacked discipline, and none of his books
     fulfills the promise of its early chapters
     (pp. 43-44). MT's concern with making money
     is typical of the age, but his books look
     back to a simpler, more innocent time; un-
     fortunately, he was an entertainer, not a
     realist, and a recognition of his lack of
     independence and his status as a writer
     helps account for his later pessimism
     (pp. 45-48). On GA as it reflected the
     times, pp. 68-72. [See also 1933.B20.]

B44 HUGHES, RUPERT. "I Heard Mark Twain Laugh,"
     Good Housekeeping, CI (November), 44-45,
     184-93.
        Hughes, who grew up in Missouri and in
     Keokuk, Iowa, later became a newspaper re-
     porter in New York. He recalls the Lotos
     Club dinner honoring MT, and the fulsome
     tributes in a succession broken by Richard
     Watson Gilder, who said: "I think I may
     claim to be one of Mark Twain's most sincere
     admirers. I doubt that any one else has
     bought more of his work or paid as much for
     it. But I must say that I can not approve
     of all he writes. I regret to find a ten-
     dency to coarseness, flippancy, irreverence,
     in much of his writing. I am often com-
     pelled to delete a great deal of what he sub-
     mits to us. Still, when he is at his best,
     he is a charming writer whom I am most happy
     to publish." MT broke the tension by assert-
     ing that he put in some passages just to
     shock Gilder--and was paid for them even
     though they were deleted. Hughes also at-
     tended MT's seventieth birthday dinner, but
     his account is limited to recollections of
     the speech, which is in print elsewhere.
     From Mary Lawton he heard the story (not in
     her 1925 book), of MT's disappointment in
     finding that his newly purchased house in
     New York faced so that the sun did not shine
     in his room: "Livy would have thought of
     that. Livy always thought of everything."
     (Includes several photographs of MT.)

B45 *KIPLING, RUDYARD. [Preface.] Tom Sawyer à
     travers le monde, traduction d'Albert Sav-
     ine. Paris: Albin Michel.
        [Source: Asselineau (1954), No. 642: "A
     translation of Tom Sawyer Abroad."]

B46 LACOSSITT, HENRY. "Hail to Hannibal, Honoring
     Mark Twain," New York Times Magazine
     (December 1), pp. 11, 16.
        A conventional portrait of the Missouri
     town where MT grew up, and briefly describ-
     ing his visit there in 1902.

B47 LAUTREC, GABRIEL DE. "Mark Twain," Mercure de France, CCLXIV (15 Novembre), 69-83.
A superficial account, apparently based on secondary material; emphasizes biography, comments briefly on some of MT's minor work, and makes the remarkable statement that MT avoided racial questions: "Chose étrange, Mark Twain ne fait jamais allusion aux nègres. On ne sait s'il partage ou non les préventions absurdes et féroces de ses contemporains. Pour un Étatsunisien pur, encore aujourd'hui, un nègre n'est pas un homme.... Mark Twain a evité prudemment de donner son opinion, qui, s'il l'avait exprimée, lui aurait fait perdre d'un coup toute sa popularité" (p. 79).

B48 LEACOCK, STEPHEN. "Mark Twain and Canada," Queen's Quarterly (Queen's University, Kingston), XLII (Spring), 68-81.
On MT's visits, made out of concern for copyright rather than any particular interest in Canada; based in part on information provided by "my friend Cyril Clemens of St. Louis, who knows more about Mark Twain than even Sam Clemens did." Includes "the main part" of an interview in the Montreal Gazette (November 29, 1881) and the text of a speech at a public dinner (Montreal Gazette, circa December 7-8, 1881). Two years later, according to Cyril Clemens, MT attended a meeting of the Royal Society. "It remains for some research scholar to open the dusty folios of that august body and see if their proceedings were enlivened by any remarks of their illustrious visitor." (Also see W., A. L. O., "More of Mark Twain in Canada," 1935.B78.)

B49 *LE BRETON, MAURICE. "Un Centenaire: Mark Twain," Revue Anglo-Américaine, XIII (June), 401-19.
On MT's limited popularity in France, his Americanism and nostalgia for his youth, accounting for the different schools of criticism. [Source: Asselineau (1954), No. 690, with a lengthy abstract; the article could not be found in a check of this issue at Duke University. It may be the same as the article listed as "Mark Twain: An Appreciation" for 1934.B15.]

B50 *LEMONNIER, LÉON. "L'Enfance de Mark Twain," Revue de France, XV (November), 130-58.
[Source: Asselineau (1954), No. 693.]

B51 ____. "Les Débuts d'un Humoriste," Grande Revue, CXLIX (November), 76-88.
Chiefly biographical; sees MT less as a man of action than as an amused witness of the adventurous life.

B52 * ____. "Les débuts d'un humoriste," Revue Anglo-Américaine, XIII (June), 401-19.
[Source: Asselineau (1954), No. 691: "Insists on the duality of Mark Twain's genius." The article could not be found in a check of this issue at Duke University-- T.A.T.]

B53 LORCH, FRED W. [Review: Minnie M. Brashear, Mark Twain: Son of Missouri (1934).] American Literature, VI (January), 460-63.
"The title of this book does not adequately suggest the serious, scholarly purpose which motivated the study. Miss Brashear does not attempt, primarily, to reclaim Mark Twain for the state of Missouri, but to deal with the more significant question, 'How is Mark Twain to be accounted for?'" This is a major study which brings MT's background into perspective.

B54 ____. [Review: Cyril Clemens, ed., Mark Twain: Wit and Wisdom.] American Literature, VII (November), 351.
Because the occasions have passed, "Many of the anecdotes appear to be nearly pointless. In some of them it is obvious that the narrator is attempting to capitalize a very slight acquaintance with Mark Twain and is hard pushed to give his slender substance the semblance of importance."

B55 ____. [Review: Fred Lewis Pattee, Mark Twain: Representative Selections.] American Literature, VII (November), 350-1.
Pattee wastes time in refuting Brooks and arguing the favorable influence of the East: "It had been better for general purposes had he developed in a more systematic way Mark Twain's social, political, and literary theories..."

B56 LOVETT, ROBERT MORSS. "Mark Twain the American," New Republic, LXXXV (November 20), 50-51.
A review article, briefly noting Cyril Clemens, ed., Mark Twain Wit and Wisdom and Albert Bigelow Paine, ed., Mark Twain's Notebook, and describing at greater length Wagenknecht's Mark Twain: The Man and His Work.

B57 M., A. N. [Review: Albert Bigelow Paine, ed., Mark Twain's Notebook.] Manchester Guardian, December 19, p. 5.
Chiefly descriptive. This is a book to be dipped into, not read straight through.

B58 MASTERS, EDGAR LEE. "Mark Twain: Son of the Frontier," American Mercury, XXXVI (September), 67-74.
MT was shaped by "the uncontaminated America of the West," and attempts by Livy to refine him were unsuccessful. Only brief discussions of specific works, except for a page on MS.

B59 ____. Vachel Lindsay: A Poet in America. New York and London: Charles Scribner's Sons, passim.
Lindsay read Adam's Diary, TS, and HF. Masters ranks Lindsay's "Three Poems about Mark Twain" below his best, although it might be put with them.

B60   MEIGS, CORNELIA. "Mark Twain," St. Nicholas,
       LXIII (November), 14-16, 50-51.
           A story for children of an escapade by
       young Sam Clemens; no source is cited.

B61   METZ, J. J. "Mark Twain Centennial," Indus-
       trial Arts and Vocational Education, XXIV
       (December), 364-65.
           Primarily biographical. "His versatility
       is truly astounding, but what is of more
       importance, Mark Twain was strictly honest.
       This characteristic should be pointed out
       specially to the shop students. The best
       craftsman, unless he be honest, cannot be
       held up as a model for the student. What
       dishonesty has done to the world is only
       too well illustrated by present-day condi-
       tions." There is an account of MT's pay-
       ment of the Webster debts: "It is this
       type of sterling honesty which is found so
       seldom, and which is, nevertheless, so
       desperately needed to cure the evils of
       the times. It is well, therefore, to em-
       phasize this admirable trait, not only in
       the school auditorium, at a formal Mark
       Twain centennial celebration, but also in
       the classroom and in the school shop."

B62   MONROE, HARRIET. "On the Great River,"
       Poetry, XLVI (August), 268-74.
           By steamboat to Hannibal; the little on
       MT is impressionistic.

B63   MORLEY, CHRISTOPHER. "Hunting Mark Twain's
       Remainders," Saturday Review of Litera-
       ture, XIII (November 2), 15-16.
           Praises HF for its humor and beauty,
       and suggests that except for this book and
       TS "the other books are fast fading out."
       Takes issue with MT's more solemn critics,
       and quotes with satisfaction a chapter
       from Don Marquis's Chapters for the Ortho-
       dox in which God tells a reporter that MT
       has been given his own river in Heaven and
       once ran a steamboat race through Hell.
       Satan once asked to borrow MT and his riv-
       er, and MT was willing, but "his wife and
       William Dean Howells wouldn't let him."

B64   PAINE, ALBERT BIGELOW, ed. "Unpublished
       Diaries of Mark Twain," Hearst's Inter-
       national, XCIX (August), 24-27, 134-36;
       (September), 48-51, 111-12.
           Excerpts from MT's notebooks, with very
       brief editorial comment by Paine.

B65   PARTRIDGE, HENRY M. "Did Mark Twain Perpe-
       trate Literary Hoaxes?" American Book
       Collector, VI (January), 20-23;
       (February), 50-53.
           Concludes a series begun in 1934, pre-
       tending to demonstrate his authorship of
       Lewis Carroll's works; includes illustra-
       tions of "The Mark Twain Club Badge" and
       the suppressed cut from LOM showing MT in
       the next world, in flames (pp. 52-53.)

B66   PAULLIN, CHARLES O. "Mark Twain's Virginia
       Kin," William and Mary College Quarterly,
       XV (July), 294-98.
           Notes errors by W. M. Clemens in Genealogy
       Magazine, XI (1923), 17-19, 65, and suggests
       that some descriptions of relatives in MT's
       Autobiography are "not to be taken serious-
       ly." Photograph: "Birthplace of Mark
       Twain's grandmother, Pamela Goggin Clemens,
       in Bedford County, Virginia."

B67   PHELPS, WILLIAM LYON. "Mark Twain," Yale Re-
       view, XXV (December), 291-310.
           He never escaped the evangelical piety of
       his time until he revolted, and "the only
       tradition or convention that he definitely
       abandoned was religious faith." Despite
       his boisterous profanity he had "a chival-
       rous reverence for the chastity of women,"
       and "in his own writings his frequent bad
       taste was equalled only by his prudishness."
       "He was not a profound thinker, but rather
       a shrewd observer.... He was a greater ar-
       tist than humorist, a greater humorist than
       philosopher." Includes the text of a let-
       ter to Mrs. Mary Hallock Foote (December 2,
       1887) about readings from Browning, and
       discusses in some detail, reproducing MT's
       schedule for an evening's reading.

B68   QUICK, DOROTHY. "A Little Girl's Mark Twain,"
       North American Review, CCXL (September),
       342-48.
           For a fuller account of MT by one of the
       "Angel Fishes," see her Enchantment
       (1961.A14).

B69   R., V. "Walter Scott and the Southern States
       of America," Notes and Queries (London),
       CLXIX (November 9), 328-30.
           Refutes MT's charges in LOM that the ro-
       manticism of Scott lay behind the Southern
       romanticism MT blames for the Civil War;
       there was an earlier attack on Scott's ro-
       mantic influence in 1851, in George Bor-
       row's Lavengro; in any case, MT should not
       be taken "seriously as a literary critic,
       while his anti-King and anti-feudal bias
       makes him suspect when he turns to social
       comment," as in his "cheap and crude" CY.

B70   ROBBINS, L. H. "Mark Twain's Fame Goes
       Marching On: His Century Which Closes this
       Year Finds Him Still the Best-Loved and
       Most Widely Read of American Authors," New
       York Times Magazine (April 21), pp. 4, 16.
           A sound but conventional account of MT's
       life and his enduring reputation.

B71   ROBERTS, R. ELLIS. "Mark Twain," Fortnightly
       Review, CXLIV (November), 583-92.
           A general discussion of the man, who put
       much of himself into the character of Huck
       Finn. Although it has been argued with
       some justice that MT "was essentially non-
       adult," the same might be said of his crit-
       ics, and "perhaps no artist ever completely
       grows up." Ellis finds MT intellectually

(ROBERTS, R. ELLIS)
beneath Ibsen, and "none of the American author's works can rank with the greatest of Dickens."

B72 *SCHÖNEMANN, FRIEDRICH. "Mark Twain--ein Freund Deutschlands," Deutsche Allgemeine Zeitung, November 24.
[Source: Asselineau (1954), No. 706.]

B73 SMITH, BERNARD. Forces in American Criticism: A Study in the History of American Literary Thought. New York: Harcourt, Brace and Company. Pp. 184, 235-37, and passim on MT.
On MT's Western truthfulness, love for the common language, but also his cynicism (p. 184); takes DeVoto's side in the controversy with Brooks (pp. 235-37).

B74 STEWART, HERBERT L. "Mark Twain on the Jewish Problem," Dalhousie Review, XIV (January), 455-58.
About "Concerning the Jews."

B75 UNDERHILL, IRVING S. "The Haunted Book: A Further Explanation Concerning Huckleberry Finn," Colophon, n.s. I (Autumn), 281-91.
On the copies of HF shipped to California and there altered to replace the offensive cut on p. 283; contains text of "Mark Twain's Altered Book" from New York Herald of November 29, 1884, on the Charles L. Webster offer of $500 for the apprehension and conviction of the person who mutilated the plate for p. 283. See Underhill's "An Inquiry into Mark Twain's Latest Book!" (1931.B31).

B76 VAN DOREN, MARK. "A Century of Mark Twain," Nation (New York), CXLI (October 23), 472-74.
On MT's growing reputation in the years since his death.

B77 VAN DYKE, TERTIUS. Henry Van Dyke: A Biography by His Son. New York and London: Harper & Brothers Publishers.
On p. 218, quotes an MT letter on the difficulty in finding the right plan for a short story that will tell itself; he usually succeeded only after several failures. On p. 259, Henry Van Dyke said MT's white suit was "all right, but I wore one long before he did."

B78 W., A. L. O. "More of Mark Twain in Canada: 1895," Queen's Quarterly (Queen's University, Kingston), XLII (Summer), 272-74.
Personal impressions of MT, whom the author met in Winnepeg. [An addendum to Stephen Leacock's "Mark Twain and Canada" in the Spring issue.]

B79 WAGENKNECHT, EDWARD. "The Mysterious Paragraph: A Reply," Saturday Review of Literature, XIII (November 16), 29.
A brief note: in his query of October 26, E. B. Foote erroneously says that MS was not published until 1922; in fact it was serialized in Harper's and then published as a book. The passage about which he inquires is not to be found there.

B80 WALSH, JAMES J. "Mark Twain and Joan of Arc," Commonweal, XXII (August 23), 408.
A letter to the editor, occasioned by the Cyril Clemens article (July 26, pp. 323-24, 1935.B23). Mentions an appreciative letter from MT to Rose Hawthorne, daughter of Nathaniel Hawthorne; also describes a conversation in which MT "told me that the Bishop of Orleans had assured him that Saint Joan had assured him that anyone who wrote so beautifully about her would get into heaven.... He seemed to be very much interested in the prospect of a hereafter that would place him near the Maid, and the good Archbishop reiterated his assurance on that prospect."

B81 WISTER, OWEN. "In Homage to Mark Twain," Harper's, CLXXI (November), 547-56.
Includes an account of a meeting with MT, and a discussion of him as thinker and critic, noting the interest he shared with Hawthorne in the problem of evil. [Reprinted frequently - see index.]

1936 A BOOKS

A1 ADE, GEORGE. Revived Remarks on Mark Twain. Also the Address of John T. McCutcheon Commemorating the Centenary of Mark Twain's Birth. Compiled by George Hiram Brownell. Chicago: Privately Printed.
Consists of reprinted tributes to MT: Oliver Wendell Holmes, "To Mark Twain on His Fiftieth Birthday"; George Ade, "Tribute to Mark Twain" (from North American Review, June, 1910); "Mark Twain and the Old-Time Subscription Book" (Review of Reviews (New York), June, 1910); "Mark Twain as Our Emissary" (Century, December, 1910); "On the Death of Mark Twain" (comment in Chicago Tribune, April 21, 1910); John T. McCutcheon, "Mark Twain's Seventieth Birthday" (an address in Chicago in honor of MT's Centennial birthday, November 30, 1935); George Hiram Brownell, "Compiler's Commentary." Also, caricatures of MT by John T. McCutcheon and others.

A2 *BENSON, IVAN. Mark Twain in the West. Sacramento: California State Printing Office.
[37-page pamphlet. Source: Asselineau (1954), No. 723.]

A3 *CLEMENS, SAMUEL L. 1601; or, Conversation by the Social Fireside as It Was in the Time of the Tudors, with Notes on Mark Twain's 1601 and a checklist of various editions and

(CLEMENS, SAMUEL L.)
reprints compiled by Irvin Haas. Chicago:
Black Cat Press.
[Source: Asselineau (1954), No. 728.]

A4 *O'CONNOR, LAUREL. Drinking with Mark Twain:
Recollections of Mark Twain and His Cronies
as Told to Me. New York: Riemsdyk Book-
service.
[Source: MHRA Annual Bibliography (1936),
No. 3599.]

1936 B SHORTER WRITINGS

B1 ANON. "He Kept His Nerve," Saturday Review of
Literature, XIII (January 11), 8.
TS, HF, PW, and LOM show as much of the
"human weakness, vice, degradation, prejudice, and superstition" as is found in
Faulkner, Caldwell, and others of the "new
school of the Mississippi valley," but MT
"did not give up humanity" or call for revolution.

B2 ANON. "Mark Twain's Favorite Music," Étude,
LIV (October), 661.
A list, sent to Mrs. Georgia Chew by MT's
daughter Clara: "I'm Awearin' Awa', Jean";
"Flow Gently, Sweet Afton"; "Annie Laurie";
"Banks and Braes of Bonnie Doon"; "Go Chain
the Lion Down"; "Swing Low, Sweet Chariot";
"Ever Lighter Grows My Slumber" (Brahms);
"Lullaby" (Brahms); "Serenade" (Schubert);
"Ave Maria" (Schubert); "Almighty Jehovah"
(Schubert).

B3 ANON. [Review: Mark Twain's Notebook
(1935).] Nation, CXLII (February 26), 258.
"The 'heresies' are rare and mild," and
the writing is often very good.

B4 BENSON, ADOLPH B. "Mark Twain in Småland,"
American Swedish Monthly, XXX (September),
4 6, 37.
MT took his daughter Jean to Sweden in
the summer of 1899 for treatment by Dr.
Heinrick Kellgren. A popular account,
based largely or entirely on such familiar
sources as Paine's 1912 Biography and 1917
edition of the Letters, and Mary Lawton's
A Lifetime with Mark Twain (1925).

B5 BRASHEAR, M[INNIE] M. "Mark Twain in Perspective," Virginia Quarterly Review, XII
(January), 127-30.
A review article, Edward Wagenknecht's
Mark Twain: The Man and His Work (1935) is
the most successful of the MT centennial
books in demonstrating the "broad human
significance in his life and writings."
MT's translation of Dr. Heinrich Hoffman's
Struwelpeter as Slovenly Peter (with an introduction by his daughter Clara), "with
its quaint illustrations...adds something
to our impression of the irrepressible
gaiety of its author."

B6 BURGESS, GELETT. "A Famous Author Tells about
His Meeting with Mark Twain," Mark Twain
Quarterly, I (Fall), 13.
Burgess met MT on a park bench in Washington Square forty years ago. MT consoled
Burgess about his name being forever linked
with his Purple Cow: "I wouldn't worry
about that, son. There's a lot of writers
trying to be humorous who are so poor they
can't keep a cow."

B7 BURKE, W. J. "Mark Twain: An Exhibition,"
Bulletin of the New York Public Library,
XL (June), 499-501.
On the centenary exhibit, which opened
November, 1935; this account is partly bio-
graphical, and lists various MT memorabilia
and manuscripts which were on exhibit. Not
illustrated.

B8 CAMPBELL, OSCAR JAMES. "Twain Versus Clemens,"
in Erich A. Walter, ed., Essay Annual (New
York: Scott, Foresman), pp. 151-68.
A reprinting of his address originally in
Anon., "The Mark Twain Commemoration"
(1935.B8).

B9 CARPENTER, C. E. "Mark Twain, 1898," Mark
Twain Quarterly, I (Fall), 4-5.
Memories of MT in Vienna: his language
was vigorous, and when Carpenter showed MT
an interview of him he had written for the
New York World MT cut out the adjectives.

B10 CHUBB, PERCIVAL. "The Two Mark Twains," The
Standard ("Issued by the American Ethical
Union"), XXII (January), 97-98.
On the darker, tragic side of MT, here attributed to his largeness and headlong impatience: "There was so much of him that he
never organized himself into any sort of
harmony or unity."

B11 CLARKE, EDWARD J. "Cynic and Humorist," Commonweal, XXIII (February 7), 415-16.
A review of Albert Bigelow Paine, ed.,
Mark Twain's Notebook (1935). Praises
Paine's "illuminating comments and efficient
editorial work," but criticizes the bad
taste, "salacity, and blasphemy" of MT, as
here revealed and in 1601 and his Stomach
Club address.

B12 CLEMENS, CYRIL. "Mark Twain's Reading," Commonweal, XXIV (August 7), 363-64.
On the authors and books MT liked--and
some he disliked. A useful summary for the
beginning student, but undocumented and
presenting familiar information.

B13 DAVIDSON, LOUIS B. "He Fell in Love with a
Picture," Reader's Digest, XXVIII (January),
9-12, "Condensed from Liberty" [November 30,
1935].
On MT's love for his wife, Olivia, from
the time her brother showed him her picture
on the Quaker City cruise; a popular account, based chiefly on Paine.

1936 - Shorter Writings

B14 DEVOTO, BERNARD. "Mark Twain and the Limits of Criticism," in his Forays and Rebuttals (New York: Little, Brown and Company), pp. 373-403.

"Read before the American Literature Section of the Modern Language Association at Cincinnati, January 1, 1936." "The purpose of this essay is to examine some of the critical judgments that have been made about the books of Mark Twain and to determine how far their results are acceptable." DeVoto argues that vocabulary studies, textual criticism, and the study of possible influences are of secondary importance at the most. "Theoretical, systematic criticism" is the most ambitious, although it may distort the work it examines.

B15 ____. "Mark Twain: The Ink of History," in his Forays and Rebuttals (Boston: Little, Brown and Company), pp. 348-72.

"An Address delivered at Columbia, Missouri December 6, 1935, as part of the concluding exercises of Mark Twain Week at the University of Missouri," insisting on MT's conscious artistry--which the literary establishment of his time had been reluctant to see.

B16 ____. [Review: Edward Wagenknecht, Mark Twain: The Man and His Work (1935).] New England Quarterly, IX (June), 332-38.

"Independence and exhaustiveness are...Mr. Wagenknecht's principal virtues: he presents little new material and does not say much that has not been said before," but he "examines all the known evidence on his own behalf. The result is a new and original study of Mark Twain--and a complete vindication of the criticism of the last few years."

B17 DRURY, WELLS. "Mark Twain, while 'Roughing It,'" in his An Editor on the Comstock Lode (New York: Farrar & Rinehart, Incorporated), pp. 220-31.

Contains anecdotes of MT told by Steve Gillis; there is also a chapter on "Dan de Quille" (William Wright).

B18 FARMER, A.-J. [Review: Fred Lewis Pattee, Mark Twain: Representative Selections (1935).] Revue Anglo-Américaine, XIII (December), 367-68.

Brief and laudatory: a good selection meriting the attention of those who are familiar with MT and of those who are not. [In French.]

B19 FERGUSON, DELANCEY. "Mark Twain and the Cleveland Herald," American Literature, VIII (November), 304-305.

In June, 1869 MT had written his mother: "I am offered an interest in a Cleveland paper.... The salary is fair enough, but the interest is not large enough, and so I must look a little further." According to letters from MT to Mary Mason Fairbanks, wife of the publisher, the paper was the Cleveland Herald.

B20 ____. "The Uncollected Portions of Mark Twain's Autobiography," American Literature, VIII (March), 37-46.

Portions of Mark Twain's Autobiography published serially in the North American Review in 1906 and 1907, and in Harper's Magazine in 1922 do not appear in the two-volume edition of 1924. Collation shows scope of the omissions, and Ferguson points to a number of "alterations which show the work of another hand, and not a skilful one."

B21 FLANAGAN, JOHN T. "Mark Twain on the Upper Mississippi," Minnesota History, XVII (December), 369-84.

On MT's trip in 1882 to collect additional materials for LOM; also about visits to Minnesota in 1886 and 1895 (quotes Duluth, Minneapolis, and St. Paul papers for July, 1895).

B22 *HAMADA, MASAJIRO. "Mark Twain's Conception of Social Justice," Studies in English Literature (Japan), XVI (October), 593-616.
[Source: Asselineau (1954), No. 753: "Naïve and superficial."]

B23 *[HAMON, LOUIS.] Cheiro's Language of the Hand. Los Angeles, n.p., pp. 169-70.

Claims to have interested MT in fingerprinting and thus to have inspired PW. [Source: Wigger (1957), p. 518, n. 1.]

B24 LAWRENCE, D. H. Preface to E. D. Dekker's Max Havelaar; reprinted in Edward D. McDonald, ed., Phoenix: The Posthumous Papers of D. H. Lawrence. London: William Heinemann Ltd. (Repr. 1961), pp. 236-39; on MT, p. 238.

Mentions Dekker's "bitter, almost mad-dog aversion to humanity," which also appears in Jean Paul Richter, "as it appears in the later Mark Twain."

B25 LEACOCK, STEPHEN. The Greatest Pages of American Humour: A Study of the Rise and Development of Humorous Writings in America with Selections from the Most Notable of the Humorists. London: Methuen & Co., Ltd., pp. 123-54.

Leacock's discussion notes MT's unevenness, prolixity, and elementary theology and history. "The book he treasured most among his works, his Joan of Arc, is worthless as history, practically without humour, utterly false in its picture of the times," but TS, RI, IA, LOM, CY, and HF "are among the world's great books" (p. 124). Selections from IA, HF, and RI on pp. 128-54. Asselineau (1954), No. 732, lists an American edition for the same year (Garden City: Doubleday, Doran & Co.).

B26 LORCH, FRED W. "Mark Twain's Orphanage Lecture," American Literature, VII (January), 453-5.

MT delivered "The American Vandal Abroad" January 22, 1869 for benefit of an orphanage of which Mrs. Fairbanks was a trustee.

(LORCH, FRED W.)
Contains text of his letter accepting the invitation to lecture and his closing words in behalf of the orphanage (reprinted from Cleveland Daily Leader).

B27 LOWE, ORTON. Our Land and Its Literature. New York, London: Harper & Brothers Publishers, passim on MT.
A high-school anthology, this includes "The Jumping Frog," two MT letters, and passages from RI, LOM, and HF. Critical judgments are derivative and not penetrating; ranks HF with The Scarlet Letter as "two really important novels of the American scene" in the century between Cooper and Dreiser (p. 93).

B28 [McCOLE, CAMILLE.] [Review: Edward G. Wagenknecht, Mark Twain: The Man and His Work (1935); Fred Lewis Pattee, ed., Mark Twain: Representative Selections (1935); and Albert Bigelow Paine, ed., Mark Twain's Notebook (1935).] Catholic World, CXLII (January), 499-500.
Wagenknecht has written "the sanest life of Twain that has yet come to my notice," fair to MT and to the various critical positions taken toward him. Pattee's anthology contains a few items that might better have been left out, but the choice is generally judicious and the background material is good. The notebooks add little to what we know from the Paine biography and MT's letters, but they do add roundness to our picture of him; notes Paine's "somewhat over-fervent commentary" and a tendency to play down "crude banalities, vaudeville jokes, inconsistencies, and attitude toward the whole 'damned human race.'" [Reviewer identified as Camille McCole in the "Index to Reviewers," p. 511.]

B29 MacMANUS, SEUMAS. "What a Famous Irishman Thinks of Twain," Mark Twain Quarterly, I (Fall), 16.
Brief comment on MT's contribution to the world's merriment.

B30 MASON, WALT. "Mark Twain the Healer," Mark Twain Quarterly, I (Fall), 3.
A poem: MT brings cheer when patent medicines fail.

B31 MASTERS, EDGAR LEE. "The House where Mark Twain Was Born," Mark Twain Quarterly, I (Fall), 5.
A poem describing Florida, Missouri and the house.

B32 *MONTENEGRO, ERNESTO. "Doble Personalidad de Mark Twain," Ateneo (Chile), October, 47-69.
[Source: Asselineau (1954), No. 756: "A summary of Brooks's theory."]

B33 *NEUBAUER, HEINZ. Amerikanische Goldgräber-literatur (Bret Harte, Mark Twain, Jack London). Grossenheim i. Sa.: H. Plasnick.
[Source: Asselineau (1954), No. 735.]

B34 ODELL, GEORGE C. D. Annals of the New York Stage. New York: Columbia University Press. Vol. VIII (1865-1870), passim.
MT gave his "Sandwich Islands" lecture at Irving Hall on May 15, 1866 (pp. 227-28), at the Athenaeum, May 10, 1866 (p. 253), and at the Bedford Avenue Reformed Church, Brooklyn on December 1, 1869 (p. 686). He gave "The American Vandals Abroad" lecture before the Newtown Y.M.C.A., Long Island City, on March 16, 1869 (p. 553).

B35 PELIKAN, HARRY R., JR. "Mark Twain and the Ozarks," Mark Twain Quarterly, I (Fall), 14.
Both will live on; let us hope the Ozarks will not be despoiled.

B36 "Poems to Mark Twain," Mark Twain Quarterly, I (Fall), 4-5.
Tributes in verse by Wm. Robert Woodburn, Robert P. Tristram Coffin, Thomas Caldecott Chubb, Wittner Bynner, Arthur Guiterman, Margaret Fishback, and Ernest Rhys.

B37 QUINN, ARTHUR HOBSON. "Mark Twain and the Romance of Youth," in his American Fiction: An Historical and Critical Survey. New York: Appleton-Century Co. (Reprinted New York: Appleton-Century Crofts, Inc., 1964), pp. 243-56.
A general survey, providing a good summary but no new information.

B38 RANDALL, DAVID A. [Review: Merle DeVore Johnson, A Bibliography of the Works of Mark Twain (1935).] Publishers' Weekly, CXXIX (February 22), 917-18.
"The work, in short, is excellent."

B39 *RATCLIFFE, S. K. [Introduction.] What Is Man? London: Watts & Co.
[Source: Asselineau (1954), No. 729.]

B40 ROLLINS, CARL PURINGTON. "A Mark Twain Item," Saturday Review of Literature, XIII (January 25), 20.
A review of MT's translation of Dr. Heinrich Hoffman's Der Struwelpeter (New York: Limited Editions Club). "The verses are not electrifying, but it is a Mark Twain 'item,' and worth perpetuating. The pictures are by far the better portion."

B41 SAKHAROV, W. [Librarian, Culture Library, Leningrad.] "Twain Exhibit in Russia," Library Journal, LXI (February 15), 157.
Describes an exhibit of MT's books and other materials collected under some difficulty in order to be ready with an exhibit by November 30; the response was good.

B42   SALLS, HELEN HARRIET. "Joan of Arc in English and American Literature," South Atlantic Quarterly, XXXV (April), 167-84.
        Passim on MT's JA, noting a "sense of the ludicrous [that] at times overlaps bounds" but is generally amusing, and his sentiment, reverence, and his charming portrait of Joan: "Sentimentalized as she is--a figure dainty as a Dresden statuette, and debonair as a princess--she appeals to us as an impulsive, lovable, very human little fighting saint after all. To Clemens, as to Michelet, her essential charm lay in her womaliness--her sensibility and her pity."

B43   *SCHÖNEMANN, FRIEDRICH. "Mark Twain und Deutschland," Hochschule und Ausland, XIV (January), 37-43; reprinted in Auslese (February).
        [Source: Asselineau (1954), No. 758: "Summary of a commemorative speech delivered in Berlin in 1935"; MHRA Annual Bibliography (1936), No. 3603.]

B44   _____. "Neue Mark-Twain-Studien," Neueren Sprachen, XLIV, Heft 6, 260-72.
        A survey of recent MT studies, chiefly descriptive, but criticizing Wagenknecht for "einem geschmacklosen Ausfall gegen unseren Führer und Reichskanzler."

B45   SCHULTZ, JOHN RICHIE. "New Letters of Mark Twain," American Literature, VIII (March), 47-51.
        Five letters MT wrote to Bayard Taylor in 1878, interesting chiefly for showing comic exasperation with the German language.

B46   SEAMAN, OWEN. "To Mark Twain," Saturday Review of Literature, XIII (February 29), 13.
        Reprints a poem which originally appeared in Punch.

B47   SMITH, BERNARD. "Van Wyck Brooks," New Republic, LXXXVIII (August 26), 69-72.
        Takes the side of Bernard DeVoto in a brief discussion of his quarrel with Brooks, who "exaggerated" MT's "potentialities."

B48   SPILLER, ROBERT E. [Review: Edward Wagenknecht, Mark Twain: The Man and His Work (1935).] American Literature, VIII (March), 96-98.
        "Mr. Wagenknecht is loath to take sides" when critics disagree. "Such lack of prejudice is honorable in the peacemaker, but even common sense seems to demand of the critic more firmness of judgment." Nonetheless, "the book is among the most useful we have on the subject" because of Wagenknecht's "humane sympathy" toward MT, and it will serve as a good introduction.

B49   TARKINGTON, BOOTH. "Mark Twain and Boys," Mark Twain Quarterly, I (Fall), 6-7.
        HF is secure as an American classic, and Tom Sawyer's character is based on the boy Mark Twain. Quotes appreciative statements by Robert Louis Stevenson and Arnold Bennett.

B50   TAYLOR, WALTER FULLER. "'Mark Twain' (Samuel Langhorne Clemens, 1835-1910)," in his A History of American Letters (Boston, New York: American Book Company), pp. 262-74.
        A general study in a survey for the undergraduate, noting MT's regionalism, weak construction, humanity and the perspective of a satirist, and his final pessimism.

B51   WALKER, FRANKLIN. "An Influence from San Francisco on Mark Twain's The Gilded Age," American Literature, VIII (March), 63-66.
        On November 3, 1870 Laura D. Fair (whom MT may have known in Virginia City) shot her married lover on the ferry from Oakland to San Francisco. She was tried, convicted of murder, and then retried and acquitted on the ground of "emotional insanity." The case attracted national attention at the time MT and Charles Dudley Warner were writing GA, and parallels the story of Laura Hawkins in that book.

B52   WINTERICH, JOHN T. "Mark Twain's Only Son," Saturday Review of Literature, XIV (October 3), 20.
        Reproduces, with brief comment, "the only known photographic print of Mark Twain's only son, Langdon Clemens," inscribed with MT's "warm regards" to Bret Harte.

B53   *_____. [Introduction.] The Adventures of Tom Sawyer, illustrated by Norman Rockwell. New York: The Heritage Press; London: The Nonesuch Press.
        [Source: Asselineau (1954), No. 727.]

1937 A BOOKS

A1   CLEMENS, SAMUEL L. Letters from the Sandwich Islands Written for the Sacramento "Union" by Mark Twain, ed. G. Ezra Dane. San Francisco: The Grabhorn Press.
        Correspondence in 1866, MT's first full-scale travel-writing. Some of these letters were later revised and incorporated in RI. This 1937 edition was limited, but there was a 1938 reprinting by Stanford University Press (by photolith, according to Ivan Benson in Mark Twain's Western Years [1938], p. 162).

A2   *LEMONNIER, LÉON. La Jeunesse aventureuse de Mark Twain. Paris: Desclée de Brouwer.
        [Source: MHRA Bibliography (1937), No. 4211, and review by M. Le Breton (1937.B22); both give year of publication as 1937. Asselineau (1954, No. 725) lists it for 1936; he describes it as "a lively and entertaining book, which, however, contains no new information on Mark Twain."]

1937 B SHORTER WRITINGS

B1   BABLER, OTTO F. "Mark Twain: An Aphorism," Notes and Queries (London), CLXXIII (July 17), 45.

(BABLER, OTTO F.)
MT's aphorism "It is not always easy to bear prosperity. Another man's, I mean" appears in autograph facsimile in a Paris bookseller's catalogue.

B2   BACON, LEONARD. "Our Golden Mark," Mark Twain Quarterly, I (Spring), 17.
A poem on MT's humor, compassion, imagination, and portrayal of his time.

B3   BALICER, HERMAN C. "Szczepanik's 'Portrait' of Mark Twain," Publishers' Weekly, CXXXI (February 20), 968-69.
On a portrait of MT (here reproduced) woven in silk on a machine designed and demonstrated by the inventor of whom MT wrote in "The Austrian Edison Keeping School Again" and "From the London Times of 1904."

B4   BENSON, ADOLPH B. "Mark Twain's Contacts with Scandinavia," Scandinavian Studies and Notes (now Scandinavian Studies), XIV (August), 159-67.
A general, but substantial and meticulously documented summary of MT's admittedly limited travel in the Scandinavian countries, reading in the literature, and acquaintance with individuals. [Not all of Benson's sources are included in the present bibliography.]

B5   BLAIR, WALTER. "Mark Twain," in his Native American Humor (1800-1900) (New York: American Book Company), pp. 147-62 [Source: 1960 paperback reprinting, San Francisco: Chandler Publishing Company, Inc., with the same pagination].
Shows MT's indebtedness to the popular humor of his formative years; for example, his portrait of his mother (so tender-hearted that before drowning kittens she warmed the water) and of Tom Sawyer's Aunt Polly may be traced to Benjamin P. Shillaber's "Mrs. Partington." "American humor, then, gave Mark Twain his materials, his methods, and his inspiration. His success was merely the working out of its attempted achievements on the level of genius." Reprinted in part in Scott (1955), pp. 236-48; (1967), pp. 221-33; in Marks (1959), pp. 19-27.

B6   BLANCK, JACOB. "Mark Twain's Sketches Old and New," Publishers' Weekly, CXXXII (October 30), 1740-41.
On the accidental inclusion of a paragraph from Jane Stuart Woolsey's Hospital Days in the first state of the first edition of Sketches New and Old; moreover, MT unconsciously borrowed from the same book phrasing (from a description of an ice-storm) which later appeared in his speech on the weather and eventually in FE.

B7   *BROWN, STERLING. The Negro in American Fiction, Washington, D.C., p. 68.
[Source: Quoted in Haslam (1967), pp. 190-91: "Sterling Brown of Howard University, himself an Afro-American and one of the first scholars in this country to study the treatment of Negro characters in our literature, claimed that 'Jim is the best example in nineteenth-century fiction...he is completely believable.' Brown was particularly moved by the 'great tenderness and truth of this portrayal.'"]

B8   *BROWNELL, EUGENE [GEORGE?] HIRAM. "Twainiana Notes," Reading and Collecting, I (June), 9-10.
[Source: MHRA Annual Bibliography (1937), No. 4205.]

B9   BURTON, RICHARD. "Mark Twain in the Hartford Days," Mark Twain Quarterly, I (Summer), 5.
MT criticized Burton's early writing and helped him get it published in The Century Magazine and elsewhere. When Burton was seeing to the publication of the Yale Lectures on Preaching delivered by his father (who had been pastor of the Park Congregational Church in Hartford), MT persuaded him to let the Charles L. Webster company handle it; the royalties were generous.

B10   CLEMENS, CYRIL. "Mark Twain's Gold Hill Hold-up," Rotarian, LI (November), 38-39.
On the joke played on MT in 1866, as described to Cyril Clemens by William R. Gillis and James W. Thompson, and described by MT in the Territorial Enterprise (November 11, 1866) and the San Francisco Bulletin (December 6, 1866); also cites an account in the Sacramento Union (November 15, 1866). Includes 1866 photographs of MT and Virginia City.

B11   COLUM, PADRAIC. "Homage to Mark Twain," Mark Twain Quarterly, I (Spring), 17.
Poem in tribute, with comments on the cave and playing pirates.

B12   CORYELL, IRVING. "Josh, of the Territorial Enterprise," North American Review, CCXLIII (Summer), 287-95.
A lively, popular account of the Territorial Enterprise and MT's connection with it; based on generally sound material (including RI), but undocumented.

B13   [DEVOTO, BERNARD.] "At the Cannon's Mouth," Saturday Review of Literature, XV (April 3), 8.
Takes issue with the comparative ranking of American authors by Dumas Malone in the current Harper's; placing MT at the head of the list is a personal choice, however.

B14   DOUGLAS, LLOYD C.   "Potatoes for Mark Twain,"
       Mark Twain Quarterly, II (Fall), 20.
              His father, a country parson, had little
       to spend on books but "always found a few
       bushels of potatoes that could be spared
       for another volume of Mark Twain."

B15   FERGUSON, DELANCEY.   "The Petrified Truth,"
       Colophon, n.s., II (Winter), 189-96.
              Ferguson's search of The Lancet, Cleve-
       land Plain Dealer, Cleveland Herald, Harp-
       er's, and Leslie's Weekly turned up no evi-
       dence to support MT's claim that many were
       taken in by his Nevada "petrified man"
       hoax.

B16   FROHMAN, DANIEL.   "Mark Twain," in his Encore
       (New York: Lee Furman, Inc.), pp. 107-108.
              Quotes The Theatre Magazine for May 31,
       1866 on the wisdom of withdrawing The Amer-
       ican Claimant from the stage; also notes
       the play was written for the humorous lec-
       turer A. E. Burback; Frohman was success-
       ful with a play based on P&P.

B17   HAGEDORN, HERMANN.   Brookings: A Biography.
       New York: The Macmillan Company, p. 178.
              Brief mention: "Men and women who count-
       ed sat at his table--Mark Twain, languid
       and casual..."

B18   HAPGOOD, NORMAN.   "My Feeling about Mark
       Twain," Mark Twain Quarterly, II (Winter),
       15.
              Brief comments on having found MT appre-
       ciated everywhere. "Some years ago, I was
       having a private chat with Sir James Bar-
       rie, and in the course of it I spoke of
       Hawthorne with The Scarlet Letter and The
       House of the Seven Gables, and Mark Twain,
       with Tom Sawyer and Huckleberry Finn, as at
       the top of American fiction. The author of
       Peter Pan agreed, but added that also those
       books are up near the top of English fic-
       tion."

B19   HERRICK, ROBERT.   "Mark Twain and the Ameri-
       can Tradition," Mark Twain Quarterly, II
       (Winter), 8-11, 24.
              "There have always been two American tra-
       ditions,--the imported and the indigenous,
       the native. Brooks tried to judge MT by
       the wrong standards, applying a criticism
       "born of European nostalgia and spurious
       psychology."

B20   JOHNSON, BURGES.   "When Mark Twain Cursed
       Me," Mark Twain Quarterly, II (Fall), 8-9,
       24.
              For a fuller version of this article see
       Johnson's "A Ghost for Mark Twain" (1952).

B21   L.   "Mark Twain Gleanings," Southwest Review,
       XXII (Winter), 212.
              A review of Cyril Clemens, ed., Mark
       Twain Wit and Wisdom (1935). "So many
       stories he never fathered have been attri-
       buted to Mark Twain that it is a pleasure

to find the names of contributors attached
to the anecdotes in this volume to vouch
for their authenticity." Some of the 150
stories were in the Paine biography, but
most are previously unpublished.

B22   LE BRETON, M.   [Review: Léon Lemonnier, La
       Jeunesse aventureuse de Mark Twain.] Études
       Anglaises, I (September), 465.
              A lively account, although there was also
       a quiet melancholy in the adventure. [In
       French.]

B23   LEISY, ERNEST E.   "Mark Twain's Part in The
       Gilded Age," American Literature, VIII
       (January), 445-47.
              On the collaboration of MT with Charles
       Dudley Warner, showing how their contribu-
       tions were interwoven; uses MT's copy of GA.

B24   L[OVEMAN], A[MY.]   "Mark Twain on the Screen,"
       Saturday Review of Literature, XVI (June 12),
       10.
              "The Prince and the Pauper must be called
       the poorest of Mark Twain's novels," yet "by
       leaving out a good deal that Mark put into
       the book and adding a good deal that he did
       not, the movies have made an excellent pic-
       ture of it.... It was possible to lift the
       events of The Prince and the Pauper out of
       the book because the events were the whole
       of the book." Though better novels, TS and
       HF can hardly be filmed without distortion,
       HF because "the events as they have meaning
       for us are inseparable from their impact on
       the mind and sympathies of Huck Finn."

B25   MALONE, DUMAS.   "Who Are the American Immor-
       tals?" Harper's, CLXXIV (April), 544-48.
              Only brief mention of MT, ranking him
       third among American writers, after Emerson
       and Hawthorne and ahead of Whitman. "Mark
       Twain and Whitman [seem] to be gaining."
       Melville is not mentioned. See DeVoto, "At
       the Cannon's Mouth," above.

B26   MARCOSSON, ISAAC F.   "Mark Twain as Collabora-
       tor," Mark Twain Quarterly, II (Winter), 7,
       24.
              MT wrote out a reminiscence of Henry H.
       Rogers for Marcosson to incorporate in an
       article he was writing on Rogers in 1904 for
       The World's Work; credit could not be given
       to MT because of his contract with Harper's.

B27   MORLEY, CHRISTOPHER.   "George Ade on Mark
       Twain," Saturday Review of Literature, XV
       (March 20), 12.
              Briefly describes and quotes Ade's Revived
       Remarks on Mark Twain (1936). Reproduces a
       sketch of MT in the book "from a drawing in
       Life (1898) by an unknown artist."

B28   N., H.   "Knowing Mark Twain," The Standard
       ("Issued by the American Ethical Union"),
       XXIII (May), 217.
              A brief review of Mark Twain's Notebook,
       which should silence the charges that MT

(N., H.)
was censored by his wife and William Dean Howells; "Still better the Notes bring the man himself before us again."

B29   ODELL, GEORGE C. D. Annals of the New York Stage. New York: Columbia University Press, Vol. IX (1870-75), passim.
"Little Mac" appeared as MT's Jumping Frog with Bryant's Minstrels, December, 1870 (p. 76). On MT with The Man Who Laughs, Steinway Hall, January 24, 1872 (p. 207). MT was going to speak on "Recollections of Some Un-Commonplace Characters I Have Met" at the Plymouth Church, Brooklyn, November 21, 1871; he spoke on Artemus Ward instead, apparently (p. 231). MT gave his Sandwich Islands lecture at Steinway Hall, February 5 and 10, 1873 (p. 335) and at the Academy of Music, Brooklyn, February 7, 1873 (p. 352). On the play from The Gilded Age (with a photograph of J. T. Raymond as Colonel Sellers), pp. 556-57.

B30   PABODY, E. F. "Mark Twain's Ghost Story," Minnesota History, XVIII (March), 28-35.
About MT's lecture with Cable in Minneapolis, January 24, 1885.

B31   *PRAZ, MARIO. ["A stimulating essay on Twain."] Studi e Svaghi inglesi. Firenze: Sansoni, pp. 157-63.
[Source: Asselineau (1954), No. 772; also MHRA Annual Bibliography (1937), No. 1540, 4216.]

B32   ROBERTSON, STUART. "Mark Twain in German," Mark Twain Quarterly, II (Fall), 10-12.
On a copy of Huckleberry Finn in Robertson's possession, badly translated into German by H. Koch (Leipzig: Hess u. Becker Verlag, n.d.).

B33   ROWE, IDA. "Mark Twain's Interest in Nature," Mark Twain Quarterly, I (Summer), 7, 9-10, 14.
On MT's interest in animals, streams, landscapes, with examples drawn from works, biography, and published reminiscences of friends.

B34   *SWAIN, LOUIS H. "Mark Twain as a Music Critic: A Case Study in Esthetic Growth," Furman Bulletin, XIX (April), 48-53.
[Source: MHRA Annual Bibliography (1937), No. 4219.]

B35   *VERDAGUER, MARIO. "Humorismo inglés y ironía yanqui," La Razón (Panama), V (July 3), 2.
[Source: "Articles on American Literature Appearing in Current Periodicals," American Literature, IX (January, 1938), 473: "Biographical sketch, stressing Mark Twain's triumph in England."]

B36   WAGGONER, HYATT HOWE. "Science in the Thought of Mark Twain," American Literature, VIII (January), 357-70.
MT had a broad and enthusiastic acquaintance with science, and a "philosophically sound, if not scientifically detailed, knowledge of the main outline of anthropology.... was ... one of the principal bulwarks of his deterministic philosophy" (p. 359).

B37   WILSON, HARRY LEON. "Mark Twain a Negligible Item," Mark Twain Quarterly, II (Winter), 13, 24.
When a boy Wilson read TS despite parental disapproval, and later discovered RI. Finally, at a testimonial dinner to Brander Matthews he saw MT and found the man, like his books, "too good to be true."

B38   WOOD, GRANT. "My Debt to Mark Twain," Mark Twain Quarterly, II (Fall), 6, 14, 24.
TS and HF were boyhood favorites he reread until they were tattered; Wood liked the adventure and the sense of fairness. "My favorite was Huckleberry Finn; probably, I realize now, because of its richness in sense impressions of the type that made my own boyhood so vivid."

B39   YEATS, WILLIAM BUTLER. "W. B. Yeats Receives the Mark Twain Medal," Mark Twain Quarterly, I (Summer), 21.
Includes three brief notes by Yeats, sending thanks for the medal and recalling that "Lady Gregory and I dined with him many years ago, and I remember vividly his talk and his stories, always admirable in matter and manner."

1938 A BOOKS

A1   BENSON, IVAN. Mark Twain's Western Years. Together with Hitherto Unreprinted Clemens Western Items. Stanford University, California: Stanford University Press, and London: Humphrey Milford, Oxford University Press.
"During his Western period he became an accomplished social satirist, and with a gradually broadening scope he wrote artistically, with a variety of effects, from the coarsest burlesque to fine descriptive and informational articles" (p. vii). Includes an extensive bibliography of MT's published writing for this period (pp. 165-74), and a generous sampling of his writings in Nevada and California papers (pp. 175-213).

A2   CLEMENS, SAMUEL L., ed G. Ezra Dane. Letters from the Sandwich Islands Written for the Sacramento "Union" by Mark Twain. Stanford University, California: Stanford University Press, and London: Humphrey Milford, Oxford University Press.
A reprint of the limited 1937 edition published by the Grabhorn Press.

A3 CLEMENS, SAMUEL L. Mark Twain's Letter to
William Bowen, Buffalo, February Sixth, 1870.
Prefatory Note by Clara Clemens Gabrilowitsch; Foreword by Albert W. Gunnison. San
Francisco: The Book Club of California.
Clara's note is descriptive and affectionate, and Gunnison's brief forward comments
on William Bowen and reprints a note Bowen
sent with a copy of the letter.

A4 _____, ed. Franklin Walker. The Washoe Giant
in San Francisco. Being Heretofore Uncollected Sketches by Mark Twain Published in
the Golden Era in the Sixties Including
Those Blasted Children, The Lick House Ball,
The Kearny Street Ghost Story, Fitz Smythe's
Horse, and Thirty-Four More Items by the
Wild Humorist of the Pacific Slope. San
Francisco: George Fields.
Contains text of MT material, helpful introduction and headnotes, a list of MT material published in the Golden Era (1863-66),
and a "Bibliographical Note" indicating the
few reprintings of this material (p. 143).

A5 *LANGDON, JERVIS. Samuel L. Clemens, Some
Reminiscences and Some Excerpts from Letters
and Unpublished Manuscripts. n.p., n.d.
(dedication dated October 7, 1938). (Pamphlet.)
[Source: Cited in Baetzhold (1970),
p. 49 and p. 330, n. 6. Baetzhold refers
to notes by MT criticizing Sir Walter Scott
for weakening his writing by vagueness and
verbosity.]

A6 *LEE, ALFRED PYLE. First and Other Editions
of Samuel L. Clemens, collected by the well-
known bibliographer, Dr. Albert P. Lee of
Philadelphia, with a few additions. New
York: F. C. Duschenes.
[31-page pamphlet. Source: Asselineau
(1954), No. 795.]

A7 MASTERS, EDGAR LEE. Mark Twain: A Portrait.
New York and London: Charles Scribner's
Sons.
A lively biographical account, shaped by
Masters' view that MT failed in his duty as
a satirist; for example, he says MT was
dabbling in trivial matters while "Ibsen
was writing An Enemy of the People and Pil-
lars of Society in which he attacked the
whole fabric of modern society, its corruption and its hypocrisy. We needed just
this surgery here in America, and the regret
is that Twain did not administer it for us.
The love of money and fear of the crowd kept
him from doing it" (p. 174). See reviews.

A8 RAMSAY, ROBERT L., and FRANCES GUTHRIE EMBER-
SON. A Mark Twain Lexicon. University of
Missouri Studies, XIII (January), cxix,
278 pp.
Based on master's theses by Margaret Sel-
lars Edwards, Ernestine Ernst, True Gaines,
Amelia Madera, Alma B. Martin, Florence
Potter Stedman, Avera Leolin Taylor, Donald

C. Thompson, Georgia House Watson, Everette
M. Webber, and Emma C. Woods, each of whom
worked with a single volume (1929-35). "The
Lexicon makes no attempt to include the whole
of Mark Twain's extraordinarily large vocabulary. Merely those elements of it have
here been brought together that seemed best
to illustrate the man and his many-sided genius...and the English language to whose
development in America he significantly contributed" (p. v). "A total of nearly eight
thousand words, combinations, and meanings
have been selected...with four aims in mind":
to collect his Americanisms, his new words
and usages, his archaisms, and "without aim-
ing at completeness, certain miscellaneous
groups of words which seemed to be significant or interesting for various reasons"
(p. vii).

A9 SEVERANCE, EMILY A. Journal Letters of Emily
A. Severance, "Quaker City," 1867. Ed. Julia
Severance Millikan. Cleveland: The Gates
Press.
Another perspective on the tour that pro-
duced IA; cited (repeatedly) in Ganzel (1968).

1938 B SHORTER WRITINGS

B1 A., E. L. "A Guest of Mark Twain," More Books:
The Bulletin of the Boston Public Library,
Sixth Series, XIII (November), 430.
Contains the text of an MT letter
(February 14, 1881, just acquired by the Boston Public Library) to Edward House, who
visited the Clemenses and spent several
months in Hartford, working on a dramatization of P&P; the project ended in acrimony
and a lawsuit.

B2 ADAMS, HENRY. Letters of Henry Adams (1892-
1918), ed. by Worthington Chauncey Ford.
Boston and New York: Houghton Mifflin Company, pp. 326-27.
Of Adam's Diary: "There are one or two
good jokes in it, but of these I am not an
expert judge. What charms my historical
soul is the point of view, which is unconsciously the same as that of the twelfth-
century mystery and of Milton, and they were
all unconscious. Is it not curious that the
man should always have represented himself as
a fool and a tool in contact with the woman?
Mark Twain's Adam is really a very interesting person. His affectation of science is
keenly true,--no one knows more about that
than I do. The Eve is not studied, of
course; the paper is a study of Adam alone;
and it is marvelous true; in fact, to own
up, it is me myself; a portrait by Boldini."
(Letter of April 8, 1901 to Elizabeth Cameron.)

B3 BEEKMAN, JUDGE DOW. "Mark Twain and the Watering Troughs," Mark Twain Quarterly, II
(Summer-Fall), 5, 24.
An anecdote told by Governor David B. Hill
of New York: on the birth of each child,

(BEEKMAN, JUDGE DOW)
MT had a stone watering trough set up beside the road, with the child's name on it.

B4   BLAIR, WALTER. "Mark Twain's Way with Words," University Review (Kansas City), V (Autumn), 60-62.
A joyous discussion of MT's vocabulary as part of a review of the Ramsay and Emberson Mark Twain Lexicon, which Blair considers sound.

B5   BLODGETT, HAROLD. "A Note on Mark Twain's Library of Humor," American Literature, X (March), 78-80.
The 1888 edition was compiled by Howells and his assistant, Charles Hopkins Clark; the 1906 edition, compiled at the Harper's offices, consists mostly of materials from other sources.

B6   BUCHNER, THOS. A. "Twain's House-Buying," Mark Twain Quarterly, III (Winter), 23.
An anecdote, vaguely recalled, of MT's purchase of a home after he decided to leave Riverdale-on-Hudson, New York.

B7   CLEMENS, CLARA. My Husband Gabrilowitsch. New York: Harper & Brothers.
Passim on MT, chiefly in passing references and comparisons of his temperament to that of Gabrilowitsch [indexed]. Declares she and her sister Jean "knew more German than our genius father" (p. 1), discusses MT's attitude toward the Jews (p. 6, in connection with her love for, and later marriage to the great pianist Ossip Gabrilowitsch, who was Jewish), and his condemnation of lynching and comment on Negroes and further comment on the Jews (pp. 12-16); texts of two letters from MT to his daughter Clara appear pp. 46-47 and 115-16.

B8   CLEMENS, KATHARINE. "My Husband and Mark Twain," in her Gardens and Books: The Autobiography of Katharine Clemens. With Foreword by Cyril Clemens [her son]. (Webster Groves, Missouri: International Mark Twain Society), pp. 205-16 and passim (indexed).
Provides family history, and describes MT in London in 1899. On p. 166, notes that Kaiser Wilhelm's memoirs mention a meeting with MT at the home of General Maximilian von Versen. Photograph of MT, p. 212.

B9   DEVOTO, BERNARD. "Mark Twain: A Caricature," Saturday Review of Literature, XVII (March 19), 5.
A review of Edgar Lee Masters, Mark Twain: A Portrait: "The worst book yet written about Mark Twain, the most inaccurate, the most wildly incomprehensible, and the stupidest.... A bad book, a false book, sometimes a vicious book, and the silliest of the now numerous books that waste time savagely assailing Mark Twain for not having been what he did not want to be, what he

could not possibly have been, what no intelligent person supposes it to have been possible for him to have been."

B10   _____. "The Mark Twain Papers," Saturday Review of Literature, XIX (December 10), 3-4, 14-15.
A description of the papers for which DeVoto has just assumed editorial responsibility, succeeding Albert Bigelow Paine. In a letter to the editor (p. 9) he says that he "cannot answer questions about the content of the papers" because of the pressure of his work and because "the terms of the agreement under which I am working forbid me to give out any information until the books on which I am working are ready."

B11   EASTMAN, MAX. "Mark Twain's Elmira," Harper's, CLXXVI (May), 620-32.
Eastman's family moved to Elmira in 1894, when he was eleven, and he describes the town and the Langdon family as he learned of them. The town was not intellectually stagnant, as Van Wyck Brooks and others suggest, and Jervis Langdon, MT's father-in-law, "was one of the most "un-coal-dealer-and-mine-owner-like characters that ever got ahead in business," generous, unaffected by his wealth, and an ardent abolitionist. [Reprinted in Eastman's Heroes I Have Known: Twelve Who Lived Great Lives (New York: Simon and Schuster, 1942,) pp. 105-42, according to MHRA Annual Bibliography (1942). No. 2137.]

B12   FERGUSON, DELANCEY. "Huck Finn Aborning," Colophon, n.s., III (Spring), 171-80.
Textual changes in the manuscript of HF show, not submission to censorship, but improvements in tone, language more suitable for Huck, and clarification of details. Reprinted in Bradley (1962), pp. 297-305; in Scott (1955), pp. 249-58; Scott (1967), pp. 234-43.

B13   H., H. W. "On Mark Twain," Manchester Guardian (April 29), p. 7.
A review of Edgar Lee Masters, Mark Twain: A Portrait, an unconvincing book. "After hearing Edgar Lee Masters on Mark Twain one cannot help regretting that it is impossible to hear Mark Twain on Edgar Lee Masters."

B14   HIBBARD, FREDERICK C. "Mark Twain From a Sculptor's Viewpoint," Mark Twain Quarterly, III (Winter), 1-3, 24.
An appreciation of MT by the sculptor who made the Hannibal group of Tom Sawyer and Huck Finn; he never met MT.

B15   JACOBS, W. W. "An Englishman's Opinion of Mark Twain," Mark Twain Quarterly, II (Summer-Fall), 1-2.
An impressionistic discussion of MT as distinctively American, a great writer, humorist, and a great personality.

1938 - Shorter Writings

B16   JORDAN, ELIZABETH. "A Silent Celebrity,"
      Christian Science Monitor, XXX (November 4),
      9.
          At a dinner she seated MT beside May Sin-
      clair in the hope that he could draw her
      into conversation; the attempt failed. [An
      excerpt from Elizabeth Jordan's Three Rous-
      ing Cheers (New York: Appleton-Century).]

B17   KANTOR, McKINLAY. "The Boy in the Dark: A
      Fantasy of the Mark Twain Country," Scholas-
      tic, XXXIII (September 17), 6, 35.
          On his nephew, Benny Fuller, who was lost
      in the cave at Hannibal and was shown un-
      known parts of the cave by a mysterious boy
      named Sammy--who then led him back to the
      tourist area and could not afterward be
      found. "Reprinted from the Mark Twain Quar-
      terly, by permission of Mr. Cyril Clemens,
      editor."

B18   LORCH, FRED W. "Mark Twain's Trip to Humboldt
      in 1861," American Literature, X (November),
      343-49.
          Includes text of an MT letter to his moth-
      er (January 30, 1862), interesting as one
      of his early literary treatments of the re-
      gion.

B19   _____. [Review: August Hüppy, Mark Twain
      und die Schweiz (1935).] American Litera-
      ture, IX (January), 488-89.
          Concerns visits to Switzerland by MT in
      1878, 1891, 1897. Appreciative, based on
      material already well known, but gives
      Swiss readers "the vigor, freshness, and
      charm" of MT.

B20   _____. [Review: Edgar Lee Masters, Mark
      Twain: A Portrait.] American Literature,
      X (November), 373-76.
          Masters distorts his portrait through
      proletarian bias; the book "has at least
      three serious faults: inaccurate report-
      ing, unwarranted assumptions, and a con-
      fused philosophy."

B21   MABBOTT, THOMAS OLLIVE. [Brief review: Ivan
      Benson, Mark Twain's Western Years.] Com-
      monweal, XXVIII (July 8), 302.
          "Well written and entertaining reading
      for all the solidity of its scholarship."

B22   _____. [Review: G. Ezra Dane, ed., Letters
      from the Sandwich Islands, Written for the
      Sacramento Union by Mark Twain.] Common-
      weal, XXVIII (September 2), 480.
          "The editing is competent," but unfortu-
      nately four letters were omitted.

B23   MacALISTER, SIR IAN. "Mark Twain, Some Per-
      sonal Reminiscences," Landmark, XX (March),
      141-47.
          "Extracts from a speech made recently
      at Dartmouth House." Comments on MT's
      gloom of the 1890's and the attempts of
      MacAlister's father "to get him out of this
      kind of neurosis" with a visit to the

Savage Club--successfully, since no demands
were made on him. Also describes a visit
to MT in New York in 1903, and seeing him
at Oxford in 1907. "My father had in his
possession hundreds of pages of manuscript"
blue-penciled by Olivia Clemens.

B24   MOORE, JOHN BASSETT. "Mark Twain and Copy-
      right," Mark Twain Quarterly, III (Winter),
      3.
          Appreciative. As "Third Assistant Secre-
      tary of State," Moore met MT at a reception
      given by Grover Cleveland in honor of au-
      thors who had come to Washington to speak
      in favor of international copyright law;
      Moore later saw MT "on several occasions and
      was always deeply impressed."

B25   MORRIS, COURTLAND P. "The Model for Huck
      Finn," Mark Twain Quarterly, II (Summer-
      Fall), 22-23.
          Boyhood memories by the boy who posed for
      the HF illustrations by E. W. Kemble, from
      May 1-October 1, 1884; he was paid four dol-
      lars per week.

B26   MOTT, HOWARD S., JR. "The Origin of Aunt Pol-
      ly," Publishers' Weekly, CXXXIV
      (November 19), 1821-23.
          Benjamin P. Shillaber's character, Mrs.
      Partington, anticipates Tom Sawyer's aunt
      in circumstances, personality, and an inci-
      dent in which she figures, and (as MT later
      described his mother) she kindly warmed the
      water before drowning the kittens. The
      frontispiece of The Life and Sayings of Mrs.
      Partington (1854) bears a strong resemblance
      to the picture of Aunt Polly on the last
      page of the first edition of TS (1876).

B27   NYE, RUSSEL B. "Mark Twain in Oberlin," Ohio
      State Archaeological and Historical Quarter-
      ly [now Ohio History], XLVII (January),
      69-73.
          On the MT-George Washington Cable reading
      there (February 11, 1885). Local press ac-
      counts ranked Cable above MT; according to
      local belief, the cold reception led MT to
      use Oberlin as his model for Hadleyburg,
      but there is only the internal evidence of
      a general similarity between the description
      of Hadleyburg and the pious town of Oberlin,
      founded some three generations earlier.
      (See Cardwell [1951].)

B28   ODELL, GEORGE C. D. Annals of the New York
      Stage. New York: Columbia University
      Press, Vol. X (1875-1879), passim.
          Mentions MT giving his "Roughing It in the
      Land of the Big Bonanza" lecture at Chicker-
      ing Hall, March 28, 29, and 31, 1876
      (p. 105), and at the Academy of Music,
      Brooklyn, March 30, afternoon (p. 136). MT
      appeared at the Academy of Music as part of
      a program that included Emma Thursby and the
      Young Apollo Club November 13, 1876 (p. 322).
      On the misfortunes of MT and Bret Harte's
      Ah Sin (pp. 370-71); it also ran for a week

(ODELL, GEORGE C. D.)
at the Grand Opera House, September 24-30, 1877 (p. 391), and at the Bowery Theatre, October 29 to early November (p. 407).

B29 PADEREWSKI, IGNACE, and MARY LAWTON. "America," Chapter IX in The Paderewski Memoirs (New York: Charles Scribner's Sons).
On p. 205, describes meeting MT at the home of Richard Watson Gilder: "The beautiful impression he made upon me abides with me still. He was a purely American product, some one that only America could have produced, in the quality of his mind, his humor and character. I think he remains an undimmed figure in your history. The years will not diminish his towering qualities and virtues."

B30 *PARKS, EDD WINFIELD. "Mark Twain as Southerner," in his Segments of Southern Thought (Athens: University of Georgia Press.)
[Source: Asselineau (1954), No. 803.]

B31 PUTNAM, SAMUEL. "The Americanism of Mark Twain," Mark Twain Quarterly, II (Fall), 13, 34.
MT was more than a humorist; he depicted his time and country for a world audience.

B32 QUICK, DOROTHY. "My Author's League with Mark Twain," North American Review, CCXLV (Summer), 315-29.
Young Dorothy was a budding writer; see her Enchantment (1961) for details of her friendship with MT.

B33 QUINN, ARTHUR HOBSON. [Review: Ivan Benson, Mark Twain's Western Years.] Pacific Historical Review, VII (September), 282-83.
Notes the book's readability, and the value of its bibliography of MT's Nevada and California writings, 1861-1865, with reprintings of some of them; agrees with Benson on the beneficial influence of Mrs. Clemens, Howells, Aldrich, "who toned Mark Twain down, and kept him from some of the banalities quoted by Mr. Benson."

B34 REYNOLDS, HORACE. "Mark Twain's Literary Beginnings," Christian Science Monitor, XXX, June 15, Magazine Section, 10.
A descriptive, uncritical review of Franklin Walker, ed., The Washoe Giant in San Francisco.

B35 ROADES, SISTER MARY TERESA. "Don Quixote and A Connecticut Yankee in King Arthur's Court," Mark Twain Quarterly, II (Summer-Fall), 8-9.
Draws a number of parallels, among them the contrast of "the modern with the antique" and the attack on books of chivalry; but "the character of Don Quixote is in marked contrast with that of the Boss."

B36 SULLIVAN, MARK. The Education of an American. New York: Doubleday, Doran & Co., pp. 230-33.
On MT in New York, Norman Hapgood's humorless description of MT in his autobiography, and Robert Collier's participation in the elaborate scheme to persuade MT that he was being sent an elephant for Christmas, to keep him company at Stormfield.

B37 TAYLOR, WALTER FULLER. "Mark Twain and the Machine Age," South Atlantic Quarterly, XXXVII (October), 384-96.
The portrayal of industrialism in GA and CY follows "a fairly simple, coherent philosophy of acquisition, control of obvious abuses, and concern for the interests of the whole people. Within him, satirist, capitalist, and democrat worked toward the same object--that of enjoying the uses of the machine, and lessening the abuses." [Reprinted in Fifty Years of the South Atlantic Quarterly (1952), according to Asselineau (1954), No. 831.]

B38 WAGENKNECHT, EDWARD. "Crucial Years for Mark Twain," New York Times Book Review (June 19), p. 2.
A review of Ivan Benson, Mark Twain's Western Years, which reflects "a very careful, judicial and exhaustive study of all the factors which influenced Mark Twain during these crucial years."

B39 _____. "Mr. Masters on Mark Twain," New York Times Book Review (May 8), p. 10.
A review of Mark Twain: A Portrait. "Masters's book is nothing more than a crude restatement of the Van Wyck Brooks theory of 1920.... What Mr. Brooks could not do with a scalpel, Mr. Masters is hardly likely to achieve with a bludgeon."

B40 WHITELEY, MRS. RICHARD P. "Interview with Mark Twain," Mark Twain Quarterly, II (Summer-Fall), 9, 24.
A headnote explains that this is about a dream her father, Robert Fitch Shepard, had about interviewing MT.

1939 A BOOKS

A1 ADE, GEORGE. One Afternoon with Mark Twain. Chicago: The Mark Twain Society of Chicago.
Describes visit to MT in "the late summer or early autumn of 1902, as nearly as I can fix the date" (p. 5). Contains no new information or critical judgment. A letter from MT to Howells (July 22, 1908), praising Ade, is reproduced in facsimile between pp. 8 and 9. "Editorial Notes" by George Hiram Brownell at end (pp. 14-15). Reprinted in Twainian, XXV (July-August, 1966), 1-4. Abstract in AES, XI (1968), 1735; reprinted in Twainian, XXVIII (January-February, 1969), 3.

1939 - Books

A2 *BLANCK, JACOB. A Supplement to "A Bibliogra-
    phy of Mark Twain." New York: Privately
    Printed (4-page pamphlet discussing the de-
    faced first issue of HF).
        [Source: Blair (1950), p. 385 and Twain-
    ian, I (May, 1939), 4.]

A3 CLEMENS, CYRIL. My Cousin Mark Twain. With
    an Introduction by Booth Tarkington. Em-
    maus, Pa.: Rodale Press.
        The first half of the book is biographi-
    cal, seasoned with anecdotes; much of this
    will be familiar to readers acquainted with
    MT's works, although sources are not very
    fully documented. The second part, also
    highly anecdotal and sometimes drawn from
    MT's work, consists of "Mark Twain as a
    Dramatist," "Some Friends of Mark Twain,"
    "Mark Twain and Smoking," "Did Mark Twain
    Say It?" (on quotations attributed to him),
    "With Mark Twain in Europe," and "The Mark
    Twain Medal" (a history of the granting of
    the medal "to show recognition for outstand-
    ing achievement in various fields of human
    endeavor"; the first recipient, in 1930,
    was Benito Mussolini (p. 205). There are
    stories here of interest for the general
    reader, although academic studies of MT
    have tended to ignore this book.

A4 *CLEMENS, SAMUEL L. Conversation As It Was at
    the Fireside of the Tudors [1601]. Embel-
    lished with an illuminating introduction,
    facetious notes and a bibliography by
    Franklin J. Meine. Chicago: Privately
    Printed for the Mark Twain Society of Chi-
    cago.
        [Source: Asselineau (1954), No. 840.]

A5 _____. Letters from Honolulu, Written for
    the Sacramento "Union" by Mark Twain. In-
    troduction by John W. Vandercook. Honolulu:
    Thomas Nickerson.
        Letters dated June 25, September 10,
    April, and March, 1866, "Excerpts from the
    Diaries of Captain Mitchell and the Fergu-
    son Brothers," and "Mark Twain's Concluding
    Remarks Reprinted from Harper's New Monthly
    Magazine, December, 1866." "The letters
    are printed exactly as they appeared in the
    SACRAMENTO UNION, typographical and editori-
    al errors included." Vandercook's intro-
    duction is general and descriptive, and the
    material in this book is now more readily
    available from other sources such as A.
    Grove Day's 1966 edition of the letters
    from Hawaii.

A6 * _____. The Prince and the Pauper, ridotto e
    annotato da G. Tacconis. Turin: Società
    ed. internazionale (Scrittori inglesi e
    americani commentati per le scuole).
        [Source: Asselineau (1954), No. 843.]

A7 * _____. Tom Sawyer, with an introduction by
    Bernard DeVoto, including as a prologue
    the "Boy's Manuscript," here first printed.
    Cambridge, Massachusetts: Printed for the

Members of the Limited Editions Club at the
University Press.
    [Source: Asselineau (1954), No. 839; the
introduction and "Boy's Manuscript" were incorporated in DeVoto's Mark Twain at Work
(1942).]

A8 *HELLMAN, FLORENCE S. List of Writings by
    Mark Twain Translated into Certain Foreign
    Languages. Washington: Library of Con-
    gress, Division of Bibliography (Selected
    list of references, No. 1450; 14 pp., type-
    written).
        [Source: Asselineau (1954), No. 834.]

A9 HEMMINGHAUS, EDGAR H. Mark Twain in Germany.
    New York: Columbia University Press [Re-
    printed New York: AMS Press, Inc., 1966].
        A survey of German interest in MT, and
    scholarly work on him, from 1874-1937, with
    appendixes listing German publication of
    his works in English, in German translations,
    and in school editions, followed by an ex-
    tensive bibliography of German scholarship.
    Because of the scope and quality of this
    work, there has been no attempt to incorpo-
    rate this material in the present bibliog-
    raphy; the Hemminghaus book should be con-
    sidered the first reference for the period
    through 1937.

A10 MENDELSON, M. Mark Tven. Fskblksm Molodaja
    Gvardija.
        [Source: Asselineau (1954), No. 838;
    confirmed by Clarence A. Manning review
    (1948.B42).

A11 *WALKER, FRANKLIN. San Francisco's Literary
    Frontier. New York: Alfred A. Knopf.
        [Source: 1969 reissue, 1969.A9. A gen-
    eral study, passim on MT.]

1939 B SHORTER WRITINGS

B1 ANON. "Mark Twain in His Proper and Profane
    Moments," New York Times Book Review
    (February 5), p. 3.
        A review of Cyril Clemens, ed., My Cousin,
    Mark Twain, which is neither distinguished
    nor valuable, "but it is lively and pleas-
    antly familiar, and thus becomes (in spite
    of some careless editing) a real addition
    to the Mark Twain library."

B2 ANON. "Mark Twain's First Lecture Tour.
    Based on the Original Newspaper Accounts,"
    Mark Twain Quarterly, III (Summer-Fall),
    3-6, 24.
        On MT's tour in October-December, 1866,
    quoting newspapers of the time.

B3 ANON. "Time and the Joke: Mark Twain To-
    Day," Times Literary Supplement, October 14,
    p. 587.
        A review of Cyril Clemens, [My Cousin,]
    Mark Twain. Primarily descriptive, calling
    the book "a commentary on what is presumed
    to be common knowledge rather than a full-
    length portrait."

B4   *ANON. [Interview with Captain Horace Bixby, 1914.] Memphis (Tennessee) Commercial Appeal, June 23, p. 4A.
      [Source: Quoted by Elmo Howell in "Mark Twain and the Civil War" (1972), p. 54, n. 4.] MT knew the river but lacked confidence: "Being a coward, he was a failure as a pilot."

B5   BEARD, DAN. "Mark Twain," in his Hardly a Man Is Now Alive: The Autobiography of Dan Beard (New York: Doubleday, Doran & Company, Inc.), pp. 334-50.
      Affectionate reminiscences by the illustrator of CY, and later, neighbor at Redding, Connecticut.

B6   BLAIR, WALTER. "Mark Twain, New York Correspondent," American Literature, XI (November), 247-59.
      About MT's correspondence for the San Francisco Alta California in New York in 1867, before he sailed on the tour that produced IA. For text of these Alta letters see Franklin Walker and G. Ezra Dane, Mark Twain's Travels with Mr. Brown (1940; reprinted New York: Russell & Russell, 1971).

B7   _____. "On the Structure of Tom Sawyer," Modern Philology, XXXVII (August), 75-88.
      MT was writing at a time of general rebellion against the model boy of earlier juvenile literature, and he produced a boy who "could play pranks at the same time he was developing qualities which would make him a normal adult." The book is well structured toward this end, with four themes: "the story of Tom and Becky, the story of Tom and Muff Potter, the Jackson's Island episode, and the series of happenings (which might be called the Injun Joe story) leading to the discovery of the treasure." Each episode begins with a boyish action and concludes with an opposing action of maturity. Reprinted in Cardwell (1963), pp. 36-45.

B8   BLAISE, BUNKER. "The Mark Twain Society," Saturday Review of Literature, XX (July 15), 11-12.
      Describes the Society, which "has only one active member--President [Cyril] Clemens. But its roster of nominal associates is more imposing than that of any organization since the Sons and Daughters of I Will Arise." Among those listed on the letterhead is the Honorary President, Benito Mussolini, a fact that has led to rejection of honorary membership by some to whom it was offered; thus, Robert Graves wrote: "My admiration for Mark Twain prevents me from accepting a vice-president to Mussolini, the enemy to all Huck Finns," and Bertrand Russell declared "Mussolini is a man I hold in utmost abhorrence!" Don Marquis rejected the offer of a vice-presidency because "It's a matter of principle not to

let a foreigner like Mussolini have a higher office than mine even if he is funnier than I am." There is a description of Cyril Clemens's lecturing and of the books published by the Society.

B9   BLEARSIDES, OLIVER. [Review: Dan Beard, Hardly a Man is Now Alive.] Mark Twain Quarterly, III (Summer-Fall), 22.
      Contains a brief account of Beard and his part in founding the Boy Scouts of America; quotes an MT note praising his Connecticut Yankee illustrations, and quotes Beard's description of MT at home.

B10   BOSTWICK, ARTHUR E. A Life with Men and Books. New York: The H. W. Wilson Company, p. 156.
      Reports that Harper & Brothers were obliged to seek an injunction against the sale of a book supposedly by the spirit of MT, but gives no further details.

B11   BRASHEAR, M[INNIE] M. [Review: Cyril Clemens, My Cousin Mark Twain.] American Literature, XI (May), 231-32.
      A "humorless retelling" of two hundred anecdotes from various sources, including earlier biographies, this is "a fairly readable book" for the uncritical. The significant parts are a frontispiece portrait of Sam Clemens at twenty-one, previously unpublished, and accounts of him in London and Vienna.

B12   [BROWNELL, GEORGE HIRAM.] "About Twain in Periodicals," Twainian, I (October), 4-5; (November), 3-4; (December), 6.
      A bibliography of secondary material, in installments that continued to the demise of the old Twainian in 1940 and was resumed in the new series beginning in 1942 and carried to completion. The installments are in alphabetical order by the names of the journals covered; the 1939 installments include Academy Magazine (London) through Collier's Weekly. This material has been incorporated in the present bibliography.

B13   _____. "Californiana," Twainian, I (December), 3-5.
      On the search by Walter Francis Frear for material in Nevada and California pertaining to MT. Among his discoveries were a number of reviews of MT lectures in 1866, with a hostile account in the Petaluma Journal and Argus and a defence in the Sonoma Democrat. There is bibliographical data on a dodger advertising his July 2, 1868 lecture on Venice, and a listing of sketches in the Overland Monthly which later appeared in IA.

B14   _____. "Concerning Cyril," Twainian, I (March), 2.
      Sarcastic reference to Cyril Clemens, prefatory to a reprinting of "The Mark Twain Tradition" from the Chicago Daily News (December 5, 1938) on The International Mark Twain Society.

B15 [BROWNELL, GEORGE HIRAM.] "Mr. Howe's 'Modest' Collection," Twainian, I (November),
4-5.
The large book collection of W. T. H.
Howe, assembled by him at a cost of between
two and three million dollars, is to be
sold on the open market and dispersed, by
his expressed wish, rather than being transferred intact to a library; the MT material
alone cost almost one hundred thousand dollars. A note in Twainian, II (November,
1940), 1, reports that the collection will
be transferred intact to the New York Public Library.

B16   . "The Real Jane Clemens," Twainian, I
(October), 2-4.
On the article, "Whitewashing Jane Clemens," by Doris and Samuel Webster (1925),
and the Van Wyck Brooks view of MT's mother.

B17   . "A Tale of 'A Dog's Tale,'" Twainian,
I (June), 2, 5-6.
Irving S. Underhill acquired the 223 mint
copies of the pamphlet from Foyle's in London; realizing he could not sell them without depressing the market, he placed them
in trust at Williams College, to be sold at
a rate of two per year, but the whole lot
is now on sale at $15.00 per copy.

B18   . "Tale of Two Twain (?) Tales," Twainian, I (April), 2-3.
On Rodman Gilder's attempts to find first
printings of "The Revised Catechism" and
"The Last Stamp," attributed to MT in clippings from unknown newspapers; they appear
to come from the late 1860's. "The Revised
Catechism" is Twainian in style.

B19   . "Twain's 'Weather' Witticism," Twainian, I (April), 3-4.
Robert Underwood Johnson's Remembered Yesterdays (Little, Brown, 1923, p. 322) quotes
MT's remark in a form Brownell finds authentic: "'We all grumble about the weather,
but' (dramatic pause) '--but--nothing is
done about it.'"

B20   . [Brief item.] Twainian, I (February),
3.
Opie Read has a series of "Mark Twain and
I" anecdotes in the Chicago Daily News:
they read well, but often place MT "at a
time and place where the facts show that
Mark just wasn't."

B21   . [Brief discussions of MT's original
pilot license.] Twainian, I (November),
1-3, 6; (December), 1-2; also see "License
Mystery Nears Solution," Twainian, II
(January, 1940), 2-3.

B22   . [Item on influence of Artemus Ward on
MT, and MT's sketch, "First Interview with
Artemus Ward."] Twainian, I (March), 1-2.
Lists a number of printings.

B23 BUTLER, NICHOLAS MURRAY. Across the Busy
Years: Reflections and Reflections. New
York and London: Charles Scribner's Sons.
I, 8-9; II, passim.
Reference in Vol. I merely notes long ac-
quaintance with MT, and there is no new in-
formation in Vol. II.

B24 CAMPBELL, OSCAR JAMES. [Review: G. Ezra
Dane, ed., Letters from the Sandwich Islands
(1938).] American Speech, XIV (February),
47-49.
Extensive passages of the speech of sea-
captains and the wife of one of them illustrate MT's "unfailing interest in all the
phenomena of living speech," as an amateur
and artist rather than a linguistic scientist.

B25   . [Review: Robert L. Ramsay and Frances
G. Emberson's A Mark Twain Lexicon (1938).]
American Speech, XIV (April), 132-33.
"A meticulously accurate and revealing
study of the way in which the American language develops its peculiar and distinctive
vocabulary and idioms. No happier choice
than the works of Mark Twain could have been
made for such an investigation."

B26 *CHASE, ROY. [Article on MT, title unknown;
contains anecdotes.] Australian National
Review, May.
[Source: Quoted by George Mackaness
(1962), pp. 6-10.]

B27 CLEMENS, CYRIL. "Mark Twain's View of '1601,'"
Saturday Review of Literature, XX
(September 30), 9.
A letter to the editor, extending his
"heartfelt congratulations on Mr. Basil Davenport's scholarly and discriminating review
of '1601'" a book which does not deserve
publication. MT "would turn in his grave if
he knew that this ephemera [sic] was em-
balmed with footnotes and critical comment.
He never meant it for publication at all."

B28   . "My Cousin, Mark Twain," Saturday Review of Literature, XIX (April 8), 9.
A reply to Bernard DeVoto's hostile review
of his book by that title (March 11). Cyril
Clemens says the similarities of his book to
the Paine biography stem from their having
talked to the same acquaintances of MT; he
does not comment on DeVoto's statement describing "the degree of cousinship involved."

B29   . "A Reply to Miss Brashear," American
Literature, XI (November), 296-97.
Takes issue with her review of his My
Cousin Mark Twain in the May issue; in detail Cyril Clemens argues the significance
of the material in the book and describes
his efforts to confirm his anecdotes.

B30 CLEMENS, SAMUEL L. "Mark Twain and John
Smith," Twainian, I (May), 2-4.

(CLEMENS, SAMUEL L.)

Fred W. Lorch has found correspondence between MT and a "John Smith" in the Quincy
(Illinois) Herald, publicizing a lecture to
be given there on April 9, 1867. The text
of the letters is reproduced.

B31   _____. "More Cemeterial Ghastliness," Mark
Twain Quarterly, III (Spring), 23.
Reprinted from Territorial Enterprise,
February 3, 1866. MT's satirical account
of a local undertaking firm owning large
shares in both the Lone Mountain Cemetery
and in the toll road leading to it: in
funeral processions, the toll is charged
even for the corpse.

B32   COWIE, ALEXANDER. "Mark Twain Controls Himself," American Literature, X (January),
488-91.
A reply to DeLancey Ferguson (Huck Finn
Aborning," 1938): MT "did like to write a
more robust style than was agreeable to his
late Victorian public," but tempered what he
said. "Whether Olivia or Howells or Mark
Twain was the censor does not much matter."

B33   *CURTIS, JOE [Article on MT as a pilot.]
Memphis Commercial Appeal, June 23.
Article quotes Captain Horace Bixby, who
said MT knew the river but lacked the self-
confidence needed to be a good pilot.
[Source: Quoted in Hutcherson (1940),
pp. 353-55.]

B34   DAVENPORT, BASIL. "1601 and All That,"
Saturday Review of Literature, XX (July 1),
19.
MT's book, recently published by the Mark
Twain Society of Chicago, is merely tedious
filth, and historically inaccurate to boot:
"One need only cite the courtier who went
into exile for seven years for the same
breach of decorum which is the beginning of
the merriment in 1601."

B35   DEVOTO, BERNARD. "Mark Twain About the Jews,"
Jewish Frontier, VI (May), 7-9.
"Under the title of '"Jewish Persecution"
A Business Passion--Mark Twain' a leaflet
is being circulated, ostensibly by one
Robert Edward Edmonson... It is based on
excerpts from an essay by Mark Twain called
'Concerning the Jews.' A vile and dishonest
misrepresentation of that essay, it is as
vicious a piece of propaganda as I have
ever seen." DeVoto sets the record
straight, partly with references to the
"Edmonson" leaflet but chiefly through a
summary of MT's essay and the known biographical details a general reader would
need.

B36   _____. "An Unpublished Chapter of Mark
Twain's Autobiography," Saturday Review of
Literature, XX (October 14), 11.
A letter to the editor, taking exception
to the strictures of Cyril Clemens and

Basil Davenport against the publication of
MT's bawdy 1601, which "people enjoy" reading. MT himself "took a naive pleasure and
even a solemn pride in having written it...
he thought of it not as an ephemeron but as
one of his lasting and most important books,"
as is shown in MT's own words, here published for the first time.

B37   _____. [Review: Cyril Clemens, My Cousin,
Mark Twain.] Saturday Review of Literature,
XIX (March 11), 16.
Begins by describing "the degree of cousinship involved: Mr. Clemens's great-
grandfather was, I believe, a cousin of Mark
Twain's father." In the book Cyril Clemens
is careless in attributing credit. Part I
is so dependent upon Paine and so similar
in phraseology that two hundred passages
ought to be placed in quotation marks.
"Part II has no close relationship with the
first part but harmonizes with it in being
dull"; it is a poor lot of anecdotes "told
to Mr. Clemens by people who either did or
did not know Mark Twain," and vapid tributes to MT "which Mr. Clemens has obtained
from various celebrities who either did or
did not know what they were talking about."

B38   DOS PASSOS, JOHN, and ALAN TATE. "The Situation in American Writing," Partisan Review,
VI (Summer), 26-92.
Dos Passos and Tate were among those answering a questionnaire question concerning
figures in a "usable past." Dos Passos says
"the best immediate ancestor (in Auden's
sense) for today's American writing is a
dark star somewhere in the constellation
containing Mark Twain, Melville, Thoreau
and Whitman." Tate: "I place Mark Twain
nearer to Augustus Longstreet than to Walt
Whitman; he was a regional writer in Huckleberry Finn, and he mastered a subtly modu-
lated style; compare this with the vulgarity of The Gilded Age, written when Mark
Twain had accepted the nationalist myth.
At his best Twain was regional and universal; toward the end of his life he became
national and parochial."

B39   *FEDERICO, P. J. "The Facts in the Case of
Mark Twain's Vest Strap," Journal of the
Patent Office Society, March.
On MT's patent applications and litiga-
tion. [Source: Reprinted in Twainian,
XVI (November-December, 1957), 1-4.]

B40   FERGUSON, DELANCEY. "The Case for Mark
Twain's Wife," University of Toronto Quarterly, IX (October), 9-21.
Livy's judgment was sometimes better than
MT's and she steered him away from several
literary blunders. What she found objec-
tionable is not his best work, and despite
her censorship he spoke more freely than
did most of his contemporaries. Moreover,
he loved her and respected her opinions.
Reprinted in Leary (1962), pp. 159-73.

B41 FERGUSON, DELANCEY. "A Letter to the Editors of American Literature," American Literature, XI (May), 218-19.

    A reply to Alexander Cowie's "Mark Twain Controls Himself" in the January issue. Cowie concedes that MT was intellectually lazy, but errs in company with Brooks when he argues that MT was censored by his wife and Howells. MT was not a frustrated satirist, and would have fought for any points he really cared about.

B42 FISCHER, W. [Review: Ramsay and Emberson, A Mark Twain Lexicon (1938).] Anglia Beiblatt, L (March), 91-94.

    A lengthy summary. [Incorrectly attributed to F. Holthausen in Asselineau (1954), No. 857.]

B43 FULLER, MURIEL. "'Mark Twain and the Middle Ages' with reply by Basil Davenport," Saturday Review of Literature, XIX (January 28), 9.

    Muriel Fuller takes issue with a statement in Basil Davenport's review of T. H. White's The Sword in the Stone that MT "hated the middle ages, knowing nothing about them." In his reply to Muriel Fuller, Davenport gives detailed reasons for saying that MT "was lacking in the historic sense"; CY states "the nineteenth-century dogma of progress...in its most naive absurdity."

B44 GATES, WILLIAM BRYAN. "Mark Twain to his English Publishers," American Literature, XI (March), 78-80.

    Four autograph letters to Chatto and Windus, dated Oct. 7, 1881, Sept. 1, 1883, Sept. 17, 1888, and Jan. 27, 1892--all on mundane business matters.

B45 GORDON, CHARLES W. (RALPH CONNOR). "Meeting Mark Twain," Mark Twain Quarterly, III (Spring), 17, 22.

    In his youth Gordon enjoyed IA, TS, and HF; years later, he was introduced to MT by George Doran, the publisher, and was pleased to find him serious-minded and sympathetic.

B46 GREET, CABELL. [Review: Robert L. Ramsay and Frances Guthrie Emberson, A Mark Twain Lexicon (1938).] American Literature, XI (May), 233.

    The excellence of this study should not surprise those familiar with the work of Ramsay and his students, but their success in transmitting Mark Twain's language is an unexpected pleasure. This is an important contribution to the study of the English language in America, with "4,342 entries for which Mark Twain gives the earliest recorded literary evidence."

B47 HAPGOOD, HUTCHINS. A Victorian in the Modern World. New York: Harcourt, Brace and Company, p. 146.

    The Hapgoods were friends of the Clemens family. Notes the secret love of Josiah Flynt for Clara Clemens, whose picture he carried everywhere he went (p. 146).

B48 HORGAN, PAUL. "News of Mark Twain," Yale Review, XXVIII (Summer), 846-49.

    A review of Ivan Benson, Mark Twain's Western Years (1938; "A...useful arrangement of much known information," with a bibliography and an appendix "which in itself makes this an important book"), and MT's Letters from the Sandwich Islands, ed. G. Ezra Dane (1938; they reveal why MT won a reputation with his combination of humor and clarity; it is unfortunate that this is not the entire series MT wrote).

B49 HULBERT, J. R. [Review: Robert L. Ramsay and Frances G. Emberson, A Mark Twain Lexicon (1938).] Journal of English and Germanic Philology, XXXVIII (April), 313-14.

    A lexicon devoted to a single author tends to suggest that he "introduced far more words and meanings of words into written literature than he really did," and "on pages x and following there is repeated evidence of the idea that by Twain's usage, regardless of other evidence, it can be determined whether an expression is an Americanism or not."

B50 LEMONNIER, LÉON. [Review: Robert L. Ramsay and Frances Guthrie Emberson, A Mark Twain Lexicon (1938).] Études Anglaises, III (January-March), 105.

    Brief and descriptive. "Un bon et solide travail, qui fait honneur à l'Université de Missouri."

B51 LORCH, FRED W. "Mark Twain's Early Nevada Letters," American Literature, X (January), 486-88.

    Corrects the sequence in Paine's edition of Mark Twain's Letters (New York, 1917) of MT's letters to his mother and sister, Sept. (?) 1861-April 2, 1862, "from which point on the sequence...seems correct."

B52 _____. [Review: G. Ezra Dane, ed. Mark Twain's Letters from the Sandwich Islands (1938).] American Literature, X (January), 511-13.

    Approves Dane's chronological arrangement of the letters, and the omission of three on commercial topics and the account of the burning of the clipper ship Hornet. Agrees on the importance of the letters as a transition from earlier crudities to the comparative polish of Innocents Abroad.

B53 OXENHAM, JOHN. "Mark Twain and The Idler," Mark Twain Quarterly, III (Spring), 8.

    Oxenham never met MT. He and Robert Barr, while planning their journal, The Idler, had hoped to get MT as editor; "Unfortunately, however, his idea of the proper division of profits left absolutely nothing for anyone else."

B54 PHELPS, WILLIAM LYON. <u>Autobiography with Letters</u>. New York, London, Toronto: Oxford University Press.

Contains numerous recollections of MT, including one of the time when Phelps in his youth mistook the great man's ducks for wild ones and killed five of them (pp. 61-63). Most of the later references to MT are incidental, and reveal only Phelps's respect for him; they add nothing to what he has said of MT elsewhere. Contains a letter from MT to a Mrs. Foote about reading from Browning (December 2, 1887, pp. 65-66) and one to Bret Harte about the <u>Jumping Frog</u> book (May 1, 1867, p. 492); both of these letters have been printed elsewhere.

B55 _____. "Mark Twain's White Ducks," <u>Mark Twain Quarterly</u>, III (Spring), 4.

As a boy in Hartford, Phelps shot some white ducks, not knowing they were domesticated and the property of MT; he never dared confess. [Phelps also tells the story in his <u>Autobiography</u>, 1940.B54.]

B56 ROBERTS, KENNETH. "The Necessity of Humor," <u>Mark Twain Quarterly</u>, III (Spring), 21.

"It is fashionable nowadays to award rich prizes to grim, gripping novels of the soil--dull books...Mark Twain, fortunately for the world, knew better."

B57 ROERICH, NICHOLAS. "Mark Twain in Russia," <u>Mark Twain Quarterly</u>, III (Spring), 7.

As a boy in Russia, Roerich found happiness in many things, among them reading <u>P&P</u>; MT was a popular author in Russia.

B58 SKINNER, OTIS. "Mark Twain in Hartford," <u>Mark Twain Quarterly</u>, III (Spring), 8.

As a boy, Skinner saw MT on Hartford streets; in later years, he enjoyed hearing him tell stories to friends at the Players' Club in New York.

B59 SMITH, GRANT H. [Review: Franklin Walker, ed., <u>The Washoe Giant in San Francisco</u> (1938).] <u>American Literature</u>, X (January), 513-18.

Smith emphasizes the crudity of these contributions to the <u>Golden Era</u> and other journals in 1863 and 1864: "their only value lies in the fact that they were written by a man who became famous."

B60 THOMSON, O. R. "How Important Is Mark Twain?" <u>Saturday Review of Literature</u>, XIX (January 7), 9.

A letter to the editor from a Williamsport, Pennsylvania librarian. <u>TS</u> and <u>HF</u> "will always be read," and there is "fine indignation" in <u>FE</u>, but MT's other books are fading. MT's humor was often "primitive" and "sadistic," and he was cautious on matters of religion and politics. "Never was a man so given to foreign stupidities; never one so silent on our own idiocies."

B61 VOGELBACK, ARTHUR LAWRENCE. "The Publication and Reception of <u>Huckleberry Finn</u> in America," <u>American Literature</u>, XI (November), 260-72.

Chiefly on the chorus of complaint that the book was "vulgar," "coarse," and "inelegant"; also tells of the mutilated cut in the first state.

1940 A BOOKS

A1 CLEMENS, SAMUEL L. <u>Mark Twain in Eruption: Hitherto Unpublished Pages about Men and Events</u>, ed. Bernard DeVoto. New York and London: Harper & Brothers Publishers.

In the 1924 edition of <u>Mark Twain's Autobiography</u>, Paine "used something less than half of the typescript in which everything Mark Twain wanted in his memoirs had been brought together. This book uses about half of the remainder. It has been selected, rearranged, and to some extent edited."

A2 _____. <u>Mark Twain's Travels with Mr. Brown. Being Heretofore Uncollected Sketches Written by Mark Twain for the San Francisco "Alta California" in 1866 & 1867, Describing the Adventures of the Author and His Irrepressible Companion in Nicaragua, Hannibal, New York, and Other Spots on Their Way to Europe</u>. Franklin Walker and G. Ezra Dane, eds. New York: Alfred A. Knopf.

These letters cover the period before the sailing of the <u>Quaker City</u>; McKeithan has collected the letters for the next period in <u>Traveling with the Innocents Abroad</u> (1958). MT later drew on parts of Letters XXIV ("A Curious Book," pp. 251-54) and XXVI for <u>Innocents Abroad</u>. Indexed and annotated.

A3 *_____. <u>Tom Sawyer Story Book</u>, retold in 96 pp. by Bennett Kline; illustrated by Henry E. Vallely. Racine, Wisconsin: Whitman Publishing Company.

[Source: Asselineau (1954), No. 887.] A letter received from William H. Larson, Senior Editor, Whitman Golden Press (April 15, 1974) cites a 1940 catalogue giving the title listed above but noting that "The cover and title page wording sometimes varied in books of this era. It has 96 pages, counting pastedowns." Apparently it is an abridgement for younger readers.

A4 *MÖHLE, DR. GUNTER. <u>Das Europabild Mark Twains</u> (Neue Deutsche Forschungen, Abt. Amerikanische Literatur- und Kulturgeschichte, Band VII). Berlin: Junker und Dünnhaupt.

[Source: MHRA Annual Bibliography (1940), No. 4108.]

A5 PROUDFIT, ISABEL. <u>River-Boy: The Story of Mark Twain</u>. New York: Julian Messner, Inc.

A biography for younger readers.

1940 - Books

A6 READ, OPIE. Mark Twain and I. Chicago:
    Reilly & Lee.
        A collection of MT anecdotes, with circum-
    stances only vaguely given.

A7 *TAYLOR, HOWARD P. Mark Twain and the Old
    "Enterprise" Gang; reminiscences of Howard
    P. Taylor and Steve Gillis. Holiday Greet-
    ings from the Watsons. San Francisco:
    The Grabhorn Press.
        [9-page pamphlet. Source: Asselineau
    (1954), No. 885: "Letters written to Joseph
    T. Goodman on the occasion of Mark Twain's
    death, edited by Douglas S. Watson."]

1940 B SHORTER WRITINGS

B1 ABRAHAMS, ROBERT D. "At Hannibal, Missouri,"
    Saturday Evening Post, CCXIII (November 30),
    66.
        A poem: Sam Clemens was a boy like other
    boys, and he and his friends live on in
    MT's books.

B2 ANON. "Hannibal Crosses Mr. Farley," Common-
    weal, XXXI (February 16), 355.
        Editorial commentary on the attack on
    MT's Civil War record by Representative
    Shannon (Missouri) when Congress was con-
    sidering the issuing of a stamp honoring
    him. [James Aloysius Farley was Postmas-
    ter-General--T.A.T.]

B3 ANON. "Mark Twain Stories," New York Times
    Book Review (April 7), p. 28.
        A descriptive review of Opie Read's Mark
    Twain and I.

B4 ANON. "Mark Twain to Young Writers" [From the
    New York Times, n.d.], Word Study (G. & C.
    Merriam Co.), XV (March), 2-4.
        MT recommends simplicity in prose, and a
    minimum of adjectives, in a letter of
    March 20, 1880 to D. W. Bowser, whose re-
    cent death is noted.

B5 ANON. "Tired Volcano," Time, XXXVI
    (December 2), 80.
        A descriptive review of Bernard DeVoto,
    ed., Mark Twain in Eruption, a weakened
    sampling from MT's late years when "he
    was utterly lonely. For most of his life
    Twain remained, as he still is, the last
    major U.S. literary voice."

B6 ANON. [Reply to the charge by Representative
    Shannon of Missouri that MT had deserted
    the Confederate Army.] New York Times
    February 7, p. 20.

B7 ANON. [Review: Edgar H. Hemminghaus, Mark
    Twain in Germany (1939).] Notes and Quer-
    ies (London), CLXXIX (July 6), 17.
        The critical estimates of MT by Germans,
    as surveyed by Hemminghaus, are often
    "plainly futile, led off to conclusions
    which are far-fetched and wholly unjusti-
    fied to anyone who has a competent

knowledge of Mark Twain's life and ways."
MT's popularity is now declining both in
Germany and in England.

B8 BLANCK, JACOB. "'The Gilded Age': A Colla-
    tion," Publishers' Weekly, CXXXVIII
    (July 20), 186-88.
        Describes variant imprints bearing 1873,
    1874, and 1875 dates.

B9 BROOKS, VAN WYCK. New England: Indian Summer.
    New York: E. P. Dutton.
        Makes no new critical comment on MT, though
    mentioning his name passim.

B10 [BROWNELL, GEORGE HIRAM.] "About Twain in
    Periodicals," Twainian, II (January), 4-5;
    (February), 6-7; (March), 3-4; (November),
    3-4; (December), 6.
        A continuation of a bibliography of sec-
    ondary material, in installments that began
    in Twainian, I (1939) and was carried to
    completion in the new series which began in
    1942. The installments are in alphabetical
    order of the journals covered; the install-
    ments for 1940 include The Colophon through
    London Quarterly Review. Brownell states
    (December, 3-4) that the coverage consists
    of known material contemporary with MT's
    early writing and, for more recent material,
    what he deems significant; he adds that
    coverage for the past ten years is incom-
    plete. This material has been incorporated
    in the present bibliography.

B11 _____. "The Chief Love and Delight of God,"
    Twainian, II (June), 1-2.
        Contains, with brief comment, the text of
    brief MT essay which appeared in Mark Twain
    in Eruption.

B12 _____. "Hannibal Honors Twain," Twainian, II
    (December), 5-6.
        On the observation of MT's 105th birthday
    anniversary in Hannibal; brief account,
    with lists of participants.

B13 _____. "Information Wanted," Twainian, II
    (February), 8.
        Reprints an MT letter from the Chicago
    Inter Ocean (December 15, 1875) on beautiful
    book illuminations produced by a girl in
    London whose vision failed just as she
    achieved recognition; may be a reprint from
    a Hartford paper.

B14 _____. "License Mystery Nears Solution,"
    Twainian, II (January), 2-3.
        On what appears to be the original pilot's
    license issued to MT, in Mariners' Museum,
    Newport News, Virginia; a news item from
    St. Louis Post-Dispatch (December 6, 1932)
    is reprinted. Earlier discussions appeared
    in Twainian, I (November, 1939), 1-3, 6, and
    (December, 1939), 1-2.

B15 _____. "Mark Twain on How Wars Start,"
Twainian, II (January), 3-4.
    Quotes a passage Brownell had been look-
ing for, finally located in MS. Brownell's
comments here are not of biographical or
critical importance.

B16 _____. "Mark Twain on Photographs," Twainian,
II (January), 6.
    Reprints, with brief comment, a portion
of a letter from MT which Walter Francis
Frear found in the Daily Hawaiian Herald
for September 5, 1866.

B17 _____. "Mark Twain on 'Woman,'" Twainian, II
(February), 4-5.
    Presents the text of MT speech "Woman:
The Pride of the Professions and the Jewel
of Ours," delivered before Correspondents'
Club, Washington, January 11, 1868; also
presents publication history of this speech
and that of "Woman: God Bless Her," delivered before the New England Society of
New York, December 22, 1882. Also see
brief correction in March issue, p. 6, and
brief note in Twainian, VI (November-December, 1947), 5.

B18 _____. "Mr. DeVoto Comes to Town," Twainian,
II (April), 1-3.
    Summarizes a talk by DeVoto, "New Light
on Mark Twain" (delivered March 5), attributing the falling-off of his creative
powers by 1890 to business troubles and
family tragedies. Describes meeting of
DeVoto and Carl Sandburg, March 6. According to DeVoto, the MT papers are in a vast
confusion, scattered through boxes and
trunks, and achieving order will take a
year or two.

B19 _____. "The Source of Mark Twain's Cigars?"
Twainian, II (February), 7-8.
    Frank C. Willson has been searching for
information on "Mark Twain Cigars" (a brand
name), and on a "Mark Twain Waltz" published
by Wm. Rohlfing & Co., Milwaukee; L. W. Her-
zog of that city is trying to locate a copy
of the sheet music.

B20 _____. "The New Mark Twain Stamp," Twainian,
II (March), 4-5.
    On the 10¢ commemorative, issued
February 13.

B21 _____. "Twain on Democracy," Twainian, II
(February), 3.
    Quotations from MT's works, submitted in
a contest for MT fans.

B22 _____. "Who's Exaggerating Now?" Twainian,
II (January), 7-8.
    Refuting Cyril Clemens's claim to have
published the "first strictly accurate" account of MT's statement about exaggerated
reports of his death, Brownell cites a half-
tone reproduction of MT's actual note appearing in Frank Marshall White's article

in The Outlook for December 24, 1910,
p. 965. There are details of the appearance
of the words in The Journal, following
White's cable from London.

B23 _____. [Brief item, describing motion picture
of MT and his daughters at Stormfield, made
by Edison in 1909.] Twainian, II (January),
1.

B24 _____. [Account of Captain Oberlin M. Carter's recollections of MT's visits to West
Point in the 1870's, and a visit to the MT
home in Hartford.] Twainian, II (February),
1-3.
    Also comments briefly on the publication
of 1601 by the West Point print-shop, under
Lieutenant Charles Erskine Scott Wood.

B25 _____. [Discussion of charges by Rep. Joseph
B. Shannon of Missouri that MT was a coward
and Confederate deserter.] Twainian, II
(March), 1-3.
    Shannon's speech in Congress, January 25,
called MT unworthy of being honored with a
commemorative postage stamp. Brownell
quotes Shannon and cites many persons defending MT; considers his "Private History
of a Campaign that Failed" and the account
by Absalom Grimes (1926) more reliable versions of MT's war experiences.

B26 _____. [Discussion of "To the Reading Public,"
ascribing it to MT.] Twainian, II (May),
1-2, 4-5.
    Text included. Appeared in first issue of
Author's Sketch Book (November, 1870), apparently an American Publishing Company
house organ to encourage the army of subscription agents. Also see Twainian for
June, p. 4.

B27 _____. [On Franklin J. Meine's speculation
that John A. Gray & Green (for whom MT
worked as a compositor in 1853, in New York)
might have been the printer for The Spirit
of the Times.] Twainian, II (June), 1.
    No evidence is given.

B28 _____. [Discussion of articles in The Ameri-
can Publisher (Hartford: American Publish-
ing Company, 1871-1872) by MT.] Twainian,
II (October), 1-3.
    For 1871, lists "Old-Time Pony Express"
(May); "A New Beecher Church" (July); "A
Brace of Brief Lectures" (September); "A
Brace of Brief Lectures" (concluded;
October); "My First Lecture" (December);
for 1872, January, "A Nabob's First Visit
to New York."

B29 _____. [Anecdote, MT's reference to Bret
Harte.] Twainian, II (November), 1-2.
    According to George Ade, at a Boston lit-
erary dinner attended by the great writers
of the day, Howells as master of ceremonies
and principal speaker reminisced about Bret
Harte, then asked MT whether he knew him.

[BROWNELL, GEORGE HIRAM]
In reply, "Mark slowly rose to his feet, facing Howells. He bit off another inch of his cigar, spat venomously, and deliberately drawled, 'Yes, I knew the son-of-a-bitch.'"

B30   _____. [Discussion of Huckleberry Finn: first-issue points and the defacement of the illustration on p. 283.] Twainian, II (December), 1-3.
Based on discussion and comparison of copies of HF by members of the Mark Twain Society of Chicago at their November meeting; inconclusive.

B31   BURLINGAME, ROGER. Engines of Democracy: Inventions and Society in Mature America. New York and London: Charles Scribner's Sons, pp. 145-48.
A discussion of James W. Paige's typesetting machine and MT's financial backing; includes reproduction of a patent drawing.

B32   CLEMENS, CYRIL. "Mark Twain and St. Louis: Address at Unveiling of Mark Twain Fountain in Forest Park, July 23, 1940," Mark Twain Quarterly, IV (Summer), 15-16.
Text of the address, quoting statements by and about MT.

B33   _____, ed. "Republican Letters," Mark Twain Quarterly, IV (Fall-Winter), passim.
An unsigned introduction (pp. 1-2) says that the reprintings here include letters to the Chicago Republican in 1868, as well as "one of Clemens' first literary efforts from the 'Hannibal Journal' edited by his elder brother Orion, and an historically interesting contribution to the Washington 'Star.'" The reprinted material is as follows: "My Trip on the Henry Chauncey" (Republican, April 9, 1868), 3-5; "Captain Ned Wakeman" (n.d.), 6-7, 13; "My Return to Virginia City" (Republican, May 19, 1868), 8-9, 14; "One or Two California Items" (n.d.), 10-11; "A Railroad Mint" (n.d.), 12-13, 21; "Hartford" (n.d.), 13; "Up Among the Clouds" (n.d.), 14; "Novel Entertainment" (n.d.; on witnessing a public hanging), 15, 17; "A Recently Discovered Twain Letter" (Washington Star, December 16, 1867), 16-17; "Historical Exhibition--A No. 1 Ruse" (Hannibal Journal, September 16, 1852), 18-19, 24.

B34   _____. [Review: Edgar H. Hemminghaus, Mark Twain in Germany.] Commonweal, XXXI (March 1), 417-18.
Descriptive and laudatory. Cyril Clemens published a similar or identical review in Mark Twain Quarterly, III (Spring), 21.

B35   DEVOTO, BERNARD. "Calling All Twainians," Twainian, II (February), 6.
Letter to the editor, appealing for help in locating the autobiography of Orion Clemens, which was not in the papers turned over to DeVoto by the MT Estate.

B36   ESKEW, GARNETT LAIDLAW. "Mark Twain, Steamboat Pilot. He Was No Great Shakes at the Wheel, Say All the Rivermen--With One Exception," Coronet, VIII (May), 100-105.
Describes talking about MT with people who remembered him, or Captain Horace Bixby, or both of them; all but one remember MT as having only a superficial knowledge of the profession. "That one exception, however, Captain [sic] Walter Blair of Davenport, Iowa--says, and follows it with an exclamation point, that Mark Twain was a pilot and a damned fine one, and adduces irrefutable evidence to back up his statement." This "Captain Walter Blair" describes meeting MT and discussing piloting with him in Davenport in 1885.

B37   GABRIEL, RALPH HENRY. The Course of American Democratic Thought. New York: The Ronald Press (Revised edition, 1956).
Contains brief and rather minor references to MT's determinism, the distortion of his work by the materialism of the period he called the "Gilded Age," and the importance of literary nativism in his works.

B38   GARLAND, HAMLIN. "Twain's Social Conscience," Mark Twain Quarterly, IV (Summer), 8-9.
Garland says that in reviewing the CY he noted the dual satire, touching past and modern times. Dan Beard's part as illustrator brought him into disfavor with editors and made commissions hard to come by, according to his autobiography.

B39   GAY, ROBERT M. "The Two Mark Twains," Atlantic Monthly, CLXVI (December), 724-726.
"There were two Mark Twains: one, the man I have called the rhetorician, the other one whom we may call the poet.... Perhaps the showman was diffident about the poet." MT was an "intuitionalist," not an intellectual, and "his at times astonishing insight and wisdom were the fruit, not of philosophy, but of human sympathy. His illuminations came through his feelings." New material in Mark Twain in Eruption provides "no soul-shaking revelations." Reprinted in Kesterson (1973), pp. 51-53.

B40   HUTCHERSON, DUDLEY R. "Mark Twain as a Pilot," American Literature, XII (November), 353-55.
Based on an article in the Memphis Commercial Appeal (June 23, 1939) by Joe Curtis, the River Editor, and on letters received from Curtis and Captain Rees V. Downs (a friend of Captain Horace Bixby, who taught Clemens the river). The accounts agree that Clemens lacked confidence, and Bixby called him "a coward, a failure as a pilot."

B41   *KLETT, ADA M. 'Meisterschaft,' or the True State of Mark Twain's German," American-German Review, VII (December), 10-11.
[Source: MHRA Annual Bibliography (1940), No. 900; also listed in "Articles on American Literature Appearing in Current

(KLETT, ADA M.)
Periodicals," _American Literature_, XIII
(March, 1941), 101: "An examination of the
manuscript of 'Meisterschaft,' a comedy,
reveals Mark Twain's ignorance of correct
and idiomatic German."]

B42 LORCH, FRED W. "A Note on Tom Blankenship
(Huckleberry Finn)," _American Literature_,
XII (November), 351-3.
Quotes reports in the Hannibal _Daily
Messenger_ in 1861 that Tom was sentenced to
thirty days in the county jail for stealing
turkeys (April 21) and suspected of stealing
onions (June 4), and two horses, a wash tub
of clothes, and a quantity of bacon, butter,
molasses, and sugar, in addition to robbing
a chicken house (June 12).

B43 MENCKEN, H. L. _Happy Days, 1880-1892_. New
York: Alfred A. Knopf, pp. 166-70.
As a boy, took _HF_ off the shelf at home:
"I had not gone further than the first in-
comparable chapter before I realized, child
though I was, that I had entered a domain of
new and gorgeous wonders"; his father saw
what he was reading and reacted with "a kind
of shy rejoicing." Mencken continued to reread _HF_ annually, "and only a few months ago
I hauled it out and read it once more--and
found it as magnificent as ever." He also
read the rest of the canon after _HF_, but
found it heavier going.

B44 ODELL, GEORGE C. D. _Annals of the New York
Stage_. New York: Columbia University Press,
Vol. XII (1882-1885), passim.
George Washington Cable was to have given
a reading at the Bedford Avenue Church on
February 6, 1884, but he was ill and remained at the MT home in Hartford (pp. 393-
94). On his readings with MT at Chickering
Hall, November 18, 19, 1884 (p. 544), and at
the Academy of Music, Brooklyn, November 22,
1884 and February 21, 1885 (pp. 571-72). MT
was listed among the authors to participate
at a reading in favor of international copyright at Madison Square Theatre, April 29,
1885 (pp. 427-28).

B45 OLIVER, ROBERT T. "Mark Twain's Views on Education," _Education_, LXI (October), 112-15.
MT was "an educational philosopher with remarkable insight," who "was before Dewey in
urging that the students be made partners in
the educational enterprise," although in part
his concern for education was the result of
"over-emphasizing the role of environment."

B46 PRICE, LAWRENCE M. [Review: Edgar H. Hemminghaus, _Mark Twain in Germany_ (1939).]
Modern Language Quarterly, I (March),
119-20.
Hemminghaus has dealt with a "formidable"
amount of criticism in a "workmanlike" manner; the work was much needed.

B47 RICE, ALICE HEGAN. _The Inky Way_. New York,
London: D. Appleton-Century Company.
Quotes statements made to her by MT concerning Bret Harte, and Richard Watson Gilder's description of MT in a letter as "most
grim and unhappy but full of life and abound-
ing in scorn of a mismanaged universe." Includes facsimile of a note from MT, and a
sketch of him (pp. 77-80).

B48 RUFF, WILLIAM. "Mark Twain in the Sixties,"
Yale Review, XXX (1940), 423-25.
A review of _Mark Twain's Travels with
Mr. Brown_, ("Worth reading for a sharp-tongued
humorist's account of American life in the
Sixties"; there is no comment on the editing.

B49 SCHRAMM, WILBUR L. [Review Article.] _Philo-
logical Quarterly_, XIX (July), 317-20.
Edgar Lee Masters, _Mark Twain: A Portrait_
(1938) is "a thin, irritating, disappointing
volume which does little credit to its distinguished author...contributes no new, and
misuses much old material. It is loaded
with errors," and apparently relies wholly
on Paine, Brooks, and Wagenknecht." Cyril
Clemens' _My Cousin, Mark Twain_ (1939) "about
his very distant cousin is a completely unimportant volume...essentially a collection
of anecdotes and tributes. Most of them are
in Paine; most of the others are not very
interesting. None of them are documented."
Franklin Walker's _The Washoe Giant in San
Francisco_ (1938) provides material of importance "beyond estimate" to scholars lacking access to files of the California papers.
Ivan Benson's _Mark Twain's Western Years_
(1938) is not stylistically graceful, but an
illuminating, solid contribution. The Ramsay and Emberson _Mark Twain Lexicon_ (1938)
is the fullest available treatment of its
subject. "It is to be regretted that the
editors of the lexicon, having consulted so
many of Twain's works, did not consult all
of them. But what has been done has been
done well." Finally, the publication of the
material in G. Ezra Dane's edition of _Letters
from the Sandwich Islands_ (1938) is extremely important to MT scholars.

B50 *SHANNON, REPRESENTATIVE, of Blue Springs,
Missouri. [Accuses MT of deserting the Confederate Army.] _Congressional Record_,
Washington, D.C. LXXXVI, Part 1.
Shannon's statement that MT "was not of
the same kidney as real Missourians" and attack on his "dismal failure as a belliger-
ent" are quoted by Fatout (1964), p. 64;
Fatout cites a reply by the New York _Times_
of February 7 (ibid., pp. 65-66).

B51 STROVEN, CARL. [Review: _Letters from Honolulu Written for the "Sacramento Union_," by
Mark Twain; introduction by John W. Vander-
cook (1939).] _American Literature_, XII
(November), 377-39.

1940 - Shorter Writings

(STROVEN, CARL)
   Describes the four letters here which were
omitted from Dane's edition of Mark Twain's
Letters from the Sandwich Islands; praises
the inclusion of these letters and the
pleasing appearance of the book.

B52   VON HIBLER, LEO. "Mark Twain und die deutsche
      Sprache," Anglia: Zeitschrift für englische
      Philologie, LXV, 206-13.
         On the gusto with which MT threw himself
      into the German language, his delight in
      the sound of the words and distress at its
      complexities, and his humorous discussion
      of the language. [In German.]

B53   WAGENKNECHT, EDWARD. "Mark Twain on Men and
      Events," New York Times Book Review
      (December 1), pp. 1, 38.
         A long but chiefly descriptive review of
      Bernard DeVoto, ed., Mark Twain in Eruption.

B54   WERNER, M. R. "Mark Twain's Philosophy," New
      Republic, CIII (December 9), 805-806.
         A review, chiefly descriptive, of Frank-
      lin Walker and G. Ezra Dane, eds., Mark
      Twain's Travels with Mr. Brown and Bernard
      DeVoto, ed., Mark Twain in Eruption.

1941 A BOOKS

A1   *CLARKE, NORMAN ELLSWORTH. Huckleberry Finn
      Again: A Bibliographical Study. Detroit.
      [Source: Asselineau (1954), No. 904:
      "On the first edition of Huckleberry Finn"
      (14-page pamphlet).]

A2   CLEMENS, SAMUEL L. Republican Letters, ed.
      by Cyril Clemens, foreword by Hugh Walpole.
      Webster Groves, Missouri: International
      Mark Twain Society. "Number Ten of the
      Society's BIOGRAPHICAL SERIES."
         Several letters by MT which appeared in
      the Chicago Republican (Spring, Summer,
      1868), one from the Washington Star
      (December 16, 1867), and excerpts from his
      works. Facts of original publication not
      always given. Introduction thanks Walter
      Blair "for reading proofs, and for sugges-
      tions." Walpole's one-page foreword is a
      rather general appreciation, praising MT's
      timeless art. The editing has been severe-
      ly criticized by reviewers. See 1942.B8,
      B41; 1943.B46; 1944.B39.

A3   HORNBERGER, THEODORE, ed. Mark Twain's Let-
      ters to Will Bowen, "My First, & Oldest &
      Dearest Friend." Austin: The University
      of Texas.
         Hornberger's introduction gives background
      on Bowen and his friendship with MT, and
      notes give background on individual letters.
      The letter of August 31, 1876 is often
      quoted in studies of MT to illustrate his
      impatience with sentimentalism; it con-
      cludes: "Well, you must forgive me, but I

have not the slightest sympathy with what
the world calls Sentiment--not the slightest." [34 page pamphlet.]

1941 B SHORTER WRITINGS

B1   ANDERSON, SHERWOOD. "Letters to Van Wyck
      Brooks" (with an introduction by Brooks),
      Story: The Magazine of the Short Story,
      XIX (September-October), 42-62.
         Anderson comments frequently on MT in
      these letters, written 1918-1938, coming to
      his defence at the time Brooks was working
      on The Ordeal of Mark Twain: "Of course
      your book cannot be written in a cheerful
      spirit. In facing Twain's life you face a
      tragedy. How could the man mean what he
      does to us if it were not a tragedy. Had
      the man succeeded in breaking through he
      would not have been a part of us. Why
      can't you take it that way?" In his intro-
      duction to the letters Brooks says that
      when the book was published, Anderson
      "showed me clearly where my study had fallen
      short. I had failed to write the most im-
      portant chapter, in which I should have
      praised Huckleberry Finn. I was too much
      concerned with the psychological problem,
      and the psychologist inhibited the poet in
      me. I regretted this as much as Sherwood,
      who loved Mark Twain above all writers."

B2   ANON. "The Art of Saying No: Mark Twain Re-
      fuses Permission to Dramatize 'Tom Sawyer,'"
      Reader's Digest, XXXVIII (March), 56.
         The text of a letter, dated "Hartford,
      Sept. 8, '87," and never mailed. There is
      no editorial comment, but a note at the bot-
      tom of the page says the letter is from A
      Treasury of the World's Great Letters, ed.
      M. Lincoln Schuster, New York: Simon &
      Schuster, Inc., 1940.

B3   ANON. "Clemens, Samuel Langhorne," in James
      D. Hart, ed., The Oxford Companion to Ameri-
      can Literature (London, New York, Toronto:
      Oxford University Press), pp. 139-41.
         Includes a brief survey of MT's life and
      works, and the nature of his literary gift;
      he was "an artist of broad understanding and
      vital, though uneven and sometimes misdi-
      rected, achievement."

B4   ANON. "Huckleberry Finn in Public Domain,"
      Publishers' Weekly, CXL (November 29), 2008.
         Copyright has finally expired. A few
      brief comments on textual problems, but
      nothing not discussed elsewhere.

B5   BELLAMY, GLADYS CARMEN. "Mark Twain's In-
      debtedness to John Phoenix," American Liter-
      ature, XIII (March), 29-43.
         Shows parallels to published works of
      George Horatio Derby ("John Phoenix") in
      "Love's Bakery," "A Full and Reliable Ac-
      count of the Extraordinary Meteoric Shower
      of Last Saturday Night," "Blanketing the

(BELLAMY, GLADYS CARMEN)
Admiral" (RI, II, Ch. XXI), "Some Learned
Fables for Good Old Boys and Girls" ("How
the Animals of the Wood Sent Out a Scientific Expedition"), "The Petrified Man," and
even the Whittier birthday dinner speech.
In this last, Miss Bellamy quotes the "John
Phoenix" treatment of Emerson's "Brahma" as
dealing with the game of euchre, with "the
red slayer" an allusion to the Right Bower.
There is a less persuasive case made that
the "solitary oesophagus" of "A Double-
Barrelled Detective Story" and Mark Twain's
dismissal of Jane Austen owe anything to
"John Phoenix."

B6   BENNETT, WHITMAN. A Practical Guide to Ameri-
can Book Collecting. New York: The Bennett
Book Studios, Inc.
Contains bibliographical descriptions of
Jumping Frog, IA, RI, TS, P&P, LOM, HF, CY,
JA, What Is Man? Captain Stormfield's Visit
to Heaven, MS, discussions of first editions
and issues, etc.

B7   BLAIR, WALTER. [Review: Edgar H. Hemminghaus, Mark Twain in Germany (1939).] American Literature, XIII (March), 87.
"The bibliography is excellent," but "Dr.
Hemminghaus has found little hitherto unknown German criticism which comments pene-
tratingly on the artistry or thought of
Twain."

B8   BLEARSIDES, OLIVER. "Mark Twain's Characters
Come From Real People," Mark Twain Quarter-
ly, IV (Summer-Fall), 16-19.
Anecdotal; contains no new information.

B9   [BROWNELL, GEORGE HIRAM.] Special issue of
Twainian, III (June).
On a meeting of MT enthusiasts planned at
George Ade's farm near Brook, Indiana,
planned for June 21. This is the only issue of the Twainian for 1941, and marks the
end of the old series. A new series begins
in 1942, and continues unbroken to the present.

B10   CLEMENS, CYRIL. "Twain and Libel," Saturday
Review of Literature, XXIV (August 30), 9.
A letter to the editor, citing a New York
Times interview (June 10, 1883) in which MT
accused C. C. Duncan (formerly captain of
the Quaker City) of fraud; in a letter MT
disavowed some of the language attributed
to him, and a news story of March 9, 1884
reports that Duncan sued MT and the Times
for damages; he was awarded six cents by
the court.

B11   _____. "Unpublished Recollections of Original Becky Thatcher," Mark Twain Quarterly,
IV (Summer-Fall), 20, 23.
Cyril Clemens "once had a long talk" with
Laura Hawkins Frazer, who passed on a number of reminiscences of MT as a boy; one of
them concerned his purchase of a copy of

Thomas Chandler Haliburton's "Sam Slick"
stories and his pleasure in the book.

B12   _____, ed. "Mark Twain's Unpublished Letters
to His English Publishers," Mark Twain Quarterly, IV (Summer-Fall), 1-2, 24.
When MT was offered either $10,000 or a
royalty for Innocents Abroad [in America]
he followed the advice of his friend A. D.
Richardson to take the royalty. The book
first appeared in England in a pirated edition published by John Camden Hotten, and
MT later arranged to have most of his works
published by Chatto & Windus; here are texts
of his letters to them October 7, 1881;
December 8, 1884; July 25, 1897; September
17, 1888; there are also two undated notes.

B13   DEVOTO, BERNARD (ed.). "Sam Clemens Tells a
Story: An Excerpt from the Recent Book,
Mark Twain in Eruption," Scholastic,
XXXVIII (February 10), 29-30.
On the telling of "His Grandfather's Old
Ram," with a brief note for high-school
students on DeVoto's editing of newly-pub-
lished material.

B14   EBY, E. H. [Review: Mark Twain in Eruption
(1940).] Modern Language Quarterly, II
(December), 654.
"These new portions of the autobiography
add nothing of vital importance to the data
already known.... Mr. DeVoto's editing
makes the material more understandable for
the general reader but makes no pretensions
to thoroughness."

B15   HORN, W. [Review: Robert L. Ramsay and Frances Guthrie Emberson, A Mark Twain Lexicon
(1938).] Archiv für das Studium der neueren
Sprachen, CLXXVIII, 57-58.
Descriptive. [In German.]

B16   JONES, HOWARD MUMFORD. [Review: Günther
Möhle, Das Europabild Mark Twains (1940),
and Bernard DeVoto, ed., Mark Twain in Eruption (1940).] Journal of English and Germanic Philology, XL (October), 448-49.
Möhle squanders eighty pages on background, leaving only fifty "to discuss a
rather intricate problem. The result is
naturally not illuminating." Moreover, the
proofreading is very poor. Mark Twain in
Eruption shows "an unfortunate monotony of
tone," because of DeVoto's choice of material to include, and biographers will still
need to go through the material that remains
unpublished. "Mr. DeVoto's introductory
analysis...is much more acute than anything
in Dr. Möhle's monograph."

B17   KRONENBERGER, LOUIS. "Now It Can Be Told,"
Nation, CLII (February 8), 161-62.
A review of Mark Twain in Eruption (1940),
previously unpublished material by MT "in
as effective a form as first-rate editing
can achieve."

1941 - Shorter Writings

B18 LORCH, FRED W. "Mark Twain and the 'Campaign that Failed,'" American Literature, XII (January), 454-70.
     Places in historical perspective MT's brief service as a Confederate irregular soldier: his conduct was fairly typical of the times. Extensively documented.

B19 McC., H. [Review: Bernard DeVoto, ed., Mark Twain in Eruption (1940).] More Books: The Bulletin of the Boston Public Library, Sixth Series, XVI (January), 22-23.
     Brief review. "Mr. DeVoto has selected and printed the best of the unused papers... it is certainly...'Mark Twain in eruption,'" but it is also amusing: "There is stuff in 'Hannibal Days' as good as anything in Tom Sawyer."

B20 ORIANS, G. HARRISON. "Walter Scott, Mark Twain, and the Civil War," South Atlantic Quarterly, XL (October), 342-59.
     Comparatively little on MT, in a lengthy refutation of his charge in LOM that Scott had filled Southern minds with romantic nonsense and thereby helped bring on the Civil War.

B21 PARRY, ALBERT. "Mark Twain in Russia," Books Abroad, XV (April), 168-75.
     A survey of changing Russian attitudes toward MT, who briefly visited and wrote about Russia and whose daughter married a Russian pianist. "In a period of three recent years Mark Twain's works sold over a million and a half copies printed in the various languages of Soviet peoples," leading all other American writers," and "his works were translated early and extensively." In translations of IA before the Revolution his description of Odessa was softened to make it less offensive, while recent versions deliberately heighten his criticism. His satire is regarded as basically kindly, a fact that some critics praise and others deplore; he is not considered a forceful social critic.

B22 POCHMANN, HENRY A. [Review: Mark Twain in Eruption (1940).] American Literature, XIII (May), 173-76.
     There is "little that is either genuinely novel or truly 'eruptive' in the book," and "like the Autobiography, of which this is properly a supplement, its chief interest lies in the inimitable witticisms and caustic comments which Mark Twain made upon men and events."

B23 PRITCHETT, V. S. "Books in General," New Statesman and Nation, CXIII (August 2), 113. Reprinted as "The American Puritan" in his In My Good Books (London: Chatto & Windus), pp. 175-82.
     A review briefly discussing PW but chiefly on HF: "although it is one of the funniest books in all literature and really astonishing in the variety of its farce and

character, we are more moved than we are amused by it" because "the particular character of American nostalgia is that it is not only harking back to something lost in the past, but suggests also the tragedy of a lost future." Reprinted, slightly abridged, as "Huckleberry Finn and the Cruelty of American Humor" in Bradley (1962), pp. 305-309, and as "Cruelty in The Adventures of Huckleberry Finn' in Lettis (1962), pp. 317-20.

B24 SLADE, WILLIAM G. "Mark Twain's Educational Views," Mark Twain Quarterly, IV (Summer-Fall), 5-10.
     Lists his reading, interest in foreign languages, mnemonic games, comments on educational goals and methods. Despite MT's lack of formal education, "some of his observations are worthy of notice and the administrator and teacher alike can profit by this layman's opinions and criticisms."

B25 STEWART, GEORGE R. "Bret Harte upon Mark Twain in 1866," American Literature, XIII (November), 263-64.
     Harte's estimate of MT's October 2, 1866 lecture about the Sandwich Islands; final paragraph in one of a series of letters to the Springfield (Mass.) Daily Republican (November 10, 1866). Harte criticized MT's coarseness but set his humor above Artemus Ward's and called him "a new star rising in this western horizon."

B26 TEMPLIN, E. H. "On Re-Reading Mark Twain," Hispania, XXIV (October), 269-76.
     With particular emphasis on CY, notes the influence of Cervantes and some parallels of Spanish works to those of MT; provides no new factual information.

B27 VON HIBLER, LEO. [Review: Ivan Benson, Mark Twain's Western Years (1938).] Englische Studien, LXXIV (January), 250-53.
     Primarily an extensive summary of the book for German readers. [In German.]

B28 WALKER, STANLEY. "The Case of Mr. Whipple's Pants," New Yorker, XVII (September 27), 58-61.
     Bob Davis's column on the editorial page of the New York Sun summarized an uncompleted MT story he had heard from Irving Bacheller, about middle-aged Henry Whipple, who returned to his old home town after an absence of many years and decided to go for a nude swim; while dressing, he heard a buggy approaching and leapt into his own buggy, and pulled a robe over his bare legs. In the other buggy were an old sweetheart and her father, who recognized him; when he hesitated to join them she climbed into his buggy and took the reins, and her father followed in the other buggy. Walker suggests several possible endings for the story.

B29   WECTER, DIXON. "Mark Twain as Translator from
       the German," American Literature, XIII
       (November), 257-63.
          In the winter of 1891 MT translated Dr.
       Heinrich Hoffman's Struwelpeter (1842);
       Harper & Brothers published the transla-
       tion as Slovenly Peter in 1935. Young
       readers still prefer the more conventional
       Winston translation.

B30   WOOLF, S. J. Here Am I. New York: Random
       House, passim.
          A more candid account of his visit to the
       Clemens home than in his 1910 Collier's ar-
       ticle. On visiting the New York apartment
       of Colonel Edward House, he saw that the
       portraits were of Woodrow Wilson, MT, Lin-
       coln, and Jackson (p. 132). Lithograph of
       MT in bed (facing p. 135; discussed
       pp. 135-36). Woolf visited President Masa-
       ryk in Prague; among the many books were
       some by MT, and Masaryk told him he had
       learned about the people of America in the
       Mississippi region from them.

1942 A BOOKS

A1   CLEMENS, CYRIL. Young Sam Clemens. Foreword
       by Hendrik Willem Van Loon and introduction
       by Grant Wood. Portland, Maine: Leon Teb-
       betts Editions.
          Biography for the general reader, enliv-
       ened by numerous anecdotes but undocumented.

A2   *CLEMENS, SAMUEL L. Adventures of Huckleberry
       Finn. New York: The Limited Editions Club,
       ed. and introduction by Bernard DeVoto.
       "The first edition in which an effort has
       been made to establish the text."
          [Source: Asselineau (1954), No. 929.]
       Introduction reprinted in Mark Twain at
       Work (1942.A4).

A3   _____. Mark Twain's Letters in the Muscatine
       Journal, ed. and introduction by Edgar M.
       Branch; foreword by George Hiram Brownell.
       Chicago: The Mark Twain Association of
       America.
          Texts of five letters, 1853-1855, to the
       newspaper of which MT's brother Orion was
       part-owner and an editor. Brownell discus-
       ses Orion Clemens, and Branch describes MT's
       early journalism before the move to Nevada.

A4   DEVOTO, BERNARD. Mark Twain at Work. Cam-
       bridge, Massachusetts: Harvard University
       Press; London: Humphrey Milford, Oxford
       University Press.
          Working from the manuscripts, DeVoto says
       "something about the actual writing" of TS
       and HF "for the first time by any critic.
       What is said...does outline the nature of
       his talent, its abundance, and its hia-
       tuses." A concluding essay, "The Symbols
       of Despair," is based "on a vast accumula-
       tion of data which Mr. Paine ignored and
       Mr. Brooks never heard about. The present

essay indicates the true ordeal of Mark
Twain. Anyone who is familiar with Mr.
Brooks's book will see at once that my interpretation of it differs altogether from
his" (pp. vii-ix). Contains text of "The
Great Dark" and early manuscript material
for TS and HF, including "Boy's Manuscript."
"The Symbols of Despair" is reprinted in
Smith (1963), pp. 140-58, and material on TS
in Scott (1955), pp. 259-71 and (1967),
pp. 244-56, and Marks (1959), pp. 28-43;
there is also an excerpt in Cardwell (1963),
pp. 46-50.

A5   MASON, MIRIAM E. Mark Twain: Boy of Old
       Missouri. Indianapolis, New York: The
       Bobbs-Merrill Company.
          A biography for younger readers, part of
       The Childhood of Famous Americans series.

A6   SHAFFER, ELLEN K., and LUCILLE S. J. HALL,
       comps. A Check List of the Mark Twain Col-
       lection Assembled by the Late Willard S.
       Morse of Santa Monica, California. Los
       Angeles, California: Dawson's Book Shop.
          Based on Morse's own "meticulous" cata-
       logue of the collection, which includes
       manuscripts, first editions, books that be-
       longed to MT, books and articles about him,
       newspaper material, as well as portraits,
       busts, etc. [The collection includes signi-
       ficant material not listed in the present
       bibliography; it is now at Yale.]

1942 B SHORTER WRITINGS

B1   ANON. "Quintus Curtius Snodgrass: His Final
       Letter in the New Orleans Crescent," Twain-
       ian, n.s., I (June), 1-3.
          Thomas Ewing Dabney found five more "Quin-
       tus Curtius Snodgrass" letters, in addition
       to the six discovered by Minnie M. Brashear
       and Ernest E. Leisy; the letter of
       March 30, 1861 is reprinted. Also see
       Twainian, V (September-October, 1946), 1-2.

B2   AUERNHEIMER, RAOUL. "Mark Twain and the Ges-
       tapo," Christian Science Monitor, XXXIV
       (October 10, Magazine Section), 6.
          Auernheimer's thoughts about MT; occasioned
       by applying for permission to emigrate at the
       Gestapo headquarters at the Hotel Metropole,
       Vienna, where MT wrote "The Man that Corrupt-
       ed Hadleyburg."

B3   BEARD, CHARLES A., and MARY R. BEARD. The
       American Spirit: A Study of the Idea of
       Civilization in the United States (Vol. IV
       in their The Rise of American Civilization).
       New York: The Macmillan Company.
          Contains little discussion of MT, quoting
       and citing him on the dubious blessings of
       civilization (pp. 49-51), on the pernicious
       influence of Sir Walter Scott on the South
       (pp. 295-96), and on American imperialism
       (pp. 589-91). There is little of interest
       here for the student of MT, with the excep-
       tion of extensive quotation from a reply to

(BEARD, CHARLES A., and MARY R. BEARD)
his criticism of Scott by Mrs. T. P. O'Connor in her My Beloved South (1913) on pp. 396-97.

B4   BERNARD, HARRY. "Lettres Américaines. Filiation de Mark Twain," Revue de l'Université d'Ottawa, XII (Juillet-Septembre), 327-41.
    MT's successors include Edgar Lee Masters (Mitch Miller), Alvin Johnson (Spring Storm), James Still (River of Earth), and Marjorie Kinnan Rawlings (The Yearling).

B5   BLAIR, WALTER. "Mark Twain, Hank, and Huck," in his Horse Sense in American Humor from Benjamin Franklin to Ogden Nash. (Chicago: The University of Chicago Press), pp. 195-217, and passim.
    On the alternation of the fool and the wise narrator, as Twain and Clemens. Hank Morgan is decent but an ignoramus, and CY attacks MT's America as well as Arthur's England. Tom Sawyer is the dupe of books and Huck and Jim follow him despite their common-sense reservations, both in HF and in TS Abroad, which contains "a whole series of dialogues which equal or surpass the dialogues in the earlier book" and a further probing of the mentality of St. Petersburg.

B6   ____. "The Methods of Mark Twain," Saturday Review of Literature, XXV (June 20), 11.
    A review of Bernard DeVoto's Mark Twain at Work, chiefly descriptive, but praising DeVoto's scholarship and "skill comparable to that of a mystery novel writer."

B7   BLANCK, JACOB. "News from the Rare Book Sellers," Publishers' Weekly, CXLII (December 26), 3536-37.
    An MT letter in the 1917 edition of his letters (pp. 182-85), which Paine says was addressed to Thomas Bailey Aldrich, previously appeared in part as "Concerning a Bear" in "The Pellet, an ephemeral newspaper" publicizing a hospital fund. The sketch tells of Bret Harte's adding railroad tracks in front of the snarling bear on the cover of the Overland, thereby providing an object for the picture.

B8   [BROWNELL, GEORGE HIRAM.] "Cyril Clemens has broken loose again," Twainian, n.s., I (February), 8.
    Describes Republican Letters as "worth its price as a piece of Twain curiosa" which apparently follows a Pacific Coast newspaper reprinting of the 1868 MT letters to the Chicago Republican and is textually inaccurate.

B9   ____. "Did Mark also Invent this Children's Game?" Twainian, n.s., II (October), 5.
    Frank C. Willson reports having purchased a game titled "Rambles through Our Country, an Instructive Geographical Game," published by The American Publishing Company in 1881. MT is not credited with the idea

for this game, which resembles one he used to teach history dates to his own children, but the illustrations include cuts from his books.

B10   ____. "Five New Letters by Sam Found in Muscatine Paper," Twainian, n.s., I (February), 7-8.
    On Edgar M. Branch's discovery of five "Letters to the Editor" from Philadelphia, Washington, and St. Louis from late 1853 to March 5, 1855; the last of these is reproduced.

B11   ____. "Hannibal Honors 106th Birthday of Mark Twain," Twainian, n.s., I (January), 1-4.
    Describes the ceremonies, names, speakers and guests.

B12   ____. "Mark Twain on Thanksgiving,' Twainian, n.s., II (December), 5-6.
    Brief prefatory material on several topics unrelated to MT, and text of MT's article in Washington Times (November 27, 1905).

B13   ____. "Musical Melange," Twainian, n.s., II (November), 1-4.
    Includes correspondence with Jerome Kern and others concerning his Mark Twain Symphony; a letter from Morris Anderson concerning the Orchestrelle from MT's home, and a number of the music rolls (MT's choices were primarily classical); the text of an MT letter about a benefit performance for the Legal Aid Society, published in a special booklet by the Metropolitan Opera Company, as quoted in the New York Evening Post (March 16, 1906); brief comment on a "Mark Twain Mazourka" and a "Mark Twain Waltz" discovered by Frank C. Willson.

B14   ____. "The Mystery of 'Jim Greeley,'" Twainian, n.s., II (December), 4-5.
    The familiar "Jim Smiley" of "The Jumping Frog" became "Jim Greeley" in The Californian for December, 1865; there is a highly conjectural attempt to show possible connections to Horace Greeley. For further brief comment see note in Twainian, VI (May-June, 1947), 6; the question remains open.

B15   ____. "A Question as to the Origin of the Name, 'Mark Twain,'" Twainian, n.s., I (February), 4-7.
    A cautious treatment of MT's account of the origin of his pen-name: the question is still open.

B16   ____. "Sam Clemens Roams Again," Twainian, n.s., II (November), 5.
    During part of 1855 SLC left Keokuk and worked as a printer in Warsaw, Illinois.

B17   ____. "Thrilling Tale of a Tall Twain Tale," Twainian, n.s., I (April), 5-6.
    On the tracing of "Millions in It," listed in Merle Johnson's 1935 Bibliography with a

[BROWNELL, GEORGE HIRAM]
cross-reference to "Mark Twain's Remarkable Gold Mine"; the tale of gold-bearing spring water first appeared as a letter to the New York Evening Post (September 16, 1880), and is here reprinted.

B18 _____. "Varied Comments on Origin of the Name: Mark Twain," Twainian, n.s. I (May), 3-6.
Cites Ernest E. Leisy's statement in American Literature (January) that a careful check of New Orleans papers for the period when SLC was a pilot revealed nothing signed "Mark Twain." A letter from Thomas Ewing Dabney argues that Captain Sellers was too illiterate to write a connected series of newspaper articles and too egotistical not to sign his own name. Quoting a letter from A. Lyle Mewhirter on a Nevada story with the pseudonym coming from SLC's habit of asking a brewery owner to "mark twain" for two beers on credit, Brownell says there were no breweries in Nevada at the time, and anyway SLC was accompanied by three friends on the occasion of the anecdote.

B19 _____. "Yale Gets Morse Twain," Twainian, n.s., II (November), 4-5.
On the purchase of the Samuel Willard Morse Collection of MT material by Judge Walter Francis Frear, who donated it to the Yale University Library.

B20 CARTER, PAUL. "Mark Twain and War," Twainian, n.s., I (March), 1-3, 7.
On the growth of MT's anti-war sentiments.

B21 CLEMENS, CYRIL. "DeVoto's Mark Twain at Work," Mark Twain Quarterly, V (Fall-Winter), 23.
Chiefly descriptive; questions an identification of "Truthful James" with Jim Gillis.

B22 _____. "Did Twain Know Whitman?" Saturday Review of Literature, XXV (September 26), 13.
A query in a letter to the editor, summarizing reasons why there ought to have been comment by one author on the other, including the fact that both were in Washington in 1868. [Answered by John G. Moore, October 31, 1942.B44.]

B23 _____, ed. "Washington in 1868," Mark Twain Quarterly, V (Summer), 1-3.
Introduction to a special issue, consisting of correspondence from MT in the Chicago Republican in 1868 (dates not given), as follows: "Congressional Poetry," pp. 3, 5; "Kalamazoo," pp. 4-7; "Defeat of the Impeachment Project," pp. 7, 24; "Senator Chandler's Party," pp. 8, 24; "St. Valentine's Day," pp. 9, 24; "Curious Legislation and Vinnie Ream," pp. 10-11; "The Illinois State Association," pp. 11-14; "A Sleeping Lion Aroused--Gideon Rampant," pp. 15-16.

B24 CLEMENS, SAMUEL L. "Letters to James Redpath," Mark Twain Quarterly, V (Winter-Spring), 19-21.
A series of letters from MT to the manager of the Redpath Lecture Bureau, 1870-1872, on current and projected lectures, and his reaction to Redpath's proposal that he write lectures for others to deliver: favorable, with a male lecturer, but "I question if a woman ever lived who could read a densely humorous passage as it should be read.... They appreciate and enjoy (you know I rely for my effects chiefly on simulated unconsciousness and intense absurdities) but they cannot render them effectively on the platform."

B25 _____. "Mark Twain on Rab," Mark Twain Quarterly, V (Fall-Winter), 19.
Letter to Fairchild, dated "Hartford, Sept. 22, 1882," on his dog Rab, who chases horses and street cars, and therefore can't be kept. "I am mighty sorry it has turned out so, for he is a noble dog."

B26 DABNEY, THOMAS EWING, and GEORGE HIRAM BROWNELL. "Mr. Dabney Reveals the Truth about Tangled 'Delta' Papers," Twainian, n.s., I (April), 7-8.
There was a New Orleans True Delta, but MT's burlesque of Captain Sellers (supposedly his source for the "Mark Twain" pseudonym) actually appeared in the New Orleans Crescent.

B27 DAVIDSON, WILLIAM EARL. "Mark Twain and Conscience," Twainian, n.s., I (April), 1-5. The "Conclusions" of Davidson's master's essay of the same title (University of Missouri).
A sense of honor and a sense of guilt influenced MT after his departure from traditional Christianity, and he retained the habit of "moral introspection." His pessimism grew in part from what he saw of man's self-deception and his own inability to find comfort in rationalization.

B28 DUFFY, CHARLES. "Three Essays on Mark Twain," South Atlantic Quarterly, XLI (October), 454.
A descriptive review of Bernard DeVoto, Mark Twain at Work, noting "this book is composed of three essays, each of which has previously been made public." See review by Haight, 1942.B36.

B29 FEINSTEIN, GEORGE W. "Vestigia in Pudd'nhead Wilson," Twainian, n.s., I (May), 1-3.
Cites a number of passages in PW which still reveal the original plan for Angelo and Luigi as Siamese twins.

B30 FERGUSON, DELANCEY. "Mark Twain's Comstock Duel: The Birth of a Legend," American Literature, XIV (March), 66-70.

(FERGUSON, DELANCEY)
MT's "How I Escaped Being Killed in a Duel," which appeared in Tom Hood's Comic Annual in 1873, is essentially just another good story of the sort the public expected from the author of RI, and in his further development of the anecdote in the Autobiography (North American Review, CLXXXIII [December 21, 1906], 1224 ff.) and the Paine biography (Mark Twain, I, p. 496) "he had honestly forgotten the original facts, and remembered only his fictional development of them."

B31 FISCHER, W. [Review: Günther Möhle, Das Europabild Mark Twains (1940).] Anglia Beiblatt, LIII, 78-80.
Fischer says the book contains more than the title suggests, in placing MT's picture of Europe in the broader context of other American authors such as Irving and Hawthorne, and less than the title suggests, in that it restricts the discussion of MT's work to IA and CY. [In German.]

B32 FLACK, FRANK MORGAN. "Mark Twain and Music," Twainian, n.s., II (October), 1-4.
Introduction and "a group of outstanding paragraphs" from Flack's master's essay (State University of Iowa). Draws heavily on published discussions and concludes that MT originally lacked sympathy or appreciation for serious music, but gradually came to enjoy it and even used it as a literary device. What appears here is conventional and derivative.

B33 *____. "Mark Twain and Wagner," Opera (December 28) (not Opera News, which has been checked).
[Source: Twainian, II (April, 1943), 6.]

B34 FULLER, JOHN G. "A Connecticut Yankee in King Arthur's Court: A New Dramatized Version of Mark Twain's Famous Novel," Scholastic, XL (March 9), 17-19.
A short adaptation for high-school students; Hank Bennett, the hero, is thrown back in time "when his hand touches the power tubes of his extra-voltage radio."

B35 GORDON, GEORGE STUART. Anglo-American Literary Relations. London: Oxford University Press, pp. 108-109.
Notes with satisfaction that English readers recognized "this authentic man of genius" while Americans still saw only the clown.

B36 HAIGHT, GORDON S. "Studies of Mark Twain's Papers," Yale Review, XXXII (Autumn), 176-78.
A review of DeVoto's Mark Twain at Work. "Strictly speaking, none of the three essays it contains is new; the first two were printed in the Tom Sawyer (1939) and Huckleberry Finn (1942) that Mr. DeVoto edited

for the Limited Editions Club; the third, outlined in Harper's Magazine for January, 1940, and again in the introduction to Mark Twain in Eruption, was a William Vaughan Moody lecture in the same year.... The most important new materials consist of a short preliminary study for Tom Sawyer and several pages of notes for Huckleberry Finn." "The third essay, 'The Symbols of Despair,' reiterates Mr. DeVoto's explanation" of MT's final pessimism through a tracing of three themes which led to MS. "One wishes Mr. DeVoto had published more of the manuscripts from which his explanation is deduced; the eight pages called 'The Great Dark'...hardly serve to substantiate it." Although "no fairer or more penetrating studies of Tom Sawyer and Huckleberry Finn have ever been written...Mr. DeVoto's work would lose none of its vigor if he were more generous towards his predecessors."

B37 JOHNSON, MERLE. Merle Johnson's American First Editions, Fourth Edition. Revised and enlarged by Jacob Blanck. New York: R. R. Bowker Co., pp. 110-15.
Includes points for various states of first editions of MT's works; also lists a number of reprintings, etc., and several books of biographical interest (listed in this bibl.).

B38 KAZIN, ALFRED. On Native Grounds; An Interpretation of Modern American Prose Literature. New York: Reynal & Hitchcock.
Discusses Brooks's The Ordeal of Mark Twain (pp. 280-85), now significant chiefly for "its effort to draw an analogy between the Gilded Age and the postwar scene; an analogy between the 'ordeal' of Mark Twain, which was dubious, and the self-consciousness of Brooks's literary generation, which was real enough."

B39 LEISY, ERNEST E. "Mark Twain and Isaiah Sellers," American Literature, XIII (January) 398-405.
In his piloting days SLC parodied the river columns by Captain Sellers in the True Delta for March 22 and May 7, 1859; the parody appeared in the Daily Crescent for May 17, signed "Sergeant Fathom." Paine gives an exaggerated account of this, claiming that it "broke the literary heart" of Sellers (Mark Twain, I, 149-50). There is a fuller reprinting of the Sellers report here than in Paine (Mark Twain, III, 1593-96). Leisy sees no reason to suppose that SLC borrowed the pen-name "Mark Twain" from Sellers, as Paine suggests.

B40 LILLARD, RICHARD G. "Hank Monk and Horace Greeley," American Literature, XIV (May), 126-34.
Documents the story in RI (I, Ch. 20) of Greeley's wild ride in a stage coach driven by Hank Monk.

B41 LORCH, FRED W. [Review: Cyril Clemens, ed., Republican Letters by Samuel L. Clemens (1941).] American Literature, XIII (January), 439-40.

A series of letters MT published in the Chicago Republican in the spring of 1868, describing his trip to San Francisco. Lorch says they actually come from some other source, probably a California paper which copied them. As they appeared in the Republican the letters are not MT's best work, but they are important to scholars. "It is regrettable, therefore, that Mr. Clemens did not present them as originally published and thus make them serviceable." Only three of the six letters in the Republican appear in the Cyril Clemens edition.

B42 "MALONE, TED" [pseud. FRANK ALDEN RUSSELL.] "Mark Twain," in his American Pilgrimage. New York: Dodd, Mead & Company, pp. 16-32 (also "Introduction," pp. xiii-xiv).

A general account of MT's life, containing no new information. One of a series of radio programs broadcast from the homes of American authors.

B43 MATTHIESSEN, F. O. "Twain into Clemens," New Republic, CVII (August 10), 179.

A review of DeVoto's Mark Twain at Work. "Bernard DeVoto continues to present his findings from the Mark Twain manuscripts. As usual he throws his weight around.... Despite all this pointless bluster and despite an equally unnecessary display of showy and rather amateur scholarship, the new material he offers us is of real interest. And...Mr. DeVoto's judgment has deepened since he wrote Mark Twain's America in 1932."

B44 MOORE, JOHN G. "Yes, Twain Knew Whitman," Saturday Review of Literature, XXV (October 31), 11.

A letter to the editor, answering a query of September 26 by Cyril Clemens, cites references in Traubel's and Frances Winwar's books on Whitman. Moreover, MT was a part owner of Charles L. Webster & Co., which in 1892 published Selected Poems by Whitman, with an unsigned preface of which Moore says that "the manner of its writing leads me to think that it might have been written by Mark Twain himself."

B45 ODELL, GEORGE C. D. Annals of the New York Stage. New York: Columbia University Press. Vol. XIII (1885-1888).

MT was a guest and made a speech at a "little supper" given by Augustin Daly after the hundredth performance of his production of The Taming of the Shrew, April 13, 1887 (p. 216). The American Claimant, or, Mulberry Sellers Ten Years Later had a "trial matinee" at the Lyceum Theatre, September 23, 1887, after earlier trials in New Brunswick, Rochester, and Syracuse; "Mark Twain was a great genius, but he simply could not write plays" (p. 426). MT was among the authors at a reading in aid of international copyright at Chickering Hall, November 28, 29, 1887 (p. 544).

B46 OLSON, JAMES C. "Mark Twain and the Department of Agriculture," American Literature, XIII (January), 408-10.

Correspondence with J. Sterling Morton, Secretary of Agriculture under Grover Cleveland, concerning MT's requests for free corn and watermelon seeds to plant for Livy in Florence (1893).

B47 POCHMANN, HENRY A. [Review: Theodore Hornberger, Mark Twain's Letters to Will Bowen: "My First, & Oldest & Dearest Friend" (1941).] American Literature, XIV (March), 94-95.

Sixteen letters over the period from May 7, 1866 to June 7, 1900, important biographically. "Professor Hornberger's notes ...are a model of good editing."

B48 POWELL, LAWRENCE CLARK. "An Unpublished Mark Twain Letter," American Literature, XIII (January), 405-407.

Letter to Sir John Adams (December 5, 1898) praising his book, The Herbartian Psychology Applied to Education (Boston, 1897). Text includes a passage deleted by MT (but legible under infrared light) expressing ideas central to his What Is Man?

B49 PROVENCAL, VALMORE. "Mark Twain as an Historian," Mark Twain Quarterly, V (Winter-Spring), 25.

A brief account of history-related writings, with praise for the "Winner of the 1941 Junior Prize."

B50 RICHARDSON, LYON N. "Men of Letters and the Hayes Administration," New England Quarterly, XV (March), 110-41.

On MT's changing view of Hayes, pp. 127-29; includes a letter from MT to Hayes (April 10, 1882), commenting on mental telegraphy and thanking him for a letter praising one of his books.

B51 ROBERTS, HAROLD: [INTRODUCTION BY THE REV. C. J. ARMSTRONG.] "Sam Clemens: Florida Days," Twainian, n.s. I (January), 7-8; (February), 1-3; (March), 4-7.

On MT's birthplace and early days, and the influence of John A. Quarles, who may have told him the "Jumping Frog" story. Insists the early influences were beneficial.

B52 TAYLOR, WALTER FULLER. "Mark Twain," in his The Economic Novel in America. Chapel Hill: The University of North Carolina Press, pp. 116-47; also passim.

"Mark Twain's, then, was a comparatively simple, coherent philosophy of acquisition, control of obvious abuses, and concern for the interests of the whole people. Within him satirist, capitalist, and democrat

(TAYLOR, WALTER FULLER)
worked toward the same object--that of enjoying the uses of the machine and lessening the abuses" (p. 146). His achievement
is valuable, despite his limited grasp of
economics and lack of discipline. Notes
that the capitalism in GA "is curiously
pre-machine" (p. 124), and ranks CY as "the
supreme work" among the economic novels of
its time, despite its flaws, because it has
abundant vitality (p. 321).

B53 TIDWELL, JAMES NATHAN. "Mark Twain's Representation of Negro Speech," American Speech,
XVII (October), 174-76.
Analysis of the pronunciations in HF reveals "honest and sincere" representation:
"His failure to systematize his spelling
allowed him to write each word as it would
sound in a given sentence, and thus he
could represent in full detail the nuances
of Jim's pronunciation."

B54 VOGELBACK, ARTHUR LAWRENCE. "The Prince and
the Pauper: A Study in Critical Standards,"
American Literature, XIV (March), 48-54.
"Critics approved of The Prince and the
Pauper because, more than any other of Mark
Twain's books up to that time, it complied
with conventional literary ideals" (p. 54).
Among the qualities praised were construction of plot, depiction of character, and
the author's capacity to deal with a serious theme. Vogelback quotes reviews in
Atlantic Monthly, Boston Transcript, Century, Critic, Harper's Monthly, and New York
Tribune, as well as the New York Herald
as quoted by Paine.

B55 WAGENKNECHT, EDWARD. "Mark Twain as He Wrote
in His Years of Trouble," New York Times
Book Review (July 5), p. 3.
A review of Bernard DeVoto's Mark Twain
at Work, "the fullest report we have yet
had concerning the unpublished Mark Twain
Papers now in Mr. DeVoto's care, and some
of the best Mark Twain criticism that has
been written" on the meaning of TS and HF,
and on MT's struggle against despair in
his late writings.

B56 *WINTERICH, JOHN T. [Foreword.] A Connecti-
cut Yankee at King Arthur's Court. New
York: The Heritage Press.
[Source: Asselineau (1954), No. 930.]

B57 WOOD, GRANT. "Letter from Grant Wood," Saturday Review of Literature, XXV
(February 28), 11.
From a letter in which Wood tells Cyril
Clemens that reading Huck's description of
Emmeline Grangerford's unfinished drawing
of a young woman about to leap from a
bridge gave him his "first intimation that
there was anything ridiculous about sentimentality." Apparently part of the letter,
not printed, praises TS.

1943 A BOOKS

A1 *CLEMENS, SAMUEL L. Las Aventuras de Huck,
traducción del inglés y prólogo por Carlos
Pereyra. Buenos Aires: Editorial Losada.
[Source: Asselineau (1954), No. 964.]

A2 CLEMENS, SAMUEL L. Washington in 1868, ed.
with an introduction and notes by Cyril
Clemens. Foreword by W. W. Jacobs. Webster Groves, Missouri: International Mark
Twain Society; London: T. Werner Laurie.
MT letters from Washington, published in
the Chicago Republican. February 8-March 1,
1868. See reviews for the severe criticism
of the editing.

A3 FERGUSON, DELANCEY. Mark Twain: Man and
Legend. Indianapolis: The Bobbs-Merrill
Company. [Also issued as a Charter Books
paperback by Bobbs-Merrill in 1963.]
A sound general study, well received by
many reviewers as one of the best works on
MT of its time and reflecting all the schol-
arship then available. The portion on the
significance of the river is reprinted in
Schmitter (1974), pp. 77-83.

A4 *VON BRANDT, RALPH VAN KIRK. Mark Twain.
Trenton: Privately Printed.
[Source: Asselineau (1954), No. 962:
"Imaginary Letters to and from Mark Twain."]

1943 B SHORTER WRITINGS

B1 ANON. "Clemens Before Twain: Prentice Steps
in Buffoonery," Times Literary Supplement
(April 24), p. 202.
A review of Cyril Clemens, Young Sam
Clemens (1942), a book which provides little
new information of interest to any but the
most dedicated students of MT; however, it
shows that even in the early period there
is evidence of the deliberate care with
which MT achieved his effects.

B2 ANON. "Mark Twain's First Curtain Speech,"
Mark Twain Quarterly, VI (Summer-Fall),
5.
Apparently a newspaper clipping, carries
the date August 2, 1877; the text of a
brief address to the audience on the New
York opening of MT's and Bret Harte's play,
Ah Sin.

B3 ANON. "Resuming the List of Writings about
Twain in Periodicals," Twainian, n.s., II.
A continuation of the bibliography begun
in The Twainian when it was published under
the auspices of the Mark Twain Society of
Chicago. Coverage is as follows:
February, 6, McClure's Magazine through
Musical Courier; March, 5, The Nation through
North American Review; April, 6, The Occi-
dent through Overland Magazine; May, 6,
Pacific Monthly through New Amstel Magazine;
June, 6, St. Nicholas through World's Work.

(ANON.)
This material has been included in the present bibliography.

B4   BENET, STEPHEN VINCENT. [Holograph tribute to MT.] Mark Twain Quarterly, VI (Winter-Spring), cover.
      Benet has been reading MT since age nine or ten, and regards him as "our great novelist."

B5   BLAIR, WALTER. [Review: Bernard DeVoto, Mark Twain at Work (1942).] American Literature, XIV (January), 447-49.
      The essays and documents concerned with the writing of TS, HF, and MS "will be important for future students of Twain...partly because, like Mr. DeVoto's earlier Mark Twain's America, they challenge previous scholarship when it seems vulnerable." "Some critics...may find Mr. DeVoto's treatment of fiction as mythology less illuminating than he feels it is, and there may be disagreements with his conclusions about structure." Praises "the meticulous study and the valuable data here available."

B6   [BROWNELL, GEORGE HIRAM.] "Billy Phelps Joins the Innumerable Caravan," Twainian, n.x., III (October), 1-4.
      Reminiscences about Phelps, who died in August, and his appreciation of the Twainian; repeats several MT anecdotes from the Phelps Autobiography with Letters (1939).

B7   ____. "Dan Beard Tells about those 'Yankee' Pictures," Twainian, n.s., III (October), 4-5.
      The text of Dan Beard's marginal notations in a copy of CY Frank C. Willson saw at a Boston book sale; comments on models, costumes; confirms Merlin's features (p. 279) as based on Tennyson's.

B8   ____. "From 'Hospital Days,'" Twainian, n.s., II (March), 1-5; (April), 4-6.
      On a brief passage attributed to MT in the first state of his Sketches New and Old (Hartford, 1875, p. 299, here reprinted), along with an erratum slip indicating that in fact he was not the author. The passage appeared in Hospital Days, the anonymous work of Jane Stuart Woolsey (1868), but Brownell argues that MT wrote and gave her the passage.

B9   ____. "Here's Another of those New-Found Mercury Tales," Twainian, n.s., III (December), 4-5.
      Includes the text of MT's "Private Theatricals" ("A Curtain Lecture Concerning Skating"), one of five MT writings discovered in the New York Mercury (see November Twainian for details).

B10   ____. "The Home of the Prodigal Son," Twainian, II (April), 1-3.

On a passage in a Holy Land letter in the Alta California (February 8, 1868) omitted from IA, although the illustration to accompany it was retained; text here reprinted, pp. 2-3.

B11   ____. "An Important Question Settled," Twainian, n.s., II (February), 1-5.
      On MT's newspaper comments on "Rock Me to Sleep" poem; located by Willard S. Morse in Cincinnati Evening Chronicle (March 9, 1868) and later by Brownell in Chicago Republican (March 15); also see "Rock Me to Sleep," Twainian, March. Also on "Sociable Jimmy," attributed to MT in an unidentified clipping in a scrapbook purchased by Irving S. Underhill; see Twainian, April, "The Home of the Prodigal Son," on the difficulty of attribution. "An Important Question Settled" and "Sociable Jimmy" are both reprinted here.

B12   ____. "I Shall Probably See Stormfield But Seldom Hereafter," Twainian, II (May), 4-6.
      Text of a letter from MT in Bermuda to Paine, Feb. 5-7, 1910, on various household arrangements; Brownell sees evidence here that MT "remained calm, patient, and kindly in his relations with others."

B13   ____. [Introduction.] "Mark Twain's Eulogy on the Reliable Contraband," Twainian, n.s., II (June), 1-3.
      Reprints one of three MT contributions to the short-lived Packard's Monthly in 1869 (the others were his "Open Letter to Commodore Vanderbilt" and "Personal Habits of the Siamese Twins"). A brief note in Twainian, n.s., III (March, 1944), 6 reports that the "Reliable Contraband" story also appeared in Greenwich Village, II, No. 1 (June 23, 1915), with an introductory note by Guido Bruno, the editor.

B14   ____. "Mark Twain's Memory Builder," Twainian, n.s., III (December), 1-4.
      A cache of 300 copies of the game MT patented in 1885 was recently discovered in Brooklyn; bibliographic description provided.

B15   ____. "Mark Twain's Tribute to Francis Lightfoot Lee," Twainian, n.s., III (November), 1-3.
      On MT's tribute (here reprinted, pp. 2-3) in The Pennsylvania Magazine of History and Biography, I, No. 3 (1877), 343. Brownell states (p. 2) that he prepared the checklist index at the back of Merle Johnson's 1935 Bibliography.

B16   ____. "New Twain Tale Found in Oxford Magazine," Twainian, n.s., II (January), 3-5.
      On the discovery of "Magdalen Tower" in the undergraduate publication, The Shotover Papers, Or, Echoes from Oxford, I (October 17, 1874); MT's text is reproduced, pp. 4-5.

B17   [BROWNELL, GEORGE HIRAM]. "Remarks on the Script of 'Mark Twain in Hawaii,'" Twain-ian, n.s., III (October), 5-6.
Brownell has been looking over Judge Frear's book in manuscript, and testifies to its accuracy and value; wartime conditions may make it difficult to find a publisher.

B18   _____. "Rock Me to Sleep," Twainian, n.s., II (March), 6.
On the authorship and original publication of the poem discussed by MT in "An Important Question Settled," Twainian, 1943.B11.

B19   _____. "Seven New Twain Tales Discovered by Chance," Twainian, n.s., III (November), 3-6.
Recent searches have turned up two MT writings in the Washington Weekly Chronicle for 1867: "A Humorist's Eloquence" (January 12, a reprint of his "Announcement to Highwaymen" in the Territorial Enter-prise of November 11, 1866) and "Mr. Sew-ard's Real Estate Transactions" (December 28). Five were discovered in the New York Sunday Mercury of 1867: "The Brand-New Yankee Gentleman" (March 3; ap-peared in May Twainian as "The Winner of the Medal"); "Private Theatricals" ("A Cur-tain Lecture Concerning Skating," March 17; reprinted in December Twainian); "Barbarous" (March 24--reprint promised, but December issue, p. 4 says it is not worth printing); "Regulation Regimen" ("Official Physic," April 21; reprinted following the present article); "Though Dead, yet Speaketh" (July 7; commonly known as "First Interview with Artemus Ward"). For further discussion see Twainian 1943.B9.

B20   _____. "Twain's Version of Hamlet," Twain-ian, n.s., II (June), 4-6.
Reprints MT's parody; source was a four-page typescript from Irving S. Underhill, taken from an unidentified newspaper clipping.

B21   _____. "The Winner of the Medal," Twainian, n.s., II (May), 1-4.
Discusses the original publication of this MT item in The American Union, A Fireside Journal (Boston: XXXVIII, May 18, 1867). Topic was an endowment of $5,000 in stocks to provide an annual medal to the "first gentleman" of each Princton graduating class (the medal was never awarded, and the funds were returned in 1873 to the donor, Leonard Jerome--whose daughter Jennie later became Lady Randolph Churchill and mother of Winston Churchill). MT text pp. 2-3.

B22   _____. [Announcement that Franklin J. Meine is at work on a collection of stories about MT, apparently by people who knew him.] Twainian, n.s., II (January), 6.

B23   _____. [Brief Item.] Twainian, n.s., II (March), 5.
In full: "On page 272 of 'Mark Twain's Notebook,' (Harper 1935) Mark states that he met a 'Mr. Gandhi' who showed him the Jain Temple. Paine comments that this man is our 'good Mahatma of later years.' Not so; Twain's Gandhi was an Indian nabob--not the hunger-striker of recent newspaper fame."

B24   CHUBB, PERCIVAL. "Mark Twain at Sundown," Mark Twain Quarterly, V (Spring), 15-16, 18.
At a small dinner party in MT's later years Chubb found him "genial and communica-tive, but...subdued in a way that surprised me" until he learned of MT's late change "from the mood of comedy to that of trage-dy."

B25   CLEMENS, CYRIL. "'The Birth of a Legend' Again," American Literature, XV (March), 64-65.
Claims that MT's account of his duel with James L. Laird (Autobiography, I, 350-61) is correct in its details--including the marksmanship of Steve Gillis. As evidence Clemens cites conversations with persons who knew MT and other individuals involved. A reply to DeLancey Ferguson (1942.B30).

B26   _____. "A Letter to the Editors," American Literature, XIV (January), 430-31.
Takes exception to the accusation by Fred W. Lorch (1942.B41) that he did not use the Chicago Tribune publication of the letters for his Republican Letters (1941) but rath-er, apparently, a reprinting from a western paper. Only three of the six letters were reprinted, to be sure, but the others were witheld for separate publication [Washington in 1868, ed. with an introduction and notes by Cyril Clemens, 1943.A2.]

B27   _____. [Review: Theodore Hornberger, ed. Mark Twain's Letters to Will Bowen (1941).] Mark Twain Quarterly, VI (Winter-Spring), 23.
Consists chiefly of the reprinting of an anecdote from the first of these "delight-ful and informative letters" (Maui, May 7, 1866).

B28   _____. "Twainiana," Hobbies--The Magazine for Collectors, XLIV (October), 96-97.
Anecdotes about MT's clothing purchases from Rogers Peet in New York; includes text of a letter from him ("Onteora, New York, August 15, 1900"), ordering what Cyril Clem-ens says was the first of his white suits.

B29   COWLEY, MALCOLM. "Mencken and Mark Twain," New Republic, CVIII (March 8) 321-22.
A review of H. L. Mencken's Heathen Days: 1890-1936, noting his tribute there to MT and commenting briefly on his earlier Happy Days: 1880-1892 (1940) and Newspaper Days: 1899-1906 (1940). "After reading his three books of memoirs, you feel that Mark Twain

(COWLEY, MALCOLM)
must have been the decisive influence in forming both his style and his picture of himself.... All his life he has been re-phrasing and modernizing the rather inno-cent bitterness of Twain's later years." MT surpasses Mencken chiefly in imagina-tion.

B30 FARRELL, JAMES T. "Twain's Huckleberry Finn and the Era He Lived In," New York Times Book Review (December 12), pp. 6, 37.
"Mark Twain was both a democrat and a cynic"; he was disillusioned, but "through his two unspoiled boys Twain forcefully em-phasized his own attitudes and values.... Tom and Huck are symbols of the possibili-ties in human beings."

B31 FERGUSON, DELANCEY. "Mark Twain's Lost Cur-tain Speeches on the Plays Gilded Age and Ah Sin," South Atlantic Quarterly, XLII (July), 262-69.
Reprints the texts of these speeches from New York papers and quotes reviews. In his speech given on the hundredth performance of the Gilded Age, MT said that the star, John T. Raymond, had shown the humor of Colonel Sellers but not the pathos.

B32 GALLAGHER, CHARLES J. [Review: DeLancey Ferguson, Mark Twain: Man and Legend.] Thought (Fordham University), XVIII (September), 534-35.
Ferguson wished "to separate his subject's life into its literary and non-literary elements; but the formula by which this is done is not apparent. It would have helped the reader somewhat had the author indicat-ed what he considered of real value in the writings of Mark Twain--an immense amount of which is pure balderdash; but from first to last there is no effort at selection." MT's "boisterous egotism was merely the intellectual superiority of the ignorant. Being a blatant atheist, he could pronounce infallibly on every subject which came his way."

B33 HEDGES, ISAAC A. "Carroll Beckwith and Mark Twain," Mark Twain Quarterly, VI (Summer-Fall), 4.
Notes two paintings and a black and white sketch of MT by Beckwith; a Mr. William L. Huse owned one of the boats on which MT was a cub pilot, and was later acquainted with him in Onteora, N.Y.

B34 JONES, HOWARD MUMFORD. [Review: DeLancey Ferguson, Mark Twain: Man and Legend.] American Speech, XVIII (December), 286-87.
Crediting journalism and the lecture platform for shaping MT "is an attractive theory, because of its simplicity, but Mr. Ferguson, in turn, becomes hobby-horsical" in that he overlooks "an art of literature, a technique, a quality of architecture that

Twain has laboriously learned"; apart from over-simplification, the book is "reliable, clear, sympathetic, and just."

B35 LILLARD, RICHARD G. "Evolution of the 'Wa-shoe Zephyr,'" American Speech, XVIII (December), 257-60.
Traces the development of tall tales about the violent desert wind to the time when MT described it in RI.

B36 *MORLEY, CHRISTOPHER. [Introduction.] Tom Sawyer and Huckleberry Finn. London: J. M. Dent & Sons (Everyman's Library). [Source: Asselineau (1954), No. 965.]

B37 PHELPS, WILLIAM LYON. "Billy Phelps Speaking," Rotarian, LXIII (July), 40.
Reviews DeLancey Ferguson, Mark Twain: Man and Legend (which he commends for its emphasis on the literary side of MT's life) and also "a little book of 119 pages, Anglo-American Literary Relations, by the late George Stewart Gordon, president of Magdalen College, Oxford, whom he quotes as regret-ting that MT was admitted "so late to his place on the summits of American literature" and calling him "this authentic man of ge-nius, the author of Huckleberry Finn--which I place, with Moby Dick, among the great books of the world, great by every test."

B38 SCHOEN, MAX. [Review: Bernard DeVoto, Mark Twain at Work (1942).] Journal of Aesthet-ics and Art Criticism, II (Fall), 97-98.
Brief, descriptive, and laudatory.

B39 SPILLER, ROBERT E. "The Phenomenon of Mark Twain," Saturday Review of Literature, XXVI (August 7), 15.
A review of DeLancey Ferguson, Mark Twain: Man and Legend, which shows a working out of the mysteries of Mark Twain's personality, a careful weighing of the evidence present-ed by Brooks and DeVoto, and an emphasis on MT's development as a writer; unfortunately, in his emphasis on this he has lost the col-or, and "the result is informative rather than entertaining or stimulating."

B40 *STOVALL, FLOYD. American Idealism. Norman: University of Oklahoma Press.
MT's youthfulness accounts for the charm of HF and the weakness of MS. [Source: Asselineau (1954), No. 967.]

B41 THOMAS, HENRY, and DANA LEE THOMAS. "Samuel Langhorne Clemens (Mark Twain), 1835-1910," in Living Biographies of Famous Novelists. Garden City, N.Y.: Garden City Publishing Co., Inc. [Reprinted Garden City, N.Y.: Halcyon House (1947).] Pp. 276-91.
Derivative and inaccurate: MT's "first child died soon after its birth. A second succumbed to pneumonia as a result of Mark Twain's absent-minded carelessness" (p. 279); "When the Civil War broke out, he enlisted in the federal army and served

(THOMAS, HENRY, and DANA LEE THOMAS)
until he was honorably discharged" (p. 285);
"He was anxious to show his father-in-law,
Mr. Rogers, that there was as much money in
writing books as there was in selling coal"
(p. 288). Critical judgments on MT's works
are less original or interesting.

B42   TROXELL, GILBERT McCOY. "Samuel Langhorne
       Clemens, 1835-1910," Yale University Libra-
       ry Gazette, XVIII (July), 1-5.
           A description of the Willard Samuel Morse
       collection of MT editions, manuscripts, and
       Twainiana, presented to the Yale University
       Library by Walter Francis Frear.

B43   VON HIBLER, LEO. [Review: Günther Möhle,
       Das Europabild Mark Twains (1940).]
       Englische Studien, LXXV (February), 259-62.
           Only the final fifty pages of this 130-
       page book concern the theme of the title,
       and much of this concerns England and the
       Middle Ages. There is much of interest,
       such as the context provided by discussion
       of Hawthorne and Irving, but this is not
       the needed comprehensive study.

B44   WAGENKNECHT, EDWARD. "A New Biography of
       Mark Twain," New York Times Book Review
       (June 13), p. 8.
           A review of DeLancey Ferguson's Mark
       Twain: Man and Legend, which "sums up vir-
       tually all that is known as of 1943," al-
       though "the best criticism is still De-
       Voto's." Describes Cyril Clemens's Young
       Sam Clemens (1942) as "unpretentious...it
       makes enjoyable reading."

B45   WILLSON, FRANK C. "That Gilded Age Again:
       An Attempt to Unmuddle the Mystery of the
       Fifty-seven Variants," Papers of the Bib-
       liographical Society of America, XXXVII
       (Second Quarter), 141-56.

B46   WILSON, EDMUND. The Shock of Recognition.
       New York: Doubleday, Doran & Company, Inc.
           Reprints MT's "Fenimore Cooper's Literary
       Offences" (1895) and William Dean Howells's
       My Mark Twain (1910), with headnotes by
       Wilson, and letters from Sherwood Anderson
       to Van Wyck Brooks (some on MT), with Wil-
       son's headnote and "Introductory Note by
       Van Wyck Brooks."

B47   WIMBERLY, LOWRY CHARLES. "Mark Twain and the
       Tichenor Bonanza," Atlantic Monthly, CLXXII
       (November), 117, 119. Condensed as "A Let-
       ter to the Editor" in Time, XLII
       (November 1), 44-45.
           Reprints with commentary a letter from
       MT datelined "Hartford, Sept. 14, 1880" to
       the New York Evening Post (n.d.), humorous-
       ly commenting on a fraudulent scheme for
       extracting gold from California spring
       waters.

1944 A BOOKS

A1   *ANON. An Exhibition of the Works of Mark
      Twain, including manuscripts, first editions
      and association items, at the Main Public
      Library, April 30 through May 31, 1944,
      sponsored by the Friends of the Detroit Pub-
      lic Library, Detroit, Michigan.
      [Source: Asselineau (1954), No. 989.]

A2   *DAVIS, SAMUEL P. The Typograhical Howitzer by
      Sam Davis with a foreword by Thomas P. Brown.
      Sacramento, California: The Meteorite
      Press. Reprinted from his Short Stories
      (San Francisco, 1886).
      [Source: Asselineau (1954), No. 991.]

1944 B SHORTER WRITINGS

B1   ADAMS, J. DONALD. "Speaking of Books," New
      York Times Book Review (April 30), p. 2.
          "While Mr. DeVoto has nursed his private
      feud with Van Wyck Brooks beyond the limits
      of one's patience, and, equally, beyond the
      pale of fair fighting...he has, neverthe-
      less, made a definite contribution to Ameri-
      can literary history." He errs in "his
      growing conviction that the region beyond
      the Mississippi is his private and untres-
      passable domain." Ibid., May 14, p. 2,
      continues a defence of Brooks, noting his
      historical sense.

B2   *ALLEN, HERVEY. "A Great American," The Maga-
      zine of Sigma Chi, George Ade Memorial Issue
      (October-November), p. 12.
          Stephen Crane's favorite MT book was LOM.
      [Source: Bridgman (1966), p. 134.]

B3   ANON. "Mark Twain," Scholastic, XLIV
      (April 17), 18-19.
          Scenes from the Warner Brothers motion
      picture on MT, starring Fredric March; the
      script by Alan LeMay draws in part on the
      stage play, Mark Twain, directed by Irving
      Rapper.

B4   ANON. "Mark Twain: Despite the Reports of
      His Death, He Lives All Over Again in New
      Film," Life, XVI (May 8), 89-99.
          On the Warner Brothers' film of his life,
      starring Fredric March. Illustrated with
      stills from the film, and with numerous
      photographs of MT, his family and homes,
      his grave at Elmira, etc.

B5   BLAIR, WALTER. [Review: DeLancey Ferguson,
      Mark Twain: Man and Legend (1943).] Ameri-
      can Literature, XVI (May), 143-45.
          It is weak on MT's writings before 1875,
      but good on later development, on "rehears-
      als and revisions," and correcting legend-
      ary aspects of the biography. The analyses
      of individual works are rather brief. "A
      book which deserves a place among the better
      studies of Mark Twain."

B6   [BROWNELL, GEORGE HIRAM.] "About Mark Twain's
      Job on the San Francisco Call," Twainian,
      n.s., III (May), 4-6.
          Reprints several Virginia City items.

B7   _____. "About the Program of that 'Babies
      Banquet,'" Twainian, IV (November), 4-6.
          E. Earl Moore has acquired a copy of the
      printed program of the Chicago banquet
      (November 13, 1879), honoring General Ulys-
      ses S. Grant, at which MT delivered his fa-
      mous speech on "The Babies." The text is
      reprinted, together with an MT letter. Also
      cites a report of the banquet in the Chicago
      Tribune.

B8   _____. "Baby vs. Burglar Alarm," Twainian,
      n.s., III (April), 6.
          Frank C. Willson has found in The Youth's
      Companion (May 18, 1882) a short MT letter,
      written in answer to a request for a gift
      tale for a fair raising money to aid abused
      children: "If you will start a society for
      the prevention of cruelty to fathers, I will
      write you a whole book."

B9   _____. "Concerning a Bear," Twainian, n.s.,
      III (April), 3-4.
          On the use by Thomas Bailey Aldrich of
      part of an MT letter without permission
      in The Pellet, an ephemeral daily. The
      topic is Bret Harte's addition of railroad
      tracks in front of the snarling bear on the
      Overland cover. MT was not named, but the
      passage is in his Letters.

B10   _____. "Everybody's Friend," Twainian, n.s.,
      III (February), 1-4.
          On the discovery by Frank C. Willson of
      an MT letter to Josh Billings in Street
      and Smith's New York Weekly (July 14, 1873)
      and reprinted by Billings in his book,
      Everybody's Friend. The item (appearing
      as a letter because publisher's contracts
      forbade MT contributing writings in other
      form) appears on p. 3; it teases Billings
      for his exaggerated misspellings.

B11   _____. "Hannibal Celebrates Twain's 108th
      Birthday," Twainian, n.s., III (February),
      5-6.
          On the celebrations, a preview showing of
      the Warner Brothers film, The Adventures of
      Mark Twain, and dedication of the building
      in which MT's father had his office as jus-
      tice of the peace.

B12   _____. "Index to The Twainian Now Being Pre-
      pared," Twainian, n.s., III (March), 6.
          The index was to cover the old and new
      series, from January, 1939 through June,
      1944; the charge would be determined some
      time before June, by the Executive Commit-
      tee. The June issue reports a delay until
      the October issue (Vol. IV), but there is
      no mention of the index in that issue and
      the matter appears to have been dropped.

B13   _____. "Mark Twain's Inventions," Twainian,
      n.s., III (January), 1-5.
          MT was granted three patents: on an ad-
      justable vest-strap (1871), on a pre-gummed
      scrap-book (1873), and on a game for learn-
      ing history dates (1885, described in
      Twainian, December, 1943). A Baltimore man
      applied for a patent on a vest-strap like
      MT's while the MT application was being con-
      sidered, and MT enlisted his brother Orion's
      aid in establishing priority.

B14   _____. "Mark Twain's Love Song," Twainian,
      n.s., III (April), 5-6.
          On a comic lyric by MT, exalting the liver
      above the passions; first appeared in The
      Medical Fortnightly, May 15, 1892, and re-
      printed in I. E. (?) Booth, ed., The Medical
      Muse, Grave and Gay (New York, 1895).

B15   _____. "New First Issue Point in Life on the
      Mississippi," Twainian, IV (November), 1-3.
          The cut of MT in flames at the foot of
      p. 441 appeared in the first copies and was
      then deleted; now, Frank C. Willson reports
      a copy in which the cut on p. 443 is titled
      "St. Louis Hotel" rather than "St. Charles
      Hotel." Brownell suggests that "it would
      appear that the earliest copies of LOM sent
      to subscribers contained both the cut of
      the St. Louis hotel legend and the cut of
      Twain in flames." Also see brief note in
      December issue, p. 5, and Brownell's "That
      Picture of 'St. Louis Hotel' in Life on the
      Mississippi," Twainian, VI (September-Octo-
      ber, 1947), 1-3.

B16   _____. "Rodman Gilder Writes of Twain and
      the Theatre," Twainian, n.s., III (March),
      4-5.
          On Gilder's article, "Mark Twain Detested
      the Theatre," Theatre Arts, February
      (1944.B34).

B17   _____. "Twain Letter Tells of 'Francis Light-
      foot Lee,'" Twainian, n.s., III (February),
      4-5.
          John W. Wholihan has found a copy of
      Volume I of the Pennsylvania Magazine of
      History and Biography with a letter signed
      by MT inserted in front of the fly-leaf;
      Brownell finds it significant as "documen-
      tary evidence in Twain's own hand that I
      had erred in my judgment that Twain wrote
      his article [on Lee] without knowledge of
      the high-brow nature of the magazine."

B18   _____. "Twain Letters to Webster," Twainian,
      IV (October), 6.
          About Samuel Charles Webster's series of
      articles, containing letters from MT, ap-
      pearing in The Atlantic Monthly; Brownell
      sees MT as almost impossible for a publish-
      er to deal with, and largely to blame for
      the failure of the Charles L. Webster Com-
      pany, but criticizes Webster as inexperi-
      enced and willing to be a yes-man.

1944 - Shorter Writings

B19   [BROWNELL, GEORGE HIRAM]. "An Unbiased Editorial," <u>Twainian</u>, n.s., III (April), 4-5.
     Reprints an MT item, "Inspired Humor," from the Buffalo <u>Express</u> (August 19, 1869); the thesis is that it is a ghastly joke for an editorial to suggest that one political party can redeem the country from the corruption of the other.

B20   _____. "'What Ought He to Have Done?' Some Remarks by Mark Twain on Child Management," <u>Twainian</u>, n.s., III (May), 1-4.
     On a letter to the editor of <u>Christian Union</u> of July 16, 1885 (reprinted, pp. 2-3); <u>See</u> Paine biography, p. 280.

B21   _____. "When and Where Were These Twain Tales First Printed?" <u>Twainian</u>, IV (December), 1-5.
     On two unidentified clippings, "The Revised Catechism" (on civic corruption) and "The Last Stamp" (probably apochryphal) in a collection bequeathed by Irving S. Underhill. <u>See</u> Rodman Gilder's letter to the editor in the next issue (January, 1945, p. 4).

B22   _____. "Who was Frank Finlay?" <u>Twainian</u>, IV (October), 1-6.
     Contains text of five letters and a postcard from MT to Finlay, over the period 1874-1900. They were acquired at an auction by Norman Bassett, without envelopes. In the attempt to identify Finlay, Bassett acquired the rare pamphlet, <u>Who Was Sarah Findlay? By Mark Twain, with a Suggested Solution by J. M. Barrie</u>. London: Clement K. Shorter, 1917. This pamphlet was pieced together by Shorter out of a preface he wrote, a brief article by Barrie, and an MT letter to the London <u>Chronicle</u> on copyright and signed "An American." The name, "Sarah Findlay" (with the "d"), is fictitious, and similarity of names mere coincidence, but Bassett was able to identify Finlay through the British War Office and correspondence with Finlay's son. Dixon Wecter provided fuller details in his "Frank Finlay; Or, 'The Thameside Tenderfoot in the Wooly West.'" <u>Twainian</u>, VI (July-August, 1947), 1-4.

B23   _____. [Brief item.] <u>Twainian</u>, III (April), 6.
     The "M'me Caprell [sic]" in the Paine biography (pp. 156-59) and MT's <u>Letters</u> (pp. 48-51) is mentioned in the New Orleans <u>Crescent</u> of February 18, 1861, with the spelling as MT gave it in a letter to his brother Orion.

B24   CLEMENS, CYRIL "Churchill and Twain," <u>Saturday Review of Literature</u>, XXVII (January 8), 13.
     A letter to the editor on the first meeting of MT and Churchill; includes text of a brief note from Churchill ("10 Downing Street, 25 October, 1943"), thanking Cyril

Clemens for the Gold Medal of the International Mark Twain Society.

B25   _____. "Contract for <u>Roughing It</u>," <u>Mark Twain Quarterly</u>, VI (Summer-Fall), 5.
     The text of an agreement dated July 15, 1870 and signed by MT and E. Bliss, Jr., concerning the book MT was to write for the American Publishing Company.

B26 * _____. "Mark Twain in St. Louis," <u>Slant</u>, I (October), 6, 16.
     [Source: Leary (1954), p. 47.]

B27 * _____. "Unique Origin of Mark Twain's Books," <u>Missouri School Journal</u>, XL (January), 16, 18-19.
     [Source: Asselineau (1954), No. 999.]

B28   _____. "Winston Churchill and Mark Twain," <u>Hobbies--The Magazine for Collectors</u>, XLIV (April), 105-107.
     Anecdotes of meetings between MT and Churchill, first in 1897 at the London home of Sir John MacAllister and a few weeks later at Sir Gilbert Parker's home. They met again in New York in 1900 and MT introduced Churchill at a Carnegie Hall lecture, and in 1907 once more in England, at another dinner given by Sir Gilbert Parker. This article was reprinted in <u>Dalhousie Review</u>, 1945, with no indication of this publication in <u>Hobbies</u>.

B29   CLEMENS, KATHARINE. "Alice James, Neglected Sister," <u>Mark Twain Quarterly</u>, VI (Summer-Fall), 6-7.
     Alice James expressed dissatisfaction with the dullness and irreverence of an MT book, apparently <u>CY</u>, but also criticized the Hon. Reginald Brett for a column in <u>Pall Mall Gazette</u> taking MT "with solemnity."

B30   CLEMENS, SAMUEL L. "The Gorki Incident: An Unpublished Fragment," <u>Slavonic and East European Review</u>, XXI (American Series III, Part 2, August), 35-36.
     A little parable of "York Minster" from Tierra del Fuego, who created a sensation by appearing before the King of England in the national costume: nude. The moral is that one must conform to local customs when traveling abroad (as Gorki failed to do when he visited America with a mistress). The text is MT's, without added commentary.

B31   _____. "Mark Differs with Mrs. Astor," <u>Mark Twain Quarterly</u>, VI (Summer-Fall), 7, 24.
     The text of MT's defense of the social graces of the self-made man; dated March, 1902, and possibly from a newspaper clipping.

B32 DUDGEON, L. W. "Twainiana," Hobbies--The
     Magazine for Collectors, XLIX (July), 98.
        "In my perusal of old family records...for
     data concerning the early history of Cane
     Valley, Ky., I find some interesting state-
     ments in the Hancock family concerning the
     grandparents of Mark Twain," Samuel Clemens
     and Pamelia [sic] Hancock.

B33 FARBER, MARJORIE. "Poisoned Pens," New York
     Times Book Review, (April 23), p. 5.
        A review of Bernard DeVoto's The Literary
     Fallacy; defends Van Wyck Brooks against
     attacks that began with DeVoto's Mark
     Twain's America.

B34 GILDER, RODMAN. "Mark Twain Detested the
     Theatre," Theatre Arts, XXVIII (February),
     109-16.
        After citing Howells on MT's expressions
     of distaste for the theater (and for lec-
     turing), traces his life-long involvement
     and concludes: "Did Mark Twain detest the
     theatre? I wonder." A popular account,
     illustrated with photographs of MT with
     actor John T. Raymond, and of Fredric March
     on the Warner Brothers' lot, made up for
     The Adventures of Mark Twain. See 1944.B16.

B35 GOHDES, CLARENCE. American Literature in
     Nineteenth-Century England. New York:
     Columbia University Press, passim.
        Contains numerous references to MT's
     popularity in England, and editions of his
     works there. Notes that despite the criti-
     cism of CY as vulgar, the new Review of Re-
     views condensed it in the second issue,
     February, 1890.

B36 JONES, JOSEPH. [Introduction and postscript
     by George Hiram Brownell.] "More Twain
     Found in New York Weekly," Twainian, n.s.,
     III (March), 1-4.
        Five of MT's letters written for the Sac-
     ramento Union were reprinted, slightly
     abridged, in the New York Weekly, March-
     June, 1867. Jones and Brownell speculate
     that MT may have allowed this publication
     as a way to publicize his forthcoming
     Jumping Frog book and Cooper Union lecture.

B37 LILLARD, RICHARD G. "Contemporary Reaction
     to 'The Empire City Massacre,'" American
     Literature, XVI (November), 198-203.
        MT's hoax story in the October 28, 1863
     Territorial Enterprise described an imagi-
     nary mass-murder so vividly that readers
     failed to note the impossibility of the de-
     tails; the result was a chorus of indigna-
     tion. [For MT's version of the story see
     "My Bloody Massacre" in Sketches New and
     Old].

B38 LORCH, FRED,W. "Albert Bigelow Paine's Visit
     to Keokuk in 1910," Iowa Journal of History
     and Politics, XLII (April), 192-98.
        Shortly after MT's death, Paine went to
     Keokuk, Iowa to collect material for his

biography. He knew of MT's brother Orion
only from MT and from what he had seen of
Orion's own autobiography, and because he
did not know how highly Orion was esteemed
in Keokuk, he provoked a lively controversy;
the result was a tempering of his portrayal
of Orion in the biography of MT.

B39 ____. "A Reply to Mr. Clemens," American
     Literature, XVI (March), 32-34.
        After comparing Cyril Clemens's edition of
     Republican Letters with photostats of the
     letters as they appeared in the Chicago Re-
     publican, Lorch says the book has only three
     of the original six and these suffer either
     from careless transcription or from altera-
     tion. "I am quite willing to accept Mr.
     Clemens's statement that he got his material
     'directly from the files of the Chicago Re-
     publican,' but his letters are not true
     copies of Mark Twain's letters; and by edit-
     ing them to the point of mutilation he has
     performed a distinct disservice."

B40 MacBRIDE, VAN DYK. "Captain Absalom Grimes--
     The Confederate Mail Carrier," The Stamp
     Specialist (New York), Maroon Book [the
     designation of the issue within a year],
     106-14.
        Describes James Bradley's The Confederate
     Mail Carrier (Mexico, Missouri: n.p.,
     1894), which gives a more flamboyant account
     of Grimes's adventures than appears in the
     1926 version edited by M. M. Quaife (See
     1944.B44); apparently the Bradley version
     does not mention MT's brief Civil War ser-
     vice. (Discussed by M. M. Quaife in "Mark
     Twain's Military Career," below.)

B41 MAYBERRY, GEORGE. "Reading and Writing,"
     New Republic, CX (May 1), 608.
        The language in the circus episode in HF
     typifies "a kind of writing no means exclu-
     sively American, but marked in modern Amer-
     ican writing at its best. Its apparent
     artlessness, emphasized by Huck's grammati-
     cal lapses and broad boy's dialect, conceals
     a structure that, if of a somewhat simpler
     order, is as consciously controlled as the
     grandiloquent prose architecture of the
     eighteenth century. It is prose that su-
     perbly fulfills its function." Hemingway
     and Sherwood Anderson have acknowledged
     their debt to MT, and the functional prose
     is also evident in Fitzgerald, Dos Passos,
     Faulkner, and Caldwell.

B42 ORCUTT, WILLIAM DANA. "From My Library
     Walls," Christian Science Monitor, XXXVI
     (November 17), 11.
        Contains an anecdote George Washington
     Cable told him about MT's response to noisy
     steam pipes while he was lecturing: "'Will
     someone in the audience,' he shouted, 'kind-
     ly go down in the basement and ask that jan-
     itor to stop gnashing his teeth?' From
     that moment, Cable concluded, Twain had the
     audience completely with him."

B43 QUAIFE, M. M. "George in Historyland," Twain-
     ian, n.s., III (January), 5-6.
        The "George" referred to is Brownell;
     Quaife questions his reference to The Penn-
     sylvania Magazine of History and Biography
     as an "obscure" publication in his article
     in the November, 1943 Twainian, "Mark
     Twain's Tribute to Francis Lightfoot Lee";
     Quaife gives no new information on MT here.
     In an introductory comment ("Dr. Quaife
     Corrects Our Remarks on Penn. Mag.")
     Brownell notes that "The Twainian has lat-
     terly become a one-man mouthpiece," as he
     recently said, with regret, in a letter to
     Quaife; this statement would support the
     attribution of unsigned material to Brown-
     ell in the present bibliography.

B44 _____. "Mark Twain's Military Career,"
     Twainian, n.s., III (June), 4-7.
        On the differing accounts in MT's "The
     Private History of a Campaign that Failed"
     and in Absalom Grimes, Confederate Mail
     Runner (Quaife, ed., 1926). Further doubt
     is cast on the Grimes account by the recent
     discovery of another treatment of his ad-
     ventures by James Bradley, in The Confeder-
     ate Mail Carrier, or, From Missouri to Ar-
     kansas, through Mississippi, Alabama,
     Georgia, and Tennessee. An Unwritten Leaf
     of the "Civil War." Being an account of
     the Battles, Marches, and Hardships of the
     First and Second Brigades, Mos. C. S. A.
     Together with the Thrilling Adventures and
     Narrow Escapes of Captain Grimes and his
     Fair Accomplice, who carried the Mail by
     "the Underground Route" from the Brigade to
     Missouri (Mexico, Missouri, 1894). Quaife
     indicates his debt to a discussion of the
     two books on Grimes in Van Dyk MacBride's
     "Absalom Grimes the Confederate Mail Carri-
     er," in The Stamp Specialist (See 1944.B40).

B45 RAYFORD, JULIAN LEE. "The Jumping Frog Jubi-
     lee," American Mercury, LIX (November),
     583-88.
        About the friendliness of the people at
     the 1929 jubilee at Angel's Camp; very
     little about MT.

B46 SHAW, BERNARD. "G. B. S.," Saturday Review
     of Literature, XXVII (August 12), 15.
        Excerpt from a letter to Cyril Clemens
     on meetings with MT.

B47 *WAGENKNECHT, EDWARD. [Introduction.] Life
     on the Mississippi, with...a number of pre-
     viously suppressed passages now printed for
     the first time, and with a note by Willis
     Wager. New York: The Limited Editions
     Club.
        [Source: Asselineau (1954), No. 990.]

B48 WEATHERLY, EDWARD H. "Beau Tibbs and Colonel
     Sellers," Modern Language Notes, LIX (May),
     310-13.

Beau Tibbs in Goldsmith's A Citizen of the
World and Colonel Sellers in The Gilded Age
show "striking parallelism...in scenes in
which each explains away an obviously cheap
and unappetizing dinner to which an unexpected guest has come."

B49 WEBSTER, SAMUEL CHARLES, ed. "Mark Twain,
     Business Man: Letters and Memoirs," Atlan-
     tic Monthly, CLXXIII (June), 37-46; CLXXIV
     (July), 72-80; (August), 71-77; (September),
     90-96; (October), 74-80; (November),
     100-106.
        Family and business correspondence, much
     of it to Charles L. Webster, who had married
     MT's niece, Annie Moffett; edited by Charles
     L. Webster's son. [Published as a book,
     1946.A6.]

B50 WEGELIN, CHRISTOF. [Review: Günter Möhle,
     Das Europabild Mark Twains (1940).] Ameri-
     can Literature, XVI (November), 255-56.
        "Dr. Möhle proposes to illustrate 'Ameri-
     can development and mentality' by comparing
     the attitudes toward England" of Irving,
     Hawthorne, and MT; the extent to which this
     is a study of the first two is unclear.
     Möhle has read comparatively little in his
     three authors: for MT, "The Innocents
     Abroad, A Connecticut Yankee, and a few
     passages from the letters and notebooks,"
     and he follows Turner to excess. "Möhle's
     contribution to scholarship is slight," but
     his book will give German readers a better
     understanding of MT and the American mind.

B51 WHITING, B. J. "Guyuscutus, Royal Nonesuch
     and Other Hoaxes," Southern Folklore Quar-
     terly, VIII (December), 251-75.
        A general discussion of practical jokes
     in the old Southwest, with some space de-
     voted to several "Guyuscutus" monster hoaxes
     and a brief discussion of the connection to
     HF.

1945 A BOOKS

A1 LILJEGREN, S[TEN] B[ODVAR]. The Revolt
     against Romanticism in American Literature
     as Evidenced in the Works of S. L. Clemens.
     Upsala: A. B. Lundequista Bokhandeln.
     [Also in Studia Neophilologica, XVII,
     207-58, according to Asselineau (1954),
     No. 1049; his No. 1094 lists a 1947 publi-
     cation, Upsala: Essays and Studies on Amer-
     ican Language and Literature. Publications
     of the American Institute of the University
     of Upsala, No. 1 (Confirmed in British Mu-
     seum Catalogue); also, reprinted, New York:
     Haskell House, 1964.]
        After a discussion of the neglect of Amer-
     ican literature by the European academic
     community, Liljegren defends MT as better
     read, more cultured and refined than his de-
     tractors will admit. As evidence of MT's
     attack on romanticism, cites his parodies of
     Gothic novels in the Weekly Occidental, and

(LILJEGREN, S[TEN] B[ODVAR])
of Longfellow's "Wreck of the Hesperus,"
Thomas Moore's "Those Evening Bells," etc.
Also briefly comments on MT's criticism of
Fenimore Cooper and Sir Walter Scott. [64-
page pamphlet, including the texts of some
of MT's parodies and the originals on which
they are based.]

A2   RODNEY, ROBERT M. Mark Twain in England: A
Study of the English Criticism of and Attitude toward Mark Twain: 1867-1940.
Unpublished Doctoral Dissertation, University of Wisconsin. The evaluations and
the bibliography in this dissertation have
been of great value in tracing material for
the present bibliography.

A3   *ROESSEL, JAMES. Mark Twain, en odölig humorist. Stockholm: Lindfors.
[Source: Asselineau (1954), No. 1021.]

1945 B SHORTER WRITINGS

B1   A., P. B. "Clemens'...Huckleberry Finn," Explicator, IV (November), Q. 7.
In Mark Twain at Work, p. 54, DeVoto says
MT disregards the fact that Jim could have
reached free soil by crossing the river to
Illinois; can any reader comment? [Answered
by DeLancey Ferguson in April, 1946 Explicator.]

B2   ADAMS, J. DONALD. "Speaking of Books," New
York Times Book Review.
June 17, p. 2: On rereading IA, he finds
the humor labored in the European portion,
better in the part on the Holy Land because
reading the Bible had made Palestine real
to MT. June 24, p. 2: TA reflects "a
much better adjustment to the European
scene" than does IA, but "it was not as a
writer of travel books that Mark Twain will
be remembered," and FE "was not good."

B3   ANON. "Mark and Baseball," Mark Twain Quarterly, VI (Winter-Spring), 12.
Text of a "St. Louis Post-Dispatch special dispatch from Bermuda, dated March 8,
1908," on MT at a baseball game.

B4   ARMSTRONG, C. J. "Sam Clemens Considered Becoming a Preacher," Twainian, IV (May), 1.
Reprinted from The Christian, June 13, 1931.
Conventional speculations, based on a
statement in the Paine biography that both
Orion and Sam Clemens had considered entering the ministry, and speculating on what
sort of minister Sam would have made, with
his lack of orthodoxy, but also with his
courage, compassion, humor, and love of
truth.

B5   BLANCK, JACOB. "News from the Rare Book
Sellers," Publishers' Weekly, CXLVIII
(August 18), 620-21.

On the recent publication by Manuscript
House of MT's A Murder, A Mystery, and A
Marriage in an edition limited to sixteen
copies, two of them deposited for copyright.

B6   [BROWNELL, GEORGE HIRAM.] "About the Origin
of that 'Weather' Epigram," Twainian, IV
(June), 4.
Although it has been suggested that the
famous saying may have originated in an
editorial by Charles Dudley Warner, the
editorial has not been found and thus the
question of who said it remains open--but it
is characteristically Twainian.

B7   _____. "Did Twain Write 'The Wrong Ashes?'"
Twainian, IV (April), 2-4.
Contains text of a macabre story in which
a man kept an urn of ashes for several years
before finding they were those of a mule,
rather than of his wife.

B8   _____. "Here's Latest News about that Great
Land-Slide Case," Twainian, IV (March),
3-4.
Corrects an erroneous statement in May,
1944 Twainian, according to which an MT
piece in the San Francisco Morning Call
later showed up in TA: actually used in RI.
Also quotes a letter from Frank C. Willson,
who has found in Nevada Reports (1865) an
account of an actual landslide case in which
the Supreme Court upheld a lower court decision that the value of a buried piece of
land was less than the cost of removing the
transplanted earth which covered it. Oliver
Barrett looked up the case and "found that
the opinion related merely to the method of
determining the amount of damages sustained
(letter, "Why Mark Twain Registered His
Name as a 'Trade Mark,'" Twainian, May, 3-4).
Also see brief note in Twainian, IX
(January-February, 1950), on a published account of the landslide case in a book of
humor in the legal profession, 1871.

B9   _____. "Mark Twain Launched the Chicago Press
Club of which George Ade Later Became a
Member," Twainian, IV (March), 1-2.
Quotes an MT letter from William H. Free-
man's The Press Club of Chicago (Chicago:
The Press Club of Chicago, 1894), declining
an invitation to visit the club (Hartford,
December 29, 1880), and passage on MT's
participation in the founding; brief adden-
dum, p. 4.

B10 _____. "Mark Twain Tells of the Daring Deed
of Professor Jenkins and His Velocipede,"
Twainian, IV (February), 1-4.
On a Canadian who crossed Niagara Falls.
Includes the following, which appeared in
the Buffalo Express, August 26 and
September 9, 1869, attributed by Brownell to
MT: "Prof. Jenkins," an unsigned news ac-
count ("with a few excisions of unimportant

([BROWNELL, GEORGE HIRAM])
text"); "In Trouble," supposedly a telegram
from an Express reporter named Michael J.
Murphy who tried to follow Jenkins but ended up stuck on the middle of the rope;
"Mark Twain in a Fix," attributing the Murphy telegram to MT (reprinted from Rochester Express by Buffalo Express; unsigned,
but "thoroughly Twainesque in its style").
Also see "More of Prof. Jenkins and his
Velocipede," March.

B11 _____. "More of Prof. Jenkins and his Veloci-
pede," Twainian, IV (March), 4.
Thomas Ollive Mabbott reports Brownell
guessed wrongly that there had never been
a Rochester (N.Y.) Express in his article,
"Mark Twain Tells of the Daring Deed of
Professor Jenkins and His Velocipede,"
Twainian, February.

B12 _____. "No Mystery Now about 'A Mystery
Cleared Up,'" Twainian, IV (May), 1-2.
The text of an interview with ex-Secretary
Stanton and Secretary Fish on the most ef-
fective means for removing warts; attributed
to MT in Wood's Household Magazine, October,
1869 (and listed in the 1935 Merle Johnson
Bibliography of MT).

B13 _____. "A Tale of Twain's Shipboard Poem,
'Good-Bye' or 'The Parting of the Ships,'"
Twainian, IV (June), 1-2.
On a poem MT wrote during the Quaker City
voyage, with the encouragement of Mrs. Solon
L. Severance; printed here with the title
"Good Bye," but listed in the 1935 Merle
Johnson Bibliography as "The Parting of the
Ships." Brownell cites a first publication
in the Cleveland Plain Dealer in 1910, and
a partial reprinting in Current Literature
(1935).

B14 _____. "That First Issue Point on Page 283
of 'Huck,'" Twainian, IV (May), 4.
A tipped-in p. 283 [replacing the mutilated "Who Do You Reckon It Is?" illustra-
tion--T.A.T.] has long been recognized as
characterizing a first-issue copy; for a
time it had been thought that this characterized the whole first edition of 30,000
copies.

B15 _____. "Twain Bibliography Owes Much to Rev.
C. J. Armstrong," Twainian, IV (April), 4.
A tribute to Armstrong, who located early
files of the Hannibal Journal containing
contributions by young Sam Clemens; he also
located a single copy of a St. Louis temperance periodical, The Saturday Evening Post;
although this contains nothing by SLC and
no other copies have been found, it ends
speculation that his statement of publishing an article or two (circa 1851) refers
to the Philadelphia journal.

B16 _____. "Twain Couldn't Take that Word 'Bogus,'" Twainian, IV (February), 4.
On the uncomplimentary connotations of the
word, as MT would see it from a printer's
view; this would explain the vindictive tone
of his letter to Thomas B. Kirby reprinted
in the January Twainian.

B17 _____. "Twain Writings Still Increase in Val-
ue," Twainian, IV (May), 2-3.
On recent Parke-Bernet auction prices of
MT manuscripts and first editions: The
Stolen White Elephant, $2,500; "On the Decay
of the Art of Lying," $400; "The Regular
Toast. Woman--God Bless Her" (delivered be-
fore the New England Society of New York,
December 23, 1882), $375; "At the Shrine of
St. Wagner," $850; "From the London 'Times'
of 1904," $875; "The Invalid's Story," $575;
"Legend of Sagenfeld, in Germany," $450; "A
Murder, A Mystery, and A Marriage," $1250;
three partial or complete chapters of A
Tramp Abroad, $250, $225, $200; "The Death-
Disk," $375; a freak copy of The Jumping
Frog with p. 198 blank, $425 (another copy
was offered by a dealer in 1932 for $25); a
fine first-issue TS sold for $950, and a fine
fine first-issue HF, with MT autograph to
U. S. Grant, Jr. and with the latter's book-
plate, $1050.

B18 _____. "Why Mark Twain Registered His Name as
a 'Trade Mark,'" Twainian, IV (April), 3-4.
On MT's problems with pirates using his
name, and his eventual solution; contains
text of a letter from Oliver R. Barrett,
who looked up details of "Clemens v. Belford,
Clarke & Co.," 14 Federal Reporter 728
(1883).

B19 CESTRE, CHARLES. La Littérature Américaine.
Paris: Librairie Armand Colin. There is
now a third ed. (1957), apparently unrevised;
pp. 103-106 on MT.
A short general study. The portion on MT
is a biographical summary, followed by brief,
conventional accounts of some of his books,
pointing to TS as his great work and HF as
comic and a valuable picture of its time.
CY displeased some readers, but its criticism of the age is not unjustified and the
anachronisms are amusing. Notes the serious
side of MT beneath the humor.

B20 *CLEMENS, CYRIL. "An Incident in Mark Twain's
Life," Slant, II (February), 7.
[Source: Leary (1954), p. 47.]

B21 _____. "F. D. Roosevelt and Mark Twain," Dalhousie Review, XXV (October), 339-41.
Describes a visit to the White House to
present the Mark Twain Gold Medal to the
President, who said that by 1900 he had read
all of MT's works then in print, and that
he took the phrase "New Deal" from CY.

B22 ____. "Mark Twain's Ancestry," Mark Twain Quarterly, VII (Winter-Spring), 8, 24.
    On some of MT's remote ancestors and his more immediate ones, with sparse documentation.

B23 ____. "Mark Twain's Exaggerated Death," Rotarian, LXVII (August), 58-59.
    Notes distorted accounts by Paine, Alexander Woolcott, and others. "Since so many different versions of the origin of this famous saying have appeared, it is high time to put on record the correct version"; a note MT wrote out for Frank Marshall White, London reporter for the New York Journal, is reproduced in facsimile.

B24 ____. "New Light on Mark Twain's Virginia Ancestors," Hobbies--The Magazine for Collectors, L (April), 104-105.
    Quotes the marriage agreement of MT's grandparents, Pamelia [sic] Goggin and Samuel Clemens, and gives other details of family history.

B25 * ____. "They Knew Mark Twain," Hobbies, L (September), 106-108.
    [Source: Asselineau (1954), No. 1035: "'They' i.e. Shaw, Helen Keller, etc."]

B26 ____. "Winston Churchill and Mark Twain," Dalhousie Review, XXIV (January), 402-405.
    An article which appeared in Hobbies--The Magazine for Collectors in 1944, with no indication of the earlier appearance.

B27 CLEMENS, SAMUEL L. "Mark on Boys," Mark Twain Quarterly, VI (Winter-Spring), 24.
    A paragraph from "an unpublished letter written by Mark Twain" (n.d.) on his reluctance to drive away some neighborhood boys who have been a nuisance.

B28 ____. "Mark's Letter to Mrs. James Ross Clemens," Mark Twain Quarterly, VI (Winter-Spring), 12.
    The text of a note from Olivia Clemens ("Hotel Krantz, Vienna, March 29, 1899") to Miss Boland, congratulating her on her engagement and adding that she considers "the marrying a Clemens the very best and happiest thing I ever did!" MT adds in a postscript that he has never married one himself, but "less particular people have taken the risk and found them well enough as a change.... I like my relative Jim very much, and as a Clemens he averages away up."

B29 ____. "Three Mark Twain Letters," Mark Twain Quarterly, VII (Summer-Fall), 24.
    Notes to [R. U.] Johnson (Hartford, March 18, and Elmira, July 28, September 8, 1885) on "that war paper" for the Century War Series; the article is not going well. [Presumably, this was "The Private History of a Campaign That Failed"--T.A.T.]

B30 ____. "Twain is 'Out of Soap,'" Mark Twain Quarterly, VII (Summer-Fall), 14.
    Text of an MT note ("Hartford, Jan. 25, 1887") to an unnamed recipient, in payment of two railroad fares from New York to Hartford.

B31 ____. "Twain to R. U. Johnson," Mark Twain Quarterly, VI (Winter-Spring), 23.
    Text of a letter ("Elmira, N.Y., Aug. 15, 1889") on "the photograph matter" and "my war article" for the Century. [Presumably the "war article" was "The Private History of a Campaign that Failed"--T.A.T.]

B32 ____. "Unpublished Letters to Dan Beard," Mark Twain Quarterly, VII (Winter-Spring), 22.
    The first, datelined "Elmira, N.Y., Aug. 28, '89," praises Beard's illustrations for A Connecticut Yankee, with particular attention to the King ("both face and figure are noble and gracious"), the "soft young grace and beauty" of Guinevere, and the Yankee himself. A letter dated December 20, 1889, to an unnamed person, expresses satisfaction with the illustrations and refers questions concerning them to Beard, who "illustrated the book throughout without requiring or needing anybody's suggestions... I merely approved of the pictures--and very heartily, too, the slave-driver along with the rest." [The slave-driver has the features of Jay Gould--T.A.T.] A letter to Beard datelined "Riverdale On The Hudson, Dec. 12, '02" agrees that "it is never too late to say the kindly word," adding that "you have done great work in great causes, and I have walked by your side."

B33 COWLEY, MALCOLM. "The Middle American Style: D. Crockett to E. Hemingway," New York Times Book Review (July 15), pp. 3, 14.
    There is a new, distinctively American style, first used seriously and at length in HF, and thereafter by Hemingway, Gertrude Stein, John Hersey, and others. It is characterized by its repetitions, flat statements about emotional response, simple diction, loose sentence structure, use of intensifying adverbs, often an excessive use of present participles to give the effect of continuing action, and the avoidance of abstract nouns.

B34 DEVOTO, BERNARD. "Mr. DeVoto Explains as to Use of the Name 'Mark Twain,'" Twainian, IV (June), 2.
    A letter from DeVoto explains that the pen-name has been registered as a protection against misuse of the name, and the Mark Twain Company regards even material on which copyright has expired as protected to the extent that it may be published with the name "Samuel L. Clemens" as author, but not "Mark Twain."

B35   FARRELL, JAMES T. "Mark Twain's Huckleberry
      Finn and Tom Sawyer," in his The League of
      Frightened Philistines and Other Papers
      (New York: The Vanguard Press), pp. 25-30.
         MT has been misunderstood, particularly
      by Lewis Mumford (in The Golden Day) and
      Van Wyck Brooks. He had a healthy sense of
      justice despite his cynicism. Tom and Huck
      can rise above MT's discouragement because
      they are boys, and Huck is "an ideal expres-
      sion of the positive side of Mark Twain."
      Today the boys "stand as a test not only of
      ourselves but of the whole of American so-
      ciety," asking why the promise has not been
      realized. Reprinted in Lettis (1962),
      pp. 321-25.

B36   FEINSTEIN, GEORGE. "Mark Twain's Regionalism
      in Fiction," Mark Twain Quarterly, VII
      (Winter-Spring), 7, 24.
         On MT's insistence that a culture or a
      dialect cannot be accurately represented
      without intimate familiarity, and that the
      national culture is too diversified to be
      described in a single novel.

B37   GIBSON, CHARLES HAMMOND. "My Last Impression
      of Mark Twain," Mark Twain Quarterly, VII
      (Winter-Spring), 5-6.
         On MT's address at the dedication of the
      Thomas Bailey Aldrich Memorial at Ports-
      mouth, New Hampshire.

B38   GILDER, RODMAN. "Rodman Gilder Writes That
      One of Those Two Twain Tales is a Forgery,"
      Twainian, IV (January), 4.
         Of two tales attributed to MT in clippings
      of uncertain provenance, reprinted in Twain-
      ian, IV (December, 1944), 1-5; accepts "The
      Revised Catechism" as "entirely Twainesque,"
      but "The Last Stamp" clipping indicates a
      date of composition (1872) when MT would
      not have had time for trivia.

B39   GRANGER, EUGENIE. "Mark Twain Versus Publici-
      ty," Mark Twain Quarterly, VII (Winter-
      Spring), 10.
         Anecdotes told by Robert Sherwood, on MT
      criticized for smoking his pipe while lec-
      turing before a university audience in New
      York and on his successful bid for publici-
      ty in London by appearing publicly in his
      bathrobe and boots, smoking a big cigar.

B40   GUEST, BOYD. "Twain's Concept of Woman's
      Sphere," Mark Twain Quarterly, VII (Winter-
      Spring), 1-4.
         MT's works and public statements reflect
      his western chivalry and his belief in
      women's rights, including the right to vote.

B41   HALL, DON E. "A Mark Twain Sales Tip," Mark
      Twain Quarterly, VII (Winter-Spring), 9.
         An anecdote, without corroborative de-
      tails, of MT's wearing out a book agent by
      inviting him to stay for dinner and for the
      night.

B42   HEMMINGHAUS, EDGAR H. "Mark Twain's German
      Provenience," Modern Language Quarterly,
      VI (December), 459-78.
         "Mark Twain's approach to the Germans,
      their language, and their literature was un-
      questionably one of great amicability and
      affectionate admiration." Hemminghaus re-
      lies largely on American sources concerning
      MT; for German views of MT, see his 1939
      book.

B43   HIFT, FRED W. "Radio in the Soviet," New York
      Times (September 2), p. 5.
         Reports that the Russian radio features
      "whole evenings of readings from Mark Twain,
      de Maupassant, and Chekov. These are espe-
      cially popular with Russian listeners because
      of the acute shortage of books."

B44   HORNBERGER, THEODORE. [Brief Review: Cyril
      Clemens, Young Sam Clemens.] American Lit-
      erature, XVII (March), 102.
         "It consists largely of a stream of sto-
      ries and anecdotes about Mark Twain, picked
      up by Mr. Cyril Clemens in the course of
      his indefatigable pursuit of Mark Twain.
      Because Mr. Clemens has visited many of the
      places where Mark Twain lived, and talked
      with people who knew Mark Twain, his anec-
      dotes are often fresh and amusing."

B45   KINNAIRD, CLARK. "Mark Twain's First Book,"
      American Mercury, LX (January), 124.
         A letter to the editor, giving a brief
      biographical sketch of Charles Henry Webb,
      "the man responsible for putting the Jumping
      Frog between book covers."

B46   LEDERER, MAX. "Mark Twain in Vienna," Mark
      Twain Quarterly, VII (Summer-Fall), 1-12.
         An extensive account of MT's stay there,
      September, 1897-May, 1899, supported by
      references to local news stories.

B47   LORCH, FRED W. "Mark Twain's Early Views on
      Western Indians," Twainian, IV (April), 1-2.
         The representation of the Goshoot Indians
      in RI reflects Nevada attitudes of the time,
      rather than careful observation or MT's
      later compassion for human suffering.

B48   O'LIAM, DUGAL. "They're Off at Angel's Camp,"
      Collier's, CXV (May 5), 21, 41.
         On the annual Jumping Frog Jubilee of Cal-
      averas County, illustrated with a cartoon of
      the jubilee and two excellent photographs of
      modern frogs.

B49   STARRETT, VINCENT. "Some Anecdotes and Fair
      Words from an Old-time Well Wisher," Twain-
      ian, IV (January), 1-2.
         Reprints two MT anecdotes from Lincoln
      Springfield's Some Piquant People (1924) and
      several reminiscences of MT in Douglas Slad-
      en's Twenty Years of My Life (date unknown).
      Barr tells of MT expressing pleasure in
      "the fact that Darwin, for a year before

(STARRETT, VINCENT)
his death, read nothing but his works. Darwin's doctors, he added, had warned him he
would get softening of the brain if he read
anything but absolute drivel."

B50   WECTER, DIXON. "Mark Twain and the West,"
Huntington Library Quarterly, VIII (August),
359-77.
The text of "An address delivered at the
Huntington Library on Founder's Day,
February 26, 1945," this is a popular ac-
count, largely biographical, for a lay au-
dience.

B51   WILLSON, FRANK C. "Mark Twain on the Old-
Fashioned Spelling-Bee," Twainian, IV
(March), 2-3.
Includes the text of an MT speech which
Brownell found in The Trumpet, I (February,
1892) an obscure journal published in New
York by Albert S. King. George Hiram Brown-
ell confirms Willson's surmise that the
speech first appeared in a Hartford paper,
and lists other printings.

B52   _____. "Twain Spanks a Government Official
for Unofficial Impertinence," Twainian, IV
(January), 2-4.
Contains the text of a letter to MT and
two letters by him, a mock-serious dispute
with Thomas B. Kirby, Private Secretary to
the Postmaster General. Willson found the
letters in Gus Williams' World of Humor
(New York: The DeWitt Publishing Company,
1880, pp. 93-95), as reprinted from the
Hartford Courant, the last of them apparently in early December, 1879. There is further comment on the use by Kirby of the
word "Bogus," and MT's response, in the
February Twainian. The MT letter to the
Courant which began the controversy appears
in Twainian, IV (March-April, 1947), 3-4.

B53   _____. "Twain Tells How to Remove Warts and
Tattoo Marks," Twainian, IV (June), 3-4.
Text of a letter to the editor of the New
York Sun (date unknown); MT states that he
removed his warts with a heated needle, and
had an anchor and rope tattooed on the back
of his left hand when he was sixteen, but
removed it nine years later as he had removed the warts.

B54   WOOLF, S. J. "How S. J. Woolf Made His Two
Portraits of Twain," Twainian, IV (June),
4.
In the course of painting MT's portrait
in 1906, Woolf made a pencil sketch one day
and later used it as the basis for a litho-
graph in late 1919 or early 1920.

1946 A BOOKS

A1   *CLEMENS, SAMUEL L. ¿Qué es el Hombre? Con una
introducción de S. K. Ratcliffe. Barcelona:
Editorial Delfos.
[What Is Man? Source: Asselineau (1954),
No. 1062.]

A2   DEVOTO, BERNARD, ed. The Portable Mark Twain.
New York: The Viking Press.
An anthology including the complete texts
of HF and MS and judicious selections from
other works, as well as a number of MT's
letters, and a valuable 34-page introduction. Still in print. Pp. 33-34, on HF,
are reprinted in Gerber (1971), p. 42.

A3   *HARNSBERGER, CAROLINE THOMAS. Mark Twain at
Your Fingertips. Chicago: Cloud, Inc.
[Source: MHRA Annual Bibliography (1946),
No. 1800; this anticipates the more familiar
1948 publication, See 1948.A2.]

A4   LEISY, ERNEST E., ed. The Letters of Quintus
Curtius Snodgrass. Dallas: Southern Methodist University Press.
A series of ten letters in the New Orleans
Daily Crescent (January-March, 1861) attributed to MT by Leisy, who credits Minnie M.
Brashear with the discovery of the first
four, as noted in Mark Twain: Son of Missouri (1934). The attribution of the letters to MT is disputed by Brinegar
(1963.B11) and discredited by Bates
(1964.B13).

A5   PELLOWE, WILLIAM C. S. Mark Twain: Pilgrim
from Hannibal. New York: The Hobson Book
Press.
About MT's inner life, with emphasis on
religion. Concludes with "An Epilogue" by
Cyril Clemens, whom Pellowe thanks for help
which included "suggestions on arrangement
of manuscript" (p. 273).

A6   WEBSTER, SAMUEL CHARLES. Mark Twain, Business
Man. Boston: Little, Brown and Company.
An Atlantic Monthly Press Book.
In part this book represents a son's defence of his father, Charles L. Webster,
MT's associate in a publishing company which
ended in bankruptcy. Webster makes a good
case for his father, but documents carefully
and does not overstate his case. The result
is an important contribution to MT biography.
Includes many MT letters (some of which Webster published in Atlantic Monthly in 1944
(See 1944.B49).

1946 B SHORTER WRITINGS

B1   ADAMS, J. DONALD. "Speaking of Books," New
York Times Book Review (March 17), p. 2.

(ADAMS, J. DONALD)
    Comments briefly on the charm of TS and
HF, and notes with pleasure that in the
preface to the Everyman's Library edition
Christopher Morley tells of a 1938 visit to
Hannibal, where he and some friends white-
washed Tom Sawyer's fence as an act of homage.

B2   ANON. "Dear Charley," Time, XLVII
      (February 11), 100-104.
    A review of Samuel Charles Webster, Mark
Twain, Business Man; largely descriptive,
citing examples of MT's poor business judgment and quoting his unreasonable demands
on the author's father, Charles L. Webster.

B3   BIDEWELL, GEORGE IVAN. "Mark Twain's Florida
      Years," Missouri Historical Review, XL
      (January), 159-73.
    On the influence of life in Florida, Mis-
souri, before the Clemens family moved to
Hannibal and during the summers of 1840-1846
the boy spent there on the farm of his uncle John A. Quarles. Through parallel passages from the Paine biography and HF, argues that the Quarles farm was the model
for the Silas Phelps farm in HF.

B4   BRANCH, EDGAR M. A Chronological Bibliog-
      raphy of the Writings of Samuel Clemens to
      June 8, 1867," American Literature, XVIII
      (May), 109-57.
    "All entries are grouped chronologically,
both under the year of writing and under
seven divisions which correspond to the
seven major regions of Clemens's literary
and professional activity during this period: (1) Hannibal, (2) the East and Midwest, (3) the Mississippi River, (4) Washoe, (5) California, (6) the Sandwich
Islands, and (7) New York City." "The
check list records, so far as the facts are
known to the compiler, four types of information: (1) the title of original publication, (2) relevant information supplied
by the compiler, (3) the place and date of
original publication, and (4) the most
generally accessible reprint."

B5   [BROWNELL, GEORGE HIRAM.] "The After-Dinner
      Speaker's Best Friend: 'Mark Twain's Pat-
      ent Adjustable Speech,'" Twainian, V
      (January-February), 1-3.
    The text of "an address by Mark Twain on
Forefathers' Day, Dec. 20, 1887, before the
Boston Congregational Club," according to
an unidentified clipping found by Frank C.
Willson in a scrapbook.

B6   _____. "'Mark Twain, Business Man,'" Twain-
      ian, V (March-April), 4.
    A favorable review of the book by Samuel
Charles Webster.

B7   _____. "Maybe this Explains Why Mark Left
      Nevada," Twainian, V (September-October),
      2-3.
    Quotes an MT letter from Carson City in
the San Francisco Morning Call (November 19,
1863): under the second article of the Nevada constitution, then being debated, former
Confederate soldiers and civil officers
would be disenfranchised. Brownell accepts
the "Quintus Curtius Snodgrass" letters as
genuine, and therefore as evidence that MT's
Confederate service was more extensive than
his brief period as an irregular in Missouri.

B8   _____. "Some Remarks on the 'Letter from the
      Recording Angel,'" Twainian, V (March-April),
      3.
    "He goes after Andrew so bitterly and min-
utely...that one is forced to the conclusion
that the entire writing was a practice piece,
the model from which he planned later to extract material for a writing of impersonal
nature."

B9   _____. "Those 'Poems' by Twain in 'The Wasp'
      of San Francisco," Twainian, V (July-August),
      3-4.
    Contains "Ye Equinoctial Storm" and "Trop-
ic Chidings," (airs of "Auld Lang Syne" and
"Say Hast Thou No Feeling"), composed by
MT on the Montana, when he sailed from San
Francisco en route to New York (via Panama)
in 1868. These poems were in the possession
of Philip Shirley, published with his brief
comment as "Some Verses by Mark Twain" in
The Wasp (the first colored cartoon paper
in America), January 19, 1884.

B10   _____. "Twain Refuses Offer of a Box of
      (Good) Cigars," Twainian, V (November-Decem-
      ber), 3-4.
    Contains text of an MT letter to the Rev.
L. M. Powers (November 1, 1905), declining
with thanks his offer of a box of cigars
and stating a preference for cheap ones.

B11   _____. "Two Hitherto Unknown Twain Tales
      Found in New York Tribune," Twainian, V
      (November-December), 1-2.
    Includes the texts of "Concerning General
Grant's Intentions" (datelined Washington,
December 8, 1868--a burlesque interview in
which MT poses a series of unanswered questions) and "Information Wanted" (concerning
MT's queries about George Francis Train;
this appeared in the Tribune for January 22,
1868, and is not to be confused with a piece
of the same title reprinted in Sketches,
New and Old).

B12   _____. "What Do You Know about the Play
      Roughing It?" Twainian, V (May-June), 6.
    On the play produced by Augustin Daly in
1873; full discussion in July-August issue,
1946.B27.

B13 ____. "Whence Came 'Well Done, Good and Faithful Servant,'" Twainian, V (January-February), 3-4.
On the concluding lines in "Riley--Newspaper Correspondent" (Buffalo Express, October 29, 1870; reprinted in Sketches New and Old, 1875); MT also used the joke in a letter from Hawaii to the Sacramento Union (September 6, 1866).

B14 ____. "Why Bibliographers are Just a Bit Daffy," Twainian, V (September-October), 3-4.
On the fruitless search for files of the Territorial Enterprise for the period when MT was connected with it. Apparently promising leads proved disappointing, but Brownell does list files for 1866, 1871, 1874-1892, and 1893-1912, scattered through several libraries.

B15 ____. "'Youths' Companion' Reveals Twain Tales and Advertisement of 'Huck Finn,'" Twainian, V (March-April), 1-3.
"How To Tell a Story" and portions of LOM. Frank C. Willson has found an advertisement for subscription agents for HF; the dates (November 20, 27, December 11, 1884) establish that the prospectus was ready by November 20. This information bears on the mutilation of the cut on p. 283, the discussion of which includes reprinted news stories from the November 29, 1884 New York Tribune ("Tampering with Mark Twain's Book") and Herald ("Mark Twain's Altered Book"); the latter quotes the caption as "What [sic] do you reckon it is?" Also see Twainian, May-June, p. 6.

B16 ____. [Brief Item: Frank C. Willson has acquired 1868-1869 volumes of the Portland (Maine) Transcript, containing a report of MT's Sandwich Islands lecture in Portland (December 30, 1869).] Twainian, V (January-February), 4.

B17 CARGILL, OSCAR. "The Ordeal of Van Wyck Brooks," College English, VIII (November), 55-61.
Only briefly mentions MT: the Brooks thesis concerning him is still not generally accepted.

B18 CASH, THELMA. "Mark Twain Goes West," Poet Lore, LII (Autumn), 256-60.
A short, vivid, popular account based on Roughing It, Paine, and DeVoto.

B19 CLEMENS, SAMUEL L. "Letter From the Recording Angel," Harper's, CXCII (February), 106-109.
Text of the previously unpublished sketch, with a headnote by Bernard DeVoto, who comments on the response to this sketch in "The Easy Chair," April, pp. 309-12 (1946.B20).

B20 DEVOTO, BERNARD. "The Easy Chair," Harper's, CXCII (April), 309-12.
MT's "intelligence was not analytical, it was intuitive," and his humor "was only the ambivalence we all share," a way of responding to inner conflict. Comments on "Letter from the Recording Angel."

B21 ____. "The Other Side of Some Mark Twain Stories: His Business Partner Was Also His Errand Boy, Broker, Detective and General Scapegoat," New York Herald Tribune Weekly Book Review (February 10), p. 3.
A review of Samuel Charles Webster, Mark Twain, Business Man, "a valuable addition to Mark Twain literature, vastly amusing to the general reader and indispensible to students," containing "the most detailed and by far the most convincing portrait of Jane Clemens ever written," with useful material on Orion Clemens and the full text of the Madame Caprell letter. The title is misleading, in that the book does not treat all of MT's business affairs but concentrates on publishing, in which MT was difficult to deal with and chiefly responsible for his own failures. Reprinted in Twainian, V (May-June), 3-5.

B22 ____. [Brief headnote to first publication of MT's "Fenimore Cooper's Further Literary Offenses."] New England Quarterly, XIX (September), 291-301.
Superseded in DeVoto, ed., Mark Twain's Letters from the Earth (1962), as "Cooper's Prose Style" (pp. 135-46).

B23 "THE EDITORS" [WALTER PILKINGTON and B. ASTERLUND.] "Mark Twain's Introductory Remarks at the Time of Winston Churchill's First American Lecture," Notes and Queries (New York), V (January), 47-48.
Includes the text of MT's brief remarks as reported in the New York Tribune, December 13, 1900. "It differs measurably from that printed in the 1910 edition of Mark Twain's Speeches. It is not a complete transcript of the speech; the only full version can be found in the unpublished Mark Twain Papers. The New York Times account (December 13, 1900) quotes Clemens only indirectly, except for two lines," a direct quotation of the conclusion, which the Tribune apparently misquoted.

B24 FEINSTEIN, GEORGE. "Mark Twain's Idea of Story Structure," American Literature, XVIII (May), 160-63.
"A tale...must grow organically, from within, or the artificiality will show" (p. 160).

B25 FERGUSON, DELANCEY. "Clemens'...Huckleberry Finn," Explicator, IV (April), Item 42. A reply to P.B.A. in Explicator, IV (November, 1945), Q. 7.

(FERGUSON, DELANCEY)

Jim could not escape directly across the river into Illinois, because he would be quickly captured for a reward; his chances would be better if he entered free territory some distance from where he had escaped.

B26 _____. [Review: Samuel Charles Webster, ed., Mark Twain, Business Man.] American Literature, XVIII (May), 169-70.

Many letters are made public for the first time, and for others the text expurgated by Paine is restored. There is comparatively little new information about SLC's connection with the Webster Publishing Company, although the difficulty of working with Clemens is elaborated. "The real additions and corrections to the record come from the family correspondence, and from the reminiscences of the editor's mother, Annie Moffett Webster.... some of Paine's most romantic details of the humorist's youth suffer a deflation which extends to the conclusions drawn from them by the psychoanalytical critics."

B27 FLACK, FRANK MORGAN. "About the Play Roughing It as Produced by Augustin Daly," Twainian, V (July-August), 1-3.

Includes letters from MT and Howells to Daly, contemporary reviews from the New York Daily Tribune, but chiefly relies on known works on Daly and his theater; the synthesis is useful. The plot of the play "related the elopement of a rich man's daughter with a poor noodle, and the father's pursuit of these fugitives from the metropolis to Simpson's Bar. A few of its situations were seen to be ingeniously constructed, and parts of its texts were smartly written. Its intention appeared to be...farcical. Its attainment was utter puerility."

B28 FLAGG, JAMES MONTGOMERY. Roses and Buckshot. New York: G. P. Putnam's Sons. Anecdotes of MT, pp. 166-70.

On p. 169, tells of MT and Howells listening to Adelina Patti at the opera. "Howells noticed the wicked leer in Mark's eye and questioned him. Mark, heaving a big sigh, said in Howells' ear: 'I would rather sleep with that woman stark naked, than with General Grant in full uniform!'"

B29 FRIEDRICH, JOHN T. "Speaking of Books about Wm. Allen White and Mark Twain," Rotarian, LXVIII (April), 47-48.

On White's Autobiography, and "a very fine and important new book, Samuel Charles Webster's Mark Twain, Business Man," here summarized.

B30 GREEN, ROGER LANCELYN. Andrew Lang: A Critical Biography. With a Short-Title Bibliography of the Works of Andrew Lang. Leicester, England: Edmund Ward, p. 167.

Lang quoted: "I have tried in an ineffective but hearty manner, to praise Mark Twain as one of the greatest of living geniuses (perhaps it is not saying much), who now use the English language." This originally appeared in Lang's "International Girlishness" in Murray's Magazine, October, 1888.

B31 *HAINES, HAROLD H., ed. The Callaghan Mail, 1821-1859. Hannibal, Missouri: n.p.
[Source: Cited by Wecter (1952) on MT's strict father (p. 284, n. 4) and the partially respectable original of Injun Joe (pp. 151, 299).]

B32 HOBEN, JOHN B. "Mark Twain's A Connecticut Yankee: A Genetic Study," American Literature, XVIII (November), 197-218.

Thoroughly documented from published critical and biographical material, this is a substantial work often cited in CY criticism. The study of MT's growing anti-English feeling in the 1870's and 1880's is continued by McKeithan in "More about Mark Twain's War with English Critics of America" (1948).

B33 HOLLENBACH, JOHN W. "Mark Twain, Story-Teller, At Work," College English, VII (March), 303-12.

MT's skill as a raconteur and fondness for the oral form has been generally recognized "for the part it has played in developing the rhythm, vividness, and sense of immediacy of his prose style. Equal recognition should also be given this habit for the part it played in giving his short stories what unity and finish of structure they did have."

B34 HUVSTEDT, S. B. "The Preacher and the Gray Mare," California Folklore Quarterly, V (January), 109-10.

In Chapter XXV of LOM, MT quotes Uncle Mumford on a steamboat calamity resulting from carrying a preacher and a gray mare, and MT adds that he knew of another such case. Huvstedt links the preacher to the Jonah motif, adding that the connection with the gray mare is more difficult to follow and asking whether readers know of California parallels.

B35 *JOHNSON, E. C. [Review: Sten B. Liljegren, The Revolt Against Romanticism in American Literature as Evidenced in the Works of Samuel L. Clemens.] Studia Neophilologica, XIX, 184-87.
[Source: MHRA Annual Bibliography (1946), No. 1804.]

B36 JONES, JOSEPH. "The Duke's Tooth-Powder Racket: A Note on Huckleberry Finn," Modern Language Notes, LXI (November), 468-69.

According to a New York paper, there really were scoundrels who sold a dentrifice that removed the enamel with the tartar. (See HF, Chapter XIX).

B37   LEDERER, MAX. "Einige Bemerkungen zu Adolph Wilbrandts Der Meister von Palmyra," Modern Language Notes, LXI (December), 551-55.
       Notes MT's interest in the play's themes of Faust and transmigration of souls, tracing them to What Is Man? and MS; cites an earlier discussion by Schönemann (1919.B19).

B38   LEISY, ERNEST E. "The Quintus Curtius Snodgrass Letters in the New Orleans Daily Crescent," Twainian, V (September-October), 1-2.
       Contains the text of "Washington Artillery Ball," one of a series of ten letters attributed to MT and now published in book form as The Letters of Quintus Curtius Snodgrass. In a following note George Hiram Brownell chides Leisy for his modest failure to note that he edited the collection and his scholar's reluctance to state firmly that the letters are MT's work. The letter that concluded the series appeared in Twainian, n.s., I (June, 1942), 1-3. According to Brinegar (1963.B11) and Bates (1964.B13), the letters are not by MT.

B39   *LILJEGREN, STEN B. [Review: Bernard DeVoto, Mark Twain at Work (1942) and DeLancey Ferguson, Mark Twain: Man and Legend (1943).] Studia Neophilologica, XIX, 187-88.
       [Source: MHRA Annual Bibliography (1946), No. 1796, 1798.]

B40   LOOMIS, C. GRANT. "Dan De Quille's Mark Twain," Pacific Historical Review, XV (September), 336-47.
       Reprints articles and sketches by William Wright ("Dan De Quille") from the Golden Era and Territorial Enterprise on MT as a room-mate, on his wedding in the East, and on the story of a drunken river pilot who had been recommended by MT as competent-- when sober.

B41   LORCH, FRED W. "Mark Twain's Philadelphia Letters in the Muscatine Journal," American Literature, XVII (January), 348-52.
       These letters, written in December, 1853, owe much to R. A. Smith's Philadelphia As It Is in 1852, but to some extent MT avoided the triteness of Smith's style. Notes publication of these letters by Edgar M. Branch in 1942.

B42   MONKSWELL, LADY MARY. A Victorian Diarist: Later Extracts from the Journals of Mary, Lady Monkswell, 1895-1909. Edited by the Hon. E. C. F. Collier. London: John Murray.
       The entry for Monday, February 15, 1897 describes MT's appearance when he visited her residence with the Poultney Bigelows (p. 23; quoted by Baetzhold [1970.A1], p. 197). A volume of extracts from her diaries for the years 1873-1895 (ed. by the Hon. E. C. F. Collier, London: John Murray, 1944), contains no reference to MT.

B43   NEWTON, JOSEPH FORT. River of Years: An Autobiography. Philadelphia, New York: J. B. Lippincott Company.
       On pp. 89-90, describes MT at a St. Louis Press Club dinner, where he told a story of St. Francis concluding: "We have been happy in the love of God and the glory of His sunlight--that is our sermon for the day." The passage is reprinted in Mark Twain Journal, XV (Winter, 1970-1971), 6.

B44   RANDEL, WILLIAM PEIRCE. Edward Eggleston: Author of "The Hoosier School-Master." Morningside Heights, New York: King's Crown Press, passim.
       Eggleston regarded MT primarily as a humorist (pp. 109, 184, 206). They met on several occasions, including Horace Greeley's sixty-fifth birthday party (p. 131) and in Washington in 1889, lobbying for changes in the copyright laws (p. 186). [Published doctoral dissertation, Columbia University.]

B45   TRILLING, LIONEL. "Mark Twain--A Dominant Genius," New York Times Book Review (February 3), pp. 1, 14.
       A review of Samuel Charles Webster's Mark Twain, Business Man. Notes MT's bullying of Webster's father: "The evidence of the letters cannot prove that there was no reason for Mark Twain to dislike Webster, but only that he was unjust to a man he disliked." MT's business ventures, though disastrous financially, may have provided a diversion, a relaxation beneficial to his writing. Reprinted in Leary (1962), pp. 177-82.

B46   WHITE, BEATRICE. [Brief Review: S. B. Liljegren, The Revolt Against Romanticism in American Literature as Evidenced in the Works of Samuel L. Clemens.] Modern Language Review, XLI (January), 89.
       "The treatment seems to be in part designed for the elementary reader," and the evidence "could, perhaps, have been more convincingly presented."

B47   WILLIAMS, STANLEY T. "Anecdotes About Mark Twain," Yale Review, n.s. XXXV (Summer), 758-60.
       A review of Samuel Charles Webster, Mark Twain, Business Man.
       The book is anecdotal, more valuable for casting light on those around MT than for clarifying his business troubles.

B48   WILLSON, FRANK C. "Twain's Tale, 'The Facts Concerning the Recent Important Resignation,'" Twainian, V (May-June), 1-3.
       One of three MT letters discovered by Willson in the New York Tribune; in this one (datelined Washington, February 9, 1868) MT pretends to have joined a House debate as an ad interim member. In concluding remarks George Hiram Brownell promises publication of the other two letters in future issues.

B49 WOOD, JAMES PLAYSTEAD. "All Out of Step but
     Mark," Saturday Review of Literature, XXIX
     (March 2), 16-17.
         A review of Samuel Charles Webster's Mark
     Twain, Business Man, which shows that MT
     was not justified in his accusations against
     Charles H. Webster, whom he burdened with
     tasks unrelated to the publishing company;
     MT was himself much to blame for the failure
     of the company. The editor shows "quiet
     but shrewd humor" in his "deft and nicely
     pointed insertions of additional informa-
     tion." Reprinted in Twainian, V (May-June),
     5.

B50 WYMAN, MARY A. "A Note on Mark Twain," Col-
     lege English, VII (May), 438-43.
         Edmund Aubrey, the Paladin in JA, and MT
     are alike "in their relationships to early
     companions who exploited their gifts and in
     their magnetism and success as public speak-
     ers." Similarities between them were noted
     in 1921 by Friedrich Schönemann, in "Mark
     Twains Weltanschauung."

1947 A BOOKS

A1   CARPENTER, EDWIN E., JR., comp.; introduction
     by Dixon Wecter. Mark Twain: An Exhibition
     Selected Mainly from the Papers Belonging to
     the Samuel L. Clemens Estate on Deposit in
     the Huntington Library. San Marino, Cali-
     fornia [Huntington Library].
         A catalogue describing the contents of
     fourteen cases containing manuscripts,
     notebooks, books belonging to MT, etc.

A2   *CLEMENS, SAMUEL L. The Adventures of Tom
     Sawyer, Pagine scelte con note di Matilde
     Bargelli. Milan: C. Signorelli.
         [Source: Asselineau (1954), No. 1097.]

A3   FREAR, WALTER FRANCIS. Mark Twain and Hawaii.
     Privately Printed. Chicago: The Lakeside
     Press.
         A very thorough treatment of his four
     months spent in Hawaii in 1865; letters MT
     wrote for the Sacramento Union later were
     incorporated in RI (they are reprinted in
     an appendix). A valuable book.

A4   *LEMONNIER, LÉON. Mark Twain. Paris: A.
     Fayard.
         [Source: Asselineau (1954), No. 1093,
     describing this as a psychological study
     of the man and works, following the Brooks
     interpretation.]

A5   MACK, EFFIE MONA. Mark Twain in Nevada. New
     York and London: Charles Scribner's Sons.
         On MT in his formative years, 1861-1864,
     with samples of his writings and those of
     contemporaries in Nevada.

A6   WRIGHT, WILLIAM ("DAN DE QUILLE"). The Big
     Bonanza: An Authentic Account of the Dis-
     covery, History, and Working of the World-
     Renowned Comstock Lode of Nevada, Including
     the Present Condition of the Various Mines
     Situated Thereon--Sketches of the Prominent
     Men Interested in Them--Incidents and Adven-
     tures Connected with Mining, the Indians,
     and the Country--Amusing Stories, Experien-
     ces, Anecdotes, etc. and a Full Exposition
     of the Production of Pure Silver. Introduc-
     tion by Oscar Lewis. New York: Alfred A.
     Knopf.
         First published Hartford: American Pub-
     lishing Company, 1876; provides useful back-
     ground information on Nevada mining, but
     nothing directly on MT. Wright and MT
     worked together on the Territorial Enter-
     prise in Virginia City, and the book incor-
     porates suggestions by MT. The introduction
     by Oscar Lewis discusses MT's involvement
     and quotes several of his letters.

1947 B SHORTER WRITINGS

B1   ANON. "Much Fresh Mark Twain Material Will Be
     Made Available," Publishers' Weekly, CLI
     (May 10), 2433.
         The Mark Twain Papers have recently been
     transferred from Harvard to the Henry E.
     Huntington Library in San Marino, California
     [and subsequently to the Bancroft Library at
     the University of California, Berkeley--
     T.A.T.]; Dixon Wecter will succeed Bernard
     DeVoto as literary editor of the MT estate.

B2   ANON. "Twain Suppressed, Russian Charges.
     Cites 'Anti-Imperialist' Essays--Editor Here
     Proves They Have Been Published," New York
     Times (July 28), p. 13.
         On the charge by M. Mendelsohn (refuted by
     Bernard DeVoto and by Frederick L. Allen of
     Harper & Brothers) that "In Defense of
     General Funston" and "To the Person Sitting
     in Darkness" had been suppressed.

B3   *BECKER, MAY LAMBERTON. [Introduction.] The
     Adventures of Huckleberry Finn. Cleveland:
     World Publishing Company (Rainbow Classics).
         [Source: Asselineau (1954), No. 1098.]

B4   BERGLER, EDMUND, M.D. "Exceptional Reaction
     to a Joke of Mark Twain," Mark Twain Quar-
     terly, VIII (Winter), 11-12.
         In his "Toast to the Babies" honoring
     General U. S. Grant (1879), "the object of
     attack was obviously hero-worship," as Berg-
     ler explains in Freudian terms; a "shuddering
     silence" then ensued, because MT was also
     touching on "the typical megalomania of the
     adult who conveniently forgets his original
     dependence in early childhood." [Bergler
     does not comment on the triumphant conclu-
     sion of the toast--T.A.T.]

B5   BLANCK, JACOB. "A Best Seller of the 70's,"
     Publishers' Weekly, CLII (July 19), Section
     II, B37.
         A brief and partial summary of Dickinson's
     article on IA, (1947.B27).

B6   BOOTH, BRADFORD. "Mark Twain's Friendship
     with Emeline Beach," American Literature,
     XIX (November), 219-30.
         Emeline was the seventeen-year-old daugh-
     ter of Moses Sperry Beach; the two were
     shipmates of MT on the Quaker City cruise.
     Booth gives us background, commentary, and
     a series of letters from MT to Miss Beach
     while he was writing IA and in later years.

B7   ____. "Mark Twain's Friendship with Emma
     Beach," Mark Twain Quarterly, VIII (Winter),
     4-10.
         The same article as 1947.B6, with no in-
     dication of the fact.

B8   BROOKS, VAN WYCK. The Times of Melville and
     Whitman. New York: E. P. Dutton & Co.,
     Inc., passim on MT (indexed).
         "Mark Twain in the West" (pp. 283-300) ar-
     gues that "Mark Twain with his fathomless
     naivity prepared the ground, as Whitman did,
     for a new and unique American art of let-
     ters, in a negative way with The Innocents
     Abroad, in a positive way with the Western
     writings in which he contributed to estab-
     lish and foster this art." TS, HF, and the
     first half of LOM "were germs of a new
     American literature with a broader base in
     the national mind than the writers of New
     England had possessed, fine as they were."
     On pp. 448-64, "Mark Twain in the East"
     shows MT as "the greatest American folk-
     writer of the time," who did not understand
     or respect his craft; thus, "He seemed all
     but indifferent to Huckleberry Finn when he
     was at work on this best of his best," and
     squandered his energies on ill-conceived
     projects; "Even Mark Twain's great books,
     with their brilliant beginnings, ended bad-
     ly"; but some of his works "were destined
     to live with the best in America." Excerpt-
     ed in Gerber (1971), pp. 29-32.

B9   [BROWNELL, GEORGE HIRAM.] "About that Helio-
     type Portrait of Mark Twain in 'Huck Finn,'"
     Twainian, VI (January-February), 1-2.
         Facing the frontispiece in first-edition
     copies of HF is a picture of the Karl Ger-
     hardt bust of MT; the plates used in the
     heliotype process by which the picture was
     reproduced were good for an average of 300
     impressions, so the process had to be re-
     peated at least 100 times, introducing
     such variants as differing dimensions and
     the presence or absence of a table under
     the bust. In many copies the edge of the
     bust bears the words, "Karl Gerhardt, Sc.,"
     apparently added on the negative, and Brown-
     ell is convinced that they cover an inscrip-
     tion chiseled on the bust itself, "To my
     Frent [sic] S. Clemens--Karl Gerdhardt."

In about half the copies Brownell has examined the inscription is simply blanked
out. Also see "That Word 'Frent' on Gerhardt Bust of Twain" (May-June), 3-4: W.
Allen DeLaney sent Brownell a list of page
references to Gerhardt in books on MT and
an encyclopedia sketch of his career; also
included is the text of a letter from Gerhardt with the word "friend" spelled correctly.

B10 ____. "The First of Series II, American
     Travel Letters, in Alta California," Twain-
     ian, VI (May-June), 1-3.
         The first of a series of fourteen letters
     by MT after his return from the Quaker City
     Tour; the series is reprinted in the Twain-
     ian through VIII (July-August, 1949).
     Franklin Walker had considered including
     these letters in his and G. Ezra Dane's
     Mark Twain's Travels with Mr. Brown (1940),
     but decided against doing so because Brown
     does not appear in these letters and the
     volume would become unwieldy. This first
     letter, datelined "New York, November 20th
     [1867]," covers the return of the Quaker
     City and a passenger list for MT's dream
     of "A Model Excursion."

B11 ____. "Second Letter of 'American Travel
     Letters, Series II,'" Twainian, VI (July-
     August), 4-6.
         Datelined "Washington, December 10th,
     1867," contains MT's comments on the Hawai-
     ian treaty; speculation by others about foul
     play in the deaths of presidents; the
     plague of office-seekers; and personal notes
     on individuals of interest to California
     readers.

B12 ____. "Third Letter of 'American Travel
     Letters, Series II,'" Twainian, VI
     (September-October), 3-4.
         Datelined "Washington, December 14, 1867,"
     on government salaries, female clerks, as-
     signment of clerkships, Seward's purchases
     of real estate, and Sutro's attempt to raise
     money for a tunnel to drain the Virginia
     City silver mines.

B13 ____. "Fourth Twain Letter in Alta First
     Printed in New York Citizen," Twainian, VI
     (November-December), 3-4.
         Datelined "Washington, D.C., Dec. 15th,
     1867," a burlesque in which MT says he was
     appointed Senate doorkeeper: he tried to
     make a speech and was squelched, joined in
     a voice vote and was impeached.

B14 ____. "Mark Twain Orates on Death of Demo-
     cratic Party in 1880(?)," Twainian, VI
     (January-February), 2-3.
         Reprint of a clipping from the Chicago
     Tribune, datelined, "Hartford, Conn.,
     Nov. 3," reporting an MT oration at a Repub-
     lican meeting the night before, and giving
     the text. It was not immediately clear that
     the speech was intended humorously, as it

1947 - Shorter Writings

([BROWNELL, GEORGE HIRAM])
followed an address by two clergymen and began with a reference to "occasions...so solemn, so weighted with the deep concerns of
life, that then even the licensed jester
must lay aside his cap and bells and remember that he is a man and mortal."

B15   ____. "Not So Good Is Mark's Effort to
Show He Can Pen a Poem Like the 'Raven' by
Poe," Twainian, VI (July-August), 3.
Contains the text of "The Mysterious Chi-
naman," written in Poe's style, "for
M. E. G.'s Album." Brownell places the
burlesque in MT's western period, and speculates that the "M. E. G." may have been a
relative of Steve Gillis.

B16   ____. "Some Figures on the 1st Edition of
'Tom Sawyer,'" Twainian, VI (March-April),
2.
On different accounts by Walter Bliss and
Merle Johnson as to the number of copies of
the first edition that were cloth-bound.
Based on Twainiana Notes from the Annotations of Walter Bliss, ed. Frances M. Edwards (1930).

B17   ____. "That Picture of 'St. Louis Hotel' in
'Life on the Mississippi,'" Twainian, VI
(September-October), 1-3.
On illustrations on pp. 441, 443 of LOM:
"In brief, the conclusion must be reached
that the correct first-state copies of LOM,
as long accepted, are those containing both
the St. Charles legend and the cut of Twain
in flames; that next in order of priority
are those copies containing the St. Louis
legend and cut of Twain; and that, third,
are the copies that contain the St. Charles
legend but lack the cut of Twain." There is
no record of a second edition published by
Osgood. A brief note in the November-December issue (p. 6) reports letters from New
York rare book dealers Gabriel Engel and
Howard S. Mott, both of whom contend that
the true first-state issue is the one with
the "St. Charles Hotel" legend on p. 443 and
MT in flames on p. 441. A letter from Mott
(Twainian, VII, January-February, 1948, 5)
corrects this statement: he had simply reported seeing a variant, making no claim
that it represented a true first state--al-
though logic would support an assumption
that it did.

B18   ____. "This German Biography Did Not Contain
Enough 'Frozen Truth' to Satisfy Twain,"
Twainian, VI (March-April), 1.
Robert Lutz in Stuttgart published a six-
volume edition of some of MT's works in
1892 and 1898; the 1898 edition included as
an appendix "Mark Twains Lebensgeschichte,"
an anonymous biography offensive to MT and
his wife. MT asked Lutz to suppress the
biography (which apparently was also issued
as a pamphlet), and offered to provide the
authorized Samuel E. Moffett biography

published first in McClure's Magazine
(October, 1899). Three MT letters to Lutz
(February 27, April 3, July 14, 1899) are
here reprinted from the January, 1947 issue
of More Books of the Boston Public Library,
1947.B21.

B19   ____. "Twain 'Ciphers' Loss from Postal De-
cree," Twainian, VI (March-April), 3-4.
Text of an MT letter to the Hartford Courant, complaining of the additional trouble
and expense of providing more complete addresses, as required by new regulations.
Also see Frank C. Willson's article on this,
with other letters, in Twainian, IV
(January, 1945), 2-4.

B20   ____. [Brief note on Clemens v. Belford
case, and the "Mark Twain" trade mark.]
Twainian, VI (March-April), 2.
Provides the legal citation: "14 Fed 728,
11 Biss 459, Table of 22 Decennial Digest
'06, p. 338, and...cited in 33 Century Digest Literary Property No. 34 and 46 Century
Digest Trade Marks No. 14." It was after
this case was decided that MT registered his
name as a trade mark in the Patent Office.

B21   C., T. "Mark Twain Protests About False German Biography," More Books: Bulletin of the
Boston Public Library, Sixth Series, XXII
(January), 30-31.
Contains three letters MT wrote in 1899
(February 27, April 3, and undated, early
summer) to Robert Lutz, the Stuttgart publisher of a six-volume collection of MT's
works, containing an introductory biography,
"Mark Twains Lebensgeschichte," of which MT
wrote: "Half of the history is true, and
the other half is not--& but little of it is
pleasant reading. According to the mainly
false 4th Chapter, my wife & I were mere
vulgar swine--& moreover that chapter is attributed to me! I never wrote a line of it."
MT asks that the offensive biography be replaced with an official one by Samuel E.
Moffett. [Letters reprinted 1947.B18.]

B22   CLEMENS, CYRIL. "Mark Twain's Southern Relative, Jeremiah Clemens," Mark Twain Quarterly, VII (Spring-Summer, "Combined with Summer, Fall, Winter, 1946"), 13; VIII (Winter),
15-17.
Only a passing reference to MT, who was
"proud to number as a relative" Jeremiah
Clemens," and "frequently referred" to him.
Born in Alabama in 1814, Jeremiah Clemens
became a member of the United States Senate,
where he spoke out in favor of slavery but
against secession. [The second installment
ended by announcing a continuation, which
finally appeared in VIII (Winter, 1950),
13-16, as "Jeremiah Clemens, Novelist and
Southern Supporter of Lincoln."]

B23   CLEMENS, SAMUEL L. "Unpublished Mark Twain
Letter," Mark Twain Quarterly, VII (Spring-
Summer, "Combined with Summer, Fall, Winter,
1946"), 19.

(CLEMENS, SAMUEL L.)
Datelined "Riverdale on the Hudson, June 17, 1902," thanks Henry Miller of the Burlington Railroad for naming a station near Hannibal, Missouri "Clemens" in his honor; unfortunately, no town materialized there.

B24 _____. [Holograph note on the report of his death as "an exaggeration."] Mark Twain Quarterly, VII (Spring-Summer, "Combined with Summer, Fall, Winter, 1946"), front cover.
This is the same note previously reproduced by Frank Marshall White in "Mark Twain as a Newspaper Reporter" (1910).

B25 COAD, ORAL S. "Mrs. Clemens Apologizes for Her Husband," Journal of the Rutgers University Library, XI (December), 30.
Text of a letter by Olivia Clemens (October 31, 1901, now in Stanton Memorial Collection, New Jersey College for Women) to Theodore Stanton, apologizing for MT's failure to offer him lunch: MT seldom ate lunch and forgot that others did.

B26 *DEVOTO, BERNARD. "Those Two Immortal Boys," Woman's Day (November), pp. 38-39, 131-34.
[Source: "Articles on American Literature Appearing in Current Periodicals," American Literature, XX (March, 1948), 98: "A critical analysis of The Adventures of Tom Sawyer and The Adventures of Huckleberry Finn, prompted by the author's hearing a 'cheap and vulgar' radio dramatization of the former."]

B27 DICKINSON, LEON T. "Marketing a Best Seller: Mark Twain's Innocents Abroad," Papers of the Bibliographical Society of America, XLI (First Quarter), 107-22.
On the subscription sale of MT's first major work. MT's publisher, Elisha Bliss, "took special pains to get out an attractive volume," and "promoted it vigorously." Describes details of this promotion. Article reprinted (without footnotes) in Twainian, X (March-April), 3-4; (May-June), 3-4.

B28 _____. "Mark Twain's Revisions in Writing The Innocents Abroad," American Literature, XIX (May), 139-157.
In 1867 MT contracted with the American Publishing Company of Hartford to make a book out of a series of some fifty travel letters he had written for the San Francisco Alta California. "Two factors--audience and form of publication--demanded that Clemens revise his travel letters. It is the purpose of this essay to show how the book differs from the letters and what exactly Clemens did to make it different. An exhibiting of these changes is instructive in revealing something of how Mark Twain operated as a writer." Reprinted (without the footnotes) in Twainian, X (January-February, 1961), 2-4; (March-April), 1-2.

B29 DONNER, STANLEY T. "Mark Twain as a Reader," Quarterly Journal of Speech, XXXIII (October), 308-11.
A general account of MT's very successful public readings from his works; documented from Paine, Howells, and other familiar sources.

B30 DUGAS, GAILE. "Mark Twain's Hannibal," Holiday, II (April), 102-107.
Hannibal, Missouri, and the Clemens house are described for the would-be tourist; there are many color photographs but no new information.

B31 FEINSTEIN, GEORGE W. "Mark Twain on the Immanence of Authors in Their Writing," Mark Twain Quarterly, VIII (Winter), 13-14.
"Twain often finds the show of personality more absorbing than the incidents."

B32 FREMERSDORFF, ELLEN H. "Mark Twain in Australia," Mark Twain Quarterly, VII (Spring-Summer, "Combined with Summer, Fall, Winter, 1946"), 20.
An anecdote concerning a visit by MT to an unnamed mining town (date not given), and his subsequent deflation of the pompous mayor.

B33 GIBSON, WILLIAM M. "Mark Twain and Howells: Anti-Imperialists," New England Quarterly, XX (December), 435-70.
On their response to the Boer War, the Boxer Rebellion, and the war in the Philippines.

B34 *GILMAN, STEPHEN. "Cervantes en la obra de Mark Twain," Cuadernos de Ínsula (Madrid), I, 202-22.
[Source: Listed in bibliography (p. 214) of Arturo Serrano-Plaja, "Magic" Realism in Cervantes: "Don Quixote" as Seen Through "Tom Sawyer" and "The Idiot." Berkeley, Los Angeles, London, 1970. (Trans. by Robert S. Rudder).]

B35 GRANT, RENA V. "The Word 'Pulu,'" American Speech, XXII (April), 150-51.
The word MT once applied to a Nevada tree in a letter to his mother (1861, in Letters, I, 54) actually is Hawaiian for a kind of silky vegetable wool; advertisements headed "PULU! PULU! PULU!" appeared regularly in the San Francisco Daily Bulletin between 1857 and 1861.

B36 HALL, FRED J. "Fred J. Hall Tells the Story of His Connection with Charles L. Webster & Co.," Twainian, VI (November-December), 1-3.
Hall succeeded Webster in managing the company, and was himself ruined in the company's bankruptcy. His letter of January 14, 1909 to Albert Bigelow Paine describes the financial over-extension, the hope placed in the Paige typesetting machine, his impression of Orion Clemens ("He seemed to have no sense of humor, and was the simplest, best natured,

(HALL, FRED J.)
most impractical and delightfully naive man
I ever met"), and a trip with MT which produced the sketch, "Traveling with a Reformer." George Hiram Brownell credits this
letter as "reproduced by courtesy of Mr.
Wesley A. DeLaney, of St. Louis, owner of
the papers left by Albert Bigelow Paine at
his death."

B37   HARRISON, JAMES G. "A Note on the Duke in
'Huck Finn': The Journeyman Printer as
Picaro," Mark Twain Quarterly, VIII (Winter), 1-2.
The Duke belongs to a literary type that
had appeared earlier in American literature, and MT referred elsewhere to the im-
providence and recklessness of journeyman
printers.

B38   HUTTON, GRAHAM. "Hawkeye, Huck Finn and an
English Boy. His Favorite Reading about a
Strange Land," Chicago Sun Book Week, V
(May 4), 2.
English boys and girls in the last centu-
ry read about the American West (very lit-
tle specifically on MT).

B39 *   ____. [Introduction.] The Adventures of
Tom Sawyer. London: Paul Eleck.
[Source: Asselineau (1954), No. 1096.]

B40   LAVERTY, CARROLL D. "The Genesis of The Mysterious Stranger," Mark Twain Quarterly,
VII (Spring-Summer, "Combined with Summer,
Fall, Winter, 1946"), 15-19.
Suggests that MT's book may owe its theme
to a story by Jane Taylor, reprinted under
that title in McGuffey's Rhetorical Guide
and Fifth Reader and New Sixth Eclectic
Reader; another source may be Adolph Wilbrandt's The Master of Palmyra.

B41   LEARY, LEWIS. Articles on American Literature Appearing in Current Periodicals,
1920-1945. Durham, North Carolina: Duke
University Press.
Superseded by his 1954 edition, "a revision and an extension" of this one.

B42 *LE BRETON, MAURICE. [Review: Léon Lemonnier,
Mark Twain.] Langues Modernes, 51e année
(September-October), A 53-54.
[Source: Asselineau (1954), No. 1103:
"The reviewer considers it an excellent
synthesis."]

B43   LEWIS, OSCAR. Silver Kings: The Lives and
Times of Mackay, Fair, Flood, and O'Brien,
Lords of the Comstock Lode. New York:
Alfred A. Knopf.
On MT, pp. 31-32, 53, 68-69, 157, brief
mention. Old-timers supposedly recall MT
with far less than their admiration for his
friend William Wright ("Dan de Quille").

B44   LORCH, FRED W. "Mark Twain's Sandwich Islands Lectures at St. Louis," American

Literature, XVIII (January), 299-307.
Includes text of the lecture from the
Missouri Republican, a letter to the editor
of the Republican by MT, and a brief report
on the lecture.

B45   ____. [Review: Ernest E. Leisy, ed., The
Letters of Quintus Curtius Snodgrass
(1946).] American Literature, XIX (March),
93-95.
Leisy "has presented in the Preface, the
Introduction, and especially in the Notes
for each of the letters impressive evidence
which is also convincing to the reader" that
MT wrote these letters, showing that he was
in New Orleans while these letters were appearing in the Daily Crescent, that he had
used the pseudonym "Snodgrass" before [but
as "Thomas Jefferson Snodgrass"--T.A.T.],
that he later spoke of having written for
the Crescent, and that there are many parallels in theme and style. Lorch adds in support of the attribution his own observations
on the letter titled "Snodgrass Dines with
Old Abe," which he says appears to be based
on the efforts of Sam's brother Orion to
secure a consulship in Germany. This series
of letters is important biographically and
for what they reveal of MT's development as
a writer: there is a greater maturity than
in the earlier series of Snodgrass letters.

B46   LOVELL, CHARLES J. "The Background of Mark
Twain's Vocabulary," American Speech, XXII
(April), 88-98.
Although Ramsay and Emberson's Mark Twain
Lexicon (1938) lists over 600 words and
phrases for which MT's use antedates the
Oxford English Dictionary, the Dictionary
of American English cites use for many of
them before MT; further research might well
show that he originated very few, although
he gave them literary currency.

B47   LYDENBERG, JOHN. "A Frontier Product," New
York Times Book Review (May 25), pp. 5, 32.
A review of Effie Mona Mack, Mark Twain in
Nevada.
"It is impossible to see the creator of
Huck Finn in these early writings for the
Territorial Enterprise." They help explain
the lack of control in MT's later writing,
but "the sources of his superb diction and
of his subtle irony are in no way visible."

B48   PARSONS, COLEMAN O. "The Devil and Samuel
Clemens," Virginia Quarterly Review, XXIII
(Autumn), 582-606.
On "the source and mythology" of the
gloom of the Promethean Samuel Clemens, as
distinct from MT: "I cannot escape the
conviction that Samuel Clemens' guilt complex was rooted in his relations with Mother Jane and Brother Henry." Not documented;
apparently draws heavily on Paine's Biography and his edition of Mark Twain's Notebook. Reprinted in Leary (1962), 183-206.

B49 ROBINSON, MARIE J. "Mark Twain: Lecturer," Mark Twain Quarterly, VII (Spring-Summer, "Combined with Summer, Fall, Winter, 1946"), 1-12.
An extensive, general discussion, fully annotated, which shows how lecturing was sometimes a burden for MT, though profitable, but also that he sometimes wrote with pleasure of his triumphs. Included are accounts of his tours, the forms of his notes and his recorded statements on the art, and discussion of his style and topics.

B50 SAMPLEY, ARTHUR M. "New Letters of Mark Twain," Southwest Review, XXXII (Winter), 101-102.
A review of Ernest E. Leisy, ed., The Letters of Quintus Curtius Snodgrass (1946). "Professor Leisy does not state categorically that Snodgrass and Clemens are the same writer, but the evidence he produces...will convince most readers.... The editing of the letters is thorough, succinct, and meticulous, and the format of the book is pleasing."

B51 *SELLERS, J. L. [Review: Effie Mona Mack, Mark Twain in Nevada.] Nebraska History, XXX, 81-82.
[Source: MHRA Annual Bibliography (1949), No. 3968.]

B52 SNELL, GEORGE. "Mark Twain: Realism and the Frontier," in his The Shapers of American Fiction, 1798-1947 (New York: E. P. Dutton & Co.), pp. 211-22 and passim.
MT was "trimmed and tamed" by his wife and Howells. "Undoubtedly this repressive influence had a great deal to do with the truncation of a career that began with such fireworks and spluttered out so dismally toward its end." His reputation as a serious writer will rest on LOM and HF, in which language is "colloquial, natural, in harmony with its content, and by long odds the clearest, easiest prose to come from any native writer." On MT's influence on the style of Hemingway, pp. 160-161, 215.

B53 WAGNER, HETTIE DEVINNY. "A Glimpse of Mark Twain in 1880," Mark Twain Quarterly, VIII (Winter), 3.
One summer day, the author met MT at Elmira and talked about wild flowers with him.

B54 WALKER, FRANKLIN. [Review: Ernest E. Leisy, ed., The Letters of Quintus Curtius Snodgrass (1946).] Modern Language Notes, LXII (November), 503.
The evidence for attributing the letters to MT "though circumstantial, is impressive.... the sketches read something like Clemens' apprentice writing, but not enough to convince this reviewer that they are indisputably his."

B55 WECTER, DIXON. "Frank Finlay; Or, 'The Thameside Tenderfoot in the Wooly West,'" Twainian, VI (July-August), 1-4.
A brief introductory note, and the text of four letters from Finlay to MT. The letter of December 20, 1877 refers to "a well-meant but imperfect sketch of one Mark Twain" in the London World of that date; apparently the sketch is not listed in MT bibliographies. See also Brownell's "Who Was Frank Finlay?" in Twainian, IV (October, 1944), 1-6.

B56 ____. "Nuggets from Washoe," Saturday Review of Literature, XXX (July 12), 26.
A review of Effie Mona Mack, Mark Twain in Nevada. It gives useful background material on Orion Clemens and on Nevada people "thinly disguised in Roughing It," but the "captious" reader will find it rambling and repetitious, and sometimes lacking in realization of the central character himself."

B57 ____, ed. "The Love Letters of Mark Twain," Atlantic Monthly, CLXXX (November), 33-39; (December), 66-72 (series ends January, 1948).
Letters from MT to Olivia, beginning with their courtship; also includes a letter from MT, December 29, 1868 to his future father-in-law in response to a very plain-spoken letter: offers character references, concedes a rough life in the West but not a shameful one, and speaks of intention to live respectably. The letters appeared in book form in 1949.A2.

B58 ____, et al. "Dixon Wecter of Huntington Library Now Literary Editor of Clemens Estate," Twainian, VI (May-June), 4-5.
On the appointment of Wecter, the transfer of the Mark Twain collection from Harvard University to the Huntington Library, and brief discussion of the material; includes Wecter's appeal for the use of any MT letters or manuscripts readers may be able to provide.

B59 WILSON, EDMUND. [Review: Effie Mona Mack, Mark Twain in Nevada.] New Yorker, XXIII (June 7), 118.
Miss Mack has turned up a wealth of material to fill in "the rather sketchy picture" by MT of his life in Virginia City. "The weakest feature of Miss Mack's performance" is her inept paraphrasing of passages from RI, ruining their effect.

1948 A BOOKS

A1 *CLEMENS, SAMUEL L. Les Aventures d'Huckleberry Finn, traduit de l'américain par Suzanne Nétillard, préface de Jean Kanapa. Paris: Éditions d'Hier et d'Aujourd'hui.

1948 - Books

(CLEMENS, SAMUEL L.)
[Source: Asselineau (1954), No. 1145, describing Kanapa's preface as "a communist interpretation of Mark Twain" which charges his bolder works are suppressed in America but that in Russia he is very popular and known for anti-imperialist views.]

A2   HARNSBERGER, CAROLINE THOMAS. Mark Twain at Your Fingertips. New York: Beechhurst Press.
Extracts from MT's published and unpublished writing, arranged alphabetically by topic from "Abroad to Ax" to "Yodeling to Youth," with a bibliography and indexes, and with a foreword by Clara Clemens. The MHRA Annual Bibliography (1946, No. 1800) cites a 1946 publication by Cloud, Inc., Chicago.

A3   SMALLEY, WEBSTER L. The Critical Reputation of Mark Twain in England: 1870-1910.
Unpublished Master's Thesis, Columbia University. The evaluations and the bibliography in this master's thesis have been of great value in locating material for the present bibliography.

A4   WECTER, DIXON, ed. Mark Twain in Three Moods: Three New Items of Twainiana. San Marino: Friends of the Huntington Library.
Previously unpublished material consisting of MT's description of Donner Lake and Lake Tahoe, his satiric description of a railroad subsidy for the Southern Pacific with the proviso that no Chinese labor be employed in the construction, and an account by Charles Erskine Scott Wood of MT's visiting and telling a story to explain why he hated babies; Wood was amused but his sister was not.

1948 B SHORTER WRITINGS

B1   ANON. "Twain Trustees Bring Suit to Halt Publication of Story," Publishers' Weekly, CLIII (January 17), 233.
A Murder, a Mystery, and a Marriage (1876) existed only as an unfinished manuscript, and "had never been intended for publication by Twain."

B2   ANON. "Owner of Mark Twain Manuscript Free to Publish Story," Publishers' Weekly, CLIII (January 24), 320.
"New York Supreme Court Justice Aron Steuer dismissed the suit brought by the trustees of the estate of Mark Twain to restrain publication of a hitherto unpublished story (Publishers' Weekly, January 17), the New York Times reported."

B3   *BECKER, MAY LAMBERTON. [Introduction.] The Prince and the Pauper. Cleveland: World Publishing Company.
[Source: Asselineau (1954), No. 1147; describes it as "a children's edition."]

B4   *BRODIN, PIERRE. Les Maîtres de la Littérature Américaine. Paris: Horizons de France.
[Source: Asselineau (1954), No. 1151: "On Mark Twain, pp. 267-306 and bibliography, pp. 472-480."]

B5   [BROWNELL, GEORGE HIRAM.] "'American Travel Letters, Series Two,' Fifth of Series in 'Alta California,'" Twainian, VII (January-February), 3-5.
The text of MT's letter datelined "Washington, Dec. 17th [1867]," on leaks of White House secrets to the press, and straight reporting of the doings of individuals of interest to western readers.

B6   _____ "'American Travel Letters, Series Two,' Sixth in Series in 'Alta California,'" Twainian, VII (March-April), 3-5.
Text of letter datelined "Washington, January 11th [1868]," describing a Dickens lecture in Steinway Hall, New York; MT found the delivery a disappointment. Brownell does not note the significance of MT's statement that "I am proud to observe that there was a beautiful young lady with me--a highly respectable young white woman"; this is Olivia Langdon, the future Mrs. Clemens, and apparently MT's first published mention of her.

B7   _____. "'American Travel Letters, Series Two,' Seventh in Series in 'Alta California,'" Twainian, VII (May-June), 3-5.
Datelined "Washington, January 16th [1868]," on Fernando Wood's speech in Congress, local gossip, and a reception by General Grant which MT later turned to comic account after Grant became President (See July-August, pp. 1-2).

B8   _____. "'American Travel Letters, Series Two,' Eighth in Series in 'Alta California,'" Twainian, VII (July-August), 3-4.
Datelined "Washington, January 12th, 1868," ordinary political and local reporting.

B9   _____. "'American Travel Letters, Series Two,' Ninth in Series in 'Alta California,'" Twainian, VII (September-October), 3-4.
Datelined "Washington, February 1st [1868]," describes girly shows on New York stage and a visit to Hartford.

B10 _____. "'American Travel Letters, Series Two,' Tenth In Series in 'Alta California,'" Twainian, VII (November-December), 5-7.
Datelined "Hartford, Conn., August, Recently, 1868," describes shipboard theatricals on a trip back east from California, praises Captain Ned Wakeman of the America, and gives a long and laudatory description of Hartford.

B11 _____. "Mark Found He Already Knew the Tricks of Professor Loisette's New Mnemonics," Twainian, VII (March-April), 1-3.

([BROWNELL, GEORGE HIRAM])

MT became so enthusiastic over a system for memorization that he wrote a testimonial, had it printed, and sent it to friends; Loisette used the testimonial in advertising until MT had second thoughts and suppressed it, and attempted to recall the copies he had mailed. The text is reproduced, together with that of a note to the Rev. John Davis, of Hannibal; at the end he expresses his regret over "that 'd'Unlap' cruelty" in "The Private History of a Campaign that Failed," adding, "I think John Robards deserved a lashing, but it should have come from an enemy, not a friend"; the statement refers to MT's ridicule of an imaginary Dunlap who changed his name to a more elegant form as Robards had to "Robards."

B12   ____. "Twain's Scrapbook Praised for Its Literary Excellence," Twainian, VII (July-August), 5-6.
Reprints "A New Book by Mark Twain," a tongue-in-cheek review of Mark Twain's Adhesive Scrap-Book in Scribner's Monthly for April, 1877; Brownell has found a statement by Robert Underwood Johnson in his Remembered Yesterdays (1923), confessing authorship of the review.

B13   ____. "Twain's Tale of the Washoe Miner at 'The Reception at the President's,'" Twainian, VII (July-August), 1-2.
A comic sketch, written for the Buffalo Express (October 1, 1870), and reprinted in the Galaxy of that month. See May-June, pp. 3-5.

B14   ____. "Unknown Twain Speech at Elmira in 1879," Twainian, VII (September-October), 5.
The text of MT's introduction of Gen. Joseph R. Hawley, who addressed a political rally in October; reprinted from an undated clipping from the Elmira Advertiser.

B15   ____. [Brief Note.] Twainian, VII (May-June), 6.
When MT's sketch, "Traveling with a Reformer," appeared in Cosmopolitan (December, 1893), an illustration by Dan Beard showed MT shaking hands with a man now identified as Fred J. Hall, who succeeded Webster as general manager of Charles L. Webster & Co.; his daughter owns the originals of this and the other Beard illustrations made for the tale.

B16   BRYNES, ASHER. "Boy-Men and Man-Boys," Yale Review, XXXVIII (Winter), 223-33.
On the accurate portrayal of boy-nature by MT and a few other American authors.

B17   CLEMENS, CYRIL. "Mark Twain's Story on the Siamese Twins,' Hobbies--the Magazine for Collectors, LIII (October), 139.
Anecdotal: "Some literalist" queried MT about the statement in Those Extraordinary Twins that "the ages of the Siamese Twins are respectively fifty-one and fifty-three years"; MT conceded that this statement was confusing and misleading: "What I meant to say was that the twins were born at the same time, but to different mothers."

B18   CLEMENS, SAMUEL L. "Ghost Life on the Mississippi: A Mark Twain Manuscript, with Foreword by Samuel C. Webster," Pacific Spectator, II (Autumn), 485-90.
The story of a steamboat taken through a difficult passage by the ghost of pilot William Jones; MT left it untitled. "The manuscript is in his handwriting and was probably left at the Moffett house when he went west to the territory of Nevada in 1861." Reprinted in Twainian, VIII (January-February, 1949), 1-2.

B19   ____. "Unpublished Twain Letter," Mark Twain Quarterly, VIII (Summer-Fall), 13.
Dated March 26, 1897, with a return address c/o Chatto and Windus in London, MT writes one "Frank" to introduce "My friend, Robert Chapin, late U. S. Consul at Johannesburg...a sterling man, but powerful quiet."

B20   COLEMAN, RUFUS A. "Trowbridge and Clemens," Modern Language Quarterly, IX (June), 216-23.
An anecdotal account of their meetings. Trowbridge, a popular poet in his time, "was critical of Clemens both as a speaker and as a writer, considering him diverting but prolix, and at times tiresome." Trowbridge was seated across the table from MT at the Whittier Birthday Dinner, but made no reference to MT's disastrous speech in his notebook, letters, or autobiography He also met MT at other public events.

B21   COWIE, ALEXANDER. "Mark Twain (1835-1910)," in his The Rise of the American Novel (New York: The American Book Company; reprinted 1951), pp. 599-652 (also, passim on MT; indexed).
A general study of MT's life and works, much of it descriptive, noting the critical fortunes of various books. Notes MT's active mind and lack of profundity, and stresses the value of his natural expression. Pp. 611-17 (on HF) reprinted in Lettis (1962), pp. 365-70.

B22   DELANEY, WESLEY A. "The Truth About That Humboldt Trip As Told by Gus Oliver to A. B. Paine," Twainian, VII (May-June), 1-3.

(DELANEY, WESLEY A.)
Judge A. W. Oliver, the "Oliphant" of RI and "The Uncomplaining Man" of IA (Ch. XXVII) adds another incident to the account in IA and describes MT, in a letter to Paine (April 24, 1910.)

B23   _____. "Twain's Last Visit to Bermuda Preceding the Final Days of His Life," Twainian, VII (January-February), 1-3.
On his visit to Bermuda in January, 1910, as a guest of Vice-Consul W. H. Allen; among the callers was Woodrow Wilson, with whom MT played miniature golf on the Allen lawn. Includes text of a letter to Allen from Paine (January 3, noting MT's mercurial temperament and the need to protect him) and extensive quotation from another (April 22, on MT's death and burial); also includes Joseph T. Goodman's letter to Paine (April 22) on hearing of MT's death.

B24   DUFFY, CHARLES. "Mark Twain Writes to Howells," Mark Twain Quarterly, VIII (Summer-Fall), 4.
Text of a letter from Hartford, February 27 (1874), on his distress over an inconvenient lecture engagement for March 5, in Boston.

B25   EIDSON, JOHN OLIN. "Innocents Abroad, Then and Now," Georgia Review, II (Summer), 186-92.
American soldiers in Europe ridicule what they cannot understand, just as MT did in Innocents Abroad.

B26   FEINSTEIN, GEORGE W. "Twain as Forerunner of Tooth-and-Claw Criticism," Modern Language Notes, LXIII (January), 49-50.
"Clearly Shaw, Mencken, DeVoto--Twainolaters all of them from their early formative years, by their own admission--and a horde of modern journalistic reviewers inherit, remotely or directly, something of Twain's flailing quality, his aggressive, epithetic line."

B27   FIEDLER, LESLIE. "Come Back to the Raft Ag'in, Huck Honey!" Partisan Review, XV (June), 664-71.
A general discussion of the Negro and homosexuality in American culture and literature, and only treating HF in passing; the title is not a quotation from HF. Reprinted in Fiedler's An End to Innocence (Boston: Beacon Press, 1952), pp. 142-51; The Collected Essays of Leslie Fiedler (New York: Stein and Day, 1971, 2 vols.), I, 142-51: Cardwell (1963), pp. 59-64.

B28   FLOWERS, FRANK C. "Mark Twain's Theories of Morality," Mark Twain Quarterly, VIII (Summer-Fall), 10.
Subtitled "Abstract," this appears to be the abstract of his 1941 doctoral dissertation for Louisiana State University, under the same title. What Is Man? illustrates

the principles and the didacticism prevalent in MT's works; but MT was not a pessimist.

B29   *GLOSTER, HUGH. Negro Voices in American Fiction, Chapel Hill, pp. 106-107.
[Source: Quoted in Gerald W. Haslam, "Huckleberry Finn: Why Read the Phelps Farm Episode?" Research Studies (Washington State University), XXXV (September), 191.] Gloster claims "that 'the foundations' of the present tendency to depict Negroes as human beings in literature 'were laid in the last quarter of the nineteenth century in the works of such writers as Albion Tourgee, G. W. Cable, and Mark Twain.'"

B30   HARNSBERGER, CAROLINE THOMAS. "Bernard Shaw Welcomes the Author of 'Mark Twain At Your Fingertips,'" Twainian, VII (November-December), 1-2.
Describes a trip to England, visit to Shaw, but says nothing interesting about MT except that his works were hard to find (as was all fiction, after the war).

B31   HART, JAMES D. [Review: Effie Mona Mack, Mark Twain in Nevada (1947).] American Literature, XIX (January), 379-80.
Dr. Mack is easily distracted from her subject and undiscriminating with sources. "Even when she senses a joke, she has an excruciating ability to ruin it. There is new information about MT and detailed social background material on RI, but "the picture that emerges is no different from that in Ivan Benson's crisper and more clearly conceived Mark Twain's Western Years."

B32   HOLLOWAY, T. E. "Mark Twain's Turning Point," Mark Twain Quarterly, VIII (Summer-Fall), 1-3.
Based on MT's own recollections, his book on Joan of Arc, and the Paine biography, discusses the Maid as his inspiration.

B33   HUTCHESON, AUSTIN E. "Twain Letter to Bob Howland Asks About Good Audience for Carson City Lecture," Twainian, VII (September-October), 1-2.
Contains the text of a brief note (October 29, 1866), as well as the text of MT's "Petrified Man" story, reprinted from George D. Lyman's The Saga of the Comstock Lode (1934).

B34   _____. "Twain Was 'News' to Other Newspapers While a Reporter on The 'Enterprise,'" Twainian, VII (November-December), 3-4.
On material relating to MT in Virginia City Evening Bulletin, still preserved in files at the University of Nevada (Reno) and elsewhere. Continued in Twainian, VIII (March-April, 1949), 2-3.

B35   HYMAN, STANLEY EDGAR. The Armed Vision: A
      Study in the Methods of Modern Literary
      Criticism. New York: Alfred A. Knopf,
      pp. 113-17, 123-25, and passim.
         Discusses a number of major critics and
      their schools. Comments at some length on
      The Ordeal of Mark Twain, and accuses
      Brooks of overrating MT's potential and un-
      derestimating his achievements (pp. 57, 110,
      113); nonetheless, it is in this work that
      Brooks is most successful in his biographi-
      cal criticism. Notes many of the changes
      made in the revised edition after DeVoto's
      Mark Twain's America, which "itself is a
      stupid and ignorant book," but in regard to
      The Ordeal "more often right than wrong...
      an irritating but valuable corrective"
      (pp. 116-17). Hyman feels that Brooks's
      revisions showed "a new caution prepared to
      discard a good part of his thesis under at-
      tack. It is not a pretty picture" (p. 116).

B36   JACOBS, STANLEY S. "Mark Twain's Strangest
      Dream," Coronet, XXIV (June), 191.
         Anecdote: premonition of his brother
      Henry's death in the explosion of the Penn-
      sylvania.

B37   JONES, HOWARD MUMFORD. The Theory of Ameri-
      can Literature. Ithaca, New York: Cornell
      University Press.
         A collection of essays on literary his-
      tory, with only passing references to MT--
      generally in lists of authors discussed by
      literary historians.

B38   LEARY, LEWIS. "Doctoral Dissertations in
      American Literature, 1933-1948," American
      Literature, XX (May), 169-230.
         Updates the Leisy and Hubbell listing in
      1933.B21. For more recent dissertations,
      see the Selby listing and Dissertation Ab-
      stracts International.

B39   _____. [Review: Effie Mona Mack, Mark Twain
      in Nevada (1947).] South Atlantic Quarter-
      ly, XLVIII (April), 265-66.
         Reflects careful scholarship and provides
      much useful background, but relies too
      heavily on Paine and RI and makes too little
      use of Ivan Benson's Mark Twain's Western
      Years. "Nevada is brilliantly there, but
      Mark Twain too often is not."

B40   _____. [Review: Dixon Wecter, ed., Mark
      Twain in Three Moods.] American Literature,
      XX (November), 362.
         Descriptive and very brief.

B41   LILLARD, RICHARD D. [Review: Effie Mona
      Mack, Mark Twain in Nevada (1947).]
      Pacific Spectator, II (Autumn), 392.
         Brief notice, merely that the book "uses
      Clemens' several years in Washoe as a
      frame for much background material."

B42   MANNING, CLARENCE A. [Review: M. Mendelson,
      Mark Twain (Moscow: Fskblksm Molodaya
      Gvardiya [Young Guard], 1939).] American
      Literature, XX (November), 358-59.
         Lively and entertaining style, but a
      straight Marxist-Leninist approach; Mendel-
      son sees MT censored by wife and friends, a
      serious critic of society treated as mere
      humorist.

B43   *MATTHEWS, BRANDER, and DIXON WECTER. [Intro-
      ductions.] The Adventures of Huckleberry
      Finn. New York: Harper's.
         [Source: Asselineau (1954), No. 1143;
      quotes Wecter's statement that "its real
      hero is Nigger Jim"--a striking realization
      for a later generation becoming aware of
      racial injustices.]

B44   McKEITHAN, DANIEL MORLEY. "A Letter from Mark
      Twain to Francis Henry Skrine in London,"
      Modern Language Notes, LXIII (February),
      134-35.
         About Kipling's switch to approving con-
      scription in the Boer War: "Why, why, why!
      has Kipling gone to satirizing Kipling?"

B45   _____. "More About Mark Twain's War With Eng-
      lish Critics of America," Modern Language
      Notes, LXIII (April), 221-28.
         Builds on Hoben's "superb article" on CY
      (1946), noting that MT had begun to show
      hostility toward British institutions in TA
      and P&P, as well as HF; agrees that "Hoben
      did well to point out that Twain was pro-
      English both at the beginning and at the end
      of his career." Reprinted in his Court
      Trials in Mark Twain and Other Essays (1958).

B46   _____. "The Occasion of Mark Twain's Speech
      'On Foreign Critics,'" Philological Quarter-
      ly, XXVII (July), 276-79.
         The immediate provocation was Matthew
      Arnold's essay, "Civilisation in the United
      States" (1888); MT mentioned by name Sir
      Henry Lepel Griffin, whose The Great Repub-
      lic he may have read (Arnold's essay quoted
      some of its harsh words for America). Re-
      printed in his Court Trials in Mark Twain
      and Other Essays (1958).

B47   *MENDELSON, M. "Mark Twain Accuses," Soviet
      Literature, May, pp. 151-61. On MT's de-
      nunciation of American imperialism.
         [Source: Asselineau (1954), No. 1183.]

B48   *NAOTARO, TATSUNOKUCHI. "Mark Twain's Views of
      American English," The Current English
      Press (November 1), p. 15.
         [Source: MHRA Annual Bibliography (1948),
      No. 3421.]

B49   *RANKIN, J. W. [Introduction.] Life on the
      Mississippi. New York and London: Harper
      & Brothers (Harper's Modern Classics).
         [Source: Asselineau (1954), No. 1146.]

1948 - Shorter Writings

B50 RUSSELL, LILLIS L. "Americanism as Typified by Mark Twain," Mark Twain Quarterly, VIII (Summer-Fall), 14.
     MT was truly American, and helped to shape and preserve our national character.

B51 SCHMITT, GLADYS. "Mark Twain Digs for Gold," Scholastic, LII (May 10), 23-25.
     A radio play for high-school students; first appeared in Scholastic in 1937.

B52 SILLEN, SAMUEL. "Dooley, Twain and Imperialism," Masses & Mainstream, I (December), 6-14.
     "It was the courage to oppose the aggressions of their own government that marked the anti-imperialist writers at the turn of the century, as it marked Thoreau and Emerson in 1846, Randolph Bourne and John Reed in 1918."

B53 SPILLER, ROBERT, WILLARD THORP, THOMAS H. JOHNSON, and HENRY SEIDEL CANBY, eds. Literary History of the United States. New York: Macmillan.
     Now in revised edition combined in 1 volume (1974), checked for present bibliography, containing Dixon Wecter, "Mark Twain" (pp. 917-39), a general biographical study; also, passim on MT (indexed). On pp. 1507-1508 there is "a reader's bibliography, and therefore highly selective." A separate bibliographical volume appeared in 1963, containing primary and secondary MT bibliography pp. 446-50 and in a supplement, pp. 94-97. According to the "Preface to the Third Edition" (p.v.), "Except for a few corrections and the omission of the index, the 1948 volume is reprinted as it appeared originally. It is followed by the 1959 Supplement, with its original Preface and no change in pagination," and a new, combined index. "Thomas H. Johnson undertook the principal work of compilation and editing of the original Bibliography and Richard M. Ludwig of the Supplement." Both the original bibliography and the supplement emphasize material available in the more familiar books and journals, and contain little or no secondary material not listed in the present bibliography; annotation is minimal.

B54 SQUIRES, J. RADCLIFFE. "Mark Twain," Accent, IX (Autumn) 32-3.
     A somewhat puzzling poem.

B55 *STONG, PHIL. "Mark Twain Cruise: Aboard a Modern River Boat, with Sam Clemens's Shade at the Wheel,"
     [Source: Asselineau (1954), No. 1187, listing publication as Holiday, V (April), 56-62, 86-87, 90, 92, 93, 95, 97. A check of Holiday reveals that Vol. V is 1949, and the article in question is not in the issue of April, 1948 or April, 1949--T.A.T.]

B56 TRILLING, LIONEL. "Introduction," The Adventures of Huckleberry Finn. New York: Rinehart & Co., pp. v-xviii.
     "In form and style Huckleberry Finn is an almost perfect work"; even the ending, though weak and too long, is important as a way of returning Huck to his anonymity (pp. xv-xvi). Trilling takes from Eliot's "The Dry Salvages" (in Four Quartets) the notion of the river as a god, and "Huck himself is the servant of the river-god," this "power which seems to have a mind and will of its own, and... appears to embody a great moral idea" (p. vii). Reprinted in Bradley (1962), pp. 310-20; Cardwell (1963), pp. 51-58; Lettis (1962), pp. 326-36; Marks (1959), pp. 44-52. Trilling published a somewhat revised version in The Liberal Imagination: Essays on Literature and Society (New York: The Viking Press, 1950), pp. 104-17; reprinted in Scott (1955), pp. 272-78 and (1967), pp. 257-63.

B57 *VAN DOREN, CARL. [Introduction.] A Connecticut Yankee in King Arthur's Court. New York: Heritage Press.
     [Source: Asselineau (1954), No. 1148.]

B58 VOGELBACK, ARTHUR L. "Mark Twain: Newspaper Contributor," American Literature, XX (May), 111-28.
     MT "was an incorrigible writer of letters to the press" on serious or trifling matters. Letters to, and comments by the editors of, a number of papers are discussed and quoted extensively.

B59 WEBSTER, SAMUEL MOFFETT. [Letter.] Twainian, VII (November-December), 4.
     MT felt he had slandered Injun Joe, who was liked, respected, and popular; also tells of MT's mother attending a play in St. Louis which had been declared immoral; she found it "all right, but not the sort of a play that a man should go to."

B60 WECTER, DIXON. "Clemens in the Ambrosial Isles," Saturday Review of Literature, XXXI (February 28), 18-19.
     A review of Frear, Mark Twain and Hawaii (1947). Wecter summarizes MT biographies, with passing reference to Paine's "four useful but sloppy volumes in 1912," Effie Mona Mack's "mediocre book on Mark Twain and Nevada," Webster's "delightful and documentary" Mark Twain, Business Man, and DeVoto's "brilliant analysis of Mark Twain's development as an artist." The present monumental study of a four-month period "makes most research in the field seem lax and uncritical by comparison," and is an "indispensable" addition to MT scholarship.

B61 ____, ed. "Mark Twain's Love Letters," Atlantic Monthly, CLXXXI (January), 83-88.

(WECTER, DIXON, ed.)
[Asselineau reports "excerpts to be found in Scholastic, vol. 51, 20, Jan. 19."] Letters from MT to his wife; completes a series beginning in 1947. They appeared in book form in 1949.A2.

B62 _____. "Mark Twain's River," Atlantic Monthly, CLXXXII (October), 45-47.
In 1947 Mr. and Mrs. Wecter went down the Mississippi on a tow-boat; passing references to MT.

B63 WEISINGER, MORT. "Listen! Mark Twain Speaking" (part of a weekly "Report to the Editors"), Saturday Evening Post, CCXX (July 3), 12.
On G. Robert Vincent's collection of recordings of famous individuals for "his unique Voice Library at Yale"; includes an MT recording, with "a voice curiously remindful of Jack Benny." [Twainian, VIII (March-April, 1949), 8, notes that the Edison film of MT and daughters at Stormfield is now at the MT Museum at Hannibal--T.A.T.]

B64 *WILLIAMS, MENTOR L. "Mark Twain's Joan of Arc," Michigan Alumnus Quarterly Review, LIV (May 8), 243-50.
[Source: Asselineau (1954), No. 1193, MHRA Bibliography (1949), No. 3977; article reprinted in Twainian, IX (September-October, 1950), 1-4, 1950.B59.]

B65 *WILLIAMS, STANLEY T. Tres Escritores Clásicos de la Literatura de los Estados Unidos, translated by Filberto Gonzales. Mexico City: Instituto Mexicano-Norteamericano de Relaciones Culturales.
[Source: Asselineau (1954), No. 1156: "Contains the text of a lecture on Twain."]

B66 *WILSON, ROBERT H. "Malory in the Connecticut Yankee," Texas Studies in English, XXVII (June), 185-205.
On MT's faithful and clever use of the Morte d'Arthur in CY. [Source: Asselineau (1954), No. 1194; MHRA Annual Bibliography (1948), No. 330, 3429.]

B67 WORKMAN, MIMS THORNBURGH. "The Whitman-Twain Enigma," Mark Twain Quarterly, VIII (Summer-Fall), 12-13.
A search for references by Whitman to MT has been fruitless; possibly Whitman "was repelled by the genial cynicism."

1949 A BOOKS

A1 *CLEMENS, CYRIL. Mark Twain and Franklin D. Roosevelt. Webster Groves, Missouri: International Mark Twain Society.
A 20-page pamphlet, reprints the interview published in Tributes to Mark Twain (1930). [Source: Asselineau (1954), No. 1201.]

A2 CLEMENS, SAMUEL L. The Love Letters of Mark Twain, ed. Dixon Wecter. New York: Harper & Brothers.
MT's letters to Olivia, 1869-1903, supplemented by letters to other members of his family and to such friends as Joseph Twichell. In addition to being a tender record of his marriage, the letters cast important light on such topics as his writing and his lecturing. Includes a "List of Persons" to identify individuals mentioned in the text, and "Check List: Mark's Letters to Livy," including letters not printed here and providing synopses.

A3 _____. Mark Twain to Mrs. Fairbanks, ed. Dixon Wecter. San Marino, California: Huntington Library.
MT's letters to Mary Mason Fairbanks, whom he met on the Quaker City in 1867. She became his confidante and literary adviser [the extent to which he followed her advice has been questioned], and the letters are a source of information about his thoughts concerning IA, CY, and other works.

1949 B SHORTER WRITINGS

B1 ANON. "Pleasure Trip," Times Literary Supplement, November 18, p. 752.
A primarily descriptive review of Dixon Wecter, ed., Mark Twain to Mrs. Fairbanks. "These are charming letters, well arranged and lucidly annotated."

B2 ANON. "The Talk of the Town," New Yorker, XXIV (January 29), 15-16.
Regrets that the trustees of the MT estate have won a court order to prevent publication of "A Murder, a Mystery, and a Marriage"; speculation on a writer's motives in putting away a manuscript, coming to the conclusion that this one may be a poor thing but MT's "amiable, disappointed ghost" might have liked to see it published.

B3 ANON. "University of California to Get Mark Twain Papers," Publishers' Weekly, CLVI (December 3), 2281.
Brief announcement: the papers are being bequeathed to the University by Clara Clemens Samossoud.

B3A *BINGAY, MALCOLM W. Of Me I Sing. Indianapolis: Bobbs-Merrill.
[Source: Twainian, VIII (September-October, 1949), 5.] On friends at the Savage Club in London keeping a supply of bourbon for MT.

B4 BLANCK, JACOB. "More Shadowy Firsts," Antiquarian Bookman, IV (December 3), 1271-72.
On a newspaper said to have been published on the Quaker City and on MT's address to the Czar: it would be good to find copies of these.

B5 *BOMPIANI. <u>Dizionario Bompiani delle Opere</u>
<u>e dei Personaggi di tutti tempi e di tutte</u>
<u>letterature.</u> Milan: Bompiani.
[Source: Asselineau (1954), No. 1207:
"Contains articles on Mark Twain's Works
in Vol. I, IV, VI, & VII."]

B6 [BROWNELL, GEORGE HIRAM.] "'American Travel
Letters Series Two,' Eleventh in Series in
Alta California," <u>Twainian</u>, VIII (January-
February), 3-6.
Datelined "Hartford, October 22, 1868."

B7 _____. "'American Travel Letters Series Two,'
Twelfth in Series in Alta California,"
<u>Twainian</u>, VIII (March-April), 5-7.
Datelined "Hartford, October 28th, 1868,"
mentions <u>IA</u> as "ready for the engravers and
electrotypers at last."

B8 _____. "'American Travel Letters Series Two,'
Thirteenth in Series in Alta California,"
<u>Twainian</u>, VIII (May-June), 3-6.
Datelined "New York, July, 1869," on a
visit to Boston as guest of "Petroleum V.
Nasby" (David Ross Locke).

B9 _____. "'American Travel Letters Series Two,'
Final (14th) in Series in Alta California,"
<u>Twainian</u>, VIII (July-August), 3-6.
Includes comments on the <u>Overland Monthly</u>
and speculation about aviation and space-
travel.

B10 _____. "Cyril Clemens Announces He'll Publish the 'Official Letters of Mark Twain,'"
<u>Twainian</u>, VIII (March-April), 3-5.
Quotes correspondence in <u>The Nation</u>
(January 22, 26, February 19) and New York
<u>Times</u> (February 13, with a reply scheduled
for the <u>New York Times Book Review</u> of
March 20). Stating that "I am universally
considered the greatest living authority on
Mark Twain," Cyril Clemens requested copies
of Mark Twain letters for an official edition; Thomas G. Chamberlain, co-trustee of
the MT estate (with the Central Hanover
Bank and Trust Company of New York) replied
that no letters could be published without
the permission of MT's daughter, Mrs. Clara
Clemens Samossoud, asked that copies of
letters be sent to the Huntington Library
in California, and then sent a letter dated
March 21 "to every important daily newspaper throughout the country...as a means of
heading off further publication of the Cyril
letter." Brownell ridicules the claims by
Cyril Clemens, adding that "As a final instance of the ghastly and almost unbeliev-
able dearth of any sense of propriety with
which Cyril is endowed, I give you: In a
recent number of his publication, The Mark
Twain Quarterly, the name of 'Clara Clemens' appears on the list of 'Honorary Members' of the International Mark Twain Soci-
ety--and there's no law that will compel
Cyril to remove that name from the list."

The following issue (May-June, p. 6) cites
a clipping from the St. Louis <u>Globe-Democrat</u>
of April 26 reporting that the MT estate has
requested a restraining order against Cyril
Clemens.

B11 _____. "Much Mystery Still Surrounds Twain
Tale of 'Carson Footprints,'" <u>Twainian</u>,
VIII (May-June), 1-3.
Speculation on MT's reasons for contribut-
ing the tale (here reprinted) in the Sacra-
mento <u>Record-Union</u> of March 25, 1885.

B12 _____. "This Tale Looks Like a Sample of
Mark Twain's Work as His Own Press Agent,"
<u>Twainian</u>, VIII (September-October), 3-4.
Text of a photostat of <u>Harry Hazel's Yan-</u>
<u>kee Blade</u> (week ending February 23, 1878),
sent by Frank C. Willson: an MT interview
(supposedly reprinted from New York <u>Sun</u>)
touches on the Whittier birthday dinner
speech and the patent scrap-book. Brownell
suggests the interview may be MT's own work.

B13 _____. "Twain's Letters in San Francisco <u>Call</u>
While a Reporter on the Enterprise," <u>Twain-</u>
<u>ian</u>, VIII (September-October), 1-2.
Datelined "Virginia City, N.T., July 5,
1863." On mines, shootings, politics;
twelve letters listed by dates. Fuller details on the content of one letter given in
the November-December issue, p. 6. Another
letter appears in <u>Twainian</u>, IX (March-April,
1950), 3-4.

B14 _____. "Twain's Tale in 'The Bazaar Record'
Based on Actual Heroic Rescue at Sea,"
<u>Twainian</u>, VIII (November-December), 1-5,
(6).
Text of MT letter to the Royal Humane Society (November 19, 1872) and memorial to
Captain Mouland of the Cunard steamship
<u>Batavia</u>. See Storkan article (1949.B43) for
details of publication.

B15 _____. [Appeal for help in locating a brief
MT item, "Soundings," which appeared in
Chicago <u>Republican</u> (May 30, 1869).] <u>Twain-</u>
<u>ian</u>, VIII (September-October), 5.

B16 _____. [Introduction to a brief note from MT
to Adolph Sutro.] <u>Twainian</u>, VIII (March-
April), 8.

B17 CARPENTER, EDWIN H., JR. "Mining Methods in
Catgut Cañon," <u>Pacific Historical Review</u>,
XVIII (February), 109-11. Reprints with
minimal comment two clippings from the New
York <u>Evening Post</u> of September 14, 17,
1880.
The first, "Gold in Solution," is a news
story about one A. C. Tichenor, who supposedly developed a process for extracting gold
from the springs at a California health re-
sort; "Millions in It" follows, a comic letter by MT who claims to have owned the
springs in the past: "I should have held on

(CARPENTER, EDWIN H., JR.)
to those springs but for the badness of the roads and the difficulty of getting the gold to market."

B18 CHAMBERLAIN, THOMAS G. "Mark Twain's Trustees," Nation, CLXVIII (February 19), 224.
Calls the letter from Cyril Clemens in the January 22 issue "false and misleading in that the official collection of the Mark Twain letters is in the Huntington Library in San Marino, California" [later moved to Bancroft Library, University of California, Berkeley--T.A.T.]. He asks that any MT letters found be sent there, and not to Cyril Clemens.

B19 CLEMENS, CYRIL. "Harry S. Truman: Mark Twain Enthusiast," Dalhousie Review, XXIX (July), 198-99.
General statements on MT's wholesomeness and vigor by Truman, who said he had read all of MT's works he could find.

B20 _____. "Margaret Mitchell and Mark Twain," Hobbies--the Magazine for Collectors, LV (October), 140.
Chiefly on Margaret Mitchell, who died August 16; reprints a letter from her (June 23, 1942) to Cyril Clemens, declining his invitation to speak at the Mark Twain Birthday Banquet but praising the "very great American."

B21 _____. [Brief letter to editor.] Nation, CLXVIII (January 22), 113.
"I am editing the official collection of Mark Twain letters, and will be happy to hear from all who have Twain letters in their possession or know of their whereabouts."

B22 _____. "Mark Twain's Kinsman," Nation, CLXVIII (February 19), 224-25.
"I am universally considered the greatest living authority on Mark Twain.... I am editing the only official collection of Mark Twain's letters, and every important journal throughout the world is being officially notified. The response has been most gratifying."

B23 _____. "Mark Twain's Opinion of the Human Body," Hobbies--the Magazine for Collectors, LIV (April), 140.
A set of undocumented quotations from MT on inadequacies of the human body, printed without editorial comment.

B24 _____. "The President: Mark Twain Enthusiast," Hobbies--the Magazine for Collectors, LIV (May), 139.
Quotes Harry S. Truman's praise of MT in speeches and letters.

B25 CLEMENS, SAMUEL L. "My Methods of Writing," Mark Twain Quarterly, VIII (Winter-Spring), 1.
A letter to an unidentified clergyman, datelined "Hartford, Oct. 15, '88," comments on style, concluding: "Doubtless I have methods, but they beget themselves; in which case I am only their proprietor, not their father."

B26 DICKINSON, LEON T. "The Sources of The Prince and the Pauper," Modern Language Notes, LXIV (February), 103-106.
The sources include J. Hammond Trumbull's The True Blue Laws of Connecticut and Richard Head and Francis Kirkman's The English Rogue. MT was careful with his sources and documentation to make clear his serious purpose: "So anxious was he for the book to be taken seriously, that he considered publishing it anonymously."

B27 FERGUSON, DELANCEY. "'Mother' to Mark Twain," New York Herald Tribune Weekly Book Review, XXV (August 14), 11.
A review of Dixon Wecter, ed., Mark Twain to Mrs. Fairbanks. "With the exception of the correspondence with William Dean Howells, this is the most revealing series of letters to any one outside the humorist's own family which has yet been published.... To all this varied record Dixon Wecter has added commentary and elucidation which make the book a little masterpiece of humane scholarship."

B28 _____. [Review: Dixon Wecter, ed., The Love Letters of Mark Twain.] New York Herald Tribune Book Review, XXVI (November 27), 1, 25.
"The husband changed the wife far more than she changed him."

B29 HALSBAND, ROBERT. "Clemens and His 'Other Mother,'" Saturday Review of Literature, XXXII (October 22), 17.
A review of Dixon Wecter, ed., Mark Twain to Mrs. Fairbanks. MT's readiness to accept Mrs. Fairbanks' recommendations undercuts the contention by Brooks that censorship by Mrs. Clemens damaged MT's work. The letters reveal "how seriously he took the problems of his craft," and "Mr. Wecter's editing is in all ways a superb job."

B30 HINKLE, GEORGE, and BLISS HINKLE. Sierra Nevada Lakes. Indianapolis and New York: Bobbs-Merrill Company.
Passim on MT and his brother Orion ("Acting Governor" of Nevada Territory, pp. 208-209); indexed.

B31 HORNBERGER, THEODORE. [Review: Dixon Wecter, ed., Mark Twain to Mrs. Fairbanks.] American Quarterly, I (Winter), 378-80.

1949 - Shorter Writings

(HORNBERGER, THEODORE)
Although Wecter rightly points out that MT was his own censor, there is evidence between the lines to support the contention by Van Wyck Brooks that Olivia Clemens tamed and diminished him. These letters show much of MT's character, though not its full exuberance, and "Mr. Wecter's editing is painstaking but restrained."

B32 HUTCHESON, AUSTIN E. "Twain Was 'News' to Other Newspapers while a Reporter on the 'Enterprise,'" Twainian, VIII (March-April), 2-3.
Continues the reprinting of comments on MT from Nevada newspapers (See Twainian, VII, November-December, 1948, 3-4): the Virginia City Bulletin on MT's "first public lecture with charged admission" (delivered January 28, 1864, his address to the "Third House" of the territorial legislature); Gold Hill Daily News on Sanitary Fund controversy and MT hoaxes.

B33 *KANAPA, JEAN. "Mark Twain, Premier Classique de l'Amérique," Lettres Françaises, January 6.
[Source: Asselineau (1954), No. 1221.]

B34 KOHT, HALVDAN. The American Spirit in Europe: A Survey of Transatlantic Influences. Philadelphia: University of Pennsylvania Press, pp. 226-28.
Cursory and impressionistic, citing only Chesterton [who did not understand MT] and Howells. Conclusion: MT was popular in Europe and an influence for freedom.

B35 LEISY, ERNEST E. [Review: Walter Francis Frear, Mark Twain and Hawaii (1947).] American Literature, XXI (May), 251-52.
Primarily a description of the material, its publishing history, and biographical significance, noting that previous editions of MT's Sacramento Union letters were inadequate. "The late Governor Frear's legal training and bibliographic contacts enabled him to supply information not available to Paine...nor to Dane. He tells for the first time the complete story of Twain's visit to Hawaii. Particularly useful are the list of Mark's lectures on the Islands and the corrections of inadequate reporting."

B36 LONG, E. HUDSON. "Sut Lovingood and Mark Twain's Joan of Arc," Modern Language Notes, LXIV (January), 37-39.
On the story of a bull-ride in George Washington Harris's "Sicily Burns's Wedding" as a source for a similar incident in JA.

B37 LORCH, FRED W. "'Doesticks' and Innocents Abroad," American Literature, XX (January), 446-49.
Two letters to MT from Mortimer Neal Thomson, a popular humorous writer who used the pseudonym "Doesticks." The letters,

dated October 21 and November 5, 1870, "reveal that Mark Twain had conceived the idea of making a book of his Quaker City letters to the Alta California prior to his departure," and correct Paine's statement (Mark Twain, I, 349) that he "was not immediately interested in book publication."

B38 *McKEITHAN, DANIEL MORLEY. "Mark Twain's Tom Sawyer Abroad and Jules Verne's Five Weeks in a Balloon," Texas Studies in English, XXVIII, 257-70.
[Source: MHRA Annual Bibliography (1949), No. 337.] Reprinted in his Court Trials in Mark Twain and Other Essays (1958).

B39 ODELL, GEORGE C. D. Annals of the New York Stage. New York: Columbia University Press, Vol. XV (1891-1894).
The play based on TS was performed at the Harlem Theatre, February 22-27, 1892 (p. 83). February 26, 27 MT and James Whitcomb Riley read from their works at Madison Square Garden Concert Hall; Odell asks, "Why did Mark Twain thus occasionally exploit himself?" (p. 762).

B40 PETERSEN, SVEND. "Splendid Days and Fearsome Nights," Mark Twain Quarterly, VIII (Winter-Spring), 3-8, 15.
Following the mock-scholarship on the Sherlock Holmes stories, Petersen investigates MT's handling of "the details of time," to which his work is "amazingly faithful," despite a few errors. As an example of his dating, he shows that the murder of Muff Potter in Tom Sawyer is given as having happened on June 17 (Chapter XXIII), which fell on a Monday (Chapters VI-IX); thus, the story took place in 1839, 1844, or 1850, and other evidence of this sort reveals the year of the story as 1844.

B41 *POCHMANN, HENRY A., and GAY WILSON ALLEN. Masters of American Literature. New York: Macmillan. 2 vol.
[Source: Asselineau (1954), No. 1206, listing "in Vol. 2, pp. 436-441, an excellent introduction to Mark Twain and a selected bibliography," with extracts from his works, pp. 441-78.] Pochmann and Allen's introductions were reprinted separately in 1969 as Introduction to Masters of American Literature, See 1969.B58.

B42 SLATER, JOSEPH. "Music at Colonel Grangerford's: A Footnote to Huckleberry Finn," American Literature, XXI (March), 108-11.
Huck's reference in Chapter XVII to the piano "that had tin pans in it" is not comic exaggeration: there were such pianos at the time. "When the Last Link Is Broken" and "The Battle of Prague" would have been appropriate selections to play.

B43 STORKAN, CHARLES J. "That Tall Twain Tale, 'A Storm at Sea,' at Last Traced to It's [sic] Printed Origin," Twainian, VIII (July-August), 1-2.

(STORKAN, CHARLES J.)

Originally published in The Bazaar Record, an ephemeral Cleveland paper (January, 1876, contributed as a favor to Mary Mason Fairbanks); a postscript by George Hiram Brownell lists reprintings in the Troy (N.Y.) Budget, March 6, 1876, and the San Francisco Alta California, April 9, 1876. Also See Twainian for September-October, pp. 5, 6 for two notes: this account is related to the Batavia rescue; the manuscript was sold at auction in 1936. Also See Twainian, VIII (November December), 1-5 for the original on which this account is based.

B44 *THOMPSON, RALPH. "In and Out of Books" column, New York Times Book Review, n.d.

[Source: Quoted in Twainian, VIII (September-October), 5.] In their love for MT the Savage Club (London) imported six cases of Kentucky bourbon; years after his death, says Malcolm W. Bingay, the cases were still there, neatly labeled with his name.

B45 WALSH, ELIZABETH P. "A Connecticut Yankee of Our Lady's Court," Catholic World, CLXIX (May), 91-97.

This article, listed in a number of MT bibliographies, does not mention him. "This is an account of the life and work of William Thomas Walsh" (her father), whose writing appeared in Catholic World for twenty-three years.

B46 WEBSTER, ANNIE (MRS. CHARLES L.); dictated to Doris (Mrs. Samuel C.) Webster. "Recollections of the Clemens Family in St. Louis when Sam was a River Pilot," Twainian, VIII (March-April), 1-2.

These recollections by MT's niece (born 1852) deal mainly with St. Louis neighbors and mention MT only in passing.

B47 WEBSTER, SAMUEL C. "Unknown Ghost Story by Twain found by Samuel C. Webster in Old Family Papers," Twainian, VIII (January-February), 1-2.

The text of "Ghost Life on the Mississippi" (about the ghost of a pilot taking a steamboat through a difficult channel at night): the Webster introduction describes MT as a story-teller and notes the popularity of ghost stories in Missouri.

B48 WEST, RAY B., JR. "Mark Twain's Idyl of Frontier America," University of Kansas City Review, XV (Winter), 92-104.

Argues MT's enduring affection for the regions of his youth: "he could damn the whole human race in theoretical terms; but the background of the country and the life he had known as a boy was always treated with nostalgia and sympathy.... Life in the Mississippi River Valley and the Far West represented for him an idyllic existence which could be treated humorously, but not with personal rancour."

B49 WILLIAMSON, SAMUEL T. "Mark's Letters to His Livy," New York Times Book Review (November 13), p. 53.

A review of Dixon Wecter, ed., The Love Letters of Mark Twain, which are interesting in four ways: as love letters, as fuel for additional debate in the tradition of Brooks and DeVoto, as the portrait of a marriage, and for what they show of "the unrealness of a realistic writer' in his very ordinary, moving response to love, death, and grief.

1950 A BOOKS

A1 ADAMS, LUCILLE. "Huckleberry Finn": A Descriptive Bibliography of the Huckleberry Finn Collection at the Buffalo Public Library. Buffalo, N.Y.: Buffalo Public Library.

"Today the Buffalo Public Library has an unusual Collection. Aside from the Manuscript, a California Salesman's Prospectus, and several U. S. first editions revealing some of the variances in the printing, it contains a number of other editions, including editions in thirteen foreign languages. The related items range from a Metro-Goldwyn-Mayer movie script, three act plays, and music, to comic and paint books for the children. There is also critical and bibliographical material". (p. 5). [There is nothing previously unknown in this critical and bibliographical material-- T.A.T.]

A2 ANDREWS, KENNETH. Nook Farm: Mark Twain's Hartford Circle. Cambridge, Massachusetts: Harvard University Press.

A carefully documented description of the immediate community in which MT lived, showing the intellectual stimulation and also the soul-searchings.

A3 BELLAMY, GLADYS CARMEN. Mark Twain as a Literary Artist. Norman: University of Oklahoma Press.

Emphasizes MT's conscious craftsmanship: torn by mental conflict, he achieved artistic distance and control by use of the Huck Finn persona, placing satiric scenes far off in time or space, reducing the race to microscopic proportions, or regarding life as a dream. There is substantial discussion of the travel books. Pp. 25-40 reprinted in Leary (1962), pp. 207-24; pp. 335-47, on HF, reprinted in Lettis (1962), pp. 338-48.

A4 BRANCH, EDGAR MARQUESS. The Literary Apprenticeship of Mark Twain. With Selections from His Apprentice Writing. Urbana: University of Illinois Press.

Primarily concerned with MT's literary career from the beginnings to the Quaker City excursion (1867), but concluding with "Apprentice and Artist: Huckleberry Finn" (pp. 195-216). Accepts the "Quintus Curtius Snodgress" letters as MT's (pp. 47-56).

1950 - Books

(BRANCH, EDGAR MARQUESS)
[Reprinted in facsimile with new title page, New York: Russell & Russell, 1966.]

A5   CLEMENS, CYRIL, ed. Mark Twain and Harry S. Truman, foreword by the Honorable Louis Johnson, Secretary of Defense. Webster Groves, Missouri: The International Mark Twain Society.
"Number eighteen of the society's biographical Series." Describes appreciation of MT by President Truman, who professes to have read the collected works by the age of twelve. (16-page pamphlet, containing brief notes from Truman).

A6   *EMRICH, DUNCAN. Comstock Bonanza: Rare Western Gallery of Mark Twain, Bret Harte, Sam Davis, James W. Gally, Dan de Quille, Joseph T. Goodman, J. Ross Browne, Fred Hart. New York: Vanguard Press.
[Source: Asselineau (1954), No. 1236; In card catalogue at Oakland (California) Public Library, but not on shelf.]

A7   *FAUST, CLARENCE L., ed. The Adventures of Huckleberry Finn. N.p.: Great Books Foundation.
[Source: Beebe and Feaster (1968), p. 113.]

A8   *HORNSTEIN, SIMON. Mark Twain: La Faillite d'un Idéal. Paris: Renée Lacoste & Cie.
[Source: Asselineau (1954), No. 1233.]
Following Brooks, an adequate, well-documented general study of MT's works, with an attempt to explain why he is not popular in France; includes bibliography of French translations and adaptations.

1950 B SHORTER WRITINGS

B1   ALTKUS, MARY. "Comet of Destiny," Coronet, XXVIII (August), 159.
Brief, popular account of MT's loss of his wife, and his belief that he could not join her until the return of Halley's Comet, which had been in the sky when he was born; his prediction was correct.

B2   ANON. "The Boy and the River," Times Literary Supplement, November 10, p. 708.
A review of the Cresset Press edition of HF with a ten-page introduction by T. S. Eliot. Sees Eliot as being at a disadvantage, having read TS and HF only as an adult and consequently unable to assess MT's achievements, including "his ability to write, simultaneously and in the same book, both as the boy of 30 or 40 years ago and as the mature man looking back on the same event." Questions the conventional account of the version of the origin of MT's pseudonym: "It is dubious as the word 'twain' was not used in counting at that time and place."

B3   ANON, as "Your Reviewer." "The Boy and the River," Times Literary Supplement, November 24, p. 747.
A letter to the editor, accepting one correction in Marcus Cunliffe's letter of November 17 (1950.B17) but holding his ground on three other points, including his statement that the leadsman's call "mark twain" was not in use when MT was a pilot. In another letter (December 8, p. 785), cites his own experience as a leadsman in European waters in support of his reservations about the assumption "that 'mark' meant a fathom, and that 'twain' meant two." [Also see Schofield letter, p. 785.]

B4   ANON. [Review: Edgar Marquess Branch, The Literary Apprenticeship of Mark Twain.] Nineteenth-Century Fiction, V (December), 247-48.
"The chief virtue of the compilation is the effective way in which the author has brought together the results of the many specialized regional studies of the past fifteen years," although "it is odd...that in the mountain of notes there should be no mention of Effie Mona Mack's Mark Twain in Nevada (1947)."

B5   ARMSTRONG, C. J. "Rev. Armstrong Reminisces on Twain's Loyalty to His Old Hannibal Friends," Twainian, IX (January-February), 1-2.
Anecdotes; asserts that John L. RoBards bore MT no ill-will for joking about his name in "The Private History of a Campaign that Failed."

B6   BLANCK, JACOB. "In Re Huckleberry Finn," New Colophon, III, pp. 153-59.
A collation of the first edition; praises Merle Johnson's "superb" description in his 1935 Bibliography of the Works of Mark Twain as "a brilliant beacon in a cloud of Underhillian fog"; Irving S. Underhill's "An Inquiry into Huckleberry Finn" (1931) and "The Haunted Book" (1935) should not have been accepted by the old Colophon: "the bibliographical problem of Huckleberry Finn was rendered an appalling disservice by their publication." Includes reproductions of "Original State of Cut on p. 283," "Corrected (Third) State of Cut," and of E. W. Kemble's note explaining the damage to Uncle Silas's trousers ("a bit of vulgarity inserted by an engraver") and "Handbill issued by Mark Twain's western agents."

B7   BOOTH, BRADFORD A. "Mark Twain's Comments on Holmes's Autocrat," American Literature, XXI (January), 456-63.
Contains 45 comments MT wrote in the margin for Livy to read while they were courting (pp. 459-63). MT liked Holmes and enjoyed his books, but Booth is cautious about suggesting the development of MT's style after Innocents Abroad could indicate influence.

B8   BRANCH, EDGAR M. "The Two Providences: The-
       matic Form in 'Huckleberry Finn,'" College
       English, XI (January), 188-95.
           Miss Watson and the Widow Douglas offer
       contrasting conceptions of heavenly provi-
       dence. From these, there follows a choice
       between conventional morality and humani-
       tarian idealism; the duality is implicit in
       the style of the novel, and provides the-
       matic unity. Reprinted in Gerber (1971),
       pp. 67-77.

B9   [BROWNELL, GEORGE HIRAM.] "Sam Webster Adds
       to the Mystery of that Cut on Page 283 of
       'Huck Finn,'" Twainian, IX (January-Febru-
       ary), 2-3.
           Quotes a letter from Samuel Charles
       Webster, who says he has a proof of p. 283
       showing the indecent cut; also reprints the
       text of a letter from MT to his brother
       Orion on General Grant's confidence in
       Charles L. Webster.

B10   _____. "Twain's Letter in San Francisco Call
       while a Reporter on The Enterprise," Twain-
       ian, IX (March-April), 3-4.
           Datelined "Virginia City, N. T., July 12,
       1863," miscellaneous local news on mines,
       horse races, a petrified man hoax, and the
       upcoming performance of "that sickest of
       all sentimental dramas, 'East Lynne.'"
       Another of these letters and a list of the
       whole series appear in Twainian VIII
       (November-December, 1949), 1-2.

B11   _____. "Who Knows about these Ghostly Twain
       Firsts," Twainian, IX (January-February),
       3-4.
           On Jacob Blanck's "More Shadowy Firsts,"
       Antiquarian Bookman (December 3, 1949), in-
       quiring about the newspaper supposedly pub-
       lished on board the Quaker City. Brownell
       adds a query as to whether the text of
       MT's address to the Russian Czar has been
       preserved.

B12   *CAHEN, JACQUES FERNAND. [On MT., pp. 42-47]
       in his La Littérature Américaine. Paris:
       Presses Universitaires (Collection Que
       Sais-Je?).
           [Source: Asselineau (1954), No. 1237.]
       Condemns his tastelessness, praises him as
       first American realist in LOM, TS, HF.

B13   CLEMENS, CYRIL. "Collecting Mark Twain,
       Eugene Field, and Harry Truman," Hobbies--
       the Magazine for Collectors, LV (November),
       141.
           On his collection; MT material includes
       letters from MT to Cyril Clemens's parents,
       "part of the manuscript of The Gilded Age,"
       "a group of twelve letters which he wrote
       in 1886 to several young friends whom he
       had met during a vacation," a letter in half
       English, half German to the Austrian drama-
       tist Schlesinger, and other letters and
       documents pertaining to MT.

B14   _____. "Hervey Allen and Mark Twain," Hob-
       bies--the Magazine for Collectors, LV
       (April), 120.
           On the life and works of Hervey Allen,
       who died December 28, 1949; notes his ad-
       miration of MT and quotes letters from him,
       praising MT, declining an invitation to
       speak, and thanking Cyril Clemens for elec-
       tion as a "Knight of Mark Twain."

B15   _____. "Recent Acquisitions of Mark Twain
       Library," Mark Twain Quarterly, VIII (Win-
       ter), 19.
           Included are three pages of manuscript of
       The Gilded Age in MT's hand and eight in ⌐
       Charles Dudley Warner's, a note from MT to
       Warner, some copies of MT's works in Polish,
       French, and Turkish, and a sheet describing
       a mock trial of MT on a North German Lloyd
       liner, with his inscription on the back:
       "A true bill, Mark Twain."

B16   _____. "Shaw and Twain," Christian Science
       Monitor, XLIII (December 5), 18.
           A letter to the editor, repeating what he
       was said elsewhere about meetings of MT and
       Shaw.

B17   CUNLIFFE, MARCUS. "The Boy and the River,"
       Times Literary Supplement, November 17,
       p. 727.
           A letter to the editor. The November 10
       review of T. S. Eliot's introduction to HF
       contains [minor] "slips and errors of em-
       phasis" pertaining to MT's life and the
       origin of his pseudonym. Defends his posi-
       tion concerning the pseudonym in another
       letter, December 8, p. 785. [Also See
       Schofield letter, p. 785 (1950.B47).]

B18   [DAVIS, CHESTER L.] "Mark Twain and Presi-
       dent Hayes," Twainian, IX (November-Decem-
       ber), 2-3.
           Letters from MT to Charles Warren Stoddard
       (September 20, 1876) and William Dean How-
       ells (February 22, 1877) mentioning Hayes,
       and to Hayes (April 10, 1882), answering his
       letter of April 6. Contains minimal edi-
       torial comment.

B19   _____. "Tom Sawyer Manuscript Purchased by
       Missouri," Twainian, IX (July-August), 1-2.
           "The State of Missouri has recently com-
       pleted a contract...for the purchase of the
       manuscript from which the English edition of
       Tom Sawyer was printed.... The main criti-
       cism of the manuscript is that it is not all
       in the hand of Mark Twain, most of the pages
       being in the hands of one or more copyists."

B20   _____. [Transitional Issue.] Twainian (May-
       June).
           Announces the death of George Hiram Brown-
       ell. Chester L. Davis, an attorney, is re-
       placing Brownell as the Secretary of the Mark
       Twain Research Association, thanks Clara
       Clemens Samossoud for her financial support

1950 - Shorter Writings

([DAVIS, CHESTER L.])
of The Twainian, discusses future editorial
policy and promises confidentiality of the
files of correspondence. There is a brief,
descriptive notice of Gladys Carmen Bellamy's Mark Twain as a Literary Artist.

B21 DECAUNES, LUC. [Review: Un Yankee à la Cour
du Roi Arthur, traduction d'Odette Ferry
et J. de Plunkett. Paris, Bruxelles,
Éditions de la Paix, 332 pp.] Paru, No. 62
(Juillet), p. 68.
Calls the novel vulgar and boring.

B22 DICKINSON, LEON T. [Review: Dixon Wecter, ed.,
Mark Twain to Mrs. Fairbanks (1949).] American Literature, XXII (May), 202-203.
Praises Wecter's editing, and in particular his including letters by other people
as a supplement to MT's. The editing adds
to the biographical significance of this
book. "And although he does not care to re-
open the question of the female-dominated
Clemens, it is clear that he believes Mrs.
Fairbanks's influence to have been for the
best, as it probably was."

B23 EDWARDS, PETER G. "The Political Economy of
Mark Twain's 'Connecticut Yankee,'" Mark
Twain Quarterly, VIII (Winter), 2, 18.
Dowley, the blacksmith in Chapter XXXIII,
could not understand that an increase in income is valuable only if prices do not rise
correspondingly, and Americans today make
the same mistake. Edwards concludes by
grumbling that "right now I'm going to go
out and buy a steak for $1.10 that would
have cost 40 cents before the war."

B24 ELIOT, T. S. [Introduction.] The Adventures
of Huckleberry Finn. New York: Chanti-
cleer Press.
"In the writing of Huckleberry Finn Mark
Twain had two elements which, when treated
with his sensibility and his experience,
formed a great book: these two are the Boy
and the River.... We come to understand the
River by seeing it through the eyes of the
Boy; but the Boy is also the spirit of the
River." Also praises the colloquial ease of
Huck's diction. Reprinted in Bradley
(1962), pp. 320-27; in Simpson (1968, condensed), pp. 107-108; in Kesterson (1973),
pp. 62-69.

B25 *ENGLEKIRK, JOHN E. A Literature Norteameri-
cano no Brasil. Privately printed in Mexico.
Distributed by Author (Tulane University).
[Source: Asselineau (1954), No. 1229*:
discusses Brazilian interest in MT, and
(presumably) lists translations of his works.]

B26 FATOUT, PAUL. "Mark Twain Lectures in Indiana," Indiana Magazine of History, XLVI
(December), 363-67.
On MT's lectures in Indianapolis and Lo-
gansport in January, 1872; documented from
contemporary newspaper accounts, some of them
unfavorable.

B27 FERGUSON, DELANCEY. [Review: Gladys Carmen
Bellamy, Mark Twain as a Literary Artist.]
New York Herald Tribune Book Review, XXVI
(August 13), 6.
Primarily descriptive, but says "Miss
Bellamy has not just written a new volume
about the humorist; she has done some new
thinking about him."

B28 _____. [Review: Edgar Marquess Branch, The
Literary Apprenticeship of Mark Twain.]
American Literature, XXII (November), 362-63.
More important as sound and detailed criticism than as biography, in which Branch is
too ready to accept Paine and the western
folklore about MT. "His criticism, which in
the major portion of the book seems too
detailed for the very slender merits of the
writing it is applied to, reaches a high
level in the closing section" with analysis
of the thematic structure of Huckleberry
Finn.

B29 _____. [Review: Dixon Wecter, ed., Mark
Twain to Mrs. Fairbanks (1949).] Modern
Language Notes, LXV (December), 568-69.
"Dixon Wecter is admirably carrying on the
work, begun by DeVoto, of bringing order out
of the chaos in which Albert Bigelow Paine
left the Mark Twain MSS, and of revealing
the biographical significance which Paine
was too indolent or too obtuse to understand."
The present volume is an indispensable companion to Mr. Wecter's edition of The Love
Letters of Mark Twain: "From now on, all
studies of Mark Twain's personality, and
therefore of his art and ideas, will have to
start from these two books."

B30 FRANCIS, RAYMOND L. "Mark Twain and H. L.
Mencken," Prairie Schooner, XXIV (Spring),
31-39.
As satirist and iconoclast, "Mencken is a
direct descendant of Mark Twain"; although
the two differed in their attitudes toward
democracy, they came from different directions
to a similar view of national institutions
and the ignorance of mobs. There are similarities in their targets and their forms of
statement.

B31 GEISMAR, MAXWELL. "High Thinking, Fine Living," New York Times Book Review, (October 8),
p. 5.
A review of Kenneth R. Andrews, Nook Farm:
Mark Twain's Hartford Circle as a good survey
of the community but "not highly successful...in telling of Mark Twain's connection
with the group" and tending to minimize his
tragedy by seeking purely psychological
causes for his bitterness.

B32 GOHDES, CLARENCE. [Review: Dixon Wecter, ed.,
Mark Twain to Mrs. Fairbanks (1949).] South
Atlantic Quarterly, XLIX (January), 118.
Although "the letters are of no importance
as literature or as humor," they add to and
correct MT biography. "The book is intended

(GOHDES, CLARENCE)
for the perusal of a Mark Twain specialist or collector--and of its kind it is a model."

B33 HART, JAMES D. The Popular Book: A History of America's Literary Taste. New York: Oxford University Press, passim.
Includes information on sales of MT's books and a discussion of their appeal as part of a general study that concerns popular tastes, subscription sale by book agents, etc. There is an extensive annotated "Bibliographical Checklist" in place of notes (pp. 289-300).

B34 HOLMAN, C. HUGH. [Review: Dixon Wecter, ed., Mark Twain to Mrs. Fairbanks (1949).] Modern Language Review, XLV (October), 541-42.
Wecter "has shown sound judgment, admirable thoroughness and knowledge, and wise discretion in annotating these letters, which are published without alteration." The non-specialist can consult DeLancey Ferguson's Mark Twain: Man and Legend, which draws on these letters, but for the MT specialist Wecter's edition is indispensable.

B35 JOHNSON, IRMIS. "Mark Twain's Only Love," American Weekly (a Sunday supplement of the Hearst newspapers) (April 23), pp. 6-7.
A popular account, following the familiar biographies.

B36 JONES, JOSEPH. "Utopia as Dirge," American Quarterly, II (Fall), 214-26.
A comparison of MT's Connecticut Yankee with Aldous Huxley's Brave New World and George Orwell's Nineteen Eighty-Four, all of which reveal "antagonism to the super-organization--a protest against or a fear of the assault of institutions against the individual," and all three reveal "the loss of wonder, the loss of the past, the loss of humanitarian culture, and the loss of responsibility in the use of power." Jones regards Hank Morgan as a protagonist, his defeat as "a trick of fate."

B37 KAPLAN, ISRAEL. "Kipling's American Notes and Mark Twain Interview," Papers of the Bibliographical Society of America, XLIV (First Quarter), 69-73.
Largely on the general question of American publication of Kipling's travel letters. "The first complete Kipling letter to appear in an American newspaper was his interview with Mark Twain, which the New York Herald printed on August 17, 1890," apparently without permission. "However, no earlier version of this letter is known, and the final paragraph, uncollected, is significant," a criticism of CY. "The paragraph in question now achieves its first American printing since August 17, 1890: 'Later.-- Oh shame! Oh shock! Oh fie! I have been reading the new book which you

will also have read by this time--the book about the Yankee animal in the court yard. It's***but I don't believe he ever wrote it; or, if he did, I am certain that if you held it up to a looking glass or picked out every third word or spelled it backward you would find that it hid some crystal clean tale as desirable as Huck Finn.'"

B38 KITZHABER, ALBERT. "Götterdämmerung in Topeka: The Downfall of Senator Pomeroy," Kansas Historical Quarterly, XVIII (August), 243-78.
Provides background for MT's treatment of the Senator's downfall in GA--here briefly noted; on p. 248, n. 8, Kitzhaber says he will discuss in detail MT's literary use of the case in a forthcoming issue of Modern Language Quarterly. (See 1954.B33.)

B39 LEISY, ERNEST E. "Mark Twain the Artist," Southwest Review, XXXV (Autumn), 295-96. A review of Edgar Marquess Branch, The Literary Apprenticeship of Mark Twain and Gladys Carmen Bellamy, Mark Twain as a Literary Artist.
"Conscientious studies both, for which every reader of Mark Twain is the wiser. We have not heretofore had as thorough an analysis of Mark Twain's various styles as Mr. Branch offers us, and we have needed the many corrections of DeVoto's and Brooks's assumptions which Miss Bellamy brings out. Her discussion of the travel books breaks new ground." Leisy suggests, however, that there should be "a more rigid appraisal of Mark Twain," whose "craftsmanship is hardly that of the born writer.... Mark Twain was an anecdotist, who by sundry apprenticeships learned the art of occasionally striking out a memorable phrase, or even of making an episode convincing, if he had heard the yarn before or had personally known the characters." Except for most of TS and HF, "and a few episodes in other books, he was not a great writer."

B40 LORCH, FRED W. "Mark Twain and the Pennsylvania Disaster," Twainian, IX (January-February), 2.
On the death of Henry Clemens, scalded in a steamboat explosion; reprints a contemporary account of SLC's grief on seeing Henry in the hospital (St. Louis News and Intelligencer, June 19, 1858; reprinted from Memphis Eagle and Inquirer of June 16).

B41 _____. "Mark Twain's Lecture from Roughing It," American Literature, XXII (November), 290-307.
Includes the text as published in the Lansing (Michigan) State Republican, December 21, 1871. For Lorch's fully developed treatment of this and other MT lectures, see his The Trouble Begins at 8 (1968.A2).

B42 MASTERS, EDGAR LEE. "The House Where Mark Twain Was Born, Florida, Missouri," Mark Twain Quarterly, VIII (Winter), 1.
A poem on the rural simplicity of the cottage.

B43 MECHLING, PHILIPP. "Mark Twain in Heidelberg," Twainian, IX (November-December), 3.
Reminiscences of MT by a guide who saw him on his visit there in 1896.

B44 MICHEL, ROBERT. "The Popularity of Mark Twain in Austria," Mark Twain Quarterly, VIII (Winter), 5-6, 19.
On MT's visits to Austria, and a meeting in his honor by the writers and journalists' club, Concordia, where a portrait of him by Gilbert Lehner was displayed; he was later received by the Emperor, Franz Joseph, and there was a great deal published by or about him in the Viennese papers.

B45 MOFFETT, WALLACE C. "Mark Twain's Lansing Lecture on Roughing It," Michigan History, XXXIV (June), 144-70.
After lecturing in Lansing in December, 1868, MT returned there in 1871, this time choosing his material to publicize his forthcoming RI. The text of his lecture is reprinted (pp. 153-70) from the Lansing State Republican (December 21, 1871), and a number of other contemporary accounts are quoted.

B46 REDDING, SAUNDERS. "Faith and Despair: The Alcotts and Mark Twain," American Scholar, XX (Winter), 112-22.
A review-article, discussing Gladys Carmen Bellamy's Mark Twain as a Literary Artist pp. 118-22. Her study falters in its attempt to demonstrate conscious artistry. She reveals MT's failure to achieve the artistic detachment needed for selection, simplification, and abstraction from the raw material of life. "This is Miss Bellamy's main thesis, and she expounds it sometimes brilliantly."

B47 SCHOFIELD, KENNETH B. "The Boy and the River," Times Literary Supplement, December 8, p. 785.
A letter to the editor, agreeing with Marcus Cunliffe in the controversy over the origin of MT's pseudonym.

B48 SMITH, HENRY NASH. "Origins of a Native American Literary Tradition," in Margaret Denny and William H. Gilman, eds., The American Writer and the European Tradition. Minneapolis: University of Minnesota Press (Reprinted: New York, Toronto, London: McGraw-Hill Book Company, 1964, paperbound, and New York: Haskell House Publishers Ltd., 1968. A comparison of indexes suggests that both of these are photographic reprints.), pp. 63-77; on MT, pp. 70-77.

On MT as influenced by southwestern humor, his repudiation of Europe, and America's literary debt to him.

B49 SPILLER, ROBERT E. "Mr. & Mrs. Clemens," Saturday Review of Literature, XXXIII (January 28), 17. A review of Dixon Wecter, ed., The Love Letters of Mark Twain (1949).
Wecter "supplies a calendar of all Mark's letters to Livy, but he wisely refrains from publishing tham all; a man in love is likely to repeat himself." The book provides no new revelations, certainly no indication that Livy's censorship was stricter than MT's own.

B50 STEVENSON, ROBERT LOUIS. "Letter from Robert Louis Stevenson to Mark Twain," Twainian, IX (September-October), 1, 4.
Undated (Chester L. Davis assumes it was during the period 1888-1893), on the possibility of Charles L. Webster & Co. handling Stevenson's work.

B51 THOMPSON, LAWRANCE. "Twain's Prelude to Fame," New York Times Book Review (July 2), p. 4.
A review of Edgar Marquess Branch, The Literary Apprenticeship of Mark Twain, which fails in an attempt to reveal a "logic of development" in MT's work: even in the "superb" HF, "the formula, or informing artistic principle, is Twain's lifelong pet, improvisation. This time it was all he needed."

B52 THORP, WILLARD. "American Writers as Critics of Nineteenth-Century Society," in Denny and Gilman, The American Writer and the European Tradition (See Smith, Henry Nash, 1950.B48), pp. 90-105; on MT, pp. 103-104.
On MT as critic of American society, his failure to speak out as he might have, and his final despair.

B53 TROMMER, MARIE. "Mark Twain and the Missing Cat Chapter," Mark Twain Quarterly, VIII (Winter), 3-4.
When she was a child in Russia, the author read a copy of Tom Sawyer from which the chapter that accompanied a picture of a cat hanging above the schoolmaster had been cut out; years later, she was able to read a complete copy in New York.

B54 WALLACE, ELIZABETH. "The Beloved Jester's Many Moods," Saturday Review of Literature, XXXIII (September 23), 30.
A review of Gladys Carmen Bellamy, Mark Twain as a Literary Artist. After having presented moralism, determinism, pessimism, and patheticism as the bases of MT's mind, Miss Bellamy discusses "with skill and clarity" the way they conflict in MT's work as one or another becomes dominant. She writes clearly and convincingly, and also "delightfully and with vigorous freshness."

B55 WATTERS, R. E. [Review: Edgar Marquess Branch, The Literary Apprenticeship of Mark Twain.] Journal of Southern History, XVI (November), 555-57.
   This is an "excellent study," and the re-printing of MT's early writings from original sources is so valuable that Watters wishes more space had been given to them, "even at the cost of curtailing the evaluations and analyses"; for example, "the sixteen-page thematic analysis of Huckleberry Finn (1884), excellent though it is, has little real connection with the rest of the book--so little, indeed that the author was able to publish a slightly abridged version of it separately in College English, XI (1950), 188-95."

B56 WEBSTER, SAMUEL C. "Here's Probably Twain's First Version of His Tale of 'Dick Baker's Cat,'" Twainian, IX (January-February), 3.
   Reprints the text of an early MS story about the cat, Tom Quartz, who later appeared in RI.

B57 *WECTER, DIXON. [Introduction.] Life on the Mississippi. New York: Harper & Brothers.
   [Source: Asselineau (1954), No. 1235.]

B58 WHICHER, GEORGE F. "The Styles of Mark Twain," New York Times Book Review (August 13), p. 6.
   A descriptive review of Gladys Carmen Bellamy's Mark Twain as a Literary Artist, which "fills a gap in the series of brilliantly able studies of Mark Twain that have been written during the past thirty years.... She has set the appropriate keystone on the arch of Mark Twain literary criticism."

B59 WILLIAMS, MENTOR L. "Mark Twain's Joan of Arc," Twainian, IX (September-October), 1-4.
   On MT's long-enduring interest in the medieval world, where he sought "the ethical core of human society. He could not find it in the modern world." (Reprinted from Michigan Alumnus Quarterly Review for Spring, 1948).

B60 WILLIAMS, STANLEY T. "The Enigma of Mark Twain," Yale Review, XL (Winter), 340-43.
   A review of Kenneth Andrews, Nook Farm: Mark Twain's Hartford Circle ("modern," in placing MT "in a pattern of American thought in a particular place at a particular time"); Gladys Carmen Bellamy, Mark Twain as a Literary Artist ("She assails the riddle of Mark Twain's mind; she tries to resolve the paradoxes.... Her theory is persuasive. It is...occasionally blurred by the manipulation of too many abstractions, as in her four 'bases' of Mark Twain's mind: moralism, pessimism, determinism, and--unhappy word--'patheticism'!"); Edgar Marquess Branch, The Literary Apprenticeship of Mark Twain ("biographically factual, rather than historical or critical").

B61 WILLSON, FRANK C. "Two Uncollected Twain Writings Found in British-Authored Books," Twainian, IX (March-April), 1-2.
   The text of letters by MT on the use of tobacco and intoxicants, and on his unconscious of half-conscious method of composition; reprinted from A. Arthur Reade, ed., Study and Stimulants (Manchester, England, and Philadelphia, 1883) and George Bainton, ed., The Art of Authorship (New York and London: D. Appleton & Co., 1890).

B62 WINKLER, JOHN A. "Tom Sawyer's Town--A Sketch," Twainian, IX (May-June), 1, 4; (July-August), 3-4.
   A popular account of MT's boyhood in Hannibal by the Chairman of the Mark Twain Municipal Board, following MT's Autobiography and adding little to this and other familiar sources.

B63 WINTERICH, JOHN T. "Clemens and Colony in the Hartford Days," Saturday Review of Literature, XXXIII (October 14), 26-27.
   A review of Kenneth Andrews, Nook Farm: Mark Twain's Hartford Circle, "a contribution of major importance," marked by "depth, judgment, shrewd and accurate appraisal, and a scholarly detachment that still has room for humor, warmth, and sympathy." MT is not allowed to overshadow the other characters, particularly his wife Olivia and their pastor Joseph Twichell (whose twelve-volume diary, covering a period of fifty years, is in the library at Yale).

1951 A BOOKS

A1 *ANON. O'Connor Auction List, Mark Twain Library Auction, April 10th, 2005 Le Brea Ave., O'Connor Auction Studios, 7949 Sunset Boulevard, Hollywood 46, Calif.
   [Source: Asselineau (1954), No. 1269.]

A2 *ANON. Zeitlin and Ver Brugge List. Books from the Library of Mark Twain, also articles from his home purchased at the sale of the library of his daughter, Clara Clemens Samassoud, April 10-14, 1951, Zeitlin and Ver Brugge, Booksellers, 815 North Cienega, Los Angeles, Calif., List No. 132, May 1951.
   [Source: Asselineau (1954), No. 1270.]

A3 CANBY, HENRY SEIDEL. Turn West, Turn East: Mark Twain and Henry James. Boston: Houghton Mifflin Company.
   Considers MT and James as representatives of their age. They are articulate, novelists of manners, come from the same moral climate, and "both are almost humorously exaggerated as representative of the Turn West and the Turn East American.... They belong, actually, in the same stream of pioneer American history, although Mark plunged in more thirstily than any of his contemporaries in literature, and Henry fought the current until he could scramble out" (p. xi). An

(CANBY, HENRY SEIDEL)
extensive index includes major works and
characteristics of their writing.
Pp. 239-57 reprinted in Scott (1955),
pp. 279-85; (1967), pp. 264-70. Pp. 249-57
reprinted in Leary (1962), pp. 225-31.

A4 *GILKEY, ROBERT. Mark Twain Voyageur et Son
Image de l'Europe. Paris (a mimeographed
dissertation for the University of Paris).
[Source: Asselineau (1954), No. 1272.]

1951 B SHORTER WRITINGS

B1   ANON. "The Characters Mark Used in His Writings," Twainian, X (September-October), 4.
Reprints an undated clipping from the
newspaper, Grit, on Joe Douglas, supposedly
the original of "Injun Joe" in Tom Sawyer,
but a harmless, gentle friend of the boys
in Hannibal. This is listed as "The First
of a Series" in The Twainian, but the series
was not continued.

B2   ANON. "Mark Twain and Anthony Trollope,
Equestrians," Mark Twain Quarterly, IX
(Winter), 14-15.
At a dinner honoring Joaquin Miller,
Trollope tried unsuccesfully to draw MT
out on the subject of horses.

B3   *ANON. "Mark Twain, J. Swift e Alphonse Daudet Presentati ai Ragazzi," La Fiera Letteraria, No. 49 (December 10), p. 8.
[Source: Asselineau (1954), No. 1306.]

B4   ANON. "New & Notable: Mark Twain," Princeton
University Library Chronicle, XII (Summer),
217-18.
The library has acquired the Thomas L.
Leeming Collection, which includes first
American editions of most of MT's works,
"the nearly complete manuscript of "The
£1,000,000 Bank-Note," one of three copies
of The Suppressed Chapter of Following the
Equator (1928), and one of sixteen copies
of A Murder, a Mystery, and a Marriage
(1945).

B5   ANON. "New England Intellectuals," Times Literary Supplement, February 16, p. 97. A
review of Kenneth R. Andrews, Nook Farm:
Mark Twain's Hartford Circle (1950).
Impressively thorough but dry, "It is a
book for the student rather than for the
general reader. Even the student may think
it too intense a culture, unless he happens
to be digging the same ground."

B6   ANON. [Brief Review: Kenneth R. Andrews,
Nook Farm: Mark Twain's Hartford Circle.]
Nineteenth-Century Fiction, V (March),
334-35.
Brief and descriptive, noting that Andrews
has shown "patience and intelligence" in
sifting the mass of material, adding to our
understanding of American thought and MT's
growing concern for values.

B7   ARNAVON, CYRILLE. "Les Humoristes: Mark
Twain," in his Les Lettres Américaines devant
la Critique Française (Paris: Société d'Édi-
tion les Belles Lettres), pp. 71-80.
Traces French criticism of MT, concluding:
"Mark Twain n'aura substantiellement enrichi
ou approfondi notre vision des Américains."

B8   BARSAMIAN, KENNETH J. "Mark Twain's Mudhen
Victory," Mark Twain Quarterly, IX (Winter),
12-13.
On the abortive duel with James Laird
which supposedly led to MT's leaving Nevada
for California; apparently based entirely on
the Paine biography.

B9   BLAIR, WALTER [Review: Kenneth R. Andrews,
Nook Farm: Mark Twain's Hartford Circle
(1950).] American Literature, XXIII (May),
258-59.
"Professor Andrews has drawn upon an impressive array of previously unused primary
sources--diaries, private papers, Hartford
newspapers, books by seventeen Hartford
writers--to learn about the Nook Farm community." The book is useful on the thought of
the time and place, but more could have been
done toward showing how they influenced The
Gilded Age and A Connecticut Yankee in King
Arthur's Court; nonetheless, the book provides "many insights and a great deal of
valuable information."

B10 _____. [Review: Gladys Carmen Bellamy, Mark
Twain as a Literary Artist (1950).] American
Literature, XXII (January), 521-24.
Provides a useful summary of Miss Bellamy's
book and her approach; notes more emphasis
on MT's ideas than on his method. Concludes:
"It is a through study of the tone of Clemens's works and of the patterns of his
thinking. It throws a great deal of light
on the content--if not, perhaps, the form--
of a great artist's writings."

B11 BLUMFIELD, RALPH D. "Twain Note," Hobbies--
the Magazine for Collectors, LVI (December),
152.
Extract from a letter to Cyril Clemens,
briefly recalling several meetings with MT.

B12 BURNAM, TOM. "Mark Twain and the Paige Typesetter: A Background for Despair," Western
Humanities Review, VI (Winter), 29-36.
To MT the typesetter was not only an in-
vestment but also a work of the imagination,
and in its failure it became a "dream" of
rational, mechanical perfection.

B13 BURNET, RUTH A. "Mark Twain in the Northwest,
1895," Pacific Northwest Quarterly, XLII
(July), 187-202.
On MT's two weeks in Washington, Oregon,
and British Columbia on his round-the-world
lecture tour to pay off his debts. A number
of contemporary newspaper accounts are cited
and quoted.

B14   CANBY, HENRY SEIDEL. "Hero of the Great Know-How: Mark Twain's Machine-Age Yankee," Saturday Review of Literature, XXXIV (October 20), 7-8, 40-41.
    Excerpted from his Turn West, Turn East ("to be published next month"). "Mark Twain had no idea whatsoever of the inner ideals or the outer responsibilities of feudalism" and the book contains some of his worst writing, but Canby's generation read CY "with passionate delight" because in Hank Morgan they saw how "the kind of fellow we see every day became the Boss by using just the kind of science we were being taught in school."

B15   CARDWELL, GUY A. "Mark Twain's Hadleyburg," Ohio State Archaeological and Historical Quarterly [now Ohio History], LX (July), 257-64.
    A detailed refutation of the suggestion by Russel B. Nye (1938) that Oberlin, Ohio was the model for Hadleyburg.

B16   CARTER, PAUL J., JR. [Review: Gladys Carmen Bellamy, Mark Twain as a Literary Artist.] Western Humanities Review, VI (Winter), 75-77.
    The analysis of MT's internal conflict "is an original and stimulating contribution to the study of Twain," though less successful when Miss Bellamy argues that with a balanced view of the duality of life MT might have been a "great" artist: "To affirm that the artist must effect some synthesis between good and evil, must achieve an inner serenity, is to ignore the experience of too many artists, who derive power and direction from their inner conflicts."

B17   CHESTER, GIRAUD. Embattled Maiden: The Life of Anna Dickinson. New York: G. P. Putman's Sons.
    On MT's advice concerning subscription publication of books (p. 131) and his letters to her (p. 156); apparently this material is now in the Anna E. Dickinson Papers in the Manuscript Division of the Library of Congress.

B18   CLEMENS, CYRIL. "Bernard Shaw and Mark Twain," Notes and Queries (London), CXCVI (March 3), 104.
    "Your readers may be interested in what Bernard Shaw wrote me on 1st April, 1937, of his meetings with Mark Twain"; reproduces without further comment the text of the note, which Cyril Clemens has also published elsewhere.

B19   _____. "Mark Twain and His Corncob," Hobbies--the Magazine for Collectors, LVI (June), 160.
    Anecdote: MT dined with Sir Bruce and Lady Seton in England, 1907; afterward, offered a cigar, he said he preferred his pipe.

B20   _____. "Mark Twain Is Entertained by Edward 7th," Hobbies--the Magazine for Collectors, LVI (March) 138-39.
    On MT's attendance at a large garden party at Windsor Castle, June 28, 1907; not documented.

B21   _____. "The Missing Mark Twain Manuscript," Hobbies--The Magazine for Collectors, LVI (May), 136. Also in Mark Twain Quarterly, IX (Winter), 13.
    The locations of most MT manuscripts are known, but "All lovers of American literature await with high anticipation the discovery of the manuscript of The Prince and the Pauper."

B22   COLLINS, CARVEL. [Review: Kenneth R. Andrews, Nook Farm: Mark Twain's Hartford Circle (1950) and Gladys Carmen Bellamy, Mark Twain as a Literary Artist (1950).] New England Quarterly, XXIV (December), 540-42.
    Although his "well-documented chapters give the reader an excellent picture of many of the influences to which Mark Twain was exposed" and Andrews "presents many new insights" into the way they acted on MT, he is less successful in "separating these influences from earlier ones and from contemporary ones not originating in the Nook Farm community." Miss Bellamy's book is confused in purpose, and "never really deals meaningfully with the over-all form of any of Twain's works, good or bad. And nowhere does a well developed aesthetic theory appear." It provides evidence of MT's craftsmanship, but "the trouble is that the book does not adequately examine that craftsmanship."

B23   COLLINS, LOUISE. "Post Cards of Mark Twain and Tom Sawyer," Hobbies--the Magazine for Collectors, LVI (November), 150-52.
    The outlook is that of a collector, not a student of MT: "At one point in Mark Twain's life he went West, and while there he wrote several interesting stories." Describes a number of post cards showing MT and places where he lived.

B24   COMMAGER, HENRY STEELE. "The Golden West," Scholastic, LVII (January 3), 10-11.
    An account for high-school students of MT's picture of the West in RI.

B25   [DAVIS, CHESTER L.] "Mark's Marginal Notes on Macaulay," Twainian, X (July-August), 1-2; (September-October), 1-4; (November-December), 3.
    On underscorings and marginal notations in MT's copy of G. Otto Trevelyan's Macaulay's Life and Letters (New York: Harper & Brothers, 1876, copyright 1875).

B26   _____. "More Background on Innocents," Twainian, X (May-June), 3.

([DAVIS, CHESTER L.])
Three letters from MT to Elisha Bliss (April 12, "April Something," and April 29, 1869) on the illustrations to IA, with minimal editorial comment.

B27 _____. "The Prince and the Pauper," Twainian, X (July-August), 3.
On unusual issues of P&P; contains MT letters (August 31, 1880 and February 23, 1882) on the writing and sales of the book.

B28 _____. "Revising the Revisor," Twainian, X (January-February), 1.
Brief comment on IA and a letter by MT to Elisha Bliss (April 20, 1869).

B29 _____. "Who Is Your Secretary?" Twainian, X (November-December), 4.
Biographical information provided by Chester Davis, an electrical engineer and later a patent lawyer, editing The Twainian by request (and as a hobby, with remuneration).

B30 DICKINSON, LEON T. [Review: Dixon Wecter, ed., The Love Letters of Mark Twain (1949).] American Literature, XXII (January), 524-25.
Notes that Wecter did not include the letters to Livy published in Paine's biography and Clara's My Father Mark Twain, "and others of apparently slight interest." The editing provides a context even for readers unfamiliar with MT's life, but the letters add little to the existing picture of MT: "It seems more and more likely that most of the evidence on Clemens is in. Further biographical studies will do well if, as this volume has done, they manage to enrich the story of Mark Twain's life."

B31 DOUGHTY, HOWARD, JR. [Review: Henry Seidel Canby, Turn West, Turn East: Mark Twain and Henry James.] Nation (New York), CLXXIII (December 8), 505.
The contrast is a useful device, but "the tensions of the question...are not altogether resolved."

B32 DOUGLAS, ROBERT. "The Pessimism of Mark Twain," Mark Twain Quarterly, IX (Winter), 1-4.
MT's pessimism sees man engaged in two different struggles: "against a controllable society" and "against a mechanistic and determined universe."

B33 EDEL, LEON. "Two Innocents at Home," New York Times Book Review (November 11), p. 8.
A review of Henry Seidel Canby's Turn West, Turn East: Mark Twain and Henry James, which reflects sympathy for MT but does injustice to James. "The blemishes of too-casual scholarship...are all the more regrettable in a book ingenious in conception," blessed with a warm and lucid prose, and "as mellow as it is worldly wise."

B34 EKSTRÖM, KJELL. "Extracts from a Diary Kept by Ozias W. Pond During the Clemens-Cable Tour of Readings in 1885," Archiv für das Studium der neueren Sprachen, CLXXXVIII (May), 109-13.
Comments by their manager on the audiences, weather, a train derailment, an interview in the Davenport (Iowa) Democrat (quoted). MT, who was reading Malory's Morte D'Arthur on the tour, gave Pond the title "Sir Sagramore, Knight of the Lake," and he went by that title for the rest of the tour.

B35 *ELIOT, T. S. "Huckleberry Finn," Bonniers Litterära Magasin (Sweden), XX (December), 751-56.
[Source: Asselineau (1954), No. 1293.]

B36 FLACK, FRANK M. "Patent Adjustable Speech," Twainian, X (November-December), 1-2.
On a proof-sheet, signed by MT, of the speech before he delivered it at the New England Dinner, Boston, December 20, 1887 (text of this version is reprinted).

B37 *FRANCIOSA, MASSIMO. "I Meriti Nacosti di Mark Twain Narratore," La Fiera Letteraria (Italy), No. 25 (June 24), pp. 4, 7.
[Source: Listed by Asselineau (No. 1294) and in "Articles on American Literature Appearing in Current Periodicals," American Literature, XXIV (March, 1952), 130. Asselineau's annotation reads: "On Mark Twain's consummate skill as a storyteller." American Literature annotation: "Apropos of an Italian translation of Tom Sawyer and Huckleberry Finn published by Einaudi in Turin, it is observed that Mark Twain is not greatly appreciated in America."]

B38 GOHDES, CLARENCE. "Mirth for the Million," in Arthur Hobson Quinn, ed., The Literature of the American People: An Historical and Critical Survey (New York: Appleton-Century Crofts), pp. 701-20.
On MT, pp. 708-20, noting his mixture of "instinctive barbarism" with an intellectual humor and a feeling for literature. "Like Emerson and Whitman, he seems to reflect the qualities of his country with unusual fullness."

B39 _____. [Review Article.] South Atlantic Quarterly, L (July), 437-39.
Summarizes the Brooks-DeVoto controversy, with eventual dominance of DeVoto's view of the importance of the frontier. Edgar Marquess Branch, The Literary Apprenticeship of Mark Twain (1950) "is a culmination of much work along this line, though it is by no means theory-ridden. In fact it delivers a severe blow to the frontier adherents." Gladys Carmen Bellamy, Mark Twain as a Literary Artist "begins where Mr. Branch leaves off. It uses as grist just about everything, good and bad, that has been written about Mark Twain.... Nevertheless, she has some

(GOHDES, CLARENCE)
very sensible opinions on her subject."
Kenneth Andrews, Nook Farm: Mark Twain's
Hartford Circle (1950) "is far more important than a mere background of Mark Twain
and stands on its own feet as an exhaustive
account of the ideas and mores prevailing
in an American community during an era
most apt to be misunderstood today."

B40   GRAY, JAMES. "Interpreting Genius," Saturday
Review of Literature, XXXIV (December 1),
27.
A review of Henry Seidel Canby, Turn West,
Turn East: Mark Twain and Henry James.
This study of two lives in the Plutarchan
manner is a fortunate use of Canby's gifts,
as he achieves "that spontaneous identification with his material which...is the
ally of moving and creative analysis."
[Canby was a founder and chairman of the
editorial board of this magazine--T.A.T.]

B41   HERZL, THEODOR. "Mark Twain in Paris"
["Translated by Alexander Behr, from Dr.
Herzl's Feuilletons"], Mark Twain Quarterly,
IX (Winter), 16-20.
Describes a reading by MT before a group
of English schoolgirls at the British Embassy; followed by a burlesque account attributed to "Hesperus M. Dark, correspondent of the Minneapolis Bluffs."

B42   HILTON, EARL. "Mark Twain's Theory of History," Papers of the Michigan Academy of
Science, Arts, and Letters, XXXVII, 445-53.
MT did not share his day's nostalgia for
the Middle Ages or hold an evolutionary
view of history. He inherited an eighteenth-
century view of which the central concepts
were "progress" and a universal "nature" of
man which made it possible. "In the years
between 1895 and 1900 Twain had come to
see external nature as malicious, and human
nature he doubted more and more. Now he
had arrived at a complete reversal of his
earlier position [as revealed, for example,
in HF]. Now it was not 'nature,' but the
cumulative human experience crystallized
in institutions, which he urged men to follow."

B43   HORNBERGER, THEODORE. [Review: Kenneth Andrews, Nook Farm: Mark Twain's Hartford
Circle (1950).] American Quarterly, III
(Summer), 188-91.
Andrews depicts the neighborhood as self-
contained and homogeneous, with standards
that influenced the writers living there.
A major source of material has been unpublished family papers, yielding considerable
color. The generalizations seem more persuasive when applied to MT and Charles Dudley Warner than when applied to the community as a whole, and there are verbal infeli-
cities and passages of fictionalized biography that seem inappropriate, but these are

minor flaws in a study that "is extraordinarily interesting and contains much that is
new."

B44   HUTCHESON, AUSTIN E. "More Tales about Twain
in Nevada, as Told by His Fellow Newspaper-
men," Twainian, X (September-October), 3-4.
Excerpts from the Gold Hill News and the
Virginia City Territorial Enterprise (1865,
1866), chiefly on MT's lectures.

B45   IRVING, LAURENCE. Henry Irving: The Actor
and His World. London: Faber and Faber,
p. 454.
Mentions MT's presence at a public banquet
honoring Irving, April 6, 1885; no details
are given.

B46   JOHNSON, MERLE. "Merle Johnson's Letters,"
Twainian, X (July-August), 3-4.
An assortment of letters in one of which
(December 23, 1924) he identified the author
of The Literary Guillotine as William Wallace
Whitelock.

B47   JONES, ALEXANDER E. "Heterodox Thought in
Mark Twain's Hannibal," Arkansas Historical
Quarterly, X (Autumn, 1951), 244-57.
Although MT's boyhood environment was
"primarily...one of Calvinistic Presbyterianism...there were also underlying currents
of liberal and unorthodox doctrine which
could have reached the boy from his uncle,
his father, his mother, and even from the
church ritual itself...an investigation of
the other members of Twain's immediate family reveals a significant fact: of those
persons who lived beyond this early Hannibal
period, not one remained orthodox in his religion." "All members...of Sam's immediate
family underwent a process of religious
development which curiously paralleled his
own."

B48   McELDERRY, B. R., JR. [Review: Kenneth R.
Andrews, Nook Farm: Mark Twain's Hartford
Circle (1950).] Personalist, XXXII (Autumn),
442-43.
Thoughtfully descriptive, noting the
book's interest as cultural history; Clemens
could have chosen worse places than Hartford
to live in the years 1871-1891. The portrayal of MT's friend Joseph Twichell is of much
interest.

B49   _____. [Review: Edgar Marquess Branch, The
Literary Apprenticeship of Mark Twain
(1950).] Personalist, XXXII (Summer),
300-301.
Chiefly descriptive, but noting the presence of "fifteen pages of really perceptive
criticism of Huckleberry Finn," although
"not sufficiently linked to what has gone before." The twenty selections from MT's apprentice writing are not powerful evidence
of its importance, and the space they take
might better have been used for a revised and

1951 - Shorter Writings

(McELDERRY, B. R., JR.)
enlarged reprinting of his bibliography of the early writings which appeared in American Literature in 1946.

B50   McGOWAN, GAULT. "Mark Twain and Heidelberg," Mark Twain Quarterly, IX (Winter), 30.
A miscellany about the Neckar, the University, and Nazi officers, but nothing of interest on MT.

B51   PARSONS, COLEMAN O. "Mark Twain--Conscious or Unconscious?" Virginia Quarterly Review, XXVII (Winter), 142-47.
A review of Kenneth R. Andrews, Nook Farm: Mark Twain's Hartford Circle (the environment was far from stultifying, but it encouraged MT to be "a professional writer rather than a deliberate artist"); Gladys Carmen Bellamy, Mark Twain as a Literary Artist (1950; generally sound, but sometimes ignores evidence contrary to the point being argued); and Edgar Marquess Branch, The Literary Apprenticeship of Mark Twain (1950; "Authoritative in all areas but one, the book throws only a fitful light on the maturing process," showing a clearer and more logical pattern than in fact existed).

B52   *RICE, HOWARD C. Kipling in New England (revised edition). Brattleboro, Vermont: n.p., p. 9. Kipling refers to MT as "the master of us all."
[Source: Quoted by Baetzhold (1970), pp. 195, 359, n. 38.]

B53   SHAW, G. BERNARD. "Mark Twain and Bernard Shaw," Mark Twain Quarterly, IX (Winter), 30.
On his meetings in London with MT, who visited his flat, lunched with him, told stories, and gave him an autographed book.

B54   STONE, EDWARD. [Review: Henry Seidel Canby, Turn West, Turn East: Mark Twain and Henry James (1950).] South Atlantic Quarterly, LI (July), 468-69.
The "juxtaposition...furnishes the reader a fresh and provocative perspective," but says little that is new: "to the James-Twain initiate...Mr. Canby's prodigious labor will seem to a great extent supererogatory."

B55   STRONG, LEAH A. "Mark Twain on Spelling," American Literature, XXIII (November), 357-59.
Text of an introductory speech by MT at a spelling-bee; reprinted from Hartford Courant, May 13, 1875.

B56   TIGERT, JOHN. "Mark Twain, Man of the People, Amidst Pomp and Circumstance at Oxford University," Mark Twain Quarterly, IX (Winter), 10-11.
On his 1907 trip to receive an honorary degree; not documented and not going beyond the familiar accounts.

B57   TRAINOR, JULIETTE A. "Symbolism in A Connecticut Yankee in King Arthur's Court," Modern Language Notes, LXVI (June), 382-85.
Equates MT with Launcelot, who with his sword ("Irreverence") assailed two giants representing monarchy and the Catholic Church. "Launcelot, in the opening Malory episode, killed his two giants, but the ending of the Yankee is inconclusive."

B58   WAGENKNECHT, EDWARD. "Twain--A Literary Lincoln," Saturday Review of Literature, XXXIV (January 20), 25-26.
MT is "still read more, I suppose, than any other standard American author," yet as one of "those who have created literature by dramatizing their own lives" he is thought of first as a personage, "the mightiest figure in the American literary mythology."

B59   WHICHER, GEORGE F. "Mark Twain, Henry James," New York Herald Tribune Book Review, XXVIII (December 2), 4.
A review of Henry Seidel Canby, Turn West, Turn East: Mark Twain and Henry James. Canby has brought "fresh insight" and written "a suggestive study," although at times he "is betrayed into laboring a trivial point."

B60   WIGGINS, ROBERT A. "The Original of Mark Twain's Those Extraordinary Twins," American Literature, XXIII (November), 355-57.
An article in the December, 1891 issue of Scientific American may have inspired MT; an account (quoted) of the different personalities of the Tocci twins resembles his description.

B61   *WILLIAMS, CECIL B. "Mark Twain, American Paradox," Bulletin of Oklahoma Agricultural and Mechanical College, XLVIII (September 30), 14-20.
[Source: Asselineau (1954), No. 1303.]

1952 A BOOKS

A1   CLEMENS, SAMUEL L. Report from Paradise. New York: Harper & Brothers Publishers.
Contains the texts of Captain Stormfield's Visit to Heaven and "Letter from the Recording Angel," together with a thorough discussion of the backgrounds in a fifteen-page introduction by Dixon Wecter.

A2   WECTER, DIXON. Sam Clemens of Hannibal. Boston: Houghton Mifflin Company.
A thorough, scholarly study of MT's early years, this is the beginning of what would have been the definitive biography of MT, but for Wecter's death. Chapter V reprinted in Cardwell (1963), pp. 65-71.

1952 B SHORTER WRITINGS

B1   *ANON. "The Mark Twain House. Clemens and
       His Fifth Avenue Years Are Recalled," New
       York Herald Tribune, February 16.
           [Source: Reprinted Twainian, XIII
       (March-April, 1954), 3-4.]

B2   ANON. "Mark Twain's Cousin, His Favorite,
       Tabitha Quarles," Twainian, XI (July-
       August), 1-2.
           A reprinting of a newspaper feature story
       of "some 35 years ago," apparently in a
       Missouri paper, containing recollections of
       MT's boyhood--many of which appear to be
       derived from the Autobiography and Paine
       biography.

B3   ANON. "Origin of Mark Twain in Flames?"
       Twainian, XI (July-August), 2.
           Text of a clipping reading "Flag of Our
       Union, July 4?? 1870." Page 448. Column
       entitled "Humors of the Day," without other
       identification; on MT as a Sunday-School
       teacher.

B4   ANON. [Brief Review: Henry Seidel Canby,
       Turn West, Turn East: Mark Twain and Henry
       James (1951).] Nineteenth-Century Fiction,
       VII (September), 146.
           No new information on MT and James for
       the serious student, who "will often quar-
       rel with Canby on matters of fact and opin-
       ion," but there is "usefulness" in a book
       that points up a significant contrast be-
       tween two American attitudes toward cul-
       ture."

B5   ANON. [Brief Review: Dixon Wecter, Sam
       Clemens of Hannibal (1950).] Nineteenth-
       Century Fiction, VII (December), 235.
           "So powerful is its combination of drama-
       tic intensity and scholarly thoroughness
       that every reader will regret again that
       its talented author did not live to carry
       his work further." Fortunately, this
       treatment of the first years is the most
       important part, because it was the forma-
       tive period and Paine had covered it inad-
       equately.

B6   BLAIR, WALTER. "Last of the Jongleurs," Sat-
       urday Review of Literature, XXXV (August 30),
       9-10.
           A review of Dixon Wecter's Sam Clemens of
       Hannibal, an "extensive study...justified by
       the close relationship between the man's
       early life and his best work." It is vastly
       superior to Paine's study of the same period
       because Wecter had a better understanding of
       MT's work, was "a trained, experienced his-
       torian," had access to material discovered
       since Paine wrote his biography, and "mas-
       tered his facts and molded them into an
       orderly and readable narrative."

B7   BROOKS, VAN WYCK. The Confident Years: 1895-
       1915. New York: E. P. Dutton & Co.
           Mentions MT's name passim, but without new
       critical statements on him.

B8   BURTIS, MARY ELIZABETH. Moncure Conway, 1832-
       1907. New Brunswick, New Jersey: Rutgers
       University Press. Passim on MT (indexed).
           Conway was MT's agent for the English
       publication of TS (pp. 158-59) and TA
       (pp. 181-82).

B9   BUTTERFIELD, ROGER. "Roger Butterfield For-
       wards Enterprise Mark Twain Item Unknown to
       Experts," Virginia City Territorial Enter-
       prise, August 1, p. 1.
           Reprints the text of an MT endorsement
       (datelined Hartford, March 3, 1873) for
       White's Patent Fly and Mosquito Net Frames:
       "A fly will stand off and curse this inven-
       tion till language utterly fails him. I
       have seen them do it hundreds of times";
       when the family uses it while dining on the
       porch "the flies have to wait for the second
       table."

B10   CARDWELL, GUY A. "Mark Twain's 'Row' with
       George Cable," Modern Language Quarterly,
       XIII (December), 363-71.
           On MT's impatience with Cable during the
       closeness of their 1884-1885 lecture tour;
       extensively quotes newspaper commentary, as
       well as MT letters, of which some are criti-
       cal and some friendly toward Cable. Differ-
       ences in temperament and philosophy explain
       why there was little contact between the
       two after their tour, as does MT's generally
       bristly relation with business associates;
       it was an achievement for Cable "to have
       traveled for four months with Mark and to
       have suffered nothing worse than half-intend-
       ed, half-regretted verbal assaults."

B11   CARTER, EVERETT. "The Meaning of, and in,
       Realism," Antioch Review, XII (March), 78-94.
           "There never was a less metaphysical man,
       at least before the hopelessness of deter-
       minism closed down upon him," and "his aim
       was to be authentic, and...to find his re-
       wards in the market-place." Huckleberry
       Finn is significant for its sustained irony,
       but it was written before 1890, when a real-
       ist could still write for Americans who be-
       lieved in a happy ending.

B12   CLEMENS, CYRIL. "Sam Clemens into Mark Twain,"
       Virginia City Territorial Enterprise,
       XCVIII (May 2), 6.
           Recollections of MT as told by Bill Gillis
       to Cyril Clemens (here incorrectly identified
       as "a direct descendant of Mark Twain").

B13   CLEMENS, SAMUEL L. [Reprint of MT letter in
       New York World.] Twainian, XI (July-August),
       3-4.

(CLEMENS, SAMUEL L.)

MT's letter to the editor (February 18, 1877) describes Captain Duncan of the Quaker City as the "head-waiter" of the Innocents Abroad cruise; he was without other authority, and, as subsequently revealed, without integrity. Includes a clipping from the New York Times (undated) on "The Ship-Owners and Mr. Duncan," and an unidentified "What an Old Shipmaster Thinks of the 'Head-Waiter.'"

B14 CUFF, ROGER PENN. "Mark Twain's Use of California Folklore in His Jumping Frog Story," Journal of American Folklore, LXV (April-June), 155-58.

Discusses previous printed versions of the story, with which he may have been familiar, as well as oral versions he heard; but the success of his story lay in the originality of his presentation.

B15 DAVIDSON, LEVETTE J. [Review: Duncan Emrich, ed., Comstock Bonanza (1950).] American Literature, XXIV (March), 107-109.

Emrich deserves thanks for this adequately annotated collection of humorous writings by MT and seven other Virginia City journalists of the boom period. Interesting in its own right, "this anthology further illustrates the contributions of 'the laughter of the West' to Mark Twain's literary development" (p. 108). The review is primarily descriptive.

B16 [DAVIS, CHESTER L.]. "First Editions--Collectors & Dealers," Twainian, XI (September-October), 1-3.

On Willard S. Morse, Irving S. Underhill, and Merle Johnson, with passages from their letters on collecting MT first editions and letters.

B17 _____. "Mark's Letters to San Francisco Call, from Virginia City, Nevada Territory, July 9th to November 19th, 1863," Twainian, XI (January-February), 1-4; (March-April), 1-4; (May-June), 1-4.

The text of the letters, prefaced by very brief editorial comment: "(Photostats from the paper itself were supplied by Dr. Austin E. Hutcheson.... We have made no corrections whatsoever, several errors in spelling being obviously overlooked by the proof-reader in the original printing)," (January-February, 1).

B18 _____. "Turn West, Turn East (A New Book)," Twainian, XI (March-April), 4.

Praises Henry Seidel Canby's 1951 book but makes no critical comment.

B19 _____. [Review: Dixon Wecter, Sam Clemens of Hannibal.] Twainian, XI (September-October), 4.

Appreciative, and concerned with Wecter as a friend and visitor to the Mark Twain

Research Foundation; says little of critical importance on the book.

B20 DEVOTO, BERNARD. "Boyhood Years that Shaped Mark Twain's Great Art," New York Herald Tribune Book Review, XXIX (August 31), 1, 9.

A review of Dixon Wecter, Sam Clemens of Hannibal. Paine was unqualified to write the story of MT's life, but Wecter "was the right man for Mark's biography: tough-minded but intuitive, a literary scholar who was also a man of letters, a brilliant historian, a first-rate writer." His new book "erases Paine. No one need ever write about the formative years again, the years on which everything in Mark Twain's books depends."

B21 FERGUSON, DELANCEY. "Mark Twain's Heaven," New York Times Book Review (September 7), p. 12.

A descriptive review of MT's Report from Paradise: "It is first-rate Mark Twain."

B22 _____. "When Mark Twain Was Young," New York Times Book Review (August 31), p. 3.

A descriptive review of Dixon Wecter's Sam Clemens of Hannibal, "which takes the humorist only to the age of 18, [but] renders obsolete all previous accounts of his formative years."

B23 FUSSELL, E. S. "The Structural Problem of The Mysterious Stranger," Studies in Philology, XLIX (January), 95-104.

"The Mysterious Stranger...was started and laid aside several times before it was finally abandoned. What is undoubtedly the final chapter was found in Twain's papers by Albert B. Paine, and attached to the uncompleted story when it was posthumously published in 1916. Because the tale was never formally completed, one cannot properly speak of Twain's formal achievement; but the very fact that Twain, even though he left the story unfinished, was able to construct the conclusion corroborates our impression that The Mysterious Stranger is somewhat unique in Twain's writings in its coherence of theme and in its adjustment of technique to the realization of that theme" (p. 95). "The solipsistic conclusion towards which Twain was apparently working is a theme embedded in the whole story, and Twain has liberally posted signs to indicate its presence."

B24 GIBSON, WILLIAM M. [Review: Henry Seidel Canby, Turn West, Turn East: Mark Twain and Henry James (1951).] American Literature, XXIV (May), 253-54.

Canby's thesis "does not sufficiently allow for Mark Twain's reputation and effect as American ambassador to the world, or the breadth of his views on race, or his late wildly bitter despair for democracy...he gives us a fresh view of Mark Twain as an

(GIBSON, WILLIAM M.)

uneasy composite of Huck and Tom. But he takes a view of the creation of living character which is too biographical and too static." Canby convincingly argues parallels in concern with independence and freedom as topics, and treatment of American innocence. Gibson credits Canby with the discovery that in The Princess Casamassima James anticipated MT's use of the term "a new deal," and Canby "has made a shrewd guess as to how Clemens got it from James."

B25 *HARDING, WALTER. "A Note on the Binding of the First Edition of Huckleberry Finn," Bibliographical Society of Virginia News Sheet, No. 20 (March), pp. 1-2.
[Source: Asselineau (1954), No. 1323.]

B26 HINZ, JOHN. "Huck and Pluck: 'Bad' Boys in American Fiction," South Atlantic Quarterly, LI (January), 120-29.
Tom and Huck belong to a literary tradition reacting against the "model" boy; unfortunately, because of pressure for adjustment and conformity, "perhaps the real boy is lost forever."

B27 JOHNSON, BURGES. "A Ghost for Mark Twain," Atlantic Monthly, CLXXXIX (May), 65-66.
As a Harper's junior editor, Johnson selected materials for a revised ed. of Mark Twain's Library of Humor. Although he received no credit on the title page or payment beyond his regular salary, Mr. Duneka told him to include some of his own work in the anthology. Later, at a dinner of newspaper cartoonists, MT was guest of honor; he was fatigued and tired of a line of autograph-seekers when Johnson introduced himself, and cursed Johnson roundly, then gained control and apologized. [A revised version of Johnson's "When Mark Twain Cursed Me" (1937.B20).]

B28 LEAVIS, F. R. "The Americanness of American Literature: A British Demurrer to Van Wyck Brooks," Commentary, XIV (November), 466-74.
On MT, pp. 471-72: "It wasn't Huck who wrote Huckleberry Finn; the mind that conceived him was mature, subtle, and sophisticated." MT, "though so unmistakably and profoundly American, writes out of a full continuity with the European past," as we also see in PW, "an ironical masterpiece" in which MT "adopts a style and a convention of sophisticated literary tradition, and handles them with the supreme skill of a writer perfectly at home with them."

B29 ____. "Introduction," in Marius Bewley's The Complex Fate: Hawthorne, Henry James, and Some other American Writers (London: Chatto & Windus; repr. New York: Gordian Press, 1967), pp. vii-xv; on MT, pp. ix-xii.

Leavis argues that the idea of a "frontier tradition" as a source of great American literature "derives an illicit respectability from the aura of Mark Twain," who belongs to "a too European past, along with Cooper, Hawthorne, Melville and James," rather than with Whitman, Dreiser, Scott Fitzgerald, and Hemingway (pp. ix-x). Compared with Hemingway's idiom, "Huck's language...is Shakespearean in its range and subtlety," despite its colloquial naturalness (p. xi).

B30 LEISY, ERNEST E. "Contrasting Craftsmen," Southwest Review, XXXVII (Winter), 80-81.
A review of Henry Seidel Canby, Turn West, Turn East: Mark Twain and Henry James. "Twain's best books have values; James's are studies about values. Canby's approach to the opposite techniques employed by his subjects is marked by rich insight and tolerance" in this Plutarchan comparison, informed by his familiarity with the writing of both men.

B31 ____. [Review: Mark Twain to Mrs. Fairbanks (1949).] Modern Language Quarterly, XIII (March), 108-109.
"This excellently printed book is an indispensible contribution to Twainiana."

B32 LORCH, FRED W. "Cable and His Reading Tour with Mark Twain in 1884-1885," American Literature, XXIII (January), 471-86.
Includes a picture of the friction between the two, and contemporary reviews. For a fuller account of this and other MT lecturing, See Lorch, 1968.A2.

B33 ____. "Mark Twain's 'Artemus Ward' Lecture on the Tour of 1871-1872," New England Quarterly, XXV (September), 327-43.
"Since relatively little is known about the Artemus Ward lecture, the purpose of this article is to show first how it was received by the public, and second to reproduce as much of it as possible by piecing together such parts of it as were found in the newspapers of the localities where Mark Twain lectured. The discussion will reveal some of the causes which operated to make the Artemus Ward lecture only moderately successful and which may have contributed to its abandonment at mid-tour. It will also supply a few glimpses of Mark Twain's estimate of his celebrated fellow humorist." A large number of contemporary newspaper accounts are quoted or cited.

B34 ____. "A Note on Mark Twain's Lecture on the Far West," American Literature, XXIV (November), 377-79.
Asserts the lecture fragment Wecter printed in Mark Twain in Three Moods (1948.A4) probably belongs to a lecture on "Curiosities of California," which he prepared in the summer or fall of 1869 but abandoned.

B35   McELDERRY, B. R., JR. [Review: Gladys Carmen Bellamy, Mark Twain as a Literary Artist
(1950).] Personalist, XXXIII (Winter), 78.
      Miss Bellamy's attribution of the medioc-
rity of much of MT's work to his alternately raging at the damned human race and the
imponderable force that damned it "is
worked out with commendable thoroughness,
a reasoned moderation, and even freshness
of approach to an almost hackneyed subject," but she treats style mechanically,
her treatments of structure in the several
books are not brought together, and she has
no answer for her question, "Why could Mark
Twain accept human nature only in boy nature?" Her approach through "moralism,
determinism, pessimism, and 'patheticism'"
provides an illuminating view of Tom Sawyer
and Huckleberry Finn.

B36   McKEITHAN, D[ANIEL] M[ORLEY]. "Mark Twain's
Story of the Bull and the Bees," Tennessee
Historical Quarterly, XI (September),
246-53.
      Traces old Laxart's story of a bull-ride
in JA, II, Chapter XXXVI to "Sicily Burns's
Wedding," by George Washington Harris. MT
had originally written his version as "The
Whipping Boy's Story" for P&P, but dropped
it because Howells said it impeded the action of the story. Reprinted in his Court
Trials in Mark Twain and Other Essays
(1958.A5).

B37   NATHAN, MONIQUE. [Review: Robert Gilkey,
Mark Twain Voyageur et Son Image de l'Europe (1951).]
      Critique, VIII (October), 893-94.

B38   REYNOLDS, HORACE. "Mark Twain's Queer Newspaper," Christian Science Monitor,
July 29, p. 9.
      On MT's unsigned "To the Reading Public"
in the recently discovered first issue of
Author's Sketch Book (a small newspaper),
here partially reproduced in facsimile and
also described and quoted. [Article reprinted in Twainian, XIV (November-December, 1955), 1-2.]

B39   ROADES, SISTER MARIA TERESA. "Was Mark
Twain Influenced by the Prolog to Don
Quixote?" Mark Twain Quarterly, IX (Winter), 4-6, 24.
      There may be reason to think that MT's
use of quotations from various languages
as chapter-headings in The Gilded Age and
his rejection of the excuses made in a
former age for having published a book may
have their origin in Cervantes, whose work
was familiar to him.

B40   SANDBURG, CARL. Always the Young Strangers.
New York: Harcourt, Brace and Company,
p. 117.
      On the books he and his friends read in
their youth: "We read Huckleberry Finn and

Tom Sawyer by Mark Twain but they didn't
get the hold on us then that other books
did. They seemed to be for a later time.
It was the same way with the novels of
Charles Dickens."

B41   SANTAYANA, GEORGE. "Tom Sawyer and Don Quixote," Mark Twain Quarterly, IX (Winter),
1-3.
      An impressionistic reaction to reading a
copy of Huckleberry Finn given him by Cyril
Clemens: both Tom and Huck show as their
deepest sentiment "kindness, humanity,
readiness to lend a helping hand to anyone
in trouble, no matter how degraded the creature may be. This is particularly clear in
Huck...a little ragamuffin... No wonder
that he should have no scruples about the
company he keeps and the means he resorts
to in his difficulties." "In the case of
Tom, the victory of pure kindness is more
difficult. Love of forms, of rules, of
making a sensation, has to be subordinated,"
although he is not mad like Don Quixote.

B42   SCHWARTZ, EDWARD. "Huckleberry Finn: The
Inward Thoughts of a Generation," Mark Twain
Quarterly, IX (Winter), 11-16, 23-24.
      A general critical article, conventionally
documented, on Huckleberry Finn as "a con-
crete expression of the life and values of
the people of the Mississippi Valley of
pre-Civil War days," and the frontier and
institutional moralities.

B43   SMITH, H[ENRY] N[ASH]. [Review: Dixon Wecter, Sam Clemens of Hannibal.] Nation,
CLXXV (September 27), 274-75.
      "We are not likely to find out much more
about Sam Clemens's first seventeen years
than is set forth in the present volume."

B44   *TRIPP, FRANK. "Tripp Recalls Mark Twain Interview. Twain's Kindly Rebuff," Port
Chester (N.Y.) Daily Item, February 27.
      As a cub reporter, met MT in a railroad
station and said his editor had said to go
to see him; reported back: "The old crab
just grunted, 'That's nice of your editor.
Run along and tell him that you did.'"
[Source: Reprinted in Twainian, XIV
(January-February, 3.]

B45   VAN DOREN, MARK. "Two Items for Mark Twain
Collectors," New York Herald Tribune Book
Review, XXIX (September 7), p. 4.
      A review of Dixon Wecter, ed., Report from
Paradise. Captain Stormfield's Visit to
Heaven is "vigorous," only mildly amusing,
and somewhat forced; "Letter from the Recording Angel" is "more successful, being
more limited in its aim; and still it will
never be one of the immortal works."

B46 WAGENKNECHT, EDWARD. "'The Lincoln of Our
Literature,'" in his The Cavalcade of the
American Novel (New York: Henry Holt and
Company), pp. 109-26.
A general study of MT, his work, and his
ideas; part of this chapter has appeared in
Wagenknecht's Mark Twain: The Man and His
Work (1935); there is an annotated bibliog-
raphy, pp. 516-20 (superseded by later bib-
liographies, including those in later edi-
tions of Mark Twain: The Man and His Work).
Pp. 114-16, classifying MT's work into the
groups of "Fiction of the Contemporary
Scene" (GA and AC); "Fiction out of Hanni-
bal" (TS, HF, TS Abroad, TS Detective, PW);
"History and Legend" (P&P, CY, JA, MS) reprinted in Kesterson (1973), pp. 60-61.

B47 WILSON, EDMUND. By the Shores of Light: A
Literary Chronicle of the Twenties and
Thirties. New York: Farrar, Straus and
Young, Inc. Passim. [A collection of es-
says by Wilson in the twenties and thirties;
most appeared in the New Republic.]
On the Brooks Ordeal of Mark Twain in
"The Delegate from Great Neck" (April 30,
1924; pp. 145-47); "The Pilgrimage of Henry
James" (May 6, 1925; pp. 226-27). On De-
Voto and the controversy with Brooks in
"Bernard DeVoto" (February 3, 1937;
pp. 650-57). In "The All-Star Literary
Vaudeville" (June 30, 1926) he says Sherwood Anderson, Hemingway, Gertrude Stein
and Ring Lardner have each "developed what
seems only a special branch of the same
colloquial language, based directly on the
vocabulary and rhythm of ordinary American
speech," in "a genre that has already produced one masterpiece in Mark Twain's Huckleberry Finn, a work to which Anderson,
Hemingway and Lardner are probably all indebted" (p. 234). In "Talking United
States" (New Yorker, date not given) Wilson
contends that "Relatively uneducated writers like Ring Lardner and Mark Twain have
had so poor a literary vocabulary that they
were likely to seem bald or thin when they
attempted straight English prose, and they
could only express themselves adequately by
having their story told by a character who
spoke some form of illiterate dialect or
special slang" (p. 638).

B48 YOUNG, JAMES HARVEY. "Anna Dickinson, Mark
Twain and Bret Harte," Pennsylvania Magazine of History and Biography, LXXVI
(January), 39-46.
The "queen of the lyceum" was a Quaker
girl born in Philadelphia, emancipated in
many respects but bearing a genteel antipathy toward MT. A friend of the Langdon
family, she wrote in 1873: "I have a fresh
wonder how the flower of their house, Olivia, as frail in body as she is clear of
mind & lovely of soul ever married the vulgar boor to whom she gave herself. -- I
hear of him all about the country at wine
suppers, & late orgies, -- dirty, smoking,

drinking--with brains no doubt, but--" On
her request MT once spent an entire day
writing letters of introduction to his acquaintances in England before she went there
on a lecture tour, but when she asked him to
do so a second time he refused; the words
"Good God!" in his letter to her are imperfectly crossed out. Not blind to Bret
Harte's failings, she esteemed him above MT,
whom she blamed for a "brutal" review of one
of his books in a New York paper in 1876.
Young shows points of similarity between
Anna Dickinson and Charles Dudley Warner's
character Ruth Bolton in GA; MT's Laura
Hawkins has something of her temperament.

B49 YOUNG, PHILIP. "Adventures of Huckleberry
Finn," Chapter VI in his Ernest Hemingway
(New York, Toronto: Rinehart & Company,
Inc.), pp. 181-212.
Compares Huck with Nick Adams, another
outsider who cannot accept the values the
world has presented him; both are honest and
sensitive, lacking in humor and intensely
serious (p. 202). Hemingway grew up as a
young Huck Finn. Unfortunately, Young draws
somewhat trustingly on MT's Autobiography as
a source of much of his biographical information.

1953 A BOOKS

A1 CARDWELL, GUY ADAMS. Twins of Genius. East
Lansing: Michigan State College Press.
On the 1884-1885 tour of public readings
by MT and George Washington Cable; includes
press notices and previously unpublished
letters (1881-1906), 18 by MT and 20 by
Cable.

A2 CLEMENS, CYRIL. Mark Twain and Dwight D.
Eisenhower. Foreword by Winston S. Churchill, Knight of Mark Twain; Mark Twain Gold
Medal, 1943. Webster Groves, Missouri:
International Mark Twain Society.
Cyril Clemens's account of Eisenhower's
enjoyment of Mark Twain, together with letters from Eisenhower and Mrs. Eisenhower.
Two of these letters (typed) are reproduced
in facsimile, together with generally accurate transcripts. "The Mark Twain Quarterly, Winter, 1953 (Volume IX, No. 3)
pages 1-4, contained some of the material
published in this book." [26-page pamphlet.]

A3 CLEMENS, SAMUEL L. Mark Twain's First Story,
ed. Franklin J. Meine. N.p.: Prairie Press,
n.d.
Text of "The Dandy Frightening the Squatter," with a foreword by Meine dated
October 15, 1952; an order slip in the copy
in the Mark Twain Papers gives the year of
publication as 1953.

A4   ENGLISH, THOMAS, ed. <u>Mark Twain to Uncle Re-</u>
      <u>mus, 1881-1885</u>. Atlanta: The Library,
      Emory University. (Emory University Publi-
      cations: Sources & Reprints, Series VII,
      No. 3).
         Letters from MT to Joel Chandler Harris.
      Discusses the way "De Woman wid de Gold'n
      Arm" ought to be read. Also includes a re-
      view of <u>The Prince and the Pauper</u> reprinted
      from the Atlanta <u>Constitution</u> of
      December 25, 1881, p. 11 (pp. 21-22).

A5   KRUMPELMANN, JOHN T. <u>Mark Twain and the Ger-</u>
      <u>man Language</u>.(Louisiana State University
      Studies, Humanities Series, No. 3). Baton
      Rouge: Louisiana State University Press.
         A general study of MT's amateurish inter-
      est in the language (21-page pamphlet, doc-
      umented almost entirely from MT's own pub-
      lished writings).

1953 B SHORTER WRITINGS

B1   ANDERSON, SHERWOOD. <u>Letters of Sherwood An-</u>
      <u>derson</u>, ed. Howard Mumford Jones and Walter
      B. Rideout. Boston: Little, Brown and Com-
      pany.
         Passim (indexed), with Anderson expressing
      profound admiration for MT in letters to a
      number of persons, among them Waldo Frank
      before the publication of <u>Our America</u>
      (1919.B12) and Van Wyck Brooks before the
      publication of <u>The Ordeal of Mark Twain</u>
      (1922). Several of the letters to Brooks
      are reprinted in Edmund Wilson, ed., <u>The</u>
      <u>Shock of Recognition</u>, with an introduction
      by Brooks (1943, pp. 1256-90).

B2   *ANON. "Dan DeQuille's Papers Given Bancroft
      Library. Rare Collection Bares Data on
      Famous Comstock Editor," Oakland <u>Tribune</u>,
      November 22, 1953.
         [Source: Reprinted in <u>Twainian</u>, XIII
      (March-April, 1954), 3.]

B3   AUDEN, W. H. "Huck and Oliver," <u>Listener</u>, L
      (October 1), 540-41.
         Contrasts attitudes toward nature in <u>HF</u>
      and <u>Oliver Twist</u>; observes Huck's stoicism
      and calls his decision to free Jim "an act
      of moral improvisation." There is in the
      book "a kind of sadness, as if freedom and
      love were incompatible." (From a BBC Third
      Programme broadcast.) Reprinted in Smith
      (1963), pp. 112-16.

B4   BEEBE, LUCIUS. "<u>Territorial Enterprise</u>,"
      <u>American Heritage</u>, IV (Spring), 20-23,
      67-68.
         A popular history of the old and the
      resurrected <u>Enterprise</u> by the modern pub-
      lisher.

B5   BLASSINGAME, WYATT. "The Use of the Lie in
      'Huckleberry Finn' as a Technical Device,"
      <u>Mark Twain Quarterly</u>, IX (Winter), 11-12.
         There are twenty-nine lies told by seven
      liars before Tom shows up at his Aunt Sal-
      ly's, with little artistic justification.

B6   BUDD, LOUIS J. [Review: Dixon Wecter, <u>Sam</u>
      <u>Clemens of Hannibal</u> (1952).] <u>American</u>
      <u>Literature</u>, XXV (May), 249-50.
         "Mr. Wecter's well-written, richly docu-
      mented chronicle of Clemens's boyhood is in
      its tentative form better than most mortals'
      final copy" (p. 250), and it is our loss
      that Wecter did not live to carry his study
      beyond 1853.

B7   CARROLL, LEWIS. <u>The Diaries of Lewis Carroll</u>.
      Now First Edited and Supplemented by Roger
      Lancelyn Green. London: Cassell & Company
      Ltd. 2 vols. II, p. 382 (entry of July 26,
      1879).
         Lewis Carroll's only comment on MT is "Met
      Mr. Clemens (Mark Twain), with whom I was
      pleased and interested." The editor supple-
      ments this with MT's reaction as it appeared
      in the <u>Autobiography</u>.

B8   CARTER, PAUL J., JR. "The Influence of William
      Dean Howells upon Mark Twain's Social Sat-
      ire," <u>University of Colorado Studies, Series</u>
      <u>in Language and Literature</u>, No. 4,
      pp. 93-100.
         Far from having weakened MT's development
      as a social critic, Howells was himself ac-
      tively interested in sociological theories,
      a reader of Tolstoy, and well aware of the
      crimes of the capitalist order. In 1887 he
      wrote a letter to the New York <u>Tribune</u>, crit-
      icizing the conviction of eight labor lead-
      ers for murder in the Haymarket Riot; al-
      though he and his wife believed that he was
      risking his career, she supported him. How-
      ells took a strong interest in the American
      labor movement, and saw more deeply into
      national and world issues than MT did. The
      two were independent in their thinking, but
      any influence of Howells on MT "should have
      proved a stimulus rather than a hindrance."

B9   CLEMENS, CYRIL. "Mark Twain and Dwight D.
      Eisenhower," <u>Mark Twain Quarterly</u>, IX (Win-
      ter), 1-4.
         On Eisenhower's admiration of MT; contains
      notes to Cyril Clemens from Eisenhower,
      thanking him for books, for being made a
      Knight of Mark Twain, etc., and from Mamie
      Doud Eisenhower thanking him for the honor
      of having been "unanimously elected a Daugh-
      ter of Mark Twain."

B10   CLEMENS, SAMUEL L. Letter to Livingston
      Wright. <u>Twainian</u>, XII (May-June), 4.
         Dated April 17, 1903, discusses an MS by
      Wright arguing that Mary Baker Eddy could
      not have written <u>Science and Health</u>. ["Re-
      printed from the New York <u>World</u>. (Contains
      an affadavit dated Boston, Oct. 31, 1906.)"]

B11   _____. "Mark Twain and the Reporter," <u>Twain-</u>
      <u>ian</u>, XII (September-October), 1-3.
         Comic, rambling interview which appeared
      in the Buffalo <u>Express</u>, April 1, 1894; a
      long introductory letter from Frank C. Will-
      son speculates that it might be reprinted

(CLEMENS, SAMUEL L.)
from a New York paper, or could be MT's own
work. [The date may be significant--T.A.T.]

B12 COLEMAN, RUFUS A. "Mark Twain in Montana,
1895," Montana Magazine of History, III
(Spring), 9-17.
On MT's visit there while lecturing,
July 31-August 5; documented from Major
James B. Pond, Eccentricities of Genius
(1900, using the 1901 London ed.) and con-
temporary newspaper accounts.

B13 _____. "Mark Twain's Jumping Frog: Another
Version of the Famed Story," Montana Magazine of History, III (Summer), 29-30.
Introduction and reprinted newspaper interview (Anaconda Standard, April 24, 1910)
of William ("Doc") Paulding, who told an
apocryphal story of a time when he and MT
tricked a man with a bet on a frog they had
loaded with shot.

B14 *COX, JAMES M. "Treasure Island and Tom Sawyer," Folio, XVIII (February), 7-21.
[Source: Leary (1970), p. 61.]

B15 [DAVIS, CHESTER L.] "Known and Unknown,"
Twainian, XII (July-August), 1-3.
An MT letter and some excerpts from his
works, reprinted in American Union (Boston),
Portland Transcript, Buffalo Express, and
elsewhere, here reprinted without significant commentary.

B16 _____. "Mark Twain in London," Twainian, XII
(September-October), 4; (November-December),
3-4; concluded XIII (January-February,
1954), 2-4.
Chiefly based on MT's copy (with his annotations) of Moncure Daniel Conway's Autobiography, Memories, and Experiences
(Houghton, Mifflin & Co., 1904). Includes
reprint of the chapter on "Mark Twain in
London" in 1872.

B17 _____. "Research Goes On," Twainian, XII
(May-June), 3-4.
Without editorial comment, reproduces the
text of correspondence between George Hiram
Brownell and The Kablegram (publication of
Kable Brothers, printers) and the Mergan-
thaler Linotype Company, concerning the
Paige typesetting machine.

B18 _____. "Studies, Research and Books on Mark
Twain," Twainian, XII (May-June), 1-2.
On the problems encountered in answering
large numbers of queries concerning MT.

B19 _____. "The Typesetting Machine and Mark's
Inventions," Twainian, XIII (July-August),
4.
"We have evidence now that the Mergan-
thaler Company acquired the patents and
Paige machines in the year 1897"; mostly
speculation on the terms of acquisition,
with little information.

B20 ELIOT, THOMAS STEARNS. American Literature
and the American Language. An Address delivered at Washington University on June 9,
1953. Washington University Studies. New
Series. Language and Literature, No. 23.
[Source: letter and photocopy from Frances Pfaff, Reference Librarian, Washington
University Library, September 22, 1975.]
In HF, MT "reveals himself to be one of
those writers, of whom there are not a great
many in any literature, who have discovered
a new way of writing, valid not only for
themselves but for others. I should place
him, in this respect, even with Dryden and
Swift, as one of those rare writers who have
brought their language up to date, and in so
doing, 'purified the dialect of the tribe.'
In this respect I should put him above Hawthorne: though no finer a stylist, and in
obvious ways a less profound explorer of the
soul." MT's Mississippi is "the universal
river of human life--more universal, indeed,
than the Congo of Joseph Conrad.... There
is in Twain, I think, a great unconscious
depth, which gives to Huckleberry Finn this
symbolic value: a symbolism all the more
powerful for being uncalculated and unconscious" (pp. 16-17). Reprinted 1966.B42.

B21 GOHDES, CLARENCE. [Review: Dixon Wecter,
Sam Clemens of Hannibal (1952).] South
Atlantic Quarterly, LII (April), 309-10.
This book "adds more details or removes
credibility from more erroneous assertions
than all its competitors," although "no
startling new disclosures turn up.... Mr.
Wecter was always an entertaining writer as
well as an industrious scholar. His last
book is delightful to read."

B22 LENNON, E. JAMES. "Mark Twain Abroad," Quarterly Journal of Speech, XXXIX (April),
197-200.
On MT's world lecture tour of 1895-1896
his audiences were impressed by the apparent
spontaneity of his speeches. It is widely
but mistakenly assumed that his performances
consisted of readings from his works; in
fact there were numerous local and topical
references.

B23 LORCH, FRED W. "Mark Twain's 'Sandwich Islands' Lecture and the Failure at Jamestown,
New York, in 1869," American Literature, XXV
(November), 314-25.
Presents the contemporary reaction, considers what it reveals of popular attitudes
concerning humorous lectures; it offers "at
least a partial explanation of his fear of
being considered a mere 'funny' man, a mere
buffoon on the platform." Includes contemporary accounts. For fuller treatment of
MT's lecturing and contemporary reactions
to it see Lorch's The Trouble Begins at
Eight (1968); in connection with one reaction at the time, See Alexander E. Jones,
(1954.B32), pp. 421-25.

B24 McCLOSKEY, JOHN C. "Mark Twain as Critic in The Innocents Abroad," American Literature, XXV (May), 139-51.

"The Innocents Abroad is not mere ridicule, not the naïve pointing of the finger of scorn at whatever the unlettered man from the backwoods does not understand.... It is satire, the product of an alert, informed, and sophisticated mind, well aware of values and ready to acknowledge them, yet complicated by prejudices and by an awareness of its professional duties as a journalistic humorist with commitments to the Alta California."

B25 McKEITHAN, D. M. "Bull Rides Described by 'Scroggins,' G. W. Harris, and Mark Twain," Southern Folklore Quarterly, XXVII (December), 241-43.

Uncle Laxart's bull-ride story in JA (II, Chapter XXXVI), originally intended for P&P, probably came from "Sicily Burns's Wedding" in Sut Lovingood's Yarns by George Washington Harris. In a letter to McKeithan, Walter Blair suggests another possible source in "Scroggins's" "Deacon Smith's Bull, or Mike Fink in a Tight Place," which MT may also have known. Reprinted in his Court Trials in Mark Twain, and Other Essays (1958).

B26 _____. "Mark Twain's Letters of Thomas Jefferson Snodgrass," Philological Quarterly, XXXII (October), 353-65.

Traces parallels between William Tappan Thompson's Major Jones's Sketches of Travel (1847) and three letters of "Thomas Jefferson Snodgrass" MT wrote for the Keokuk Saturday Post (November 1, 1856) and Daily Post (November 29, 1856 and April 10, 1857); the "Major Jones" and "Snodgrass" material is quoted at length. After having established MT's familiarity with Thompson's "Major Jones" material, McKeithan suggests that parallels in Innocents Abroad and Roughing It may also be derivations; he is more cautious about a possible derivation in A Tramp Abroad. Reprinted in his Court Trials in Mark Twain and Other Essays (1958).

B27 * _____. "Mark Twain's Tom Sawyer, Detective," Studia Neophilologica, XXV, 161-79.

[Source: MHRA Annual Bibliography (1953-1954), No. 6567.] Reprinted in his Court Trials in Mark Twain and Other Essays (1958).

B28 MARBERRY, M. M. Splendid Poseur: Joaquin Miller--American Poet. New York: Thomas Y. Crowell Company. Passim on MT (indexed).

On Miller introducing MT to Richard Monckton Milnes (Lord Houghton), pp. 114-15; Charles Warren Stoddard introduced MT and Ambrose Bierce in 1873 (p. 134).

B29 MARX, LEO. "Mr. Eliot, Mr. Trilling, and Huckleberry Finn," American Scholar, XXII (Autumn), 423-40.

Replying to their defense of the ending, Marx argues that "it jeopardizes the significance of the entire novel. To take seriously what happens at the Phelps farm is to take lightly the entire downstream journey." When Huck says to Jim on Jackson's Island "They're after us!" he identifies himself with Jim's flight from slavery; yet in the end, although Jim is free, it was not the journey that took him to freedom. The symmetry of structure that some critics see is imposed on the novel from outside; in fact, the journey was doomed to failure, but "Clemens did not acknowledge the truth his novel contained," the inevitability of a partial defeat. Reprinted in Marks (1959), pp. 53-64; Bradley (1962), pp. 328-41; Lettis (1962), pp. 350-64; Cardwell (1963), pp. 72-81; Simpson (1968), pp. 26-40.

B30 MEYER, GEORGE W. "Days of Innocence," American Scholar, XXII (Winter), 112-14.

A review of Dixon Wecter's Sam Clemens of Hannibal (1952), "a monumental work of scholarship whose every page will be read with delight."

B31 PARSONS, COLEMAN O. "Sam Clemens in Mythland," Virginia Quarterly Review, XXIX (Winter), 152-55.

A review of Dixon Wecter, Sam Clemens of Hannibal (1952); discusses MT's youth and his temperament, making little evaluation of the book.

B32 PARTRIDGE, HENRY M. "Was Sam Clemens 'Lewis Carroll'?" Mark Twain Quarterly, IX (Winter), 19-20.

MT's fondness for hoaxes suggests that "he must have sought secret outlets for his overproduction" under several pseudonyms; moreover, "he was intrigued by acrostics and ciphers and was a master of the Morse code. His enthusiasm for short-hand led him to suggest the use of the short-hand alphabet in place of the Latin. He was proficient in the use of sign-language and dactylology, adept at making up anagrams and writing backwards, 'mirror writing.'" There is no documentation of these statements, which will surprise students of MT, nor is reason given for identifying MT as author of "Lewis Carroll's" works. A parenthetical note says that this was "Written in 1936," seventy years before the year 2006 [sic], and a promise at the end, "To be continued," was not kept--perhaps fortunately.

B33 SCHMIDT, PAUL. "Mark Twain's Satire on Republicanism," American Quarterly, V (Winter), 344-56.

(SCHMIDT, PAUL)

MT ridicules Eastern political orthodoxy and the eighteenth-century republicanism on which it is based, together with its characteristic emphasis on ideals of Individualism, Freedom, and Progress; his response to genteel charges of Western savagery and "loutish stupidity" is to burlesque them. His depiction of politics in the mining-camps, his sometimes approving accounts of irregular justice, and his portrayal in RI of the outlaw Slade neither glamorized nor condemned (but seen through the admiring eyes of a tenderfoot) are at odds with Eastern gentility.

B34 SCOTT, ARTHUR L. "The Innocents Abroad Revaluated," Western Humanities Review, VII (Summer), 215-23.

"It cannot be denied that Mark Twain wrote of Europe from the viewpoint of an American Westerner who was ignorant of many cultural values. He did not, however, lack the humility of his ignorance, as most critics would have us believe." A number of such critics are listed (without facts of publication and generally without titles of their studies); to balance their portrait of MT Scott cites examples of appreciation and sensitivity in IA. Article reprinted in Kesterson (1973), pp. 117-25.

B35 _____. "Mark Twain Looks at Europe," South Atlantic Quarterly, LII (July), 399-413.

MT's attitude matured after IA, though even there he betrayed "a deep romantic vein." MT represented "national culture in human terms.... As other writers had drawn America closer to Europe, Mark Twain drew Europe closer to America."

B36 _____. "Mark Twain's Revisions of The Innocents Abroad for the British Edition of 1872," American Literature, XXV (March), 43-61.

More than four hundred revisions produced a work more literary, more conventional in style, less positive in its judgment of things foreign. "The English edition is less wordy, less free in its comic spirit, less outrageous in its buffoonery, and less fun to read--at least for the average American."

B37 STEPHENS, H. B. "Mark Twain's 'Dorg,'" Twainian, XII (July-August), 3.

A mildly humorous account of MT's dog "Burns," with a note from MT and a few doggerel lines; reprinted from Every Other Saturday, I (December 20, 1884), 457-58.

B38 TRAUBEL, HORACE. With Walt Whitman in Camden, January 21 to April 7, 1889, ed. Sculley Bradley. Philadelphia: University of Pennsylvania Press.

Traubel quotes Whitman on MT: "I think he mostly misses fire: I think his life misses fire: he might have been something:

he comes near to being something: but he never arrives" (p. 208). "I have always regarded him as friendly, but not warm: not exactly against me: not for me either." Letters from Rudolph Schmidt to Whitman in 1874, 1875 are less gentle: "As representants for mental power and intellectual vigor such people as Bret Harte and Mark Twain are fading away into ridiculousness" (p. 337); "But your humorists of the day I don't like. Mark Twain has been translated into Danish this year. He is a detestable fool" (p. 464).

B39 "TWARK MAIN," "Archimedes," Twainian, XII (November-December), 2-3.

Contains the text of thoughts on land monopoly which could well have come from MT himself. An introductory note credits Caroline Harnsberger with having helped find the essay, and asks whether MT and Henry George were friends; the answer is not conclusive.

B40 WIGGINS, ROBERT A. "Mark Twain and the Drama," American Literature, XXV (November), 279-86.

MT was exposed to the theater even in his youth, later wrote reviews, had a kind of theatrical experience in his lecturing, appeared in private theatricals, and made attempts at writing for the stage. "The form of Twain's fiction recalls his practice in playwriting of concentrating on the scene or episode as his chief structural element" (p. 282).

B41 WILLIAMS, STANLEY T. [Review: Dixon Wecter, Sam Clemens of Hannibal (1952).] Yale Review, XLII (March), 475-78.

The details make the book heavy going, but "we must, however, admire both his tireless investigation and his courage in making his account so complete."

B42 WULIGER, ROBERT. "Mark Twain on King Leopold's Soliloquy," American Literature, XXV (May), 234-37.

Describes one letter and contains text of three others from MT to officials of the Congo Reform Association: October 15, 1904 (described), April 11, 1905, and (circa) January 12, 1906 to E. D. Morel; to Thomas S. Barbour, January 8, 1906. Adds no new information.

1954 A BOOKS

A1 ALLEN, JERRY. The Adventures of Mark Twain. Boston: Little, Brown and Company.

"Although he never completed his biography, the story of his life was written, and by him. He gave it in snatches, sometimes in the guise of fiction, sometimes in the guarded privacy of his notes and letters.... The clues he furnished to his fiction have been traced back to parent facts, and the people, the places, the incidents, have here been taken out of the fictional dress he

1954 - Books

(ALLEN, JERRY)
gave them and put back into the life he
lived" (p. ix).

A2   ASSELINEAU, ROGER. The Literary Reputation of
Mark Twain from 1910 to 1950: A Critical
Essay and a Bibliography. Paris: Marcel
Didier.
Consists of an introductory critical essay
on the growth of MT criticism in the United
States and an annotated bibliography of secondary material on MT for this period, as
well as a few items for 1951-1952 and for
the years before 1910. The introductory
essay is a sound and valuable survey of
criticism for the years 1910-1950. The bibliography, including a number of items by
foreign critics, has been of great assistance in the compilation of the present bibliography, for some items in which it is
the only source.

A3   PEARE, CATHERINE O. Mark Twain: His Life.
New York: The Junior Literary Guild and
Henry Holt and Company.
A biography for young readers, based pri-
marily on Paine.

A4   STONG, PHIL. Mississippi Pilot: With Mark
Twain on the Great River. Garden City,
N.Y.: Doubleday & Company.
A work of fiction for young readers, in
which MT is a character.

1954 B SHORTER WRITINGS

B1   ANON. "Expressive Voices: The Emergence of
a National Style," Times Literary Supplement, September 17, pp. xii-xiii.
Passim on MT, praising the "instinctive
casualness and realism" of his colloquial
style and citing him as an examplar of the
emerging American style.

B2   ANON. "University Gets Mark Twain Items,"
New York Times, September 19, p. 120.
Reports the acquisition by the University
of California (Berkeley) of "about 1600
family letters," 134 of them signed by MT,
from the estate of his grandniece Anita
Moffett; also briefly describes other MT
acquisitions by the university.

B3   ANON. [Brief Review: Roger Asselineau, The
Literary Reputation of Mark Twain from 1910
to 1950.] Times Literary Supplement,
September 24, p. 614.
Asselineau deserves the gratitude of scholars who "will henceforth be saved the trouble of searching through library catalogues
and indexes of periodicals."

B4   APPEL, JOHN J. "Mark Twain's View of Jews,"
Congress Weekly (December 6), pp. 16-18.
A popular account, describing MT's com-
ments on the Jews in IA, his notebooks, and
"Concerning the Jews"; concludes that he was
sympathetic and tolerant, and "seems to have

understood the historical necessity behind
such a movement as Zionism," but was essentially superficial in his outlook.

B5   BAETZHOLD, HOWARD G. "Mark Twain's 'The Prince
and the Pauper,'" Notes and Queries (London), CXCIX, n.s. I (September), 401-403.
Although Paine gives Charlotte M. Yonge's
The Prince and the Page as inspiration for
The Prince and the Pauper, "the story and
characters...bear no resemblance whatever."
Her The Little Duke may be another matter,
since MT's book "contains parallels...which
must be more than coincidental" in characters, relationships, and situations.

B6   BOOTH, BRADFORD A. "Mark Twain's Comments on
Bret Harte's Stories," American Literature,
XXV (January), 492-95.
Consists primarily of 435 words of manuscript marginalia by MT in his copy of The
Luck of Roaring Camp, and Other Sketches
(1870). "Though he is always alert to
Harte's carelessness and inattention, particularly in the dialogue, he has a lively
sense of his friend's merits as a writer of
vigorous and colorful narrative"
(pp. 492-93).

B7   BROOKS, VAN WYCK. Scenes and Portraits: Memories of Childhood and Youth. New York:
E. P. Dutton & Co., Inc.
Describes seeing MT for the first and only
time--lying in his coffin at the Fifth Avenue church (p. 158 in the reprint of the
book as the first section of Van Wyck Brooks:
An Autobiography, 1965).

B8   BROWN, GLENORA W., and DEMING B. BROWN. A
Guide to Soviet Russian Translations of
American Literature. New York: King's
Crown Press, Columbia University.
Lists translations of MT's works, Nos.
1540-1632 (pp. 199-208).

B9   BURNHAM, TOM. "Mark Twain and the Austrian
Edison," American Quarterly, VI (Winter),
364-72.
On Jan Szczepanik and MT's interest in
him as reflected in "The Austrian Edison
Keeping School Again" and "From the 'London
Times' of 1904," both of which appeared in
Century Magazine (October, November, 1898).

B10   CARTER, EVERETT. Howells and the Age of Realism. Philadelphia and New York: J. B. Lippincott Company, passim.
Many references to MT's writing and specific works.

B11   *CLEMENS, CYRIL. "Mark Twain and Eugene Field,"
Hobbies--The Magazine for Collectors, LVIII
(April), 128.
[Source: Leary (1970), p. 60.]

B12 CLEMENS, SAMUEL L. "Mark Twain's War Experiences: His Graphic Recital of them at the Dinner to the Boston Ancient and Honorable Artillery Company," Twainian, XIII (March-April), 1-2.

Reprint of a clipping sent by Caroline Thomas Harnsberger from the New York Times, October 7, 1877; MT is quoted in an account of the Civil War experiences which he described elsewhere in "The Private History of a Campaign that Failed."

B13 _____. "Rev. Charles Kingsley and 'Mark Twain,'" Twainian, XIII (January-February), 1.

Text of an MT address in Boston, 1874, apparently following an introduction by Charles Kingsley. A brief headnote by Chester L. Davis says this appeared in The Commonwealth, Boston, February 28, 1874, p. 4; he adds: "Johnson's Bibliography reports 'Introducing Charles Kingsley--Speech, Boston, February 17, 1874: 'Modern Eloquence 2, 1901.'" (sic). Caroline Thomas Harnsberger corrects this with a copy of Modern Eloquence with the relevant material reprinted in the following issue (March-April), 2.

B14 COX, JAMES M. "Remarks on the Sad Initiation of Huckleberry Finn," Sewanee Review, LXII (July-September), 389-405.

On Tom and Huck and their antithetical values, and MT's fascination with Tom. Reprinted in Marks (1959), pp. 65-74.

B15 *CUNLIFFE, MARCUS. "American Humour and the Rise of the West: Mark Twain," in his The Literature of the United States (London: Penguin Books), pp. 149-69.

[Source: Beebe and Feaster (1968), p. 98. Also in 1964.B32 revised ed., pp. 149-69.]

B16 [DAVIS, CHESTER L.] "The Anita Moffet[t] Collection of Mark Twain Materials," Twainian, XIII (November-December), 1.

A brief description of the collection of letters by MT and relatives, and ten scrapbooks of clippings, recently acquired by the University of California, Berkeley.

B17 _____. "Dogberry," Twainian, XIII (July-August), 1-4.

"From our correspondence files your Secretary has found four newspaper stories by "Dogberry," The Golden Era's Distressed Novelist, together with correspondence by and between Morse and Brownell which in the opinion of your Secretary most likely establishes the fact that they were written by Mark Twain." The texts from The Golden Era (December 17, 1865-January 14, 1866) follow, with a conclusion in the following issue of the Twainian (September-October).

B18 _____. "Johnson's Bibliography," Twainian, XIII (September-October), 2.

On the Merle Johnson bibliography of MT's works and its continuation by various editors after his death.

B19 _____. "Life as I Find It," Twainian, XIII (September-October), 2.

A sketch in Agricultural Almanac attributed to MT; place is either New York or Lancaster, Pennsylvania, and date appears to be 1874.

B20 _____. "Mark Twain in London," Twainian, XIII (January-February), 2-4.

Conclusion of extracts from MT's own annotated copy of Moncure Daniel Conway's autobiography; for beginning of series see Twainian, 1953.

B21 _____. "Mark Twain's 'Author's Sketch Book,'" Twainian, XIII (November-December), 2-4.

On a four-page newspaper published in Hartford in November, 1870; reprints much of the contents, attributing to MT material which may or may not be his. (Continued in the next issue of Twainian, January-February, 1955, but with nothing more relating to MT).

B22 _____. "Orion Clemens and the American Publisher," Twainian, XIII (September-October), 3-4.

"The issue of May 1871 contains what appears to be pages 70-72 of the book 'Roughing It' but under the title 'The Old-Time Pony Express of the Great Plains, ['] by Mark Twain, and an editorial which bears the handwritten legend on the photostat we have 'By Orion Clemens, Editor.'" This turns out to be a veiled advertisement for a seed company in the text, which is reproduced.

B23 _____. "A Woman's Part in a Revolution, By Mrs. John Hays Hammond," Twainian, XIII (May-June), 1-2.

On MT's marginal comments in his copy of that book about the Boer War. "Some of the words written by Mark as notations, especially concerning the brutalities, is better left out of this printing.... Your Secretary cannot see the necessity of printing in bold type any obscene words in the Twainian, the circulation being as general as it has become."

B24 _____. [Review: Roger Asselineau, The Literary Reputation of Mark Twain from 1910 to 1950: A Critical Essay and a Bibliography.] Twainian, XIII (September-October), 3.

Uncritical, consisting chiefly of a lengthy quotation from the portions of Asselineau's "Foreword" which describe the plan of the bibliography and extend thanks for grants, the assistance of libraries, etc.

1954 - Shorter Writings

B25 FERGUSON, DELANCEY. "Mark Twain, Impresario," New York Times Book Review (February 7), p. 4.
    A descriptive review of Guy A. Cardwell, Twins of Genius (1953) as thorough, "informative," and "valuable and pleasant reading."

B26 FUSSELL, EDWIN. "Hemingway and Mark Twain," Accent, XIV (Summer), 199-206.
    Noting Philip Young's essay in comparative biography and psychology in the "Adventures of Huckleberry Finn" chapter of his Ernest Hemingway (1952), Fussell says that "Young's view of the Mark Twain-Hemingway connection and mine are not really contradictory; they are more like Marvell's lovers, so parallel they never meet." Fussell discusses the treatment of emotional, imaginative, and literary integrity in Huckleberry Finn, and Hemingway's concern with these matters in In Our Time, The Sun Also Rises, and other works.

B27 GERBER, HELMUT E. "Twain's Huckleberry Finn," Explicator, XII (March), Item 28.
    There is geographical, chronological, and thematic unity, and also a five-part "structural unity based on the pattern or rhythm of the alternating settings," but "organically asymmetrical or irregular." Huck has solved a problem and is changed by it.

B28 GOOLD, EDGAR H., JR. "Mark Twain on the Writing of Fiction," American Literature, XXVI (May), 141-53.
    Cites MT's observations on the work of other writers to illustrate the importance to him of realism, probability, concrete details, and suitable motivation and consistency on the part of the characters; notes a decorum that puts him in the company of Howells and Thackeray, rather than Thomas Hardy or George Moore.

B29 HENDERSON, ARCHIBALD. "Mark Twain and Bernard Shaw," Mark Twain Journal, IX (Summer), 1-3.
    On his appreciation of both MT and Shaw, whom he introduced to each other at St. Pancras Station in London, and of whom he wrote biographies.

B30 HOELTJE, HUBERT H. "When Mark Twain Spoke in Portland," Oregon Historical Quarterly, LV (March), 73-81.
    On MT's 1895 visit, during his world lecture tour. The cordial newspaper reception is summarized, and the interview in the Sunday Oregonian reprinted. In it, MT speaks favorably of governmental monopolies he has seen in Europe, reveals his plans for casual assembling of impressions for his next book (FE), and discusses the naming of Tom Sawyer and Huckleberry Finn; he denies the claim in recent San Francisco papers that a bartender named Tom Sawyer was his inspiration, and is reported as saying that "Finn was the name of the other boy, but I

tacked on the 'Huckleberry'"; Hoeltje points out that in the Autobiography MT said Tom Blankenship was the model for Huck. [In the North American Review serialization, August or September, 1907, MT said Huck was based on Frank Finn, son of Jimmy Finn (Source: Summary in Review of Reviews, London, XXXVI, September, 1907, 288)--T.A.T.]

B31 JONES, ALEXANDER E. "Mark Twain and Freemasonry," American Literature, XXVI (November), 363-73.
    MT became a Mason in 1861, a Master Mason on July 26; his interest lapsed when he went west, but he was reinstated before the Quaker City tour and "it is not surprising that Twain's renewed preoccupation with Masonic lore is reflected in The Innocents Abroad" (p. 365). Moreover, some of his philosophical views have Masonic parallels.

B32 _____. "Mark Twain and the 'Many Citizens' Letter," American Literature, XXVI (November), 421-25.
    Points out that a letter supposedly attacking MT's "Sandwich Islands" lecture in Jamestown, New York is in reality "not a serious attack but an example of tongue-in-cheek humor," the ostensible work of "a person who was often pompous, ordinarily gullible, and invariably ready to take a determined stand on an indefensible position." For the text of this letter and the circumstances surrounding it, see Lorch (1954.B40), pp. 314-25.

B33 KITZHABER, ALBERT R. "Mark Twain's Use of the Pomeroy Case in The Gilded Age," Modern Language Quarterly, XV (March), 42-56.
    Traces the parallel scandals of Senator Dilworthy in GA and Samuel Clarke Pomeroy, Republican Senator from Kansas: in addition to an absence of scruples, Pomeroy displayed "a convenient flair for prayer meetings and temperance movements...Twain's account in The Gilded Age, far from being overdrawn, is a surprisingly exact copy."

B34 KRUTCH, JOSEPH WOOD. "Speaking of Books," New York Times Book Review (May 23), p. 2.
    HF "conclusively...proves that a great work of fiction does not need to be what is called a 'good novel' or, indeed, a merely 'good' anything else." It is melodramatic and badly structured, "a botched job," but "uniquely delightful" in the same way as is the last quarter of LOM. HF has epic "largeness of plan...and there are ways in which an epic is better than even a 'good' novel." Reprinted in Bradley (1962.A2), pp. 362-63.

B35 LEARY, LEWIS. Articles on American Literature, 1900-1950. Durham, North Carolina: Duke University Press.
    Lists articles on MT, pp. 43-55; it has been a valuable source of information for the present bibliography; and all entries have been checked or listed as "not seen."

B36 _____. "Tom and Huck: Innocence on Trial," Virginia Quarterly Review, XXX (Summer), 417-30.
The structure and theme of TS express "a deeply underlying principle which haunted Mark Twain." In three sections, TS shows that adventure "leads innocently to knowledge of evil...wins out over prosaic adult methods of doing things," and, "compounded in part of the spirit of make-believe, imagination, illusion--that adventure, not common sense, leads to the wiping out of evil." In HF, Huck's response to evil was fear, repulsion, a desire to escape, but Tom's imaginative actions at the end, like Huck's attempt to flee, fail to end the evil. In sum, HF is the finer book, and "the contrived innocence of Tom fails," while "the questing spirit of Huck, who would be impatient at our even raising the spirit of innocence, lives on."

B37 LEASE, BENJAMIN. "Mark Twain and the Publication of Life on the Mississippi: An Unpublished Letter," American Literature, XXVI (May), 248-50.
Contains the text of a letter (January 6, 1883) to Osgood and Company about the plates and the proof-reading; adds little to the existing picture of MT.

B38 LENNON, E. JAMES [Review: Guy A. Cardwell, Twins of Genius (1953).] Quarterly Journal of Speech, XL (October), 339.
Descriptive and uncritical.

B39 LORCH, FRED W. "Mark Twain's 'Morals' Lecture during the American Phase of His World Tour in 1895-1896," American Literature, XXVI (March), 52-66.
Includes "as complete a text of the lecture as can be constructed from newspapers which reported it," quotations of contemporary reactions, and remarks by MT in interviews. For more about MT's lecturing, see Lorch's The Trouble Begins at Eight (1968.A2).

B40 _____. "Reply to Mr. Jones," American Literature, XXVI (November), 426-27.
Lorch says he himself considered the possibility that the "Many Citizens" letter was not a serious attack, but there is nothing else in the Jamestown Journal, apart from Coleman Bishop's article, which could have called forth MT's angry response. Lorch's main objection, however, is to a misinterpretation of his article by Jones: he did not assert that the attack contributed to a decision by MT to quit the lecture platform.

B41 McKEITHAN, D. M. "A Conjecture: Mark Twain and Winston Churchill," Notes and Queries (London), CXCIX, n.s. I (January), 39.
The words "blood and sweat and poverty" appear in Chapter X of The American Claimant, and in his essay "My Boyhood Dreams"

MT speaks of "blood and tears"; could these words have inspired Churchill's famous "blood, sweat, and tears"?

B42 P., L. [Brief Review: John T. Krumpelmann, Mark Twain and the German Language (1953).] English Studies (Amsterdam), XXXV (1954), 46.
"Mark Twain's peculiar brand of humor" may console "those who have no talent for foreign languages," but it seems unnecessary to "publish in a scientific and elaborate study every particular step on a road leading to...next to nothing."

B43 SHAW, BERNARD. "My Encounters with Mark Twain," Mark Twain Journal, IX (Summer), 24.
A reprinting, not indicated as such, of "Mark Twain and Bernard Shaw" in Mark Twain Quarterly, IX (Winter, 1951), 30.

B44 STALLMAN, ROBERT WOOSTER. "Come Back to the Raft!" Sewanee Review, LXII (July-September), 441-42.
A poem on the cleverness of Huck and the wisdom of the river.

B45 *SÜHNEL, RUDOLPH. "Huckleberry Finn," in Karl Brunner, ed., Anglo-Americana: Festschrift für Leo von Hibler (Wiener Beiträge zur engl. Philologie, LXII), pp. 150-56.
[Source: MHRA Annual Bibliography (1954), Nos. 658, 6572.]

B46 TURNER, ARLIN. "Notes on Mark Twain in New Orleans," McNeese Review, VI (Spring), 10-22.
On MT in New Orleans in 1861 in his river-piloting days, and in 1882 while gathering material for LOM. Quotes an interview with Horace E. Bixby (who taught MT piloting) in the Times-Democrat, May 7, 1882.

B47 _____. [Review: Guy A. Cardwell, Twins of Genius (1953).] American Literature, XXVI (May), 266-67.
Chiefly descriptive rather than evaluative. The book "parallels and supplements" Fred W. Lorch in American Literature for January (1952.B32). Lorch and Cardwell have examined newspaper reports "and have reached much the same conclusions: that preferences among reporters and audiences were about even; that Mark Twain made better copy for the newspapers but often Cable's stories and his rendering of them received the higher praise; that Cable's literary reputation was as great as Mark Twain's before they went on the road and was enhanced by the publication of another novel, Dr. Sevier, on the eve of the tour and his highly controversial article on Negro rights midway of the tour. Huckleberry Finn was not off the press until the tour was nearly over."

B48 VOGELBACK, ARTHUR L. "Mark Twain and the Fight for Control of the Tribune," American Literature, XXVI (November), 374-83.
Not primarily about MT, but includes the

(VOGELBACK, ARTHUR L.)
text of his "New Cock Robin," which appeared
in the Hartford Evening Post and Chicago
Tribune (January 2, 1873).

B49 WAGENKNECHT, EDWARD. "World of Huck's Dad,"
Saturday Review of Literature, XXXVII
(May 29), 15.
     A review of Jerry Allen, The Adventures
of Mark Twain. "Though it is absorbingly
interesting throughout, it is not all of a
piece." There is heavy use of secondary
material, using paraphrase legitimately but
relying perhaps too much on what she considers autobiographical in MT's own writing.
There is something of a novelist's license
in this, "one of the most readable books
about Mark Twain."

B50 WECTER, DIXON. [Untitled: Excerpts from
MT's correspondence of 1867-1868, concerning his relations with the New York Herald
and New York Tribune.] Twainian, XIII
(March-April), 4.

1955 A BOOKS

A1 SCOTT, ARTHUR L., ed. Mark Twain: Selected
Criticism. Dallas: Southern Methodist
University Press.
     Reprints a number of useful critical ar-
ticles and excerpts from books, 1867-1951;
a revised edition appeared in 1967. The
material reprinted is listed in the present
bibliography and cross-referenced.

1955 B SHORTER WRITINGS

B1 *ADERMAN, RALPH M. "When Mark Twain Came to
Town," Historical Messenger (Milwaukee),
XI (December), 2-5.
     [Source: Beebe and Feaster (1968),
p. 93.]

B2 *ANICETTI, M. "Mark Twain a Venezia," Ateneo
Veneto, CXXXIX (July-December), 97-111.
     [Source: MHRA Annual Bibliography
(1955), No. 8006.]

B3 ANON. "'Mark Twain's Quest' (A Rare Book),"
Twainian, XIV (March-April), 1-2.
     Reprint of an undated Hartford Courant
article on MT's unsuccessful attempt to ob-
tain a copy of The Enemy Conquered; or,
Love Triumphant, and a letter to the editor
of The Palladium giving further details
(signed Thomas H. Pease, New Haven,
April 23, 1884).

B4 *BAETZHOLD, HOWARD G. "Mark Twain's 'First
Date' with Olivia Langdon," Missouri Historical Society Bulletin [formerly Glimpses
of the Past], XI (January), 155-57.
     [Source: Beebe and Feaster (1968),
p. 94.]

B5 BAILIN, GEORGE. "Tom Sawyer: In Memoriam,"
Colorado Quarterly, III (Winter), 288-90.
     A poem on Tom and his boyhood world.

B6 BALDANZA, FRANK. "The Structure of Huckleberry Finn," American Literature, XXVII
(November), 347-55.
     "I propose to show that without advanced
planning, and spurred by momentary impul-
ses--in all probability unconsciously--Mark
Twain constructed whole passages of Huckleberry Finn on an aesthetic principle of repetition and variation." Reprinted in Marks
(1959), pp. 75-81; in Lettis (1962),
pp. 371-79.

B7 BELL, ROBERT E. "How Mark Twain Comments on
Society Through Use of Folklore," Mark Twain
Journal, X (Summer), 1-8, 24-25.
     MT preserved folk histories and dialect,
and represented the flavor of a region in
his work; he was close to his materials, and
in his work showed "what I consider the
three central patterns of Mississippi Valley
folklore.... 1. the folk-hero pattern;
2. the tall-tale pattern, and 3. the supernatural pattern."

B8 BLAIR, WALTER. [Review: Jerry Allen, The
Adventures of Mark Twain (1954).] American
Literature, XXVII (March), 124-25.
     Calls Miss Allen "credulous" in trusting
MT for biographical details, and the book
"unsatisfactory" as an account of his life.

B9 BLANCK, JACOB. "'Hospital Days' in 'Sketches
Old and New,'" Twainian, XIV (March-April),
4.
     On p. 299 of the first edition of Sketches
Old and New (1875) appears a paragraph headed "From 'Hospital Days'"; there is also an
erratum slip indicating that the sketch
should not have been included, and bibliographers have long argued the source. Blanck
points to a recently discovered copy of
Jane Stuart Woolsey's Hospital Days, privately and anonymously published New York,
1868, and suggests that the passage is part
of an MT book review accidentally included;
Blanck also cites another passage from the
Woolsey book which turned up in Following
the Equator. Reprinted from Publishers'
Weekly, October 30, 1937; ends with note:
"To Be Continued"--but there was no continuation.

B10 *BROOKS, CLEANTH. "Teaching the Novel: Huck-
leberry Finn," Proceedings of the First Yale
Conference on the Teaching of English.
     [Source: cited by Edward J. Gordon, in
"What's Happened to Humor?" (1958.B34).]

B11 BROWNELL, FRANCES V. "The Role of Jim in
Huckleberry Finn," Boston University Studies
in English, I (Spring-Summer), 74-83.

(BROWNELL, FRANCES V.)

Jim is passive or absent in most of the episodes involving physical action, and his main role is that of "moral catalyst...it is my thesis that Jim's primary function is to further the characterization of Huckleberry Finn: by his presence, his personality, his actions, his words, to call forth from Huckleberry Finn a depth of tenderness and moral strength that could not otherwise have been fully and convincingly revealed to the reader."

B12   BRUNEAU, JEAN. [Review: Roger Asselineau, The Literary Reputation of Mark Twain from 1900 to 1950 (1954).] Revue de Littérature Comparée, XXIX, No. 1, 136-37.

"Il est peut-être regrettable que l'auteur n'ait cru devoir inclure les éditions et traductions des oeuvres de Mark Twain ne comportant ni introduction, ni préface,' and more might have been done with MT's critical fortunes in France since 1917 (Cyrille Arnavon had covered the earlier period in Les lettres américaines devant la critique française [1888-1917], Paris: Les Belles-Lettres, 1952), but "le livre de M. Asselineau, qui se termine par un excellent Index, constitue donc une mine des documents très précieuse pour la littérature comparée."

B13   CLEMENS, CYRIL. "The Model for Huckleberry Finn," Hobbies--the Magazine for Collectors, LIX (February), 106-109.

"Not long before his death," Courtland P. Morris told Cyril Clemens about posing as model for all the characters in HF in the illustrations by Edward Windsor Kemble.

B14   COWLEY, MALCOLM. "Introduction," in Van Wyck Brooks, The Ordeal of Mark Twain. New York: Meridian Books (paperbound).

A balanced description of the background of Brooks's book and the debate with Bernard DeVoto, whose Mark Twain's America (1932) was less temperate than his later writing; the two critics gained from their confrontation. Brooks had produced a seminal book, whose first appearance in 1920 "is one of the true events in American literature, comparable with the publication of Emerson's The American Scholar, which announced and helped to produce the renaissance of the 1850's."

B15   CUNLIFFE, MARCUS. [Brief Review: Nils Erik Envist, American Humor in England before Mark Twain (Abo: Acta Academiae Aboensis. Humaniora, XXI, 1953).] Modern Language Review, L (July), 364.

"An excellent scholarly investigation of British responses to American humor as represented by such writers as 'Sam Slick,' Oliver Wendell Holmes, J. R. Lowell (in The Bigelow Papers), Artemus Ward, and Charles Godfrey Leland ('Hans Breitmann')." [As the title suggests, the book is not about

MT; the book itself has been examined, but is not listed in the present bibliography --T.A.T.]

B16   [DAVIS, CHESTER L.] "Background on Autobiography. Valuable Letters to Paine," Twainian, XIV (September-October), 1.

The Mark Twain Research Foundation has acquired "more than 200 letters which were sent to Albert Bigelow Paine during the last few years of Mark Twain's life and for several years afterwards." Paine has been criticized for suppressing information available to him; some of these letters may be published in future issues of the Twainian.

B17   _____. "Mark Twain Manuscript," Twainian, XIV (January-February), 1-3.

On the exhibit at the Pierpont Morgan Library, New York, November 19, 1954-February 28, 1955; the Huckleberry Finn MS was included, on loan. Quotes Antiquarian Bookman account of the event (date of the issue not given).

B18   _____. "Mark Twain's Religious Beliefs, as Indicated by Notations in His Books," Twainian, XIV (May-June), 1-4; (July-August), 1-4; (September-October), 1-4; (November-December), 3-4.

On MT's personal copy of William Edward Hartpole Lecky's History of European Morals (New York: D. Appleton & Company, 1879). Includes long quotations of Lecky's text and MT's marginal comments, interspersed with comments by Chester Davis.

B19   _____. "Steve Gillis Letter to Albert Bigelow Paine (Background on 'Biography')," Twainian, XIV (November-December), 1.

Text of the letter, merely appreciative.

B20   FADIMAN, CLIFTON. "A Note on Huckleberry Finn," in his Party of One: The Selected Writings of Clifton Fadiman (Cleveland and New York: The World Publishing Company), pp. 129-31.

HF is our national epic, important for the language, the rebellion against civilization. (Originally written as the introduction to a 1940 Heritage Press edition of HF).

B21   FIEDLER, LESLIE A. "'As Free as Any Cretur...'," New Republic, CXXXIII (August 15), 17-18; (August 22), 16-18.

"Pudd'nhead Wilson is, after all, a fantastically good book, better than Mark Twain knew or his critics have deserved. Morally, it is one of the most honest books, in our literature, superior in this one respect to Huckleberry Finn; for here Twain permits himself no sentimental relenting, but accepts for once the logic of his own premises." When the real Tom Driscoll is freed at the end there is an ironic echo of Tom Sawyer's declaration that Nigger Jim was "as free as any cretur that walks this earth," and the

1955 - Shorter Writings

(FIEDLER, LESLIE A.)
indictment of the community's racism becomes "a local instance of some universal
guilt and doom." Reprinted in Smith
(1963.A5), pp. 130-39.

B22   FORD, THOMAS W. "The Miscegenation Theme in
Pudd'nhead Wilson," Mark Twain Journal, X
(Summer), 13-14.
Through "skillful handling of the subject" and a refusal to "condemn or condone"
miscegenation," MT escaped public criticism, even though Ford says the theme "was
totally avoided in nineteen-century American literature."

B23   GERBER, JOHN. "Mark Twain's 'Private Campaign,'" Civil War History, I (March),
37-60.
MT's "The Private History of a Campaign
that Failed" (here reprinted, pp. 45-60)
"is primarily a literary rather than an
historical document," entertaining to read
but inconsistent with MT's brief service in
the "Marion Rangers." There is an account
of this service, based on the available
data. Gerber also reproduces from the Congressional Record an attack on MT on
January 25, 1940, by Congressman Joseph B.
Shannon of Missouri for his unheroic service, and a reply in a New York Times editorial of February 7.

B24   G[OHDES], C[LARENCE]. [Very brief mention of
Roger Asselineau, The Literary Reputation
of Mark Twain from 1910 to 1950: A Criti-
cal Essay and a Bibliography (Paris: Marcel
Didier, 1954).] American Literature, XXVII
(May), 290-91.

*HAMADA, MASAJIRO. Mark Twain: His Character
and Works. Tokyo: Kenkyusha.
[Source: Facts of Publication from MHRA
Annual Bibliography (1955), No. 8028; sub-
title from Shunsuke Kamei, "Mark Twain in
Japan" (1963).]

HERRICK, GEORGE H. "Mark Twain, Reader and
Critic of Travel Literature," Mark Twain
Journal, X (Summer), 9-10, 22-23.
MT was familiar with travel books, and
his own standards called for accuracy,
brevity, and literary artistry.

HEUER, HERMANN. [Review: John T. Krumpelmann, Mark Twain and the German Language
(1953).] Archiv für das Studium der neueren
Sprachen, CXCII (June), 71-72.
Brief and descriptive, noting MT's residence in German-speaking countries and his
comic way of describing the language. [In
German.]

IGNATIEFF, LEONID. "American Literature in
the Soviet Union," Dalhousie Review, XXXV
(Spring), 55-66.
"10,000,000 copies of the works of Jack
London and 3,000,000 copies of the works of

Mark Twain circulated in the USSR between
the early twenties and 1940, these two authors being consistently the favourite American writers in that country." Although
Soviet critics have tried to exploit the
social criticism of these authors, "Jack
London...was too inconsistent to be of much
help. Mark Twain offered greater promise....
Unfortunately for them, it was not the later
works at all, but Tom Sawyer, The Prince and
the Pauper, and Huckleberry Finn that interested the Soviet public."

B29   LANE, LAURIAT, JR. "Why Huckleberry Finn is
a Great World Novel," College English, XVII
(October), 1-5.
It is authentic, with real human figures,
a real society, genuine moral and ethical
problems, with a generally direct and realistic treatment; it transcends national
limitations, it is epical in form, and contains the allegory of Huck's journey
"through the world of spirit, ever working
out a pattern of increasing involvement with
the world of reality and with his own self,
both cast aside at the beginning of the
journey." Reprinted in Marks (1959.A5),
95-100; in Bradley, et al. (1962.A2),
364-71.

B30   LONG, E. HUDSON. [Review: Roger Asselineau,
The Literary Reputation of Mark Twain from
1910 to 1950]. Études Anglaises, VIII
(October-December), 369-70.
The result of "a comprehensive investigation of criticism devoted to Twain," the
book contains "a sound appraisal" of the
Brooks-DeVoto controversy and "a perceptive
study" of MT's literary reputation.

B31   LORCH, FRED W. "Mark Twain's Lecture Tour of
1868-1869: 'The American Vandal Abroad,'"
American Literature, XXVI (January), 515-27.
Liberally documented with quotations
from contemporary newspaper accounts. For
further treatment of MT's lecturing, see
Lorch's The Trouble Begins at Eight (1968.A2).

B32   O'CONNOR, WILLIAM VAN. "Why Huckleberry Finn
Is Not the Great American Novel," College
English, XVII (October), 6-10.
"The critical acumen of Eliot and Trilling
notwithstanding, there are a number of flaws
in Huckleberry Finn, some of them attributable to Twain's refusal to respect the 'work
of art' and others attributable to his imperfect sense of tone." Twain is hardly
the "Lincoln of our literature" that Howells
called him: "If Lincoln had written novels,
he would, without doubt, have been a greater
novelist than Twain. His virtues include
Twain's and surpass them." Huck's appeal is
through an immature sort of innocence, and
thus of limited usefulness as a symbol; "If
we refuse to over-value him as a symbol, we
may be less inclined to over-value the novel,
or to over-value the language in which it is
written." Reprinted in Marks (1959.A5),

(O'CONNOR, WILLIAM VAN)
100–106; Bradley, et al. (1962.A2), 371–78; Lettis, et al. (1962.A11), 379–83.

B33   RAVITZ, ABE C., and NORRIS YATES.   "Mark Twain, Cable, and the Philistine," <u>Mark Twain Journal</u>, X (Summer), 14, 23.
A reprinting of a story from Elbert Hubbard's <u>The Philistine</u> ("Heart to Heart Talks with Philistines by the Pastor of His Flock," XII [April, 1901], 146–49), about an explosion on a lecture tour when George Washington Cable implored MT to give up smoking, drinking, and swearing, and was told to mind his own affairs; Ravitz and Yates add that the story "cannot be dismissed as completely incredible," although much of it is obviously fabricated.

B34   REMES, CAROL.   "The Heart of Huckleberry Finn," <u>Masses & Mainstream</u>, VIII (November), 8–16.
A popular account, not obtrusively Marxist. "One does not think of Huck as a boy. He seems to be the embodiment of the conscience of a decent humanity confronted with the evils in society and wanting to right them."

B35   REYNOLDS, HORACE.   "Author's Sketch Book," <u>Twainian</u>, XIV (November–December), 1–2.
A reprinting from the <u>Christian Science Monitor</u> of July 29, 1955 [misprinted as 1952] of reaction to "Author's Sketch Book" in <u>Twainian</u> for November–December, 1955; chiefly descriptive, adding little to material in that issue of <u>Twainian</u>.

B36   *RICHIE, DONALD.   "Mark Twain," <u>Study of Current English</u> (Tokyo), X (September), 33–40.
[Source: Leary (1970), p. 72.]

B37   *SCHONFELDER, KARL-HEINZ. [Review: Roger Asselineau, <u>The Literary Reputation of Mark Twain</u> (1954). <u>Zeitschrift für Anglistik und Amerikanistik</u>, III, 212–14.
[Source: MHRA <u>Annual Bibliography</u> (1955–1956), No. 8007.]

B38   SCHORER, C. E.   "Mark Twain's Criticism of <u>The Story of a Country Town</u>," <u>American Literature</u>, XXVII (March), 109–112.
The text of a letter from MT to E. W. Howe, February 13, 1884.

B39   SCOTT, ARTHUR L.   "The <u>Century Magazine</u> Edits <u>Huckleberry Finn</u>, 1884–1885," <u>American Literature</u>, XXVII (November), 356–62.
Describes alterations made in the interest of genteel taste by Richard Watson Gilder in publishing more than a quarter of the novel in the <u>Century</u>.

B40   _____.   "Mark Twain: Critic of Conquest," <u>Dalhousie Review</u>, XXXV (Spring), 45–53.
A heated response to the Communist charge (summarized in New York <u>Times</u>, July 28,

1947, p. 13) that America has suppressed MT's attacks on imperialism. Summarizes his anti-imperialist statements, noting his shift to an attack on American expansionism. Extensively researched, but based on familiar material and thinly documented, without facts of publication.

B41   _____.   "Mark Twain Revises <u>Old Times on the Mississippi</u>, 1875–1883," <u>Journal of English and Germanic Philology</u>, LIV (October), 634–38.
When the seven installments which had appeared in the <u>Atlantic</u> in 1875 were incorporated as Chapters IV-XVII of <u>Life on the Mississippi</u>, a number of purely mechanical changes were made, of the sort "which might be the work of a conscientious proofreader." In addition, there were 45 changes involving style or facts--but MT's dislike of the chore of revision is evident.

B42   SHAIN, CHARLES E.   "The Journal of the <u>Quaker City</u> Captain," <u>New England Quarterly</u>, XXVIII (September), 388–94.
The Patten Free Library of Bath, Maine recently acquired the journal of the captain of the ship which took MT on the tour described in <u>Innocents Abroad</u>. Included are "121 pages of almost daily entries, followed by 24 newspaper clippings, some of which draw on the captain's notes, which were evidently written for the New York <u>Sun</u> by Moses S. Beach." "Clemens evidently saw something of Captain and Mrs. Duncan in New York, and he soon became an intimate in the Beecher circle to which the Duncans belonged." MT and Duncan later quarreled, publicly and bitterly.

B43   SMITH, HENRY NASH.   "'That Hideous Mistake of Poor Clemens's,'" <u>Harvard Library Bulletin</u>, IX (Spring), 145–80.
A thorough account of MT's speech at the 1877 dinner given by the publishers of the <u>Atlantic Monthly</u> in honor of John Greenleaf Whittier's seventieth birthday. MT and Howells mistakenly considered the speech a disaster, but only because they "churned themselves into a state of mind which bore little relation to external reality at the time and distorted their memories of what happened." In fact, the reception when the speech was delivered was mixed rather than entirely cold, and there was favorable comment in Boston papers the next day, although there were later second thoughts and there were hostile comments from papers in Springfield, Chicago, and elsewhere; a survey of newspaper comment "suggests that indignation over Mark Twain's speech was greater in upcountry Massachusetts and in the Middle West than in Boston." There is extensive documentation from newspapers, and published reminiscences and correspondence of several persons involved, and several documents are reproduced, including part of the holograph manuscript, MT's letter of apology to his

(SMITH, HENRY NASH)
victims, and a seating plan for the dinner autographed by those present. [Much of the material cited is not included in the present bibliography.]

B44 _____. [Review: Roger Asselineau, The Literary Reputation of Mark Twain from 1910 to 1950.] Modern Language Notes, LXX (May), 383–85.
"Belongs to a very useful genre and is excellent of its kind," with a bibliography in which "the list is selective rather than complete, but the selection is intelligently made, and in reading it through I have not been reminded of any important items that are omitted." The introductory essay provides a survey of MT's reputation which "neatly analyzes the issues raised by Bernard DeVoto's attack on Brooks in Mark Twain's America (1932) and describes with restrained amusement the sectional pieties" that led scholars to claim him for various regions. "Scholars interested in Mark Twain will long be grateful for this admirable manual."

B45 SPILLER, ROBERT. The Cycle of American Literature: An Essay in Historical Criticism. New York: The Macmillan Company.
Contains a perceptive general discussion of MT and his works, pp. 150-62; also frequent brief comments on him, passim.

B46 STONE, ALBERT E., JR. "The Twichell Papers and Mark Twain's A Tramp Abroad," Yale University Library Gazette, XXIX (April), 151-64.
The Yale library has been given the papers of the Reverend Joseph Hopkins Twichell by the Twichell family. In the collection are inscribed books and 67 letters from MT, and two notebooks he kept during the travels on which A Tramp Abroad was based and later presented to his friend, on whom the character "Harris" in that book is based. There are also ten volumes of Twichell's private journal, including the period of his travels with MT.

B47 TRIPP, FRANK. "Tripp Recalls Mark Twain Interview," Twainian, XIV (January-February), 3.
Reprinted from Port Chester (New York) Daily Item, February 27, 1952 (1952.B44).

B48 TURNER, ARLIN. "James Lampton, Mark Twain's Model for Colonel Sellers," Modern Language Notes, LXX (December), 592-94.
The character in GA was based on a cousin of MT's mother.

B49 _____. "Mark Twain, Cable, and 'A Professional Newspaper Liar,'" New England Quarterly, XXVIII (March), 18-33.
During the joint lecture tour of 1884-1885, MT's patience wore thin, partly because of fatigue and partly from occasional

chagrin at seeing Cable's readings better received. His feelings were expressed in letters to his wife, Olivia, and apparently in a letter which fell into the hands of a correspondent for the Boston Herald: on May 7, 1885 the "New York Literature" column detailed complaints, chiefly involving pettiness in financial matters. Cable demanded and received a published retraction, while MT took the lofty view that "the slander of a professional newspaper liar" was beneath the dignity of notice. There was a temporary coolness but no estrangement between the two, and Cable thereafter had nothing but kind words for MT.

B50 VOGELBACK, ARTHUR L. "Mark Twain and the Tammany Ring," Publications of the Modern Language Association, LXX (March), 69-77.
Provides a brief history of the Tammany Ring and its downfall, together with an annotated text of MT's "The Revised Catechism" (reprinted from New York Tribune, September 27, 1871), an indictment of municipal corruption, based on the form of the Westminster Catechism.

B51 WARREN, WILLIAM G., M.D. "On the Naming of Tom Sawyer," Psychoanalytic Quarterly, XXIV (July), 424-36.
The wood-sawyer was proverbially independent, and sawing is considered as a way to freedom in the escapes with which HF begins and ends. Sawing and cutting are further significant in that "Twain's works are rich in sadistic fantasies of death and mutilation." The name "Tom" is significant in that its derivatives "describe: 1, maleness; 2, the common man, in a derogatory sense; 3, foolishness (amateur and professional!), nonsense, stupidity and madness; 4, smallness; 5, untruthfulness; 6, the quality of being typical." Moreover, the term "Peeping Tom" suggests MT's exhibitionism. There are other significant Toms in P&P and PW, works involving twinship. "It would be interesting to know whether Clemens was familiar with the derivation of the name 'Tom' from the Aramaic, meaning 'twin.'.... The selection of the name 'Tom Sawyer'...springs from deep sources basic to the lifelong psychic conflicts of the author, Mark Twain."

B52 WELLAND, DENNIS S. R. "Mark Twain the Great Victorian." Chicago Review, IX (Fall), 101-109.
"In Huckleberry Finn Mark Twain did something that Arnold never achieved with equal success: he fused, for once, art and morality in such a way that the morality is the inevitable outcome of the characters and situations of the story." Also treats CY, IA, and MT's views of the Byron scandal.

B53 WILLIAMS, STANLEY T. The Spanish Background of American Literature. New Haven: Yale University Press; reprinted "in an unaltered

(WILLIAMS, STANLEY T.)
and unabridged edition" by Archon Books
(n.p.), 1968. 2 Vol.
Contains a number of brief references to
MT, passim.

B54 _____. [Review: Roger Asselineau, The Literary Reputation of Mark Twain (1954).]
Books Abroad, XXIX (Spring), 223.
Brief and descriptive: it "will be very
useful."

B55 WILLSON, FRANK C. "Mark Twain and the Foster
Murder Case," Twainian, XIV (March-April),
2-3.
Presents a summary of the murder case as
introduction to an MT letter to the editor
of the New York Tribune of March 10, 1873;
a reply by one H.K. criticizes his "ghastly
flippancy."

B56 WRIGHT, WALDO CARLTON. "The Mark Twain I Remember," American Mercury, LXXX (February),
123-25.
Recollections by the son of an Elmira,
New York contractor, not named, "as told to
Waldo Carlton Wright"; anecdotal and somewhat inaccurate.

1956 A BOOKS

A1 *CLEMENS, CLARA. Awake to Tomorrow. New York:
Harper and Row.
[Source: Thomas J. Smith, "Mark Twain's
Last Years at Redding," Yankee, XXXI
(June, 1967), 139.]

A2 *CLEMENS, SAMUEL L. Life on the Mississippi.
Mit Einleitung, Bibliographie und Kommentar
von Karl-Heinz Schönfelder (Englisch-
Amerikanische Bibliothek Band·VII). Halle
(Saale): VEB Max Niemeyer Verlag.
[Source: MHRA Annual Bibliography (1959),
No. 4578.]

1956 B SHORTER WRITINGS

B1 ADAMS, RICHARD P. "The Unity and Coherence
of Huckleberry Finn," Tulane Studies in
English, VI, 87-103.
After summarizing much of the debate over
the structure of HF, concentrates on Huck's
moral growth in a context of the evil of
slavery itself, of "the pseudo-aristocratic
society which fosters and depends on slavery," and "the sentimental culture veneer
with which that society conceals that evil
from itself, if not from others." A happy
ending in which Huck is reconciled to the
values of his society is clearly impossible,
but in terms of Huck's maturation and of
the portrayal of a society there is "a remarkably high degree of consistency, coherence, and unity." Reprinted in Marks
(1959.A5), pp. 82-94; Bradley (1962.A2),
pp. 342-57; Lettis (1962.A11), pp. 384-400;
Simpson (1968.A5), pp. 41-53.

B2 ALLEN, JERRY. "Tom Sawyer's Town," National
Geographic, CX (July), 120-40.
On present-day Hannibal, Missouri; with
map and 22 illustrations.

B3 BAETZHOLD, HOWARD G. "Mark Twain: England's
Advocate, American Literature, XXVIII
(November), 328-46.
A Connecticut Yankee represents views
quite different from those MT held in the
1870's, when he visited England twice and
so admired the English government that he
favored adopting some of its features in
the United States. Baetzhold traces MT's
admiration through the early period.

B4 BERGMAN, HERBERT. "The Whitman-Twain Enigma
Again," Mark Twain Journal, X (Winter),
22-23.
Referring back to Mims Thornburgh Workman's
"The Whitman-Twain Enigma" (1948) on the lack
of references by the two to each other, suggests that MT's "distaste for poetry and possible dislike of Whitman's frankness regarding sex and the body" and his flippancy and
lack of spirituality and optimism that were
important to Whitman would have kept the two
apart--although statements by the two are
quoted, showing they were at least well disposed toward each other. [Continued in
1957.]

B5 BLAIR, WALTER. "Why Huck and Jim Went Downstream," College English, XVIII (November),
106-107.
William Van O'Connor has criticized as a
flaw the trip on the raft, since free territory lay across the river in Illinois; the
objection has been made before, by DeVoto
and by Dixon Wecter, but takes no account of
the activity of slave-catchers there, or the
fact that Huck's father had got money from
Judge Thatcher "to hunt for the nigger all
over Illinois with."

B6 BUDD, LOUIS J. [Review: Arthur L. Scott, ed.,
Mark Twain: Selected Criticism (1955).]
South Atlantic Quarterly, LV (July), 390-91.
"The essays...are soundly and fairly chosen.... For anyone who knows current commentary well enough, the most interesting
evaluations are those written between 1890
and 1920, between the first rush of serious
respect for Twain and the first outbreak
of active controversy."

B7 CARTER, PAUL. [Review: Arthur L. Scott, ed.,
Mark Twain: Selected Criticism (1955).]
American Quarterly, VIII (Winter), 388-89.
"Criticism before 1900 is well represented
in thirteen of the selections, which remind
us that Twain's contemporaries had a keen
appreciation of his literary skill and significance. Haweis, Lang, and Howells are
especially perceptive and their critical
judgments have held up well." The value of
such a collection is doubtful, since the
scholar knows the material and can find it

(CARTER, PAUL)
in any good library, while the general reader will find the material confusing, even dull.

B8   CLARK, GEORGE PEIRCE. "The Devil that Corrupted Hadleyburg," Mark Twain Journal, X (Winter), 1-4.
"'The Man that Corrupted Hadleyburg'...belongs to those years when Mark Twain increasingly was turning his mind to the problem of the demonic in the nature of things," during the period when he was writing The Mysterious Stranger. In each story a bag of money is a danger to an honest poor man, and there is serious or humorous reference to casual killing. The stranger in Hadleyburg at one point is referred to as a "poor devil." The theme of an untested virtue as unreliable may be traced to Milton's Areopagitica.

B9   CLARK, HARRY HAYDEN. "Mark Twain," in Floyd Stovall, ed., Eight American Authors: A Review of Research and Criticism (New York: Modern Language Association).
[Source: Reprinted 1963, New York: W. W. Norton & Company, Inc., 319-63. Superseded by 1971 revised edition (1971.B11).] A substantial bibliography of writings by and about MT, with some annotation. Not systematically checked for the present bibliography.

B10   CLEMENS, CLARA. Awake to a Perfect Day: My Experience with Christian Science. New York: Citadel Press. Briefly mentions her father passim.
"Had my father lived longer and witnessed the phenomenal spread of Christian Science and its benefactions throughout the world," he would have thought more highly of Mary Baker Eddy.

B11   CLEMENS, CYRIL. "The True Account of Mark Twain's Exaggerated Death," Virginia City Territorial Enterprise, November 16, pp. 9-10.
"It is high time to put the correct version on record." The report grew out of the illness of James Ross Clemens, father of Cyril Clemens.

B12   COYKENDALL, JAMES B., with JACK DENTON SCOTT. "My Friend Mark Twain," American Mercury, LXXXIII (August), 103-109.
A 94-year-old man reminisces. Coykendall says he was a friend of Frank Beecher, adopted son of Henry Ward Beecher, and was present when Kipling visited MT "one bleak winter day in 1889"; he also remembers that Olivia Clemens was a great comfort to her husband when their daughter Jean died. At MT's funeral the undertaker "was openly crying."

B13   COYLE, LEO P. "Mark Twain and William Dean Howells," Georgia Review, X (Fall), 302-11.
Chiefly a repetition of material available in Paine and other familiar sources. Suggests that friendship may have influenced Howells's reviews of some of MT's works. His influence on MT's writing was "considerable," but "that it was profound is less certain."

B14   CRANE, SUSAN. "Letters from Susan Crane," Twainian, XV (September-October), 1-4; (November December), 3-4.
Reminiscences by MT's sister-in-law in letters to Paine, 1906-1913. There are touching recollections of the death of Jean Clemens. On Olivia, she says that "Livy's letters always make her so alive--her life and her loving so worth while. It is no wonder that Mr. Clemens was so crushed, so changed by her going away from us all. Whatever her own estimates of herself may have been at times, she was very great..." In 1911 Susan Crane asked Paine for an MT autograph to give to a friend: I could find nothing among my letters, as they were never signed in full. Samuel S. [sic], 'S. L. C.' or 'Holy Samuel.' I asked Mr. Langdon, but he was situated as I am--no letters are signed." A concluding note by Chester L. Davis observes that the Twainian "reaches many different readers, including many school children. We have no secrets from our members, however we must use discretion as to what appears in our publication.... In the Susan Crane correspondence we have not published all of it, likely we never will, but it is available for inspection by our members."

B15   NO ENTRY

B16   [DAVIS, CHESTER L.] "The 'Mock Robbery' of Mark Twain,'" Twainian, XV (January-February), 2-4.
Based on letters to Paine from Mrs. Alf Doten (quoting her late husband's diary) and Steve Gillis, on the mock robbery of MT on the road between Virginia City and Gold Hill, Nevada, in 1868.

B17   _____. [Review: Clara Clemens, Awake to a Perfect Day.] Twainian, XV (November-December), 2-3.
Contains extensive quotation and praises, but scant critical discussion.

B18   FATOUT, PAUL. "Mark Twain's First Lecture: A Parallel," Pacific Historical Review, XXV (November), 347-54.
MT's story of his San Francisco lecture debut (October 2, 1866) in RI does not agree with contemporary newspaper accounts, and similarities to Washington Irving's description of the opening of She Stoops to Conquer

(FATOUT, PAUL)
in his Life of Goldsmith (New York, 1881, pp. 315-16) suggest that MT's source was literary rather than experience.

B19 FRANTZ, RAY W., JR. "The Role of Folklore in Huckleberry Finn," American Literature, XXVIII (November), 314-27.
     For Huck, folklore is the equivalent of a religion governing his actions, values and virtues; in the book folklore supports much of the thematic development and serves as a device for foreshadowing events.

B20 FULLER, FRANK. "Letters from Frank Fuller," Twainian, XV (July-August), 1-3; (September-October), 4.
     To Paine, answering queries in connection with the biography; provides very little information, but mentions the American Grocer, which supposedly printed MT's first speech; of an occasion when Governor James W. Nye was to introduce MT to a lecture audience but failed to appear, Fuller reports hearing him say twenty years later, "I never intended to introduce him. He is nothing but a damned Secessionist anyway."

B21 GILLIS, STEVEN E. "Jumping Frog Story; Gillis on Bret Harte; The Great Oak Plan," Twainian, XV (March-April), 1-4.
     Letters to Paine in 1907, providing material for the biography. Gillis denies that Bret Harte had any part in editing the "Jumping Frog" story, reproduces a letter from MT recalling the time they first heard of it (and comments on "The Burning Shame," which was to become "The Royal Nonesuch" of HF, and also on his imminent marriage). Another letter comments on MT's gifted profanity, and jokes about a scheme to become rich selling acorns from the live oak tree that sheltered MT on Jackass Hill.

B22 GOODMAN, JOSEPH T. "Joseph Goodman's Assistance on the 'Biography,'" Twainian, XV (May-June), 2-4; (July-August), 3-4.
     Letters to Paine, 1907-1911. Mentions enclosing some reminiscences not here reproduced: "The only justification I can offer for talking about him so freely is that the 'News' pays me $15.00 a column for anything I may write, and the struggle for maintenance has got down to a groundhog case with me" (May-June, 3; city not given for the News).

B23 _____. [Letter to Albert Bigelow Paine, March 13, 1908.] Twainian, XV (January-February), 1.
     Takes issue with a statement by MT that his copies of Territorial Enterprise material were destroyed and suggests a careful search for them; also, describes MT saying grace at table while living in Buffalo.

B24 _____. "Letters from Joseph T. Goodman," Twainian, XV (March-April), 4.
     To Paine, providing material for the biography. A letter of December 7, 1911 shares MT's cavalier attitude toward mere facts and criticizes Paine's choice of words as stilted and vague; a letter of December 17 comments on his description: "I recall but one thing in your portraiture of Mark that seems to me incorrect. You repeatedly insist on endowing him with physical vigor and activity. To my notion, he never had either. It was always a source of wonder and admiration to me, the contrast between his bodily helplessness, so to speak, and his mental power. But perhaps it would have been impossible to picture him that way without conveying the idea that he was a weakling--which he wasn't--and so, probably you have chosen the better parts."

B25 HEADRICK, MRS. C. L. "Mining Days Sweetheart of Mark Twain," Twainian, XV (May-June), 1-2.
     As a little girl she was Carrie Pixley, a friend of MT in Nevada (reminiscences sent to Paine for the biography).

B26 HOBEN, JOHN B. "Mark Twain: On the Writer's Use of Language," American Speech, XXXI (October), 163-71.
     Although not a professional linguistic scholar, MT had a good ear and "put his language theory to practice in a cadence passionate and alive"; he contributed greatly to "making the vernacular a respected and appropriate medium for literary expression."

B27 HOELTJE, HUBERT L. [Review: Arthur L. Scott, ed., Mark Twain: Selected Criticism (1955).] Oregon Historical Quarterly, LVII (December), 357-58.
     Questions the value of some of the essays, such as those by V. F. Calverton and Lionel Trilling, which he quotes, "the one being a foolish judgment and the other a cliquish one indeed." There are also some more interesting selections, such as Bret Harte's review of IA and an appraisal of MT by Gamaliel Bradford. The extract from Van Wyck Brooks's psychological interpretation represents "an effort which once created a sensation but which must now seem strange even to Mr. Brooks."

B28 JELLIFFE, ROBERT A., ed. Faulkner at Nagano. Tokyo: Kenkyusha Ltd., p. 88.
     "In my opinion Mark Twain was the first truly American writer and all of us since are his heirs, we descended from him...Whitman was an experimenter with the notion that there could be an American literature. Twain was the first that grew up in the belief that there is an American literature and he found himself producing it. So I call him the father of American literature, though he is not the first one." Reprinted in Meriwether and Millgate (1968.B78), p. 137.

1956 - Shorter Writings

B29 JONES, ALEXANDER E. "Mark Twain and Sexuality," Publications of the Modern Language
Association, LXXI (September), 595-616.
     There may be a sexual element in MT's
feelings of guilt. Youthful indiscretions,
though unprovable, must not be ruled out;
certainly, MT felt strongly about feminine
purity but also believed in a double standard. He was more reticent in print than
most authors, and his HF represents a sex-
less, masculine Eden "until the King and
the Duke dash panting into the story,
bringing to Eden a hint of the Fall with
their presentation of that phallic beast--
the Royal Nonesuch." Reprinted in Leary
(1962.A10), pp. 232-56, followed by a reprinting of Allen (1957.B1), who disagrees
with Jones.

B30 KAPLAN, CHARLES. "Holden and Huck: The Odys-
seys of Youth," College English, XVIII
(November), 76-80.
     "In addition to being comic masterpieces
and superb portrayals of perplexed, sensitive adolescence," The Catcher in the Rye
and Huckleberry Finn "deal obliquely and
poetically with a major theme in American
life, past and present--the right of the
nonconformist to assert his nonconformity."
In a concluding note, Kaplan says that his
article was accepted for publication before
the appearance of Arthur Heiserman and
James E. Miller, Jr., "Some Crazy Cliff,"
in Western Humanities Review, (Spring,
1955), 129-137, and "the numerous parallels
between the two can be attributed only to
coincidental simultaneous generation."

B31 KERR, AGNES ROGERS. "Happy Hours with Mark
Twain," Mark Twain Journal, X (Winter),
11-13, 24.
     Childhood memories of reading MT's books,
naming a kitten after him, whitewashing a
fence, and playing with a raft.

B32 KESTEN, HERMANN. "Der Humorist und die Gesellschaft: Das gross Gelächter des Mr.
Samuel Langhorne Clemens," Akzente: Zeitschrift für Dichtung, III (October),
467-79.
     Notes MT's role as moralist and satirist.

B33 LANE, LAURIAT, JR. "Letters to the Editor,"
College English, XVIII (November), 108-109.
     A reply to Gilbert M. Rubenstein's criti-
cism of his article on Huckleberry Finn;
Lane calls Rubenstein's approach "both
'moral' in the wrong sense and unduly sentimental," and briefly answers his objections. There are also a letter by William
Van O'Connor (1956.B42), and a concluding
word by the editor.

B34 LEAVER, FLORENCE B. "Mark Twain's Pudd'nhead
Wilson," Mark Twain Journal, X (Winter),
14-20.
     A general study, noting the bitterness,
the treatment of slavery, the village,

human cruelty, the structural defects, and
the style.

B35 LEAVIS, F. R. "Mark Twain's Neglected Classic: The Moral Astringency of Pudd'nhead
Wilson," Commentary, XXI (February), 128-36.
     "The present essay appears as an introduc-
tion to a new edition of Pudd'nhead Wilson
that Grove Press is bringing out this
month" (editor's note, p. 128). "A classic
in its own right...for all the unlikeness,
it bears a very close relation to Huckleberry Finn; a relation of such a kind that
to appreciate the lesser work is to have a
surer perception of the workings of the
greater." There is power in the central
irony of the exchange of the babies and
their lives, although the book is not faultless. Article reprinted in Cardwell
(1963.A3), pp. 82-91, and in Kesterson
(1973), pp. 108-12. Excerpt from the 1955
printing as introduction to PW (London:
Chatto & Windus, Ltd.) in Simpson (1968.A5),
pp. 109-11 (noting that the article was also
reprinted in Leavis, Anna Karenina and Other
Essays, London: Chatto & Windus, 1967).

B36 LEISY, ERNEST E. "Mark Twain Seminar," Southwest Review, XLI (Spring), ix-x, 203. A review of Arthur L. Scott, Mark Twain: Selected Criticism (1955).
     "One of the more useful undertakings in
the field of criticism in recent years has
been the assembling on one volume of articles that represent divergent points of
view in regard to an author.... herewith is
a good one for the most popular of American
writers." Leisy summarizes some of the
views toward MT represented in this volume.

B37 *LORCH, FRED W. "Julia Newell and Mark Twain
on the Quaker City Holy Land Excursion,"
Rock County Chronicle, II (June), 15-25.
     [Source: "Current Bibliography," American
Literature, XXX (March, 1958), 152; on
glimpses of MT in her letters to the Janesville (Wisconsin) Gazette.]

B38 MARX, LEO. "The Pilot and the Passenger:
Landscape Conventions and the Style of
Huckleberry Finn," American Literature,
XXVIII (May), 129-46.
     As in Tom Sawyer and Life on the Mis-
sissippi, MT uses landscape as "a primary
source of unity and meaning." The superiority of Huckleberry Finn lies in its
style, and "the distinguishing mark of
style is language." It is in Huck that
MT can strike a balance between the ex-
tremes of elevated description common in
travel literature, on the one hand, and
too harsh a reality on the other: "It
does not occur to Huck to choose between
beauty and utility." Reprinted in Smith
(1963.A5), pp. 47-63.

B39 McKEITHAN, D[ANIEL] M[ORLEY]. [Review: Arthur L. Scott, Mark Twain: Selected Criticism (1955).] American Literature, XXVIII (May), 243-44.
Scott has achieved a balance of early and late criticism, favorable and unfavorable, general and specific, with emphasis on MT. "This excellent volume concludes with a useful four-page annotated guide to the best bibliographies of writings by and about Mark Twain."

B40 MOSTECKY, VACLAV. "The Library Under Communism: Czechoslovak Libraries from 1948 to 1954," Library Quarterly, XXVI (April), 105-17.
On pp. 114-15, reproduces annotation on a catalog card distributed by the National and University Library, Prague: "CLEMENS, SAMUEL LANGHORNE. Adventures of Huckleberry Finn.--Mark Twain, the well-known American humorist, rejected in this work the false romanticism of worthless murder stories and sharply criticized American racism and the excesses of Puritan morality."

B41 O'BRIEN, DEAN. "Tom Sawyer in Maturity," Mark Twain Journal, X (Winter), 9-10, 24.
Working from Philip Young's suggestion that Huck Finn is the prototype of Hemingway, O'Brien adds that F. Scott Fitzgerald was Tom Sawyer: "Denial of Free Will produces a Hemingway, a Huck Finn, who tries to act as best he can in the face of a predetermined future. Emphatic acceptance of Free Will creates the romantic, Fitzgerald, Tom Sawyer, who is convinced that he is master of his fate."

B42 O'CONNOR, WILLIAM VAN. "Letters to the Editor," College English, XVIII (November), 108.
Stands firmly on the ground he took when he "tried to relate the Huck cult to our American desire to live in a state of innocence," and adds as a postscript: "I have discovered that criticizing Twain is apparently as irreverent and sacrilegious as criticizing Mother's Day." The letter is in answer to the strictures of Gilbert M. Rubenstein (1956.B44) and Walter Blair (1956.B5), and is followed by a letter by Lauriat Lane, Jr. in answer to Rubenstein, and concluding remarks by the editor concerning the flight down the river.

B43 PERCY, WALKER. "The Man on the Train: Three Existential Modes," Partisan Review, XXIII (Fall), 478-94.
On alienation in literature, with passing reference to Huck, Jim, and Tom (pp. 478, 484-85).

B44 RUBENSTEIN, GILBERT M. "The Moral Structure of Huckleberry Finn," College English, XVIII (November), 72-76.
Lauriat Lane, Jr. and William Van O'Connor (in the October, 1955 College English) ob-

scure or deny the greatness of the book; Lane extends the moral realism "into fantastic patterns of allegory and symbolism" and O'Connor "commits the graver fault of misreading the realities of the book entirely." What the book is actually about is "nothing that the ordinary reader--not given to supersubtle speculations and distortions, but possessed only of common sense and a responsive heart--would fail to understand and appreciate": clear, direct insight, and "the humorous but sharp exposure of human failings on the one hand and the warm faith in human goodness and equality on the other." Reprinted in Bradley (1962.A2), 378-84; Simpson (1968.A5), 54-60.

B45 SCHMIDT, PAUL. "The Deadpan on Simon Wheeler," Southwest Review, XLI (Summer), 270-77.
In "The Jumping Frog," Simon Wheeler is not a comic butt as the narrator believes: "He is relaxed and friendly, in contrast to the efforts of his visitor to be imposing and superior.... Wheeler polarizes the values generated by community as against the inept and grotesque isolation of individualism. What the genteel 'Mark Twain' carelessly dismisses in the last lines is fraternity. He rudely walks out..."

B46 SCHÖNEMANN, FRIEDRICH. "Mark Twains "Huckleberry Finn' (Zum 70. Geburtstag, 1885-1955)," Archiv für das Studium der neueren Sprachen, CXCII, 273-89.
Discusses the book's realism, structure, and portrayal of character; the secondary sources cited are chiefly book-length general studies of MT. [In German.]

B47 *SCHÖNFELDER, KARL-HEINZ. "Mark Twain und die Indianer," Zeitschrift für Anglistik und Amerikanistik, IV, 88-101.
[Source: MHRA Annual Bibliography (1955-1956), No. 8043.]

B48 STEIN, JEAN. "The Art of Fiction XII: William Faulkner," Paris Review, XII (Spring), 28-52.
An interview: "This conversation took place in New York City, mid-winter, early 1956." On Sherwood Anderson, p. 46: "He was the father of my generation of American writers and the tradition of American writing which our successors will carry on.... Dreiser is his older brother and Mark Twain the father of them both." On favorite characters in literature (p. 47): "Huck Finn, of course, and Jim. Tom Sawyer I never liked much--an awful prig."

B49 TORCHIANA, DONALD T. "Will Huck Hang? The Individual and Society in Huckleberry Finn," Mark Twain Journal, X (Winter), 5-8.
After examining the hairball oracle, Jim warns Huck to avoid water and all risks, "'kase it's down in de bills dat you's gwyne to git hung," and MT "seldom fails to exploit a lie, a sign, or a conversation as a

(TORCHIANA, DONALD T.)
means of shepherding his flow of narrative."
Huck avoids neither water nor other risks,
and a possible death by hanging is consistent with the book's theme of death and
violence. His evasion of social rules and
his plans to "light out for the territory"
may make him a victim of "the lynch law of
the West."

B50 TURNER, ARLIN. George W. Cable: A Biography.
Durham, North Carolina: Duke University
Press, passim.
Cable went on lecture tour with MT, and it
was in part his introducing MT to Malory's
Morte D'Arthur that led to CY. There are
many page-references to MT in the index.

B51 WALKER, PHILLIP. "Mark Twain, Playwright,"
Educational Theatre Journal, VIII (October),
185-93.
A factual history of MT's partially successful attempts to write for the stage;
providing no new information or interpretations, this is a useful summary of known
material.

B52 WOLFE, THOMAS. The Letters of Thomas Wolfe.
Collected and Edited, with an Introduction
and Explanatory Text, by Elizabeth Nowell.
New York: Charles Scribner's Sons, p. 656.
In a letter to Sherwood Anderson
(September 22, 1937): "I think of you with
Whitman and Twain--that is, with men who
have seen America with a poet's vision, and
with a poetic vision of life--which to my
mind is the only way it actually can be
seen."

B53 WOODFIELD, DENIS. "The 'Fake' Title-Page of
The Gilded Age: A Solution." Papers of
the Bibliographical Society of America, L
(Third Quarter), 292-6.
A variant title-page tipped in to some
copies of The Gilded Age may indicate that
Elisha Bliss, Jr. and his son Frank Bliss
misrepresented sales figures in their reports to MT and Warner.

B54 WOUK, HERMAN. "America's Voice Is Mark
Twain's," San Francisco Chronicle, August 5,
"This World" section, p. 20.
On MT as "the archetype of American writers," an exact observer whose novels are
"extravagant romances." In HF he "established at a stroke the colloquial style
which has swept American literature, and
indeed spilled over into world literature."
HF is "a jerky, uneven, patchwork tale...
jerry-built...yet it is the crown of our
literature." The modern writers "are hardly
conceivable except coming after Twain."

1957 A BOOKS

A1 CLEMENS, CYRIL, ed. Mark Twain Jest Book.
With an introduction by Carl Sandburg. Kirkwood, Missouri: Mark Twain Journal.
Consists of a number of anecdotes; the 94-
word introduction by Sandburg praises MT as
philosopher and storyteller. In the same
year there was a second edition titled Mark
Twain's Jest Book, containing a few more
stories and in facsimile, MT's note in which
he first said "the report of my death is an
exaggeration" (facing p. 1). [32 and 27-
page pamphlets, respectively.]

A2 CLEMENS, SAMUEL L. The Complete Short Stories
of Mark Twain. Now Collected for the First
Time. Edited with an introduction by Charles
Neider. Garden City, N.Y.: Hanover House.
Sixty stories, of which five are extracts
from RI, two from TA, three from LOM, and
three from FE; includes texts of "The Man
that Corrupted Hadleyburg" and MS. In his
introduction Neider says that MT buried fictional sketches in longer works, was aware
of the formlesness of his writings, and
"rarely bothered about the niceties of fiction."

A3 LONG, E. HUDSON. Mark Twain Handbook, New
York: Hendricks House.
An extensive and valuable survey of biographical and critical works, with a good summary of MT's life, thought, and works, and
annotated bibliography of books and articles
about him. [Not cross-checked for the present bibliography.]

A4 MIERS, EARL SCHENCK. Mark Twain on the Mississippi. New York: World Publishing Company; reprinted New York: Collier Books,
1963.
A fictionalized biography for young readers.

A5 SMITH, HENRY NASH, and FREDERICK ANDERSON, eds.
Mark Twain of the "Enterprise": Newspaper
Articles & Other Documents 1862-1864.
Berkeley and Los Angeles: University of
California Press.
Texts of MT's newspaper correspondence, as
well as some personal letters and texts of
writings by other parties in newspaper controversies, as in the dispute over the Sanitary Fund which resulted in MT's leaving
Nevada for California. This book is meticulously edited, with useful introductory
material and with a "Biographical Directory"
briefly describing forty individuals prominent in MT's correspondence (pp. 225-31).

B1   ALLEN, CHARLES A.   "Mark Twain and Conscience," Literature and Psychology, VII (May), 17-21.
      "In this essay I will examine Twain's struggle against the orthodox conscience, speculate on the motives for the struggle, and suggest that the conflict helps account for both the strength and weakness of the fiction." Allen attacks Alexander E. Jones's "Mark Twain and Sexuality" (1956.B29) as "warping the central insight of depth psychology." Reprinted in Leary (1962.A10), pp. 257-68, immediately after the reprinted Jones essay.

B2   ANON.   "Mark Twain Toasts the Scotch," Twainian, XVI (November-December), 4.
      Reprint of a clipping provided by Paul Fatout from the Lafayette (Indiana) Daily Courier of January 14, 1874, giving MT's toast at a dinner of the St. Andrews Society in London, November 29, 1873.

B3   ANON.   "Mark Twain's Courtship" and "Mark Twain's Brother," Twainian, XVI (November-December), 4.
      Clippings provided by George H. Town from the Utica (N.Y.) Saturday Globe of September 26, 1891 and May 21, 1892 containing anecdotes; neither contains important information, and the first refers to Olivia Langdon as "Miss Lizzie" and her father as a judge. MT's daughter Clara disputed the first of these in a letter to Chester Davis reprinted in "Clara, a Great Person in Her Own Right," Twainian, XXII (January-February, 1963), 1-2.

B4   *ANON.   "Mark Twain's Piloting," Missouri Historical Society Bulletin, XIII (July), 403-405.
      [Source: Beebe and Feaster (1968), p. 94; a note received from Missouri Historical Society adds: "From the St. Louis Republican, June 13, 1875."]

B5   *ANON.   [Editorial criticizing the dropping of HF from the approved reading lists in New York City public schools.] Christian Science Monitor, September 14.
      [Source: Reprinted in Twainian, XVI (September-October), 1.]

B6   ANON.   [Review: Charles Neider, ed., The Complete Short Stories of Mark Twain.] New York Herald Tribune Book Review, XXXIII (February 17), 13.
      One paragraph, descriptive and non-critical.

B7   ANON.   [Review: Henry Nash Smith and Frederick Anderson, eds. Mark Twain of the "Enterprise".] New York Herald Tribune Book Review, XXXIII (July 7), 9.
      Short paragraph, descriptive rather than critical and with no evaluation.

B8   *BAETZHOLD, H. G.   "The Encaenia of 1907," Oxford Magazine, LXXV (February 28), 322.
      [Source: Leary (1970.B51), p. 57.]

B9   BERGMAN, HERBERT.   "The Whitman-Twain Enigma Again," Mark Twain Journal, X (Fall-Winter), 3-9.
      Summarizes critical discussions that may bear on the scant interest of the two in each other and notes that there are now three statements by each to consider. [Continues a discussion Bergman began in 1956.]

B10   BLAIR, WALTER.   "The French Revolution and Huckleberry Finn," Modern Philology, LV (August), 21-35.
      In addition to A Tale of Two Cities, of which the influence on Huckleberry Finn has been previously noted (and is here discussed), MT was familiar with a number of other books dealing with the French Revolution; of these, Thomas Carlyle's seems particularly influential, not only for its depiction of royalty and as a source for elements of the burlesque escape of Jim, but also for its portrait of the cruelty and the cowardice of mobs.

B11   BLANCK, JACOB.   "Samuel Langhorne Clemens (Mark Twain), 1835-1910," in Bibliography of American Literature, Compiled by Jacob Blanck for the Bibliographical Society of America (New Haven: Yale University Press, and London: Oxford University Press), II, 173-254.
      "It has been thought useful to present this list in three sections as follows: Section One: Primary books; and books by authors other than Clemens but containing first edition material by him. Section Two: Collections of reprinted material issued under the Clemens name or pseudonym; separate editions (i.e., books reprinted from one of Clemens's books and issued in separate form); undated reprints; and ana. Section Three: Books by authors other than Clemens which contain material reprinted from Clemens's earlier books. Books containing letters by Clemens are not listed. Books containing letters written for publication are listed. Formal collections of letters are listed in Section One. Letters published in separate form which may be properly described as first book publication are listed in Section One." [Not cross-checked for the present bibliography.]

B12   BRANCH, EDGAR.   "Mark Twain and J. D. Salinger: A Study in Literary Continuity," American Quarterly, IX (Summer), 144-58.
      Without attempting to show influence or "to compare the 'then' and 'now' of American society through the illustrative use" of Huckleberry Finn and The Catcher in the Rye, Branch reveals parallels in "narrative pattern and style, characterization and critical import.... Independently and in his own right each author has probed beneath surface

(BRANCH, EDGAR)
facts--so dramatically contrasted in Huck's and Holden's environments--to the experiential continuity of American life."

B13   BROOKS, VAN WYCK. Days of the Phoenix: The Nineteen-Twenties I Remember. New York: E. P. Dutton and Company, Inc., pp. 104, 170-74, 188-89 (also minor, passing references to MT on pp. 108, 111, 119, 125, 138, 193, 166).
      While writing The Ordeal of Mark Twain Brooks felt emotionally that America had long been "a kind of limbo" for the writer, and he allowed psychology to crowd out literary and human appreciation. Sherwood Anderson tried to show him where he had fallen short: "I should have sung the praises of Huckleberry Finn." Brooks stands by his book, conceding it reveals "perhaps only half of the real Mark Twain, but certainly much, if not the whole, of a well-known abstract character, the typical American author as we knew him at the moment" (pp. 170-74). Later, during "a season in hell" of mental illness a doctor disagreed with Brooks on whether "reason" or "emotion" had been more influential in his writing; in time, Brooks came to understand that he generally "felt things out" rather than thinking them out, and wrote intuitively (pp. 188-89). The revised edition of The Ordeal of Mark Twain (1933) came out after this period, and, while it takes account of the factual information on the West provided by DeVoto in Mark Twain's America (1932), the basic argument in the book remains substantially as before. Days of the Phoenix also appears as the central section of Van Wyck Brooks: an Autobiography (New York: E. P. Dutton, Inc., 1965), 249-445, but the index to the volume is sharply reduced.

B14   [BROWNELL, GEORGE HIRAM?] "Sam Slick, The Connecticut Clockmaker, Original of Uncle Sam and Source of Inspiration for Dickens, Mark Twain, and Other Humorists," Twainian, XVI (March-April), 3-4; (May-June), 4.
      Reprinted from Dearborn Independent, XXV (October 10, 1925.B11)

B15   BUDD, LOUIS J. "Mark Twain Plays the Bache-or," Western Humanities Review, XI (Spring), 157-67.
      The conventional view that MT was inhibited in treating sex in his writing is more valid for the time after he met Olivia Langdon than for the preceding years; a different picture emerges from the earlier work, "particularly the newspaper letters and columns in which from 1864 to 1868 he played the manly bachelor."

B16   *CADY, EDWIN S. [On Huckleberry Finn], pp. 8-10 in Richard S. Kennedy, Edwin S. Cady, Stewart C. Dodge, and Perry D. Westbrook, "The Theme of the Quest," English Record, VIII (Winter), 2-17.

[Source: Leary (1970), p. 60; AES, II (1959), Item 169: Huck seeks his moral identity, learning that the morality of his society is false and corrupt.]

B17   CARTER, PAUL J., JR. "Mark Twain and the American Labor Movement," New England Quarterly, XXX (September), 382-88. [Reprinted in Twainian, XIX (September-October, 1960), 1-4.
      MT's championship of organized labor in Connecticut Yankee is also reflected in "The New Dynasty," an article he read to the Monday Evening Club in Hartford on March 22, 1886, here published for the first time.

B18   _____. "Mark Twain Describes a San Francisco Earthquake," Publications of the Modern Language Association, LXXII (December), 997-1004.
      MT's "The Great Earthquake in San Francisco" (here reprinted, pp. 999-1004), not listed by his bibliographers, appeared in the New York Weekly Review November 25, 1865--a week after the New York Saturday Press published his "Jim Smiley and His Jumping Frog." It shows his growing reputation in the East, and is a kind of writing he considered superior to the "Jumping Frog" story; he introduced burlesque when reworking it for Roughing It (Vol. II, Chapter XVII). Abstract in AES, I (1958), 209.

B19   _____. "Mark Twain: 'Moralist in Disguise,'" University of Colorado Studies, Series in Language and Literature, No. 6, pp. 65-78.
      "Twain's morality, like Huck's, was emotive, intuitive, and uncertain. It was a morality which could be both militant and tolerant. It prompted his sharpest satiric judgments and his most trivial diatribes.... he could seldom see life without raging or moralizing, and the detachment necessary to art was lost.... This innate conflict was the price he paid for his sensitivity."

B20   CHASE, RICHARD. "Mark Twain and the Novel," in his The American Novel and Its Tradition. Garden City, New York: Doubleday Anchor Books, pp. 139-56.
      On HF (pp. 139-49), praises the language, Huck's clear vision, notes the mythic quality previously mentioned by DeVoto--it takes the forms of initiation and the ritual of exorcism; discusses the attack on romantic falsifications. On PW (pp. 149-56). Only in HF and first part of LOM is there anything really first rate by MT, and Fiedler and Leavis over-praise PW. "But what keeps this book from being a great novel is that the characters and their relationships are not adequate to the moral action." Pp. 138-49 (on HF) reprinted in Lettis (1962.A11), pp. 401-409; pp. 144-45 reprinted in Simpson (1968.A5), pp. 111-12.

B21 *CLEMENS, CYRIL. "Mark Twain at Oxford," Hobbies, LII (May), 108.
   [Source: Leary (1970), p. 60; volume and
   year seem inconsistent.]

B22 CLEMENS, KATHARINE (Mother of Cyril Clemens).
"I Knew Mark Twain," Mark Twain Journal, X
(Fall-Winter), 15-16.
   On dining with MT in London and New York,
   and visiting him at his "Stormfield" home
   in Redding, Connecticut; includes the text
   of a note to her from MT in Bermuda,
   March 24, 1910.

B23 CLEMENS, SAMUEL L. "Samuel L. Clemens on
'Die Lorelei,'" Georgia Review, XI (Spring),
50-52.
   An excerpt from TA, with no commentary or
   indication of the source.

B24 _____. "Two Civil War Letters," American
Heritage, VIII (October), 62-64.
   Texts of letters by MT and Walt Whitman
   on the prospects for survival of the Union.
   MT, writing his friend Billy Claggett on
   September 9, 1862, was pessimistic following
   the second battle of Bull Run.

B25 CUMMINGS, SHERWOOD. "Mark Twain's Social Darwinism," Huntington Library Quarterly, XX
(February), 163-75.
   "Thirty years of reading in current science" bore fruit in MT's later years when,
   crushed by business reverses and the loss
   of those he loved, he turned to a view of
   man as a Darwinian animal driven by nature's
   law to eat or be eaten.

B26 DA PONTE, DURANT. "Some Evasions of Censorship in Following the Equator," American
Literature, XXIX (March), 92-95.
   "While following the equator, Clemens
   found an Oriental word with which to
   strengthen the English language: lingam,
   the Hindu word for phallus. The term appears ten times within the space of thirty-
   nine pages in the second volume of his travel book.... Some of the references are
   clearly humorous; others seem to border upon
   the downright prurient, as though the author, relatively secure in the knowledge
   that the meaning of the word in question
   would be likely to escape most readers,
   were taking obvious delight in seeing how
   far he could go."

B27 [DAVIS, CHESTER L.] "American Bar Association
Recognizes Mark Twain's Contribution to Our
Copyright Laws," Twainian, XVI (July-Au-
gust), 1.
   On the passage of a resolution to that
   effect introduced by Chester L. Davis at
   the Annual Meeting in New York City. There
   is further commentary on p. 4 under "Mark
   Twain's Letters to Sylvester Baxter of the
   Boston Herald."

B28 _____. "Biography [sic] of American Litera-
ture, Released," Twainian, XVI (November-
December), 1.
   A review of the second volume of Jacob
   Blanck's monumental work; descriptive and
   laudatory.

B29 _____. "Mark Twain's Burglar," Twainian, XVI
(January-February), 1-2.
   Extensively quotes two letters from Henry
   Williams, one of two men convicted of break-
   ing into MT's "Stormfield" home. Williams
   claims a previous connection with MT in having "worked for a certain company in which
   he was a stockholder," and Davis suggests he
   may have illustrated some of MT's books.

B30 _____. "Mark Twain's Copyright Lobbying,"
Twainian, XVI (July-August), 1-3.
   Chiefly on MT in Washington in 1906; lit-
   tle more than extensive quotation from the
   Paine biography.

B31 _____. "Mark Twain's Letters to Sylvester
Baxter of the Boston Herald," Twainian, XVI
(July-August), 4.
   On tottering thrones in Brazil and Portu-
   gal, and his CY; apparently these letters
   of late 1889 were not for publication.

B32 _____. "New York City Schools 'Banning' Huck
Finn! Mark Twain and the Negro Race.
Champion for Organized Labor," Twainian,
XVI (September-October), 1-4.
   A defense of MT, consisting chiefly of
   various reprints: Associated Press dispatch
   on the dropping of HF from approved reading
   lists in New York; a Christian Science Monitor editorial (September 14, as reprinted
   in the Hannibal Courier-Post of September 17);
   an MT letter from Paine's 1917 edition; William Dean Howells's My Mark Twain.

B33 _____. "Original Preface for 'Yankee' in
1889 Mentions 'Twin Civilizations of Hell
and Russia'; Soviet Using Mark Twain's 'Yankee' for Satellite Propaganda; Mark Twain
and Atomic Energy," Twainian, XVI (May-June),
1-4.
   A lengthy, rambling answer to a recent
   paperbound edition of CY published in Leipzig: Davis reprints the original preface to
   CY from the 1912 Paine biography (Vol. III,
   Appendix S) and the Leipzig preface (noting
   such factual errors as MT's place of birth
   and which of his books was his first).
   Davis then quotes extensively from CY passages in Caroline Thomas Harnsberger's Mark
   Twain at Your Fingertips, and concludes with
   vague references to "Sold to Satan" in Europe and Elsewhere (Satan is made of radium).
   The article is of scant critical or biographical interest.

1957 - Shorter Writings

B34 [DAVIS, CHESTER L.] [Review: Henry Nash
      Smith, Mark Twain of the "Enterprise."]
      Twainian, XVI (March-April), 1-3.
           Laudatory, but with no specific, critical
      discussion; chiefly descriptive, with a list
      of the contents.

B35 EDWARDS, OLIVER. "Hilarious Days,' The Times
      (London), September 19, p. 13.
           On MT in Nevada; a popular account, pro-
      viding no new information or interpretation.

B36 ELCONIN, VICTOR A. [Review: Arthur L. Scott,
      ed., Mark Twain: Selected Criticism.
      (1955).] Books Abroad, XXXI (Winter), 83.
      Brief and descriptive.

B37 FATOUT, PAUL. "The Twain-Cable Readings in
      Indiana," Indiana Magazine of History, LIII
      (March), 19-28.
           On the lecture tour of 1884-1885, docu-
      mented from contemporary New York and Indi-
      ana newspaper accounts; Indiana papers re-
      garded MT the more highly of the two, both
      in genius and in versatility.

B38 FEDERICO, P. J. "Mark Twain's Inventions and
      Patents," Twainian, XVI (November-December),
      1-4.
           Federico was an official in the Patent
      Office, and apparently used material in the
      files as well as biographical information
      from Paine. Reprints MT correspondence and
      quotes patent applications. [Originally
      appeared in Journal of the Patent Office
      Society, March, 1939, with illustrations
      not here reproduced.]

B39 FERGUSON, DELANCEY. "Sam Clemens Was the By-
      Line," New York Times Book Review (May 5),
      p. 10.
           A brief, descriptive review of Henry Nash
      Smith and Frederick Anderson, eds., Mark
      Twain of the "Enterprise." MT's early writ-
      ing printed there is "apprentice work," in
      which the good "lines are far between. Per-
      haps it is just as well that the Enterprise
      files are lost."

B40 _____. [Review: Henry Nash Smith and Fred-
      erick Anderson, eds., Mark Twain of the
      "Enterprise."] American Scholar, XXVI (Au-
      tumn), 515-16.
           Makes no complaint about the editing, but
      "no other of our major writers, not even
      Walt Whitman, had to cleanse himself of
      more trash before achieving artistic maturi-
      ty. It is unlikely that any masterpieces
      perished with the Enterprise files."

B41 GOODMAN, JOSEPH T. "Goodman O.K.'s Paine In-
      accuracies," Twainian, XVI (January-Febru-
      ary), 2 (incorrectly marked "Page Four").
           Two letters to Paine, of which the first
      (December 7, 1911) had already appeared in
      Twainian, XV (March-April, 1956) and appar-
      ently printed again through carelessness;

the second (December 25, 1909) sends condo-
lences on the death of Jean Clemens.

B42 GULLASON, THOMAS ARTHUR. "The 'Fatal' Ending
      of Huckleberry Finn," American Literature,
      XXIX (March), 86-91.
           The concluding episode, "based on Tom's
      lie, cannot be considered fatal because Huck
      settles conflicts presented earlier in the
      novel. Important themes, which are repeated
      and varied, furnish the key." In the last
      chapters Huck rejects "Tom's romantic irre-
      sponsibility...and society's cruel nature...
      understands Jim's true worth"; and Huck's
      honest and humble facing and resolving of
      the conflicts shows his developing strength
      of character (p. 91). Reprinted in Bradley
      (1962.A2), pp. 357-61.

B43 JONES, ALEXANDER E. "Mark Twain and the Deter-
      minism of What Is Man?" American Literature,
      XXIX (March), 1-17.
           This is not a pessimistic tract in the
      vein of The Mysterious Stranger; MT had been
      pondering determinism since 1880, and indeed
      had encountered it during his piloting days.
      "What Is Man? is not, then, a mere cry of
      despair. True, it does represent Twain's
      attempt to smother a burning sense of guilt;
      but it is even more important as an attack
      upon human pride."

B44 KEATING, L. CLARK. "Mark Twain and Paul Bour-
      get," French Review, XXX (April), 342-49.
           In a discussion of their depiction of each
      other's countries, considers the background,
      development, and attitudes of the two.
      There are persistent, minor errors of detail
      by Clark concerning MT; for example, he is
      said to have written "The Jumping Frog"
      while a reporter for the "Virginia City Ga-
      zette," and he is misquoted as having said
      that in France "adultery is the rule.
      Frenchmen do not seek to know their grand-
      father." Abstract in AES, XIV (1970-1971),
      2840; reprinted in Twainian, XXXI (March-
      April, 1972).

B45 *KLAUS, ROSMARIE. "Mark Twain und die Neger-
      frage: Huckleberry Finn," Zeitschrift für
      Anglistik und Amerikanistik, V, 166-81.
           [Source: MHRA Annual Bibliography (1959),
      No. 4560.]

B46 KOHN, JOHN S. VAN E. "Mark Twain's 1601,"
      Princeton University Library Chronicle,
      XVIII (Winter), 49-54.
           Provides a brief history of the writing
      and publication of the work. John Hay wrote
      three letters about the book to his friend
      Alexander Gunn (the one of June 24, 1880 is
      here reproduced in facsimile). "The holo-
      graph originals of these letters form a por-
      tion of a collection of letters and docu-
      ments pertaining to Mark Twain's 1601 assem-
      bled by the late Frank H. Ginn of Cleveland
      that has recently been presented to the

(KOHN, JOHN S. VAN E.)
Library by Mr. Ginn's children...'." There
are also notes from MT in the collection.

B47   LEISY, ERNEST E. "Mark Twain in Nevada,
1862-1864," Southwest Review, XLII (Summer),
247-48.
A review of Henry Nash Smith and Frederick
Anderson, eds., Mark Twain of the "Enterprise," which is "carefully edited.... It
contains thirty newly discovered letters and
dispatches plus background material, and it
makes numerous corrections in the record."

B48   LORCH, FRED W. "Mark Twain's Public Lectures
in England in 1873," American Literature,
XXIX (November), 297-304.
"The purpose of this article is to offer
a complete schedule of dates for Mark
Twain's lecture engagements in England and
to give a more detailed report of the reception which his lectures received there
than Paine has given" (p. 297). MT was
generally well received as a droll lecturer,
but not taken as seriously as he would have
wished. As always, Lorch documents liberally with citations from the contemporary
press. For further treatment of MT's lecturing by Lorch, see his The Trouble Begins
at Eight (1968). Abstract in AES, I (1958),
8.

B49   MERIWETHER, LEE. "Me and Mark Twain," Mark
Twain Journal, X (Fall-Winter), 17-19.
Anecdotes of a visit to the MT home in
Hartford in 1875, a jumping frog contest
there in 1955 [sic], MT and an effusive
drunk at a St. Louis luncheon in 1902.

B50   _____. "Our Struggle with the Internal Revenue Bureau," Mark Twain Journal, X (Fall-
Winter), 1-2, 9.
A member of the Mark Twain Memorial Association, Harry Williams, without authoriza-
tion "prepared a letterhead bearing the
names of seven presidents of the United
States, several Justices of the U.S. Supreme
Court; Winston Churchill and Sir Anthony
Eden, Britain's Prime Ministers; Attaturk,
President of Turkey and a score of other
world famous people.... That letterhead was
used by Williams in soliciting contributions
from lovers of Mark Twain in all parts of
the world except St. Louis, Missouri, and
near-by states. They were excluded in order
to prevent the Society's members and friends
from learning what he was doing." He deposited $31,000 in the bank in the name of the
Society, and at the time of his death had
withdrawn all but $11,000; when the facts
became known "the Internal Revenue Bureau
claimed the Mark Twain Society owed
$11,309.96 income taxes and to secure that
claim it seized all of the Mark Twain's as-
sets [sic], $8,765.00," of which it later
returned $4,427.

B51   _____. "A Short History of the Mark Twain
Memorial Association," Mark Twain Journal,
X (Fall-Winter), 10-11, 19.
Chiefly on the celebrities whose names
have been associated with the organization
(and Benito Mussolini's contribution of
$250 toward a bust of MT in St. Louis), Cy-
ril Clemens's relation to MT, and his successful suit against Harper & Brothers, resulting in an out-of-court settlement in
which they paid him $1250 after having
called him a "Faker and a liar" and having
denied that he was related to MT.

B52   MILLER, WILLIAM C. "Mark Twain at the Sanitary Ball--and Elsewhere?" California Historical Society Bulletin, XXXVI (March),
35-40.
The text of "The Sanitary Ball," reprinted
from the Territorial Enterprise of January
10, 1863, and here attributed to MT.

B53   PAUL, RODMAN WILSON. [Review: Henry Nash
Smith and Frederick Anderson, eds., Mark
Twain of the "Enterprise."] Mississippi Valley
Historical Review, XLIV (September), 368-69.
Chiefly descriptive, noting that "the bulk
of the present volume" consists of "thirty
letters and dispatches to the Enterprise"
from a scrapbook of clippings. Lacking the
art of Roughing It, "these articles are samples of a man's day-to-day journalistic out-
put." Smith's introduction is "excellent,"
and he "has added a twenty-page section that
prints all known correspondence dealing with
the question of whether Mark Twain had to
leave Virginia City in order to avoid having
to fight a duel."

B54   REINFIELD, GEORGE. "Huckleberry Finn, Candi-
date for Greatness," Mark Twain Journal, X
(Fall-Winter), 12-14.
The book is a great novel, which reveals
"the barefaced duplicity of fortune tellers,"
the cowardice of lynch mobs, and "the growth
of character of Huck and Jim as they entrust
each other with their freedom and form a fast
friendship"; in the portrayal of the King and
Duke "royalty comes in for a sound thrash-
ing."

B55   ROGERS, FRANKLIN R. "Washoe's First Literary
Journal," California Historical Society Quarterly, XXXVI (December), 365-70.
On the Weekly Occidental (described in RI),
the first literary paper in Nevada; it died
after four issues, a victim of insufficient
audience, insufficient time on the part of
the staff, and competition from the influen-
tial Golden Era.

B56   RUBIN, LOUIS D., JR. "Tom Sawyer and the Use
of Novels," American Quarterly, IX (Summer),
209-16.
The book is important, not as a document
that describes its times, but as a novel
which helps explain them. Tom has won

(RUBIN, LOUIS D., JR.)
success, wealth, and fame, at the cost of "something impractical and spiritual.... It took a Mark Twain to show us how the meaning of success, and of loss, lies at the heart of American experience" (p. 216). Reprinted in Hennig Cohen, ed. The American Experience: Approaches to the Study of the United States (Boston: Houghton Mifflin Company, 1968), 106-14. In an "Afternote" to the reprinted article (p. 114) Rubin says that he would have "written the essay very differently" if he had had the benefit of Henry Nash Smith's Mark Twain: The Development of a Writer (1962), "a superb demonstration of just how the work of a major writer may profitably be used to interpret a culture."

B57 *SCHÖNFELDER, KARL-HEINZ. "Kriege im Leben und Werk von Mark Twain," Zeitschrift für Anglistik und Amerikanistik, V, 414-32.
[Source: MHRA Annual Bibliography (1959), No. 4574.]

B58 SMITH, HENRY NASH. "Mark Twain as an Interpretor of the Far West: The Structure of Roughing It," in Walker D. Wyman and Clifton B. Kroeber, eds., The Frontier in Perspective. Madison: The University of Wisconsin Press (paperback ed., 1967), pp. 205-28. (Also quotation from LOM and extensive quotation from RI on pp. 201-203 of Frederic G. Cassidy, "Language on the American Frontier," pp. 185-204).
The first half of the book recounts the gradual development of the tenderfoot narrator (p. 210), and in the second half, "structurally distinct...the narrative scheme is loosely autobiographical, and the narrative is merely a framework within which more or less fully developed anecdotes are placed. The second half, that is, answers closely to the description of the entire work given by Mr. Fried and other critics" (p. 224). Also treats MT's turn to Eastern gentility though affirming frontier comradeship and freedom, influence of vernacular on style, and narration by a tenderfoot. The West had considerable influence on American literary development, if not on our democracy (editors' headnote, pp. 205-206).

B59 STALLMAN, R. W. "Huck Finn Again," College English, XVIII (May), 425-26.
"Everything in the novel goes by pairs. Doubleness is the dominant leitmotif, notably in the two Hucks," torn between conscience and conformity. "The structure of Huckleberry Finn, as I see it, consists of a recurrent counterpointing of the real or true event with the juxtaposed parody of it. Nothing is not parodied." The journey southward on the raft, masking the true intention to go northward, is "justifiable both at the literal and the thematic level.... Everything in the novel goes masked, even Moses in the bullrushes; that's what

saved him." The article is followed by: "Note: This letter ends the discussion of Huckleberry Finn begun by Professor O'Connor's attack two years ago.--Ed." Reprinted as "Reality and Parody in Huckleberry Finn," in Bradley (1962.A2), 384-87.

B60 STEGNER, WALLACE. "Yarn-Spinner in the American Vein," New York Times Book Review (February 10), pp. 1, 25.
A review of Charles Neider, ed., The Complete Short Stories of Mark Twain, "an entertaining volume," but much of its content can be called short stories "only by stretching definition to its elastic limits.... Mark Twain is less a short-story writer than a fabulist, satirist, parodist," although his fables and yarns reveal artistic intelligence and sensibility.

B61 TOWN, GEORGE H. [Letter to Chester L. Davis.] Twainian, XVI (January-February), 4.
Cites an article in the Utica (New York) Saturday Globe of February 11, 1899, according to which the original of Colonel Sellers (in The Gilded Age) was one James W. Wardner.

B62 WASIOLEK, EDWARD. "The Structure of Make-Believe: Huckleberry Finn," University of Kansas City Review, XXIII (October), 97-101.
"The river, and life on the river, is fluid, sinuous, unpredictable. The shore, and life on the shore, is still rigid, and predictable," as in the Arkansas crowd's watching the daily spectacle of Boggs's drunkenness and in the feud whose origins are forgotten and which has become ritual; Huck can predict Tom Sawyer's actions and feelings because "Tom's behavior is a regulated show." The controversial ending is consistent with his world and one of grown-ups: "Both worlds are indifferent to real human situations; both entranced with the rules of their play-acting."

B63 WHITE, WILLIAM. "One Man's Meat: Societies and Journals Devoted to a Single Author," American Book Collector, VIII (November), 22-24.
Lists Mark Twain Journal and Twainian, with addresses and names of editors, but provides no other information on MT. Abstract in AES, I (1958), 235.

B64 WIGGER, ANNE P. "The Composition of Mark Twain's Pudd'nhead Wilson and Those Extraordinary Twins: Chronology and Development," Modern Philology, LV (November), 93-102.
The manuscript in the Morgan Library and materials in the Mark Twain Papers reveal "a remarkable literary metamorphosis" during the composition of the book; they reveal MT's intentions, "particularly in the characterization of Tom Driscoll, which becomes rather obscured through the revisions," and originally was a much more dramatic treatment of the effects of inherited training and particularly of the legacy of slavery. Abstract in AES, I (1958), 93.

B65   . "The Source of Fingerprint Material
in Mark Twain's Pudd'nhead Wilson and Those
Extraordinary Twins." American Literature,
XXVIII (January), 517-20.
    The evidence indicates that MT's source
was Sir Francis Galton's Finger Prints (London), a copy of which Chatto & Windus apparently sent him. Disputes the claim by Louis
Hamon (a palmist who used the pseudonym
"Cheiro") to have provided MT with the interest in fingerprinting.

B66 WILLSON, FRANK C. "Hartford 'Tom Sawyer'
Club," Twainian, XVI (January-February), 4.
    On the formation of the club by respect-
able Hartford citizens in 1881; prints an
MT letter of February 11, 1882 declining an
invitation to their first annual dinner.

B67 WINTERICH, JOHN T. "Mark Twain, Reporter,"
Saturday Review, XL (July 27), 26.
    A brief, favorable review of Henry Nash
Smith and Frederick Anderson, eds., Mark
Twain of the "Enterprise" as "this colorful
material, here admirably presented and an-
notated."

1958 A BOOKS

A1 CLEMENS, SAMUEL L. Traveling with the Innocents Abroad: Mark Twain's Original Reports
from Europe and the Holy Land, ed. Daniel
Morley McKeithan. Norman: University of
Oklahoma Press.
    The texts of MT's newspaper letters to
the San Francisco Daily Alta California and
the New York Herald and Tribune, which
formed the basis for Innocents Abroad. This
picks up the correspondence where Franklin
Walker and G. Ezra Dane stopped in Mark
Twain's Travels with Mr. Brown (1940); parts
of two letters in that volume also found
their way into Innocents Abroad. McKeithan's editing is careful and thorough, not
only in showing backgrounds for MT's writing but also in showing some of the changes
the material underwent for Innocents Abroad.

A2 DARBEE, HENRY, ed. Mark Twain in Hartford.
Hartford: The Mark Twain Library and Memorial Commission.
    A pamphlet including Hartford scenes, pic-
tures and floor-plans of MT's home, and excerpts from published sources (not all cited
in the present bibliography) bearing on MT
in Hartford.

A3 EATON, JEANETTE. America's Own Mark Twain.
New York: William Morrow and Company.
Biography of MT for young readers.

A4 FONER, PHILIP S. Mark Twain: Social Critic.
New York: International Publishers.
    A Marxist interpretation, carefully docu-
mented and supported by liberal quotation
from MT to an extent that makes it a useful

source of materials elsewhere unpublished
or difficult of access.

A5 McKEITHAN, DANIEL M[ORLEY]. Court Trials in
Mark Twain and Other Essays. 'S-Gravenhage
[The Hague]: Martinus Nijhoff.
    "The major section of this volume, dealing
with court trials in Mark Twain, is here
published for the first time with the exception of the discussion of the trial of Silas
Phelps. The account of this trial and the
essay entitled 'The Origin of Mark Twain's
Tom Sawyer, Detective' were originally published together as 'Mark Twain's Tom Sawyer,
Detective' in Studia Neophilologica in 1953
(XXV, 161-179). In this section I have
tried to retain at least a little of the
quality of Twain in retelling the stories
and on this basis alone it should be judged.
The other essays appeared, respectively, in
the Philological Quarterly for October, 1953
(XXXII, 353-365), the Tennessee Historical
Quarterly for September, 1952 (XI, 246-253),
the Southern Folklore Quarterly for December, 1953 (XVII, 241-243), the Philological
Quarterly for July, 1948 (XXVII, 276-279),
Modern Language Notes for April, 1948
(LXIII, 221-228), and the University of
Texas Studies in English for 1949 (XXVIII,
257-270).... The major themes here dealt
with are Twain's interest in the administration of justice in the United States, his
use of court trials as elements in his plots,
his debt to frontier American literature,
his reply to foreign critics of America, and
his ability to use foreign sources for details of plot while remaining thoroughly
American in style, spirit, and point of
view" (pp. ix-x). For commentary on the
previously published materials see the years
of original publication.

A6 SMITH, HENRY NASH, ed. Adventures of Huckleberry Finn. Boston: Houghton Mifflin Company.
    Appendices give the text of the "Raft Pas-
sage" from LOM and examples of MT's revisions
of the text of HF. In his introduction Smith
discusses the importance of language in HF,
the use of Huck as innocent narrator, the
gain and the loss in MT's rejection of cultural tradition, and structural questions in
the flight downstream (Jim's escape is not
always a central concern) and culminating at
the Phelps farm. Smith disputes the notion,
increasingly popular among critics, that Huck
learns to see the evils of slavery or the
society that condones it: "When Huck says
he means to set out ahead of the others,
there is nothing in the text to indicate that
his intention is more serious than Tom's."

1958 B SHORTER WRITINGS

B1 ANON. [Miscellaneous material from December
Harper's Magazine]. Twainian, XVII (November-December), 1-4.

(ANON.)
Statement by Charles Neider on MT's auto-biography, followed by statements by MT on various topics. Quoted in Twainian, XXXII (November-December, 1973), 4.

B2   ASSELINEAU, ROGER. [Review: Arthur L. Scott, Mark Twain: Selected Criticism (1955) and Huckleberry Finns Abenteuer, translated in-to German by Barbara Cramer-Nauhaus, and with an afterword by F. W. Schulze (1956).] Études Anglaises, VIII (April-June), 183-84.
Scott's great fault is giving undue space to the favorable notices MT received in his lifetime, many of them superficial, with the result that the book is more interest-ing as history than as criticism. It would have been more useful to present texts clarifying a certain number of important points, such as the Brooks-DeVoto contro-versy, or the discussions of HF by Lionel Trilling, T. S. Eliot, and Leo Marx. F. W. Schulze's afterword to the German transla-tion of HF provides an excellent analysis of the characters of Tom, Huck, and, espe-cially, Jim; it is unfortunate that, prob-ably for want of space, he did not attempt to define the particular flavor of MT's humor in this book. [In French.]

B3   BARROWS, HERBERT. [Review: Daniel Morley McKeithan, ed., Traveling with the Inno-cents Abroad.] Antioch Review, XVIII (Win-ter), 515-22.
No comment on the editing, but calls this "just possibly a better book than The Inno-cents Abroad," revealing the "ebullient spirit" of the letters before they were toned down "into a self-conscious literary production."

B4   BECK, WARREN. "Huck Finn at Phelps Farm: An Essay in Defense of the Form of Mark Twain's Novel," Archives des Lettres Modernes, Nos. 13-15 (Juin-Septembre), pp. 1-31.
"What makes the Phelps farm episode con-clusively relevant, therefore, in spite of its juvenile flavor, is the constant pres-ence of the realistic and increasingly re-sponsible Huck, and his repeated interpola-tions as the half-detached and more than half-skeptical foil to Tom's fancifulness and enslavement to tradition" (p. 22). [32-page pamphlet, with an abstract in French on p. 32.]

B5   BERRY, MABEL F. E. "Mark Twain in Hartford," Mark Twain Journal, X (Spring-Summer), 16.
She saw MT in church there and once de-livered stationery to his house by bicycle.

B6   BLAIR, WALTER. "When Was Huckleberry Finn Written?" American Literature, XXX (March), 1-25.
Contends that Paine is nearer the truth in giving periods of composition as 1876, 1880, and 1883 than is DeVoto in giving only 1876 and 1883. "Furthermore, I believe that both, with most other students of Twain, overestimate the influence of Clem-ens's Mississippi River trip of 1882 on the novel. If my beliefs prove to be well founded, significant revisions of the story of the genesis of the book will be necessa-ry." The evidence includes letters and re-corded conversations, MT's notes, notebooks, and the surviving MS material. Most of the evidence not available to DeVoto is in Web-ster's Mark Twain, Business Man or in tran-scripts in the Mark Twain Papers in Berke-ley. Abstract in AES, I (1958), 546.

B7   BOOMKAMP, LEEUWEN. "A Dutch Admirer Meets Mark Twain," Mark Twain Journal, X (Spring-Summer), 8.
In the summer of 1900, he was reading and laughing over TS on a New York bus, and got into "quite a pleasant argument, pro and contra," with a man who called it "kid stuff"; Boomkamp eventually recognized the man as MT.

B8   BUDD, LOUIS J. [Review: Henry Nash Smith and Frederick Anderson, eds., Mark Twain of the "Enterprise."] South Atlantic Bulletin, LVII (Winter), 145-46.
Thirty newspaper letters and dispatches from scrapbooks recently added to the Mark Twain Papers at Berkeley, "definitively edited, handsomely printed...it is a valu-able as well as an interesting book," both for the MT scholar and for the "absorbing Americana" it contains.

B9   CARTER, PAUL J. "Mark Twain Material in the New York Weekly Review," Papers of the Bib-liographical Society of America, LII (First Quarter), 56-62.
Reveals eight MT items appearing there, one of them (on a San Francisco earthquake) previously unknown.

B10   _____. "Olivia Clemens Edits Following the Equator," American Literature XXX (May), 194-209.
Consists primarily of the text of Livy's comments and MT's responses, as preserved in the Mark Twain Papers. She did urge some changes for the sake of propriety, but her main role was that of skilful proofreader; MT appreciated her suggestions, but did not accept them all. [See Da Ponte, 1957.] Ab-stract in AES, I (1958), 762.

B11   CLARK, GEORGE PEIRCE. "Mark Twain and Bret Harte," Mark Twain Journal, X (Spring-Sum-mer), 12-13.
Reprints the text of MT's comments to How-ells in letters of April 15, 1879 and Decem-ber 4, 1903; "neither of these letters is printed in full, but nothing pertaining to Harte is omitted from them." See 1958.B12.

B12 _____. "Mark Twain on Bret Harte: Selections from Two Unpublished Letters," Journal of English and Germanic Philology, LVII (April), 208-10.
Letters from Paris (April 15, 1879) and Florence (December 4, 1903), attacking Harte as a man of no integrity and an author whose latest book MT read "through tears of rage over the fellow's inborn hypocrisy & snobbishness, his apprentice-art, his artificialities, his mannerisms, his pet phrases...his laboriously acquired ignorance, & his jejeune anxiety to display it. O my God!" Abstract in AES, III I (1960), 1453; reprinted in Twainian, XIX (November-December, 1960).

B13 CLEMENS, CYRIL. "Sir Max Beerbohm and Mark Twain," Hobbies--the Magazine for Collectors, LXIII (November), 110.
Prints several notes from Beerbohm, one of them (February 14, 1953) recalling a luncheon with MT at Bernard Shaw's home: "He was then very old, but very beautiful to look at, and to listen to. A lovely voice, lovely manners, and, among other attributes, wonderfully eloquent hands."

B14 COCTEAU, JEAN. Sketch (not resembling MT), bearing the legend: "Mark Twain n'est pas un humoriste c'est un poète et je l'aime Jean Cocteau* 1958." Mark Twain Journal, X (Spring-Summer), front cover.

B15 CONSIGLIO, CARLA. "La Fortuna di Mark Twain in Italia: Nota Bibliografica di Carla Consiglio." Studi Americani, IV, 198-208.
An annotated bibliography of translations and criticism, 1891-1957.

B16 _____. "La Prosa di Mark Twain e i Suoi Influssi" ["Mark Twain's Prose and Its Influences"], Studi Americani, IV, 175-97.
A detailed examination of MT's influence on Gertrude Stein, Sherwood Anderson, and Ernest Hemingway. In his "superb adaptation of the vernacular to the purposes of art" MT "has forged a classic prose that moves according to the canons of simplicity, grace, and limpidness." Gertrude Stein knew his works, and "it would be interesting...to know if Stein was completely conscious of the affinity of her prose with that of Mark Twain." In turn, she helped shape Hemingway and Anderson. "All that Anderson and Hemingway proposed to say was similar to that which Mark Twain had said"; they shared his interest in the life of the common people, aversion to formal education, and, especially, a wish to depict reality objectively and without distortion.

B17 COOPER, M. LOVINA. "I Remember Mark Twain," Mark Twain Journal, X (Spring-Summer), 5.
Recollection of MT's appearance when he spoke at the University of Minnesota. "We listened with wrapped [sic] attention while the famous Mark Twain talked. No, I can't tell you what he said."

B18 COSBEY, ROBERT C. "Letter to the Editor," College English, XIX (April), 320.
Tom Sawyer's fence has horizontal boards, as described in Tyrus Hillway's note in the January issue (1958.B35), but Tom is described as easily scrambling over it; the extremely high fence "is the creation of impressionistic humor, not of carpenters."

B19 *CUMMINGS, SHERWOOD. "Memories of Mark Twain," North Dakota Quarterly, XXXVI (Spring), 65-66.
[Source: Leary (1970), p. 62.]

B20 _____. "Science and Mark Twain's Theory of Fiction," Philological Quarterly, XXXVII (January), 26-33.
"The idea of scientific determinism was...implicit in Mark Twain's earliest reading and thinking"; the influence of Darwin and Taine is evident. MT's theory applies in TS and HF, where "the power of place...is at once pervasive and unobtrusive" and in PW, where "the exposition of environmental influence upon Tom Driscoll and Chambers is worked out with the neatness of a sociologist's case history." Abstract in AES, I (1958), 1048.

B21 CURRIE, H. MacL. "Aristophanes and Mark Twain," Notes and Queries (London), CCIII, n.s. V (April), 165-68.
Compares the attitude of the two as revealed in the latter part of the Thesmophoriazusae and in chapters XXXVI-XXXIX of Huckleberry Finn. They were "not dissimilar in spirit," and if there is no evidence that MT had read Aristophanes, he did read widely and the plays were readily available in the Bohn classical series. Abstract in AES, I (1958), 890.

B22 [DAVIS, CHESTER L.]. "Mark's Copy 'Origin of Religions-Aryan Sun-Myths,'" Twainian, XVII (September-October), 1-3.
"Mr. Victor Jacobs...has sent us photostatic copies of certain pages from the above book, pages having marginal notations in the handwriting of Mark Twain, the book being one which was in the last public dispersal of Mark's library." Reproduces passages from the book with some of MT's comments (author of book not named). Quoted in Twainian, XXXII (November-December, 1973.B15), 4.

B23 _____. "Mark Twain and John Hays Hammond," Twainian (January-February), 1-3.
On MT's marginalia in his copy of Mrs. John Hays Hammond's A Woman's Part in a Revolution (New York and Bombay: Longmans, Green & Co., 1897); Mrs. Hammond describes MT's visit to the prisoners at Pretoria on p. 152 of her book. Quoted in Twainian, XXXII (November-December, 1973.B15), 1.

B24   [DAVIS, CHESTER L.] "Mark Twain and Space Travel," Twainian, pp. 3-4.
      Quotations from his published works with no new information.

B25   _____. "Mark Twain Coinage of Words," Twainian, p. 4.
      On Robert L. Ramsay and Frances Guthrie Emberson's A Mark Twain Lexicon (1938): excerpts, with no new information or useful comment. Quoted in Twainian, XXXII (November-December, 1973.B15), 1-2.

B26   _____. "Mark Twain Memorial--Future Home of Twainian," Twainian, (May-June), 1-4.
      On the plans for the building, to be erected at Florida, Missouri, and on the Mark Twain Research Foundation and its predecessors. Quoted in Twainian, XXXII (November-December, 1973.B15), 2-3.

B27   _____. "Mark Twain's Personal Library to Be Collected and Contained in Mark Twain Memorial to Be Erected at His Birthplace in Florida, Missouri," Twainian, (July-August), 2-4; (September-October), 3-4.
      Lists titles of books containing MT's marginalia; "Those which we do not have or which we have not located approximates about half of the total items listed." Quoted in Twainian, XXXII (November-December, 1973.B15), 3-4.

B28   _____. "A Visit to Florida in the Year Paine Published the 'Biography' 1912," Twainian, (March-April), 1-4.
      Headnote to reprint of T. V. Bodine, "Birthplace of Mark Twain. The Story of the Great Humorist and Philosopher and His Equally Whimsical Uncle--Judge John S. Quarles," in Kansas City Star, May 19, 1912: "(The following article is not generally available and has been referred to by many writers. Repeated inquiries justify the republication of the article almost in it's entirety. Parts which are not reprinted herein have definitely been of little value to later writers and historians, parts largely speculative and not proven, or better treated by later writers such as Paine, DeVoto and Wecter.)" Quoted in Twainian, XXXII (November-December, 1973.B15), 2.

B29   _____. [Review: E. Hudson Long's Mark Twain Handbook (1958),] Twainian, (November-December), 1.
      Descriptive and laudatory.

B30   ELLIOTT, GEORGE P. "Wonder for Huckleberry Finn," in George P. Shipiro, ed., Twelve Original Essays on Great American Novels. (Detroit: Wayne State University Press), pp. 69-95.
      A general study of MT and his book; notes the entertainment value of MT's books, his sensitivity to words and their sound and arrangement, his poor critical judgment of his own work, and "his acceptance of standards of value--moral, social, literary-- which in his heart he disbelieved in." It is our good fortune that he came to write HF as he did.

B30A ELLISON, RALPH. "Change the Joke and Slip the Yoke," Partisan Review, XXV (Spring), 212-22; reprinted in his Shadow and Act (1964), pp. 45-59.
      An answer to an essay by Stanley Edgar Hyman on Negro American literature and folklore (immediately preceding). On HF, Ellison argues that "Twain fitted Jim into the outlines of the minstrel tradition, and it is from behind this stereotype mask that we see Jim's dignity and human capacity-- and Twain's complexity--emerge." MT was still too close to the Reconstruction to escape "the white dictum that Negro males must be treated either as boys or 'uncles'-- never as men. Jim's friendship for Huck comes across as that of a boy for another boy rather than as the friendship of an adult for a junior; thus there is implicit in it not only a violation of the manners sanctioned by society for relations between Negroes and whites, there is a violation of our concept of adult maleness." Ellison suggests that it was concern over this question that led Leslie Fiedler to argue a homosexual relationship in "Come Back to the Raft Ag'in, Huck Honey!" Fiedler was "so profoundly disturbed by the manner in which the deep dichotomies symbolized by blackness and whiteness are resolved that, forgetting to look at the specific form of the novel, he leaped squarely into the middle of that tangle of symbolism which he is dedicated to unsnarling and yelled out his most terrifying name for chaos."

B31   FIEDLER, LESLIE A. "Boys Will be Boys!" New Leader, XLI (April 28), 23-26.
      HF conformed to the 19th century taboo on any intimations of sex in books about children, although MT faced violence frankly; however, in TS Tom takes both the punishment and the blame for Becky's damaging the schoolmaster's book: "It is as necessary to him that Becky retain her mythical Goodness as it is for her that he retain his equally mythical Badness." Reprinted in his No! In Thunder (1960), and The Collected Essays of Leslie Fiedler (1971.B22).

B32   _____. "Good Good Girl and Good Bad Boy," New Leader, XLI (April 14), 22-25.
      On the literary Cult of the Child: the portrayal of the boy must reject the aristocratic "little gentleman," like Sid Sawyer. HF exists on a superficially comic and deeper tragic level; it is "an astonishingly complicated novel, containing not one image of the boy-child as a symbol of the good life of impulse, but a series of interlocking ones: boys within boys." Reprinted in his

(FIEDLER, LESLIE A.)
No! In Thunder (1960) and The Collected Essays of Leslie Fiedler (1971.B22). Abstract in AES, I (1958), 1800.

B33 GERBER, JOHN C. "The Relation between Point of View and Style in the Works of Mark Twain," in Style in Prose Fiction, English Institute Essays, 1958; New York: Columbia University Press (1959), pp. 142-71.
    "Twain's style is so intimately dependent upon his point of view that it flourishes only to the extent that the point of view is detached and sharply restricted," providing psychological distance and "forcing him to focus upon a specific and concrete situation" (p. 143). This accounts for the superiority of HF to TS and CY. In IA MT is more detached as storyteller than as observer or satirist, and as a result "The details are more specific and the incidents far better shaped for climax" (p. 149). Abstract in AES, VIII (1965), 2571; reprinted in Twainian, XXV (January-February, 1966). Article reprinted in Lettis (1962.A11), pp. 410-18.

B34 GORDON, EDWARD J. "What's Happened to Humor?" English Journal, XLVII (March), 127-33.
    Huck Finn sees through the self-deceptions of others; he is contrasted with John Marquand's character George Apley, who deceives himself.

B35 HILLWAY, TYRUS. "Tom Sawyer's Fence," College English, XIX (January), 165-66.
    The planks were horizontal, rather than vertical; moreover, it was a nine-foot fence, "an unusually high one, unless Mark Twain was intentionally exaggerating." Abstract in AES, I (1958), 271. For further commentary see Robert C. Cosbey (April), B. R. McElderry, Jr. (May), and Robert H. Woodward (October, with another letter by Hillway).

B36 _____, and Robert H. Woodward. "Rebuttal: Tom Sawyer's Fence," College English, XX (October), 32.
    Hillway replies to Robert C. Cosbey's note in April (1958.B18) that climbing a nine-foot fence is no great feat, particularly with a toehold on horizontal boards. The Woodward letter notes an illustration "in The Book of Knowledge (1953 ed., VI, 2132), which pictures exactly the style of fence described in the novel"; he does not describe this illustration, but argues that the boards are vertical on the basis of a photograph taken in 1902, showing MT at the house; moreover, a guidebook on sale at Hannibal describes the fence as "just like" the original. [A photograph accompanying Henry M. Wharton's "The Boyhood Home of Mark Twain" in Century, LXIV (September, 1902), 674, shows the house with a fence on the right of a viewer facing toward the

house from the street, which slopes downhill to the right; the fence appears to be almost six feet high, with vertical boards. To the left, less than three feet from the house, appears a substantial brick building. According to the caption, "There was a high board fence on the left, for the whitewashing of which he sold privileges to one or more of his youthful companions, somewhat as related in 'Tom Sawyer.'"--ed.]

B37 HINZ, JOHN. "A No. 1 Ruse," Mark Twain Journal, X (Spring-Summer), 14.
    Disputes the statement by Edgar M. Branch that this early sketch is "disappointing," merely "a long diffuse tale."

B38 HUNTING, ROBERT. "Mark Twain's Arkansaw Yahoos," Modern Language Notes, LXXIII (April), 264-68.
    Chapters XXI-XXII ("An Arkansaw Difficulty" and "Why the Lynching Bee Failed") "in point of view and in tone...stand apart from the rest of the novel.... the mask slips and...the reporter in these two chapters looks suspiciously like Mark Twain himself," lacking in Huck's compassion. (See reply by E. Arthur Robinson, 1960.B95.) Abstract in AES, I (1958), 867.

B39 KELLER, HELEN. "My Friend Mark Twain," Mark Twain Journal, X (Spring-Summer), 1.
    On her admiration and affection for MT, whom she first met when she was fourteen; "It seemed to me that his pessimism was rather superficial. I thought he enjoyed exercising his wonderful gift of making sardonic aphorisms," although they were incisive and arrested attention.

B40 LAING, DILYS. "His Own Bowdler," Nation, CLXXXVII (July 19), 37-38.
    A review of Daniel Morley McKeithan, ed., Traveling with the Innocents Abroad. MT toned the letters down for the book.

B41 LORCH, FRED W. "Hawaiian Feudalism and Mark Twain's A Connecticut Yankee in King Arthur's Court," American Literature, XXX (March), 50-66.
    Suggests supplementing John B. Hoben's "genetic study" (1946) with a "pre-genetic study": it was in Hawaii that MT first encountered the remnants of a feudal society, and his reading about the islands supplemented his vivid personal impressions. There is particularly clear evidence of the influence of James Jackson Jarves's History of the Sandwich Islands (Honolulu, 1847), with which MT was familiar and which anticipates the Yankee not only in the broad picture of the society, but also in such details as the interdict (Javes describes the effects of taboo, and draws attention to its similarity to the interdict of the Roman Church). Abstract in AES, I (1958), 549.

B42 LORCH, FRED W. [Review: Henry Nash Smith and Frederick Anderson, ed., Mark Twain of the "Enterprise" (1957).] American Literature, XXX (March), pp. 125-27.

The two great contributions to MT scholarship are the clear detailing of MT's kinds of reporting for the Enterprise (straight reporting signed "Sam" or "SLC" and humorous material signed "Mark Twain"), and the documented explanation of why MT suddenly left Nevada--not to avoid arrest for violation of the dueling laws, but because of his tasteless assertion that money being collected for the Sanitary Fund was being sent to support miscegenation societies. There are no serious inaccuracies evident, and Smith provides valuable supplementary data in the headnotes.

B43 LOWENHERZ, ROBERT J. "Mark Twain Laughs at Death," Mark Twain Journal, X (Spring-Summer), 2-5, 16.

On comic treatments of death in MT's works; reprints the text of a burlesque obituary he wrote for the "Contributors' Club" of the Atlantic Monthly (November, 1884).

B44 _____. "Mark Twain on Usage," American Speech, XXXIII (February), 70-72.

A brief introductory note by Lowenherz precedes an abridged reprinting of MT's unsigned reply to "A Boston Girl" in "The Contributors' Club" of Atlantic, XLV (June, 1880), 849-60; MT's topics are grammar and the accurate rendering of speech.

B45 LUNDY, ROBERT W. "Mark Twain and Italy." Studi Americani, IV, 135-49.

"His two travel books which include sections on Italy confirm the impression that he learned little about or from it" (p. 137), because he had no real interest in the country or its history.

B46 LYNN, KENNETH S. "Huck and Jim," Yale Review, XLVII (March), 421-31.

MT's early interest in Joan of Arc grew from reading about her in her prison cell, and "in a sense Twain spent all his lifetime writing about Joan; the tension between the nightmare of being locked up and forgotten and the dream of liberation is in all his best work." In HF there is a succession of Biblical themes, especially that of Moses--and a parallel in that when Moses led the Israelites toward freedom he moved toward death, and the movement carrying Jim to freedom will separate the two friends. Huck undergoes rebirths in a cycle of initiations culminating in deaths, and Jim passes through successive bondages. Abstract in AES, I (1958), 755. Article reprinted in Kaplan (1967), pp. 123-33.

B47 McELDERRY, B. R., JR. "Tom Sawyer's Fence-- Original Illustrations," College English, XIX (May), 370.

In answer to the note by Tyrus Hillway in the January issue and the letter by Robert C. Cosbey in May, calls attention to the illustrations in the first edition by True Williams, presumably with MT's approval: "Three illustrations (pp. 17, 28, 30) show a fence along the street, made of four wide boards, well spaced, and nailed horizontally to square posts set six or eight feet apart. The height of the fence is about four feet.... the fence is shown extending to the left of the house. The fence shown in Hannibal today as a 'replica' stands about fifteen feet to the right of the house, and is, as Mr. Hillway remarks, a solid board fence about six feet high, the boards nailed vertically."

B48 McGRAW, WILLIAM CORBIN. "Polyanna Rides Again," Saturday Review, XLI (March 22), 37-38.

Illustrates the thesis that censorship by children's librarians stultifies the writing of children's books with a skit, "If Sam Clemens Had Been Born Sixty Years too Late (A Near-Tragedy in One Act)," with dialogue between MT and "Cordelia Minor, juvenile editor, harassed and fiftyish," who explains why HF cannot be published. This is followed by "An Answer to Mr. McGraw," by Frances Lander Spain, Coordinator, Children's Services, New York Public Library, who points out that HF did encounter censorship when it was new, and the taboos McGraw cites are those of society and not only of libraries; moreover, if authors and editors seek advice from librarians before publication they share the guilt of "emasculating a manuscript."

B49 *MACK, EFFIE [MONA]. "Mark Twain in Nevada. A Leaf from the Civil War Story," Oakland (California) Tribune, November 16.

[Source: Reprinted in Twainian, XIX (March-April), 4.] On the glorious sight of the flag on Mt. Davidson on the day Vicksburg fell to Union forces; adds little to the account in RI.

B50 MESERVE, WALTER J. "Colonel Sellers as a Scientist: A Play by S. L. Clemens and W. D. Howells," Modern Drama, I (December), 151-56.

On the collaboration of MT and Howells, and later use of portions of the play in The American Claimant. Abstract in AES, II (1959), 288.

B51 MILLER, JAMES E., JR. [Brief review: Charles Neider, ed., The Complete Short Stories of Mark Twain.] Prairie Schooner, XXXII (June), 88.

"Mr. Neider's collection not only makes pleasurable reading but also calls significant attention to Twain's mastery of the art of the short fictional form."

B52   MIRIZZI, PIERO. "Il Mondo di Mark Twain"
      ["The World of Mark Twain"], Studi Ameri-
      cani, IV, 151-74.
          A general and somewhat derivative por-
      trayal of MT's life and works, noting the
      influences by which he was shaped, his at-
      titudes, and the quality of his authorship.

B53   MONTGOMERY, MARION. "The Old Romantic vs. the
      New: Mark Twain's Dilemma in Life on the
      Mississippi," Mississippi Quarterly, XI
      (Spring), 79-82.
          MT's attack on the romanticism of Sir
      Walter Scott contrasts with his own por-
      trait in LOM of the romance of a pilot's
      life twenty years earlier, "and, more ex-
      asperating, his mystical glorification of
      the industrial life of the late nineteenth
      century." Abstract in AES, I (1958), 1461.
      Article reprinted in Kesterson (1973),
      pp. 113-16.

B54   MORRIS, WRIGHT. "The Available Past: Mark
      Twain," in his The Territory Ahead: Criti-
      cal Interpretations of American Literature.
      (New York: Harcourt, Brace & World),
      pp. 79-90.
          [Source: 1963 paperback reprinting, New
      York: Athenaeum; the pagination is the
      same as that reported in Beebe and Feaster
      (1968), p. 106, where the year of publica-
      tion is given as 1958.] Contrasts MT and
      Hemingway in their treatment of innocence
      and "the corruption and abuse of America's
      green promise," and MT and Henry James as
      "the supremely unconscious natural talent"
      and "the supremely self-conscious artist."
      "Hemingway's exile is a judgment on things
      as they are" in a spoiled America, that of
      Henry James is an attempt to re-possess his
      inheritance and share its culture with the
      new world, but MT was simply an innocent
      abroad who resisted foreign culture. His
      preference for facts over ideas left him
      at the end with "staleness and disenchant-
      ment.... And what was he? Stripped of his
      imagination, Henry James could have told
      him, he was not much." Reprinted in Leary
      (1962), pp. 269-76.

B55   *MUELLER, HAROLD L., ed. "Mark Twain Library
      Golden Anniversary" special edition of
      Redding (Connecticut) Times, December 4.
          Includes article apparently by Mueller on
      history of the library, with a speech by MT
      at the dedication of the library at its
      first, temporary quarters. [Source: Re-
      printed in Twainian, XVIII (January-Febru-
      ary, 1959), 1-3.]

B56   NEIDER, CHARLES, ed. "Mark Twain Speaks
      Out," Harper's, CCXVII (December), 36-41.
          Previously unpublished writings by MT on
      the freedom of writing as from the grave,
      honorary degrees, amateur writing, and hu-
      mor; from dictations of 1906-1907. Abstract
      in AES, II (1959), 171.

B57   OLIVER, EGBERT S. "The Pig-Tailed China Boys
      Out West," Western Humanities Review, XII
      (Spring), 159-78.
          On the mistreatment of Chinese immigrants
      in the West; on pp. 174-77, describes the
      insight and sympathy with which they are
      portrayed by MT and Bret Harte.

B58   PAINE, ALBERT BIGELOW. "Mark Twain at Eighty-
      Eight," Redding (Connecticut) Times, Decem-
      ber 4, pp. 14-15, 23.
          Written in Chinon, France, according to a
      headnote by his daughter, Louise Paine
      Moore. On MT's birthdays, his billiard-
      playing, and his international popularity.

B59   PELLEGRINI, ALMA. "Mark Twain alla Scoperta
      dell'Europa: The Innocents Abroad" ["Mark
      Twain on the Discovery of Europe: The Inno-
      cents Abroad"], Studi Americani, IV, 109-33.
          A general discussion of MT's perspective
      in IA and attitudes toward his material.
      From a position of practical, independent
      common sense he sometimes used the mask of
      the fool, sometimes turned to burlesque,
      and sometimes understated; he often took a
      moralist's view of the follies and vices of
      the Old World. His was almost a dual per-
      sonality, and his inner defects sometimes
      appear in his works as well as determining
      the structure and defects of the self. Only
      in HF does he achieve "an almost perfect
      equilibrium of his expressive means"; in this
      aspect IA "is in essence an uneven book
      which lacks an intimate core that can assure
      continuity of tone and results, and furnish
      Twain a valid perspective in which to frame
      Europe."

B60   SANFORD, CHARLES. "Classics of American Re-
      form Literature," American Quarterly, X
      (Fall), 295-311.
          Includes a discussion of Connecticut Yan-
      kee (302-305) as MT's "symbolic attempt to
      persuade himself that all was right in the
      American garden after all," although sug-
      gesting that "the industrial order lacks
      the symbols to captivate the imagination and
      that the new American may have lost the
      sense of heart which characterized the sim-
      pler, agrarian past." Abstract in AES, II
      (1959), 129.

B61   SMITH, HENRY NASH. "Mark Twain's Image of
      Hannibal: From St. Petersburg to Eseldorf,"
      Texas Studies in English, XXXVII, 3-23.
          "Villagers of 1840-3," part of MT's memo-
      ries which Smith collectively terms the
      "Matter of Hannibal," "embraced the glory of
      boyhood but it also embraced the terror and
      the guilt." From the idyllic portrayal of
      the small town in TS there is a decline in
      the image through HF, CY, PW and other works.
      "Mark Twain came nearer registering in fic-
      tion the death of nineteenth-century culture
      than did such contemporaries as Howells...or
      James." Unable from the 1890's to ignore
      his insights into the corruption of democracy

(SMITH, HENRY NASH)
by money and into war as a natural human
condition, he was also unable to embody
them successfully into his work. Nonetheless, "as we have slowly become aware, the
development of twentieth-century American
literature, its dominant themes and above
all its language, began on the day in 1876
when Mark Twain conceived the idea of treating the Matter of Hannibal from the viewpoint of the outcast, Huckleberry Finn."
Abstract in AES, II (1959), 1556; reprinted in Twainian, XIX (January-February,
1960). Article reprinted in Bradley
(1962), pp. 410-21; in Cardwell (1963),
pp. 92-103.

B62 *STARTSEV, A. "Something New about Young
Twain," Inostrannaja Literatura [Foreign
Literature], IV, 261-263.
A review of Mark Twain of the "Enterprise" (1957); Startsev notes the "abundant
historical commentary as well as interesting details describing an important period
in Twain's literary work." Source: Abstract in AES, I (1958), 1263.

B63 STEWART, RANDALL. "Dreiser and the Naturalistic Heresy," Virginia Quarterly Review,
XXXIV (Winter), 100-116.
On HF: despite What Is Man? MT does not
belong among the naturalists, "if for no
other reason than the fact that Huck Finn
is one of the most responsible of fictional
mortals." Reprinted in his American Literature & Christian Doctrine (1958),
pp. 120-21. Abstract in AES, I (1958), 233.

B64 WILKINS, THURMAN. Clarence King: A Biography. New York: The Macmillan Company.
Brief references to MT passim (indexed),
but no useful information.

1959 A BOOKS

A1 BRASHEAR, MINNIE M., and ROBERT M. RODNEY,
eds., The Art, Humor and Humanity of Mark
Twain. Norman: University of Oklahoma
Press.
An anthology of extracts from MT's published works, with commentary and notes,
in three parts: "Mark Twain, Master Story-
teller and Descriptive Artist"; Mark Twain,
Missouri Humorist"; "Mark Twain, Epigrammat-
ist." Includes an introduction by Edward
Wagenknecht, "an extensive "Chronology of
Mark Twain's Life and Literary Career,"
and a useful "Selected Bibliography."

A2 CLEMENS, SAMUEL L. Concerning Cats: Two
Tales by Mark Twain. With an Introduction
by Frederick Anderson. San Francisco: The
Book Club of California.
The texts of "A Cat Tale" and "The Autobiography of Belshazzar," with a generous
introduction on the Clemens family's

affection for cats and a discussion of the
care expended on these unfinished manuscripts, which he apparently considered
publishing. "The Autobiography of Belshazzar" is of interest as a portrait of the
Clemens family at Quarry Farm, and in MT's
self-description (later struck out): "He
was a kind of author, and made books, but
was afraid to print them in his own name,
for they were mainly nonsense and the rest
was lies. It was his idea that if he
changed his name he would not be found out,
and some innocent person would get the
blame; for he was of a malicious disposition
and had not much sense."

A3 *____. Mark Twain Tonight! An Actor's Por-
trait: Selections from Mark Twain. Edited,
Adapted, and Arranged with a Prologue, by
Hal Holbrook. New York: Ives, Washburn.
[Source: "Brief Mention," American Lit-
erature, XXXII (May), 227.]

A4 LYNN, KENNETH S. Mark Twain and Southwestern
Humor. Boston and Toronto: Little, Brown
and Company.
Many readers have misunderstood MT's mask
of innocence, and more have confused the
Southwestern humorists with the backwoods
mind they described. "My belief, however,
is that Mark Twain was a conscious and deliberate creator, and one of the purposes of
this book is to treat him as such.... As
with Mark Twain, my primary assumption about
the humorous tradition behind him is that it
is a self-conscious art, and not an expression of American mindlessness." Chapter IX,
Sections iii, vii, and viii are reprinted in
Bradley (1962), pp. 421-36. A part of Chapter V, dealing with RI, is reprinted in
Smith (1963), pp. 40-46. The portion dealing with "The Jumping Frog," pp. 144-48, is
reprinted in Cardwell (1963), pp. 113-15.

A5 MARKS, BARRY R. Mark Twain's Huckleberry Finn
(Problems in American Civilization). Boston: D. C. Heath and Company.
A collection of critical essays on HF, all
of which are listed in the present bibliography, cross-referenced to this collection.

A6 NEIDER, CHARLES, ed. The Autobiography of
Mark Twain, Including Chapters Now Published
for the First Time. New York: Harper &
Brothers, Publishers.
Material left by MT at his death, here for
the first time arranged in chronological order. "For the first time the whole manuscript is being used as the source, not
parts or selections of it. Also, the present volume contains from 30,000 to 40,000
words which have never before seen print."
Also available in paperback, New York:
Washington Square Press, 1961.

1959 B SHORTER WRITINGS

B1 ALTENBERND, LYNN. "Huck Finn, Emancipator," Criticism, I (Fall), 298-307.
"The purpose of this article is to show that the final episode is the thematic climax of the novel because the rescue of Jim from the cabin is an allegory representing the Civil War": although the South could have freed the slaves voluntarily, romantic nonsense (represented by that of Tom Sawyer) interfered. "What actually frees Jim, and what will actually free the nominally emancipated slave, is a voluntary act of human love," first from Huck, then from Miss Watson, who gives him his freedom in her will. Abstract in AES, IX (1966), 1584; reprinted in Twainian, XXVI (January-February, 1967).

B2 ANDERSON, DAVID. "Twain Estate Up $65,000 in Year. Accounting in Connecticut Discloses $22,000 Came from Royalties," New York Times, April 18, p. 25.
A half-column description of the annual accounting.

B3 ANDERSON, FREDERICK. "Twain Papers a Fount of Biographical Studies," Manuscripts, XI (Fall), 14-15.
Describes the Mark Twain Papers in the University of California Library at Berkeley, the materials that have been published, and plans for further publication. Followed by "A Note on Copyrights," explaining that "The Trustees of the Mark Twain Estate control the right to publish any previously unpublished writing by Mark Twain whether the manuscript is in the possession of the Estate or not (according to common-law copyright)." [Permissions to publish are now arranged through Frederick Anderson, Editor, The Mark Twain Papers, The University of California Library, Berkeley, California 94720--T.A.T.]

B4 *ANON. "De Tom Sawyer à Mark Twain," Informations et Documents, No. 113 (November 15), pp. 31-35.
[Source: Leary (1954), p. 56.]

B5 ANON. "Mark Twain in Tarrytown," The Chronicle of the Historical Society of the Tarrytowns, Inc., No. 4 (September), pp. 3-4.
Quotes at length from a letter from Mrs. Samuel C. Webster and records in the files of Ernest F. Griffin on his purchase of a property at Tarrytown, later sold after a successful suit to have the tax assessment reduced.

B6 ANON. "Two Letters Solve a Bitter Dispute," Manuscripts, XI (Fall), 13.
As Walter Blair points out in Mark Twain & Huck Finn, soon to be published, letters to MT from Charles L. Webster show that HF was sold in England and Canada before it was sold in the U.S., but copies existed in the U.S. first. The letters, of March 16 and 18, 1885, are in the Mark Twain Papers in Berkeley.

B7 BAENDER, PAUL. "Mark Twain and the Byron Scandal," American Literature, XXX (January), 467-85.
Includes the text of six unsigned editorials in the Buffalo Express in August and September, 1869, attributed by Baender to MT, discussing them in the light they cast on MT's thought. Abstract in AES, II (1959), 389.

B8 BERTHOFF, WERNER. "The Country of Jewett's Pointed Firs," New England Quarterly, XXXII (March), 31-53.
Only brief mention of MT: quotes Willa Cather's grouping of HF with The Scarlet Letter and The Country of the Pointed Firs as the "three American books which have the possibility of a long life" and suggests that Miss Jewett came around to a narrative technique more Twainian than Jamesian or Flaubertian. Abstract in AES, II (1959), 1255; reprinted in Twainian, XIX (January-February, 1960).

B9 *BRUNNER, KARL. "Dickens und Mark Twain in Italien," in Festschrift für Walter Fischer, Heidelberg, pp. 112-16.
[Other details not available. Source: MHRA Annual Bibliography (1959), Nos. 3930, 4552.]

B10 BUDD, LOUIS J. "Southward Currents under Huck Finn's Raft," Mississippi Valley Historical Review, XLVI (September), 222-37.
"Perhaps no analysis of Huckleberry Finn can fix its proportions of escape, abstract moralizing, basic human warmth, nostalgia, clowning, and social commentary. The debate over the course of the New South, however, was an important factor in the novel's genesis," and it "was revised and finished between 1880 and 1883, when Twain was an active and sometimes angry commentator on the southerner's way of life and his peculiar institutions." Abstract in AES, VIII (1965), 2995; reprinted in Twainian, XXV (March-April, 1966).

B11 _____. "Twain, Howells, and the Boston Nihilists," New England Quarterly, XXXII (September), 351-71.
While Howells was reading Tolstoy, MT was profoundly impressed by George Kennan's accounts of conditions in Siberia. Both were sympathetic toward the efforts of Sergei Kravchinski, who, as "Sergius Stepniak," organized the Society of American Friends of Russian Freedom, with headquarters in Boston; MT was one of the original members, and more of a firebrand than Howells. Later, when Gorky's mission to America was compromised by the disclosure that the woman with whom he was traveling was not his wife, Howells withdrew partly because his support had been

(BUDD, LOUIS J.)
lukewarm from the outset; "as for Twain, his retreat was more grudging and orderly than anyone has granted." Abstract in AES, III (1960), 94; reprinted in Twainian, XIX (January-February, 1960).

B12   CARDWELL, GUY A. "Mark Twain's Failures in Comedy and The Enemy Conquered," Georgia Review, XIII (Winter), 424-36.
Traces MT's reading of the thin, sentimental story published in 1845 by Samuel Watson Royston. MT's attack on it in "A Cure for the Blues" (1893) "betrays characteristic excess," but "it was his allegorizing habit to look through the immediate offence to the universal unreason behind it and in this instance he moved into the genre of satiric allegory, as Dryden did in Mac Flecknoe." MT failed to equal Dryden's achievement because of "technical inexpertness" and failure to limit his scope to the reasonable. His humor fails when his anger and pessimism exceed reasonable bounds, or conversely, when he lapses into sentimentalism, as in P&P; HF succeeds because it is controlled: "the edge of MT's satiric contempt for man's feeble mind and corrupt heart is softened by pity." Abstract in AES, III (1960), 1216; reprinted in Twainian, XIX (November-December, 1960). Article reprinted in Cardwell (1963), pp. 104-12.

B13   *CARTER, PAUL J., JR. "The Influence of the Nevada Frontier on Mark Twain," Western Humanities Review, XIII (Winter), 61-70.
[Source: Abstract in AES, II (1959), 991; reprinted in Twainian, XIX (January-February, 1960).]
Although Hannibal and Virginia City were not really frontier settlements, the frontier humor and burlesque tradition in journalism helped shape MT's writing--generally to its detriment, both in taste and form and, more seriously, in diverting MT's attention away from genuinely important topics.

B14   CLARK, HARRY HAYDEN. [Review: E. Hudson Long, Mark Twain Handbook (1958).] American Literature XXX (January), 543-44.
"On the whole...granting the lack of use of dissertations and the lack of full-length analysis of individual major books by Twain, and the omission of a few pertinent studies, this Handbook provides a wealth of information conveyed in a pleasing and even-tempered manner."

B15   CLEMENS, CYRIL. "Mark Twain's Mother," Hobbies--The Magazine for Collectors, LXIV (March), 107-109, 120-21.
A popular account, not documented but drawn in part from MT's published reminiscences; describes the misunderstanding that led MT's mother to marry John Marshall Clemens rather than young Dr. Barrett.

B16   COSBEY, ROBERT C. "Mark Twain's Joan of Arc--Not So Anonymous," Mark Twain Journal, XI (Summer), 10, 14, 16.
The scholarly tradition that MT successfully concealed his authorship when Joan of Arc appeared serially in Harper's is undercut by a teasing announcement in the March, 1895 issue that the next issue will begin the serial "by one of the most successful among America's writers of fiction," and by the recognizable style. The serialization ended in April, 1896, and in May MT's friend Joseph Twichell included it in a list of MT's works; the first edition in book form appeared the same month, with MT's name omitted from the title page but boldly stamped on the front cover and spine. Abstract in AES, III (1960), 353.

B17   COX, JAMES M. "Pudd'nhead Wilson: The End of Mark Twain's American Dream," South Atlantic Quarterly, LVIII (Summer), 351-63.
This is MT's "last American novel," foreshadowing "the corrosive disillusion so apparent in his late work"; it "precariously holds together...neither cynical nor sentimental." "Because miscegenation could culminate in the problem of mistaken identity, his arbitrary fictional device was justified and became the organic means of dramatizing the last phase of a society trapped by its secret history." Roxana, "one of Twain's greatest creations," has the strength, passion, and fertility lacking in the fragile white women.

B18   DA PONTE, DURANT. "Life Reviews Huckleberry Finn," American Literature, XXXI (March), 78-81.
The unsigned review, "Mark Twain's Blood-Curdling Humor," appeared in the old comic magazine, Life, V (February 26, 1885), 119; it was probably written by Robert Bridges, and one month later Life expressed satisfaction at the news that the Concord (Massachusetts) Library Committee had banned the book. The mention of "a polite version of the 'Gyascutus'" story indicates that an analogue of "The Royal Nonesuch" was familiar to Bridges and some of his readers. Abstract in AES, II (1959), 1376, reprinted in Twainian, XIX (January-February, 1960), 3. Life review reprinted in Anderson (1971), pp. 126-27.

B19   DARBEE, HENRY (ed.) "Mark Twain in Hartford: The Happy Years," American Heritage, XI (December), 65-80.
"This is the story of twenty happy and productive years in the life of Mark Twain, told by the author himself and by those who knew him. Portions of it were published earlier as a guide to the Mark Twain Memorial, the house now being restored in Hartford..." Contains photographs and extensive excerpts from various sources about MT in Hartford.

B20   [DAVIS, CHESTER L.] "General Grant and the National Publishing Company: Imitation of Mark Twain's 'Innocents Abroad,'" <u>Twainian</u>, XVIII (September-October), 1-4.

Passages from a travel book copyrighted by a subscription publishing company in 1879, credited to a General Grant (no first name given), "but in fact...mostly a series of letters by Mr. John Russell Young of the New York <u>Herald</u>. We also find many items of one Mr. Smalley of the New York <u>Tribune</u>." Abstract in <u>AES</u>, III (1960), 450.

B21   _____. "Jumping Frog and N.Y. <u>Saturday Press</u>; Boston and the N.Y. Bohemians; W. D. Howells and 'Literary Friends,'" <u>Twainian</u>, XVIII (March-April), 1-4.

On the New York <u>Saturday Press</u>, which first published MT's "Jumping Frog" about November 18, 1865; the greater part of this issue is devoted to quotation from William Dean Howells's <u>Literary Friends and Acquaintance</u> [sic], partly on a visit to the <u>Saturday Press</u> but chiefly on topics with no relation to MT. Abstract in <u>AES</u>, III (1960), 446.

B22   _____. "Mark Twain's Copy 'Life of Pasteur'; Background on 'What Is Man?' and 'The Adventures of a Microbe - - - By a Microbe'; Mark's Writing, Machinery Hiding Secret," <u>Twainian</u>, XVIII (November-December), 1-4.

On MT's personal copy of R. Vallery-Radot's 2-volume work, with marginal comments; Davis apparently means that this could have influenced the works named, and he quotes a marginal note in which MT comments on his view of authorship while praising Vallery-Radot: "A past-master of the pathetic, this author; he keeps one's tears near the surface all the time, yet hides his machinery so well that he never seems to be trying to do it."

B23   _____. "Mark Twain's Personal Marked Copy of John Bunyan's 'Pilgrim's Progress'; Value of First Editions," <u>Twainian</u>, XVIII (May-June), 1-4.

Contains MT letter of April 20, 1869 reprinted from Paine's 1912 biography, and criticizes Paine for saying in the 1917 edition of the <u>Letters</u> after a letter of February 27, 1869 that "No further letters have been preserved until June." Davis is chiefly concerned with description of MT's copy of a facsimile edition, and quotation from it, with almost nothing on MT. Abstract in <u>AES</u>, III (1960), 447.

B24   _____. "Mark Twain's 'Things Not Generally Known' as Background for His Writings," <u>Twainian</u>, XVIII (July-August), 1-4.

Quotes long passages and some of MT's marginal annotations from the book of scientific miscellany edited by John Timbs (London: Lockwood & Co., 1867), suggesting that it may have helped form his ideas. Abstract in <u>AES</u>, III (1960), 448.

B25   DONNER, STANLEY T. [Review: Philip S. Foner, <u>Mark Twain: Social Critic</u>.] <u>Quarterly Journal of Speech</u>, XLV (February), 95.

A brief review, calling the opening portrait "one of the best short biographies of Mark Twain ever written." The book shows "comprehensive scholarship" and insight; it is "easily readable...a useful as well as delightful volume."

B26   DREISER, THEODORE. <u>Letters of Theodore Dreiser: A Selection</u>. Ed. with Preface and Notes by Robert H. Elias. Philadelphia: University of Pennsylvania Press. 3 vols. Passim.

TS and HF were among the few American books Dreiser cared for (I: 121). Both appealed to him "immensely, especially <u>Huckleberry Finn</u>. I never believed of Twain, however, that he gave forth in philosophic form his inmost convictions. His country overawed him I think" (June 17, 1918, to Frank Harris; I: 253). There is also a letter to Mencken (December 2, 1920) in which Dreiser says he was introduced to MT by Henry M. Alden some time in 1905-1907. Later, he encountered MT in the back of a saloon, "lit up--and alone." In the conversation that ensued he said that he was unhappy in his marriage, as most men are, but had to keep up appearances (pp. 305-306).. See 1935.B33.

B27   EATON, VINCENT L. "Mark Twain, Washington Correspondent," <u>Manuscripts</u>, XI (Fall), 16-26.

On MT's stay in Washington, November, 1867-March, 1868, with a lengthy passage quoted from the <u>Reminiscences</u> of Senator William M. Stewart on MT as the despair of his landlady. Describes MT's somewhat informal correspondence for several newspapers.

B28   FATOUT, PAUL. "Mark Twain: Litigant," <u>American Literature</u>, XXXI (March), 30-45.

On the lawsuit brought against MT and others by Edward House, who claimed an agreement gave him rights to produce a dramatization of <u>The Prince and the Pauper</u>; the resulting legal maneuverings reflect little credit on either party. Liberally documented with citations from New York newspapers of 1890. Abstract in <u>AES</u>, II (1959), 1371; reprinted in <u>Twainian</u>, XIX (January-February, 1960), 3. The article is reprinted as "Daniel Frohman Production of 'Prince and the Pauper'" in <u>Twainian</u>, XXII (September-October, 1963), 1-4; (November-December), 3-4, without footnotes.

B29   FERGUSON, DELANCEY. "Some Nuggets from Tailings Left Behind," <u>New York Times Book Review</u> (February 8), p. 5.

A review of Charles Neider, ed., The <u>Autobiography of Mark Twain</u>. The scholar would appreciate an appendix listing sources, and "even for the general reader Mr. Neider has not always met his full editorial responsibilities," as in his acceptance of texts bowdlerized by Albert Bigelow Paine rather

(FERGUSON, DELANCEY)
than the versions in the North American Review, "chosen, proofread, and passed for press by Mark Twain himself." Moreover, Neider ought to have annotated MT's inaccurate and sometimes unjust statements, such as his accusations against Charles L. Webster.

B30 FIEDLER, LESLIE A. "Love Letter from the Grave," New Republic, CXL (May 18), 18-19.
A review of Charles Neider, ed., The Autobiography of Mark Twain. MT's clowning was part of a concealment of his inner beliefs, and "it is his hopeless submission... his conviction (half-wish, perhaps) that all men submit as he which make the Autobiography one of the saddest books ever written, a book terrible in a way possible only in America." Death is a recurring theme, and after the death of Jean "Twain's lover-letter is finally readdressed, directed no longer to his dead, but to Death itself."

B31 FRIEDRICH, OTTO. "Mark Twain and the Nature of Humor," Discourse: A Review of the Liberal Arts, II (April), 67-86.
Preceded by "Editor's Note: This article is based on a longer essay concerning Mark Twain, and his concept and use of humor. Mr. Friedrich's study of Twain is part of a projected book, The Dark Tradition, an analysis and re-evaluation of American literature from Jonathan Edwards to William Faulkner, based on the particular writer's recognition of evil in the universe and his efforts to come to grips with it. Mark Twain, who seems to see this evil as a kind of absurdity, chooses humor as his weapon and defense against fears of the utter void." Abstract in AES, II (1959), 679; reprinted in Twainian, XIX (January-February, 1960).

B32 GORDAN, JOHN D. "New in the Berg Collection: 1957-1958," Bulletin of the New York Public Library, LXIII (April), 205-15.
On p. 214, describes copies of The Gilded Age, Tom Sawyer, 1601 (West Point Edition), and a copy of Sir Granville George Greenwood's Shakespeare Problem Restated (London and New York: John Lane, 1908), with heavy annotations by MT. Abstract in AES, II (1959), 1608; reprinted in Twainian, XIX (January-February, 1960).

B33 GROSS, SEYMOUR L. "Mark Twain and Catholicism," Critic (Chicago), XVII (April-May), 9, 12, 88-91.
Although MT included the Catholic Church in his attack on formal religion, criticizing what he viewed as superstition and oppression, he was not a bigot and he did not ridicule the sacraments; he praised Catholic acts of courage and self-sacrifice. Abstract in AES, II (1959), 1408.

B34 _____. "Mark Twain on the Serenity of Unbelief: An Unpublished Letter to Charles Warren Stoddard," Huntington Library Quarterly, XXII (May), 260-62.
A warm, gentle letter ("Hartford June 1/85," here reproduced) which MT wrote after reading A Broken Heart (1885), a spiritual autobiography in which Stoddard describes his conversion to Roman Catholicism; MT says he went through similar soul-searchings before settling down to his own disbelief: "Both of us are certain now; & in certainty there is rest. Let us be content. May your belief & my unbelief never more be shaken in this life!" Abstract in AES, VI (1963), 1653; reprinted in Twainian, XXIII (January-February, 1964).

B35 *HALL, ROBERT A. "Cultural Symbolism in Mark Twain's Connecticut Yankee," Annali dell' Istituto Orientale di Napoli, Sezione Germanica, II, 127-40.
[Source: Leary (1970), p. 64.]

B36 HERZL, THEODOR. "Mark Twain and the British Ladies: A Feuilleton," trans. by Alfred Werner, Commentary, XXVIII (September), 243-45.
From the second volume of Herzl's Feuilletons (Berlin, 1903), an account written in 1894 of a reading by MT before an audience of English schoolgirls at the British Embassy in Paris; his appearance and reading style are described. Abstract in AES, II (1959), 1618; reprinted in Twainian, XIX (January-February, 1960). See 1951.B41.

B37 HICKS, GRANVILLE. "Mark Twain's Self-Portrait," Saturday Review, XLII (February 7), 16.
A review of Charles Neider's version of The Autobiography of Mark Twain, which has the advantage over Paine's version in that "it consistently holds the attention," and over DeVoto's in that "it tells the story of Twain's life." Chiefly descriptive, contending that "the best of the book is to be found at the beginning and in the end." Abstract in AES, II (1959), 802; reprinted in Twainian, XIX (January-February, 1960).

B38 HUDSON, RUTH. "A Literary 'Area of Freedom' Between Irving and Twain," Western Humanities Review, XIII (Winter), 47-60.
[Source: Abstract in AES, II (1959), 990; reprinted in Twainian, XIX (January-February, 1960).] Apparently places emphasis on twenty-five minor writers on the West between 1834 and 1862; they worked in a genre which began with Washington Irving's Tour on the Prairies and ended in the burlesque exemplified by RI.

B39 JOHNSON, JAMES WILLIAM. "The Adolescent Hero: A Trend in Modern Fiction," Twentieth Century Literature, V (April), 3-11.

(JOHNSON, JAMES WILLIAM)
Compares Huckleberry Finn and Catcher in the Rye (p. 5) as illustrating "the difference between the nineteenth- and twentieth-century use of the adolescent," in that Huckleberry Finn is external in its emphasis: Huck looks at the world and it is Huck's world that Twain is concerned with." Moreover, Huck's choices are determined by his character, which shows compassion, candor, honesty, and humor from the first: "His is an adult intelligence masquerading as an adolescent."

B40   KENNY, HERBERT A. [Review: Charles Neider, The Autobiography of Mark Twain.] Critic (Chicago), XVII (April-May, 12, 68.
Neither Paine nor DeVoto "set the material in chronological order which Neider has done here and which should have been done in the first place. The book is in general first-rate Twain and consequently first-rate reading."

B41   KLINGELHOFER, HERBERT E. "Mark Twain, Edited and Bowdlerized," Manuscripts, XI (Fall), 2-12.
On the correspondence between MT and T. Douglas Murray over "Saint Joan of Arc," which MT wrote by Murray's request as an introduction to a book on her, then withdrew when Murray tampered with the text (MT did change one minor word, on Murray's suggestion).

B42   *KLOTZ, GÜNTHER. [Review: Karl-Heinz Schönfelder, intro., bibliography, and notes, Life on the Mississippi (1956).] Zeitschrift für Anglistik und Amerikanistik, V, 222-24.
[Source: MHRA Annual Bibliography (1959), No. 4578.]

B43   KLOTZ, MARVIN. "Mark Twain and Socratic Dialogue," Mark Twain Journal, XI (Summer), 1-3.
"An April 10, 1951 auction sale checklist of books from Mark Twain's library lists 'Dialogues of Plato, by B. Jowett, 4 vols'"; although a lack of marginalia makes it uncertain whether MT read them, the device of Socratic dialogue appears in his works, particularly in Huckleberry Finn, Joan of Arc, and What Is Man? Abstract in AES, III (1960), 349.

B44   KNOX, GEORGE. "The Mysterious Stranger: Mark Twain's Last Laugh?" Mark Twain Journal, XI (Summer), 11-12.
The story may be "a kind of intellectual practical joke," in which "the humor is double-edged...because Twain is not only castigating the reader who swallows the 'philosophy' of the story but is lashing himself for being intellectually committed against his emotional sympathies." Abstract in AES, III (1960), 354.

B45   KOMROFF, MANUEL. "How I Shook Hands with Mark Twain," Mark Twain Journal, XI (Summer), 4-5.
As a boy, Komroff had a minor part in an amateur performance of the P&P play; afterward, MT autographed his program and shook his hand. Abstract in AES, II (1960), 350.

B46   KRAUSE, SYDNEY J. "Twain's Method and Theory of Composition," Modern Philology, LVI (February), 167-77.
"Although Twain minimized conscious craftsmanship in theory, he was in practice a most avid reviser." "He discovered his subject not before, but as he wrote." Abstract in AES, II (1959), 736; reprinted in Twainian, XIX (January-February, 1960).

B47   KRUMPELMANN, JOHN T. "Schiller's Rehabilitation of Jeanne d'Arc," American-German Review, XXVI (December, 1959-January, 1960), 8-9, 38.
Devotes some space to the impression Joan of Arc made on MT and the possibility that Schiller's Jungfrau von Orleans may have influenced his book on her. Abstract in AES, III (1960), 2560.

B48   LA COUR, TAGE (trans. by Poul Ib Liebe). "The Scandinavian Crime-Detective Story," American Book Collector, IX (May), 22-23.
Tom Sawyer, Detective shows points of similarity in plot to Praesten i Vejlby (The Vicar of Vejlby, 1829) by the Danish novelist, Steen Steensen Blicher, but in a letter to a Danish reviewer who noted the resemblance, MT's secretary, I. V. Lyon, denied that MT had read the earlier work. Abstract in AES, II (1959), 1365; reprinted in Twainian, XIX (January-February, 1960).

B49   LYNN, KENNETH S. "The Actor Who Made Mark Twain Live Again on the Stage and in Our Minds," New York Herald Tribune Book Review, XXXVI (December 20), p. 5.
A review of Hal Holbrook's book, Mark Twain Tonight! "The reason his pastiche of Twain's work is so effective--both on the stage and within hard covers--is that he knows Marks Twain's books backwards and forwards...he is familiar with the whole range of critical and biographical works about Twain, which is considerable."

B50   _____. "Mark Twain Miscellany," New York Herald Tribune Book Review, XXXVI (September 27), 13. A review of Minnie M. Brashear and Robert M. Rodney, eds., The Art, Humor and Humanity of Mark Twain.
Miss Brashear's Mark Twain, Son of Missouri (1934) was "a reliable study," but the reliability of the present work is closer to that of Charles Neider: names and dates are rendered inaccurately, and the editors mistake MT's fiction for autobiography. They have rendered a service in making some of MT's neglected short pieces more widely available, but when they condensed CY and MS "the decision...was a miserable one."

B51 McKEITHAN, DANIEL MORLEY. "Madame Laszowska Meets Mark Twain," Texas Studies in Literature and Language, I (Spring), 62-65.

The text of three letters from Jean Emily (Gerard) de Laszowska and one from MT (October-November, 1897) to William Blackwood, whose note of introduction made possible a meeting in Vienna. She was impressed by MT as "at first an excessively serious almost solemn person," by Olivia Clemens as "also very intelligent and charming in manner but looks delicate," and by the two daughters as "pretty--the eldest one [Clara] remarkably so in a dark Creole style"; the family were still in mourning for Susan Clemens. Abstract in AES, II (1959), 1952; reprinted in Twainian, XIX (January-February, 1960).

B52 McINTOSH, BERYL HOBSON. "A Seamstress Remembers Mark Twain," Mark Twain Journal, XI (Summer), 7, 16.

Recollections by Annie Courtney, who worked in the MT house in Hartford when she was eighteen. Abstract in AES, III (1960), 351.

B53 MARKS, BARRY A. "Mark Twain's Hymn of Praise, English Journal, XLVIII (November), 443-48.

On meaning and structure in TS, in which the action is "a series of withdrawals and returns," by which Tom matures from sentimental individualism (self-love) to the joy of other-love. The first half of the book satirizes "both the romanticism of childhood and the conventionality of adulthood," followed by a growth in "the town's ability to experience joy and love simultaneously." Abstract in AES, III (1960), 758; reprinted in Twainian, XIX (November-December, 1960).

B54 MARX, LEO. "Two Kingdoms of Force," Massachusetts Review, I (October), 62-95.

On HF and the destruction of the raft, pp. 69-71. "Clemens provides his hero with an Arcadian landscape, a profound sense of unity with nature, and then he causes the sudden, menacing intrusion of the machine." [Revised, this essay became a part of Marx's The Machine in the Garden (1964).]

B55 MENDELSON, M. "'Novaya Dynastiya' Marka Tvena [Mark Twain's 'New Dynasty']," Voprosy Literatury, No. 7 (July), pp. 156-67.

MT's support for the American working class is revealed in his 1886 address by this title. Abstract in AES, III (1960), 2548; reprinted in Twainian, XIX (November-December, 1960).

B56 *MITCHELL, JOHN. [Review: A Connecticut Yankee in King Arthur's Court. Leipzig: Paul List Verlag, 1956--an East German edition.] Zeitschrift für Anglistik und Amerikanistik, VI, 203-207.

[Source: MHRA Annual Bibliography (1959), No. 4577.]

B57 MOORE, LOUISE PAINE. "Mark Twain as I Knew Him," Twainian, XVIII (January-February), 3-4.

Reminiscences by the daughter of Albert Bigelow Paine, one of the young girls MT called his "Angel-Fish"; includes an MT letter on the death of his cat Tammany, naming her survivors: "two children by her first marriage--Billiards and Babylon; and three grandchildren by her second--Amanda, Annanci and Sindbad." Abstract in AES, III (1960), 445.

B58 MOSES, W. R. "The Pattern of Evil in Adventures of Huckleberry Finn," Georgia Review, XIII (Summer), 161-66.

There is a progression of types of evil, similar to that of Dante's Inferno, from Pap's incontinence to the violence of the feuding Shepherdsons, and finally to the fraud of the King and Duke. A comic ending is needed because MT could not leave Huck in Hell or raise him to a Purgatory (unless one chooses so to interpret Aunt Sally's threat to adopt and civilize him). Abstract in AES, II (1959), 1644; reprinted in Twainian, XIX (January-February, 1960). Article reprinted in Bradley (1962), pp. 387-92.

B59 MUELLER, HAROLD L. "Redding [sic] Connecticut [sic] Mark Twain Library Observes 50th Birthday," Twainian, XVIII (January-February), 1-3.

Reprinted from Redding Times, December 4, 1958 (1958.B55). Abstract in AES, III (1960), 444.

B60 NEWARK, F. H. [Review: Daniel Morley McKeithan, Court Trials in Mark Twain, and Other Essays.] Modern Language Review, LIV (July), 423-4.

"This collection of essays, which have previously appeared in periodicals, is not, it must be confessed, very weighty. The pattern of each essay is the same--a long résumé of the plot with extracts from the work to illustrate the more exciting parts, and in conclusion a brief--very brief--attempt at a critical appreciation." However, McKeithan has made a solid contribution in showing the probable influence of Jules Verne's Five Weeks in a Balloon on Tom Sawyer Abroad.

B61 ORNSTEIN, ROBERT. "The Ending of Huckleberry Finn," Modern Language Notes, LXXIV (December), 698-702.

Miss Watson's freeing of Jim in her will is not a sacrifice, but "perhaps the crowning act of selfishness and pious greed: the desire to make the best of all possible worlds." Tom's childish intervention can be explained in personal terms: he could free a slave, as MT could attack slavery, when it had become safe to do so. Abstract in AES, V (1962), 2627.

B62   PODHORETZ, NORMAN. "The Literary Adventures of Huck Finn," New York Times Book Review (December 6), pp. 5, 34.
        Seventy-five years after the publication of HF, surveys its reputation among critics and argues that MT "was asserting through the image of life on the raft that the State of Nature is a reality, and he was asserting through the character of Huck that the distinction between the individual and society is a true distinction and a necessary one." Abstract in AES, III (1960), No. 585; reprinted in Twainian, XIX (November-December, 1960).

B63   REXROTH, KENNETH. "Humor in a Tough Age," Nation (New York), CLXXXVIII (March 7), 211-13. A review of Charles Neider, ed., The Autobiography of Mark Twain.
        "Mark Twain was just a very wise nineteenth-century man," and "an eminently normal man." The Neider edition of MT's autobiography is more coherent than those edited by Paine and DeVoto, but omits important political and social criticism that DeVoto included. [Reprinted in Rexroth's Assays (New York: New Directions, 1962), pp. 95-98.]

B64   *SARUKHANYAN, A. "Mark Twain in the Soviet Union," Redding (Connecticut) Times, June 18. Source: Reprinted, Twainian, XVIII (July-August), 4; (September-October), 4.
        On MT's great popularity in the Soviet Union. Lists some Russian editions of his works and notes his personal acquaintance with I. S. Turgenev, S. M. Stepnyak-Kravchinsky, and Maxim Gorky; quotes Gorky's description of MT and mention of his visit to Russia in 1867 on the Quaker City, "and the name of Samuel Langhorne Clemens in the list of passengers of that American ship was published in the 'Odessky Vestnik.'" Notes considerable publication of MT's works and notes about him, and quotes an obituary of him by A. I. Kuprin. More recently, "A Mark Twain Memorial Meeting was held at Moscow's Central Writers' Club, on April 26, 1950. A report on the work of Mark Twain was delivered by the Soviet writer Valentin Katayev. It is noteworthy that the materials published for the 120th anniversary of Mark Twain's birth [sic] marked by a special literary evening included [a] bibliographical reference book covering the Russian translations of his productions." The article is introduced by two letters to the editor of the Redding Times by A. Kuznetsov, Vice Chairman of the Committee for Cultural Relations with Foreign Countries. Abstract in AES, III (1960), 449, 451.

B65   *SCHÖNFELDER, KARL-HEINZ. [Review: Charles Neider, ed., The Complete Short Stories of Mark Twain (1957).] Zeitschrift für Anglistik und Amerikanistik, VI, 98-100.
        [Source: MHRA Annual Bibliography (1959), No. 4570.]

B66   SCOTT, WINFIELD TOWNLEY. "A New Editor Brings Order to Mark Twain's Chaotic 'Autobiography,'" New York Herald Tribune Book Review, XXXV (February 8), 3.
        A review of Charles Neider, ed., The Autobiography of Mark Twain. "The best ordered ...far and away the most important and most satisfactory text of the 'Autobiography' we have; and yet there are reasons for believing that it is not--it cannot be--the final text." Neider has made "a valiant, mostly intelligent, largely successful attempt to shape this material to the greatness which is in it."

B67   SPACKS, BARRY B. "The Thematic Function of the 'Rescue' in Huckleberry Finn," Mark Twain Journal, XI (Summer), 8-9.
        Unlike Odysseus, Huck is alienated, fleeing from home. The ending represents a seduction back to "Tom's frame of reference, into the culture of Miss Watson and Aunt Sally," but despite the fraud "Huck emerges from it still resisting the false gods of sentiment and complacency." Abstract in AES, III (1960), 352.

B68   STONE, ALBERT E., JR. "Mark Twain's Joan of Arc: The Child as Goddess," American Literature, XXXI (March), 1-20.
        "At a particular moment in his life Twain found that the Maid of Orleans gave him a means of dramatizing his own, and his age's, spiritual dilemma without the embarrassing obligation to solve the dilemma.... To the aging man who was both a realist and romantic in his writing, a determinist and a moralist in his thinking, an agnostic and yet a deist in his worship, Joan of Arc provided a temporary haven....in the timeless past of childhood" (pp. 19-30). Abstract in AES, II (1959), 1369; reprinted in Twainian, XIX (January-February, 1960), 3. The article later became a part of his The Innocent Eye: Childhood in Mark Twain's Imagination (1961).

B69   STRONG, LEAH A. [Review: Philip S. Foner, Mark Twain: Social Critic.] Books Abroad, XXXIII (Spring), 217.
        Brief, says the third and longest section "is a real contribution to the ever-growing body of Twainiana."

B70   ____. [Review: Daniel Morley McKeithan, Court Trials in Mark Twain, and Other Essays.] Books Abroad, XXXIII (Autumn), 467.
        "A gallimaufry of plot summary and sketchy discussion."

B71   *VITZ, CARL. "J. B. Pond and Two Servants," Historical and Philosophical Society of Ohio Bulletin, XVII (October), 277-84.
        During their 1884-1885 reading tour, MT and G. W. Cable concealed their names when they registered at the St. Nicholas Hotel, Cincinnatti, January 2, 1885. [Source: Abstract in AES, XI (1968), 3214; reprinted in Twainian, XXVIII (January-February, 1969).]

B72   WALDHORN, ARTHUR. "Twain: The Adventures of Huckleberry Finn," in J. Sherwood Weber, Jules Alan Wein, Arthur Waldhorn, and Arthur Zeiger, eds., From Homer to Joyce: A Study Guide to Thirty-Six Great Books (New York: Holt, Rinehart and Winston, Inc.), pp. 244-52.
       Includes a survey of the book's critical reputation, "Questions for Study and Discussion," and a short annotated bibliography of critical discussions of MT.

B73   WALSH, WILLIAM. The Use of Imagination: Educational Thought and the Literary Mind. London: Chatto & Windus. "Huck in Huckleberry Finn" (pp. 139-48) in "The Writer and the Child: Mark Twain, Henry James, D. H. Lawrence and Walter de la Mare" (pp. 137-182); also, passim on MT.
       Huck is a voice of sanity and integrity, in contrast to Tom Sawyer and to the people he meets along the river; the river "represents life unconstrained by artifice, and value uncomplicated by pretence" (p. 145).

B74   WEBER, CARL J. The Rise and Fall of James Ripley Osgood: A Biography. Waterville, Maine: Colby College Press.
       Passim on MT's business relations with Osgood, the publisher (indexed); there is an extensive list of acknowledgements but scanty documentation.

B75   *WIRZBERGER, KARL-HEINZ. [Review: Henry Nash Smith and Frederick Anderson, eds., Mark Twain of the "Enterprise" (1957).] Zietschrift für Anglistik und Amerikanistik, VI, 317-18.
       [Source: MHRA Annual Bibliography (1959), No. 8224.]

1960 A BOOKS

A1   BLAIR, WALTER. Mark Twain & Huck Finn. Berkeley and Los Angeles: University of California Press.
       Blair calls this his "attempt to define the forces which gave Adventures of Huckleberry Finn its substance and its form." While considering the importance of MT's boyhood and piloting on the river, he feels that the way they were transmuted into fiction is more important; "therefore I discuss in greater detail the forces shaping such modifications--the man's life, his reading, his thinking, and his writing between 1874 and 1884" (p. vii). This definitive study concludes with a discussion of HF's popularity abroad in translation, and there is an appendix titled "First New York Edition, First Issue," discussing the bibliographical points and the damaged plate on p. 283 (pp. 385-87). Chapter V ("Tom and Huck"), pp. 71-76 is reprinted in Bradley (1962), pp. 392-96; pp. 131, 134-44 are reprinted in Simpson (1968), pp. 61-70; the

portion dealing with TS in Smith (1963), pp. 64-82; "Raft and Shore: Wish and Belief," pp. 334-46 in Gerber (1971), pp. 90-101.

A2   DOUBLEDAY, NEAL FRANK, ed. Mark Twain's Picture of His America: Selected Source Materials for College Research Papers. Boston: D. C. Heath and Company.
       Selections from MT's works, with brief introductions, and with an eight-page introduction of suggestions on writing research papers.

A3   FATOUT, PAUL. Mark Twain on the Lecture Circuit. Bloomington: Indiana University Press (as reprinted, Gloucester, Massachusetts: Peter Smith, 1966).
       "This book attempts to view, chiefly, his platform performances and to glance, though less intensely, at his dinner speaking." Traces his life-long career as speaker, arguing that his oral gifts rivaled his talents as a writer. Cites numerous contemporary newspaper reviews.

A4   *GIBSON, WILLIAM M., ed. A Connecticut Yankee in King Arthur's Court. New York: Harper.
       [Source: MHRA Annual Bibliography (1960), No. 4794.]

A5   HARNSBERGER, CAROLINE THOMAS. Mark Twain: Family Man. New York: The Citadel Press.
       An enthusiast's account of MT's family life, enlivened by profuse quotation; the quotation includes "20,000 words heretofore unpublished," according to the front flap of the dust jacket. The author joined the Mark Twain Association while working on her "Twain reference book, Mark Twain at Your Fingertips," and through this connection met Clara Clemens, whom she visited in her Hollywood home and came to know as a friend (pp. 9-10). There is much charm in the book, but the scholar may want to confirm statements of fact from other evidence.

A6   LEARY, LEWIS. Mark Twain. Minneapolis: University of Minnesota Press (University of Minnesota Pamphlets on American Writers, No. 5); also London: Oxford University Press. Reprinted in Richard Foster, ed., Six American Novelists of the Nineteenth Century: An Introduction, Minneapolis: University of Minnesota Press, 1968, pp. 118-54. Condensed as "Mark Twain and the Comic Spirit" in Leary's Southern Excursions: Essays on Mark Twain and Others (1971), pp. 3-41.
       In a general study of his life and works Leary notes the importance of recognizing "Mark Twain" as a mask for Clemens. He was not a buffoon, but "a comic realist," in the end pessimistic because he was tired.

A7 *LONG, E. HUDSON, ed. A Connecticut Yankee in King Arthur's Court. New York: Dodd, Mead.
  [Source: Beebe and Feaster (1968), p. 124.]

A8 MELTZER, MILTON. Mark Twain Himself: A Pictorial Biography. New York: Thomas Y. Crowell.
  Over 600 contemporary photographs and drawings of MT and his surroundings, intelligently chosen and with a judicious text. More than a coffee-table ornament, this is of real interest to the student of MT; a Bonanza Books reprinting is frequently offered for sale at approximately six dollars by such remainder dealers as Marboro Books and Publishers Clearing House.

A9 *MINTON, HAROLD, ed. The Adventures of Huckleberry Finn. New York: Washington Square Press.
  [Source: Beebe and Feaster (1968), p. 113.]

A10 NEIDER, CHARLES Mark Twain and the Russians: An Exchange of Views. New York: Hill and Wang; London: Paterson.
  "This exchange of letters between the distinguished American critic Charles Neider and Y. Bereznitsky, editor of the official Soviet publication Literary Gazette, constitutes a fascinating official discussion of Mark Twain" (p. 3). It consists of a charge in Literaturnaya Gazeta that Neider's edition of The Autobiography of Mark Twain (1959) represents an official censorship of MT's social criticism, Neider's somewhat intemperate response, a reply to Neider in Literaturnaya Gazeta, and a last word by Neider which the Russian journal declined to publish. [29-page pamphlet.]

A11 PETERSON, SVEND (comp.). Mark Twain and the Government. Caldwell, Idaho: Caxton Printers, Ltd.
  An anthology of remarks by MT on topics ranging from "Americanism" (p. 13) to "World Power, America as a" (p. 138). Cross-referenced. Contains no significant commentary or new information.

A12 ROGERS, FRANKLIN R. Mark Twain's Burlesque Patterns as Seen in the Novels and Narratives 1855-1885. Dallas: Southern Methodist University Press.
  "The focus of the study is Twain's structural patterns derived from burlesque"; as a general principle, the term is restricted in this study to "literary burlesque, a humorous imitation and exaggeration of the conventions in plot, characterization, and style peculiar to a literary type, the works of a certain author, or a particular book, short story, play, or poem" (p. v).

A13 SMITH, HENRY NASH, and WILLIAM M. GIBSON, eds., Mark Twain-Howells Letters: The Correspondence of Samuel L. Clemens and William D. Howells, 1872-1910. Cambridge, Massachusetts: The Belknap Press of Harvard University Press. 2 Vols.
  The correspondence, meticulously edited and annotated, casting significant light on the personal and professional friendship of the two. [The dust jacket gives the years of correspondence as 1869-1910, but the first letter is dated January 7, 1872.]

A14 *STEGNER, WALLACE, ed. The Adventures of Huckleberry Finn. New York: Dell.
  [Source: MHRA Bibliography (1960), No. 4832.]

A15 TURNER, ARLIN, ed. Mark Twain and George W. Cable: The Record of a Literary Friendship. [East Lansing]: Michigan State University Press.
  Consists chiefly of letters by Cable and some by MT during their lecture tour of 1884-1885, excluding materials already in print. Reprints texts of Cable's column on MT and Josh Billings in the New Orleans Picayune (1870.B5) and a sketch of MT in The Letter of February 1, 1896, and Cable's speeches honoring MT at the Seventieth Birthday Dinner and the memorial service in New York on November 30, 1910.

1960 B SHORTER WRITINGS

B1 ADAMS, J. DONALD. "Speaking of Books," New York Times Book Review (May 29), p. 2.
  Describes the controversy between Charles Neider and Y. Bereznitsky of the Literary Gazette [Printed in Neider's pamphlet, 1960.A10] as "a tempest in a teapot": although the Russians now portray MT as a critic of America, he was popular with them before the Revolution. "Russian humor is not far removed from our own, and Russians could also understand a boyhood like Mark Twain's"; but they err in regarding him as a thinker.

B2 American Book Collector, X (June). Special Mark Twain Number.
  Also available as Twainian, stamped: "THIS SPECIAL ISSUE OF THE AMERICAN BOOK COLLECTOR HAS BEEN PROCURED BY US, IS AVAILABLE ONLY TO MEMBERS WHO HAVE PAID MEMBERSHIP DUES, AND CONSTITUTES THE ISSUE OF 'THE TWAINIAN' FOR JULY-AUGUST, 1960, NINETEENTH YEAR, NO. 4. THE MARK TWAIN RESEARCH FOUNDATION. PERRY, MO."

B3 ANON. "The Artist's Mind in Action," Times Literary Supplement, October 28, p. 686.
  A review of Charles Neider, ed., The Autobiography of Mark Twain (1959), criticizing the imposition of chronological order on the material. "Furthermore, in his pursuit of order Mr. Neider has not hesitated to alter the text in ways which will not commend his work to readers who respect an author's

(ANON.)

right to speak in his own voice. He has inserted his own sentences or has transferred
words from other Twain writings to fill in
the cracks in his structure; he has omitted
passages without indicating where he has
done so; he has dropped the titles and dates
of composition which Twain attached to his
sections; and he has improved Twain's punctuation."

B4   ANON. "Innocence and Experience," Times Literary Supplement, August 12, p. 512.
A review-article on Henry Nash Smith and
William M. Gibson, eds., Mark Twain-Howells
Letters (praising the editing); Walter
Blair, Mark Twain and Huck Finn (HF is "an
open book...much of Professor Blair's devoted scholarship is simply supererogatory");
and Kenneth S. Lynn, Mark Twain and Southwestern Humor (the part on MT is "instructive and compelling reading," but the section on minor humorous writers "is virtually a separate book, and a far less interesting one"). There is also a general discussion of MT, who "is not taken seriously
enough outside the academies," but within
them "is perhaps taken a bit too seriously."
On HF, suggests that Huck's journey is "a
process of self-discovery through experience...the Huck who emerges at the end
realizes that he cannot return to the Tom
Sawyer world of innocence and romantic
games." Cf. reply by Donald MacRae
(1960.B76).

B5   ANON. "Magazine Articles about Mark Twain
During Past Year," Twainian, XIX (January-
February), 1-4; continued as "Articles Published Elsewhere during Past Year about
Mark Twain" (November-December), 1-3.
Abstracts of material on MT from Abstracts
of English Studies, II (1959), III (1960).
This reprinting is continued as an annual
feature of the Twainian hereafter, and may
be used with much confidence since individual abstracts are reprinted with very few
errors and in full (including the original
AES numbering). Unfortunately, some of the
reprinted abstracts are of peripheral interest, with only passing reference to MT,
and not all AES abstracts are reprinted;
for example, abstracts of Twainian articles
are not always reprinted, and Mark Twain
Journal material is always excluded. The
present bibliography notes these and other
abstracts in the annotation of entries describing books and articles on MT.

B6   ANON. "Mark Twain," Look (May 10), pp. 40-51.
A popular, general account, illustrated.
"The pictures and Twain's words are taken
from Mark Twain Himself, by Milton Meltzer,
to be published in October by Thomas Y.
Crowell Company." Notes an NBC television
production of RI, starring Hal Holbrook,
scheduled for May 13.

B7   ANON. "Mark Twain Birthplace Shrine Dedication," Twainian, XIX (May-June), 1-4.
Consists of the news story reprinted from
the Perry (Missouri) Enterprise of June 9,
1960, with added photographs; the dedication
took place June 5, with a crowd of 7,000
persons. Abstract in AES, IV (1961), 676.

B8   ANON. "A Soviet View of Six Great Americans,"
American Heritage, XI (October), 64-74.
The article, "Twain, Mark," is "translated
in full from the current Large Soviet Encyclopedia" and followed by a discussion by
Henry Nash Smith, who describes the article
as determinedly fitting all "the facts of
history into a neat pattern.... of the class
struggle." MT's work in some ways invites
such interpretation because "he often invites the reader to adopt the viewpoint of a
low or humble character who is at odds with
the mores and conventions of society," but
the encyclopedia article "overinterprets
this recurrent theme" and ignores contrary
evidence.

B9   ANON. [Review: Henry Nash Smith and William
M. Gibson, eds., Mark Twain-Howells Letters.]
New Mexico Quarterly, XXX (Winter), 422.
Brief and descriptive.

B10   BAENDER, PAUL. [Review: Kenneth S. Lynn,
Mark Twain and Southwestern Humor.] Modern
Philology, LVII (May), 285-86.
Lynn fails to prove his "neat" but "too
categorical" thesis that the humorists wrote
in a declining Whig tradition, from which MT
departed by turning the Clown into a vernacular spokesman, without adopting his coarseness. "Lynn's indifference to probabilities
is especially evident from his analyses of
texts, which are usually sophistical except
when he paraphrases the work of other men....
The chapters on Clemens are the most defective," either oversimplified, glib, or unoriginal. The book may be well received by
newspapers and may awaken student interest
in its field, but it "has little other than
cautionary value for the professional scholar and critic."

B11   *BAY, ANDRÉ. "Voici Mark Twain, Père de la
Littérature Américaine," Figaro Littéraire,
No. 731 (April 23), p. 4.
[Source: Leary (1970), p. 58.]

B12   BEHRMAN, S. N. Conversations with Max. London:
Hamish Hamilton, pp. 19-20.
On Bernard Shaw's rudeness: he had invited Sir J. M. Barrie, Max Beerbohm, and
others to lunch to meet MT, but after lunch
he rushed off to a dentist appointment,
leaving his guests at a loss.

B13   BLAIR, WALTER. "A Long Friendship Filled With
Light and Laughter," New York Herald Tribune
Book Review (May 8), p. 1.
A review of Henry Nash Smith and William

(BLAIR, WALTER)
M. Gibson, eds., Mark Twain-Howells Letters. Praises the editing and describes the letters, more from MT in the early years and later more from Howells. The editors are probably too optimistic in hoping to "complete the destruction" of outmoded views of the MT-Howells relationship, as in Brooks's The Ordeal of Mark Twain, long disproved but still accepted by some critics. Abstract in AES, XI (1968), 2970; reprinted in Twainian, XXVIII (March-April, 1969).

B14 BOLOGNA, SANDO. "Marked for Twain," Travel, CXIII (May), 48-50.
On MT shrines and memorabilia in Hannibal and Florida, Missouri; Virginia City, Nevada; Hartford, Connecticut; and Elmira, New York. The emphasis is on hours and admission charges for the benfit of those planning pilgrimages on the 125th anniversary of MT's birth.

B15 BRIDGMAN, RICHARD. [Review: Walter Blair, Mark Twain & Huck Finn.] Moderna Språk, LIV (September), 305-306.
"Mr. Blair has examined Twain's various literary projects, his reading, social life, business problems, travels, family affairs, and general state of mind throughout the decade 1874-1884, so that we might observe Huckleberry Finn growing into the misshapen giant we know today," and he has reviewed its present reputation and the criticism and censorship over the years. "Of central interest in Mr. Blair's study is that he has discovered or collected hundreds of sources, relationships, similarities, coincidences, and even instances of plagiarism with a bearing upon Huckleberry Finn.... Always alert, patient, and knowledgeable," Blair sometimes guesses (as he admits), even "stretches his material precariously thin. On the other hand, the very inclusiveness of his work makes one aware of the variety of impulses that acted upon the conception of Huckleberry Finn."

B16 BROWNELL, GEORGE HIRAM. "Reprinting of George Hiram Brownell's First Issue--January 1939," Twainian, XIX (January-February), 4.
Material from the first issue of the original series of the Twainian.

B17 BUDD, LOUIS J. [Review: Kenneth S. Lynn, Mark Twain and Southwestern Humor.] South Atlantic Quarterly, LIX (Autumn), 580-81.
Like MT's own work, this is "uneven but always interesting, boldly venturesome rather than deliberate, more persuasive in snatches than in total effect, challenging but also vulnerable." Beginning with William Byrd of Westover, Lynn makes a useful point of showing antebellum humorists and Whig political tradition. Unfortunately, he sometimes stretches the texts to fit

his argument, and neglects some of the relevant scholarship.

B18 CAMBON, GLAUCO. "What Maisie and Huck Knew." Studi Americani, VI, 203-20.
MT and James both faced problems of showing reality through the eyes of a child, although Maisie's world is that of society while for Huck freedom can only be achieved by escape; yet both characters are saved by experience rather than coarsened by it. In a postscript Cambon points out that MT's "imaginative withdrawal is a simpler solution than James's."

B19 CARDWELL, GUY A. [Review: Walter Blair, Mark Twain and Huck Finn.] American Quarterly, XII (Fall), 428-29.
"The intention here is 'to define the forces which gave Adventures of Huckleberry Finn its substance and form,' but this intention is pursued in a conventional and, it must be confessed, at times a rather exhausting manner." Although there is useful information on the chronology of composition and the circumstances surrounding it, "Mr. Blair works with his eye perhaps excessively close to the object" and he fails to "settle Mark Twain largely and firmly in his times, which surely were the great 'influence' on him." Review listed in AES, IV (1961), 225, with brief comment.

B20 CARPENTER, FRANK G. Carp's Washington, Arranged and Edited by Frances Carpenter. New York: McGraw-Hill Book Company, Inc.
Washington newspaper correspondence in the Cleveland Leader; on pp. 130-32, an undated column describes MT lecturing with George Washington Cable.

B21 CARTER, PAUL J., JR. "Mark Twain and the American Labor Movement," Twainian, XIX (September-October), 1-4. Reprinted from New England Quarterly (1957.B17). Abstract in AES, III (1964), 1570.

B22 CLEMENS, CYRIL. "Mark Twain and the Man from Maine," Mark Twain Journal, XI (Summer), 17.
A brief review of Carl J. Weber, The Rise and Fall of James Ripley Osgood (Waterville, Maine: Colby College Press, 1959). "In this book Mark Twain's association with James R. Osgood is given careful treatment, with a special chapter about Life on the Mississippi and about Osgood's trip down the river with Mark Twain a year before the publication of the famous book"; a trip to Montreal, other meetings and trips, and Osgood's literary advice are also described. Abstract in AES, IV (1961), 515.

B23 COHEN, MORTON N. "Mark Twain and the Philippines: Containing an Unpublished Letter." Journal of the Central Mississippi Valley American Studies Association, I (Fall), 25-31; also, inside back cover.
About MT's anti-imperialism. Contains

(COHEN, MORTON N.)
facsimiles of holograph letters: MT's "A salutation-speech from the Nineteenth Century to the Twentieth," first published in the New York Herald, December 30, 1900 (reproduced on inside back cover), a letter of December 30, 1900 to MT from Abner C. Goodell, and MT's reply of December 31 (pp. 26-27).

B24 COVICI, PASCAL, JR. (ed.). "'Dear Master Wattie': The Mark Twain-David Watt Bowser Letters," Southwest Review, XLV (Spring), 104-21.
The texts of MT's correspondence (1880-1882) with a Texas schoolboy. The letters, some here reproduced in facsimile, are "destined for eventual deposit in the manuscript archives of the University of Texas"; they cast light on MT's views of writing, piloting, the river, and boyhood at a time halfway between the publication of TS and HF. Abstract in AES, III (1960), 2059; reprinted in Twainian, XIX (November-December, 1960).

B25 COX, JAMES M. "A Connecticut Yankee in King Arthur's Court: The Machinery of Self-Preservation," Yale Review, L (Autumn), 89-102.
"The Yankee, Pudd'nhead, and Philip Traum all insist that man is a machine who must obey the laws of his 'make,' that he cannot fully create anything." CY represents MT's "turning away from business and machinery, and Hank Morgan is perhaps the unmasked genius of Twain's comic art"; his death is thus a personal statement. Abstract in AES, X (1967), 752; reprinted in Twainian, XXVII (January-February, 1968). Article reprinted in Smith (1963), pp. 117-29, with a revised final paragraph.

B26 CUMMINGS, SHERWOOD. "Mark Twain and the Sirens of Progress." Journal of the Central Mississippi Valley American Studies Association, I (Fall), 17-24.
"Up to 1898 he gloried in the material progress of the nineteenth century," then "suffered a dramatic change of mind. From then on material progress seemed to him futile and meaningless inasmuch as man himself had not improved. But even to the end of his life...he was capable of marveling at its material achievements."

B27 CUNLIFFE, MARCUS. "A Lost American Masterpiece?" Encounter, XV (October), 71-74.
On MT's autobiographical writings, as edited by Paine, DeVoto, and, now, by Charles Neider (1959), whose version "has the distinct merit of arranging the material in a rough chronological sequence," although "a less casual editor" might have taken the trouble to distinguish between the factual and the fictious portions--"to distinguish, that is, between Mark Twain and Samuel L. Clemens." These writings are

not an MT masterpiece, because they lack the detachment with which he used autobiographical material in his best works, such as HF and parts of LOM, as well as in IA and RI. Abstract in AES, IV (1961), 1793; reprinted in Twainian, XXI (January-February, 1962, incorrectly attributing the review to Durham University Journal).

B28 DAICHES, DAVID. [Review: Charles Neider, ed., The Autobiography of Mark Twain (1959).] Listener, LXIV (December 15), 1111-12.
Questions Neider's use of a chronological order. "The crudities, sentimentalities, preposterousnesses in this book...stand beside the humour, the moralizing, the savagery, the thrashings at the limitations imposed by respectability, to reveal one of the most remarkable Americans of his time."

B29 [DAVIS, CHESTER L.] "Manuscript Transferred," Twainian, XIX (March-April), 2. On the acquisition of the manuscript for the English edition of TS.
"The manuscript--654 handwritten pages--is mainly in the script of several secretaries of the author. Mark Twain, however, wrote the preface, conclusion and 300 corrections. This manuscript was used to set type for the first printing of 'The Adventures of Tom Sawyer' in London in 1876," and is being placed in the Mark Twain Birthplace Memorial Shrine at Florida, Missouri.

B30 _____. "Personal Memoirs of U. S. Grant," Twainian, XIX (November-December), 3-4.
Quotes from MT's copy of the Grant memoirs on service in Missouri (I, 246 ff.), apparently with the implication that "The Private History of a Campaign that Failed" was written with Grant in mind.

B31 DRAKE, ROBERT Y., JR. "Huck Among the Doctors," National Review, IX (November 19), 320-22.
Critics have often misread HF, either because of Freudian preconceptions (as in the case of Leslie Fiedler) or through an inability to understand the Southwestern "intuitive apprehension that paradox inevitably lies at the heart of reality," as in the "paradox of slavery in the midst of a people so historically committed to the quest for freedom." Huck himself is always concerned "with the individual...never with society and institutions, which, all too often degenerate into a mob. (Unlike the sociologist or the 'enlightened' legislator, he is not concerned with class or race as such.)" Abstract in AES, IV (1961), 92; reprinted in Twainian, XXI (January-February, 1962).

B32 DUROCHER, AURELE A. "Mark Twain and the Roman Catholic Church." Journal of the Central Mississippi Valley American Studies Association, I (Fall), 32-43.
Throughout his life MT consistently "saw the Church as a very human institution which

(DUROCHER, AURELE A.)
had made many grave mistakes but had also
several redeeming features--both of which
he referred to in his writings."

B33 EASTMAN, MAX. "Mark Twain: Representative
American," New Leader, XLIII (September 26),
18-21.
An "amplification" of his keynote speech
at the opening banquet of the MT festival
in Elmira, New York (September, 1954). MT
was indeed a humorist, and in America "humor stands more on a level with serious art
and mixes more naturally with serious thinking" than in other countries. Eastman,
formerly from Elmira, tells of his own acquaintance with MT, describes MT's courtship
of Olivia Langdon, and argues that her influence benefited him; local accounts are
cited, among them that of Jervis Langdon,
son of Olivia's brother Charles. Abstract
in AES, IV (1961), 98; reprinted in Twainian, XXI (January-February, 1962).

B34 EBY, CECIL D., JR. "Mark Twain's 'Plug' and
'Chaw': An Anecdotal Parallel," Mark Twain
Journal, XI (Summer), 11, 25.
The joke by an Arkansas loafer "was in
circulation in the mining camps of Colorado
(and perhaps Nevada) for at least twelve
years before it was printed in The Adventures of Huckleberry Finn (1885)," as is
attested in an unpublished journal of David
Hunter Strother, who "was a noted raconteur," and could have told MT the story in
Philadelphia, in 1876. Abstract in AES, IV
(1961), 512.

B35 FATOUT, PAUL. "Mark Twain: A Footnote,"
Columbia University Forum, III (Fall),
51-52.
On Jap Herron: A Novel Written from the
Ouija Board (New York: Mitchell Kennerley,
1917). "In a long introduction, Mrs. Emily
Grant Hutchings of Hannibal, Missouri explains that the novel was written in 1915 by
the other-wordly essence of the humorist."
Fatout summarizes the story of Jasper (Jap)
Herron, adding: "Full of a lamentable mor-
tality, continual agonizing over coffins,
and people as wooden as puppets, the book
is alien to the robust manner of the living
Mark Twain. Snuffling and sobbing drench
the pages, so much tearful sobbing that, to
echo Huck Finn, the story is 'that damp I
never see anything like it.' Reviewers, to
a man, condemned." Legal action to halt
publication or suppress the book ended when
the New York Supreme Court refused to hear
the case. Abstract in AES, IV (1961), 36;
reprinted in Twainian, XXI (January-February,
1962).

B36 FEINSTEIN, HERBERT. "Mark Twain at the Bar,"
Journal of the State Bar of California,
XXXV (March-April), 192-96.
A review of D. M. McKeithan's Court Trials
in Mark Twain and Other Essays (1958).

Largely descriptive. "Mr. McKeithan is a
first-rate court reporter in relating six
trials by Mark Twain in that many novels."

B37 _____. "Two Pair of Gloves: Mark Twain and
Henry James," American Imago, XVII (Winter),
349-87.
On phallic and other symbolism of gloves
in The Turn of the Screw and the incident at
Gibraltar in IA. Abstract in AES, V (1962),
1811; reprinted in Twainian, XXII (January-
February, 1963).

B38 FERGUSON, DELANCEY. "How Sam Clemens Grew
into Mark Twain," New York Herald Tribune
Book Review, XXXVI (January 24), 5.
A review of Kenneth S. Lynn, Mark Twain
and Southwestern Humor, which points out
political backgrounds, clash of the Whigs
on the seaboard and Jacksonian democracy on
the frontier, and the literary consequences.

B39 _____. "The Legacy of Letters," American
Scholar, XXIX (Summer), 406-18.
A review-article, discussing the Mark
Twain-Howells Letters pp. 410, 412, 414; the
rest of the review article concerns the cor-
respondence of Swinburne, Melville, and
Stephen Crane.

B40 _____. "Many Faces of a Photogenic Man," New
York Times Book Review (November 20), p. 43.
A review of Milton Meltzer, Mark Twain
Himself. "This book would have delighted
Mark Twain." The many pictures of him and
his world are valuable, and the text is "no
perfunctory job. Mr. Meltzer has drawn
widely from contemporary newspapers and from
uncollected items in the files of long-for-
gotten magazines, as well as from volumes of
scholarly research."

B41 FIEDLER, LESLIE A. "Duplicitious Mark Twain,"
Commentary, XXIX (March), 239-48.
"Love and Death in the American Novel,
from which this essay has been adapted, will
be published this month." "The persona
called Mark Twain...is, first of all, a funny man, but more particularly, one who is
funny at the expense of culture: an anti-
literary writer, whose best books are trav-
esties of others." Nevertheless, "he is
not an open rebel," but "at worst a genteel
Noble Savage, the friend of enlightened
clergymen." "He was a man fitfully intelligent when he did not know he was thinking, a
spottily skillful stylist when he was not
aware he was writing artistically." "To
make of Twain a cult or a case...is...to lose
the sense of him as a poet, the possessor of
deep and special mythopoetic power, whose
childhood was contemporaneous with a nation's." If we consider TS and HF "not as
sequels but as alternative versions of the
same themes, these themes will reveal themselves in their mythic significance...dreamed
twice over, the second time as nightmare."
Abstract in AES, III (1960), 1871; reprinted

(FIEDLER, LESLIE A.)
in Twainian, XIX (November-December, 1960). Article reprinted in Kaplan (1967), pp. 134-51; in revised form in Fiedler's Love and Death in the American Novel (1960.B42).

B42 * ____. Love and Death in the American Novel. New York: Criterion Books.
[Source: 1966 revised edition, New York: Stein and Day.] On MT, pp. 269-90, 402-408, 456-68, and passim (partly accessible through the index). Places heavy emphasis on HF and PW, on themes of the child, sexuality, race, and Gothic traditions. Includes material which appeared as "Duplicitous Mark Twain" in Commentary (1960.B41). Pp. 553-74 of the 1960 edition reprinted in Leary (1962), pp. 277-300 as "Faust in The Eden of Childhood." "Accommodation and Transcendence" (pp. 575-91, on HF) reprinted in Gerber (1971), pp. 78-90.

B43 ____. "Travels with a Literary Source-Hunter," New York Times Book Review (April 3), p. 10.
A review of Walter Blair, Mark Twain & Huck Finn. "There is no really satisfactory book-length study of Mark Twain," although the texts and criticism are now available. As a history of HF Blair's study is "clearly reasonable, reasonably clear," but as criticism it is weakened by Blair's "desire to avoid risky speculation in favor of safe facts" of dates of editions, possible sources, etc.

B44 *FRAIBERG, LOUIS. "Van Wyck Brooks versus Mark Twain versus Samuel Clemens," in his Psychoanalysis and American Literary Criticism (Detroit: Wayne State University Press), pp. 120-33.
[Source: Beebe and Feaster (1968), p. 100; also, cited in James R. Vitelli, Van Wyck Brooks (New York: Twaine Publishers, Inc., 1969), p. 171, n. 3.]

B45 FRENCH, BRYANT MOREY. "The Gilded Age Manuscript," Yale University Library Gazette, XXXV (July), 35-41.
About one-fifth of the manuscript, 284 pages, survives, the greater part of it at Yale University. "Not only is the extant manuscript representative, but fortunately for students of Mark Twain's writing methods it is highly revealing in its interpolations, additions, deletions, and renumberings of pages and chapters." Marginal annotations reveal "a greater interweaving of the collaborators' work than would appear from the basic assignment of chapters," and concessions to gentility by both MT and Charles Dudley Warner. Article reprinted in Twainian, XX (March-April, 1961), 1-3, and reprinting abstracted in AES, VII (1964), 1571.

B46 FRIEDRICH, GERHARD. "Erosion of Values in Mark Twain's Humor," CEA Critic, XXII (September), 1, 7-8.
MT's development from humorist to pessimist may be explained in other than Freudian terms, in his technique of sententious buildup followed by deflation. Ultimately, "Twain's technique of humor became a cancerous habit of laughing any and all values to pieces," and "left him at last with nothing but debris--cosmic debris." Abstract in AES, VIII (1965), 1899; reprinted in Twainian, XXV (January-February, 1966).

B47 GARGANO, JAMES W. "Disguises in Huckleberry Finn," University of Kansas City Review, XXVI (March), 175-78.
"The 'disguises' in Huckleberry Finn...are the vehicle of Twain's indictment of human dissimulation and gullibility," but Huck and Jim use disguises as protection, the King and Duke as "predator's tools in their ceaseless battle to gull and exploit mankind." "Perhaps it is as a disguise that the author's much-discussed prefatory 'notice' can best be understood. Only too aware of the Swiftian implications of Huckleberry Finn, he attempted to disarm his readers by insisting that his literary intentions were altogether innocent." Abstract in AES, III (1960), 1353; reprinted in Twainian, XIX (November-December, 1960).

B48 GERSTENBERGER, DONNA. "Huckleberry Finn and the World's Illusions," Western Humanities Review, XIV (Autumn), 401-406.
The consistent metaphor of disguise and pretense may reveal "a significance for the novel not unlike that which an examination of the dramatic metaphor in Hamlet has provided." Huck (who can join society only through one disguise or another, but never as himself) gradually learns that "it is the elaborate illusion that the world insists is reality which causes man's moral confusion." Abstract in AES, IV (1961), 2786; reprinted in Twainian, XXI (January-February, 1962).

B49 GIBB, CARSON. "The Best Authorities," College English, XXII (December), 178-83.
Tom and Huck "believe niggers and people are two different things," but MT is not ending HF "with a burst of spleen" aimed at "two likable youngsters"; his target is the culture which has shaped their attitudes. Abstract in AES, IV (1961), 248; reprinted in Twainian, XXII (January-February, 1962). Article reprinted in Lettis (1962), pp. 429-37.

B50 GRENANDER, M. E. "Ambrose Bierce and Charles Warren Stoddard: Some Unpublished Correspondence," Huntington Library Quarterly, XXIII (May), 261-92.
Contains several references to MT, including the account of a meeting in early September, 1872 between John Camden Hotten and MT,

(GRENANDER, M. E.)
whom Tom Hood the Younger introduced as
"Mr. Bryce"; Hotten was not deceived, and
both he and Hood told the story to Bierce.
Abstract in AES, VI (1963), 1665; reprinted
in Twainian, XXIII (January-February, 1964).

B51 GROSS, SEYMOUR L. "Sherwood Anderson's Debt
to Huckleberry Finn," Mark Twain Journal,
XI (Summer), 3-5, 24.
Places particular emphasis on "I Want to
Know Why," which Anderson said was popular
because it was "a story of immaturity...
much like Mark Twain at his best." Gross
adds that "both boys are morally finer than
the adult world which they are describing,"
but distrust their own judgments. There
are similarities in irony, criticism of society, and use of the Negro as "a kind of
moral center." Abstract in AES, IV (1961),
509.

B52 *GUIDI, AUGUSTO. "L'Italia di Mark Twain,"
Revista di Letterature Moderne e Comparante
(Firenze), XIII (December), 284-89.
[Source: MHRA Annual Bibliography (1960),
No. 4796.]

B53 GULYEV, LEONID, and NELLI GULYEV. "Mark
Twain about Russia," USSR Illustrated
Monthly, No. 12 (December), pp. 50-51.
A popular account, noting his observations on the Quaker City tour, his praise
of revolution in CY, "The Czar's Soliloquy,"
his [initial] cordiality to Maxim Gorky,
etc. This is competent work for its purpose but provides no new information or insight.

B54 GUTTMAN, ALLEN. "Mark Twain's Connecticut
Yankee: Affirmation of the Vernacular Tradition?" New England Quarterly, XXXIII
(June), 232-37.
Arguing that "most critics...have seen
the novel as a fierce attack upon Arthurian
England and a thorough-going affirmation of
nineteenth-century America (and of New England's technological triumphs)," Guttman
warns that MT himself described Hank Morgan
as "an ignoramus" and portrayed him in the
book, not like Huck, but "more and more
like an enlarged version of Colonel Sherburn." His conduct is increasingly dicta-
torial and ultimately destructive. Abstract
in AES, III (1960), 1967; reprinted in
Twainian, XIX (November-December, 1960).
Article reprinted in Kesterson (1973),
pp. 103-107.

B55 HANSER, RICHARD. "Mark Twain's America."
Coronet, XLVIII (May), 111-45.
A minimal amount of text accompanies contemporary photographs illustrating the age,
with no particular emphasis on what MT saw
and described.

B56 HICKS, GRANVILLE. "The Mail of Two Men of
Letters," Saturday Review, XLIII (April 23),
20.
A review of Henry Nash Smith and William
M. Gibson, eds., The Mark Twain-Howells
Letters. The "superlative job" of editing
unobtrusively gives the reader "all he
needs to know" without "fussiness over triv-
ialities"; the correspondence reveals Howells as the better critic, with "everything
but genius." Abstract in AES, III (1960),
2481; reprinted in Twainian, XIX (November-
December, 1960).

B57 *HOBBIE, DIANA POTEAT. "Mark Twain's Letter to
the Texas Schoolboy," Houston Post, February 7.
[Source: Reprinted in Twainian, XIX
(March-April), 2-4.] With explanatory comments, provides the text of a letter from
MT to young Watt Bowser of Dallas, March 20,
1880. MT comments on piloting, unwilling-
ness to be a boy again, report cards, and
the value of "plain, simple language, short
words, and brief sentences." Abstract in
AES, III (1960), 1614.

B58 HOFFMAN, DANIEL G. "Jim's Magic: Black or
White?" American Literature, XXXII (March),
47-54.
Jim's "superstitions are used structurally
to indicate his slavery while a slave and
his spiritual freedom with Huck"; freed from
credulity with his escape from bondage, "he
becomes a magician able to read the mysterious signs of nature." Abstract in AES, III
(1960), 1620; reprinted in Twainian, XIX
(November-December, 1960), 3. Hoffman substantially rewrote this article for the
chapter, "Black Magic--and White--in Huckleberry Finn," in his Form and Fable in American Fiction (1961.B39).

B59 JACOBSON, DAN. "Devilishness," Spectator, CCV
(November 25), 846, 848.
A review of Charles Neider, ed., The Autobiography of Mark Twain (1959). Although
"much of the book is banal and conventional," there are "spasmodic but unmistakable
irruptions of his genius."

B60 _____. "Mark Twain and the Calm Squatter,"
Spectator, CCV (August 5), 219-20.
A review-article on Kenneth S. Lynn's
Mark Twain and Southwestern Humor and Henry
Nash Smith and William M. Gibson, eds., Mark
Twain-Howells Letters, neither of which is
discussed critically. Adopting the vernacular of his society was not a surrender by
MT, but "the condition of his freedom from
either shame or boastfulness in writing
about it"; nonetheless, he blundered in his
life and work, "was at once a vulgarian and
the victim of the worst gentilities of his
time...debased his own gifts for the sake of
money and applause...was a clown, a show-off
and a coward," as he sadly admitted. His

(JACOBSON, DAN)
highest aspirations produced "an unreadable book like The Personal Recollections of Joan of Arc," but there is evidence of his "prodigious talent" in several of his works, and sustainedly in Huckleberry Finn, where Huck and Jim show a degree of civilization uncommon elsewhere because "it demands mutual responsibility, self-abnegation, and moral choice." Abstract in AES, III (1960), 2502; reprinted in Twainian, XIX (November-December, 1960).

B61   JEFFERIES, WILLIAM B. "The Montesquiou Murder Case: A Possible Source For Some Incidents in Pudd'nhead Wilson," American Literature, XXXI (January), 488-90.
A murder in St. Louis in 1849 involving two French brothers parallels the murder in Pudd'nhead Wilson; accounts in the St. Louis papers (cited) were available to MT in his youth. Abstract in AES, III (1960), 703, reprinted in Twainian, XIX (November-December, 1960), 1-3.

B62   JONES, LLEWELLYN. "Mark Twain--a Humanist Too," Humanist, XX (November-December), 365-67.
A review-article, somewhat impressionistic and descriptive, of Minnie M. Brashear and Robert M. Rodney, eds., The Art, Humor, and Humanity of Mark Twain; The Adventures of Huckleberry Finn, with an Afterword by George Elliott, who discusses the "moral grandeur" of Huck's character (A Signet Classic: New York, The New American Library); The Adventures of Tom Sawyer, with an Afterword by George Elliott (A Signet Classic: New York, The New American Library); A Connecticut Yankee in King Arthur's Court, Introduction by Charles Neider, who "tells us that the book was read by Mark Twain's wife Libby who did a little editing in the interests of propriety of speech" (New York: Hill & Wang); Charles Neider, Mark Twain and the Russians: an Exchange of Views (New York: Hill & Wang).

B63   KARL, FREDERICK R. "Joseph Conrad and Huckleberry Finn," Mark Twain Journal, XI (Summer), 21-22.
MT matured between Tom Sawyer and Huckleberry Finn as Conrad did between Youth and Heart of Darkness; there are similar treatments of river and shore in the two mature works, which "as studies in human degradation surrounded by the possibilities of regeneration...symbolize an era." Abstract in AES, IV (1961), 517.

B64   KLOTZ, MARVIN. "Goethe and Mark Twain," Notes and Queries (London), CCV, n.s. VII (April), 150-151.
The possibility that the equating of madness with lasting happiness at the end of The Mysterious Stranger is derived from The Sorrows of Young Werther adds "to the overwhelming evidence that Mark Twain was not a

genius-in-the-rough, but a well-read and erudite author." Abstract in AES, III (1960), 1761; reprinted in Twainian, XIX (November-December, 1960).

B65   *KOSTER, DONALD N. "Mark Twain, Mysterious Stranger," Adelphi Quarterly, III (Summer), 16-26.
[Source: Beebe and Feaster (1968), p. 103.]

B66   KRISTOL, IRVING. "D-a-v-y Da-vy Crockett," Commentary, XXIX (February), 169-71. A review of Kenneth S. Lynn, Mark Twain and Southwestern Humor.
The importance of MT's almost-forgotten predecessors lies "in their eventual radical impact on serious American writing and in their status as witnesses to a transformation of the democratic idea in America." "The triumph of the vernacular over the trans-Atlantic rhetoric of the genteel tradition was a momentous event in American letters, American politics, American culture. It meant the victory of the masculine tone in the novel, hitherto regarded as a feminine entertainment--the way was open for Stephen Crane, Dreiser, Sherwood Anderson." Abstract in AES, III (1960), 963; reprinted in Twainian, XIX (November-December, 1960).

B67   KRUTCH, JOSEPH WOOD. "The Kremlin Claims Mark Twain," New York Times Magazine Section (March 6), pp. 16, 68-69.
The official Russian critical view misrepresents American criticism in assuming that here, too, there is an "official line" and that it attempts to suppress MT's social criticism. The error of this view is revealed by disagreement among American critics. The Russians err, too, in the "tacit assumption that...he might have turned his bitterness into faith in a People's Democracy." However, it is also reported that Russian children (and probably adults as well) read TS and HF "simply as the delightful tales they have always seemed to English-speaking children."

B68   LAING, NITA. "The Later Satire of Mark Twain," Midwest Quarterly, II (October), 35-48.
On the devastating influence of MT's despair on his later work, which, however, shows traces of his old brilliance; based on the familiar scholarship, to which the debt is acknowledged. Abstract in AES, VIII (1965), 1663; reprinted in Twainian, XXV (January-February, 1966).

B69   LOOMIS, C. C., JR. "Twain's Huckleberry Finn," Explicator, XVIII (January), Item 27.
Tom Sawyer "lacks Huck's realism, toughness, and moral sensitivity," but his romanticism offers a means of seeing the often brutal world as adventure. Abstract in AES, III (1960), 778; reprinted in Twainian, XIX (November-December, 1960).

B70 *LOOMIS, EDWARD W. "Three Notes on Plot,"
     Spectrum, IV (Spring-Summer), 94-99.
         The absurd ending of HF follows the ab-
     surdity of the novel's prose. (Also on
     plot in James Gould Cozzens and as described
     in The Notebooks of Henry James.) [Source:
     AES, III (1960), 1610; reprinted in Twain-
     ian, XIX (November-December, 1960).]

B71 LONG, E. HUDSON. [Review: Charles Neider, ed.,
     The Autobiography of Mark Twain.] American
     Literature, XXXI (January), 494-95.
         Neider's organization adds to the enter-
     tainment value at the expense of the in-
     sights provided by the editing of Paine
     and DeVoto. The general reader will enjoy
     the great passages by MT, but "there is
     still the need for a complete scholarly
     edition of Mark Twain's autobiographical
     writings which Mr. Neider's popular, abbre-
     viated version does not fill."

B72 LYNN, KENNETH S. "Case History of Huckleberry
     Finn," New York Herald Tribune Book Review,
     (May 22), p. 8.
         A review of Walter Blair, Mark Twain &
     Huck Finn, which clears up the chronology
     of the book's composition and shows that
     MT was not henpecked by his wife. The book
     "pathetically fails," however, in its ob-
     jective of illuminating MT's life and times,
     and the quality of HF, because Blair does
     not know how to use the material he has un-
     earthed, is "abjectly dependent on the in-
     sights of other critics," and "draws paral-
     lels by the hundreds, but he cannot con-
     nect."

B73 MACDONALD, DWIGHT. "Mark Twain: An Unsenti-
     mental Journey." New Yorker, XXXVI
     (April 9), 160-96. Reprinted as "Mark
     Twain" in his Against the American Grain
     (New York: Random House, 1962), 80-122
     (incorrectly giving the date of publication
     in the New Yorker as April 2); also reprint-
     ed in part in Kaplan (1967), 91-122, and in
     Cardwell (1963), pp. 116-30.
         A thoughtful and informed discussion of
     MT, his works, and the editors and critics.
     The occasion is the recent publication of
     The Autobiography of Mark Twain, assembled
     by "Charles Neider, a literary Jack-of-all-
     trades whose interests have ranged from
     Kafka to the diaries of Mrs. Robert Louis
     Stevenson.... One's first reaction is:
     why?... If there is any need for a new edi-
     tion, it is for a complete one, edited by
     a specialist in Mark Twain," (p. 160). Mac-
     donald discusses the editing of MT biograph-
     ical material by Paine and DeVoto, the con-
     troversy between DeVoto and Brooks (in
     which he takes the side of Brooks as the
     more perceptive, but notes that in later
     years the two practically exchanged posi-
     tions), and summarizes some of the important
     scholarship. In his own discussion of MT,
     Macdonald admits that for him "the great
     bulk of Mark Twain's work is no longer

readable"-- IA, CY, JA, and much of the
trivia. TS is important as a forerunner of
HF: Tom became the matrix of a stereotype
and "his rebellion is phony...while Tom is
a sentimental abstraction, Huck is Huck"
(p. 173). The autobiographical ramblings
are less revealing than MT thought, "the
tone is that of the public performer"
(p. 181), and "the tragedy of Mark Twain, I
think, is this peculiar inability to speak
in his own voice" (p. 183).

B74 MACK, EFFIE [MONA]. "Mark Twain in Nevada.
     A Leaf from the Civil War Story." Twainian,
     XIX (March-April), 4; reprinted from Oakland
     (California) Tribune, November 16 (1958.B49).
         Describes the flag on Mt. Davidson. (See
     RI, II, Ch. XIV.) Abstract in AES, III
     (1960), 1615.

B75 McKEE, JOHN DEWITT. "A Connecticut Yankee as
     a Revolutionary Document," Mark Twain Jour-
     nal, XI (Summer), 18-20, 24.
         On the book's attack on institutions. Ab-
     stract in AES, IV (1961), 516.

B76 MacRAE, DONALD. "Huck and Experience," Times
     Literary Supplement, August 26, p. 545.
         A letter to the editor, arguing that Huck
     "learns nothing whatever from his experience"
     because, contrary to what he thinks, he was
     indeed "started right" and is spontaneously
     right in the crucial points in the book. [A
     reply to a statement in the anonymous "Inno-
     cence and Experience," (August 12), p. 512,
     1960.B4.]

B77 *MALONE, DAVID H. "Analysis of Mark Twain's
     Novel Life on the Mississippi," in Hans
     Galinsky, ed., The Frontier in American His-
     tory and Literature (Frankfurt a/M [Diester-
     weg, Beiheft 7 of N.S.?]), pp. 80-93.
     [Source: Beebe and Feaster (1968),
     p. 132.]

B78 *_____. "Mark Twain and the Literature of the
     Frontier," ibid., pp. 65-79.
     [Source: MHRA Annual Bibliography (1961),
     5292.]

B79 MAYFIELD, JOHN S. [Review: Svend Petersen,
     Mark Twain and the Government.] American
     Book Collector, X (June), 3-4.
     [Also available as Twainian, XIX (July-
     August).] Chiefly descriptive, favorable.

B80 MEINE, FRANKLIN J. "Some Notes on the First
     Editions of 'Huck Finn,'" American Book Col-
     lector, X (June), 31-34 [Also available as
     Twainian, XIX (July-August)].
         Chiefly concerned with the mutilation of
     the cut on p. 283; six illustrations on
     pp. 32-33 show various states of the cut,
     before and after the picture was defaced.
     The documentation is based on Walter Blair's
     Mark Twain & Huck Finn. Abstract in AES,
     III (1960), 1856.

B81 MESERVE, WALTER J., ed., The Complete Plays of William Dean Howells. New York: New York University Press, pp. 205-41 and passim.
   Contains the text of Colonel Sellers as a Scientist, by MT and Howells (not previously published), with an introduction (pp. 205-208) discussing their collaboration.

B82 MILLER, WILLIAM C. "Mark Twain's Source for 'The Latest Sensation' Hoax?" American Literature, XXXII (March), 75-78.
   On MT's "Dutch Nick Massacre" story: "A Twain item copied from the columns of the Virginia City Territorial Enterprise for 'July 22d' (1863) and unnoticed until now, appears to be the source for the famous hoax"; the story, apparently factual, is here reproduced from a reprinting in the Sacramento Daily Union of July 24, 1863. Abstract in AES, III (1960), 1622, reprinted in Twainian, XIX (November-December, 1960), 3.

B83 MOYNE, ERNEST J. "Mark Twain Meets a Lady from Finland," Mark Twain Journal, XI (Summer), 9-10, 25.
   On MT's meetings with Baroness Alexandra Gripenberg. An expanded version of this article appeared in American Literature as "Mark Twain and Baroness Alexandra Gripenberg" (1973.B43). Abstract in AES, XI (Summer, 1960), 511.

B84 PARKE, RICHARD H. "Soviet Edition of Mark Twain Given to Connecticut Library," New York Times, (December 11), p. 88.
   Datelined "Reddington [sic: presumably Redding], Conn., Dec. 10" reports that "a resident of this town who has been exchanging books by and about Mark Twain with a Soviet library gave a Russian book to the Mark Twain Library here today"; it is titled Mark Twain Collections.

B85 PARSONS, COLEMAN O. "The Background of The Mysterious Stranger," American Literature, XXXII (March), 55-74.
   On the originals for setting and some of the characters, and on literary sources and analogues,; "These background materials will be grouped under five headings: Title, Setting, Characters, Plot, and Ideas." Abstract in AES, III (1960), 1621, reprinted in Twainian, XIX (November-December, 1960), 3.

B86 PEARSON, NORMAN HOLMES. "Mark Twain--Genius or Jokesmith? Fifty Years After His Death, the Critics Are Still Bemused," Saturday Review, XLIII (June 25), 24-25.
   A review-article, summarizing Charles Neider's Mark Twain and the Russians, Svend Petersen's Mark Twain and the Government, Kenneth S. Lynn's Mark Twain and Southwestern Humor, and Walter Blair's Mark Twain & Huck Finn ("a brilliant parallel to J. L. Lowes's 'The Road to Xanadu' in reconstructing the road from Hannibal").

B87 _____. "The Mark Twain Memorial in Hartford, Connecticut." Journal of the Central Mississippi Valley American Studies Association, I (Fall), 10-16.
   Describes the house as "a document," tracing its ownership since MT's death and describing in some detail the restoration. Among resources being collected for scholars are a facsimile of his library, a log of his Hartford years (based in part on "a combing of Hartford newspapers"), and as complete a collection as possible of "all known photographs of Mark Twain," in addition to manuscript material.

B88 PIPER, HENRY DAN. "Fitzgerald, Mark Twain and Thomas Hardy," Fitzgerald Newsletter, No. 8 (Winter), pp. 1-2.
   Fitzgerald admired MT, and called the Paine biography "excellent." A member of the International Mark Twain Society, he sent a note to the 1935 banquet: "Huckleberry Finn took the first journey back. He was the first to look back at the republic from the perspective of the West. His eyes were the first eyes that ever looked at us objectively that were not eyes from overseas." (Hardy is not mentioned in connection with MT; in a letter he expressed admiration for Fitzgerald.) Abstract in AES, IV (1961), 1830. Fitzgerald's tribute is reprinted in Simpson (1968), p. 107.

B89 POCHMANN, HENRY A. Introduction to "Mark Twain Anniversary Number," Journal of the Central Mississippi Valley American Studies Association, I (Fall), 1.
   MT's reputation is secure in 1960, the 125th anniversary of his birth and the 50th of his death; he is commemorated by a dozen convocations and conferences, and a number of magazines and learned journals honor him with special issues.

B90 PRATT, WILLIS C. (as told to Grace Valliere King). "The Last Time I Saw Mark Twain," Mark Twain Journal, XI (Summer), 6-8, 23.
   Pratt interviewed MT at his Fifth Avenue home for the New York Herald. MT was in bed, recovering from bronchitis, but he spoke at length on political bossism, revealing considerable knowledge of Richard Croker, and he complained of a humorist's difficulty in being taken seriously. Abstract in AES, IV (1961), 510.

B91 PRITCHETT, V. S. "First Person Singular," New Statesman, LX (November 26), 848-49.
   Includes a review of Charles Neider, ed., The Autobiography of Mark Twain.
   The material MT left is "a huge and disastrous ragbag of shaggy anecdotes. Mr. Neider is the latest editor to attempt an

(PRITCHETT, V. S.)
arrangement of it. Twain set out to tell the whole truth and we can certainly deduce his inner terror and insecurity from it, but characteristically his notion of telling the truth was simply never to stop talking."

B92   RANDOLPH, VANCE. "A Treasury to Draw Upon," New York Times Book Review (February 28), pp. 6, 42.
A descriptive review of Kenneth S. Lynn's Mark Twain and Southwestern Humor, a book "full of splendid stuff."

B93   RAYFORD, JULIAN LEE. "The Mississippi River Leadline Chant," American Book Collector, X (June), 6-10 [also available as Twainian, XIX (July-August)].
The chant as Rayford heard it on a towboat in 1946; not directly related to MT.

B94   REED, JOHN Q. "Mark Twain: West Coast Journalist," Midwest Quarterly, I (January), 141-61.
A critical survey of MT's journalistic writings, 1861-1866, based on familiar, published material. Although his writing for the Territorial Enterprise "displays course [sic] humor, ineffective satire, florid style, and chaotic form, it also shows a steady advance in quality," which continued in his later Western writings; nonetheless, "when he left the West in 1866 he was still a journalist and not a literary artist." Abstract in AES, VIII (1965), 1660; reprinted in Twainian, XXV (January-February, 1966).

B95   ROBINSON, E. ARTHUR. "The Two 'Voices' in Huckleberry Finn," Modern Language Notes, LXXV (March), 204-208.
The authorial intrusion in HF is not limited to Chapters XXI-XXII (discussed by Robert Hunting, 1958.B38); rather, "not infrequently, Huck seems oblivious of implications which are clear to the reader," as in the passage where Jim talks of stealing his wife and children out of slavery: "the thoughts are Huckleberry Finn's, but the significance is Mark Twain's." As Huck matures, he becomes more able to carry the irony himself. Abstract in AES, X (1967), 3063; reprinted in Twainian, XXVII (January-February, 1968).

B96   ROPER, GORDON. "Mark Twain and His Canadian Publishers," American Book Collector, X (June), 13-29 [also available as Twainian, XIX (July-August)].
A detailed account of authorized and pirated editions of MT's works in Canada; concludes with "Check List of Canadian Editions of Mark Twain's Work" (pp. 28-29). Abstract in AES, III (1960), 1855. Also see Roper's "Mark Twain and His Canadian Publishers: A Second Look" (1966.B92).

B97   RYAN, PAT M., JR. "Mark Twain: Frontier Theatre Critic," Arizona Quarterly, XVI (Autumn), 197-209.
"Though ready enough to present himself to his public as a fairly unsophisticated chap capable of immense enjoyment at the theatre, Twain was also a critic, in the true sense, of American culture." Examples of his theater criticism in California papers are quoted, as are passages from his later books, indicating that his interest in the theater was life-long. Abstract in AES, IV (1961), 1296; reprinted in Twainian, XXI (January-February, 1962).

B98   SCHMIDT, PAUL. "River vs. Town: Mark Twain's Old Times on the Mississippi," Nineteenth-Century Fiction, XV (September), 95-111.
"Speaks eloquently and often of a tragic split in life and mind. The bleached lifelessness of the town and the dark dramatic color of the river and the boat spell out Clemens's version of this conflict. At the heart of his best work lies a rich registration of this conflict and his solid conviction that in the steamboat and what it represents lies its creative resolution." Abstract in AES, IV (1961), 1655; reprinted in Twainian, XXI (January-February, 1962).

B99   SCOTT, ARTHUR L. "Mark Twain Today." Journal of the Central Mississippi Valley American Studies Association, I (Fall), 2-10.
Portions of a talk delivered in Hannibal on October 15. Scott briefly lists recent books on MT; describes holdings in the Mark Twain Papers at the University of California in Berkeley, and comments on other significant collections of MT material in this country: the Berg Collection in the New York Public Library, Buffalo Public Library (most of the Huckleberry Finn manuscript), Houghton Library at Harvard, Huntington Library at San Marino, California, Lilly Collection at the University of Indiana, the private collections of C. Walter Barrett and Samuel Charles Webster, and the Hartford Memorial Library and the Mark Twain Research Foundation. Concludes by discussing current popularity of MT's works, and their translations and film adaptations.

B100   SCOTT, WINFIELD TOWNLEY. "Hannibal and the Bones of Art," New Mexico Quarterly, XXX (Winter), 339-46.
On a two-day visit to the town of MT's boyhood Scott saw houses and memorabilia, but "I was not as moved as I expected to be.... I had been closer when I was not here." The town is more vivid in MT's books than in its present-day actuality. Abstract in AES, IV (1961), 2416. Article reprinted in Kaplan (1967), pp. 152-60.

B101   SHOCKLEY, MARTIN STAPLES. "The Structure of Huckleberry Finn," South-Central Bulletin, XX (Winter), 3-10.
"I propose that Huckleberry Finn is thematically coherent and structurally unified.

1960 - Shorter Writings

(SHOCKLEY, MARTIN STAPLES)
I propose a logical, ordered, five-part structure, with introduction, rising action, climax, falling action, conclusion. I propose proportion and balance among these parts, achieving a total aesthetic harmony." Thus, the Phelps farm chapters, though unsatisfactory as a conclusion, may be interpreted as falling action; the true conclusion is the brief "Chapter the Last: Nothing More to Write," in which Huck, having repudiated the civilization he has seen, "is ready to live by innate morality, a free man." Abstract in AES, IV (1961), 1272; reprinted in Twainian, XXI (January-February, 1962). Article reprinted in Kesterson (1973), pp. 70-81.

B102 SMITH, HENRY NASH. "Mark Twain's World Restored in Words and Pictures," New York Herald Tribune Book Review, XXXVII (November 6), 1. A review of Milton Meltzer, Mark Twain Himself.
"Mr. Meltzer has done his work well"--but, paradoxically, the accumulation of pictorial data adds to our sense of the remoteness of MT's time from our own.

B103 ____. "Old Mark Loved an Audience," New York Herald Tribune Book Review, XXXVII (December 18), 36. A review of Paul Fatout, Mark Twain on the Lecture Circuit.
Fatout "has found an abundance of material and put it together in a clear, workmanlike narrative"; he "has dug out hundreds of reviews of Mark Twain's lectures in newspapers all over the world."

B104 SOLOMON, ERIC. "Huckleberry Finn Once More," College English, XXII (December), 172-78.
Both critics and defenders of the thematic unity of HF assume that MT's intention "was either to show Huck's growth to maturity, to hail the joys of freedom on the river, or to depict the escape from civilization and slavery." Judged under this assumption, the ending is a failure; but the book may also be viewed in terms of the major theme of a search for security, as exemplified by Huck's invention of various family patterns for himself. Abstract in AES, IV (1961), 247; reprinted in Twainian, XXI (January-February, 1962). Article reprinted in Bradley (1962), pp. 436-43; in Lettis (1962), pp. 420-28.

B105 STARRETT, VINCENT. "Shaking Hands with Immortality," American Book Collector, X (June), 9-12. [Also available as Twainian, XIX (July-August).]
On the discovery in Rome of a statuette of MT from the studio of Luigi Amici; the statuette (illustrated) and a medallion portrait (apparently lost) were described to Starrett as "both taken from life," but he notes problems with provenance and documentation. Abstract in AES, III (1960), 1854.

B106 ____. [Review: Walter Blair, Mark Twain & Huck Finn.] American Book Collector, X (June), 3. [Also available as Twainian, XIX (July-August).]
"Literary detection at its liveliest and best," reflecting thorough familiarity with the book and its genesis, and the influence of MT's life and reading.

B107 TEITELBAUM, HAROLD. "Samuel Langhorne Clemens (Mark Twain)," Book Bulletin of the Chicago Public Library, XLII (September), 123-26.
A very brief estimate of MT, followed by summaries and estimates of major books by and about him; introductory.

B108 VITELLI, J. R. "The Innocence of Mark Twain," Bucknell Review, IX (December), 187-98.
A conscious craftsman and stylist, MT created an American Innocent as "a composite--as all such images are--of two character-types of the Innocent: the Innocent as complacent fool, and the Innocent as wise-seeker, both merged by and with the informing presence of their creator, that is, the personality of Mark Twain."

B109 VITTORINI, ELIO. "An Outline of American Literature (1941)," Sewanee Review, LXVIII (July), 423-37.
MT was "the chief and most typical" of the authors who created "an American legend of the son of the West, the symbol of the new man." Abstract in AES, XIV (1970-1971), 1609; reprinted in Twainian, XXXI (January-February, 1972).

B110 VON KREBS, MARIA. "'Rache' Is the German for 'Revenge,'" Baker Street Journal, X, n.s. (January), 12-14.
Six years before A Study in Scarlet, MT in TA commented on the inscription Rache in a cell at the college prison at Heidelberg University; "It is clear that Doyle, like Twain, recognized the inherent dramatic possibilities of the scrawled word on the wall, and...incorporated his famous story around it." Both books contain illustrations (here reproduced) of walls with the inscription. Abstract in AES, III (1960), 1163.

B111 WEBB, HOWARD W., JR. "Mark Twain and Ring Lardner," Mark Twain Journal, XI (Summer) 13-15.
A comparison between the two, showing no evidence of influence or other contact except for Lardner's statement in the New York Times Magazine (March 25, 1917, p. 44) that he felt George Ade had superceded MT as our national humorist and Booth Tarkington's Penrod had replaced Huckleberry Finn: "I've known Booth Tarkington's boys, and I've not known those of Mark Twain. Mark Twain's boys are tough and poverty-stricken and they belong to a period very different from that of our own boys." Abstract in AES, IV (1961), 514.

B112 WELLS, ARVIN R. "Huck Finn and Holden Caulfield: The Situation of the Hero," Ohio
University Review, II, 31-42.
Examines in the books by MT and Salinger
"the marked dissimilarities as contributory
to the ultimately very different effects
produced by these two novels," to reveal
"the essential qualities and fundamental attitudes found in each" and emphasize "the
fact that these novels are, after all, the
products of two unique creative imaginations
responding to quite different milieux."
Abstract in AES, IV (1961), 578; reprinted
in Twainian, XXI (January-February, 1962).

B113 YATES, NORRIS W. "The 'Counter-Conversion'
of Huckleberry Finn," American Literature,
XXXII (March), 1-10.
On the phenomenon of conversion to and
away from religion--in Huck's case to "wickedness" as an alternative to betrayal of
Jim. Abstract in AES, III (1960), 1616; reprinted in Twainian, XIX (November-December,
1960), 3.

1961 A BOOKS

A1 BALDANZA, FRANK. Mark Twain: An Introduction
and Interpretation. New York: Barnes &
Noble, Inc.; London: Constable.
"This study of the life and works of Mark
Twain is intended for both the general
reader and the student. The aim has been
to take into account all the biographical
research that has been done since A. B.
Paine's monumental authorized biography."
The chapters on MT's works "have been organized in a unique manner, treating the
autobiographical, the travel, the historical, the juvenile, the American, and the
polemical writings as units in themselves,"
in order to concentrate on "fresh insights
to be drawn from the inter-relations of the
work themselves" (p. v.). The portion on
CY is reprinted in Schmitter (1974),
pp. 117-21.

A2 *BRADLEY, SCULLEY, RICHMOND CROOM BEATTY, and
E. HUDSON LONG, eds. Samuel Langhorne
Clemens: Adventures of Huckleberry Finn:
An Annotated Text. Backgrounds and Sources,
Essays in Criticism. New York: W. W. Norton & Company, Inc.
A standard casebook for classroom use; it
was copyrighted in 1961 and reviewed at
least once (in Twainian), but the copies
now available also carry a 1962 copyright
date and the present bibliography lists the
volume under both years to prevent possible
loss of material cross-referenced to this
important reprinting.

A3 CLEMENS, SAMUEL L. Contributions to "The
Galaxy" 1868-1871 by Mark Twain (Samuel
Langhorne Clemens). Facsimile Reproductions,
Edited with an Introduction and Notes by
Bruce R. McElderry, Jr., Gainesville, Flori-
da: Scholars' Facsimiles & Reprints.

In a "Bibliographical Note" (p. xxi)
McElderry points out that "Only a few of
Twain's Galaxy sketches have never appeared
elsewhere, and these uncollected items are
chiefly brief paragraphs." Nonetheless,
McElderry's careful editing and the bibliographical data he provides make this an extremely useful source for students of this
period in MT's life.

A4 _____. "My Dear Bro": A Letter from Samuel
Clemens to His Brother Orion, Foreword by
Frederick Anderson. Berkeley, California:
The Berkeley Albion.
"In this previously unpublished letter
[San Francisco, October 19, 1865] sent to
his brother, Orion, and Orion's wife, Mol-
lie, Samuel Clemens expresses the ambiguous
attitude toward his view of himself as a
writer that would trouble him throughout his
life.... it was not until the fall of 1865,
when he was nearly thirty, that Mark Twain
concluded he must commit himself to a literary career, and even then his decision was
reluctant." He hesitated to become a professional humorist.

A5 _____, and BRET HARTE. "Ah Sin," a Dramatic
Work by Mark Twain and Bret Harte, ed.
Frederick Anderson. San Francisco: The
Book Club of California.
Anderson's preface describes the growth
and decline of the two men's friendship and
traces the fortunes of the play, of which
"much, perhaps most, of the initial material...came from Bret Harte," while MT's contribution lay in turning Harte's stilted
dialogue to "the rhythms and vocabulary of
actual speech." The play was a failure and
has since received little critical attention, "since while Ah Sin is not the poor-
est work by either man, it is not far from
it."

A6 FONER, PHILIP. Mark Tven-Socialny Kritik.
Moskva: Izdatelstvo Inostrannoi Literatur.
A Russian translation of Foner's Mark
Twain: Social Critic (1958).

A7 FRIED, M[ARTIN] B. Mark Twain on the Art of
Writing. Buffalo [N.Y.]: The Salisbury
Club.
A brief foreword gives the background for
MT's "Report to the Buffalo Female Academy"
(Buffalo Express, June 18, 1870), "A General
Reply" (Buffalo Express, November 12, 1870,
and Galaxy, X [November, 1870], 732-34), and
"A Good Letter: Mark Twain's Idea of It"
(Buffalo Express, November 10, 1869). [41
page pamphlet.]

A8 HARNSBERGER, CAROLINE THOMAS. Mark Twain's
Views of Religion. Evanston, Illinois:
The Schori Press.
A general study, annotated from MT's pub-
lished and unpublished writings. In 1906
Rufus K. Noyes gave him a copy of his Views
of Religion. "Mark Twain did not agree

1961 - Books

(HARNSBERGER, CAROLINE THOMAS)
with every doctrine expressed in the volume. His extensive marginal notes, printed
here for the first time, are the inspiration for this résumé of his views of religion." His extensive annotations of Jonathan Edwards' Freedom of the Will are noted
in passing but not quoted.

A9   LEARY, LEWIS, ed. Mark Twain's Letters to
Mary. New York: Columbia University Press.
The text of MT's letters to Mary Benjamin
Rogers, the wife of Henry Huttleston Rogers,
Jr. Leary's account is a useful contribu-
tion to MT biography for the years 1900-
1910.

A10 McKEITHAN, DANIEL MORLEY. The Morgan Manuscript of Mark Twain's "Pudd'nhead Wilson."
Uppsala: A.-B. Lundequistska Bokhandeln
(Essays and Studies on American Language
and Literature, 12).
"In 1909 the manuscript was purchased by
J. Pierpont Morgan [from MT]. I shall describe the manuscript, call attention to
the revisions in it, and point out the differences between it and the book" (p. 14);
there is also a general discussion of PW,
with attention to the racial theme.

A11 *NEIDER, CHARLES, ed. The Complete Humorous
Sketches and Tales of Mark Twain. Garden
City, New York: Hanover House.
[Source: MHRA Annual Bibliography
(1961), No. 5302.]

A12 ____, ed. Life as I Find It: Essays, Sketches,
Tales, and Other Material, the Majority of
Which is Now Published in Book Form for the
First Time. Garden City, New York: Hanover
House.

A13 ____, ed. The Travels of Mark Twain. New
York: Coward-McCann, Inc.
Excerpts from MT's travel books with an
introduction (largely biographical, and
useful only to the general reader) and a
few background footnotes by Neider.

A14 QUICK, DOROTHY. Enchantment: A Little Girl's
Friendship with Mark Twain. Norman: University of Oklahoma Press.
Dorothy Quick was almost eleven years old
in 1907 when she met MT, a lonely old man
who missed his family of young daughters.
This book is the record of the friendship of
the two, and is interesting for the record
of MT by one of his "Angel-Fishes" and for
his advice to a very young writer. A number of letters from MT are included, with
four photographs of him in the text and
another on the dust-jacket.

A15 ROGERS, FRANKLIN R., ed. The Pattern for Mark
Twain's "Roughing It": Letters from Nevada
by Samuel and Orion Clemens 1861-1862.
Berkeley and Los Angeles: University of
California Press.

Correspondence published in the Keokuk
(Iowa) Gate City and St. Louis Missouri
Democrat, valuable as background for RI and
interesting as early writing by MT. Rogers
questions Ernest E. Leisy's attribution of
the Quintus Curtius Snodgrass letters to MT.

A16 SALOMON, ROGER B. Twain and the Image of History. New Haven: Yale University Press
(Yale Studies in English, 150).
"Twain's images of history reflect the
interaction of a writer's private insights
with a major facet of his cultural tradition, an interaction that was to have a radical influence on the form and content of
most of his work." Commonly, "behind the
ambiguity, the divided intentions, the stylistic lapses of even his best books lies a
confused and bitter conflict between his
conception of history and his conception of
human nature; behind them also lies a pas-
sionate desire to escape the moral and
aesthetic implications of both through some
sort of transcendent dream" (p. 4).

A17 SCHÖNFELDER, KARL-HEINZ. Mark Twain: Leben,
Persönlicheit und Werk. Halle (Saale):
VEB Verlag Sprache und Literatur.
A brief, general study with a section on
his life followed by chapters titled "Humor
und Satire," "Gesellschaftskritik," "Pessi-
mismus," "Lokalkolorit," and a concluding
"Mark Twain in Spiegel der Kritik," which
summarizes the criticism of MT.

A18 STONE, ALBERT E., JR. The Innocent Eye:
Childhood in Mark Twain's Imagination. New
Haven: Yale University Press.
[Source: 1970 reprinting "in an unaltered
and unabridged edition," Hamden, Connecticut: Archon Books.] Placing MT in a context of the developing interest in childhood as a theme after the Civil War, reveals
his fascination with immaturity. Treats the
portrayal of childhood in TS, HF, JA, and
other works, distinguishing in the discussion
of CY between the kind of innocence that is
laudable and the kind that is merely a limitation. Pp. 153-58, dealing with HF, reprinted in Bradley (1962), pp. 444-48.

A19 WAGENKNECHT, EDWARD. Mark Twain: The Man and
His Work. Norman: University of Oklahoma
Press.
"A completely new and revised edition" of
the 1935 book, with a new bibliography drop-
ping entries which may readily be found in
LHUS and elsewhere, but also with some not
listed in the present bibliography.
Pp. 164-73 are reprinted as "Literature and
Love" in Leary (1962), pp. 301-310.

1961 B SHORTER WRITINGS

B1 ANDERSON, DAVID D. "Melville and Mark Twain in Rebellion," Mark Twain Journal, XI (Fall), 8-9.
On parallels between The Mysterious Stranger and The Confidence Man. Abstract in AES, V (1962), 1277.

B2 ANON. [Review: Gladys Brooks, Gramercy Park: Memories of a New York Girlhood (Dent).]. Times Literary Supplement, January 27, p. 54.
Book not seen. Reviewer notes that MT was a friend of the Brooks family [unrelated to Van Wyck Brooks]: "As the children ate their corned beef hash and codfish cakes he would prowl round the table talking on and on."

B3 ASSELINEAU, ROGER. [Review: E. Hudson Long, Mark Twain Handbook (1957), and Lewis Leary, Mark Twain 1960).] Études Anglaises, XIV (January-March), 83-84.
The full and accurate bibliographies following the chapters constitute an unequaled and valuable documentation, and the Handbook is marked by good sense and objectivity. Despite a greater emphasis on the biographical part of MT studies than is perhaps justified, the book gives a judicious choice of the superabundant literature on MT and it will be indispensable for the student of MT; its inadequacies are the inadequacies of the existing criticism itself. Lewis Leary gives a very good description of the work of MT and sensibly refuses to see a great thinker in him. [In French.]

B4 BABCOCK, C. MERTON. "Mark Twain: A Heretic in Heaven," ETC: A Review of General Semantics, XVIII (July), 189-96.
On "Mark Twain's concern for facts and judgments, and for the tendency of people to confuse the two"; notes MT's own "semantic sophistication." Abstract in AES, V (1962), 744; reprinted in Twainian, XXII (January-February, 1963).

B5 BAETZHOLD, HOWARD G. "'The Autobiography of Sir Robert Smith of Camelot': Mark Twain's Original Plan for A Connecticut Yankee," American Literature, XXXII (January), 456-61.
Reprints accounts from New York newspapers of MT's reading an early version of the first three chapters before the Military Service Institute, November 11, 1886; the conception of the book changed sharply thereafter, and the discovery of this early fragment supports the conjecture by John B. Hoben in 1946 that MT broke off his composition at this point. Abstract in AES, IV (1961), 709; reprinted in Twainian, XXI (January-February, 1962).

B6 _____. "The Course of Composition of A Connecticut Yankee: A Reinterpretation," American Literature, XXXIII (May), 195-214.
John B. Hoben (1946) and Fred W. Lorch (1958) "have contributed important insights into the genesis of A Connecticut Yankee. But new evidence--unpublished materials in the Mark Twain Papers and in the Berg Collection of the New York Public Library...suggests a reassessment of the shaping forces" and chronology; Baetzhold lists a number of literary sources apparently not previously noted. Abstract in AES, V (1962), 1824; reprinted in Twainian, XXII (January-February, 1963).

B7 *BARUCCA, PRIMO. "Mark Twain e l'Italia," La Fiera Letteraria, XVI (May 21), 4.
[Source: AES, IV (1961), 1828; reprinted in Twainian, XXI (January-February, 1962).] Cites Agostino Lombardo's comment on IA as a pessimistic contrast to The Marble Faun: MT sees tradition, conformity, and the past as destructive.

B8 BELL, NEIL. "Mark Twain's Joan of Arc," Mark Twain Journal, XI (Fall), 4-6.
Personal response to MT's treatment of the story. Abstract in AES, V (1962), 1274.

B9 BOOTH, WAYNE C. The Rhetoric of Fiction. Chicago and London: The University of Chicago Press.
Very brief comments on Huck Finn as a narrator, passim (indexed).

B10 BOWDEN, EDWIN T. The Dungeon of the Heart: Human Isolation and the American Novel. New York: The Macmillan Company, pp. 30-43 and passim.
Huck is detached, but sympathetic, and has a deep sense of ethics (p. 35). He gradually comes to form a commitment to Jim.

B11 BRITTAIN, SIR HARRY. "My Friend Mark Twain," Mark Twain Journal, XI (Fall), 1-3.
On MT's 1907 visit to England. Abstract in AES, V (1962), 1273.

B12 BROWNE, RAY B. "Mark Twain and Captain Wakeman," American Literature, XXXIII (November), 320-29.
On Edgar ("Ned") Wakeman, whom MT first met in 1866 and who served as a model for the hero in Captain Stormfield's Visit to Heaven and less familiar works by MT; based in part on 1878 California newspaper material and on The Log of an Ancient Mariner, Being the Life and Adventures of Captain Edgar Wakeman, Written by Himself and Edited by His Daughter [Minnie Wakeman-Curtis], (San Francisco, 1878). Abstract in AES, V (1962), 1831, reprinted in Twainian, XXII (January-February, 1963).

B13 *BURHANS, CLINTON S., JR. "Mark Twain's View of History," Papers of the Michigan Academy of Science, Arts and Letters, XLVI, 617-27.
On the conflict between his belief in progress and his view of history as repetitious and decadent. [Source: MHRA Annual Bibliography (1961), No. 5268, and abstract in AES, IV (1961), 2712; reprinted in Twainian, XXI (January-February, 1962).]

B14 CARPENTER, KENNETH E. "An Unrecorded Mark Twain," Papers of the Bibliographical Society of America, LV (Third Quarter), 236-39; reprinted Twainian, XXI (January-February, 1962), 3-4.
The first appearance of "The Czar's Soliloquy" in book form was an eight-page pamphlet, in Russian translation, published in Geneva by the Socialist Revolutionary Party, 1905. Abstract in AES, V (1962), 843; reprinted in Twainian, XXII (January-February, 1963).

B15 CARSTENSEN, BRODER. "The Adventures of Huckleberry Finn: Die Problematik des Schlusses," Neueren Sprachen, XII (December), 541-51.
Explains the weak ending of HF in terms of MT's use of his unfinished novel, The Mysterious Chamber, also dealing with a prisoner. [In German]. Abstract in AES, V (1962), 1105; reprinted in Twainian, XXII (January-February, 1963); article reprinted in 1968.B19.

B16 CLEMENS, SAMUEL L. "A Boston Girl," Harper's, CCXXII (June), 52-53.
Text of an MT reply to a letter criticizing his grammar. Followed by a brief note by Charles Neider: "This article was published anonymously in the June, 1880 issue of The Atlantic Monthly.... The article, which is slightly cut here, will be published next fall in my new collection, Life as I Find It." Abstract in AES, VIII (1965), 2004; reprinted in Twainian, XXV (January-February, 1966).

B17 COLTON, HAROLD S[ELLERS]. "Mark Twain's Literary Dilemma and Its Sequel," Arizona Quarterly, XVII (Autumn), 229-32.
The author's great-uncle, George Escol Sellers, was a businessman and mechanical engineer; an attempt to raise money in Philadelphia to build up a coal industry at Sellers Landing, Illinois was unsuccessful because people thought he was the prototype for the impractical Colonel Escol Sellers of The Gilded Age. He was said to have received the middle name "Escol" because on the night he was born, his father dreamed of four men carrying a large bunch of grapes, recalling the brook of Eschol (Numbers XIII:23). Abstract in AES, V (1962), 4; reprinted in Twainian, XXII (January-February, 1963).

B18 COX, JAMES M. "Walt Whitman, Mark Twain, and the Civil War," Sewanee Review, LXIX (Spring), 185-204.
"Mark Twain's Civil War was never the historical Civil War but an emotional equivalent of that war in which Mark Twain was perpetually involved as he created for himself and for his nation an image of the past which could contain the war instead of being destroyed by it," but for MT the cost "was ultimately to be overtaken by the chaos of the inner war that all the stratagems and evasions of humor, burlesque, and parody could not resolve." He was the novelist--or poet-- of Reconstruction, "for in Huckleberry Finn he brought not the old south but an entirely new south back into the Union." Abstract in AES, XI (1968), 1563; reprinted in Twainian, XXVIII (January-February, 1969).

B19 CUMMINGS, SHERWOOD. "What's in Huckleberry Finn?" English Journal, L (January), 1-8.
An analysis geared to teaching in high school. Students are accustomed to television dramas in which the moral values are clear and nothing is left to inference; but MT tells the story through Huck, who himself is unaware of what MT is implying. The two major themes are Huck's rejection of society and his struggle with his conscience. Abstract in AES, V (1962), 1479; reprinted in Twainian, XXII (January-February, 1963).

B20 DAHL, CURTIS. "Mark Twain and the Moving Panoramas," American Quarterly, XIII (Spring), 20-32.
MT must have seen the moving panoramas in his youth; he had "a primarily visual imagination...absorbed much of their technique into his writing," and the fact helps explain both the defective structure of his works and their vitality. There were panoramas of the Mississippi, and of journeys to the West and to Europe and the Near East, with subclasses depicting the Gold Rush, Classical antiquity, and the Holy Land, all of which have parallels in MT's writings. In such set-pieces as the description of Lake Tahoe in Chapter XXIII of Roughing It "one can practically see the changing diorama and hear the lecturer's spiel." Abstract in AES, V (1962), 1173.

B21 [DAVIS, CHESTER L.] "The Adventures of Huckleberry Finn (annotated)," Twainian, XX (September-October), 3-4.
Praises the footnotes of the edition of HF incorporated in the current The American Tradition in Literature edited by Sculley Bradley, Richard Croome Beatty, and E. Hudson Long (New York: W. W. Norton).

B22 _____. "Twentieth Year of 'The Twainian' Begins: Review of Shrine accomplishment," Twainian, XX (January-February), 1-4.

([DAVIS, CHESTER L.])
A chatty reminiscence of the Mark Twain Research Foundation and the Shrine at MT's birthplace in Florida, Missouri. Reproduces text of a feature story by Jack Rice in the St. Louis Post-Dispatch of May 22, drawing heavily on an interview with Davis on the same topic and quoting him on the policy concerning use of unpublished material: "I don't show notes that haven't been printed in the Twainian, Keeps up the interest." Also reprints article by Davis in the Perry (Missouri) Enterprise on the Foundation and Memorial Park (June 23, apparently paid for as an advertisement).

B23   DICKINSON, LEON T. [Review: Daniel Morley McKeithan, Court Trials in Mark Twain, and Other Essays (1958).] English Studies (Amsterdam), XLII, 325-27.
A disappointing treatment of a promising topic, this consists mostly of summaries with little analysis or commentary. The other essays in the book, reprinted from journals, "pinpoint specific borrowings" from various sources, but might be enriched if the critical comment were more extensive.

B24   DYSON, A. E. "Huckleberry Finn and the Whole Truth," Critical Quarterly, III (Spring), 29-40; reprinted in his The Crazy Fabric: Exercises in Irony (New York: St. Martin's Press, 1965), pp. 96-111.
Argues against simplistic readings: for example, there is not a simple contrast between corrupt society and virtuous outsiders, since "the Duke, the King, and Huck's father...are all far further away from the 'respectable' folk than Huck himself is," and they "are all failures, who stand outside society...simply because they are lazy, vicious, and by nature parasitic." In contrast, the respectable people do not wholly lack the virtues embodied in Huck and Jim. The disputed ending of the story is consistent with "the logic and texture of the whole book," in that "actual human progress does come about...through muddled insights, muddled kindliness, muddled actions as much as from the straightforward vindication of ideals." Abstract in AES, V (1962), 1443; reprinted in Twainian, XXII (January-February, 1963). Article reprinted from the 1965 book in Schmitter (1974), pp. 95-107.

B25   EASTMAN, MAX. "Mark Twain and Socialism," National Review, X (March 11), 154-55.
MT's "feelings toward the underprivileged and the working class were not sharply different from those of the socialists," but his "casual observation and shrewd common sense" kept him from embracing socialist doctrine. Abstract in AES, IV (1961), 1628; reprinted in Twainian, XXI (January-February, 1962).

B26   FERGUSON, DELANCEY. "Honorary Grandfather," New York Times Book Review (October 8), p. 22.
A review of Dorothy Quick's Enchantment: A Little Girl's Friendship with Mark Twain. The letters from MT make the book essential for every MT collector, and "it has genuine charm as a record of a friendship. But its essentials could have been conveyed in fewer pages."

B27   *FIGUERA, ANGELA. Tres Escritores Norteamericanos: Mark Twain, Henry James, Thomas Wolfe. Madrid: Gredos.
[Source: MHRA Annual Bibliography (1962), Nos. 5108, 5668.

B28   FLANAGAN, JOHN T. [Review: Henry Nash Smith and William M. Gibson, eds., The Mark Twain-Howells Letters (1960).] Journal of English and Germanic Philology, LX (April), 342-44.
The 680 surviving letters, written over 41 years, cover the range of literary, business, and personal matters. "Twain's letters, as might be expected, are more charged with spirit and show the wider emotional range." The editing is impeccable, but not obtrusive, making this a book for the scholar and the general reader.

B29   FRIEDMAN, ROBERT P. [Review: Paul Fatout, Mark Twain on the Lecture Circuit (1960).] Quarterly Journal of Speech, XLVII (April), 206-207.
A product of "diligent research and able writing," this book "corrects mistaken ideas and clarifies hazy aspects of Twain's lecture career"; it is "a genuine contribution."

B30   FRIEDRICH, GERHARD. [Brief Review: Brashear and Rodney, eds., The Art, Humor, and Humanity of Mark Twain (1959).] Books Abroad, XXXV (Autumn), 389.
"An entertaining assortment."

B31   GERBER, JOHN C. [Review: Franklin R. Rogers, Mark Twain's Burlesque Patterns.] Modern Language Notes, LXXVI (December), 902-904.
"Unfortunately, while this is a helpful work, it is not a great one. And in some respects it is not even a very good one." There are "oversimplifications," "strained connections," "an oppressive over-use of awkward terms," and "unconvincing conclusions." "More fundamentally, the book is weakened by a procedure that hardens into a routine and by a conclusion that comes much too soon."

B32   HAMBLEN, ABIGAIL ANN. "Uncle Tom and 'Nigger Jim': A Study in Contrasts and Similarities," Mark Twain Journal, XI (Fall), 13-17.
"Because of lack of opportunity for development, Jim's mentality and his moral nature cannot be matched with those of Uncle Tom," but the two slaves are similar in loyalty and in the loyalty and love they inspire in the white people around them. Abstract in AES, V (1962), 1279.

B33 HEYM, STEFAN. [Introduction.] King Leopold's Soliloquy, New York: International Publishers, and Berlin (D.D.R), Seven Seas Books, pp. 11-26.

   The booklet is an East German reprinting of the 1906 edition of the pamphlet MT wrote for the Congo Reform Association; the contemporary illustrations are supplemented by nine pages of photographs showing Patrice Lumumba, the United Nations debate on the Congo, a shooting in Leopoldville, a school and shanties in the Congo, etc. Heym's introduction emphasizes MT's social criticism, his understanding of imperialism based on what he had seen, since although "he knew Gorki...he did not know Lenin or Lenin's thoughts on the subject." In his pamphlet MT shows his customary discipline in his craft, even though he feels strongly: "Mark Twain the artist remains an artist even when a propagandist."

B34 HIGHFILL, PHILIP H., JR. "Incident in Huckleberry Finn," Mark Twain Journal, XI (Fall), 6.

   When Huck was revealed as a boy in girl's clothes when he clapped his knees together to catch a lump of lead (Chapter XI), MT could have been following an English source "in the grab-bag of scholarly argument, ana, and country custom called Literary Anecdotes...Of Professor Porson and Others; from the Manuscript Papers of the Late E. H. Barker...London, 1852 (Anecdote No. CCXXXIV The Two Thieves, p. 282)." Abstract in AES, V (1962), 1276.

B35 HILL, HAMLIN. "The Composition and Structure of Tom Sawyer," American Literature, XXXII (January), 379-92. Reprinted in Twainian, XX (May-June), 1-4.

   After briefly summarizing the views of Blair, Wecter, Gladys Bellamy, E. H. Long, Ferguson, Cowie, and Asselineau, cites the manuscript at Georgetown University, as "convincing evidence to corroborate Blair's interpretation of the book" as a structured account of a boy's maturation. Abstract in AES, IV (1961), 702.

B36 _____. "Mark Twain's Book Sales, 1869-1879," Bulletin of the New York Public Library, LXV (June), 371-89.

   Elisha Bliss published MT's works through the American Publishing Company during this period. His shrewd (and occasionally unscrupulous) promotion of MT's books, sold by subscription, contributed to the sale of 337,902 volumes in the 1870's; MT's books continued to sell over the years, in contrast with most subscription books, which became unmarketable after a year. Sales of Sketches New and Old were disappointing, and sales of TS still more so; TA was more successful, but MT switched to a new publisher, James R. Osgood, who had no experience in subscription publishing and botched the sales of P&P and LOM. Abstract in AES,

VI (1964), 718; reprinted in Twainian, XXIII (January-February, 1964).

B37 _____. "Mark Twain's 'Brace of Brief Lectures on Science,'" New England Quarterly, XXXIV (June), 228-39.

   Reprints for the first time the text of MT's "A Brace of Brief Lectures on Science," which appeared in The American Publisher (edited by his brother, Orion) in September and October, 1971 as "I. Paleontology" and "II. Paleontology Concluded--Primeval Man." They reveal a shifting tone: "How is it possible to explain the somewhat forced and repetitious irony of the first half, the rollicking burlesque of the second half, and the apologia in the last paragraph?" The answer may lie in a "conflict between propriety and personal opinion, which caused both the unusual attitude toward science and the mixture of comic techniques." Abstract in AES, IV (1961) 1944; reprinted in Twainian, XXI (January-February, 1962).

B38 _____. [Review: Franklin R. Rogers, Mark Twain's Burlesque Patterns as Seen in the Novels and Narratives 1855-1885 (1960.] Prairie Schooner, XXXV (March), 8-9.

   "In spite of minor points of argument, I think Mr. Rogers' skillful tracing of the dominent structural patterns in Twain's major works from Innocents Abroad through Huckleberry Finn, benefitted by the examination of hitherto unpublished Twain materials, is a major achievement and a cohesive analysis that cannot be ignored by future Twain scholars."

B39 HOFFMAN, DANIEL. "Mark Twain," in his Form and Fable in American Fiction (London and New York: Oxford University Press).

   On pp. 317-42, "Black Magic--and White-- in Huckleberry Finn," showing three attitudes toward life, indicated in supernatural terms: both "the conventional piety of the villagers" and "the irrelevant escape of the romantic imagination" are "morally inadequate," but "the third--which pays homage to the river god--gives dignity to human life" through the world of supernatural omens understood by Jim; Jim, too, undergoes growth in the story. This article is a complete revision of "Jim's Magic: Black or White?" (1960.B58). This 1961 revision is reprinted in part in Bradley (1962), pp. 396-409; Leary (1962), pp. 311-334; Smith (1963), pp. 101-11. On pp. 343-50, "Huckleberry Finn: His Masquerade," on his disguises, his several identities, and his problem of preserving his essential self. In the end, as in the beginning, his only safety lies in flight.

B40 HOWARD, ROBERT WEST. "The Mark Twain Story," Twainian, XX (July-August), 1-4.

   A popular account of MT's life, reprinted from the house organ (name not given) of the Inland Steel Company (Summer, 1961); emphasizes the significance of the Middle West in

(HOWARD, ROBERT WEST)
shaping him. Abstract in AES, VII (1964), 1573.

B41 *KAMEI, SHUNSUKE. "On Interpretations of The Adventures of Huckleberry Finn," Comparative Literature and Comparative Culture (1961).
[Source: Kamei, Shunsuke, "Mark Twain in Japan," Mark Twain Journal, XII (Spring), 20.]

B42 KENDALL, LYLE H., JR. "The Walter Scott Episode in Huckleberry Finn," Nineteenth-Century Fiction, XVI (December), 279-81.
The organization of Huckleberry Finn is based on "Huck's emancipation, from Pap Finn, from the King and the Duke, and from Tom Sawyer's darkly humorous influence." In the cabin Pap had called Huck the "Angel of Death," and this is "precisely what Huck becomes on board the Walter Scott six chapters later." Kendall identifies Pap Finn with "Old Hatfield," murdered by Jim Turner, and "ironically, Pap Finn's evil existence is to be closed out by Huck's exacting retribution for his father's murder" as Huck strands the robbers on the wrecked steamboat. Abstract in AES, V (1962), 818; reprinted in Twainian, XXII (January-February, 1963).

B43 LAKIN, R. D. "Mark Twain and the Cold War," Midwest Quarterly, II (January), 159-67.
Summarizes the debate between Charles Neider and Yan Bereznitsky, of the Russian Literary Gazette, as published in Neider's Mark Twain and the Russians (1960); both reflect the conventional thinking of their societies, and MT himself would feel out of place in either camp. Abstract in AES, VIII (1965), 1665; reprinted in Twainian, XXV (January-February, 1966).

B44 LAVIGNE, GARY W. "The Day Mark Twain Came to Geneseo, New York," Twainian, XX (November-December), 1-4.
MT was originally scheduled to give his "American Vandals in the Old World" lecture on February 18, 1869, but an error in booking caused a delay until March 1. LaVigne's account draws partly on local sources and partly on such familiar material as letters to Livy and to Mrs. Fairbanks. Abstract in AES, VII (1964), 1577.

B45 LEARY, LEWIS. "Mark Twain at Barnard College." Columbia Library Columns, X (May), 12-17.
About MT as "the belle of New York," speaking before women's college groups in the spring of 1906. According to an editor's note the article is an expansion of material collected by Leary for his edition of Mark Twain's Letters to Mary.

B46 LONG, E. HUDSON. "Tom Sawyer's 'Pitchiola,'" Twainian, XX (September-October), 4.
When the captive Jim was urged in Chapter XXXVII of HF to raise a flower, MT's source was Picciola; the Prisoner of Fenestrella, or Captivity Captive, by Joseph Xavier Saintine (pseudonym for Boniface), 1798-1865.

B47 _____. [Review: Walter Blair, Mark Twain & Huck Finn (1960.] American Literature, XXXII (January), 467-68.
Blair "has apparently neglected nothing in the way of published material, and the minute notes testify that he has been equally thorough in using available manuscripts. His book is a storehouse of information, all of it based on sound, documented evidence," and "furnishes a perceptive account of Samuel Clemens the creative artist from 1876 through 1883"; it is a "major contribution to our knowledge of Mark Twain as a man and writer."

B48 _____. [Review: Milton Meltzer, Mark Twain Himself (1960).] American Quarterly, XIII (Fall), 438-39.
This is "an informative pictorial biography of Samuel Clemens" and of his times, 1835-1910, in which Meltzer lets MT tell his own story, setting the record straight where necessary. The information is accurate, and "the more than six hundred illustrations will attract anyone interested in photography."

B49 LORCH, FRED W. [Review: Henry Nash Smith and William M. Gibson, eds., Mark Twain-Howells Letters (1960).] American Literature, XXXIII (March), 78-80.
This is "a superb job of editing" 681 notes and letters, 385 of them previously unpublished.

B50 LOWE, WILLIAM J. "The Mountain Shakes," College English, XXIII (October), 62-63.
Eric Solomon (1960.B104) and Carson Gibb (1960.B49) in their investigations of HF "are trying to bolster the weak ending of a fine novel with materials drawn from today's frame of reference"--MT was tired when he wrote it, and modern psychology and portraits of Tom as a modern playboy are inappropriate to a novel of an earlier age. In a brief rebuttal, Carson Gibb says that Lowe's premise would reduce literature of the past to mere relics. Abstract in AES, V (1962), 731; reprinted in Twainian, XXII (January-February, 1963).

B51 *LYDENBERG, JOHN. "American Novelists in Search of a Lost World," Revue des Langues Vivantes, XXVII, 306-21.
MT is one of a number of American authors discussed in an essay dealing with the theme of loss, betrayal, and vain searching. [Source: Abstract in AES, IX (1966), 2407; reprinted in Twainian, XXVI (January-February, 1967).]

B52 LYNN, KENNETH S. [Review: Franklin R. Rogers, Mark Twain's Burlesque Patterns: As Seen in the Novels and Narratives 1855-1885 (1960).] American Literature, XXXIII (November), 384-86.

A witty review, depicting contemporary criticism of MT as "that age-old American struggle between the Dandies and the Squatters" [the terms are taken from an 1852 sketch by MT]; the former show imagination but "a tendency to be carried away by their theories, especially the psychological variety," and the latter work hard but launch few speculative flights with their ideas. The Rogers book reflects patient research but "considerable faults," including a "failure to deal with A Connecticut Yankee, surely the most interesting of Twain's major works from the point of view of burlesque. But its main flaw is its Squatterishness.... The best one can say for Mark Twain's Burlesque Patterns is that it may well prove useful to more imaginative critics."

B53 McELDERRY, B[RUCE] R., JR. "Who Was Sarah Findlay?" Twainian, XX (September-October), 3.

On a rare pamphlet by that title, "By Mark Twain, with a Suggested Solution of the Mystery by J. M. Barrie. London: Privately Printed by Clement Shorter, April 1917." Contains an MT letter to the London Daily Chronicle (written November 18, 1896, but not printed) chiding Barrie for failure to protect his books by copyright in America; the "Sarah Findlay" name was invented by Barrie to substitute for a real one in an MT inscription quoted from a copy of HF.

B54 McKEITHAN, D. M. "The Morgan Manuscript of The Man that Corrupted Hadleyburg," Texas Studies in Literature and Language, II (Winter), 476-80.

The autograph MS in the Pierpont Morgan Library in New York reveals that at the outset MT was uncertain concerning his trap to catch the leading citizens; "The fact that nearly all the revisions concerned details of plot points to one other conclusion: that whenever Twain had clearly in mind what he wanted to say, the style and diction in the first draft were so excellent that few changes were necessary." Abstract in AES, VII (1964), 1240.

B55 MALIN, IRVING. "Mark Twain: The Boy as Artist," Literature and Psychology, XI (Summer), 78-84.

MT's "fiction is boyish and incomplete" because "he does not face squarely the emotional patterns which are involved" in his treatment of "authoritarianism and rebellion in the family and outside." Bixby and Brown in LOM, and Jim and Pap in HF, represent good and bad fathers, and an ambivalent view on MT's part. In CY, the Boss is "a good, powerful father-image for the dark ages." PW, like CY, "is a cruel book written by an immature author," and in Hadleyburg and MS "we enter a new world, where we meet the triumphant bad father." As Americans we have made MT, with his hatred and love of power, "a national father after all. Perhaps some day we will grow up." Abstract in AES, V (1962), 1978; reprinted in Twainian, XXII (January-February, 1963).

B56 MENDELSON, M. O. "Mark Twain's Unpublished Literary Heritage," Soviet Review: A Journal of Translations, II (September), 33-53.

"An authority on Mark Twain takes his literary executors to task for allowing a significant part of Twain's literary heritage to remain unpublished. Izvestia Akademii Nauk SSR, Otdeleniye Literatury i Yazyka (Bulletin of the USSR Academy of Sciences, Literature and Languages Section), 1961, Vol. XX, No. 1." Abstract in AES, V (1962), 872; reprinted in Twainian, XXII (January-February, 1963).

B57 MICHAELSON, L. W. "Four Emmeline Grangerfords," Mark Twain Journal, XI (Fall), 10-12.

Possible literary models for the "Ode to Stephen Dowling Bots, Dec'd" In Chapter XVII of Huckleberry Finn are in the poetry of Julia A. Moore, Bloodgood H. Cutter, William McGonagall (1830-189?), and Seba Smith. Abstract in AES, V (1962), 1278.

B58 MILLGATE, MICHAEL. [Review: Lewis Leary, Mark Twain (1960) and Henry Nash Smith and William M. Gibson, eds., Mark Twain-Howells Letters (1960).] Modern Language Review, LVI (July), 417-18.

Leary's University of Minnesota pamphlet is "a pleasant introduction to Mark Twain's work." The MT-Howells letters are well-edited, not all of them important in their own right but valuable as a collection that adds to our understanding of the men and their times; their publication enhances the stature of Howells as friend and critic, although MT's letters are the more lively.

B59 MILLER, WALLACE C. "Mark Twain's Account of the Goodman-Fitch Duel," Twainian, XX (September-October), 1-2; reprinted from Nevada Historical Society Quarterly, II, No. 3, "The Back Number" (unexplained, and year, pp. not given).

MT's account of the duel between Joseph T. Goodman and Thomas S. Fitch is given as reprinted in Myron Angel, ed., History of Nevada (Oakland: Thompson and West, 1881) and in a fuller reprint from the Sacramento Union, "probably copied word for word from the Enterprise." Abstract in AES, VII (1964), 1574.

B60   MONTIERO, GEORGE. "A Note on the Mark Twain-
       Whitelaw Reid Relationship," Emerson Society
       Quarterly, XIX (Second Quarter, 1960), 20-21.
         MT dropped his plans to write a hostile
       biography of Reid after deciding he had
       erred in thinking that the New York Tribune
       had been campaigning against him in late
       1881; moreover, the Tribune had printed a
       long, enthusiastic review by Howells of The
       Prince and the Pauper on October 25, 1881.
       MT's hostility toward Reid would not have
       cooled if he had known that the editorial
       decision to print the Howells review was
       made independently by John Hay, despite a
       letter from Reid expressing disapproval on
       the ground that "it isn't good journalism
       to let a warm personal friend & in some
       matters literary partner, write a review of
       him in a paper wh. [sic] has good reason
       to think little of his delicacy and highly
       of his greed." Abstract in AES, IV (1960),
       2610; reprinted in Twainian, XXI (January-
       February, 1962).

B61   MOSER, CHARLES A. "A Nihilist's Career:
       S. M. Kravchinskij," American Slavic and
       East European Review, XX (February), 56-71.
         Contains a brief reference to MT's sup-
       port for an appeal expressing sympathy with
       the cause of a Russian revolution
       (pp. 68-69).

B62   MUELLER, HAROLD L. "Mark Twain's Stormfield
       Days" [title appears as "The Stormfield-
       Redding Library" on p. 1], Twainian, XX
       (March-April), 3-4.
         On MT's pleasure in the Redding, Connec-
       ticut home where he passed his last years,
       and the part he played in founding a town
       library. As the Mark Twain Library, the
       institution now houses a rich collection of
       portraits and memorabilia. "Among the
       2,000-odd books that Twain gave are hundreds
       that are autographed. Some are distin-
       guished with marginal markings and nota-
       tions, underlinings, exclamation points,
       question marks, and pages turned-down at
       the corners. In some are bits of tobacco
       spilled from the pipe he smoked as he read
       them at Stormfield or elsewhere." Abstract
       in AES, VII (1964), 1572.

B63   PARSONS, COLEMAN O. "Mark Twain in Australia,"
       Antioch Review, XXI (Winter), 455-68.
         Traces the itinerary of MT's lecture tour
       from September 16, 1895-January 4, 1896,
       and quotes speeches and interviews (without
       dates) in which MT commented in general
       terms on his works, criticized prohibition
       and Bret Harte, and praised Australia for
       having the modern conveniences. Abstract
       in AES, VIII (1965), 602; reprinted in
       Twainian, XXV (January-February, 1966).

B64   PICKETT, CALDER M. "Mark Twain as Journalist
       and Literary Man: A Contrast," Journalism
       Quarterly, XXXVIII (Winter), 59-66.

       "A comparison of Samuel Clemens' Holy Land
       letters for newspaper publication and The
       Innocents Abroad shows a transition from
       journalist to literary writer, and recogni-
       tion of his larger and differing audience"
       (headnote). Shows a number of the changes
       made, and notes that IA reveals not only
       more restraint, but also an increase in the
       amount and the sophistication of the humor.

B65   PIZER, DONALD. "Late Nineteenth-Century Real-
       ism: An Essay in Definition," Nineteenth-
       Century Fiction, XVI (December), 263-69.
         The realism discussed is diverse in sub-
       ject matter and "ethically idealistic.
       Three texts will illustrate my thesis:
       Howells' The Rise of Silas Lapham (1885),
       Twain's Adventures of Huckleberry Finn
       (1884), and James's What Maisie Knew (1897)."
       In the first two books "the social world is
       the embodiment of evil," and the latter two
       "juxtapose a child and an evil world....
       The three writers...dramatize a vision of
       experience in which individuals achieve that
       which is still a goal for mankind at large."
       Abstract in AES, V (1962), 815.

B66   POCHMANN, HENRY A. [Review: Caroline Thomas
       Harnsberger, Mark Twain: Family Man (1960).]
       American Literature, XXXIII (March), 86-87.
         The 20,000 words of previously unpublished
       material will give this book "a place of
       modest importance among students of Mark
       Twain," but "the documentation is inadequate"
       and "the author's too feminine and domestic
       point of view" is irritating. Because MT's
       daughter Clara was a prime source of infor-
       mation she tends to become a major concern
       of the book, but her "reminiscences...are
       germane and of prime importance. Herein lies
       the book's essential worth."

B67   _____. [Review: Arlin Turner, Mark Twain and
       George W. Cable: The Record of a Literary
       Friendship (1960).] American Literature,
       XXXIII (May), 233-34.
         Turner's editing of these MT-Cable letters
       "is faultless. The interchapters and notes,
       supplying relevant facts and continuity,
       make an interesting and complete chapter in
       the lives of both men" and commentary on the
       audience.

B68   POLI, BERNARD. [Review: Blair, Mark Twain &
       Huck Finn (1960) and Rogers, Mark Twain's
       Burlesque Patterns (1960).] Étude Anglaises,
       XIV (April-June), 175-76.
         Blair's is a basic book for the special-
       ist, written with the inflexible objectiv-
       ity of the historian; but, although we
       doubtless know MT better after this "gi-
       gantesque autopsie d'un chef-d'oeuvre," we
       may not always be sufficiently aware of
       the distance Huck always kept between him-
       self and "Mr. Mark Twain." The "excellent
       study of literary technique" by Franklin
       Rogers might nonetheless take more note of
       the part improvisation and fantasy played
       in MT's art. [In French.]

1961 - Shorter Writings

B69   POWER, WILLIAM. "Huck Finn's Father," Uni-
       versity of Kansas City Review, XXVIII (Win-
       ter), 83-94.
            "Mark Twain minimizes, even conceals, the
       force of Huck's animus against his father,"
       who "is responsible for Huck's moral dev-
       elopment"; "Huck's strength, finally, is
       Finn's." Abstract in AES, V (1962), 446;
       reprinted in Twainian, XXII (January-Feb-
       ruary, 1963).

B70   REYES, PEDRO A., JR. "A Difference of Gram-
       mar," Diliman Review (University of the
       Philippines, Quezon City), IX (January),
       117-23.
            Comparing HF with Joyce's A Portrait of
       the Artist as a Young Man, finds "the state-
       ment of revolt in different grammars," with
       Huck's "WE" contrasted to Stephen's inward-
       turning "I."

B71   RUBIN, LOUIS D., JR., and JOHN REES MOORE, eds.
       The Idea of an American Novel. New York:
       Thomas Y. Crowell Company.
            Passim on MT (indexed); on pp. 258-72,
       reprints statements on him by Howells, Sher-
       wood Anderson, Van Wyck Brooks, Henry Nash
       Smith, and Lionel Trilling; these are ex-
       tracts from material generally available
       in the original publications (listed in the
       present bibliography), and for this reason
       they are not here cross-referenced.

B72   SALOMON, ROGER R. "Escape from History: Mark
       Twain's Joan of Arc," Philological Quarter-
       ly, XL (January), 77-90.
            Like others of the eighteenth and nine-
       teenth centuries, MT substituted faith in
       history for faith in God, but what he saw
       of man and "the oligarchic and imperialist-
       ic drift of America" made his "a tenuous
       faith--tormented by a dream of freedom and
       innocence outside the grip of time." For
       this reason, A Connecticut Yankee is "ul-
       timately an artistic failure because of its
       ambivalence," and "Joan of Arc can be most
       fruitfully examined as a final, desperate
       attempt to establish values apart from the
       futile treadmill of sin and suffering which
       was the life of man on earth." Although MT
       took essentially a Catholic view of Joan,
       he wrote "a deeply pessimistic book. If it
       is an affirmation of the existence and pow-
       er of innocence, it is also a scathing rec-
       ord of its betrayal." Abstract in AES, IV
       (1961), 1944; reprinted in Twainian, XXI
       (January-February, 1962).

B73   SCHULMAN, IVAN A. "José Martí and Mark Twain:
       A Study of Literary Sponsorship," Symposium:
       A Quarterly Journal in Modern Literatures,
       XV (Summer), 105-13.
            The Cuban poet of the modernista period
       "first popularized the literary productions
       of Samuel L. Clemens throughout the Spanish-
       speaking world. There is even evidence to
       believe that Martí may have been the first

to disseminate the popular humorist's name
in Spanish literary circles." He admired MT
as stylist and satirist, and praised a number of his books, among them A Connecticut
Yankee, which he compared to Don Quixote.
In a footnote (p. 112, n. 5) Schulman reports that "Our investigations failed to un-
cover a single study on Twain by outstanding
Spanish American writers who might conceivably have been acquainted with his work,
either because they lived in the United
States for a period of time or because they
were familiar with our culture and literature" during this period. Schulman lists a
few articles on MT, including one by the
poet Rubén Darío, who commented on the limited awareness of MT in the Spanish-speaking
world. Abstract in AES, V (1962), 2144;
reprinted in Twainian, XXII (January-February, 1963).

B74   SCOTT, WINFIELD TOWNLEY. "Mark Twain Revisit-
       ed," New York Times Book Review (December 3),
       p. 48.
            A review of Lewis Leary, ed., Mark Twain's
       Letters to Mary (the letters are of minor
       importance, but "Leary has surrounded them
       with a knowledgeable account of the last of
       Mark Twain's decades") and Albert E. Stone,
       Jr.'s The Innocent Eye: Childhood in Mark
       Twain's Imagination ("a model of what such
       academic work should be...its subject is of
       genuine importance, it is analyzed with
       great intelligence," Stone has done exten-
       sive research, "and--Heaven be praised--he
       writes well").

B75   SMITH, HENRY NASH. "The Backwoods Bull in the
       Boston China Shop," American Heritage, XII
       (August), 32-33, 108-12.
            A popular account of MT's disastrous Whit-
       tier Birthday Dinner speech of December 17,
       1877; illustrated with a full-page color
       reproduction of the Carroll Beckwith por-
       trait of MT, now in the Hartford house.
       The text of MT's speech introducing Winston
       Churchill to an audience at the Waldorf As-
       toria, December 12, 1900 is printed for the
       first time.

B76   _____. "Mark Twain on Tour," New York Herald
       Tribune Book Review, XXXVII (April 23), 32.
            A review of Charles Neider, ed., The Trav-
       els of Mark Twain. "Given the inexorable
       limitations of space, the selections are
       sensible enough."

B77   _____. "Mr. Clemens to 'Niece,'" New York
       Herald Tribune Book Review, XXXVII (May 21),
       27.
            A review of Lewis Leary, ed., Mark Twain's
       Letters to Mary. "The letters to Mary Rog-
       ers hold little interest for the student of
       his literary career. But the biographical
       interest is high."

B78 STEWART, PAUL R. [Review: Kenneth S. Lynn, ed., "Huckleberry Finn": Text, Sources, and Criticism]. College English, XXIII (October), 70.
   A brief, harsh notice: there is little justification for the book, and "the collateral materials are too thin and spotty."

B79 STONE, ALBERT E., JR. "Mark Twain and the Story of the Hornet," Yale University Library Gazette, XXXV (April), 141-57.
   While traveling in the Sandwich Islands as a correspondent for the Sacramento Union, MT had the opportunity to interview the survivors of the clipper ship Hornet, which had burned at sea; he later rewrote the story for Harper's, and in 1899 published the account and described his own involvement in "My Debut as a Literary Person." In the writing he drew on the journals of the ship's captain, and accounts by two passengers, Samuel and Henry Ferguson. These journals, privately printed, have been given to the Yale Library, together with correspondence, including four unpublished letters from MT. Ferguson criticized MT for not having allowed him to edit the journal material before it appeared in Harper's: "What was published did do harm, I am informed, to one man of the party & caused great grief to another," and he asked that names be changed or deleted before the account was given the permanence of publication in a book.

B80 TANNER, TONY. "The Literary Children of James and Clemens," Nineteenth-Century Fiction, XVI (December), 205-18.
   MT used a boy, a first-person vernacular narrator, whose own bewilderedness produced moral clarity, but James used girls as protagonists, maintained his omniscience and ironic detachment, and "worked out a literary style...as far removed from the vernacular as possible"; there is "an increasing moral ambiguity in his work." James found innocence endearing, but to be outgrown, while MT "saw no dividend in the exchange of innocence for maturity." Abstract in AES, V (1962), 810; reprinted in Twainian, XXII (January-February, 1963).

B81 ____. "The Lost America--the Despair of Henry Adams and Mark Twain," Modern Age, V (Summer), 299-310.
   Their growing move toward despair "argues concurrence rather than coincidence.... this despair is in a slow process of incubation from their earliest work, and...it is finally hatched by the growing discords, conflicts, and problems of the age. It is not a despair of personal bereavement but of country--ultimately of man." Abstract in AES, IV (1961), 2387. Article reprinted in Smith (1963), pp. 159-74.

B82 ____. [Review: Charles Neider, ed., The Autobiography of Mark Twain (1960).] Critical Quarterly, III (Autumn), 284-85.
   Contains an appreciation of MT and concludes by thanking Neider "for bringing this work to the attention of the general reader in a form which will attract him," but criticizing "Neider's scissors and paste method which has wrenched the material into a pseudo-chronological sequence it was never intended to have in the first place."

B83 WALDRON, ELI. "Mark Twain: The World He Left Behind. Hannibal, Missouri Keeps the Great Writer's Reputation Alive, in Ways both Lovable and Weird," Holiday, XXX (July), 54-55, 72-75, 97-99.
   A popular account of a visit to Hannibal, Missouri; provides no new information, but is enlivened by sketches by Ronald Searle, two depicting MT.

B84 WALLACE, ROBERT D. "Mark Twain on the Great Lakes," Inland Seas, XVII (Fall), 181-86.
   On MT's lecturing in 1895 in Cleveland, Sault St. Marie, Mackinac, Petosky, and Duluth; documented from contemporary newspapers and Major J. B. Pond's Eccentricities of Genius (1900.B33). Abstract in AES, IX (1966), 792; reprinted in Twainian, XXVI (January-February, 1967).

B85 WARREN, LUCIAN C. "Mark Twain on the Income Tax," New York Times Magazine Section, (April 9), pp. 16, 69.
   A brief headnote on the history of the income tax, as introduction to a reprinting of MT's "A Mysterious Visit" from Sketches New and Old.

B86 WHITE, WILLIAM. "Mark Twain to the President of Indiana University," American Literature, XXXII (January), 460-63.
   Contains the text of a letter from William L. Bryan, asking whether a loved and admired author may "somehow sense the innumerable friendships which he has made?" MT's reply ("Mar 29/07," apparently not mailed) follows, speaking of the comfort of receiving such letters in his lonely old age. Abstract in AES, IV (1961), 710; reprinted in Twainian, XXI (January-February, 1962).

B87 *WIRZBERGER, KARL-HEINZ. [Review: Henry Nash Smith and William M. Gibson, eds., Mark Twain-Howells Letters (1960).] Zeitschrift für Anglistik und Amerikanistik, IX, 431-33.
   [Source: MHRA Annual Bibliography (1961), No. 4729.]

B88 WOUK, HERMAN. "Huck Finn Pumped Vigor into American Literature," Twainian, XX (November-December), 4; XXI (January-February, 1962), 4.

(WOUK, HERMAN)
Described by Chester Davis as "written as a special feature for the Associated Press. It appeared in the 'Sacramento Union,' issue of August 5, 1956." A general discussion, noting MT's chaotic structure and underlying strength. Abstract in AES, VII (1964), 1578.

1962 A BOOKS

A1   BLAIR, WALTER, ed. Selected Shorter Writings of Mark Twain. Boston: Houghton Mifflin Company (Riverside Editions.)
A comprehensive anthology, from the early writings to The Man that Corrupted Hadleyburg and The Mysterious Stranger. Blair's introduction is a substantial treatment of MT's literary career, the forces that shaped it, and the style and perspective he developed.

A2   BRADLEY, SCULLEY, RICHMOND CROOM BEATTY, and E. HUDSON LONG, eds. Samuel Langhorne Clemens, Adventures of Huckleberry Finn. An Annotated Text   Backgrounds and Sources. Essays in Criticism. New York: W. W. Norton & Company, Inc. (also copyrighted 1961).
A classroom casebook, with text of HF (including the "Raft Passage" from LOM), plus significant background and source material and excerpts from MT's autobiography, the Paine biography, etc. Also contains a valuable set of reprinted critical essays from periodicals and excerpted from books, all of which are listed in the present bibliography with cross-references to the reprinting here. The bibliography of primary and secondary material at the end is intelligently selective (it does not contain material not listed in the present bibliography).

A3   BUDD, LOUIS J. Mark Twain, Social Philosopher. Bloomington: Indiana University Press.
Approaches MT's social attitudes through his habit of taking interest in topical matters and personalities; emerges with view of him as essentially allied in politics with the business community and, more broadly, with nineteenth-century Liberalism and its commitment to rationalism and the doctrine of progress though he could sincerely appeal to romantic democracy; reviewers handled the book respectfully though several held it understated his ambivalences and his sympathies for the underdog.

A4   CLEMENS, CYRIL. Mark Twain and John F. Kennedy. Kirkwood, Missouri: Mark Twain Journal.
Consists of several letters from John F. Kennedy as Senator and later as President, thanking Cyril Clemens for honorary membership in the International Mark Twain Society, a complimentary life subscription to the Mark Twain Journal, and the gift of

Mark Twain and Dwight D. Eisenhower. There are also tributes to MT by Kennedy, Eisenhower, William Howard Taft, Herbert Hoover, and Harry S. Truman (previously published, for the most part). [4-page pamphlet.]

A5   CLEMENS, SAMUEL L. The Adventures of Tom Sawyer. Boston: Houghton Mifflin Company (Riverside Literature Series).
Includes a scholarly introduction by Walter Blair well directed toward younger readers, and stimulating "Suggestions for Reading and Discussion" by Frank Townsend.

A6   _____. Letters from the Earth, ed. Bernard DeVoto, with a Preface by Henry Nash Smith. New York and Evanston: Harper & Row, Publishers.
Consists of a section of writings on Biblical themes and a section of shorter pieces and The Great Dark. This book was edited by DeVoto in 1939, but MT's daughter Clara witheld permission to publish it until recently.

A7   COVICI, PASCAL, JR. Mark Twain's Humor: The Image of a World. Dallas: Southern Methodist University Press.
"My concern is primarily with the use of humor in what Twain wrote.... That Twain's attempts to perform a multiple function through his humor did not always succeed will be obvious to the reader: 'One can deliver a satire with telling force through the insidious medium of a travesty,' Twain warned, 'if he is careful not to overwhelm the satire with the extraneous interest of the travesty.' Twain's attacks on the spirit of his times are often obscured by his delight in 'travesty.'" This book is an attempt to "show what Twain was attempting, to suggest its importance, and to re-examine a few of his works in the light of the artistry organized and given meaning by the humor" (Preface, p. ix).

A8   GRANT, DOUGLAS. Mark Twain. Edinburgh, Scotland: Oliver and Bond, Ltd. and New York: Grove Press, Inc.
A good introduction for the general reader. The portion on IA is reprinted in Schmitter (1974), pp. 71-76.

A9   HILL, HAMLIN, and WALTER BLAIR, eds. The Art of Huckleberry Finn: Text, Sources, Criticisms. San Francisco: The Chandler Publishing Company.
The text is a facsimile of the first edition, and the biographical and literary source material includes excerpts from writings by Dixon Wecter, John Marshall Clemens, (MT's father), William Wright, Charles Dickens, Thomas Carlyle, Julia A. Moore, Johnston J. Hooper, Richard M. Johnston, and W. E. H. Lecky; the criticism is less extensive, consisting of the 1885 Brander Matthews review, Lionel Trilling's introduction to the 1948 Rinehart edition, and 1955 articles by

(HILL, HAMLIN, and WALTER BLAIR, eds.)
William Van O'Connor and Frank Baldanza
(these criticisms are listed in the present
bibliography, but are not cross-referenced
to this collection, and the source materials are not listed). There is also useful
classroom material on the writing of HF,
with suggestions for use of sources and
criticisms, and a short bibliography; this
is an excellent teaching text.

A10 LEARY, LEWIS. A Casebook on Mark Twain's
Wound. New York: Thomas Y. Crowell Company
   A collection of critical essays from periodicals and excerpted from books, tracing
the Brooks-DeVoto controversy and the response of other critics. These essays and
excerpts are listed in the present bibliography, with cross-references to the reprintings here. Leary opens with a summary of
the debate in an essay, "Standing with Reluctant Feet," pp. 3-32; reprinted in his
Southern Excursions: Essays on Mark Twain
and Others (1971), pp. 42-74.

A11 LETTIS, RICHARD, ROBERT F. McDONNELL, and
WILLIAM E. MORRIS. Huck Finn and His Critics. New York: The Macmillan Company.
   A casebook for students, consisting of
the text of HF (including the "Raftsmen
Passage" published in LOM), a generous assortment of critical articles from periodicals and excerpted from books (all of
which are cross-referenced in the present
bibliography, with the exception of a brief
passage from the Paine biography). Includes
questions for students, topics and suggestions for research, "Notes on the Critics,"
and a bibliography which lists a number of
studies of J. D. Salinger's The Catcher in
the Rye but nothing on MT not listed in
the present bibliography.

A12 McNEER, MAY. America's Mark Twain. Boston:
Houghton Mifflin Company.
   A juvenile biography, apparently based on
Paine and on MT's works. "Previews" of
his works appear in the order of composition
as an encouragement to young readers, and
there are attractive illustrations by Lynd
Ward (1953 winner of the Caldecott Award for
The Biggest Bear) which reflect an intelligent familiarity with the times and with
existing photographs.

A13 SCHOLES, JAMES B. (ed. by Walter Harding).
Samuel L. Clemens "The Adventures of Huckleberry Finn." A Study Guide. Bound Brook,
New Jersey: Shelley Publishing Company.
   This is similar to the guides currently
on the market, but differs from others in
asking the student to do more of the work
of interpretation for himself.

A14 SIOUI, TAK. "Huckleberry Finn": More Mole-
cules. N.p.: privately printed. [Copyright
by John Hakac.]
   Attributes the mutilation of the illustration on p. 283 of the first ed. of Hucklebe-
ry Finn to E. W. Kemble, the illustrator.
Two states of the offending engraving are reproduced, with the portrayal of Uncle Silas
(saying, "Who do you reckon it is?") made
more clearly indecent after a first alteration which could have been considered innocent. It is also argued that the illustration on p. 290 ("A Pretty Long Blessing") is
also indecent: "If one is hesitant about de-
ciding on the artist's intention, he should
try blotting out the false leg-line in the
table cloth with a finger in order to simpli-
fy the view" (p. 25). MLA Bibliography (1964)
No. 6286, gives place as Tucson, Arizona.

A15 SMITH, HENRY NASH. Mark Twain: The Development
of a Writer. Cambridge, Massachusetts: The
Belknap Press of Harvard University Press.
   "This book considers first the problems of
style and structure Mark Twain faced at the
outset of his career, and then traces his
handling of these problems in nine of his
principal works [TS, HF, CY, IA, LOM, Hadleyburg, MS, PW, RI]. Since questions of
technique necessarily involve questions of
meaning, I have dealt also with his ethical
ideas. The inquiry leads ultimately to the
consideration of how his writing reveals a
conflict between the dominant culture of
his day and an emergent attitude associated
with the vernacular language of the native
American humorists." The concluding chapter
previously appeared in Massachusetts Review
(1962.B68). The chapter titled "A Sound
Heart and a Deformed Conscience" is reprinted, more or less completely, in Smith (1963),
pp. 83-100; Simpson (1968), pp. 71-81;
Gerber (1971), pp. 43-67; Kesterson (1973),
pp. 82-86. The section on TS is reprinted
in Schmitter (1974), pp. 85-94.

A16 SMITH, JANET, ed. and introduction. Mark
Twain on the Damned Human Race. Preface by
Maxwell Geismar. New York: Hill and Wang.
   A popular anthology excerpted from MT's
published writing on such topics as war,
race, imperialism, national vanity, and
religion. A good introduction to MT as satirist and advocate.

1962 B SHORTER WRITINGS

B1 ANON. "Digest of Mark Twain Items Published
Elsewhere," Twainian, XXI (January-February),
1-3.
   A reprinting of abstracts from Abstracts
of English Studies, IV (1961). The reprinting is accurate, except for the omission
(in this one year) of the AES abstract numbers, but a number of abstracts (including
those involving Mark Twain Journal) are silently omitted.

1962 - Shorter Writings

B2 ANON. "Double Bill," Times Literary Supple-
    ment, May 18, p. 358.
        A short review of Guy A. Cardwell's Twins
    of Genius, which provides little new infor-
    mation. The MT-George Washington Cable
    letters of 1881-1906 "are not many in number
    or particularly interesting, as Twain's cor-
    respondence goes, but Mr. Cardwell manages
    to compensate for their weakness by his
    ample introduction and commentary."

B3 ANON. [Brief Review: Harold Beaver, ed.,
    Life on the Mississippi. London: Oxford
    University Press; World's Classics Series.]
    Times Literary Supplement, October 5,
    p. 782.
        Praises Beaver's introduction to LOM,
    "one of Mark Twain's most important books"
    despite its dull parts.

B4 ANON. [Review: Bernard DeVoto, ed., Letters
    from the Earth.] Time, LXXX (September 21),
    91.
        Descriptive, emphasizing MT's despair as
    here revealed.

B5 ANON. [Review: Charles Neider, ed., Mark
    Twain: Life as I Find It (1961).] Missouri
    Historical Review, LVII (October), 116-17.
        "Charles Neider is a well-known authority
    on Mark Twain," and in collecting the
    sketches (of varying quality) in this vol-
    ume he "has done a service to those who
    appreciate the literary efforts of Mark
    Twain whatever his mood."

B6 ASHMEAD, JOHN. "A Possible Hannibal Source
    for Mark Twain's Dauphin," American Litera-
    ture, XXXIV (March), 105-107.
        Reprints "A Visit from Our Bourbon" from
    the Hannibal Journal for May 12, 1853; this
    hard-drinking pretender visiting a newspa-
    per office may explain why MT's notes de-
    scribe the Duke and Dauphin in HF as "print-
    ers." Abstract in AES, VI (1963), 1957;
    reprinted in Twainian, XXIII (March-April,
    1964), 3.

B7 ASPIZ, HAROLD. "Lecky's Influence on Mark
    Twain," Science & Society, XXVI (Winter),
    15-25.
        In writing CY, MT used William E. H.
    Lecky's History of European Morals from
    Augustus to Charlemagne (1869) for three
    purposes: "as a source, conscious or other-
    wise, of characters, incidents, and bits of
    'local color'"; for the novel's unifying
    "theme of training and of those dedicated
    souls who attempt to raise the level of hu-
    manity and the mass of men unwilling to
    think for themselves. Finally, Mark Twain
    translated the thematic concepts developed
    with Lecky's help into the fictional frame-
    work of the novel," thus achieving "a well-
    defined theme and a large measure of artis-
    tic unity." Abstract in AES, XII (1969),
    1328; reprinted in Twainian, XXIX (January-
    February, 1970).

B8 BABCOCK, C. MERTON. "Mark Twain and the Free-
    dom to Tell a Lie," Texas Quarterly, V
    (Autumn), 155-60.
        On MT's interest in the lie--in the uncon-
    scious lie, and in the willful lie as a top-
    ic and as a literary device. Abstract in
    AES, VI (1963), 1906; reprinted in Twainian,
    XXIII (March-April, 1964).

B9 BAKER, CARLOS. "Two Rivers: Mark Twain and
    Hemingway," Mark Twain Journal, XI (Summer),
    2.
        Shows similarities in descriptions of riv-
    ers by Huck (Chapter XIX) and by Frederick
    Henry in A Farewell to Arms (Chapter XXXI);
    many more such parallels could be drawn,
    though not as evidence of direct influence;
    the two writers share a directness and ap-
    pearance of simplicity. Abstract in AES,
    VIII (1965), 1052.

B10 BLAIR, WALTER. [Review: Albert E. Stone, Jr.,
    The Innocent Eye: Childhood in Mark Twain's
    Imagination (1961).] American Literature,
    XXXIV (May), 296-97.
        Stone provides valuable background in Amer-
    ican writing about children as he defines
    MT's achievements, and "he is particularly
    enlightening when he relates Twain's concept
    of youthful innocence to portrayals of the
    protagonists in Huckleberry Finn and Joan of
    Arc." His discussions of Huck Finn and Tom
    Sawyer among the Indians, Tom Sawyer's Con-
    spiracy, and the Hannibal version of MS "add
    important biographical data and round out
    Mr. Stone's valuable survey."

B11 BROOKS, ROGER L. "A Second Possible Source
    for Mark Twain's 'The Aged Pilot Man,'"
    Revue de Littérature Comparée, XXXVI (July-
    September), 451-53.
        Although MT said in Roughing It that the
    poem was probably suggested by an old song,
    'The Raging Canal,' it more closely resem-
    bles Coleridge's The Rime of the Ancient
    Mariner in language and structure, and "there
    are over thirty similarities" in rhymes.
    [In English]. Abstract in AES, VIII (1965),
    1189.

B12 BROWN, DEMING. Soviet Attitudes toward Ameri-
    can Writing. Princeton, N.J.: Princeton
    University Press.
        This is a general study in which most of
    the references to MT are in lists of Ameri-
    can authors long popular with Russian read-
    ers. There is an account of more interest
    describing Communist reaction when HF was
    removed from New York City schools in 1958,
    after Negro protests. Clearly, said Inos-
    trannaya Literatura, in this day of Little
    Rock and McCarthy MT was removed because he
    fought for racial equality (p. 197). Yel.
    Romanovna was even more misled in describing
    the Mark Twain Society, which had long oper-
    ated "under the aegis of Truman, Churchill,
    and DeGaulle"--and now there were plans for
    an affiliate of the society in Western Ger-
    many, with a membership of 50,000! (p. 165).

B13 BROWNELL, GEORGE HIRAM. "Shrine Builders,"
Twainian, XXI (May-June), 3-4.
     Text of a letter (June 21, 1931) to Wil-
lard S. Morse and apparently also intended
for Franklin J. Meine and Merle Johnson,
concerning bibliography of material by and
about MT (title apparently provided by
Chester L. Davis).

B14 BRUMM, URSULA. [Review: Roger B. Salomon,
Twain and the Image of History (1961).]
Archiv für das Studium der neuren Sprachen
und Literaturen, CXCIX, 197-98.
     Surveys the scholarship on the topic, not-
ing that Salomon is one of Henry Nash
Smith's students. "Das schmale Buch von
Roger B. Salomon ist insofern ein Ereignis,
als hier zum erstenmal konsequent und mit
weiter gestecktem Blickfeld die Unge-
reimtheiten, Bruch und Widersprüche in Mark
Twains Werk nicht primär psychologisch
sondern geistesgeschichtlich durchleuchtet
werden."

B15 BUDD, LOUIS J. [Review: Roger B. Salomon,
Twain and the Image of History (1961) and
Albert E. Stone, Jr., The Innocent Eye:
Childhood in Mark Twain's Imagination
(1961).] South Atlantic Quarterly, LXI
(Winter), 109-10.
     Both books "trace a theme or value that
doubled as a narrative device in Mark
Twain's writing. Stone exaggerates the
technique and intellectual depth in TS,
"achieves an original analysis of both the
sources and the emotional patterns behind
The Prince and the Pauper," makes JA more
interesting than MT did, and "superbly
lights up the nightmare world of The Mysterious Stranger." Salomon's book is
"first-rate" on broad perspective, very
good on P&P and JA, but less helpful on GA
and CY.

B16 BURHANS, CLINTON S., JR. "The Sober Affirmation of Mark Twain's Hadleyburg," American
Literature, XXXIV (November), 375-84.
     Affirmation of a virtue tested by temptа-
tion "places Twain within a great and positive tradition." Abstract in AES, VI
(1963), 1972, reprinted in Twainian, XXIII
(March-April, 1964), 3-4.

B17 CADY, EDWIN H. "Howells and Twain: The World
in Midwestern Eyes," Ball State Teachers
College Forum, III (Winter), 3-8.
     The two were alike in their Ohio and Mis-
souri backgrounds and outlooks. "The realism and penetration of Twain and Howells
sprang from their sense of strangeness, of
isolation, of cultural relativity between
the middle West and the otherwise civilized
world. That coincidence of view was a
source of strength and renewal in their
friendship as it was of significance in
their work." Abstract in AES, VI (1963),
2404; reprinted in Twainian, XXIII (March-
April, 1964).

B18 CAMBON, GLAUCO. "Mark Twain and Charlie Chaplin as Heroes of Popular Culture," Minnesota
Review, III (Fall), 77-82.
     Both dramatized "the tramp as mythical fig-
ure.... And, certainly, both Twain's and
Chaplin's late productions are attempts to
get behind their respective mythical masks,
to converse with them, to explain or reform
them...whatever the results." Both maintained their artistic standards while reaching "the largest audience an artist can get,"
but "our two pilgrims' progress from humor to
disenchantment and horror is similar, and
testifies to their basically naive thinking."
Abstract in AES, IX (1966), 1739; reprinted
in Twainian, XXVI (January-February, 1967).

B19 CLEMENS, CYRIL. "Mark Twain's Impressions of
the Play 'Palmyra,'" Hobbies--The Magazine
for Collectors, LXVII (August), 124.
     Reprints from "an old newspaper that I re-
cently came across" MT's praise of Adolph
Wilbrandt's play, The Master of Palmyra.

B20 COFFEE, JESSIE A. "Mark Twain's Use of
'Hain't' in Huckleberry Finn," American
Speech, XXXVII (October), 234-36.
     The form ain't, used 305 times, commonly
represents the present am not, is not, and
are not; the form hain't is used 74 times,
where the word have or has is indicated, as
in the present perfect, or in the expression
he has not got.

B21 *COHEN, HENNIG. "Mark Twain's Sut Lovingood,"
in Ben Harris McClary, ed. The Lovingood Papers, 1962 (Athens, Tenn.: The Sut Society;
1962.) [1st vol. of an annual.]
     [Source: MLA Bibliography (1962),
No. 5199.]

B22 CROWE, CHARLES. "Mark Twain's Huckleberry
Finn and the American Journey," Archiv für
das Studium der neuren Sprachen und Literaturen, CXCIX, 145-58.
     Summarizes critical views of the book;
argues that it must be recognized as "a
great comic novel and a boy's tale," with
Huck as "the single authentic American folk
hero and...the voyage down the river as a
mythic representation of the fundamental
national experience." Abstract in AES, VIII
(1965), 2804; reprinted in Twainian, XXV
(January-February, 1966).

B23 CUMMINGS, SHERWOOD. "Mark Twain's Acceptance
of Science," Centennial Review, VI (Spring),
245-61.
     MT read Darwin and often treated science
favorably, using its findings to attack
religion, but he also played several roles
as detractor of science, as "Swiftian satirist" and "common sense 'common man,'" and
"twice he wrote in a white heat of moral indignation against what he thought were abo-
minations and frauds of science" (in "A
Dog's Tale" and in a letter to Twichell,
condemning physicians and surgeons as "shams
and humbugs"). Abstract in AES, VI (1963),
240; reprinted in Twainian, XXIII (January-
February, 1964).

B24 [DAVIS, CHESTER L.]. "Foundation Receives Gift from Julian and Helene Sprague Foundation. Shrine Builders Brownell, Ade, Cities of Denver and Elmira," Twainian, XXI (March-April), 1-4.
Publishes correspondence of George Hiram Brownell and Anna B. Morse, 1935-1938 concerning the Willard S. Morse Collection; the MT material went to the library at Elmira, New York. Abstract in AES, VIII (1965), 1843; reprinted in Twainian, XXV (January-February, 1966). The following issue of Twainian begins with a correction: the Morse collection went to Yale, not to the Elmira library.

B24A *DEVOTO, BERNARD. "Introduction to Mark Twain," in Literature in America: An Anthology of Literary Criticism, selected and introduced by Philip Rahv. New York: World Publishing Company. Copyright 1957.
[Source: Cited by D. E. S. Maxwell (1965), p. 219; full title and facts of publication are from LC-NUC Author Lists, 1942-1962.]

B25 EBY, E. H. "Mark Twain's Testament," Modern Language Quarterly, XXIII (September), 254-62.
In MS, only the "presumed final chapter" creates the solecism and places the story in a dream-frame; in other respects the story is implicitly and explicitly "a testament to man's imagination as a creator." Satan personifies the artist, and "can free man from the bonds of necessity"; man may be saved through imagination. Abstract in AES, VII (1964), 850.

B26 _____. [Review: Henry Nash Smith and William M. Gibson, eds., Mark Twain-Howells Letters.] Modern Language Quarterly, XXIII (March), 90-91.
Well edited, "a valuable reference work for almost any study of Howells or Mark Twain" in the organization of data, but "the letters themselves are disappointing.... One can see that the most meaningful exchanges came not in their letters but in their face-to-face talks."

B27 EDEL, LEON. Henry James: The Conquest of London, 1870-1883. London: Rupert Hart-Davis, p. 186.
James in 1875 "had clearly been reading Mark Twain's Mississippi installments in the Atlantic, for he on one occasion observes that 'in the day of Mark Twain there may be no harm in being reminded that the absence of drollery may, at a stretch, be compensated by the presence of sublimity.'"

B28 ESS, KARL. "Shooting Pool with Mark Twain. Billiards Was More than a Game to the Great Humorist--It Was the Obsession of His Later Years," Sports Illustrated, XVI (February 26), 57-58.

Presents no new information, but blends such sources as Paine, Willie Hoppe, and Katy Leary to produce a readable and accurate popular account.

B29 FATOUT, PAUL. "Mark Twain's Nom de Plume," American Literature, XXXIV (March), 1-7.
According to western newspapers, the "Mark Twain" pseudonym was derived from Clemens's custom of chalking up drinks in local saloons. Abstract in AES, VI (1963), 1947; reprinted in Twainian, XXIII (March-April, 1964), 3; article reprinted (without footnotes) in Twainian, XXV (September-October, 1966), 2-4; also (with footnotes) in Kaplan (1967), 161-68.

B30 FEINSTEIN, HERBERT. "Mark Twain & the Pirates," Harvard Law School Bulletin, XIII (April), 6-18.
Reprinted as "Mark Twain and the Copyright Pirates," Twainian, XXI (May-June), 1-3; (July-August), 1-4; (September-October), 1-4; (November-December), 3-4. On MT's extensive litigation to prevent unauthorized publication of his works, use of his name with the works of others, and re-sale in stores of his works sold by subscription; also treats his efforts to promote more favorable copyright legislation and to prolong copyright of his collected works by leaving material in manuscript to be released over a period of years. Abstract in AES, VIII (1965), 1844-1847, reprinted in Twainian, XXV (January-February, 1966); not noted in the abstracts are details of MT's resentment of John Wanamaker's actions in sales of his subscription books, but later kind words in connection with reform in the Congo. Contains quotations from Philadelphia Press (May 15, August 4, 1886), Philadelphia Times (July 28, August 3, 1886), New York Herald (November 12, 1905).

B31 FRANTZ, RAY W., JR. "Sam Clemens's Belt," Twainian, XXI (July-August), 1.
The picture of Sam Clemens at age fifteen in Wecter's Sam Clemens of Hannibal and, more recently, in Meltzer's Mark Twain Himself shows what appears to be a belt-buckle; closer inspection reveals a compositor's stick with "SAM" in type.

B32 GANZEL, DEWEY. "Samuel Clemens and Captain Marryat," Anglia (Tübingen), LXXX, No. 4, 405-16.
MT used Marryat's A Diary in America in LOM; moreover, his descriptions in HF of a camp meeting and the moral cowardice condemned by Colonel Sherburn also suggest Marryat's influence. Abstract in AES, VIII (1965), 942.

B33 _____. "Twain, Travel Books, and Life on the Mississippi," American Literature, XXXIV (March), 40-55.

(GANZEL, DEWEY)

On MT's extensive use of earlier travelers' accounts for information, direct quotation, and for indirect use (here shown
through parallel passages). Significantly,
MT's apparent use in HF of notes taken in
1882 for LOM supports DeVoto's dating of
the composition of parts of HF later than
the 1880 date given by Blair. Abstract in
AES, VI (1963), 1950; reprinted in Twainian, XXIII (March-April, 1964), 3.

B34   GELB, ARTHUR. "Witheld Work by Twain is Due,"
New York Times (August 24), p. 23.
On the forthcoming publication of MT's
Letters from the Earth (ed. Bernard DeVoto).
Describes attempts by Charles Neider to ob-
tain permission from MT's daughter Clara
to publish five chapters by MT on religion
in his edition of the Autobiography; permission was finally granted, although "two
magazines have already rejected the chapters
as being 'too inflammatory.'" [They eventually appeared both in Hudson Review (1963.B64)
and in Letters from the Earth (1962.A6).]

B35   GERBER, JOHN C. "Mark Twain's Use of the
Comic Pose," Publications of the Modern
Language Association, LXXVII (June),
297-304.
"Mark Twain" is not a consistent persona
employed by Samuel Clemens: the pseudonym
is not used with consistency. The point of
view taken may be MT's own, a pose, or an
alternation between the two. The pose was
aesthetically useful, though seldom used
"to give a work tonal and structural unity";
it was personally useful to Clemens "because its restricted point of view simplified life and made it more tolerable."
Abstract in AES, VIII (1965), 2336; reprinted in Twainian, XXV (January-February,
1966). Article reprinted in Scott (1967),
pp. 271-85.

B36   HIGGINS, WILLIAM. "I Try to Do It Another
Way and Am Sorry," Ball State Teachers College Forum, III (Winter), 13-14.
In the manner of Chapter XIV of HF, a
dialogue in which Huck tries to explain
symbolism, myth, and structure in the book
to Jim, but fails in the attempt: "I never
saw a nigger so down on critics. Anyway,
maybe Jim was right and they are all like
that fellow Percrusty Aunt Polly told me
about.... But making a book over is harder
than the first time, so I guess I won't
tackle it."

B37   HILL, HAMLIN. "Eschol Sellers from Uncharted
Space: A Footnote to The Gilded Age,"
American Literature, XXXIV (March), 107-113.
Publishes correspondence of Charles Dudley Warner with one George Escol Sellers
(with whom he was acquainted through a
friend) on use of his name in GA; the facts
given here refute three incorrect versions

related by MT. Abstract in AES, VI (1963),
1958; reprinted in Twainian, XXIII (March-
April, 1964), 3.

B38   _____. "Mark Twain's Quarrels with Elisha
Bliss," American Literature, XXXIII (January), 442-56.
"The purpose of this study is to recon-
struct the most serious altercations between
Bliss and Twain...to show that Twain's statements about Bliss in Mark Twain in Eruption
were surprisingly accurate, and to estimate
...Twain's actual loss on his American Publishing Company books." Subscription publication was profitable, both to Bliss and
to MT, but Bliss misrepresented costs, as
when he concealed the fact that he used the
same (or slightly modified) engravings for
MT's and other books he published. There
are also details of the involvement of Bliss
and MT's brother Orion in the short-lived
journal, The American Publisher. Abstract
in AES, V (1962), 1838; reprinted in Twainian, XXII (January-February, 1963).

B39   HINER, JAMES. [Review: Charles Neider, Mark
Twain and the Russians (1960).] American
Quarterly, XIV (Summer), 217.
This series of letters between Neider and
Y. Bereznitsky of the Literary Gazette about
Neider's edition of The Autobiography of
Mark Twain now has an added introduction
"reviewing the facts of the exchange and
justifying the present publication." The
debate is ideological, with Neider taking a
somewhat dogmatically liberal stand, and
"the editors of the Literary Gazette were
correct in punctuating the exchange when
they did."

B40   HOLMES, CHARLES S. "A Connecticut Yankee in
King Arthur's Court: Mark Twain's Fable of
Uncertainty," South Atlantic Quarterly, LXI
(Autumn), 462-72.
"Ultimately destructive of all value,"
the book expresses MT's "deep contraditions
in his feelings about his own career, about
American culture, and, finally, about life
itself." Hank Morgan's character is ambiguous, and the dream-framework of the book
undercuts the values of both the earlier
time and the bustling nineteenth century.
Abstract in AES, VI (1963), 658; reprinted
in Twainian, XXIII (January-February, 1964).

B41   HOLTZMAN, FILIA. "A Mission that Failed:
Gor'kij in America," Slavic and East European Journal, VI (Fall), 227-35.
On the 1906 visit of Gorki to the United
States to raise money for the Bolshevik
Party; he spoke at the "A Club," and a photograph of Gorki seated beside MT is preserved. Unfortunately, a newspaper released
the news that the woman traveling with him
was not his legal wife, and MT, Howells,
and others withdrew their support.

B42 JONES, HOWARD MUMFORD. "The Other Face of
the Humorist," New York Times Book Review
(September 23), pp. 7, 53.
A review of Letters from the Earth (ed.
DeVoto) as "the most impressive contribution
to books by Mark Twain since The Mysterious
Stranger of 1916, the imaginative grandeur
of which it shares."

B42A KAZIN, ALFRED. "Almost Perfect," Library
Journal, LXXXVII (November 15), 4243-45
(also numbered as Children's Section,
23-25).
Although HF deteriorates in the horse-
play of the last chapters, the ending is a
way of returning the action to TS, where it
began. Modern critics are more conscious
of such blemishes than was MT, who did not
necessarily notice--or care: HF "is the
product of a mind whose lapses were virtually necessary to his imaginative strength.
For he had above all to feel easy to write
at all, and if he had had to check himself
every time he was in danger of displeasing
the unnaturally severe taste of our time he
wouldn't have found himself in the unexpected depths of Huckleberry Finn." Abstract
in AES, XVII (1973-1974), 853; reprinted in
Twainian, XXXIV (March-April, 1975).

B43 LORCH, FRED W. [Review: Paul Fatout, Mark
Twain on the Lecture Circuit (1960).]
American Literature, XXXIII (January),
540-541.
The chronological organization of the book
is at the expense of "comprehensive, unified
discussion" of MT's platform art, his theory
of lecturing and reading, and significant
criticism; comments on these matters are
scattered and hard to find, and source references are inadequate. Fatout writes vigorously, "with here and there a tendency
toward exaggeration for the sake of effect," and he "is no inordinate admirer of
Mark Twain." [Note: Lorch had already
published a number of articles on MT as a
lecturer, and in 1968 published his own
book on the subject, The Trouble Begins at
Eight--T.A.T.]

B44 LYNN, KENNETH S. [Review: Henry Nash Smith
and William M. Gibson, eds., Mark Twain-
Howells Letters (1961).] New England Quarterly, XXXV (March), 110-11.
"The most spectacular exhibition afforded
by these volumes is that of Mark Twain blowing his top," but we also see "how Mark
Twain's feeling for the American language
gradually has become a literary style. In
this epochal development--from the colloquial flair of the early stories to the
vernacular perfection of Huckleberry Finn
to the breakdown of narrative tone in A
Connecticut Yankee--Twain was enormously
aided by the advice and encouragement of
Howells." The editing is superb, both in
accuracy and in thoroughness, dating letters, identifying references, and the notes

are "often capsule essays which set Twain's
friendship with Howells in the broader perspective of his total career."

B45 McALEER, JOHN J. "Noble Innocence in Huckleberry Finn," Ball State Teachers College
Forum, III (Winter), 9-12.
On the use of nakedness to reveal both innocence and a gross exploitation of it, taking examples from MT, Sherwood Anderson,
Hemingway, and Swift; also shows parallels
between Anderson and MT in depicting the destructive power of the machine. Abstract in
AES, VI (1963), 2405; reprinted in Twainian,
XXIII (March-April, 1964).

B46 MACKANESS, GEORGE. "Mark Twain's Visit to
Australia," American Book Collector, XII
(May), 6-10.
A popular account of MT's 1895 visit,
quoting his reactions to what he saw (but
only vaguely documented); also quotes anecdotes in an article [title not given] by Roy
Chase in Australian National Review, May,
1939. Illustrations: photo of MT and facsimiles of title pages of first Australian
editions of IA and Jumping Frog books. Abstract in AES, V (1962), 1399; reprinted in
Twainian, XXII (January-February, 1963).

B47 McKEITHAN, D. M. [Review: Frank Baldanza,
Mark Twain: An Introduction and Interpretation (1961).] American Literature, XXXIV
(November), 424-25.
Largely descriptive; questions some of
Baldanza's interpretations but notes his
familiarity with his subject and enthusiastic writing, "and his study is interesting
and at times quite stimulating."

B48 MESERVE, WALTER J. [Review: Roger B. Salomon, Twain and the Image of History (1961)
and Albert E. Stone, Jr., The Innocent Eye:
Childhood in Mark Twain's Imagination
(1961).] American Quarterly, XIV (Spring),
100-101.
An uncritical summary of the two books.

B49 MILLGATE, MICHAEL. [Review: Franklin R. Rogers, ed., The Pattern for Mark Twain's
Roughing It" (1961).] Modern Language Review, LVII (January), 147.
"The intrinsic interest of the letters is
not great," but the commentary is useful
and the "effect of the volume is...to rein-
force the work of other recent critics who
have increasingly challenged the view, particularly associated with the late Bernard
DeVoto, that Twain, far from being a craftsman, was essentially a natural and instinctive writer."

B50 MILNE, W. GORDON. [Brief review: Roger B.
Salomon, Twain and the Image of History
(1961).] Books Abroad, XXXVI (Winter),
76-77.
"Carefully balanced...perceptive."

B51   MONTEIRO, GEORGE. "Publication of Mark Twain in Canada," American Notes and Queries, I (October), 20-21.

To the list of unauthorized publications of MT's works may be added translations of his sketches, "Running for Governor" and "About Barbers," which appeared in L'Opin-ion Publique, Montreal, as "Une Candida-ture" (October 20, 1881) and "Les Barbiers" (January 26, 1882). Abstract in AES, VI (1963), 2002; reprinted in Twainian, XXIII (March-April, 1964).

B52   *MORIOKA, SAKAE. "Huckleberry Finn and A Fare-well to Arms." Kyusha American Literature, No. 5 (April), pp. 27-35.
[Source: MHRA Annual Bibliography (1962), No. 5689.]

B53   *____. "Pudd'nhead Wilson and the Racial Problem," Studies in English Language and Literature (Kyushu University), No. 12, pp. 1-11.
[Source: MHRA Annual Bibliography (1962), No. 5688.]

B54   MUNFORD, HOWARD. [Review: Roger B. Salomon, Twain and the Image of History (1961).] Mississippi Valley Historical Review, XLIX (September), 360-61.

"In this reworking of a dissertation done under Henry Nash Smith, the student does credit to his mentor." Salomon shows how MT came to anticipate twentieth-century thinking as a result of the conflict be-tween his inherited assumptions and his in-tuitive sense of American life; Salomon's failure to consider scientific thinking of the age is not a defect, because the subject has been treated elsewhere.

B55   MURADIAN, THADDEUS. "Huckleberry Finn: an Approach to Literature in the High School," The Independent School Bulletin (National Association of Independent Schools, Boston). Series of 62-63 (November), pp. 6-9.

On the successful teaching of HF, the questions raised, and the ways of discussing it in relation to other books. Considers the question of censorship at some length. "This article won the 1961-62 prize for the best article in a specific subject field."

B56   *NARAIN, S. K. "Mark Twain: A Consideration of His Realism," Literary Criterion (Mysore, India), V, 66-71.
[Source: MHRA Annual Bibliography (1963), No. 4737.]

B57   *OBA, HIROYOSHI. "An Essay on Mark Twain," Kamereon, No. 5 (August), pp. 50-63.
[Source: Leary (1970), p. 71.]

B58   O'CONNOR, WILLIAM VAN. "Huckleberry Finn and the Great American Novel," in his The Gro-tesque: An American Genre (Carbondale: Southern Illinois University Press), pp. 109-18.

This appears to be essentially the same text as appears in O'Connor's "Why Huckle-berry Finn Is Not the Great American Novel" (1955; reprinted in Bradley, 1962).

B59   *OKAMOTO, KATSUMI. "The Tragedy of Mark Twain, the Man and Artist," Geibun (Kinki Univer-sity), III (August), 1-32.
[Source: Leary (1970), p. 71.]

B60   PARSONS, COLEMAN O. "Mark Twain in New Zea-land," South Atlantic Quarterly, LXI (Win-ter), 51-76.

On the 38 days MT spent there in November-December, 1895, his itinerary, his lectures, and his reception; abundantly documented from the New Zealand press. Abstract in AES, V (1962), 1156; reprinted in Twainian, XXII (January-February, 1963).

B61   POCHMANN, HENRY A. [Review: Karl-Heinz Schönfelder, Mark Twain: Leben, Persönlich-keit und Werk (1961).] American Literature, XXXIII (January), 541-42.

In four times the length of one of the University of Minnesota Pamphlets, this East German booklet does half as well: there are significant inaccuracies, and MT's at-tacks on capitalism are overemphasized, everything he said taken "with heavy-handed seriousness."

B62   *POIRIER, RICHARD. "Huckleberry Finn: Atti-tudes Toward Tricks and Adventure," Exer-cise Exchange, X (November), 23-34.
[Source: Beebe and Feaster (1968), p. 119.]

B63   ____. "Mark Twain, Jane Austen, and the Imagination of Society," in Reuben A. Brower and Richard Poirier, eds., In Defence of Reading: A Reader's Approach to Literary Criticism (New York: E. P. Dutton & Co., Inc.), pp. 282-309.

Criticisms of Jane Austen by Emerson, Henry James, and MT "reveal a significantly American dissatisfaction with the novel of manners." MT's fantasy in PW and MS moves "toward a saturnalia of repudiation," but HF, "more complicated than anything in James before The Bostonians," has MT's "af-fection for a character whose longings are a curious and inseparable blend of Isabel Archer's dream of 'freedom' with some of Mark Twain's own nostalgic desire for commu-nity." [According to Leo Marx's "Selected Bibliography" in the Bobbs-Merrill ed. of HF, this article was revised as Chapter IV of Poirier's A World Elsewhere: The Place of Style in American Literature (1966).]

B64   POMMER, HENRY F. "Mark Twain's 'Commissioner of the United States,'" American Literature, XXXIV (November), 385-92.

Pommer describes William Gibson, M.D., the original of this character, as "a pompous windbag" and publishes some of Gibson's sci-entific correspondence and MT's descriptions

(POMMER, HENRY F.)
of him in letters to show why his satire took
the form it did. Abstract in AES, VI (1963),
1973 (item number incorrectly given as 1873
in the volume index); reprinted in Twainian,
XXIII (March-April, 1964), 4.

B65 *RICE, JACK. [Article on MT's Letters from The
Earth and his marginal notations in W. E. H.
Lecky's History of European Morals, with
passing comment on Chester L. Davis and the
Twainian.] St. Louis Post-Dispatch, Octo-
ber 14.
[Source: Reprinted in Twainian, XXI
(November-December), 1-3.]

B66 *ROBERTS, THOMAS. "Huckleberry Finn: Understanding Comic Devices," Exercise Exchange,
X (November), 22-23.
[Source: Beebe and Feaster (1968),
p. 120.]

B66A ROSS, JOHN F. [Review: Salomon, Twain and the
Image of History; Stone, The Innocent Eye
(both 1961).] Nineteenth-Century Fiction,
XVI (March), 366-69.
Salomon provides "a valuable account" of
what history meant to MT, but may overestimate his later disillusionment with it. Ross
praises CY, questions whether structure or
unity of tone are essential, and criticizes
Stone's view that it is a falling-off after
HF and his picture of Hank Morgan.

B67 SCOTT, ARTHUR L. "'Review of Holiday Literature,'" College English, XXIII (February),
385-87.
A spoof under this title in the Buffalo
Express of Christmas Eve, 1870, signed
"Carl Byng" (here reprinted) may be by MT; it
anticipates the New Criticism "with its detailed textual analysis, its admiration for
subtlety, imagination, audacity, ambiguity,
conceits, and allegory." Also comments
on MT's sending twenty dollars to Walt Whitman, but no evidence of familiarity with
his work. Abstract in AES, V (1962), 2577.

B68 SMITH, HENRY NASH. "Pudd'nhead Wilson and
After," Massachusetts Review, III (Winter),
233-53.
"This essay is the last chapter of a book
to be called Mark Twain the Writer: A
Study in Method and Meaning [Mark Twain:
The Development of a Writer], to be pub-
lished in the autumn of 1962." Abstract in
AES, V (1962), 2300; reprinted in Twainian,
XXII (January-February, 1963).

B69 STARTSEV, A. "Problema Pozdnego Tvena [The
Problem of the Later Twain]," Voprosy Literatury, VI:11 (November), 138-59.
In the pessimism of his late years MT mistook the defects of American society for
universal attributes of the human condition.
Abstract in AES, VI (1963), 1207; reprinted
in Twainian, XXIII (January-February, 1964).

B70 TANNER, TONY. "Samuel Clemens and the Progress of a Stylistic Rebel," Bulletin of the
British Association for American Studies,
n.s., No. 3 (December, 1961), pp. 31-42.
On MT's vernacular style, used successfully in HF, but not in TS Abroad and TS
Detective, where his use of Huck as narrator "never escapes the trivial because the
naive vernacular style is not being applied
to anything calculated to call its deepest
ironic potentialities into play."

B71 _____. [Review: Henry Nash Smith, Mark Twain:
The Development of a Writer, and Bernard De-
Voto, ed., Letters from the Earth.] Critical Quarterly, IV (Winter), 380-83.
With "an extensive knowledge of nineteenth-
century American culture as well as an un-
paralleled intimacy with Twain's work,"
Smith has confronted questions of the relation of language and style to vision. There
is a "really masterly chapter on Innocents
Abroad," and "Smith's book is indispensable
and will remain so for a long while." In
Letters from the Earth "there is nothing
childish in a man agonising over the suffer-
ings of mankind. This is not great literature, but it is a remarkable example of the
anguished turbulence of the late nineteenth-
century mind--crucified on a childhood of
Calvinism and an adulthood of Darwinism,
collapsing under the weight of a Determinism
which argued either an atrociously cruel God
or a terrifyingly meaningless universe."

B72 THORP, WILLARD. "A Bittersweet Treasury of
Posthumous Twain," New York Herald Tribune
Book Review, XXXIX (September 30), 4, 15.
A review of Letters from the Earth, ed.
Bernard DeVoto: a description, with com-
mentary, of the selections.

B73 VAN WHY, JOSEPH S. "Nook Farm," The Stowe,
Beecher, Hooker, Seymour, Day Foundation
Bulletin for 1962, I, i-iii, 1-36.
On MT's Hartford neighborhood and neighbors, with map and key (pp. ii-iii), table
of "Nook Farm Residents and their Relationships" (p. 34), and photographs of MT's
and other houses (pp. 35-36). Includes the
text of MT's humorous sketch, "Fearful Calamity in Forest St.," which first appeared as
a letter to the editor of the Hartford Courant (March 31, 1871; not previously reprinted).

B74 WELSH, DONALD H. "Sam Clemens' Hannibal:
1836-1838 [sic]," Midcontinent American
Studies Journal, III (Spring), 28-43.
On the town as described by local newspapers, 1846-1848 [sic]; describes business
activity, public health, patent-medicine advertising, problems with vice and dogs, and
resentment over the presence of free Negroes.
This town, "which in some ways demonstrated
its Southern heritage and in others seemed
to be a child of New England," gave MT "many

(WELSH, DONALD H.)
impressions from which he drew in later
years." Abstract in AES, VI (1963), 345;
reprinted in Twainian, XXIII (January-
February, 1964).

B75 *ZAPULLA, GIUSEPPE. "Gli Inediti di Mark
Twain," La Fiera Letteraria, XVII (October
14).
[Source: Leary (1970), p. 77.]

1963 A BOOKS

A1 CAMP, JAMES E., and X. J. KENNEDY. Mark
Twain's Frontier: A Textbook of Primary
Source Materials for Student Research and
Writing. New York: Holt, Rinehart and
Winston, Inc.
A generous selection from MT's writings
about Nevada, together with "Memoirs and
Tales by Twain's Contemporaries," selec-
tions from Brooks and DeVoto, a brief bib-
liography, and suggested topics for short
and long papers.

A2 CARDWELL, GUY A. Discussions of Mark Twain.
Boston: D. C. Heath and Company.
A collection of critical essays, from
periodicals and excerpted from books; all
are cross-referenced in the present bibliography.

A3 DUSKIS, HENRY, ed. The Forgotten Writings of
Mark Twain. New York: Philosophical Library; paperbound edition by The Citadel
Press. London: Peter Owen.
Reprinted material from the Buffalo Express 1869-71, signed by MT or attributed
to him by Duskis. Unfortunately, this material consists of excerpts rather than
complete texts, dates are given vaguely or
not at all, and many of the attributions
to MT are questionable.

A4 ROGERS, FRANKLIN R., ed. and introduction.
Simon Wheeler, Detective. New York: The
New York Public Library.
Makes an interesting MT piece more ac-
cessible and provides background through a
lengthy introduction.

A5 SMITH, HENRY NASH, ed. Mark Twain: A Collection of Critical Essays. Englewood
Cliffs, New Jersey: Prentice-Hall, Inc.
Contains essays by critics over a period
of years, from periodicals and excerpted
from books, dealing broadly with MT's life
and several of his works; all of these essays are cross-referenced in the present
bibliography.

A6 *STARTSEV, A. Mark Tven i Amerika [Mark
Twain and America], Moskva: Sovietskii
Pisatel.
[Source: MHRA Annual Bibliography, 1963,
No. 4751, and review by A. Elistratova,
1963.B27.]

A7 STOUTENBURG, ADRIEN, and LAURA NELSON BAKER.
Dear, Dear Livy: The Story of Mark Twain's
Wife. New York: Charles Scribner's Sons.
Written as a story for the general reader,
drawing on primary sources for details.

A8 TAPER, BERNARD, ed. Mark Twain's San Francisco. New York, Toronto, London: McGraw-
Hill Book Company, Inc.
A collection of MT's writings which appeared in the Nevada and California papers,
1863-66. There are a good introduction and
introductory head-notes, both directed primarily toward the general reader. The introduction also appears in American Heritage 1963.B82 and Twainian 1963.B83.

A9 TUCKEY, JOHN S. Mark Twain and Little Satan:
The Writing of "The Mysterious Stranger."
West Lafayette, Indiana: Purdue University
Studies.
Establishes time of composition of several
versions from 1897 to 1908, with "the actual
order...very nearly the reverse of the one
that was assumed by DeVoto" (pp. 76-77); the
conflation of the different versions has
been a source of confusion to scholars. An
extensive portion of this book is reprinted
in Tuckey's Mark Twain's "The Mysterious
Stranger" and the Critics (1968),
pp. 127-54.

1963 B SHORTER WRITINGS

B1 ABEL, DARREL. "Mark Twain," in his Master-
works of American Realism: Twain, Howells,
James (vol. III in his American Literature).
Great Neck, New York: Barron's Educational
Series. Pp. 10-121.
A general work for school use, this consists primarily of biography and plot summaries; there is very little of critical
significance.

B2 *ANDERSSON, THOMAS. "Mark Twain's Views on
Politics, Religion and Morals," Moderna
Språk, LVII (September), 283-89.
[Source: MHRA Annual Bibliography (1963),
No. 4703; abstract in AES, VIII (1964),
1098.]

B3 ANON. "Articles Published Elsewhere During
Past Year," Twainian, XXII (January-February), 2-4.
Reprints a number of abstracts from Abstracts of English Studies, V (1962).

B4 ANON. "The Bear and Huckleberry Finn: Heroic
Quests for Moral Liberation," Mark Twain
Journal, XII (Spring), 12-13, 21.
Ike McCaslin and Huck lack parents and
find substitute fathers in older Negroes;
they undergo initiations in isolation, and
both novels end on an affirmative note:
"Both boys have transformed their knowledge
and ability into charity and humility, and
both are now guided by a moral vision."
Abstract in AES, VIII (1965), 1059.

B5   ANON. "Collections," Mark Twain Journal, XII
      (Spring), back cover.
         "As founder of the Mark Twain Society and
      Editor of the Mark Twain Journal since
      1936, Cyril Clemens has had occasion to
      correspond with literary figures of note.
      His correspondence has been acquired by the
      following libraries: George Santayana--
      Duke University Library, Durham, N.C.;
      John Cowper Powys--Northwestern University
      Library, Evanston, Ill.; George Bernard
      Shaw--University of North Carolina Library,
      Chapel Hill; Robert Frost--Boston Public
      Library; Edgar Lee Masters--Berg Collection,
      New York Public Library; Margaret Mitchell--
      University of Georgia Library, Athens;
      George Ade--University of Indiana Library,
      Bloomington; Wendell Willkie--University of
      Indiana Library, Bloomington; H. L. Menck-
      en--University of Pennsylvania Library,
      Philadelphia; James Branch Cabell-Universi-
      ty of Pennsylvania Library, Philadelphia;
      Sinclair Lewis--University of Minnesota
      Library, Minneapolis; Willa Cather--Willa
      Cather Memorial, Red Cloud, Nebraska; Ezra
      Pound--Hamilton College Library, Clinton,
      N.Y.; Arthur Machen--Houghton Library,
      Harvard University; Will and Wallace Irwin--
      Stanford University, California; Walter de
      la Mare--Gordon T. Banks, Esq., Boston;
      Albert Einstein--George T. Goodspeed, Esq.,
      Boston."

B6   ANON. "Missouri Boy," Times Literary Supple-
      ment, January 4, p. 5.
         A review of Douglas Grant's Mark Twain,
      praising the concise biography, good use of
      Charles Neider's edition of the Autobiogra-
      phy, and a course steered with "dexterity
      and fairness" between Brooks and DeVoto.

B7   AUSTIN, JAMES C. "Artemus Ward, Mark Twain,
      and the Limburger Cheese," Midcontinent
      American Studies Journal, IV (Fall), 70-73.
         MT's friend anticipated "The Invalid's
      Story" with an earlier tale of the odor of
      Limburger cheese in a baggage-car being
      mistaken for that of a corpse. The differ-
      ence between the two versions "illustrates
      brilliantly the difference between the
      Southwestern yarn and the Yankee anecdote,
      and it also shows Twain's manner of develop-
      ing a story." Abstract in AES, VII (1964),
      1416.

B8   BABCOCK, C. MERTON. "Mark Twain's Seven
      Lively Sins," Texas Quarterly, VI (Autumn),
      92-97.
         On MT's accounts of his stealing, gam-
      bling, laziness, smoking, drinking, swear-
      ing, and lying: "When one considers the
      consecration and devotion with which he
      pursued his lively vices, it is quite ap-
      parent that he had a 'damned good moral
      character.'" Abstract in AES, VIII (1965),
      2401; reprinted in Twainian, XXV (January-
      February, 1966).

B9   BAENDER, PAUL. "The 'Jumping Frog' as a Come-
      dian's First Virtue," Modern Philology, LX
      (February), 192-200.
         "The critical tradition has sometimes gone
      astray" concerning MT, as is the case when
      "The Jumping Frog" is used in portraying
      him as a frontiersman; the southwestern
      frame-story on which such interpretations
      are based was declining in popularity, and
      MT's intention is revealed in what he said
      ironically of an inept tragic actor who had
      "the first virtue of a comedian, which is
      to do funny things with grave decorum and
      without seeeming to know that they are fun-
      ny." Abstract in AES, VI (1963), 2512;
      reprinted in Twainian, XXIII (March-April,
      1964).

B10   BLAIR, WALTER. [Review: Roger B. Salomon,
      Twain and the Image of History (1961).]
      American Literature, XXXIV (January),
      578-80.
         "Mr. Salomon sees Clemens's faith in prog-
      ress foredoomed by disillusionment about
      human nature...wavering between a belief
      that progress was at best temporary and a
      belief that it was merely an illusion."
      Salomon's "over-all history of Twain's
      shifting ideas is accurate, sufficiently
      complex, and convincingly documented," and
      his insights are "both sensible and sensi-
      tive."

B11   BRINEGAR, CLAUDE S. "Mark Twain and the
      Quintus Curtius Snodgrass Letters: A Sta-
      tistical Test of Authorship," Journal of
      the American Statistical Association, LVIII
      (March), 85-96.
         Ten letters in the New Orleans Daily
      Crescent in 1861, often attributed to MT,
      have been interpreted as casting light on
      his service in the Civil War; "this study
      applies an old, though little used statis-
      tical test of authorship--a word-frequency
      test--to show that Twain almost certainly
      did not write these 10 letters." Reprinted
      in Twainian, XXIII (July-August, 1964),
      1-2; (September-October, 1964), 4. An un-
      signed headnote by Chester L. Davis notes
      "some necessary cutting...most of the text
      minus the charts, tables, graphs and foot-
      notes follows," but "for those who want the
      complete scientific story the original arti-
      cle should be consulted and studied." Ab-
      stract in AES (1965), 1855; reprinted in
      Twainian, XXV (January-February, 1966), 3.

B12   BUCCO, MARTIN. "Mark Twain to the Editor of
      the Columbia Missouri Herald," Missouri
      Historical Review, LVII (July), 398-99.
         Text of a letter to Walter Williams
      (March 4, 1894), declining what is apparent-
      ly an invitation to speak in Columbia.

B13   BUDD, LOUIS J. "Twain Could Mark the Beat,"
      Midcontinent American Studies Journal, IV
      (Spring), 39-44.

(BUDD, LOUIS J.)

Biographical accounts, letters, and passages in his works reveal that MT "found a deep release in dancing that comes only to the enthusiast, and never felt the need to justify it." Abstract in AES, VI (1963), 2490; reprinted in Twainian, XXIII (March-April, 1964).

B14 _____. [Review: Pascal Covici, Mark Twain's Humor: The Image of a World (1962).] American Literature, XXXIV (January), 581-82.

Covici is "better on Twain's artistry than ideas," and "the force of [his] book is cumulative. Its sum is greater than its parts, and it builds steadily toward a major insight."

B15 CARDWELL, GUY A. [Review: Louis J. Budd, Mark Twain: Social Philosopher (1962).] Nineteenth-Century Fiction, XVIII (September), 197-200.

"So far as large social matters are concerned, Budd's evidence makes incidentally plain that Mark Twain had a frowsy, superficial mind. He expressed muddled opinions on such matters as determinism, the capacities of the Negro, and social Darwinism." Compared to Philip S. Foner's Mark Twain: Social Critic (1958), Budd's book reflects a "more objective, better informed, and more critical" view, and familiarity with recent criticism, but the chapters often become chaotic because of various interests of MT's in the material under discussion. This is one of the better recent studies of MT, and will be valuable to future scholars.

B16 CARTER, PAUL J. [Review: Henry Nash Smith, Mark Twain: The Development of a Writer (1962).] American Literature, XXXV (May), 248-50.

Notes Smith's treatment of MT's efforts to develop "a consistent fictional persona which would allow him to evade the cult of gentility while defining his own role in society," and praises this "major contribution to scholarship," which "focuses attention upon style, upon the role of language in the writer's achievement."

B17 CHAPIN, HENRY B. "Twain's Pudd'nhead Wilson, Chapter VI," Explicator, XXI (April), Item 61.

"The Italian twins' reception in Dawson's Landing is...an essential element of the novel's exploration of the relativity of good and evil": the citizens readily submit to their spell but in turn the twins become the property of the widow Cooper and of Rowena. Abstract in AES, VI (1963), 2085; reprinted in Twainian, XXIII (March-April, 1964).

B18 _____. [Review: Charles Neider, ed., The Complete Essays of Mark Twain (1963).] New Mexico Quarterly, XXXIII (Winter), 474.

"Nieder [sic] has six books to his credit-- all of them written by Twain. This one does not contain Twain's complete essays contrary to the title...it omits all essays not collected in Twain's lifetime and in that of his chief literary executor, Albert Bigelow Paine. Twain's papers have been ignored completely. Of the essays that have been included, the notes are scanty and erratic.... Some more-revealing notes begin 'Paine says ...' which is Nieder's [sic] way of borrowing not only the author's work but his editor's as well."

B19 CLEMENS, SAMUEL L. "A Twain Letter," Southwest Review, XLVIII (Autumn), 348.

Dated "Farmington Avenue, Hartford. Dec. 21," to Howells, explaining that he didn't invite Thomas Bailey Aldrich to stay with him because he thought he was living in town. The letter is reproduced in facsimile on the front cover; the original is in the Ferguson collection of the Bridwell Library, Southern Methodist University.

B20 COHEN, HENNIG. "Twain's Jumping Frog: Folktale to Literature to Folktale," Western Folklore, XXII (January), 17-18.

The story of a frog filled with shot was common in oral tradition and had appeared in newspapers several times before MT wrote his famous sketch. The account of a gamecock filled with rifle balls (here reprinted from the San Francisco Evening Bulletin of December 11, 1867, with credit to the Territorial Enterprise) conjectures that the trickster got his idea from MT, but the story may well have existed independently as a folk tale. Abstract in AES, VI (1963), 2674; reprinted in Twainian, XXIII (March-April, 1964).

B21 COX, JAMES M. "The Muse of Samuel Clemens," Massachusetts Review, V (Autumn), 127-41.

MT made his wife Olivia his editor, "defining the much deeper role her image played in his creative memory. She was, by virtue of his imagination, part of his identity as a man and as a writer." Abstract in AES, VIII (1965), 101; reprinted in Twainian, XXV (January-February, 1966).

B22 COYLE, WILLIAM. "Never the Twain," CEA Critic, XXVI (November), 1, 3.

On school adaptations of HF, some American and some British, which he saw on sale in Brazil when he was a Fulbright lecturer there. Simplified classics have their value to foreign students, but HF is a poor choice, with the language destroyed and with it the characterization. "Little remains but the plot, which some have defended but few have praised." Abstract in AES, XI (1968), 2794; reprinted in Twainian, XXVIII (March-April, 1968).

B23 [DAVIS, CHESTER L.] "Clara, a Great Person in Her Own Right," Twainian, XXII (January-February), 1-2.

On MT's daughter, who died November 19, 1962, and her assistance to the Mark Twain

([DAVIS, CHESTER L.])
Research Foundation, while declining to
act as censor; "The files, [sic] of your
Foundation, [sic] must necessarily be made
public solely in the manner and to the extent that your Secretary believes it in
the furtherance of scholarship relating to
the life and writings of Mark Twain. It
can now be said that at no time during the
past 20 years had Clara given to your foundation any substantial money to defray expenses of operation, she very early taking
the position that to do so during her lifetime would be improper." Quotes a letter
from Clara dated January 8, 1958, denying
"so palpably false an untruth as that described in the Utica Globe" (reprinted
as "Mark Twain's Courtship" in Twainian,
XVI, November-December, 1957, 4, 1957.B28).

B24   ____. "Edward H. House Correspondence.
'Prince and the Pauper' Dramatization,"
Twainian, XXII (March-April), 1-3; (May-
June), 2-4.
Letters by MT and others on a variety of
topics, including the participation of
House in a stage version of The Prince and
the Pauper. There is a letter from MT to
his sister Pamela touching this topic, and
other letters include one from M. E. (Mary
Elenor?) Clemens, concerning Pamela's ill-
ness in her later years. MT letters to
House concern The Prince and the Pauper,
Colonel Mulberry Sellers in Age, the publication of Grant's Memoirs, "An Imaginary
Conversation between Mr. & Mrs. Clemens"
(delightfully profane), the Paige type-setting machine, and the text of "S'klk!
G'lang!," a 25-line poem by MT "apparently
unpublished." Abstract in AES, VIII (1965),
1849, 1851; reprinted in Twainian, XXV
(January-February, 1966), 3.

B25   DUNNE, FINLEY PETER. "On Mark Twain," in his
Mr. Dooley Remembers, ed. Peter Dunne (Boston: Little, Brown and Company),
pp. 239-68.
Dunne's comments on MT in December, 1935,
praising him, recalling personal acquaintance, and recounting anecdotes. On p. 242,
tells of MT dining in London with Edwin Abbey and repeating his talk originally given
in Paris before the Stomach Club [text in
Playboy, 1974.B11]. Some time later, on Abbey's urging, MT repeated it before a larger
audience at a dinner given at the Lyceum by
Henry Irving; the response was one of general embarrassment. Also tells of the time
when "Henry James, the flawless, the sedate,
the impeccable Henry asked him, 'Do you know
Bret Harte?' 'Yes,' Mark replied readily,
'I know the son of a bitch.'" [Excerpts are
reprinted as "Mr. Dooley's Friends: Teddy
Roosevelt and Mark Twain," in Atlantic
Monthly, CCVII (September), 78-80, 88-99 and
abstracted in AES, X (1967), No. 1592; reprinted in Twainian, XXVII (January-February,
1968).]

B26   DURHAM, PHILIP. [Brief review: Pascal Covici, Mark Twain's Humor: the Image of a
World (1962).] Western Folklore, XXII
(July), 217.
"Such an ambitious project must lose direction at times and become thin on occasion, but the result is a fairly sensible
interpretation," much preferable to "those
recently coming from prominent academic
psychologists."

B27   ELISTRATOVA, A. "Mark Tven--Nepoiukhshii
Vulkan [Mark Twain--an Unextinguished Vol-
cano]," Voprosy Literatury, VII (August),
224-28.
A review of A. Startsev, Mark Tven i Amerika [Mark Twain and America]. Contemporary
American biographers describe MT's life as
a triumph of individualism in a land of
equal opportunity; this is "using the name
and fame of a great writer to promote American capitalism," in the opinion of A. Startsev, who tries to present the writer's life
as an American tragedy and stresses his pas-
sionate hostility toward capitalist America.
[In Russian.]

B28   *FAIRLEY, BARKER. "Raabe and Mark Twain: A
Point of Contact," Jahrbuch der Raabe-
Gesellschaft, nv: 76-77.
[Source: Leary (1970), p. 63.]

B29   FEUCHTWANGER, LION. The House of Desdemona;
or, the Laurels and Limitations of Historical Fiction, Detroit: Wayne State University Press. On MT and his historical fiction
(CY, GA, HF, Hadleyburg, MS, JA, P&P),
pp. 97-108.
"The greatest of American poets, Samuel
Langhorne Clemens...is scarcely less bitter
at heart than Herman Melville. But for most
of his life he bound his bitterness up in
his breast." He is a romantic, moved by
human suffering, but a good reporter and
"thoroughly and completely honest."

B30   FITZGERALD, F. SCOTT. The Letters of F. Scott
Fitzgerald, ed. Andrew Turnbull. New York:
Charles Scribner's Sons.
On p. 593, acknowledges his debt to "the
great central parts of Huckleberry Finn" in
a letter to Morton Kroll (August 9, 1939).

B31   GALE, ROBERT L. "The Prince and the Pauper
and King Lear," Mark Twain Journal, XII
(Spring), 14-17.
MT read widely in preparation for writing
P&P; among his sources may have been Shake-
speare, whom he had occasionally mentioned.
Several parallels to Lear are noted, includ-
ing speeches on mercy by the boy-king and by
Lear. Abstract in AES, VIII (1961), 1060.

B32   GERBER, JOHN C. "Mark Twain," in James Wood-
ress, ed., American Literary Scholarship:
An Annual/1963 (Durham, North Carolina:
Duke University Press, 1965), pp. 53-63.

(GERBER, JOHN C.)

The first of what has become an annual survey of MT scholarship (and as the first, covering some material earlier than 1963). Contents: "i. Texts and Editions"; "ii. Biography"; "iii. Criticism." Although Gerber does not list everything written about MT in 1963, he provides extremely valuable brief descriptions and frank estimates of a number of items he lists. [Contents have not been cross-checked for this and succeeding years, but most of the material appears also to be incorporated in the present bibliography. The chief value of Gerber's survey lies in the annotations, which are important individually and for placing many items within a broader context of Mark Twain scholarship; the survey may also prove useful as an independent check of published material, and, in case of error, on facts of publication. This has been responsible and thoughtful work from the first, and, if anything, has shown a steady growth in sophistication with passing years. It was the work of John Gerber through the coverage for 1968 (published in 1970), and since then it has been the very able work of Hamlin Hill; both are known MT scholars and familiar with trends in their field of study.]

B33   GIBSON, WILLIAM M. [Review: Louis J. Budd, Mark Twain: Social Philosopher (1962).] American Literature, XXXV (May), 250-51.

"Adds much new evidence for the understanding of Clemens's social commitments and political forays." "If the tenor of Mr. Budd's book occasionally seems restrictively modern, the analysis...is new and authentic."

B34   GILENSON, BORIS. "Mark Twain--An Accuser," Soviet Literature, XII, 152-56.

Surveys Russian editions and criticisms of MT, who is very popular in Russia. Principal emphasis is on Abel Startsev's Mark Twain and America, which emphasizes the relation of the writer and his society, and is supported by new data made available in recent years. Also observes that Van Wyck Brooks's The Ordeal of Mark Twain, "despite its obviously mistaken, Freudian treatment of Mark Twain as an individual, presented the fruitful thesis of the hostility of American society to the full creative development of the writer." Abstract in AES, VII (1964), 1523.

B35   GIPSON, LAWRENCE H. "Reminiscences of a Rhodes Scholar at Oxford in the Edwardian Era," The American Oxonian, L (April), 64-72.

On pp. 70-72, describes MT receiving his Oxford degree in 1907 and his solemn disregard of the friendly comments by students in the galleries.

B36   GREEN, MARTIN. "Twain and Whitman: the Problem of 'American' Literature," in his Re-Appraisals: Some Commonsense Readings in American Literature (London: Hugh Evelyn).

Considers MT as an entertainer and Huckleberry Finn "a charming children's book, with some beautiful passages," but not a major novel (pp. 142-43). However, "in ways that transcend the limits of humour, Twain was a fine lyric poet, a master of spoken language in print, and a beautiful ironist. The first two talents are best exemplified in Huckleberry Finn, but the third becomes major in A Connecticut Yankee; and this book represents Twain's true achievement perhaps better than the more famous one.... The important part of the book is the friendly, uncritical but lively irony it directs at the Yankee himself and what he stands for."

B37   GRUNDY, J. OWEN. "R. L. S. in Greenwich Village," Bulletin of the New York Public Library, LXVII (March), 152-54.

When Stevenson came to America in 1887 he and MT "spent several restful hours together" in Washington Square Park; a watercolor of them by Luis Mora, National Arts Club, 15 Gramercy Park is reproduced in black-and-white, facing p. 154. Abstract in AES, VI (1963), 1567; reprinted in Twainian, XXIII (January-February, 1964).

B38   GUIDO, JOHN FOOTE. "King Leopold's Soliloquy," Papers of the Bibliographical Society of America, LVII (Third Quarter), 351-52.

The Bibliography of American Literature (II, No. 3485) describes a copy in the New York Public Library as intermediate between the first two issues of the first edition. "I have recently come upon what is apparently another intermediate in the Cornell University Library. This copy is identical to that described in the BAL, with the exception that page 32 is in the early state, that is, consistent with the first, second, and third issues of the first published edition." Abstract in AES, VII (1964), 197; reprinted in Twainian, XXIV (January-February, 1965).

B39   HANSEN, CHADWICK. "The Character of Jim and the Ending of Huckleberry Finn," Massachusetts Review, V (Autumn), 45-66.

Jim was Huck's "moral burden," in that "by his constant presence, and his constant decency, and his constant humanity he forces Huck to do something more than drift with the river. He forces Huck to come to grips with that part of himself which belongs to society"; in the ending Huck and Jim both allow themselves to be drawn into Tom's romantic schemes, but not without reservations. The closing sentences represent "for Huck an emotional, if not an intellectual rejection of civilization," and an escape both for Huck and for Jim. Abstract in AES, VIII (1965), 100; reprinted in Twainian, XXV (January-February, 1966).

1963 - Shorter Writings

B40 *HAYASHI, TETSUMARO. "Mark Twain's The Adven-
        tures of Huckleberry Finn: Hope for Man-
        kind," Lumina, No. 3 (1960).
        [Source: Kamei, Shunsuke, "Mark Twain in
        Japan," Mark Twain Journal, XII (Spring,
        1963), 20.]

B41 HAYS, JOHN Q. "Twainiana: Two Studies of
        Mark Twain's Art," Southwest Review, XLVIII
        (Summer), iv-v, 296-300.
        A review article on Pascal Covici, Mark
        Twain's Humor: The Image of a World and
        Henry Nash Smith, Mark Twain: The Develop-
        ment of a Writer. The approach is chiefly
        descriptive, summarizing and comparing the
        intentions and conclusions in the two books.

B42 *HIETSCH, OTTO. "Mark Twain and Johann
        Strauss," Jahrbuch für Amerikastudien,
        VIII, 210-11.
        A letter from MT to Strauss's widow in
        the Vienna City Library shows that MT visit-
        ed him May 26, 1899. [Source: MHRA Annual
        Bibliography (1963), No. 4723, and abstract
        in AES, VIII (1965), No. 1397, reprinted in
        Twainian, XXV (January-February, 1966).]

B43 HILL, HAMLIN. "Mark Twain: Audience and
        Artistry," American Quarterly, XV (Spring),
        25-40.
        On the influence of subscription publica-
        tion on MT's writing, and particularly on
        his padding, sensationalsim, and moralizing.
        Abstract in AES, VI (1963), 1552; reprinted
        in Twainian, XXIII (January-February, 1964).
        Article reprinted in Scott (1967),
        pp. 286-302. Reprinted without footnotes as
        "The Business and Social Influence of The
        Subscription Book," Twainian, XXII (May-
        June).

B44 HOFSTADTER, RICHARD. Anti-Intellectualism in
        American Life. New York: Alfred A. Knopf,
        pp. 241-44.
        Van Wyck Brooks is right to consider MT's
        enthusiasm for machinery over-done, but MT
        "was too much a moralist and a pessimist to
        imagine that mechanical progress was an all-
        sufficient end." Even in CY, MT recognized
        Hank Morgan's limitations. With other Amer-
        icans, MT ambivalently shared "a robust
        faith in the patent office and the future"
        and a regard for genteel Eastern culture.

B45 HUNTER, JIM. "Mark Twain and the Boy-Book
        in 19th-Century America," College English,
        XXIV (March), 430-38.
        This genre consists of works "composed
        about children for the amusement of adults,"
        but MT's writing overlaps with the genre of
        children's tales. "The moral impulse in
        Twain's books is toward maturity," but he
        remained "intensely nostalgic for his own
        childhood."

B46 JACOBS, ROBERT D. [Review: Louis J. Budd,
        Mark Twain: Social Philosopher (1962).]
        Journal of Southern History, XXIX (August),
        410-12.
        Praises the examination of neglected ma-
        terial to demonstrate that MT never became
        a liberal democrat.

B47 KAMEI, SHUNSUKE. "Mark Twain in Japan," Mark
        Twain Journal, XII (Spring), 10-11, 20.
        On MT's reputation in Japan, and transla-
        tions of his works. His reputation as a
        funny man, and the Japanese emphasis on
        British culture and lack of a frontier tra-
        dition have reduced his literary influence,
        despite his wide popularity. Cites Masajiro
        Hamada's Mark Twain: His Character and
        Works (1955) as the only "notable book on
        Mark Twain" he knows, "and of recent works
        on Twain I can cite only two articles:
        Tetsumaro Hayashi's 'Mark Twain's The Adven-
        tures of Huckleberry Finn: Hope for Man-
        kind' in Lumina No. 3 (1960) and Shunsuke
        Kamei's 'On Interpretations of The Adventures
        of Huckleberry Finn' in Comparative Litera-
        ture and Comparative Culture (1961)." Ab-
        stract in AES, VIII (1965), 1058.

B48 KANELLAKOU, CHRIS. "Mark Twain and the Chi-
        nese," Mark Twain Journal, XII (Spring),
        7-9, 20.
        Chiefly on his reaction to mistreatment of
        the Chinese in the West, and his respect for
        their honest, orderly conduct. Abstract in
        AES, VIII (1965), 1057.

B49 KAUFFMANN, STANLEY. "Mark Twain from Under
        Ground," New Republic, CXLVIII (April 6),
        20-22. A review of Bernard DeVoto, ed.,
        Letters from the Earth (1962).
        The fact that MT did not publish freely in
        his own time shows that he "was an artistic
        genius but morally an average man," although
        "he told as much truth as any American writ-
        er of his generation, more than most." Ab-
        stract in AES, VII (1964), 2726; reprinted
        in Twainian, XXIV (January-February, 1965).

B50 KAUL, A. N. "Huckleberry Finn: A Southwest-
        ern Statement," in his The American Vision:
        Actual and Ideal Society in Nineteenth-Cen-
        tury American Fiction. New Haven and Lon-
        don: Yale University Press, pp. 280-304.
        On the community of the raft.

B51 *KLOTZ, GÜNTHER. [Review: Bernard DeVoto, ed.,
        Letters from the Earth (1962).] Zeitschrift
        für Anglistik und Amerikanistik, XI (July),
        281-87.
        [Source: Abstract in AES, IX (1966), 342;
        reprinted in Twainian, XXVI (January-Febru-
        ary, 1967).]

B52 LEARY, LOUIS. "On Diminishing Mark Twain," Virginia Quarterly Review, XXXIX (Spring), 334-39.

A review-article covering Janet Smith's Mark Twain on the Damned Human Race (with remarks by MT which "can be as arresting today as they must have been fifty years ago"); DeVoto's Letters from the Earth ("much of Mark Twain's fulmination is dull indeed"); Budd's Mark Twain: Social Philosopher ("a hard-headed, informed, and reliable study," showing, in Budd's words that despite MT's "outrageous irony and his impulses toward nonconformity he was usually, at heart, in tune with his times"); and Henry Nash Smith's "carefully wrought Mark Twain: The Development of a Writer, which goes over much of the same ground, but draws less generously on topical writings." The collections of MT's later writings will give pleasure, but they diminish MT by diverting attention from a great artist to an ordinary thinker.

B53 LITTLE, GAIL B. "Three Novels for Comparative Study in the Twelfth Grade," English Journal, LII (October), 501-505.

On examining narrative technique, the three protagonists, and literary achievement in HF, The Catcher in the Rye, and Intruder in the Dust.

B54 LONG, E. HUDSON. "Mark Twain's Ordeal in Retrospect," Southwest Review, XLVIII (Autumn), 338-48.

Brooks undertook his study in order to show that MT was defeated by his environment, but more recent studies vitiate many of his arguments. MT's pessimism may best be explained, not as a consequence of an artist's surrender to materialism, but of personal tragedy; "moreover, there were national and international events in the making that a person of Twain's prescience could not face with optimism. Once he warned of the possibility of 'an inundation of Russian and German political degradations which would envelop the globe and steep it in a sort of Middle-Age night and slavery which would last till Christ comes again." Abstract in AES, VII (1964), 591; reprinted in Twainian, XXIV (January-February, 1965). The article is reprinted in Twainian, XXIII (May-June, 1964), 3-4; (July-August), 2-4.

B55 LOWENHERZ, ROBERT J. "The Beginning of Huckleberry Finn," American Speech, XXXVIII (October), 196-201.

In the opening 108 words, "Mark Twain firmly establishes the vernacular speech of his narrator, Huck, characterizes him, enunciates one of the major themes of the story [truth and falsehood], provides a frame of reference for the action, and even works in some free advertisement [sic] for his earlier novel The Adventures of Tom Sawyer." Here, as in the rest of HF, MT used

phonetic spelling of dialect "sparingly" and "functionally." Abstract in AES, VIII (1964), 1290.

B56 LYDENBERG, JOHN. [Review: Louis J. Budd, Mark Twain: Social Philosopher (1962) and Henry Nash Smith, Mark Twain: The Development of A Writer (1962).] American Quarterly, XV (Spring), 101-103.

In these "more stately and sophisticated structures...Henry Nash Smith shows the ordeal of Mark Twain to be more complex than Van Wyck Brooks had thought, and Louis Budd makes clear that Mark Twain's vision of America was more complicated than Bernard DeVoto had imagined." These new books present "almost diametrically opposed views of the same man," where Budd's emphasis on what MT said about particular social questions reveals "a comparatively simple man" and Smith "tells us more about Twain's underlying social philosophy."

B57 LYON, PETER. Success Story: The Life and Times of S. S. McClure. New York: Charles Scribner's Sons.

Mentions MT passim (indexed); on the abortive plan to have him edit a new magazine, pp. 180-86.

B58 McCLARY, BEN HARRIS. "Melville, Twain, and the Legendary 'Tennessee Poet,'" Tennessee Folklore Society Bulletin, XXIX (September), 63-64.

"The poor poet of Tennessee" in Moby Dick (Chapter I) has not been identified, but in Captain Stormfield's Visit to Heaven MT describes "that tailor Billings, from Tennessee, [who] wrote poetry that Homer or Shakespeare couldn't begin to come up to; but nobody would print it"; Billings cannot be traced. Abstract in AES, VII (1964), 1564.

B59 McCURDY, FRANCES L. [Review: Pascal Covici, Mark Twain's Humor: The Image of a World (1962).] Quarterly Journal of Speech, XLIX (February), 92-93.

"An occasional symbolic interpretation is strained and unconvincing, and psychological insights generally associated only with trained psychiatrists are ascribed to Clemens, but the writer's thesis is, on the whole, interestingly supported by illustrations and quotations."

B60 MACINNES, COLIN. "Everything on Our Raft," New Statesman, LXV (June 21), 933-34.

Notes MT's portrayal of his times, and his language and his controlled balance of the tragic and the idyllic. "Huckleberry Finn is one of those stories, rare even among masterpieces, on which grace has descended absolutely; and this is because the narrative, so charming and arresting in itself, is constantly and effortlessly sustained by underlying theme and symbol." For example, "the raft is a birth-life symbol, and therein lies its fascination." Abstract in AES, VII (1964), 1109.

1963 - Shorter Writings

B61 McNAMARA, EUGENE. "A Note on 'My Platonic
     Sweetheart,'" Mark Twain Journal, XII
     (Spring), 18-19, 21.
          "The cohesion of the dream-world and the
     child-world is most clearly seen" in this
     sketch of a recurring dream; dreams offered
     a means of escape to child-like innocence
     after failures in the adult world. Ab-
     stract in AES, VIII (1965), 1061.

B62 MAXWELL, D. E. S. "Twain as Satirist," in
     his American Literature: The Intellectual
     Background. London: Routledge & Kegan
     Paul, pp. 192-235.
          Traces MT's satire through his various
     works, relating it to other traditions of
     satire. On pp. 292-93, praises the collo-
     quial language of HF as well as MT's more
     formal prose, "capable...of a piercing
     simplicity."

B63 MILNE, W. GORDON. [Review: Bernard DeVoto,
     ed., Letters from the Earth (1962).] Books
     Abroad, XXXVII (Summer), 336-37.
          Brief and primarily descriptive. The
     average reader "will appreciate the oppor-
     tunity to read some vintage Twain."

B64 NEIDER, CHARLES, ed. "Mark Twain: 'Reflec-
     tions on Religion.'" Hudson Review, XVI
     (Autumn), 329-52.
          The text of previously unpublished mate-
     rial, now released by MT's daughter Mrs.
     Clara Clemens Samossoud, with brief intro-
     duction and notes by Neider. Abstract in
     AES, VII (1964), 355; reprinted in Twain-
     ian, XXIV (January-February, 1965), 3.

B65 O'CONNOR, WILLIAM VAN. [Review: Henry Nash
     Smith, Mark Twain, The Development of a
     Writer (1962).] Nineteenth-Century Fic-
     tion, XVIII (December), 291-95.
          "For a long time now, Twain scholars have
     been a strange breed in the study of liter-
     ature, American or otherwise. They direct
     their concern less at the work than at the
     man.... It is everywhere evident in Smith's
     work that he is very knowledgeable about
     Mark Twain. I am critical of Mark Twain,
     The Development of a Writer only because it
     seems representative of the whole Twain
     mystique." O'Connor devotes over a page to
     the imperfections of Pudd'nhead Wilson and
     concludes: "My main point ought to be per-
     fectly clear. Twain--a very imperfect writ-
     er--was no true novelist, and we ought to
     quit saying or implying that he was." Ab-
     stract in AES, VIII (1964), 2235; reprinted
     in Twainian, XXIV (January-February, 1965).

B66 OLAN, LEVI A. "The Voice of the Lonesome:
     Alienation from Huck Finn to Holden Caul-
     field," Southwest Review, XLVIII (Spring),
     143-50.
          Begins with the Brooks thesis, chiefly on
     the destructive influence of surroundings
     on MT, though warning that his "posing and
     childish self-adulation" and the probability

that "the major part of his literary produc-
tivity is of a low grade" should not blind
the reader to the merits of Huckleberry
Finn, in which "he responded to the human
situation as a total being, an artist who
apprehends by a mysterious talent and creates uninhibited by either logic or purpose," anticipating the theme of alienation
in modern literature. Abstract in AES, VII
(1964); reprinted in Twainian, XXIV (January-February).

B67 PARSONS, COLEMAN O. "Mark Twain in Ceylon,"
     Twainian, XXII (January-February), 4;
     (March-April), 3-4.
          On MT's 1896 visit during the lecture tour
     described in Following the Equator. Con-
     cludes: "My materials are chiefly drawn
     from the great newspaper collection of the
     British Museum: The Times of Ceylon, Colum-
     bo, January 16, 22, and April 1, 9, 1896;
     The Ceylon Observer, Columbo, January 16,
     April 1, 9, 1896; and The Ceylon Examiner,
     Columbo, April 2, 4, 6, 1896" (liberally
     quoted, together with other local material).
     Abstracts in AES, VIII (1965), 1848, 1850;
     reprinted in Twainian, XXV (January-February,
     1966), 3.

B68 _____. "Mark Twain: Sightseer in India,"
     Mississippi Quarterly, XVI (Spring, 1963),
     76-93.
          A detailed account of MT's 1896 visit to
     India while on the world lecture tour that
     was the basis for FE; documented from con-
     temporary Indian newspapers, published works
     by and about MT, and MT's unpublished pa-
     pers. Abstract in AES, VII (1964), 844.

B69 PEARCE, ROY HARVEY. "'The End. Yours Truly,
     Huck Finn': Postscript," Modern Language
     Quarterly, XXIV (September), 253-56.
          The territory for which Huck was going to
     "light out" was Indian Territory (now Okla-
     homa); although he sought to escape civili-
     zation, he would be only "one step ahead of
     the rest: boomers, dukes and dauphins, Aunt
     Sallies, Colonel Sherburns, and Wilkses--
     civilizers all." Abstract in AES, VII
     (1964), 1795; reprinted in Twainian, XXIV
     (January-February, 1965).

B70 *RIZZARDI, A. "Anglo-American Literature,"
     Convivium (Bologna?), XXX (May-June),
     370-71.
          A review of DeVoto, ed., Letters from the
     Earth. [Source: Abstract in AES, VII
     (1964), 727.]

B71 ROGERS, FRANKLIN R. "The Road to Reality:
     Burlesque Travel Literature and Roughing
     It," Bulletin of the New York Public Libra-
     ry, LXVII (March), 155-68.
          After tracing the tradition from William
     Combe's The Tour of Dr. Syntax in Search of
     the Picturesque (which began appearing se-
     rially in 1809), with the development of a
     companion who "constantly reminds the reader

(ROGERS, FRANKLIN R.)
and the traveler himself of those unpictur-
esque elements of the actuality which the
traveler has chosen to ignore," Rogers
shows MT's experiments with point of view.
From using the imaginary companion "Mr.
Brown" in his travel letters in California
papers, MT went on to the portrayal of a
narrator in Roughing It who links the old-
timer and the tenderfoot. Abstract in AES,
VI (1963), 1568; reprinted in Twainian,
XXIII (January-February, 1964).

B72 ROVIT, EARL. [Review: Pascal Covici, Mark
Twain's Humor: The Image of a World
(1962).] Books Abroad, XXXVII (Summer),
333-34.
"In a sense, an extension of Kenneth
Lynn's argument in Mark Twain and Southwestern Humor." The argument for conscious
artistry in the ending of HF is "ingenious,
but to me unconvincing." Despite "the in-
trusive clumsiness of Covici's thesis-
machinery, there is much perception on
Twain and his organic relation to the American tradition."

B73 RUBIN, LOUIS D., JR. "Mark Twain and the
Language of Experience," Sewanee Review:
LXXI (Autumn), 664-73.
A review of Henry Nash Smith's Mark Twain:
The Development of a Writer (1962), which
applies to Huckleberry Finn the critical approach suggested by Erich Auerbach in Mime-
sis: The Representation of Reality in Western Literature (1946). "One great merit of
Henry Nash Smith's study is its demonstration of the way in which for Twain the
problem of idea and image, of form and meaning, is always one of fictional technique.
The successes and failures of Huckleberry
Finn clearly and matchlessly reflect its
author's struggle to give meaning to his
experience."

B74 SCHROEDER, FRED. "America's First Literary
Realist: Horatio Alger, Jr.," Western Hu-
manities Review, XVII (Spring), 129-37.
Includes comparisons of Alger's books to
Huckleberry Finn. Abstract in AES, VII
(1964) 691; reprinted in Twainian, XXIV
(January-February, 1965).

B75 SCOTT, ARTHUR L. "The Innocents Adrift Edited by Mark Twain's Official Biographer,"
Publications of the Modern Language Association, LXXVIII (June), 230-37.
What was originally the beginning of a
book was trimmed by Paine to produce "Down
the Rhône" for Europe and Elsewhere; what
disappeared was a wealth of anecdote and
digression, four companions, and MT's spelling and punctuation. The irresponsible
editing is of the sort also to be found in
Paine's version of MS, which, with other
posthumously published manuscripts, has
"given us an exaggerated picture of Mark
Twain's bitterness and pessimism at the turn

of the century." Abstract in AES, VIII
(1965), 1497; reprinted in Twainian, XXV
(January-February, 1966).

B76 SMITH, BRADFORD. "Mark Twain and the Mystery
of Identity," College English, XXIV (March),
425-30.
"The key to Mark Twain's mind is the concept of identity": MT focuses on the identity of the individual, and "nearly everybody in Mark Twain's books, consciously or
unconsciously, is playing a part." There
is a consistent pattern in which the hero
solves or attempts to solve problems involving choices "by a change of identity and
a change of place."

B77 SPILLER, ROBERT E. "Columnist's Chats,"
Saturday Review of Literature, XLVI (April
27), 39, 44.
A review of Charles Neider, ed., The Complete Essays of Mark Twain. "These pieces
in Mr. Neider's latest collection are neither 'essays,' nor is the book 'complete';
they are simply some more miscellaneous
writings that deserve republication and that
didn't get into the two earlier volumes...
Mr. Neider's books are well-printed, well-
bound, and well-indexed, and they fill in
the gaps for the Mark Twain enthusiast...
even though there are annoying elements of
misrepresentation."

B78 STARTSEV, A. "Mark Tven i Russkie [Mark Twain
and the Russians]," Voprosy Literatury, VII
(December), 116-21.
American publishers suppress MT's criticism of the political, religious, and moral
views of the American capitalist society.
The protests of Soviet literary critics and
their discussion with Charles Neider have
led to improvement, as has the publication
in the Soviet Union of a complete edition
of MT's works in Russian translation, with
none of his anti-American writings omitted.
[In Russian.]

B79 STEWART, D. H. "Myth and Truth in Criticism,"
Minnesota Review, III (Summer), 452-60.
Condemns "the critics' pilfering of modern
anthropological and psychological apparatus,"
and makes only passing mention of HF criticism: "A critic who tells me I am somehow
rehearsing a bear-myth or making sacrifice
to a River God when I read Huckleberry Finn
forfeits my trust immediately." Abstract in
AES, IX (1966), 1742; reprinted in Twainian,
XXVI (January-February, 1967).

B80 STRONKS, JAMES B. "Mark Twain's Stage Debut
as Seen by Hamlin Garland," New England
Quarterly, XXXVI (March), 85-6.
Garland heard MT and George Washington
Cable lecture in Boston, either November 13
or 15, 1884, and recorded his impressions in
a notebook which has not been published; his
comments appear here for the first time, describing MT's voice as "flexible and with a

(STRONKS, JAMES B.)
fine compass. Running to very fine deep notes easily. He hits off his most delicious things with a raspy, dry 'rosen' voice" and he never smiles. Abstract in AES, VI (1963), 2530; reprinted in Twainian, XXIII (March-April, 1964).

B81 TANNER, TONY. "Mark Twain and Wattie Bowser," Mark Twain Journal, XII (Spring), 1-6.
MT's letter of March 20, 1880, in answer to a Dallas schoolboy who had asked him whether he would be a boy again if he could. MT's comments on boyhood are interesting in view of the problems he was currently having with HF; there is also commentary on style, and a discussion by Tanner of the question of youth for MT and his reaction to Howells's Indian Summer. Abstract in AES, VIII (1965), 1056.

B82 TAPER, BERNARD. "Mark Twain's San Francisco," American Heritage, XIV (August), 50-53, 93-94.
A brief popular account consisting largely of familiar biographical material. "A revised version of 'Mark Twain's San Francisco' will serve as the introduction to his edition of Twain's San Francisco journalism to be published by McGraw-Hill this fall under the same title." Abstract in AES, VI (1963), 2388; reprinted in Twainian, XXIII (March-April, 1964). Article reprinted in Twainian, 1963.B83.

B83 _____. "Mark Twain's San Francisco, Introduction by Taper," Twainian, XXII (November-December), 1-3 (concluded in the following issue).
Reprinting of the introduction to Taper's new book, a description of the city and its literati in the 1860's.

B84 TAYLOR, NANCY DEW. "The River of Faulkner and Mark Twain," Mississippi Quarterly, XVI (Fall), 191-99.
Parallels in character suggest that Faulkner had HF in mind as he wrote The Old Man, and his tall convict may be "a composite of the outstanding characteristics of Huck, Jim, and Tom." There are also parallels in theme and in symbolic use of the river. Abstract in AES, VIII (1965), 2642; reprinted in Twainian, XXV (January-February, 1966).

B85 Van Der BEETS, RICHARD. "A Note on Henry James' 'Western Barbarian,'" Western Humanities Review, XVII (Spring), 175-78.
There is evidence of a possible influence in "some rather curious parallels of both incident and phrase that exist between the characterization of The American's central figure, Christopher Newman, and the early persona, or projected image, of Mark Twain as revealed primarily in his early writings and The Innocents Abroad (1869)," providing "characterization, details, and background"

not available from James's personal experience. Abstract in AES, VII (1964), 695; reprinted in Twainian, XXIV (January-February, 1965).

B86 WAGENKNECHT, EDWARD. [Review: Louis J. Budd, Mark Twain: Social Philosopher (1962) and Henry Nash Smith, Mark Twain: The Development of a Writer (1962).] English Language Notes, I (September), 75-77.
Budd lets his materials take him where their own logic leads, and shows MT as "essentially a good, intelligent Republican"; this portrait contrasts with Philip Foner's depiction of MT as rather more radical, although Foner has not distorted his materials. Smith "studies primarily his author's style but he studies it not in isolation but rather in full consciousness that 'questions of meaning' and 'ethical ideas' are involved." Smith's approach is essentially sound, although his contention that Huck is "a mask for the writer, not a fully developed character...is valid only if one believes the reactions and judgments of Huck himself unconvincing"; Smith overstates the matter when he says that MT's Whittier Birthday Speech manifests in MT "a latent hostility" toward the New England writers he burlesqued.

B87 WERMUTH, PAUL C. "Santayana and Huckleberry Finn," New England Quarterly, XXXVI (March), 79-82.
Summarizes Santayana's "Tom Sawyer and Don Quixote" (Mark Twain Quarterly, IX [Winter, 1952], 1-3; 1952.B41), observing that from all other evidence "Santayana seems to have been monumentally uninterested in Twain." Having been given a copy of Huckleberry Finn by Cyril Clemens, he dutifully read it; but "in his wonderfully polite and subtle way," Santayana seems to be saying between the lines: "Well, here I am, an old man; I have taken my precious time to read this man's books because everybody said I should; and all I found was that I was right in the first place not to have read them years ago."

B88 WHITFORD, KATHRYN. "Rough Spots in 'Roughing It,'" Mississippi Quarterly, XVI (Spring), 94-96.
A hoax article, citing inconsistent details [in Chapters XXXII-XXXIII] as evidence that "Mark Twain is a hoax--any work composed after Roughing It cannot be other than the work of an imposter, for young Samuel Clemens died one night in a snowstorm on the Nevada desert." Abstract in AES, VII (1964), 845.

B89 WIGGINS, ROBERT A. "Pudd'nhead Wilson: A Literary Caesarian Operation," College English, XXV (December), 182-86.
Disagreeing with recent praise of the book, follows the contention by Richard

(WIGGINS, ROBERT A.)
Chase that "the characters and their relationships are not adequate to the moral
action"; even Chase might have made more of
the flawed structure of the work. Abstract
in AES, VII (1964), 299; reprinted in
Twainian, XXIV (January-February, 1965).

B90 WINTEROWD, W. ROSS. [Review: Pascal Covici,
Jr., Mark Twain's Humor: The Image of a
World (1962).] Western Humanities Review,
XVII (Spring), 194.
"Covici's work does not constitute an informing theory, but rather an extended ex-
plication, and in most instances a good
one," revealing the transformation of humor
from an end in itself to a tool of the artist. There is a weakness in Covici's shifting view of the hoax from a stylistic device
to one of plot, but the book contains "insight and sound judgment...above all, a
fresh and usually acute look at several of
Mark Twain's most provocative works."

1964 A BOOKS

A1 CLEMENS, SAMUEL L. Pudd'nhead Wilson. New
York: New American Library (A Signet Classic).
Includes a brief foreword by Wright Morris, dealing sensibly with MT's life but
not examining PW in depth. There is a
"Selected Bibliography" in which the section
devoted to "Other Works by Mark Twain" emphasizes Signet editions and the "Selected
Biography and Criticism" stresses well-known
books without consideration of their avail-
ability, relevance, or value; it lists no
articles in journals, and gives no indication of where a reader might find material
dealing specifically with PW.

A2 DUCKETT, MARGARET. Mark Twain and Bret Harte.
Norman: University of Oklahoma Press.
An attempt to put the relationship of the
two in perspective: "though the break in
the friendship has frequently been alluded
to by critics hostile to Harte, there is
another side of the story which has never
been told" (p. viii). Notes that Bret
Harte's diary, 1881-1888, is now in the New
York Public Library. (p. ix).

A3 FATOUT, PAUL. Mark Twain in Virginia City.
Bloomington: Indiana University Press.
A valuable work on this formative period
in MT's life. Fatout has found previously
unknown writing by MT; cites contemporary
newspaper material about MT not listed in
the present bibliography.

A4 HILL, HAMLIN. Mark Twain and Elisha Bliss.
Columbia: University of Missouri Press.
"The present volume concentrates on
Twain's business relationship with Bliss and
the American Publishing Company. The decade
during which Twain was Bliss's most important

author was germinal, I think, to Twain's
later career as a publisher and businessman
and significant, in ways that have never
been fully explored, to his aims, techniques, and development in writing" (p. vii).

A5 SMITH, HENRY NASH. Mark Twain's Fable of
Progress: Political and Economic Ideas in
"A Connecticut Yankee." New Brunswick, N.J.:
Rutgers University Press.
Places MT's book in context by comparing
it to Charles Dudley Warner's A Little Journey in the World and William Dean Howells's
A Hazard of New Fortunes as contemporary
portrayals of industrialism, then traces the
development of the novel and concludes with
a treatment of ideas in the book, including
MT's growing distaste for the human costs of
the machine. Meticulously documented.

A6 VARBLE, RACHEL M. Jane Clemens: The Story of
Mark Twain's Mother. Garden City, N.Y.:
Doubleday & Company, Inc.
Written as a popular account, without spe-
cific documentation for individual state-
ments of fact.

A7 WIGGINS, ROBERT A. Mark Twain: Jackleg Novelist. Seattle: University of Washington
Press.
Begins with the disastrous Whittier Birthday Dinner speech of 1877 as "traumatic for
Twain's literary psyche," revealing "his
deep-seated insecurity as a writer and...
especially relevant to his career as a novelist." Wiggins argues that "limited understanding of realism and humor," together
with effective technical equipment, helped
shape MT's personal approach to writing, and
that "his difficulties as a novelist began
when he became self-conscious about the novel." He traces the twelve novels, from GA
through MS, explaining their success or relative failure in terms of MT's fidelity to
a realistic approach. Wiggins argues that
MT's popularity grew in part from "a strong
and pervasive American folk tradition," and
in him "the public was approving an image of
itself."

1964 B SHORTER WRITINGS

B1 ALTER, ROBERT. Rogue's Progress: Studies in
the Picaresque Novel. Cambridge, Massachusetts: Harvard University Press. Pp. 117-21.
Places Huck in a tradition of picaroons,
with compassion but a sufficiently "thick
skin to prevent experience from paralyzing
him or torturing him excessively," while rejecting society's hypocrisies. HF is superior to the traditional picaresque novels in
its language, which reflects Huck's moral
position.

B2 ANDERSON, JAMES BRUCE. "Mark Twain in Shawneetown, Illinois, Home of Tom Sawyer and Colonel Sellers," Charlatan (Iowa City, Iowa),
No. 2, [pp. 1-8].

1964 - Shorter Writings

(ANDERSON, JAMES BRUCE)

Although TS is generally thought to be based on memories of Hannibal, Missouri, a case may be made that MT's more immediate source was Shawneetown; he was acquainted with one Thomas Sawyer Spivey of that city. The Eschol Sellers who threatened suit over use of his name in GA is probably the individual of that name from Bowlesville, Illinois, three miles from Shawneetown. Among sources cited on the acquaintance of MT and Thomas Sawyer Spivey are a Spivey family history and Geo. P. Dent, ed., Four Score and More (n.p., n.d.; Chapter VII, "Looking Backward," is here extensively quoted). MT may have found inspiration not only for locale, but also for such incidents as being lost in a cave. Abstract in AES, IX (1966), 2870.

B3   ANON. "Juvenilia," Times Literary Supplement, January 16, p. 41. Includes a review of Henry Duskis, The Forgotten Writings of Mark Twain (1963).

This material from the Buffalo Express is not MT's best work, and the material is fragmentary and inconvenient to read.

B4   ANON. "Mark Twain Items Published Elsewhere from 'Abstracts of English Studies, Vol. 6,'" Twainian, XXIII (January-February), 3-4; (March-April), 3-4.

Reprints all the abstracts of articles pertaining to MT from Abstracts of English Studies, VI (1963), accurately and with AES numbering.

B5   ANON. "Mark Twain Letter Found," Mark Twain Journal, XII (Winter), 15.

While the library of the late Walter Williams was being catalogued at the University of Missouri, a letter from MT was found (March 4, 1894, here reprinted), declining an unspecified invitation from Williams, then editor of the Columbia Herald and later founder and dean of the School of Journalism, and finally president of the University of Missouri.

B6   ANON. "Twain Goes West," Times Literary Supplement, November 19, p. 1041.

A review article, covering Robert A. Wiggins, Mark Twain: Jackleg Novelist; Henry Nash Smith, Mark Twain's Fable of Progress; Paul Fatout, Mark Twain in Virginia City. Descriptive and laudatory.

B7   *ARIKAWA, SHOJI. "Mark Twain's Sense of Equilibrium in The Prince and the Pauper," Kyusha American Literature, No. 7, pp. 13-20.

[Source: MHRA Annual Bibliography (1965), No. 6957.]

B8   BABCOCK, C. MERTON. "Mark Twain, Mencken and 'The Higher Goofyism,'" American Quarterly, XVI (Winter), 587-94.

Compares the satire of these two moralists and gifted users of the language.

B9   ____. "Mark Twain's Map of Paris," Texas Quarterly, VII (Autumn), 92-97.

On MT's 1870 map of Paris as a mirror-image: "The trouble with a great many readers of Mark Twain is that they forget to read him backwards. They might as well try to find their way about the city of Paris with the author's Map--but no mirror. Like Swift, Mark Twain employed irony so masterfully in his writings as, frequently, to defeat his own purposes." Abstract in AES, VIII (1965), 2413; reprinted in Twainian, XXV (January-February, 1966).

B10   BAENDER, PAUL. "The Date of Mark Twain's 'The Lowest Animal,'" American Literature, XXXVI (May), 174-79.

MT apparently began the essay "around August 13, 1896, shortly before Susy's death on the 18th," rather than in 1897 or 1905, as DeVoto speculates; "What helped Twain complete 'The Lowest Animal' in those heavy days was his familiarity with its opinions, not an infatuation with them because of the circumstances." Abstract in AES, VIII (1965), 5; reprinted in Twainian, XXV (January-February, 1966).

B11   ____, and FREDERICK ANDERSON. "Twain in Progress: Two Projects," American Quarterly, XVI (Winter), 621-23.

Baender briefly describes the forthcoming edition of MT's previously published works and lists the editors, and Anderson describes plans for the materials previously unpublished or only "published in such inadequately prepared editions as to be unacceptable by contemporary scholars."

B12   BASSAN, MAURICE. "The Poetaster and the Horse-Doctors," Midcontinent American Studies Journal, V (Spring), 55-59.

"Will Carleton is one of the more deservedly obscure of our nineteenth-century poetasters"; as a member of the Authors' Club in New York, MT was dragged into the controversy over Carleton's election to membership, and subsequently resigned. Abstract in AES, VII (1964), 2183; reprinted in Twainian, XXIV (January-February, 1965).

B13   BATES, ALLAN. "The Quintus Curtius Snodgrass Letters: A Clarification of the Mark Twain Canon," American Literature, XXXVI (March), 31-37.

A series of travel letters published in the New Orleans Daily Crescent in 1861 have been tentatively attributed to MT. Minnie M. Brashear published four of these letters in Mark Twain, Son of Missouri (1934), and Ernest E. Leisy and Thomas Ewing Dabney published these and six more letters in The Letters of Quintus Curtius Snodgrass (1946). These letters cannot be the work of MT, because they involve a running exchange with another reporter and discuss events in Louisiana at a time when MT was in St. Louis.

(BATES, ALLAN)
Abstract in AES, VII (1964), 1993; reprinted in Twainian, XXIV (January-February, 1965), 4.

B14   BAUMRIND, SHELDON, D.D.S. "Mark Twain Visits the Dentist," Journal of the California Dental Association, December.
[Source: reprint in Mark Twain Papers.]
On MT's unfinished and unpublished "Happy Memories of the Dental Chair," which described his lengthy and painful treatment of Riggs' Disease by Dr. John M. Riggs of Hartford, Connecticut.

B15   BAYLEN, JOSEPH O. "Mark Twain, W. T. Stead, and 'The Tell-Tale Hands,'" American Quarterly, XVI (Winter), 606-12.
On MT's interest in palmistry, and Stead's publication of pictures of his hands, together with palmists' readings of them in Borderland, 1894.B2, 1895.B2.

B16   *BENNETT, JAMES R. "The Thematic Importance of Chapter One of Huckleberry Finn," Exercise Exchange, XII (November), 23-25.
[Source: Beebe and Feaster (1968), p. 112.]

B17   BIGNAMI, MARIALUISA. "La Letteratura Americana in Italia," Studi Americani, X, 443-95.
On pp. 454-55 there is a brief list of Italian translations of MT's works and secondary material about him; the secondary material is listed in the present bibliography.

B18   BOGGAN, J. R. "That Slap, Huck, Did It Hurt?" English Language Notes, I (March), 212-15.
Huck's concern over "the plain hand of Providence slapping me in the face and letting me know my wickedness was being watched all the while from up there in heaven" has been exaggerated by the critics: his statements elsewhere show that "hell has no emotional meaning for Huck...the force of his exclamation is much diminished...Twain's attempt to win an added Christian sympathy for his good 'bad boy' is unconvincing." Abstract in AES, VIII (1965), 1279; reprinted in Twainian, XXV (January-February, 1966).

B19   BORST, CHARLES V. S. [Introduction.] Mark Twain's A Cure for the Blues. With "The Enemy Conquered; or, Love Triumphant" by G. Ragsdale McClintock. Rutland, Vermont: Charles E. Tuttle Co.
Borst's introduction is primarily factual, following Paine. He identifies the author of The Enemy Conquered as Samuel Watson Royston, a native of Cumming, Georgia, who was graduated from the Yale Law School in 1845.

B20   BRATCHER, JAMES T. "Twain's Tom Sawyer," Explicator, XXII (January), Item 40.
Although MT sometimes used the generic noun sawyer to denote independence, the term

was also used on the river to denote drifting trees--a hazard of which the ex-pilot was fully aware; hence, the name has a dual significance. Abstract in AES, VII (1964), 1369.

B21   BRIDGMAN, RICHARD. [Brief Review: Henry Duskis, ed., The Forgotten Writings of Mark Twain (1963).] Western Folklore, XXIII (October), 276-77.
The material reprinted from the Buffalo Express is fragmentary, and there is inadequate basis for attribution of some of it to MT. "It could contribute to our understanding of Twain, except that, to be of value, the editorial work would have to be done afresh. This edition has effectively lessened the chance of that happening for some time."

B22   BROWN, CLARENCE A. "Huckleberry Finn: A Study in Structure and Point of View," Mark Twain Journal, XII (Spring), 10-15, 5.
The novel "must be read as a 'pastoral,' albeit one on which a nightmare world of human injustice and brutality constantly impinges"; thus, "the concluding episode in the novel is simply Huck's return to the world of Tom Sawyer." The core of the narrative is not Jim's flight to freedom, "but, quite simply, the adventures of Huckleberry Finn," and too much can be made of his moral growth--at the Phelps farm he returns to the world from which he set out. "While Huck functions as a sensitive center of consciousness, he does not function as a direct voice for Twain," and MT's style, though unlike that of Henry James, is equally effective in conveying to the reader the consciousness of the central character. Abstract in AES, VIII (1965), 1066.

B23   BUDD, LOUIS J. "Mark Twain on Joseph the Patriarch," American Quarterly, XVI (Winter), 577-86.
On MT's comic portrayal of Joseph in IA and later treatment of him as an embodiment of the laissez-faire capitalist with a corner in the grain market.

B24   _____. [Review: Henry Nash Smith, Mark Twain's Fable of Progress.] Nineteenth-Century Fiction, XIX (December), 304-306.
Smith's "thesis is that A Connecticut Yankee in King Arthur's Court signaled 'something like a negative conversion' for Twain which 'all but paralyzed his powers of imagination and condemned him to the relative sterility of his last twenty years.'" "Mark Twain and Smith make a very rewarding pair, all the more because their minds are so dissimilar"; that readers may disagree in part with Smith's argument seems likely, because of the book's originality and because he "evades no challenges."

B25 CALDWELL, DOROTHY. [Review: Paul Fatout, Mark Twain in Virginia City.] Missouri Historical Review, LVIII (July), 541-43.

An extensive but uncritical summary of the book, which reflects extensive research and the discovery of much new material.

B26 ____. [Review: Albert E. Stone, Jr., The Innocent Eye (1961); Roger B. Salomon, Twain and the Image of History (1961); Louis J. Budd, Mark Twain: Social Philosopher (1962).] Missouri Historical Review, LVIII (April), 398-401.

Chiefly descriptive, praising the scholarly thoroughness of the three works.

B27 CARSTENSEN, VERNON. "The West Mark Twain Did Not See," Pacific Northwest Quarterly, LV (October), 170-76.

On the early days of Washington and Oregon: "It is a pity that Mark Twain did not see the Pacific Northwest in the third quarter of the last century." [This article has been listed in other bibliographies of MT, but does not concern him.]

B28 CHARBONNEL, AVIS BLIVEN. "My Friend Clara Clemens," Mark Twain Journal, XII (Spring), 16-17.

The author knew MT's daughter when they both studied piano in Vienna under Theodor Leschetizky; here she recalls anecdotes about Clara and Ossip Gabrilowitsch.

B29 CHARD, LESLIE F., II. "Mark Twain's 'Hadleyburg' and Fredonia, New York," American Quarterly, XVI (Winter), 595-601

Unpleasant experiences turned MT's early favorable view of the town to a hostility which may have led him to pillory Fredonia in "The Man that Corrupted Hadleyburg"; "Even today it is commonly supposed in Fredonia that the community was the original for Hadleyburg and that many of the characters in the story were based on prominent Fredonians of the past."

B30 CLEMENS, CYRIL. "Mark Twain and Lyndon B. Johnson," Hobbies--The Magazine for Collectors, LXIX (April), 112, 122, 126.

Quotes the praise of several presidents for MT, in conversation with Cyril Clemens or in letters to him.

B31 CUMMINGS, SHERWOOD. "What is Man?: The Scientific Sources," in Sydney J. Krause, ed., Essays on Determinism in American Literature. (Kent, Ohio: Kent State University Press), pp. 108-16.

What Is Man? has been treated as a curiosity, and comments on it have been casual and impressionistic, but "the formation of Mark Twain's deterministic ideas, far from being peculiar, was in the classical pattern." MT read widely, and in particular he was influenced by Holmes, Darwin, Lecky, Lubbock, and Huxley. MT "swam during his whole career in the mainstream of ideas that produced the naturalistic writers." He did not join their number partly because determinism did not dominate his thinking until the later years and partly because his best writing was unconscious rather than doctrinal; in any case there is an influence of environment in P&P, CY, and PW.

B32 CUNLIFFE, MARCUS. "American Humour and the Rise of the West (Mark Twain)," in his The Literature of the United States (Harmondsworth and Baltimore: Penguin Books), pp. 157-78.

This book is described as a revised edition, with original publication in 1954, and the bibliography lists a number of more recent studies of MT. Cunliffe's discussion is for the general reader, beginning with treatment of western humor and showing how MT transcended it though not entirely escaping it. Cunliffe notes unevenness in CY, which is weakened by burlesque. "At moments, instead of indicting King Arthur's England, he speaks of it nostalgically in much the same terms as when he recalls the Missouri of his boyhood.... At other times, perhaps unwittingly, he implies that the industrial order is cruel, greedy, and destructive." Posterity will remember MT for "Tom Sawyer, Life on the Mississippi,--and, above all-- Huckleberry Finn. In them he wrote with warmth and accuracy of the life he most vividly knew."

B33 DAICHES, DAVID. "Mark Twain as Hamlet," Encounter, XXII (February), 70-76.

A review-article, with passing reference to Douglas Grant's Mark Twain as "a useful little book" and dismissing Caroline Thomas Harnsberger's Mark Twain's Views of Religion (1961) as "a rather scrappy little book...in which a somewhat perfunctory introduction is followed by a collection of extracts from Mark Twain's notebooks, marginal notes in books, essays, letters, and the autobiography." There is extensive and laudatory discussion of Henry Nash Smith's Mark Twain: The Development of a Writer. Daiches calls HF MT's "greatest work," but CY "in some respects his most interesting one...because in the latter we see him trapped in the ambiguous implications of modern industrial civilisation in a way that illuminates a whole area of modern history, British as well as American." The mask of humor is a necessary defense: MT "is not like the traditional comedian who longs to play Hamlet; he is rather Hamlet who puts on an antic disposition in order to save his reason." Abstract in AES, VII (1964), 1341.

B34 [DAVIS, CHESTER L.] "'Mark Twain and Longfellow' in 'Life' Magazine," Twainian, XXIII (September-October), 2-4.

Reprints Dora Jane Hamblin's "Mark (Ye) (the) Twain" from Life (July 10), p. 13; in

([DAVIS, CHESTER L.])
an unsigned headnote Chester L. Davis says the story is reprinted "only to let our members see how utterly ridiculous it is. If it were a light sort of thing, some story in a magazine of small circulation, we likely would let it pass. Things being as they are we are reprinting it as a far-fetched assertion, a speculation by one who should have checked the facts (and thus killed the story before it was ever written), but how else can a million or so readers be enlightened except through our serious student members saying 'maybe so', but 'highly unlikely'." Abstract in AES, VIII (1965), 1855, reprinted in Twainian, XXV (January-February, 1966), 3. The following issue acknowledges a letter from the editors of Life "with an explanation as useless and futile as that given by Orson Wells [sic] for his 'Invasion from Mars' program, never to be forgotten, but only because it too was a 'Special Report,' without warning."

B35   _____. "'Simon Wheeler, Detective' Published," Twainian, XXIII (March-April), 1-3.
On the MT manuscript recently published by the New York Public Library: discusses significance of the Missouri milieu and reprints the first pages of Chapter I. Abstract in AES, VIII (1965), 1852; reprinted in Twainian, XXV (January-February, 1966).

B36   _____. "Writings on Mark Twain, Average in Top Ten," Twainian, XXIII (May-June), 2.
"For the past three years we have been publishing annually, usually with the January-February 'Twainian', [sic] an abstract of all articles which have been published during the past year or so relating to the life and writings of Mark Twain"; the source of these abstracts is Abstracts of English Studies, a study of which reveals that MT is among the leaders in the number of articles published about him. [The opening statement must be qualified: not everything written about MT is abstracted in AES, and Twainian does not reprint all the AES abstracts (abstracts of material from Mark Twain Journal, for example, are silently passed over)--T.A.T.] Abstract in AES, VIII (1965), 1853; reprinted in Twainian, XXV (January-February, 1966).

B37   _____. [Review: Bradley, Beatty, Long, eds., The Adventures of Huckleberry Finn (Norton Critical Edition, 1962).] Twainian, XXIII (November-December).
Laudatory; describes contents, then quotes extensively from the introduction.

B38   _____. [Review: Hamlin Hill, Mark Twain and Elisha Bliss.] Twainian, XXIII (September-October), 1.
Descriptive and laudatory.

B39   _____. [Review: Rachel M. Varble, Jane Clemens: The Story of Mark Twain's Mother.] Twainian, XXIII (November-December), 1-3.
Laudatory, more analytical than usual in Twainian reviews; contains much quotation.

B40   _____. [Statement on Mark Twain Research Foundation.] Twainian, XXIII (March-April), 1.
"We have had and now have quantities of material including intimate letters which we believe good taste justified witholding from publication. We will continue to publish what we believe to be in the interest of research into the life and writings of Mark Twain, and this statement must stand as the sole reply to the many letters of inquiry which are continually received and seldom answered by us. Again we believe we are reacting as Mark himself would have done and we like to think, as he would have expected of us."

B41   DEKKER, GEORGE. "Lilies that Fester: The Last of the Mohicans and The Woman that Rode Away," New Left Review, No. 28 (November-December), pp. 75-84.
On p. 79, contrasts Cooper's Leatherstocking Tales with "two of the central masterpieces of American fiction. Although Moby Dick and The Adventures of Huckleberry Finn are concerned with racial relations, they do not invite us to ask: what will become of the white, red, and black races in North America--what in fact will become of North America? In Cooper's Leatherstocking Tales these questions are almost automatically raised..." and D. H. Lawrence's novel brings them up to date. Abstract in AES, VIII (1965), 2656; reprinted in Twainian, XXV (January-February, 1966).

B42   DILLINGHAM, WILLIAM B. "Setting and Theme in Tom Sawyer," Mark Twain Journal, XII (Spring), 6-8.
"The principal tensions in Tom's growth are those between freedom and involvement, illusion and reality," as represented by Jackson's Island and St. Petersburg, Cardiff Hill and the cave. Tom's "'salvation' and new growth, even though represented in terms of Christian rebirth [three days and nights in an underworld] are in Twain's view no cause for jubilation," since they cost him his boyish illusion. Abstract in AES, VIII (1965), 1064. Article reprinted in Kesterson (1974), pp. 87-91.

B43   DUFFY, MYRTLE M. "Twain in Howells' A Modern Instance," American Quarterly, XVI (Winter), 612-14.
Squire Gaylord resisted his wife's efforts to change his agnosticism, and eventually her own faith declined; Howells had seen the same thing happen in the Clemens family, and described it in his My Mark Twain (1910) and "Editor's Easy Chair" (Harper's Monthly, CXXXVI [March, 1918], 603).

B44 ELLISON, RALPH. _Shadow and Act_. New York: Random House.

Includes "The Seer and the Seen" (1946; published in _Confluence_, December, 1953), pp. 24-44; "Change the Joke and Slip the Yoke" (_Partisan Review_, Spring, 1958), pp. 45-59; "The Art of Fiction: An Interview" (_Paris Review_, Spring, 1955), pp. 167-83; "Some Questions and Some Answers" (_Preuves_, May, 1958), pp. 261-72. On Huck who, "like Prometheus...embraces the evil implicit in his act in order to affirm his belief in humanity," and the recognition of Jim's humanity (and on "Hemingway's blindness to the moral values of _Huckleberry Finn_ despite his sensitivity to it technical aspects"), pp. 29-36. On MT's failure to represent Jim as an adult, pp. 50-51; again on the central moral question in HF, pp. 182-83. On language, Ellison speaks of "having inherited the language of Shakespeare and Melville, Mark Twain and Lincoln and no other," although American Negro speech has been important to our language (pp. 266-67). Pp. 58-59, on Ellison's own use of folklore, and his ability to imagine himself as Huck Finn more readily than as Jim, reprinted in Simpson (1968), pp. 112-13.

B45 FLORY, CLAUDE R. "Huck, Sam and the Small-Pox," _Mark Twain Journal_, XII (Winter), 1-2, 8.

MT was well acquainted with Harriet Beecher Stowe, and--as Walter Blair has pointed out--there are parallels between _Uncle Tom's Cabin_ and _Huckleberry Finn_. There is a further parallel in Mrs. Stowe's _Sam Lawson's Oldtown Fireside Stories_ (1871), in which pretended smallpox is used to frighten away a man who came to collect a debt, just as Huck evaded the slave-catchers in Chapter XVI. Abstract in AES, VIII (1965), 1067.

B46 FRENCH, BRYANT MOREY. "Mark Twain, Laura D. Fair, and the New York Criminal Courts," _American Quarterly_, XVI (Winter), 545-61.

"That the trial and acquittal of Laura Hawkins [in GA] was intended by Mark Twain primarily as an exposé of the American jury system and only secondarily as a parody of the Fair case is made abundantly clear by the play he based on the novel." Describes the trial and the climax of the play, and praises Franklin Walker's "well-documented pioneering article" (1936) on MT's use of the trial.

B47 FRENCH, WARREN. [Review: _Simon Wheeler, Detective_, ed. Franklin R. Rogers (1963).] _American Notes and Queries_, III (September), 14-15.

This is very poor MT stuff, and the interests of scholars and collectors might better have been served by simply reproducing the manuscript in facsimile. The editing, introduction, and printing are admirable, but was it worth the time and expense?

B48 GANZEL, DEWEY. "Samuel Clemens, Sub Rosa Correspondent," _English Language Notes_, I (June), 270-73.

The greater part of MT's correspondence from the _Quaker City_ tour has been collected in Daniel Morley McKeithan's _Traveling with the Innocents Abroad_ (1958); to these Ganzel adds two brief dispatches from Naples (here reprinted) and a longer one probably from Constantinople (summarized) to the New York _Herald_. These are unsigned, because MT was under contract to the _Tribune_. He also notes a dispatch in the _Herald_ from Captain Duncan and an unsigned letter by Dr. Abraham Reeves Jackson. Abstract in AES, VIII (1965), 1954; reprinted in _Twainian_, XXV (January-February).

B49 *GARVENKO, F. (ed.). _Vēstules No Zemes: Antireligisku Rakstu Krājums_. Trans. by I. Melnbrade. Riga: Latvijas Valsts Izdevnieciba. [_Letters from the Earth_.]
[Source: MHRA _Annual Bibliography_ (1965), No. 6978.]

B50 GERBER, JOHN C. "Mark Twain," in James Woodress, ed., _American Literary Scholarship: An Annual/1964_ (Durham, North Carolina: Duke University Press, 1966), pp. 50-61.

The second annual survey of MT scholarship; See 1963 entry for coverage.

B51 _____. "The Mark Twain Edition," _Books at Iowa_ (October), pp. 15-17.

On the need for an accurate edition of MT, because "there is not a single major work of Mark Twain's in print that is as he wrote it. There has never been a complete and correct edition of his works, or of any one of his major works. Minor errors have crept into the works through printers' errors and major errors through the ill-advised activity of his editors. Sometimes the changes seem almost incredible," as in MS. Describes plans for a new, authoritative edition to be edited by scholars at several major universities, with Gerber as Chairman of the Editorial Board.

B52 _____. [Review: Bernard DeVoto, ed., _Letters from the Earth_, by Mark Twain, with a Preface by Henry Nash Smith (1962).] _American Literature_, XXXVI (May), 220-22.

"The first half of the book, containing 'Letters from the Earth' and 'Papers of the Adam Family,' is by far the more interesting part," with the vigor of MT's journalism of the sixties, but also with its unevenness and occasional coarseness. Paul Baender, currently working on some of this material, "tells me that Bernard DeVoto's editing is quite careless," with "misreadings of the manuscript" as a result of DeVoto's apparently having allowed a typist to establish text.

B53 HAGOPIAN, JOHN V., and MARTIN DOLCH, with the assistance of W. Gordon Cunliffe and Arvin Wells. Insight I: Analyses of American Literature. Frankfurt am Main: Hirschgraben-Verlag.

The second edition of a 1952 text for German schools. On pp. 248-53 contains a brief account of MT's life and works, and summaries of "The Jumping Frog" and "Traveling with a Reformer," with questions for students.

B54 HAMBLEN, ABIGAIL ANN. "The American Scene: Dickens and Mark Twain," Mark Twain Journal, XII (Winter), 9-11, 16.

A comparison of Martin Chuzzlewit and GA as portraits of the vulgarity and corruption in American life. Abstract in AES, VIII (1965), 1070.

B55 HAMBLIN, DORA JANE. "Mark (Ye) (the) Twain," Life, LVII (July 10), 13.

A spoof, attributing the authorship of MT's works to Henry Wadsworth Longfellow: the July 31 issue contains letters to the editors (p. 12) from deceived readers seeking to refute her argument and by Sherwood Cummings, Paul Fatout, and Henry Morgan, who enjoyed the joke. Article reprinted with comment in Twainian, XXIII (September-October), 2-4, 1964.B34.

B56 HAVARD, WILLIAM C. "Mark Twain and the Political Ambivalence of Southwestern Humor," Mississippi Quarterly, XVII (Spring), 95-106.

On MT's treatment of man and society in GA, HF, and CY, tracing his thought from early days as a frontier humorist to the despair of later years. Abstract in AES, VIII (1965), 2993; reprinted in Twainian, XXV (January-February, 1966).

B57 HEMINGWAY, LEICESTER. "Ernest Hemingway's Boyhood Reading," Mark Twain Journal, XII (Spring), 4-5.

The author heard from his mother that his much older brother, years ago, "said Mark Twain had the real stuff." What he learned from MT is uncertain, "but it must have been plenty." Abstract in AES, VIII (1965), 1063.

B58 HENDERSON, ROSWELL P., and RALPH GREGORY. "Judge John Marshall Clemens," Missouri Historical Society Bulletin, XXI (October).

[Source: Missouri Historical Society price list of publications.]

B59 HILL, HAMLIN. "Barnum, Bridgeport and The Connecticut Yankee," American Quarterly, XVI (Winter), 615-16.

Hank Morgan's references in Chapter I to Bridgeport and circuses, and his casual acceptance of a knight and a turreted fortress, may be explained simply: P. T. Barnum had his headquarters in Bridgeport, Connecticut, and he built a series of "castles" there.

B60 HINCHCLIFFE, ARNOLD P. [Review: Douglas Grant, Mark Twain (1962).] Critical Quarterly, VI (Winter), 376-77.

This is a corrective to "Van Wyck Brooks' unfortunate volume The Ordeal of Mark Twain." Grant does not resolve the contradictions in MT's psyche and art, but "the puzzle...is at least given a comprehensible and sane form."

B61 HINER, JAMES. "Mark Twain: Ambivalence Not Disjunction," American Quarterly, XVI (Winter), 620-21.

The conflicts in HF between raft and shore, the real and the romantic have been misread by critics who seek in MT an allegiance to either side. "Head and heart are not merely opposed...but self contradictory. The heart goes toward suicide, and the head to madness. Those are the ultimate conditions of each drive."

B62 HOUGH, ROBERT L. [Review: John S. Tuckey, Mark Twain and Little Satan (1963).] College English, XXV (January), 310.

"An important study," containing "convincing evidence to overthrow the established assumptions concerning the dates and order of the three versions of The Mysterious Stranger" and "some indication of the editorial tinkering done by Albert Paine and Frederick Duneka."

B63 JENSEN, FRANKLIN L. "Mark Twain's Comments on Books and Authors," Emporia State Research Studies, XII (June), 5-53.

"This study originated as a Master's thesis at Kansas State Teachers College of Emporia"; based on published material generally available and familiar. Abstract in AES, VIII (1965), 341; reprinted in Twainian, XXV (January-February, 1966).

B64 KAPLAN, JUSTIN. [Introduction.] The Gilded Age: A Tale of Today. New York: Trident Press. pp. v-xxiv.

Considers MT's own views toward money and power after settling into Eastern respectability. The book reflects "a casual attitude toward the power of fiction to digest an immense amount of raw topical material and still have the wholeness of fiction." In this first sustained fiction, MT "found a matrix for the materials of his past" which would characterize all of his major books.

B65 KAZIN, ALFRED. "The Scholar Cornered: A Progression of Children" [From A Critic's Notebook], American Scholar, XXXII (Spring), 171-83.

On TS and HF, pp. 176-77, 180-81; notes "the indulgent, arch, patronizing tone that Mark Twain adopts in Tom Sawyer" as typical of boy stories until Crane's Whilomville Stories of 1900 and Tarkington's Penrod of 1914. "Only once, actually, did Mark Twain break through this all-too-twinkly, chuckly

(KAZIN, ALFRED)
softness," in HF, where the boy's "experience is not middle-class, not comfortable, not an exclusive concern with fun and games." Abstract in AES, VII (1964), 2003; reprinted in Twainian, XXIV (January-February, 1965).

B66 KOMPASS, ARTHUR M. "Twain's Use of Music: a Note on Life on the Mississippi," American Quarterly, XVI (Winter), 616-19.
Gives the text of the hymn, "Last Beam," a line of which the pilot Bixby sang in the chapter "A Cub-Pilot's Experience" in LOM; dealing with fears of the dark, it is an effective device for mocking both the cub and the genteel culture.

B67 KRAUSE, S. J. "The Art and Satire of Twain's 'Jumping Frog' Story," American Quarterly, XVI (Winter), 562-76.
Although recent studies have emphasized evidence the story provides of conflict between genteel, civilized values of the East and those of the western frontier, the question of form has been neglected. In eight levels of point of view MT "employs an order of increasing detail and of ascending absurdity and fantasy," and "the structure of the Jim Smiley story is that of a moral satire in the classical mold."

B68 LEVY, LEO B. "Society and Conscience in Huckleberry Finn," Nineteenth-Century Fiction, XVIII (March), 383-91.
The critical view that equates what Huck calls "conscience" with the views of the society in which he lives are basically correct, but "criticism of the novel has suffered from too much insistence upon its schematic or doctrinal aspects. "Natural man is not necessarily innocent--vide the degraded Pap--and the growing closeness of Huck and Jim is "the recognition and fulfillment of mutual needs so strong that they can transcend racial barriers"; hence, Huck's decision to help Jim escape may be, not "rebellious and isolating," but "a socializing decision through which he begins to discover a deeper bond with society than any he has known." Abstract in AES, VII (1964), 2240; reprinted in Twainian, XXIV (January-February, 1965).

B69 *LONG, E. HUDSON. [Introduction.] Pudd'nhead Wilson and The Man that Corrupted Hadleyburg. New York: Harper & Row
Provides useful biographical, textual, and critical background. [Source: Extensively quoted in Twainian, XXIV (May-June, 1965), 4.]

B70 LYDENBERG, JOHN. "New Books on Twain," American Quarterly, XVI (Winter), 624-28.
A review of Bernard Taper, ed., Mark Twain's San Francisco (1963; only moderately amusing, and inadequate for the serious scholar); Hamlin Hill, Mark Twain and Elisha

Bliss (meticulously detailed, "a scholarly contribution of the most orthodox and approved variety"); Henry Nash Smith, Mark Twain's Fable of Progress ("this one I confess to finding slender in substance as well as in form"); and Robert A. Wiggins, Mark Twain, Jackleg Novelist (Wiggins forgets his title and concentrates instead on MT's concentration on a single story, that of the folk hero).

B71 McELDERRY, BRUCE R., JR. "Wolfe and Twain," in his Thomas Wolfe (New York: Twayne Publishers), pp. 64-66.
Compares Wolfe's autobiographical method to that of MT, who, however, did little with "the painful years of adolescence"; Wolfe shows "a serious treatment of intimate personal relationships he never attempted in his successful books."

B72 McNULTY, JOHN BARD. Older than the Nation: The Story of the Hartford "Courant." Stonington, Connecticut: The Pequot Press, Inc.
On MT's friendship with Charles Dudley Warner, rivalry over pay rates, sorrow at Warner's death, pp. 104-106, 143; also includes MT's comments when his telephone was being installed ("The voice carries too far as it is. If Bell had invented a muffler or a gag, he would have done a real service") and his introductory remarks at an 1875 spelling-bee (pp. 104-106).

B73 MANIERRE, WILLIAM R. "'No Money for to Buy the Outfit': Huckleberry Finn Again," Modern Fiction Studies, X (Winter), 341-48.
The pragmatic Huck is "a natural born joiner. He 'joins' Tom's gang; he 'joins' Jim; later, he 'joins' the Grangerfords; later still he 'joins' Mary Jane Wilks and her cause; finally, he 'joins' society, presumably for good.... Huck's 'moral growth' has, I believe, been vastly overestimated." Abstract in AES, IX (1966), 1748; reprinted in Twainian, XXVI (January-February, 1967).

B74 MARX, LEO. The Machine in the Garden: Technology and the Pastoral Ideal in America. New York: Oxford University Press, pp. 319-40 and passim.
In HF the pastoral mode "for the first time...is wholly assimilated to a native idiom." The motif of the intruding machine "has as much to do with the defects as with the merits of the work," and MT's "ingenious efforts to contrive an affirmation virtually break his masterpiece in two" (p. 319). In between the perspective of the innocent traveler who sees only beauty and that of the pilot to whom lovely details stand for hidden dangers stands Huck, with a "willingness to accept the world as he finds it, without anxiously forcing meanings on it" (p. 334).

B75 *MENDELSON, M. Mark Tven (new issue). Mos-
kva: Molodaja Gvardija.
[Source: MHRA Annual Bibliography (1964),
No. 6569.]

B76 METZGER, CHARLES R. "The Adventures of Huckleberry Finn as Picaresque," Midwest Quarterly, V (April), 249-56.
Unlike the romantic Tom Sawyer, "Huck...
is doomed to play the picaresque role, as
are possibly all pícaros, because he is an
essentially honest person living in a dishonest world." MT knew the literary character Gil Blas de Santillana, and Huck
embodies attributes of the pícaro. Abstract in AES, IX (1966), 2321; reprinted
in Twainian, XXVI (January-February, 1967).

B77 MILLGATE, MICHAEL. [Review: Henry Nash
Smith, Mark Twain: The Development of a
Writer (1962).] Modern Language Review,
LIX (July), 469-70.
"Professor Smith, in this admirable study,
has come as close as anyone to a succesful
penetration of Mark Twain's intricate mech-
anisms of defence," through close familiarity with his subject, "the nice management
of differing critical strategies," and a
"strict critical scrupulosity" which has
confined his claims to what can be fully
sustained.

B78 MILLS, BARRISS. "Old Times on the Mississippi
as an Initiation Story," College English,
XXV (January), 283-89.
Here, for once, MT found unity in his
story, by using "the motif...of the initiation story--the account of a boy's becoming
a man as he moves from innocence and ignorance, through the difficult process of ac-
quiring knowledge of the world, to the
practical but somewhat disillusioning wisdom of adulthood." MT "characteristically"
destroyed the unity when he padded out the
shorter work to make LOM. Abstract in AES,
VII (1964), 974.

B79 MOBLEY, LAWRENCE E. "Mark Twain and the
Golden Era," Papers of the Bibliographical
Society of America, LVIII (First Quarter),
8-23.
Includes an annotated list of sixty con-
tributions by MT up to April 17, 1868, and
reprints several of them. Abstract in AES,
VII (1964), 1843; reprinted in Twainian,
XXIV (January-February, 1965).

B80 PARSONS, COLEMAN O. [Review: John S. Tuckey,
Mark Twain and Little Satan: The Writing
of "The Mysterious Stranger" (1963).] American Literature, XXXVI (March), 92.
Tuckey has reversed DeVoto's chronology,
convincingly, but he conspicuously qualifies
his statements and might better have waited
until material in the Mark Twain Papers at
the University of California (Berkeley) is
made available.

B81 PERKINS, GEORGE. "Death by Spontaneous Combustion in Marryat, Melville, Dickens, Zola,
and Others," Dickensian, LX (Winter), 57-63.
MT's reference in LOM to the death of Jimmy Finn "of a combination of delirium tremens and spontaneous combustion" [Author's
National Edition, n.d., p. 453] follows a
long-standing literary tradition of a grisly
death of drunkards. Abstract in AES, VIII
(1965), 1915; reprinted in Twainian, XXV
(January-February, 1966).

B82 RATNER, MARC L. "Two Letters of Mark Twain,"
Mark Twain Journal, XII (Spring), 9, 17.
Contains texts of two previously unpublished letters from the Boyesen Collection,
Columbia University Library (April 23, 1880
and January 11, 1882) to Hjalmar Hjorth
Boyesen, the Norwegian-American writer and
teacher, reflecting their personal friendship and MT's current involvement with TA
and P&P; MT mentions having read from TA one
evening in Twichell's "chapel." Abstract in
AES, VIII (1965), 1065.

B83 RODNON, STEWART. "Mark Twain's Get-Rich-Quick
Schemes: A Balance Sheet," Mark Twain Journal, XII (Winter), 3-5.
Although early poverty and his latent romanticism led MT into schemes in which he
lost money, his "use of get-rich-quick projects in his novels was consistently successful." In addition to his portrayal of Colonel Sellers, MT "employed the easy-money
motif in three general ways: occasionally
money is passively received, sometimes it is
gained through a quirk of fate and manipu-
lated to extend the luck, and often it is
won by chicanery." Abstract in AES, VIII
(1965), 1068.

B84 ROGERS, FRANKLIN R. "Mark Twain and Daudet:
A Tramp Abroad and Tartarin sur les Alpes,"
Comparative Literature, XVI (Summer), 254-
63.
Suggests "a substantial debt on Daudet's
part to Mark Twain": his itinerary follows
the travels in TA rather than those of Daudet himself--but Daudet's treatment shows
originality and we should not be too quick
to join those who dismiss him as a mere
plagiarizer from MT--as well as from Cha-
teaubriand, Balzac, Flaubert, Zola, Goncourt,
and Charles Dickens. Abstract in AES, IX
(1966), 1095; reprinted in Twainian, XXVI
(January-February, 1967).

B85 SALOMON, ROGER B. "Realism as Disinheritance:
Twain, Howells, and James," American Quarterly, XVI (Winter), 531-44.
A foe of romance, MT was intellectually
a realist; yet such works as CY and even IA
reflect a longing for the past. "Twain alternately fondled and violated the past de-
pending on the mode that was uppermost at any
given time. Only occasionally--the great

(SALOMON, ROGER B.)
example is, of course, Huckleberry Finn--
did the modes come into any kind of fruitful equilibrium."

B86   SAMUELS, THOMAS CHARLES. "Mr. Trilling, Mr.
Warren, and An American Tragedy," Yale Review, LIII (Summer).
Pp. 637-39 concern Leo Marx and the debate over HF: "Since he had demonstrated
that the ending is a cruel travesty of the
book's human, un-illusioned attack on hypocrisy and discrimination, Marx neatly
proves that Trilling and Eliot had stressed
form and ignored morality. He then shrewd-
ly speculates that so egregious a blunder
in critics so eminent could only result
from an indifference to the book's moral
point." Abstract in AES, XIII (1969-1970),
672; reprinted in Twainian, XXIX (January-
February, 1970).

B87   SCHELL, EDGAR T. "'Pears' and 'Is' in Pudd'n-
head Wilson," Mark Twain Journal, XII (Winter), 12-15.
Two major characters "stand outside the
world of Dawson's Landing: Roxy because
she is a Negro and a slave, Pudd'nhead because he is an outsider and apparently a
fool. In a sense they frame that world.
Roxy is a focus for all the attitudes, good
and bad, of the Southern past, Pudd'nhead
represents the Northern future; Roxy acts,
Pudd'nhead observes; Roxy obscures reality,
Pudd'nhead uncovers it. Their association
with opposing attitudes and values is reflected in their rolls [sic] as principal
antagonists." The book "is a far more unified, more balanced novel than many of its
critics have been willing to grant...an exposition of the extremely fine line between
appearance and reality." Abstract in AES,
VIII (1965), 1071.

B88   SCOTT, ARTHUR L. "Letters from Mark Twain to
William Walter Phelps, 1891-1893," Hunting-
ton Library Quarterly, XXVII (August),
375-81.
Describes and quotes from six letters to
Phelps, American minister in Berlin, and one
to his daughter Marian; their light-hearted
tone gives no hint of his fears and anxie-
ties of the time. "These letters are part
(HM 27353-59) of the William Walter Phelps
Correspondence, a recent acquisiton of the
Huntington Library." Abstract in AES, VIII
(1965), 1378; reprinted in Twainian, XXV
(January-February, 1966).

B89   SHARP, EUGENE. [Review: Paul Fatout, Mark
Twain in Virginia City.] Journalism Quarterly, XLI (Summer), 446-47.
Brief and descriptive: journalists will
be interested to see the picture of their
profession in Nevada.

B90   SMITH, HENRY NASH. "The Search for a Capitalist Hero: Businessmen in American Fiction,"
in Earl F. Cheit, ed., The Business Establishment (New York: John Wiley & Sons,
Inc.), pp. 77-112.
Passim on GA and CY (indexed).

B91   SMITH, PAUL. "The Infernal Reminiscence:
Mythic Patterns in Mark Twain's 'The Celebrated Jumping Frog of Calaveras County,'"
Satire Newsletter, I (Spring), 41-44.
A critical spoof: "In this dark and nearly tragic story...Mark Twain seems to have
first become aware of the archetypal and
mythic, the deeply autochthonic qualities of
his fictional material."

B92   SORIA, REGINA. "Mark Twain and Vedder's Medusa," American Quarterly, XVI (Winter),
602-606.
Chiefly on the artist Elihu Vedder, whose
picture of Medusa MT bought at his studio in
Rome in 1878.

B93   TAPER, BERNARD. "Mark Twain's San Francisco,
Introduction by Taper," Twainian, XXIII
(January-February), 1-3.
The second of two installments reprinting
the introduction to Taper's book.

B94   *TIRUMALAI, C. K. "Father-Son Relationships in
Huckleberry Finn," Exercise Exchange, XII
(November), 22-23.
[Source: Beebe and Feaster (1968),
p. 121.]

B95   TRILLING, DIANA. "Tom Sawyer, Delinquent, in
her Claremont Essays (New York: Harcourt,
Brace & World, Inc.), pp. 143-52.
The book is a celebration of boyhood by an
author who had small use for the adult
world. And yet, after all, Tom makes compro-
mises Huck does not; this is "a town book,"
and the world of the Mississippi still lies
ahead. (This first appeared in 1962 as the
introduction to the Crowell-Collier Publishing Company ed. of TS.)

B96   *TUTTLETON, JAMES W. "Twain's Use of Theatrical Traditions in the Old Southwest," College Language Association Journal, VIII
(December), 190-97.
On the dramatic declaration and the camp
meeting, as seen in HF. [Source: MHRA Annual Bibliography (1964), No. 6589; Abstract
in AES, X (1967), 416, and reprinted in
Twainian, XXVII (January-February, 1968).]

B97   *VAGTS, ALFRED. "Mark Twain at the Courts of
the Emperors" [Also listed as "Mark Twain at
the Courts of Europe"], Jahrbuch für Amerikastudien, IX, 149-51.
On MT's visits to Czar Alexander II and
Emperor Wilhelm II; passages on the meeting
with Alexander II at Yalta were censored
before and after the Revolution in Russian
editions of IA, first for flippancy and then
for too friendly a portrayal. [Source:

(VAGTS, ALFRED)
MHRA Annual Bibliography (1964), No. 6590; Abstract in AES, VIII (1965); 1402, and reprinted in Twainian, XXV (January-February, 1966).]

B98 WILLIAMS, JAMES D. "Revision and Intention in Mark Twain's A Connecticut Yankee," American Literature, XXXVI (November), 288-97.

"The notebook entries, the manuscript, and the published novel do not support the thesis that A Connecticut Yankee began simply as a humorous contrast and then--because of a conscious change in intention-- became at a specific point an 'inverted satire.'" MT had been thinking about "chivalry, slavery, and progress" for twenty years, but "his Anglophobia...had shallow roots and was poor in associations." Abstract in AES, VIII (1965), 1555, reprinted in Twainian, XXV (January-February, 1966).

1965 A BOOKS

A1 CLEMENS, SAMUEL L. The Adventures of Colonel Sellers. Being Mark Twain's Share of "The Gilded Age," a Novel which He Wrote with Charles Dudley Warner. Now Published Separately for the First Time and Comprising, in Effect, a New Work. Ed. Charles Neider. Garden City, N.Y.: Doubleday.

The introduction includes a useful account of the reception of GA, quoting a number of reviews (many of them English) not listed in the present bibliography. Neider argues that "It was an error for Mark Twain to seek Warner's help.... As it happens, his share of The Gilded Age is the central share and the text is cohesive and extensive enough to be printed separately if certain sections by Warner are synopsized to carry the story along" (p. xiii).

A2 FRENCH, BRYANT MOREY. Mark Twain and "The Gilded Age": The Book that Named an Era. Dallas: Southern University Press.

On the backgrounds of the novel, models on whom characters are based, with discussion of the play Colonel Sellers and appendices on copyright and details of publication, Colonel Sellers' Railroad Map, and the chapter mottoes. Extensively documented.

A3 GREGORY, RALPH. Mark Twain's First America: Florida, Missouri, 1835-1840. Florida, Missouri: Friends of Florida.

A brief history of the town and the connection of the Clemens family with it; documentation includes local accounts (34-page pamphlet).

A4 McKEITHAN, DANIEL MORLEY. A Mark Twain Notebook for 1892. Uppsala: A.-B. Lundquista Bokhandeln. (Essays and Studies on American Language and Literature, XVII.)

On a notebook kept by MT, mainly in Florence and Bad Nauheim; quotes passages of the text, which is in the Miriam Lutcher Stark Library, University of Texas.

A5 MIRIZZI, PIERO. Mark Twain. (Biblioteca di Studi Americani, 10). Rome: Edizioni di Storia e Letteratura.

A general study, attempting to strike a balance between the "admiring critics" and the "dissenting critics." Contains a brief survey of Italian criticism (pp. 302-303). [In Italian.]

A6 PFLUG, RAYMOND J. The Adventures of Huckleberry Finn: The Evolution of a Classic. Boston: Ginn and Company.

A school "Casebook for Objective Writing."

A7 POLI, BERNARD. Mark Twain: Écrivain de l'Ouest. Régionalisme et Humour. Paris: Presses Universitaires de France.

A major study by one of the few French scholars currently concerned with MT as an important author. [In French.]

A8 SALSBURY, EDITH COLGATE, ed. Susy and Mark Twain: Family Dialogues. New York: Harper & Row, Publishers.

"The family, their friends, and their servants tell the story of Susy Clemens and her father, Mark Twain.... In some cases I have combined two versions of the same story...In a few cases anecdotes have been shifted chronologically." Mrs. Salsbury tells the story by editing the actual words of MT, Susy, Olivia Clemens, Howells, and others, and as "Narrator" provides the needed commentary.

A9 STEARNS, MONROE. Mark Twain. New York: Franklin Watts, Inc.

A biography for young readers, with full index and a bibliography; carefully researched and generally reliable, though sometimes perhaps too trusting of sources.

1965 B SHORTER WRITINGS

B1 ANDERSON, FREDERICK. [Review: Bryant Morey French, Mark Twain and "The Gilded Age."] Nineteenth-Century Fiction, XXI (June), 106-108.

French has made a valuable contribution in tracing background material, identifying figures portrayed, and assessing the respective contributions made by MT and Charles Dudley Warner, but the book should have been "edited so that the valid points made by its author would appear with greater economy and force"; the failure by the Southern University Press to provide such help "does little credit to the author it publishes or to the reputation of the publisher."

B2   ANON. "The Cow Tracks Stop at the Tree,"
Times Literary Supplement (May 6), p. 344.
      A review of MT's Simon Wheeler, Detective
(1964), a poor specimen of his writing
somewhat redeemed by "the handsome production and impeccable editing." The reviewer
adds his own interesting comments on PW, in n
which the fact that he was dealing with
Negro characters allowed MT to master some
of his literary taboos, among them the fact
"that a mother may be hated by her son."

B3   ANON. "Mark Twain Items Appearing Elsewhere,"
Twainian, XXIV (January-February), 3-4.
      Reprints several abstracts from AES, VII
(1964).

B4   ANON. "Mark Twain's First 'Literary Venture,'" Missouri Historical Review, LX
(October), 75-76.
      Reprints without editorial comment MT's
letter signed "A Dog-Bedevilled Citizen"
from the Hannibal Journal of September 16,
1852, followed by his comment on it in "My
First Literary Venture" (Sketches New and
Old).

B5   ANON. [Review: Charles Neider, ed., The Adventures of Colonel Sellers.] Choice, II
(June), 225.
      "Warner has suffered enough among critics
for daring to collaborate with the master
humorist, but this is literary snobbery
and opportunistic publishing at its worst."

B6   ANON. [Brief Review: Edith Colgate Salsbury, Susy and Mark Twain: Family Dialogues.] Choice, II (December), 685.
      "The reader's interest lags, as each
chapter...becomes bogged down in insignifi-
cant and often very personal details of
family life."

B7   *ARIKAWA, SHOJI. "Huck and Death," Kyusha
American Literature, No. 8, pp. 19-24.
      [Source: MHRA Annual Bibliography (1965),
No. 6956.]

B8   BABCOCK, C. MERTON. "Mark Twain and Mencken:
A Literary Kinship," Menckeniana, XIV (Summer), 4-5.
      Menken began reading MT's writings at the
age of nine, came to develop an outlook
like MT's, and was unmistakably influenced
by him, although there is no evidence that
they ever met. Menken's "A Prayer for Puri-
tans" (Smart Set, XLV, March, 1915, p. 228,
here quoted at length) is strikingly similar to MT's "The War Prayer"--which, however, was first published in Europe and
Elsewhere in 1923. Abstract in AES, XII
(1969), 462; reprinted in Twainian, XXIX
(January-February, 1970).

B9   BALDANZA, FRANK. [Review: Robert A. Wiggins,
Mark Twain: Jackleg Novelist (1964).]
American Literature, XXXVI (January), 535.
      The approach with little note of other

critics is "refreshing," as Wiggins depicts
in MT "a man who dreams of, and succeeds in,
performing an action which will embody values and aspirations of the primitive folk
mind. Huckleberry Finn is the unquestioned
masterpiece of this genre," but MT's later
"pessimistic determinism jarred disastrously
against the folk values and the realistic
and colloquial style" and resulted in an
artistic decline. Wiggins makes "a reasoned
and--within the confines of his thesis--
sympathetic assessment," and one may hope it
will not stir bitter controversy.

B10 BARNES, DANIEL R. "Twain's The Adventures of
Huckleberry Finn, Chapter I," Explicator,
XXIII (April), Item 62.
      Biblical prototypes cast light on the por-
trayal of the lives of the major characters,
as in the parallel between Huck and Moses
in the "bullrushers." Abstract in AES, IX
(1966), 2605.

B11 BERTHOFF, WARNER. The Ferment of Realism:
American Literature 1884-1919. New York:
The Free Press, and London: Collier-Macmil-
lan Ltd.
      MT's art was that of the performer, and
his "great influence on subsequent American
writing has been in the main a technical and
not an imaginative influence." Like Poe,
also schooled as a journalist, "Twain conceived of the writer's work as pre-eminently
a manipulation of responses, a staging of
irresistible effects"; this resulted in an
art which was often mechanical, but both
writers also achieved "a trance-like directness and integrity of enacted vision that
comes upon us with the force of unarguable
revelation," with an effect "that compels us
to rank both men among the few original
masters of our literature." In the effort
to explain their artistry, criticism of both
authors is inclined to turn to psychoanalysis which, however, is adequate only with
their less successful works (p. 63).

B12 BOESER, LINDA. "Two Comstock Journalists:
Samuel L. Clemens and William L. Wright,"
Missouri Historical Review, LIX (July),
428-38.
      On MT and his friend (who used the pseudo-
nym "Dan De Quille") and their work on the
Territorial Enterprise; Wright, born a Quaker, was quieter and more retiring than MT,
and less successful; "Apparently the very
conservatism and high regard for facts which
made De Quille such an able reporter, also
ironically worked against him as an author."

B13 BOOTH, BRADFORD A. [Review: Margaret Duckett,
Mark Twain and Bret Harte (1964).] Nineteenth-Century Fiction, XX (June), 101-102.
      The evidence that has become available,
revealing MT's "egregious slanders" of
Harte, "has been sifted by Margaret Duckett
with painstaking thoroughness, ingenuity,
and skill," and we now see Harte "as an

(BOOTH, BRADFORD A.)
essentially honorable, if sometimes thought-
less man, often calumniated and much misunderstood." This book "admirably" refutes
the slanders, and impartial critics will
appreciate "its informed scholarship and
its essential objectivity in the face of
controversial material."

B14 BROOKS, VAN WYCK. Van Wyck Brooks: An Autobiography. Foreword by John Hall Wheelock;
Intro. by Malcolm Cowley. New York: E. P.
Dutton & Co., Inc.
Consists of Scenes and Portraits (1954),
Days of the Phoenix, and From the Shadow of
the Mountain (1961); the indexes of those
works are less extensive than in their original publication.

B15 BROWNE, RAY B. "Huck's Final Triumph," Ball
State Teachers College Forum, VI (Winter),
3-12.
After summarizing the debate over the
ending of HF, argues that the book's theme
is "Huck's search for personal liberation,"
for the maturity that will allow him to
proclaim that he is his own master. The
novel's theme develops in three strands as
Huck outgrows Tom, Jim and Pap, and in the
end he can be true to himself rather than
to society. Abstract in AES, IX (1966),
715; reprinted in Twainian, XXVI (January-
February, 1967).

B16 *BUTCHER, PHILIP. "Mark Twain Sells Roxy Down
the River," College Language Association
Journal, VIII (March), 225-33.
The portrait of the slave-woman in PW is
a caricature, reflecting "popular notions
about the Negro's emotional instability and
lack of profound feeling." [Source: MHRA
Annual Bibliography (1965), No. 6963; Abstract in AES, X (1967), 417, and reprinted
in Twainian, XXVII (January-February,
1968).]

B17 CALLAN, RICHARD J. "The Burden of Innocence
in Melville and Twain," Renascence, XVII
(Summer), 191-94.
A comparison of Billy Budd and Huckleberry
Finn, whose authors were skeptics about man
and "in the matter of religiosity...shook
and shocked us into attention. Finally, the
leading characters of those fictions and
some of their predicaments have a surprising
similarity." Abstract in AES, VIII (1965),
3077; reprinted in Twainian, XXV (March-
April, 1966).

B18 CARTER, PAUL J. [Review: Robert A. Wiggins,
Mark Twain: Jackleg Novelist (1964).]
Western Humanities Review, XIX (Summer),
277-78.
Wiggins contends that uneasiness in his
role as novelist led MT to reliance primarily on instinct rather than conscious craftsmanship, to an emphasis on realism, and to
an overestimation of the potentialities of

humor to allow him to write almost anything,
so long as it was entertaining. Application
of this thesis to MT's novels illustrates
it but adds little knowledge or critical insight.

B19 CHAPUT, DONALD. "Mark Twain: Copied Originality," Mark Twain Journal, XII (Summer),
20-21.
"Twain's debt to others is enormous. Almost every important work or character by
Twain had been suggested by someone he knew
or something he read"; for example, Huck
Finn is merely Tom Blankenship renamed, Jim
is Uncle Dan'l, and Sid is MT's brother
Henry. "Twain was ready for the ideas. He
was ready to write." Abstract in AES, IX
(1966), 2656.

B20 CLARK, WILLIAM G. "Mark Twain's Visual and
Aural Descriptions," Mark Twain Journal, XII
(Summer), 1-9, 16.
MT's ear was better than his eye: descriptions of what he has seen read like derivative set-pieces, but his "aural descriptions
...usually seem to represent a real understanding of the person, place or event being
described." Abstract in AES, IX (1966),
2652.

B21 COX, JAMES M. [Review: Henry Nash Smith,
Mark Twain's Fable of Progress (1964).]
American Literature, XXXVII (March), 81-82.
Smith includes "a fine analysis of Charles
Dudley Warner's A Little Journey in the World
and William Dean Howells' A Hazard of New
Fortunes" to provide context; his "argument
is persuasive, yet one wonders whether it is
not a more heroic effort to come to terms
with the novel than the novel was to create
a capitalist hero."

B22 [DAVIS, CHESTER L.] "The Adventures of Colonel Sellers, by Neider," Twainian, XXIV
(March-April), 1-4.
A "review," consisting of introductory
comments on the theory of patents and copyright, an estimate of Twainian readership at
30,000 (for 300 members of the Mark Twain
Research Foundation), and description of
Neider's edition of MT's part of The Gilded
Age as "a fine contribution of lasting merit...something new and useful.... We now
reprint from the book what would normally be
the introduction, which Neider calls 'A Novelist's Debut,' a great part of it, and a
short sketch from the 'Sellers' story to remind our readers how fine it is." Reprint
follows, pp. 2-4, extensively citing contemporary newspaper reviews.

B23 _____. "Contemporary Newspaper Accounts of
Mark Twain's Lectures," Twainian, XXIV
(November-December), 1-3.
Reprints accounts of MT lectures in Keokuk
(Iowa) Gate City and Paris Kentuckian
(1885.B8, B10). This is followed by a list
of "the worthwhile collection of complete

([DAVIS, CHESTER L.])
newspaper accounts now in the possession of one of our members," for some of which information is apparently lacking, but which appears to represent a valuable contribution to MT secondary bibliography. Chester Davis writes of acting as a clearing-house for further information of this sort, but cautions that its value is uneven: "We know of one report which is hardly worth reprinting in our publication, because it is so prejudiced against the man and so contrary to the facts." Abstract in AES, XI (1968), 1728; reprinted in Twainian, XXVIII (January-February, 1969).

B24 _____. "Hannibal Boy-hood Home, Mahan Correspondence with Albert Bigelow Paine," Twainian, XXIV (September-October), 1-3.
One letter to F. A. Duneka of Harper's (September 16, 1911) and six to Paine (October 18, 1911-July 13, 1916) from George A. Mahan, a Hannibal attorney, on purchase of the MT home as a memorial; notes accounts in St. Louis Republic and New York Herald of September 2, 1911. Abstract in AES, XI (1968), 1726; reprinted in Twainian, XXVIII (January-February, 1969).

B25 _____. "Jervis Langdon and Other Correspondence with Paine on 'Biography,'" Twainian, XXIV (July-August), 1-4.
A miscellany of letters, 1910-1912, on topics relating to business affairs rather than the Paine biography of MT. Includes letters by Charles T. Lark on the estate of Jean L. Clemens, and Jervis Langdon on funeral expenses, pictures, bequests by MT, sale of "Stormfield" and the billiard table there, etc. Abstract in AES, XI (1968), 1724, reprinted in Twainian, XXVIII (January-February, 1969).

B26 _____. [Review: Edith Colgate Salsbury, Susy and Mark Twain.] Twainian, XXIV (November-December), 1.
Fitting together the actual words of MT, Susy, and others "in an interesting and novel manner," the editor has produced "a very scholarly work," although the readability could be improved.

B27 DICKINSON, LEON T. [Review: Hamlin Hill, Mark Twain and Elisha Bliss (1964).] American Literature, XXXVII (November), 334-35.
Recapitulates the history of the business raltionship and observes that "Mr. Hill tells his story well. He presents much new evidence--letters, sales figures, publishing records--to support his contention that for twelve years Elisah Bliss exerted a great influence in determining the direction of Mark Twain's literary development."

B28 DIXON, ELIZABETH WHITE. "Mark Twain Dresses Up," Mark Twain Journal, XIII (Winter), 17-20.
Loosely and confusedly biographical. MT's love of fine clothing is a compensation for a childhood in which his parents could not "afford to buy toys like those of other children.... to provide for his own amusement during his formidable years [sic], he was forced to hold the world up by the tail, so to speak, and laugh at it."

B29 EDISON, THOMAS A. [Letter to Cyril Clemens, dated "Orange, N. J., January 12, 1927"; signed typescript, here reproduced in facsimile.] Mark Twain Journal, XIII (Winter), front cover.
Describes a visit to the Edison Laboratory by MT, who made a recording (destroyed in a fire in 1914).

B30 EMBERSON, FRANCES GUTHRIE, and ROBERT L. RAMSAY. A Mark Twain Lexicon (1938), partially reprinted in Twainian, XXIV (May-June), 1-4; (July-August), 4; (September-October), 3-4; (November-December), 3-4.
A headnote by Chester L. Davis expresses the wish that it were possible to reprint the entire book, but "we must content ourselves, at least at the start of this series, with only a part of the some 500 pages." Abstracts in AES, XI (1968), 1723, 1725, 1727, 1729; reprinted in Twainian, XXVIII (January-February, 1969).

B31 FALK, ROBERT. "Mark Twain and the Earlier Realism," in his The Victorian Mode in American Fiction, 1865-1885.(East Lansing: Michigan State University Press), pp. 157-66.
Although MT was both a realist and a Victorian, he lies outside the mainstream. His contributions lay in his attack on romanticism and insistence on the authentic. "The association of realism with local color and especially with the western story was Twain's one positive contribution to theoretical criticism of the novel" (p. 163).

B32 GAINES, ERVIN J. [Review: Margaret Duckett, Mark Twain and Bret Harte (1964).] Library Journal, XC (January 1), 123.
The book fails to answer the central question of what caused the fatal rupture between the two men. "Facts are loosely interpreted throughout, and the expository skills demanded by an undertaking like this are unfortunately absent."

B33 GANZEL, DEWEY. "Clemens, Mrs. Fairbanks, and Innocents Abroad," Modern Philology, LXIII (November), 128-140.
Scholarly legend exaggerates the influence Mary Mason Fairbanks exerted on MT while he was touring Europe and the Holy Land on the Quaker City and writing newspaper correspondence. She was a good friend, but not a mentor, and she was helpful chiefly in proofreading and in reminding him of topics--particularly after MT discovered fourteen of his letters had been lost in the mails. Abstract in AES, IX (1966), 2672.

B34 GANZEL, DEWEY. "Samuel Clemens and John Camden Hotten," The Library, Fifth Series, XX (September), 230-42.

Although MT reviled Hotten for publishing his books without permission and without paying royalties, Hotten was a strong advocate of better international copyright and had in fact written MT to ask permission to reprint Innocents Abroad but received no answer; he did pay Bret Harte and Artemus Ward for works of theirs he reprinted, and presumably would have been willing, as he claimed, to pay MT. Abstract in AES, XI (1968), 495; reprinted in Twainian, XXVIII (January-February, 1969).

B35 _____. "Samuel Clemens, Guidebooks, and Innocents Abroad," Anglia (Tübingen), LXXXIII, No. 1, pp. 78-88.

MT used several familiar guidebooks not only for information but also for some of his organization and perspectives. Abstract in AES, X (1967), 827; reprinted in Twainian, XXVII (January-February, 1968).

B36 GERBER, JOHN C. "Mark Twain," in James Woodress, ed., American Literary Scholarship: An Annual/1965. (Durham, North Carolina: Duke University Press, 1967), pp. 57-68.

A survey of MT scholarship for the year; See 1963.B32. Contents: "i. Texts and Editions"; "ii. Biography"; "iii. Criticism"; "iv. Innocents Abroad"; "v. The Gilded Age"; "vi. Tom Sawyer"; "vii. Huckleberry Finn"; "viii. A Connecticut Yankee"; "ix. Short Selections."

B37 GOODER, R. D. "One of Today's Best Little Writers?" Cambridge Quarterly, I (Winter), 81-90.

On J. D. Salinger; contrasts Catcher in the Rye and Huckleberry Finn, observing that Holden "calls the tune, and proves himself morally and spiritually superior to everyone except his little sister...Holden judges all, but is not judged.... Where do we ever find Holden in a position of admitted moral inferiority, as we find Huck when he admits he has played a mean trick on Jim? Where does Holden have to make the difficult choice between what he has been taught and what he knows in himself is right, as Huck has to do when he decides to shield Jim?" Abstract in AES, XV (1971-1972), 1248.

B38 GORDAN, JOHN D. "An Anniversary Exhibition. The Henry W. and Albert A. Berg Collection 1940-1965," Bulletin of the New York Public Library, LXIX (December), 665-677.

Concludes a three-part series. On pp. 675-76, describes a dedication copy of P&P presented to Susie Clemens and notes the rich holdings in the Berg Collection of MT material, including the manuscript of CY, the corrected typescript of FE, and almost four hundred letters. The remainder of the installment and the series does not concern

MT. Abstract in AES, IX (1966), 2851; reprinted in Twainian, XXVI (January-February, 1967).

B39 _____. "Novels in Manuscript: An Exhibition from the Berg Collection," Bulletin of the New York Public Library, LXIX (May), 317-29.

On p. 325, briefly summarizes MT's career and notes: "The manuscript of A Connecticut Yankee, here displayed, is over nine hundred pages long. These pages show considerable correction, from the very first line..." A continuation of this article in the following issue contains nothing further on MT. Abstract in AES, IX (1966), 45; reprinted in Twainian, XXVI (January-February, 1967).

B40 *GORDON, JOSEPH T. "The Gilded Age and Democracy: A Literary View of Post-Civil War America," Forum (Houston), VI (Winter-Spring), 4-9.

[Source: AES, X (1967), 2695, reprinted in Twainian, XXVII, January-February, 1968; facts of publication confirmed by note from Forum.] AES abstract notes the satire of the corruption of the day in the novels of MT and Warner, and by Henry Adams.

B41 GREENLEAF, RICHARD. "Mark Twain and the Bishop of Woolwich," Religion in Life: A Christian Quarterly of Opinion and Discussion (Nashville: Abington Press), XXXV (Winter).

[Source: unpaged offprint in Mark Twain Papers]. Arranged as a dialogue, consisting of quotations from MT's "Reflections on Religion" (edited by Charles Neider in Hudson Review, 1963) and Honest to God by John A. T. Robinson, Bishop of Woolwich; concludes that most atheists are opposed merely to false images of God, "a way of conceiving him which has become an idol."

B42 HALVERSON, JOHN. "Patristic Exegesis: A Medieval Tom Sawyer," College English, XXVII (October), 50-55.

When Tom is slighted by Becky and broods in the woods (Chapter VIII) he follows the example of The Man in Black in Chaucer's The Book of the Duchess, which MT probably "knew and understood" (Halverson's italics). The underlying doctrine is Augustinian, and in TS "underneath the apparently frivolous cortex of this extraordinary work there is a profound condemnation of the foolishness and vice to which unbridled concupiscence leads."

B43 HARDING, WALTER. "Mark Twain's Blue Jays and the Red-Headed Woodpeckers," Twainian, XXIV (January-February), 1.

Compares Jim Baker's story in TA of a blue jay attempting to fill a knot-hole in a cabin roof to a similar account in Arthur Cleveland Bent's Life History of North American Woodpeckers (Smithsonian Institution, U. S. National Museum Bulletin 174, 1939, pp. 202-203) of a woodpecker poking acorns in a hole extending through a telephone pole:

1965 - Shorter Writings

(HARDING, WALTER)
"On the ground under the pole was about a double handful of acorns that had fallen out." Contains no information on MT.

B44 *HENDERSON, ROSWELL P. "Judge John Marshall Clemens," Bulletin of the Missouri Historical Society, XXI (October), 25-30.
Reveals a more impressive figure than depicted by his son, MT. [Source: Abstract in AES, XI (1968), 1842; Leary (1970), p. 65 lists this for 1964.]

B45 HILL, HAMLIN. "Toward a Critical Text of The Gilded Age," Papers of the Bibliographical Society of America, LIX (Second Quarter, 1965), 142-49.
"Over 170 variants, then, belong by best judgment in the copy-text which represents the closest version to Mark Twain's intended one, almost half of them substantive readings. And derived texts of The Gilded Age almost without exception corrupt the text further." Abstract in AES, IX (1966), 924; reprinted in Twainian, XXVI (January-February, 1967).

B46 _____. "Two Mark Twain Heresies," Modern Language Quarterly, XXVI (June), 327-32.
A review article. Margaret Duckett's Mark Twain and Bret Harte (1964) is too long. "Duckett demonstrates admirably that Bret Harte was an extremely important influence on the early Mark Twain," but later she "becomes an apologist for Harte; and on several occasions the defense is inadequate." Robert A. Wiggins's Mark Twain: Jackleg Novelist (1964) "would have been immeasurably more useful if it had assimilated some of the critical and scholarly studies written during the past decade and a half."

B47 HOROWITZ, FLOYD R. "Mark Twain's Belle Lettre in 'The Loves of Alonzo Fitz Clarence and Rosannah Ethelton,'" Mark Twain Journal, XIII (Winter), 16.
This story, written in 1878, accurately represents the first commercial model of the telephone (1877). Abstract in AES, XI (1968), 2263.

B48 JAUCH, CLEVELAND E., JR. "The Huckleberry Finn Exhibition," Grosvenor Society Occasional Papers, I (January), 27-35.
An appreciative discussion of HF and the manuscript of it exhibited by the Buffalo and Erie County Public Library, October 12-17 [1964?]; for the general reader.

B49 JOHNSON, ROBERT L. "The Road Out in Australian and American Fiction: a Study of Four Spokesmen," Southern Review: An Australian Journal of Literary Studies (University of Adelaide), I:3, pp. 20-31.
Uses HF and Cooper's Leatherstocking Tales as a basis of comparison for the discussion of Australian authors Joseph Furphy and Henry Lawson. Abstract in AES, X (1967), 3158; reprinted in Twainian, XXVII (January-February, 1968).

B50 JORDAN, PHILIP D. [Review: Margaret Duckett, Mark Twain and Bret Harte (1964).] American Notes and Queries, IV (October), 29.
Miss Duckett provides a useful record of the relationship of the two men but fails to explain the break in their friendship: "She records symptoms, but ignores causes.... It might have been profitable had Miss Duckett shown her manuscript to a psychiatrist." Nonetheless, "the volume as it stands is sound and will no doubt become the definitive work on a pair of talented but abnormal men of letters."

B51 KAHN, SHOLOM J. "Mark Twain's Final Phase." Studi Americani, XI, 143-62.
The last twenty years of MT's literary career constitute a phase of his development which has been somewhat neglected and perhaps misunderstood: after FE in 1897 he was no longer pressed by financial obligations and he turned his attention increasingly to commenting on man, religion, and society, and recording his own past.

B52 KEELEY, MARY PAXTON. [Review: Rachel M. Varble, Jane Clemens: The Story of Mark Twain's Mother (1964).] Missouri Historical Review, LX (October), 120-21.
Chiefly descriptive; praises the book as "delightful...well documented; some of the material, such as family letters, is new," presenting "a more realistic and less eulogistic picture of Mark Twain" than most books on him.

B53 KELLY, JAMES J. "They're Trying to Kill Huckleberry Finn," Mark Twain Journal, XIII (Winter), 13-14.
On the removal of HF from New York schools as racially offensive, and (briefly) on past bannings of the book. Kelly defends the portrayal of Jim and the representation of Negro speech, adding: "For any individual or organization to deny the fact that the American Negro generally, and with the exception of a small minority, speaks a limited and lower-vulgate English is ridiculous.... It is hardly the fault of Samuel Clemens if the average American Negro remains inarticulate in English after being in this country for three-hundred years."

B54 KRAUSE, SYDNEY J. "Cooper's Literary Offences: Mark Twain in Wonderland," New England Quarterly, XXXVIII (September), 291-311.
The assault on Cooper is delivered by a literary persona, rather than the responsible Samuel Clemens. "Actually, he is an unabashable hack and in his baccanal of sophistry latches on to just enough fact to silence doubt. Thus, over the long haul,

(KRAUSE, SYDNEY J.)
what this creature has gotten away with on the basis of gall alone is literary mayhem pure and simple" in his successful misrepresentation of Cooper, as may be seen by returning to what Cooper actually said; for example, MT's "account of the ambush is almost a complete canard." Abstract in AES, IX (1966), 2675.

B55 _____. "Huck's First Moral Crisis," Mississippi Quarterly, XVIII (Spring), 69-73.
Huck's moral awareness of Jim does not come in the fog episode in Chapter XV (as Lionel Trilling suggests), since his reponse there is psychological rather than moral; apologizing to Jim and recognizing him as a person prepares Huck for the following chapters, in which he "saves Jim by dint of courage and wit" from slave hunters. Abstract in AES (1966), 2328; reprinted in Twainian, XXVI (January-February, 1967).

B56 _____. "Twain and Scott: Experience versus Adventures," Modern Philology, LXII (February), 227-36.
MT "felt that unsound social views yielded an unsound literature and that bad writing sprang from a stultification of experience. Both situations he regarded as excesses of romanticism, and he tried to combat them by injecting critical analogues of romantic fiction into his books. In Adventures of Huckleberry Finn there is a group of such analogues that implicate Sir Walter Scott's representation of history as adventures." Abstract in AES, IX (1966), 399; reprinted in Twainian, XXVI (January-February, 1967).

B57 KUBICEK, EARL C. "Becky Thatcher Grants an Interview," American Book Collector, XV (Summer), 37-38.
Recollections of Sam Clemmens [sic] by Laura Hawkins Frazer, whom Kubicek visited in 1928; she conversed politely and told him nothing she had not told other interviewers. Abstract in AES, IX (1966), 12; reprinted in Twainian, XXVI (January-February, 1967).

B58 LAWRENCE, MARY MARGARET. "A Low Comedian," North American Review, n.s. II (May), 14-15.
"Low comedian" is MT's term for the Indian crow, the subject of this article. There is nothing of critical or biographical interest on MT, although Following the Equator (II, Ch. II) is quoted extensively.

B59 LEITER, LOUIS H. "Dawson's Landing: Thematic Cityscape in Twain's Pudd'nhead Wilson," Mark Twain Journal, XIII (Winter), 8-11.
Although Dawson's Landing is superficially a typical American small town, it is symbolically given greater significance through references to other cities and countries (suggesting that it is a microcosm), to "one- and two-storey frame dwellings" (life there

may have "more than one 'story,' more than one meaning"), and "climbing tangles of rose-vines, honeysuckles, and morning glories" (implying complication, concealment, and "the rosy view, the honeyed view, the glorious view of existence--the superficial, communal view of the status quo"). "Twain exposes theme by forcing descriptions of houses to suggest ethical attitudes (superficial) and species of plants (old-fashioned) to suggest traditional beliefs." Abstract in AES, XI (1968), 2261.

B60 LEWIS, R. W. [Review: Hamlin Hill, Mark Twain and Elisha Bliss (1964).] College English, XXVI (March), 492.
Brief, chiefly descriptive. "Thoroughly researched and carefully documented, the book still reads easily and it makes a convincing case for Bliss's indirect influence."

B61 LILLARD, RICHARD G. [Review: Paul Fatout, Mark Twain in Virginia City (1964).] Journal of American History, LI (December), 511-12.
"The author presents here a long article's worth of new material in a book that reorganizes much that historians already have access to. ...the approach is descriptive rather than analytical," giving a full and accurate picture of MT's twenty months with the Enterprise.

B62 LINNEMAN, WILLIAM R. "Punch and Huckleberry Finn," English Language Notes, II (June), 293-94.
The weekly "Roundabout Readings" column for January 4, 1896 tells of the author's eleven year old nephew's "keen and appreciative enjoyment" of Huckleberry Finn and adds his own praise of "this Homeric book--for Homeric it is in the true sense, as no other English book is, that I know of." Abstract in AES, X (1967), 1199; reprinted in Twainian, XXVII (January-February, 1968).

B63 LYDENBERG, JOHN. [Review: Bryant Morey French, Mark Twain and "The Gilded Age."] American Quarterly, XVII (Winter), 768.
"Mr. French has assiduously collected almost all the facts about The Gilded Age that one could conceivably find, or want to find," and although he "tells us little that is new," he makes a good case for the political criticism and gives persuasive evidence that the sentimentalism and melodrama "are in large part intentional...as burlesques of the popular fiction of the time."

B64 McKEE, JOHN DeWITT. "Three Uses of the Arming Scene," Mark Twain Journal, XII (Summer), 18-19, 21.
MT's description of the dressing of a knight [Chapter XI: "The Yankee in Search of Adventures"] has no counterpart in Malory's "Le Mort D'Arthur"; it is here compared to an account in Chaucer's "Sir Thopas," and to one in Sir Gawain and the Green Knight, which

1965 - Shorter Writings

(McKEE, JOHN DeWITT)
"could have served as sources for both Chaucer and Twain." Abstract in AES, IX (1966), 2655.

B65 MANN, CHARLES W. [Review: Charles Neider, ed., The Adventures of Colonel Sellers.] Library Journal, XC (March 1), 1120-21.
The book is "a bibliographical curiosity. ...Twain and Warner, whatever their differences in temper and genius, did it their way, not Mr. Neider's."

B66 MANSFIELD, LILLIAN M. "Early Members, Parishioners, and Mark Twain," in her The History of Asylum Hill Congregational Church, Hartford, Connecticut (Hartford: Asylum Hill Congregational Church), pp. 12-22.
Passim on MT, his friendship for the pastor Joseph Twichell, and his renting a pew at the church although he and his wife did not become members officially; elsewhere, notes the church was more liberal than it had been in former times.

B67 MAXWELL, D. E. S. "Twain as Satirist," in his American Fiction: The Intellectual Background (New York: Columbia University Press; London: Routledge and Kegan Paul), pp. 192-235; also, p. 292 on HF.
A major study, beginning with eighteenth-century conceptions of satire, then treating MT's satire as an assault on the failure of institutions as seen in HF and other works.

B68 MILLER, F. DeWOLFE. "Whitman Bibliography in Russia," Walt Whitman Review, XI (September), 77-79.
MT receives more space than any other American author in a bibliography of Russian criticism of American writers in G. P. Zlobin, ed., "Studies in American Literature (more literally, Problems in the History of the Literature of the U.S.A.)," Moscow: Izdatelstvo "Hayka" (n.d.).

B69 MORGAN, H. WAYNE. "Mark Twain: The Optimist as Pessimist," in his American Writers in Rebellion from Mark Twain to Dreiser (New York: Hill and Wang), pp. 1-36.
Begins with a long biographical summary, using the Paine biography rather trustingly and MT's own accounts more cautiously. Without dismissing MT's pessimism and determinism, Morgan argues that "their hidden purpose weakened them; it was always that of the humanist, to lift, to cleanse, and to create as well as to criticize.... the shock of his losses late in life did not make him a pessimist"; rather, the outlook of his last years was the result of youthful freethinking and the "profound social changes of his lifetime."

B70 MORRIS, WRIGHT. "The Lunatic, the Lover, and the Poet," Kenyon Review, XXVII (Autumn), 727-37.
On the element of the grotesque in American literature, noting that "neither Mark Twain nor the times was ripe for the gallow's [sic] humor beneath his smiling platform manner, but he was too much of an artist, and he suffered too deeply, to conceal his feelings completely. The story of Pudd'nhead Wilson charts this personal crisis," although MT abandoned his original topic of Siamese twins (pp. 732-33). Abstract in AES, IX (1966), 2968; reprinted in Twainian, XXVI (January-February, 1967).

B71 PEDERSON, LEE A. "Negro Speech in The Adventures of Huckleberry Finn," Mark Twain Journal, XIII (Winter), 1-4.
An expanded version of a paper read to the American Dialect Society at the 1964 meeting of the Modern Language Association, this "preliminary report on a projected study of all the literary dialects in the novel" is a "brief account...limited to phonology," revealing close correspondence between the speech in HF and that still in use. Abstract in AES, XI (1968), 2260.

B72 *POWERS, RICHARD H. "To Mark Twain's Missionary Defenders," Forum (Houston), VI (Winter-Spring), 10-16.
[Source: AES, X (1967), 2696; reprinted in Twainian, XXVII, January-February, 1968; facts of publication confirmed by note from Forum. AES abstract notes that MT was restricted by his lack of formal education, although he learned of the human problem and the difficulty of its solution.]

B73 REGAN, ROBERT. [Review: Edith Colgate Salsbury, Susy and Mark Twain: Family Dialogues.] Library Journal, XC (September 15), 3605.
Brief review: Making a book of excerpts from books, journals, and letters, allowing people to speak for themselves, still tells us "nothing very interesting" about MT's books, "but for that shortcoming and others, Mrs. Salsbury's book compensates abundantly by conveying the reality of Mark Twain's family life with remarkable immediacy."

B74 RIDLAND, J. M. "Huck, Pip, and Plot," Nineteenth-Century Fiction, XX (December), 286-90.
Huck struggles with his conscience, and his decision to help Jim parallels that of Pip in Great Expectations to help the escaped convict Magwitch; Pip has learned morality from a "tall and bony" older sister comparable to Miss Watson, and in each book there is a collision with a steamboat on a river. Abstract in AES, XI (1968), 2329.

B75 ROGERS, FRANKLIN R. [Review: Paul Fatout, Mark Twain in Virginia City (1964).] American Literature, XXXVI (January), 534.
Because of a too-severe limitation in the scope of the book, Fatout "is unable to add anything to our understanding of the author's development as a writer"; moreover, he misrepresents MT as "a flamboyant feature writer who expended his major effort on hoaxes and humorous squibs"; and, finally, he has paid insufficient attention to original sources or the scholarship concerning them.

B76 ____. [Review: Robert A. Wiggins, Mark Twain: Jackleg Novelist (1964.] Nineteenth-Century Fiction, XIX (March), 412-13.
This brief book "deserves and will reward the reader's careful attention" as it follows "Twain's development from a humorist thoroughly untutored in the art of the novel to the novelist who wrote Huckleberry Finn and struggled with the complexities inherent in later conceptions." Wiggins finds MT's strength as located in the folk mind, which he later partially deserted, to his cost, since there was not an offsetting in sophisticated self-control. Although Wiggins does not come to grips with contrary critical opinions he is aware of them, and his own thesis is "worth considering"; he has written "a quite refreshing book."

B77 ROSSKY, WILLIAM. "The Reivers and Huckleberry Finn: Faulkner and Twain," Huntington Library Quarterly, XXVIII (August), 373-87.
As a young man Faulkner once disparaged MT, but he later praised his work and influence. The two humorous boys' books here discussed are alike in relations of boys to companions, their protective attitude toward young women, struggles with conscience, a revolt against conventional morality leading to higher morality, and "similar use of the tramp pattern with its variations." Abstract in AES, IX (1966), 1691; reprinted in Twainian, XXVI (January-February, 1967).

B78 *SCANLON, LAWRENCE E. "Unheroic Huck," East-West Review, II (Winter, 1965-1966), 99-114.
A passive character, Huck is further alienated from society by events beyond his control. [Source: Abstract in AES, XI (1968), 1219.]

B79 SMITH, HENRY NASH. "Mark Twain, The Adventures of Huckleberry Finn," in Wallace Stegner, ed., The American Novel from James Fenimore Cooper to William Faulkner (New York, London: Basic Books, Inc.), pp. 61-72.
"Huck's habit of moral improvisation, his antinominian attitude toward established authorities and institutions, his tolerance of a wide disparity between theory and practice" stem from what MT called his "sound heart and a deformed conscience." The book's structure reveals basic American attitudes, from near farce at the start to a growing richness in the quest for freedom, and then a "tragic realization that freedom cannot be attained in this or any world," and MT apparently "taking refuge from tragedy in a joke."

B80 ____. [Review: Hamlin Hill, Mark Twain and Elisha Bliss (1964).] Nineteenth-Century Fiction, XX (June), 96-98.
Hill has supported his "modest but clear thesis" that MT was shaped as a writer by the demands of subscription publication. Hill furnishes "a number of fresh insights into how Mark Twain's imagination functioned," and the book should be "permanently useful."

B81 SMITH, J. HAROLD. "Mark Twain's Basic Political Concepts: Men, Parties, Democracy," Missouri Historical Review, LIX (April), 349-54.
MT's generally derogatory portrait of political life derived both from a bitterness growing out of personal sorrows and from disillusionment founded on his own observations of a corrupt age.

B82 SMITHLINE, ARNOLD. [Review: Bryant Morey French, Mark Twain and "The Gilded Age."] Library Journal, XC (September 15), 3604.
"Rather clumsy and pedantic," but useful in showing the degree of collaboration between MT and Warner.

B83 *STEWART, VINCENT. "Out of the Looking Glass: Illusion and Reality in Tom Sawyer," Missouri English Bulletin, XXII (January), 1-8.
[Source: Beebe and Feaster (1968), p. 123; Leary (1970), p. 74; MHRA Annual Bibliography (1969), No. 7988.]

B84 SWAN, JON. "Innocents at Home," American Heritage, XVI (February), 58-61, 97-101.
On the 1906 visit of Maxim Gorky to New York, raising funds for a Russian revolution. MT and Howells lent enthusiastic support but withdrew upon public revelation that the woman traveling with Gorky was not his wife. A photograph shows MT with Gorky and others at a banquet at Club A in Manhattan. Abstract in AES, VIII (1965), 2181; reprinted in Twainian, XXV (January-February, 1966).

B85 TANNER, TONY. "Mark Twain" in his The Reign of Wonder: Naivety and Reality in American Literature (Cambridge: Cambridge University Press). pp. 97-183.
Beginning with the Simon Suggs and Sut Lovingood perspective, Tanner examines "the way in which the vernacular supplanted the official rhetoric in Clemens's writing," then turns to "examine some of the details

(TANNER, TONY)
of this important stylistic shift" (p. 127).
In MT's inversion of oratory and of the pastoral situation, "the low uneducated figure
is in fact wiser than the educated tourist,
and he speaks more tellingly." His early
works show him looking for appropriate
speakers (p. 129). He found such a speaker
in Huck Finn, and "The young vernacular
rebel is alone with his wonder, his candour,
and his sound heart" (p. 154); he stands in
contrast to Tom Sawyer, who accepts the
rules and outlook of society (Ch. X, passim).
"The Pond of Youth" is reprinted in Schmitter (1974), pp. 29-39.

B86   _____. "Versions of Pastoral," Encounter,
XXIV (June), 59-62.
A review-article, chiefly concerned with
Leo Marx, The Machine in the Garden; a
briefer account of Henry Nash Smith's Mark
Twain's Fable of Progress accepts and describes the detailed exploration of "one of
the most important early attempts to celebrate the technological age positively,"
only to culminate in "an orgy of embittered
destruction."

B87   TAYLOR, J. GOLDEN. [Introduction.] "The
Celebrated Jumping Frog of Calaveras County," American West, II (Fall), 73-76.
Provides the general reader an account of
the first publication of the sketch (here
reprinted, pp. 76-79) and the part it played
in MT's development as vernacular stylist.
"The literary significance...lies in the
authenticity and artistry with which a humorous incident in an early western mining-
camp is made to yield fable-like insights
into certain universal traits in human nature." Abstract in AES, XIV (1970-1971),
2541 ("adapted from 'Abstracts of Folklore
Studies' [Canada], 8:1, Sp., 1970, 13");
reprinted in Twainian, XXXI (January-February, 1972).

B88   TEDESCHINI LALLI, BIANCA MARIA. "Il Piccolo
Satana di Mark Twain" [Mark Twain's Little
Satan], Studi Americani, XI, 163-80.
On The Mysterious Stranger, taking into
account current American scholarship. Concludes that the Stranger is imperfectly delineated, representing an anti-God, invol-
untary cruelties, a symbol of sorrow but
at the same time creator of joy: "He made
birds out of clay and he set them free,
and they flew away singing" (p. 180).

B89   TODD, WILLIAM B. "Problems in Editing Mark
Twain," Books at Iowa (April), 3-8.
A paper read at the meeting of the Modern
Language Association in New York, December
27, 1964, on textual difficulties created
by variants and by MT's carelessness and
his readiness to allow friends to make
textual decisions for him.

B90   *TOEBASCH, WIM. "Der Neger in de Amerikaanse
Literatuur" [The Negro in American Litera-
ture], Vlaamse Gids, XLIX (September), 602-15.
[Source: Abstract in AES (1965), 2825.]
Notes the important character Jim in HF.
[In Flemish.]

B91   TULIP, JAMES. "Huck Finn--The Picaresque
Saint," Balcony/The Sydney Review, No. 2
(Winter), pp. 13-18.
[Source: photocopy provided by kindness of
Professor Stephen Knight, University of Sydney.] A broad and provocative criticism of
HF. "I been there before," the concluding
sentence, dramatically involves both Huck
and MT, whose "deepest response is, then to
the past even at the moment when he appears
to be sending his hero off into a hopeful
future.... Huck's run for the future is
really a race from the past," and his "most
vital image" is the lies he tells. They
"have a saving effect, but their cause and
their content imply a world that is damned:
his family are dead, the farm has been sold
up, there's smallpox on the raft." It is
"the effervescence of the picaresque" that
"establishes a moral order in the narrative," but one "which in its very quality of
continual moments of release from the past
is in no sense a triumph over that past."
MT's "imagination is reaching out to a reality far beyond the capacity of Huck's imagination," and "the most dramatic writing in
the book is to be found in those passages
where Twain 'takes over' from Huck the role
of hero-cum-narrator." Abstract in AES,
XVII (1973-74), 2836.

B92   TURNER, MARTHA ANNE. "Mark Twain's '1601'
Through Fifty Editions," Mark Twain Journal,
XII (Summer), 10-15, 21.
A discussion for the general reader, with
data culled from familiar sources. Abstract
in AES, IX (1966), 2653.

B93   TWICHELL, JOSEPH H. Letter to Albert Bigelow
Paine (June 1, 1911), Twainian, XXIV (May-
June), 1.
According to F. E. Bliss, Charles Dudley
Warner received no share in the profits from
the Gilded Age play, and there was consequent
ill-feeling between Warner and MT. In a
headnote Chester Davis comments on policy of
the Mark Twain Research Foundation: "We
often are blamed for not permitting the general public to inspect and make copies of
material in our Foundation files, which material we have not yet published in The
Twainian. As such material is published by
us, the original material is then available
and not before." Abstract in AES, XI (1968),
1722; reprinted in Twainian, XXVIII (January-February, 1969).

B94 WARNER, DEANE M. "Huck and Holden," CEA Critic, XXVII (March), 4a-4b.
"I propose to show, through a discussion of Huckleberry Finn, The Red Badge of Courage, and The Catcher in the Rye, the evolution of American reaction to initiation, and how the perspective of pre-initiation innocence is an indication, and even an indictment, of contemporary attitudes." Abstract in AES, XIII (1969-1970), 1754; reprinted in Twainian, XXX (January-February, 1971).

B95 WEISHERT, JOHN J. "Once Again: Mark Twain and German," Mark Twain Journal, XII (Summer), 16.
First reprinting of an MT letter dated "Hotel Metropole, Wien, March 15, 1898," from the Louisville Anzeiger (May 1, 1910); contains an amusing mixture of German and English, tells of distant past when he used to trade a German-language weekly received in the exchange "to our German baker every week for a slab of gingerbread as big as a flagstone," and concludes by mentioning his prized acquaintance with Carl Schurz.

B96 WELLAND, DENNIS. "Mark Twain's Last Travel Book," Bulletin of the New York Public Library, LXIX (January), 31-48.
On the publication of the book in America as Following the Equator and in England as More Tramps Abroad. Andrew Chatto, the English publisher, took considerable pains with the book; by contrast, the American publisher, Frank Bliss "seems to have made so many textual changes on his own authority that it might not be unreasonable to see More Tramps Abroad as the editio princeps, and to describe Following the Equator as an abridged variant of it." The differences in chapter division are tabulated, and there is a list of maxims not used in the English edition, together with the texts of those used only there. Abstract in AES, IX (1966), 30; reprinted in Twainian, XXVI (January-February, 1967).

B97 WERGE, THOMAS. "Huck, Jim and Forty Dollars," Mark Twain Journal, XIII (Winter), 15-16.
The generosity of the slave-hunters who give Huck forty dollars, which he promptly shares with Jim (Chapter XVI) underscores Huck's sense of guilt in not betraying Jim; it contrasts with the action of the King, who sells Jim for forty dollars and keeps the money for himself. The concluding episode repeats the theme, when Tom Sawyer gives Jim forty dollars for his trouble as a prisoner. "This forty dollars is freely given and freely accepted, and this act of generosity recalls and reaffirms Huck's values while denying those predatory hunters whose lust for money is surpassed only by their absolute moral corruption." Abstract in AES, XI (1968), 2262.

B98 WHITE, WILLIAM. "Teaching Huck Finn in Korea," Mark Twain Journal, XIII (Winter), 5-7.
As a visiting professor under a Fulbright grant, White found his students at three different colleges unprepared for college-level work in English.

B99 WILLIAMS, JAMES D. "The Use of History in Mark Twain's A Connecticut Yankee," Publications of the Modern Language Association, LXXX (March), 102-10.
MT learned of medieval life chiefly from secondary sources, among them Lecky and Carlyle, but drew more heavily on post-Renaissance history; "Since for the most part he was collecting examples of misery and injustice the modernity of his material implied increasingly narrow chronological limits for his theme of social and moral progress." Abstract in AES, IX (1966), 525; reprinted in Twainian, XXVI (January-February, 1967).

B100 *WILSON, COLIN. "Madach's Tragedy of Man and Mark Twain's Mysterious Stranger," in his Eagle and Earwig (London: John Baker), pp. 162-70.
[Source: Beebe and Feaster (1968), p. 133.]

B101 WINKELMAN, DONALD A. "Goodman Brown, Tom Sawyer and Oral Tradition," Keystone Folklore Quarterly, X (Spring), 43-48.
An early member of the American Folklore Society, MT uses folklore "as a series of psycho-physical functions which often motivate and always affect the actions of Tom and Huck," but he does not allow it to interrupt a mood, such as that established with Tom and Becky in the cave. "This paper was read at a meeting of the American Folklore Society in Washington, D.C., December, 1963."

B102 _____. "Three American Authors as Semi-Folk Artists," Journal of American Folklore, LXXVIII (April-June), 130-35.
On folklore in the works of MT, Charles W. Chesnutt, and Manley Wade Welman. MT's folklore, centered around a locale, lets him "demonstrate that a man can interpret but never control nature"; but MT "used folklore chiefly as a device for portraying local color or setting the stage for future action." Abstract in AES, IX (1966), 1880 ["Reprinted from Abstracts of Folklore Studies, III:4 (December, 1965)"]; reprinted in Twainian, XXVI (January-February, 1967).

B103 WOODWARD, ROBERT W. "'Personating Mark Twain': a Folk Story," Mark Twain Journal, XIII (Winter), 12, 20.
Reprints an anecdote by this title from The Californian: A Western Monthly Magazine; IV (July, 1881), about a temperance lecturer who took the stage when MT failed to appear for a lecture; the audience was unaware of the substitution and laughed at every word.

1966 - Books

1966 A BOOKS

A1　BRASHEAR, MINNIE M., and ROBERT M. RODNEY,
　　　eds. The Birds and Beasts of Mark Twain.
　　　Norman: University of Oklahoma Press.
　　　　An anthology of anecdotes and descrip-
　　　tions of animals from MT's works.

A2　COX, JAMES M. Mark Twain: The Fate of Hu-
　　　mor. Princeton, New Jersey: Princeton
　　　University Press.
　　　　On the role of humor in shaping MT's lit-
　　　erary identity as it appears in his major
　　　works. "Southwestern Vernacular"
　　　(pp. 167-84, on HF) reprinted in Simpson
　　　(1968), pp. 82-94.

A3　DAY, A. GROVE, ed. Mark Twain's Letters from
　　　Hawaii. New York: Appleton-Century.
　　　　VAluable chiefly for putting a complete
　　　text of Mark Twain's letters to the Sacra-
　　　mento Union in 1866 back in print. Con-
　　　tains a sensible introduction explaining
　　　the circumstances under which the letters
　　　were written, but no notes or introductions
　　　to the individual letters.

A4　GORDON, EDWIN. Mark Twain. New York: Crow-
　　　ell-Collier Press.
　　　　Popular biography for teenage readers.

A5　KANE, HARNETT T. Young Mark Twain and the
　　　Mississippi. New York: Random House.
　　　　A reliable biography for young readers.

A6　KAPLAN, JUSTIN. Mr. Clemens and Mark Twain:
　　　A Biography. New York: Simon and Schus-
　　　ter.
　　　　Covering the period from 1866, when MT
　　　left the West, emphasizes his inner ten-
　　　sions as exemplified in a dual nature.
　　　Incorporating previously unpublished mate-
　　　rials, Kaplan's book is dramatically pre-
　　　sented and was enthusiastically greeted by
　　　many reviewers, though more temperately in
　　　some academic journals. It received the
　　　National Book Award and Pulitzer Prize for
　　　Biography in 1967. The reviews by Day,
　　　DeMott, Blair, and Krause (1966-1967) are
　　　summarized by Robert H. Woodward in ALA, I
　　　(December, 1967), 125-26.

A7　NEIDER, CHARLES, ed. The Complete Travel
　　　Books of Mark Twain. The Early Works:
　　　"The Innocents Abroad" and "Roughing It."
　　　Garden City, N.Y.: Doubleday & Company, Inc.
　　　　Consists of the two books, introduced by
　　　"Mark Twain's Travels" by Charles Neider
　　　(pp. vii-xxix), which includes a letter
　　　MT wrote the night before the Quaker City
　　　sailed but is otherwise of interest only
　　　as background for the general reader.
　　　Does not contain editorial matter or notes,
　　　except for "A Note on the Text," which
　　　states that the text is that of the first
　　　American edition, with only minor changes
　　　and with the chapter numbers changed from
　　　Roman to Arabic (p. xxxi).

A8　REGAN, ROBERT. Unpromising Heroes: Mark
　　　Twain and His Characters. Berkeley and Los
　　　Angeles: University of California Press.
　　　　Takes the theme of the Unpromising Hero
　　　from folklore (though not dealing with spe-
　　　cific folktales). "Tom Sawyer, little
　　　Prince Edward and his pauper double, the
　　　Connecticut Yankee, and Pudd'nhead Wilson
　　　are among the many characters in Mark
　　　Twain's books who are significantly related
　　　to this familiar figure of folk literature,"
　　　as is the character of "Mark Twain"
　　　(pp. viii-ix).

A9　SCOTT, ARTHUR L. On the Poetry of Mark Twain.
　　　With Selections from His Verse. Urbana and
　　　London: University of Illinois Press.
　　　　"Let no one mistake this book as an effort
　　　to establish a reputation for Mark Twain in
　　　the realm of poetry. It is no such thing.
　　　Nor is it a critical study of Mark Twain's
　　　poetry. It is, rather, a survey of the
　　　life-long interest of Mark Twain in poetry--
　　　a form of writing which almost everyone
　　　thinks he detested" (p. vii). Includes
　　　poetry previously published, as well as
　　　some from the Mark Twain Papers. There is
　　　a 39-page discussion of MT's poetry, and
　　　there are bibliographical and other comments
　　　on the poems.

A10　SPENGEMANN, WILLIAM C. Mark Twain and the
　　　Backwoods Angel: The Matter of Innocence in
　　　the Works of Samuel L. Clemens. Kent, Ohio:
　　　The Kent State University Press.
　　　　"As Clemens presents it, the myth of Amer-
　　　ican innocence entails three distinguishable
　　　but obviously related problems": "the moral
　　　drama" of the innocent hero confronting
　　　evil; "the conflict between agrarian and
　　　urban, industrial values"; and an examina-
　　　tion of the reliability of MT's faith "by
　　　putting it to the imaginative test of set-
　　　ting, character, and action.... This ten-
　　　sion between faith and fact engenders the
　　　conflict which makes his best work more
　　　than a mere reflection of popular sentiment
　　　and raises Huckleberry Finn to the level of
　　　prophecy" (pp. xi-xii). Among the works
　　　treated are the travels with Brown and IA;
　　　RI and Captain Stormfield's Visit to Heaven;
　　　GA and TS; Old Times on the Mississippi;
　　　P&P and "A Campaign that Failed"; HF; CY;
　　　JA, and MS.

A11　STRONG, LEAH A. Joseph Hopkins Twichell:
　　　Mark Twain's Friend and Pastor. Athens:
　　　University of Georgia Press.
　　　　The friendship of "Joe" Twichell and MT
　　　extended from their meeting in the winter
　　　of 1867-1868 until MT's death in 1910, and
　　　in warmth is comparable to that of MT and
　　　Howells. Twichell was MT's traveling com-
　　　panion on trips to Bermuda and to Europe
　　　(where he was the original of "Harris" in
　　　A Tramp Abroad), and the broadly tolerant
　　　friend for whom MT wrote the naughty 1601
　　　(Dr. Strong also recounts MT's disastrous

(STRONG, LEAH A.)
   miscalculation in reading it years later before Twichell's wife, Harmony, and the next
   day to a literary club consisting of some
   of the grandes dames of Hartford
   [pp. 138-39]). The book begins with a biography of Twichell revealing him as an interesting man in his own right, but major
   emphasis is on his friendship with MT and
   his influence on MT's thought and writing.
   Reviews by Mann (1966) and Branch (1967)
   are summarized by Robert B. Hausmann in ALA,
   I (December, 1967), 132-33.

1966 B SHORTER WRITINGS

B1   ADE, GEORGE, "One Afternoon with Mark Twain,"
     Twainian, XXV (July-August), 1-4.
        Reprint of a pamphlet which appeared in
     1939 under this title, 1939.A1. Abstract in
     AES, XI (1968), 1735; reprinted in Twainian,
     XXVIII (January-February, 1969).

B2   ALLEN, GERALD. "Mark Twain's Yankee," New
     England Quarterly, XXXIX (December),
     435-46.
        "In its ragged but surprisingly complete
     way, CY expresses more consistently and en-
     gagingly than any other work the seminal
     attitude of American writers between 1870
     and 1910. In a time when the old ideals of
     progress were being subjected to the ex-
     periences of the Civil War, political cor-
     ruption, and massive industrialization,
     Twain is completely in tune." The artistic
     failure and indication "that Twain is con-
     fused and unsure of this thesis" is valu-
     able, because "successes put forth answers,
     while failures define the questions more
     precisely." Abstract in AES, X (1967),
     2027; reprinted in Twainian, XXVII (January-
     February, 1968).

B3   ALLISON, JOHN M. "Victorian View of Honolu-
     lu," Saturday Review, XLIX (March 19), 33.
        A review, largely descriptive, of A.
     Grove Day (ed.), Mark Twain's Letters from
     Hawaii.

B4   ALTER, ROBERT. "The Apocalyptic Temper,"
     Commentary, XLI (June), 61-66.
        Includes passing mention of MS in a tra-
     dition beginning with Melville's The Con-
     fidence-Man—a tradition that R. W. B.
     Lewis calls "savagely comical apocalypse."

B5   ALTIERI, JOANNE. "The Structure of 'The
     Private History of a Campaign That Failed,'"
     Mark Twain Journal, XIII (Winter), 2-5.
        Behind the apparent rambling and digres-
     sion lies "a relatively tight structure
     which achieves simultaneously a narrative
     crisis and affective climax, unobtrusively,
     with seeming ease." A better case may be
     made for the architectonics in MT's short
     works than in his long ones. Abstract in
     AES, XII (1969), 1234.

B6   ANON. "Gutting the Gilded Age," Times Liter-
     ary Supplement, June 16, p. 539.
        A review of Charles Neider, ed., The Ad-
     ventures of Colonel Sellers (1965), MT's
     share of GA with the contributions by
     Charles Dudley Warner omitted. "There is
     something to be said for this rather ruth-
     less act of salvage," but it might have been
     better to reprint the entire novel. "But
     the most notable thing is Mark Twain's com-
     pulsive interest in voices. He never analy-
     ses characters--he imitates them speaking."

B7   ANON. "Innocent Abroad," Time, LXXXVII
     (March 18), 114, 116.
        A descriptive review of A. Grove Day, ed.,
     Mark Twain's Letters from Hawaii.

B8   ANON. "Mark Twain Items Published Elsewhere,"
     Twainian, XXV (January-February), 1-4;
     (March-April), 4.
        Reprints most of the abstracts of material
     relating to MT from AES, VIII (1965). Ab-
     stract in AES, XI (1968), 1730, 1732; re-
     printed in Twainian, XXVIII (January-Februa-
     ry, 1969).

B9   ANON. [Review: Peter Coveney, ed. and intro-
     duction, The Adventures of Huckleberry Finn,
     1966.B31).] Times Literary Supplement,
     September 29, p. 901.
        Criticizes Coveney's heavy-handed inter-
     pretation and excessive annotation of the
     obvious. Coveney's "Suggestions for Further
     Reading" following the introduction "Sur-
     prisingly...does not include Lionel Tril-
     ling's essay on Huckleberry Finn. Especial-
     ly surprising, because Mr. Coveney's essay
     is at times so similar to Mr. Trilling's."
        On November 17 (p. 1052) Coveney defends
     himself in a letter to the editor: his sug-
     gested reading list included Barry Marks's
     Mark Twain's Huckleberry Finn: Problems in
     American Civilization, which contains the
     Trilling essay. In a reply that follows,
     the reviewer points to close verbal paral-
     lels between the texts of Coveney and Tril-
     ling. "Surely when Mr. Coveney is in such
     substantial and detailed agreement with Mr.
     Trilling's essay it deserved mention in its
     own right by name, rather than silently as
     part of a collection of articles," especial-
     ly since The Liberal Imagination is far more
     generally available than the Marks anthology.

B10 ANON. [Review: Justin Kaplan, Mr. Clemens
     and Mark Twain.] Time, LXXXVII (June 24),
     108, 110.
        Descriptive and approving, emphasizing
     MT's pessimism.

B11 ANON. [Brief review: Edith Colgate Salsbury,
     Susy and Mark Twain (1965).] Times Literary
     Supplement, July 28, p. 692.
        Criticizes the format but notes interest-
     ing family details and "some enchanting pho-
     tographs"; Mrs. Salsbury has handled her ma-
     terial (some of it previously unpublished)
     "with respect."

B12   ARVIN, NEWTON. American Pantheon, ed. Daniel
Aaron and Sylvan Schendler. New York:
Delacorte Press.
      Contains "Mark Twain Simplified" (1932.B4)
and "The Friend of Caesar" (1933.B6).

B13   BABCOCK, C. MERTON. "Mark Twain and the Dictionary," Word Study (G. & C. Merriam Co.),
XLII (October), 1-6.
      On MT's painstaking choice of words; in-
cludes facsimile reproduction of an MT letter (Hartford, March, 1891) to G. & C. Merriam & Co., praising their dictionary and
thanking them for the copy they sent him.

B14   _____. "Mark Twain's Religious Creed,"
Southern California Quarterly, XLVIII
(June), 169-74.
      On MT's comments on theology and organ-
ized religion, as revealed in his Notebook
(1935, ed. Paine) and Letters from the
Earth (1962, ed. DeVoto). Abstract in AES,
X (1967), 490; reprinted in Twainian, XXVII
(January-February, 1968).

B15   BAENDER, PAUL. "Alias Macfarlane: A Revision of Mark Twain Biography," American
Literature, XXXVIII (May), 187-97.
      Passages in Paine's 1912 Biography (I,
115) and 1924 ed. of the Autobiography
(I, 143-47) have been taken as evidence
that MT acquired his pessimistic doctrine
in 1856-1857 from a laboring man and self-
taught philosopher named Macfarlane; a more
convincing case can be made that Macfarlane
is a character, like the "Mr. Brown" of
MT's early travel sketches, used to deflate
pretension; "but by the 1890's Mark Twain
was most concerned with the premises of
societies, not their manners." Abstract in
AES, X (1967), 790; reprinted in Twainian,
XXVII (January-February, 1968).

B16   BARCHILON, JOSE, and JOEL S. KOVEL. "Huckleberry Finn: A Psychoanalytic Study," Journal of the American Psychoanalytic Association, XIV (October), 775-814.
      Deliberately limited to evidence in HF,
excluding biographical data and evidence
from MT's other works. "The essential
feature of the method is that we treat the
novels as if they were the life histories
of real people." Sub-sections are "The
Structure of Huck's Personality"; "The
Wish to be Dead: Reunion with the Dead
Mother"; "The Wish to Kill the Mother and
Its Resolution through Passivity"; "The
Theme of Moses and the Wish to Live: The
Nile and the Mississippi"; "Jim's Charac-
ter"; "Sexuality In Huckleberry Finn"; "Tom
Sawyer's Character"; "Huck's Growth through
the Relationship with Jim"; "Children's
Games: The Three Orphans Reborn as Sib-
lings"; "The Wish to Have a Negro Mother?"
"The Relationship of the Moses' Myth to the
Story of Huck"; "A Wanderer on the American
Frontier"; and a "Postcript" on "Method"

and "Goals." Reprinted (in part:
pp. 799-808) in Gerber (1971), pp. 113-21.

B17   BEWLEY, MARIUS. "Split in Twain," New York
Review of Books, VII (September 8), 19-22.
Reprinted in Bewley's Masks & Mirrors: Essays in Criticism (New York: Athenaeum,
1970), pp. 180-90.
      A review of Justin Kaplan, Mr. Clemens
and Mark Twain: "The best life of Twain
that we possess...in his treatment of Twain's
work Kaplan shows himself to be a thoroughly
reliable and astute critic."

B18   BRANCH, EDGAR M. [Review: Leah A. Strong,
Joseph Hopkins Twichell: Mark Twain's Friend
and Pastor (1966).] American Literature,
XXXIX (May, 1967), 228-30.
      Summarizes the book, which would benefit
from fuller use of the Mark Twain Papers,
and which "in effect demonstrates the unim-
portance of Twichell's influence upon
Twain's writing."

B19   BRIDGMAN, RICHARD. "Henry James and Mark
Twain," in his The Colloquial Style in America. New York: Oxford University Press,
pp. 78-130; also passim.
      The chief difference between the two is in
subject-matter: "Huck and the other characters in his book talk about things, whereas
the Jamesian characters discuss states of being" (p. 78). Quotes Alice B. Toklas as saying that MT was Gertrude Stein's favorite
American writer--whom "she was continuously
reading," but recognizes possible hyperbole,
since this was in a letter to MT's biographer
Miss Jerry Allen, and transcribed in a copy
of her book given to Miss Isabel Lyon
(pp. 166-7, and 243 n. 8).

B20   *BROWN, MAURICE. "Mark Twain as Proteus:
Ironic Form and Fictive Integrity," Papers
of the Michigan Academy of Science, Arts
and Letters, LI, 515-27.
      [Source: MHRA Annual Bibliography (1967),
No. 7098.]

B21   *BRUNVAND, JAN HAROLD. "The Western Folk Humor in Roughing It," The Western Folklore
Conference: Selected Papers (ed. by Austin
E. Fife and J. Golden Taylor. Monograph
Series, IX, iii). Logan: Utah State University Press, 1964, pp. 53-65.
      [Source: Beebe and Feaster (1968),
p. 137; additional details from MLA Bibliography (1966), Nos. 14, 8028.]

B22   BUDD, LOUIS J. "Camaraderie," South Atlantic
Bulletin, XXXII (March), 21-22.
      A review of Leah A. Strong's Joseph Hop-
kinds Twichell: Mark Twain's Friend and
Pastor, in which she draws heavily on Twichell's fourteen volumes of scrapbooks on his
church but passes over The Mark Twain-Howells Letters (1960). She trusts some reminiscences too much, but makes a good case
for the steadying influence of Twichell.

B23   ____. "Mark Twain and the Upward Mobility of Taste," in Ray B. Browne, Donald M. Winkelman, and Allen Hayman, eds., New Voices in American Studies (West Lafayette, Indiana: Purdue University Studies, pp. 21-34.
       After the iconoclasm of IA, MT showed a growing interest in the arts. He bought paintings, took painting lessons, and subsidized the study abroad of sculptor Karl Gerhardt, but "he pondered dismayingly little about art in any form as making a unique kind of discourse and, most of his life, shied away from conceiving of his writing in such terms."

B24   BURGESS, ANTHONY. "Mark Twain and James Joyce," Mark Twain Journal, XIII (Winter), 1-2.
       Although James Joyce "did not read either Tom Sawyer or Huckleberry Finn very thoroughly, if at all," in Finnegans Wake he punningly links MT with Arthurian legend through King Mark of Cornwall, Tom with peeping Tom ("Tom saw-yer"), and Huck with the revived Finnegan, "Finn again." Abstract in AES, XII (1969), 1233.

B25   NO ENTRY

B26   *CLEMENS, CYRIL. "A Chat with Joseph Conrad," Hobbies (January), pp. 85, 88, 92. [Source: Reprinted in Conradiana, II (Winter, 1969-1970), 97-103.]
       In the course of the interview, Conrad mentions his pleasure in reading Life on the Mississippi and his thoughts about MT while piloting a steamboat on the Congo. The Conradiana reprint is abstracted in AES, XIV (1970), 2140.

B27   CLEMENS, SAMUEL L. "Mark Twain's Last Letter, Written the Editor's Mother, Mrs. James Ross Clemens," Mark Twain Journal, XIII (Winter), front cover.
       From Bermuda, March 24, 1910 (reproduced in facsimile), on his loss of Jean, Livy, and Susy; expresses his heavy sorrow but says he would not bring them back if he could: "Death is the most precious of all the gifts this life has for us."

B28   ____. [Letter to Governor David R. Francis of Missouri.] Mark Twain Journal, XIII (Winter), 21.
       Publishes without comment MT's letter from Florence (May 26, 1904), expressing regret that circumstances do not allow him "to exhibit myself at the great St. Louis Fair and get a prize."

B29   CLOUGH, WILSON O. [Review: Margaret Duckett, Mark Twain and Bret Harte (1964).] American Literature, XXXVII (January), 491-92.
       "Less a literary evaluation than a study in divergent characters.... while not denying Harte's limitations as man and artist, and while not greatly shifting critical verdicts on either man, does round out the portrait of Harte more conformably to fact." MT's bitterness and perhaps "a sense of guilt, remains the enigma still, a part of the more complex of the two characters."

B30   COCKERILL, DONALD J. [Review: Henry Duskis, ed., The Forgotten Writings of Mark Twain (1963).] Denver Quarterly, I (Summer), 128-29.
       Duskis "edits the wildly impromptu melange of comment (often silly or saccharine) on woman's suffrage, gold mine exploiters, etc., plus all the contemporary trivia a journalist can contrive, into snippets bridged by synopses and running commentary. The result is not unlike gargling bourbon instead of drinking it." The material is "essentially third-rate Twain," and "the lack of an index makes the book a major publishing disaster for the scholar since Duskis' technique favors simple chronology."

B31   COVENEY, PETER. [Introduction.] The Adventures of Huckleberry Finn. Harmondsworth, Middlesex, England: Penguin Books, pp. 9-41.
       Provides an over-view of the book and summary of the published criticism, but no new insights. See 1966.B9.

B32   [DAVIS, CHESTER L.] "Mark Twain's Marginal Notes on 'The Queen's English,'" Twainian, XXV (March-April), 1-4.
       Extensively discusses and quotes G. Washington Moon's Learned Men's English: The Grammarians (London, 1867; revised ed. London: George Routledge & Sons, 1892), and reproduces some of MT's marginal notations in a copy he gave his daughter Clara; the comments reveal MT's views of the English language and of Moon. In a concluding note Chester L. Davis announces that the copy annotated by MT may be examined by members of the Mark Twain Research Foundation: "It is only after we have printed the material in The Twainian that it is released and is then generally available. Our planning of future issues is often governed by such requests for information.... We welcome inquiries from authors while they are working on articles or on entire books...such inquiries might cause us to publish items which otherwise might be released years later. Certainly there is no desire to deprive the world of any material in our files which rightfully adds to enrichment of literature, however we alone must be the judge of what we do release, and once again, only after publication in The Twainian, later the same material and perhaps some related material we decided not to use, is open for examination in our offices." Among such material Davis is prepared to publish in part and then release are letters by Laura Frazer (the original for Becky Thatcher)

([DAVIS, CHESTER L.])
and letters to Albert Bigelow Paine. "There
are some definite restrictions however. Inquiries for information and the release of
material which could serve no worthwhile
purpose, get no attention from us. An example would be what our files contain relating to Nina, the granddaughter of Mark
Twain having recently died. We do not propose to ever release any material concerning
Nina, no member should ever ask for it."
Incorrectly attributed to James B. Stronks
in MHRA Annual Bibliography (1966), No. 7046;
Abstract in AES, XI (1968), 1731; reprinted
in Twainian, XXVIII (January-February,
1969).

B33   _____. "New Edition of Mark Twain Books,"
Twainian, XXV (September-October), 2.
Begins: "Many of the serious students of
Mark Twain have known for the past several
years that a group of capable authors are
getting together a new set of Mark Twain
books for the publishing firm Harper & Row;"
mentions having been written or visited by
some of the editors, and readiness "to co-
operate and permit the use in our office of
the valuable card-index compiled by George
Hiram Brownell." Davis urges readers with
useful material to send it to the Foundation
or to the editors themselves. There follows a list of the editors and the works for
which they are responsible [this seems to
be essentially the same as the edition being
published by the University of California
Press in cooperation with the Center for
Editions of American Authors--T.A.T.]. Abstract in AES, XI (1968), 1737; reprinted
in Twainian, XXVIII (January-February,
1969).

B34   _____. "The Transition from Wisconsin to
Missouri in 1950," Twainian, XXV (November-
December), 3-4.
On the transfer of the files of the Mark
Twain Research Foundation from Elkhorn,
Wisconsin to Perry, Missouri.

B35   _____. "'Twainian' First Published in 1939--
Regular Series Began in 1941. 'Our Silver
Anniversary'--An Appraisal and Review,"
Twainian, XXV (November-December), 2-3.
Highlights of the history of the Mark
Twain Research Foundation and of some of
the 1939 issues.

B36   _____. "Why 'Research' Is in Our Corporate
Name," Twainian, XXV (May-June), 1-2.
On MT material filed at the Mark Twain
Research Foundation, and the continuing
search for first publication of his writings, etc. Abstracted in AES, XI (1968),
1733; reprinted in Twainian, XXVIII (January-February, 1969).

B37   DAY, A GROVE. "He Was His Own Best Character,"
Saturday Review, XLIX (June 18), 31-33.
A review of Mr. Clemens and Mark Twain: A
Biography, by Justin Kaplan, who "has read
all the books and articles, all the letters
and notes. He has sifted all the biographical grains and blown away the chaff of leg-
ends and lies. He has listened to all the
theories but has swallowed none." The book
"supersedes previous accounts of its subject's later years.... It is the book that
Dixon Wecter, had he lived, could have written."

B38   DEMOTT, BENJAMIN. "In the American Vein,"
New York Times Book Review (July 3), pp. 1,
16-17.
A review of Justin Kaplan's Mr. Clemens
and Mark Twain as "the closest biographical
approach yet made to the writer," revealing
MT's limitations in temperament, taste, and
ideas in "a book of dignity, evenhandedness
and grace."

B39   *DE SCHWEINITZ, GEORGE W. "Huck and Holden,"
Proceedings of Conference of College Teach-
ers of English at Texas, XXXI (September),
27-28.
[Source: MHRA Annual Bibliography (1967),
No. 7102, with annotation: "(Abstract)."]

B40   DICKINSON, LEON T. [Review: Arthur L. Scott,
On the Poetry of Mark Twain.] English Studies (Amsterdam), LII (1971), 82-83.
This is verse, rather than poetry, and
"the serious pieces are interesting and moving, though more, one feels, because one
knows the circumstances that prompted them
than for the power of the verse itself";
this is interesting only because it is by
MT. Scott's editing has included meticulous
proof-reading, but for some of the selections better copy-texts could have been used,
as for "Good-Bye."

B41   _____. [Review: Henry Nash Smith, Mark
Twain's Fable of Progress (1964).] English
Language Notes, III (March), 234-37.
With a lengthy summary, declares "this
short study...is truly admirable in its multiple approach to the study and evaluation
of a puzzling work, and the clarity with
which it sorts out and yet relates the various strands of a complex literary problem."
Says Smith "dates Mark Twain's decline as a
writer from the composition of this fable."

B42   ELIOT, T. S. "American Literature and the
American Language," Sewanee Review, LXXIV
(January-March), 1-20. See 1953.B20.
On pp. 11-13, links MT with Poe and Whitman as one of his "landmarks I have chosen
for the identification of American literature"; in HF, MT "reveals himself to be one

(ELIOT, T. S.)
of those writers, of whom there are not a
great many in any literature, who have discovered a new way of writing, valid not
only for themselves but for others. I
should place him, in this respect, even with
Dryden and Swift, as one of those rare writers who have brought their language up to
date, and in so doing, 'purified the dialect
of the tribe.'" Abstract in AES, IX (1966),
2434; reprinted in Twainian, XXVI (January-
February, 1967); annotation: "(reprinted
from To Criticize the Critic, 1965)."

B43   FATOUT, PAUL. "Mark Twain's Nom de Plume,"
Twainian, XXV (September-October), 2-4.
Reprinted from American Literature, XXXIV
(March, 1962), 1-7.
        Prefaced by Chester L. Davis: "Again we
regret that it is difficult for us to reprint reference characters and notes. This
article is well documented and the original
publication should be studied for details."
Abstract in AES, XI (1968), 1738; reprinted
in Twainian, XXVIII (January-February,
1969).

B44   _____. [Review: Edith Colgate Salsbury,
Susy and Mark Twain: Family Dialogues
(1965).] American Literature, XXXVIII
(May), 251-52.
        "The record sharpens general impressions
of the life of Mark Twain," and "the materials of this book are copious and authentic, but the method of using them causes
distracting incoherence and a failure to
follow through."

B45   FIEDLER, LESLIE A. "An American Abroad,"
Partisan Review, XXXIII (Winter), 77-91.
        On IA, in which MT to some extent embodied
the limitations of his time but also recognized and satirized them. "Yet, over and
over, he was to return to the themes of The
Innocents Abroad: not only in other self-
declared travel books like A Tramp Abroad or
Following the Equator," but also in P&P, CY,
JA, TS Abroad, MS, and even in HF. Abstract
in AES, X (1967), 241; reprinted (incorrectly attributed to Notes and Queries) in
Twainian, XXVII (January-February, 1968).

B46 * _____. "Toward a Centennial: Notes on Innocents Abroad," New American Review (as reprinted in The Collected Essays of Leslie
Fiedler, 1971, 2 vols., II, 296-311).
        Notes MT's inability to throw away con-
ventional outlooks entirely, despite his
professed irreverence under the protection
of an assumed boyishness.

B47   FOX, MAYNARD. "Two Primitives: Huck Finn
and Tom Outland," Western American Literature, I (Spring), 26-33.
        The character in Willa Cather's The Pro-
fessor's House (1925) followed Huck in a
tradition in which nature is not necessarily benevolent; but both boys "found

independence, spontaneity, freedom, and an
energizing vitality in their retreats from
the center of population." Abstract in AES,
XI (1968), 2772; reprinted in Twainian,
XXVIII (January-February, 1969).

B48   FRANKLIN, H. BRUCE. "Mark Twain and Science
Fiction," in his Future Perfect: American
Science Fiction of the Nineteenth Century.
New York: Oxford University Press,
pp. 374-79.
        An anthology, with critical introductions.
Franklin briefly discusses several of MT's
imaginative works, among them CY and The
Great Dark, and reprints his "From the 'Lon-
don Times' of 1904" (pp. 380-90; this first
appeared in The Century Magazine, 1898).

B49   FRIEDRICH, GERHARD. [Review: Bryant Morey
French, Mark Twain and "The Gilded Age"
(1965).] Books Abroad, XL (Spring), 205.
        More abstract than review; uncritical.

B50   GAFFNEY, W. G. "Mark Twain's 'Duke' and
'Dauphin,'" Names: Journal of the American
Dialect Society, XIV (September), 175-78.
        After the embarrassment over having used
the name of a real Eschol Sellers in GA, MT
was careful in naming characters; he could
call a rascal in HF the Duke of Bridgewater
because the actual Dukedom was extinct;
moreover, Francis Egerton, third Duke of
Bridgewater, had been one of the wealthiest
men in the world, and his son, from whom
MT's character claimed descent, died a bach-
elor and without issue. The Dauphin could
not claim descent from the English or other
active European thrones, because they were
well occupied; "Literally the only way to
outrank the Duke of Bridgewater was to be
the (equally disinherited) rightful King of
France."

B51   GERBER, JOHN C. "Mark Twain," in James Wood-
ress, ed., American Literary Scholarship:
An Annual/1966 (Durham, North Carolina:
Duke University Press, 1968), pp. 48-64.
        A survey of MT scholarship for the year;
See 1963.B32. Contents: "i. Texts and
Editions"; "ii. Biography"; "iii. Criti-
cism"; "iv. Travel Books"; "v. Tom Sawyer
and Tom Sawyer Abroad"; "vi. Huckleberry
Finn"; "vii. A Connecticut Yankee"; "viii.
Pudd'nhead Wilson"; "ix. Miscellaneous."

B52   GILHOOLEY, LEONARD. [Review: Justin Kaplan,
Mr. Clemens and Mark Twain.] America, CXV
(July 16), 71-72.
        Kaplan explores MT's duality "with such
depth and force and grace that Clemens/Twain
emerges in whole and in part as he has
from no other biography." The book is "a
product of intense and scrupulous research,"
and Kaplan does not allow personal feelings
to distort it.

1966 - Shorter Writings

B53 GILL, BRENDAN. "The Confidence Man," New
Yorker, XLII (September 3), 114-17.
A review of Justin Kaplan's Mr. Clemens
and Mark Twain, in which Kaplan "has proved
in every respect worthy of his great subject. It must be a very pleasant feeling
to begin one's career as a biographer with
a work that is sure to be read as long as
Twain is read." Abstract in AES, XII
(1969), 975.

B54 *GOWDA, H. H. ANNIAH. "Mark Twain in India,"
Literary Half-Yearly, July, 17-23.
[Source: Abstract in AES, XII (1969),
928; reprinted in Twainian, XXIX (January-
February, 1970), with author's name spelled
"Gooda" and title of journal given as "Li-
brary Half-Yearly."]

B55 GRAUMAN, LAWRENCE, JR. "Mark Twain Beside
Himself," New Republic, CLV (July 16),
31-34.
A review of Justin Kaplan, Mr. Clemens
and Mark Twain, a book which "represents a
prodigious accumulation of data, selected
and shaped from both a biographical and a
critical perspective, and presented without much style," or rather in a style which
attempts to be both popular and scholarly.

B56 GURIAN, JAY. "Literary Convention and the
Mining Romance," Journal of the West, V
(January), 106-14.
Our picture of the West is colored by
literary conventions. For example, MT's
description of the Comstock was meant to
entertain, and "the purposes of DeVoto and
Mack are to instruct, yet their use of literary conventions prevents them from doing
so.... The problem is that the Comstock's
historians and Twain's critics have tacitly
accepted the burlesque as reality, the caricature as character."

B57 HAMBLEN, ABIGAIL ANN. "The Best-Known Teen-
ager: Huck Finn," Mark Twain Journal,
XIII (Winter), 15-19.
"Huck Finn's is a sensitive imaginative
mind," though practical rather than philosophical; he matures in the book but still
cannot accept the shackles of civilization.

B58 *HARPER, MARION. "The West of Twain and Cather," Diliman Review, XIV (January), 60-80.
MT's West is masculine, Cather's feminine; contrasts their tone and values, and
the names of characters. [Source: Abstract in AES, XIV (1970-1971), 584;
reprinted in Twainian, XXXI (January-February, 1972).]

B59 HILL, HAMLIN. [Review: Bryant Morey French,
Mark Twain and "The Gilded Age" (1965).]
American Literature, XXXVIII (March),
134-35.

"In effect a comprehensive handbook to
Mark Twain and Charles Dudley Warner's novel...explores more thoroughly than anyone
else previously the transformation of raw
material and biographical data into a nov-
el--or something deceptively similar to a
novel, at any rate."

B60 HOROWITZ, FLOYD R. "'The Invalid's Story':
an Early Mark Twain Commentary on Institutional Christianity," Midcontinent American
Studies Journal, VII (Spring), 37-44.
In his story of the exchange of a box of
rifles and a Limburger cheese sandwich for
a coffin in an express car MT satirizes institutional religion: "Center of the structure, then, is a Christ-like body which is
actually no body, but guns and odiferous
[sic] cheese hidden from sight." Abstract
in AES, X (1967), 507; reprinted in Twainian, XXVII (January-February, 1968).

B61 HOWELL, ELMO. "Mark Twain, William Faulkner,
and the First Families of Virginia," Mark
Twain Journal, XIII (Summer), 1-3, 19.
Although MT's PW lacks Faulkner's reverence toward Virginia and the South, both
authors abhor "the violence and the injustice inherent in the social system of the
South" but respect the tranquility, courage,
and integrity of the Southern gentleman.
Abstract in AES, XI (1968), 2264.

B62 *HUDON, EDWARD. "Mark Twain and the Copyright
Dilemma," American Bar Association Journal,
LII (January), 56-60.
An account of MT's troubles with British
and Canadian pirate publishers, and his efforts to promote copyright legislation more
favorable to authors. [Source: Reprinted
in Twainian, XXV (May-June), 2-4; (July-
August), 4; a headnote by Chester L. Davis
adds: "It is with regret that our form of
publication makes it difficult to print
reference notes, the article being well
supplied with authoritative references."]
Abstracts in AES, XI (1968), 1734, 1736;
reprinted in Twainian, XXVIII (January-
February, 1969).

B63 JONES, HOWARD MUMFORD. "James, Howells, Mark
Twain," in his Jeffersonianism and the
American Novel. New York: Teachers College
Press, Teachers College, Columbia University, pp. 35-47.
Only the last section of the chapter
(pp. 44-47) concerns MT who, despite his
humanitarianism and anti-imperialism, dis-
trusted the common man: see Colonel Sherburn face down the mob in HF, and note Hank
Morgan as enlightened despot in CY; note
also MT's attack on the Moral Sense, and
his deterministic philosophy. Thus, MT may
be considered anti-Jeffersonian.

B64 KOHN, JOHN S. VAN E. "The Doubly Suppressed Chapter of Following the Equator," Princeton University Library Chronicle, XXVII (Spring), 156-58.

The copy of this rarity acquired by the library from the collection of Thomas F. Leeming contains a statement by Jacob Blanck (December, 1939) that made it possible to describe it as one of three extant copies, although in the Bibliography of American Literature, II (1959) Blanck had described the publication under BAL 3546: "Privately Printed for Merle Johnson. Not published. The entire edition, save for two copies preserved for the printer, destroyed by Jacob Blanck by order of Merle Johnson." Olivia Clemens had originally asked that the chapter be dropped because of indelicacy; it was suppressed the second time because of serious typographical errors in the printed copy.

B65 KRUSE, HORST. "Die Literaturkritischen Elementen in Mark Twains Life on the Mississippi," Neueren Sprachen, XV (July), 297-309; (August), 355-63.

On MT's conception of a writer's social responsibility, and his duty to avoid bias or mere tradition, as revealed in his literary criticism in LOM. Abstract in AES, X (1967), 184, 186; reprinted in Twainian, XXVII (January-February, 1968).

B66 LAHOOD, MARVIN I. "Huck Finn's Search for Identity," Mark Twain Journal, XIII (Winter), 11-14.

"Huck Finn is one of a handful of classic American frontier heroes...who are able to find their identity only in opposition to the society that threatens their freedom. All are essentially anarchic, and must 'light out for the territory ahead of the rest.'" Huck sees through the hypocrisy of those around him, including Tom and the Phelpses, and he seeks "a society with a heart as good as his." Abstract in AES, XII (1969), 1236.

B67 LEE, ROBERT EDSON. "From West to East: Mark Twain," in his From West to East: Studies in the Literature of the American West (Urbana and London: University of Illinois Press), pp. 82-111.

Argues that MT's backgrounds were basically of the East rather than the West, and traces his development through IA and RI. "The East seemed determined that the West should be romantic, and Twain concurred, and romantic it therefore was."

B68 "Letters to Paine--Early Days of 'The Mark Twain Company,'" Twainian, XXV (September-October), 4; (November-December), 1.

Letters from E. E. Loomis, Charles T. Lark, and Jervis Langdon on business matters and the forthcoming Mark Twain and the Happy Island (1913) by Elizabeth Wallace.

Abstract in AES, XI (1968), 1739, 1741; reprinted in Twainian, XXVIII (1969).

B69 LEWIS, MERRILL. [Review: Margaret Duckett, Mark Twain and Bret Harte (1964).] Western Humanities Review, XX (Winter), 85-86.

Professor Duckett is admittedly partisan, and her attribution of MT's hostility toward Harte to professional jealousy and later feelings of guilt is "intriguing but not very well supported." Moreover, "emphasis as well as thesis seem to me to distort the personalities and literary stature of both men." In any case, not all the stories about Harte began with MT.

B70 McNAMARA, EUGENE. "Huck Lights Out for the Territory: Mark Twain's Unpublished Sequel," University of Windsor Review, II (Fall), 68-74.

Huck's concluding statement has received undue attention from critics who ignore Tom Sawyer's suggestion, noted "a scant nine paragraphs before it," that the boys go off for adventures in the territory among the Indians; MT's intention was simply to leave the way open for a sequel, such as the unfinished Huck Finn and Tom Sawyer Among the Indians, here discussed. Abstract in AES, X (1967), 3250; reprinted in Twainian, XXVII (January-February, 1968).

B71 MALE, ROY R. "The Story of the Mysterious Stranger in American Fiction," Criticism, III (Fall), 281-94.

A study of examples from MT, Hawthorne, Melville, Harte, Howells, and others, in which "the settings are...isolated in place, time, or both. And they are circumscribed." "The problem of the ending results chiefly from the character of the stranger." Abstract in AES, IX (1966), 2523.

B72 MATTHEWS, JACK. "Mark Twain, 'Cartographer,'" ETC: A Journal of General Semantics, XXIII (December), 479-84.

On the contrast between Tom's abstract thinking and the literal-mindedness of Huck and Jim, who cannot understand why the countries over which they pass are not the colors by which they are represented on maps. Abstract in AES, X (1967), 1243; reprinted in Twainian, XXVII (January-February, 1968).

B73 MEINE, FRANKLIN J. [Review: Arthur L. Scott, On the Poetry of Mark Twain.] American Book Collector, XVI (Summer), 5.

"A sensitive and competent account" of MT's poems, more than 120 of which Scott has located, giving texts of 65 of them. "Twain's poetry gives the reader and the Twain collector an entirely different feeling and insight into this complex personality."

1966 - Shorter Writings

B74　MILLER, JIM WAYNE. "Pudd'nhead Wilson's Calendar," Mark Twain Journal, XIII (Winter),
8-10.
　　Refuting the contention by Richard Chase
(in The American Novel and Its Tradition)
that the aphorisms are inappropriate to
Wilson's character, shows that they fall
into four groups: "1) Death 2) Religion
3) The Fall 4) Pessimistic View of Man,"
and argues that they add to the portrait of
Wilson's character either directly or by reflecting the contradictions inherent in his
position as an outsider. Abstract in AES,
XII (1969), 1235.

B75　MILNE, GORDON. "Expertise: Twain, De Forest,
and Adams," in his The American Political
Novel (Norman: University of Oklahoma
Press), pp. 40-64; pp. 40-45 on MT.
　　Notes the unevenness of GA, the indictment
of corruption, lively portrayal of the leg-
islative sessions, and some well-drawn characters; J. W. De Forest covers some of the
ground, "and, on the whole, more penetrat-
ingly" (p. 46).

B76　MOERS, ELLEN. "The 'Truth' of Mark Twain,"
New York Review of Books, V (January 20),
10-15.
　　Begins as a review article, covering
Edith Colgate Salsbury, Susy and Mark Twain:
Family Dialogues (1965: "the best possible
memorial to the improbable Clemens establishment"); Margaret Duckett, Mark Twain and
Bret Harte (1964: "a rougher, nastier Mark
Twain"); Robert A. Wiggins, Mark Twain:
Jackleg Novelist (1964, briefly dismissed);
and Bryant Morey French, Mark Twain and
"The Gilded Age": The Book that Named an
Era (1965: "a more useful approach to the
assessment of Twain as a spokesman for American values and delineator of the American
character"). There follows a more general
discussion of MT's work: on Tom and Huck
as town boys, the justified stealing in HF
as opposed to the corruption in GA, and MT's
racial views.

B77　*MUGGERIDGE, MALCOLM. [Review: Charles Neider, ed. The Adventures of Colonel Sellers
(1965).] Observer, August 14, p. 19.
　　[Source: MHRA Annual Bibliography (1966),
No. 7024.]

B78　*NIELSEN, VENETA. "The Savage Prophet; or,
Who's Afraid of Samuel Twain?" Proceedings
of the Utah Academy of Science, Arts, and
Letters, XLIII, 1-7.
　　[Source: Leary (1970), p. 71.]

B79　NYREN, DOROTHY, comp. "Twain, Mark (1835-
1910)," in her A Library of Literary Criticism (Third Edition. New York: Frederick
Ungar Publishing Co.), pp. 489-93.
　　Excerpts from criticisms by Frank R. Stockton (1893), Henry Dwight Sedgwick (1908),

Stuart P. Sherman (1910), Brander Matthews
(1910), Hamlin Garland (1910), Henry M. Alden (1910), William Dean Howells (1910),
Edith Wyatt (1917), Van Wyck Brooks (1920),
Theodore Dreiser (1935), Henry Seidel Canby
(1951), Dixon Wecter (1952), Leslie A. Fiedler (1955), Kenneth S. Lynn (1958), and, on
HF, Edgar Marquess Branch (1950) and F. R.
Leavis (1956). Also, passim on HF, TS, PW,
LOM (as "autobiography"), and MS (as "short
story").

B80　O'CONNOR, RICHARD. Bret Harte: A Biography.
Boston, Toronto: Little, Brown and Company,
passim.
　　The numerous references to MT are based on
his own statements in his Autobiography and
elsewhere, and on other material familiar to
students of MT. There is no new light on
the causes for the break in friendship between MT and Harte.

B81　PECK, RICHARD E. "On Three Mark Twain Poems,"
Mark Twain Journal, XIII (Winter), 10-11.
　　The C. Walter Barrett Collection at the
Alderman Library, University of Virginia has
autograph manuscripts of three poems, of
which two differ textually from the versions
in Arthur L. Scott's On the Poetry of Mark
Twain and one is not included there. One
differs only in the spelling of a single
word, and Peck gives the texts of "Be Good,
Be Good. A Poem" and a short poem previously unpublished.

B82　*PILKINGTON, JOHN. "About this Madman Stuff,"
University of Mississippi Studies in English,
VII, 65-75.
　　Like Huck Finn, Holden Caulfield in Catcher
in the Rye is sane, idealistic, individual-
istic, and compassionate. [Source: MHRA
Annual Bibliography (1966), No. 7027; abstract in AES, X (1967), 723; and reprinted
in Twainian, XXVII (January-February,
1968).]

B83　PIZER, DONALD. Realism and Naturalism in Nineteenth-Century American Literature. Carbondale and Edwardsville: Southern Illinois
Press; London and Amsterdam: Feffer & Simons, Inc., pp. 3-10, 134-35, 141.
　　Uses HF, The Rise of Silas Lapham, and
What Maisie Knew to illustrate his thesis
that late nineteenth-century American realism does not always stress the representative, and it is subjective and ethically
idealistic (pp. 3-10); briefly comments on
statements by Leo Marx on the destruction of
the raft in HF as illustrating MT's hostility
toward the coming of the machine, and W. F.
Taylor on MT's stated approval of the machine.

B84　PLANTE, PATRICIA R. "Mark Twain, Ferber and
the Mississippi," Mark Twain Journal, XIII
(Summer), 8-10.

(PLANTE, PATRICIA R.)
  Edna Ferber's Show Boat "reveals marked
resemblances to both Twain's Life on the
Mississippi and Huckleberry Finn," espe-
cially in the symbolic use of the river.
Abstract in AES, XI (1968), 2267.

B85 POIRIER, RICHARD. "Transatlantic Configura-
     tions: Mark Twain and Jane Austen," in his
     A World Elsewhere: The Place of Style in
     American Literature. (New York: Oxford
     University Press. pp. 144-?07; also passim
     on MT.
       "An enlarged and considerably revised
     version of an essay first printed in In De-
     fense of Reading" (p. x.). Pp. 183-95 re-
     printed, abridged as "Huck Finn and the
     Metaphors of Society," in Simpson (1968),
     pp. 95-101.

B86 PRICE, LAWRENCE MARSDEN. The Reception of
     United States Literature in Germany. Chapel
     Hill: The University of North Carolina
     Press.
       On MT, pp. 11-19 and passim; a consider-
     ably more extensive treatment may be found
     in Hemminghaus, Mark Twain in Germany
     (1939), which Price cites, but there is
     also some material updating Hemminghaus.

B87 PRITCHETT, V. S. "Chicaneries," New States-
     man, LXXII (July 8), 56. A review of
     Charles Neider, ed., The Adventures of Colo-
     nel Sellers (1965).
       "Neither Mark Twain nor his collaborator,
     C. D. Warner, was capable of getting a real
     novel out of their material.... Twain was
     a cocky, peddling traveller and autobiogra-
     pher who never saw below the surface of
     reality: his genius lay in his gift for
     escaping from it." Abstract in AES, X
     (1967), 1324; reprinted in Twainian, XXVII
     (January-February, 1968).

B88 *RODD, LEWIS CHARLES. The Bad Boy from the
     Mississippi: The Story of Mark Twain.
     Melbourne: Cheshire. (Know Your Author;
     28-pp. pamphlet).
       [Source: MHRA Annual Bibliography (1966),
     No. 7134.]

B89 ROGERS, FRANKLIN R. "Mark Twain's First Ven-
     ture into Fiction," Southwest Review, LI
     (Winter), 97-98.
       A review of Bryant Morey French, Mark
     Twain and "The Gilded Age" (1965) as "an
     exhaustive study...Mr. French discusses in
     an impressively detailed fashion the compo-
     sition of the novel, the nature of the col-
     laboration between the two authors, and the
     specific targets of the satire. He provides
     useful information on such matters as the
     play based on the novel, the manuscript, and
     copyright problems," and the scattered work
     by other scholars on GA. By astute detec-
     tive work he has collected evidence support-
     ing his claim that GA is a roman à clef.

Unfortunately, GA itself lacks "an artistic
grace...a timelessness of theme or characterization," as is revealed by French's "attempt...to resurrect the satiric targets."

B90 ROLLINS, RONALD G. "Huckleberry Finn and
     Christie Mahon: The Playboy of the Western
     World," Mark Twain Journal, XIII (Summer),
     16-19.
       MT's novel and Synge's play show parallels
     in that the fathers are "cruel, arbitrary
     and despotic tyrants," and when Huck and
     Christy escape "both flights are similar in
     that they involve fake or symbolic murders,"
     after which the boys hide their true identi-
     ties or personalities and later are reborn
     to new maturity. Abstract in AES, XI (1968),
     2269.

B91 ROOT, ROBERT. [Review: A. Grove Day, ed.,
     Mark Twain's Letters from Hawaii.] Journal-
     ism Quarterly, XLIII (Winter), 793.
       Brief and descriptive: "These are person-
     al essays...will meet some needs of journal-
     ism students looking into the conjunction of
     literature and journalism."

B92 ROPER, GORDON. "Mark Twain and His Canadian
     Publishers: A Second Look," Papers of the
     Bibliographical Society of Canada, V, 30-89.
       Supplements Jacob Blanck's Bibliography
     of American Literature on MT editions.
     "This essay is an expansion of an article
     entitled 'Mark Twain and His Canadian Pub-
     lishers' in the 'Special Mark Twain Number'
     of The American Book Collector, X (June,
     1960), pp. 13-29" (p. 84, n. 2). On MT's
     problems with Canadian pirates and eventual
     success in arranging for authorized publica-
     tion. Includes "Check List of Canadian Edi-
     tions of Mark Twain's Work," with references
     to Blanck and with 27 editions not listed in
     Blanck (pp. 82-84).

B93 ROSE, MARILYN GADDIS. "Pudd'nhead Wilson: A
     Contemporary Parable," Mark Twain Journal,
     XIII (Summer), 5-7.
       The racial theme is still relevant: "In
     fact, Twain's fluctuating boundaries of Ne-
     gro and white and master and slave are as
     intricate and relevant as, say, Jean Genet's
     in Les Negres (1962)." Wilson is "a Thoreau
     with practical ambitions" and, "incidentally,
     one year younger than Hawthorne" on his ar-
     rival at Dawson's Landing in 1830. Abstract
     in AES, XI (1968), 2266.

B94 ROSENTHAL, RAYMOND. "Bohemian from the Sage-
     Brush," New Leader, XLIX (July 18), 15-16.
     A review of Justin Kaplan's Mr. Clemens and
     Mark Twain.
       MT's "influence on his wife and on Howells
     was much greater than theirs on him. He
     turned his wife Livy from a strait-laced
     Puritan into a tippler, an unbeliever and al-
     most a cynic.... Kaplan's account is more
     subtle and more convincing than Brooks'.

1966 - Shorter Writings

(ROSENTHAL, RAYMOND)
Mark Twain was a forceful artist, a compelling personality, who carried his conflicts within him."

B95   NO ENTRY

B96   ROTHBERG, ABRAHAM. "The Flawed Dream: American Novels of Politics," London Magazine, VI (April), 17-33.
Briefly mentions GA as having anticipated the attitudes and approaches in political novels of the present day. Abstract in AES, IX (1966), 3004; reprinted in Twainian, XXVI (January-February, 1967).

B97   SABITH, BARNEY. "All Things to All Men," Chicago Tribune, "Books Today" (June 26), Section 9, p. 10.
A review of Justin Kaplan, Mr. Clemens and Mark Twain. Uncritical, basically a description of the book; but, "Kaplan's examination of Clemens's life is compelling. His sources include material made public only recently, as well as letters not previously used in analysis of Clemens' work and personality. Kaplan's special gift is his analysis of events and relationships."

B98   *SACHS, VIOLA. "Wedrujaca Granica a Literatura Amerykanska," Przeglad Humanistyczny, X, No. 1, 43-57.
[Source: AES, X (1967), 2861; reprinted in Twainian, XXVII (January-February, 1968).] Includes discussion of the character Jim in HF. [In Polish.]

B99   SAMOSSOUD, CLARA CLEMENS. "One of the Last Letters from Clara Samossoud to Our Foundation," Twainian, XXV (November-December), 1.
A letter of January 15, 1961, thanking Chester L. Davis for a copy of a letter sent to a person (not named) being considered as president of the Mark Twain Research Foundation, Inc.; this is of no biographical or critical interest. Abstract in AES, XI (1968), 1740; reprinted in Twainian, XXVIII (January-February, 1969).

B100   SAN JUAN, PASTORA. "A Source for Tom Sawyer," American Literature, XXXVIII (March), 101-102.
The Hartford Courant of April 21, 1873 contained a story of boys lost in a Hannibal cave; this "is probably Mark Twain's source for the episode in The Adventures of Tom Sawyer"; moreover, "the style of the news item is reminiscent of Twain," who may have written it. Abstract in AES, X (1967), 781; reprinted in Twainian, XXVII (January-February, 1968).

B101   *SAPOSHNIKOV, G. "Sholem Aleichem and Mark Twain," Zukunft, LXXI, 174-76.
[In Yiddish. Source: MLA Bibliography (1966), No. 15039.]

B102   SCANLON, LAWRENCE E. "'They're After Us' Again," Mark Twain Journal, XIII (Summer), 20-21.
In "Mr. Eliot, Mr. Trilling, and Huckleberry Finn," Leo Marx puts undue stress on Huck's words to Jim; in fact he is as much a fugitive as Jim is, but has not yet come to identify his own flight with Jim's. Abstract in AES, XI (1968), 2270.

B103   SCHLESINGER, ARTHUR, JR. "Mark Twain; or, the Ambiguities," Atlantic Monthly, CCXXVIII (August), 61-64.
Based on Justin Kaplan's Mr. Clemens and Mark Twain, this is essentially a review and summary. Kaplan's "remarkable...book is nonportentous and nonideological, concerned with telling Clemens' story rather than with making points about America. He has mastered the Mark Twain scholarship (even if he is something less than generous in acknowledging debts to those who went before) but has moved beyond the familiar Mark Twain controversies." Schlesinger discusses MT's lifelong inner tensions, emphasizing the later years, and follows Kaplan's view of him as a divided personality. He takes exception to the Howells description of MT as "the Lincoln of our literature," comparing him, rather, to Grant: "Like Grant, Mark Twain was a flawed man who never composed his inner schisms, never purged himself of bitterness, never distilled serenity out of torment."

B104   SCOTT, WINFIELD TOWNLEY. "Combed All to Hell," Book Week (Washington Post), III (June 26), 4, 15.
A review of Justin Kaplan, Mr. Clemens and Mark Twain, "a brilliant biography." Kaplan's "vast research and his scholarly intelligence are impeccable but never heavy, for he writes extremely well--with verve, wit, penetration, compassion," and revealing MT's inner conflicts. "This is not a theory-ridden book," as are those by Brooks and De-Voto, and the criticism of MT's works is "superb."

B105   SMITH, HENRY NASH. [Review: Bernard Poli, Mark Twain, Écrivain de l'Ouest: Regionalisme et Humour (1965).] Études Anglaises, XIX, 457-58.
Meeting his responsibilities in this first full-length introduction of MT to French readers, Poli provides essays on MT as "béotien au royaume des lettres," his religious and moral thought, his humor, and his style, as well as "a discriminating guide to relevant American scholarship. The European reader may turn to this book with confidence. It is a thoroughly reliable introduction to its subject." It is also an interpretation "with a fresh and arresting thesis" that MT's West was his experiences and remembered past which he attempted to use through "a surrogate narrator capable of mediating between reality and fantasy in the author's reminiscences"; thus, the loss of his

(SMITH, HENRY NASH)
creative powers in the later years may be attributed to a solidification of thoughts and consequent loss of "the delicate ambiguities of statement made possible by the use of a fully dramatized narrator." [In English.]

B106 STEIN, RUTH. "The ABC's of Counterfeit Classics: Adapted, Bowdlerized, and Condensed," English Journal, LV (December), 1160-63.
Exemplified by HF, in classroom editions and other adaptations. Generally the book is cut to "the mere story of a runaway slave," language is changed, and descriptions are reduced. Great stories so distorted are of doubtful value, and "in the 'popular' editions school children may actually learn to tolerate mediocrity."

B107 STEPHENS, GEORGE D. "Huckleberry Finn as a Journey," Mark Twain Journal, XIII (Summer), 11-15.
MT himself was an inveterate traveler, and "at one time or another Twain read LeSage, Rabelais, Fielding, and Smollett. Don Quixote was an early and lasting favorite. He read and admired the work of Dickens." HF follows some of the traditions of the picaresque novel in the journey and adventures, and in the use of an anti-hero as the central character. Abstract in AES, XI (1968), 2268.

B108 STOWELL, ROBERT F. "Notes on Geography in Huckleberry Finn," Mark Twain Journal, XIII (Summer), front cover, 22.
Stowell's map on the front cover shows Huck and Jim's route, with state boundaries and approximate distances; in his "Notes" Stowell asks for any needed corrections, as the map is to be incorporated in an Atlas for American Literature being compiled.

B109 STRONKS, JAMES B. [Review: Hamlin Hill, Mark Twain and Elisha Bliss (1964).] Modern Philology, LXIII (May), 369-71.
The subscription publisher who helped MT achieve wide sales (but may have underpaid him by some $50,000 in royalties) influenced his form of writing for an uncritical market; but the book is not primarily about him: "What Hill has actually written is a step-by-step history of the composition and publication of the six books that Bliss marketed for Twain: The Innocents Abroad (1869), Roughing It (1872), The Gilded Age (with C. D. Warner, 1873), the Sketches, New and Old (1875), Tom Sawyer (1876), and A Tramp Abroad (1880). The approach is solidly factual, sometimes tediously so, and some of the ground has been covered before; "and if the present book is not invariably interesting or unified it is because the author, skirting the claims of these previous prospectors, often mines lower-grade ore in scattered pockets."

B110 TRILLING, LIONEL, RAY B. WEST, and LYMAN BRYSON. "Mark Twain: The Adventures of Huckleberry Finn," in George D. Crothers, ed., Invitation to Learning: English & American Novels. New York, London: Basic Books, pp. 242-51.
One of a series of radio conversations on great novels; laudatory and somewhat general. Notes the terror in the book, and the significance of Huck's Pap; four kinds of authority: convention, nature, the supernatural, and (what counts with Huck) affection. There is brief comment on the importance of the language, and a concluding word on Huck's rejection of both convention and of romance: Tom does his rebelling in conventional terms, Huck does not.

B111 VALES, ROBERT T. "Thief and Theft in Huckleberry Finn," American Literature, XXXVII (January), 420-29.
"Huck has decided to steal Jim, and it is theft and its related synonyms which united all aspects of the novel. It is also through theft that we learn about the nature of man and society." Abstract in AES, X (1967), 767; reprinted in Twainian, XXVII (January-February, 1968).

B112 WALCUTT, CHARLES CHILD. "Freedom Afloat--and Adrift," pp. 131-44 in his Man's Changing Mask: Modes and Methods of Characterization in Fiction. Minneapolis: University of Minnesota Press.
"There is no firm theme to be realized in the plot; hence the action must turn into melodrama and the characters, having no firm beginnings, do not develop in great problems and decisions but recede into deeper obscurity as the melodramatic conclusion takes over."

B113 *WILLIAMS, PHILIP. "Mark Twain and Social Darwinism," Essays and Studies in English Language and Literature (Tohoku Gakuin University Review, Sendai, Japan), No. 49-50, pp. 143-72.
[Source: MHRA Annual Bibliography (1966), No. 7057; Leary (1970), p. 77.]

B114 WOODWARD, ROBERT H. "More on Mark Twain and the Dictionary," Word Study (G. & C. Merriam Co.), XLII (December), 8.
Repeats "a story--probably apocryphal: such anecdotes generally are--that appeared in one of the early issues of Word Study and was reprinted in the Word Study deskside reader entitled Vocabulary Building, Bibliography, and Word Study (1937). Over the name of the contributor, George A. Posner, and under the title 'Plagiarism'" appeared the story of MT's telling a speaker that "I have a book at home (and a very old book) that contains every word of that speech you just delivered"--and sending him a dictionary.

1966 - Shorter Writings

B115   WOODWARD, ROBERT H. "Teaching Huckleberry Finn
        to Foreign Students," Mark Twain Journal,
        XIII (Winter), 5-7.
            Students from the Republic of Mali, West
        Africa responded well to selections from HF
        in a class at San Jose State College.

B116   *YOUNG, PHILIP. Ernest Hemingway: A Recon-
        sideration. University Park, Pennsylvania:
        Pennsylvania State University Press.
            [Source: pp. 228-29, on HF, reprinted in
        Simpson (1968), pp. 113-14.] Describes Huck
        as hurt by his experiences, and not amused
        even by such nominally funny encounters as
        that with the Duke and Dauphin: "But Huck
        is not amused; they disgust him with man-
        kind in general. He is wounded, and bitter,
        and suffering from both insomnia and night-
        mare, and he finally rebels." Faced with a
        decision on whether to betray Jim, "off on
        his own, and exposed to the violence and
        evil of society as a whole, he renounces
        it.... If it is good, he is wicked. And if
        it aims for heaven, he will go elsewhere."

B117   ZIFF, LARZER. "Literary Absenteeism: Henry
        James and Mark Twain," pp. 50-72 in his The
        American 1890s: Life and Times of a Lost
        Generation (New York: Viking).
            "The lessons that the nineties slowly and
        painfully brought home to Howells and James
        came on [MT] more swiftly, like a thunder-
        clap. The decade...had battered Twain so
        severely that his art was never to recover."

1967 A BOOKS

A1   ANDERSON, FREDERICK, WILLIAM M. GIBSON, and
        HENRY NASH SMITH, eds. Selected Mark Twain-
        Howells Letters, 1872-1910. Cambridge,
        Massachusetts: The Belknap Press of Harvard
        University Press.
            "The text of the letters we have included
        reproduces the text in the two-volume edi-
        tion, except that we have omitted canceled
        words...and have condensed many letters by
        deleting passages having small interest or
        relevance for readers who are not special-
        ists in American literature"; includes two
        additional letters from MT to Howells (p. v).
        The letters reveal the literary influence
        of Howells as beneficial (p. xii), and "help
        to clarify the outlines of a vernacular tra-
        dition in the Gilded Age, which has exerted
        a powerful influence on a number of the
        best writers of tales and novels in the
        twentieth century. Howells fostered the
        tradition," both through his editing of the
        Atlantic Monthly, and in his own writing
        (p. xiii).

A2   ANON. Mark Twain in Romania: Bibliography of
        the Romanian Translations Published in Vol-
        ume and in Magazines. Bucharest: Romanian
        Institute for Cultural Relations with For-
        eign Countries.

In English. Includes Introduction and
Bibliographical Presentation by Dorothea
Sasu-Timerman, bibliography (annotated
briefly, and indexed), and "Number of Mark
Twain's Works Editions Published in the Socialist Republic of Romania, 1949-1966," giving the number of copies in each edition.
Introduction names several of "the foremost
fifty translators attracted by Mark Twain's
deep genuine creation," but notes the difficulty in dealing with his style. "That is
why till 1944 translations have been made
after French or German versions." More recent translations "have a high aesthetic
value; those realized after the English original, are often accompanied by biographical
presentations or studies, and bibliographical notes, which introduce the readers in
the atmosphere and the social political
events which generated a lot of incidents
evoked with such a wit and irony in his
books" (pp. 4-5). "The translations published in volumes and Romanian reviews, presented us the often dramatic action of his
writings, the funny part and sharp irony
covering his ideas as fighter against bondage, hypocrisy, superstition, lie and corruption, ever being in search for honesty,
truth and justice. That is why Mark Twain
is one of the most appreciated foreign
writers in Romania" (p. 5).

A3   BALDWIN, MARY AUSTIN, ed. William Dean How-
        ells, My Mark Twain: Reminiscences and
        Criticisms. Baton Rouge: Louisiana State
        University Press.
            This reprint of the 1910 edition (1910.A3)
        contains a useful ten-page introduction,
        twenty pages of notes to the text, and an
        index. It should be the new standard edi-
        tion of a work important for the critical
        judgment of the author and for his close
        friendship with MT. Available hardbound and
        in paperback.

A4   CLEMENS, CYRIL. Mark Twain and Lyndon B. John-
        son. Foreword by Adlai E. Stevenson. Kirk-
        wood, Missouri: Mark Twain Journal.
            Consists of letters from Lyndon Johnson
        thanking Cyril Clemens for a newspaper clip-
        ping, an invitation to address the Mark
        Twain Birthday Banquet, etc., together with
        letters from Hubert Humphrey and Mrs. John-
        son. The introduction by Adlai E. Stevenson
        does not mention this 23-page pamphlet, but
        tells of the time when MT wrote a bit of
        doggerel on the back of a menu for Steven-
        son's father, on the pronunciation of "Ad-
        lai" (p. 9).

A5   CLEMENS, SAMUEL L. "A Curtain Lecture Concern-
        ing Skating"; Being an Unusual Example of
        Mark Twain's Early Journalistic Humor, Writ-
        ten Entirely in Dialogue, and Reprinted for
        the First Time in Book Form as it Originally
        Appeared in the New York Sunday Mercury of
        March 17, 1867; and, the Later, Unauthorized
        Revision, Mrs. Mark Twain's Shoe; Being a

(CLEMENS, SAMUEL L.)
Facsimile Taken from the Pages of Beadle's
The Dime Dialogues No. 10: For Homes,
Schools and Exhibitions. New York: Beadle
and Company, Publishers, 98 William Street.
First Published in April, 1871. Edited by
Donald M. Kunde. Denver, Colorado: Pri-
vately Printed by Ralph Baldwin.
A contribution to a column titled "Table-
Talk" in the Sunday Mercury. Unfamiliar
with this early version, Merle Johnson dis-
missed the Beadle's distorted reprinting:
"I cannot think Mark Twain wrote it."

A6 ____. Mark Twain's Letters to His Publishers, 1867-1894, ed. Hamlin Hill. Berkeley,
Los Angeles, London: University of California Press.
A volume in the CEAA edition of the MT
Papers. Texts of 290 letters, 28 of them
reprinted from earlier book publications
because the originals are no longer available. "A few letters not addressed to
Mark Twain's official publishers--letters
to Orion Clemens, Charles Dudley Warner,
T. B. Pugh, Thomas Bailey Aldrich, and Moncure Conway, for example--are included because their major substance concerns publishing."

A7 ____. Mark Twain's Satires & Burlesques,
ed. Franklin R. Rogers. Berkeley and Los
Angeles: University of California Press.
A volume in the CEAA edition of the MT
Papers. Includes the Simon Wheeler and
Hellfire Hotchkiss sequences, the burlesque
Hamlet, and other unpublished manuscript
materials.

A8 ____. Mark Twain's "Which Was the Dream?"
and Other Symbolic Writings of the Later
Years, ed. John S. Tuckey. Berkeley and Los
Angeles: University of California Press.
A volume in the CEAA edition of the MT
Papers. "All of the selections in this
volume were composed between 1896 and 1905,"
after the death of his daughter Susy and
heavy financial disasters. "Their principal fable is that of a man who has been
long favored by luck while pursuing a dream
of success that seemed about to turn into
reality." Following sudden reverses, he
takes refuge in the thought that he may be
living in a nightmare from which he will
awaken; but his nightmares may be the actuality of his life.

A9 ____, and C. D. WARNER. The Gilded Age, ed.
by Herbert Van Thal, with an introduction
by Richard Church. London: Cassell. The
First Novel Library.
Van Thal's introduction concerns novels
in general, and Church's is biographical
rather than critical.

A10 KAPLAN, JUSTIN, ed. and Introduction. Great
Short Works of Mark Twain. New York: Harper & Row.
Kaplan's introduction gives brief biography
and conventional description of MT as author.

A11 ____, ed. Mark Twain: A Profile. New York:
Hill and Wang.
A collection of articles on MT (cross-
referenced to this anthology in the present
bibliography) and extracts from books (not
cross-referenced where more readily available in their original form). Includes the
account by Henry Nash Smith (from Mark
Twain: The Development of a Writer) of the
Whittier Birthday Dinner and its consequences, and Kaplan's own "The Yankee and the
Machine: The Perfectable World" ("Adapted
from Mr. Clemens and Mark Twain...1966").

A12 *KASYAN, A. K. Mark Tven v Rossii. (1872-
1966). [Mark Twain in Russia]. Leningrad:
Leningradskii Pedagogicheskii Institut Imeni
A. I. Gertsena.
[Source: MHRA Annual Bibliography (1967),
No. 7118.]

A13 KRAUSE, SYDNEY J. Mark Twain as Critic.
Baltimore: Johns Hopkins Press.
Traces MT's critical approach from his
early innocent mask of "Muggins" to the
later, more worldly "Grumbler," noting his
treatment of Goldsmith, Cooper, Scott, and
Harte, and its relation to his anti-roman-
ticism; also considers at length his appreciation of Macaulay, Howells, Howe, Zola,
and Adolph Wilbrandt. MT was a sensitive
reader and a serious student of his literary
craft. Reviews by Wiggins, Budd, Gerber,
Regan, Fatout, and an anonymous reviewer for
Choice (1967-1968) are summarized by Warren
B. Benson in ALA, II (June, 1969), 337-39.

A14 MARX, LEO., ed. Adventures of Huckleberry
Finn. Indianapolis and New York: The
Bobbs-Merrill Company, Inc.
Introduction describes MT's life, backgrounds and composition of HF, and summarizes the critical controversy. There are
also aids to the student and an appendix of
excerpts from LOM.

A15 NEIDER, CHARLES, ed. The Complete Travel
Books of Mark Twain. The Later Works: "A
Tramp Abroad," "Life on the Mississippi,"
"Following the Equator." Garden City, N.Y.:
Doubleday & Company, Inc.
Consists of the three books, with no introduction, editorial matter, or notes, except for "A Note on the Text," which states
that the texts are those of the first American editions of the books with only minor
changes and with the chapter numbers changed
from Roman to Arabic (p. ix).

1967 - Books

A16   NEIDER, CHARLES. Mark Twain. New York:
      Horizon Press.
         According to a "Prefatory Note" (p. ix),
      "The majority of these chapters were pub-
      lished as introductions to volumes of Mark
      Twain's work. 'On Mark Twain Censorship'
      and 'The Notebooks' have not been published
      previously." The chapters on MT are "The
      Novels" (1964), "The Adventures of Colonel
      Sellers," (1964), "The Travel Books and
      Travels" (1966), "The Essays" (1962), "The
      Autobiography" (1958), "Mark Twain and the
      Russians" (1959), "On Mark Twain Censor-
      ship" (1966), "The Notebooks" (1966), "The
      Sketches" (1961), "The Stories" (1956), and
      "Life as I Find It" (1961). "Mark Twain
      and the Russians" is subtitled "An Exchange
      of Views," and consists of Neider's corres-
      pondence with Literaturnaya Gazeta (Mos-
      cow), concerning the Russian charges that
      Neider's edition of MT's autobiography
      represented deliberate suppression of at-
      tacks on the establishment of his day;
      Neider reports this exchange (originally
      published by Hill and Wang in 1959), was
      later included in the Washington Square
      Press edition of the Autobiography (p. v).

A17   SCOTT, ARTHUR L., ed. Mark Twain: Selected
      Criticism. Dallas: Southern Methodist
      University Press.
         A revised edition of a 1955 collection of
      critical articles and excerpts from books,
      1867-1963. The material reprinted is in-
      cluded in the present bibliography and
      noted in cross-references to both editions.

A18   SIMON, JOHN Y., ed. and introduction. "Gen-
      eral Grant" by Matthew Arnold, with a Re-
      joinder by Mark Twain. Carbondale and Ed-
      wardsville: Southern Illinois University
      Press (1966).
         Contains the text of Arnold's two-part
      essay on Grant originally published in
      Murray's Magazine (repr. 1887, 1888) and
      the reply by MT in a speech at the Annual
      Reunion of the Army and Navy Club of Con-
      necticut, April 27, 1887. Simon's intro-
      duction describes Arnold's article as "a
      graceful tribute" to Grant, intended "to
      strengthen trans-Atlantic good will" (p. 4).

A19   WAGENKNECHT, EDWARD. Mark Twain: The Man
      and His Work, Third Edition. Norman:
      University of Oklahoma Press.
         Essentially the same as the 1961 edition,
      with an added thirty-page "Commentary on
      Mark Twain Criticism and Scholarship Since
      1960" (not systematically incorporated in
      the present bibliography). Excerpt (bio-
      graphical summary) reprinted in Schmitter
      (1974), pp. 11-18.

1967 B SHORTER WRITINGS

B1   ANON. "German Reds Use Mark Twain Work. Play
     Makes the Connecticut Yankee G.I. Slain in
     [Vietnam] War." New York Times, February 26.
        The play by Claus Hemmel, a warning to
     those who advocate socialism as a middle
     way, made its premiere in Erfurt the previ-
     ous week. This article is based on a review
     in the national Communist party newspaper.
     "The Yankee's cardinal sin, according to
     Rainier Kerndl, the Neues Deutschland thea-
     ter critic, is that he 'ignores the obvious
     signs of class conflict and believes that
     the telephone, mirror, fire insurance and
     postal service can benefit everyone without
     affecting the relationships between the
     classes.'"

B2   ANON. "Mark Twain Items Published Elsewhere,"
     Twainian, XXVI (January-February), 1-4.
        Reprints a number of abstracts from AES,
     IX (1966) of material relating to MT; some
     involve only passing mention, and a number
     of abstracts in AES are not here reprinted.
     Abstract in AES, XII (1969); 674; reprinted
     in Twainian, XXIX (January-February, 1970).

B3   ATHERTON, JAMES S. "To Give Down the Banks
     and Hark from the Tomb!" James Joyce Quar-
     terly, IV (Winter), 75-83.
        On quotations from HF incorporated in
     Finnegans Wake.

B4   BABCOCK, C. MERTON. "Mark Twain and the
     Belles of San Francisco," San Francisco, IX
     (November), 38.
        A popular account, consisting chiefly of
     MT's comments on women in his days as a San
     Francisco newspaperman and in RI.

B5   BAILEY, ROGER B. "Twain's Huckleberry Finn,
     Chapters 1 and 2," Explicator, XXVI (Septem-
     ber), Item 2.
        The fact that Huck trips over a root but
     Tom Sawyer steps on and snaps a dry twig
     (like a Fenimore Cooper character) reveals
     the contrast between Huck's realism and
     Tom's romancing. Abstract in AES, XII
     (1969), 823; reprinted in Twainian, XXIX
     (January-February, 1970).

B6   BATES, ALLAN. "Sam Clemens, Pilot-Humorist
     of a Tramp Steamboat," American Literature,
     XXXIX (March), 102-109.
        Reprints the text of a burlesque river re-
     port from the Missouri Republican of August
     30, 1860, signed by MT and J. W. Hood; MT
     was pilot on the Arago July 28-September 9.
     Bates suggests that some of the references
     were bawdy, and MT was not taking his

(BATES, ALLAN)
profession seriously at the time. Extracts appeared in the New Orleans Daily Delta September 2, with credit and praise for MT as the author. Abstract in AES, X (1967), 2250; reprinted in Twainian, XXVII (January-February, 1968). Also abstracted in ALA, I (December, 1967), 43-44.

B7   BENJAMIN, WILLIAM EVARTS. "Letters from William Evarts Benjamin to Paine," Twainian, XXVI (November-December), 4.
Four letters of May-June, 1910; the first is interesting because it notes that Benjamin is sending Paine the texts of an MT speech at the opening of the Virginian Railway (n.d., paying tribute to Benjamin's father-in-law Henry H. Rogers) and "Mark Twain," an article by Charles Lancaster in the Liverpool Daily Post and Mercury, May 5, 1910. Abstract in AES, XIII (1969-1970), 1356; reprinted in Twainian, XXX (January-February, 1971).

B8   BENNETT, JAMES R. "The Adventures of Huck Finn in Chapter One," Iowa English Yearbook, XII, 68-72.
"The opening chapter suggests all the major motifs of the novel--freedom, the slave society, religion, money, illusion, the family, superstition, loneliness, death, and moral growth. Chapter One presents a series of concise scenes which epitomize the book." Abstract in AES, XI (1968), 470; reprinted in Twainian, XXVIII (January-February, 1969).

B9   BERTOLOTTI, D. S., JR. "Mark Twain Revisits the Tailor," Mark Twain Journal, XIII (Summer), 18-19.
MT's contention in CY that men are distinguished more by their clothes than by their characters may be derived from Carlyle's Sartor Resartus. There are "many philosophic parallels" between the two authors, although MT was never able to progress beyond Carlyle's "Everlasting No."

B10   ____. "Structural Unity in 'The Man that Corrupted Hadleyburg,'" Mark Twain Journal, XIV (Winter), 19-21.
The episodes are linked by the letters from Howard L. Stephenson, which comment ironically on the supposed integrity of the "holy nineteen" and initiate the action which follows. Abstract in ALA, I (June, 1968), 188-89.

B11   BLAIR, WALTER. "Mark Twain," American Book Collector (Chicago), XVIII (November), 7.
Announces that the University of California has begun publishing the Mark Twain Papers, and, probably joined by the University of Iowa, will publish definitive editions of his works.

B12   ____. [Review: Justin Kaplan, Mr. Clemens and Mark Twain (1966).] American Literature, XXXIX (May), 220-23.
Kaplan's book is titillating, rich in lurid or sexy quotations or bits of gossip, but inadequately documented and often inaccurate, and questionable in its interpretations; it is unworthy of the praise it has received.

B13   BOWEN, JAMES K., and RICHARD VanDerBEETS, eds., American Literature Abstracts, I (December), pp. 43-47, 125-26, 132-33.
Contains abstracts more extensive than those in the present bibliography, often prepared by the authors of the articles abstracted; however, these abstracts represent only part of a year's work and a large proportion of them are from journals such as American Literature, which are more readily available than the abstracts. A useful feature is the "Book Review Consensus," summarizing at some length the reviews of individual books; again, the emphasis is on major (and hence readily available) journals. The abstracts and book review summaries are noted in the present bibliography.

B14   BRANCH, EDGAR M. "Major Perry and the Monitor Camanche: An Early Mark Twain Speech," American Literature, XXXIX (May), 170-79.
Reprints from the San Francisco Alta California of June 13, 1864 the text of MT's second earliest extant speech: "It honored Major Edward C. Perry, who had helped to raise the ship Aquila and its cargo, the dismantled monitor Camanche, from the floor of the San Francisco harbor," and shows MT's growing skill and reputation as a popular lecturer. Abstract in AES, X (1967), 2255; reprinted in Twainian, XXVII (January-February, 1968). Also abstracted in ALA, I (December, 1967), 44-45.

B15   ____. "'My Voice Is Still for Setchell': A Background Study of 'Jim Smiley and His Jumping Frog,'" Publications of the Modern Language Association, LXXXII (December), 591-601.
Some of the episodes, characters, and names may be traced to MT's experiences, as shown in his 1864-1865 journalism; it was probably written in the period October 16-25, 1865. Branch relates the tale's "compelling appeal and its poetic unity" to MT's development as a writer. Abstract in AES, XI (1968), 646; reprinted in Twainian, XXVIII (January-February, 1969). Also abstracted in ALA, I (June, 1968), 189.

B16   ____. "Samuel Clemens and the Copperheads of 1864," Mad River Review (Wright State Campus, Dayton, Ohio), II (Winter-Spring), 3-20.

(BRANCH, EDGAR M.)

In his four months with the San Francisco Morning Call MT wrote hundreds of unsigned items, from brief notices to long articles on local events. "Among these, in my opinion, were several political meetings held that summer in San Francisco during the Lincoln-McClellan election campaigns. This article reprints three of these reports, all unsigned but all bearing distinctive marks of Clemens' authorship. They help us to gauge Clemens' political feelings in 1864, and they preface the more active interest he took in politics in later times." Abstract in AES, X (1967), 3301; reprinted in Twainian, XXVIII (March-April, 1969).

B17   BROWN, SPENCER. "Huckleberry Finn for Our Time: A Re-Reading of the Concluding Chapters," Michigan Quarterly Review, VI (Winter), 41-46.

The "uneasy amusement" and "irritation" intelligent readers feel over the ending are "the reactions Mark Twain deliberately provoked" in an attack on slavery through showing its effect on ordinary, kind people, and most of all, its effect on Huck and Jim: "Thus slavery has corrupted and rendered selfish the best character in the novel" and reduced the manly Jim to a clown. Abstract in AES, X (1967), 1999; reprinted in Twainian, XXVII (January-February, 1968).

B18   BUDD, LOUIS J. [Review: Hamlin Hill, ed., Mark Twain's Letters to His Publishers, 1867-1894; Franklin R. Rogers, ed., Mark Twain's Satires & Burlesques; John S. Tuckey, ed., Mark Twain's "Which was the Dream?" and Other Symbolic Writings.] New England Quarterly, XL (December), 583-86.

The editing of these volumes should "satisfy the needs of all but those who would have gone to the original manuscripts in any case," and "the Mark Twain Papers are off to the glittering start that Samuel Langhorne Clemens craved for any of his enterprises." Hill's edition of the letters shows MT's wholehearted dedication to making money from his books, but there is comfort in the evidence that he "was mostly right about the incompetence of Charles Webster. Among some "richly suggestive passages" is one in 1881 beginning "Howells don't have no taste." Mark Twain's Satires & Burlesques "run the gamut of quality with fewer of his total misfires than usual," although they will not raise MT's stature: "No matter how important burlesque was to his creative circuits, it is usually tedious unless muted or integrated with other purposes. On the contrary Mark Twain's "Which Was the Dream?" and Other Symbolic Writings of the Later Years prints items of major interest and appeal, at present anyway," revealing humor and playfulness rather

than unrelieved gloom; Tuckey assumes that MT's darkening outlook was a result of his personal tragedies and reverses.

B19   _____. [Review: James M. Cox, Mark Twain: The Fate of Humor (1966).] Modern Philology, LXV, 420-21.

"Cox is continually lucid, incisive, fresh, and persuasive and has come closer than anyone else to explicating Twain within his own frame of mind. I feel major qualms only when Cox reproves Twain for not keeping a total commitment to humor and thus letting all good causes slide."

B20   CARDWELL, GUY A. [Review: Richard Bridgman, The Colloquial Style in America (1966).] American Literature, XXXIX (March), 124-25.

"Mr. Bridgman's chief contribution...is perhaps his view of the stylistic relationships" of MT (with the boy-narrator), James, Hemingway, and Gertrude Stein.

B21   CARTER, EVERETT. [Review: Bernard Poli, Mark Twain, Écrivain de l'Ouest: Régionalisme et Humour (1965).] Criticism, IX (Winter), 98-100.

MT "has found a commonsensical, shrewd cultural historian in Bernard Poli, who has presented this most representative of American writers to his countrymen with sympathy and understanding," presenting a judicious synthesis of MT's work and the criticisms it.

B22   CASEY, DANIEL J. "Universality in Huckleberry Finn: A Comparison of Twain and Kivi," Mark Twain Journal, XIV (Winter), 13-18.

Argues the case for the book's universal appeal by comparing it to Aleksis Kivi's Seven Brothers, which portrays the Finnish national character; does not suggest influence. Abstract in ALA, I (June, 1968), 189-90. See 1968.B20.

B23   CHRISTIAN, SHELDON. "The Day the Hornet Burned," Yankee XXXI (May), 74-5, 118-23.

Adds little or nothing to MT's account in the Sacramento Union, which it credits.

B24   COYNE, BERNARD V. "Mark Twain and the Transatlantic Mail," New Mexico Philatelist (Official Organ of the New Mexico Philatelic Association), XX (October-November), 1, 4-5.

An attempt to calculate the speed of surface mail, based on MT's correspondence of 1892-93.

B25   CRANE, SUSAN. "Letters from Susan Crane to Albert Bigelow Paine," Twainian, XXVI (July-August), 3-4.

Seven 1912 letters from Olivia Langdon Clemens's sister, chiefly interesting for their mention of family matters, including letters from Olivia, hostility toward MT's secretary Isobel Lyon ("how sure she was, how wiley [sic], and how she hastened the

(CRANE, SUSAN)
good man out of this life!"), and praise for Paine's work as official biographer. Brief abstract in AES, XII (1969), 687.

B26 CUMMINGS, SHERWOOD. [Review: Justin Kaplan ed., Mark Twain: A Profile.] American Literary Realism, I (Summer), 69-70.
    Many of the essays in Kaplan's collection are a joy to read, but they do not bear on MT's realism and they have appeared in print before.

B27 [DAVIS, CHESTER L.]. "'All Right!' from 'The Carpet-Bag'--Possibly Twain?" Twainian, XXVI (November-December), 1-2.
    This sketch from The Carpet-Bag (Boston, June 14, 1851) antedates MT's first known published story, "The Dandy Frightening the Squatter," which appeared there May 1, 1852; it is on file at the Mark Twain Research Foundation as part of "a large accumulation of material the identification of which was in dispute between Morse, Underhill, Johnson and others at the time your secretary took over the duties of Brownell." Abstract in AES, XIII (1969-1970), 1335.

B28 ____. [Comment on holdings of Mark Twain Research Foundation and policy concerning their disclosure.] Twainian, XXVI (July-August), 1.
    The Foundation "has many unpublished letters, some of which would undoubtedly have been of some value to the authors of those books [reviewed in the March-April Twainian]. Certainly we would not throw open our files to permit the indiscriminate selection and publication of material which we ourselves would refuse to publish. We have often thought that perhaps what we consider should not be published, should be destroyed, yet we are not 'book burners' nor are we unofficial protectors of anyone, past or present, whether an unknown or a famous personality. It is hard to draw the line, but in the opinion of your Secretary certain things have been published by others, often out of context, and to say the least, add little or nothing to our knowledge of Mark Twain and quite often merely disclosing the exercise of bad taste." Pays tribute to Paine for his monumental achievement, and recognizes his situation, his love for MT and the difficulty in dealing with a mass of contradictory material.

B29 ____. "Identification of Mark Twain Material," Twainian, XXVI (September-October), 4.
    General comments on the problems involved with passages vaguely remembered, oddities such as part of a letter by Olivia but in MT's hand (apparently copied by him for Paine's use in the biography), and material collected by Paine but not used. Brief abstract in AES, XIII (1969-1970), 1347.

B30 ____. "1838 Letter from Florida, Missouri Found," Twainian, XXVI (November-December), 2-3.
    Text of a letter from MT's uncle John A. Quarles to another uncle, James T. Quarles; adds to family history. Abstract in AES, XIII (1969-1970), 1355; reprinted in Twainian, XXX (January-February, 1971).

B31 ____. "Mark Twain on Lynching," Twainian, XXVI (November-December), 3.
    On MT's visit to Paris, Missouri, June 3, 1902, a speech he made there, and his condemnation of lynching on being told of the recent hanging of Abe Witherup there; apparently this article is based on a contemporary account, but the source is not given. Abstract in AES, XIII (1969-1970), 1343.

B32 ____. "Mark Twain's Room-Mate in St. Louis--Burrough," Twainian, XXVI (May-June), 1.
    A letter to Paine from "Ida Burrough Coil (Coit?)" and one from Mary Burrough, establishing that MT's room-mate in St. Louis (as listed in Paine's biography, p. 103) was not Frank E. Burrough, but his father, Jacob Hutchinson Burrough. Abstract in AES, XII (1969), 680; reprinted in Twainian, XXIX (January-February, 1970).

B33 ____. "Progress in the Mark Twain Region," Twainian, XXVI (September-October), 1.
    On the improvements made to Mark Twain shrines in Missouri in recent years. Abstract in AES, XIII (1969-1970), 1358; reprinted in Twainian, XXX (January-February, 1971).

B34 ____. "Three New Books Released Under Direction of 'Mark Twain Papers,'" Twainian, XXVI (March-April), 1-2.
    Review article, briefly commenting on Mark Twain's Letters to His Publishers, ed. Hamlin Hill; Mark Twain's "Which Was the Dream?" ed. John S. Tuckey; Mark Twain's Satires & Burlesques, ed. Franklin R. Rogers. The comments by Davis note the value of indexes and appendixes and quote extensively from the books, but are not a detailed critical commentary.

B35 DAVIS, SAM. "Letter from Sam Davis to Paine," Twainian, XXVI (July-August), 2.
    Expresses regret for the financial losses of MT, Joseph T. Goodman, and others. Abstract in AES (1969), 685.

B36 DENNIS, LARRY R. "Mark Twain and the Dark Angel," Midwest Quarterly, VIII (January), 181-97.
    On the varied perspectives toward death in HF; they are all denied to Edwards in The Great Dark. Abstract in AES, XI (1968), 1477; reprinted in Twainian, XXVIII (January-February, 1969).

B37   DIAS, EARL J. "Mark Twain in Fairhaven,"
Mark Twain Journal, XIII (Summer), 11-15.
On MT's visit there as guest of Henry
Rogers, and his address at the dedication
of the new town hall on February 22, 1894.
The text of the address and an MT letter to
the officials of the Millicent Library are
printed here, from manuscripts in the library collection.

B38   DUNLAP, JOSEPH R. "Future Times," Independent Shavian, V (Spring), 44.
Both MT (in "From the London Times of
1904") and Shaw published satiric sketches
supposedly from the London Times of later
dates. Abstract in AES, X (1967), 3295;
reprinted in Twainian, XXVIII (March-April,
1969).

B39   ENSOR, ALLISON. "Twain's The Adventures of
Huckleberry Finn, Chapter 37," Explicator,
XXVI (November), Item 20.
MT had already quoted in IA from Acts
XVII, and would have known Paul's statement
that God "hath made of one blood all nations of men for to dwell on all the face
of the earth"; thus, the fact that Uncle
Silas Phelps was preparing next week's ser-
mon from the same chapter may be an ironic
thrust at his dual role as minister and
slave-owner. Abstract in AES, XII (1969),
840 (incorrectly attributing the passage to
Acts XXVII), also abstracted in ALA, I
(June, 1968), 190.

B40   EXMAN, EUGENE. The House of Harper: One
Hundred and Fifty Years of Publishing. New
York, Evanston, London: Harper & Row, Publishers, passim.
Contains brief references to MT and his
relations with his publishers, but very
little not already in print elsewhere.

B41   FATOUT, PAUL. [Review: Sydney J. Krause,
Mark Twain as Critic.] Journal of American
History, LIV (December), 689-90.
The book is heavily researched and useful, but ponderous and verbose: "compres-
sion could have made room for criticism of
writers not discussed--Cable, Harris, Riley,
Holmes, Ward, and so forth," and the topic
of public speaking.

B42   FEINBERG, LEONARD. Introduction to Satire.
Ames: The University of Iowa Press, passim.
MT is among the authors noted as examples
in a study of the nature, material, technique, and results of satire.

B43   FIFIELD, WILLIAM. "Joyce's Brother, Lawrence's Wife, Wolfe's Mother, Twain's
Daughter," Texas Quarterly, X (Spring),
69-87.
On great writers as described in books
by relatives; describes Clara Clemens
Gabrilowitsch as having had "something too

sweet about her overrefined," and tells of
a visit to her California home. Fifield
finds "Twain, a conscious artist, linked
more really to Joyce than to Wolfe."

B44   FRASER, JOHN. "In Defence of Culture: Huckleberry Finn," Oxford Review, No. 6 (Michael-
mas), pp. 5-22.
Summarizing and answering a number of critics' statements on HF, argues that in many
ways the book is "soothing," and "Huck's
progress through the ostensible dangers of
the trip downstream is largely that of the
kind of superboy of Tom Sawyer's imaginings."
The depiction of slavery is not a central
theme, but consists of set-pieces; in general
the treatment of the Negro is validated rather than attacked. Huck is not a coherent and
developing character, just as Gulliver is not,
because, like Swift, MT was concentrating on
the local and the immediate. Abstract in
AES, XI (1968), 2024; reprinted in Twainian,
XXVIII (January-February, 1969).

B45   GALE, ROBERT L. [Review: Justin Kaplan,
Mr. Clemens and Mark Twain (1966).] Books
Abroad, XLI (Autumn), 472-73.
"A study that should prove to be a major
contribution to American literary scholarship and biography.... Kaplan rides hard
his thesis that Clemens was self-divided,
and he neglects no opportunity to make full
use of all evidence supporting Mark Twain's
doubts, rages and disappointments. The book
is...incidentally packed with casual aesthetic insights of the most provocative sort."

B46   _____. [Review: Edward Wagenknecht, Mark
Twain: The Man and His Work.] Studies in
Short Fiction, V (Summer), 399.
This is "one of the finest general, introductory volumes on Twain," but "the only
thing new about the third edition...is the
bibliographical essay." The book "remains
what it was in 1961, that is, a sane, balanced biographical but not literary study,
organized by psychographic topics but not
chronologically."

B47   GANZEL, DEWEY. "Samuel Clemens' Correspondence in the St. Louis Missouri Republican,"
Anglia (Tübingen), LXXXV, 390-403.
Supports John Camden Hotten's biographical
sketch of MT in The Choice Humorous Works
of Mark Twain (London, [1872]), which contains verifiable data apparently approved
by MT himself. Ganzel reprints with commentary the texts of river correspondence
which suggest MT's expertise as a pilot, reveal his membership in the Western Boatmen's
Benevolent Association, and cast light on
his movements during the piloting years, but
give no hint of his future career as a writer.

B48 GERBER, JOHN C. "Mark Twain," in James Wood-
     ress, ed., American Literary Scholarship:
     An Annual/1967 (Durham, North Carolina:
     Duke University Press, 1969), pp. 56-72.
         A survey of MT scholarship for the year;
     See 1963.B32. Contents: "i. Texts and
     Editions"; "ii. Biography"; "iii. General
     Criticism"; "iv. Earlier Works"; "v. Huck-
     leberry Finn"; "vi. Later Works."

B49 GIBSON, WILLIAM M. [Review: Robert Regan,
     Unpromising Heroes: Mark Twain and His
     Characters (1966) and James M. Cox, Mark
     Twain: The Fate of Humor (1966).] Ameri-
     can Literature, XXXIX (November), 412-14.
         Regan proposes to examine the "psycholo-
     gical imperatives" of the folklore type im-
     portant in MT's works, buttressing his case
     by showing MT's portrayal of real heroes
     such as General Grant and Anson Burlingame;
     fortunately, "he employs his thesis only
     where it works." Cox's book contains a few
     oversights and factual errors, but "easily
     overrides all such flaws. It brings Clem-
     ens's humor into sharp focus and will remain
     a powerful study of his imagination."

B50 GILMORE, T. B. "Critic of What?" North
     American Review, n.s., V (September),
     39-40.
         A review of Sydney J. Krause, Mark Twain
     as Critic, which devotes too much space to
     MT's criticism of Sir Walter Scott and Bret
     Harte, but provides a clear, readable, tho-
     rough treatment of its subject for those
     already familiar with MT's work--as Krause
     obviously is.

B51 GOODMAN, JOSEPH T. "Letters from Joe Good-
     man," Twainian, XXVI (May-June), 3-4.
         Three letters to Paine from MT's editor
     on the Territorial Enterprise; one indi-
     cates that Goodman was checking text of
     biographical material for Paine, and anoth-
     er comments on Howard Taylor, once a print-
     er on the Enterprise, who secured MT's
     permission to dramatize CY--but the language
     was hopelessly bad--and now Taylor writes
     Goodman that he has prepared a book of rec-
     ollections concerning MT and hopes [in vain--
     T.A.T.] to have it published. The remaining
     material in the letters chiefly concerns
     Goodman himself, and his declining health.
     Appended is what Chester Davis describes as
     the full text of the review of MT's profes-
     sional lecture debut with his Sandwich Is-
     lands address, copied by Goodman from the
     Daily Alta California, April 3, 1866. Ab-
     stract in AES, XII (1969), 682; reprinted
     in Twainian, XXIX (January-February, 1970).

B52 GRIMM, CLYDE L. "The American Claimant:
     Reclamation of a Farce," American Quarterly,
     XIX (Spring), 86-103.
         This novel, though hastily and crudely
     written, is interesting for what it shows

of "Twain's imaginative conversion of pointless humor into meaningful satire" and because the political and social themes reflect a mature statement of views MT had
long held. The increasingly sympathetic
portrait of Colonel Sellers reflects MT's
understanding of "the American disparity between noble motives and opportunities for
their fulfillment." Abstract in ALA, I
(December, 1967), 45.

B53 HALL, FRED J. "Letters from Fred J. Hall to
     Paine," Twainian, XXVI (July-August), 2.
         Hall, who took over the management of Web-
     ster and Company, owns several letters from
     MT and Olivia, speaks of her loyal and gen-
     erous attitude, and says MT made the final
     decisions as to what books should be pub-
     lished after Hall took charge of the compa-
     ny; thanks Paine for describing the Webster
     & Company failure "skilfully, justly, and
     honestly." Abstract in AES, XII (1969),
     686.

B54 HALL, ROBERT A. "The Innocents Abroad a Hun-
     dred Years Later," Annali dell'Istituto
     Orientale di Napoli, Sezione Germanica, X
     217-32.
         [Source: Reprint in Mark Twain Papers.]
     A general criticism; IA is still signifi-
     cant, both as a picture of its time and be-
     cause it treats the relation between Eu-
     ropean and American culture.

B55 HARDING, DOROTHY STURGIS. "Mark Twain Lands
     an Angel-Fish," Columbia Library Columns,
     XVI (February), 2-12.
         The friendship of a little girl with MT,
     whom she met on the S.S. Bermudian in 1908;
     tells of having done the lettering of MT's
     "Notice. To the Next Burglar" (reproduced
     in Meltzer, Mark Twain Himself, 1960,
     p. 283). Reprints the story of a joke
     played on MT at the Tavern Club (January 15,
     1901), from club records. Photographs of
     MT, pp. 2, 5. Abstract in AES, XII (1969),
     64; reprinted in Twainian, XXIX (January-
     February, 1970).

B56 HASLAM, GERALD W. "Huckleberry Finn: Why
     Read the Phelps Farm Episode?" Research
     Studies (Washington State University), XXXV
     (September), 189-97.
         Although the ending of HF is weakened by
     stylistic excesses, and defenses based on
     form are unsatisfactory, it can be justified
     "as a logical extension of the often-empha-
     sized moral texture of the novel...the dis-
     sonance one senses in the final episodes of
     the novel is largely a product of Twain's
     fictional projection of the seminal moral
     dilemma of a slave-holding society: human
     beings viewed as commodity." Abstract in
     AES, XII (1969), 1310; also abstracted in
     ALA, I (June, 1968), 190-91.

B57 HILL, JOHN S. "Huck Finn's Reaffirmation of Rejection," Mark Twain Journal, XIII (Summer), 16-17.

The concluding episode exploits both Jim and Huck, reflecting "the view that a white person of a lower class may also be duped, be used for sport." Huck has already gone through successive stages under the rule of the South, as a rebel, and again under the rule of the South, and in the end he rebels once more against the old order and Tom Sawyer, its symbol. Abstract in AES, XII (1960), 1238.

B58 HOLLAND, LAURENCE B. [Review: Richard Bridgman, The Colloquial Style in America (1966).] Yale Review, LVI (Spring), 438-42.

Notes "Huckleberry Finn's central position in advancing 'the movement toward an American prose.'"

B59 HOWE, IRVING. "Anarchy and Authority in American Literature," Denver Quarterly, II (Autumn), 5-30.

On HF (pp. 22-25): on the raft, "itself so wonderful a symbol of the isolation, purity and helplessness on which the anarchist vision rests," Huck and Jim "create a community of equals," but the idyllic existence is constantly threatened by the world and it cannot last. Abstract in AES, XI (1968), 1882; reprinted in Twainian, XXVIII (January-February, 1969).

B60 INGLIS, K. S. "Mark Twain and The Gilded Age: Some Suggestions for Comparative Study," Australian Economic History, VII (March), 19-37.

On MT's portrayal of the brutality and corruption of his time, with particular attention to his symbolic use of the railroads.

B61 IRWIN, ROBERT. "The Failure of Tom Sawyer and Huckleberry Finn on Film," Mark Twain Journal, XIII (Summer), 9-11.

The reluctance of producers to give offence has resulted in false interpretations, despite pains taken to achieve authenticity in casting, costumes, and scenery. A number of film versions are discussed, and there is a bibliography of reviews.

B62 JONES, HOWARD MUMFORD. "The Pessimism of Mark Twain," in his Belief and Disbelief in American Literature. Chicago & London: The University of Chicago Press; Toronto: The University of Toronto Press, pp. 94-115.

MT's pessimism was philosophical and temperamental, a blend of eighteenth-century rationalism and romantic sensibility. In his works "some human beings totally escape the inglorious human predicament.... In fact it would be easy to go through his writings and cull out instance after instance of human generosity, saintliness,

self-sacrifice, and humility that totally contradict his officially cynical attitude toward altruism.... He judged Christianity not by its performance but by its principle. He appealed from Christian fact to Christian idealism" (p. 110). Reprinted in Schmitter (1974), pp. 41-56.

B63 JORDAN-SMITH, PAUL. "Mark Twain of Nevada," American Book Collector (Chicago), XVII (March), 7.

A review of James M. Cox's Mark Twain: the Fate of Humor (1966) as a "scholarly-entertaining study of the greatest American humorist.... In a brief review of this scholarly work it is not needful to point out all the by-paths followed by its author," but the book takes the reader on "a joyous journey."

B64 *KASYAN, A. K. "Iz Istorii Perevodov Marka Tvena v Rossii" ["The History of Translations of Mark Twain in Russia"], Irkutskii Pedagogicheskii Institut, Irkutsk, XXVI, 185-97.

[Source: MHRA Annual Bibliography (1967), No. 7117.]

B65 *_____. "Mark Twain v Rossii (1917-1965 gg.)" ["Mark Twain in Russia"], Irkutskii Pedagogicheskii Institut, Irkutsk, XXVI, 162-85.

[Source: MHRA Annual Bibliography (1967), No. 7119.]

B66 KRAUS, W. KEITH. "Huckleberry Finn: A Final Irony," Mark Twain Journal, XIV (Winter), 18-19.

The supposedly genuine Wilks heirs are a second set of frauds, who probably "met the same young man, or someone as equally well informed about the Wilks' family, as the King and Duke." The "lost" luggage and William's broken arm are clever ruses, but suspicion is raised by their lack of grief at Peter's death, by Harvey's "poor grammar and lapses into colloquial speech," and by the vagueness of his description of the tattoo on Peter's chest. Abstract in ALA, I (June, 1968), 191.

B67 KRAUSE, SYDNEY J. "Olivia Clemens's 'Editing' Reviewed," American Literature, XXXIX (November), 325-51.

MT respected his wife's suggestions, of which some were innocuous and others useful, but he did not always follow her advice, as is revealed in the manuscript of More Tramps Abroad (the British edition of Following the Equator). Not only did some indecorous and irreverent material slip by, but MT added still more, as in his account of the phallic worship in Benares (a city he referred to as "Lingamburg"). The editorial suggestions by Olivia Clemens are listed and classified. Abstract in AES, XI (1968), 1789; reprinted in Twainian, XXVIII (January-February, 1969). Also abstracted in ALA, I (June, 1968), 191-92.

B68   ____. [Review: Justin Kaplan: Mr. Clemens and Mark Twain (1966) and James M. Cox, Mark Twain: The Fate of Humor (1966).] New England Quarterly, XL (September), 441-45.
   Agreeing that Cox may be right in calling Kaplan's book "the decisive work on Mark Twain in our time," Krause praises it as "eminently readable," though exaggerated in some of its interpretations. The portrait of MT is painful, emphasizing his obsession with money, his vanity, his "incurably selfish motives" and "unfounded paranoia." Cox has written "a book that is at once wholly basic and wholly new," with the thesis that Clemens discovered his artistic imagination when he discovered Mark Twain, was effective when he followed the strategies of humor, but failed when he tried to be serious; however, some passages which have been interpreted in that light are actually instances where MT appropriated the conventions he parodied--but many readers will find such an interpretation difficult to accept.

B69   KRUSE, HORST H. "Annie and Huck: A Note on The Adventures of Huckleberry Finn," American Literature, XXXIX (May), 207-14.
   MT's "A Complaint About Correspondents" (written in late 1865 or early 1866) contains what purports to be a letter from his niece Annie. "It is...safe to conclude that in writing Annie's letter Mark Twain realized what could be done with the combination of the first-person narrator and the child perspective," a forerunner of Huck, who is "perfectly suited for his purposes both as a humorist and as a social and moral critic." Abstract in AES, X (1967), 2261; reprinted in Twainian, XXVI (January-February, 1968). Also abstracted in ALA, I (December, 1967), 45-46.

B70   LEE, CHARLOTTE I. [Review: Hamlin Hill, ed., Mark Twain's Letters to His Publishers, 1867-1894; Franklin S. Rogers, ed., Mark Twain's Satires and Burlesques; John S. Tuckey, ed., Mark Twain's "Which Was the Dream?"] Quarterly Journal of Speech, LII (December), 390-91.
   Chiefly descriptive, praising the scholarship but noting that there is little here of great interest to members of the speech profession.

B71   "Letters from Susan Crane, Skrine, Webb, Goodman," Twainian, XXVI (September-October), 1-4.
   For the most part this is correspondence concerning the transmission of material to Paine for his biography of MT, and contains very little biographical information of interest. The letter from Elizabeth Webb, abstracted in AES, XIII (1969-1970), 1336, mentions her possession of various photographs and correspondence of her father, C. H. Webb, publisher of The Celebrated

Jumping Frog of Calaveras County; among the material is a play based on this MT story, and an incomplete article about MT in San Francisco by her father. Abstracts of the remaining material in AES, XIII (1969-1970), 1352, 1353, 1354, and reprinted in Twainian, XXX (January-February, 1971).

B72   LANGDON, CHARLES J. "Letters to Paine from Charles J. Langdon," Twainian, XXVI (July-August), 1-2.
   On the day his sister Olivia married MT, Charles Langdon was in Calcutta on his world tour. Abstract in AES, XII (1969), 684.

B73   *LONG, ELEANOR. "Superstitious Belief in Huckleberry Finn," Northern California Folklore Society, II (July), 51-55.
   [Source: Leary (1970), p. 68.]

B74   MacALISTER, J. Y. W. "Letters from J. Y. W. MacAlister to Paine," Twainian, XXVI (May-June), 4.
   MacAlister says he has "something like 200 letters, of all kinds,--many of them of too intimate and personal a nature to print," but others which he may copy and send; also tells of MT receiving two letters, addressed "Mark Twain--God knows where" and "Mark Twain--devil knows where." Abstract in AES, XII (1969), 683.

B75   MANIERRE, WILLIAM R. "Parallel Scenes in Tom Sawyer and Huck Finn," CEA Critic, XXX (November), 1, 4, 6-7.
   Carries further Walter Blair's discussion in Mark Twain & Huck Finn (Chapter V), to show that TS contains "rehearsals" of three scenes in HF dealing with Huck's inner debate (documented from the Riverside Edition of HF and the Signet Classic ed. of TS). Abstract in ALA, I (June, 1968), 192.

B76   MARTIN, JAY. "Adding up the Double," Nation, CCV (July 3), 24-26.
   A review of Justin Kaplan, Mr. Clemens and Mark Twain (1966). Generally favorable: although the book "should be supplemented by those of Walter Blair, Henry Nash Smith, and James Cox, still it provides a rich understanding of Twain's life that none of these can give."

B77   ____. "Mark Twain: The Dream of Drift and the Dream of Delight," in his Harvests of Change: American Literature 1865-1914. Englewood Cliffs, N.J.: Prentice-Hall, Inc., pp. 165-201.
   Presents an extensive discussion of MT's gauging of the popular taste, his treatment of foreign travel, and his use of history. "Emphasizing the true importance of creation above memory" in the apparent formlessness of his Autobiography, "Twain reasserted his potency as an artist to the last. His revelation of creativity preserved the man--perhaps from the madness that in the late 1890s Twain hovered near.... he made his drift a dream of delight."

B78   MENCKEN, H[ENRY] L[OUIS]. A Mencken Chresto-
       mathy. Edited and Annotated by the Author.
       New York: Alfred A. Knopf.
           On pp. 485-89, reprints the texts of Menck-
       en's "Credo" (1913.B12) and "The Man Within"
       (1919.B17) from Smart Set, for which Mencken
       was the book reviewer.

B79   MIZENER, ARTHUR. "Mark Twain: Huckleberry
       Finn," in his Twelve Great American Novels
       (New York: The New American Library),
       pp. 37-48.
           Mizener's preface describes his book as
       being intended "for the reader who...does
       not feel entirely at home with novels when
       he tries to read them seriously" (p. x).
       The discussion of HF is sensible but breaks
       no new ground.

B80   *NASU, YORIMASA. "Mark Twain's 'Horseshoe
       Pattern' and Huckleberry Finn," Jimbungaku,
       XLIII (January), 70-84.
           [Source: Leary, 1970), p. 71.]

B81   NEIDER, CHARLES. "Major Author in a Minor
       Key," Saturday Review of Literature, L
       (March 25), 34-35.
           A review-article, chiefly descriptive
       (but deriding excessive scholarly serious-
       ness in the editors) of John S. Tuckey,
       ed., Mark Twain's "Which Was the Dream?"
       and Other Symbolic Writings of the Later
       Years; Hamlin Hill, ed., Mark Twain's Let-
       ters to His Publishers, 1867-1894; and
       Franklin R. Rogers, ed., Mark Twain's Sat-
       ires and Burlesques.

B82   OLIVER, A. W. "Letter from Judge A. W.
       ('Gus') Oliver," Twainian, XXVI (January-
       February), 4.
           Letter to Albert Bigelow Paine, April 24,
       1910, recalling incidents in RI by a friend
       MT recorded there as "Oliphant." Abstract
       in AES, XII (1969), 675; reprinted in
       Twainian, XXIX (January-February, 1970).

B83   PICKERING, JAMES H. [Review: Hamlin Hill,
       ed., Mark Twain's Letters to His Publish-
       ers.] New York History, XLVIII (October),
       399-400.
           An "impeccable job of editing and anno-
       tating," reveals MT's growing involvement
       in the publishing business and the impos-
       sible demands he made on his publishers.

B84   POCHMANN, HENRY A. [Review: Hamlin Hill,
       ed., Mark Twain's Letters to His Publish-
       ers; Franklin R. Rogers, ed., Mark Twain's
       Satires and Burlesques; John S. Tuckey,
       ed., Mark Twain's "Which Was the Dream?"]
       American Literature, XXXIX (November),
       397-400.
           Hill's edition of the letters "provides
       altogether engaging reading" and gives
       evidence for choosing between MT's portrait
       of himself as victim and the less flatter-
       ing one drawn by S. C. Webster. "There

is as yet no agreement with Mr. Rogers that
burlesque was the chief vehicle by which
Mark Twain learned the art of authorship."
Pochmann notes the bitterness and sense of
personal failure in MT's late writings edited by Tuckey, but they "may be regarded as
steps in the process of literary self-heal-
ing by which he achieved a dramatic recovery
of his literary powers near the end." There
is also evidence of an interest on MT's part
in "the implications of depth psychology,
especially with respect to the role and function of the unconscious for the creative
literary artist."

B85   PRITCHETT, V. S. "Twainship and Twinship,"
       New Statesman, LXXIII (June 23), 876. A
       review-article, describing Justin Kaplan,
       Mr. Clemens and Mark Twain (1966); A. Grove
       Day, Mark Twain's Letters from Hawaii (1966);
       John S. Tuckey, ed., Mark Twain's "Which Was
       the Dream?"; Hamlin Hill, ed., Mark Twain's
       Letters to His Publishers; and Franklin R.
       Rogers, ed., Mark Twain's Satires and Bur-
       lesques.
           The more valuable part is a probing dis-
       cussion of MT and his works, emphasizing his
       Ego, foundation in myth, and idealist's jeer-
       ing at both raw experience and bland hypo-
       crisy. Abstract in AES, XI (1968), 3291.

B86   REGAN, ROBERT. "Mark Twain's 'Unfinished
       Properties,'" Virginia Quarterly Review,"
       XLIII (Summer), 494-99.
           A review-article, praising the editing of
       the previously unpublished, fragmented ma-
       terial in Hamlin Hill, ed., Mark Twain's
       Letters to His Publishers, 1867-1894;
       Franklin R. Rogers, ed., Mark Twain's Sat-
       ires and Burlesques; John S. Tuckey, ed.,
       Mark Twain's "Which Was the Dream?" and Oth-
       er Symbolic Writings of the Later Period.

B87   _____. [Review: James M. Cox, Mark Twain:
       The Fate of Humor (1966).] South Atlantic
       Quarterly, LXVI (Summer), 473-74.
           "On the identity of 'Mark Twain' and on
       other matters of primarily biographical in-
       terpretation, few scholars have been so il-
       luminating.... Cox demonstrates, for ex-
       ample, that Olivia Clemens served not only
       as censor but also as muse for her husband
       and that she contributed positively in both
       capacities to his artistic success." Cox
       is more successful in discussing MT's pure-
       ly humorous works than those which, like
       HF and CY, "combine humorous and satiric
       modes."

B88   REINITZ, NEALE. "'Mark Twain Tonight,'"
       Colorado Quarterly, XVI (Summer), 71-80.
           As a Fulbright lecturer in Jyväskylä,
       Finland, Reinitz made the arrangements for
       publicity and for the properties and stage-
       lighting for a performance of Hal Holbrook's
       "Mark Twain Tonight" program in Jyväskylä.
       After lecturing to a small audience at

(REINITZ, NEALE)
Turku, Holbrook was concerned about the inadequate lighting and difficulties with the
Finnish workmen, but here the audience was
far larger than expected. Holbrook found
them unresponsive and later said the preparation had been inadequate; Reinitz says in
rebuttal that "The applause was not tumultu-
ous, but it was warm enough. The show was
a success." A Finnish senior colleague who
had earlier argued against bringing Holbrook
to the small, provincial city later conceded, "I was entirely wrong. It was a
great day for Finnish-American relations."
Abstract in AES, XVI (1972-1973), 2937.

B89 REXROTH, KENNETH. "Classics Revisited--
XLVI: Huckleberry Finn," Saturday Review,
L (May 13), 14-15.
An anti-Odyssey: "It would have been
quite impossible for Mark Twain not to have
had Homer constantly in mind, as he must
also have had Robinson Crusoe, the travels
of Peter and Paul, Pilgrim's Progress, and
dozens of others, not the least Marco Polo.
He carefully contradicts them all." The
raft carries Huck and Jim "through a universe of moral chaos," but in the controversial ending "the social lie wins again
against the brotherhood of man." Abstract
in AES, X (1967), 3141; reprinted in Twainian, XXVII (January-February, 1968).

B90 ROBINSON, TRACY. "Letter from Tracy Robinson," Twainian, XXVI (January-February), 4;
(March-April), 4.
To Paine, dated February 10, 1912; remembers meeting MT in Aspinwall, Panama in
1869, and the pleasure with which he read
MT's books. Abstract in AES, XII (1969),
676, 679; reprinted in Twainian, XXIX
(January-February, 1970).

B91 ROTH, MARTIN. [Review: Bernard Poli, Mark
Twain: Écrivain de l'Ouest (1965).]
Modern Philology, LXV (November), 171-72.
An exhaustive study which, unfortunately,
distorts the picture of MT. There are
valuable synthetic chapters throughout the
book for the benefit of French readers.
"The first chapter is a cogent discussion
of the American West. One of the final
chapters admirably sorts out the various
metaphors used by Twain to define his art."

B92 RUBIN, LOUIS D., JR. "Mark Twain Tonight,"
in his The Teller in the Tale (Seattle,
London: University of Washington Press),
pp. 52-82; also, in "Concerning Cide Hamete
Benengeli and Others," pp. 17-21 on HF.
The book is concerned with the authorial
presence in the novel. Rubin notes different uses of MT's presence when Huck decides
to risk his soul for Jim and later on, at
Phelps Farm (pp. 17-21), and takes up the
matter at greater length in "Mark Twain
Tonight" (which is not a review of Hal Holbrook's stage impersonation of MT).

B93 _____. "Tom Sawyer and the Use of Novels,"
in his The Curious Death of the Novel: Essays in American Literature (Baton Rouge:
Louisiana State University Press), pp. 88-99.
"It took a Mark Twain to show us how the
meaning of success, and of loss, lies at
the heart of American experience.... Documentation can tell us what, but fiction
tells us why."

B94 RULAND, RICHARD. The Rediscovery of American
Literature: Premises of Critical Taste,
1900-1940. Cambridge, Massachusetts: Harvard University Press, pp. 129-31 and passim.
Passing references to the consideration
given MT by such critics as Brooks, Sherman,
Matthiessen, and others. There is a useful
summary of Mencken's views of MT (pp. 129-
31): MT was a Philistine, insensitive to
art and afraid of public opinion, but one
of "the five first-rate artists that America has produced," in the company of Emerson, Hawthorne, Poe, and Whitman.

B95 RULON, CURT M. "Geographical Limitation of
the Dialect Areas in The Adventures of Huckleberry Finn," Mark Twain Journal, XIV
(Winter), 9-12.
Internal evidence suggests that "the
Phelps farm is probably located well south
of Memphis rather than above Memphis as
Stowell would have it but still in southern
Arkansas rather than in northern Louisiana
as Marx maintains." "What is important for
the linguistic geographer is that the general location is in the proximity of the
Mississippi River below Cairo, Illinois,
which point is the heel of an overturned
boot configuration delimiting known contemporary dialect areas: Midland and Southern,
respectively." Abstract in ALA, I (June,
1968), 192-93.

B96 SALOMON, ROGER B. "Mark Twain and Victorian
Nostalgia," in Marston LaFrance, ed., Patterns of Commitment in American Literature.
Published in Association with Carleton
University by University of Toronto Press.
Sees in MT a "double vision" which "manifests itself in the differing points of view
of the invader and the worlds he invades,"
and "involves an ambivalent relation between
the author and even his most sympathetic
characters" (p. 74).

B97 SIDNELL, M. J. "Huck Finn and Jim: Their
Abortive Freedom Ride," Cambridge Quarterly,
II (Summer), 203-11.
MT was more perceptive than his critics
who view the ending of HF as flawed: "Life
on the raft has offered a beautiful vision
of what might be the relationship of negro
and white, but the vision is not, and cannot be, a representation of America as it
really is." Huck "must return to the triv-
ially vicious world of Tom Sawyer's America," at the end "utterly changed not in
itself but in our perception of it."

1967 - Shorter Writings

(SIDNELL, M. J.)
Abstract in AES, XV (1971-1972), 1496; reprinted in Twainian, XXXII (January-February, 1973). Also abstracted in ALA, I (December, 1967), 46-47.

B98   SIMMS, HENRY H. [Review: John Y. Simon, "General Grant" by Matthew Arnold, with A Rejoinder by Mark Twain (1966).] Ohio History, LXXV, 178-79.
Descriptive and mildly favorable.

B99   SKLAR, ROBERT. F. Scott Fitzgerald: The Last Laocoön. New York: Oxford University Press.
Passim on Fitzgerald's interest in MT and familiarity with his works (indexed).

B100   SMITH, H. ALLEN. "Humorous Critic of the Human Race," Saturday Review of Literature, L (February 11), 37.
A descriptive, appreciative review of Charles Neider's Mark Twain, complaining only of the price.

B101   SMITH, THOMAS J. "Mark Twain's Last Years at Redding," Yankee, XXXI (June), 68-73, 128-39.
A popular account providing no new information or insights.

B102   STANCHFIELD, CLARA. "Letters from Clara Stanchfield," Twainian, XXVI (May-June), 1-3.
Two letters to Paine from "the 'Clara Spaulding', close friend of Olivia, after whom Clara Clemens was named," about traveling in Europe twice with MT and Olivia (1873 and a second time for which the year is not given). Unfortunately, Clara Stanchfield destroyed her diaries of the tours, but she remembers being present at meetings of MT with Robert Browning, Turgenev, Sir Charles Dilke, Henry Stanley, Lord Houghton, Sir John Millais, "the artists Abbey and Frank Millet, whose wedding we afterwards attended in Paris," Joaquin Miller, Charles Kingsley ("I remember a delightful luncheon he gave for Mr. Clemens"), and "Lord Dunraven who brought Mr. Hume, the medium with him for an evening with Mr. Clemens." There is also a brief note from John Brown (the son of the author of Rab and His Friends) testifying to MT's "honest manliness" and "warm heartedness." Abstract in AES, XII (1969), 681; reprinted in Twainian, XXIX (January-February, 1970).

B103   STONE, ALBERT E., JR. "Later, Lesser Twain," New York Times Book Review, (July 30), p. 8.
A review of Hamlin Hill, ed., Mark Twain's Letters to His Publishers, 1867-1894; Franklin R. Rogers, ed., Mark Twain's Satires and Burlesques; and John S. Tuckey, ed., Mark Twain's "Which Was the Dream?"

And Other Symbolic Writings of the Later Years ("the most interesting of these three volumes, for it reveals the most about the myth of Mark Twain").

B104   _____. [Review: James M. Cox, Mark Twain: The Fate of Humor (1966).] Nineteenth-Century Fiction, XXII (December), 304-307.
"A model of literary criticism: sensitive, judicious, beautifully written. Wiser than anyone who has yet tackled this thorny subject, Cox...joins that small group of writers--Paine, Brooks, DeVoto, Smith, Andrews, Blair, Kaplan--who have contributed most to our understanding of Mark Twain."

B105   _____. [Review: Robert Regan, Unpromising Heroes (1966).] Nineteenth-Century Fiction, XXII (December), 304-307.
"Regan's study, at times illuminating and original, remains at bottom partial because its thesis does not sufficiently acknowledge the sovereignty of character (not plot) and style (not belief) in the work of Mark Twain." The characters are fit "too exclusively into the pattern of an archetypal plot."

B106   STRONG, LEAH A. "Mark Twain and Frontier Folklore," Pacific Northwest Quarterly, LVIII (July), 113-18.
MT incorporated themes from the folklore of the past (as in the chapter from HF transferred to LOM, incorporating "the tall tale, the exaggeration, the gigantic lie, the anticlimactic ending...the contest, the defeat of the bully..."), and he used superstition as a device in HF.

B107   STUBBLEFIELD, CHARLES. "Mark Twain's Unpublished Works," Denver Quarterly, II (Autumn), 113-17.
A review of Franklin R. Rogers, ed., Mark Twain's Satires and Burlesques; Hamlin Hill, ed., Mark Twain's Letters to His Publishers; John S. Tuckey, ed., Mark Twain's "Which Was the Dream?" Praises the editing, but adds: "These volumes are not disappointing; it is just that they contain nothing very interesting....they contain little that is not already known."

B108   STURDEVANT, JAMES R. "Mark Twain's Unpublished Letter to Tom Taylor--an Enigma," Mark Twain Journal, XIV (Winter), 8-9.
An MT letter acquired by Sturdevant (January 5, 1874, here printed for the first time) refers to Taylor as "the author of the only play I ever appeared in on any stage." Taylor (1817-1880) became editor of Punch shortly after MT ended his 1874 trip to England, and remained in that post until 1880; he also wrote almost one hundred plays, among them Our American Cousin, the play Abraham Lincoln was watching when he was assassinated. Abstract in ALA, I (June, 1968), 193-94.

B109   SYKES, ROBERT H. "A Source for Mark Twain's
       Feud," West Virginia History, XXVIII
       (April), 191-98.
          The Shepherdson-Grangerford feud in HF
       is probably not based on a Darnell-Watson
       feud (described in LOM but not mentioned
       elsewhere); however, there are "ten signi-
       ficant points of similarity" to the actual
       feud of the Hatfields and McCoys. Abstract
       in AES, X (1967), 3614; reprinted in Twain-
       ian, XXVIII (March-April, 1969).

B110   TANNER, TONY. "Two Men at War in a Great
       Writer," Sunday Times (London), February 5,
       p. 48.
          A review of Justin Kaplan, Mr. Clemens
       and Mark Twain (1966). "It is an excellent
       biography. The clarity and intelligence
       it brings to bear on this most fascinating
       American writer make it immediately indis-
       pensible, even though it avails itself of
       the crucial pioneer work of such people as
       Albert Bigelow Paine, Bernard DeVoto, Henry
       Nash Smith, and others. (Kaplan is very
       thin on acknowledging his indebtedness to
       secondary sources)."

B111   THAYER, EMMA B., and SEVERANCE, S. L. "Let-
       ters from Emma B. Thayer and S. L. Sever-
       ance," Twainian, XXVI (March-April), 2-3.
          Three letters from companions on the
       Quaker City tour which MT recorded in IA.
       Emma B. Thayer's letter (June 22, 1907) re-
       members the influence of Mary Mason Fair-
       banks on MT's newspaper letters written on
       the trip, his taking the side of young
       Charles Langdon when the boy was teased by
       other passengers, and MT's asking her (then
       only 17) to sit up with him under the stars:
       "He would call my attention to the beauty
       of Curtis' language in The Howaji in Syria,
       reading passages aloud." S. B. Severance
       comments on MT's "intense likes and dis-
       likes" in his letter of November 23, 1911,
       and his letter of March 13, 1912 passes on
       a number of details: "the talk on ship-
       board ran to the effect that Dan Leary was
       going to try to sell the ship to the Khe-
       dive of Egypt and we all wished that he
       could do so," because the food was becoming
       uninteresting on board; a letter from a
       friend named Fairbanks says his mother
       [presumably Mary Mason Fairbanks--T.A.T.]
       received a letter from MT before publica-
       tion of Innocents Abroad, listing possible
       titles, and Fairbanks says the book was
       written, not in Washington, but in Elmira
       and Hartford [this is only partially cor-
       rect: by the time MT was visiting in Elmira
       the book had reached the proofreading
       stage--T.A.T.]. Severance also notes an is-
       sue of the Portland Sunday Oregonian of
       July 3, 1910 containing "some very good
       pictures." Abstract in AES, XII (1969);
       reprinted in Twainian, XIX (January-Febru-
       ary, 1970).

B112   THURMOND, MARGARET E. [Review: Franklin R.
       Rogers, ed., Mark Twain's Satires and Bur-
       lesques.] Journal of the West, VI (April),
       341-42.
          Roger's "Introduction, Editor's Notes, and
       annotations may well be the most valuable
       parts of the entire book," and he makes an
       important point in showing the hard work and
       trial and error in MT's creative process.

B113   _____. [Review: John S. Tuckey, ed., Mark
       Twain's "Which Was the Dream?" and Other
       Symbolic Writings of the Later Years.]
       Journal of the West, VI (April), 342-43.
          "Professor Tuckey has met this challenge
       gracefully and well," and the book will be
       of interest both to the specialist and to
       the general reader.

B114   _____. [Review: Hamlin Hill, ed., Mark
       Twain's Letters to His Publishers.] Journal
       of the West, VI (April), 343-44.
          "Hamlin Hill, who...is well-versed in
       Twainiana, does a truly James Bondsmanlike
       piece of detective work with his precise and
       painstaking footnoting following immediately
       upon the printing of each letter." The let-
       ters show MT's financial motivation, and the
       general reader will enjoy his explosions at
       publishers.

B115   VOLLMER, JOHN P. "Letter from John P. Voll-
       mer," Twainian, XXVI (March-April), 3-4.
          The letter, to Albert Bigelow Paine (De-
       cember 26, 1911), tells of MT playing "Sev-
       en Up" with a card-shark on shipboard in
       1868 on the way to San Francisco; earlier
       on the same trip he saw MT as one of a party
       who had chosen to make part of the trip
       across the Isthmus carried by porters--but
       the breech-clout of MT's porter had slipped,
       making a spectacular picture: "There he
       was perched in a chair on the back of his
       human ship of the Isthmus, his legs dangling
       in unison with each step of his carrier.
       As his position was such that he could look
       only backwards, he was unaware of the scene
       in front." Brief abstract in AES, XII
       (1969), 678; reprinted in Twainian, XXIX
       (January-February, 1970).

B116   WELLAND, DENNIS. "A Note on Some Early Re-
       views of Tom Sawyer," Journal of American
       Studies, I (April), 99-103.
          Moncure Daniel Conway took the manuscript
       of TS to England, negotiated its publica-
       tion, and apparently wrote the lengthy fa-
       vorable unsigned review in the Examiner
       (here summarized, together with a patroniz-
       ing review in the Athenaeum). Welland shows
       points of similarity between the Examiner
       review and one Conway wrote for the Cincin-
       atti Commercial when TS appeared in America
       six months later; other newspapers drew on
       this for their own reviews of TS. Ab-
       stract in AES, XI (1968), 2216; reprinted
       in Twainian, XXVIII (January-February, 1969).

1967 - Shorter Writings

B117   WHITE, WILLIAM. "Roger Butterfield and the
       Earliest Mark Twain," Mark Twain Journal,
       XIII (Summer), 20.
          "In an attractive folio, privately print-
       ed for the 18th annual meeting of the Anti-
       quarian Booksellers' Association of America,
       Roger Butterfield tells the story of 'Sam
       Clemens and the American Courier,'" in
       which an MT sketch appeared; however, the
       issue bears two dates, May 1 and May 8,
       1852, so priority for MT's first publication
       remains with "The Dandy Frightening the
       Squatter" in The Carpet-Bag.

B118   WIGGINS, ROBERT A. [Review: Sydney J.
       Krause, Mark Twain as Critic.] New England
       Quarterly, XL (December), 609-11.
          "Probably the most original and creative
       contribution to Twain scholarship in the
       past decade.... This is a good book. It
       might have been a better book." Still
       needed is a treatment of MT as self-critic,
       although Krause has done admirably in col-
       lecting MT's critical statements from vari-
       ous sources. Wiggins agrees that "there is
       more critical substance in him than has
       generally been recognized," but insists
       that "Mark Twain was not a literary critic
       in the usual meaning of the term."

B119   WYATT, BRYANT N. "Huckleberry Finn and the
       Art of Ernest Hemingway," Mark Twain Jour-
       nal, XIII (Summer), 1-8.
          "Aside from the purely stylistic affini-
       ties between Finn and the writings of Hem-
       ingway, there are certain affinities of
       subject-matter," among them the opposition
       of reality and illusion, the loss of illu-
       sion, the use of superstition, the symbolic
       use of rivers, and self-realization through
       experience. Abstract in AES, XII (1969),
       1237.

B120   *YU, BEONGCHEON. "The Ending of the Adven-
       tures of Huckleberry Finn," Phoenix (Seoul),
       II (Spring), 23-30.
          [Source: Leary (1970), p. 77.]

B121   ____. "The Immortal Twins: An Aspect of
       Mark Twain," The English Language and Lit-
       erature (The English Literary Society of
       Korea), XXIII (Summer), 48-77.
          [Source: Photocopy in Mark Twain Pa-
       pers.] "There is singular persistence in
       Mark Twain's interest in identical twins,
       changelings, impostors, and claimants--
       something we cannot dismiss as symptoms of
       his weakness for burlesque and melodrama.
       These motifs and devices are there where
       apparently uncalled for, and are often cen-
       tral in many of his works." Tracing MT's
       treatment of doubles through three succes-
       sive periods shows "his central concern
       progressing from the moral-psychological
       to the metaphysical to the psychical direc-
       tion, and, likewise, his art developing
       from the realistic to the allegorical to

the symbolic realm. On the whole, his is a
drama unfolding an artist's quest for identity in terms of duality--beyond appearance
and reality--at each of three levels with
deepening implications."

1968 A BOOKS

A1   GANZEL, DEWEY. Mark Twain Abroad: The Cruise
      of the "Quaker City." Chicago and London:
      The University of Chicago Press.
         A detailed study of the 1867 tour of Eu-
      rope and the Holy Land described by MT in IA.
      Documentation includes the log of Captain
      Duncan of the Quaker City (in the Patten
      Free Library, Bath, Maine) and published ac-
      counts of the trip by Mary Mason Fairbanks
      (1892), Mrs. Stephen Griswold (1871), and
      Emily Severance (1938), as well as The Long
      Island Farmer's Poems (n.d.) by Bloodgood
      Cutter (the "Poet Lariat" of the party), and
      a number of newspaper letters, not listed in
      the present bibliography, by other passen-
      gers.

A2   LORCH, FRED W. The Trouble Begins at Eight:
      Mark Twain's Lecture Tours. Ames: Iowa
      State Universtty Press.
         Traces MT's lifetime career as a lecturer,
      with a discussion of his manners and tech-
      niques, audiences and reception, and prof-
      its; includes "Texts of Tour Lectures," from
      manuscript and newspaper sources; some are
      composites from several sources.

A3   RABAN, JONATHAN. Mark Twain: "Huckleberry
      Finn," London: Edward Arnold. Studies in
      English Literature No. 36.
         One of a series of studies intended for
      "the advanced sixth-former and the universi-
      ty student" (p. 5). The study concludes:
      "Huckleberry Finn is a masterpiece of equi-
      vocation: its humour suddenly switches into
      tragic realism; its two languages, vernacu-
      lar and rhetoric, are perpetually opposed;
      its situations are largely unresolved; its
      characters, so important for brief periods,
      fade into the passing blur of the crowd.
      It tells two truths, and they will not be
      reconciled" (pp. 59-60).

A4   ROSA-COLT, PAOLA. L"Angoscia di Mark Twain
      [The Anguish of Mark Twain]. Milan: M.
      Ursia & Co.
         Sections titled "La Crisi Ideologica"
      ("The Ideological Crisis," emphasizing CY);
      "Fra Realismo E Simbolismo" ("Between Real-
      ism and Symbolism"); "Verso Il Racconto
      Filosofico" ("Toward Philosophical Narra-
      tion"); "La Fase Finale" ("The Final Phase,"
      on MS, CS, Captain Stormfield's Visit to
      Heaven, etc.); "Conclusione: Opera Aperta"
      ("Conclusion: Unfinished Work"). [In Ital-
      ian.]

A5   SIMPSON, CLAUDE M., ed. Twentieth Century Interpretations of "Adventures of Huckleberry Finn": A Collection of Critical Essays. Englewood Cliffs, N.J.: Prentice-Hall, Inc.
        Includes discussions of HF by major authors and critics; contains some articles not readily obtained elsewhere. All of this material is listed in the present bibliography and cross-referenced to Simpson's reprinting.

A6   TUCKEY, JOHN S. Mark Twain's "The Mysterious Stranger" and the Critics. Belmont, California: Wadsworth Publishing Company.
        The text of MS, followed by a selection of critical discussions reprinted from books and scholarly journals. These reprintings are not cross-referenced in the present bibliography because their original printings are generally accessible, although Professor Tuckey has done the student a service in bringing them together here. Also included are Tuckey's "The Mysterious Stranger: Mark Twain's Texts and the Paine-Duneka Edition," here published for the first time (pp. 85-89) and "Mark Twain and Little Satan: The Writing of The Mysterious Stranger" (pp. 126-54), an extensive excerpt from his Mark Twain and Little Satan (1963). "It is now clear that Albert Bigelow Paine and Frederick A. Duneka, who edited the story as it was published six years after Mark Twain's death, actually wrote into the tale a character--the astrologer--who did not appear at all in the manuscript as Mark Twain had written it; they also deleted thousands of Mark Twain's own words.... For the text of The Mysterious Stranger I have followed the 1916 edition of Paine and Duneka. I have, however, corrected an obvious misprint.... I have also annotated the text to give some indication of the ways in which the 1916 edition differs from the manuscript on which it is based" (Preface, p. v).

A7   WILSON, EDMUND. The Fruits of the MLA. New York: A New York Review Book.
        A reprinting of material which previously appeared in the New York Review of Books; Part II, pp. 21-35 is the part on MT (1968. B116).

A8   WOOD, JAMES PLAYSTED. Spunkwater, Spunkwater! A Life of Mark Twain. Illustrated with Photographs. New York: Pantheon Books.
        A biography for teenage readers; accurate and interesting.

1968 B SHORTER WRITINGS

B1   American Literature Abstracts, I (June); II (December).
        Contains a number of abstracts of articles on MT; many are by the authors of the articles abstracted, and all are longer than abstracts in the present bibliography; however, in many cases the journal articles are more readily available than the abstracts, and coverage for the year's scholarship is not complete.

B2   ANON. "Grumblings," Times Literary Supplement, March 28, p. 311.
        A review of Sydney J. Krause, Mark Twain as Critic (1967), chiefly descriptive. MT "really cannot be considered seriously as a critic. Mr. Krause is a good scholar and a discriminating one and cannot be held responsible for the sorry stuff [MT] turned out under this title."

B3   ANON. "Mark Twain Items from 'Abstracts of English Studies' in 1967," Twainian, XXVII (January-February), 1-4.
        Most of the abstracts related to MT from AES, X (1967), plus one entry from AES, IX (1966), 3352; Items 3295, 3301, and 3614 from AES, X appear in Twainian, XXVIII (March-April, 1969). Abstract in AES, XIII (1969-1970), 1360; reprinted in Twainian, XXX (January-February, 1971).

B4   BAENDER, PAUL. "Review Article: Two Books on Mark Twain," Philological Quarterly, XLVII (January), 117-35. On Justin Kaplan, Mr. Clemens and Mark Twain and James M. Cox, Mark Twain: The Fate of Humor (both 1966).
        Kaplan has done extensive research, has avoided "the sentimental nostalgia that has stultified so many of the accounts since Paine," and successfully "conveys Clemens's sense that the past, present and future were all unsure," but he rides too hard his thesis that explains MT as a parvenu, confused and unstable. Many of Kaplan's contentions are merely "slipshod, smarty, unimaginative," there are annoying inaccuracies of fact, and Kaplan frequently quotes "misleading extracts designed to prove what they do not prove when read in context." Cox seeks in MT a "depth and consistency of intention he did not have," through two main points: "that 'Mark Twain' served Samuel L. Clemens as a means of emotional economy and pleasure" and that the Freudian process may be reconstituted as an ideological struggle. Unfortunately, Cox has taken a rigid approach which leads to some serious misinterpretations of MT's work.

B5   BANTA, MARTHA. "Escape and Entry in Huckleberry Finn," Modern Fiction Studies, XIV (Spring), 79-91.
        Huck's flight to the river and his failure to escape thereby from society must be explained, not by the reader's moral preconceptions, but by Huck's "loose-hung code that is beholden only to what provides the free, the easy, and the comfortable." Huck's experiences reflect MT's own discovery that there can be no escape from the

(BANTA, MARTHA)
consequences of heredity and environment: novelty may offer man a free choice of new routes, "or may simply show him driven by yet one more compulsive thrust into predetermined paths of action." Abstract in AES, XII (1969), 1263; reprinted in Twainian, XXIX (January-February, 1970). Abstracted by Martha Banta in ALA, II (December), 47.

B6   BEEBE, MAURICE, and JOHN FEASTER. "Criticism of Mark Twain: A Selected Checklist," Modern Fiction Studies, XIV (Spring), 93-139.
"Part I consists of general studies of Twain's life and work. Part II lists discussions of his individual works in the following order--(A) editions of the works containing some kind of critical apparatus, Introductions, Afterwords, etc., (B) an index to the general studies listed in Part I, and (C) special studies not previously listed.... we have listed in Part II only the better known works, thus omitting many short topical pieces and his lesser works of non-fiction.... As usual, we have omitted foreign criticism, unpublished theses or dissertations, and routine discussions in encyclopedias, handbooks, and histories of literature." This is a valuable and responsible piece of work, of which one especially useful feature is the lists of page references showing where particular works by MT are treated in the longer studies of his thought and writing; these lists of page references have not been transferred to the present bibliography. The compilers have also found a number of articles in books, material not readily to be found through bibliographies which emphasize periodical articles and books devoted entirely to MT. Comparatively few errors in other bibliographies are here repeated. This checklist has been invaluable as a finding-list for the present bibliography, which incorporates the major part of its listings (but not the indexes to general studies). Listed in AES, XII (1969), 1264, and in Twainian, XXIX (January-February, 1970).

B7   BEIDLER, PETER G. "The Raft Episode in Huckleberry Finn," Modern Fiction Studies, XIV (Spring), 11-20.
MT dropped the episode, which had already appeared in LOM, on the advice of his publisher, Charles Webster; the intention was to make the book shorter, as a companion volume to TS. In the excision MT lost a passage important technically as the explanation of how Huck learned that the raft had passed Cairo, and psychologically for revealing his "generally morbid outlook on life, his repeated identification with dead and suffering human beings." Huck's lies add to the psychological portrait, since

"in many of them Huck casts himself in the role of a boy who is alone in the world and whose family is dead, sick, or in grave danger." Abstract in AES, XII (1969), 1256; reprinted in Twainian, XXIX (January-February, 1970). Abstracted by Beidler in ALA, II (December), 47-48. Article reprinted in Gerber (1971), pp. 101-12.

B8   BENARDETE, JANE JOHNSON. "Huckleberry Finn and the Nature of Fiction," Massachusetts Review, IX (Spring), 209-26.
"It is the thesis of this essay that Huckleberry Finn is a book about the nature of fiction (which epitomizes the deceptive power of language, for fiction is told or written and heard or read although it is known to be untrue): that each episode illustrates some quality of fiction; that the major theme of Huck's development is his increasing preference for fiction over fact; and that the novel itself is deliberately devised to exemplify fiction's power to distort life."

B9   BERCOVITCH, SACVAN. "Huckleberry Bumppo: A Comparison of Tom Sawyer and The Pioneers," Mark Twain Journal, XIV (Summer), 1-4.
Despite MT's ridicule of Cooper, the two books are similar in structure and such characters as the town patriarchs Judge Thatcher and Judge Temple, who stand at opposite poles from Huck and Natty; other parallels are evident as well, but there are also significant differences in the treatment of the frontier myth and the Indian. Abstract in ALA, II (December), 48.

B10   BERGMANN, FRANK. "Mark Twain and the Literary Misfortunes of John William DeForest," Jahrbuch für Amerikastudien (Heidelberg), XIII, 249-52.
Text of a letter to MT (July 31, 1874), in which DeForest asks, "Could we not publish a conjoint volume by subscription" of their short stories; the letter appears to be the first contact between the two, and nothing came of the proposal. Abstract in AES, XII (1969), 1551; reprinted in Twainian, XXIX (January-February, 1970).

B11   *BERKOVE, LAWRENCE I. "The 'Poor Players' of Huckleberry Finn," Papers of the Michigan Academy of Science, Arts and Letters, LIII, 291-310.
[Source: MHRA Annual Bibliography (1968), No. 7709.]

B12   BIER, JESSE. The Rise and Fall of American Humor. New York: Holt, Rinehart and Winston.
On MT, pp. 117-61, with a valuable discussion of HF and the reasons why it is "inaccessible" to foreigners.

B13 BLANCK, JACOB. "BAL Addendum 3479: Twain's 'A Dog's Tale,'" Papers of the Bibliographical Society of America, Vol. LXII (Fourth Quarter), 617.
Reports 3,000 copies of the pamphlet were were printed by Harper and Brothers, New York for use by the National Anti-Vivesectionist Society, London: the order to print was issued January 26, 1904. Abstract in AES (1969), 2041; reprinted in Twainian, XXIX (January-February, 1970).

B14 BLUES, THOMAS. "The Strategy of Compromise in Mark Twain's 'Boy Books,'" Modern Fiction Studies, XIV (Spring), 21-31.
"The heroes of Tom Sawyer, The Prince and the Pauper, and Huckleberry Finn harbor aggressive designs against the community," but each hero achieved his victory in a way that left the community's stability intact, through "a compromise solution that had the important value of permitting triumph without isolation." Abstract in AES, XII (1969), 1257; reprinted in Twainian, XXIX (January-February, 1970). Abstract in ALA, II (December), 48-49.

B15 BOLAND, SALLY. "The Seven Dialects in Huckleberry Finn," North Dakota Quarterly, XXXVI (Summer), 30-40.
MT's use of dialect is not an end in itself, but a literary tool to delineate characters. The speech of the Negro and backwoodsman is represented phonetically, in a conspicuous "eye-dialect," but there is no such representation of the pronunciation of more educated persons. The dialects are used to represent regional and social differences in the characters, and there is also "a childhood lingo that cuts across all other distinctions." "The study was limited to the text of the novel...no conclusions were drawn as to the relation of the novel to linguistic realities."

B16 BROWN, CLARENCE A. [Review: Sydney J. Krause, Mark Twain as Critic (1967).] Thought, XLIII (Autumn), 445-46.
"In spite of the magnitude of its achievement, this book is weakened somewhat by its failure to develop in sufficient detail Twain's theoretical statements concerning literature...the treatment of Twain's criticism would have been enhanced by a concluding chapter in which some formulation and evaluation of Twain's theory and criticism was attempted."

B17 BUDD, LOUIS J. "Mark Twain and the Quaker City," Southern Literary Journal, I (Autumn), 112-16.
A review of Mark Twain Abroad: The Cruise of the "Quaker City," by Dewey Ganzel, who "has gone just about as far as possible in nailing down the facts...he wavers between scholarliness and gusto, between cross-examination and joining the laughter....whenever possible, Ganzel pushes on to Twain's development as an artist."

B18 ____. [Review: Sydney J. Krause, Mark Twain as Critic (1967).] South Atlantic Quarterly, LXVII (Winter), 184-85.
Worth the money but perhaps not worth the time, this book "sometimes deals with minor or worn items" and most readers should "let the specialists isolate and subsume the many useful insights of this book."

B19 CARSTENSEN, BRODER. "The Adventures of Huckleberry Finn: Die Problematik des Schlusses," in Franz H. Link, ed., Amerika, Vision und Wirklichkeit: Beiträge deutscher Forschung zur amerikanischen Literaturgeschichte. Frankfurt am Main, Bonn: Athenäum Verlag, pp. 199-210. First appeared in Neueren Sprachen (1961.B15).
Finds the last fifth of HF inappropriate to the rest of the book. Concludes: "Huckleberry Finn is no Ulysses, Faust, Don Quixote, Don Juan and no Hamlet, and Huckleberry Finn does not belong in the library of great books of world literature." [In German.]

B20 CASEY, DANIEL J. "Huckleberry in Finland: A Comparison of Twain and Kivi," Moderna Språk, LXII (December), 385-94.
MT's universal appeal is attested by the ease with which Casey has been able to introduce HF to students in the United States, Italy, and Finland; moreover, HF is much like the book portraying the Finnish national character, Kivi's Seven Brothers, in that both books concern the independence, self-reliance, and compassion of outcast characters. Abstract in AES, XIV (1970-1971), 583; reprinted in Twainian, XXXI (January-February, 1972). See 1967.B22.

B21 CLERC, CHARLES. "Sunrise on the River: The 'Whole World' of Huckleberry Finn," Modern Fiction Studies, XIV (Spring), 67-78.
A rhetorical analysis of a 400-word paragraph at the beginning of Chapter XIX. Its strength lies not in mere accurate imitation of an uneducated boy's speech, but in a sophisticated art: "Any suggestion of sloppiness in the passage may be dispelled...by a consideration of the wide variety of rhetorical forms and grammatical techniques used to achieve vividness and vivacity." Abstract in AES, XII (1969), 1262; reprinted in Twainian, XXIX (January-February, 1970). Abstract by Clerc in ALA, II (December), 49.

B22 COARD, ROBERT L. "The Dictionary and Mark Twain," Word Study (G. & C. Merriam Co.), XLIII (February), 1-4.
"On the basis of the numerous and frequently specific references to dictionaries in his works, one must conclude that Mark Twain, like so many other authors, was something of a dictionary buff."

1968 - Shorter Writings

B23   COX, JAMES M. "The Approved Mark Twain: The Beginning of the End," Southern Review, n.s. IV (April), 542-50.

A review-article on the first three volumes of the Mark Twain Papers: Rogers's Mark Twain's Satires and Burlesques, Hill's Mark Twain's Letters to His Publishers, 1867-1894, and Tuckey's Mark Twain's "Which Was the Dream?" and Other Symbolic Writings of the Later Years. Though ably edited, the newly published writings "reveal how little of value remains among the unpublished papers." There is some question of whether the editors should "continue publishing the letters by category rather than chronology," since the effect is misleading.

B24   CUMMINGS, SHERWOOD. [Review: Sydney J. Krause, Mark Twain as Critic (1967).] Western Humanities Review, XXII (Summer), 272-73.

Krause divides MT's critical approach into three periods, in which he successively posed as "muggins," as "grumbler," and, finally, spoke without a mask. The analysis of examples of MT's criticism generally leads to "an informative study which produces a steady sparkling of illuminations," but some topics are so limited that the method becomes tedious. The chapters on Macaulay, Howells, Howe, and Zola are "pithier and more convincing" than the chapter on Harte, and Macaulay's influence on Twain's theory of realism is "important news."

B25   [DAVIS, CHESTER L.] "'Life as I Find It' or 'Poor Little Stephen Girard,'" Twainian, XXVII (July-August), 1.

On the confusion concerning early publication of this story by MT, here reprinted from the Boston Evening Transcript, "Magazine Section," April 27, 1935. Abstract in AES, XIII (1969-1970), 1341.

B26   _____. "Mark Twain's Marginal Notations on 'Life, Letters and Journals of George Ticknor,'" Twainian, XXVII (July-August), 4; (September-October), 1-4; (November-December), 1-4.

On George S. Hillard (?), comp., The Life, Letters, and Journals of George Ticknor, Boston: James R. Osgood and Company, 1876, 2 vols. Follows the copy from MT's personal library, liberally quoting the text of the book, with MT's underlinings and notations. The series continues in Twainian through XXIX (March-April, 1970); the first installment noted that the second volume was unavailable, but it was found and reported in XXVIII (November-December, 1969), 1, and reprinting continued through this volume. The series is significant for what it reveals of MT's interests in a variety of topics. Abstracts in AES, XIII (1969-1970), 1350 (not reprinted in

Twainian; 1351, reprinted in Twainian, XXX (January-February, 1971); in AES, XIV (1970-1971), 585, reprinted in Twainian, XXXI (January-February, 1972).

B27   _____. "Mark Twain's Marginal Notes on Girard College," Twainian, XXVII (May-June), 1-4; (July-August), 2-4.

On MT's personal copy of Richard B. Westbrook, Girard's Will and Girard College Theology (Philadelphia, 1888). Reprints passages concerning Girard's desire that the students not be exposed to warring orthodox theologies, and the failure of the officers to follow his wishes; many of MT's underscorings are noted and marginal comments reproduced. Abstract in AES, XIII (1969-1970), 1348, 1349.

B28   _____. "Modern Language Association Center for Editions of American Authors, Works on Mark Twain," Twainian, XXVII (March-April), 2-4.

Provides a brief description and history of the CEAA, followed by "some random quotations especially significant in Mark Twain work" from the CEAA Statement of Editorial Principles: A Working Manual for Editing Nineteenth Century American Texts (1967). Abstract in AES, XIII (January-February), 1359; reprinted in Twainian, XXX (January-February, 1971).

B29   _____. "University of California Collection--Howe 'Story of a Country Town,'" Twainian, XXVII (January-February), 4; (March-April), 1-2.

On a visit by Davis to the Mark Twain collection at the University of California, Berkeley. The March-April installment reprints the text of MT's letter of February 12, 1884 to Edgar Watson Howe on his The Story of a Country Town. Abstract in AES, XIII (1969-1970), 1357; reprinted in Twainian, XXX (January-February, 1971).

B30   DOYNO, VICTOR A. "Over Twain's Shoulder: The Composition and Structure of Huckleberry Finn," Modern Fiction Studies, XIV (Spring), 3-9.

"Twain created in Huckleberry Finn three parallel sequential patterns of action. Each pattern involves first the meeting of Huck with someone who thinks him dead, the formation or renewal of a partnership to free the slave which ends in failure, and finally, the exchange of forty dollars." This pattern extends through "the natural world [of] the Mississippi...the picaresque adventures and deceptions of the King and Duke; and, finally, the burlesque romanticism of Tom's plot on the Phelps's farm. This pattern, and the ultimate impossibility of winning the slave's freedom," become increasingly evident: "for Huck freedom exists, if at all, in the process of seeking freedom." The disputed ending is an

(DOYNO, VICTOR A.)
appropriate framing element. Abstract in AES, XII (1969), 1255; reprinted in Twainian, XXIX (January-February, 1970). Abstract by Doyno in ALA, II (December), 49-50.

B31 EBY, E. H. "Gold in the Slag Heap: More Mark Twain Material," Pacific Northwest Quarterly, LIX (January), 45-47.
A review of Hamlin Hill, ed., Mark Twain's Letters to His Publishers, 1867-1894; Franklin R. Rogers, ed., Mark Twain's Satires and Burlesques; John S. Tuckey, ed., Mark Twain's "Which Was the Dream?" and Other Symbolic Writings of the Later Years (all 1967). These books are not for the general reader, but for the scholar they are "indispensable. Here is a rich and enormously complex store of material ably edited both as to text and essential background." The greater part of the review is on MT as revealed in these volumes of his unpublished writings; the approach is more descriptive than critical.

B32 ELLIS, HELEN E. "Mark Twain: The Influence of Europe," Mark Twain Journal, XIV (Winter), 12-18.
Although MT spent more than ten years abroad, he was never out of America longer than eighteen months and he developed a perspective for judging Europe and America in terms of each other, a broader understanding of Man, and view of the world's future; "In consequence of his expanding vision, Twain altered from a young, naive and proud young American to an old, embittered and disillusioned man." Abstract by Ellis in ALA, II (June, 1969), 250-51.

B33 ENSOR, ALLISON. "The Contributions of Charles Webster and Albert Bigelow Paine to Huckleberry Finn," American Literature, XL (May), 222-27.
The captions for the illustrations and the titles of the chapters in the original Huckleberry Finn are the work of Charles L. Webster, and somewhat inconsistent with the narrative voice of Huck. Chapter titles introduced in 1912 in the Author's National Edition have been attributed by Charles Neider to Albert Bigelow Paine; they "offer no striking divergence from the tone and point of view of the work itself." Abstract in AES, XIII (1969-1970), 1339. Abstract by Ensor in ALA, II (December), 50.

B34 _____. "The 'Opposition Line' to The King and The Duke in Huckleberry Finn," Mark Twain Journal, XIV (Winter), 6-7.
Answering W. Keith Kraus, "Huckleberry Finn: A Final Irony" (1967), points out that the language of the second set of brothers appears only as reported by Huck, their lack of visible grief may be the result of shock at having their identity disputed, the point of the tattoo was not

worth making unless some benefit might come of it, and the broken arm could be a device of the author, rather than the character; in sum: the second set of brothers are not proven to be frauds. Abstract by Ensor in ALA, II (June, 1969), 251.

B35 *ERICKSON, MILDRED. "Our Paths Have Crossed," University College Quarterly, XIII (January), 17-23.
A list of miscellaneous information concerning Hannibal, Missouri, circa 1820-1850, may illuminate MT's boyhood. [Source: Abstract in AES, XI (1968), 2424.]

B36 *FILCEV, PETAR. "Princat i Prosekat" ["The Prince and the Pauper"], Narodna Kultura (Sofia), No. 4 (January), p. 24.
[Source: MHRA Annual Bibliography (1968), No. 7727.]

B37 FOSTER, EDWARD F. "A Connecticut Yankee Anticipated: Max Adeler's Fortunate Island," Ball State University Forum, IX (Autumn), 73-76.
The 1881 novel by "Max Adeler" (Charles Heber Clark) "contains an identical theme and numerous parallels" in the story of a sociology professor and his daughter shipwrecked on a floating island that had broken loose from Arthurian England; after a stunning blow on the head the hero awoke to find the experience had been a dream. There is no evidence that MT had read the book, although in 1915 Adeler felt it necessary to point out that his book appeared before CY. Abstract in AES, XIV (1970-1971), 2838; reprinted in Twainian, XXXI (March-April, 1972).

B38 FREIMARCK, JOHN. "Pudd'nhead Wilson: A Tale of Blood and Brotherhood," University Review (Kansas City), XXXIV (Summer), 303-306.
Ranks the book with HF in importance, above it in "unity of theme and general organization," though "at times mechanical." The most important criticisms are by Leslie Fiedler (1955) and F. R. Leavis (1956). "Richard Chase soon followed with the caution that these were extravagant estimates, The American Novel and Its Tradition (New York, 1957)." Both Tom Driscoll and Valet de Chambre are victims of society; they have their counterpart in the more harmonious Italian twins, with circumstances and conduct serving as a contrast. Abstract in AES, XIII (1969-70), 3090.

B39 GANZEL, DEWEY. [Review: Franklin R. Rogers, ed., Mark Twain's Satires & Burlesques (1967); John S. Tuckey, ed., Mark Twain's "Which Was the Dream?" and Other Symbolic Writings of the Later Years (1967); Hamlin Hill, ed., Mark Twain's Letters to His Publishers, 1867-1894 (1967).] Modern Philology, LXVI (August), 83-87.

(GANZEL, DEWEY)

In a detailed discussion, notes the value of primary materials such as these to scholarship increasingly concerned with MT's aesthetic and his mode of composition. "Both the specialist and the non-specialist will find much to interest them in Clemens' correspondence; the manuscripts, on the other hand, will be of interest chiefly to the scholar." Unfortunately, the editing of the manuscript material to produce "readable text" for a general reader (who will find the abortive attempts disappointing) has produced "not the manuscript transcriptions one might have hoped them to be, but, rather, edited versions of those manuscripts." Hill's edition of MT's letters contains much of value, though Ganzel criticizes the selection.

B40   GARDNER, JOSEPH H. "Gaffer Hexam and Huck Finn," Modern Philology, LXVI (November), 155-56.

Although A Tale of Two Cities has often been suggested as a source for Pap's attack on Huck for learning to read and write, there is a closer analogue in Our Mutual Friend; Gardner documents MT's familiarity with Dickens' work. Abstract in AES, XII (1969), 1280; reprinted in Twainian, XXIX (January-February, 1970).

B41   GARLAND, HAMLIN. Hamlin Garland's Diaries, ed. by Donald Pizer. San Marino, California: The Huntington Library, passim.

At a memorial meeting to MT, April 30, 1910, among the old guard, one intoxicated and "Opie Read purple-visaged walking sedately and talking a lot of 'guff'" (p. 17). Dined with Clarence Darrow (November 4, 1920), who "particularly dwelt upon Mark Twain and his savage attacks on the Christian religion. It was all rather wearisome to me" (p. 123). Says Howells inspired MT with reform ideas, and P&P and CY "were due to Howells almost directly" (p. 152). Went to see Will Rogers on the film set for CY (December 28, 1930; pp. 181-82). Describes MT at a dinner honoring Henry James (December 9, 1904): "When Mark Twain's humor vanishes he is tragic. His wife is dead, one daughter is dead, another is in a sanitarium" (p. 191). At a lunch with Colonel Harvey (March 13, 1906) "Twain looked old and sluggish and congested, his purplish face and bushy yellow-white hair making him a picturesque figure. He drank more than he should and ate more than he should. He is old and his work is nearly done" (pp. 191-92). On MT's friendship for Howells and the differences between them, MT's coarse anecdotes-- "His profanity was oriental in its richness and power" (pp. 192-93).

B42   GEISMAR, MAXWELL. "Mark Twain on U. S. Imperialism, Racism & Other Enduring Characteristics of the Republic," Ramparts, VI (May), 64-71.

Defends the late writings of social protest as part of MT's most important work and far from an artistic failure. According to an editorial headnote, "Maxwell Geismar, the distinguished literary critic and historian, is presently at work on a study of Mark Twain [Mark Twain: An American Prophet (1970)]. This essay is excerpted from his chapter on the political radicalism of Twain's later writings." The front cover of this issue shows the American flag as MT suggested it might be remade, with black stripes and with skulls and crossbones instead of stars. Abstract in AES, XI (1968), 2642; reprinted in Twainian, XXVIII (March-April, 1969).

B43   GERBER, JOHN C. "Mark Twain," in J. Albert Robbins, ed., American Literary Scholarship: An Annual/1968 (Durham, North Carolina: Duke University Press, 1970), pp. 66-83.

A survey of MT scholarship for the year; See 1963.B32. Contents: "i. Textual and Bibliographical Matters"; "ii. Biography"; "iii. General Criticism"; "iv. Earlier Works"; "v. Huckleberry Finn"; "vi. Later Works."

B44   _____. [Review: Sydney J. Krause, Mark Twain as Critic (1967).] American Literature, XL (November), 408-409.

"The book is divided into three parts: Twain's Early Criticism: The Critic as Muggins, Twain's Later Criticism: The Critic as Grumbler, and Twain's Appreciative Criticism: From History into Life. As these titles reveal, there is an over-neatness about the division between the first two, and a confusion about the relation of the third to the other two. These difficulties are at the heart of the troubles that beset what could have been an important work." The third section of the book represents an improvement, and the section on Macaulay is particularly good.

B45   GIBSON, DONALD B. "Mark Twain's Jim in the Classroom," English Journal, LVII (February), 196-99, 202.

On the twentieth-century problems arising from the stereotyped portrayal of Jim in HF, and from MT's ambivalent attitude toward him.

B46   GIBSON, WILLIAM M. "Mark Twain's Mysterious Stranger Manuscripts: Some Questions for Textual Critics," Bulletin of the Rocky Mountain Modern Language Association, XXII (December), 183-91.

(GIBSON, WILLIAM M.)

"The following paper was delivered at the annual meeting of the RMMLA in October 1968 at Colorado Springs. It is an abbreviation of a paper given at the Dublin meeting of the International Association of University Professors of English." A description of the three texts cobbled together by Paine and Duneka as MS; Paine "secretly tried to fill Mark Twain's shoes, and he tampered with the faith of Mark Twain's readers." Gibson discusses "the scholarly, esthetic, and moral questions" he has had to face in his turn.

B47   GRAVES, WALLACE. "Mark Twain's 'Burning Shame,'" Nineteenth-Century Fiction, XXIII (June), 93-98.
The "Royal Nonesuch" of HF appears in the typescript as "The Burning Shame." Graves repeats a Swedish version as he heard it told in the thirties. "Interesting for its sustained drama as well as its obscenity," the story involves two destitute actors who performed for an audience from which women and children were excluded. One actor appeared on hands and knees, naked, while his partner introduced the act: "'And now, gentlemen, you are about to see The Tragedy of the Burning Shame.' He inserted a candle in the naked man's posterior, and lit it. When nothing further happened, the audience shouted for something more; the man said the performance was over...'have you ever seen a better example of a "Burning Shame"?'" And the actors fled with the receipts. Abstract by Graves in ALA, II (December), 50-51.

B48   HART, JOHN E. "Heroes and Houses: The Progress of Huck Finn," Modern Fiction Studies, XIV (Spring), 39-46.
Identifies the term "house" broadly, to include "sheds and rafts, huts and mansions," and even steamboats. A view of Huck's journey as a progression from house to house gives the story unity; "in one way or another, the house stands for civilization, a container of ambiguities: of freedom and bondage, of mystery and insight, of good and evil, of life and death." Abstract in AES, XII (1969), 1259; reprinted in Twainian, XXIX (January-February, 1970). Abstract by Hart in ALA, II (December), 51.

B49   HILL, HAMLIN. "Mark Twain and His Enemies," Southern Review, n.s. IV (April), 520-29.
"Towering rages" were "quite possibly an ingredient in the essential Mark Twain." Often, what he attacked in his enemies were aspects of himself: "His bitterness and vitriol were, then, as often touchstones to Mark Twain's self-doubts, recriminations, and inadequacies as to his enmities." He was motivated chiefly by fear--of failure, of success, of offending, of being laughed at. "He was a man most flawed by his fear of revealing his flaws."

B50   ____. [Review: Sydney J. Krause, Mark Twain as Critic (1967).] Modern Language Quarterly, XXIX (June), 236-38.
"Twain was a literary cat toying with pathetically unimportant mice. Mark Twain as Critic will impress any reader with the scope and the range of its subject's critical writings--which are all the more impressive because they lacked a solid basis or a theoretical depth."

B51   HOUGH, ROBERT L. "Mark Twain as Traveler," Prairie Schooner, XLII (Winter), 360-61.
A review of Dewey Ganzel, Mark Twain Abroad, which he praises for showing the effect which the pressure of time and lost letters had on the correspondence making up the latter half of Innocents Abroad, for showing that the influence of Mrs. Fairbanks on MT has been exaggerated, and for the portrayal of the other passengers on the Quaker City. Although "Ganzel sometimes pushes his evidence too far," the "lapses...are minor and do not seriously impair the informational or critical insights of the book."

B52   ____. "Twain's Double-Dating in 'A Connecticut Yankee,'" Notes and Queries, CCXIII, n.s. XV (November), 424-25.
MT uses two sets of dates for Hank Morgan's scheduled execution and his exploitation of the solar eclipse: that of Sir Kay and the mistaken dating of Clarence; Hank's first full day in prison is the 21st, so Clarence's advancing the date of execution to the 20th is impossible. Abstract in AES, XII (1969), 1998; reprinted in Twainian, XXIX (January-February, 1970).

B53   HOWELL, ELMO. "Huckleberry Finn in Mississippi," Louisiana Studies, VII (Summer), 167-72.
On the locations in Mississippi of some of the incidents in HF, in which MT's "purpose is to give a kindly rendering of a country and a civilization" he loved. Abstract in AES, XII (1969), 936; reprinted in Twainian, XXIX (January-February, 1970).

B54   ____. "Uncle John Quarles' Watermelon Patch," Midwest Quarterly, IX (April), 271-82.
On the tender recollections in HF of MT's own boyhood days on his uncle's farm: "He had been in Eden and he knew whereof he spoke." (Documentation is from familiar works on MT). Lengthy abstract by Howell in ALA, II (December), 52.

B55   ____. "Uncle Silas Phelps: A Note on Mark Twain's Characterization," Mark Twain Journal, XIV (Summer), 8-12.
"Mark Twain was a friend of the Negro... and he never failed to speak out against the injustice he suffered, particularly in the South," but he "also loved those Valley people who enslaved Jim.... Thus Huckleberry Finn is built around a paradox," the Phelps

(HOWELL, ELMO)
family "are among Mark Twain's favorite people, and Uncle Silas Phelps is his finest portrait of a good man," kindly and decent rather than clever. Lengthy abstract by Howell in ALA, II (December), 52-53.

B56 *IVANOVA, ELKA. "Mădăr Urok. Piesata 'Prinčăt i Prosekăt v Nar. teatar za mladežta" ["A Good Lesson. 'The Prince and the Pauper' as Staged by the Nat. Theatre of Youth"], Teatăr (Sophia), XXI, No. 3, 40-41.
    [Source: MHRA Annual Bibliography (1968), No. 7745.]

B57 JONES, JOSEPH. "Mark Twain's Connecticut Yankee and Australian Nationalism," American Literature, XL (May), 227-31.
    Although the book met a hostile reception from English reviewers, Australians found it attuned to their own sentiments. Among Australian reviews quoted is one from the Sydney Bulletin (March 8, 1890), titled "Mark Twain's New Book. A Crusher for Royalty." Abstract in AES, XIII (1969-1970), 1337. Also abstracted in ALA, II (December), 53.

B58 KAPLAN, JUSTIN. "What Really Happened to the Innocents Abroad," Chicago Tribune, "Book World," II (October 6), 5.
    A review of Dewey Ganzel's Mark Twain Abroad; primarily descriptive, with limited evaluation: "In trying to set the record straight to tell what actually happened, Ganzel has taken on a thankless task. He is up against a brilliant entertainer. Ganzel's synoptic version may be 'truer' than Mark Twain's, more historical and evenhanded, but it is inevitably drabber and less acute."

B59 KIMBALL, WILLIAM J. "Samuel Clemens as a Confederate Soldier: Some Observations About 'The Private History of a Campaign That Failed,'" Studies in Short Fiction, V (Summer), 382-84.
    MT's account of his brief service in an irregular Confederate unit is not wholly accurate. Abstract in AES, XII (1969), 1404; reprinted in Twainian, XXIX (January-February, 1970). Abstract by Kimball in ALA, II (December), 54.

B60 *KOHLI, RAJ K. "Huck Finn and Isabel Archer: Two Responses to the Fruit of Knowledge," in Banasthali Patrika (Rajasthan), XI (July), 73-82. Special Number on American Literature, ed. by Rameshwar Gupta. [Proceedings of the Seminar on American Literature, 2-3 March 1968 at Banasthali Vidyapath.]
    [Source: MLA Bibliography (1968), Nos. 78, 10284.]

B61 *LAIDLAW, R. P. "More Huck Finn in Finnegans Wake," A Wake Newsletter, V (October), 71-73.
    On references to HF not listed in Atherton's The Books at the Wake (1960), Hosty, introduced on p. 40, is described as, like Huck, having "no slouch of a name." [Source: Abstract in AES, XIII (1969-1970), 577; reprinted in Twainian, XXIX (January-February, 1970).]

B62 LEARY, LEWIS. "The Bankruptcy of Mark Twain," The Carrell: Journal of the Friends of the University of Miami Library, IX (June), 13-20.
    Describes MT's failure in publishing, and his friendship with Henry Rogers, who put MT's business affairs in order and retrieved his fortune. Also, describes use of the MT mask to conceal inner weakness. As a writer "he had great successes and horrible failures—how marvelous he can be at his best... but how jejune and embarrassing he can be at his worst, when he becomes serious or tries to think." It is "our brother, Mark Twain, who speaks for us because he is human and fallible," but he fails to go beyond "to something we had not thought to say. And that which he nor we do not say defines the artist."

B63 _____. "On Writing about Writers: Mark Twain and Howells," Southern Review, n.s. IV (April), 551-57.
    A review article; the portion on MT deals with James M. Cox, Mark Twain: The Fate of Humor (1966), on "Mark Twain" as a creation of Samuel Clemens, and the achievement of Cox in distinguishing between the two. When "Mark Twain" fails it is because Samuel Clemens intrudes, and "the fate of humor is that it becomes platitude...becomes serious at last." An aging, bitter Clemens "allowed Mark Twain to speak as an agent rather than a catalyst."

B64 LEHAN, RICHARD. [Review: Edward Wagenknecht, Mark Twain: The Man and His Work (revised ed., 1967).] Nineteenth-Century Fiction, XXIII (June), 133-24.
    "Much of this book is trivial and irrelevant." MT's views on religion, politics, love, and "preoccupation with nakedness—are important subjects superficially treated," but Wagenknecht is "disarmingly honest" about the limits of the book as it originally appeared, and he now "makes at times excellent use of recent criticism... and appends a superb 'Commentary on Mark Twain Criticism and Scholarship Since 1960.'"

B65 LEVIN, DAVID. "Mark Twain and Samuel L. Clemens," Yale Review, LVII (Spring), 434-37.
    A review of James M. Cox, Mark Twain: The Fate of Humor (1966). Cox begs a few questions, but the book "gives great pleasure along with serious instruction" and reveals "a shrewd use of scholarship...a scrupulous respect for the complexity of unpublished texts...and an admirable combination of biographical and literary intelligence."

B66 McDERMOTT, JOHN FRANCIS. "Mark Twain and the Bible," Papers on Language and Literature (Journal of the Midwest Modern Language Association for Scholars and Critics of Language and Literature), IV (Spring), 195-98.

Contains the text of a letter to MT from C. F. Davis, of Keokuk, Iowa (May, 1882) asking for reminiscences, reminding him of the time as a child when he was accidentally left behind when the Clemenses moved from Florida, Missouri, to Hannibal (and was found asleep in a flour barrel), and inquiring about "your familiar quotations from the Bible, when you were never known to read that book." MT's reply on July 8 enclosed a "manuscript scrap" (here printed), confessing that "I did manufacture a lot of bogus biblical 'quotations' & play them off on Patterson & the others, knowing that they would not be able to detect the swindle." McDermott concludes the article with a list of the books in the estate of John Marshall Clemens on his death in 1847. Abstract in ALA, II (December), 55.

B67 McINTYRE, JAMES P. "Three Practical Jokes: A Key to Huck's Changing Attitude Toward Jim," Modern Fiction Studies, XIV (Spring), 33-37.

Beginning with Chadwick Hansen's 1963 study, traces Huck's growing awareness of Jim's humanity: first Tom hung Jim's hat on a tree, then Huck nearly killled him in a joke involving a rattlesnake skin, but it was only through offending Jim's human dignity in the "trash" episode that Huck fully recognized his companion as an individual rather than a type. McIntyre's interpretation contrasts with Hansen's picture of Jim as developing from a minor figure to a symbol of man. Abstract in AES, XII (1969), 1258; abstract by McIntyre in ALA, II (December), 55.

B68 McMILLAN, DOUGLAS J. [Brief Review: Robert Regan, Unpromising Heroes: Mark Twain and His Characters (1966).] Western Folklore, XXVII (July), 223.

"The psychological interpretation (interwoven with the folkloristic, but not so detailed) of Twain's view of himself--as an unpromising hero mirrored in his fictional alter egos--is convincingly and entertainingly presented, provided one accepts its Freudian bases."

B69 *MALHOTRA, M. L. "The Question of Unity in Huckleberry Finn," The Banasthali Patrika (Rajasthan), No. 11 (July), pp. 69-72.

[Source: MHRA Annual Bibliography (1968), 7753. Additional publication facts in MLA Bibliography (1969), Nos. 78, 10288.]

B70 MANIEERE, WILLIAM R. "Huck Finn, Empiricist Member of Society," Modern Fiction Studies, XIV (Spring), 57-66.

The opening chapters do not represent Tom's point of view, or that of society; rather, the first three prepare for the story and define "the moral standards which give it meaning. The values of St. Petersburg--money, church, 'aristocracy,' to name only the most important--are equated with untruth, Tom Sawyer's 'lies,' and, for the moment at least, are rejected"; the fourth chapter introduces Pap and gives portents of future troubles. These first four chapters juxtapose opposing concepts, and Huck pragmatically tests and either accepts or rejects various ways of dealing with experience; but in the end his pragmatism has become "merely verbal." Abstract in AES, XII (1969), 1261; reprinted in Twainian, XXIX (January-February, 1970). Also abstracted in ALA, II (December), 54.

B71 _____. "On Keeping the Raftsmen's Passage in Huckleberry Finn," English Language Notes, VI (December), 118-22.

Removal of the passage to serve as padding for LOM damages HF structurally by obscuring Huck's responses to Jim's imminent freedom; the passage should be restored. Abstract in AES, XIV (1970-1971), 1542; reprinted in Twainian, XXXI (January-February, 1972). Abstract by Manierre in ALA, II (July, 1969), 252.

B72 MANN, CAROLYN. "Innocence in Pudd'nhead Wilson," Mark Twain Journal, XIV (Winter), 18-21, 11.

The influence of temperament and environment is stressed as a means of absolving characters of responsibility for their conduct, and in the end Wilson is not embittered. The author's "sympathy with those of his characters in Pudd'nhead Wilson who mean no harm is...proof that Mark Twain's nature profoundly desired innocence in man, or that he was willing to forgive man wherever possible."

B73 MATTSON, J. STANLEY. "Mark Twain on War and Peace: the Missouri Rebel and 'The Campaign that Failed,'" American Quarterly, XX (Winter), 783-94.

In October, 1884 the Century Magazine began a three-year series of "Battles and Leaders of the Civil War," the major part of which was written by celebrated leaders from both sides; their approach was serious, though not sentimental. In contrast to the general picture of the war as rational and important is MT's "The Private History of a Campaign that Failed" (Century, XXXI [December, 1885], 255-82), which portrays both the war and his own participation as inglorious. "In all, Mark Twain left to posterity no less than four major and five minor disparate versions of his career with the Confederate Army" (here listed). Mattson describes MT's anti-war sentiments and notes his correspondence with Robert Underwood Johnson, co-editor of the series.

B74   MATTSON, J. STANLEY. "Twain's Last Months
       on the Mississippi," Missouri Historical
       Review, LXII (July), 398-409.
          Tracing MT's movements in 1861, concludes
       that "both Twain and Paine were considerably
       more careful of the facts than we have here-
       tofore been led to believe."

B75   MAYBERRY, GEORGE. "Huckleberry Finn Enriched,"
       Nation, CCVII (August 26), 154-57.
          Discusses in some detail several of the
       more than twenty paperbound editions of HF
       intended for classroom use; most of those
       here considered contain useful introduc-
       tions, and several include biographical
       summaries, critical essays, and, in some
       cases, materials for class study. The Nor-
       ton Critical Edition and the Harbrace
       Sourcebook contain a wealth of supplementary
       material, as does The Art of Huckleberry
       Finn (Chandler), in which the text is a fac-
       simile of the first American edition, with
       the original Kemble illustrations. The Vik-
       ing, Bobbs-Merrill, Riverside, and Rinehart
       editions range from good to superb, and a
       simple Chandler edition using a facsimile
       of the first edition (with the Kemble il-
       lustrations) and an introduction and bib-
       liography by Hamlin Hill is "my favorite
       among paperback editions and...possibly the
       'best buy.'" Editions published by Pocket
       Books, Bantam, Dell, and Signet reveal
       small concern by their editors for MT's
       text and vary in the quality of the added
       material. The poorest of these is the
       Reader's Enrichment edition (Pocket Books:
       Washington Square Press), in which the back-
       ground material is "barely adequate" and
       "the sections on writing skills, vocabulary
       development and spelling include the fasci-
       nating suggestion to study such words as
       'ingots,' 'nabob,' and 'reticule,' 'because
       they are popular with good writers and
       speakers.'" The Bantam, Dell, and Signet
       editions are considerably better, and some
       of the supplementary material is quite
       good. Very brief abstract in AES, XII
       (1969), 1955; reprinted in Twainian, XXIX
       (January-February, 1970).

B76   MAYNARD, REID. "Mark Twain's Ambivalent Yan-
       kee," Mark Twain Journal, XIV (Winter), 1-5.
          Summarizes the "one-sided" interpreta-
       tions of the book, in which "the Yankee's
       overt attitude and actions are taken at
       face value while his moments of admiration
       for certain elements in Arthur's kingdom are
       either overlooked or conveniently neglect-
       ed." After summarizing various other criti-
       cal views, Maynard concludes that the book
       is "a thematically uneven novel" in which
       various aspects of MT's "damned human race,"
       past and present, "are satirized intention-
       ally and unintentionally." Abstract by
       Maynard in ALA, II (June, 1969), 252-53.

B77   *MELNIKOV, I. "Raskoldovannoe Leto" ["Disen-
       chanted Summer"; on HF.] Detskaya Litera-
       tura, VII, 41-43.
          [Source: MHRA Bibliography (1968), No.
       7760.]

B78   MERIWETHER, JAMES B., and MICHAEL MILLGATE,
       eds. Lion in the Garden: Interviews with
       William Faulkner. New York: Random House.
       Passim on MT (indexed).
          HF is "too loose" to be called a novel,
       "just a series of events" (p. 56); Hawthorne
       and James were not strictly American authors
       as MT, Whitman, and Sandburg were
       (pp. 167-68). The passage in Faulkner at
       Nagano (1956.B28) appears on p. 137.

B79   MILLER, J. HILLIS. "Three Problems of Fiction-
       al Form: First-Person Narration in David
       Copperfield and Huckleberry Finn," in Roy
       Harvey Pearce, ed., Experience in the Novel:
       Selected Papers from the English Institute
       (New York and London: Columbia University
       Press), pp. 21-48.

B80   MORRISON, CLAUDIA C. "Van Wyck Brooks's Analy-
       sis of Mark Twain," in her Freud and the
       Critic: The Early Use of Depth Psychology
       in Literary Criticism (Chapel Hill: The
       University of North Carolina Press).
          Traces Brooks's argument, frequently tak-
       ing issue with him; nonetheless, The Ordeal
       of Mark Twain, despite the thesis ridden
       too hard and the occasionally false psycholo-
       gizing, "is a provocative and, in its broad
       outlines at least, an essentially sound in-
       terpretation of Mark Twain's character"
       (p. 189). Brooks's success can be attribut-
       ed to his intelligence and critical sophisti-
       cation (p. 191). Suggests (pp. 112-13) that
       a more rounded psychological portrait may be
       found in O'Higgins and Reede: The American
       Mind in Action (1924.B25).

B81   MURRAY, DONALD. "Hong Kong Letter: Bombs,
       Books, and Hemingway," American Book Col-
       lector (Chicago), XVIII (March), 16-21.
          In a Mandarin Chinese translation, Huck
       Finn's language is stiff and formal. "I
       haven't yet found out about the 'complete
       edition' of Mark Twain, with propaganda
       prefaces, reportedly published on the Main-
       land." Abstract in AES, XI (1968), 2449;
       reprinted in Twainian, XXVIII (January-
       February, 1969).

B82   MYERS, MARGARET. "Mark Twain and Melville,"
       Mark Twain Journal, XIV (Summer), 5-8.
          "In thematic development, Melville seems
       to begin where Twain left off": MT goes
       from the "fond nostalgia" of HF to the bit-
       ter disillusionment of MS, while "Melville
       seems to seize Twain's disenchantment for
       the source of Ahab's defiance in Moby-Dick,
       then renounces the struggle in the submis-
       sion of Billy Budd." Lengthy abstract by
       Myers in ALA, II (December), 55-56.

B83 NOBLE, DAVID W. "The Realists: Mark Twain, William Dean Howells, Henry James," in his The Eternal Adam in the New World Garden: The Central Myth in the American Novel Since 1830. (New York: George Braziller), pp. 49-98; on MT, pp. 51-67.
On the decline of MT's optimistic belief in New World innocence and the possibility of progress: "It is man who imposes evil upon his social environment rather than the other way around" (p. 66).

B84 PECK, RICHARD E. "A Mark Twain 'Literary Offence,'" Mark Twain Journal, XIV (Winter), 7-9.
In HF, MT commits literary offences of which he accused Fenimore Cooper, particularly in violation of rules on the relevancy of incidents to the development of the plot, and on the use of language appropriate to the characters.

B85 *PETROVA, E. N. "Bor'ba Vokrug Tvorcheskogo Naslediya Marka Tvena v Literaturnoi Kritike Ameriki 1910-1920 Godov" ["The Controversy Surrounding the Creative Legacy of Mark Twain in the Literary Criticism of 1910-1920"], Leningradskii Pedagogicheskii Institut Imeni A. I. Gertsena (Leningrad) CCCXVI, 29-45.
[Source: MHRA Annual Bibliography (1970), No. 8271.]

B86 PICKETT, CALDER M. Ed Howe: Country Town Philosopher. Lawrence and London: University Press of Kansas, pp. 75-77 and passim.
Contains the text of MT's letter of February 13, 1884 to Howe about The Story of a Country Town, which MT and Cable liked; the letter is in two parts, the first to be made public if Howe chose and the second making some pointed suggestions for improvement (pp. 75-77). Also, quotes Howe in the Atchinson Globe of June 2, 1902 (1902. B18; quoted p. 123).

B87 RAVITZ, ABE C. [Review: Sydney J. Krause, Mark Twain as Critic (1967).] Mississippi Quarterly, XXI (Spring), 160-63.
Praises Krause's "gracefully-written, thoroughly-searched study," with the reservation that he does not adequately reveal the haste and shallowness of MT's judgments; however, his book is significant in showing that MT approached criticism "with wit and sensitivity," and "It is Twain's standard for Twain that one can now evaluate with keener understanding."

B88 REES, ROBERT A. "Mark Twain and Lucius Fairchild," Wisconsin Academy Review, XV (Spring), 8-9.
On the friendship of "Wisconsin's famous Civil War hero and ex-governor" and "the Twains," who missed an opportunity for a joint balloon ascension in Paris in 1879. Notes further meetings and a performance of Die Meisterschaft by the German

Conversation Club of Madison. Documented from the Fairchild Papers at the Wisconsin Historical Society, Madison, and other sources; quotes MT correspondence.

B89 _____. [Review article.] Nineteenth-Century Fiction, XXIII (June), 113-16.
John S. Tuckey, ed., Mark Twain's "Which Was the Dream?" (1966) is "interesting from a biographical-critical viewpoint." MT witheld these pieces, not because they were bad work, but because "his soul is here laid so bare"; Hamlin Hill, ed., Mark Twain's Letters to His Publishers (1967) is 290 letters which "in their totality give a rare and candid view of one of the more complex personalities in American letters," and "Hill's excellent introduction and notes unify the narrative." In Mark Twain's Satires and Burlesques Franklin R. Rogers "continues his excellent work on Twain's burlesque patterns with the eight pieces he edits with introductions...while these pieces tend to be uneven and unfinished, there is an occasional flash of Twainian brilliance, as in the burlesque of Victor Hugo's Les Travailleurs de la Mer."

B90 REEVES, PASCHAL, et al. "A Checklist of Scholarship for 1968." Mississippi Quarterly, XXII (Spring, 1969); on MT, pp. 160-62.
The first appearance of what has become an annual checklist. This is considerably less extensive than the annual bibliographies published by the MLA and MHRA, but has the advantage of appearing at least two years earlier.

B91 RICKELS, MILTON. "Samuel Clemens and the Conscience of Comedy," Southern Review, n.s. IV (April), 558-68.
A review-article on Fatout's Mark Twain in Virginia City, Hill's Mark Twain and Elisha Bliss, Wiggins's Mark Twain: Jackleg Novelist, and Smith's Mark Twain's Fable of Progress (all 1964). Rickles praises Fatout's and Hill's "careful research," adding that "by doing only the most modest violence to their authors' intentions it is possible to examine elements of the developing conscience of Samuel Clemens," which he then traces. Wiggins's depiction of MT as improviser is weak in the portrayal of the moral basis of MT's art and in support through analysis of a charge that MT did not understand the nature of humor. Finally, Smith's book is rich in insights and critical implications, showing that "subtle analysis of characterization, form, style, and humorous technique reveal how Mark Twain's imagination confronted profound ethical questions."

B92 RUST, RICHARD DILWORTH. "Americanisms in A Connecticut Yankee," South Atlantic Bulletin, XXXIII (May), 11-13.
The language is used partly to amuse, and partly to characterize Hank Morgan; there is

(RUST, RICHARD DILWORTH)
ambivalence in such terms as "The Boss" and
"Yankee," and Hank's drawing the majority
of his Americanisms from baseball, the stock
market, and poker shows his limitations.
In the end, the failure of his technology
is marked by "his breakdown in communication and his ultimate reliance on the language he originally ridiculed." Abstract in
AES, XII (1969-1970), 1338; reprinted in
Twainian, XXX (January-February, 1961).

B93 SALOMON, ROGER B. "Mark Twain Today," Case
Western Reserve University Magazine: A
Quarterly Publication for Alumni and Other
Friends, I (Winter), 7-11.
Surveys his current status and the criti-
cism; for the general reader.

B94 SCHONHORN, MANUEL. "Mark Twain's Jim: Solomon on the Mississippi," Mark Twain Journal,
XIV (Winter), 9-11.
Defending the portrayal of Jim in Chapter
XIV against the contention of Daniel Hoffman
(Form and Fable in American Fiction, 1951,
p. 321) and Chadwick Hansen ("The Character
of Jim and the Ending of Huckleberry Finn,"
1963), that he is shown as a minstrel-show
comic, argues that in the passage discussing Solomon's wisdom Jim and Huck are taking the roles previously given to Huck and
the romantic Tom Sawyer; subsequently, when
the lost raft is found by the Grangerford
slaves, Jim amicably settles the question
of its ownership with an ease and grace
that contrast with the bloody feud over a
trifling lawsuit thirty years in the past.

B95 SHARMA, MOHAN LAL. "Mark Twain's Passage to
India," Mark Twain Journal, XIV (Summer),
12-14.
On his visit there in 1896, as reflected
in Following the Equator, his notebooks,
and "old press clippings of the period"
(quoted, but naming only the Bombay Gazette
and giving no dates). Lengthy abstract by
Sharma in ALA, II (December), 56-57.

B96 SIMPSON, LOUIS P. "Mark Twain: Critical
Perspectives," Southern Review, n.s. IV
(April), 491-92.
Introduces a section of this issue collecting essays and review-essays by Arlin
Turner, Hamlin Hill, Robert Tracy, James
M. Cox, Lewis Leary, and Milton Rickels.
The question of the Clemens-Mark Twain
identity "involves the identity of us all,"
as people and as a nation. "By virtue of
his Southern environment, Mark Twain had
the most fertile education nineteenth-
century America afforded in the dilemma of
being an American."

B97 SOLOMON, JACK. "Huckleberry Finn and the
Tradition of the Odyssey," South Atlantic
Bulletin, XXXIII (March), 11-13.
In the debated ending of HF, Tom's and
Huck's use of disguises is in the tradition

of the homecoming of Odysseus; there are
other parallels, among them the journey,
Huck's imprisonment in the hut, the destruction of the raft, and even--in Huck's faking
his own death and later hiding gold in a
coffin--a sort of descent into a world of
the dead. Abstract in AES, XIII (1969-1970),
1340.

B98 SPENGEMANN, WILLIAM C. [Review: Sydney J.
Krause, Mark Twain as Critic (1967).]
Criticism, X (Spring) 166-68.
"The first book to present Clemens' critical theories in a way which might help us
to fix his position on a line stretching
from the Romantic subjectivism of Emerson to
the Romantic objectivism of Eliot."
Krause's effect is occasionally vitiated by
a tendency "to emphasize the object Clemens
criticized instead of the mind of Clemens
the critic," but the book "will prove a rich
source of information and inspiration to
American scholars."

B99 STEWART, GEORGE R. "Travelers by 'Overland':
Stagecoaching on the Central Route, 1859-
1865," American West, V (July), 4-12.
On the journeys by Horace Greeley (1859),
Richard Burton (1860), MT (1861), and Samuel
Bowles and Schuyler Colfax (1865). With a
map on pp. 8-9 showing the various routes,
this is interesting chiefly as general background, but has little direct interest for
the study of MT.

B100 STOEHR, TAYLOR. "Tone and Voice," College
English, XXX (November), 150-61.
On pp. 157-61, "Sam Clemens and Mark
Twain: Finding a Voice," discusses his
gradual development of a persona, most suc-
cessfully in HF.

B101 TANSELLE, G. THOMAS. "Anderson, Annotated by
Brooks," Notes and Queries (London),
CCXIII, n.s. XV (February), 60-61.
A copy of A Story Teller's Story in Tanselle's possession carries the marginal
notation by Brooks: "Paul R. [Rosenfeld]
thought I was a traitor attacking artists
Mark Twain etc." Tanselle also notes
Brooks's statement on Anderson's admiration
of MT in Story magazine (1941.B1). Abstract
in AES, XI (1968), 61; reprinted in Twainian, XXVIII (January-February, 1969).

B102 TATE, ALLEN. "Faulkner's Sanctuary and the
Southern Myth," Virginia Quarterly Review,
XLIV (Summer), 418-27.
(Apparently this was the introduction to
an edition of Sanctuary). Links HF with
Augustus Baldwin Longstreet's Georgia Scenes
as "a second crucial novel"; it is "the
first Southern novel in which the action is
generated inside the characters. It is not
perhaps the masterpiece that the academic
Mark Twain 'industry' has made it out to
be; yet for the reason I have indicated, it
is a work of great originality and historical

(TATE, ALLEN)
importance. These two works are the beginning of modern Southern literature; they are also important for American literature as a whole."

B103   . "A Southern Mode of the Imagination," in his Essays of Four Decades (Chicago: The Swallow Press, Inc.), pp. 577-92.
    On HF, pp. 591-92; calls this "the first modern novel by a Southerner," with the mode of progression no longer that of rhetoric but with the action "generated inside the characters...Mark Twain seems not to have been wholly conscious of what he had done; for he never did it again." He was "a forerunner who set an example which was not necessarily an influence," and "the shift from the rhetorical mode to the dialectical mode had to be rediscovered by the twentieth-century novelists of the South." (The date "1959" appears at the end, but there is no indication of where this was previously published.)

B104 TATHAM, CAMPBELL. "'Dismal and Lonesome' A New Look at Huckleberry Finn," Modern Fiction Studies, XIV (Spring), 47-55.
    "The Huck Finn who takes part in the events at the Phelps farm is a logical projection of the Huck Finn who at three crucial moments based his actions on his pathological fear of loneliness and his personal need for acceptance and comfort. The book ends where it began because that is what the book is all about. Twain simply did not have the confidence in man's ability to effect a moral progression to pose Huck as a conventional hero"; this reflects the outlook MT expressed in What Is Man? Abstract in AES, XII (1969), 1260; reprinted in Twainian, XXIX (January-February, 1970). Abstract by Tatham in ALA, II (December), 57-58.

B105 TIECK, WILLIAM A. Riverdale, Kingsbridge, Spuyten Duyvil: A Historical Epitome of the Northwest Bronx. Old Tappan, New Jersey: Fleming H. Revell Company.
    On "Wave Hill," the Riverdale house MT rented, with photograph of the house, pp. 53-54.

B106 TRACY, ROBERT. "Myth and Reality in The Adventures of Tom Sawyer," Southern Review, n.s. IV (April), 530-41.
    In TS "Mark Twain attempts a subtle interplay of reality, bookish romance, and myth in order to express an ambiguous attitude to both American civilization and the savage American wilderness." Tom expresses both freedom and conformity, and MT conceals the evasion through melodrama.

B107 TURNER, ARLIN. "Mark Twain and the South: An Affair of Love and Anger," Southern Review, n.s. IV (April), 493-519.

MT criticized in the South what he saw in mankind, but more severely because the blame lay nearer himself. There is extensive discussion of MT's maturing views on race, the influence of Cable, and the treatment of Southern themes in MT's works, especially in PW. The part on PW is reprinted in Schmitter (1974), pp. 123-32.

B108   . [Review article.] South Atlantic Quarterly, LXVII (Summer), 566-67.
    John S. Tuckey, Mark Twain's "Which Was the Dream?" And Other Symbolic Writings of the Later Years (1966) shows the editor's conviction that MT retained his creative powers; Franklin R. Rogers, ed., Mark Twain's Satires and Burlesques (1967) shows MT's fondness for the mode and insists perhaps too emphatically on the influence of burlesque in shaping his satire; Hamlin Hill, ed., Mark Twain's Letters to His Publishers, 1867-1894 (1967) "provides sounder bases than we have ever had for judging the wrath Mark Twain poured upon his publishers."

B109 *TURNER, MARTHA ANNE. "Was Frank Dobie a Throwback to Mark Twain?" Western Review, V (Winter), 3-12.
    [Source: MHRA Annual Bibliography (1968), No. 7776.]

B110 VANDERSEE, CHARLES. "The Mutual Awareness of Mark Twain and Henry Adams," English Language Notes, V (June), 285-92.
    Joseph Gilder's "Glimpses of John Hay" (Critic, XLVII [September, 1905], 248) records a meeting in January, 1886 between Adams (then depressed over his wife's recent suicide) and MT; although a closer acquaintance failed to develop, references by the two to each other are favorable and Gilder's recollection "does seem to establish that the two were more at ease than 'at odds' with each other. And the clear awareness that each man had of the other forms a more solid basis on which to study further the analogies in their thought and art." Abstract in AES, XII (1969), 1518; reprinted in Twainian, XXIX (January-February, 1970). Abstract by Vandersee in ALA, II (December), 58.

B111 WAGER, WILLIS. "Mainly the Novel, Amateur to Professional: Twain to James," in his American Literature: A World View (New York: New York University Press, and London: University of London Press, Limited), pp. 129-84 (On MT, pp. 131-39).
    A solid general study, providing no new information or interpretation.

B112 WALKER, I. M. [Review: James M. Cox, Mark Twain: The Fate of Humor (1966).] Review of English Studies, n.s., XIX (August), 331-32.
    "It is the development and final betrayal of Mark Twain's identity as a humorous writer that Professor James Cox argues in this

(WALKER, I. M.)
stimulating and often persuasive book....
It is...in his discussion of Twain's satire
that Mr. Cox is least satisfactory," and
the fact explains "his failure fully to
come to terms with Huckleberry Finn, for
the novel involves satiric dimensions
which he virtually ignores. Nevertheless
he has written a valuable and suggestive
study which deserves careful reading."

B113 WARD, HARRY M. [Review: Edward Wagenknecht,
Mark Twain: The Man and His Work (1967).]
Journal of the West, VII (October), 573.
Chiefly descriptive. "If the author
might have given more weight to the Gilded
Age and the travel books as self-revealing
of the man, he has, nevertheless, given us
a sharper glance of Twain through his
dichotomous character."

B114 WEEKS, LEWIS E., JR. "Mark Twain and Hemingway: 'A Catastrophe' and 'A Natural History of the Dead,'" Mark Twain Journal,
XIV (Summer), 15-17.
The descriptions of makeshift hospitals
by MT in LOM and by Hemingway are similar
in circumstances but different in that MT
is merely reporting, without advancing a
thesis.... "In some ways, too, Twain's writing in this chapter is ironically similar
to the very style and treatment that Hemingway is satirizing."

B115 WELSH, JOHN R. [Review: Sydney J. Krause,
Mark Twain as Critic.] Georgia Review,
XXIII (Summer), 244-45.
Chiefly descriptive, but suggests the
book "could stand some tightening up, for
it occasionally borders on the tedious";
by undue emphasis on the critic as "muggins" and "grumbler," Krause fails to show
how these masks related to the unmasked
critic.

B116 WILSON, EDMUND. "The Fruits of the MLA: II.
Mark Twain," New York Review of Books, XI
(October 10), 6-14.
On the University of California edition
of the MT Papers and works, which are useful to the biographer; but the vastness of
the project is essentially "boondoggling."
In passing, notes "the serious shortcomings" of Justin Kaplan's Mr. Clemens and
Mark Twain," which "rather indecently" ignores the work of Brooks, Dixon Wecter, and
Effie Mona Mack. For what made MT attractive to his public "we are obliged to go
back to Albert Payson Terhune's [sic] old
biography, written in the spirit of the
period."

B117 WINTERICH, JOHN T. "Missouri Yankee: Mark
Twain," in his Writers in America 1842-
1967: An Informal Glance at Some of the
Authors Who Have Flourished Since the Establishment of the Davey Company One Hundred

and Twenty-Five Years Ago (Jersey City,
N.J.: The Davey Company), pp. 55-59.
A general discussion to entertain the general reader. The book is a gift volume to
celebrate the 125th anniversary of a firm
manufacturing binder's board for the book
industry.

B118 WYSONG, JACK P. "Samuel Clemens' Attitude
Toward the Negro as Demonstrated in Pudd'n-
head Wilson and A Connecticut Yankee in
King Arthur's Court," Xavier University
Studies, VII (July), 41-57.
The difference in the portrayal of slaves
in the two books lies in the fact that in
CY they are white, and they show courage and
the ability to benefit from education. "In
Pudd'nhead Wilson we see that all Negroes
steal and are humble.... All whites are in-
herently noble and magnanimous," and even
Tom and Chambers, though exchanged, act ac-
cording to their race. The contrast with
CY strengthens the evidence that MT retained
the racial attitudes of his youth.

1969 A BOOKS

A1 CLEMENS, SAMUEL L. Clemens of the "Call":
Mark Twain in San Francisco, ed. Edgar M.
Branch. Berkeley and Los Angeles: University of California Press.
A selection of 200 contributions by MT
during his four months' employment on the
San Francisco Daily Morning Call in 1864;
arranged topically rather than chronologically.

A2 _____. Mark Twain's Correspondence with Henry
Huttleston Rogers, 1893-1909, ed. Lewis
Leary. Berkeley and Los Angeles: University
of California Press.
A volume in the CEAA edition of the MT
Papers. Continues the account of MT's business affairs from where Hamlin Hill left it
in Mark Twain's Letters to His Publishers,
1867-1894 (1967), and also "illuminates a
friendship which Clemens came to value
above all others, and...suggests a profound
change in his patterns of living," from that
of family man to a life more like that of
the California and Nevada days, as "a man
among sporting men."

A3 _____. Mark Twain's Hannibal, Huck & Tom,
ed. Walter Blair. Berkeley and Los Angeles:
University of California Press.
A volume in the CEAA edition of the MT
Papers, consisting of unpublished material
on Hannibal and the villagers, and manu-
script material dealing with Huck and Tom;
includes the texts of Huck Finn and Tom
Sawyer Among the Indians, and Tom Sawyer:
A Play.

A4   _____. Mark Twain's Mysterious Stranger Manuscripts, ed. William M. Gibson. Berkeley
and Los Angeles: University of California
Press.
    A volume in the CEAA edition of the MT
Papers. Presents, meticulously edited, the
texts of the manuscript material from which
Albert Bigelow Paine and Frederick A. Duneka assembled their "editorial fraud," the
1916 edition of MS.

A5   ENSOR, ALLISON. Mark Twain and the Bible.
Lexington: University of Kentucky Press.
    MT knew the Bible well, "raged against it
as wicked, obscene, and damnatory; but he
could never ignore it.... It has often
been recognized that Twain was more influenced by the Bible than by any other book
and that he drew upon it uniquely for
ideas, subjects, and imagery.... During
two periods of his life he made extensive
use of it: in his Quaker City excursion to
the Holy Land and his courtship of Olivia
Langdon, roughly 1867-1870, and in the final
years of his life, roughly 1893-1909, when
biblical fantasies and criticism flowed
freely from his pen" (pp. 1-2). Reviews are
summarized by Elmer F. Suderman in ALA, IV
(June, 1971), 117-18.

A6   SCOTT, ARTHUR L. Mark Twain at Large. Chicago: Henry Regnery Company.
    "This book is about Mark Twain's travels
and his opinions concerning the entire foreign scene. The fun-loving Westerner of
1867 slowly grew into the international
personage of 1897.... He had not become
global in his fame without becoming global
in his thinking as well. And because Mark
Twain symbolized the American spirit to
millions of people the world over, his
voice seemed truly to be that of an unofficial Ambassador.... How Mark Twain became such an Ambassador-at-Large and finally a kind of oracle and how he served in
these capacities are the subjects of the
present study" (Preface, vii).

A7   SELBY, P. O. Chronology of the Life of Mark
Twain. Kirksville: Missouriana Library,
Northeast Missouri State College.
    Lists a number of events in MT's life and
publications of works, by dates. The
sources are in a list at the end, and include familiar works on MT, but sources for
individual dates are not given. [Mimeo-
graphed 67-page pamphlet.]

A8   _____. Mark Twain Namesakes and Memorials.
Kirksville: Missouriana Library, Northeast
Missouri State College.
    A letter received from Dr. Selby explains
the method of compilation: "To make a list
of Mark Twain's namesakes and memorials, I
wrote to superintendents of public instruc-
tion in the various states to get information about schools named for Mark Twain.

I examined city directories in a hundred
cities to see where the name Mark Twain was
being used. And I have visited Hannibal,
Hartford, Redding, Elmira, and Jackass Hill,
where he lived." [Mimeographed 5-page pamphlet.]

A9   WALKER, FRANKLIN. San Francisco's Literary
Frontier. Seattle and London: University
of Washington Press.
    The 1939 edition, with corrections and a
new introduction by the author. On MT in
California and Nevada, his travels, and his
later writings, passim (indexed).

A10   WILSON, WILLARD. Mark Twain Returns to Hawaii.
Honolulu: University of Hawaii Press.
    Contains facsimile reproductions of MT
letters to Gilder (July 8, 1900) and to
Frank E. Bliss (February 2, 1900, about the
forthcoming uniform edition of his works,
and the importance of having Brander Matthews do the "re-arranging"). The "return"
consisted of the acquisition of these two
letters and a first edition of TS. [15-
page pamphlet.]

1969 B SHORTER WRITINGS

B1   ALLEN, WALTER. The Urgent West: The American
Dream and Modern Man. New York: E. P. Dutton & Co., Inc., pp. 168-79 and passim.
    MT brought native American speech to lit-
erature, preparing the way for writers who
have followed. He was influenced by Calvinism, his mother, and his wife (whose literary influence was negative), but in HF he
wrote "the classic of boyhood everywhere.
It dramatises every man's dream of freedom"
(p. 172). "Huck's sweetness of mind and
common sense, which is the product of seeing
truly, irradiate the book. He is, in fact,
that rarest of characters in fiction, the
human being who convinces us as being positively good" (p. 177).

B2   ANDERSON, KENNETH. "The Ending of Mark
Twain's A Connecticut Yankee in King Arthur's Court," Mark Twain Journal, XIV
(Summer), 21.
    As a metaphor, the ending can be taken as
a statement of "an unknown character (fate,
determinism, or something in human nature)
which works against human aspirations and
thereby corrupts and destroys them." "On
an artistic level, the melodramatic ending
...fails to provide the reader with the
author's ultimate judgment of Hank Morgan,"
who appears as both liberator and dictator,
the dichotomy making him an ultimately tragic figure, "but the nature and intensity of
that tragedy are never defined."

B3   ANON. "Clemens, S. L.," in American Literature Abstracts, II (June), 250-53 (also includes a survey by Warren B. Benson of reviews of Krause, Mark Twain as Critic
[1967], 337-39); III (December), 21-23.

1969 - Shorter Writings

(ANON.)
Abstracts of several journal articles on MT; the abstracts are longer than in the present bibliography and a number of them are by the authors themselves.

B4   ANON.   "'Huck Finn' Banned from Reading List," Philadelphia Evening Bulletin, January 15, p. 12.
An Associated Press dispatch on the dropping of HF from the required reading list at Miami Dade Junior College, Florida because of complaints by Black students.

B5   ANON.   "Mark Twain Items Published Elsewhere," Twainian, XXVIII (January-February), 1-4; (March-April), 4.
Reprints a number of abstracts of material about MT or mentioning him in passing, from AES, XI (1968) and three from AES, X (1967). Abstracts in AES, XIV (1970-1971), 593, 594.

B6   ANON.   "Samuel L(anghorne) Clemens (1835-1910), (Mark Twain)," in The American Writer in England: An Exhibition Arranged in Honor of the Sesquicentennial of the University of Virginia, with a Foreword by Gordon N. Ray and an Introduction by C. Waller Barrett (Charlottesville: The University Press of Virginia), pp. 69-75.
A list of some first editions, inscriptions, text of a previously unpublished letter inviting Charles Kingsley and his family for a visit (February 13, 1874), and reproductions of a caricature of MT by "Fudge" and an oil portrait of him in his Oxford robe by Mrs. Edward A. Ward.

B7   BABCOCK, C. MERTON.   "'Dusting Off' Mark Twain, the Incorrigible," New England Galaxy (Old Sturbridge, Inc., Sturbridge, Massachusetts), XXX (Winter), 3-8.
A popular account of MT's courting Olivia Langdon, and her later trials with his profanity and her editing of his manuscripts; undocumented, this adds nothing to material available from familiar sources.

B8   BANTA, MARTHA.   "Rebirth or Revenge: The Endings of Huckleberry Finn and The American," Modern Fiction Studies, XV (Summer), 191-207.
"Huck Finn and Christopher Newman meet head-on with the forces of conscience well past mid-way in their quests," and neither heaven nor Claire de Cintré is a real loss; both heroes make the decisions that result in personal satisfaction. Abstract in AES, XIII (1969-70), 2075; reprinted in Twainian, XXX (January-February, 1971). Abstract by Banta in ALA, III (December), 21.

B9   BARSNESS, JOHN A.   "Platform Manner in the Novel: A View from the Pit," Midcontinent American Studies Journal, X (Fall), 49-56.
MT's early works reveal the style of the platform, often with "scarcely any change from the lecture to the printed page"; consciousness of the created persona continues in HF, CY, MS, and other works. Abstract by Barsness in ALA, IV (December, 1970), 22.

B10   BIRCHFIELD, JAMES.   "Jim's Coat of Arms," Mark Twain Journal, XIV (Summer), 15-16.
MT's criticism of romantic foolishness appears often in HF, where the wrecked steamboat is named the Walter Scott, and Tom and Huck both display "unlikely bits of historical and antiquarian book learning." Tom Sawyer's confused description of a coat of arms shows him "possessed by the aristocratic delusions which infect the South...fascinated by the ceremony, the trappings and externalities of the chivalric code"; Huck, on the other hand, thinks of the old nobility as "regular rapscallions."

B11   BRADBURY, MALCOLM.   "Mark Twain in the Gilded Age," Critical Quarterly, XI (Spring), 65-73.
Surveys recent criticism of MT and takes issue with the excessive emphasis on psychology; describes MT as "very much at the centre of the Gilded Age, in all its energies and contradictions, and he is surely very much made by the literary and professional opportunities it threw up--for, like Dickens, Twain very much created himself against a newly emerging audience." Abstract in AES, XIII (1969-1970), 1024; reprinted in Twainian, XIX (January-February, 1970). Abstract by Bradbury in ALA, III (December), 21-22.

B12   BRANCH, EDGAR M.   "Mark Twain Reports the Races in Sacramento," Huntington Library Quarterly, XXXII (February), 179-86.
On MT's attendance at the Thirteenth Annual Fair of the California State Agricultural Society, with reprinted passages from the Sacramento Daily Union of September 13 and 14, 1866; though unsigned, they "have the familiar ring of Mark Twain's early manner and the stamp of his imagination."

B13   BUNGERT, HANS.   [Review: Bernard Poli, Mark Twain, Écrivain de l'Ouest: Régionalisme et Humour (1965).] Archiv für das Studium der neuren Sprachen und Literatur, CCV, 405-407.
Notes Poli's contention that Hannibal, Virginia City, and the Mississippi are central to MT's best work, and that it was between 1870 and 1885 that his great work was possible. [In German.]

B14   *BUTCHER, PHILIP.   "'The God-fathership' of A Connecticut Yankee," College Language Association Journal, XII (March), 189-98. [Source: MHRA Annual Bibliography (1969), Nos. 6358, 7929.
A lengthy abstract by Butcher in ALA, III (December), 22 says that the inspiration was

(BUTCHER, PHILIP)
considerably broader than George Washington
Cable's giving him a copy of Malory's Morte
D'Arthur, as Cable claimed after MT's death
(later supported by Paine). Citing notebook entries, Butcher concedes that MT indeed drew on Malory, but also on "articles
on contemporary Russia and a book on slavery
in the United States.... So conscious was
he of the multitude of influences that
helped to shape his book and so disenchanted
did he become with Cable that he refrained
from conferring on him in public the honor
of 'the godfathership.'"] Also abstracted
in AES, XIX (1975-1976), 236.

B15   _____. "Mark Twain's Installment on the National Debt," Southern Literary Journal, I
(Spring), 48-55.
On MT's concern over the injustice done
Negroes by slavery and racism; traces the
career of Warner Thornton McGuinn, whose
expenses he paid at Yale Law School.

B16   CARSON, HERBERT L. "Mark Twain's Misanthro-
py," Cresset, XXXIII (December), 13-15.
"According to Twain, all of mankind is
sick, and that sickness is his normal condition." MT had something of Huck's sensitivity, but the sheltered world of the raft
could not last.

B17   CECIL, L. MOFFITT. "Tom Sawyer: Missouri
Robin Hood," Western American Literature,
IV (Summer), 125-31.
Like Robin Hood, Tom successfully stands
against the establishment (p. 130). "Tom
Sawyer is a better book, a truer book, than
The Mysterious Stranger. It is Mark
Twain's happiest and most hopeful novel"
(p. 131). Abstract in AES, XV (1971-1972),
536; reprinted in Twainian, XXXII (January-
February, 1973). Abstract by Cecil in ALA,
III (June, 1970), 113-14.

B18   CHELLIS, BARBARA A. "Those Extraordinary
Twins: Negroes and Whites," American Quarterly, XXI (Spring), 100-12.
On racial themes in Pudd'nhead Wilson:
the real Tom Driscoll, though completely
white, acquired all the characteristics of
a slave from his twenty-three years of slavery, while Valet de Chambers, taking his
place, learned hatred of the Negro. Roxy,
though a slave, has learned the values of
the community and she largely accepts them.
Abstract by Chellis in ALA, III (December),
22.

B19   COARD, ROBERT L. "Huck Finn and Mr. Mark
Twain Rhyme," Midwest Quarterly, X (July),
317-29.
"A study of Huck Finn's rhymes, placed in
the larger context of Mark Twain's rhymes
in his other prose, should shed considerable light on the exuberant word-play that,
perhaps as much as any unified theme,

helped to shape an American masterpiece."
Abstract by Coard in ALA, III (June, 1970),
114.

B20   [DAVIS, CHESTER L.] "Life, Letters and Journals of George Ticknor," Twainian, XXVIII
(January-February), 4; (March-April), 1-4;
(May-June), 1-4; (July-August), 1-4; (September-October), 1-4; (November-December),
1-4.
Continues a series of MT's underlinings
and marginal annotations in this two-volume
work; series begins July-August, 1968.
Abstracts in AES, XIV (1970-1971), 586-592;
reprinted in Twainian, XXXI (January-February, 1972).

B21   DUCKETT, MARGARET. [Review: Fred W. Lorch,
The Trouble Begins at Eight (1868).] Western Humanities Review, XXIII (Summer),
175-76.
Lorch is justified in asserting that MT
was one of the most successful of American
lecturers and that he owed his fame more
to his lectures than to his writing. Although this book covers much the same ground
as Fatout's Mark Twain on the Lecture Circuit (1960), uses the same sources, and
reaches similar conclusions, the focus here
is on "physical appearance, mannerisms,
voice inflection, and carefully calculated
emphases and pauses." Structural weaknesses
in the book lead to repetitiousness, but the
reworking of old ground has produced "valuable nuggets."

B22   ENSOR, ALLISON R. "The Birthplace of Samuel
Clemens: A New Mark Twain Letter," Tennessee Studies in Literature, XIV, 31-34.
Text of MT's note to George H. Morgan (December 16, 1882), correcting the story told
in Tennessee that he was born in either
Gainesboro or Jamestown, Tennessee, rather
than Florida, Missouri; MT enclosed a reprint of a biographical sketch from the
British reference work, The Men of the Time.
Abstract by Ensor in MLA Abstracts (1970),
6774.

B23   _____. "The Location of the Phelps Farm in
Huckleberry Finn," South Atlantic Bulletin,
XXXIV (May), 7.
After summarizing guesses by various schol-
ars, concludes "that Pikesville and the
Phelps farm are located in the extreme
southeastern part of Arkansas," citing MT's
Autobiography and TS, Detective. Abstract
in AES, XV (1971-1972), 3022; reprinted in
Twainian, XXXII (January-February, 1973).

B24   FREDERICK, JOHN T. "Mark Twain," in his The
Darkened Sky: Nineteenth-Century American
Novelists and Religion (Notre Dame, London:
University of Notre Dame Press), pp. 123-76.
"Closely examined...the evidence fails to
support the legend that Calvinism had a trau-
matic impact on Mark Twain in childhood"
(p. 129).

B25 GARDNER, JOSEPH H. "Mark Twain and Dickens,"
     Publications of the Modern Language Associ-
     ation, LXXXIV (January), 90-101.
          Traces a thorough familiarity with Dick-
     ens from MT's youth; fear of him as a rival
     made MT reluctant to praise Dickens or ex-
     press critical judgments. Abstract in AES,
     XIII (1969-70), 229 (condensed from Gard-
     ner's own abstract on contents page); re-
     printed in Twainian, XXIX (January-February,
     1970).

B26 GIBSON, WILLIAM M. [Review: Fred W. Lorch,
     The Trouble Begins at Eight: Mark Twain's
     Lecture Tours (1968).] American Litera-
     ture, XLI (November), 440-41.
          Lorch wrote this book independently of
     Fatout's Mark Twain on the Lecture Circuit
     (1960), "a more truly critical work"; but
     the two books are complementary. "Lorch
     is interesting...for a group of analytic
     concluding chapters on platform manners
     and techniques, the vexed question of sub-
     stance versus manner, good and bad audi-
     ences, and profits," and he has reconstruct-
     ed texts of tour lectures from various news-
     paper sources.

B27 GLICK, WENDELL. "The Epistomelogical Theme
     of The Mysterious Stranger," in Ray B.
     Browne and Donald Pizer, eds. Themes and
     Directions in American Literature (West
     Lafayette, Indiana: Purdue University
     Studies), pp. 130-47.
          "The bitterness...derives, not so much
     from Twain's conviction that man is irra-
     tional, as from Twain's impatience with
     man's presumption that he is not" (p. 130).
     "To argue as this paper does that Twain's
     theme is the ubiquitous twentieth century
     idea of the breakdown of epistomelogical
     certainty is to argue for a continuity in
     Twain's thought between The Adventures of
     Huckleberry Finn and The Mysterious Strang-
     er and for the emergence of similar episto-
     melogical themes in the two works" (p. 131).

B28 GREENAGEL, FRANK J. [Review: Dewey Ganzel,
     Mark Twain Abroad: The Cruise of the
     "Quaker City."] Quarterly Journal of
     Speech, LV (April), 204.
          "The reconstruction of the journey is
     thorough, and only occasionally tedious,"
     although MT never comes to life. The in-
     fluence of Mary Mason Fairbanks is treated
     with unusual perception, and there is good
     analysis of MT's use of guidebooks, "al-
     though Ganzel curiously omitted any dis-
     cussion of two apparent sources [not here
     identified] of Twain's often-quoted descrip-
     tion of the Sphinx."

B29 *GREGORY, RALPH. "John A. Quarles: Mark
     Twain's Ideal Man," Missouri Historical
     Society Bulletin, XXV (April), 229-35.
          On the influence of the uncle with whom
     MT spent two or three months a year, as a
     boy. Quarles was known for his freethink-

ing and story-telling, and may even have
been a source for the "Jumping Frog."
[Source: Abstract in AES, XVI (1972-1973),
1773; reprinted in Twainian, XXXIII (January-February, 1974.)]

B30 HARWOOD, C. EDWIN. "Twain's Huckleberry Finn,
     Chapter XIV," Explicator, XXVIII (December),
     Item 36.
          The debate between Huck and Jim on why a
     Frenchman speaks French is "no digression
     at all but an ingenious statement of a main
     theme of the book...the brotherhood of man."
     The insight revealing the point was that of
     Miss Laura Helton, while writing an examina-
     tion.

B31 HILFER, ANTHONY CHANNELL. "Mark Twain: The
     Southwest and the Satirist," in his The
     Revolt from the Village 1915-1930 (Chapel
     Hill: The University of North Carolina
     Press), pp. 64-83.
          "Twain's conception is that what holds
     the small town together is communal fear....
     No later writer surpassed the ferocity of
     Twain's assault on the conformist mass
     mind" (p. 83). Hilfer shows complete fam-
     iliarity with the work of Neider, Brooks,
     DeVoto, Kaplan, and other students of Mark
     Twain, but adds comparatively little to
     this secondary material.

B32 HILL, HAMLIN. "Mark Twain," in J. Albert
     Robbins, ed., American Literary Scholarship:
     An Annual/1969 (Durham, North Carolina:
     Duke University Press, 1971), pp. 77-88.
          A survey of MT scholarship for the year,
     begun by John C. Gerber in 1963.B32 and con-
     tinued by him through coverage for 1968.
     Contents: "i. Textual and Bibliographical";
     "ii. Biography"; "iii. General Criticism";
     "iv. Earlier Works"; "v. Huckleberry Finn";
     "vi. Later Works." [Contains material not
     listed in the present bibliography.]

B33 _____. [Review: Leah A. Strong, Joseph Hop-
     kins Twichell: Mark Twain's Friend and
     Pastor (1967).] American Literary Realism,
     1867-1910, I (Spring), 97-98.
          "Miss Strong's bibliographical record is
     scanty. She ignores a multitude of histori-
     cal information published since she first
     explored this topic in her 1953 doctoral
     dissertation. No use whatsoever is made of
     the Mark Twain-Howells Letters, for example,
     nor of the unpublished storehouse in the
     Mark Twain Papers at Berkeley. Although
     the Yale University holdings of Twichell
     papers (which includes seventy letters from
     Twain to Twichell) are included in the bib-
     liography, no quotation, paraphrase, or
     reference is made based upon them." The
     evidence that Twichell influenced MT's
     writing is tenuous at best, and in any case
     "if the friendship between Twain and Twich-
     ell deserves study, it is for biographical
     and psychological reasons, not literary
     ones."

B34 HOFFMANN, MICHAEL J. "Huck's Ironic Circle," Georgia Review, XXIII (Fall), 307-22.
     HF "is not a novel about a boy's moral awakening, nor a polemic against slavery, nor a book about how good instincts are stronger than an evil society. We have always overestimated Huck Finn and have likewise underestimated his creator.... The dynamic theme that runs throughout Huckleberry Finn is an unresolved dialectic between the moral responsibility of the individual and the morality of the society in which he moves and against which he must function." Huck does not share the perceptiveness of MT and the reader; he never truly learns to regard Jim as an equal, but believes in property rights and the institution of slavery, and he follows the leadership of Tom Sawyer. The ending is consistent with this unimaginative Huck: "The irony of the book has now come full circle in that Huck has not rejected society's standards at all. He just feels personally inconvenienced by things like school, and clothes. But he still believes just as strongly that society is right."

B35 JAMES, STUART B. "The Politics of Personal Salvation: The American Literary Record," Denver Quarterly, IV (Autumn), 19-45.
     On Huck Finn as "another Tocquevillean democrat...yet another American fictional character at odds with and fleeing from the culture in which he grew up. But when we ask the question, What are his responsibilities to this culture, we hit a snag," because of its nature as a brutalizing, slave-holding society. There is a danger however, that such portraits of society by MT and others will breed in the young contempt for all laws and encourage the "very idealistic and self-righteous role of the Holy Revolutionary"; Huck's answer was to escape, deserting Jim (pp. 34-39). Abstract in AES, XIII (1969-1970), 2734; reprinted in Twainian, XXX (January-February, 1971).

B36 KAHN, SHOLOM J. "The Real Mark Twain: School of Tuckey," Jahrbuch für Amerikastudien, XIV, 301-307.
     A review-article, on Hamlin Hill, ed., Mark Twain's Letters to His Publishers, 1867-1894 (1967); Franklin A. Rogers, ed., Mark Twain's Satires and Burlesques (1967); John S. Tuckey, ed., Mark Twain's "Which Was the Dream?" (1967). Contains comparatively little on the editing and criticism, though hailing Tuckey's volume as the most important of the three: "What not enough of the Mark Twain scholars seem to realize is that Tuckey's findings render obsolete most of the earlier criticisms of The Mysterious Stranger and other later writings." Kahn's main emphasis is on MT's works, as here revealed and as seen by the critics; publication of full and reliable editions of MT will force reassessment, and Tuckey does much to point the way.

B37 KAPLAN, JUSTIN. "Never Quite Sane in the Night," Psychoanalytic Review, LVI (Spring), 113-27.
     On MT's self-castigation, given focus by the death of his daughter Susan. [From Chapter XVI of the 1968 Pocket Book edition of Mr. Clemens and Mark Twain, pp. 396-412.]

B38 KIRKHAM, E. BRUCE. "Huck and Hamlet: An Examination of Twain's Use of Shakespeare," Mark Twain Journal, XIV (Summer), 17-19.
     The Duke's speech in Chapter XXI combines garbled lines from Hamlet and Macbeth, in which "indecision...prevents Hamlet from acting when he should and keeps Macbeth from acting when he shouldn't," and from Richard III, in which Richard acts without regard for moral questions. As a confidence man, the Duke "is required to have the ability to shift ground on a moment's notice and channel his activities in another vein," and he is a man of action, in contrast to the passive Huck. "It is ironic that a man with his moral character on the raft should give the very moral advice that Huck, the innocent aboard, most needs," but "after Huck has heard and memorized the speech on action from 'Hamlet,'" after he has seen the Duke operate on the Wilkses and Jim sold into slavery again, he...rebels against his environment...and says he will 'go to work and steal Jim out of slavery again.'"

B39 KOLB, HAROLD H., JR. The Illusion of Life: American Realism as a Literary Form. Charlottesville: The University Press of Virginia, passim.
     On realism in the works of MT, Howells, and Henry James. The extensive listing of MT in the index includes such topics as point of view, author-narrator, complexity, ambiguity, morality, and Huck's pragmatism and his freedom.

B40 KRUSE, HORST H. "'Gatsby' and 'Gadsby,'" Modern Fiction Studies, XV (Winter), 539-41.
     The name "Gatsby" may derive from a Washington, D.C. hotel-owner named "Gadsby" in TA; "Although there is no direct evidence that Fitzgerald read A Tramp Abroad," he is known to have been "a lifelong admirer of Mark Twain."

B41 LEHAN, RICHARD. [Review: Dewey Ganzel, Mark Twain Abroad (1968); Sydney J. Krause, Mark Twain as Critic (1967); and Fred W. Lorch, The Trouble Begins at Eight (1968).] Nineteenth-Century Fiction, XXIV (December), 377.
     Brief and descriptive, with a short commendation of the usefulness of each book.

B42 LONG, ROBERT EMMET. [Review: Lewis Leary, ed., Mark Twain's Correspondence with Henry Huttleston Rogers; Walter Blair, ed., Mark Twain's Hannibal, Huck & Tom; William M. Gibson, ed., Mark Twain's Mysterious Stranger Manuscripts.] Saturday Review, LII (June 21), 49-50.

(LONG, ROBERT EMMET)
"One has the impression...that this edition answers a need for enlarged information about its subject, but that there is nothing about it to suggest an urgency such as to pre-empt the editions of American authors proposed by Edmund Wilson." [See Wilson's "The Fruits of the MLA," 1968.] The three volumes are described, favorably, but "the scholarship that went into them is far more impressive than the revelations they contain."

B43 M McELDERRY, BRUCE R., JR. [Review: James Playstead Wood, Spunkwater, Spunkwater! A Life of Mark Twain (1968).] Modern Fiction Studies, XV (Winter), 554.
"A commendable simplification...as the younger reader proceeds to a mature interest in the author, there is little that he will have to unlearn. In fact, the scholar may spend a pleasant hour with this volume."

B44 MARTIN, JAY. "Mark Twain: The Fate of Primitivity," Southern Literary Journal, II (Fall), 123-37.
A review article, covering Walter Blair, ed., Mark Twain's Hannibal, Huck & Tom (briefly described); William M. Gibson, ed., Mark Twain's Mysterious Stranger Manuscripts (briefly described); Allison R. Ensor, Mark Twain and the Bible ("Ensor writes well and almost entirely avoids the pedantry which such studies threaten," but he misunderstands MT's awareness that unorthodoxy was a saleable commodity); Lewis Leary, ed., Mark Twain's Correspondence with Henry Huttleston Rogers (described); and Arthur L. Scott, Mark Twain at Large ("A remarkably detailed account not only of Twain's travel writing but also of the special place which the non-American scene occupied in his imagination." Unfortunately, Scott over-simplifies, and "there is reason to suspect that he has not kept pace with the recent Mark Twain studies--his notes refer to few works published after 1960--which have made his simple view an old-fashioned one.")

B45 MASEFIELD, JOHN. [Holograph note reproduced in facsimile.] Mark Twain Journal, XIV (Summer), front cover.
On his delight in HF, which he has read at least once a year since he was fourteen.

B46 MEWS, SIEGFRIED. "German Reception of American Writers in the Nineteenth Century," South Atlantic Bulletin, XXXIV (March), 7-9.
Notes MT's great popularity in Germany, chiefly as a humorist rather than as a serious writer; not documented (pp. 8-9). Abstract in AES, XV (1971-1972), 3015; reprinted in Twainian, XXXII (January-February, 1973).

B47 MILLER, HENRY. The Books in My Life. New York: New Directions, pp. 41, 318.
Lists TS and HF among books he read as a boy and longs to re-read--along with Rider Haggard, G. A. Henty, Fenimore Cooper. [An earlier ed., undated, is mentioned by Walter Blair in Mark Twain and Huck Finn (1960), pp. 7, 390.]

B48 MORSBERGER, ROBERT E. "Pap Finn and the Bishop's Candlesticks: Victor Hugo in Hannibal," CEA Critic, XXXI (April), 17.
Jim's elaborate escape at the end of HF includes several elements borrowed from Dumas: from The Man in the Iron Mask, The Count of Monte Cristo, and Twenty Years After. Less evident is the conversion and downfall of Pap Finn, patterned on the conversion of Jean Valjean in Les Miserables. These incidents in HF parody their romantic models.

B49 *NAGEL, JAMES. "Huck Finn and The Bear: The Wilderness and Moral Freedom," English Studies in Africa, XII (March), 59-63.
Each work pairs an adult male with a young white boy, but Faulkner is less optimistic because the frontier has diminished. [Source: Abstract in AES, XIV (1970-1971), No. 1543; reprinted in Twainian, XXXI (January-February, 1972).]

B50 ORTH, MICHAEL. "Pudd'nhead Wilson Reconsidered; or, The Octoroon in the Villa Viviani," Mark Twain Journal, XIV (Summer), 11-15.
There are numerous parallels to the octoroon fiction from before the Civil War; even the device of the fingerprints is anticipated by the use of photography in Mayne Reid's The Quadroon (1856), and its dramatization by Dion Boucicault as The Octoroon (1859), and "in both cases the accidental discovery of the true identity of a murderer comes through the novel and scientific-gadgeteering hobby of a fool Yankee, who rights all wrongs by defending the innocent in a climactic trial at the end of the story." The novel has been overpraised, but it deserves critical attention for what it shows of MT's mind and art. Abstract by Orth in ALA, III (June, 1970), 114.

B51 PARSONS, COLEMAN O. "Down the Mighty River with Mark Twain," Mississippi Quarterly, XXII (Winter), 1-18.
On MT's 1882 trip to gather material for LOM. Abstract by Parsons in ALA, III (December), 22-23.

B52 PATRICK, WALTON R. [Review: Edward Wagenknecht, Mark Twain: The Man and His Work (Third Edition, 1967), and James M. Cox, Mark Twain: The Fate of Humor (1966).] Southern Humanities Review, III (Summer), 293-95.

(PATRICK, WALTON R.)
Wagenknecht's 1935 study, "substantially revised in 1960, has already won its place among reputable commentaries on Mark Twain," and this third edition is new chiefly in the updating of its "excellent bibliography." Cox, arguing that the "Mark Twain" pseudonym exposed and freed the writer in Clemens, passes too lightly over the fact that even some of MT's humorous works are poorly written; moreover, there is insufficient evidence to support the contention that MT's humor was frequently a compensation for his failings. It often appears "that any resemblance between the Mark Twain of Mr. Cox's book and the real Mark Twain is purely coincidental."

B53 PEDERSON, LEE A. "Mark Twain's Missouri Dialects: Marion County Phonemics," _American Speech_, XLII (December, 1967), 261-78.
A study based on tape-recorded interviews with six Caucasian and six Negro informants in 1964, using "more than 1,300 specific items, to which I added almost 300 words and phrases from the novel" (_HF_); the emphasis is on description of current speech rather than with MT's representation in _HF_. Abstract in _AES_, XIV (1970-71), 1544; reprinted in _Twainian_, XXXI (January-February, 1972).

B54 PETERSON, CLARENCE. [Brief Review: Justin Kaplan, _Mr. Clemens and Mark Twain_ (1968).] _Book World_ (Chicago _Tribune_), I (May 12), 19.
"Justin Kaplan's great biography...is available in paperback at last.... The book is so deeply researched and so intelligent that it stands as the definitive Clemens biography and it is almost as rich and readable as Twain himself."

B55 PICKETT, CALDER M. [Review: Edgar M. Branch, _Clemens of the "Call."_] _Journalism Quarterly_, XLVII (Summer), 383-84.
Descriptive and uncritical, except for observing that "It is a valuable compilation, even though it is something rather dull and a bit inconsequential"; this is not MT's best work and Branch's language is sometimes pedantic.

B56 _____. [Review: Justin Kaplan, ed., _Mark Twain: a Profile_ (1968) and Dewey Ganzel, _Mark Twain Abroad_ (1968).] _Journalism Quarterly_, XLVI (Summer), 385-86.
"Ganzel's book is always fun, but it's not Mark Twain.... this new book becomes mere recitation of what the travelers were doing and where they were at certain times," and shows that MT wrote differently, and for a wider audience, when he revised his travel letters into _IA_. Kaplan's collection of essays runs from the "slashing iconoclasm" of Dwight MacDonald to the "treacly" sentimentalism of Howells. "Most

of the essays are good," especially Kaplan's at the end, but they add little to our understanding of MT.

B57 _____. [Review: Arthur L. Scott, _Mark Twain at Large._] _Journalism Quarterly_, XLVI (Autumn), 628-29.
Brief summary. "Much has been done in recent years...on Mark Twain as world traveler-commentator. Here is one of the better books."

B58 POCHMANN, HENRY A., and GAY WILSON ALLEN. "Samuel L. Clemens (Mark Twain) (1835-1910)," in their _Introduction to Masters of American Literature_. Carbondale and Edwardsville: Southern Illinois University Press; London and Amsterdam: Feffer & Simons, Inc. [Copyright 1949 under the title _Masters of American Literature_.]
This book consists of the introductions in the two-volume anthology of 1949. The treatment of MT is a sound general discussion, and the titles of his works discussed are listed by page number in the index on p. 155.

B59 *POPA, IOAN. "Opera Nepublicată a lui Mark Twain" ["Mark Twain's Unpublished Works"], _Familia_, No. 5 (March), p. 15.
[Source: MHRA _Annual Bibliography_ (1969), No. 7976.]

B60 REES, ROBERT A., and RICHARD DILWORTH RUST. "Mark Twain's 'The Turning Point of My Life,'" _American Literature_, XL (January), 524-35.
On MT's last work written for publication; traces the extensive revisions after MT's daughter Jean and biographer Paine gave the first version a chilly reception which "brought Twain's acute self-criticism into play and caused him to discard a mediocre piece of writing and to turn out something fine instead." As published in _Harper's Bazaar_ it incorporated changes apparently made by editor Elizabeth Jordan to improve MT--as she did for letters of Henry James in the _Bazaar_. Abstract in _AES_, XIII (1969-1970), 1342; reprinted in _Twainian_, XXX (January-February, 1971).

B61 REEVES, PASCHAL, et al. "A Checklist of Scholarship on Southern Literature for 1969," _Mississippi Quarterly_, XXIII (Spring, 1970); on MT, pp. 189-93.
Annotated.

B62 REXROTH, KENNETH. "Mark Twain, _Huckleberry Finn_," in his _Classics Revisited_ (New York: Avon Books), pp. 280-85.
"Mark Twain's judgment of that life [on shore] is very different from Homer's, and not unlike that of Saint Paul in the _Book of the Acts of the Apostles_--if Saint Paul had been an atheist."

B63 RUBIN, LOUIS D., JR. "Mark Twain: The Adventures of Tom Sawyer," in Hennig Cohen, ed., Landmarks of American Writing (New York, London: Basic Books, Inc.), pp. 157-71. ["These essays were originally prepared for the Voice of America for presentation as lectures to audiences abroad through its Forum series" (p. x).]

TS would have made MT a reputation even without HF, which overshadows it. The presence of the adult storyteller in TS deprives us of Huck's voice but allows MT to provide a sense of time and its passage (p. 165).

B64 RULE, HENRY B. "The Role of Satan in The Man that Corrupted Hadleyburg," Studies in Short Fiction, VI (Fall), 619-29.

Traces MT's interest in Satan, then shows Satanic parallels to the stranger in Hadleyburg "(Hadesburg?)" and possible allegorical significance of the names of characters. Ultimately, "Satan is Hadleyburg's greatest benefactor," purging the town of hypocrisy. Abstract in AES, XIV (1970-1971), 1835; reprinted in Twainian, XXXI (January-February, 1972).

B65 SCOTT, ARTHUR L. [Review: Dewey Ganzel, Mark Twain Abroad: The Cruise of the "Quaker City" (1968).] American Literature, XLI (March), 124-25.

"A charming, informative volume, carefully researched and presented in an easy descriptive manner," useful both as an account of the trip and the passengers and for correcting misconceptions in the Paine biography and in studies of IA.

B66 SEELYE, JOHN. "'De Ole True Huck': An Introduction," Tri-Quarterly, XVI (Autumn), 5-19.

The introduction and the final chapters of Seelye's The True Adventures of Huckleberry Finn (1970). In the introduction Seelye summarizes objections to MT's HF by librarians, pressure groups, and critics; this version will retell the story as the "crickits" would have it. Abstract in AES, XV (1971-72), 2144.

B67 SPANGLER, GEORGE M. "Locating Hadleyburg," Mark Twain Journal, XIV (Summer), 20.

The theme of the story is not a Miltonic echo that untried virtue is meaningless; rather, "the tale demonstrates the distressingly crude proposition that all men have their price," and the real target is Gilded Age America. Abstract by Spangler in ALA, III (June, 1970), 114-15.

B68 SPENCER, BENJAMIN T. "Sherwood Anderson: American Mythopoetist," American Literature, XLI (March), 1-18.

Passing references to MT, pp. 4-6, noting the statements in Dark Laughter of regret that MT's America stunted his literary development and that his moving to the genteel East was an acquiescence. Abstract in AES,

XIII (1969-1970), 1365; reprinted in Twainian, XXX (January-February, 1971).

B69 STANDART, PHOEBE. "Introduction," in Your Personal Mark Twain: In Which the Great American Ventures an Opinion on Ladies, Language, Liberty, Literature, Liquor, Love, and Other Controversial Subjects (New York: International Publishers, and Berlin (D.D.R.): Seven Seas Books), pp. 9-14.

An East German anthology of short pieces by MT and selections from his works, very few of them with any political overtones whatever and none of them especially startling. Phoebe Standart's introduction stresses his personal humor and warmth, commenting only in passing on his social criticism. [In English.]

B70 *STARTSEV, A. [Introductory article to Russian translation of "The United Lynching States" ("The United States of Lyncherdom").] Moscow: Khudozhestvennaya Literatura.

[Source: MHRA Annual Bibliography (1970), No. 8284.]

B71 STERN, MADELEINE B. "Mark Twain Had His Head Examined," American Literature, XLI (May), 207-18.

On a phrenological examination of MT in 1901, probably by Dr. Edgar C. Beall, described in the Phrenological Journal and Science of Health, CXI (April, 1901), 103-106; following MT's death the Phrenological Journal paid tribute to his character as revealed in "the organs of Mirthfulness, Comparison, Combativeness, Benevolence, and Human Nature" [CXXIII (June, 1910), 190]. Both articles are here reprinted. Abstract in AES, XIII (1969-1970), 1345; reprinted in Twainian, XXX (January-February, 1971). Abstract by Stern in ALA, III (December), 23.

B72 STESSIN, LAWRENCE. "The Businessman in Fiction," Literary Review (Fairleigh Dickinson University), XII (Spring), 281-89.

A Professor of Management, Stessin complains against frequently unsympathetic portrayals and praises CY as an exception, "an imaginative chronicle in which the glorified days of knight errantry are exposed as a form of childish barbarism. Beneath a layer of wonderful wit, Twain defends the cause that a society which is not business and technology oriented leaves its people abused and impoverished.... Using the 4-M's of management—money, men, materials, and motivation—his protagonist, Hank Morgan, galvanizes the backward nation into a beehive of builders, whose collective handiwork appreciably raises the standard of living.... Hank Morgan anticipates the rise of the new professional manager who takes textbook examples of good management—direction, coordination, delegation, staffing, and control—and unifies them to bring both material and social wealth to society." Abstract in AES, XV (1971-72), 2243; reprinted in Twainian, XXXII (January-February, 1973).

B73 *SYKES, MADELENE McEUEN. "Mark Twain's Atti-
tudes Toward Women as Revealed Through His
Writings," Missouri English Bulletin, XXII
(May), 1-9.
[Source: MHRA Annual Bibliography
(1969), No. 7991.]

B74 TUCKEY, JOHN S. [Review: Fred W. Lorch, The
Trouble Begins at Eight (1968).] Journal
of Popular Culture, III (Summer), 172-74.
Compares Lorch's book with Paul Fatout's
Mark Twain on the Lecture Circuit. Lorch
provides the "comprehensive, unified discussion of the celebrated humorist's platform art, his theory of the humorous lecture, his theory and practice of the art of
reading, [and] the major critical apprais-
als of Mark Twain's lectures" which his review in American Literature (1962) accused
Fatout of neglecting. Tuckey notes the
value of this material, but also praises
"Mr. Fatout's more chronological and better
integrated narrative presentation." This
new book "does not supersede it," although
it "comes off very well as what it was intended to be, Fred Lorch's major contribution." Tuckey observes that Lorch mentions
Fatout's works in the bibliography but not
in his notes.

B75 *VALČEV, TODOR. [Introduction.] "Neugasnal
Vulkan" ["An Inextinct Volcano"], in Mark
Tven, Avtobiografija [Mark Twain's Auto-
biography]. Sofia: Narodna Mladež,
pp. 5-10.
[Source: MHRA Annual Bibliography
(1969), No. 7994.]

B76 VITELLI, JAMES R. Van Wyck Brooks. New
York: Twayne Publishers, Inc., pp. 38,
87-95, 113, and passim.
Mentions the attempt by Randolph Bourne
to persuade Brooks to revise his view of
American writers, and of MT in particular
(p. 38). On The Ordeal of Mark Twain,
pp. 87-95.

B77 WHITE, RAY LEWIS, ed. Sherwood Anderson's
Memoirs: A Critical Edition. Chapel Hill:
The University of North Carolina Press.
Passim on MT (indexed), whom Anderson
admired; on p. 342, describes HF as "that
amazingly beautiful book," but notes MT's
reticence concerning sex in his books.

B78 WILLIAMSON, JERRY M. "Winslow Homer and Mark
Twain," Mark Twain Journal, XIV (Summer),
2-7.
Compares them as local colorists, in attitudes toward the Negro, and in their
artistic careers, but gives no indication
they were aware of each other.

B79 ZARASPE, RAQUEL SIMS. "The Picaresque Tradition in Mark Twain," Diliman Review (University of the Philippines, Quezon City),
XVII (July), 218-43.

"The intention of this paper is to trace
the development of the picaresque hero in
Mark Twain." Contrasts Huck Finn with Hank
Morgan, who lacks Huck's ability to form
"a more vital and enduring fraternity with
Jim and the river." Shows parallels of
Spanish character types, values, and conditions in Lazarillo de Tormes and in TS, HF,
and CY. Abstract in AES, XIV (1970-1971),
2139; reprinted in Twainian, XXXI (March-
April, 1972).

B80 *ZIL!BERBROD, B. A. "Oblichenie Monarkhii
Dollara v Publitsistike Marka Tvena. (An
accusation of a dollar monarchy in the
journalistic writings of Mark Twain.)"
Vestnik Khar'kovskogo Universiteta, 1969
[Seriya Inostrannykh Yazykov] (2), pp. 26-30.
[Source: MHRA Annual Bibliography (1970),
No. 8295.]

1970 A BOOKS

A1 BAETZHOLD, HOWARD G. Mark Twain and John Bull:
The British Connection. Bloomington and
London: Indiana University Press.
Discusses MT's many visits to England, his
popular lectures there, the influence on him
of British thought and writing, and the
shifts in the warmth of his feelings toward
things British.

A2 BLUES, THOMAS. Mark Twain & the Community.
Lexington: The University Press of Kentucky.
In GA, TS, P&P, and HF the protagonists
are committed to the community although MT
repudiates its values and stability; he was
"deeply distrustful of the character and
fearful for the fate of the individual who
attempts to triumph over the community."
CY fails because MT could no longer use this
commitment as a structural device. In developing Hank Morgan, MT "faced the fact that
the individual is in no sense the superior
of the community he triumphs over," but the
community "is in no sense a worthy refuge
for the individual" (pp. x-xi).

A3 BROWNE, RAY B., ed. and introduction. Mark
Twain's Quarrel with Heaven: "Captain
Stormfield's Visit to Heaven and other
Sketches." New Haven: College & University
Press.
An unpretentious and attractive edition
for the general reader. Also contains texts
of "The Late Reverend Sam Jones's Reception
in Heaven," "Mental Telegraphy?" "Appendix
A: Old Abe's 'Slap' at Chicago [Lincoln,
from a popular humorous collection published in 1864]": "Appendix B: Alternate
Passage [by MT, but alternate to "Stormfield," rather than to Appendix A]." There
is a good introduction (pp. 11-32) for the
reader encountering this aspect of MT's
thought for the first time.

A4   CLEMENS, SAMUEL L. <u>Mark Twain's Letters to</u>
     <u>the Rogers Family (The Millicent Library</u>
     <u>Collection)</u>. Edited with Notes and an In-
     troduction by Earl J. Dias. New Bedford,
     Massachusetts: Reynolds-DeWalt Printing,
     Inc.
        Forty letters from MT and Olivia Clemens,
     plus background information on the individ-
     uals involved and the friendship of MT and
     Henry Rogers, and a chapter on "Mark Twain
     and the Millicent Library" (in Fairhaven,
     Massachusetts; named for the deceased
     daughter of Henry Rogers).

A5   GEISMAR, MAXWELL. <u>Mark Twain: An American</u>
     <u>Prophet</u>. Boston: Houghton Mifflin Company.
        MT had "the double soul of a great art-
     ist" rather than a split personality, and
     he was not destroyed by materialism or cen-
     sorship (pp. 4-5). "A whole area of Twain's
     social criticism of the United States has
     been repressed or avoided by Twain scholars
     precisely because it is so bold, so bril-
     liant, satirical, and prophetic. He was one
     of the most mature American artists precisely
     because he had, so to speak, such a long,
     deep childhood" (p. 6). <u>See</u> Index for nu-
     merous reviews of this book, most of them
     hostile.

A6   GROVER, GURU DAYAL. <u>Mark Twain: The Adven-</u>
     <u>tures of Huckleberry Finn (A Critical</u>
     <u>Study)</u>. Delhi, Doaba House.
        A very general treatment, with no speci-
     fically Indian perspectives. "My method has
     been to arrive at an eclectic synthesis of
     several approaches to the novel, and to con-
     centrate on a close reading of the text, and
     to assess whatever contributions the text
     itself demands from folklore, myth, ritual,
     biographical, and literary antecedents."

A7   *KRUSE, HORST H. <u>Mark Twains "Life on the Mis-</u>
     <u>sissippi": Eine Entstehungs- und Quellenges-</u>
     <u>chichtliche Untersuching zu Mark Twains</u>
     <u>"Standard Work."</u> <u>Kieler Beiträge zur Ang-</u>
     <u>listik und Amerikanistik</u>, VIII. Neumünster:
     Karl Wachholz.
        [Source: <u>MLA Bibliography</u> (1971), No.
     6987 and Eichelberger review (1972.B39).]

A8   *MENDELSOHN M. <u>Mark Tven</u>. Erevan: Aiastan.
     (In Armenian,; biography for children.)
        [Source: MHRA <u>Annual Bibliography</u> (1971),
     No. 8859.]

A9   SEELYE, JOHN. <u>The True Adventures of Huckle-</u>
     <u>berry Finn</u>. Evanston, Illinois: Northwest-
     ern University Press.
        A retelling of <u>HF</u> as the critics would
     like to have it, with the sex and profanity
     put in and a more acceptable ending provided;
     an amusing <u>tour de force</u>.

A10 *TUCKEY, JOHN S., ed. <u>Mark Twain's "The Myste-</u>
     <u>rious Stranger" and the Critics</u>. Belmont,
     California: Wadsworth.
        [Source: MHRA <u>Annual Bibliography</u> (1970),
     No. 8886.]

A11 WALKER, I[AN] M[ALCOLM]. <u>Mark Twain</u>. London:
     Routledge & Kegan Paul.
        Extracts from MT's work, intended to in-
     troduce him to the general reader. Contains
     brief introduction and commentary, emphasiz-
     ing his humor.

1970 B SHORTER WRITINGS

B1   ANDERSON, KENNETH. "Mark Twain, W. D. How-
     ells, and Henry James: Three Agnostics in
     Search of Salvation," <u>Mark Twain Journal</u>,
     XV (Winter), 13-16.
        All three believed that heaven was dubious
     and looked for salvation on earth; <u>CY</u>, <u>A</u>
     <u>Hazard of New Fortunes</u>, and <u>The Ambassadors</u>
     "provide three different conclusions to this
     quest for salvation." Abstract in <u>AES</u>, XIII
     (1969-70), 3088.

B2   ANON. "Huckleberry Jam," <u>Time</u>, XCV (March 2),
     80.
        A review of John Seelye, <u>The True Adven-</u>
     <u>tures of Huckleberry Finn</u> as "one of the
     best literary stunts in a long while."

B3   ANON. "Mark Twain Items Published Elsewhere,"
     <u>Twainian</u>, XXIX (January-February), 1-4.
        Contains a number of abstracts from <u>AES</u>,
     XII (1969) and a few from <u>AES</u>, XIII (1969-
     1970). Abstract in <u>AES</u>, XIV (1970-1971),
     1840.

B4   *BABCOCK, C. MERTON. "Mark Twain as 'A Major-
     ity of One,'" <u>University College Quarterly</u>,
     XV (May), 3-7.
        On his attitudes toward moral courage,
     and toward brutality and violence. [Source:
     Abstract in <u>AES</u>, XIV (1970-1971), No. 1272;
     reprinted in <u>Twainian</u>, XXXI (January-Febru-
     ary, 1972).]

B5   _____. "Mark Twain's Chuck-Wagon Special-
     ties," <u>Western American Literature</u>, V (Sum-
     mer), 147-51.
        MT appreciated good food, but described
     unappetizing concoctions in his <u>Notebook</u>,
     the Buffalo <u>Express</u>, <u>TA</u>, and "A Majestic
     Literary Fossil." Abstract by Babcock in
     <u>ALA</u>, IV (June, 1971), 91.

B6   BELSON, JOEL JAY. "The Nature and Conse-
     quences of the Loneliness of Huckleberry
     Finn," <u>Arizona Quarterly</u>, XXVI (Autumn),
     243-48.
        Huck is an outcast from a society which
     "by denying the rightness of every truly
     humane impulse he seeks to express...by
     convincing him of his own intellectual and
     moral inadequacy and by providing no ap-
     proval or positive satisfactions...isolates
     him finally and absolutely as nature, as
     Twain presents it, does not do." He is a
     fugitive, victim, and observer, and his
     chief protection is concealment from an un-
     intelligible and hostile world. Abstract

(BELSON, JOEL JAY)
in AES, XVI (1972-1973), 2053. Abstract by Belson in MLA Abstracts (1970), 6754; in ALA, IV (June, 1971), 92.

B7   BICKLEY, R. BRUCE, JR. "Humorous Portraiture in Twain's News Writing," American Literary Realism, III (Fall), 395-98.
      After listing Nevada and California papers for which MT wrote, and his varied subject matter, gives examples of portraiture in legislative and local reporting as anticipating the depiction of character in his later work. Abstract in AES, XVIII (1974-1975), 2589, with name listed as "Beckley."

B8   BOWEN, JAMES K., and RICHARD VAN DER BEETS, eds. American Literature Abstracts, III (June), 113-15; IV (December), 22-25.
      Contains sixteen abstracts by the authors of articles on MT.

B9   BUDD, LOUIS J. [Very brief, descriptive review: Lewis Leary, ed., Mark Twain's Correspondence with Henry Huttleston Rogers, 1893-1909; William M. Gibson, ed., Mark Twain's "Mysterious Stranger" Manuscripts; Walter Blair, ed., Mark Twain's Hannibal, Huck & Tom (all 1969).] South Atlantic Quarterly, LXIX (Winter), 164-65.

B10   BURNS, STUART R. "St. Petersburg Re-Visited: Helen Eustis and Mark Twain," Western American Literature, V (Summer), 99-112.
      The Fool Killer (1954) is a deliberate imitation of TS and HF. "Perhaps because she had the advantage of retrospect, Helen Eustis faces squarely the fact that Mark Twain hinted at but backed away from: that there can be no escape from society" (p. 111). Abstract in AES, XVII (1973-1974), 2106; reprinted in Twainian, XXXIV (March-April, 1975).

B11   CARTER, PAUL J. [Review-Article: Lewis Leary, ed., Mark Twain's Correspondence with Henry Huttleston Rogers (1969); Walter Blair, ed., Mark Twain's Hannibal, Huck & Tom (1969); William M. Gibson, ed., Mark Twain's "Mysterious Stranger" Manuscripts (1969).] American Literature, XLII (March), 105-107.
      In the letters to Rogers, "unfortunately, the one-sided correspondence is dull reading," dealing largely with business matters, including "the rectification of Clemens's repeated idiocies. He is a pathetic figure" as his dreams fail "and his family life shatters; the letters are full of his illnesses, despair, and self-pity. But there are occasional bits of humor and of good companionship." "Walter Blair shows us Mark Twain struggling to exploit the 'Matter of Hannibal'.... These are flawed pieces, interesting primarily as illustrations of the author's personality and method

of composition, although they do serve to refute the view that Clemens in this period was interested only in sales." Gibson's edition of the MS material "reveals glaringly the extent of the bowdlerization of the edition put together by Albert B. Paine and Frederick A. Duneka," who, nonetheless, "did make use of the best material in the manuscripts, including the only ending.... The student will have rich hunting in the fragments."

B12   CHAMBLISS, AMY. "The Friendship of Helen Keller and Mark Twain," Georgia Review, XXIV (Fall), 305-10.
      When Helen Keller met MT she was 14, the age of Jean Clemens. MT admired her character and talents, and persuaded Henry Rogers to sponsor her. Their friendship and correspondence are heart-warming. Abstract in AES, XIV (1970-1971), 3162; reprinted in Twainian, XXXI (March-April, 1972). Abstract by Chambliss in MLA Abstracts (1970), 6764.

B13   COBURN, MARK D. "'Training is Everything': Communal Opinion and the Individual in Pudd'nhead Wilson," Modern Language Quarterly, XXXI (June), 209-19.
      Wilson shares the town's views on "the rightness of slavery, the supremacy of white men, and the glory of the code duello," and "his desire to be a 'person of consequence' in the town is as strong as that of any other character"; conditioned by the same antebellum society that formed his neighbors, he sees truths of his own only in the calendar entries. Abstract in AES, XVI (1972-73), 536; reprinted in Twainian, XXXIII (January-February, 1974). Abstract by Coburn in MLA Abstracts (1970), 6768.

B14   COOK, DORIS E. Sherlock Holmes and Much More; or, Some of the Facts about William Gillette. Hartford: The Connecticut Historical Society.
      On Gillette in the GA play, pp. 12-13; on MT's part in bringing the play, The Professor, to the New York stage, pp. 19-20; living at Nook Farm in Hartford, p. 32; rejecting MT sketches as material for a radio series in 1935, pp. 87-88.

B15   COPLIN, KEITH. "John and Sam Clemens: A Father's Influence," Mark Twain Journal, XV (Winter), 1-6.
      The father-figures in MT's major novels are almost all failures, either weak and ineffectual or tyrannical and overpowering (the discussion emphasizes TS and HF). The reasons can be traced back to MT's own cold, austere father, whose integrity and authority he respected but toward whom he felt basically hostile. This essay is heavily indebted to secondary material. Abstract in AES, XIII (1969-1970), 3089.

1970 - Shorter Writings

B16 COX, JAMES M. "Mark Twain's Mysterious
Stranger," Virginia Quarterly Review, XLVI
(Winter), 144-50.
A review-article on Walter Blair, ed.,
Mark Twain's Hannibal, Huck & Tom; William
M. Gibson, ed., Mark Twain's "Mysterious
Stranger" Manuscripts; Lewis Leary, ed.,
Mark Twain's Correspondence with Henry Hut-
tleston Rogers (all 1969). After praising
the editing of all three, Cox goes on to a
discussion of the periods they cover in
MT's life.

B17 ____. "Toward Vernacular Humor," Virginia
Quarterly Review, XLVI (Spring), 311-330.
A discussion chiefly in terms of MT's
HF, and Ring Lardner and J. D. Salinger.
Extensive abstract in AES, XIV (1970-1971),
2611; reprinted in Twainian, XXXI (March-
April, 1972.

B18 DAVIS, CHESTER L. "'Harper's New Monthly
Magazine,' May, 1896, No. 552 (Article by
Joseph H. Twichell)," Twainian, XXIX
(September-October), 1-4; November-December), 1-3.
Describes the issue of Harper's, with
comments on advertisements, other articles,
etc., and quotes long passages from Twichell's article (1896.B13). Abstracts in
AES, XV (1971-1972), 1509, 1510; reprinted
in Twainian, XXXII (January-February,
1973).

B19 ____. "Life, Letters and Journals of George
Ticknor," Twainian, XXIX (January-February),
4; (March-April), 1-4.
Concludes a series of MT's underlinings
and marginal annotations in this two-volume
work; series begins July-August, 1968.B25.
Abstracts in AES, XIV (1970-1971), 1836,
1837; reprinted in Twainian, XXXI (January-
February, 1972).

B20 ____. "Mark Twain and Dan Beard and Boy
Scouts of America (Illustrations and Philosophies as Revealed in 'Connecticut Yankee', 'American Claimant', Etc.)," Twainian, XXIX (May-June), 1-4; "(Illustrations
and Philosophies as Revealed in 'American
Claimant', 'Tom Sawyer Abroad' and''Following the Equator')" (July-August), 1-4.
Dan Beard, one of the founders of the Boy
Scouts of America, illustrated these books
in whole or in part, as well as The Million-
Pound Bank-Note; a number of his illustrations incorporate the fleur-de-lis or the
scroll now familiar as Boy Scout insignia.
Davis discusses the Scouts, merit badges,
and Scout principles at some length; he
argues that MT's works reveal a number of
these principles, and that MT and Beard had
similar philosophies: "disgust with sham
and hypocrisy, with insincerity, with slavery and lack of care for the downtrodden";
he is also at pains to argue that MT "was
not anti-religious, he was anti-doctrine or

anti-dogma perhaps, but he did believe in
God as a divine being." Abstracts in AES,
XIV (1970-1971), 1838; reprinted in Twain-
ian, XXXI (January-February, 1972); AES, XV
(1971-1972), 1505; reprinted in Twainian,
XXXII (January-February, 1973).

B21 ____. "Review of Foundation Activities During Past Twenty Years," Twainian, XXIX
(May-June), 1.
Contains no new critical or biographical
material on MT. Abstract in AES, XIV (1970-
1971), 1839; reprinted in Twainian, XXXI
(January-February, 1972).

B22 DEMOTT, BENJAMIN. "Maxwell Geismar in Eruption," New York Times Book Review, (November 8), pp. 4-5, 47.
A review of Maxwell Geismar's Mark Twain:
An American Prophet. "Likable traits of
earnestness and embattled forthrightness
do appear at moments.... But for most of
its length it is too disheveled, self-right-
eous and simplistic to secure sympathetic
hearing of its (to this reviewer) doubtful
cause."

B23 DICKINSON, LEON T. [Review: Dewey Ganzel,
Mark Twain Abroad: The Cruise of the "Quaker City" (1968).] Modern Philology, LXVIII
(August), 117-19.
"Ganzel has done a good job of historical
recovery. His book is lively, well written,
and essentially accurate. It is well indexed." Dickinson argues, however, that
Ganzel states inferences as though they were
facts, and is "misleading" in his representation of some of the persons on the tour,
incidents in which they are involved, and
MT's relation to them; in particular, he
underestimates the influence on MT's writing
of Mary Mason Fairbanks, who indeed persuaded him to tone down some of his statements. In support, Dickinson here prints
for the first time a letter to John Russell
Young of the New York Tribune (November 22,
1867; it is in the Young Correspondence in
the Library of Congress), in which MT mentions "some twenty letters, which have sur-
vived the examination of a most fastidious
censor on shipboard." Dickinson concludes
his review by suggesting that Ganzel's study
provides a "detailed and convincing account
of MT's writing of his letters en route...it
will be a useful companion" to IA.

B24 DOYLE, PAUL A. "Henry Harper's Telling of a
Mark Twain Anecdote," Mark Twain Journal,
XV (Summer), 13.
"In a recently discovered letter of Henry
Harper's, written to the journalist and author Edward Sandford Martin" (May 20, 1895--
location not given), Harper repeats MT's account of an Australian impostor who profitably impersonated him on stage. When the
impostor died a friend of MT's served as
pallbearer and sent Mrs. Clemens his condo-
lences--which MT read. Abstract in AES,
XIV (1970-71), 912.

B25 DUSKIS, HENRY A. "Serious Wilkins in Boston: A Previously Unpublished Manuscript by Mark Twain," Yankee, XXXIV (June), 78-79, 179-83.
 The text of a piece attributed to MT by Duskis, here printed with minimal editorial comment; includes photograph of MT by George Kendall Warren.

B26 EARNEST, ERNEST. The Single Vision: The Alienation of American Intellectuals. New York: New York University Press; London: London University Press, pp. 14-20.
 On Brooks' The Ordeal of Mark Twain (chiefly summary, with objections) and the prudery of William Dean Howells. Provides no new material on MT.

B27 ELSBREE, LANGDON. "Huck Finn on the Nile," South Atlantic Quarterly, LXIX (Autumn), 504-10.
 On his experiences and observations as a Fulbright teacher of American literature in Cairo, 1966-67. He felt that although the Nile was not the Mississippi, Huck "might have stopped earlier and hoped to grow up in a community that was not too far from home." Abstract in AES, XV (1971-72), 1205; reprinted in Twainian, XXXII (January-February, 1973). Abstract by Elsbree in ALA, IV (June, 1971), 92.

B28 ENSOR, ALLISON. "A Clergyman Recalls Hearing Mark Twain," Mark Twain Journal, XV (Winter), 6.
 Reprints the account of an MT talk at a St. Louis Press Club dinner in his honor from River of Years, the autobiography of Joseph Fort Newton (1946.B43). Abstract in AES, XV (1971-72), 270. Abstract by Ensor in ALA, IV (June, 1971), 92.

B29 _____. "Mark Twain's 'The War Prayer': Its Ties to Howells and to Hymnology," Modern Fiction Studies, XVI (Winter), 535-39.
 Shows a number of parallels to Howells' "Editha," and argues that MT's choice of hymn reveals an ironic contrast in that "it does not fit the mood of the service Twain describes." Abstract by Ensor in ALA, IV (June, 1971), 93; in MLA Abstracts (1971), 7970.

B30 _____. "The 'Tennessee Land' of The Gilded Age: Fiction and Reality," Tennessee Studies in Literature, XV, 15-23.
 Si Hawkins in GA dreamed that his thousands of acres would make his children rich, but schemes failed and offers were refused and the land was finally sold for taxes. Ensor discusses the acquisition of 75,000-100,000 acres over a period of years by MT's father, John Marshall Clemens: "The total price was apparently $400-$500." Like Hawkins, MT's brother Orion turned down better offers and the land eventually brought "ten to fifty cents an acre--much more than John Clemens had paid for it, but far short of his

expectations." Abstract in AES, XIV (1970-1971), 3138; reprinted in Twainian, XXXI (March-April, 1972). Abstract by Ensor in MLA Abstracts (1970), 6776.

B31 FATOUT, PAUL. [Review: Allison Ensor, Mark Twain and the Bible (1969).] Indiana Magazine of History, LXVI (March), 89-90.
 Ensor is zealous, but solemn, and might have probed more deeply ("An unexplored topic is [MT's] appreciation of the sound and rhythm of biblical language"). The book is "a scholarly exposition of the shifting emotions, gentle and explosive of a paradoxical genius who could neither take the Bible nor let it alone."

B32 GEISMAR, MAXWELL. "Mark Twain and the Robber Barons," Scanlan's Monthly, I (March), 32-36.
 On MT's criticism of Gould, Rockefeller, et al., with an attack on other scholars for slighting his social commentary.

B33 *GERVAIS, RONALD J. "The Mysterious Stranger: The Fall as Salvation," Pacific Coast Philology, V (April), 24-33.
 [Source: Data provided by letter from R. S. Meyerstein, Secretary-Treasurer, Pacific Coast Philology.]

B34 GRIMES, GEOFFREY ALLEN. "Vagrancy, Vagabondage, and Vigilance: Periods of Vice in the Style of Mark Twain," Journal of the American Studies Association of Texas, I (June), 34-42.
 Emphasizes topic rather than style: "Samuel Clemens was severely criticized throughout his literary career for sins against good taste, for his inability to discern the dust and chaff in his works, and for his usual habit of flaunting much well intended and often well deserved criticism, which he considered superfluous and an imposition on his genius as an artist." His early journalism often exploited "sordid, squeamish, or risque matters," and "In spite of much high-minded criticism, Mark Twain continued to employ throughout his lifetime the trademarks of his western brand of humor."

B35 HAKAC, JOHN. "Huckleberry Finn: a Copy Inscribed in 1903," American Book Collector (Chicago), XX (January), 7-9.
 A copy at the University of Texas is inscribed: "None genuine without this label/ on the bottle Mark Twain/ Oct 23/03." Abstract in AES, XV (1971-72), 1494; reprinted in Twainian, XXXII (January-February, 1973).

B36 *HAMSUN, KNUT, ed. and translated by Barbara Morgridge. The Cultural Life of Modern America. Cambridge, Massachusetts: Harvard University Press.
 [Source: Anon. review, "Thirty Years Before Main Street," Book World (Chicago Tribune), June 7, p. 17, which states that

1970 - Shorter Writings

(HAMSUN, KNUT)
"He correctly described Mark Twain as no creative artist, but a 'wily wag who gets the world to laugh while he himself sits sobbing.'"]

B37   HARKEY, JOSEPH H. "When Huck Finn Smouched that Spoon," Mark Twain Journal, XV (Summer), 14.
About a class discussion of the word "smouch," which a freshman looked up in the O.E.D.; with some amusement at the discomfiture of a Jewish friend sitting next to him, he reported meanings of "Jew" and "filch." There is no evidence that MT's use of the term was anti-Semitic. Abstract in AES, XIV (1970-71), 909.

B38   HILL, HAMLIN. "Mark Twain," in J. Albert Robbins, ed., American Literary Scholarship: An Annual/1970 (Durham, North Carolina: Duke University Press, 1972), pp. 77-89.
A survey of MT scholarship for the year, begun by John C. Gerber in 1963.B32 and continued by him through 1968. Contents; "i. Textual and Bibliographical"; "ii. Biography"; "iii. General Criticism"; "iv. Earlier Works"; "v. Huckleberry Finn"; "vi. Later Works."

B39   _____. [Review: Allison Ensor, Mark Twain and the Bible (1969).] American Literary Realism, 1870-1910, III (Winter), 83-85.
A brief but thorough analysis of the book, which might have been more effective had Ensor either confined himself more rigorously to his central thesis or else followed up references for a fuller consideration of What Is Man?, JA, and Hadleyburg. "There is too much attention to mechanical borrowings from the Bible and not enough to the possibility of Biblical influence on the cadence, tone, and rhythm of Mark Twain's prose style. The attempt to correlate the humorist's attitude toward the Bible with a dominant culture vs. vernacular value dichotomy seems to me unconvincing. In short, Mark Twain and the Bible is synopsis and prolegomenon only."

B40   *HOOK, ANDREW. "Huckleberry Finn and Scotland," English Record, XXI (December), 8-14.
Scots respond to Huck's religion and language. [Source: MHRA Annual Bibliography (1970), No. 8254. Abstract in AES, XIV (1970-1971), 2542; reprinted in Twainian, XXXI (January-February, 1972).]

B41   HOWELL, ELMO. "In Defense of Tom Sawyer," Mark Twain Journal, XV (Winter), 17-19.
On Tom as a representative of those aspects of the aristocratic Old South which MT admired and expressed through such characters as Colonel Driscoll in PW. Huck Finn, by contrast, is "the mouthpiece

of Twain's views...not easy to envision, since his role is essentially passive." Abstract in AES, XIII (1969-70), 3091. Abstract by Howell in ALA, III (June), 114.

B42   _____. "Mark Twain's Arkansas," Arkansas Historical Quarterly, XXIX (Autumn), 195-208.
"Although he falls into the easy manner of his time of using Arkansas to suggest frontier raucousness, his generalizations belie his treatment of Arkansas people, which is uniformly kind."

B43   *JANKOVIĆ, MIRA. "Formativna Funkcija Sitnog Oblika Književnosti" [About Mark Twain's Short Stories.] Umjetnostrijeci (Zagreb), XIV, 1-2, 107-13.
[Source: MHRA Annual Bibliography (1970), No. 8256.]

B44   JOHNSON, ELLWOOD. "Mark Twain's Dream Self in the Nightmare of History," Mark Twain Journal, XV (Winter), 6-12.
A discussion of MS as illustrating a double consciousness MT shared with Emerson, of seeing the world in terms of freedom and fate. The central figure in MT's later works is "the 'dream self' in the prison of history." Abstract in AES, XIII (1969-70), 3092. Abstract by Johnson in ALA, IV (December), 23.

B45   *KAPOOR, S. D. "Tradition and Innovation in Huckleberry Finn," Modern Review, No. 762 (June), pp. 409-13.
[Source: Abstract in AES, XVII (1973-1974), 1806; reprinted in Twainian, XXXIV (March-April, 1975).] Treats American identity, confrontation with reality, and speech, as revealed in MT's portrayal of social reality against a historical background.

B46   KEGEL, PAUL. "Henry Adams and Mark Twain: Two Views of Medievalism," Mark Twain Journal, XV (Winter), 11-21.
A comparison of Mont Saint-Michel and Chartres with CY and P&P: "Adams extolls the beautiful while ignoring the unpleasant; Twain flails away at all he finds wrong with medievalism while ignoring the positive aspects." Abstracts in AES, XV (1971-72), 156.

B47   KIRALIS, KARL. "Two Recently Discovered Letters by Mark Twain," Mark Twain Journal, XV (Winter), 1-5.
Letters to Jerome B. Stillson (January 19, 25, 1875, here printed for the first time) charge that a statement in the New York Tribune praising the performance of Kate Field in the Gilded Age play are an edited and distorted version of comments in a private letter and published without his consent; moreover, his remarks were based only on hearsay evidence, since "in truth I never have seen the lady play at all." Abstract in AES, XV (1971-72), 271.

360

B48 KOLIN, PHILIP. "Mark Twain, Aristotle, and Pudd'nhead Wilson," Mark Twain Journal, XV (Summer), 1-4.
     The tragic success of PW can be explained in terms of Aristotle's Poetics, which MT may have known either directly or through literary histories; a number of his statements on drama and books parallel Aristotle. Abstract in AES, XIV (1970-71), 911. Abstract by Kolin in ALA, IV (December), 23.

B49 *LANINA, T. [Afterword to Lettish translation of P&P.] Riga: Liesma.
     [Source: MHRA Annual Bibliography (1970), No. 8260.]

B50 *____. [Afterword to Russian translation of P&P.] Moscow: Detskaya Literatura.
     [Source: MHRA Annual Bibliography (1970), No. 8261.]

B51 LEARY, LEWIS. Articles on American Literature, 1950-1967. Durham, North Carolina: Duke University Press.
     Lists articles on MT, pp. 56-77; this material has been included in the present bibliography.

B52 ____. "More Letters from the Quaker City," American Literature, XLII (May), 197-202.
     Three letters written on the 1867 tour by one of the owners, Daniel Leary, who describes the passengers as "nothing but a common lot of western people" and mentions plans to sell the ship, if possible. Abstract in AES, XIV (1970-1971), 1547; reprinted in Twainian, XXXI (January-February, 1972). Abstract by Leary in ALA, IV (December), 23; in MLA Abstracts (1970), 6790.

B53 LEGATE, DAVID M. Stephen Leacock: A Biography. Toronto: Doubleday Canada Limited, and Garden City, New York: Doubleday & Company, Inc., passim.
     Leacock "never cared for" TS (p. 13). His Mark Twain (1932) is described as "in the main a succession of endearing generalities," and inadequately researched (p. 180).

B54 LEWIS, STUART A. "Pudd'nhead Wilson's Election," Mark Twain Journal, XV (Winter), 21.
     Wilson's election as mayor in PW suggests only that the office was "so unrewarding and trivial that only the town fool was fit for it," but the abortive Those Extraordinary Twins from which PW was derived shows him taking the office in triumph when the Whigs had no candidate strong enough to run against him; "thus Wilson's election, which makes little sense in the final version, can be seen as an example of Twain's carelessness in matters of detail, and should not be taken as an example of genuine Missouri political life." Abstract in AES, XIII (1969-70), 3093.

B55 LOWERY, CAPTAIN ROBERT E. "The Grangerford-Shepherdson Episode: Another of Mark Twain's Indictments of the Damned Human Race," Mark Twain Journal, XV (Winter), 19-21.
     The names of the feuding families in HF allegorically represent the roots of the conflict: grange suggests a farmer, "particularly a gentlemen farmer with large holdings," and a "'ford'--a river crossing or a port--implies settlement, stability, and permanence in a specific area." The Shepherdsons, by contrast, represent nomads, and, significantly, "are always on horseback." Other details, such as the artificial fruit with which the Grangerfords decorate their home, reveal them as "only imitations of the noble and cultured society which established itself in the South." Abstract in AES, XIII (Winter), 3094.

B56 McCARTHY, HAROLD T. "Mark Twain's Pilgrim's Progress: The Innocents Abroad," Arizona Quarterly, XXVI (Autumn), 249-58.
     When MT wrote about Nevada, California, and the Sandwich Islands there was some serious social criticism; "but his criticism applied to local ills and often to specific personalities and did not pretend to have touched upon any fundamental disorder in American society." The Quaker City tour of 1867 gave him a chance to observe the educated, respectable and devout, and in the Holy Land to see their inability to distinguish between reality and their preconceptions; moreover, the biblical precepts to which they assented verbally were not evident in their personal conduct. Abstract in AES, XVI (1972-1973), 2054. Abstract by McCarthy in MLA Abstracts (1970), 6795; in ALA, IV (June, 1971), 93.

B57 McKEE, JOHN DEWITT. "Roughing It as Retrospective Reporting," Western American Literature, V (Summer), 113-19.
     MT caught the spirit of the flush times in Virginia City because "he was more than an observer. He was a participant" (p. 118). Abstract in AES, XVII (1973-1974), 2087; reprinted in Twainian, XXXIV (March-April, 1975). Abstract by McKee in ALA, IV (June, 1971), 94.

B58 McKEITHAN, D. M. [Review: Allison Ensor, Mark Twain and the Bible (1969).] American Literature, XLII (November), 410-11.
     Summarizes MT's attitudes, calls Ensor's book "a useful, fascinating, and thorough survey of the subject."

B59 MENDELSOHN M. "Strannaia Sud'ba 'Tainstvennogo Neznakomtsa' [The Strange Fate of The Mysterious Stranger]," Voprosy Literatury, XIV (September), 158-64.
     The publication of MS six years after MT's death came as a shock to American readers, most of whom knew him as a joker and

(MENDELSOHN, M.)
author of popular books for children. In the mid-sixties the University of California began publishing a complete edition of MT's letters and unpublished writings; one volume is W. M. Gibson, ed., Mark Twain's "Mysterious Stranger" Manuscripts, which Mendelsohn discusses in great detail. MS is a "creation of a writer who until his last minute of life continued to scourge cruelty, exploitation and false inventions of priests."

B60 *MILLER, RUTH. "But Laugh or Die: The Mysterious Stranger and Billy Budd," Literary Half-Yearly, XI:1.
[Source: Abstract in AES, XV (1971-1972), 250; reprinted in Twainian, XXXII (January-February, 1973). MLA Bibliography (1970), No. 6798 gives Mysore as place of publication.]

B61 MILLS, NICOLAUS C. "Prison and Society in Nineteenth-Century American Fiction," Western Humanities Review, XXIV (Autumn), 325-31.
On Cooper, Hawthorne, Melville, and MT, all of whom found the structure of society imprisoning. "Throughout Huckleberry Finn slavery is seen imprisoning whites as well as blacks," and CY shows that MT "saw exploitation characteristic of society as a whole, not merely the antebellum South." Abstract in AES, XIV (1971-1972), 1450.

B62 _____. "Social and Moral Vision in Great Expectations and Huckleberry Finn," Journal of American Studies, IV (July), 61-72.
A meticulously detailed and documented comparison of the two books, noting the boys' "outward allegiance to a society whose values they instinctively oppose," in which home is dominated by women, the values are those of an oppressive economic and legal system, and religion has been reduced to a defence of the corrupted society. The boys face similar psychological and moral decisions, and there is even a parallel in final betrayal by the River: "At the moment when it should lead to freedom it leads to the capture of Magwitch and Jim." Abstract in AES, XV (1971-1972), 1089; reprinted in Twainian, XXXII (January-February, 1973).

B63 MORROW, PATRICK. [Review: Edgar M. Branch, Clemens of the "Call" (1969).] Western American Literature, V (Summer), 155-56.
"Branch's book, quite simply, is a beautiful job. He took the fifty-four hundred or so local items printed in the Call during Clemens's tenure there, and...selected the best two hundred that can reasonably be attributed to Clemens." Their value lies in what they show of 19th-century attitudes and in particular of MT's views concerning race, although they lack any great literary merit.

B64 MOTT, BERTRAM, JR. "Twain's Joan: A Divine Anomaly," Études Anglaises, XXIII (July-September), 246-55.
After comparing portrayals of Joan by Shaw and Anouilh, treats MT's Joan of Arc in terms of Calvinist views on the nature of God, divine grace, and private interpretation of the Bible. His Joan is like the Calvinists' Christ, saving the predestined elect, but she does not transform men. If in Joan MT "was seeking a model, a Christ, salvation from the Calvinist limitations of depravity and predestination, he failed...he could not respond to the divine half of the elusive Maid of Orleans.... She is a divine anomaly; and mortal man is still both willess and depraved."

B65 PARKER, GAIL. "Mary Baker Eddy and Sentimental Womanhood," New England Quarterly, XLIII (March), 3-18.
Frequent, passing reference to MT, who attacked Christian Science, "was outspoken in his repugnance for sentimentalism in all its forms, and felt particularly uncomfortable about the notion that women were the conscience of the nation." Mrs. Eddy was not a "monster of American success"; to the contrary, she failed, because "the combination pope and holy mother of Christian Science consolidated an empire and healed thousands without ever really integrating her own conflicted personality."

B66 PAVESE, CESARE. American Literature: Essays and Opinions. Translated by Edwin Fussell. Berkeley, Los Angeles, London: University of California Press, pp. 28, 83, 147-48.
Pavese gradually came to appreciate MT's use of the American idiom, regarding it first only as local color (p. 28), or a concession to his public (p. 83), then recognizing the poetry and original language in HF (pp. 147-48). The essays involved first appeared in 1930, 1932, and 1934.

B67 PETTIT, ARTHUR GORDON. "Mark Twain, Unreconstructed Southerner, and His View of the Negro, 1835-1860," Rocky Mountain Social Science Journal, VII (April), 17-27.
"The experiences of his first twenty-five years were responsible in large part for the fact that neither Clemens, the private man, nor Mark Twain, the writer of Huckleberry Finn and of Pudd'nhead Wilson, ever completely outlived his earliest impressions of the Negro."

B68 _____. "Mark Twain's Attitude Toward the Negro in the West," Western Historical Quarterly, I (January), 51-62.
MT's expressed views in his formative years and during the time when he lived in the West were consistently racist, and he often joked about the inferiority of the Negro. His outlook on racial matters was

(PETTIT, ARTHUR GORDON)
not modified significantly by a shift in
his political allegiance from South to
North, but when he moved to the East,
worked to establish himself as a national
writer, and married the daughter of "a
leading conductor on the New York under-
ground railway before the war," his views
began to change. He "left most (not all,
but most) of his more violent prejudice
behind him in the West."

B69   REED, KENNETH T. "Mirth and Misquotation:
Mark Twain in Petosky, Michigan," Mark
Twain Journal, XV (Summer), 19-20.
Supplements the sparse details in Fred
W. Lorch's The Trouble Begins at Eight
(1968) of MT's lecture delivered July 20,
1895 in Petosky. When the Daily Resorter
[sic] attributed to him statements bearing
on its feud with a "volunteer newspaper"
sponsored by a Dr. Hall of a local summer
school, MT denied them in a note published
in the Petosky Record: "I don't like being used as a waste-pipe for the delivery
of another man's bile." Abstract in AES,
XIV (1970-71), 913.

B70   REES, ROBERT A. "Captain Stormfield's Visit
to Heaven and The Gates Ajar," English Language Notes, VII (March), 197-202.
Elizabeth Stuart Phelps's The Gates Ajar
(1868) anticipates Captain Stormfield in
suggesting that halos, wings, and a life
of singing and prayers may be unsatisfactory; that in Heaven a person can follow what
career he chooses, with increased intellect, and with a recognition of abilities
that may have been denied in his earthly
life; and that in a vast Heaven the celebrities may find it an imposition to greet
everybody who has been looking forward to
meeting them. Although, as Franklin Rogers points out, MT was not burlesquing The
Gates Ajar in Captain Stormfield, he did
so in "The Story of Mamie Grant, the Child
Missionary." Rees also quotes "an unpublished fragment entitled 'Captain Stormfield Resumes,'" which mentions The Gates
Ajar.

B71   REEVES, PASCHAL, et al. "A Checklist of
Scholarship on Southern Literature for
1970," Mississippi Quarterly, XXIV (Spring,
1971), 175-222; on MT, pp. 186-89.

B72   RODNON, STEWART. "The Adventures of Huckleberry Finn and Invisible Man: Thematic
and Structural Comparisons," Negro American
Literature Forum, IV (July), 45-51.
There are similarities in "the journey
concept, the education motif, and the essential theme," as well as something deeper
than "a satiric examination of...American
society" and a "basic-goodness-of-the-heart
theme," and "the novels are stylistically
alike in at least four areas: language,

folklore, humor, and narrator point-of-view."
In Shadow and Act (1964), Ellison has commented on Jim's role as a symbol of humanity
for Huck, whose decision to help him escape
represents MT's acceptance of a personal responsibility.

B73   RUBIN, LOUIS D. "Southern Local Color and the
Black Man," Southern Review, n.s. VI (October), 1011-30; on HF, 1026-30.
Huck provides a voice, and Jim a basis for
evaluating "the moral worth of the town and
the countryside along the river." MT may
not have recognized the importance of his
theme of Jim's yearning for freedom; Ralph
Ellison has argued that Jim's character
could be more fully rounded, though he is a
triumph of characterization and understanding, a symbol of humanity. Abstract in AES,
XIV (1970-1971), 3140; reprinted in Twainian, XXXI (March-April, 1972).

B74   ____. "Three Installments of Mark Twain,"
Sewanee Review, LXXVIII (August), 678-84.
A review article covering three volumes
of the MT papers published in 1969 by the
University of California Press, Berkeley:
Walter Blair, ed., Mark Twain's Hannibal,
Huck & Tom ("The most interesting document
is... 'Villagers of 1840-3,'" with MT's
1897 recollections of Hannibal people);
William M. Gibson, ed., Mark Twain's "Mys-
terious Stranger" Manuscripts (this shows
what Paine did in splicing together dispar-
ate material to make a book, and destroys
DeVoto's argument that MT came back from
the edge of insanity to a restoration of
his creative powers); Lewis Leary, ed., Mark
Twain's Correspondence with Henry Huttleston
Rogers, 1893-1909 ("The truly interesting
book of the three volumes," revealing that
MT was less noble than he has been depicted
in his settlement of his financial affairs).
The effect of publishing MT's papers is to
support his portrait by Van Wyck Brooks.
Abstract in AES, XIV (1970-1971), 1548; reprinted in Twainian, XXXI (January-February,
1972).

B75   SAPPER, NEIL G. "'I Been There Before':
Huck Finn as Tocquevillian Individual,"
Mississippi Quarterly, XXIV (Winter),
35-45.
Tocqueville used the terms of individualism and conformity to denote prevalent American qualities. Huck had a strong sense of
the community of the raft, but he rejected
the civilization on shore and thereby "demonstrated finally and conclusively that he
was a Tocquevillian individual. Perhaps he
was the only one that we have had." Abstract in AES, XVII (1973-1974), 2408; reprinted in Twainian, XXXIV (March-April,
1975). Abstract by Sapper in MLA Abstracts
(1971), 8007.

1970 - Shorter Writings

B76   SEELYE, JOHN. "Mark Twain as Grumbler," New Republic, CLXIII (November 28), 21-24.
        A review of Maxwell Geismar, Mark Twain: An American Prophet. The book is enlivened by extensive quotation from MT. "Geismar's method is to slap down a few choice paragraphs, applaud, slap down some more, applaud, and then slap down a page and a half for emphasis, boot Justin Kaplan with a footnote, and burst into cheers. Well, it's lots of fun, and though Maxwell Geismar may be full of prunes, his book is full of plums--mostly Mark Twain's."

B77   SERRANO-PLAJA, ARTURO. "Magic" Realism in Cervantes: "Don Quixote" as Seen Through "Tom Sawyer" and "The Idiot." Translated by Robert S. Rudder. Berkeley, Los Angeles, London: University of California Press.
        Also treats HF, passim, although the emphasis is on Cervantes. Serrano-Plaja says he did not read MT until he was in his thirties. One afternoon during the Civil War in Spain, in a cafe with Hemingway, "I learned about two things from the Anglo-Saxon world: whiskey and the importance of Mark Twain.... Hemingway told me it was absolutely impossible to understand anything about the United States without knowing Mark Twain in depth; and he, Hemingway, considered him the most important writer of his country" (pp. 2, 3). [MLA Bibliography (1968), No. 16226 lists the Spanish publication as: "Realismo 'magoci' en Cervantes: 'Don Quixote' dese 'Tom Sawyer' y 'El Idiota.' Madrid: Gredos, 1967."]

B78   SHRELL, DARWIN H. "Twain's Owl and His Bluejays," in Thomas Austin Kirby and William John Olive, eds., Essays in Honor of Esmond Linworth Marilla (Baton Rouge: Louisiana State University Press), pp. 283-90.
        MT was still distressed and puzzled over the apparent failure of his Whittier Birthday Dinner speech when he was writing TA, and "Jim Baker's Bluejay Yarn" in Chapter III parallels the address in that "the settings for both stories are in a California mining camp, and each story is told by a California miner. In both there are clearly polarized and contrasting cultural standards reflecting eastern and western attitudes or values. In each story the easterners are on a pilgrimage to Yosemite. The literary methods in each story are essentially the same: the use of learned and vernacular language for humorous effect; the use of quasi-dramatic form to illustrate a point." Moreover, "the ambitious intentions and comic frustrations of the first jay are in no small way similar to [MT's] own motives and reactions at that famous Atlantic dinner," while the humorless owl allows MT "to re-create--with artistic detachment--another situation in which grotesque or audacious western humor failed to be understood."

B79   SIMONSON, HAROLD R. "Huckleberry Finn as Tragedy," Yale Review, LIX (Summer), 532-48; reprinted (revised) in his The Closed Frontier: Studies in American Literary Tragedy. New York: Holt, Rinehart and Winston, pp. 57-76; also, pp. 129-33 on Connecticut Yankee.
        The concluding section is "a dramatic travesty of this rebirth, of Huck's becoming Tom. The tragedy rests in the irony that only as Tom can Huck survive" (p. 60). On the CY, 129-33: "Culminating in an Armageddon...does not concern the triumph of modern technology over medieval feudalism as much as it damns this same technology." Article abstracted by Simonson in ALA, IV (December), 23.

B80   SKOW, JOHN. "Quarter Twain," Time, XCVI (November 30), 80, 82.
        A review of Maxwell Geismar's Mark Twain: An American Prophet. "This latest critical appreciation of Mark Twain is not without blemish, being sloppy, narrow, quarrelsome, doctrinaire, vague, repetitive," but it is redeemed by Geismar's love for MT and frequent quotations from him and by the "modest patches of solid ground" in the criticism.

B81   *SOLOMON, PETRE. "Verva Postumă a lui Mark Twain" ["Mark Twain's Posthumous Verve"], Romania Litară (Bucharest), III (April), 21.
        [Source: MHRA Annual Bibliography (1970), 8281.]

B82   SPANGLER, GEORGE M. "Pudd'nhead Wilson: A Parable of Property," American Literature, XLII (March), 28-37.
        Traditional interpretations in terms of racial themes and environmental determinism do not reflect the unity that may be found in a view of the book as illustrating "the perils of an obsession with property to the exclusion of all other human values and needs." Abstract in AES, XIV (1970), 1546; reprinted in Twainian, XXXI (January-February, 1972). Abstract by Spangler in ALA, IV (December), 24; in MLA Abstracts (1970), 6807.

B83   SPILLER, ROBERT E., ed. The Van Wyck Brooks-Louis Mumford Letters: The Record of a Literary Friendship, 1921-1963. New York: E. P. Dutton & Co., Inc., pp. 84-87, 218-19.
        Letters between Mumford and Brooks discussing DeVoto as a fool and his Mark Twain's America as providing little information of value (December 27, 30, 1932; pp. 84-87); letter from Mumford to John Chamberlain commenting on The Golden Day, Waldo Frank's Our America, and about DeVoto on MT's reticence concerning sex (August 6, 1942; pp. 218-19).

B84 SPOFFORD, WILLIAM K. "Mark Twain's Connecticut Yankee: An Ignoramus Nevertheless," Mark Twain Journal, XV (Summer), 15-18.
MT "never intended the revolution to succeed," as he shows through "Hank's 'practical' and insensitive character and by endowing the Boss with a warped notion of democracy, and an incomplete comprehension of the significance of training. Throughout the novel Twain thus implicitly and explicitly undermines the Yankee's goal." Abstract in AES, XIV (1970-71), 908. Abstract by Spofford in ALA, IV (December), 24.

B85 STEVENSON, ADLAI E. [Typed, signed letter of November 20, 1951 to Cyril Clemens, reproduced in facsimile.] Mark Twain Journal, XV (Summer), back cover.
Declines with thanks and regrets an invitation to address the Mark Twain Birthday Banquet, and recalls doggerel by MT on the pronunciation of "Adlai."

B86 *STRELNIKOV, BORIS, and ILYA SHATUNOVSKII. "V Avtomobile po Amerike [O poeshchenii g. Hannibala--rodiny M. Tvena: Iz putevogo dnevnika]." "[Through America by Car (a visit to Hannibal--the birthplace of M. Twain: a diary).]" Zhurnalist, I, 71-73.
[Source: MHRA Annual Bibliography (1970), No. 8285.]

B87 *TOLCHARD, CLIFFORD. "Mark Twain's Australia," Walkabout, XXXVI (July), 52-55.
[Source: MHRA Annual Bibliography (1970), No. 8286.]

B88 TRACHTENBERG, ALAN. "The Form of Freedom in Adventures of Huckleberry Finn," Southern Review, n.s. VI (October), 954-71.
"Huckleberry Finn became a cultural object of special intensity" as a view of freedom, "the precise negation of all the forces felt as oppressive in the 1950s.... Huck's freedom...requires that he achieve a conscious moral identity," but his role as narrator helps to define him, and in any case MT "seriously doubted the possibilities of personal freedom within a social setting." The cost of Huck's freedom and survival is high: "he pays with his chance to grow up." Abstract in AES, XIV (1970-1971), 3137; reprinted in Twainian, XXXI (March-April, 1972).

B89 TUCKEY, JOHN S. "Hannibal, Weggis, and Mark Twain's Eseldorf," American Literature, XLII (May), 235-40.
Examination of MT's notebook shows that "in The Mysterious Stranger his first portrayal of village boys...reflects his recent observations of Weggis [near Lake Lucerne, in Switzerland] more directly and immediately than it evidently does any recollection of Hannibal in the 1840's," as DeVoto had asserted. Abstract by Tuckey in ALA, IV (December), 24; in MLA Abstracts (1970), 6810.

B90 ____. "Mark Twain's Later Dialogue: The 'Me' and the Machine," American Literature, XLI (January), 532-42.
The frequent despair of MT's last years was leavened by "expressions of faith and hope" which "were something more than occasional and random." Even in Three Thousand Years Among the Microbes, MS, and What Is Man? there are indications of a readiness to believe in an immortal self. Abstract in AES, XIV (1970-1971), 1549; reprinted in Twainian, XXXI (January-February, 1972). Abstract by Tuckey in ALA, III (June), 115; in MLA Abstracts (1970), 6811. Article reprinted in Schmitter (1974), pp. 57-67.

B91 ____. [Review: Arthur L. Scott, Mark Twain at Large (1969) and Allison Ensor, Mark Twain and the Bible (1969).] Modern Fiction Studies, XVI (Autumn), 214-17.
Scott's book is solidly founded in the MT papers and available scholarship, and "careful and modest, perhaps even stinted, in its conclusions," since there is evidence here that MT's "marked shift in tone and treatment" may be the result of a loss of contrasts as the freshness of experiences wore off. Mark Twain and the Bible, treating "the theme of a lost Eden as it applies to Twain's works," is "a good beginning," but the subject requires a bigger book; however, Chapter III provides a valuable treatment of MT's use of the Biblical images of the Prodigal Son; Adam, Eve, and the fall; and Noah and the flood.

B92 TWICHELL, JOSEPH H. "Letters from Twichell to Paine," Twainian, XXIX (September-October), 4; (November-December), 3-4.
Ten letters, 1908-1911, chiefly concerning the transmission of material pertinent to the forthcoming Biography; Twichell relies on Paine's judgment in guarding MT's privacy while discussing MT letters, some of which should not be preserved. There is also mention of Twichell letters written during the tour with MT which led to TA, a series of photographs of MT in the Hartford Courant (apparently either taken in Dublin, N.H., or annotated there), and a talk and a Harper's article on MT by Twichell; Twichell also comments on MT's wedding, and his "deep humilities." There is a final installment of these letters in the next issue of Twainian (January-February, 1971). Abstracts in AES, XV (1971-1972), 1506, 1507; reprinted in Twainian, XXXII (January-February, 1973).

B93 WAGENKNECHT, EDWARD. "Huckleberry Finn as the Devil's Disciple," Boston University Studies, XVIII (Spring), 20-24.
On Huck's decision to go to Hell for Jim's freedom: "What he knows as God is only a cruel caricature of God. If this were what God is like, He would deserve no obedience," and religious history is filled with examples of defiance of church and state by

(WAGENKNECHT, EDWARD)
"those who truly love God...The Devil's
Disciple becomes God's own child" (p. 23).

B94 _____. [Review: William M. Gibson, ed.,
Mark Twain's "Mysterious Stranger" Manuscripts; Walter Blair, ed., Mark Twain's
Hannibal, Huck & Tom; Lewis Leary, ed.,
Mark Twain's Correspondence with Henry Huttleston Rogers (all 1969).] Studies in the
Novel, II (Spring), 88-95.
Includes not only a useful, general discussion of the materials, but also a summary of the history of the unpublished papers of Mark Twain, commenting on Paine's
trusteeship and his editing of The Mysterious Stranger; he observes in passing that
the new knowledge about the composition
"makes it necessary to scrap Bernard De-
Voto's brilliant essay, 'The Symbols of
Despair' (Mark Twain at Work), which is
probably the most moving thing that has
ever been written about Mark Twain....
Chronology can be very cruel to literary
theories." Abstract in AES, XIV (1970-
1971), 1273; reprinted in Twainian, XXXI
(January-February, 1972).

B95 WERGE, THOMAS. "Mark Twain and the Fall of
Adam," Mark Twain Journal, XV (Summer),
5-13.
On MT's continuing use of Adam to represent child-like innocence and yielding to
temptation, whether through direct portrayal or allusion. "Twain measures Adam's
significance for his own time not by his
pre-lapsarian goodness, but by his fallen
state, which is, finally, the state of all
men." Abstract in AES, XIV (1970-71),
910. Abstract by Werge in ALA, IV (December), 24.

B96 WHEELOCK, C. WEBSTER. "The Point of Pudd'n-
head's Half-a-Dog Joke," American Notes and
Queries, VIII (July), 150-51.
When Wilson expressed the wish that he
owned half of a barking dog so he could
kill his half, he was considered a fool in
the small Southern community. There is a
major satiric point here, in that a white
person cannot be enslaved, but a person
with some Negro blood and a preponderance
of white blood can be, as were Roxy and her
natural son Valet de Chambers: "Men who
are aghast at the prospect of the newcomer's killing a creature that may be only
partially his--a moral and legal crime,
clearly--are daily accustomed to dealing
with their own species on precisely the
same terms."

1971 A BOOKS

A1 ANDERSON, FREDERICK, ed. With the assistance
of Kenneth M. Sanderson. Mark Twain: The
Critical Heritage. London: Routledge &
Kegan Paul, and New York: Barnes & Noble.

Reprints reviews of MT's books and evaluations of his writing, in his lifetime and
for the period immediately after his death,
in chronological order, with an extensive
introduction (pp. 1-19); an MT letter to
Andrew Lang and a previously unpublished
letter to Andrew Chatto (16 July 1889) are
also included. The present bibliography indicates reprintings of listed material in
this book.

A2 ANON. Hartford as a Publishing Center in the
Nineteenth Century. Hartford: Stowe-Day
Foundation.
A pamphlet issued for an exhibit, listing
works by MT, contracts, salesman's prospec-
tuses, etc.

A3 GERBER, JOHN C., ed. Studies in "Huckleberry
Finn." Columbus, Ohio: Charles E. Merrill
Publishing Company.
Contains early reviews, excerpts from various sources concerning "The Fracas Created
by the Concord Public Library" in 1885, and
articles and excerpts from books by nine
critics since MT's death. All of this material is listed in the present bibliography,
with cross-references to Gerber's reprintings.

A4 LEARY, LEWIS. Southern Excursions: Essays
on Mark Twain and Others. Baton Rouge:
Louisiana State University Press. On MT,
pp. 3-110.
Contains the following essays on MT, with
previous publication as indicated: "Mark
Twain and the Comic Spirit" (pp. 3-41), a
slightly shortened version of his Mark
Twain pamphlet (1960); "Mark Twain's Wound:
Standing with Reluctant Feet" (pp. 42-74),
reduced from the introduction to his A Casebook on Mark Twain's Wound (1960); "The
Bankruptcy of Mark Twain" (pp. 75-86) in
Carrell (1968) and as "Mark Twain among the
Malefactors" in Brom Weber's Sense and Sensibility in Twentieth-Century Writing
(1970), with other material derived from
Leary's ed. of Mark Twain's Correspondence
with Henry Huttleston Rogers (1969); "On
Writing about Writers: Especially Mark
Twain" (pp. 87-95), in Southern Review
(1968); "Tom and Huck: Innocence on Trial"
(pp. 96-110), in Virginia Quarterly Review
(1954). For details, see the original publication of this material.

A5 ROWLETTE, ROBERT. Mark Twain's "Pudd'nhead
Wilson": The Development and Design. Bowling Green, Ohio: Bowling Green University
Popular Press.
"The present study will examine the form
and substance of Pudd'nhead Wilson. In
particular it will examine what I consider
to be Twain's structural achievement of
integrating the novel's three apparently
disparate themes and the plots that drama-
tize them: slavery, detection, and twin-
hood" (p. ix).

B1 ALLEN, MARTHA. "Train Travel in the Mississippi West, 1869-1900 as Seen by Travelers,"
Journal of the American Studies Association
of Texas, II, 5-14.
    On p. 8, briefly cites MT's complaint
about railroad-station dining, with little
time to consume the "Bare Stake and Dear
Meet" (from San Francisco Daily Examiner,
May 25, 1869).

B2 ANDERSEN, DAVID M. "Basque Wine, Arkansas
Chawin' Tobacco: Landscape, and Ritual
in Ernest Hemingway and Mark Twain," Mark
Twain Journal, XVI (Winter), 3-7.
    The social ritual at Berguete of sharing
wine, described in The Sun Also Rises, has
its parallel in the dispute over chewing
tobacco in HF: "Reciprocity, beginning
even with such material symbols as wine
and tobacco, is not just essential to civilization, it is civilization." Abstract in
AES, XVI (1972-1973), 1768.

B3 ANON. "Mark Twain Items Published Elsewhere
During Past Year," Twainian, XXX (January-
February), 1-3.
    Reprints a number of abstracts from AES,
XIII (1969-1970). Abstract in AES, XV
(1971-1972), 1512; reprinted in Twainian,
XXXII (January-February, 1973).

B4 *ARIKAWA, SHOJI. "Huckleberry Finn in Japan,"
English Record (Japan), XXI (February), 20-26.
    Japanese students respond to Huck's Ameri-
can character and status as fugitive, and
gain insight into American racial problems
through his book. [Source: MHRA Annual
Bibliography (1971), No. 8815, and abstract
in AES, XIV (1970-1971), 2839; reprinted in
Twainian, XXXI (March-April, 1972).]

B5 *BOBROVA, M. [Afterword to Moldavian translation (from Russian) of Connecticut Yankee.]
Kishinev: Kartya Moldovenyaskë.
    [Source: MHRA Annual Bibliography
(1971), No. 8820.]

B6 BOWEN, JAMES K., and RICHARD VAN DER BEETS,
eds. American Literature Abstracts, IV
(June), 91-94, 117-18; V (December), 135.
    Contains eleven abstracts by the authors
of articles on MT, and (June, 117-18) Elmer
F. Suderman's summary of reviews of Allison Ensor's Mark Twain and the Bible
(1969.A5).

B7 BUGLIARI, JEANNE. "The Picaresque as a Flaw
in Mark Twain's Novels," Mark Twain Journal, XV (Summer), 10-12.
    P&P, RI, LOM, TS, and CY "are diminished
as serious literary efforts because either
their characters are more or less flat,
static, and insufficiently drawn or because
their themes are not purposefully directed";

HF suffers from its "curious admixture of
style and content," but gains stature in
departing from the picaresque mode. Abstract in AES, XV (1971-72), 1498.

B8 BYERS, JOHN R., JR. "Miss Emmeline Grangerford's Hymn Book," American Literature,
XLIII (May), 259-63.
    The "Ode to Stephen Dowling Bots, Dec'd"
from HF and Isaac Watts's "Alas! and did my
Saviour Bleed!" are printed in parallel columns to show a possible derivation; particularly significant are parallels in the first
and second lines, the common bathos, and similar structure of questions and answers concerning death. Abstract in AES, XVI (1972-
1973), 1121; reprinted in Twainian, XXXIII
(January-February, 1974). Brief abstract by
Byers in ALA, V (December), 135; in MLA Abstracts (1971), 7963.

B9 CADY, EDWIN H. "Huckleberry Finn by Common
Day," in his The Light of Common Day: Realism in American Fiction. Bloomington, London: Indiana University Press, pp. 88-119;
also, pp. 36-39 on "A True Story,"
pp. 79-84 on IA, and passim on MT.
    In HF morality is based on the value of
the individual (p. 32); notes an element of
the mock-heroic (pp. 65-66). On HF as picaresque and anti-romantic, pp. 88-119. "A
True Story" summarized and praised for its
language and the vivid portrayal of Aunt
Rachel (pp. 36-39). IA treated as an assault on romantic, dishonest perceptions by
travel writers (pp. 79-84).

B10 CAMPBELL, FRANK, and INA CAMPBELL. "Mark
Twain's Florentine Villas in 1964-1965,"
Mark Twain Journal, XV (Summer), 12-14.
    Describes the Villa Quarto and Villa Vi-
viani, which have been changed but resemble
MT's descriptions of them; a search for the
"Villa Paulhof" summer home in Kaltenleut-
geben was unsuccessful. Abstract in AES,
XV (1971-72), 1502.

B11 CLARK, HARRY HAYDEN. "Mark Twain" (with corrections and additions by Howard G. Baetzhold), in James B. Woodress, ed., Eight
American Authors: A Review of Research and
Criticism (New York: W. W. Norton & Company, Inc.), pp. 273-320.
    A revised edition of the bibliography ori-
ginally published by the Modern Language
Association in 1956 and reprinted by Norton
in 1963. Contents: "Bibliography," "Editions and Texts," "Biographies," "Criticism"; annotated. [Not systematically
checked for the present bibliography.]

B12 CLEMENS, CYRIL. "Bernard Shaw Meets Mark
Twain," Mark Twain Journal, XVI (Winter),
back cover.
    Facsimile of a typed, signed letter (Lon-
don, n.d., text previously published) from
Shaw to Cyril Clemens on two meetings with
MT in London; in a note below, Cyril Clemens

1971 - Shorter Writings

(CLEMENS, CYRIL)
quotes Shaw's gracious refusal of permission to dedicate a book to him. Briefly described in AES, XVI (1972-1973), 1746.

B13   COLWELL, JAMES L. "Huckleberries and Humans: on the Naming of Huckleberry Finn," Publications of the Modern Language Association, LXXXVI (January), 70-76.
MT did not see huckleberries until he went to Hartford in 1868; the name suggests rusticity and wildness. "Finn" came from a Hannibal drunkard, like the father of Tom Blankenship, the boy on whom Huck was modeled. Moreover, "To the nonpsychologically trained ear, 'Huck' is to 'Mark' about as 'Finn' is to 'Twain,' and the resemblance seems both striking and deliberate." Abstract (condensed from Colwell's own abstract) in AES, XV (1971-1972), 269; reprinted in Twainian, XXXII (January-February, 1973). Abstract by Colwell in ALA, IV (June), 92; in MLA Abstracts (1971), 7965.

B14   CRACROFT, RICHARD H. "The Gentle Blasphemer: Mark Twain, Holy Scripture, and the Book of Mormon," Brigham Young University Studies, XI (Winter), 119-40.
Although MT "obviously" had not read the Book of Mormon, he ridiculed it, as he ridiculed the Bible, Mary Baker Eddy's Science and Health, and the religious practices of Moslems and Hindus; but he did so without malice. "On reading Mark Twain's gentle blasphemies, whether concerning the Almighty or His foible-prone creatures, everybody, including the victim, has a good time." Abstract in AES, XV (1971-1972), 2143. Abstract by Cracroft in MLA Abstracts (1971), 7967.

B15   CRONIN, FRANK C. "The Ultimate Perspective in Pudd'nhead Wilson," Mark Twain Journal, XVI (Winter), 14-16.
"The moral center...is the omniscient narrator who...unfolds before the reader some of the darker ironies of life to which Pudd'nhead is tragically blind." The real subject is "the terrifying discrepancy between appearance and 'reality' which reveals the ultimate uncertainty of man's identity." Abstract in AES, XVI (1972-1973), 1771.

B16   [DAVIS, CHESTER L.] "Paine, Book Publishing, Dispersal of Mark Twain Manuscripts," Twainian, XXX (March-April), 4; (May-June), 1-4, with added sub-title, "Letters from Langdon, Laura Frazer (Becky Thatcher) and (July-August), 1-4, as "Letters from Laura Frazer (Becky Thatcher) to Paine, 1907-1912"; (September-October), 1-4, as "Letters from Laura Frazer (Becky Thatcher), Helen K. Garth, Fee, Fuller, RoBards and Mahan."

This series, with varying titles, reprints correspondence received by Paine while he was working on his biography of MT. Abstracts in AES, XV (1971-1972), 1511, reprinted in Twainian, XXXII (January-February, 1973); AES, XVI (1972-1973), 788, 789, 790, reprinted in Twainian, XXXIII (January-February, 1974).

B17   ____. "Walter F. Frear, Willard S. Morse, Yale University Collection. M. T. Bibliographies Started 'Foundation' and 'Mark Twain and Hawaii,'" Twainian, XXX (November-December), 1-4.
A general discussion of the Mark Twain Research Foundation, and Mark Twain collecting, bibliography, and scholarship. Contains the text of an address given by Frear before The Social Science Association of Honolulu, October 6, 1947, on MT's visit to Hawaii in 1866. Abstract in AES, XVI (1972-1973), 791; reprinted in Twainian, XXX (January-February, 1974). A confusing entry in the 1971 MHRA Annual Bibliography, No. 8833, lists this as "Mark Twain in Hawaii. Twainian (6), 1-4."

B18   DENTON, LYNN W. "Mark Twain and the American Indian," Mark Twain Journal, XVI (Winter), 1-3.
MT's early prejudice aginst the Indian "eventually changed to toleration and then finally to idealism." Although MT's views of other national and racial groups are well known, "Maxwell Geismar, in Mark Twain, an American Prophet, is one of the very few critics to even mark Twain's attitudes toward the Indian." Abstract in AES, XVI (1972-1973), 1772.

B19   DONALDSON, SCOTT. "Pap Finn's Boy," South Atlantic Bulletin, XXXVI (May), 32-37.
Although Huck matures, he remains a loner, like his Pap, though rejecting society rather than being rejected by it. In matters of religion, as in those of race, Huck maintains a view like his father's--little more than a set of superstitions.

B19A   *DURAM, JAMES C. "Mark Twain and the Middle Ages," Wichita State University Bulletin, University Studies. XLVII (August), 1-16.
[Source: Abstract in AES, XVIII (1974-1975), 591.] JA, CY, P&P, and MS criticized and accurately represented the Middle ages, and embody MT's view that Church and feudalism dehumanize man; gradually, however, MT turned from his belief in progress to a cyclic view of history, with institutions rooted in human nature.

B20   EBÓN, MARTIN. "Mark Twain's 'Mental Telegraphy,'" in his They Knew the Unknown, New York: The World Publishing Company, pp. 79-87.

(EBON, MARTIN)
A summary of MT's psychic experiences, drawn from the autobiographical material, the Paine Biography, and other familiar sources.

B21 FETTERLEY, JUDITH. "The Sanctioned Rebel," Studies in the Novel, III (Fall), 293-304.
Tom Sawyer's escapades break the tedium of life in St. Petersburg for the adults, who in turn furnish prohibitions against which to rebel. MT was exposing the hypocrisy of the Bad Boy fiction of his day, in which the Bad Boy is just the Good Boy in disguise, in the same category with the adults Tom Sawyer exposes. Basically, the tone of TS is positive and the focus is on the benefits of the symbiotic relationship between Tom and the adults. Abstract in AES, XVI (1972-1973), 245; reprinted in Twainian, XXXIII (January-February, 1974). Article reprinted in Kesterson (1973), 92-102.

B22 FIEDLER, LESLIE. The Collected Essays of Leslie Fiedler. New York: Stein and Day. 2 vols., passim.
There are frequent insights into MT in essays not specifically about him, as in the observation that he represents a Folk, rather than Pop tradition, and thus "has become ever more remote from an urban, industrialized world" (II, 470), and in the sadness in IA (I, 91-92). Among the essays dealing extensively with MT are "Come Back to the Raft Ag'in, Huck Honey!" (I, 142-51, originally in Partisan Review, June, 1948); a lengthy treatment of the "Good Good Girl and Good Bad Boy" and "Boys Will Be Boys!" (I, 481-94, passim on MT; originally in The New Leader, April 14, 28, 1958); and "Toward a Centennial: Notes on Innocents Abroad" (I, 296-311, originally in New American Review, 1966). The two volumes are well indexed.

B23 FLECK, RICHARD L. "Mark Twain in the American Wilderness," Nature Study: A Journal of Environmental Education and Interpretation (Verbank, New York), XXV (Summer), 12-14; (Autumn), 10-11.
On RI, noting MT's spirit of freedom in his writings, his growing love for the West, and his portrayal of Hawaii. "While the landscape passages are not, by any means, the whole of Roughing It, they must be considered as a significant element in that they not only illustrate Twain's techniques in language, but they also serve as a subtle barometer of his varying emotional attitudes toward the land."

B24 _____. "Mark Twain's Social Criticism in The Innocents Abroad," Bulletin of the Rocky Mountain Modern Language Association, XXV (June, 1971), 39-48.
"Twain had to swallow his national pride when it came to judging the welfare of the common man." After tracing the social criticism in IA and recent criticism of the book, concludes by noting the awareness MT had gained of social injustices throughout the world. Regardless of what social system might be at fault, foreign or American, "the effects were always the same--the loss of human dignity.... that man should be reduced to the animal state was for Mark Twain insufferable."

B25 FORTENBERRY, GEORGE. "The Unnamed Critic in William Dean Howells' Heroines of Fiction," Mark Twain Journal, XVI (Winter), 7-8.
In the chapter "Scott's Jeanie Deans and Cooper's Lack of Heroines," when discussing Cooper Howells says he "turned to a literary friend who had made rather a special study of him"; Howells's "use of the word 'females' and his reference to The Last of the Mohicans almost makes it a certainty that his critic is Mark Twain." Abstract in AES, XVI (1972-1973), 1763.

B25A FRENCH, BRYANT MOREY. "James Hammond Trumbull's Alternative Chapter Headings for The Gilded Age," Philological Quarterly, L (April), 271-80.
The mottoes chosen by Trumbull parodied the contemporary over-use of chapter mottoes and added satirical running commentary on the plot. Trumbull also furnished alternative mottoes (here printed) which "vie in cleverness with and sometimes exceed" the mottoes used in GA. Abstract by French in MLA Abstracts (1971), 7974.

B26 GERBER, JOHN C. [Review: Maxwell Geismar, Mark Twain: An American Prophet (1970).] American Literature, XLIII (May), 296-98.
"A long, repetitious, highly personal biography that creates a Mark Twain most of us do not recognize...something of a corrective for many of the mucky analyses" of MT in recent years, "yet the fact remains that this is an inept work. Its facts are not always correct, its organization is confusing, its style is irritating, and its thesis is at times absurd." Nonetheless, Gerber agrees with Geismar's view that the last two decades were not a time when MT, on the verge of psychic collapse, wrote works of unrelieved gloom.

B27 GIBSON, WILLIAM M. [Review: Thomas Blues, Mark Twain & the Community (1970).] American Literary Realism, 1870-1910, IV (Summer), 291-92.
"Professor Blues concerns himself...with the subject...how is the individual to fulfill himself in a democracy, by resistance or accommodation, withdrawal or leadership? Unhappily his treatment of this great topic is mostly inadequate" because he tries to cover too much and because his rejection of old views and quest for new ones lead him astray.

B28 GOAD, MARY ELLEN. "The Image and the Woman in the Life and Writings of Mark Twain," _Emporia State Research Studies_, XIX (March), 5-70.

Traces the influence of MT's wife, his mother, and Mary Mason Fairbanks, among others, with particular emphasis on the question of whether he made serious concessions to propriety because of them. "This study originated as a partial fulfillment of the requirements for the degree Master of Arts, Kansas State Teachers College, Emporia, Kansas." Based on familiar, published sources. Abstract in _AES_, XV (1971-1972), 537; reprinted in _Twainian_, XXXII (January-February, 1973).

B29 GOLDSTIEN, NEAL L. "Mark Twain's Money Problem," _Bucknell Review_, XIX (Spring), 36-54.

"Twain thought of things in terms of money and profit," and "the confusion over money which permeates his books is the result, not the cause, of his lack of art." _RI_ and _CY_ furnish useful examples, because "the dominant tones of each are those which rule the author as well," and because the seventeen years between their publication shows a ubiquitous money theme which "almost suggests...an outpouring, an unburdening, and a confession." Abstract in _AES_, XV (1971-1972), 1207; reprinted in _Twainian_, XXXII (January-February, 1973). Abstract by Goldstien in _MLA Abstracts_ (1971), 7976.

B30 GOODYEAR, RUSSELL H. "Huck Finn's Anachronistic Double Eagles," _American Notes and Queries_, X (November), 39.

Although the book was published in 1885 and the preface says "Time: forty to fifty years ago," Chapters XVI and XXII mention twenty-dollar gold pieces--which were first minted in 1849.

B31 GRIMM, CLYDE L., JR. [Review: Howard G. Baetzhold, _Mark Twain and John Bull: The British Connection_ (1970) and Maxwell Geismar, _Mark Twain: an American Prophet_ (1970).] _Studies in the Novel_, III (Spring), 118-21.

Baetzhold's book reflects long and close familiarity with MT, "so much so, indeed, that Baetzhold has had some difficulty in bringing his material into steady focus"; a number of connections are explored, and "in summary, Professor Baetzhold has provided a comprehensive and detailed account of a shaping force on the works of Mark Twain at least as significant as the Missouri frontier or the frontier humorists." The first seventy pages of Geismar's book were enough for Grimm, who tired of the factual inaccuracies, awkward phrasing, amateur psychology, and "distortions of Clemens' social and political views," and refused to read further.

B32 HILL, HAMLIN. "Mark Twain," in J. Albert Robbins, ed., _American Literary Scholarship: An Annual/1971_ (Durham, North Carolina: Duke University Press, 1973), pp. 75-85.

A survey of MT scholarship for the year (See 1963.B32). Contents: "i. Textual and Bibliographical"; "ii. Biographical"; "iii. General Criticism"; "iv. Earlier Works"; "v. _Huckleberry Finn_"; "vi. Later Works."

B33 HOUSMAN, A[LFRED] E[DWARD]. _The Letters of A. E. Housman._ Cambridge, Massachusetts: Harvard University Press, pp. 246-47, 277, 388-89.

Contains the texts of three notes from Housman to Cyril Clemens. He declines the office of honorary Vice-President in the Mark Twain Society, and refers to the elegy on Stephen Dowling Bots in _HF_ as "one of the poems I know by heart" (2 February 1927, pp. 246-47), and permits him to reprint his words about _HF_ although he does not remember what he said (16 February 1929, p. 277). He declines with thanks the Silver Medal of the Mark Twain Society, adding that he has also declined honors offered by two Universities and by the King (2 March 1936), pp. 388-89).

B34 HOWELL, ELMO. "Mark Twain's Indiantown," _Mark Twain Journal_, XV (Summer), 16-19.

The village of a short sketch and the longer _Which Was It?_ appears to be based on Napoleon, Arkansas; the nostalgic excursion is evidence that MT "always felt at home only in the deep South." Abstract in _AES_, XV (1971-72), 1497.

B35 KING, BRUCE. "Huckleberry Finn," _Ariel: A Review of International English Literature_ (University of Calgary), II (October), 69-77.

The "absolute internalization of moral values is peculiarly American," and "_Huckleberry Finn_ is a spiritual autobiography. Its main themes are the development of Huck's acceptance of Jim as an equal...and his willingness to be rejected by society and risk damnation so that Jim may escape." The trip down the river has as its archetype "the traditional allegory of the soul's pilgrimage through this world." It is a radical book, though not in the sense that it would substitute populism: _vide_ Pap Finn. "Huck, isolated, uncorrupted, true to himself, could never be assimilated into any society." Reprinted in Schmitter (1974), pp. 109-16.

B36 KOLIN, PHILIP C. "Mark Twain's Pudd'nhead Wilson: A Selected Checklist," _Bulletin of Bibliography_, XXVIII (April-June), 58-59.

In preparing this checklist of criticism, "I have used the resources of the bibliographies found in _PMLA_ and _American Literature_ as well as such useful tools as

(KOLIN, PHILIP C.)
Dissertation Abstracts and Stovall's guide to research in Eight American Authors. I have excluded earlier, incorrect readings of the novel that don't even follow the plot and I have concentrated on those studies which stay well within the mainstream of useful criticism."

B37 LEARY, LEWIS. [Review: Howard G. Baetzhold, Mark Twain and John Bull: The British Connection (1970) and Thomas Blues, Mark Twain and The Community (1970).] Modern Fiction Studies, XVII (Summer), 276-78.
"Mr. Baetzhold has told just about everything that there is to tell about Clemens and his relations with and attitudes toward Britain," in a book of lasting value for its revelation of how the "readings, reflections, prejudices, and long-toed resentments" of Clemens became the pronouncements of the persona MT. Thomas Blues leaves the term community somewhat unclear, and his book is annoying and puzzling, but the more stimulating of the two, demanding that the reader return to MT with a fresh vision; and for this Blues deserves gratitude.

B38 LEHAN, RICHARD. [Review: William M. Gibson, ed., Mark Twain: "The Mysterious Stranger" Manuscripts (1969) and John S. Tuckey, ed., Mark Twain's "The Mysterious Stranger" and the Critics (1970).] Nineteenth-Century Fiction, XXV (March), 502-508.
The two complementary books "in some ways are central to all Twain criticism." There is an important theme in MT's work of a physical and a spiritual self, an "essential self" and an alter ego, and the topic needs further exploration.

B39 _____. [Review: Arthur L. Scott, Mark Twain at Large (1969), and Howard G. Baetzhold, Mark Twain and John Bull: The British Connection (1970).] Nineteenth-Century Fiction, XXVI (September), 248-50.
Chiefly descriptive, praising both books as well written and valuable additions to MT scholarship.

B40 LONG, E. HUDSON. [Review: Howard G. Baetzhold, Mark Twain and John Bull (1970).] American Literature, XLII (January), 579-81.
A thorough investigation and full documentation make this "a significant contribution to scholarship"; moreover, there are "careful analyses" of a number of MT's works and his mind, which was "free and flexible," though impulsive. There is a useful discussion of the influence on MT of English writers, especially W. E. H. Lecky.

B41 McCULLOUGH, JOSEPH B. "Mark Twain and Journalistic Humor Today," English Journal, LX (May), 591-95.
Iconoclasm is characteristic of American literature, particularly of humor. It is not uncommon for one of our outstanding humorists to end in despair, no longer "able to cope with those aspects of melancholy, terror, violence, and death that he at one time found fit to deal with comically." Abstract in AES, XVI (1972-1973), 870; reprinted in Twainian, XXXIII (January-February, 1974).

B42 _____. "Mark Twain and the Hy Slocum-Carl Byng Controversy," American Literature, XLIII (March), 42-59.
Comic sketches in the Buffalo Express, 1868-1871 under the pseudonyms "Carl Byng" and "Hy Slocum" have been linked to MT. In The Forgotten Writings of Mark Twain (1963) Henry Duskis identifies this and other material as the work of MT, but "his reasons for attribution are usually tenuous and conjectural, and he offers little evidence to support his contentions"; moreover, he does not reprint material in its original form, and misses some sketches, making identification difficult. It appears that MT wrote the sketches signed "Byng" but not those signed "Slocum." Abstract in AES, XV (1971-1972), 1208; reprinted in Twainian, XXXII (January-February). Abstract by McCullough in ALA, IV (June), 93; in MLA Abstracts (1971), 7990.

B43 McMAHAN, ELIZABETH E. "The Money Motif: Economic Implications in Huckleberry Finn," Mark Twain Journal, XV (Summer), 5-10.
Money provides plot motivation and is a means of characterization; it also "serves to focus the reader's attention on the central theme: the indictment of human greed and hypocrisy in a corrupt, profit-oriented society." Abstract in AES, XV (1971-72), 1495.

B44 MALHOTRA, M. L. Bridges of Literature: 23 Critical Essays in Literature. Mayur Colony, Ajmer (India): Sunanda Publications, pp. 25-36, 45-54.
"Notes on Mark Twain's Humour" (pp. 25-37) considers MT as frontiersman and newspaperman, primarily a humorist, though conceding that he was more. In HF emphasizes the humorous aspects of Pap, and the King and Duke. The essay ends by noting that Hal Holbrook, "who physically resembles him a great deal in every detail," has shown the durability of MT's humor by "making huge money" out of stage appearances. ["Read at the All-Rajasthan Universities Seminar on American Literature, sponsored by the USEFI, at Government College, AJMER (1968)."]

1971 - Shorter Writings

(MALHOTRA, M. L.)

"Is Huckleberry Finn a Flawed Work?" (pp. 45-54) argues that "the book fails to tell how [Huck's] non-conformism is a pragmatic approach to life"; Huck's decision to run away at the end and the "evasion of the issues" illustrate this failure. The book survives because of its vitality and humor (pp. 52-53). ["Read at the Regional Seminar on American Literature held at Nainital (1969)."]

B45   MATTHEWS, BRANDER. "The Penalty of Humor," Twainian, XXX (March-April), 1-4, reprinted from Harper's, May, 1896 (1896.B10). Abstract in AES, XV (1971-1972), 1504; reprinted in Twainian, XXXII (January-February, 1973).

B46   MAY, JOHN R. "The Gospel According to Philip Traum: Structural Unity in The Mysterious Stranger," Studies in Short Fiction, VIII (Summer), 411-22. Reprinted in his Toward a New Earth: Apocalypse in the American Novel. Notre Dame, London: University of Notre Dame Press, 1972, pp. 74-91.

"The structural unity of The Mysterious Stranger develops out of Philip Traum's mission of salvation to Theodor Fischer." Abstract by May in ALA, V (December), 135. Reprinted in Schmitter (1974), pp. 133-43.

B47   *MENDELSOHN, M. [Introduction to Russian edition of TS and HF.] Moscow: Khudozhest-vennaya Literatura.

[Source: MHRA Annual Bibliography (1971), No. 8858.]

B48   MILLER, BRUCE E. "Huckleberry Finn: the Kierkegaardian Dimension," Illinois Quarterly, XXXIV (September), 55-64.

In TS, MT portrays boyish egotism and pursuit of excitement and pleasure. "In Huckleberry Finn he examines another side-- the tentative reaching towards companionship, the sorting out of responsibilities, and the troubled investigation of oneself and one's surroundings," and "Huck's final move to the Indian Territory, like Abraham's pilgrimage to Mount Moriah in Soren Kierkegaard's account expresses a unique spiritual adjustment which replaces the norms of social intercourse with a transcedent and terrifyingly immediate acquaintance with supernatural force." Abstract in AES, XV (1971-1972), 2692; reprinted in Twainian, XXXII (January-February, 1973).

B49   MILLICHAP, JOSEPH R. "Calvinistic Attitudes and Pauline Imagery in The Adventures of Huckleberry Finn," Mark Twain Journal, XVI (Winter), 8-10.

Presbyterianism has been predominant as subject matter and ideological influence in Southern literature (although Baptist and Methodist churches are more common), because it insists on human limitations.

St. Paul's influence on the thinking of John Calvin is reflected in HF, especially in the treatment of Huck's father, a figure of the "fallen Adam in the New World." This role is underscored by Huck's references to him as "the old man," who became drunk and "raised Cain...A body would a thought he was Adam--he was just all mud," and by the illusory snakes and devils of his delirium tremens. Abstract in AES, XIV (1972-1973), 1769.

B50   NEBEKKER, HELEN E. "The Great Corrupter or Satan Rehabilitated," Studies in Short Fiction, VIII (Fall), 635-36.

Henry B. Rule's argument in "The Role of Satan in 'The Man That Corrupted Hadleyburg'" (1969) can be further strengthened if we remember that the town had already feared burglars before Satan arrived; in the "Calvinist ethos which Twain both knew and detested," man is already corrupt and the stranger therefore no corrupter.

B51   PEARCE, ROY HARVEY. "Huck Finn in His History," Études Anglaises, XXIV (July-September), 283-91.

Hawthorne's Hester Prynne and Melville's Ishmael will ultimately come to terms with their society, but Huck by his nature cannot: "His function, it turns out, is to demonstrate the absolute incompatability of the sort of self he is and the sort of world in which he tries so hard to live. He gains no sense of his own history and has no future.... He exists not to judge his world but to furnish us the means of judging it-- and also our own world as it develops out of his."

B52   PETTIT, ARTHUR G. "Mark Twain and the Negro, 1867-1869," Journal of Negro History, LVI (April), 88-96.

On MT's ambivalent attitudes. In the West he learned that he could be both pro-Northern and anti-Negro, and for a long time he was prone to make jokes about such topics as the odor of sweating Negroes; but by 1867 he was attacking the dead issue of slavery and reconciled to the idea of Negro citizenship. He later condemned lynching, and eventually learned the need to depict Black men and women "with certain emotional and intellectual attributes long denied the Negro in American literature." The change in his attitudes was partly the result of environment--Nevada was pro-Union and his father-in-law Jervis Langdon was pro-abolition--but MT also was becoming more liberal in his outlook with greater experience of the world.

B53   _____. "Mark Twain, the Blood-Feud, and the South," Southern Literary Journal, IV (Fall), 20-32.

MT's published works and late, unpublished manuscripts reveal "that there were clearly

(PETTIT, ARTHUR G.)
two Souths in Mark Twain's literary imagination--one of nostalgia, the other of nausea and nightmare...the unfallen Eden of his boyhood" and "a Waste Land of murder, miscegenation, blood-feuding, dueling, smalltown depravity, lynching, and white race guilt." He became disenchanted with the South because he changed, but he "remained a Southerner to the end." Abstract in AES, XVI (1972-1973), 246; reprinted in Twainian, XXXIII (January-February, 1974). Abstract by Pettit in MLA Abstracts (1971), 7999.

B54   PICKETT, CALDER M. [Review: Maxwell Geismar, Mark Twain: An American Prophet (1970) and Howard G. Baetzhold, Mark Twain and John Bull (1970).] Journalism Quarterly, XLVIII (Summer), 355-56.
Geismar's "long and curious work which is not really a biography" follows the pattern of his Henry James and the Jacobites, "a brutal commentary not only of [sic] Henry James but on all his admirers." Geismar devotes less than half of his book to what have been considered the major works, emphasizing instead "the diatribes, the disquisitions, the criticisms of contemporary affairs"; nonetheless, it is refreshing to see the attention given to the Autobiography (seen as one of the major works) and FE. Baetzhold's book is briefly described, with the comment that "it is pure scholarship, and it is not as much fun to read as angry old Geismar, but it is a much better book."

B55   RACKHAM, JEFF. "The Mysterious Stranger in 'The Campaign that Failed,' Southern Humanities Review, V (Winter), 63-67.
"A mysterious stranger murdered at night by arcadian boys playing soldier is an imaginative creation inserted into what otherwise would have been only a humorous recollection," indicting war not only for its destruction of human life but also because it turns innocent boys into killers. Abstract in AES, XV (1971-1972), 535; reprinted in Twainian, XXXII (January-February, 1973).

B56   *RAKNEM, INGVALD. Joan of Arc in History, Legend and Literature. Oslo: Universitetsforlaget.
[Source: MHRA Annual Bibliography (1971), 2004, 8869; other details not given.]

B57   REEVES, PASCHAL, et al. "A Checklist of Scholarship on Southern Literature for 1971," Mississippi Quarterly, XXV (Spring, 1972), 199-246. On MT, pp. 209-13.

B58   RITUNNANO, JEANNE. "Mark Twain vs. Arthur Conan Doyle on Detective Fiction," Mark Twain Journal, XVI (Winter), 10-14.
A Double-Barreled Detective Story burlesques A Study in Scarlet, a similar story of revenge, which it follows in plot and several details; however, they differ in that Doyle leads through a series of ordered events to a triumph of justice, while MT's chaotic story "makes no effort to balance the scales of justice." Abstract in AES, XVI (1972-1973), 1767.

B59   ROWLETTE, ROBERT. "Mark Twain's Barren Tree in The Mysterious Stranger: Two Biblical Parallels," Mark Twain Journal, XVI (Winter), 19-20.
Satan's creating and blighting of a tree in Chapter X is a "blending of two of Christ's miracles--the feeding of the five thousand and the cursing of the fig tree"; previously in MS Satan merely pointed to man's shabby nature, but "here, he is shifted from observer to participant, with the result that the scene grows taut with dramatic interest." Abstract in AES, XVI (1972-1973), 1770.

B60   RUBIN, LOUIS D., JR. "How Mark Twain Threw off His Inhibitions and Discovered the Vitality of Formless Form," Sewanee Review, LXXIX (July-September), 426-33.
A review of Maxwell Geismar's Mark Twain: An American Prophet, hostile, and in its vigor reminiscent of some of MT's own criticisms. Geismar, who "frequently can't tell the difference between a novel and a political pamphlet," is mainly interested in MT's anti-imperialism, and distorts his subject to emphasize this point. In this opinionated book, "the list of Mr. Geismar's dislikes constitutes almost a Who's Who of intellectual distinction in our time. Name a good mind, and the chances are that Mr. Geismar dislikes him. Name a good book, and the chances are that Mr. Geismar dislikes it." ("This review is an expanded version of one which originally appeared in the Washington Star.")

B61   SCHIECK, WILLIAM J. "The Spunk of a Rabbit: An Allusion in Huckleberry Finn," Mark Twain Journal, XV (Summer), 14-16.
Shortly before saving Jim from the slave-hunters, Huck wrote, he couldn't speak up because he lacked courage, "the spunk of a rabbit"; but he drove them away by pleading with them to come on the raft to help his father, ill with small-pox. Asking for the opposite of what he wants repeats a device in Uncle Remus, His Songs and Sayings (1880), where Brer Rabbit begs Brer Fox not to throw him in the briar patch. Abstract in AES, XV (1971-72), 1499.

B62   SCHMITZ, NEIL. "The Paradox of Liberation in Huckleberry Finn," Texas Studies in Literature and Language, XIII (Spring), 125-36.
"The freedom Huck strives to attain is his right to be a child, not an impertinent manikin like Tom Sawyer, but the unregenerate poetic child alive in his body and sensitive to the mystery of being in the world."

(SCHMITZ, NEIL)
For Jim, however, the question is one of his manly independence, and he shows his recognition of a slave's position in his attack on Solomon's proposal to divide the child--he has seen "black families dismembered on the [auction] block." The ending throws away the character, Jim "after he has served as a 'moral burden.'" The emancipations of Huck and Jim were different and conflicting in nature. Abstract by Schmitz in MLA Abstracts (1971), 8009.

B63 ____. "Twain, Huckleberry Finn, and the Reconstruction," American Studies (Kansas; formerly Midcontinent American Studies Journal), XII (Spring), 59-67.
"Jim's situation at the end of Huckleberry Finn reflects that of the Negro in the Reconstruction, free at last and thoroughly impotent, the object of devious schemes and a hapless victim of constant brutality." Abstract by Schmitz in MLA Abstracts (1971), 8010.

B64 SKINNER, OTIS. "Mark Twain at the Players' Club," Mark Twain Journal, XV (Summer), back cover.
Facsimile reproduction of a signed typescript; Skinner briefly recalls MT in rather general and conventional terms. Abstract in AES, XV (1971-72), 1501.

B65 SMITH, LUCIAN R. "Sam Clemens: Pilot," Mark Twain Journal, XV (Summer), 1-5.
From MT's published statements and discussions by Paine, DeLancey Ferguson, Dudley R. Hutcherson, and others, concludes that MT "did not enjoy piloting nearly as much as he said he did. From the outset it has been apparent that piloting was not an end in itself, but merely a means to another end: wealth and prestige." Abstract in AES, XV (1971-72), 1500.

B66 STEIN, ALLEN F. "Return to Phelps Farm: Huckleberry Finn and the Old Southwestern Framing Device," Mississippi Quarterly, XXIV (Spring), 111-16.
"The events at Phelps Farm combine with the opening of the novel at St. Petersburg to enclose the account of the trip down the river in a frame which works in much the same way as did the framing device traditionally used by writers in this school of humor," but MT "subtly adds to the functions of the frame, thus enhancing the effectiveness of the novel." Abstract by Stein in MLA Abstracts (1971), 8014; in ALA, V (June, 1972), 183.

B67 STEIN, GERTRUDE. "Unique Tribute to Mark Twain from the Inimitable Gertrude Stein," Mark Twain Journal, XV (Summer), front cover.
Facsimile reproduction of a hand-written note comparing MT to the Mississippi River,
with the signature of Alice Toklas in the margin. "Written for her fellow members of the Mark Twain Society when she visited St. Louis and now published for the first time." Abstract in AES, XV (1971-1972), 1503.

B68 STERN, MADELEINE B. Heads & Headlines: The Phrenological Fowlers. Norman: University of Oklahoma Press.
On the family of phrenologists. Passim on MT, with an account of Jessie Fowler's phrenograph of MT (pp. 253-54; reprinted from Phrenological Journal of April, 1901).

B69 STONE, ALBERT E. [Review: Arthur L. Scott, Mark Twain at Large (1969).] American Literature, XLIII (November), 459-60.
"This is a brisk, informative, but not very profound survey of Twain's career from 1866, when he sailed to Hawaii, to 1910, when he returned from Bermuda to die.... Scott offers no radically new interpretation of the man, the career, the work"; he "jousts with writers of a bygone day...on points no longer moot," but might have made fuller use of recent scholarship.

B70 TWICHELL, JOSEPH H. "Twichell's Letters to Paine," Twainian, XXX (January-February), 3-4.
Twelve letters, 1911-1913, concerning the Paine biography of MT, currently appearing serially in Harper's, making a minor correction and commenting on notebooks, letters, etc. Concludes a series beginning in 1970, (1970.B92). Abstract in AES, XV (1971-1972), 1508; reprinted in Twainian, XXXII (January-February, 1973).

B71 VORPAHL, BEN M. "'Very Much Like a Fire-Cracker': Owen Wister on Mark Twain," Western American Literature, VI (Summer), 83-98.
Based on Wister's "In Homage to Mark Twain," which appeared in Harper's in 1935, summarizes Wister's comments and gives background on Wister and his slight acquaintance with MT. Abstract in AES, XVII (1973-1974), 2151; reprinted in Twainian, XXXIV (March-April, 1975).

B72 WEBER, BROM. [Review: Maxwell Geismar, Mark Twain: An American Prophet (1970).] Saturday Review, LIV (February 27), 27-28.
"Shrouded in a paranoid fog that blurs the book's positive contributions." [Saturday Review editor's note: "Brom Weber has praised Mark Twain's social criticism in The Art of American Humor (1962, 1970) and reprinted it in American Literature: Tradition and Innovation (1969)."]

B73 ZWAHLEN, CHRISTINE. "Of Hell or Hannibal?" American Literature, XLII (January), 562-63.
The title of MT's juvenile poem, "Love Concealed: to Miss Katie of H--L" (Hannibal

(ZWAHLEN, CHRISTINE)
Journal, May 6, 1853) represents a deliberate ambiguity for humorous effect and not
an abbreviation to fit a limited space;
a photostat of the Journal shows room to
write out "Hannibal" in full. MT later
asked his brother about events in "H--L,"
and recalled the reaction to this poem with
amusement. Abstract in AES, XV (1971-1972),
1206; reprinted in Twainian, XXXII (January-
February, 1973). Christine M. Zwahlen's abstract in ALA, V (December), 135, reads in
full: "A pica count of the headline, 'To
Miss Katie of H...L,' suggests that Mark
Twain intended an ambiguous reading"; identical text of this abstract is in MLA Abstracts (1971), 8017.

1972 A BOOKS

A1 CLEMENS, SAMUEL L. The Adventures of Tom Sawyer. New York: Washington Square Press.
Enriched Classics Edition.
A "Reader's Supplement" in the center (as
in other books in this series) includes biographical data and study aids, among them
brief extracts from published criticism.
Contains fifteen stills from the 1938 film
of the novel by Selznick International Pictures, released through United Artists,
with Tommy Kelly as Tom. [A paperbound
popular edition.]

A2 _____. Fables of Man, ed. John S. Tuckey.
Berkeley, Los Angeles, London: University
of California Press.
A volume in the CEAA edition of the MT
Papers. "This collection offers Mark
Twain's pieces on such large topics as God,
providence, Christianity, and human nature,
gathered from the unpublished writings in
the Mark Twain Papers. Although Albert
Bigelow Paine and Bernard DeVoto printed
some of the works included here and various
scholars have quoted extracts in support
of their arguments, none of these texts
has ever appeared in an authoritative printing and few are currently accessible."

A3 _____. The Great Landslide Case: Three Versions, With Editorial Comment by Frederick
Anderson and Edgar M. Branch. Berkeley:
Friends of the Bancroft Library, University
of California.
On the lawsuit described in RI, Chapter
XXXIV. Includes a tipped-in full-size reproduction of the San Francisco Daily Morning Call, August 20, 1863, p. 1.

A4 _____, ed. Frederick Anderson. A Pen Warmed-
Up in Hell: Mark Twain in Protest. New
York, London: Harper & Row, Publishers,
Toronto: Fitzhenry & Whiteside, Ltd.
An anthology of MT's anger, in published
writings and in material from the Mark Twain
Papers. An introduction (pp. x-xviii) de-
scribes MT's "bitterness about the terrors

imposed by useless war, the squalor of racial injustice, the fraudulent distribution
of wealth, and the exploitation of their
citizens by indifferent governments."

A5 _____, and CHARLES DUDLEY WARNER, ed. Bryant
Morey French. The Gilded Age: A Tale of
To-Day. Indianapolis and New York: The
Bobbs-Merrill Company, Inc.
Introduction gives MT and Warner biography,
and background, composition, and criticism
of GA. Appendixes include "Author's Preface
to the London Edition"; "The British Copyright"; "Colonel Sellers's Improvised 'Railroad Map'"; "The Given Name of Colonel Sellers"; a discussion of the chapter-head mottoes.

A6 HARNSBERGER, CAROLINE THOMAS, ed. Everyone's
Mark Twain. South Brunswick and New York:
A. S. Barnes and Company; London: Thomas
Yoseloff Ltd.
Like her Mark Twain at Your Fingertips
(1948), this is a collection of quotations
from MT's published works with a small amount
of material published for the first time.
Arranged alphabetically by categories from
"ABROAD See also ASS, FORGETFULNESS, OPINION"
to "ZEAL See RELIGION," with an extensive
bibliography (pp. 686-92) and a "Correlated
Subjects Index" (pp. 693-703). "Foreword"
by Clara Clemens (pp. 7-8).

A7 SMITH, JANET, ed. Mark Twain on Man and Beast.
New York, Westport: Lawrence Hill & Co.
"What we have here are forty-four of Mark
Twain's highly emotional comments on life,
distinguished from his other comments only
because in each of them birds or beasts or
fish or insects play a part. And so do people," and his animals are often human types,
though true to nature (p. 13). The standard
of selection was the editor's taste, and
"Out of all the Mark Twain that could, by
any definition, be called an animal story,
I discarded nine because they seemed to me
inferior. I made no effort to concentrate
on the obscure, although eleven of these
selections are not in print elsewhere"
(p. 14).

A8 *YOSHIDA, HIROSHIGE. Mark Twain Kenkyu--Shiso
to Gengo no Tenkai [Study of Mark Twain--
Development of Thought and Language]. Tokyo:
Nanundo.
[Source MLA International Bibliography
(1972), 8804.]

1972 B SHORTER WRITINGS

B1 ALSEN, EBERHARD. "Pudd'nhead Wilson's Fight
for Popularity and Power," Western American
Literature, VII, 135-43.
Wilson pretends to support the aristocratic code "because he knows that this will
help his career" (p. 140). The themes of
power and property, evolving out of the

1972 - Shorter Writings

(ALSEN, EBERHARD)

stories of the protagonist and antagonist
help create a "structural and thematic symmetry" which makes PW "Mark Twain's most
tightly constructed novel" (p. 143).

B2 ANAND, SHALINE. "Huckleberry Finn and the
Hemingway Hero," in C. D. Narasimhaiah,
ed., Student's Handbook of American Litera-
ture. Ludhiana, India: Kalyani Publish-
ers. [Papers presented at the All India
Postgraduate Student Seminar in American
Literature held at Mysore University in
December, 1968; organized by the U. S.
Educational Foundation in India.]
A comparison of Huck Finn and Nick Adams;
this is based on Philip Young and Sheridan
Baker, according to the bibliography, and
reflects their thinking.

B3 ANDERSON, FREDERICK, and HAMLIN HILL. "How
Samuel Clemens Became Mark Twain's Publisher: A Study of the James R. Osgood Contracts," Proof, II, 117-43.
A discussion of the terms under which
MT's books were published with Osgood, and
facsimile reproductions of actual contracts.
Abstract by Anderson and Hill in MLA Abstracts (1972), 8742.

B4 ANDERSON, SHERWOOD. "Four American Impressions," in Horace Gregory, ed., The Portable Sherwood Anderson (rev. ed.). New
York: The Viking Press, pp. 428-33.
("These sketches were written in 1919 and
published in The New Republic.") Compares
Ring Lardner to MT, pp. 430-31.

B5 ANON. "Mark Twain Items Published Elsewhere," Twainian, XXXI (January-February),
1-4; (March-April), 3-4.
Reprints a number of abstracts from AES,
XIV (1970-1971).

B6 ANON. "More Mark Twain," Bancroftiana (Bancroft Library, University of California,
Berkeley), No. 52 (April), p. 7.
New acquisitions by the Mark Twain Papers
include manuscript of a chapter in TA and
two leaves of GA, prospectuses of four
books, and an annotated copy of CY showing
passages MT omitted in readings.

B7 ARNER, ROBERT D. "Acts Seventeen and Huckleberry Finn: A Note on Silas Phelps' Ser-
mon," Mark Twain Journal, XVI (Summer), 12.
Allison Ensor's note on Chapter XXXVII of
HF in Explicator (1967) should be expanded:
not only does the Biblical chapter refer to
the brotherhood of all men in verse 26, but
in verse 29 it cautions against the worship
of Mammon, "the chief reason the Souther-
ers...continue to hold slaves"; moreover,
"the fact that one of the preachers mentioned in Acts Seventeen, the man who accompanies Paul to Athens, is named Silas
seems further evidence that this is no

casual allusion on Twain's part." Abstract
in AES, XVI (1972-1973), 2364.

B8 ASPIZ, HAROLD. "Mark Twain and 'Doctor' Newton," American Literature, XLIV (March),
130-36.
On James Rogers Newton, the faith doctor
who successfully treated Olivia Langdon (future wife of MT) for a partial paralysis.
Abstract in AES, XVIII (1974-1975), 1904.
Abstract by Aspiz in ALA, V (June), 182; in
MLA Abstracts (1972), 8745.

B9 BAETZHOLD, HOWARD G. "Found: Mark Twain's
'Lost Sweetheart,'" American Literature,
XLIV (November), 414-29.
The short story "My Platonic Sweetheart"
(1898), originally titled "My Lost Sweet-
heart," is based on MT's fond memories of
Laura M. Wright (not to be confused with
Laura Frazer, the original of Becky Thatch-
er); she was the subject of a recurring
dream by MT, and the dream of a lost sweet-
heart recurs in his works. Abstract by
Baetzhold in MLA Abstracts (1972), 8746.

B10 BARNES, BARBARA LAMKIN. "Mark Twain's Family
Christmas," Yankee, XXXVI (December),
106-109, 136-41.
Based in part on material in the Mark
Twain Papers; includes a description of the
Clemens home in Hartford, with two color
photographs by Willis L. Lamkin.

B11 BARTON, MARION. "Shavian Mirth Recalled.
Shaw and Mark Twain in 1907 Laughed in House
of Commons," Independent Shavian, X
(Spring), 48.
A letter to the editor of the New York
Times (New York, April 19, 1933; appeared
in issue of April 24, p. 14, column 7). A
very brief comment on seeing MT and Shaw at
a distance. Abstract in AES, XVI (1972-
1973), 742; reprinted in Twainian, XXXIII
(January-February, 1974).

B12 BELLAMY, JOE D. "Two Eras, Two Epitaphs:
Steamboating Life in the Works of Mark
Twain and Richard Bissell," Ball State University Forum, XIII (Autumn), 48-52.
MT portrayed the grandeur of the age of
steamboating he had known; Bissell writes
with similar love about the decline of another age of steamboating.

B13 BIE, WENDY A. "Mark Twain's Bitter Duality,"
Mark Twain Journal, XVI (1972-1973), 14-16.
"Many critics have dealt with duality in
Twain's works as the psychological expression of Clemens/Twain or the Polemicist/
Humorist schizophrenia, or as a narrative
device which Twain very nearly overworked";
in fact it is an expression of the duality
MT recognized in human nature, the product
of "the disparity between man's 'low' impulses, drives, and instincts and his 'high'
social and moral code." Abstract in AES,
XVI (1972-1973), 2367.

B14 BONAZZI, ROBERT. [Review: Maxwell Geismar, Mark Twain: An American Prophet (1970).] New Orleans Review, III, 95-97.
Discusses Geismar's debates with other critics, among them Brooks, DeVoto, Leavis, and biographers and editors Paine, Neider, Kaplan. Praises the "very intelligently detailed appraisal of Twain's work," and finds the book "well detailed and gracefully written," though thin on the early period and too detailed on Christian Science and MT's speeches.

B15 BOWEN, JAMES K., and RICHARD VAN DER BEETS, eds. American Literature Abstracts, V (June), 183.
Contains four abstracts by the authors of articles on MT. Discontinued publication with this issue; superseded by MLA Abstracts.

B16 BRACK, O. M., JR. "Mark Twain in Knee Pants: The Expurgation of Tom Sawyer Abroad," Proof, II, 145-51.
This book first appeared serially in St. Nicholas: An Illustrated Magazine for Young Folks, edited by Mrs. Mary Elizabeth Mapes Dodge (author of Hans Brinker; or, The Silver Skates), who made extensive changes to make Huck's dialect more genteel and to soften or remove references to sweating and other bodily functions, to alcohol, to death, and to Negroes and to religious groups in terms which might offend. For book publication in America the expurgated text from St. Nicholas was used for the first two-thirds and the authoritative typescript for the remainder; the English edition published by Chatto & Windus is closer to MT's intentions, apparently set from a carbon copy of the original typescript.

B17 BRAND, JOHN M. "The Incipient Wilderness: A Study of Pudd'nhead Wilson," Western American Literature, VII, 125-34.
A way of entering the setting of PW is through Cooper's The Prairie, which has a "zest and flair" MT's book lacks (p. 125); in both works "existing law proves insufficient to reorder a threatened society" (p. 126), and even if there were a Divine Law which could change the laws of society, "it is doubtful that even Wilson, the best in his community, would have eyes to see and the will to apply it" (p. 134).

B18 BRODWIN, STANLEY. "The Humor of the Absurd: Mark Twain's Adamic Diaries," Criticism, XIV (Winter), 49-64.
"For Twain, humor ultimately derives from contradiction, absurdity and incongruity, the principle of irony triumphant; it functions as a theological sign of man's fall but at the same time enables him to deal with that pathetic state.... Twain's perception of the nature and role of humor in relation to his theological determinism has not been delineated.... I propose to confront this problem in theological-literary terms," showing how MT's diaries of Adam, Eve, and Satan reflect "a variety of ideas illuminating one central concept: that humor is a theological element that binds God's creation to man's fall." Abstract by Brodwin in MLA Abstracts (1972), 8750.

B19 BROGUNIER, JOSEPH. "An Incident in The Great Gatsby and Huckleberry Finn," Mark Twain Journal, XVI (Summer), 1-3.
Compares the killings of Myrtle Wilson and Boggs, with the reactions by Nick and Huck and by the morbidly curious neighbors. Fitzgerald admired MT and expressed his indebtedness to the influence of HF in a letter of August 9, 1939. Abstract in AES, XVI (1972-1973), 2386.

B20 BRONSON, DANIEL ROSS. [Review: Frederick Anderson, ed., Mark Twain: The Critical Heritage (1971).] American Literary Realism, V (Summer), 323-25.
"As a scholarly tool...cannot be faulted.... The selection of criticisms is ample, representative, and without a hint of manipulation for the sake of argument.... For the student just approaching Twain seriously this book is a valuable guidepoint; for the Twain scholar it is a handy reference and a source of continuing conjecture." Anderson makes it clear that the reviews influenced later criticism more than they influenced MT's writing.

B21 *BRUMM, URSULA. "Amerikanische Dichter und europäische Geschichte: Nathaniel Hawthorne und Mark Twain," in Alfred Weber and Harmut Grandel, eds. Geschichte und Fiktion: Amerikanische Prosa im 19 Jahrhundert/History and Fiction: American Prose in the 19th Century (Göttingen: Vanderhoeck & Ruprecht), pp. 85-108.
[Source: MLA Bibliography (1972), Nos. 117, 8236.]

B22 BUDD, LOUIS J. "Did Mark Twain Write 'Impersonally' for the New York Herald?" Library Notes (Duke University Library), No. 43 (November), pp. 5-9.
"Gossip at the National Capital" (February 3, 1868) and two "Washington Gossip" letters (February 10, p. 8 and February 18, p. 3) are unsigned and "do not sound all that much like Mark Twain.... the problem is to judge how Mark Twain would sound when he was trying not to project his breezy, raucous, and witty persona."

B23 BURNS, GRAHAM. "Time and Pastoral: The Adventures of Huckleberry Finn," Critical Review (Melbourne), No. 15, pp. 52-63.
Extends the approach of Leo Marx in The Machine in the Garden (1964); but where Marx "concentrates almost exclusively on

(BURNS, GRAHAM)

the technological subversion of the pastoral ideal.... I want to argue, myself, that the lyrical river journey in Huckleberry Finn, while splendidly realized as a naturalistic re-creation, it is also felt, as we experience it, as a kind of analogue for life itself; and that the characteristic pacing of Twain's writing in the central lyrical episodes creates a sense of timelessness central to its pastoral qualities." Abstract in AES, XVI (1972-1973), 2935.

B24 BUSH, ROBERT. "Grace King and Mark Twain," American Literature, XLIV (March), 31-51.

On the New Orleans author (1851-1932), who visited the Clemenses repeatedly in Hartford (after meeting them there in 1887), and was their guest in Florence in 1892. In addition to her reminiscences of MT in Memories of a Southern Woman of Letters (1932), there are "impressions" of MT and impressions about the Clemens family in her notebooks and letters (here liberally quoted, by permission of Mr. John M. Coxe and the Department of Archives, Louisiana State University, Baton Rouge). Three MT letters are here published, and one appeared in her 1932 Memories. Abstract in AES, XVIII (1974-1975), 1903. Abstract by Bush in ALA, V (June), 182.

B25 CHRISTOPHER, J. R. "On the Adventures of Huckleberry Finn As a Comic Myth," Cimarron Review, No. 18 (January), pp. 18-27 ["This paper was read at a meeting of the South Central Modern Language Association in Memphis, Tennessee, on October 30, 1970."]

Northrop Frye's Anatomy of Criticism (1957) mentions HF three times; "The purpose of this essay is simply to investigate the ways in which Northrop Frye's Theory of Myths is applicable to this Twain fiction."

B26 CLEMENS, OLIVIA and SAMUEL L. CLEMENS. [Facsimile reproduction of joint letter by Olivia Clemens and MT.] Mark Twain Journal, XVI (Winter), front cover.

To the mother of Cyril Clemens, expressing good wishes on her engagement to James Ross Clemens.

B27 COARD, ROBERT L. "Mark Twain's The Gilded Age and Sinclair Lewis's Babbitt," Midwest Quarterly, XIII (April), 319-33.

"Although there seems to be no question of any specific indebtedness of the latter book to the earlier, a comparison...may illuminate the satirical techniques of the two celebrated practitioners and say something about the continuity of American satirical tradition." (Based on texts of the Signet Classic Edition for the two works). Abstract in AES, XVI (1972-1973), 787; reprinted in Twainian, XXXIII (January-February, 1974).

B28 CROWLEY, JOHN W. "A Note on The Gilded Age," English Language Notes, X (December), 116-18.

"A recently discovered Charles Dudley Warner letter" about GA "indicates that the book was completed more quickly than generally supposed" and "supports B. M. French's contention that Warner and Mark Twain were reacting to specific Washington scandals such as the Credit Mobilier affair." The letter (here reprinted) is to Edward Burlingame, who had reviewed the book in Appleton's Journal, XI (January 10, 1874), 59. Abstract in AES, XVII (1973-1974), 1808; reprinted in Twainian, XXXIV (March-April, 1975).

B29 D'AVANZO, MARIO L. "In the Name of Pudd'nhead," Mark Twain Journal, XVI (Summer), 13-14.

The name may be traceable to the reward, the "solid Pudding," which Benjamin Franklin said he received for Poor Richard's Almanac--to which the aphorisms of "Pudd'nhead Wilson's New Calendar" have been compared. Abstract in AES, XVI (1972-1973), 2365.

B30 [DAVIS, CHESTER L.] "Annie Moffett Webster and Charles Noel Flagg Letters to Paine (Pictorial Mark Twain)," Twainian, XXXI (March-April), 1-3.

Chiefly concerned with paintings of MT; Davis speaks of "our promise to print substantially all of the letters written to Paine." Abstract in AES, XVII (1973-1974), 2089; reprinted in Twainian, XXXIV (March-April, 1975).

B31 _____. "Financial Support for Worthy Studies and Publications Supplied by Private, Foundation and Government Sources (Writing and Publication of 'Mark Twain and Hawaii')," Twainian, XXXI (July-August), 1-4; (September-October), 1-4.

A general discussion of the collecting of Twainiana and the contributions made by various individuals; reprints correspondence between Walter Francis Frear and George Hiram Brownell. Abstract in AES, XVII (1973-1974), 2091; reprinted in Twainian, XXXIV (March-April, 1975). The abstract of the September-October installment, "Frear's 'Mark Twain and Hawaii,'" in AES, XVII (1973-1974), 2282 is not yet reprinted in Twainian; see later issues.

B32 _____. "Francis D. Millet, James Montgomery Flagg and Spiridon Portraits (pictorial Mark Twain)," Twainian, XXXI (May-June), 1-4.

On paintings of MT; factual, chiefly indebted to published material. Abstract in AES, XVII (1973-1974), 2090; reprinted in Twainian, XXXIV (March-April, 1975).

B33 _____. "'The Letters of Madame de Sevigne' (17th Century History); (Mark Twain's Marked Copy)," Twainian, XXXI (November-December), 1-4.

([DAVIS, CHESTER L.])

On MT's personal copy of The Letters of Madame de Sevigne to Her Daughter and Friends, Edited by Mrs. Hale...(Revised Edition, Boston: Roberts Brothers, 1878). Begins a series of extensive reprinting of the text of the book (both letters and editorial background), with underscorings and comments by MT; this series in Twainian continues into 1974. Abstract in AES, XVIII (1974-1975), 2274.

B34 ____. [Editor's comment on holdings.] Twainian, XXXI (May-June), 1.

"Many of our members have asked us to give them some idea as a rough estimate how much UNPUBLISHED material we have in our files and our reply is that we have enough, or enough available on call, to fill our four-page 'Twainian' every two months for the NEXT FIFTY YEARS. Some arrangement may be worked out to permit a more rapid use of this material, yet as new material comes to us or the several other depositories in the United States and abroad, we are quite certain that our subtitle 'Mark Twain--Yesterday and Today' was wisely chosen."

B35 ____. [Review: Franklin R. Rogers, ed., Roughing It.] Twainian, XXXI (September-October), 3-4.

Provides useful description of book and editing.

B36 ____. [Review: John S. Tuckey, ed., Fables of Man.] Twainian, XXXI (September-October), 4.

Provides useful description of book and editing.

B37 DINAN, JOHN S. "Hank Morgan: Artist Run Amuck," Massachusetts Studies in English, III (Spring), 72-77.

"The Arthurian world is cruel and unacceptable," but "Hank's art does not illumine, it mystifies. It does nothing to purge his audience of the characteristics that make them slaves.... Without his being aware of it, Hank's Great Artifact, his New World, is but a change in form, not spirit." Abstract in AES, XVIII (1974-1975), 244.

B38 [EICHELBERGER, CLAYTON L.] [Review: Samuel L. Clemens, The Great Landslide Case: Three Versions, ed. Frederick Anderson and Edgar M. Branch.] American Literary Realism, V (Fall), 497.

Brief notice of "an impressively designed and printed publication which reproduces Twain's three versions of a single episode, accompanied by well-documented historical background and comment."

B39 ____. [Review: Horst H. Kruse, Mark Twains "Life on the Mississippi": Eine Entstehungs- und Quellengeschichtliche Untersuchung zu Mark Twains "Standard Work" (1970).] American Literary Realism, V (Spring), 179.

A brief description of this "detailed examination" of the chapters added in 1882.

B40 FETTERLEY, JUDITH. "Disenchantment: Tom Sawyer in Huckleberry Finn," Publications of the Modern Language Association, LXXXVII (January), 69-74.

In TS Tom was a leader, but in HF he has nothing to offer, is pointlessly cruel in his jokes, and becomes a minor tyrant. He has counterparts throughout HF, as in his sharing with Miss Watson "the syndrome of moralism, aggression, and hypocrisy"; the Grangerford-Shepherdson feud reveals a false code of honor when "Southern chivalry is exposed as sneaking up behind a couple of kids and shooting them in the back. But the exposure of that cruelty is not so important as the exposure of the connection between that cruelty and the language of honor. What Mark Twain is recording in Huckleberry Finn, through the Grangerfords, through Miss Watson, and through Tom Sawyer, is his sense of the inevitable connection between moralism, the language of right and wrong with its inevitable concomitant of self-righteousness, and the fact, the act, of aggression." Abstract in AES, XV (1971-1972), 2455 [condensed from Judith Fetterley's own abstract on contents page (p. 5)]; reprinted in Twainian, XXXII (January-February, 1973). Abstract by Judith Fetterley in ALA, V (June), 182; in MLA Abstracts (1972), 8760. [See reply by Anna Mary Wells, 1972.B84.]

B41 NO ENTRY

B42 FISHER, MARVIN, and MICHAEL ELLIOTT. "Pudd'nhead Wilson: Half a Dog is Worse than None," Southern Review, n.x., VIII (July), 533-47.

Wilson is not the hero of the story or "a largely sympathetic character reflecting the author's own feelings"; although an underdog, "he is essentially unfeeling and only superficially perceptive." In a sense a slave's "more than spectral fear of being sold down the river, the precarious condition of a dog's life, and Wilson's fateful remark solving the problem of a barking dog by killing half are symbolic equivalents." Dogs take on a new symbolic value in this book, chiefly as victims. Abstract by Fisher and Elliott in MLA Abstracts (1972), 8762.

B43 GASSAWAY, BOB M. "Tom Sawyer is Back on the River," Contempora (Atlanta, Georgia), II (August-December), 36-40.

1972 - Shorter Writings

(GASSAWAY, BOB M.)
An illustrated account of the filming of TS by APJAC Productions in Arrow Rock, Missouri, noting the expense and logistical complexity: "Mark Twain would have liked it."

B44   GERBER, JOHN C. "Practical Editions: Mark Twain's The Adventures of Tom Sawyer and The Adventures of Huckleberry Finn," Proof, II, 285-92.
MT's concern with precise degrees of emphasis in his writing is revealed by his attention to both conventional punctuation and liberal use of dashes, parentheses, brackets, italics, and exclamation points, and his linking by hyphens words not customarily joined; "as a result, the exact accidental in one of his novels can be almost as crucial for meaning as the right word." Unfortunately, there is no single text of TS that can be used as printer's copy for a new edition, and even HF presents problems because the manuscript used by the printer is lost. School and college texts of both books introduce large numbers of variants and "are unsatisfactory, in some instances dramatically so. At best, our students are reading approximations of what Mark Twain wanted them to read." Abstract by Gerber in MLA Abstracts (1972), 8765.

B45   GOTTFRIED, LEON. "The Odyssean Form: An Exploratory Essay," in Peter Uwe Hohendahl, Herbert Lindenberger, and Egon Schwarz, eds., Essays on European Literature in Honor of Liselotte Dieckmann (St. Louis: Washington University Press), pp. 19-43, passim.
On the Odyssey, Don Quixote, Joseph Andrews, and Huckleberry Finn. In each there is a contrast of "home" and "road," with problems in the final homecoming (p. 29), "pattern of flight and return," and "a symbolic death" for the hero; and "at some point he is rescued naked or nearly so from pit, ditch, river, or sea. In each work, finally, there is an initiation, that is, a significant transmission of values from an older, wiser, or higher ranking central figure to his junior" (p. 33). HF "is the least hopeful" of the four books, because MT "found (or presented) no social reality of any sort that he could affirm as being worthy of his heroes."

B46   GRIBBEN, ALAN. "Mark Twain, Phrenology and the 'Temperaments': A Study of Pseudoscientific Influence," American Quarterly, XXIV (March), 44-68.
"In the following essay I wish to demonstrate that his fascination with this pseudoscience actually had begun by the time he was nineteen years old; that he made use of its terminology and tenets in a minor but persistent manner in his literature; that while he scorned its practitioners, he displayed a lifelong uncertainty about the

soundness of its theories; and that one of the fundamental doctrines which he absorbed from his early study of phrenology--the notion of 'temperaments'--not only shaped his self-concept, but also influenced his choice of language in expressions of his later deterministic philosophy." Abstract by Gribben in MLA Abstracts (1972), 8766.

B47   HARRELL, DON W. "A Chaser of Phantoms: Mark Twain and Romanticism," Midwest Quarterly, XIII (January), 201-12.
MT's dream fragments "The Enchanted Sea Wilderness," "An Adventure in Remote Seas," and The Great Dark "employ identical protagonists and frame stories, and they echo strangely the best of Twain's earlier writing" such as RI and HF; parallels may be traced back as far as his newspaper correspondence from the Sandwich Islands. Abstract in AES, XV (1971-1972), 3023; reprinted in Twainian, XXXII (January-February, 1973). Abstract by Harrell in MLA Abstracts (1972), 8767.

B48   HARRISON, STANLEY R. "Mark Twain's Requiem for the Past," Mark Twain Journal, XVI (Summer), 3-10.
Explanations of MT's early optimism and late cynicism in terms of his personal experiences tend to overlook the obvious fact that his life paralleled that of his country: the growth of a more sober, disillusioned national outlook is reflected in his works. Abstract in AES, XVI (1972-1973), 2368.

B49   HILL, HAMLIN. "Mark Twain," in J. Albert Robbins, ed., American Literary Scholarship: An Annual/1972.
A survey of MT scholarship for the year (See Gerber 1963.B32). Contents: "i. Textual and Bibliographical"; "ii. Biographical"; "iii. General Criticism"; "iv. Earlier Works"; "v. Huckleberry Finn"; "vi. Later Works."

B50   HOWELL, ELMO. "Mark Twain and the Civil War," Ball State University Forum, XIII (Autumn), 53-61.
On MT's slight involvement in the War, the importance of the South in his writings, and, as exemplified in his river piloting, his self-doubts.

B51   _____. "Tom Sawyer's Mock Funeral: A Note on Mark Twain's Religion," Mark Twain Journal, XVI (Winter), 15-16.
MT "seemed emancipated, but the best of his work reflects the spirit of Missouri fundamentalist faith," as in the emotional scene in the church: "In his most moving moments Mark Twain turned instinctively to the values derived from religious faith."

B52 HUBBELL, JAY B. Who Are the Major American Writers?: A Study of the Changing Literary Canon. Durham, North Carolina: Duke University Press, pp. 135-44 and passim.
        Traces the growth of MT's reputation in an extended study ("Mark Twain," pp. 135-44), with a number of significant comments on him elsewhere in the volume, as in references to him in literary histories and the standing he achieved in various polls to determine who were the nation's major writers. Includes references to anthologies and critical surveys which are not listed in the present bibliography. Article reprinted in Schmitter (1972), pp. 19-28.

B53 KAPLAN, HAROLD. "Huckleberry Finn: What It Means to Be Civilized," in his Democratic Humanism and American Literature (Chicago and London: University of Chicago Press), pp. 225-52.
        "Huck is demonstrably a frontier Thoreau, who has a ritualistic need for isolation, and whose escape from his social role is dramatized by his false death and funeral" (p. 237); but "for Huck this isolation won't sustain itself" and he needs Jim (p. 238). Huck and Jim continually face the community on shore, and thereby discover the primary values that might redeem its existence" (p. 242). As in Melville's The Confidence Man, "the issue...remains the question of whom to trust" (p. 251); in the end Huck has been civilized: he "lives in the civilized imagination of his society."

B54 KERR, HOWARD. "'Sperits Couldn't A Done Better': Mark Twain and Spiritualism," in his Mediums, and Spirit-Rappers, and Roaring Radicals: Spiritualism in American Literature, 1850-1900 (Urbana, Chicago, London: University of Illinois Press), pp. 155-89.
        A thorough treatment of spiritualism in MT's life and works. Includes his visits to mediums in San Francisco, seances in the Nook Farm colony, and visiting mediums in London with Olivia after Susan's death-- although he was not a believer. Kerr relies principally on the familiar published material about MT, but has discovered interesting parallels between the tricks of Tom and Huck at the Phelps farm and the activities of a spirit at the home of the Reverend Eliakim Phelps in 1850: in each case there were straw-stuffed dummies, anonymous letters, mysterious writings in unknown symbols, and wandering sheets, spoons, nails, and candlesticks; and details of the Eliakim Phelps haunting were available to MT (pp. 173-80).

B55 KIM, YONG-KWON. "Teaching and Survey of American Literature in Korea: A Survey," in C. D. Narasimhaiah, ed., Asian Responses to American Literature (Delhi, London: Vikas Publications), pp. 395-98.
        The Periodical Index published by the Republic of Korea National Assembly Library in 1970 lists eight articles on MT out of 101 on American literature for the period 1963-1969 (p. 397), and five master's theses were written on MT in Korean universities between 1945 and 1968.

B56 KRAUS, W. KEITH. "Mark Twain's 'A Double-Barreled Detective Story': A Source for the Solitary Oesophagus," Mark Twain Journal, XVI (Summer), 10-12.
        Compares the famous passage to a descriptive passage in Conan Doyle's A Study in Scarlet, of which MT's story is a parody and to which he appears to have referred previously, in "Hadleyburg," Abstract in AES, XVI (1972-1973), 2363.

B57 "Letters to Paine from Samuel E. Moffett, S. L. Severance and Annie M. Webster in Years 1906-1917," Twainian, XXXI (May-June), 4.
        Contain little information directly pertaining to MT. Abstract in AES, XVII (1973-1974), 2088; reprinted in Twainian, XXXIV (March-April, 1975).

B58 LEWIS, STUART. "Twain's Huckleberry Finn, Chapter XIV," Explicator, XXX (March), Item 61.
        While Huck takes the traditional view of Solomon's wisdom in proposing to divide a baby, "Jim realizes the terror of one man's holding absolute power over another.... The test is too close for comfort." Abstract by Lewis in MLA Abstracts (1972), 8776.

B59 *LLOYD, JAMES B. "The Nature of Twain's Attack on Sentimentality in The Adventures of Huckleberry Finn," University of Mississippi Studies in English, XIII, 59-63.
        Characters cry a total of 71 times in HF, for the right reason, or sentimentally, or hypocritically; this crying is one of MT's ways of demonstrating a proper balance of head and heart. [Source: Abstract by Lloyd in MLA Abstracts (1973), 8876.]

B60 LYCETTE, RONALD. "Mark Twain Mapping His Territory," ETC: A Review of General Semantics, XXIX (June), 155-64.
        MT's "works reveal a persistent effort to understand the process that enables a man to grow emotionally and intellectually," as is revealed in Old Times on the Mississippi and HF.

B61 McCULLOUGH, JOSEPH B. "A Listing of Mark Twain's Contributions to the Buffalo Express, 1869-1871," American Literary Realism, 1870-1910, V (Winter), 61-70.
        Lists a total of 134 items, grouped as "Sketches," "Sketches and Poems Signed Carl Byng," "Editorials," "People and Things," and "Miscellaneous."

1972 - Shorter Writings

B62 *MELLARD, JAMES. "Prolegomena to a Study of the Popular Mode in Narrative," Journal of Popular Culture, VI (Summer), 1-19. [Source: Abstract in AES, XVIII (1974-1975), 2512. As part of a broader study, treats MT's assimilation of formulaic material from the "folk."

B63 MEYER, HORST E. "An Unnoticed Twain Letter," Mark Twain Journal, XVI (Winter), back cover. To Christian Bernard, first Baron Tauchnitz (September 14, 1876), on the German publication of Tom Sawyer; MT had learned through "my friend, Bret Harte" that Tauchnitz was interested in the book.

B64 MILLER, LEO. "Huckleberries and Humans," Publications of the Modern Language Association, LXXXVII (March), 314, (letter). MT's choice of the Christian name "Eschol" for his Colonel Sellers in GA may be significant, referring to the Hebrew word for "a bunch of grapes" and to an incident in Numbers XIII, 23-24; it could have been suggested by MT's friend, the Reverend Joseph Twichell.. See 1961.B17; 1962.B37.

B65 MURRAY, DONALD, CHAN WAI-HUENG, and SAMUEL HUANG. "A Checklist of American Books in Chinese Translation," American Book Collector (Chicago), XXII (March-April), 15-37. On pp. 28-29, lists 37 books by MT, most of them published in the '30's and '40's, or in Hong Kong or on Taiwan.

B66 OSTROM, ALAN. "Huck Finn and the Modern Ethos," Centennial Review, XVI (Spring), 162-79. It is a misreading to see HF in terms of our day, as "a socially liberal/radical Bildungsroman": the novel's structure reveals a denial of the perfectability of man, and Huck, no Noble Savage, is merely "trying his best, a man of good will trapped in a world he never made." Abstract in AES, XVI (1972-1973), 2936.

B67 REEVES, PASCHAL, et al., comps. "A Checklist of Scholarship on Southern Literature for 1972," Mississippi Quarterly, XXVI (Spring 1973), 201-203 (portion on MT.) Fifth annual checklist, including about two dozen books and articles on MT published in 1972; annotated. Generally duplicates other standard bibliographies.

B68 *ROBINSON, FRED C. "Appropriate Naming in English Literature," Names, XX (June), 131-37. [Source: Abstract in AES, XVIII (1974-1975), 1013.] As part of a broader study, discusses the names of Tom Sawyer and Huck Finn.

B69 ROWLETTE, ROBERT. "Mark Twain, Sarah Grand, and The Heavenly Twins," Mark Twain Journal, XVI (Summer), 17-18. "Hundreds of notations" in MT's copy of Sarah Grand's popular novel, shows his interest in a book burdened, like his own Those Extraordinary Twins, with "a sub-plot featuring twins...who interfered with the main line of action." MT's harsh judgments, as he must have recognized, "were apropos not only of her book but essentially of the uncut version of his," which he revised into PW. "Internal evidence indicates that he revised his book before reading hers," although it is still possible that he was already familiar with Sarah Grand's book and influenced by it. Abstract in AES, XVI (1972-1973), 2366.

B70 ROYOT, DANIEL. "Éléments Phonologiques du Dialect Noir dans 'Huckleberry Finn,'" Langues Modernes, LXVI, No. 1, 79-83. This examination of Negro dialect in Huckleberry Finn consists chiefly of three lists: "Graphonologie: Système Vocalique" (on the pronunciation of specific phonemes); "Phonétique et Morphologie" (on the structure of words, as in the adding or dropping of sounds); "Valeur de la Transcription" (notes that Jim's speech is a synthesis of "Low Colloquial," "Southern Speech," and Negro dialect).

B71 RUBIN, LOUIS D., JR. "Mark Twain and the Post-War Scene," in his The Writer in the South: Studies in a Literary Community. Athens: University of Georgia Press. Mercer University Lamar Memorial Lectures, No. 15. Only MT and George W. Cable "were able to escape the trauma of the Lost Cause," and Cable did so only through lifetime struggle against it; "Thus it is Mark Twain, and Mark Twain alone, whose imagination was sufficiently free to look within himself" (p. 48), but he never fully broke away. "It seems to me that in A Connecticut Yankee the whole ambivalent love-hate relationship of Sam Clemens with the South is dramatized and laid out plainly. That the Arthurian England which Hank Morgan, master mechanic from Connecticut, sets out to reform is in effect the South of Clemens's youth, is clear from the very outset" (p. 69).

B72 SACKETT, S. J. E. W. Howe. New York: Twayne Publishers, Inc., passim. Contains numerous quotations from correspondence between MT and Howe, little of it particularly revealing. Quotes Howe's estimate in 1881 that MT's literary career was almost over (Atchinson Globe, December 31, p. 3, 1881.B6; quoted p. 74).

B73 SCHERTING, JACK. "Poe's 'The Cask of Amontillado': A Source for Twain's 'The Man That Corrupted Hadleyburg,'" Mark Twain Journal, XVI (Summer), 18-19.

(SCHERTING, JACK)

Although the story's theme is that of Milton's Areopagitica, which "cannot praise a fugitive and cloistered virtue...that never sallies out and sees her adversary," the structural parallels are closer to Poe's story of a delayed revenge for an unspecified offence; moreover, both Montresor and Stephenson "exploit human vanity by challenging the reputation of their victims." Although MT probably did not deliberately pattern his story on Poe's, he was sometimes unconsciously influenced by his reading; "In this connection it is also worth noting that Poe's story 'William Wilson' may have provided Twain with some of the ingredients for his novel with a similar title, Pudd'nhead Wilson." Abstract in AES, XVI (1972-1973), 2357.

B74   SHETTY, NALINI V. "A Case for the Study of Twain's Pudd'nhead Wilson," in C. D. Narasimhaiah, ed., Asian Response to American Literature (Delhi and London: Vikas Publications), pp. 207-14.

Expresses surprise that there is so little interest displayed in PW, important for its treatment of the Negro and the theme of miscegenation; this is especially relevant to India, with its phenomenon of the Anglo-Indian.

B75   SIMPSON, LOUIS P. "Mark Twain and the Pathos of Regeneration: A Second Look at Geismar's Mark Twain" Southern Literary Journal, IV (Spring), 93-106.

Defends Maxwell Geismar's Mark Twain: An American Prophet (1970) against the charge by Brom Weber (Saturday Review, February 27, 1971) that it is merely a continuation of Geismar's "ugly political attack" against "American literary intellectuals." In reply, Simpson calls it a "big, ill-organized, clumsily written--but in its way important-- book," in which Geismar appeals less to our view of MT as radical than "to the image of an aged prophet speaking to us out of the depths of the Old Republic about an American pastoral destiny that could never be." Abstract in AES, XVI (1972-1973), 1447; reprinted in Twainian, XXXIII (January-February, 1974). Article reprinted in Simpson's The Man of Letters in New England and the South: Essays on the History of the Literary Vocation in America (1973), pp. 150-66.

B76   SKERRY, PHILIP J. "The Adventures of Huckleberry Finn and Intruder in the Dust: Two Conflicting Myths of the American Experience," Ball State University Forum, XIII (Winter), 4-13.

Compares MT's and Faulkner's novels on "the basic narrative level, the psychological level, the sociological level, and the symbolic level," with opposing interpretations of the American experience and the American hero.

B77   SOLOMON, ANDREW. "Jim and Huck: Magnificent Misfits," Mark Twain Journal, XVI (Winter), 17-24.

Despite the damage done to the ending by MT's amateurishness, HF is "a brilliantly warm and comic portrait of two human beings, one white and one black, who fall outside of and above their society." Abstract by Solomon in MLA Abstracts (1972), 8792.

B78   TARIQ, AZIZUDDIN. "Mark Twain and the Damned Human Race," in C. D. Narasimhaiah, ed., Asian Response to American Literature (Delhi and London: Vikas Publications), pp. 20 pp. 201-207.

Beneath the scathing commentator there was a man of great warmth. "No American writer has been more dedicated, to the welfare of mankind, and at the same time, more grievously wounded by its follies" (p. 206).

B79   TAYLOR, ROBERT, JR. "Sounding the Trumpets of Defiance: Mark Twain and Norman Mailer," Mark Twain Journal, XVI (Winter), 1-14.

On their social criticism and questioning of the American myth.

B80   VANDERBILT, KERMIT. "Mark Twain Writes to Poet Longfellow," Mark Twain Journal, XVI (Summer), front cover.

Facsimile reproduction of MT letter (June 4, 1877), asking Longfellow's support (together with that of Lowell, Whittier, and Holmes) in urging President Hayes to appoint William Dean Howells to a government mission in Switzerland. Abstract in AES, XVI (1972-1973), 2369.

B81   _____. "Correction and Further Note on Mark Twain and Longfellow," Mark Twain Journal, XVI (Winter), 24.

MT's letter to Longfellow reproduced on the front cover of the preceding issue helps reveal his inner conflict in viewing the Eastern literary establishment a few months before the Whittier Birthday Dinner speech in Boston. The date of a Howells letter, misprinted in the preceding issue, is here corrected.

B82   WALTERS, THOMAS N. "Twain's Finn and Alger's Gilman: Picaresque Counter-Directions," Markham Review, III (May), 53-58.

"Whereas Huck struggles with questions of what morality is, Jed [in Horatio Alger, Jr.'s Jed, The Poorhouse Boy, 1900] conforms to the morality of the society he wishes to join," and is a less successful, imaginative creation than Huck. Abstract in AES, XVIII (1974-1975), 1546.

B83   WARREN, ROBERT PENN. "Mark Twain," Southern Review, n.s. VIII (July), 459-92.

A study of MT's incoherent character and his major works, with particular emphasis on HF.

B84 WELLS, ANNA MARY. "Huck Finn, Tom Sawyer, and Samuel Clemens," Publications of the Modern Language Association, LXXXVII (October), 1130-31.

A reply to Judith Fetterley's article in the January PMLA: Huck Finn is not Mark Twain or Samuel Clemens; what he "finally sees in Tom is unendurable, and if the function of art is to make us endure the unendurable, it is still hard to do it in a book for boys." Huck's decision to abandon civilization was not that of Clemens, who in his letters to Howells "was clearly identifying with Tom."

B85 WELSH, JOHN R. [Review: Lewis Leary, Southern Excursions: Essays on Mark Twain and Others (1971).] Southern Literary Journal, IV (Spring), 128-32.

MT isn't really a Southerner, and perhaps the book's title is misleading: "Southern Excursions is really a book about the national literature, and a very good one."

B86 WHITE, RAY LEWIS. Sherwood Anderson/Gertrude Stein: Correspondence and Personal Essays. Chapel Hill: University of North Carolina Press, pp. 45, 73, 97, 104.

Contains brief, laudatory comments on MT by Gertrude Stein.

B87 YOUNG, PHILIP. "Huckleberry Finn: The Little Lower Layer," in his Three Bags Full: Essays in American Fiction (New York: Harcourt Brace Jovanovich, Inc.), pp. 136-53.

HF represents a national dream of escape, but Huck is wounded by his experiences on shore and has grown up out of MT's control; it is for this reason that the story is turned over to Tom Sawyer. The date "1952" appears at the end of the essay, but there is no indication that this is from Young's book on Ernest Hemingway of that year. Young also discusses the wounded Huck in his Ernest Hemingway: A Reconsideration (1966).

1973 A BOOKS

A1 BISSELL, RICHARD. My Life on the Mississippi; or, Why I am Not Mark Twain. Boston: Little, Brown and Company.

Bissell, who was formerly a Mississippi River pilot and still holds a license, had been reading and thinking for years about MT and brings a professional's interest to speculations about him as a pilot, describes MT as "a nut," but respects his strengths.

A2 CLEMENS, SAMUEL L., ed. Paul Baender. The Works of Mark Twain: "What is Man?" And Other Philosophical Writings. Berkeley, Los Angeles, London: Published for the Iowa Center for Textual Studies by the University of California Press.

A volume in the standard edition of MT's works: "An Approved Text, Center for Editions of American Authors, Modern Language Association of America."

A3 GALE, ROBERT L. Plots and Characters in the Works of Mark Twain. With a foreword by Frederick Anderson. Hamden, Connecticut: Archon Books, 1973. 2 vol.

Vol. I summarizes book and "notebook material, autobiographical dictation (including Mark Twain in Eruption), and collected letters." Vol. II alphabetically lists "all fictional characters and all real-life people as well, provided they move, speak, or otherwise have a part in action which Twain vivifies (except where indicated in footnotes after certain titles). Well over seven thousand characters are collected from Twain's works and identified here..." (I, xi). Meticulously prepared and invaluable to students of MT.

A4 GEISMAR, MAXWELL, ed. and introduction. Mark Twain and the Three R's: Race, Religion, Revolution--and Related Matters. Indianapolis and New York: The Bobbs-Merrill Company, Inc.

"This is an anthology of Mark Twain's radical social commentary," from 1869. "I claim that, far from being the embittered old man of the scholarly legend, Twain was a revolutionary temperament from the very beginning of his literary career (or his life) to the end. Indeed, it is true that his best polemics and social satires were written after 1900, in the closing decade of his life" (p. xv). "In this book I have tried to keep editorial comment to a minimum. As usual Mark Twain speaks for himself better than anybody can speak for him, and that is what he is doing in these pages" (p. xxvi). This is not new material, and it overlaps Foner's Mark Twain: Social Critic (1958) and Janet Smith's Mark Twain on the Damned Human Race (1962), but the selections are intelligently made and the introduction is an interesting portrayal of MT as a man of his time.

A5 HILL, HAMLIN. Mark Twain: God's Fool. New York: Harper & Row, Publishers.

A meticulously documented picture of the tragic last ten years of MT's life, based on original material, most of it unpublished, in the Mark Twain Papers and other collections. Hill reveals the disintegration of a family, struggles for the favor of "The King," and rages and alienations, and he suggests that these years were the culmination of a life of guilt and uncertainty: "Fear had been the controlling interest of his life: fear of poverty, fear of offending and alienating his family and friends, fear of being mistaken by his audience. He moved insecurely in all the worlds he inhabited, much like the mysterious stranger in a dream world who obsessed him in his fiction" (p. 269).

A6 KESTERSON, DAVID B. Critics on Mark Twain: Readings in Literary Criticism. Coral Gables, Florida: University of Miami Press.
"Critics on Mark Twain: 1882-1940" (pp. 13-36) and "Critics on Mark Twain Since 1940" (pp. 37-50) consist largely of very brief excerpts from 31 sources; because of their brevity and the ease with which they may be found elsewhere most of these are not cross-referenced in the present bibliography. There are also longer or complete reprintings of critical material, in the remainder of the book, and in most cases these are cross-referenced in the present bibliography.

A7 SMITH, J. HAROLD. Mark Twain: Rebel Pilgrim. New York: Heath Cote Publishing Corp.
A study of MT's skepticism and his search for understanding. "The aim of this analysis of Mark Twain's life and thought is two-fold: (1) to provide a human-interest account of the events and experiences in the life of a fascinating man. (2) To illuminate the thought of the author by arranging his views, attitudes, and concepts under distinctive topical areas of consideration." Two appendixes tabulate his references to God, Jesus Christ, and Heaven, and "Subject-Areas of Major Writings in Relation to Time-Pattern of Publication."

A8 _____. Women in Mark Twain's World. New York: Carlton Press, Inc.
On women in MT's domestic, social, romantic, love, literary, and political worlds, including extensive quotation from his works in the text of 23 pages.

1973 B SHORTER WRITINGS

B1 ANON. "Mark Twain Items Published Elsewhere," Twainian, XXXII (January-February), 1-4. Reprints a number of abstracts from AES, XV (1971-1972).
"Actually our reprinting each year starts with the issue of A.E.S. last carried by us, not necessarily opening and closing the calendar year but only from such issues as have been received by us before going to press for this issue. Attention is also called to the fact that many of the items appeared in their original printing much earlier than the past year however they had not been abstracted and available to us. We make no attempt to read or reprint everything mentioning Mark Twain" (unsigned headnote by Chester L. Davis). Of the 29 abstracts, nine concern material in past issues of Twainian, a few involve only passing mention of MT, and (following what appears to be an unstated Twainian policy) abstracts of material from Mark Twain Journal are silently passed over. Abstract in AES, XVIII (1974-1975), 2283.

B2 ARMS, GEORGE. [Review: John S. Tuckey, ed., Mark Twain's Fables of Man, (1972).] American Literature, XLV (March), 122.
"Mr. Tuckey has perceptively observed th three major motifs in his collection and grouped the manuscripts accordingly.... 'The Myth of Providence'... 'The Dream of Providence'... 'The Nightmare of History.'" They include some of MT's better work, and the editing (with full textual apparatus) is excellent.

B3 *BRODWIN, STANLEY. "Blackness and the Adamic Myth in Mark Twain's Pudd'nhead Wilson," Texas Studies in Literature and Language, XV, 167-76.
On the two "falls" in PW: that of America, as exemplified by slavery, and the fall of Roxana and her son Tom; Wilson links the falls and provides revelation through his fingerprinting. [Source: Abstract by Brodwin in MLA Abstracts (1973), 8837.]

B4 _____. "Mark Twain's Masks of Satan: The Final Phase, American Literature, XLV (May), 206-27.
MT cast Satan in four basic roles: "the conventional tempter and 'Father of Lies,'" "a sympathetic commentator on the tragedy of man's fall," "a mischievous, sarcastic questioner of God's ways," and "a force of spiritual though amoral 'innocence' charged with divine-like creative power"; he ultimately came "to the 'position' that salvation lay outside of man, in the inevitable triumph of Satan." Abstract by Brodwin in MLA Abstracts (1973), 8838.

B5 BYERS, JOHN R., JR. "Mark Twain's Mary Jane Wilks: Shamed or Shammed?" Mark Twain Journal, XVII (Winter), 13-14.
Huck writes in Chapter XXVII of "them devils laying right there under her own roof, shaming her and robbing her"; the word "shaming" is probably misspelled. Abstract in AES, XVIII (1974-1975), 2932.

B6 CARDWELL, GUY A. "Life on the Mississippi: Vulgar Facts and Learned Errors," ESQ: A Journal of the American Renaissance, XIX (4th Quarter), 283-93.
Discusses a number of factual errors in accounts of the inception, writing, and publication of LOM. Abstract by Cardwell in MLA Abstracts (1973), 8840.

B7 CARY, RICHARD. "In Further Defence of Harriet Shelley: Two Unpublished Letters by Mark Twain," Mark Twain Journal, XVI (Summer), 13-15.
Texts of two MT letters (July 17, 30, 1901, from Ampersand, near Lower Saranac Lake, N.Y.) to Elizabeth Akers Allen (author of the sentimental song, "Rock Me to Sleep, Mother"), responding to letters in which she defended Percy Shelley's conduct. Abstract in AES, XVIII (1974-1975), 595. Abstract by Cary in MLA Abstracts (1973), 8842.

MARK TWAIN: A REFERENCE GUIDE

1973 - Shorter Writings

B8   CATHER, WILLA. "Willa Cather's Tribute to
     Mark Twain," Mark Twain Journal, XVII (Win-
     ter), back cover.
         Facsimile of a signed typescript with her
     corrections (n.d.), here published for the
     first time, relating how a Russian violin-
     ist enjoyed HF in translation. Asking how
     this is possible, with MT's virtually un-
     translatable language, she concludes: "The
     only answer seems to be that if a book has
     vitality enough, it can live through even
     the brutalities of translators." Abstract
     in AES, XVIII (1974-1975), 2937.

B9   CLEMENS, SAMUEL L. "Complete Text of Letter
     to Mark Twain's Kinsman, Dr. James Ross
     Clemens, the Editor's Father, Whom the Hu-
     morist Nicknamed 'Doctor Jim,'" Mark Twain
     Journal, XVI (Summer), front cover.
         Facsimile reproduction of letter from
     Hotel Krantz, Vienna (March 5, 1899) on
     various family matters; urges him to keep
     his moustache. Abstract in AES, XVIII
     (1974-1975), 597.

B10 CLOUTIER, ARTHUR C. "'Dear Mr. Seelye...Yours
     Truly, Tom Sawyer,'" College English, XXXIV
     (March), 849-53.
         A reply to Seelye's The True Adventures of
     Huckleberry Finn (1970); written in boy-
     dialect by Tom Sawyer, who discusses ques-
     tions of style, the debated ending of HF,
     and his own place in the novel. Abstract by
     Cloutier in MLA Abstracts (1973), 8844.

B11 CLYMER, KENTON J. "John Hay and Mark Twain,"
     Missouri Historical Review, LXVII (April),
     397-406.
         On their personal and literary friendship
     of 38 years. MT never criticized Secretary
     of State Hay, although sharing with Howells
     a disagreement with Hay's social and politi-
     cal philosophy, and opposition to his for-
     eign policy. It was John Hay who assented
     to a proposal by Howells to review P&P in
     the New York Tribune, supporting him in the
     face of Whitelaw Reid's objections to the
     ethics of allowing "a warm personal friend
     & in some matters literary partner, write a
     critical review of him in a paper."

B12 COX, JAMES M. "Mark Twain, the Height of Hu-
     mor," in Louis D. Rubin, Jr., ed., The Comic
     Imagination in American Literature (New
     Brunswick, New Jersey: Rutgers University
     Press), pp. 139-48 (also passim on MT; in-
     dexed).
         A rebel against the Union and a deserter
     from Confederate forces, MT remained a
     troublemaker when he went to Nevada. As a
     humorist he dealt with a less reputable
     genre, but learned a balance between affront
     to his audience and a bland predictability;
     thus, we can laugh at the townspeople duped
     by the "Royal Nonesuch" in HF, where "the
     image of a naked King which reduces us to a
     wail of pain in King Lear, finally reduces
     us to helpless laughter."

B13 _____. "Mark Twain: The Triumph of Humor,"
     in Matthew J. Bruccoli, ed., The Chief Glory
     of Every People (Carbondale and Edwardsville:
     Southern Illinois University Press; London
     and Amsterdam: Feffer & Simmons, Inc.),
     pp. 211-30.
         Past criticism has dismissed MT as a "mere"
     humorist or praised him for being something
     more; Cox argues in favor of the importance
     of the humor itself. He also sees in MT's
     Civil War experiences "treason" in joining
     Confederate forces and "desertion" in leav-
     ing them: "He had in the space of a month
     committed two capital crimes," and there was
     a streak of the outlaw in the man and his
     humor (p. 215).

B14 [DAVIS, CHESTER L.] "The Letters of Madame de
     Sevigne," Twainian, XXXII (January-February),
     1; (March-April), 3-4; (May-June), 1-4;
     (July-August), 1-4; (September-October), 1-4;
     (November-December), 4.
         Continues a series begun in 1972 and con-
     tinuing into 1974, extensively reprinting
     the text of this book from MT's library with
     his annotations and underlinings. Abstracts
     through July-August in AES, XVIII (1974-
     1975), 2275-2278.

B15 _____. "Mark Twain's Reading, His Library and
     Our Foundation," Twainian, XXXII (July-Au-
     gust), 4; (September-October), 1-2; (Novem-
     ber-December), 1-3.
         On the disposition of MT's estate through
     various heirs; eventually, after the death
     of his daughter Clara and her daughter Nina,
     the assets of more than one million dollars
     were divided between Yale University and The
     American Red Cross; the latter "has refused
     our request to earmark their bequest for the
     furtherance of Mark Twain knowledge, saying
     that there was no restriction." Various
     trusts were also created by Clara, one of
     them establishing a Mark Twain Foundation
     apparently distinct from the Mark Twain Re-
     search Foundation although Davis says that
     "Clara had our Foundation in mind at the
     time." There is also discussion of MT mate-
     rials but little specifically relating to
     his reading and his library, as mentioned in
     the title. The third issue in this series
     consists of extensive quotations from the
     six 1958 issues of Twainian. Abstract of
     July-August installment in AES, XVIII (1974-
     1975), 2281.

B16 THE EDITORS. "Here Comes Tom Sawyer!" Read-
     er's Digest, CIII (July), 16-22.
         About the making of a film version by the
     Reader's Digest. Laudatory.

B17 THE EDITORS, comp. "The Many Sides of Mark
     Twain," Reader's Digest, CIII (August),
     191-205, 210-31.
         Brief excerpts from MT's published works
     and familiar works written about him, com-
     piled for a popular audience.

386

B18 EMBLEN, D. L. "Mark Twain Alive and Well--
     Very Well Indeed--in Sweden," Mark Twain
     Journal, XVI (Summer), 16-18.
        MT's works have been in print and popular
     in Sweden since their first appearance; the
     major libraries also have his works in Eng-
     lish, together with some of the major sec-
     ondary material about him. There is a list
     of recent publications of translations of
     his works. Abstract in AES, XVIII (1974-
     1975), 592.

B19 ESCHOLZ, PAUL A. "Mark Twain and the Lan-
     guage of Gesture," Mark Twain Journal, XVII
     (Winter), 5-8.
        On non-verbal communication, some of it
     unconscious, in CY, TA, HF, and PW. Ab-
     stract in AES, XVIII (1974-1975), 2935.

B20 ____. "Twain's The Tragedy of Pudd'nhead
     Wilson," Explicator, XXXI (April), Item 67.
        The tragedy of Wilson is revealed in the
     ironic conclusion, in which he becomes a
     member of the Dawson's Landing community
     which had ridiculed him: he is no longer
     the independent person he had once been.
     Abstract by Escholtz in MLA Abstracts
     (1973), 8871.

B21 FETTERLEY, JUDITH. "Yankee Showman and Re-
     former: The Character of Mark Twain's
     Hank Morgan," Texas Studies in Literature
     and Language, XIV (Winter), 667-79.
        A Connecticut Yankee "offered Mark Twain
     the opportunity of indulging in a fantasy
     of omnipotence," but "Hank as a character
     is ambiguous," because his power can be
     creative or destructive. Much of his at-
     titude is aggressive, even in his humor,
     and in the end his betrayal "is ultimately
     a self-betrayal"; he has been a violent
     man who entered Arthurian England as a re-
     sult of a blow suffered in a fight, and
     there he felt insufficiently appreciated.
     Abstract by Fetterley in MLA Abstracts
     (1972 [sic]), 8761.

B22 FULLER, DANIEL J. "Mark Twain and Hamlin Gar-
     land: Contrarieties in Regionalism," Mark
     Twain Journal, XVII (Winter), 14-18.
        "Both of them were influenced by the dic-
     tates of Hippolyte Taine, and he helped
     them gain the spirit to portray common and
     familiar scenes as settings for their nov-
     els and stories." HF and PW reveal a con-
     trast between MT's social criticism and his
     portrayal of a region. Concluding Note:
     "From the Editor, We regret that the foot-
     notes for this article have been misplaced.
     If you desire any reference information,
     please write the author." Abstract in AES,
     XVIII (1974-1975), 2936.

B23 GOGOL, J. M. "Nikolai Aseev and Mark Twain,"
     Mark Twain Journal, XVI (Summer), 15-16.
        A brief biography of the Russian Futurist
     poet, with the text of his 1949 poem, "Mark
     Twain" (translated by J. M. Gogol). Ab-
     stract in AES, XVIII (1974-1975), 594.

B24 *GORDON, CAROLINE. "The Shape of the River,"
     Michigan Quarterly Review, XII (Winter),
     1-10.
        Notes the role of the central intelligence
     as protagonist and narrator in LOM. [Source:
     Abstract in AES, XVIII (1974-1975), 1028;
     part of a general study and perhaps dealing
     only tangentially with LOM.]

B25 GOUDIE, ANDREA. "'What Fools These Mortals
     Be!' A Puckish Interpretation of Mark
     Twain's Narrative Stance," Kansas Quarterly,
     V (Fall), 19-31.
        "Both Twain and Puck are keenly perceptive
     auditors, actors too when they see cause,"
     "and humor for both Twain and Puck is fre-
     quently an involuntary response" (p. 20).
     Abstract in AES, XIX (1975-1976), 237. Ab-
     stract by Goudie in MLA Abstracts (1973),
     8857.

B26 HAMILTON, MAXWELL. "'Tom Sawyer' Lives Again.
     Filmed on Location in the Missouri Country-
     side, the New Musical, 'Tom Sawyer,' Prom-
     ises Warm Authenticity," Holiday Inn Inter-
     national Magazine, July/August, pp. 48-50.
        Adds no information to the Reader's Digest
     account of the film (1973.B16), but provides
     an additional nine stills of the film (five
     in color).

B27 HANSEN, CHADWICK. "The Once and Future Boss:
     Mark Twain's Yankee," Nineteenth-Century
     Fiction, XXVIII (June), 62-73.
        In CY, the Yankee anticipates the 20th-
     century dictator with his love of mob scenes,
     his mixture of sentimentality and insensitiv-
     ity, and his destructiveness on an apocalyp-
     tic scale. "We have all seen him. But it
     was Mark Twain, in this brilliant nightmare
     of a novel, who saw him first." Abstract by
     Hansen in MLA Abstracts (1973), 8858.

B28 HANSON, R. GALEN. "Bluejays and Man: Twain's
     Exercise in Understanding," Mark Twain Jour-
     nal, XVII (Winter), 18-19.
        Summarizes the bluejay yarn in RI, in
     which MT "makes light of human collective
     behavior, of human deceptions, of the range
     of ways that are human ways." Abstract in
     AES, XVIII (1974-1975), 2934.

B29 KAHN, SHOLOM J. "Mark Twain as American Rabel-
     ais," Hebrew University Studies in Litera-
     ture, No. 1 (Spring), pp. 47-75.

(KAHN, SHOLOM J.)
Provides several definitions of "Rabel-aisianism" in the sense of indelicacy, satire, in a literary world that is "not only anatomical and geographical...but also historical, folkloristic, legendary, and ultimately metaphysical." Draws on Rabelais scholarship, and suggests that "to be an 'American Rabelais' implies performing a satiric, or more broadly literary, function for the United States comparable, or parallel, to that of Rabelais in sixteenth-century France." Abstract by Kahn in MLA Abstracts (1973), 8866.

B30 *KARPOWITZ, STEVEN. "Tom Sawyer and Mark Twain: Fictional Women and Real in the Play of Conscience with the Imagination," Literature and Psychology, XXIII, No. 1, 5-12.
[Source: Abstract in AES, XVIII (1974-1975), 1554.] Because of the women in MT's life, his thought often linked thoughts of fame and death with woman's suffering, in his Nevada writing and in TS where the humor masks murderous wishes; Tom's fantasies blend sadism and fame.

B31 KETTERER, DAVID. "Epoch-Eclipse and Apocalypse: Special 'Effects' in A Connecticut Yankee," Publications of the Modern Language Association, LXXXVIII (October), 1104-14.
Hank Morgan is defective in his perception of reality, unaware of symbolism and imagery; he does not see, as the reader does, the nature of MT's statement on Arthurian England and nineteenth-century America through the eclipse, and succeeding episodes involving solar images, leading to the concluding battle of the sandbelt. Abstract in AES, XVIII (1974-1975), 1274. Abstract by Ketterer in MLA Abstracts (1973), 8870.

B32 KINGHORN, NORTON D. "E. W. Kemble's Misplaced Modifier: A Note on the Illustrations for Huckleberry Finn," Mark Twain Journal, XVI (Summer), 9-11.
On MT's reactions to the HF illustrations by Kemble. On p. 322 his illustration of Uncle Silas Phelps with a brass warming pan that "belonged to one of his ancestors with a long wooden handle" showed a wooden handle on the pan and on the ancestor, a wooden leg--which might have been called a "handle" in contemporary slang. Abstract in AES, XVIII (1974-1975), 588.

B33 KIRALIS, KARL "Two More Recently Discovered Letters by S. L. Clemens," Mark Twain Journal, XVI (Summer), 18-20.
Contains background data and texts of two brief notes. The first, to the Clover Club (January 2, 1891) declines with thanks a dinner invitation, and the second (May 8, 1894) asks Fred J. Hall (general manager

and part-owner of the defunct Webster and Company) to speak to Mr. Rogers about an unnamed project. Abstract in AES, XVIII (1974-1975), 596. Abstract by Kiralis in MLA Abstracts (1973), 8872.

B34 KRAUSE, SYDNEY J. "Steinbeck and Mark Twain," Steinbeck Quarterly, VI (Fall), 104-11.
Although there is no external evidence as to whether Steinbeck read MT "with the kind of attention that would have invited borrowing," there are parallels in thinking--especially in The Pearl and "Hadleyburg" (which Krause proposes to treat in a sequel to this article). Abstract in AES, XVIII (1974-1975), 1966.

B35 *LANGLEY, DOROTHY. Tom Sawyer Comes Home. Chicago: The Traumwald Press.
[Source: Advertisement in Mark Twain Journal, XVI (Summer), back cover.] "Stemming not only from the Tom Sawyer-Huck Finn series but particularly from The Mysterious Stranger, the book takes Tom, Huck and Jim on a ride through history on Satan's ticket, and brings them back to Missouri around 1950."

B36 LINDBORG, HENRY J. "A Cosmic Tramp: Samuel Clemens's Three Thousand Years Among the Microbes," American Literature, XLIV (January), 652-57.
In this rambling novel which personifies the universe as the body of the tramp Blitzowski, MT reveals a dual view of a God of "unthinkable grandeur and majesty," but indifferent to man. Notes possible sources and influences in W. H. Conn's The Life of the Germ (1897) and C. W. Saleeby's The Cycle of Life According to Modern Science (1904). Abstract by Lindborg in MLA Abstracts (1973), 8875.

B37 *MAURANGES, J.-P. "Aliénation et Châtiment chez Mark Twain et Heinrich Böll," Revue des Langues Vivantes, XXXIX, No. 2, 131-36.
[Source: Abstract in AES, XVII (1973-1974), 1807; reprinted in Twainian, XXXIV (March-April, 1975).]
In Böll's Der Bahnhof von Zimpren, as in "Hadleyburg," a small town is duped by the promise of easy riches, those in power perpetuate the swindle, and the society disintegrates in fear and distrust. Although MT is the more pessimistic, there remains hope for Hadleyburg. [In French.]

B38 MENDELSOHN, EDWARD. "Mark Twain Confronts the Shakespeareans," Mark Twain Journal, XVII (Winter), 20-21.
MT ridicules cultural pretension in his "Is Shakespeare Dead?" and shows Shakespeare's name cheapened by grasping impostors in HF. Though no scholar, MT put first emphasis on the works; he also observed that his society regarded Shakespeare as a symbolic fetish, as it regarded Satan as a symbolic bugbear. Abstract in AES, XVIII (1974-1975), 2933.

B39   MILLER, WILLIAM C. "Samuel L. and Orion
      Clemens vs. Mark Twain and His Biographers
      (1861-1862)," Mark Twain Journal, XVI
      (Summer), 1-9.
          On the early days of the two Clemens
      brothers in Nevada Territory, the regula-
      tions governing the duties of Orion as Sec-
      retary, his employment of Samuel for sixty
      days as an assistant, and Samuel's early
      newspaper work: he was the Aurora corres-
      pondent for the Carson City Silver Age and
      tried to obtain the same post with the Sac-
      ramento Union, in the time before he joined
      the Territorial Enterprise; an item from
      the Silver Age, possibly by MT, was copied
      by the San Francisco Daily Alta California
      (here reprinted). There is also a discus-
      sion of MT's contributions to the Enter-
      prise over the pseudonym "Josh." It would
      appear that Orion Clemens "may have been
      in large part responsible for Samuel Clem-
      ens' becoming Mark Twain"--far more than
      MT or his biographers acknowledge. Abstract
      in AES, XVIII (1974-1975), 593.

B40   MILLS, NICOLAUS. "Charles Dickens and Mark
      Twain," in his American and English Fiction
      in the Nineteenth Century: An Antigenre
      Critique and Comparison. Bloomington and
      London: Indiana University Press.
          Compares Great Expectations and HF in
      their division into three sections dealing
      with childhood and the home, with society
      as a whole, and with psychological and moral
      decisions. [Incorporates parts of "Social
      and Moral Vision in Great Expectations and
      Huckleberry Finn," Journal of American Stud-
      ies, July, 1970.]

B41   *MIXON, WAYNE. "Mark Twain, The Gilded Age,
      and the New South Movement" Southern Human-
      ities Review, VII, 403-409.
          In 1873 MT could see the beginning of the
      movement which would become evident in the
      next decade, to make the South like the in-
      dustrial North; although MT believed in
      such progress he condemned the means used
      to achieve it. [Source: Abstract by Mixon
      in MLA Abstracts (1973), 8880.]

B42   MONTEIRO, GEORGE. "'Such as Mother Used to
      Make': An Addition to the Mark Twain Can-
      on," Papers of the Bibliographical Society
      of America, LXVII (Fourth Quarter), 450-52.
          Reprints a sketch by this title in the
      "Contributors' Club" in the Atlantic Month-
      ly for January, 1903. Abstracted by Mon-
      teiro in MLA Abstracts (1973), 8881. Also
      abstracted in AES, XVIII (1974-1975), 2279.

B43   MOYNE, ERNEST J. "Mark Twain and Baroness
      Alexandra Gripenberg," American Literature,
      XLV (November), 370-78.
          On MT's meeting and subsequent corres-
      pondence with the Finnish author and leader
      in Finnish woman suffrage and temperance

movements; she recorded the meeting and a
dialect story he told in her A Half Year in
the New World: Miscellaneous Sketches of
Travel in the United States (trans. and ed.
Ernest J. Moyne, Newark, Delaware, 1954) and
in articles for the Scandinavian press. A
letter to the editor of the Stockholm Nya
Dagligt Allehanda accused MT of plagiarism
from Boccaccio's Decameron, and MT wrote
the Baroness a letter of explanation: his
own source had been Hopkinson Smith's "Gin-
ger and the Goose" in Harper's Monthly, LXIV
(March, 1882), 138-40. Moyne includes the
text of two MT letters and cites pertinent
material in Finnish and Swedish newspapers
of 1888-1889, as well as Alexandra Gripenberg's diary and letters. [This is a re-
written and expanded version of Moyne's
"Mark Twain Meets a Lady from Finland,"
which appeared in Mark Twain Journal in
1960.B84.] Abstract by Moyne in MLA Abstracts (1973), 8882.

B44   NIBBELINK, HERMAN. "Mark Twain and the Mor-
      mons," Mark Twain Journal, XVII (Winter),
      1-5.
          Contrasts their portrayal in RI with ac-
      counts by other writers of the time. Ab-
      stract in AES, XVIII (1973-1975), 2937.
      Abstract by Nibbelink in MLA Abstracts
      (1974), 9635.

B45   *PARK, MARTHA M. "Mark Twain's Hadleyburg:
      A House Built on Sand," College Language
      Association Journal, XVI, 508-13.
          MT may have had in mind the New Testament
      parable of the two houses, one built on rock
      and one on sand, when he wrote the story,
      in which there are frequent references to
      crumbling foundations. [Source: Abstract
      by Park in MLA Abstracts (1973), 8884.]

B46   PAULY, THOMAS H. "Directed Readings: The
      Contents Tables in Huckleberry Finn,"
      Proof, III, 63-68.
          Critical discussions of Huckleberry Finn
      have often quoted and been influenced by
      one of two tables of contents; they are
      presumably the work of Charles L. Webster
      and Albert Bigelow Paine, but in any event
      are not by MT. Abstract by Pauly in MLA
      Abstracts (1973), 8885.

B47   POCHMANN, HENRY A. [Review: Franklin R.
      Rogers and Paul Baender, eds., Roughing It
      (1972).] American Literature, XLIV (Janu-
      ary), 687-89.
          Includes a lengthy discussion of editori-
      al principles involved in the Center for
      Editions of American Authors publications,
      with praise for the introduction by Frank-
      lin R. Rogers as "superb" and his Explana-
      tory Notes as "especially full, as they
      need to be for a book like Roughing It."
      Paul Baender's textual notes are "succinct
      but adequate," though they might well have
      been expanded to cover MT's idiosyncratic
      spellings and unusual words.

B48 *POWERS, LYALL H. "The Sweet Success of Twain's Tom," Dalhousie Review, LIII, 310-24.

The popularity of TS derives from its structure and narrative development of the themes of death, treasure-hunting, and romantic adventure, with growing seriousness and respectability; MT skilfully underscores his theme by his management of time. [Source: Abstract by Powers in MLA Abstracts (1973), 8886.]

B49 REGAN, ROBERT. [Review: John S. Tuckey, ed., Mark Twain's Fables of Man (1972) and Franklin R. Rogers, ed., Roughing It (1972).] American Literary Realism, 1870-1910, VI (Winter), 82-84.

The introductions and textual apparatus of the two volumes are quite different, because one consists of previously unpublished material, left in manuscript, calling for considerable analysis, and the other is a book which was never revised and for which no manuscript survives. There is a marked disparity of the promise in RI and "the literary ruins of his declining years" in Fables of Man: "The Mark Twain of Roughing It had--rightly or wrongly--respected himself and respected his audience; the Mark Twain of Fables of Man had come to despise both." There is an extensive and valuable discussion of the Iowa-California edition of MT's published and previously unpublished writing.

B50 REEVES, PASCHAL, et al., comps. "A Checklist of Scholarship on Southern Literature for 1973," Mississippi Quarterly, XXVII (Spring, 1974), 235-39 (portion on MT).

Sixth annual checklist, including about three dozen books and articles on MT published in 1973; annotated. Generally duplicates other standard bibliographies.

B51 RODGERS, PAUL C., JR. "Artemus Ward and Mark Twain's 'Jumping Frog,'" Nineteenth-Century Fiction, XXVIII (December), 273-86.

MT's use of the frame structure and deadpan narrator are a result of his desire to employ Ward's lecture technique in a story, or a need to make the story conform to the context of Ward's Travels (1865), of which it was originally intended to be a part. Abstract by Rodgers in MLA Abstracts (1973), 8887.

B52 ROGERS, RODNEY O. "Twain, Taine, and Lecky: The Gensis of a Passage in A Connecticut Yankee," Modern Language Quarterly, XXXIV (December), 436-47.

On a passage MT originally wrote for TA after reading Taine's L'Ancien Régime; he did not use the passage there, but later revised it for CY under the influence of Lecky's History of European Morals. Abstract by Rogers in MLA Abstracts (1973), 8888.

B53 *ROSS, MICHAEL. "Mark Twain's Pudd'nhead Wilson: Dawson's Landing and the Ladder of Nobility," Novel, VI (Spring), 244-56.

On MT's indictment of mankind, here shown in a feudal society. [Source: Abstract in AES, XVIII (1974-1975), 928.]

B54 ROWLETTE, ROBERT. "'Mark Ward on Artemis Twain': Twain's Literary Debt to Ward," American Literary Realism, VI (Winter), 13-25.

Quotes passages revealing a number of parallels, some fairly persuasively indicating "that Twain borrowed considerably from Ward, far more than DeVoto would allow. Mostly he borrowed the staples of the comicwriters' trade--jokes, anecdotes, catchphrases, snappers, one-liners--for use in his Sandwich Islands letters, The Innocents Abroad, Life on the Mississippi, and several sketches," as well as ideas for the form of RI. "After Roughing It, except for striking correspondences in Life on the Mississippi, it virtually ceased." Abstract by Rowlette in MLA Abstracts (1973), 8890.

B55 SEARS, ROBERT R. "Episodic Analysis of Novels," Journal of Psychology, LXXXV, 267-76.

[Source: Offprint in Mark Twain Papers.] Among the novels analyzed are Captain Stormfield's Visit to Heaven, TS, HF, CY, PW, MS, IA, and P&P. Episodes are used as a basis for investigation of the growth of MT's personality.

B56 SIMPSON, LOUIS P. "Mark Twain: The Pathos of Regeneration," in his The Man of Letters in New England and the South: Essays on the History of the Literary Vocation in America. Baton Rouge: Louisiana State University Press, pp. 150-66. Reprinted from Southern Literary Journal, 1972.B75.

B57 STOWELL, ROBERT F. "River Guide Books and Mark Twain's Life on the Mississippi," Mark Twain Journal, XVI (Summer), 21.

LOM makes no mention of a number of guidebooks useful both to the apprentice learning the river and to the working steamboat pilot. With the maps available, "there was no necessity for him to attempt to keep the multitude of details of eleven hundred miles of river constantly in mind when he could readily turn to such books as The Western Pilot." Abstract in AES, XVIII (1974-1975), 589.

B58 TRUMAN, HARRY S. [Letter to Chester L. Davis (July 30, 1957), expressing admiration for MT: "He has quite a record; in fact, I believe he was the first newspaper columnist to be run out of Washington. His Civil War record is also highly interesting."] Twainian, XXXII (March-April), 1-2. Abstract in AES, XVIII (1974-1975), 2280.

B59 WEXMAN, VIRGINIA. "The Role of Structure in Tom Sawyer and Huckleberry Finn," American Literary Realism, 1870-1910, VI (Winter), 1-11.
In the dual world of TS, comic incidents involving boyish innocence prepare the way for incidents of a more somber kind, as in Tom's playing Robin Hood with Joe Harper before the murder of Dr. Robinson by Injun Joe, the search for treasure by Tom and Huck in a haunted house soon found by Injun Joe and a companion, and Huck's following the two villains through a maze of streets reminiscent of the cave in which the village children had been playing. The alternation of light and dark scenes "helps to preserve our sense of the comic in this book" and permits a conclusion which, "in true comic spirit, reaffirms social unity." HF takes a different course, as Huck's imagination is educated by experience, and his "creativity cannot be harmless as Tom's had been, for he finds himself in a world where innocence is immoral rather than merely premoral." Again, MT parallels incidents from the dark and light worlds, but here the effect is to heighten the portraits of human depravity. Abstract by Wexman in MLA Abstracts (1973), 8896.

B60 WILSON, JAMES D. "Hank Morgan, Philip Traum, and Milton's Satan," Mark Twain Journal, XVI (Summer), 20-21.
CY and MS bear out Milton's prediction of increasingly deadly machines of war. Abstract by Wilson in MLA Abstracts (1973), 8897.

1974 A BOOKS

A1 ANON. Nook Farm Genealogy. [Hartford, Connecticut]: Stowe-Day Foundation.
Part I: "Alphabetical Listing of Nook Farm residents, a partial listing of their ancestors and descendants, and a cross-section of their contemporaries as they pertain to Library materials"; Part II: "ADDENDA. Chronological listing of major Nook Farm families." Provides useful data on MT's neighbors, but no new material on his own family. (Typescript).

A2 KAPLAN, JUSTIN. Mark Twain and His World. New York: Simon and Schuster.
A life of MT for the general reader, attractively illustrated with color prints revealing the man and his age.

A3 PETTIT, ARTHUR G. Mark Twain & the South. Lexington: University Press of Kentucky.
Describes MT's evolving racial and regional views, the mingled love and loathing he felt for the South. MT "reflected and expressed some of the most advanced thoughts and entrenched prejudices of his time,"

mirroring the changing national attitudes; he "came to look upon his personal lot and that of the country, especially that of the South, as similar and tragic."

A4 SCHMITTER, DEAN MORGAN, ed. Mark Twain: A Collection of Critical Essays. New York: McGraw-Hill Book Company.
Essays from journals and excerpted from books; all are listed in the present bibliography, with cross-references to Schmitter's reprintings. The material is in two sections, the first on MT's life, literary career, and the themes of humor and pessimism, and the second devoted to criticism of major works. There is a bibliography (with brief annotations) of books about MT.

A5 WALKER, FRANKLIN. Irreverent Pilgrims: Melville, Browne, and Mark Twain in the Holy Land. Seattle and London: University of Washington Press.
Traces the 1851 travels of John Ross Browne as recorded in his Yusef; or, the Journey of the Frangi (New York, 1853), Melville's 1857 visit as described in Clarel (1876), and the 1867 tour MT portrayed in newspaper letters and IA.

A6 WATKINS, T. H. Mark Twain's Mississippi. Also Selected Excerpts from Mark Twain's "Life on the Mississippi." Palo Alto, California: American West Publishing Company.
Consists of appropriate material from LOM and many contemporary and modern pictures of the river and the scenes MT described.

1974 B SHORTER WRITINGS

B1 ALSEN, EBERHARD. "The Futile Pursuit of Truth in Twain's What Is Man? and Anderson's 'The Book of the Grotesque,'" Mark Twain Journal, XVII (Winter), 12-14.
Sherwood Anderson's correspondence with Van Wyck Brooks in 1918-1919 shows that he often thought of MT while writing Winesburg, Ohio. "The introductory sketch, 'The Book of the Grotesque,' revolves around a conception of truth which is very similar to the one developed in 'What Is Man?'" and in A Story Teller's Story, 1924, p. 189) Anderson shows familiarity with this late work. Derivation is suggested by the self-portrait in the "old man" and the conception that there are no absolute truths and that pursuit of a single idea can turn a man into a grotesque.

B2 BAUM, JOAN. "Mark Twain on the Congo," Mark Twain Journal, XVII (Summer), 7-9.
Describes MT's 1905 pamphlet, King Leopold's Soliloquy, recently reissued by International Publications (New York) and Seven Seas Press (East Berlin). Abstract by Baum in MLA Abstracts (1974), 9589.

B3   BEBB, BRUCE. [Review: Paul Baender, ed., "What Is Man?" and Other Philosophical Writings (1973).] American Literary Realism 1870-1910, VII (Summer), 283-86.
        "It is a big, solid, handsome book, and should be a source of pride to the many people associated with its production. Most of the more than two dozen pieces of Mark Twain's writings that make up this volume have appeared in print before, though at...diverse times and places.... They are a heterogeneous lot." Bebb criticizes the editing; in particular "the textual notes are next to impossible to work with." However, "What is Man? is done right, basically," avoiding some of the errors in the editing of RI, the first volume in this edition, and "Paul Baender's introduction is a thoughtful and lucid guide to the development of Mark Twain's ideas."

B4   BERGER, SIDNEY. "New Mark Twain Items," Papers of the Bibliographical Society of America, LXVIII (Third Quarter), 331-35.
        Chatto & Windus used the best copy-text available for the English editions of TS Abroad and PW; for the latter they apparently were forced to use the Century serialization, but for TS Abroad they had a carbon copy of the typescript sent to St. Nicholas and hence had a text free of emendations by Mary Mapes Dodge. Quotes letters from Chatto & Windus to MT (August 15, 1893) and to Frederick Hall of Charles L. Webster & Company (January 16, 1894). Abstract by Berger in MLA Abstracts (1974), 9591.

B5   BLEI, NORBERT. "Marking Twain in Hannibal-- a Trip to Missouri to Learn What Influence Mark Twain has Had upon His Boyhood Home," American Libraries, V (March), 128-34.
        On the town of Hannibal, memorials, use of the MT name for local businesses; photographs.

B6   BRIDEN, E. F. "Samuel L. Clemens and Elizabeth Jordan: An Unpublished Letter," Mark Twain Journal, XVII (Summer), 11-13.
        Text of a letter (December 4, 1908) in which MT declines to write something for Miss Jordan because he lacks interest and would do it badly, and "The Harpers would flay me for destroying my commercial value." Also quotes from her autobiography, Three Rousing Cheers (New York and London: D. Appleton-Century, 1934) a letter of August 4, 1906 in which MT declines to contribute a chapter to a composite novel, The Whole Family, which failed despite the contributions by Howells, Henry James, Mary E. Wilkins Freeman, and others. Briden also quotes Miss Jordan's autobiography on meetings with MT at the Harpers' offices in New York, and breakfasts with him during visits to Colonel George Harvey's summer home, "Jorjalma," at Deal Beach, New Jersey.

B7   *BRUNVAND, JAN HAROLD. "Western Folk Humor in Roughing It," The Western Folklore Conference: Selected Papers, Utah University Press Monograph Series, XI, ed. Austin Fife and J. Golden Taylor (June), 53-65.
        [Source: Citation provided by kindness of D. K. Wilgus, Folklore and Mythology Group, U.C.L.A., adding that it is cited by Barrick (1975.B3).]

B8   BUDD, LOUIS J. "Mark Twain Talks Mostly about Humor and Humorists," Studies in American Humor, I (April), 4-22.
        MT's theoretical statements about humor, liberally documented both from the familiar published works and from newspaper interviews. Includes the texts of interviews in the New York Sun (January 27, 1895), Sydney (Australia) Morning Herald (September 17, 1895), and Auckland New Zealand Herald (November 21, 1895).

B9   CHURCH, SAMUEL HARDEN. [Facsimile reproduction of letter to Cyril Clemens, February 19, 1942, on three meetings with MT at the home of Andrew Carnegie.] Mark Twain Journal, XVII (Winter), back cover.
        Mentions having written MT to ask about his statement that the Siamese Twins were of different ages; in reply MT wrote that the statement was "an egregious blunder... What I meant to say was that the twins were born at the same time but of different mothers."

B10   CLEMENS, SAMUEL L. "Mark Twain Approves the Staging of Huckleberry Finn," Mark Twain Journal, XVII (Winter), front cover.
        Facsimile reproduction, without comment, of an MT letter on hotel stationery of Marshall House, York Harbor, Maine (the printed year is "190_," with the last figure not filled in) to Klaw & Erlanger; he is completely satisfied with the stage adaptation by Lee Arthur.

B11   _____. "Some Thoughts on the Science of Onanism," Playboy, XXI (September), 157.
        The text of a humorous talk delivered by MT before the Stomach Club, in Paris, 1879.

B12   CRACROFT, RICHARD H. "Distorting Polygamy for Fun and Profit: Artemus Ward and Mark Twain among the Mormons," Brigham Young University Studies, XIV (Winter), 272-88.
        "Twain's was the greater fictional imagination," but in portraying the Mormons he was "the lesser artist of the two" (p. 287). Both knowingly perpetuated falsehoods about the Mormons for humorous effect.

B13   DENTON, L. W. "Mark Twain on Patriotism, Treason, and War," Mark Twain Journal, XVII (Summer, 4-7.
        Undated quotations from various published writings by MT, on a citizen's responsibility to oppose his country's policies when they are wrong.

B14 ENSOR, ALLISON. "The Downfall of Poor Richard: Benjamin Franklin as Seen by Hawthorne, Melville, and Mark Twain," Mark
Twain Journal, XVII (Winter), 14-18.
Like most writers of the nineteenth century MT--somewhat unjustly--criticized
Franklin's sententiousness in his epigrams
on industry and frugality.

B14A HILL, HAMLIN. "Mark Twain," in James Woodress, ed., American Literary Scholarship:
An Annual/1974. Durham, North Carolina:
Duke University Press, 1976, pp. 75-85.
The annual survey of MT scholarship (begun by John Gerber in 1963.B32). Includes
material not listed in the present bibliography. Contents: "i. Textual and Bibliographical"; "ii. Biographical"; "iii. General Criticism"; "iv. Earlier Works";
"v. Huckleberry Finn"; "vi. Later Works."

B15 _____. "Who Killed Mark Twain?" American
Literary Realism, 1870-1910, VII (Spring),
119-24.
"The major problem with the current state
of Mark Twain studies is that most of it is
written by humorless, dull pedants whose
prose style alone would be enough to petri-
fy an unwary reader as comprehensively as
Ice-9." They occupy themselves with trivia, and some of the work done is perfunctory
and careless: "It somehow does not inspire
confidence in a scholar's own estimate of
the importance of his research to see him
cite a Dell paperback as his documentation."
It is time to revive MT with a new assessment, and the publication of his previously
unpublished writings by the University of
California Press will provide the opportunity. Hill points to some of the new insights
made possible; for example, "there is evidence that he terrorized most of the people
who knew him well, that he was if not impotent at least unable to satisfy his wife
Olivia sexually, and that much of their tension and her frustration arose from his ob-
sessive absences from her bed. There is
evidence that his fixation on teen-age girls
in his last years was the result of a love
affair with Laura Wright when he was twenty-
one and she was fifteen." Some of the useful criticism of recent years is described,
and there are suggestions of fruitful topics
for investigation. Abstract by Hill in MLA
Abstracts (1974), 9614.

B16 HOOD, ROBERT E. "Mark Twain's Huck Finn,"
Scouting (published eight times a year by
Boy Scouts of America for adult leaders),
LXII (March-April), 28-31, 68.
A popular account, largely descriptive,
praising the book for its humor. Illustrated by Mary Ellen Mark's color photographs
during the filming of the current musical
treatment (the cover illustration is also
from the filming).

B17 HYDE, JAMES H. (told to Cyril Clemens).
"Mark Twain and Colonel George Harvey,"
Mark Twain Journal, XVII (Winter), 21.
Brief and superficial. "The first time
I met Mark Twain was at a dinner given at
the Metropolitan Club shortly after 1900
by Colonel George Harvey" in honor of Admiral Lord Charles Beresford, who dined too
well and fell asleep under a table. MT
spoke after dinner on his bad investments
and the help he had received from Henry
Rogers in putting his affairs in order.
Hyde later invited MT to a large dinner and
found him "perfectly charming."

B18 ILLIANO, ANTONIO. "'Italian Without a Master':
A Note for the Appreciation of Mark Twain's
Undictionarial Translation as Exercise in
Humor," Mark Twain Journal, XVII (Summer),
17-20.
Reprints the Italian passages and MT's
comic translations, together with literal
translations.

B19 JAGER, RONALD B. "Mark Twain and the Robber
Barons: A View of the Gilded Age Businessman," Mark Twain Journal, XVII (Winter),
8-12.
Personally inept in business, MT admired
the productive genius of Andrew Carnegie and
his friend Henry Rogers, but could not "dis-
associate personal moral integrity from the
more impersonal, corporate standards that
were coming to apply in this new age of industrialization." He deplored the money-
grubbing of Jay Gould and his kind.

B20 KIBLER, JAMES, et al. "A Checklist of Scholarship on Southern Literature for 1974,"
Mississippi Quarterly, XXVIII (Spring, 1975),
228-32 (portion on MT).
Seventh annual checklist, including about
three dozen books and articles on MT published in 1974; annotated. Generally duplicates other standard bibliographies.

B21 LEARY, LEWIS. "Mark Twain Did Not Sleep Here:
Tarrytown, 1902-1904," Mark Twain Journal,
XVII (Summer), 13-15.
A meticulously detailed account of Olivia
Clemens's purchase of a house and nineteen
acres in Tarrytown, New York after the
death of Susan, when the family could no
longer bear to live in the Hartford house;
problems over the tax assessment were settled, but repairs were needed, the family
went to Florence (where Mrs. Clemens died),
and MT apparently visited the place but
never lived there; he leased it in May, 1903,
and sold it in January, 1905. Abstract by
Leary in MLA Abstracts (1974), 9622.

B21A _____. "Troubles with Mark Twain: Some Con-
siderations on Consistency," Studies in
American Fiction, II, 89-103.
Briefly discusses the pitfalls of enumera-
tive bibliography, but is primarily concerned

(LEARY, LEWIS)
with the textual problems of IA and the raft passage MT removed from HF to pad LOM: the difficulties are compounded by the fact that MT was not always a sound critic of his own work or uniformly conscientious in decisions concerning his text.

B22 LIGHT, MARTIN. "Sweeping out Chivalric Silliness: The Example of Huck Finn and The Sun Also Rises," Mark Twain Journal, XVII (Winter), 18-20.
Tom Sawyer and Robert Cohn are romantic and Quixotic, and Huck Finn and Jake Barnes, "linked by their adherence to common sense and the lessons of experience, bear a likeness to Sancho Panza." Hemingway follows MT in the attack on romantic folly once swept away by Cervantes but restored by Sir Walter Scott.

B23 LONG, TIMOTHY. "Mark Twain's Speeches on Billiards," Mark Twain Journal, XVII (Summer), 1-3.
On MT's speech, delivered when he visited a tournament in 1906, describing his defeat by a left-handed player. Paine gives different texts in the 1912 biography and 1929 edition of the speeches; Willie Hoppe's Thirty Years of Billiards (1925, quoted in "Mark Twain as a Billiard Fan," Literary Digest, July 25, 1925, p. 55) quotes verbatim the version in the biography. Long also cites accounts in the New York Times of April 10, 12, 18, 20, 23, and 25, 1906, as well as Newsweek (February 24, 1941, p. 56), Time (November 20, 1937, p. 50), and New Yorker (November 16, 1940, pp. 27-28), in which Hoppe quotes MT. Abstract by Long in MLA Abstracts (1974), 9626.

B24 *McELRATH, JOSEPH R., JR. "Mark Twain's America and the Protestant Work Ethic," CEA Critic, XXXVI (March), 42-43.
[Source: Abstract in AES, XVIII (1974-1975), 2588.] In CY, Hank Morgan harnesses a bowing pillar saint to a sewing machine; thereby he demonstrates attitudes of MT's bourgeois, Protestant America.

B25 MONTEIRO, GEORGE. "New Mark Twain Letters," Mark Twain Journal, XVII (Summer), 9-10.
Three brief notes to Atlantic Monthly (January 5, 6, 1875, and February 12, year not given) from the Houghton Library, Harvard University; MT asks that the Atlantic be sent to his brother Orion and sends his check, thanks them for a complimentary subscription, and declines with thanks a suggestion of theirs (not described) which he likes but thinks would not be profitable.

B26 PRINCE, GILBERT. "Mark Twain's 'A Fable': The Teacher as Jackass," Mark Twain Journal, XVII (Winter), 7-8.
On MT's short tale as an attack on the long-established notion that it is a teacher's function to interpret a subject for his

students; as a consequence they tell him what he wants to hear and they fail to experience for themselves.

B27 RACHAL, JOHN. "Scotty Briggs and the Minister: An Idea from Hooper's Simon Suggs?" Mark Twain Journal, XVII (Summer), 10-11.
In HF, MT drew on Hooper's "Simon Attends a Camp-Meeting," which also anticipates the passage in RI in which a clergyman is puzzled by card-game lingo.

B28 REQUA, KENNETH A. "Counterfeit Currency and Character in Mark Twain's Which Was It?" Mark Twain Journal, XVII (Winter), 1-6.
On his unfinished novel, with its "variations on important themes found in other late works of Mark Twain: money as the irresistible temptation, hypocrisy, and existence as a dream." Despite flaws of structure and tone, "Mark Twain had found a center for his novel: the idea of counterfeits, through which he brought together action, method, character, preaching, and had he gone further, he could also have successfully integrated the dream-frame of the novel."

B29 SIMPSON, LEWIS P. [Review: Paul Baender, ed., "What Is Man?" And Other Philosophical Writings (1973).] American Literature, XLV (January), 617-18.
"Reservations about some aspects of selection and methodology...can only be incidental in the face of yet another demonstration by the Iowa-California edition of the sophistication and maturity Mark Twain scholarship has attained." Baender's Introduction is "carefully constructed, well-written, and thoughtful," though prone to find "more structure or pattern" in MT's philosophical inquiries than is truly present; Baender rightly takes issue with reviewers who criticized "Letters from the Earth" in the light of the present-day assumption that Christian literalism is of no significance," rather than as a fiction "which presents the story of the modern fall from faith in reason."

B30 TUCKEY, JOHN S. [Review: Hamlin Hill, Mark Twain: God's Fool (1973).] American Literature, XLVI (March), 116-18.
Chiefly following the journal of Isabel V. Lyon, MT's secretary (1902-1909), but also other unpublished material, including the Ashcroft-Lyon MS, Hill "sees Clemens in the classic role of the domestic tyrant, self-centered and vindictive, who makes psychological cripples of his wife and children." Here, as in Hill's argument that MT was unjustified in dismissing Miss Lyon and his financial secretary Roger Ashcroft, Tuckey disagrees with Hill.

B31 TUCKEY, JOHN S. [Review: Hamlin Hill, _Mark Twain: God's Fool_ (1973).] _American Literary Realism, 1870-1900_, VII (Spring), 175-77.

Tuckey appears reluctant to accept a portrait of MT as domestic tyrant in his last decade, noting that Hill also gives evidence to show Olivia as "all-dominating mother," leaving the reader to reconcile the two diagnoses. "In his previous works Mr. Hill has abundantly demonstrated that he is capable of the most rigorous scholarship and critical analysis." Hill's "searching look at, mainly, the domestic Clemens of the final decade" draws on "the splendid resources of the Mark Twain Papers collection and especially the diary of Isabel V. Lyon, Clemens' secretary from November 1902 until the spring of 1909," and breaks new ground.

B32 WEAVER, WILLIAM. "Mark Twain and Kate Field Differ on Constitutional Rights," _Mark Twain Journal_, XVII (Summer), 16-17.

Reproduces from Lilian Whiting, _Kate Field: A Record_ (Boston, 1899) an MT letter of March 8, 1886, apparently declining to publish one of her books; MT shares her antipathy toward Mormonism, and he "would like to see it extirpated, but always by fair means" and not by oppressive laws, "by arguments and facts, not brute force."

B33 _____. "Samuel Clemens Lectures in Kentucky," _Mark Twain Journal_, XVII (Summer), 20-21.

On MT's lecture in Paris, Kentucky and two lectures on Louisville during his 1884-1885 tour with George Washington Cable; based chiefly on familiar studies but also quoting reports from contemporary newspapers. Abstract by BLW in _MLA Abstracts_ (1974), 9646.

B34 WILSON, MARK K. "Mr. Clemens and Madame Blanc: Mark Twain's First French Critic," _American Literature_, XLV (January), 537-56.

MT's hostility toward the French may be attributed in part to "snide" and "condescending" statements about the man and his books by Marie-Thérèse Blanc (writing as "Th. Bentzon") in "Les Humoristes américains" and "L'Âge doré en Amérique," which appeared in the _Revue des Deux Mondes_ July 15, 1872 and July 15, 1875. Madame Blanc, who translated "The Jumping Frog" and included it as a part of the first article, confused the poses MT assumed with his own attitudes; her estimates are not always perceptive or just. The first article treats _IA_ in some detail and _RI_ in passing, and the second devotes considerable space to a plot-summary of _GA_, a lesser amount of space to a critique (unsympathetic to the structure and to the portrait of Colonel Sellers); these were the first French criticisms of MT and have affected subsequent estimates of his work. The Clemenses met Madame Blanc in Paris in 1879. Abstract by Wilson in _MLA Abstracts_ (1974), 9648.

1975 A BOOKS – NONE

1975 B SHORTER WRITINGS

B1 ANDREWS, WILLIAM L. "The Source of Mark Twain's 'The War Prayer,'" _Mark Twain Journal_, XVII (Summer), 8-9.

On Henry Clay Dean (portrayed in _LOM_, Chapter LVII) as the original of the stranger who took the pulpit.

B2 ASPIZ, HAROLD. "The Other Half of Pudd'nhead Wilson's Dog," _Mark Twain Journal_, XVII (Summer), 10-11.

Reveals a possible source in _The Life of P. T. Barnum, Written by Himself_ (New York: Redfield, 1854), describing a dispute between two owners of an elephant and the threat of one to kill his half.

B3 *BARRICK, Mac E. "The Hat Ranch: Fact, Fiction or Folklore?" _Western Folklore_, XXXIV (April), 149-53.

[Source: Citation provided by kindness of D. K. Wilgus, Folklore and Mythology Group, U.C.L.A., with the annotation: "Discusses use of the story (X1611.1) by Peter B. Kyne, Earl Stanley Gardner, Dan De Quille, and Mark Twain."]

B4 BRANCH, EDGAR M. "Samuel Clemens: Learning to Venture a Miracle," _American Literary Realism, 1870-1910_, VIII (Spring), 91-99.

["This essay, appearing here in slightly revised form, was read at the 89th annual convention of the Modern Language Association, December 1974."] MT attacked romance in Scott and Cooper, satirized other popular romance in his apprentice writing, but submitted experience to a literary ordering of his own. "In Clemens's fiction, Huck's realistic language is the medium that best realizes the romantic ideal seeking to unify subject and object while it simultaneously and faithfully presents each, sacrificing neighter one to the other--but that is another and a better known story of Clemens's later years."

B5 DITSKY, JOHN M. "Mark Twain and 'The Great Dark': Religion in _Letters from the Earth_," _Mark Twain Journal_, XVII (Summer), 12-19.

On conceptions of the Moral Sense and the Deity, and the relevance of "The Great Dark" to conclusions made possible by other portions of the volume.

B6 GERBER, JOHN C. [Review: Franklin Walker, _Irreverent Pilgrims: Melville, Browne, and Mark Twain in the Holy Land_ (1974).] _American Literary Realism_, VIII (Spring), 173-75.

"Specialists in American literature may find the Browne chapters in _Irreverent Pilgrims_ mildly interesting because Browne's life and works are relatively unknown. But they will find nothing new in the accounts of Melville and Mark Twain: the facts recorded in them have been recorded elsewhere,

(GERBER, JOHN C.))
and Mr. Walker seems disinclined to specu-
late freshly or even to draw the comparisons
that the material constantly invites. As in
all his works, Mr. Walker's style here is
clear and easy to read," but the parts dealing with Melville and MT "can be read most
profitably by those relatively unfamiliar
with both authors.

B7   GRANANDER, M.E. "Mark Twain's English Lectures and George Routledge & Sons," Mark
Twain Journal, XVII (Summer), 1-4.
Contains texts of two receipts for pay-
ments from Routledge (July 10, 1872 for IA
and November 10, 1875 for GA), and a brief
note (July 10, 1872) on writing a preface
for IA; also describes MT's arranging for
GA copyrights when he was in London.

B8   GROVE, NOEL. "Mark Twain: Mirror of America,"
National Geographic, CXLVIII (September),
300-37.
A popular account, but following modern
scholarship in giving a balanced view that
includes MT's fears and despair as well as
the humor and local color in his works.
Illustrated with modern photographs of Hannibal and other river towns, Virginia City,
and the MT house in Hartford, by James L.
Stanfield, and by contemporary photographs,
including a color photograph of MT in his
Oxford gown, here published for the first
time.

B9   HARRIS, HELEN L. "Mark Twain's Response to
the Native American," American Literature,
XLVI (January), 495-505.
MT described the Indian unsympathetically
in his early writings, later recognized
both "the American treachery toward the Indian" and his own guilt in having helped
to shape attitudes; "in his silence then he
gave consent to that injustice."

B10   SCHINTO, JEANNE M. "The Autobiographies of
Mark Twain and Henry Adams: Life Studies
in Despair," Mark Twain Journal, XVII (Summer), 5-7.
They regretted the loss of a simpler age
of the past and condemned materialism.

B11   SCRIVNER, BUFORD, JR. "The Mysterious
Stranger: Mark Twain's New Myth of the
Fall," Mark Twain Journal, XVII (Summer),
20-21.
"The Mysterious Stranger is the working-
out of a kind of restoration, or anti-fall,
which reverses the baneful consequences of
the fall of man by negating altogether the
Christian world view which established and
sustains such a belief."

B12   WARREN, ROBERT PENN. "Bearers of Bad Tidings:
Writers and the American Dream," New York
Review of Books, XXII (March 20), 12-19.
On pp. 12-14 discusses MT's deep embodi-
ment of the tensions of his age and his
pessimistic ambivalences, as revealed in
HF, CY, and elsewhere.

Addenda

No Date

FITZROY, SIR ALMERIC. Memoirs. London: Hutchinson & Co., 2 vols., I, 236.
  "July 6th [1907].--We dined with the Clintons last night, and went to Lady Portsmouth's party, at which 'Mark Twain' was a prominent figure."

RIDGE, W. PETT. A Story Teller: Forty Years in London. London: Hodder and Stoughton, pp. 43-44.
  Tells story of being introduced to MT as "the Mark Twain of London" [also in 1910.B99]. At dinners only two days apart, MT delivered the same speech, with the story about a watermelon--but Ridge says "economy is permissible when a man is called on to speak frequently," and gives examples of English speakers who do the same.

1939

*HOLTHAUSEN, F. [Review: Frances Guthrie Emberson, Mark Twain's Vocabulary: A General Survey (1935.A8) and Robert L. Ramsay and Frances Guthrie Emberson, A Mark Twain Lexicon (1938.A8).] Anglia Beiblatt, L, 91-95.
  [Source: MHRA Annual Bibliography (1939), Nos. 4395, 4406.]

1948

*WEST, VICTOR ROYCE. "Mark Twain's Idyl of Frontier America," University of Kansas City Review, XV, 92-104.
  [Source: MLA Bibliography (1948), p. 52.]

1949

*SAINT-PIERRE, MARCEL. "Mark Twain," Action Universitaire, XV (July), 42-51.
  [Source: MHRA Annual Bibliography (1949), No. 3972.]

1950

*FERGUSON, DELANCEY. [Review: Kenneth R. Andrews, Nook Farm: Mark Twain's Hartford Circle (1950.A2).] New York Herald Tribune Book Review (December 31), p. 5.]
  [Source: MHRA Annual Bibliography (1950-1952), No. 9381.]

1952

FELHEIM, MARVIN. [Incorrect attribution.] 1952.B33 is correctly attributed in the present bibliography to Fred W. Lorch. The 1952 MLA Bibliography incorrectly attributes it to Marvin Felheim, author of an article which immediately precedes the Lorch article in New England Quarterly, XXV (September, 1952). The incorrect attribution is also in Beebe and Feaster (1968), p. 100.

1953

PAUL, RODMAN. "Introduction," Roughing It. New York: Rinehart, pp. iii-xvi.
  [Source: Tenth Printing, 1966.] A biographical and critical account of the background and perspective shaping RI. "This text omits the last eighteen chapters and the three appendixes of the original edition.... The omitted chapters and appendixes occupy 147 of the original 591 pages."

1955

*ASSELINEAU, ROGER. [Review: Jerry Allen, The Adventures of Mark Twain (1954.A1).] Études Anglaises, IX, 281.
  [Source: MHRA Annual Bibliography (1955-1956), No. 8005.]

*SCHÖNFELDER, KARL-HEINZ. [Review: Jerry Allen, The Adventures of Mark Twain (1954.A1).] Zeitschrift für Anglistik und Amerikanistik, III, 490-91.
  [Source: MHRA Annual Bibliography (1955-1956), No. 8005.]

1956

*CADY, E. H., FREDERICK J. HOFFMAN, and ROY HARVEY
PEARCE. "Notes on Reading Huckleberry Finn, in
The Growth of American Literature (New York), I,
856-58. [Publisher not named in source.]
[Source: Blair (1960.A1), p. 425.]

*JONES, HOWARD MUMFORD. The Frontier in American
Fiction: Four Lectures on the Relationship of
Landscape to Literature. Jerusalem: Magness
Press. [On Cooper, MT, Cather.]
[Source: MLA Bibliography (1957), No. 4137.]

*ROMM, A. C. Rannie Iumoristitseskie Raskazi Marka
Tvena (K Voprosyo Iumore Tvena.) Utsenie Zapiku
Leningradskogo Pedagogitseskogo Instituta, m. 18:
Fakultet Iazika i Literatury, 1956, vp. 5,
str. 125-39. [Various Humorous Short Stories by
Mark Twain (About Problems of Twain's Humor).
Scholarly Publications of the Leningrad Pedagogi-
cal Institute, Vol. XVIII: Department of Lan-
guage and Literature, 1956, No. 5, pp. 125-39.]
[Source: MHRA Annual Bibliography (1955-1956),
No. 8039.]

1957

*CAMPBELL, WALTER STANLEY, ed. Life on the Missis-
sippi. With Introduction. New York: Sagamore
Press.
[Source: MLA Bibliography (1957), No. 4590.]

NEVIUS, BLAKE. [Review: Henry Nash Smith and
Frederick Anderson, eds., Mark Twain of the "Enterprise" (1957.A5).] Nineteenth-Century Fiction, XII (September), 164-66.
Most of this newspaper material is of little
value, although the compilation is useful for
showing the difference between "Sam. L. Clemens,"
the political reporter, and "Mark Twain," and for
casting light on MT's sudden departure from Nevada in May, 1864. "For the most part the humor
has evaporated, along with the personalities and
conditions at which it was aimed. What remains,
happily, is the local color, admittedly less distinct than in Roughing It, but also less subject
to embroidery."

1958

*FREDDI, GIOVANNI. Mark Twain. Brescia: La Scuola.
[Source: MLA Bibliography (1959), No. 4953.]

*MARX, LEO. "The Vernacular Tradition in American
Literature: Walt Whitman and Mark Twain," Die
neueren Sprachen, pp. 46-57.
[Source: MLA Bibliography (1959), No. 5150.]

1959

*EGRI, PÉTER. "Mark Twain ifjusági regenyei."
[Mark Twain's Novels for Young People.] Filológia
Közlöny, V, 198-208.
[Source: MHRA Annual Bibliography (1962),
No. 5664.]

ELLIOTT, GEORGE P. "Afterword: A Game of Truth,"
in The Adventures of Huckleberry Finn. New York:
New American Library (A Signet Classic),
pp. 284-88.
Like TS, HF is "a game," but motives are different: the questions are serious ones, and, as in
the "trash" episode in Chapter XV, Huck learns
human truths.

_____. "Afterword: Vacation into Boyhood," The
Adventures of Tom Sawyer. New York: New American
Library (A Signet Classic), pp. 220-24.
Treats TS as a vacation escape from sex, work,
tedium, and money, and an escape to MT's style and
unpretentiousness. [The text has been silently
altered, beginning on the first page, where Aunt
Polly asks, "What's wrong with that boy, I wonder?"]

*FRIED, MARTIN B. "Mark Twain in Buffalo," Niagara
Frontier, V (Winter), 89-110.
[Source: MLA Bibliography (1959), No. 4954.]

*HAMSUN, KNUT Drei Amerikaner: Mark Twain, Ralph
Waldo Emerson, Walt Whitman--Essays. München:
Albert Langen, Georg Müller. [German translation
of an essay on MT published in a Norwegian periodical in 1885; the other two were in Hamsun's first
book, 1888.]
[Source: MLA Bibliography (1961), No. 5190.]

HUGHES, LANGSTON. [Introduction.] Pudd'nhead Wilson. New York: Bantam Books.
"In this book the basic theme is slavery, seriously treated, and its main thread concerns the
absurdity of man-made differentials, whether of
caste or 'race.' The word race might properly be
placed in quotes for both of Twain's central Negroes are largely white in blood and physiognomy,
slaves only by circumstance..." but "Mark Twain,
in his presentation of Negroes as human beings,
stands head and shoulders above the other Southern
writers of his times, even such distinguished ones
as Joel Chandler Harris, F. Hopkins Smith [sic],
and Thomas Nelson Page."

*SCHMIDT-HIDDING, WOLFGANG. Sieben Meister des lit-
erarischen Humors in England und Amerika. Heidelberg: Quelle und Meyer. [Chaucer, Shakespeare,
Fielding, Sterne, Lamb, Dickens, MT.]
[Source: MLA Bibliography (1961), No. 2371.]

*SMITH, HENRY NASH, ed. Roughing It. With Intro-
duction. New York: Harper.
[Source: MLA Bibliography (1959), No. 4976.]

1960

*DAVIS, CURTIS CARROLL. "His Name Was Diomed," Vir-
ginia Cavalcade, X, ii (1960), 42-47.
[Source: MLA Bibliography (1960), No. 5430.]

*MARX, LEO. "The Vernacular Tradition in American
Literature," Die neueren Sprachen, Beiheft 3, n.d.
46-57. Reviewed by *HANS BUNGERT in Archiv für
d. Studien der neueren Sprachen (Herrig), CXCVI,
342.
[Source: MHRA Annual Bibliography (1960),
Nos. 1318, 4811.]

NEIDER, CHARLES. "Introduction," A Connecticut
Yankee in King Arthur's Court. New York: Hill
and Wang, pp. ix-xii.
    Neider's brief introduction notes MT's "humani-
tarianism and savage satire."

1961

BRANCH, EDGAR M. [Review: Walter Blair, Mark
Twain & Huck Finn (1960.A1).] Modern Language
Notes, LXXVI (June), 562-64.
    Blair provides a useful record of influences on
the writing of HF (including MT's personal life
at the time), but "the accumulation of sources
cannot replace the insight essential to a genuine
synthesis of meaning."

*HOWARD, LEON. [Review: Walter Blair, Mark Twain &
Huck Finn (1960.A1).] Western Folklore, XX,
136-37.
    [Source: MHRA Annual Bibliography (1961),
No. 5262.]

KRIEGEL, LEONARD. "Afterword," Life on the Mississippi. New York: New American Library (A Signet
Classic), pp. 375-81.
    Kriegel ranks LOM with TS and HF "as one of the
indisputably great works in the Twain canon"; the
lack of structure is part of the appeal.

*LYNN, KENNETH S., ed. "Huckleberry Finn": Text,
Sources, and Criticism. New York: Harcourt,
Brace & World.
    [Source: MHRA Annual Bibliography (1961),
No. 5921.]

TANNER, TONY. "Samuel Clemens and the Progress of
a Stylistic Rebel," See 1962.B70.

*VANČURA, Z. [Review: Walter Blair, Mark Twain &
Huck Finn (1960.A1).] Časopis pro Moderni Filogii,
XLIII, 180.
    [Source: MHRA Annual Bibliography (1961),
No. 5262.]

1962

*ARVIN, NEWTON. [Introduction.] Adventures of
Huckleberry Finn. New York: Collier Books.
    [Source: MLA Bibliography (1962), No. 5468.]

*BEAVER, HAROLD. [Introduction.] Life on the Mis-
sissippi. London: Oxford University Press.
    [Source: MLA Bibliography (1962), No. 5471;
for review See 1963.B3.]

CLEMENS, SAMUEL L. Adventures of Huckleberry Finn:
A Facsmile of the First Edition. Introduction by
Hamlin Hill. San Francisco: Chandler Publishing
Company.
    With the original illustrations, this is an at-
tractive reading edition of HF. Hill's introduction provides a sound foundation for the reader
unfamiliar with HF; among the topics considered
are the course of composition, reputation, themes,
and structure of the book, and the character of
Huck in his role as narrator. Hill provides a
carefully-selected bibliography of books and articles for further reading; it is classified,

annotated where necessary, and far more useful
than the lists in many popular editions of HF.

*MARSHALL, PERCY. Masters of the English Novel.
London: Dennis Dobson. [Section on MT.]
    [Source: MLA Bibliography (1963), No. 2674.]

*REISS, EDMUND. [Foreword.] "The Mysterious
Stranger" and Other Stories. New York: New American Library.
    [Source: MLA Bibliography (1962), No. 5472.]

RUBIN, LOUIS. "The South and the Faraway Country,"
Virginia Quarterly Review, XXXVIII (Summer),
444-59.
    Treats MT in passing as "the prototype of the
Southern writers of our own time. Like them he
grew up in a tranquil, contained community, and
like them he was propelled by his art and his
times far beyond that community." Like MT, the
modern Southern writers symbolize the disintegration of the smalltown life before the forces of
the twentieth century.

*WAGENKNECHT, EDWARD. [Introduction.] The Innocents
Abroad. New York: Heritage Press.
    [Source: MLA Bibliography (1963), No. 5501.]

1963

*BUNGERT, HANS. [Review: Kenneth S. Lynn, Mark
Twain and Southwestern Humor (1959.A4).] Archiv
für d. Studium d. neueren Sprachen (Herrig), CC,
466-68.
    [Source: MHRA Annual Bibliography (1963),
No. 4734.]

CLEMENS, SAMUEL L. A Connecticut Yankee in King
Arthur's Court: A Facsimile of the First Edition.
San Francisco: Chandler Publishing Company. "Introduction," "A Note on the Text," and "Bibliography" by Hamlin Hill.
    This is the most interesting of the Chandler Fac-
simile Editions of MT's books, because of Dan
Beard's added satiric comments through his illustrations [and the likenesses of Sarah Bernhardt
(p. 38), Tennyson (pp. 41, 279), Edward, Prince of
Wales and the Emperor of Germany (p. 297), and Jay
Gould (p. 465).] Hill's bibliography is well selected and annotated to lead the student into a
fruitful investigation of the background and critical problems. His introduction gives the general
reader a good foundation for understanding the intentions, confusions, and achievements of MT in
this remarkable book.

*NEIDER, CHARLES, ed. The Complete Essays of Mark
Twain. With Introduction. Garden City, New York:
Doubleday.
    [Source: MLA Bibliography (1963), No. 5524.]

REISS, EDMUND. "Afterword," in A Connecticut Yankee
in King Arthur's Court. New York: New American
Library (A Signet Classic), pp. 321-31.
    In a sound discussion for the general reader
Reiss follows the major criticism, recognizing the
ambiguous nature of Hank Morgan and of the modern
benefits he brought to Arthurian England. "The
ambiguous presentation of good and evil leads to

(REISS, EDMUND)
Twain's major difficulty in the book," and, faced
with man's dual nature, "Twain never decides anything."

1964

*ARNOLD, ARMIN. "Friedrich Dürrenmatt und Mark
Twain: Zur Methode der vergleichenden Inter-
pretationen," in Jost, François, ed., Proceedings
of the IVth Congress of the International Comparative Literature Association, 1964. 2 vols. (The
Hague: Mouton), II: 1097-1104.
[Source: MLA Bibliography (1967), Nos. 64,
17544.]

1965

ANON. [Contemporary Newspaper Accounts.] Twainian, XXIV (January-February), 1-3.
Reprints 1895.B6 and 1895.B13, on MT lecturing
in Washington.

*ANON. [Review: Ralph Gregory, Mark Twain's First
America: Florida, Missouri, 1835-1840
(1965.A3).] Missouri Historical Review, LIX, 523.
[Source: MHRA Annual Bibliography (1965),
No. 6982.]

COHEN, RALPH, ed. The Adventures of Huckleberry
Finn. New York: Bantam Books.
Added matter for the student includes a critical discussion, "Games and Growing Up: a Key to
understanding Huckleberry Finn"; "Is Huckleberry
Finn a Great Novel? Opinions, Reviews, and Comments (reprints excerpts from 1939.B61; 1955.B29,
32); "Huckleberry Finn and The Catcher in the Rye
(reprints part of 1956.B30); "Mark Twain: A Biographical Sketch."

WILLOUGHBY, JOHN, ed. Life on the Mississippi.
New York: Airmont Publishing Company.
Willoughby's brief introduction is descriptive
and appreciative.

1966

ANON. [Brief Review: A. Grove Day, ed., Mark
Twain's Letters from Hawaii (1966.A3).] Nineteenth-Century Fiction, XXI (December), 302.
Brief description: Day's "editing" consists of
"an introduction rehearsing the contents of the
letters"; there are no notes or index.

*ANON. [Review: John Y. Simon, ed., "General Grant"
by Matthew Arnold, with a Rejoinder by Mark Twain
(1967.A18).] Lincoln Herald, LXVIII, 54.
[Source: MHRA Annual Bibliography (1966),
Nos. 5432, 7039.]

*ASPIZ, HAROLD. [Review: Robert Regan, Unpromising
Heroes: Mark Twain and His Characters (1966.A8);
Justin Kaplan, Mr. Clemens and Mark Twain
(1966.A6).] Studies in Scottish Literature, IV,
241-42.

[Source: MHRA Annual Bibliography (1967),
Nos. 7116, 7131. This review could not be located
in the copy of Studies in Scottish Literature, IV,
examined at Sir George Williams University.]

CLEMENS, SAMUEL L. The Adventures of Tom Sawyer,
ed. Robert D. Spector. New York: Bantam.
"The World of Tom Sawyer" (pp. 221-27) follows
the familiar critics, describing Tom as symbolic
of all boys, but individual and complex; follows
Blair's interpretation of the structure (1939.B7).
"The Making of Tom Sawyer" (pp. 228-36) includes
passages from MT's Autobiography and "Boy's Manuscript." "Tom's Readers and Critics" (pp. 238-42)
includes excerpts from Howells (1876.B6) and Kipling (1899.B19). "Islands of Good and Evil: Tom
Sawyer and Lord of the Flies" (pp. 243-45) contrasts idyllic and frightening views of nature.
"Mark Twain: A Biographical Sketch" (pp. 246-49)
is conventional, helpful to the reader unfamiliar
with MT, but very brief.

*ELLIS, ALLAN B., and F. ANDRÉ FAVAT. "From Computer
to Criticism: An Application of Automatic Content
Analysis to Literature, pp. 628-38 in The General
Inquirer: A Computer Approach to Content Analy-
sis, eds. Philip J. Stone, Dexter C. Dunphy, Mar-
shall S. Smith, and Daniel M. Ogilvie (Cambridge,
Mass.: MIT).
[Source: MLA Bibliography (1966), No. 4678.]

FIEDLER, LESLIE A. "Afterword," The Innocents
Abroad. New York: New American Library (A Signet
Classic), pp. 477-92.
Provides a context for IA through an extensive
and perceptive examination of popular travel writing of the nineteenth century, with attention to
the interests and prejudices of the travelers,
most of them Anglo-Saxon Protestants; also, considers the use of travel in developing perspective
toward one's own country.

*WAGENKNECHT, EDWARD. [Introduction.] A Tramp
Abroad. New York: Heritage.
[Source: MLA Bibliography (1967), No. 9389.]

1967

BABCOCK, C. MERTON. "Mark Twain's Adventures in
Art," Art in America, LV (March-April), 66-71.
For the general reader, a summary of MT's comments on art, with a mock-serious discussion of
his sketches, which, "clearly in a class by themselves, had the power of soliciting comments previously unheard in temples of art." Illustrated
with 21 drawings by MT.

*DURAM, JOHN M., Jr. "Mark Twain Comments on Reli-
gious Hypocrisy," Revista de Letras da Faculdade
de Filosofia Ciencias e Letras de Assis, X, 60-75.
[Source: MLA Bibliography (1970), No. 6772.]

*KAPLAN, JUSTIN. [Review: Hamlin Hill, ed., Mark
Twain's Letters to His Publishers (1967.A6);
Franklin R. Rogers, ed., Mark Twain's Satires &
Burlesques (1967.A7).] Book Week/World, March 5,
p. 4.

(*KAPLAN, JUSTIN)
    [Source: MHRA Annual Bibliography (1967), Nos.
7112, 7135. The attribution is unclear, but is
probably to the Washington Post Book World, in
which Kaplan published another review in 1973
(See p. 405, below.]

*LEFCOURT, CHARLES R. "Dürrenmatt's Güllen and
Twain's Hadleyburg: The Corruption of Two Towns,"
Revue des Langues Vivantes (Bruxelles), XXXIII,
303-308.
    [Source: MHRA Annual Bibliography (1967),
No. 7123; MLA Bibliography (1967), No. 17549.]

*SMITH, HENRY NASH. "The Morals of Power: Business
Enterprise as a Theme in Mid-Nineteenth-Century
American Fiction," in Clarence Gohdes, ed., Essays
on American Literature in Honor of Jay B. Hubbell
(Durham, N.C.: Duke University Press), pp. 90-
107. [On GA and The House of the Seven Gables.]
    [Source: MLA Bibliography (1967), Nos. 105,
9052.]

*WILLIAMS, PHILIP. "Huckleberry Finn and the Dialec-
tic of History," Essays and Studies in English
Language and Literature (Tohoku Gakuin University,
Sendai, Japan), 51-52, pp. 59-98.
    [Source: MLA Bibliography (1971), No. 8016.]

1968

*ANDERSON, FREDERICK. "Hazards of Photographic
Sources," Center for Editions of American Authors
Newsletter (MLA), I, 5.
    [Source: MLA Bibliography (1968), No. 10260.]

* ____. "Overlapping Texts," Center for Editions of
American Authors Newsletter (MLA), I, 6-7.
    [On MS. Source: MLA Bibliography (1968),
No. 10261.]

*BAETZHOLD, HOWARD. "An Emendation in A Connecticut
Yankee," Center for Editions of American Authors
Newsletter (MLA), I, 10.
    [Source: MLA Bibliography (1968), No. 10263.]

*BURRISON, JOHN A. "The Golden Arm": The Folk Tale
and Its Literary Use by Mark Twain and Joel C.
Harris. (Research Paper 19). Atlanta: Georgia
State University.
    [Source: MLA Bibliography (1970), No. 6763.]

*CLEMENS, SAMUEL L. "An Unpublished Letter: Mark
Twain to Chatto & Windus, 25 July 1897," Center
for Editions of American Authors Newsletter (MLA),
I, 1.
    [Source: MLA Bibliography (1968), No. 10305.
See Hart, James D., 1969, p. 402, below.]

____. Pudd'nhead Wilson and Those Extraordinary
Twins, Facsimile of the First Edition, with Introduction, Note on Text, and Bibliography by Frederick Anderson. San Francisco: Chandler Publishing Company.
    Drawing on his close familiarity with the schol-
arship and on the rich resources of the Mark Twain
Papers, Anderson describes the backgrounds and
composition of GA and the associated Those Extraordinary Twins, and the critical reception they

received; he discusses their relation to MT's concern with the problem of identity and his conflicting attitudes toward the South. The brief bibliography is annotated and chosen for its appropriate-
ness to this particular book. The reader will appreciate the clear type and illustrations of the
original edition.

* ____. Tom Sawyer and Huckleberry Finn. Introduction by Andrew Sinclair and Notes by Michael Ler-
ner. London: Pan. (Best-Sellers of Literature).
    [Source: MHRA Annual Bibliography (1968),
No. 7777.]

*CRIŞAN, CONSTANTIN. [Introduction.] "Viaţa lui
Mark Twain" [The Life of Mark Twain], in Mark
Twain, Aventurile lui Tom Sawyer [The Adventures
of Tom Sawyer]. Bucureşti: Editura timeretuli,
pp. 5-15.
    [Source: MHRA Annual Bibliography (1968),
No. 7718.]

*DAVIDSON, LOREN K. "The Darnell-Watson Feud," Du-
quesne Review, XIII, 76-95.
    [Source: MLA Bibliography (1969), No. 6462.]

LINDEMAN, JACK, ed. The Conflict of Convictions:
American Writers Report the Civil War. A Selection and Arrangement from the Journals, Correspondence and Articles of the Major Men and Women
of Letters Who Lived through the War. Philadelphia: Chilton.
    Listed in one of the major bibliographies, this
is simply an anthology containing MT's "The Private History of a Campaign that Failed."

*REST, JAIME. "Huckleberry Finn como Innovación en
la Técnica Narrativa," in Actas de las Terceras
Jornadas de Investigación de la Historia y Literatura Rioplatense y de los Estados Unidos. Mendoza
(Argentina): Universidad Nacional de Cuyo,
pp. 257-62.
    [Source: MLA Bibliography (1971), No. 8003.]

*YOSHIDA, HIROSHIGE. "Huckleberry Finn ko," Eigo
Seinen [The Rising Generation] (Tokyo), CXIV,
84-86.
    [Source: MLA Bibliography (1970), No. 6816.]

1969

*ANDERSON, FREDERICK. "Team Proofreading: Some
Problems," Center for Editions of American Authors
Newsletter (MLA), II, 15. [On MT Papers.]
    [Source: MLA Bibliography (1969), No. 6448.]

ANON. [Review: Justin Kaplan, ed., Mark Twain: A
Profile (1967.A12).] Civil War History, XV, 86.
Only a brief mention.

*DMITRIEV, V. G. Pod Chuzim Imenem (Under Another's
Name). Moscow: Nauka.
    [Source: MHRA Annual Bibliography (1969),
No. 7939.]

*DOUGHTY, NANELIA S. "Realistic Characterization in
Postbellum Fiction," Negro American Literature
Forum, III, 57-62, 68.
    [Source: MLA Bibliography (1969), No. 6418.]

FELHEIM, MARVIN. "Introduction," The Gilded Age.
New York: New American Library (A Signet Classic), pp. vii-xviii.
A sound general discussion of the backgrounds
of MT's and Warner's composition of GA, and their
satiric portrait of the age.

GERBER, JOHN C. "Mark Twain's Search for Identity," in Max F. Schulz, William D. Templeman, and
Charles R. Metzger, eds., Essays in American and
English Literature. Presented to Bruce Robert
McElderry, Jr. (Athens, Ohio: Ohio University
Press), pp. 27-47.
MT's inner contradictions are revealed in the
variety of forms in which he signed his name, in
his dress, in his cheerfulness and melancholy; he
was torn by an ambivalence of decorum and rebellion, of admiration for the rich and great, and
his native democracy. "On reflection it almost
seems as though there were two consciousnesses at
work in Twain, one constantly sensing personal
opportunity, the other constantly sensing human
need and aspiration. Ultimately, however, MT's
"search for identity was the search of every
thoughtful man, and his failures were the failures of his age--and ours."

*GOTO, AKIO. "Seijuku no Kyozetsu--M. Twain no
Amerikateki Seikaku," Eigo Seinen [The Rising
Generation] (Tokyo), CXV, 286-87. [Rejection of
Maturity--MT's American character.]
[Source: MLA Bibliography (1970), No. 6783.]

*HART, JAMES D. "On an 'Unpublished Letter' by Mark
Twain," Center for Editions of American Authors
Newsletter (MLA), II, 15.
[Source: MLA Bibliography (1969), No. 6475;
reference is to an entry for 1968 (See p. 401,
above).]

KOHLI, RAJ K. "Isabel Archer and Huck Finn": Two
Responses to the Fruit of Knowledge," in Sujit
Mukherjee and D. V. K. Raghavacharyulu, eds.,
Indian Essays in American Literature: Papers in
Honour of Robert E. Spiller (Bombay: Popular
Prakashan), pp. 167-78.
[Source: MLA International Bibliography (1969),
Nos. 82, 6666.] See 1968.B60.

*ODESSKY, MARJORY H. "The Impartial Friend: The
Death of Mark Twain," Journal of Historical Stud-
ies, II, 159-60.
[Source: MLA Bibliography (1969), No. 6484.]

*PLESSNER, MONIKA. "Huckleberry Finns wirkliches
Ende," Frankfurter Hefte, XXIV, 441-46.
[Source: MLA Bibliography (1969), No. 6486.]

SELBY, PAUL OWEN. Theses on Mark Twain, 1910-1967.
Kirksville, Missouri: Missouriana Library, Northeast Missouri State College.
A letter from Dr. Selby says this is based on
the replies to his requests for data from the
graduate institutions where the theses were written.

*TALBOTT, LINDA H. "Huck Finn: Mark Twain at Mid-
stream," Nassau Review (Nassau Community College),
I, v, 44-60.
[Source: MLA Bibliography (1969), No. 6496.]

*ANON. "A Certain Private Letter--Author's Reading,"
Yankee (November), pp. 126-31.
[Source: Quoted by Charles R. Duke (1974); See
p. 406, below.] An 1887 letter from a young man
to his fiancée describes MT at a reading with
Hale, Aldrich, Howells, Higginson, Holmes, and
Longfellow.

*BOWEN, JAMES K., and RICHARD VAN DER BEETS, eds.
Adventures of Huckleberry Finn. Glenview, Illi-
nois: Scott, Foresman. [Includes Edgar M.
Branch, "Mark Twain Scholarship: Two Decades."]
[Source: MLA Bibliography (1970), No. 6759.]

*BUDD, LOUIS J. "Baxter's Hog: The Right Mascot for
an Editor (with CEAA Standards) of Mark Twain's
Political and Social Writings," Center for Editions of American Authors Newsletter (MLA), III,
3-10.
[Source: MLA Bibliography (1970), No. 6762.]

_____. [Review: Walter Blair, ed., Mark Twain's
Hannibal, Huck & Tom (1969.A3); William M. Gibson,
ed., Mark Twain's "Mysterious Stranger" Manuscripts (1969.A4); Lewis Leary, ed., Mark Twain's
Correspondence with Henry Huttleston Rogers
(1969.A2).] South Atlantic Quarterly, LXIX (Winter), 164-65.
A brief review, describing the books and praising the editing.

*CLEMENS, SAMUEL L. "Mark Twain to Chatto & Windus:
Two Unpublished Letters," Center for Editions of
American Authors Newsletter (MLA), III, 1-2.
[Source: MLA Bibliography (1970), No. 6794.]

*ENGLISH TEACHERS' ASSOCIATION OF NEW SOUTH WALES.
Reading and Teaching the Novel. Ashfield, New
South Wales: English Teachers' Association of New
South Wales.
[Source: MHRA Annual Bibliography (1970),
Nos. 2502, 8239.]

*LEARY, LEWIS. "Mark Twain among the Malefactors,"
in Brom Weber, ed., Sense and Sensibility in
Twentieth-Century Writing: A Gathering in Memory
of William Van O'Connor (Carbondale and Edwardsville: Southern Illinois University Press; London:
Feffer & Simons), pp. 109-17.
Extensively revised from 1968.B62. On MT in his
last years, enjoying the luxuries of a millionaire
in the company of Henry H. Rogers and Andrew Carnegie; in turn, being seen with MT improved their
public image. The Brooks "reasoned explanation of
what Clemens had allowed to be done to the genius
of Mark Twain...has needed only small revision in
the almost fifty years since it was first made.
Like many of his countrymen, before or since,
Clemens did sell out."

*RAO, B. RAMACHANDRA. "Structural Devices in The Ad-
ventures of Huckleberry Finn," Banasthali Patrika,
XIV, 23-29.
[Source: MLA Bibliography (1971), No. 8001.]

*SHEPPERSON, WILBUR S. Restless Strangers: Nevada's Immigrants and Their Interpretors. Reno: Nevada University Press.
  [Source: MHRA Annual Bibliography (1972), Nos. 6425, 8745.]

*SHULTS, DONALD. "On The Gilded Age," Kyushu American Literature (Fukuoka, Japan), XII, 1-13.
  [Source: MLA Bibliography (1970), No. 6805.]

*TOWERS, TOM H. "Mark Twain's Connecticut Yankee: The Trouble in Camelot," in Ray B. Browne, Larry N. Landrum, and William K. Bottorff, eds., Challenges in American Culture. (Bowling Green, Ohio: Bowling Green University Popular Press), pp. 190-98.
  [Source: MLA Bibliography (1971), Nos. 58, 8015.]

1971

*ATCHITY, KENNETH JOHN. [Review: Arturo Serrano-Plaja, "Magic" Realism in Cervantes (1970.B77).] Western Humanities Review, XXV, 182-83.
  [Source: MHRA Annual Bibliography (1971), No. 8881.]

BAETZHOLD, HOWARD. [Review Article.] Modern Fiction Studies, XVII (Winter), 645-49.
  Maxwell Geismar's Mark Twain: An American Prophet (1970.A5) providing some insights, is marred by misstatements and the caustic tone. Mary Ellen Goad's The Image and the Woman in the Life of Mark Twain (1971.B28) needs modification in some specific arguments, but provides the foundation for "a much more accurate assessment of the role of women in Mark Twain's life and works than we heretofore have had." Lewis Leary's Southern Excursions (1971.A4) is a pleasure to read for the style alone, and "Mark Twain and the Comic Spirit" is "still one of the best brief introductions to Mark Twain. 'Mark Twain's Wound: Standing with Reluctant Feet' is also an exceptionally good summary of the Van Wyck Brooks-Bernard DeVoto controversy."

*BONAZZI, ROBERT. [Review: Maxwell Geismar, Mark Twain: An American Prophet (1970.A5).] Southwest Review, LVI, 202-206.
  [Source: MHRA Annual Bibliography (1971), No. 8840.]

COX, JOHN F. "On the Naming of Huckleberry Finn," Publications of the Modern Language Association, LXXXVI (October), 1038.
  A brief letter to the editor in response to Colwell (1971.B13): "The boy was a 'hick' who loved to have 'fun,' or a 'fun hick.' The transposition of letters would not have been all that difficult."

DETWEILER, ROBERT. "Articulate Scholarship," South Atlantic Bulletin, XXXVI (March), 60-62.
  A review, primarily descriptive, of Allison Ensor's Mark Twain and the Bible (1969.A5), as "well-structured and clearly written.... The subject of Twain and the Bible is worth precisely the size and kind of book that Ensor has provided."

*DURAM, JAMES C. "Mark Twain and the Middle Ages," Wichita State University Bulletin, XLVII, iii, 3-16.
  [Source: MLA Bibliography (1974), No. 9603.]

EBY, E. H. [Review: Howard G. Baetzhold, Mark Twain and John Bull: The British Connection (1970.A1).] Pacific Northwest Quarterly, LXII, 156-57.
  [Source: MHRA Annual Bibliography (1972), No. 8687.]

*HAUCK, RICHARD BOYD. "The Prisoner at the Window: Mark Twain," in his A Cheerful Nihilism: Confidence and "The Absurd" in American Humorous Fiction (Bloomington, London: Indiana University Press), pp. 133-66.
  Treats ambiguity of meaning in CY (MT's "masterpiece of the absurd"), IA, RI, HF, and shows that the late works demonstrate a belief "that the imagination to create meaning in a meaningless universe was not one of man's gifts"; certainly, it had not been a gift of Huck Finn or Hank Morgan. In CY, MT used the satirist's shifting points of view, but he also satirized the perception process that makes satire possible--thereby experimenting in the comedy of the absurd. "The process is emblemized by Hank Morgan's analysis of his conscience."

*JUSTUS, JAMES H. [Review: Thomas Blues, Mark Twain & The Community (1970.A2).] Indiana Magazine of History, LXVII, 84-85.
  [Source: MHRA Annual Bibliography (1971), No. 8819.]

*LANINA, T. [Afterword to Russian translation of TS and HF.] Moscow: Detskaya Literatura.
  [Source: MHRA Annual Bibliography (1971), No. 8850.

*LO-JOHANSSON, IVAR. "Mark Twains Resa i Sverige" [Mark Twain's Swedish Journey]. Böckernas Värld, VI, No. 5, 49-54.
  [Source: MHRA Annual Bibliography (1971), No. 8852.]

*RIGAUX, JACQUES. Ces Écrivains-Vagabonds: Borrow, Twain, Kipling, London, Cendrars, Stevenson, Conan Doyle, Hemingway, Leurs Vies, Leurs Oeuvres. Liège: Editions Jalis.
  [Source: MHRA Annual Bibliography (1971), Nos. 6746, 8872.]

*ROBINSON, VIRGINIA P. "The Double Soul: Mark Twain and Otto Rank," Journal of the Otto Rank Association, VI, 32-53.
  [Source: MLA Bibliography (1971), No. 8005.]

*SAWEY, ORLAN. "The Consistency of the Character of Nigger Jim in Huckleberry Finn," TAIUS (Texas A&I), IV, 35-41.
  [Source: MLA Bibliography (1974), No. 9641.]

*TOMISCH, JOHN. A Genteel Endeavor: American Culture and Politics in the Gilded Age. Palo Alto, California: Stanford University Press.
  [Source: MHRA Annual Bibliography (1971), No. 6481; (1972, with name spelled "Tomsich"), Nos. 6450, 8749.]

*WILCOX, EARL. "Jake and Bob and Huck and Tom: Hemingway's Use of Huck Finn," in Matthew J. Bruccoli and C. E. Frazer Clark, eds., Fitzgerald/ Hemingway Annual, 1971 (Washington, D.C.: NCR Microcard Editions), pp. 322-24.

In Chapter II of The Sun Also Rises, Jake Barnes and Robert Cohn are juxtaposed as realist and romantic, like Huck and Tom; Barnes observes that Cohn believes too much in the books he has read. There is a verbal parallel to Huck's opening statement on TS in Barnes's comment on Cohn's reading of a W. H. Hudson book: "You understand me, he made some reservations, but on the whole the book to him was sound." Hemingway's chapter reflects both a major theme in HF and his own respect for MT.

1972

BABCOCK, C. MERTON. [Review: John S. Tuckey, ed., Mark Twain's "Which Was the Dream?" and Other Symbolic Writings of the Later Years (1967.A8).] Etc.: A Review of General Semantics, XXIX (March), 101-103.

Largely descriptive; praises the editing.

BAZERMAN, CHARLES. "Toward the End, an Effete Snob," Nation, CCXV (September 18), 215-16.

A review, chiefly descriptive, of Frederick Anderson, ed., A Pen Warmed-Up in Hell: Mark Twain in Protest (1972.A4); defends the polemics of the late years: "Directness and clarity are achievements, whether or not we are pleased with our portraits."

BLUEFARB, SAM. "Huckleberry Finn: Escape from Conscience and the Discovery of the Heart," in his The Escape Motif in the American Novel: Mark Twain to Richard Wright (Columbus: Ohio State University Press), pp. 12-24.

HF is "the first modern American novel in which the theme is dominant," anticipating later novels is the genre in "violence, the difference between the uses of rhetoric and the contrasting realities, conscious and unconscious hypocrisy, gratuitous cruelty...but in amounts that may seem immodest or overplayed when we compare the work with the novels that follow it."

*CHELIDZE, V. [Introductory article to Georgian translation of TS and HF.] Tbilisi: Sabchota Sakartvelo.

[Source: MHRA Annual Bibliography (1972), No. 8697.]

CLEMENS, SAMUEL L. Roughing It. With an Introduction and Explanatory Notes by Franklin R. Rogers. Text Established and Textual Notes by Paul Baender. Berkeley, Los Angees, London. Published for the Iowa Center for Textual Studies by the University of California Press. A CEAA approved text.

*COLEMAN, ALEXANDER. "Notes on Borges and American Literature," Tri-Quarterly, XXV, 356-77.

[Source: MHRA Annual Bibliography (1973), Nos. 2260, 8700.]

*GIDNEY, JAMES B. [Review: Maxwell Geismar, Mark Twain: An American Prophet (1970.A5).] Ohioana Quarterly, XV:1, 29-31.

[Source: MHRA Annual Bibliography (1972), No. 8712.]

*JEFFERSON, DOUGLAS W. "Mark Twain: Adventures of Huckleberry Finn," in Hans-Joachim Lang, ed., Der amerikanische Roman: Von den Anfang bis zur Gegenwart (Düsseldorf: August Bagel), pp. 142-67.

[Source: MLA Bibliography (1973), Nos. 132, 8864.]

*LIBMAN, Z. [Introductory article to Ukrainian translation of stories and pamphlets.] Kiev: Dnipro.

[Source: MHRA Annual Bibliography (1972), No. 8729.]

McCARRY, CHARLES, and DAVID L. ARNOLD. "Yesterday Lingers along the Connecticut," National Geographic, CXLII (September), 334-68.

Includes a photograph of MT's Hartford home, p. 366.

*MOORE, RAYBURN S. [Review: Lewis Leary, Southern Excursions (1971.A4).] Georgia Review, XXVI (Summer), 237-40.

The essays on MT "offer considerable information in compact form...gracefully marshal materials on important topics [and] provide valuable critical insights into problems old and new." Leary "has provided information, insight, and understanding sufficient to satisfy the interest he has aroused."

*ORLOVA, R. [Afterword to Kornei Chukovsky's translation of TS.] Kaliningrad: Knizhnoe Izdatel'- stvo.

[Source: MHRA Annual Bibliography (1972), No. 8736.]

*ÖVERLAND, ORM. [Review: Walter Blair, ed., Mark Twain's Hannibal, Huck & Tom (1969.A3); William M. Gibson, ed., Mark Twain's "Mysterious Stranger" Manuscripts (1969.A4); Lewis Leary, ed., Mark Twain's Correspondence with Henry Huttleston Rogers (1969.A2).] English Studies (Amsterdam), LIII, 372-74.

[Source: MHRA Annual Bibliography (1972), Nos. 8690, 8714, 8726.]

TERRY, CLIFFORD. [Review: Frederick Anderson, ed., A Pen Warmed-Up in Hell: Mark Twain in Protest (1972.A4).] Book World (Chicago Tribune), June 4, p. 8.

[Source: MHRA Annual Bibliography (1972), No. 8682.]

1973

*AGRAWAL, I. N. "Mark Twain's Visit to Allahabad," Indian Journal of American Studies, III, i, 104-108.

[Source: MLA Bibliography (1974), No. 9587. Abstract in 1974 MLA Abstracts.]

*ANON. "Mark Twain's Last Manuscript," Bancroftiana (Berkeley), LV (June), 9.

[Source: MLA Bibliography (1973), No. 8877.]

CARDWELL, GUY A. "Mark Twain, James R. Osgood, and Those 'Suppressed' Passages," New England Quarterly, XLVI (June), 163-88.

(CARDWELL, GUY A.)
Chapter XLVIII of LOM was not dropped out of consideration for Southern readers, as has been suggested, but because the book was becoming too long. That this and some of the other portions removed are more interesting than some that remained "is almost surely indicative of nothing more than slapdash editing."

*CATE, HOLLIS L. "Two American Bumpkins," Research Studies (Washington State University), XLI, 61-63.
[Source: MLA Bibliography (1973), No. 8911.]

*COHEN, EDWARD H. "The Return to St. Petersburg," Iowa English Bulletin: Yearbook, XXIII, 50-55.
[Source: MLA Bibliography (1973), No. 8845.]

*ENANG, S. D. "The Deceptive Simplicity of Mark Twain's Novels," Horizon (Ibadan), IX, 55-61.
[Source: MLA Bibliography (1973), No. 8850.]

*FREESE, PETER. "Adventures of Huckleberry Finn und The Catcher in the Rye: exemplarischen Deutung der Romananfänge," Die Neueren Sprachen (LLBA), XXII, 658-68.
[Source: MLA Bibliography (1974), No. 9606.]

GASTON, GEORG MERI-AKRI. "The Function of Tom Sawyer in Huckleberry Finn," Mississippi Quarterly, XXVII (Winter), 33-39.
"Tom, a true child of his society, is capable of terrible selfishness and cruelty," and serves as a foil in the portrayal of Huck's moral development. Abstract by Gaston in 1974 MLA Abstracts, No. 9608.

*GEISMAR, MAXWELL. Mark Twain: An American Prophet. New York: McGraw-Hill.
Geismar's own abridgement of 1970.A5. Source: MLA Bibliography (1974), No. 9609.

*HANSEN, CHADWICK. "There Warn't No Home Like a Raft Floating Down the Mississippi, or Like a Raft Floating Down the Neckar, or Like a Balloon Ballooning Across the Sahara: Mark Twain as Improviser," in Stanley Weintraub and Philip Young, eds., Directions in Literary Criticism: Contemporary Approaches to Literature. Festschrift for Henry W. Sams (University Park and London: Pennsylvania State University Press), pp. 160-67.
[Source: MLA Bibliography (1973), Nos. 64, 8859.]

*KAPLAN, JUSTIN. "Never the Twain," Washington Post Book World (July 29), pp. 2-3.
[Source: Bray, 1974; See p. 405, below.] A review of Hamlin Hill, Mark Twain: God's Fool (1973.A5), which Kaplan calls "moralistic and even hostile," too "preoccupied with the obvious aspects of aging--escalating narcissism coupled with physical and psychic degeneration."

*KARITA, MOTOJI. "Mark Twain Mikan no Isaku," Eigo Seinen [The Rising Generation] (Tokyo), CXIX, 462-64. [MT's Unfinished Piece.]
[Source: MLA Bibliography (1973), No. 8867.]

*LANG, H. JACK. "Mark Twain A.L.S. More Valuable than Lincoln," Manuscripts, XXV, 187-91.
[Source: MLA Bibliography (1973), No. 8874.]

*MAURANGES, J.-P. "Aliénation et Châtiment chez Mark Twain et Heinrich Böll," Revue des Langues Vivantes (Bruxelles), XXXIX, 131-36.
[Source: MLA Bibliography (1974), No. 9630.]

ROEMER, KENNETH M. "The Yankee(s) in Noahville," American Literature, XLV (November), 434-37.
Franklin H. North's The Awakening of Noahville (1898) is "an obvious attempt to rewrite" CY, which it resembles not only in plot and characters, but even in specific illustrations. North's Yankees show his awareness of "the ingenuity, the power, the cruelty, and the ridiculousness of Twain's hero." Abstract by Roemer in 1973 MLA Abstracts, No. 9145.

*SCHÄFER, JÜRGEN. "Huckleberry, U.S.," English Studies, LIV, 334-35.
[Source: MLA Bibliography (1973), No. 8891.]

*SMITH, LAURA. "Fictive Names in Mark Twain's Pudd'nhead Wilson," pp. 91-94 in Fred Tarpley, ed., Love and Wrestling, Butch and O.K. (So. Central Names Inst. Pub. 2.) Commerce, Texas: Names Inst. P. [Order from ed. Dept. of Lit. and Lang., E. T. Station, Commerce, Texas 75428.]
[Source: MLA Bibliography (1973), Nos. 171, 8893.]

1974

*ANON. "The Appert Collection of Mark Twain," Bancroftiana (University of California, Berkeley), LVII (January), 5-6.
[Source: MLA Bibliography (1974), No. 9643. On new acquisition of letters, clippings, etc.]

*BANKS, R. JEFF. "Mark Twain: Detective Story Writer. An Appreciation," Armchair Detective, VII, 176-77.
[Source: MLA Bibliography (1974), No. 9588.]

BEAVER, HAROLD. "Run, Nigger, Run: Adventures of Huckleberry Finn as a Fugitive Slave Narrative," Journal of American Studies, VIII (December), 339-61.
Jim is an adult and a slave, and his situation is not Huck's: "If young Huck is taken in by that river-born camaraderie between black and white on a Mississippi raft, it does not follow that his friend (and victim) was equally taken in."

BERGER, SIDNEY. "New Mark Twain Items," Papers of the Bibliographical Society of America, LXVIII (July-September), 331-35.
Chatto & Windus correspondence reveals that the first English edition of PW was based on serial publication in the Century Magazine; "The variants in it, then, have no authority--a fact which greatly reduces my work" [as editor of the CEAA edition of PW]. Abstract by Berger in 1974 MLA Abstracts, No. 9591.

BRAY, ROBERT. "Mark Twain Biography: Entering a New Phase," Midwest Quarterly, XV (Spring), 286-301.
On the depiction of MT by Paine, Brooks, DeVoto, Howells, more recently by Justin Kaplan, and now

(BRAY, ROBERT)
by Hamlin Hill; who has "superbly" corrected the portrayal of MT's last years fabricated by Paine and Clara Clemens. The debunking is well documented and prepares the way for a new interpretation of MT and his works. Lengthy abstract in AES, XVIII (June, 1975), 3294.

*BROGAN, HOWARD O. "Early Experience and Scientific Determinism in Twain and Hardy," Mosaic: A Journal for the Comparative Study of Literature and Ideas, VII, iii, 99-105.
[Source: MLA Bibliography (1974), No. 9595. Abstract by Brogan in 1974 MLA Abstracts, No. 9595.]

BURG, DAVID F. "Another View of Huckleberry Finn," Nineteenth-Century Fiction, XXIX (December), 299-319.
The ending of HF is not the failure described in "largely moralistic interpretations which argue its shortcomings"; on the contrary, "it constitutes both a valid formal completion of the novel and an emphatic declaration of the author's metaphysics." HF "is, in fact, a revolutionary novel. It dispels the conventional morality and the conventional wisdom of its own time and ours. And in its joining of a vision of life's absurdity with a circular structure, Huckleberry Finn comprehends and manifests the essence of literary modernity." Huck "is the first absurd hero in our literature, and his story is the prototype of the American novel of black humor." Abstract by Burg in 1974 MLA Abstracts, No. 9597.

CROWLEY, JOHN W. "The Sacerdotal Cult and the Sealskin Coat: W. D. Howells in My Mark Twain," English Language Notes, XI (June), 287-92.
"All of My Mark Twain may be regarded as a tale in the Southwestern humor tradition in which the antics of a 'vernacular hero' (Mark Twain) are related by a self-consciously distanced 'genteel narrator' (Howells).... Howells as narrator betrays divided feelings toward his vernacular hero," and with his own Midwestern background was not wholly at ease in Boston. The disastrous Whittier Birthday Dinner address is discussed at length.

DAVID, BEVERLY R. "The Pictorial Huck Finn: Mark Twain and His Illustrator, E. W. Kemble," American Quarterly, XXVI (October), 331-51.
Reprints 20 illustrations from HF, including the mutilated p. 283 cut and the replacement that was tipped in. Concerned with potential sales, MT was attentive to the book's illustration, making it "a tool that converted the cruelty and sexuality of the story into a series of boyish adventures." Abstract by David in 1974 MLA Abstracts, No. 9599.

*DELANEY, PAUL. "The Avatars of The Mysterious Stranger: Mark Twain's Images of Christ," Christianity and Literature, XXIV, i, 25-38.
[Source: MLA Bibliography (1974), No. 9600.]

DUKE, CHARLES R. "Mark Twain: Speaker at Large," English Record (New York State English Council), XXV (Spring), 43-52.
A general discussion of MT as lecturer, based largely on Paine, Lorch, and other familiar

sources; also, quotes the description of an 1887 MT reading in Boston from a private letter published in Yankee (November, 1970; See p. 402, above).

HENDERSON, HARRY B., III. "Twain: The Varieties of History and A Connecticut Yankee," in his Versions of the Past: The Historical Imagination in American Fiction (New York: Oxford University Press), pp. 175-97.
CY is "perhaps the most magnificent failure of all American historical fiction," and "as a progressive historical novel...terribly divided against itself." Henderson attributes the confusion of CY to a lack of control by MT. There is also a briefer discussion of P&P and JA.

*HSU, C. Y. "Mark Twain and the Chinese," Asian Student, XVI (March), 6-7.
[Source: MLA Bibliography (1974), No. 9615.]

*KAMEI, SHUNSUKE. "Mark Twain no Ie," [Mark Twain's House], Eigo Seinen [The Rising Generation] (Tokyo), CXIX, 738-39.
[Source: MLA Bibliography (1974), No. 9617.]

KETTERER, DAVID. "Epoch-Eclipse and Apocalypse: 'Special Effects' in A Connecticut Yankee," Chapter IX (pp. 213-32) in his New Worlds for Old: The Apocalyptic Imagination, Science Fiction, and American Literature (Bloomington and London: Indiana University Press).
This previously appeared in Publications of the Modern Language Association (1973.B31).

*KLASS, PHILIP. "An Innocent in Time: Mark Twain in King Arthur's Court," Extrapolation, XVI, 17-32.
[Source: MLA Bibliography (1974), No. 9620.]

KRAUTH, LELAND. "Mark Twain: At Home in the Gilded Age," Georgia Review, XXVIII (Spring), 105-13.
"Domesticity was the key to Twain's identity, and it became a touchstone within his fiction"; it is "the heart of The Gilded Age," where in effect corruption is sanctioned for the sake of home and family. Abstract by Krauth in 1974 MLA Abstracts, No. 9621.

*LEE, L. L. "Mark Twain's Assayer: Some Other Versions," Markham Review, IV, 47-48.
[Source: MLA Bibliography (1974), No. 9624; abstract by Lee in 1974 MLA Abstracts.]

*LIVINGSTON, JAMES L. "Names in Mark Twain's The Mysterious Stranger," American Notes and Queries, XII, 108-109.
[Source: MLA Bibliography (1974), No. 9625.]

McELRATH, JOSEPH R., Jr. "Mark Twain's America and the Protestant Work Ethic," CEA Critic, XXXVI (March), 42-43.
In CY, Hank Morgan hitched the pillar saint, St. Simeon Stylites, to a sewing-machine; thus, MT reveals his view of the work ethic as part of the American national character.

*MANIERRE, WILLIAM R. "Contemporary Relevance of Huckleberry Finn," pp. 77-94 in Klaus Lanzinger, ed., Americana Austriaca: Beiträge zur Amerikakunde. Band 3. Wien und Stuttgart: Braumüller.
[Source: MLA Bibliography (1974), Nos. 102, 9629.]

PAULY, THOMAS H. "'The Science of Piloting' in Twain's 'Old Times': The Cub's Lesson on Industrialization," Arizona Quarterly, XXX, 229-38.
    On the increasingly complex understanding of the age of industrialization gained by MT's narrator. Abstract by Pauly in 1974 MLA Abstracts, No. 9636.

*ROHDE, REGITZE. "St. St. Blicher og Mark Twain," in Felix Nørgaard, ed., Omkring Blicher 1974. Copenhagen: Gylendal, pp. 58-66.
    [Source: MLA Bibliography (1974), No. 9639.]

*SCHUBERT, KARL. "Mark Twain: Adventures of Huckleberry Finn," in Edgar Lohner, ed., Der amerikanische Roman im 19. und 20. Jahrhundert (Berlin: Erich Schmidt), pp. 70-91.
    [Source: MLA Bibliography (1974), Nos. 103, 9642.]

*TOWERS, TOM H. "Hateful Reality: The Failure of the Territory in Roughing It," Western American Literature, IX, 3-15.
    [Source: MLA Bibliography (1974), No. 9644.]

*WEINTRAUB, RODELLE, ed. "Mental Telegraphy?: Mark Twain on G. B. S.," Shaw Review, XVIII, 68-70.
    [Source: MLA Bibliography (1974), No. 8419.]

*WILSON, JAMES D. "Adventures of Huckleberry Finn: From Abstraction to Humanity," Southern Review, X (January), 80-94.
    "The pragmatic Huck encounters a series of ideal codes of behavior" of the Widow Douglas, Tom Sawyer, his father, the Grangerfords, and Sherburn, "before discovering each one inadequate to meet the demands of his intuitive moral nature, his environment, and his companions." Ironically, in his personal life MT could put abstract intellectual concepts ahead of human needs, as in the painful destruction of his wife's religious faith. Abstract by Wilson in 1974 MLA Abstracts, No. 9647.

1975

ANDERSON, DAVID M. "A Mark Twain Practical Joke: An Unpublished Anecdote," Mark Twain Journal, XVIII (Winter), 20-21.
    An apocryphal tale about MT on a train, heard at third hand in Finland.

CLEMENS, CYRIL. "Tributes to Mark Twain, by Sax Rohmer, Will Rogers, and W. Somerset Maugham," Mark Twain Journal, XVIII (Winter), outside back cover.
    Rohmer briefly remembers meeting MT in London; Rogers and Maugham express conventional appreciation.

CLEMENS, SAMUEL L. [Letters to James Ross Clemens.] Mark Twain Journal, XVIII (Winter), front cover.
    Brief notes to James Ross Clemens, January 12, 1903 and June 25 [1897], reproduced in facsimile.

HOY, JAMES F. "The Grangerford-Shepherdson Feud in Huckleberry Finn," Mark Twain Journal, XVIII (Winter), 19-20.
    Stresses the importance of the names, which represent "wandering herders versus settled gardeners."

KESTERSON, DAVID B. "The Mark Twain-Josh Billings Friendship," Mark Twain Journal, XVIII (Winter), 5-9.
    Both lectured for Redpath's bureau, and there were similarities of temperament, but MT was less outgoing toward his friend and seldom mentioned him--possibly out of professional jealousy.

MARTIN, WILLARD E., Jr. "Letters and Remarks by Mark Twain from the Boston Daily Journal," Mark Twain Journal, XVIII (Winter), 1-5.
    Reprints with explanatory footnotes the text of a long letter on "A Rescue at Sea" by the Cunard steamship Batavia (February 7, 1873), on the Jubilee Singers (March 13, 1875), his Civil War experiences (news report, October 3, 1877, on his remarks at a banquet); a letter on money for the preservation of battle-flags (September 12, 1879); and his remarks on introducing Henry M. Stanley, the explorer, to a lecture audience (December 10, 1886).

MOTT, BERTRAM. "The Turn-of-the-Century Mark Twain: A Revisit," Mark Twain Journal, XVIII (Winter), 13-16.
    On the several versions of The Mysterious Stranger, and on "The Man that Corrupted Hadleyburg" and What Is Man? "Though it is easy to overstate the case, surely there is copious evidence that the pessimism of the turn-of-the-century Mark Twain...has been somewhat exaggerated."

WEEKS, ROBERT P. "The Captain, the Prophet, and the King: A Possible Source for Twain's Dauphin," Mark Twain Journal, XVIII (Winter), 9-12.
    The character in HF may be modeled on George J. Adams, whom MT mentioned in IA; he and the King had more in common than their rascality. There is a survey of attempts by other scholars to suggest models for the character, but some of the documentation is inconsistent and hard to follow.

WERGE, THOMAS. "The Sin of Hypocrisy in 'The Man that Corrupted Hadleyburg' and Inferno XXIII," Mark Twain Journal, XVIII (Winter), 17-18.
    MT and Dante treat hypocrisy as a sin of fraud and incontinence, and both use "gilded lead as an image of hypocrisy," and "a pervasive tone and imagery of weight, weariness, and oppressiveness to dramatize the external and inner life of the hypocrite."

1976

BERGER, ARTHUR ASA. "Huck Finn as an Existential Hero: Making Sense of Absurdity," Mark Twain Journal, XVIII (Summer), 12-17.
    Central to our national literature for its humor and use of the vernacular, HF is marked by its realism and by "absurdity and alienation and other existential concerns."

CLEMENS, CYRIL. "Two Presidents and the Journal," Mark Twain Journal, XVIII (Summer), back cover.
    Facsimile reproductions of brief notes by Lyndon B. Johnson and Gerald R. Ford thanking Cyril Clemens for sending them his publications; both were vice-presidents when they wrote.

CLEMENS, SAMUEL L. "The Mammoth Cod," and Address to The Stomach Club, with an Introduction by G. Legman. Milwaukee: Maledicta: 25 pages.

The text of a bawdy poem and letter, apparently written to be read aloud during a 1902 cruise on Henry Rogers's yacht, the Kanawha; also includes the text of MT's eight-line poem, "A Weaver's Beam" (about "the Penis mightier than the Sword," now stilled by the impotence of old age) and "Some Remarks [sic] on the Science of Onanism" (See 1974.B11). The greater part of this book consists of an introduction by Gershon Legman, who traces the surviving record of MT's bawdy writings, suggesting that "perhaps the impotence that tormented Twain for so many decades was only the physical counterpart of his self-achieved literary castration, like that of his penultimate image on the subject: the spoutless teapot." Legman argues, however, that "it may be suspected that Twain's much-lamented impotence was in part imaginary, as were some of the other masochistic and hypochondriacal complaints that made him take to his bed and wear only white daytime clothing." Legman's psychological discussion and bibliographical information will be of considerable interest to the students of this aspect of MT.

EVANS, ELIZABETH. "Thomas Wolfe: Some Echoes from Mark Twain," Mark Twain Journal, XVIII (Summer), 5-6.

Documents statements by Wolfe showing that he had read MT. "It is not unexpected then to find echoes from Mark Twain in Wolfe. Even though the proof of the echoes rests in similarities, those similarities are strong." The evidence here adduced is subjective.

FELLOWS, LAWRENCE. "Sketch of Huck Finn Returning to Twain's Home," New York Times (January 19).

The original E. W. Kemble drawing of Huck holding a dead rabbit has been donated to the Mark Twain Memorial in Hartford by Lessing Whitford Williams, whose sister had received it as a gift from MT when she was a baby.

GAYLIN, WILLARD. "Two Routes to Unselfish Behavior. From Twain to Freud: an Examination of Conscience," Hastings Center Report (Institute of Society, Ethics, and the Life Sciences), VI (August), 5-8.

Chiefly on the broader topic of conscience, but opens with an example from HF, when Huck sees the King and Duke ridden on a rail. "The words that Twain uses in an attempt to dissect the emotions of conscience are enormously sophisticated and not redundant. They are the words that only a student of conscience, or an intuitive genius,

would have used: 'ornery,' 'humble,' and 'to blame.'" ["Willard Gaylin, M.D., is President of the Institute, a practicing psychiatrist, and professor of psychiatry and law at Columbia University. This article is adapted from his book, Caring, to be published in October by Alfred A. Knopf, Inc."]

GREGORY, RALPH. "Joseph P. Ament--Master-Printer to Sam Clemens," Mark Twain Journal, XVIII (Summer), 1-4.

On the owner of the Hannibal Courier and for a time Samuel Clemens's employer; includes useful documentation.

ISLER, CARL. "Mark Twain's Style," Mark Twain Journal, XVIII (Summer), 18-19.

Primarily on TS Abroad and HF, briefly commenting on dialogue and contrasting personalities. In discussing point of view, states incorrectly that "Tom Sawyer is told by Tom."

KEETCH, BRENT. "Mark Twain's Literary Sport," Mark Twain Journal, XVIII (Summer), 7-10.

"The purpose of this paper is to advance the view that Huck Finn has a fully logical structure that enhances the theme of a boy's quest for freedom." The title of this essay is derived from a misreading of Henry Nash Smith (in p. 72 of 1965.B 1965.B79); Smith calls HF "a literary sport," in the sense that it does not belong to any literary tradition, has "no connections with the past, no history." Misunderstanding the sense in which Smith used the word, Keetch refers to "the literary sport played by Twain" (p. 7) and concludes: "Such sport as this evokes the laughter of the gods" (p. 10).

KRAVEC, MAUREEN T. "Huckleberry Finn's Aristocratic Ancestry," Mark Twain Journal, XVIII (Summer), 19-20.

"One of the most subtle instruments of semantic irony concern's Huck's surname," which may be linked with the Fin MacCool of James MacPherson's "Ossian" forgeries; the root "fiona" means "white" or "fair." MT has shown "the pernicious effect of a culturally-imposed notion of nobility upon natural mankind," though Pap is evidence that Huck's natural nobility was not hereditary; moreover, the Ossian poems were fabrications.

SHUTT, RANDALL, ed. "Of Mark Twain and Hannibal," Mark Twain Journal, XVIII (Summer), 21.

Excerpts from the unpublished memoirs of Wallace Bruce Amsbary, actor and Chautauqua lecturer; Amsbary remembered a world like that described in TS, but never met MT.

Index

A

Antiquarian Booksellers' Association of America, 1967.B117
Appel, John J., 1954.B4
Appleton's Journal, 1972.B28
Archer, William, 1899.B10; 1900.B16; 1910.B133
Arikawa, Shoji, 1964.B7; 1965.B7; 1971.B4
Aristophanes, 1958.B21
Aristotle, 1970.B48
Arms, George, 1973.B2
Armstrong, C. J., 1930.B1; 1931.B2-3; 1932.B7; 1942.B51; 1945.B4, B15; 1950.B5
Arnavon, Cyrille, 1951.B7
Arner, Robert D., 1972.B7
Arnold, Matthew, 1882.B16; 1888.B3-4; 1948.B46; 1967.A18
Arthur, Lee, 1974.B10
Arvin, Newton, 1932.B4; 1933.B6; 1934.B6; 1935.B15; 1966.B12
Aseev, Nikolai, 1973.B23
Ashcroft, R. W., 1912.B27; 1921.B6; 1974.B30
Ashe, F. M., 1902.B4
Ashmead, John, 1962.B6
Ashton, J. W., 1931.B4
Aspiz, Harold, 1962.B7; 1972.B8; 1975.B2
Asselineau, Roger, 1954.A2; 1958.B2; 1961.B3
    Works, Reviewed: The Literary Reputation of Mark Twain (1954), 1954.B3, B24; 1955.B12, B24, B30, B37, B44, B54
Asterlund, B., 1946.B23
Astor, Mrs., 1944.B31
Atlanta Constitution, 1953.A4
Atlantic Monthly, 1961.B16; 1973.B42
Auden, W. H., 1953.B3
Auerbach, Erich, 1963.B73
Auernheimer, Raoul, 1942.B2
Augustine, St., 1965.B42
Austen, Jane, 1933.B15; 1962.B63; 1966.B85
Austin, James C., 1963.B7
Austin, L. F., 1890.B15
Australia, 1947.B32; 1953.B39; 1961.B63; 1962.B46; 1970.B87
Austria, 1971.B10
Authors' Club, 1933.B29; 1964.B12
Ayers, Col. James, 1922.B8

B

B., L., 1922.B9
B., R. C., 1896.B6
Babler, Otto, 1937.B1
Babcock, C. Merton, 1961.B4; 1962.B8; 1963.B8; 1964.B8-9; 1965.B8; 1966.B13-14; 1967.B4; 1969.B7; 1970.B4-5
Bacheller, Irving, 1905.B7; 1912.B17; 1926.B2; 1941.B28
Bacon, Leonard, 1937.B2
Bad Nauheim, 1911.B16; 1965.A4
Baender, Paul, 1959.B7; 1960.B10; 1963.B9; 1964.B10-11; 1966.B15; 1968.B4; 1973.A2
    Works, Reviewed: What Is Man? and Other Philosophical Writings by Mark Twain (1973), 1974.B3, B29
Baetzhold, Howard G., 1954.B5; 1955.B4; 1956.B3; 1957.B8; 1961.B5-6; 1970.A1; 1971.B11; 1972.B9
    Works Reviewed: Mark Twain and John Bull: The British Connection (1970), 1971.B31, B37, B39-40, B54
Baker, Carlos, 1962.B9

Baker, Laura Nelson, 1963.A7
Bailey, Elmer James, 1909.B8
Bailey, Roger B., 1967.B5
Bailey, Temple, 1929.B45
Bailin, George, 1955.B5
Bainton, George, 1890.B16; 1950.B61
Baldanza, Frank, 1955.B6; 1961.A1; 1965.B9
    Works, Reviewed: Mark Twain: An Introduction and Interpretation (1961), 1962.B47
Baldwin, Charles C., 1931.B5
Baldwin, Mary Austin, 1967.A3
Balicer, Herman C., 1937.B3
Balini, Laura, 1926.A1
Ball, Sir Robert, 1915.B3
Bangs, John Kendrick, 1902.B4; 1905.B7; 1910.B75
Banta, Martha, 1968.B5; 1969.B8
Barchilon, Jose, 1966.B16
Bargelli, Matilde, 1947.A2
Barnard College, 1961.B45
Barnes, Barbara Lamkin, 1972.B10
Barnes, Daniel R., 1965.B10
Barnes, George E., 1887.B1
Barnes, L. Call, 1906.B7
Barnes, W. W., 1915.B4
Barnett, Walter, 1904.B1
Barnum, P. T., 1964.B59; 1975.B2
Barr, Amelia E., 1905.B7
Barr, Robert, 1898.B15-16; 1932.B5; 1939.B53; 1945.B49
Barrado, A., 1912.A2
Barrett, C. Waller, 1969.B6
Barrett, Oliver R., 1945.B18
Barrett, William G., M.D., 1955.B51
Barrick, Mac E., 1975.B3
Barrie, James M., 1917.A1; 1937.B18; 1960.B12; 1961.B53
Barrows, Herbert, 1958.B3
Barrus, Clara, 1925.B5
Barsamian, Kenneth J., 1951.B8
Barsness, John A., 1969.B9
Barton, Sir Dunbar Plunket, 1928.B2
Barton, Marion, 1972.B11
Barucca, Primo, 1961.B7
Bassan, Maurice, 1964.B12
Bassett, Norman, 1944.B22
Batavia rescue, 1949.B43
Bates, Allan, 1964.B13; 1967.B6
Baum, Joan, 1974.B2
Baumrind, Sheldon, D.D.S., 1964.B14
Baxter, Sylvanus, 1889.B2
Baxter, Sylvester, 1957.B31
Bay, Andre, 1960.B11
Bay, J. Christian, 1929.B4
Baylen, Joseph O., 1964.B15
Bazaar Record (Cleveland), 1949.B14, B43
Beach, E. E., 1900.B17
Beach, Emeline, 1947.B6-7
Beach, Rex E., 1905.B7
Beall, Dr. Edgar C., 1969.B71
Beard, Charles A., 1942.B3
Beard, Daniel Carter, 1890.B1, B10, B13, B17; 1910.B69-70; 1939.B5, B9; 1940.B38; 1943.B7; 1945.B32; 1948.B15; 1970.B20
Beard, Mary R., 1942.B3
Beatty, Richard Croom, 1961.A2; 1962.A2
Beaver, Harold, 1962.B3
Bebb, Bruce, 1974.B3
Beck, Warren, 1928.B3; 1958.B4
Becker, May Lamberton, 1935.B16; 1947.B3; 1948.B3
Beckwith, Carroll, 1891.B7; 1920.B23; 1943.B33
Beebe, Lucius, 1953.B4
Beebe, Maurice, 1968.B6

Boer War, 1930.B5; 1948.B44
Boeser, Linda, 1965.B12
Boggan, J. R., 1964.B18
Bok, Edward, 1921.B3
Boland, Sally, 1968.B15
Böll, Heinrich, 1973.B37
Bologna, Sando, 1960.B14
Bolton, Sarah H., 1887.B2
Bombay Gazette, 1968.B95
Bompiani, 1949.B5
Bonazzi, Robert, 1972.B14
Book of Mormon, 1971.B14
Boomkamp, Leeuwen, 1958.B7
Booth, Bradford A., 1947.B6-7; 1950.B7; 1954.B6; 1965.B13
Booth, Edwin, 1910.B135
Booth, Wayne C., 1961.B9
Borderland, 1964.B15
Borges, Jorge Luis, 1935.B18
Borrow, George, 1935.B69
Borst, Charles V. S., 1964.B19
Borzi, Professor, 1907.B31
Bosc, R., 1919.B6
Boston, 1949.B8
Boston Advertiser, 1949.B43
Boston Ancient and Honorable Artillery Company, 1954.B12
Boston Congregational Club, 1946.B5
Boston Herald, 1955.B49; 1957.B31
Boston Transcript, 1873.B9; 1879.B3; 1909.B6; 1949.B43; 1968.B25
Bostwick, Arthur E., 1939.B10
Boucicault, Dion, 1969.B50
Bourget, Paul, 1895.B3, B18; 1957.B44
Bourne, Randolph, 1969.B76
Bowden, Edwin T., 1961.B10
Bowen, Edwin W., 1916.B2
Bowen, William, 1938.A3; 1941.A3; 1943.B27
Bowser, David Watt, 1940.B4; 1960.B24, B57; 1963.B81
Boyesen, Hjalmar Hjorth, 1881.B5; 1964.B82
Boynton, Henry Walcott, 1903.B11
Boynton, Percy H., 1919.B7; 1920.B10; 1924.B11; 1932.B6; 1933.B8
Boy Scouts of America, 1970.B20
Brack, O. M., Jr., 1972.B16
Bradford, Gamaliel, 1920.B11; 1922.B10; 1924.B11; 1933.B9
Bradbury, Malcolm, 1969.B11
Bradley, 1919.B15
Bradley, James, 1944.B40, B44
Bradley, Sculley, 1953.B38; 1961.A2, B21; 1962.A2; 1964.B37
Bragman, Louis J., 1925.B9
Branch, Edgar Marquess, 1942.A3, B10; 1946.B4; 1950.A4, B8; 1957.B12; 1958.B37; 1966.B18; 1967.B14-16; 1969.A1, B12; 1972.A3; 1975.B4
Works, Reviewed: The Literary Apprenticeship of Mark Twain (1950), 1950.B4, B28, B39, B51, B55, B60; 1951.B39, B49, B51
Clemens of the "Call" (1969), 1969.B55; 1970.B63
Brand, John M., 1972.B17
Brandl, Alois, 1925.B10
Brashear, Minnie M., 1929.B5; 1930.B3; 1934.A1; 1936.B5; 1939.B11; 1959.A1; 1964.B13; 1966.A1
Works, Reviewed: Mark Twain: Son of Missouri (1934), 1934.B5-6, B11, B16; 1935.B5, B53
The Art, Humor and Humanity of Mark Twain (Ed., with Robert M. Rodney, 1959), 1959.B50; 1960.B62; 1961.B30

Bratcher, James T., 1964.B20
Brereton, Austin, 1908.B6
Brett, Reginald, 1944.B29
Briden, E. F., 1974.B6
Bridges, Horace James, 1919.B8; 1923.B7
Bridges, Robert, 1885.B15; 1959.B18
Bridgman, L. J., 1900.B20
Bridgman, Richard, 1960.B15; 1964.B21; 1966.B19
Works, Reviewed: The Colloquial Style in America (1966), 1967.B20, B58
Briggs, John Ely, 1929.B6
Bright, John, 1934.B19
Brinegar, Claude S., 1963.B11
Brittain, Sir Harry, 1961.B11
Broadley, A. M., 1910.B72
Brodin, Pierre, 1948.B4
Brodwin, Stanley, 1972.B18; 1973.B3-4
Brogunier, Joseph, 1972.B19
Bronson, Daniel Ross, 1972.B20
Bronson, Walter C., 1900.B21
Brookings, Robert, 1937.B17
Brooklyn Public Library, 1935.B31
Brooks, Cleanth, 1955.B10
Brooks, Gladys, 1961.B2
Brooks, Noah, 1898.B19-20; 1899.B11
Brooks, Roger L., 1962.B11
Brooks, Sydney, 1907.B18-19; 1910.B71
Brooks, Van Wyck, 1919.B12; 1920.A1, B12-15, B21; 1921.B17; 1923.B8, B12, B24, B32; 1924.B11, B32; 1925.B38; 1927.B8; 1929.B10, B38; 1930.B10; 1932.A2, B4, B10, B15, B21, B34; 1933.A1, B17, B24, B28; 1935.B18, B20, B73; 1936.B47; 1937.B19; 1938.B39; 1939.B16; 1940.B9; 1941.B1; 1942.B38; 1943.B46; 1944.B1, B33; 1945.B35; 1946.B17; 1947.B8; 1948.B35; 1949.B31; 1952.B7, B28, B47; 1954.B7; 1955.B14; 1957.B13; 1960.B13, B44, B73; 1963.B34, B54, B66; 1965.B14; 1968.B80, B101; 1969.B76; 1970.B26
Works, Reviewed: The Ordeal of Mark Twain (1920; revised 1932), 1920.B2, B5, B7, B33; 1921.B4; 1922.B2; 1923.B19; 1925.B25; 1933.B6, B22, B25; 1934.B4, B20
Brown, Clarence A., 1964.B22; 1968.B16
Brown, Deming B., 1954.B8; 1962.B12
Brown, George Rothwell, 1908.B11; 1930.B4
Brown, Glenora W., 1954.B8
Brown, John, 1967.B102
Brown, Maurice, 1966.B20
Brown, Robert, 1883.B7
Brown, Spencer, 1967.B17
Brown, Sterling, 1937.B7
Brown, Thomas P., 1944.A2
Browne, Charles Farrar. See "Artemus Ward"
Browne, John Ross, 1974.A5
Browne, Ray B., 1961.B12; 1965.B15; 1970.A3
Browne, Sir Thomas, 1910.B118
Brownell, Frances V., 1955.B11
Brownell, George Hiram (Unsigned material in Twainian is here attributed to him as Editor), 1925.B11; 1932.B7; 1933.B10-13; 1934.B7; 1936.A1; 1937.B8; 1939.B12-22; 1940.B10-30; 1941.B9; 1942.A3, B8-19, B26; 1943.B6-23; 1944.B6-23, B36, B43; 1945.B6-18, B51; 1946.B5-16, B38; 1947.B9-20; 1948.B5-15; 1949.B6-16, B43; 1950.B9-11, B20; 1953.B17; 1954.B17; 1957.B14; 1960.B16; 1962.B13, B24; 1972.B31
Browning, Robert, 1911.B5; 1934.A3; 1935.B67; 1939.B54; 1967.B102
Brumm, Ursula, 1962.B14; 1972.B21
Bruneau, Jean, 1955.B12

Cather, Katherine Dunlap, 1925.B12
Cather, Willa, 1959.B8; 1963.B5; 1966.B47, B58;
    1973.B8
Cecil, L. Moffitt, 1969.B17
Century Company, 1923.B17
Century Magazine, 1912.B28; 1917.B1; 1945.B29, B31;
    1955.B39; 1968.B73
Cervantes, Miguel de, 1922.B25; 1932.B23; 1938.B35;
    1941.B26; 1947.B34; 1952.B39, B41; 1961.B73;
    1970.B77; 1972.B45
Cestre, Charles, 1926.B3; 1931.B9; 1945.B19
Ceylon Examiner, 1963.B67
Ceylon Observer, 1963.B67
Chamberlain, Thomas G., 1949.B10, B18, B22
Chambers, E. K., 1894.B6
Chambliss, Amy, 1970.B12
Chapin, Adèle le Bourgeois (Mrs. R. W. Chapin),
    1931.B10
Chapin, Christina, 1931.B10
Chapin, Henry B., 1963.B17-18
Chapin, Robert, 1948.B19
Chaplin, Charlie, 1962.B18
Chapman, Helen Post, 1928.B5
Chapman, John W., 1932.B12
Chaput, Donald, 1965.B19
Charbonnel, Avis Bliven, 1964.B28
Chard, Leslie F., II, 1964.B29
Charles, Ernest, 1910.B10
Charpentier, John, 1935.B21
Chase, Mary Ellen, 1933.B14
Chase, Richard, 1957.B20; 1963.B89; 1966.B74
Chase, Roy, 1939.B26; 1962.B46
Chatto and Windus, 1929.A1; 1939.B44; 1941.B12
Chaucer, Geoffrey, 1965.B42
Chellis, Barbara A., 1969.B18
Chenoweth, Mrs., 1917.B8; 1919.B14
Chester, Giraud, 1951.B17
Chesterton, Gilbert Keith, 1903.B7; 1910.B5, B77;
    1922.B24; 1930.A4; 1934.A2; 1949.B34
Chicago Daily News, 1939.B14, B20
Chicago Inter ocean, 1940.B13
Chicago Republican, 1940.B33; 1941.A2; 1942.B23;
    1943.A2, B11; 1949.B15
Chicago Tribune, 1875.B3; 1979.B3; 1944.B7;
    1947.B14
Childs, Marquis W., 1926.B4
Christian, Sheldon, 1967.B23
Christian, The, 1945.B4
Christian Science Monitor, 1955.B35; 1957.B32
Christian Union, 1944.B20
Christopher, J. R., 1972.B25
Chubb, Percival, 1910.A1; 1936.B10; 1943.B24
Chubb, Thomas Caldecott, 1936.B36
Church, Richard, 1967.A9
Church, Samuel Harden, 1974.B9
Churchill, Lady Randolph, 1943.B21
Churchill, Winston S., 1930.B5; 1944.B24, B28;
    1945.B26; 1946.B23; 1954.B41; 1961.B75
Cicero, 1924.B22
Cincinnati Commercial, 1876.B5
Cincinnati Evening Chronicle, 1943.B11
Claggett, Billy, 1957.B24
Clarion, The, 1921.B1
Clark, Champ, 1910.B32
Clark, Charles Heber (see "Adeler, Max")
Clark, Charles Hopkins, 1885.B16; 1938.B5
Clark, George Peirce, 1956.B8; 1958.B11-12
Clark, Harry Hayden, 1956.B9; 1959.B14; 1971.B11
Clark, William G., 1965.B20
Clarke, Edward J., 1936.B11
Clarke, Norman Ellsworth, 1941.A1

Clemens Family (General), 1888.B5; 1972.B24
Clemens, Clara, 1909.B3; 1910.B54; 1923.B9;
    1924.B14; 1926.A3; 1930.B6; 1931.A3, B11;
    1932.B19; 1936.B5; 1938.A3, B7; 1939.B47;
    1948.A2; 1949.B3, B10; 1950.B20; 1956.A1, B10,
    B17; 1959.B51; 1961.B66; 1962.B34; 1963.B23;
    1964.B28; 1966.B99; 1967.B43; 1973.B15
    Works, Reviewed: My Father, Mark Twain (1931),
    1931.B1, B24, B32; 1932.B2, B6, B17, B25
Clemens, Cyril, 1929.A1-2, B7-11, B16, B40;
    1930.B7; 1932.A1, B13; 1933.A2, B15; 1934.A2,
    B3, B8; 1935.A2-3, B11, B22-23, B48; 1936.B12;
    1937.B10; 1938.B8; 1939.A3, B8, B14, B27-28,
    B36-37; 1940.B22, B32-34; 1941.A2, B10-12;
    1942.A1, B8, B21-23, B44, B57; 1943.A2, B25,
    B27-28; 1944.B24-28, B46; 1945.B20-26; 1946.A5;
    1947.B22; 1948.B17; 1949.A1, B10, B18, B20-24;
    1950.A5, B13-16; 1951.B11, B18-21; 1952.B12;
    1953.A2, B9; 1954.B11; 1955.B13; 1956.B11;
    1957.A1, B21, B51; 1958.B13; 1959.B15;
    1960.B22; 1962.A4, B19; 1963.B5, B87; 1964.B30;
    1966.B26; 1967.A4; 1971.B12, B33; 1974.B17
    Works, Reviewed: Mark Twain The Letter Writer
    (1932), 1933.B5, B7
    Mark Twain Wit and Wisdom (1935), 1935.B3, B54,
    B56; 1937.B21
    My Cousin Mark Twain (1939), 1939.B1, B3, B11,
    B29, B37; 1940.B49
    Republican Letters (1941), 1942.B41; 1943.B26;
    1944.B39
    Young Sam Clemens (1942), 1943.B1, B44;
    1945.B44
Clemens, Florence, 1929.B21
Clemens, Henry, 1858.B1; 1889.B3; 1929.B32;
    1950.B40
Clemens, Dr. James Ross, 1929.B12-13; 1933.B16;
    1935.B11; 1938.B8; 1973.B9
Clemens, Jane, 1885.B7-8; 1925.B38; 1939.B16;
    1946.B21; 1948.B59; 1959.B15; 1964.A6, B39
Clemens, Jean, 1932.B19; 1936.B4; 1957.B41;
    1959.B51; 1965.B25; 1969.B60
Clemens, Jeremiah, 1947.B22
Clemens, John Marshall, 1946.B31; 1964.B58;
    1965.B44; 1968.B66; 1970.B15, B30
Clemens, Katharine, 1938.B8; 1944.B29; 1945.B28;
    1957.B22
Clemens, Langdon (photograph), 1936.B52
Clemens, M. E., 1963.B24
Clemens, Mildred Leo, 1917.B7
Clemens, Molly, 1917.B13; 1929.B27, B29, B32
Clemens, Olivia, 1897.B21; 1904.B7; 1918.B8;
    1919.B10; 1920.B1, B3, B16; 1922.B19; 1929.B10,
    B24; 1930.B20; 1932.B19, B21; 1933.B27;
    1935.A14, B19; 1936.B13; 1939.B32, B40;
    1945.B28; 1947.B25, B57; 1948.B6, B61; 1949.A2;
    1950.B35; 1952.B48; 1955.B4; 1956.B14; 1957.B26;
    1958.B10; 1959.B26, B51; 1960.B33; 1963.A7, B21,
    B24; 1967.B25, B29, B53, B67, B72, B87; 1969.B7;
    1970.A4; 1972.B8, B26; 1974.B21
Clemens, Orion, 1917.B2; 1928.A1; 1929.B6, B27-28,
    B30, B32-33, B40; 1940.B35; 1942.A3; 1944.B38;
    1946.B21; 1947.B36; 1949.B30; 1950.B9; 1954.B22;
    1961.A4, A15, B37; 1962.B38; 1970.B30; 1973.B39
Clemens, Pamela Goggin, 1935.B66; 1963.B24
    (also see Goggin, Pamelia [sic])
Clemens, Samuel L.
--Autographs, 1916.B8; 1956.B14; 1970.B35
--Birthday Dinners, 1902.B9; 1903.A1; 1922.B29;
    1925.B5; 1926.B17
--Birthplace, 1896.B1; 1919.B18; 1923.B2;
    1942.B51; 1960.B7

(Clemens, Samuel L.)

--Civil War Experience, 1910.B12; 1919.B11; 1922.B4; 1940.B6, B50; 1944.B40; 1946.B7; 1968.B59, B73

--Death (See also 1910 passim), 1948.B23

--Duel (Abortive), 1942.B30; 1943.B25; 1951.B8

--"Exaggerated Death" story, 1910.B136; 1929.B10, B12; 1931.B28; 1940.B22; 1945.B23; 1947.B24; 1956.B11; 1957.A1

--Fiction about MT, 1954.A4

--First Editions, 1910.A7; 1911.A2; 1933.B27; 1938.A6

--Foreign Editions, Translations, Critical Reputation (Also see Bibliographies, works by individual critics, and names of countries),

--Australia, 1962.B46; 1968.B57

--Austria, 1950.B44

--China, 1968.B81; 1972.B65

--Czechoslovakia, 1956.B40

--England, 1876.B8; 1891.B11; 1898.B29; 1907.B18-19; 1935.B5; 1942.B35; 1945.A2; 1948.A3

--Finland, 1968.B20; 1973.B43

--France, 1886.B3; 1895.B3; 1900.A1; 1910.B10; 1914.B7; 1918.B13; 1922.A3; 1950.A8; 1951.B7; 1965.A7

--Germany, 1896.B5; 1897.B6, B18; 1898.B25, B30; 1900.B24; 1901.B16; 1912.B30; 1913.B9; 1914.B2, B9; 1915.B7; 1922.B21; 1924.B38; 1936.B44; 1937.B32; 1939.A9; 1964.B53; 1966.B86; 1969.B46, B69; 1972.B63

--India, 1972.B78

--Italy, 1901.B18; 1904.B15; 1949.B5; 1951.B37; 1958.B15; 1959.B9; 1964.B17; 1965.A5

--Japan, 1963.B47; 1971.B4

--Korea, 1972.B55

--Romania, 1967.A2

--Russia, 1916.B9; 1936.B41; 1939.A10, B57; 1941.B21; 1945.B43; 1947.B2; 1954.B8; 1955.B28; 1957.B33; 1959.B64; 1960.A10, B8, B67, B83; 1961.B56; 1963.B34; 1964.B75; 1965.B68; 1967.A12, B64-65; 1968.B85; 1970.A8; 1971.B47; 1973.B23

--Scandinavian Countries, 1937.B4; 1973.B18, B43

--Spain and Latin America, 1912.A2; 1918.B5; 1950.B25; 1961.B73

--Yugoslavia, 1970.B43

--Unclassified, 1910.B91, B118; 1911.B3; 1939.A8; 1960.A1

--Genealogy and Family History, 1924.B12; 1944.B32; 1945.B22, B24; 1967.B30

--Homes

--Hartford, 1872.A1; 1878.B2; 1879.B4; 1885.B16; 1888.B5; 1895.B16; 1904.B7; 1920.B6; 1922.B18; 1926.B2; 1928.B4; 1932.B19; 1935.B31; 1950.A2; 1958.A2; 1959.B19; 1960.B87; 1962.B73; 1972.B10; 1974.A1

--"Stormfield" (Redding, Connecticut), 1908.B2; 1909.B3, B5, B7, B19, B21; 1914.B4; 1961.B62

--Burglary, 1922.B11; 1935.B25; 1957.B29; 1967.B55

--Other Homes, 1885.B16; 1926.B2; 1931.B17; 1968.B105

--Humor and Pessimism, 1960.B46; 1966.A2; 1967.B62; 1972.B48

--Interviews with MT, 1878.B1; 1879.B2; 1895.B5-6, B8; 1896.B3; 1900.B2; 1904.B3, B11-12; 1916.B9; 1935.B33, B48; 1951.B34; 1952.B44; 1954.B39; 1961.B63; 1974.B8

--Interests and Attitudes

--Baseball, 1945.B3

--Bicycles, 1928.B5

--Billiards, 1925.B2, B22, B26; 1935.B39; 1958.B58; 1962.B28

--Cats, 1959.B57

--Copyright, 1882.B20; 1888.B7; 1899.B19; 1905.B3, B13; 1923.B17; 1927.B2; 1932.B1; 1934.B19; 1935.B48; 1957.B27, B30; 1961.B53; 1962.B30; 1966.B62, B92

--Dogs, 1884.B13; 1942.B25

--Folklore, 1930.A5; 1946.B34; 1952.B14; 1955.B7; 1956.B19; 1963.B20; 1965.B102; 1966.B21; 1967.B73, B106; 1974.B7

--German Language, 1897.B14; 1936.B45; 1938.B7; 1940.B41, B52; 1941.B29; 1946.B37; 1953.A5; 1954.B42; 1965.B95

--Graphology, 1895.B2

--Intoxicants and Smoking, 1950.B61

--Inventions, 1901.B20; 1925.B15; 1939.B39; 1942.B9; 1944.B13; 1957.B38

--Jews, 1924.A3; 1935.B74; 1938.B7; 1954.B4

--Music, 1922.B17; 1923.B9; 1936.B2; 1937.B34; 1942.B13; 1943.B32; 1949.B42; 1964.B66

--Negroes, 1937.B7; 1938.B7; 1942.B53; 1948.B29; 1957.B32; 1958.B30A; 1965.B2; 1967.B56; 1968.B118; 1969.B15, B18; 1970.B67-68, B72; 1971.B52; 1972.B70

--Palmistry, 1894.B2; 1895.B2; 1964.B15

--Phrenology, 1901.B3; 1910.B16; 1971.B68; 1972.B46

--Profanity, 1937.B20; 1952.B27; 1956.B21

--Telephone, 1931.B8; 1964.B72; 1965.B47

--Theater, 1919.B10; 1922.B16; 1923.B21; 1927.B12; 1935.B11; 1937.B16; 1938.B1, B28; 1943.B31; 1944.B16, B34; 1946.B37; 1948.B9-10; 1953.B40; 1956.B51; 1959.B28; 1960.B81, B97; 1967.B71; 1969.A3; 1970.B14

--Women and Girls, 1912.B8; 1922.B19; 1945.B40; 1969.B73; 1971.B28; 1973.A8

--Investments and Estate, 1910.B34, B36; 1932.B5; 1959.B2

--Lack of Physical Vigor, 1956.B24

--Lawsuits, 1935.B39; 1941.B10; 1945.B18

--Lectures, Readings, Speeches, 1867.B2; 1873.B1-7; 1874.B3; 1875.B2; 1881.B2; 1885.B8, B10; 1886.B1-2; 1895.B13; 1896.B6; 1898.B17; 1900.B23, B33; 1901.B11; 1903.B2, B15; 1904.B7; 1905.B7; 1906.B9, B11; 1907.B18; 1910.B79, B96, B133, B135; 1911.B5; 1912.A1, B8, B28; 1913.A1; 1918.B7; 1921.B5; 1923.A2, B33; 1924.B20, B29; 1928.B4; 1929.B29; 1930.B5; 1931.B23; 1934.A3, B25; 1935.B11, B31, B48, B67, B77; 1936.B26; 1937.B30; 1938.B27; 1939.B2, B13, B30; 1940.B16, B17, B44; 1942.B24, B45; 1943.B2, B31; 1944.B7, B42; 1945.B51; 1946.B5, B16, B23, B33; 1947.B4, B14, B29, B44, B49; 1948.B14, B24, B33, B46; 1949.B39; 1950.B26, B41, B45; 1951.B34, B36, B41, B44, B55; 1952.B10, B32-34; 1953.A1, A4, B22-23; 1954.B12-13, B30, B32, B39; 1956.B18, B20, B50; 1957.B37, B48; 1958.B55; 1959.B36, B71; 1960.A3, B20; 1961.B5, B44, B63, B75, B84; 1962.B60; 1963.B67, B80; 1965.A1, B23; 1967.B14, B31, B37, B51; 1968.A2, B66; 1970.B28, B69; 1972.B6; 1973.B54; 1974.B23, B33

--Letters and Notes: Personal, Business, and Newspaper, 1866.B1; 1867.B2; 1869.B4; 1871.B4; 1872.B8-10; 1873.B9-11, B14; 1874.B3; 1875.B3; 1877.B5; 1879.B3; 1883.B13; 1884.B13; 1885.B17; 1888.B7; 1890.B16; 1892.B6; 1894.B8; 1895.B2; 1896.B6; 1900.B23, B33, B37; 1901.B6; 1905.B9, B15; 1906.B1; 1908.B7; 1910.B24, B46, B72, B90, B99, B118, B135-136; 1912.B27; 1915.B5; 1917.A2,

(Clemens, Samuel L.)
  B5, B10; 1918.B7, B16; 1919.B9, B10, B22;
  1920.B16, B18, B29; 1921.B3, B5; 1922.B15, B18;
  1924.B15, B37; 1925.A1, B2; 1926.A3, B1;
  1929.A1, B5, B10, B13, B29, B40; 1930.B12, B19;
  1931.A3, B2; 1932.A1, B1, B12, B19, B24;
  1933.B1, B4, B27, B32; 1934.A3, B1, B10;
  1935.B4, B11, B25, B80; 1936.B19, B26, B45;
  1938.A3, A5, B1, B7, B18; 1939.A1, B30, B44,
  B51, B54; 1940.B13, B47; 1941.A3, B2, B12;
  1942.B7, B13, B24-25, B46, B48, B50; 1943.B12,
  B28, B47; 1944.B7-8, B10, B17, B20, B22, B31,
  B49; 1945.B9, B27-32, B52-53; 1946.A6, B7, B10,
  B27, B41, B48; 1947.A6, B6-7, B18-19, B21,
  B23, B44, B57; 1948.B11, B19, B24, B33, B44,
  B58, B61; 1949.A2, B10, B16-18, B21-22, B25,
  B37; 1950.B9-10, B13, B15, B32, B61; 1951.B17,
  B26-28; 1952.B9-10, B13; 1953.A1, A4, B10, B12,
  B15, B42; 1954.B16, B37, B50; 1955.B31, B38,
  B46, B55; 1957.A5, B22, B24, B31, B46, B66;
  1958.B12; 1959.B23, B34, B51, B57; 1960.A13,
  A15, B23-24, B57; 1961.A4, A9, A14, A16, B53,
  B79, B86; 1962.B23, B64, B73; 1963.B12, B19,
  B24, B42, B81; 1964.B5, B82, B88; 1965.B38, B95;
  1966.A3, A7, B13, B27-28; 1967.A1, A6, B37, B47,
  B53, B74, B108; 1968.B29, B86, B88; 1969.A10,
  B6, B22, B33; 1970.A4, B12, B23, B47, B69, B92;
  1971.A1; 1972.B24, B26, B63, B80-81; 1973.B7,
  B9, B33, B43; 1974.B4, B6, B9-10, B25; 1975.B7
--Manuscripts, 1911.A1; 1938.A5, B23; 1950.B13, B15;
  1955.B17; 1961.A10; 1965.A4; 1967.B29
  --"Mark Twain" persona and pseudonym, 1871.B3;
  1877.B4; 1910.B51; 1919.B9; 1942.B15, B18, B26,
  B39; 1950.B2-3, B17, B47; 1962.B29, B35;
  1968.B100
--As Mason, 1928.B1; 1954.B31
--Memorials to MT, 1910.B90; 1924.B5, B33; 1925.B39;
  1934.B21; 1958.B26; 1967.B33
--Negroes , As Seen and Depicted by MT, 1937.B7;
  1938.B7; 1942.B53; 1948.B29; 1957.B32;
  1958.B30.1; 1965.B2; 1967.B56; 1968.B118;
  1969.B15, B18; 1970.B67-68, B72; 1971.B52;
  1972.B70
--Photographs, 1892.B9; 1894.B2; 1895.B2; 1896.B1;
  1897.B17, B21, B27; 1898.B16, B26-27;
  1900.B22-23, B28; 1901.B4, B6, B11, B25, B28;
  1902.B2, B8, B22; 1903.B2, B12, B14; 1904.B1,
  B3, B15; 1905.B7; 1907.B6, B16, B18-19, B25,
  B27; 1908.B1-2, B13; 1909.B7, B21; 1910.B3-4,
  B6, B15, B30, B38-39, B54, B63, B69, B81, B84,
  B88, B94, B97, B103, B115, B136; 1911.A3, B2;
  1912.B8, B27; 1913.A1; 1914.B3; 1915.B8;
  1916.B7; 1918.B16; 1919.B16; 1920.B23, B32;
  1923.B17; 1924.B2, B21, B30, B44; 1925.A2,
  B13, B17; 1926.B1, B12; 1929.B23; 1931.A3;
  1935.B6, B19, B44; 1937.B10; 1938.B8; 1940.B16;
  1944.B4, B34; 1950.B44; 1960.B6; 1961.A14;
  1962.B31, B46; 1965.B84; 1968.A8; 1970.B25,
  B92; 1975.B8
--Piloting on River, 1899.B2; 1909.B2; 1910.B12;
  1915.B1; 1927.B15; 1939.B4, B21, B33;
  1940.B14, B40; 1954.B46; 1957.B4; 1967.B47;
  1971.B65; 1972.B50; 1973.A1
--Portraits: Cartoons, Paintings, Sculptures, and
  other Non-Photographic Representations,
  1872.B7; 1874.B8; 1882.B20; 1884.B2; 1891.B7-8;
  1892.B8, B10; 1893.B6; 1896.B13; 1897.B19;
  1900.B19, B31, B33-35; 1901.B7; 1902.B4, B17;
  1903.B5-6, B13; 1904.B4, B9-10, B13; 1905.B15,
  B19; 1906.B4, B6; 1907.B17, B19, B23; 1908.B4,
  B7; 1910.B28, B52, B59, B74, B100, B115, B118,

B138; 1912.B27; 1914.B9; 1915.B10; 1919.B15;
  1922.B5; 1923.B10; 1924.B21; 1928.B1; 1929.A1;
  1932.B18; 1935.B2, B9; 1936.A1; 1937.B3, B27;
  1941.B30; 1943.B33; 1945.B54; 1947.B9; 1960.A8,
  B105; 1963.B37; 1969.B6; 1972.B30, B32
--Psychological Interpretations of MT (Also see
  Brooks, Van Wyck, passim), 1921.B12; 1924.B25;
  1938.B23; 1955.B51; 1956.B29; 1961.B55; 1968.B80
--Reading, Literary Influences
  --General, 1925.A3; 1934.A1; 1936.B12; 1941.B24;
  1960.B78, B85; 1961.B6; 1964.B63; 1973.B15
  --Bible, 1968.B66; 1969.A5; 1971.B49, B59;
  1972.B7
  --Personal Library and Marginalia, 1914.B11;
  1954.B6, B23; 1955.B18; 1958.B22-23, B27;
  1959.B22-24, B32; 1961.A8, B62; 1966.B32;
  1968.B26-27; 1969.B20; 1970.B19; 1972.B33;
  1973.B14-15
--Recordings of MT's Voice, 1929.B16; 1948.B63;
  1965.B29
--Robbery (Mock), 1956.B16, B21
--Satire, 1935.A14; 1960.B68; 1963.B62; 1967.B42
--Structure, 1939.B7; 1946.B24; 1955.B6; 1961.B35;
  1962.A15; 1966.B5; 1968.B30
--Style, 1884.B9; 1890.B16; 1892.B6; 1898.B21;
  1899.B10; 1920.B22; 1936.B9; 1945.B33; 1954.B1;
  1956.B38, B54; 1958.B16, B33; 1963.B81;
  1968.B21; 1969.B1; 1970.B17
--Subscription Sales of Books, 1874.B9; 1881.B1;
  1963.B43
--Themes and Topics
  --American Indians, 1945.B47; 1971.B18; 1975.B9
  --Chinese Immigrants, 1933.B18; 1958.B57;
  1963.B48
  --Conscience, 1899.B19; 1942.B27; 1957.B1;
  1974.B32
  --Court Trials, 1958.A5; 1959.B28
  --Duality, 1972.B13
  --Education, 1940.B45; 1941.B24
  --History, Science, 1937.B36; 1951.B42; 1959.B24;
  1960.B26; 1961.A16, B13
  --Immaturity, 1961.B55
  --Innocence, 1965.B85
  --Organized labor, 1957.B17
  --Philosophy, Ethical Ideas, Determinism,
  1899.B19; 1937.B36; 1958.B20; 1962.A15
  --Race, 1935.B47; 1957.B45; 1961.A10; 1962.B53;
  1966.B76, B93; 1968.B45, B107; 1969.B15
  --Religion, 1912.B21; 1914.B5; 1925.B18, B20;
  1929.B27; 1934.B8; 1935.A2, B80; 1942.B27;
  1945.B4; 1946.A5; 1951.B47; 1952.B3; 1956.B23;
  1959.B33; 1960.B32; 1961.A8; 1963.B2; 1965.B41;
  1966.B14; 1968.B66; 1969.A5, B24; 1970.B20, B90,
  B93; 1971.B14; 1972.B51; 1973.A7; 1974.B12, B32;
  1975.B5
  --Social Criticism, 1900.B5; 1910.B24; 1924.B6;
  1936.B22; 1947.B33; 1948.B47, B52; 1953.B8;
  1955.B40; 1958.A4; 1962.A3; 1963.B2; 1966.B113;
  1968.B42; 1969.B80
  --Small town, 1958.B61
  --Socialism, 1961.B25
  --South, 1931.B19; 1935.B11; 1938.B30; 1968.B107;
  1974.A3
--Typesetting Machine: See Paige, James W.
--Vocabulary and Usage, 1888.B2; 1935.A8; 1938.A8;
  1944.B41; 1947.B35, B46; 1948.B48; 1956.B26,
  B38; 1958.B25, B44; 1965.B30; 1966.B32, B42;
  1968.B92
--Wedding, 1946.B40
--White Suit, 1935.B77

(Clemens, Samuel L.)
--(Works and Attributed Works)
  --Colonel Sellers as a Scientist (Play), 1911.B7;
    1958.B50; 1960.B81
  --"A Complaint About Correspondents," 1967.B69
  --"Concerning a Bear," 1944.B9
  --"Concerning General Grant's Intentions,"
    1946.B11
  --"Concerning the Jews," 1899.B5, B20; 1935.B74;
    1939.B35
  --A Connecticut Yankee in King Arthur's Court,
    1886.B1-2; 1889.B1-2; 1890.B1-3, B6-13, B15,
    B17-18, B20-22; 1891.B4, B11; 1892.B2; 1894.B6;
    1897.B10, B26; 1898.B16; 1907.B3, B24, B35;
    1910.A6, B27, B70, B77, B112, B125; 1913.B10, B12;
    1918.B6; 1921.B15; 1926.B16; 1932.B3, B20, B34;
    1933.B3; 1934.B3; 1935.B19, B69; 1938.A5, B35;
    1939.B5, B9, B43; 1940.B38; 1941.B6, B26;
    1942.B5, B34, B52; 1943.B7; 1944.B29, B35;
    1945.B19, B32; 1946.B32; 1948.B45, B57, B66;
    1949.A3; 1950.B21, B23, B36-37; 1951.B14, B57;
    1955.B52; 1956.B3, B50; 1957.B17, B33; 1958.B33,
    B41, B60; 1959.B35, B56; 1960.A4, A7, B25, B54,
    B75; 1961.B5-6, B52, B55, B72-73; 1962.A15, B7,
    B15, B40, B66A; 1963.B29, B36, B44; 1964.A5,
    B24, B33, B56, B59, B85, B90, B98; 1965.B21,
    B36, B39, B64, B86, B99; 1966.A10, B2, B48, B51;
    1967.A11, B1, B9, B51; 1968.A4, B37, B41,
    B52, B57, B76, B92, B118; 1969.B2, B9, B14, B72,
    B79; 1970.A2, B1, B20, B46, B61, B79, B84;
    1971.B5, B7, B19A, B29; 1972.B37, B71; 1973.B21,
    B27, B31, B52, B60; 1974.B24; 1975.B12
  --Conversation as It Was by the Social Fireside
    in the Time of the Tudors [Date, 1601], 1906.B12;
    1925.A1, B28; 1936.A3, B11; 1939.A4, B27, B34,
    B36; 1940.B24; 1957.B46; 1959.B32; 1965.B92
  --"A Cure for the Blues," 1959.B12; 1964.B19
  --The Curious Republic of Gondour, and Other
    Whimsical Sketches, 1919.B1
  --"A Curtain Lecture Concerning Skating,"
    1943.B9; 1967.A5
  --"The Czar's Soliloquy," 1905.B1; 1961.B14
  --"The Dandy Frightening the Squatter,"
    1931.B26; 1933.B12; 1953.A3
  --"The Death-Disk," 1945.B17
  --"The Death of Jean," 1924.B22
  --"Dick Baker's Cat," 1950.B56
  --"A Dog's Tale," 1911.B6; 1932.B30; 1939.B17;
    1968.B13
  --"A Double-Barreled Detective Story," 1902.B11-13,
    B17; 1932.B14, B24; 1971.B58; 1972.B56
  --"Down the Rhône," 1963.B75
  --"Dutch Nick Massacre," 1944.B37; 1960.B82
  --"The Enchanted Sea Wilderness," 1972.B47
  --Europe and Elsewhere, 1923.B1, B6; 1924.B37
  --Eve's Diary, 1932.B34
  --Extracts from Adam's Diary, 1897.B11; 1901.B8;
    1904.B2-3, B14; 1938.B2; 1972.B18
  --Eye Openers, 1876.B8
  --"A Fable," 1974.B26
  --Fables of Man, 1972.A2
  --"The Facts Concerning the Recent Important
    Resignation," 1946.B48
  --"The Facts in the Case of George Fisher,
    Deceased," 1931.B25
  --"Fearful Calamity in Forest St.," 1962.B73
  --"Fenimore Cooper's Literary Offences," 1895.B15;
    1965.B54; 1968.B84
  --"Fenimore Cooper's Further Literary Offences,"
    1946.B22

  --"First Interview with Artemus Ward," 1939.B22
  --Following the Equator, 1897.B1, B8-9, B15;
    1898.B3-5, B7-10, B28; 1899.B7; 1937.B6;
    1945.B2; 1954.B30; 1955.B9; 1957.B26; 1958.B10;
    1963.B67-68; 1965.B58, B96; 1966.B54, B64;
    1967.A15, B67; 1970.B20
  --"Fortifications of Paris," 1915.B2; 1964.B9
  --"From 'Hospital Days'" (Apocryphal), 1943.B8;
    1955.B9
  --"From the London 'Times' of 1904," 1945.B17;
    1954.B9; 1967.B38
  --"Ghost Life on the Mississippi," 1948.B18;
    1949.B47
  --The Gilded Age (With Charles Dudley Warner),
    1873.B8; 1874.B1, B4-7, B9; 1875.B1; 1899.B8;
    1919.B22; 1921.B5; 1927.B8, B12; 1930.A3;
    1935.B43; 1936.B51; 1937.B23; 1938.B37;
    1940.B8; 1942.B52; 1943.B45; 1944.B48; 1950.B15,
    B38; 1952.B39, B48; 1954.B33; 1955.B48;
    1956.B53; 1957.B61; 1958.B33; 1959.B32; 1960.B45;
    1961.B17; 1962.B15, B37; 1963.B29; 1964.B2,
    B46, B54, B56, B64, B90; 1965.A1-2, B22, B36,
    B40, B45; 1966.B6, B75-76, B87, B96; 1967.A9,
    B60; 1970.A2, B30; 1971.B25A; 1972.A5, B27-28,
    B64; 1973.B41; 1974.B34; 1975.B7
  --The Gilded Age (Play), 1897.B25; 1910.B135;
    1925.B40; 1927.B12; 1937.B29; 1943.B31;
    1964.B46; 1965.A2, B93; 1970.B47
  --"The Golden Arm," 1918.B7
  --"Gorki Incident," 1944.B30
  --"The Great Dark," 1942.A4; 1966.B48; 1967.B36;
    1972.B47; 1975.B5
  --"The Great Earthquake in San Francisco,"
    1957.B18
  --The Great Landslide Case: Three Versions,
    1972.A3
  --Hamlet (Burlesque), 1943.B20; 1967.A7
  --"Happy Memories of the Dental Chair," 1964.B14
  --"How To Remove Warts and Tattoo Marks,"
    1945.B53
  --"How To Tell A Story," 1946.B15
  --Huck Finn and Tom Sawyer Among the Indians,
    1966.B70; 1969.A3
  --Huckleberry Finn. See Adventures of Huckleberry
    Finn
  --"An Important Question Settled," 1943.B11, B18
  --"Information Wanted," 1946.B11
  --"In Defense of General Funston," 1947.B2
  --The Innocents Abroad, N.D.A3; 1867.B1; 1868.B1;
    1869.B1-3, B5-6; 1870.B2-3, B7-8; 1871.A1, B2;
    1882.B4; 1887.B3; 1892.B6; 1898.B13, B23;
    1899.B15; 1907.B2, B21; 1910.A8, B89, B106;
    1912.B9; 1913.B10; 1918.B12; 1919.B7; 1920.B25;
    1925.B1; 1928.B7; 1929.B46; 1930.B21; 1935.B43;
    1938.A9; 1941.B6; 1942.B5; 1943.B10; 1945.B2;
    1947.B5-6, B27-28; 1948.B22, B25; 1949.A3, B7,
    B27, B37; 1951.B26, B28; 1952.B13, B24, B26,
    B34, B36; 1954.B31; 1955.B42, B52; 1956.B37;
    1958.A1, B33, B59; 1959.B20, B23; 1960.A12, B37;
    1961.B7, B64; 1962.A8, A15, B64; 1964.B23, B48,
    B85, B97; 1965.B33, B35-36; 1966.B45-46, B67;
    1967.B54, B111; 1968.A1, B51, B58; 1969.A5;
    1970.B52, B56; 1971.B9, B22, B24; 1974.A5,
    B21A, B34; 1975.B7
  --The Innocents Adrift, 1963.B75
  --"Inspired Humor," 1944.B19
  --"In Trouble," 1945.B10-11
  --"The Invalid's Story," 1882.B10, B13; 1945.B17;
    1963.B7; 1966.B60
  --Is Shakespeare Dead? 1909.B1, B6, B14, B17;
    1912.B29; 1928.B2; 1973.B38

(Clemens, Samuel L.)
--(Works and Attributed Works)
  --(Poems)
    --"The Mysterious Chinaman," 1947.B15
    --"Ode To Stephen Dowling Botts," 1971.B33
    --"Tropic Chidings," 1884.B12; 1946.B9
    --"Ye Equinoctial Storm," 1884.B12; 1946.B9
  --The Prince and the Pauper, 1881.B3-5, B7;
    1882.B5-10; 1895.B9; 1898.B16; 1902.B14;
    1909.B8; 1910.A6, B46; 1913.B10; 1916.B9;
    1920.B28; 1925.B41; 1928.B14; 1935.B25;
    1938.A5; 1939.A6; 1941.B6; 1942.B54; 1948.B3,
    B45; 1949.B26; 1951.B21, B27; 1952.B36;
    1953.A4, B25; 1954.B5; 1955.B51; 1959.B12;
    1962.B15; 1963.B24, B29, B31; 1964.B7;
    1965.B38; 1966.A8, A10; 1968.B14, B36;
    1970.A2, B46, B49-50; 1971.B7, B19A; 1973.B11
    --Dramatization, 1890.B14; 1900.B34; 1911.B11;
      1925.B40; 1935.B39; 1937.B16, B24; 1938.B1;
      1959.B28; 1968.B56
  --"The Private History of a Campaign that Failed,"
    1926.B9; 1940.B25; 1941.B18; 1944.B44; 1945.B29,
    B31; 1948.B11; 1950.B5; 1954.B12; 1955.B23;
    1960.B30; 1966.B5; 1968.B59, B73; 1971.B55
  --"The Private History of the Jumping Frog Story,"
    1894.B7
  --"Private Theatricals." See "A Curtain Lecture
    Concerning Skating."
  --"Prof. Jenkins," 1945.B10-11
  --Pudd'nhead Wilson. See The Tragedy of
    Pudd'nhead Wilson.
  --"The Recent Carnival of Crime in Connecticut,"
    1882.B13
  --"The Reception at the President's," 1948.B13
  --"Reflections on Religion," 1963.B64; 1965.B41
  --"The Reliable Contraband," 1943.B13
  --"The Remarkable Sagacity of a Cat," 1950.B56
  --Republican Letters (Ed. Cyril Clemens),
    1942.B8; also see Clemens, Cyril, for reviews
  --"Review of Holiday Literature," 1962.B67
  --"The Revised Catechism," 1939.B18; 1944.B21;
    1945.B38; 1955.B50
  --"Riley - Newspaper Correspondent," 1946.B13
  --Roughing It, 1867.B2; 1872.B3-4, B13; 1893.B7,
    B10; 1901.B21; 1903.B9; 1915.B9; 1917.B7, B13;
    1927.B8; 1929.B14; 1937.A1; 1938.A2, B18, B28;
    1939.B51; 1941.B6; 1942.B40; 1943.B25, B35;
    1944.B25; 1945.B8, B47; 1947.A3, B44; 1948.B22,
    B31; 1950.B41, B45, B56; 1951.B24; 1953.B26;
    1954.B22; 1956.B18; 1957.B58; 1959.A4; 1960.A12,
    B6; 1961.A15, B20; 1962.A15, B11; 1963.B71, B88;
    1964.A3; 1966.B21, B67; 1967.B82; 1970.B57;
    1971.B7, B23, B29; 1972.A3; 1973.B39, B44;
    1974.B7, B27, B34; 1975.B3
  --"Running For Governor," 1962.B51
  --"Saint Joan of Arc," 1959.B41
  --[Sandwich Islands Letters], 1944.B36
  --"The Sanitary Ball," 1957.B52
  --[Savage Club, Description], 1925.B37
  --Screamers, 1872.B5, B8, B12
  --"Serious Wilkins" (Apocryphal), 1970.B25
  --Simon Wheeler, Detective, 1963.A4; 1964.B35,
    B47
  --"Sir Robert Smith of Camelot," 1886.B1-2;
    1961.B5
  --1601. See Conversation as it Was By the Social
    Fireside in the Time of the Tudors.
  --[Sketch in London World], 1877.B7; 1947.B55
  --Sketches, New and Old, 1875.B4; 1876.B1;
    1937.B6; 1943.B8; 1955.B9

--Slovenly Peter (Mark Twain's Translation of Dr.
  Heinrich Hoffman's Struwelpeter), 1935.A6,
  B13-14; 1936.B40; 1941.B29
--Snodgrass, Quintus Curtius. See Letters of
  Quintus Curtius Snodgrass (Apocryphal).
--Snodgrass, Thomas Jefferson. See Adventures of
  Thomas Jefferson Snodgrass.
--"Sociable Jimmy," 1943.B11
--"Some Rambling Notes of an Idle Excursion,"
  1910.B118
--"Some Thoughts on the Science of Onanism,"
  1936.B11; 1963.B25; 1974.B11
--"Soundings," 1949.B15
--The Stolen White Elephant, 1882.B10-15, B22;
  1899.B13; 1901.B10; 1945.B17
--Stomach Club Address. See "Some Thoughts on
  the Science of Onanism."
--"A Storm at Sea," 1949.B14, B43
--"Such as Mother Used to Make," 1973.B42
--The $30,000 Bequest, and Other Stories, 1907.B32
--Those Extraordinary Twins. (Also see The
  Tragedy of Pudd'nhead Wilson), 1942.B29;
  1948.B17; 1951.B60; 1970.B54; 1972.B69
--"3,000 Years Among the Microbes," 1918.B3;
  1970.B90; 1973.B36
--Tom Sawyer. See The Adventures of Tom Sawyer.
--Tom Sawyer Abroad, 1894.B3-6, B11; 1929.B3;
  1935.B45; 1942.B5; 1949.B38; 1966.B51, B72;
  1970.B20; 1972.B16; 1974.B4
--Tom Sawyer, Detective, 1897.B10-12; 1929.B4;
  1953.B27; 1959.B48
--"To the Person Sitting in Darkness," 1901.B2,
  B5, B9; 1947.B2
--"To the Reading Public," 1940.B26
--The Tragedy of Pudd'nhead Wilson (Also see
  Those Extraordinary Twins), 1894.B1-2, B9;
  1895.B10-12; 1902.B20; 1912.B11; 1936.B23;
  1941.B23; 1942.B29; 1952.B28; 1955.B21-22, B51;
  1956.B34-35; 1957.B20, B64-65; 1958.B20;
  1959.B17; 1960.B25, B42, B61; 1961.A10, B55;
  1962.A15, B53, B68; 1963.B17, B65, B89; 1964.A1,
  B31, B69, B87; 1965.B2, B16, B59, B70; 1966.A8,
  B51, B61, B74, B93; 1968.B38, B72, B107, B118;
  1969.B18, B50; 1970.B13, B48, B54, B82, B96;
  1971.A5, B15, B36; 1972.B1, B17, B29, B42, B69,
  B73-74; 1973.B3, B20, B22, B53; 1974.B4;
  1975.B2
--A Tramp Abroad, 1880.B3-7; 1883.B7; 1901.B23;
  1902.B15; 1903.B16; 1905.B14; 1922.B28; 1925.B41;
  1935.A11; 1945.B2, B17; 1952.B8; 1955.B46;
  1960.B110; 1964.B84; 1967.A15; 1969.B40;
  1970.B78, B92; 1973.B28, B52
--"Traveling with a Reformer," 1947.B36; 1948.B15
--"A True Story," 1971.B9
--"The Turning Point of My Life," 1969.B60
--"The United States of Lyncherdom," 1969.B70
--[Unsigned Newspaper Writing], 1972.B22
--"The War Prayer," 1965.B8; 1970.B29; 1975.B1
--"Washington Artillery Ball," 1946.B38
--"Weather" Epigram, 1939.B19; 1945.B6
--What Is Man? 1911.B1; 1913.B4-5; 1919.B2, B5,
  B7, B12, B17, B19; 1921.B15; 1934.B1; 1936.B39;
  1941.B6; 1942.B48; 1946.A1, B37; 1948.B28;
  1957.B43; 1959.B22, B43; 1964.B31; 1968.B104;
  1970.B90; 1973.A2; 1974.B1
--"What Ought He to Have Done?" 1944.B20
--"Which Was the Dream?" 1967.A8
--Which Was It? 1971.B34; 1974.B28

Daily Hawaiian Herald, 1940.B16
Daily Resorter, 1970.B69
Daly, Augustin, 1942.B45; 1946.B12, B27
Dane, G. Ezra, 1937.A1; 1938.A2; 1940.A2
    Works, Reviewed: Letters From the Sandwich
    Islands (ed., 1937, 1938), 1938.B22; 1939.B24,
    B48, B52; 1940.B49
Danziger, Samuel, 1918.B6
Da Ponte, Durant, 1957.B26; 1959.B18
Darbee, Henry, 1958.A2; 1959.B19
Darió, Rubén, 1961.B73
Darrow, Clarence, 1968.B41
Darwin, Charles, 1899.B16; 1924.B36; 1933.B29;
    1945.B49; 1958.B20; 1962.B23; 1964.B31
Daudet, Alphonse, 1951.B3; 1964.B84
Daulton, Major Frank, 1917.B12
D'Avanzo, Mario L., 1972.B29
Davenport, Basil, 1939.B27, B34, B36, B43
Davidson, Levette J., 1952.B15
Davidson, Louis B., 1935.B27; 1936.B13
Davidson, William Earl, 1942.B27
Davis, Arthur Kyle, Jr., 1931.B12
Davis, Bob, 1941.B28
Davis, C. F., 1968.B66
Davis, Chester L. [Most of this material is un-
    signed, and here attributed to Davis as Editor
    of The Twainian], 1854.B19; 1899.B8; 1925.B11;
    1950.B18-20; 1951.B25-29; 1952.B16-19;
    1953.B15-19, B39; 1954.B13, B16-18, B20-24;
    1955.B16-19; 1956.B14, B16-17; 1957.B14,
    B27-34, B61; 1958.B22-29; 1959.B20-24;
    1960.B29-30; 1961.B21-23; 1962.B24, B30;
    1963.B11, B23-24; 1964.B34-40; 1965.B22-26,
    B93; 1966.B32-36, B99; 1967.B27-34, B71;
    1968.B25-29; 1969.B20; 1970.B18-21; 1971.B16-17;
    1972.B30-36; 1973.B1, B14-15, B58
Davis, Rev. John, 1948.B11
Davis, Sam, 1967.B35
Davis, Samuel P., 1944.A2
Day, A. Grove, 1966.A3, B37
    Works, Reviewed: Mark Twain's Letters From
    Hawaii (1966), 1966.B3, B7, B91; 1967.B85
Dean, Henry Clay, 1975.B1
Deane, The Rev. Canon Anthony, 1935.B28
Dearborn Independent, 1957.B14
DeCasseres, Benjamin, 1934.A3
Decaunes, Luc, 1950.B21
DeForest, John William, 1968.B10
Dekker, George, 1964.B41
de Laguna, Theodore, 1898.B21
de la Mare, Walter, 1929.B45; 1930.A4; 1963.B5
DeLaney, Wesley A., 1947.B9, B36; 1948.B22-23
De Leon, Daniel, 1905.B11
DeMott, Benjamin, 1966.B38; 1970.B22
Dennis, Larry R., 1967.B36
Denslow, Ray V., 1928.B1
Densmore, Gilbert S., 1923.B21
Denton, Lynn W., 1971.B18; 1974.B13
"De Quille, Dan" (pseud. Wright, William),
    1862.B1; 1880.B1; 1893.B8-10; 1910.B82;
    1911.B13; 1936.B17; 1946.B40; 1947.B43;
    1953.B2; 1965.B12
Derby, George Horatio: see "Phoenix, John"
De Schweinitz, George W., 1966.B39
De Voto, Bernard, 1929.B14; 1931.B13-15; 1932.A2,
    B15-17; 1933.A1, B2, B17, B25; 1935.B18,
    B29-30, B73; 1936.B14-16; 1937.B13; 1938.B9-10;
    1939.A7, B28, B33, B36-37; 1940.A1, B18, B35;
    1941.B13; 1942.A2, A4; 1944.B1, B33; 1945.B34;
    1946.A2, B19-22; 1947.B1-2, B26; 1948.B26, B35,
    B60; 1952.B20, B47; 1960.B27, B73; 1962.A6,

B24A, B33; 1964.B10; 1966.B56; 1970.B83, B89,
    B94
    Works, Reviewed: Mark Twain's Letters From the
    Earth (Ed., 1962), 1962.B4, B71; 1963.B49, B52;
    1964.B52
    Mark Twain At Work (1942), 1942.B6, B21, B28,
    B36, B43, B55; 1943.B5, B38; 1946.B39
    Mark Twin in Eruption (Ed., 1940), 1940.B5, B39,
    B53-54; 1941.B14, B16-17, B19, B22
    Mark Twain's America (1932), 1932.B4, B10, B28,
    B33; 1933.B7-8, B14, B24, B28, B30; 1935.B16
Dias, Earl J., 1967.B37; 1970.A4
Dickens, Charles, 1934.B14; 1948.B6; 1953.B3;
    1957.B10; 1964.B54; 1965.B74; 1968.B40;
    1969.B25; 1970.B62; 1973.B40
Dickey, Marcus, 1922.B15
Dickie, J. F., 1910.B83
Dickinson, Anna, 1951.B17; 1952.B48
Dickinson, Asa Don, 1935.B31
Dickinson, Leon T., 1947.B5, B27-28; 1949.B26;
    1950.B22; 1951.B30; 1961.B23; 1965.B27;
    1966.B40-41; 1970.B23
Diederich, B., 1903.B8; 1905.B12; 1906.B8
Dilke, Sir Charles, 1967.B102
Dillingham, William R., 1964.B42
Dinan, John S., 1972.B37
Ditsky, John M., 1975.B5
Dixon, Elizabeth White, 1965.B28
Dobie, Frank, 1968.B109
Dodge, Mrs. Mary Elizabeth Mapes, 1972.B16
Dodge, Peter Mapes, 1897.B27
"Dogberry," 1954.B17
Dolch, Martin, 1964.B53
Donaldson, Scott, 1971.B19
Donner, Stanley T., 1947.B29; 1959.B25
Donovan, M. M., 1926.B5
Dos Passos, John, 1939.B38
Dostoyevsky, Fyodor, 1970.B77
Doten, Alf, 1899.B12; 1910.B51; 1956.B16
Doten, Mrs. Alf, 1956.B16
Doubleday, Neal Frank, 1960.A2
Doughty, Howard, Jr., 1951.B31
Douglas, Gilbert, 1934.B10
Douglas, Joe, 1951.B1
Douglas, Lloyd C., 1937.B14
Douglas, Robert, 1951.B32
Doumic, René, 1899.B13; 1901.B10
Doyle, Sir Arthur Conan, 1960.B110; 1971.B58;
    1972.B56
Doyle, Paul A., 1970.B24
Doyno, Victor A., 1968.B30
Drake, Eric, 1931.B16
Drake, Robert Y., Jr., 1960.B31
Dredd, Firmin, 1910.B84
Dreiser, Theodore, 1935.B32-33; 1956.B48; 1959.B26
Drew, John, 1922.B16
Drinkwater, John, 1934.A2
Drury, Wells, 1936.B17
Dryden, John, 1959.B12
Duckett, Margaret, 1964.A2; 1969.B21
    Works, Reviewed: Mark Twain and Bret Harte
    (1964), 1965.B13, B32, B46, B50; 1966.B29,
    B69, B76
Dudgeon, L. W., 1944.B32
Duffie, Myrtle M., 1964.B43
Duffy, Charles, 1942.B28; 1948.B24
Dugas, Gaile, 1947.B30
Dugmore, A. Radclyffe, 1909.B7
Duncan, Captain Charles, N.D.A3; 1867.B1; 1877.B1,
    B5; 1941.B10; 1952.B13; 1955.B42; 1964.B48
Duneka, Frederick A., 1952.B27; 1965.B24; 1968.A6

(Ferguson, DeLancey)
   1952.B21-22; 1954.B25; 1957.B39-40; 1959.B29;
   1960.B38-40; 1961.B26
   Works, Reviewed: Mark Twain: Man and Legend
   (1943), 1943.B32, B34, B37, B39, B44; 1944.B5;
   1946.B39
Ferris, George T., 1874.B8
Ferry, d'Odette, 1950.B21
Fetterley, Judith, 1971.B21; 1972.B40, B84;
   1973.B21
Feuchtwanger, Lion, 1963.B29
Field, Eugene, 1902.B8; 1954.B11
Field, Kate, 1900.B37; 1970.B47; 1974.B32
Fiedler, Leslie A., 1948.B27; 1955.B21; 1957.B20;
   1958.B30A-32; 1959.B30; 1960.B41-43; 1966.B45-46;
   1971.B22
Fielder, Elizabeth Davis, 1899.B14
Fielding, Henry, 1972.B45
Fields, Mrs. James T., 1904.B8; 1922.B18-19
Fifield, William, 1967.B43
Figaro, Le, 1895.B3
Figuera, Angela, 1961.B27
Filčev, Petăr, 1968.B36
Films on MT's Life and Works, 1930.B11;
   1940.B23; 1944.B4, B11; 1967.B61
Finger, Charles J., 1924.A3, B13; 1926.A3
Finlay, Frank, 1944.B22; 1947.B55
Finn, Frank, 1954.B30
Finnegans Wake, 1966.B24
Fischer, M., 1909.B9
Fischer, Walther, 1926.B6; 1935.B37; 1939.B42;
   1942.B31
Fishback, Margaret, 1936.B36
Fisher, Henry W., 1922.A2
   Works, Reviewed: Abroad with Mark Twain and
   Eugene Field (1922), 1922.B5-7, B26
Fisher, Marvin, 1972.B42
Fisher, Samuel J., 1923.B12
Fitch, George Hamlin, 1916.B3
Fitch, Thomas S., 1903.B9; 1919.B11; 1961.B59
Fitzgerald, F. Scott, 1923.B13; 1956.B41; 1960.B88;
   1963.B30; 1967.B99; 1969.B40; 1972.B19
Flack, Frank Morgan, 1942.B32-33; 1946.B27;
   1951.B36
Flagg, Charles Noël, 1897.B19; 1972.B30
Flagg, James Montgomery, 1946.B28; 1972.B32
Flanagan, John T., 1936.B21; 1961.B28
Fleck, Richard L., 1971.B23-24
Florence, Italy, 1932.B19; 1965.A4
Florida, Missouri, 1912.B19; 1919.B18; 1946.B3;
   1958.B28; 1965.A3
Flory, Claude R., 1964.B45
Flowers, Frank C., 1948.B28
Floyd, John B., 1931.B25
Flynt, Josiah, 1939.B47
"Folio, Tom," 1869.B5
Foner, Philip S., 1958.A4; 1961.A6; 1963.B15, B86
   Works, Reviewed: Mark Twain: Social Critic
   (1958), 1959.B25, B69
Foote, E. B., 1935.B38, B79
Foote, Mary Hallock, 1934.A3; 1935.B67; 1939.B54
Ford, James L., 1900.B25
Ford, Sewell, 1910.B121
Ford, Thomas W., 1955.B22
Forgues, Eugène, 1886.B3
Fortenberry, George, 1971.B25
Foss, Sam Walter, 1910.B129
Foster, Edward F., 1968.B37
Foster, William (Murder Case), 1873.B11; 1955.B55
Foulke, W. D., 1930.B19
Fraiberg, Louis, 1960.B44
France, Clemens J., 1901.B13

Franciosa, Massimo, 1951.B37
Francis, Raymond L., 1950.B30
Frank, Waldo, 1919.B12; 1933.B17; 1970.B83
Franklin, Benjamin, 1972.B29; 1974.B14
Franklin, H. Bruce, 1966.B48
Frantz, Ray W., Jr., 1956.B19; 1962.B31
Fraser, Horatio N., 1901.B11
Fraser, John, 1967.B44
Frazer, Laura Hawkins, 1899.B14; 1910.B81;
   1913.B1; 1918.B2; 1920.B4; 1925.B21; 1927.B15;
   1929.B2, B7; 1935.B25; 1965.B57; 1966.B32;
   1971.B16
Frear, Walter Francis, 1939.B13; 1940.B16;
   1942.B19; 1943.B17, B42; 1947.A3; 1971.B17;
   1972.B31
   Works, Reviewed: Mark Twain and Hawaii (1947),
   1948.B60; 1949.B35
Frederick, John T., 1969.B24
Fredonia, New York, 1964.B29
Freeman, Mary E. Wilkins, 1922.B24
Freeman, William H., 1894.B8; 1945.B9
Freimarck, John, 1968.B38
Fremersdorff, Ellen, 1947.B32
French, Bryant Morey, 1960.B45; 1964.B46; 1965.A2;
   1971.B25A; 1972.A5
   Works, Reviewed: Mark Twain and "The Gilded
   Age" (1965), 1965.B1, B63, B82; 1966.B49, B59,
   B76, B89
French, Mrs. Daniel Chester, 1928.B9
French, Warren, 1964.B47
Fried, Martin B., 1961.A7
Friedman, Robert P., 1961.B29
Friedrich, Gerhard, 1960.B46; 1961.B30; 1966.B49
Friedrich, John T., 1946.B29
Friedrich, Otto, 1959.B31
Frisbee, George S., 1934.B27
Frohman, Daniel, 1911.B7; 1935.B39; 1937.B16
Frost, Robert, 1963.B5
Frye, Northrop, 1972.B25
Fuller, Daniel J., 1973.B22
Fuller, Frank, 1956.B20; 1971.B16
Fuller, John G., 1942.B34
Fuller, Muriel, 1939.B43
Fuller, Thomas, 1892.B6
Fulton, Robert, 1914.B3
Fussell, E. S., 1952.B23; 1954.B26; 1970.B66

G

Gabriel, Ralph Henry, 1940.B37
Gabrilowitsch, Ossip, 1909.B3; 1938.B7; 1964.B28
Gaffney, W. G., 1966.B50
Gagnot, B., 1926.B3
Gaines, Clarence H., 1910.B88
Gaines, Ervin J., 1965.B32
Gaither, Rice, 1929.B18
Galaxy, 1870.B6; 1948.B13; 1961.A3
Gale, Robert L., 1963.B31; 1967.B45-46; 1973.A3
Gallagher, Charles J., 1943.B32
Galsworthy, John, 1930.A4; 1934.A2
Galton, Sir Francis, 1957.B65
Gandhi, 1943.B23
Gannon, William, 1932.B31
Ganzel, Dewey, 1962.B32-33; 1964.B48; 1965.B33-35;
   1967.B47; 1968.A1, B39
   Works, Reviewed: Mark Twain Abroad (1968),
   1968.B17, B51, B58; 1969.B28, B41, B56, B65;
   1970.B23

Grimes, Geoffrey Allen, 1970.B34
Grimm, Clyde L., 1967.B52
Grimm, Clyde L., Jr., 1971.B31
Grinstead, Frances, 1934.B11
Gripenberg, Baroness Alexandra, 1888.B5;
    1894.B7; 1960.B83; 1973.B43
Griswold, Stephen, 1907.B21; 1910.B89
Griswold, Mrs. Stephen, 1871.A1
Grit (newspaper), 1951.B1
Gross, Seymour L., 1959.B33-34; 1960.B51
Grove, Noel, 1975.B8
Grover, Guru Dayal, 1970.A6
Grundy, J. Owen, 1963.B37
Guerra, Angel, 1912.A2
Guest, Boyd, 1945.B40
Guidi, Augusto, 1960.B52
Guido, John Foote, 1963.B38
Guild, James, 1930.B4
Guiterman, Arthur, 1936.B36
Gullason, Thomas Arthur, 1957.B42
Gulyev, Leonid, 1960.B53
Gulyev, Nelli, 1960.B53
Gunn, Alexander, 1906.B12; 1957.B46
Gunnison, Albert W., 1938.A3
Gurian, Jay, 1966.B56
Guthrie, F. Anstey, 1910.B99
Guttman, Allen, 1960.B54
"Gyascutus," 1959.B18

H

H., H. W., 1938.B13
H., W. J., 1900.B26
Haas, Irvin, 1936.A3
Hagedorn, Hermann, 1937.B17
Hagopian, John V., 1964.B53
Haight, Gordon S., 1935.B40; 1942.B36
Haines, Harold H., 1946.B31
Hakac, John, 1962.A14; 1970.B35
Haldeman-Julius, Emanuel, 1926.B10
Haliburton, Thomas Chandler ("Sam Slick"),
    1925.B11; 1941.B11; 1957.B14
Hall, Don E., 1945.B41
Hall, Fred J., 1947.B36; 1948.B15; 1967.B53;
    1973.B33
Hall, Lucille S. J., 1942.A6
Hall, Robert A., 1959.B35; 1967.B54
Halleck, Reuben Post, 1911.B8
Halsband, Robert, 1949.B29
Halsey, Francis W., 1902.B17
Halstead, Murat, 1901.B14; 1910.B135; 1919.B22
Halverson, John, 1965.B42
Ham, George H., 1921.B6
Hamada, Masajiro, 1936.B22; 1955.B25; 1963.B47
Hamblen, Abigail Ann, 1961.B32; 1964.B54; 1966.B57
Hamblin, Dora Jane, 1964.B34, B55
Hamilton, Maxwell, 1973.B26
Hammond, John Hays, 1958.B23
Hammond, Mrs. John Hays, 1897.B20; 1954.B23;
    1958.B23
Hamon, Louis T. ("Cheiro"), 1912.B11; 1931.B21;
    1936.B23; 1957.B65
Hamsun, Knut, 1929.B45; 1930.A4; 1970.B36
Hancock, Pamelia, 1944.B32
Hannibal, Missouri, 1899.B14; 1902.B26; 1905.B16;
    1913.B1; 1914.B10; 1916.B1; 1917.B12;
    1924.B43; 1926.B4; 1929.B34; 1935.B9, B12, B34,
    B46; 1946.B1; 1947.B30; 1951.B47; 1956.B2;

1958.B61; 1960.B100; 1961.B83; 1962.B74;
    1965.B24; 1968.B35; 1970.B86; 1974.B5
Hannibal Courier-Post, 1957.B32
Hannibal Journal, 1929.B5; 1932.B7; 1965.B4
Hannigan, D. F., 1895.B15
Hansen, Chadwick, 1963.B39; 1968.B67, B94;
    1973.B27
Hanser, Richard, 1960.B55
Hanson, R. Galen, 1973.B28
Hapgood, Hutchins, 1939.B47
Hapgood, Norman, 1930.B9; 1937.B18; 1938.B36
Harbeck, Hans, 1927.B7
Harding, Dorothy Sturgis, 1967.B55
Harding, Walter, 1952.B25; 1965.B43
Hardy, Thomas, 1929.B12, B38
Harkey, Joseph H., 1970.B37
Harkins, E. F., 1901.B15
Harland, Henry, 1899.B15
Harnsberger, Caroline Thomas, 1946.A3; 1948.A2,
    B30; 1953.B39; 1954.B12-13; 1957.B33; 1960.A5;
    1961.A8; 1972.A6
    Works, Reviewed: Mark Twain: Family Man
    (1960), 1961.B66
    Mark Twain's Views of Religion (1961), 1964.B33
Harper, Henry, 1970.B24
Harper, Joseph Henry, 1934.B12
Harper, Marion, 1966.B58
Harper & Brothers, 1910.B45
Harper's Bazaar, 1969.B60
Harper's Magazine, 1891.B3; 1958.B1; 1970.B18;
    1971.B45
Harper's Weekly, 1904.B3
Harrell, Don W., 1972.B47
Harris, Frank, 1921.B7; 1923.B14
Harris, George Washington, 1949.B36; 1952.B36;
    1953.B25
Harris, Helen L., 1975.B9
Harris, Joel Chandler, 1885.B18; 1905.B7; 1918.B7;
    1931.B22; 1953.A4; 1971.B61
Harris, Julia Collier, 1931.B22
Harrison, James G., 1947.B37
Harrison, Stanley R., 1972.B48
Harry Hazel's Yankee Blade, 1949.B12
Hart, James D., 1941.B3; 1948.B31; 1950.B33
Hart, John E., 1968.B48
Hart, John S., 1873.B12
Harte, Bret, 1866.B1; 1868.B1; 1870.B7; 1871.B1-2;
    1872.B11; 1876.B8; 1877.B2; 1882.B18; 1903.B7,
    B17; 1905.B15; 1908.B7, B9; 1910.B100, B112;
    1912.B31; 1915.B9; 1916.B6; 1919.B7; 1923.B14,
    B24; 1926.A2; 1927.A1, B8; 1931.B30; 1933.B18;
    1936.B52; 1938.B28; 1940.B29, B47; 1941.B25;
    1942.B7; 1943.B2; 1944.B9; 1952.B48; 1954.B6;
    1956.B21; 1958.B11-12, B57; 1961.A5, B63;
    1963.B25; 1964.A2; 1966.B80; 1967.A13; 1972.B63
Hartford, Connecticut, 1948.B9-10
Hartford Courant, 1884.B14; 1945.B52; 1947.B19;
    1955.B3; 1962.B73; 1966.B100
Harvard Law School Bulletin, 1962.B30
Harvey, Colonel George, 1910.B45; 1968.B41;
    1974.B17
Harwood, C. Edwin, 1969.B30
Harwood, H. C., 1925.B20
Haslam, Gerald W., 1967.B56
Hatton, Bruce, 1892.B9
Havard, William C., 1964.B56
Hawaii, 1922.B8; 1937.A1; 1938.A2; 1939.A5;
    1947.A3; 1966.A3; 1972.B31
Haweis, Hugh Reginald, 1882.B18; 1883.B9; 1887.B3;
    1900.B23
Hawkins, Laura (Frazer), 1941.B11; also see Frazer,
    Laura

Howe, Julia Ward, 1910.B55, B129
Howe, W. T. H. (collection), 1939.B15
Howell, Elmo, 1966.B61; 1968.B53-55; 1970.B41-42;
    1971.B34; 1972.B50-51
Howell, John, 1926.A2; 1927.A1
Howells, William Dean, 1869.B6; 1872.B13; 1875.B4;
    1876.B6; 1880.B7; 1882.B19; 1890.B17; 1896.B8;
    1900.B29; 1901.B17-18; 1902.B4, B19; 1905.B7;
    1908.B1; 1909.B14; 1910.A3, B32, B93-96; B129;
    1911.B5, B7; 1913.B7-8; 1918.B8-9; 1920.B3;
    1922.B19, B24, B29; 1923.A2, B14; 1924.B11;
    1928.B11; 1929.B38; 1930.B20; 1931.B20;
    1934.B13; 1935.B33; 1938.B5; 1940.B29; 1943.B46;
    1946.B27; 1947.B33; 1948.B24; 1953.B8; 1954.B10;
    1956.B13; 1958.B12, B50; 1959.B11, B21;
    1960.A13, B81; 1961.B60, B65; 1962.B17;
    1963.B81; 1964.A5, B43, B85; 1965.B21, B84;
    1966.B83; 1967.A1, A3, A13; 1968.B41; 1970.B1,
    B26, B29; 1971.B25; 1972.B80; 1973.B11
Howland, Alice G., 1902.B16
Howland, Robert M., 1948.B33
Huang, Samuel, 1972.B65
Hubbard, Elbert, 1901.B19; 1955.B33
Hubbell, Jay B., 1933.B21; 1972.B52
Hudon, Edward, 1966.B62
Hudson, Ruth, 1959.B38
Huendgren, 1905.B14
Hughes, Robert M., 1931.B25
Hughes, Rupert, 1929.B45; 1935.B44
Hugo, Victor, 1969.B48
Hulbert, J. R., 1939.B49
Hulbert, Mary Allen, 1926.B12
Hume (the Medium), 1967.B102
Humphrey, Hubert, 1967.A4
Huneker, James Gibbons, 1899.B17; 1922.B20
Hunter, Jim, 1963.B45
Hunting, Robert, 1958.B38; 1960.B95
Hüppy, August, 1935.A11; 1938.B19
Huse, William L., 1943.B33
Hutcherson, Dudley R., 1940.B40
Hutcheson, Austin E., 1948.B33-34; 1949.B32;
    1951.B44; 1952.B17
Hutchings, Emily Grant, 1917.A3, B8; 1918.B10;
    1919.B14; 1960.B35
Hutchinson, George, 1910.B100
Hutchison, Percy A., 1923.B16
Hutton, Graham, 1947.B38-39
Hutton, Lawrence, 1905.B15; 1920.B23
Huvstedt, S. B., 1946.B34
Huxley, Aldous, 1950.B36
Huxley, Thomas, 1964.B31
Hyatt, Edward, 1910.A4
Hyde, James H., 1974.B17
Hyman, Stanley Edgar, 1948.B35; 1958.B30A
"Hy Slocum," 1971.B42
Hyslop, James Hervey, 1917.B8; 1918.B10;
    1919.B13-14

I

Ib Liebe, Poul, 1959.B48
Idler, 1939.B53
Ignatieff, Leonid, 1955.B28
Illiano, Antonio, 1974.B18
India, 1898.27; 1966.B54
Inglis, K. S., 1967.B60
Inglis, Rewey Belle, 1925.B23
Inland Steel Company, 1961.B40

Ireland, Mrs. W. E., 1935.B12
Irving, Henry, 1893.B6; 1906.B14; 1908.B6;
    1951.B45; 1963.B25
Irving, Laurence, 1951.B45
Irving, Washington, 1956.B18
Irwin, Robert, 1967.B61
Irwin, Wallace, 1910.B121; 1963.B5
Irwin, Will, 1963.B5
Ish-Kishor, Sulamith, 1910.B46
Italy, 1955.B2; 1959.B9; 1960.B52
Ivanova, Elka, 1968.B56

J

Jackson, Dr. Abraham Reeves, 1964.B48
Jacobs, Robert D., 1963.B46
Jacobs, Stanley S., 1948.B36
Jacobs, Victor, 1958.B22
Jacobs, W. W., 1929.B45; 1930.A4; 1938.B15; 1943.A2
Jacobson, Dan, 1960.B59-60
Jager, Ronald B., 1974.B19
James, Alice, 1944.B29
James, George Wharton, 1910.B97; 1915.B6; 1919.B15
James, Henry, 1910.B11, B104; 1930.B10; 1931.B20;
    1935.B42; 1951.A3; 1958.B54; 1960.B18, B37;
    1961.B65, B80; 1962.B27; 1963.B25, B85;
    1964.B85; 1966.B19, B83; 1968.B41, B60;
    1969.B8; 1970.B1
James, Oliver Clemens, 1929.B21
James, Stuart B., 1969.B35
James, William, 1920.B20
Jan, Eduard von, 1928.B12
Janesville (Wisconsin) Gazette, 1956.B37
Janković, Mira, 1970.B43
Jantzen, H., 1926.B13
Jarves, James Jackson, 1958.B41
Jauch, Cleveland E., Jr., 1965.B48
Jefferies, William B., 1960.B61
Jefferson, Thomas, 1966.B63
Jehlen, Myra, 1934.B15
Jelliffe, Robert A., 1956.B28
Jensen, Franklin L., 1964.B63
Jensen, Johannes V., 1910.B98
Jerome, Jerome K., 1910.B99
Jerome, Leonard, 1943.B21
Jerrold, Walter, 1910.B100
Jewett, Sarah Orne, 1959.B8
Johannesburg, 1925.B7
Johnson, Alvin, 1920.B21
Johnson, Burges, 1937.B20; 1952.B27
Johnson, Clifton, 1905.B16
Johnson, E. C., 1946.B35
Johnson, Ellwood, 1970.B44
Johnson, Irmis, 1950.B35
Johnson, James William, 1959.B39
Johnson, Louis, 1950.A5
Johnson, Lyndon B., 1967.A4
Johnston, Colonel Richard Malcolm, 1906.B9
Johnson, Merle, 1910.A5, B43, B68; 1914.A1; 1930.A1;
    1935.A12; 1936.B38; 1942.B37; 1943.B15; 1945.B13;
    1947.B16; 1950.B6; 1951.B46; 1952.B16; 1954.B18;
    1962.B13; 1967.A5
Johnson, Robert L., 1965.B49
Johnson, Robert Underwood, 1877.B6; 1923.B17;
    1939.B19; 1945.B29, B31; 1948.B12; 1968.B73
Jones, Alexander E., 1951.B47; 1954.B31-32, B40;
    1956.B29; 1957.B43

Kruse, Horst, 1966.B65; 1967.B69; 1969.B40;
    1970.A7; 1972.B39
Krutch, Joseph Wood, 1954.B34; 1960.B67
Kubicek, Earl C., 1965.B57
Kunde, Donald M., ed., 1967.A5
Kuprin, A. I., 1959.B64
Kuznetsov, A., 1959.B64
Kwest, Dr. Franz, 1922.B21
Kyne, Peter B., 1912.B23

L

Labadie-Lagrave, 1895.B3
Lacey, Alex, 1917.B12
LaCossitt, Henry, 1935.B46
La Cour, Tage, 1959.B48
Lafayette (Indiana) Daily Courier, 1957.B2
LaHood, Marvin I., 1966.B66
Laidlaw, R. P., 1968.B61
Laing, Dilys, 1958.B40
Laing, Nita, 1960.B68
Laird, James, 1951.B8
Lakin, R. D., 1961.B43
Lamond, Hammond, 1905.B18
Lampton, James, 1919.B22; 1955.B48
Lancaster, Charles, 1910.B102; 1967.B7
Landon, Melville D. ("Eli Perkins"), 1891.B10
Lane, Lauriat, Jr., 1955.B29; 1956.B33, B44
Lang, Andrew, 1885.B2; 1886.B4; 1888.B6; 1889.B4;
    1891.B11; 1907.B23-24; 1932.B22; 1946.B30
Langdon, Charles J., 1967.B72, B111; 1971.B16
Langdon, Jervis, 1892.B12; 1922.B8; 1935.A13;
    1938.A5, B11; 1947.B57; 1960.B33; 1965.B25;
    1966.B68
Langley, Dorothy, 1973.B35
Lanina, T., 1970.B49-50
Lans, Matthew Irving, 1900.B30
Lapidus, Deborah, 1973.B55
Lardner, Ring W., 1917.B4; 1960.B111; 1970.B17;
    1972.B4
Large Soviet Encyclopedia, 1960.B8
Lark, Charles T., 1965.B25; 1966.B68
Larom, Walter H., 1924.B15
Larowe, Nina, 1910.B48, B97
Laszowska, Jean Emily Gerard de, 1959.B51
Lautrec, Gabriel de, N.D.A4; 1900.A1, B13;
    1922.A3; 1935.B47
Laverty, Carroll D., 1947.B40
LaVigne, Gary W., 1961.B44
Law, Frederick Houk, 1926.B15
Lawrence, D. H., 1936.B24; 1964.B41
Lawrence, Mary Margaret, 1965.B58
Lawton, Mary, 1925.A2, B24; 1938.B29
    Works, Reviewed: A Lifetime With Mark Twain
    (1925), 1925.B4
Leacock, Stephen, 1922.B24; 1929.B45; 1932.A3;
    1933.B29; 1934.B14; 1935.A3, B48; 1936.B25;
    1970.B53
    Works, Reviewed: Mark Twain (1932), 1932.B3;
    1933.B6, B26
Leary, Daniel, 1970.B52
Leary, Katy, 1925.A2, B4, B24
Leary, Lewis, 1947.B41; 1948.B38-40; 1954.B35-36;
    1960.A6; 1961.A9, B45; 1962.A10; 1963.B52;
    1967.B111; 1968.B62-63; 1969.A2; 1970.B51-52;
    1971.A4, B37; 1974.B21, B21A
    Works, Reviewed: Mark Twain (1960), 1961.B3,
    B58

Mark Twain's Correspondence With Henry Huttleston
    Rogers (ed., 1969), 1969.B42, B44; 1970.B9, B11,
    B16, B74, B94
Mark Twain's Letters To Mary (ed., 1961),
    1961.B77
Southern Excursions (1971), 1972.B85
Lease, Benjamin, 1954.B37
Leathers, Jesse, 1932.B12
Leaver, Florence B., 1956.B34
Leavis, F. R., 1952.B28-29; 1956.B35; 1957.B20
Le Breton, Maurice, 1934.B15-16; 1935.B49; 1937.B22;
    1947.B42
Lecky, William Edward Hartpole, 1955.B18; 1962.B7,
    B65; 1964.B31; 1965.B99; 1973.B52
Lederer, Max, 1945.B46; 1946.B37
Lee, Alfred Pyle, 1938.A6
Lee, Charlotte I., 1967.B70
Lee, Francis Lightfoot, 1943.B15; 1944.B17, B43
Lee, Robert Edson, 1966.B67
Leeming, Thomas L., 1951.B4; 1966.B64
Legal Aid Society, 1942.B13
Le Gallienne, Richard, 1896.B9
Legate, David M., 1970.B53
Lehan, Richard, 1968.B64; 1969.B41; 1971.B38-39
Lehner, Gilbert, 1950.B44
Leisy, Ernest Edwin, 1924.B16; 1929.B26; 1933.B21;
    1937.B23; 1942.B18, B39; 1946.A4, B38; 1949.B35;
    1950.B39; 1952.B30-31; 1956.B36; 1957.B47;
    1961.A15; 1964.B13
    Works, Reviewed: The Letters of Quintus
    Curtius Snodgrass (Ed., 1946), 1947.B45, B50,
    B54
Leiter, Louis H., 1965.B59
LeMay, Alan, 1944.B3
Lemmon, Leonard, 1891.B9
Lemonnier, Léon, 1935.B50-52; 1937.A2; 1939.B50;
    1947.A4
    Works, Reviewed: La Jeunesse Aventureuse de
    Mark Twain (1937), 1937.B22
    Mark Twain (1947), 1947.B42
Lennon, E. James, 1953.B22; 1954.B38
Leslie, Elsie, 1890.B14; 1925.B40
Lessing, O. E., 1927.B9
Letter, The, 1960.A15
Lettis, Richard, 1962.A11
Leupp, Francis E., 1901.B20
Levering, Albert, 1903.B13
Levin, David, 1968.B65
Levy, Leo B., 1964.B68
Levy, M. S., 1899.B20
Lewis, C. B. ("M. Quad"), 1910.B121
Lewis, Dudley Payne, 1913.B17
Lewis, Merrill, 1966.B69
Lewis, Oscar, 1931.A4; 1947.A6, B43
Lewis, R. W., 1965.B60
Lewis, Sinclair, 1963.B5; 1972.B27
Lewis, Stuart, 1970.B54; 1972.B58
Lewisohn, Ludwig, 1932.B21
Light, Martin, 1974.B22
Likens, Mrs. J. W., 1874.B9
Liljegren, S[ten] B[odvar], 1945.A1; 1946.B39
    Works, Reviewed: The Revolt Against Romanticism
    in American Literature as Evidenced in the Works
    of Samuel L. Clemens (1945), 1946.B35, B46
Lillard, Richard S., 1942.B40; 1943.B35; 1944.B37;
    1948.B41; 1965.B61
Lindborg, Henry J., 1973.B36
Lindsay, Vachel, 1917.B9; 1935.B59
Linneman, William R., 1965.B62
Literary Guillotine, The, 1902.B27

M

N

O

P

Portland (Maine) Transcript, 1946.B16; 1953.B15
Port Chester (N.Y.) Daily Item, 1952.B44; 1955.B47
Popa, Ioan, 1969.B59
Posner, George A., 1966.B114
Potter, John K., 1932.A4
Potter-Frissell, E., 1898.B24
Pound, Ezra, 1963.B5
Powell, Lyman P., 1930.B17
Power, William, 1961.B69
Powers, L. M., 1946.B10
Powers, Lyall H., 1973.B48
Powers, Richard H., 1965.B72
Powys, John Cowper, 1963.B5
Pratt, Willis C., 1960.B90
Praz, Mario, 1937.B31
Press Club of Chicago, 1894.B8; 1945.B9
Price, Lawrence M., 1940.B46; 1966.B86
Prince, Gilbert, 1974.B26
Pritchett, V. S., 1941.B23; 1960.B91; 1966.B87;
    1967.B85
Proudfit, Isabel, 1940.A5
Provencal, Valmore, 1942.B49
Purcell, E., 1881.B7
Putnam, Samuel, 1938.B31
Punch, 1909.B15; 1965.B62

Q

Quaife, M. M., 1926.B9; 1929.B40; 1944.B40, B43-44
Quaker City and Quaker City Excursion, 1867.B1;
    1877.B5; 1892.B6; 1907.B21; 1910.B48, B89;
    1938.A9; 1941.B10; 1945.B13; 1947.B10;
    1950.B11; 1955.B42; 1956.B37; 1959.B64;
    1964.B48; 1967.B111; 1970.B52
Quarles, James T., 1967.B30
Quarles, John A., 1942.B51; 1946.B3; 1967.B30;
    1969.B29
Quarles, Judge John S., 1912.B19; 1958.B28
Quarles, Tabitha, 1952.B2
Quick, Dorothy, 1935.B68; 1938.B32; 1961.A14
    Works, Reviewed: Enchantment: A Little Girl's
    Friendship With Mark Twain (1961), 1961.B26
Quincy (Missouri) Whig Journal, 1923.B2
Quinn, Arthur Hobson, 1920.B28; 1927.B12; 1936.B37;
    1938.B33

R

R., V., 1920.B29; 1935.B69
Raabe, 1963.B28
Raban, Jonathan, 1968.A3
Rabelais, François, 1973.B29
Rachal, John, 1974.B27
Rackham, Jeff, 1971.B55
Raknem, Ingvald, 1971.B56
Ramsay, Robert L., 1930.A3; 1935.A8; 1938.A8;
    1947.B46; 1958.B25; 1965.B30
    Works, Reviewed: A Mark Twain Lexicon (with
    Frances G. Emberson, 1938), 1938.B4; 1939.B25,
    B42, B46, B49-50; 1940.B49; 1941.B15
Ramsay, W., 1901.B27
Randall, A. W. G., 1925,B29
Randall, David A., 1936.B38
Randolph, Vance, 1960.B92
Rankin, J. W., 1923.B27; 1948.B49

Rankin, Scott, 1892.B8
Raoul, Margaret Lente, 1931.B28
Rapper, Irving, 1944.B3
Rascoe, Burton, 1932.B26
Ratcliffe, S. K., 1936.B39; 1946.A1
Ratner, Marc L., 1964.B82
Ravitz, Abe C., 1955.B33; 1968.B87
Ray, Gordon N., 1969.B6
Rayford, Julian Lee, 1944.B45; 1960.B93
Raymond, E. T., 1924.B28
Raymond, John T., 1910.B135; 1925.B40; 1943.B131;
    1944.B34
Read, Opie, 1930.B18; 1939.B20; 1940.A6, B3;
    1968.B41
Reade, A. Arthur, 1883.B13; 1950.B61
Redding (Connecticut) Times, 1959.B59
Redding, Saunders, 1950.B46
Redpath, James, 1900.B23; 1942.B24
Reed, John Q., 1960.B94
Reed, Kenneth T., 1970.B69
Reed, Thomas, 1919.B10
Reede, Edward H., M.D., 1921.B12; 1924.B25;
    1968.B80
Rees, Robert A., 1968.B88-89; 1969.B60; 1970.B70
Reeves, Paschal, 1968.B90; 1969.B61; 1970.B71;
    1971.B57; 1972.B67; 1973.B50
Regan, Robert, 1965.B73; 1966.A8; 1967.B86-87;
    1973.B49
    Works, Reviewed: Unpromising Heroes (1966),
    1967.B49, B105; 1968.B68
Regan, W. A., 1900.B34
Reid, Mayne, 1969.B50
Reid, Whitelaw, 1921.B5; 1961.B60; 1973.B11
Reinfield, George, 1957.B54
Reinitz, Neale, 1967.B88
Remes, Carol, 1955.B34
Repplier, Agnes, 1905.B7
Requa, Kenneth A., 1974.B28
Resor, Alice, 1907.B17
Review of Reviews (London), 1954.B30
Revista, La, 1920.B17
Rexroth, Kenneth, 1959.B63; 1967.B89; 1969.B62
Reyes, Pedro A., Jr., 1961.B70
Reynolds, Horace, 1938.B34; 1952.B38; 1955.B35
Rhys, Ernest, 1936.B36
Rice, Alice Hegan, 1940.B47
Rice, Clarence C., M.D., 1924.B29
Rice, Dan, 1929.B36
Rice, Howard C., 1951.B52
Rice, Jack, 1961.B22; 1962.B65
Rice, James, 1932.B14
Richards, P., 1907.B19; 1912.B27; 1914.B9;
    1929.B41; 1933.B29
Richardson, A. D., 1941.B12
Richardson, Charles F., 1886.B5; 1913.B16
Richardson, Lyon N., 1942.B50
Richepin, Jean, 1920.B30
Richie, Donald, 1955.B36
Rickels, Milton, 1968.B91
Rideing, William Henry, 1910.B119; 1912.B28
Rideout, Walter B., 1953.B1
Ridge, W. Pett, 1910.B99
Ridland, J. M., 1965.B74
Ries, Theresa Feodorowna, 1898.B26; 1910.B115
Riggs, Kate Douglas [Wiggin], 1905.B7
Riley, J. H., 1933.B32
Riley, James Whitcomb, 1910.B55, B120-121; 1922.B15;
    1930.B19; 1946.B13
Rinaker, Clarissa, 1921.B14
Ritunnano, Jeanne, 1971.B58
Rizzardi, A., 1963.B70

Roades, Sister Mary Teresa, 1938.B35; 1952.B39
RoBards, John L., 1910.B90; 1931.B2; 1948.B11;
  1950.B5; 1971.B16
Robbins, L. H., 1935.B70
Roberts, Carl Eric Bechhofer, 1923.B28
Roberts, Harold, 1942.B51
Roberts, Kenneth, 1939.B56
Roberts, R. Ellis, 1935.B71
Roberts, Thomas, 1962.B66
Robertson, J. M., 1912.B29
Robertson, Stuart, 1937.B32
Robinson, E. Arthur, 1960.B95
Robinson, Fred C., 1972.B68
Robinson, John A. T. (Bishop of Woolwich),
  1965.B41
Robinson, Sir John R., 1904.B16
Robinson, Kenneth Allan, 1910.B123
Robinson, Marie J., 1947.B49
Robinson, Tracy, 1967.B90
Rochester (N.Y.), Post Express, 1932.B24
Rockwell, Norman, 1936.B53
Rockwood (Artist), 1907.B17
Rodd, Lewis Charles, 1966.B88
Rodgers, Cleveland, 1924.B30
Rodgers, Paul C., Jr., 1973.B51
Rodney, Robert M., 1945.A2; 1959.A1; 1966.A1
Rodnon, Stewart, 1964.B83; 1970.B72
Roerich, Nicholas, 1939.B57
Roessel, James, 1945.A3
Rogers, Cameron, 1924.B31
Rogers, Franklin R., 1957.B55; 1960.A12; 1961.A15;
  1963.A4, B71; 1964.B84; 1965.B75-76; 1966.B89;
  1967.A7
  Works, Reviewed: Mark Twain's Burlesque
  Patterns (1960), 1961.B31, B38, B52, B68
  Mark Twain's Satires & Burlesques (ed., 1967),
  1967.B18, B34, B70, B81, B84-86, B103, B107,
  B112; 1968.B23, B31, B39, B89, B108; 1969.B36
  The Pattern For Mark Twain's "Roughing It"
  (1961), 1962.B49
  Roughing It (ed., with Paul Baender, 1972),
  1972.B35; 1973.B47, B49
  Simon Wheeler, Detective (ed., 1963), 1965.B2
Rogers, Henry Huttleston, 1917.B3; 1919.B16;
  1925.B5; 1926.B12; 1937.B26; 1967.B7, B37;
  1968.B62; 1969.A2; 1970.A4; 1973.B33; 1974.B19;
Rogers, Mrs. Henry, 1925.B2
Rogers, Mary, 1961.A9
Rogers Peet (N.Y. clothing store), 1943.B28
Rogers, Rodney O., 1973.B52
Rogers, Will, 1968.B41
Rollins, Carl Purington, 1936.B40
Rollins, Ronald G., 1966.B90
Roosevelt, Franklin Delano, 1933.B3; 1934.A2, B3;
  1945.B21; 1949.A1
Roosevelt, Theodore, 1905.B7; 1910.B55
Root, Robert, 1966.B91
Roper, Gordon, 1960.B96; 1966.B92
Rosa-Clot, Paola, 1968.A4
Rose, Marilyn Gaddis, 1966.B93
Rosenberger, Edward G., 1928.B16
Rosenfeld, Paul, 1924.B32
Rosenthal, Raymond, 1966.B94
Rosewater, Victor, 1916.B8
Ross, John F., 1962.B66A
Ross, Michael, 1973.B53
Rossky, William, 1965.B77
Roth, Martin, 1967.B91
Rothberg, Abraham, 1966.B96

Roughing It (Play, not based on MT's novel),
  1946.B12, B27
Rourke, Constance, 1931.B29
Routledge, George, & Sons, 1872.B10; 1975.B7
Rovit, Earl, 1963.B72
Rowe, Ida, 1937.B33
Rowlette, Robert, 1971.A5, B59; 1972.B69; 1973.B54
"Royal Nonesuch," 1902.B4; 1944.B51; 1959.B18
  (also see "Burning Shame")
Royot, Daniel, 1972.B70
Royston, Samuel Watson, 1959.B12; 1964.B19
Rubenstein, Gilbert M., 1956.B33, B42, B44
Rubin, Louis D., Jr., 1957.B56; 1961.B71; 1963.B73;
  1967.B92-93; 1969.B63; 1970.B73-74; 1971.B60;
  1972.B71
Ruff, William, 1940.B48
Ruffner, Ann Virginia, 1914.B10
Ruland, Richard, 1967.B94
Rule, Henry B., 1969.B64; 1971.B50
Ruloff murder case, 1871.B4
Rulon, Curt M., 1967.B95
Russell, Bertrand, 1939.B8
Russell, Frances Theresa, 1933.B30
Russell, Lillis L., 1948.B50
Russell, Walter, 1935.B2, B9
Rust, Richard Dilworth, 1968.B92; 1969.B60
Ryan, Pat M., Jr., 1960.B97

S

S., E. OE, 1885.B9
Sabith, Barney, 1966.B97
Sachs, Viola, 1966.B98
Sackett, S. J., 1972.B72
Sacramento Union, 1893.B12; 1937.B10; 1938.A2;
  1939.A5; 1946.B13; 1947.A3; 1949.B11; 1961.B59;
  1969.B12; 1973.B39
Sadleir, Michael, 1927.B13
San Andreas Independent, 1915.B4; 1929.B36
St. Andrews Society (London), 1874.B2; 1957.B2
St. Gaudens, Augustus, 1931.B5
St. Louis Globe-Democrat, 1923.B2; 1949.B10
St. Louis Missouri Democrat, 1961.A15
St. Louis Missouri Republican, 1947.B44; 1967.B6, B47
St. Louis News and Intelligencer, 1858.B1; 1950.B40
St. Louis Post-Dispatch, 1945.B3; 1961.B22
St. Louis Post-Standard, 1916.B1
St. Louis Press Club, 1946.B43; 1970.B28
St. Louis Republic, 1965.B24
St. Louis Republican, 1871.B3; 1957.B4
St. Nicholas Magazine, 1972.B16
Saintsbury, George, 1893.B13
Saintine, Joseph Xavier, 1961.B46
Sakharov, W., 1936.B41
Salinger, J. D., 1956.B30; 1957.B12; 1959.B39;
  1960.B112; 1963.B53, B66; 1965.B37, B94;
  1966.B39, B82; 1970.B17
Salls, Helen Harriet, 1936.B42
Salomon, Eric, 1961.B50
Salomon, Ludwig, 1905.B19
Salomon, Roger B., 1961.A16, B72; 1964.B85;
  1967.B96; 1968.B93
  Works, Reviewed: Twain and the Image of
  History (1961), 1962.B14-15, B48, B50, B54,
  B66A; 1963.B10; 1964.B26; 1966.B95
Salsbury, Edith Colgate, 1965.A8
  Works, Reviewed: Susy and Mark Twain (1965),
  1965.B6, B26, B73; 1966.B11, B44, B76

Sampley, Arthur M., 1947.B50
Samuels, Thomas Charles, 1964.B86
Sanborn, Professor, 1885.B11
Sandberg, Carl, 1935.B11; 1952.B40
Sanderson, Kenneth M., 1971.A1
Sanford, Charles, 1958.B60
San Francisco, 1939.A11; 1963.B83; 1969.A9
San Francisco Alta California, 1939.B6; 1940.A2;
    1943.B10; 1947.B10-13; 1948.B5-10; 1949.B7-9,
    B14, B43; 1958.A1; 1967.B14, B51
San Francisco Argonaut, 1910.B57
San Francisco Bulletin, 1937.B10; 1963.B20
San Francisco Call, 1887.B1; 1922.B8; 1944.B6;
    1945.B8; 1949.B13; 1950.B10; 1952.B17;
    1969.A1
San Francisco Call-Bulletin, 1934.B21
Sanitary Fund, 1949.B32
San Juan, Pastora, 1966.B100
Santayana, George, 1952.B41; 1963.B5, B87
Sapozhnikov, G., 1966.B101
Sapper, Neil G., 1970.B75
Saranac Lake, New York, 1924.B15
Sarukhanyan, A., 1959.B64
Sasu-Timerman, Dorothea, 1967.A2
Saturday Evening Post, 1945.B15
Saturday Morning Club (Hartford), 1912.A1;
    1919.B10; 1928.B5
Savage Club, 1904.B7; 1907.B34; 1925.B37; 1933.B29;
    1938.B23; 1949.B3A, B44
Savine, Albert, 1935.B45
Scanlon, Lawrence E., 1965.B78; 1966.B102
Scheick, William J., 1971.B61
Schell, Edgar T., 1964.B87
Scherting, Jack, 1972.B73
Schiller, Friedrich, 1959.B47
Schinto, Jeanne M., 1975.B10
Schlesinger, Arthur, Jr., 1966.B103
Schlesinger, Sigmund, 1935.B11; 1950.B13
Schliech, K. L., 1898.B25
Schmidt, Paul, 1953.B33; 1956.B45; 1960.B98
Schmidt, Rudolph, 1953.B38
Schmitt, Gladys, 1935.B9; 1948.B51
Schmitter, Dean Morgan, 1974.A4
Schmitz, Neil, 1971.B62-63
Schneider, Otto, 1923.B10
Schoen, Max, 1943.B38
Schofield, Kenneth B., 1950.B47
Scholastic, 1948.B61
Scholes, James B., 1962.A13
Schönfelder, Karl-Heinz, 1955.B37; 1956.A2, B47;
    1957.B57; 1959.B65; 1961.A17
    Works, Reviewed: Life On the Mississippi
    (ed., 1956), 1959.B42
    Mark Twain: Leben, Persönlichkeit und Werk
    (1961), 1962.B61
Schönemann, Friedrich, 1919.B19-20; 1920.B31;
    1921.B15; 1922.B27-28; 1923.B29-30; 1925.A3,
    B30; 1935.B72; 1936.B43-44; 1956.B46
    Works, Reviewed: Mark Twain Als Literarische
    Persönlichkeit (1925), 1925.B10, B14, B25,
    B29; 1926.B6, B13-14
Schonhorn, Manuel, 1968.B94
Schorer, C. E., 1955.B38
Schramm, Wilbur L., 1940.B49
Schroeder, Fred, 1963.B74
Schulman, Ivan A., 1961.B73
Schultz, John Richie, 1936.B45
Schulze, F. W., 1958.B2
Schurz, Carl, 1965.B95
Schwartz, Edward, 1952.B42
Scientific American, 1951.B60

Scots Observer, 1890.B5
Scott, Arthur L., 1953.B34-36; 1955.A1, B39-41;
    1960.B99; 1962.B67; 1963.B75; 1964.B88;
    1966.A9, B81; 1967.A17; 1969.A6, B65
    Works, Reviewed: Mark Twain At Large (1969),
    1969.B44, B57; 1970.B91; 1971.B39, B69
    Mark Twain: Selected Criticism (1955),
    1956.B6-7, B27, B36, B39; 1957.B36; 1958.B2
    On the Poetry of Mark Twain (1966), 1966.B40,
    B73
Scott, Jack Denton, 1956.B12
Scott, Sir Walter, 1913.B14; 1921.B1, B8; 1935.B69;
    1938.A5; 1941.B20; 1942.B3; 1965.B56; 1967.A13
Scott, Winfield Townley, 1959.B66; 1960.B100;
    1961.B74; 1966.B104
Scottish Rite Progress, 1928.B1
Scrivner, Buford, Jr., 1975.B11
"Scroggins," 1953.B25
Seabaugh, Samuel, 1915.B4; 1929.B36
Seabright, J. M., 1924.B33
Seaman, Owen, 1907.B30; 1910.B99, B133; 1936.B46
Searle, Ronald, 1961.B83
Sears, Robert R., 1973.B55
Sedgwick, Henry Dwight, 1908.B10
Seelye, John, 1969.B66; 1970.A9, B76; 1973.B10
    Works, Reviewed: The True Adventures of
    Huckleberry Finn (1970), 1970.B2
Seitz, Don C., 1919.B21; 1924.B34
Selby, P. O., 1969.A7-8
Seldes, Gilbert, 1932.B27
Sellers, Captain Isaiah, 1871.B3; 1942.B15, B26
Sellers, George Escol, 1961.B17; 1962.B37;
    1964.B2(?); 1972.A5(?)
Sellers, J. L., 1947.B51
"Sergeant Fathom," 1942.B39
Serrano-Plaja, Arturo, 1970.B77
Severance, Emily A., 1938.A9; 1945.B13
Severance, S., 1967.B111; 1972.B57
Sévigné, Madame de, 1972.B33; 1973.B14
Shaffer, Ellen K., 1942.A6
Shain, Charles E., 1955.B42
Shakespeare, William, 1959.B32; 1963.B31; 1969.B38
Shannon, Representative (of Missouri), 1940.B2,
    B6, B25, B50; 1955.B23
Sharma, Mohan Lal, 1968.B95
Sharp, Eugene, 1964.B89
Sharp, Luke, 1892.B9
Shatunovskii, Ilya, 1970.B86
Shaw, George Bernard, 1924.B35; 1925.B33; 1929.B16;
    1934.A2; 1944.B46; 1945.B25; 1948.B26, B30;
    1950.B16; 1951.B18, B53; 1954.B29, B43;
    1960.B12; 1963.B5; 1967.B38; 1970.B64;
    1971.B12; 1972.B11
Shaw, Henry Wheeler. See "Billings, Josh"
Shawneetown, Illinois, 1964.B2
Shelley, Harriet, 1973.B7
Shepard, Odell, 1928.B6
Shepard, Robert Fitch, 1938.B40 ·
Sherman, Stuart P., 1910.B122-123; 1921.B16;
    1927.B14
Sherwood, Robert Edmund, 1926.B19; 1945.B39
Shetty, Nalini V., 1972.B74
Shillaber, Benjamin P., 1937.B5; 1938.B26
Shinn, Everett, 1900.B35
Shirley, Philip, 1884.B12; 1946.B9
Shockley, Martin Staples, 1960.B101
Shoemaker, Floyd Calvin, 1918.B15
Shrell, Darwin H., 1970.B78
Shuster, George Nauman, 1917.B11
Siamese Twins, 1974.B9
Sidgwick, Henry, 1906.B13; 1910.B119

Stoehr, Taylor, 1968.B100
Stoker, Bram., 1906.B14
Stone, Albert E., Jr., 1955.B46; 1959.B68;
    1961.A18, B79; 1967.B103-105; 1971.B69
    Works, Reviewed: The Innocent Eye (1961),
    1961.B74; 1962.B10, B15, B48, B66A; 1964.B26
Stone, Edward, 1951.B54
Stong, Phil, 1948.B55; 1954.A4
Storkan, Charles J., 1949.B43
Stoutenburg, Adrien, 1963.A7
Stovall, Floyd, 1943.B40
Stowe, Harriet Beecher, 1905.B15; 1961.B32;
    1964.B45
Stowell, Robert F., 1966.B108; 1967.B95; 1973.B57
Strate, Jessie B., 1924.B40
Strauss, Johann, 1963.B42
Street, Julian, 1914.B10
Strelnikov, Boris, 1970.B86
Strindberg, August, N.D.B1
Strong, Leah A., 1951.B55; 1959.B69-70; 1966.A11;
    1967.B106
    Works, Reviewed: Joseph Hopkins Twichell
    (1966), 1966.B18, B22; 1969.B33
Stronks, James B., 1963.B80; 1966.B32, B109
Stroven, Carl, 1940.B51
Strunsky, Simeon, 1910.B128
Stuart, J., 1892.B11
Stubblefield, Charles, 1967.B107
Sturdevant, James R., 1967.B108
Suderman, Elmer F., 1971.B6
Sühnel, Rudolph, 1954.B45
Sullivan, Mark, 1938.B36
Summary, The, 1885.B11
Sunset (San Francisco), 1910.B137
Sutro, Adolph, 1949.B16
Swain, Louis H., 1937.B34
Swan, Jon, 1965.B84
Swift, Jonathan, 1935.A15; 1951.B3
Swinburne, Algernon Charles, 1912.B12
Switzerland, 1935.A11
Swoboda, Wilhelm, 1903.B16
Sydney (Australia) Bulletin, 1890.B3
Sykes, Robert H., 1967.B109
Sykes, Madelene McEuen, 1969.B73
Synge, John Millinton, 1966.B90
Szczepanik, Jan, 1937.B3; 1954.B9

T

T., S., 1898.B30
Tacconis, G., 1939.A6
Taft, William Howard, 1910.B50, B55, B129
Taine, Hippolyte, 1958.B20; 1973.B22, B52
"Tak Sioui," 1962.A14
Tammany Hall, 1955.B50
Tandy, Jennette, 1925.B32
Tanner, Tony, 1961.B80-82; 1962.B70-71; 1963.B81;
    1965.B85-86; 1967.B110
Tanselle, G. Thomas, 1968.B101
Taper, Bernard, 1963.A8, B82-83; 1964.B70, B93
Tarbell, Ida, 1929.B45
Tariq, Azizuddin, 1972.B78
Tarkington, Booth, 1910.B55, B75, B120; 1922.B24;
    1933.B31; 1936.B49; 1939.A3
Tarrytown, New York, 1959.B5; 1974.B21
Tassin, Algernon, 1923.B31
Tate, Alan, 1939.B38; 1968.B102-103
Tatham, Campbell, 1968.B104

Tavern Club, 1967.B55
Taylor, Annie Elizabeth, 1926.B1
Taylor, Bayard, 1936.B45
Taylor, Coley Banks, 1935.A15
Taylor, Howard P., 1940.A7; 1967.B51
Taylor, J. Golden, 1965.B87
Taylor, Jane, 1947.B40
Taylor, Nancy Dew, 1963.B84
Taylor, Robert, Jr., 1972.B79
Taylor, Tom, 1967.B108
Taylor, Walter Fuller, 1936.B50; 1938.B37;
    1942.B52
Taylor, William Desmond, 1930.B11
Tedeschini Lalli, Bianca Maria, 1965.B88
Teichmann, E., 1907.B32
Teitelbaum, Harold, 1960.B107
Templin, E. H., 1941.B26
Ten Eyck, Andrew, 1920.B32
Tennessee land, 1928.B17; 1970.B30
Tennyson, Alfred Lord, 1943.B7
Territorial Enterprise, 1901.B22; 1937.B10, B12;
    1939.B31; 1946.B14, B40; 1948.B34; 1949.B13,
    B32; 1951.B44; 1953.B4; 1956.B23; 1957.A5, B52;
    1960.B94; 1961.B59; 1963.B20; 1967.B51;
    1973.B39
Tesla, Nikolai, 1923.B17
Thackeray, William Makepeace, 1935.A15
Thayer, Emma B., 1967.B111
Theatre Magazine, 1937.B16
Thomas, Dana Lee, 1943.B41
Thomas, Frederick Moy, 1904.B16
Thomas, Henry, 1943.B41
Thompson, Charles Miner, 1897.B4, B28
Thompson, James Westfall, 1910.B130; 1937.B10
Thompson, Lawrance, 1950.B51
Thompson, Paul, 1909.B21
Thompson, Ralph, 1949.B44
Thompson, Vance, 1907.B33
Thompson, William Tappan, Major Jones's Sketches of
    Travel (1847), 1953.B26
Thomson, Mortimer Neal, 1949.B37
Thomson, O. R., 1939.B60
Thorp, Willard, 1950.B52; 1962.B72
Thurmond, Margaret E., 1967.B112-114
Tichenor, A. C., 1949.B17
Tichenor Bonanza, 1943.B47
Ticknor, Caroline, 1914.B11; 1922.B29
Ticknor, George, 1968.B26; 1969.B20; 1970.B19
Tidwell, James Nathan, 1942.B53
Tieck, William A., 1968.B105
Tigert, John, 1951.B56
Timbs, John, 1959.B24
Times of Ceylon, The, 1963.B67
Tirumalai, C. K., 1964.B94
Tisdale, Jimmy, 1917.B12
Tocqueville, Alexis de, 1970.B75
Todd, William B., 1965.B89
Toebasch, Wim, 1965.B90
Toklas, Alice B., 1966.B19; 1971.B67
Tolchard, Clifford, 1970.B87
Tomlinson, H. M., 1929.B45; 1930.A4
"Tom Sawyer Club," 1957.B66
Tom Sawyer's fence, 1946.B1; 1958.B18, B35-36, B47
Torchiana, Donald T., 1956.B49
Tormes, Lazarillo de, 1969.B79
Torrey, Charles L., 1910.B131
Town, George H., 1899.B8; 1957.B61
Towner, Ausburn, 1892.B12
Townsend, Frank, 1962.A5
Trachtenberg, Alan, 1970.B88
Tracy, Robert, 1968.B106

U

V

W

Y

Z